D1738041

CAMBRIDGE CLASSICAL TEXTS AND
COMMENTARIES

EDITORS
J. DIGGLE E. W. HANDLEY H. D. JOCELYN
M. D. REEVE D. N. SEDLEY R. J. TARRANT

31

ALEXIS: THE FRAGMENTS

A COMMENTARY

ALEXIS: THE FRAGMENTS,

A COMMENTARY

BY

W. GEOFFREY ARNOTT

Emeritus Professor of Greek, University of Leeds

CAMBRIDGE
UNIVERSITY PRESS

Published by the Press Syndicate of the University of Cambridge
The Pitt Building, Trumpington Street, Cambridge CB2 1RP
40 West 20th Street, New York, NY 10011–4211, USA
10 Stamford Road, Oakleigh, Melbourne 3166, Australia

First published 1996

Printed in Great Britain at the University Press, Cambridge

A catalogue record for this book is available from the British Library

Library of Congress cataloguing in publication data

Arnott, W. G.
Alexis – the fragments: a commentary/by W. Geoffrey Arnott.
p.   cm. – (Cambridge classical texts and commentaries:31)
Includes bibliographical references (pp. xi–xxi) and index.
ISBN 0 521 55180 3
1. Alexis, ca. 372–270 BC – Criticism, Textual.
2. Greek drama (Comedy) – Criticism, Textual.
3. Manuscripts, Greek (Papyri). 4. Lost literature – Greece.
I. Title. II. Series.
PA3864.A54Z52   1996
882'.01 – dc20   95 12774 CIP

ISBN 0 521 55180 3 hardback

CE

TO MY WIFE

CONTENTS

vii

LIST OF CONTENTS

PREFACE

When I started research on the fragments of Alexis in 1953 it soon seemed to me that this poet's impact on the world of comedy was greater than anyone else's between the periods of Aristophanes and Menander, and a detailed commentary on the frs. appeared both desirable in itself and the best way to test that hypothesis. *Quod iuuenis temere susceperam senex denique ad finem perduxi*; I plagiarise E. Bethe's words at the beginning of the second volume of his edition of Pollux. The appearance of R. Kassel and C. Austin's magisterial edition of the comic frs. (Alexis in 2 (Berlin and New York 1991) 21–195) meanwhile has removed any need for me to print a separate text, and this commentary is accordingly linked to that in Kassel–Austin, although there are many places where I take issue with their decisions, and a few also with their readings.

Over the last forty years or so I have received assistance, advice and information from many scholars and institutions. I should like to express my gratitude to them all, and to apologise if any name has been omitted by error. I benefited from research funds in the Universities of London and Newcastle upon Tyne, and the award of a research fellowship at Gonville and Caius College, Cambridge. Photographs of manuscripts and papyri were supplied to me by libraries and museums in Venice, Florence, Paris and a now united Berlin, photocopies of dissertations and other material otherwise inaccessible by libraries in Amsterdam, Cambridge, Göttingen, Leiden, London, Munich and Regensburg. Individuals who have responded to queries and requests are too many to name, but I should like particularly to acknowledge here my debts to Dr C. Austin, Professor C. O. Brink, Dr R. W. Brock, Professor P. B. Corbett, Professor J. Diggle, N. Dunbar, Professor K. Gaiser, A. F. Garvie, Professors M. Gigante, E. W. Handley, Dr R. L.

PREFACE

Hunter, Professors R. Janko, H. D. Jocelyn, Dr E. Jenkinson, Professor R. Kassel, Dr P. Maas, Professor R. H. Martin, Dr J. Th. M. F. Pieters, M. Platnauer, Professors S. L. Radt, F. H. Sandbach, B. B. Shefton, Dr W. Stockert, T. H. Tarver, Professor T. B. L. Webster, N. G. Wilson and Professor G. Zuntz. I must not forget the help and encouragement that I have received from Pauline Hire and Caroline Murray at Cambridge University Press, and from my sub-editor Nigel Hope. I should like to thank Professors E. W. Handley and F. Williams for their assistance with proof-reading. The greatest debt, however, is owed to my family and above all my wife, to whom this work must have seemed a never-vanishing incubus, but they have had the grace not to show it. Without their support I should never have achieved the goal.

W. G. A.
Leeds 1994

ABBREVIATIONS AND
SELECT BIBLIOGRAPHY

1. *Periodicals.* The abbreviations are generally those prescribed by *L'Année Philologique.*

2. *Ancient texts.* Normally I use the abbreviations of LSJ[9] and the *Oxford Latin Dictionary*, but where these are condensed into incomprehensibility I follow the more expansive lead of *OCD*[2]. The following special points should be noted:

(i) Pl. = Plato, Plaut. = Plautus.

(ii) The frs. of Euripides are cited in the numeration of Nauck[2], other tragic frs. in that of *TrGF.*

(iii) The frs. of identified comic poets other than Menander are cited in the numeration of Kassel–Austin, with that of Kock appended in brackets (thus Alexis 103(98K) = fr. 103 Kassel–Austin, fr. 98 Kock). Anonymous fragments are numbered either as in Kock (book frs.) or as in C. Austin, *Comicorum graecorum fragmenta in papyris reperta* (Berlin and New York 1973) (papyrus frs.). The book frs. of Menander are numbered as in Körte–Thierfelder, *Menandri quae supersunt* 2 (Leipzig 1959[2]), the papyrus texts have the line-numberings of F. H. Sandbach's Oxford Classical Text (1990[2]).

(iv) Standard modern commentaries are referred to by the commentator's name only, e.g. 'Barrett on Eur. *Hipp.* 100' or 'Barrett, comm. on Eur. *Hipp.* p. 140'.

3. All three-figure dates are BC unless otherwise indicated.

4. The following abbreviations are used throughout this commentary:

André	J. André
Alimentation	*L'alimentation et la cuisine à Rome* (Paris 1961)
Lexique	*Lexique de termes de botanique en latin* (Paris 1956)
Oiseaux	*Les noms d'oiseaux en latin* (Paris 1967)
Audollent, *Defix.*	A. Audollent, *Defixionum tabellae, quotquot innotuerunt tam in graecis orientis quam in totius occidentis partibus praeter atticas in corpore inscriptionum atticarum editas* (Diss. Paris 1904)
Austin	C. Austin
CGFP	*Comicorum graecorum fragmenta in papyris reperta* (Berlin and New York 1973)
NFEP	*Nova fragmenta Euripidea in papyris reperta* (Berlin and New York 1968)
Bachmann, *Anecd.*	L. Bachmann, *Anecdota graeca* (Leipzig 1826)

Bailey, *CGF*   J. Bailey, *Comicorum graecorum fragmenta* (Cambridge 1840)
Bain, *Actors*   D. Bain, *Actors and Audience. A Study of Asides and Related
                       Conventions in Greek Drama* (Oxford 1977)
Baiter–Sauppe   J. G. Baiter and H. Sauppe, *Oratores Attici* (Zurich
                       1839–50)
Bayer   E. Bayer, *Demetrios Phalereus der Athener* (Stuttgart and
                       Berlin 1942, reprinted Darmstadt 1969)
Beazley   J. D. Beazley
  ABV   *Attic Black-Figure Vase-Painters* (Oxford 1956)
  *ARV*²   *Attic Red-Figure Vase-Painters*, 2nd ed. (Oxford 1963)
Bechtel   F. Bechtel
  Frauennamen   *Die Attischen Frauennamen* (Göttingen 1902)
  Personennamen   *Die historischen Personennamen des Griechischen bis zur
                       Kaiserzeit* (Halle 1917)
  Spitznamen   *Die einstämmigen männlichen Personennamen des Griechischen,
                       die aus Spitznamen hervorgegangen sind* (*Abh.* Göttingen
                       2.5, Berlin 1898)
Bekker, *Anecd.*   I. Bekker, *Anecdota graeca* 1–3 (Berlin 1814–21)
Bentley   R. Bentley
  Phalaris   *A Dissertation upon the Epistles of Phalaris. With an Answer
                       to the Objections of the Honourable Charles Boyle, Esquire,*
                       cited in the paginations of the London editions of 1699
                       and (edited by A. Dyce) 1836.
  Emend. Men. et   *Emendationes in Menandrum et Philemonem post Petrum
   Phil.*   Burmannum*, ed. A. Meineke, *Men. et Phil.* 437–561.
Bilabel, *Ops.*   F. Bilabel, *OΨAPTYTIKA und Verwandtes* (*SB* Heidel-
                       berg 23.1920)
Björck, *Alpha*   G. Björck, *Das Alpha Impurum und die tragische Kunst-
  Impurum*   sprache* (Uppsala 1950)
Blass–Debrunner–   F. Blass and A. Debrunner, *A Greek Grammar of the New
  Funk   Testament and Other Early Christian Literature*, translated
                       and revised by R. W. Funk from the 9th and 10th
                       German eds. (*Grammatik des neutestamentlichen Griechisch*)
                       (Cambridge and Chicago 1961)
Blaydes   F. H. M. Blaydes
  Adv.   *Adversaria in comicorum graecorum fragmenta* (Halle 1 =
                       1890, 2 = 1896)
  Anal.   *Analecta comica graeca* (Halle 1905)
  Misc. Crit.   *Miscellanea critica* (Halle 1907)
Blümner,   H. Blümner, *Technologie und Terminologie der Gewerbe und
  Technologie*   Künste bei Griechen und Römern* 1, 2nd ed. (Leipzig and
                       Berlin 1912)

Bothe   F. H. Bothe
   Griech. Kom.   *Die griechischen Komiker. Eine Beurteilung des neuesten Aufgabe ihrer Fragmenten* (Leipzig 1844)
   PCGF   *Poetarum comicorum graecorum fragmenta* (Paris 1855)
Breitenbach   H. Breitenbach, *De genere quodam titulorum comoediae atticae* (Diss. Basle 1908)
Bruhn, *Wortschatz*   C. Bruhn, *Über den Wortschatz des Menanders* (Diss. Kiel 1910, printed at Jena)
Buck–Petersen, *Reverse Index*   C. D. Buck and W. Petersen, *A Reverse Index of Greek Nouns and Adjectives arranged by Terminations with Brief Historical Introductions* (Chicago 1945)
CHCL   *The Cambridge History of Classical Literature, 1: Greek Literature*, ed. P. E. Easterling and B. M. W. Knox (Cambridge 1985)
CMG   *Corpus Medicorum Graecorum* (Leipzig 1908–)
CSHB   *Corpus scriptorum historiae Byzantinae: Editio emendatior et copiosior, consilio B. G. Niebuhrii instituta* (Bonn 1828–97)
Campbell, *Guide*   A. C. Campbell, *The Hamlyn Guide to the Flora and Fauna of the Mediterranean Sea* (London 1982)
Canter   Th. Canter
   Nov. Lect.   *Novarum lectionum libri quatuor* (Basle 1564)
   Paris MS   Paris, Bibliothèque Nationale, suppl. gr. 1013, containing conjectures by Canter and Scaliger; cf. Kassel–Austin, ii.xxiii
Casaubon, *Animadv.*   I. Casaubon, *Animadversionum in Athenaei Dipnosophistas libri XV*, 2nd ed. (Paris 1621)
Chantraine   P. Chantraine, *Dictionnaire étymologique de la langue grecque* (Paris 1 = 1968–70, 2 = 1974–80)
Charitonidis and others, *Mosaïques*   S. Charitonidis, L. Kahil, R. Ginouvès, *Les mosaïques de la maison du Ménandre à Mytilène* (*Antike Kunst* Beiheft 6, Berne 1970)
Cobet   C. G. Cobet
   NL   *Novae lectiones* (Leiden 1858)
   VL[2]   *Variae lectiones*, 2nd ed. (Leiden 1873)
Collitz, *GDI*   H. Collitz and others, *Sammlung der griechischen Dialekt-Inschriften* (Göttingen 1884–1915)
Coulon, *Essai*   V. Coulon, *Essai sur la méthode de la critique conjecturale appliquée au texte d'Aristophane* (Paris 1953)
CPG   See Leutsch–Schneidewin, *CPG*
Cramer, *Anecdota graeca*   J. A. Cramer, *Anecdota graeca e codicibus manuscriptis bibliothecarum Oxoniensium* (Oxford 1835)

Daléchamp, *Annot.* J. Daléchamp, *Annotationes et emendationes in Athenaeum* = pp. 705–811 of Casaubon's 2nd ed. of Athenaeus (Paris 1612), with *Adnotationes* on the title page but *Annota-* on the page headings

Dar.–Sag. C. V. Daremberg and E Saglio, edd., *Dictionnaire des antiquités grecques et romaines d'après les textes et les monuments* (Paris 1877–1919)

Davidson, *Seafood* A. Davidson, *Mediterranean Seafood*, 2nd ed. (Harmondsworth 1981)

Davies, *APF* J. K. Davies, *Athenian Propertied Families* (Oxford 1971)

Denniston, *GP* J. D. Denniston, *Greek Particles*, 2nd ed. (Oxford 1954)

Descroix J. Descroix, *Le trimètre iambique des iambographes à la comédie nouvelle* (Diss. Paris 1931, printed at Macon)

Desrousseaux, A. M. Desrousseaux, *Observations critiques sur les livres*
Obs. *III et IV d'Athénée* (Paris 1942)

Diels–Kranz H. Diels, *Die Fragmente der Vorsokratiker*, 6th ed. revised by W. Kranz (Berlin 1951–2)

Diggle, *Studies* J. Diggle, *Studies on the Text of Euripides* (Oxford 1981)

Dittenberger W. Dittenberger
OGIS *Orientis graeci inscriptiones selectae* (Leipzig 1903–5)
SIG[3] *Sylloge inscriptionum graecarum*, 3rd ed. (Leipzig 1915–24)

Dobree, *Adv.* P. P. Dobree, *Adversaria*, ed. J. Scholefield (Cambridge 1831–3)

Dohm, *Mageiros* H. Dohm, *Mageiros* (*Zetemata* 32, Munich 1964)

Dover, *GPM* Sir Kenneth Dover, *Greek Popular Morality in the Time of Plato and Aristotle* (Oxford 1974)

Durham, D. B. Durham, *The Vocabulary of Menander, Considered in*
Vocabulary *its Relation to the Koine* (Diss. Princeton 1913)

EAA *Enciclopedia dell'arte antica classica e orientale* (Rome 1958–84)

Edmonds J. M. Edmonds, *The Fragments of Attic Comedy* (Leiden 1957, 1959, 1961)

Emperius A. Emperius, *Opuscula philologica et historica*, ed. F. G. Schneidewin (Göttingen 1847)

Enk, *Handboek* P. J. Enk, *Handboek der latijnse letterkunde* (Zutphen 1 = 1928, 2 = 1937)

Erfurdt, *Obs.* C. G. A. Erfurdt, *Observationes criticae maxime in Athenaei Deipnosophistas, Königsberger Archiv für Philosophie, Theologie, Sprachkunst und Geschichte* 1 (1812) 424–72

FGrH F. Jacoby, *Die Fragmente der griechischen Historiker* (Berlin 1923–30, Leiden 1940–58)

FHG C. and Th. Müller, *Fragmenta historicorum graecorum* (Paris 1841–70)

LIST OF ABBREVIATIONS AND SELECT BIBLIOGRAPHY

Fick–Bechtel A. Fick, *Die griechischen Personennamen*, 2nd ed. revised by F. Bechtel and A. Fick (Göttingen 1894)

Flores *La critica testuale greco-latina, oggi: metodi e problemi*, ed. E. Flores (Rome 1981)

Forbes, *Technology* R. J. Forbes, *Studies in Ancient Technology* (Leiden) 1 1955^1 1964^2, 2 1955^1 1965^2, 3 1955^1 1965^2, 4 1956^1 1964^2, 5 1957^1 1966^2, 6 1958^1 1966^2, 7 1963^1 1966^2, 8 1964^1 1971^2, 9 1964^1 1972^2)

Fraenkel E. Fraenkel

Beob. *Beobachtungen zu Aristophanes* (Rome 1962)

EP *Elementi Plautini in Plauto* (Florence 1960)

Kl. Beitr. *Kleine Beiträge zur klassischen Philologie* (Rome 1964)

MNC *De media et nova comoedia quaestiones selectae* (Diss. Göttingen 1912)

Frisk H. Frisk, *Griechisches etymologisches Wörterbuch* (Heidelberg 1 = 1954–60, 2 = 1961–70)

Gil L. Gil, *Estudios Clásicos* 14 (1970) 311–45

Gildersleeve, *Syntax* B. L. Gildersleeve (with C. W. E. Miller), *Syntax of Classical Greek* (New York, Cincinnati and Chicago 1 = 1900, 2 = 1911)

Göbel, *Ethnica* M. Göbel, *Ethnica* (Diss. Wroclaw 1915)

Gomme–Sandbach A. W. Gomme and F. H. Sandbach, *Menander: A Commentary* (Oxford 1973)

Goodwin, *MT* W. W. Goodwin, *Syntax of the Moods and Tenses of the Greek Verb*, 2nd ed. (London 1889)

Grotius H. Grotius

Dict. Poet. *Dicta poetarum quae apud Ioannem Stobaeum exstant* (Paris 1623)

Exc. *Excerpta ex tragoediis et comoediis graecis* (Paris 1626)

Gruter, *Lampas* J. Gruter, *Lampas sive fax artium liberalium* (Frankfurt 1602–34)

Hähnle A. Hähnle, ΓΝΩΡΙΣΜΑΤΑ (Diss. Tübingen 1929)

Hehn, *Kulturpflanzen* V. Hehn, *Kulturpflanzen und Haustiere in ihrem Übergang aus Asien nach Griechenland und Italien sowie in das übrige Europa*, 8th ed. (Berlin 1911)

Heimsoeth F. Heimsoeth

Comm. Crit. *Commentatio critica de diversa diversorum mendorum emendatione* (Index schol. Bonn 1866)

Comm. Alt. *De diversa diversorum mendorum emendatione commentatio altera* (Index Schol. Bonn 1867)

Hermann–Blümner, *Privatalterthümer* K. F. Hermann, *Lehrbuch der griechischen Privatalterthümer*, 3rd ed. revised by H. Blümner (Freiburg and Tübingen 1882)

Hertel	J. Hertel, *Vetustissimorum et sapientissimorum comicorum quinquaginta, quorum opera integra non extant, sententiae quae supersunt, graece et latine collectae* (Basle 1560)
Herwerden	H. van Herwerden
Anal. Crit.	*Analecta critica ad Thucydidem, Lysiam, Sophoclem, Aristophanem, et comicorum graecorum fragmenta* (Utrecht 1868)
Coll. Crit.	*Collectanea critica, epicritica, exegetica, sive Addenda ad Theodori Kockii opus comicorum atticorum fragmenta* (Leiden 1903)
NAC	*Nova addenda critica ad Meinekii opus, quod inscribitur fragmenta comicorum graecorum* (Leiden 1864)
Obs. Crit.	*Observationes criticae in fragmenta comicorum graecorum* (Diss. Leiden 1855)
Hirschig	G. A. Hirschig
Annot.	*Annotationes criticae* (Utrecht 1849)
Diss.	*Dissertatio ... qua continentur selecta Alexidis comici fragmenta* (Diss. Leiden 1840)
Hunter	R. L. Hunter, *Eubulus: The Fragments* (Cambridge 1983)
Jackson, *Marg. Scaen.*	J. Jackson, *Marginalia Scaenica* (Oxford 1955)
Jacobi	H. Jacobi in Meineke, 5.v–ccclxxvi
Jacobs	F. Jacobs
Addit.	*Additamenta animadversionum in Athenaei Deipnosophistas* (Jena 1809)
Spic.	*Spicilegium observationum et emendationum ad novissimam Athenaei editionem* (Altenburg 1805)
VS	*Vermischte Schriften* (Leipzig 4 = 1830)
Jaeger, *Paideia*	W. W. Jaeger, *Paideia: The Ideals of Greek Culture*, translated by G. Highet (Oxford 1939–45)
Kaehler, *Annot.*	O. Kaehler, *Annotationes ad comicos graecos, Wissenschaftliche Beilage zum Jahresberichte des Weimarischen Gymnasiums von 1902* (Weimar 1901)
Kaibel, *CGF*	G. Kaibel, *Comicorum graecorum fragmenta* 1.1 (Berlin 1899, reprinted with addenda 1958)
Kann, *De iteratis*	S. Kann, *De iteratis apud poetas antiquae et mediae comoediae atticae* (Diss. Giessen 1909)
Kassel–Austin	R. Kassel and C. Austin, *Poetae comici graeci* (Berlin and New York: 2 = 1991, 3.2 = 1984, 4 = 1983, 5 = 1986, 7 = 1989)
Kirchner, *PA*	J. Kirchner, *Prosopographia attica* (Berlin 1901–3)
K (or Kock)	T. Kock, *Comicorum atticorum fragmenta* (Leipzig 1880–8)

xvi

LIST OF ABBREVIATIONS AND SELECT BIBLIOGRAPHY

Körte–Thierfelder   A. Körte, *Menandri quae supersunt, pars altera*, posthumously edited by A. Thierfelder, 2nd ed. (Leipzig 1959)

K.B.   R. Kühner, *Ausführliche Grammatik der griechischen Sprache: I Elementar- und Formenlehre*, 3rd ed. by F. Blass (Hanover and Leipzig 1890–2)

K.G.   R. Kühner, *Ausführliche Grammatik der griechischen Sprache: II Satzlehre*, 3rd ed. by B. Gerth (Hanover and Leipzig 1898–1904)

Lang–Crosby,   M. Lang and M. Crosby, *The Athenian Agora, X:*
Agora x   *Weights, Measures and Tokens* (Princeton 1964)

Legrand, *NGC*   P. E. Legrand, *The New Greek Comedy*, translated by J. Loeb (London and New York 1917)

Leo, *Plaut. Forsch.*[2]   F. Leo, *Plautinische Forschungen*, 2nd ed. (Berlin 1912)

Leopardus, *Emend.*   P. Leopardus, *Emendationum et miscellaneorum libri viginti* (1 Antwerp 1568, 2 Frankfurt 1604)

Lesky, *HGL*   A. Lesky, *A History of Greek Literature*, 2nd ed. translated by J. Willis and C. de Heer (London 1966)

Leutsch–   E. Leutsch and F. G. Schneidewin, *Corpus paroemiogra-*
Schneidewin,   *phorum graecorum* (Göttingen 1 = 1839, 2 = 1851)
CPG

Lobeck   C. A. Lobeck
Paralipomena   *Paralipomena grammaticae graecae* (Leipzig 1837)
Prol. Path.   *Pathologiae sermonis graeci prolegomena* (Leipzig 1843)

LSJ   H. G. Liddell and R. Scott, *A Greek–English Lexicon*, 9th ed. by Sir Henry Stuart Jones (Oxford 1940) and *A Supplement*, ed. E. A. Barber (Oxford 1968)

Madvig, *Adv. Crit.*   J. N. Madvig, *Adversaria critica ad scriptores graecos et latinos* (Copenhagen 1 = 1871, 3 = 1884)

Mayser   E. Mayser, *Grammatik der griechischen Papyri aus der Ptolemäerzeit* (Berlin 1926–38)

Mayser–Schmoll   Mayser I.1, *Einleitung und Lautlehre*, 2nd ed. revised by H. Schmoll (Berlin 1970)

Meineke   A. Meineke, *Fragmenta comicorum graecorum* (Berlin 1839–57)
Anal. Crit.   *Analecta critica ad Athenaei Deipnosophistas* (Leipzig 1867)
Cur. Crit.   *Curae criticae in comicorum fragmenta ab Athenaeo servata* (Berlin 1814)
ed. min.   *Fragmenta comicorum graecorum, editio minor* (Berlin 1847)
FCG   See Meineke
Men. et Phil.   *Menandri et Philemonis reliquiae* (Berlin 1823)
Quaest. Men.   *Quaestionum Menandrearum specimen primum* (Berlin 1818)

xvii

Quaest. Scen.	*Quaestionum scenicarum specimen tertium* (Berlin 1830)
Meisterhans–Schwyzer	K. Meisterhans, *Grammatik der attischen Inschriften*, 3rd ed. by E. Schwyzer (Berlin 1900)
Mette	H. J. Mette, *Urkunden dramatischer Aufführungen in Griechenland* (Berlin and New York 1977)
MGR	*Mélanges Gréco–Romaines tirés du Bulletin de l'Académie Impériale des Sciences de St.-Pétersbourg*
Miller, *Mélanges*	E. Miller, *Mélanges de littérature grecque* (Paris 1868)
G. Morel	G. Morel, *Ex veterum comicorum graecorum fabulis, quae integrae non extant, sententiae* (Paris 1553)
Nauck²	A. Nauck, *Tragicorum graecorum fragmenta*, 2nd ed. (Leipzig 1889)
Nesselrath	H.-G. Nesselrath
LP	*Lukians Parasitendialog* (Berlin and New York 1985)
MK	*Die attische Mittlere Komödie* (Berlin and New York 1990)
OGIS	W. Dittenberger, *Orientis graeci inscriptiones selectae* (Leipzig 1 = 1903, 2 = 1905)
Pack	R. A. Pack, *The Greek and Latin Literary Texts from Greco–Roman Egypt*, 2nd ed. (Ann Arbor 1965)
Page	D. L. Page
FGE	*Further Greek Epigrams* (Cambridge 1984)
GLP	*Greek Literary Papyri* = *Select Papyri III: Literary Papyri, Poetry* (London and Cambridge, Mass. 1941)
PMG	*Poetae melici graeci* (Oxford 1962)
Palombi–Santorelli	A. Palombi and M. Santorelli, *Gli animali commestibili dei mari d'Italia*, 2nd ed. (Milan 1960)
Peppink, *Observ.*	S. P. Peppink, *Observationes in Athenaei Deipnosophistas* (Leiden 1936)
Pickard-Cambridge	Sir Arthur Pickard-Cambridge
*DFA*²	*The Dramatic Festivals of Athens*, 2nd ed. revised by J. Gould and D. M. Lewis (Oxford 1968, reprinted with select addenda 1988)
*DTC*¹ *DTC*²	*Dithyramb Tragedy and Comedy*, 1st ed. (Oxford 1927); 2nd ed. revised by T. B. L. Webster (Oxford 1962)
GCP	*Select Fragments of the Greek Comic Poets* (Oxford 1900)
TDA	*The Theatre of Dionysus in Athens* (Oxford 1946)
Porson	R. Porson
Adv.	*Adversaria* (Cambridge 1812)
Misc.	*Tracts and Miscellaneous Criticisms of the late Richard Porson Esq.*, ed. T. Kidd (London 1815)

Powell, *Coll. Alex.* J. U. Powell, *Collectanea Alexandrina: Reliquiae minores poetarum graecorum aetatis Ptolemaicae 323–146 A.C.* (Oxford 1925)

Preisigke, F. Preisigke, *Wörterbuch der griechischen Papyruskunden*
Wörterbuch (ed. E. Kiessling 1–3 Berlin 1923–31, 4.1–4 Marburg 1944–71, *Supplement* 1 Amsterdam 1971, ed. H.-A. Rupprecht and A. Jördens *Supplement* 2 Wiesbaden 1991)

Preller–Robert, L. Preller and C. Robert, *Griechische Mythologie* I⁴
GM (1 and 2: Berlin 1894)

RAC *Reallexikon für Antike und Christentum* (Stuttgart 1950–)

Rankin, E. M. Rankin, *The Role of the* ΜΑΓΕΙΡΟΙ *in the Life of the*
ΜΑΓΕΙΡΟΙ *Ancient Greeks* (Chicago 1907)

RE *Real-Encyclopädie der classischen Altertumswissenschaft* (Stuttgart and Munich 1893–1978),

Suppl. with *Supplementbände* I–XV (Stuttgart and Munich 1903–78)

Rehdantz–Blass, C. Rehdantz, *Demosthenes' neun Philippische Reden,* II.2:
Index *Indices,* 4th ed. revised by F. Blass (Leipzig 1886)

Ribbeck O. Ribbeck, *CRF³*

Alazon *Alazon. Ein Beitrag zur antiken Ethologie* (Leipzig 1882)

CRF³ *Scaenicae romanorum poesis fragmenta,* II: *Comicorum romanorum praeter Plautum et Syri quae feruntur sententias fragmenta,* 3rd ed. (Leipzig 1898)

Kolax *Kolax. Eine ethologische Studie (Abh.* Leipzig 9.1, 1883)

TRF³ *Scaenicae romanorum poesis fragmenta,* I: *Tragicorum romanorum fragmenta,* 3rd ed. (Leipzig 1897)

Richards, *AO* H. Richards, *Aristophanes and Others* (London 1909)

Richter–Milne, G. M. A. Richter and M. J. Milne, *Shapes and Names of*
Shapes *Athenian Vases* (New York 1935; reprinted Washington 1973)

Robert, *GH* C. Robert, *Griechische Heldensage* (Berlin 1 1920, 2 1921, 3.1 1921, 3.2.1, 3.2.2 1926)

Roscher W. H. Roscher, ed., *Ausführliches Lexikon der griechischen und römischen Mythologie* (Leipzig 1884–1937)

Rutherford, *NP* W. G. Rutherford, *The New Phrynichus* (London 1881)

Saint-Denis, E. de Saint-Denis, *Le vocabulaire des animaux marins en*
Vocabulaire *latin classique* (Paris 1947)

Sandbach See Gomme–Sandbach

Scaliger   See Canter, Paris MS

Schanz–Hosius   M. Schanz, *Geschichte der römischen Literatur* (Munich I and II 4th ed. revised by C. Hosius 1927–35, III 3rd ed. revised by C. Hosius and G. Krüger 1922, IV.1 2nd ed. 1914, IV.2 with C. Hosius and G. Krüger 1920)

Schmid–Stählin   W. Schmid, *Geschichte der griechischen Literatur* (Munich I.i–v 1929–48, II.i–ii with the help of O. Stählin 1920–4)

Schmidt, *Krit. Stud.*   F. W. Schmidt, *Kritische Studien zu den griechischen Dramatikern*, I-III (Berlin 1886–7)

Schulze   W. Schulze

Kl. Schr.   *Kleine Schriften* (Berlin 1934)

QE   *Quaestiones epicae* (Gütersloh 1892)

Schweighaeuser, *Animadv.*   J. Schweighaeuser, *Animadversiones in Athenaei Deipnosophistas* (Strasbourg 1801–7)

Schwyzer   E. Schwyzer, *Griechische Grammatik* (Munich 1939–50)

SH   H. Lloyd-Jones and P. Parsons, *Supplementum Hellenisticum* (London and New York 1983)

Sicking, *Annotationes*   L. J. Sicking, *Annotationes ad Antiatticistam* (Diss. Amsterdam 1883)

SIG[3]   W. Dittenberger, *Sylloge inscriptionum graecarum*, 3rd ed. (Leipzig 1915 1, 1917 2, 1920 3, 1924 4, with revisions by F. Hiller von Gaertringen and others)

Sittl, *Gebärden*   C. Sittl, *Die Gebärden der Griechen und Römer* (Leipzig 1890)

Sparkes–Talcott, *Agora* XII   B. A. Sparkes and L. Talcott, *The Athenian Agora, XII: Black and Plain Pottery* (Princeton 1970)

Stefanis   'Ι. 'Ε. Στεφανής, Διονυσιακοὶ Τεχνῖται (Heraklion 1988)

Strömberg   R. Strömberg

Fischnamen   *Studien zur Etymologie und Bildung der griechischen Fischnamen* (Göteborg 1943)

Greek Proverbs   *Greek Proverbs: A Collection of Proverbs and Proverbial Phrases which are not Listed by the Ancient and Byzantine Paroemiographers* (Göteborg 1954)

TGL   *Thesaurus graecae linguae* ed. W. and L. Dindorf and others (Paris 1831–65)

Thompson   D'A. W. Thompson

Birds[2]   *A Glossary of Greek Birds*, 2nd ed. (London and Oxford 1936)

Fishes   *A Glossary of Greek Fishes* (London 1947)

Thompson–Wycherley, *Agora* XIV   H. A. Thompson and R. E. Wycherley, *The Athenian Agora, XIV: The History, Shape and Uses of an Ancient City Center* (Princeton N.J. 1972)

Threatte	L. Threatte, *The Grammar of Attic Inscriptions*, 1: *Phonology* (Berlin and New York 1980)
Thumb–Kieckers	A. Thumb, *Handbuch der griechischen Dialekte*, 2nd ed.
Thumb–Scherer	(Heidelberg 1 revised E. Kieckers 1932, 11 A. Scherer 1959)
Trendall, *Phlyax Vases*	A. D. Trendall, *Phlyax Vases*, 2nd ed. (*BICS Suppl.* 19, 1967)
TrGF	B. Snell, R. Kannicht, S. Radt, *Tragicorum graecorum fragmenta* (Göttingen 1971–)
Tsirimbas, *Sprichwörter*	D. A. Tsirimbas, *Sprichwörter und sprichwörtliche Redensarten bei den Epistolographen der zweiten Sophistik* (Diss. Munich 1936)
Usener, *Kl. Schr.*	H. Usener, *Kleine Schriften* (Leipzig and Berlin 1912–14)
Veitch, *Greek Verbs*[4]	W. Veitch, *Greek Verbs Irregular and Defective*, 4th ed. (Oxford 1887)
Wakefield, *Silv. Crit.*	G. Wakefield, *Silva critica, sive in auctores sacros profanosque commentarius philologus* (Cambridge and London 1789–95)
Walde–Hofmann	A. Walde, *Lateinisches etymologisches Wörterbuch*, 3rd ed. revised by J. B. Hofmann (Heidelberg 1938 1, 1954 2)
Webster	T. B. L. Webster
IM	*An Introduction to Menander* (Manchester 1974)
MINC	*Monuments Illustrating New Comedy*, 1st ed. (*BICS Suppl.* 11, 1961), 2nd ed. (*BICS Suppl.* 24, 1969
MIOMC	*Monuments Illustrating Old and Middle Comedy*, 3rd ed., revised by J. R. Green (*BICS Suppl.* 39, 1978)
SLGC	*Studies in Later Greek Comedy*, 2nd ed. (Manchester 1970)
SM	*Studies in Menander*, 2nd ed. (Manchester 1960)
Wehrli, *Motivstudien*	F. Wehrli, *Motivstudien zur griechischen Komödie* (Leipzig 1936)
West, *Greek Metre*	M. L. West, *Greek Metre* (Oxford 1982)
Wilamowitz	U. von Wilamowitz-Moellendorf
Glaube	*Der Glaube der Hellenen* (Berlin 1 = 1931, 2 = 1932)
Kl. Schr.	*Kleine Schriften* (Berlin 1935–69)
Schiedsg.	*Menander, Das Schiedsgericht* (Berlin 1925)
Wilcken, *UPZ*	U. Wilcken, *Urkunden der ptolemäischer Zeit* (Berlin and Leipzig 1927–57)
Wycherley, *Agora* iii	R. E. Wycherley, *The Athenian Agora*, iii: *Literary and Epigraphical Testimonia* (Princeton N.J. 1957)

INTRODUCTION

I ALEXIS' CAREER

The more substantial discussions – but of unequal value – include Meineke 1.374ff., 3.382ff., Hirschig, *Diss.* 5f., Kock 2.297ff., Th. Bergk, *Griechische Literaturgeschichte* 4 (Berlin 1887) 150ff., G. Kaibel in *RE* s.v. *Alexis* 9, 1468.22ff., E. Capps in *RE Suppl.* 1 s.v. 56.59ff. and *AJP* 21 (1900) 59ff., Kirchner, *PA* 1.39f. no. 549, A. Olivieri, *Dioniso* 7 (1939) 279ff., Webster, *SLGC* index s.v. *Alexis* 252[1] = 272[2] and *CQ* 2 (1952) 16ff., G. Schiassi, *RFIC* 79 (1951) 222, W. G. Arnott, *CQ* 5 (1955) 211 n. 2, *Rh. Mus.* 102 (1959) 255ff., *OCD*[2] 44f. s.v. *Alexis* and *Studi di filologia classica in onore di Giusto Monaco* 1 (Palermo 1991) 327ff., Edmonds 2.372ff., R. Argenio, *Riv. Stud. Class.* 12 (1964) 237ff., 13 (1965) 5ff., Gil 311ff., C. Austin, *ZPE* 14 (1974) 201, W. Kraus in *Der Kleine Pauly* s.v. *Alexis* 254.57ff., M. Gigante in G. Pugliese Carratelli and others, *Megale Hellas: Storia e civiltà della Magna Grecia* (Milan 1983) 602ff., Nesselrath, *MK* 50 n. 52, 58f., 198f. and index 377, Kassel–Austin 2.21ff. (*testimonia*).

(i) *Testimonia*

The *testimonia* are given (up to 16) in the numbering of Kassel–Austin. An asterisk denotes doubt whether the reference is to the comic poet.

1 *Suda* α 1138 Adler Ἄλεξις Θούριος, ὅστις πρότερον Σύβαρις ἐκαλεῖτο, κωμικός, ἐδίδαξε δράματα σμε΄ (= 245)· γέγονε δὲ πάτρως Μενάνδρου τοῦ κωμικοῦ (*test.* 5 Körte–Thierfelder): {ἔσχε δὲ υἱὸν Στέφανον, καὶ αὐτὸν κωμικόν} (*test.* 1 Kassel–Austin, cf. 7.614).

ἔσχε – κωμικόν was deleted by H. Flach, *Hesychii Milesii Onomatologi quae supersunt* (1882) 9.16 after H. F. Clinton, *Fasti Hellenici* 2 (Oxford 1834) 155; see below (1.iii).

3

The *Suda* contains 86 entries[1] devoted to named drama-tists who produced comedies on the Athenian stage. They reveal a structure, patterns of phrasing and types of infor-mation which suggest a common source (cf. D. Volkmann, *De Suidae biographicis quaestiones selectae* (Bonn 1841) 1ff., F. Leo, *Die griechisch–römische Biographie nach ihrer literarischen Form* (Leipzig 1901) 31f., A. Adler in *RE* s.v. *Suidas* 1, 706.42ff., 707.21ff.). Four of these recurrent elements can be identified in the entry for Alexis.

(a) The name is accompanied by an adjective indicating place of origin (elsewhere most often Athens, but cf. Camirus or Colophon for Anaxandrides, Cius or Smyrna or Rhodes for Antiphanes, Gela for one of the two Apollodori, Thasos for Hegemon, Syracuse for Philemon, Cassandrea for Posidippus, Sicyon or Thebes for Sophilus).

(b) The poet is normally identified as κωμικός, but for a number of cases that classification is subdivided according to the tripartite division of comedy that emerged in Hellenistic scholarship (cf. Hunter 4ff., Nesselrath, *MK* 1ff.); thus 16 dramatists are assigned to Old Comedy, 9 to Middle, 4 to New and 1 (Eubulus) 'on the boundary between Middle and Old'.

(c) γέγονε is one of several words (γεγονώς, ἤκμαζε/-ασεν, ἦν, σύγχρονος) used to indicate *floruit* (R. Bentley, *Phalaris* 56 (London 1699) = 1.123 (Dyce, London 1836), E. Rohde, *Rh. Mus.* 33 (1878) 161ff., 638f., 34 (1879) 620ff. = *Kleine Schriften* 1 (Tübingen and Leipzig 1901) 114ff., J. T. Allen, *California Publications in Classical Philology* 11(6) (1932) 144f., R. Pfeiffer, *History of Classical Scholarship* 1 (Oxford 1968) 256, W. G. Arnott, *Studi Monaco* 329).

---

[1] They are conveniently assembled by A. Westermann, ΒΙΟΓΡΑΦΟΙ: *Vitarum scriptores graeci minores* (Brunswick 1845) 160f. and 164ff., although the text needs to be checked against that in Adler's edition of the *Suda*.

4

(d) In the entries for the major dramatists the number of plays that each wrote/produced is added; here γράφω and ποιῶ are the verbs commonly used, but for διδάσκω see also the entries for Eubulus, Hermippus, Pherecrates, the younger Philemon, Theopompus.

2 Anon. *De comoedia* (II.12, 17 p. 9 Kaibel, III p. 10 Koster) τῆς μὲν οὖν μέσης κωμῳδίας εἰσὶ ποιηταὶ νζ´ (57) ... τούτων δὲ ἀξιολογώτατοι Ἀντιφάνης καὶ (?) Ἄλεξις (so Dobree, *Adv.* 2.159, Meineke, *Quaest. Scen.*, *Specimen III* 51: στέφανος MSS, note that Ἀντιφάνης μὲν οὖν Στεφάνου directly follows). ... Μένανδρος δὲ (*test.* 2 Körte–Thierfelder) Διοπείθους υἱὸς Ἀθηναῖος, λαμπρὸς καὶ βίῳ καὶ γένει, συνδιατρίψας δὲ τὰ πολλὰ Ἀλέξιδι ὑπὸ τούτου δοκεῖ παιδευθῆναι.

3 *Canones comicorum* ed. O. Kroehnert in *Canonesne poetarum scriptorum artificum per antiquitatem fuerunt?* (Diss. Königsberg 1897), catalogue M p. 6 = C p. 12 κωμῳδοποιοὶ ... μέσης κωμῳδίας β´· Ἀντιφάνης (*test.* 3 Kassel–Austin), Ἄλεξις Θούριος (ἀλεξιθουριος or ἀλφιθ- MSS).

4 Plut. *Mor.* 420d (opposing the Epicurean view ὡς οὐ δυνατόν ἐστι φαύλους καὶ ἁμαρτητικοὺς ὄντας μακαρίους καὶ μακραίωνας εἶναι) οὕτω γὰρ Ἐπίκουρός τε χείρων Γοργίου φανεῖται τοῦ σοφιστοῦ καὶ Μητρόδωρος Ἀλέξιδος τοῦ κωμῳδοποιοῦ· διπλάσιον γὰρ ἔζησε Μητροδώρου. According to Diog. Laert. 10.23 φασὶ δὲ (sc. Μητρόδ-ωρον) ... τελευτῆσαι πεντηκοστὸν τρίτον ἔτος ἄγοντα.

5 Plut. *Mor.* 785b Φιλήμονα δὲ τὸν κωμικὸν (*test.* 8 Kassel–Austin) καὶ Ἄλεξιν ἐπὶ τῆς σκηνῆς ἀγωνιζομένους καὶ στεφανουμένους ὁ θάνατος κατέλαβε.

6 *IG* ii².2318.278 = 1 col. 14.64 Mette (list of victors, Dionysia 347 BC)

Ἄ]λεξις ἐδ[ίδασκε

7 *IG* ii². 2322.92 = III B 1 col. 3.5 Mette (list of comedies, either Dionysia or Lenaea, date uncertain)

INTRODUCTION

"Αλεξις δε[ύ:(τερος)
ὑπε:(κρίνετο) Καλλ[

Supplemented by A. Wilhelm, *Urkunden dramatischer Aufführungen in Athen* (Vienna 1906) 42. For the actor Call-, see no. 268 O'Connor, 1320 Stefanis.

8 *IG* ii².2325.150 = v c i col. 3.11 Mette (list of victors and their number of victories at the Lenaea)

"Αλεξις | | [

In acrophonic notation for numbers a break on the Attic inscription after | | indicates that Alexis won 2, 3 or 4 victories at the Lenaea.

*9 *IG Urbis Romae* 222 L. Moretti (Rome 1968) = vi a 8 Mette (victories of comic poets)

1   ]μουσ[
        'Ε]πιδαυρ[
        ]σην λι[
4   ]ωι 'Αλεξ[

2 'Ε]πιδαυρ[ίωι is the obvious supplement, but this need not refer to Alexis' play (see introduction to 'Επιδαύριος)   3 Λή[ναια Moretti   4 "Αλεξ[ις or 'Αλέξ[ανδρος (*test.* *5 Kassel–Austin) Moretti

*10 *Marmor Parium, FGrH* 239 a 78 ἀφ' οὗ [* * * 'Αθήνησιν] ἐνίκησεν, ἔτη ΓᐩΔΔΔΔΙΙΙ, ἄρχοντος 'Αθήνησιν 'Αγαθοκλέους (356 bc)

E. Capps, *AJP* 21 (1900) 60 filled the gap with ἀφ' οὗ ['Αλεξις 'Αθήνησιν] ἐνίκησεν, sc. gained his first victory in Athens, but although the date 356 would be conceivable for Alexis (cf. on *test.* 8 above), many other names could be supplied with equal plausibility. See F. Jacoby, comm. *ad loc.*, 2D (Berlin 1930) p. 698.

11 Aulus Gellius 2.23.1 *comoedias lectitamus nostrorum poetarum sumptas ac uersas de Graecis Menandro aut Posidippo* (*test.* 4

Kassel–Austin) *aut Apollodoro* (Car., *test.* 4 Kassel–Austin) *aut Alexide et quibusdam item aliis comicis.*

Alexis' Δημήτριος seems to have been adapted by Turpilius' *Demetrius*, Καρχηδόνιος by Plaut. *Poen.*, perhaps his Λέβης by Plaut. *Aul.*; attempts have also been made to link Alexis' Ἐπιστολή, Συρακόσιος and Φυγάς with plays by Caecilius, Θηβαῖοι with Plaut. *Capt.*, Ψευδόμενος with Plaut. *Pseud.* and an unidentified play with Plaut. *MG*; see introductions to the Alexis titles, Appendix I, and section I.vi of the general introduction.

12 Ath. 8.344c καὶ Ἄλεξις δ' ὁ ποιητὴς ἦν ὀψοφάγος, ὡς ὁ Σάμιός φησι Λυγκεύς· καὶ σκωπτόμενος ὑπό τινων σπερμολόγων εἰς ὀψοφαγίαν ἐρομένων τε ἐκείνων τί ἂν ἥδιστα φάγοι, ὁ Ἄλεξις "σπερμολόγους" ἔφη "πεφρυγμένους". Cf. H. Wankel on Dem. 18.127 pp. 677f. The joke plays on two meanings of σπερμολόγος: 'gossip' (LSJ s.v. III) and a seed-eating bird, including rook (*Corvus frugilegus*: κολοιῶδες ζῷον Hesych. s.v., cf. Thompson, *Birds*² 265f.) and possibly other species.

13 Ath. 2.59f Ἄλεξις ὁ χαρίεις citing fr. 263(261K).

Athenaeus normally adds to the names of cited authors only tags of identification (place of origin, e.g. Callixeinus ὁ Ῥόδιος 5.196a, Xanthus ὁ Λυδός 8.346e; profession, e.g. Aristoxenus ὁ μουσικός 12.545a, Calliades ὁ κωμικός 13.577c, Menippus ὁ κυνικός 14.664e), but he occasionally varies the practice by adding a laudatory adjective or phrase (e.g. Antiphanes ὁ χαρίεις 1.27d, ὁ ἡδύς 4.156c, ὁ ἥδιστος 4.161e, 14.622f, Agathon ὁ καλός 5.185a, Menander ὁ καλός 8.364d, Homer ὁ τῶν ποιητῶν βασιλεύς 2.40a, Plato the philosopher ὁ ἱερώτατος 15.670f). Cf. Bergk 4.152 n. 104.

*14 Diog. Laert. 3.31 (citing 'Aristippus Περὶ παλαιᾶς τρυφῆς' 4 on the boys loved by Plato: a 3rd-century-BC forgery, cf. *FHG* 2.79, G. Giannantoni, *I Cirenaici* (Florence 1958) 59f.) ἀλλὰ καὶ Ἀλέξιδος, φασίν, ἐρασθεὶς καὶ Φαίδρου ...τοῦτον ἐποίησε τὸν τρόπον (= *Anth. Pal.* 7.100, Apuleius, *Apologia* 10)·

7

1 νῦν, ὅτε μηδὲν Ἄλεξις ὅσον μόνον εἴφ' ὅτι καλός,
     ὦπται καὶ πάντῃ πᾶς τις ἐπιστρέφεται.
     θυμέ, τί μηνύεις κυσὶν ὀστέον; εἶτ' ἀνιήσῃ
4   ὕστερον; οὐχ οὕτω Φαῖδρον ἀπωλέσαμεν;

2 πᾶς τις ἐπιστρέφεται Diog. Laert., πᾶσι πὲριβλέπεται *Anth.*
Pal., Apul.   3 ἀνιήσῃ H. Stephanus: -σει Apul., -σεις Diog., *Anth. Pal.*

The attribution to Plato is accepted by Wilamowitz,
Platon 1 (Berlin 1920²) 362; considered doubtful by
J. Geffcken, *Griechische Epigramme* (Heidelberg 1916) 32,
R. Lagerborg, *Die platonische Liebe* (Leipzig 1926) 75,
C. Ritter, *Platonische Liebe* (Tübingen 1931) 71, 79; and
totally rejected by R. Reitzenstein, *Nachr. Gött.* (1921) 60,
W. Ludwig, *GRBS* 4 (1963) 69ff., D. L. Page, *Further Greek
Epigrams* (Cambridge 1981) 164f. Cf. also H. Leisegang in
RE s.v. *Platon* 1, 2537.4ff. and J. M. Raines, *TAPA* 77 (1946)
85. Page's summing-up is admirable:

Diogenes Laertius, in the paragraph preceding his quotation of the
pseudo-Platonic epigrams ... gives the text of two passages concerning
Plato from the Comic poet Alexis, and it is highly probable that Diogenes
identified 'Alexis' in this epigram with that poet; it is certain that he
identified 'Phaedrus' with the pupil of Socrates who appears as a young
man in the *Symposium* and in the dialogue named after him. He was surely
right; and, if so, it follows that the epigram is a deliberate forgery.
Phaedrus was at least twenty years older than Plato, and cannot possibly
have been his 'boy'; when Alexis was eighteen,[1] Plato was seventy-three.
The author has chosen names connected with Plato in one way or
another, without considering whether those names are appropriate to his
subject.

15 Stob. *Anth.* 4.50b.83 (5. p. 1049 Hense, MSS SMA:
also *Gnomologium Vindobonense* no. 36 (C. Wachsmuth in
Festschrift zur Begrüssung der in Karlsruhe tagenden XXXVI.

---

[1] Although this calculation ignores the '*c.*' prefixed to the birth dates
   suggested for Alexis in my *OCD²* entry, it cannot be far out; cf. Kaibel
   1468.67f., E. Capps, *AJP* 21 (1900) 59f.

Philologen-Versammlung, Freiburg i. B. 1882), and *Gnom. Vaticanum* no. 46 (L. Sternbach, reprinted Berlin 1963 = *Wien. Stud.* 9 (1887) 197) ἐκ τῶν Ἀριστοτέλους Χρειῶν· Ἄλεξις ὁ τῶν κωμῳδιῶν ποιητής, ἐπειδή τις αὐτὸν ὄντα πρεσβύτην ἑώρα μόλις πορευόμενον καὶ ἠρώτα 'τί ποιεῖς;', ἔφη "κατὰ σχολὴν ἀποθνήσκω".

MS S of Stob. omits ἐκ τῶν Ἀρ. Χρ., *Gnom. Vind.* and *Vat.* substitute Ἀλέξιδος ὁ τῆς κωμῳδίας *Gnom. Vind.* τὸ τί ποιεῖ(ς) MA of Stob. κατὰ σχολὴν φησὶν *Gnom. Vat.*, ἔφη κ. σχ. φησὶν *Gnom. Vind.*

Cf. V. Rose, *Aristoteles pseudepigraphus* (Leipzig 1863) 612f., O. Hense on Stob. *Ecl.* 3.5. 42 (p.269) and *RE* s.v. *Ioannes (Stobaios)* 18, *Nachtrag* 2572.1ff. Aristotle could not have been the source of this anecdote; he died before Alexis was sixty.

16 Psellus *Laud. Matr.* (p. 60 K. N. Sathas, Μεσαιωνικὴ Βιβλιοθήκη 5 (Venice 1876)) ἐῶ λέγειν ὁπόσα μοι παρέχουσι πράγματα, τίς ὁ Ἄλεξις καὶ ὁ Μένανδρος καὶ ὁ αὐτόσιτος Κρόβαλος, reprinted in P. Maas, *Kleine Schriften* (Munich 1973) 476 = *Byz.-neugriech. Jahrb.* 15 (1938/9) 1f.

Κρόβαλος is an error for Κρωβύλος, cf. Maas *ad loc.* and Kassel–Austin 4.350 (Crobylus fr. 1).

*17 Stephanus of Byzantium s.v. Οἶον· δῆμος τῆς Λεοντίδος φυλῆς. ἐξ Οἴου. Ἄλεξις Ἀλέξιδος ἐξ Οἴου Λεοντί[δο]ς.

Identification of this Alexis as the comic poet is unlikely, cf. Kaibel in *RE* s.v. *Alexis* 9, 1468.37ff.

*18 *IG* ii².10631. A marble lekythos (mid-4th century) portrays an armed bearded man named Ὀλύμπιχος on the right stretching out his hand to a woman Θεοδώρα standing on the left; behind her is a bearded man Ἄλεξις. Presumably Theodora's funeral monument, with Olympichus and Alexis most probably her sons. The date fits Alexis the comic poet, but he was not alone with this name in Athens at the time (Kirchner, *PA* 1.40, e.g. no. 552).

(ii) Datable plays

Sometimes references in the frs. of Alexis to people or events provide clues (usually ill-defined, occasionally precise) to the production dates of some 37 comedies. Plays whose titles alone suggest a particular stage in Alexis' career (e.g. myth travesties: cf. Webster, *SLGC* 82ff., Nesselrath, *MK* 188ff.) here are excluded, as also those where references to people give too wide a range of possible dates (e.g. Θεοφόρητος mentioning 'Ptolemy' in fr. 92(88K)). Evidence for the datings given in the following list is provided in introductions to the individual plays.

?354–338	Ἀρχίλοχος
350s–347	Ἀγκυλίων, Παράσιτος, not necessarily Ἰμίλκων, Μεροπίς
350s–*c*.330	Μίνως
late 350s–*c*.340	Ἀποβάτης
c.350–*c*.330 (?early 330s)	Ἀγωνίς
c.350–*c*.300	Μιλήσιοι, Ὀδυσσεὺς ὑφαίνων, Ὀλυνθία
c.345–*c*.335	Τίτθη
c.345–*c*.320	Παγκρατιαστής, Ταραντῖνοι
?*c*.345–*c*.320	Φαῖδρος
c.345–318	Δορκίς, Ἰσοστάσιον, Κράτεια (1st production), Μανδραγοριζομένη, Ποντικός, Συντρέχοντες, Φαίδων
?*c*.345–*c*.305	Δημήτριος (2nd production), Ποιηταί
342–340	Ἀδελφοί, Στρατιώτης
before 340	Ὀλυμπιόδωρος
c.340–late 320s	Σπονδοφόρος
c.340–*c*.315 (?335–320)	Λυκίσκος
c.328–*c*.321	Ἐπιδαύριος
?327–325	Λέβης
c.325–*c*.310	Συναποθνῄσκοντες, Φυγάς
before *c*.310	Θεσπρωτοί
early 306	Ἱππεύς
305	Κράτεια (2nd production)
c.305–*c*.295	Πύραυνος
?beginning 3rd century	Ἐρετρικός
279–268	Ὑποβολιμαῖος

(iii) Facts and problems

The *Suda* (*test.* 1) says that Alexis came from Thurii in Magna Graecia, produced 245 plays as a comic poet, was the paternal uncle of one comic poet (Menander) and the father of another (Stephanus). None of these statements is confirmed by any other independent authority (Alexis' identification as Θούριος in Kroehnert's Byzantine *Canones*, *test.* 3, presumably derives from the *Suda* or a common source). Only the ascription of a son Stephanus to Alexis can be totally discounted. The words ἔσχε δὲ υἱὸν Στέφανον, καὶ αὐτὸν κωμικόν, which stand at the end of the *Suda* entry, come from a passage in the middle of the entry for Antiphanes (α 2735 Adler, παῖδά τε ἔσχε Στέφανον, καὶ αὐτὸν κωμικόν = *test.* 1 Kassel–Austin), where the statement is in place. The *Suda* says that Antiphanes was 'the son of Demophanes, but some say of Stephanus', while the anonymous tractate on comedy (cf. *test.* 2 above; 13 p. 9 Kaibel, p. 10 Koster) names Antiphanes' father unequivocally as Stephanus. A male child in Athens often took the name of his paternal grandfather. The tractate goes on to say that some of Antiphanes' comedies were produced by Stephanus; Aristophanes' two last plays were produced by his son Araros (*Plut.*, hypothesis 4 = Kassel–Austin 3.2 p.33.iv). It is possible that a scribe who had carelessly omitted the seven words about Stephanus from the *Suda*'s Antiphanes entry added them in a margin or at the foot of the page, leaving a later scribe in doubt over their correct positioning.

The allegations that Alexis came from Italy and was Menander's uncle need to be discussed together.

(a) Menander was an Athenian citizen of the deme Cephisia and son of a Diopeithes who was a public arbitrator in the city in the year 325/4 BC (*IG* xiv. 1 184, ii².1926.19 = *test.* 3, 4 Körte–Thierfelder). This dates Diopeithes' birth to 385/4, a few years before that of Alexis.

(b) Apart from the *Suda* entry we have no information

about Alexis' family background. If he was born in Thurii to a local family, he would have come to Athens as a metic. Some comic poets from outside Attica who distinguished themselves on the comic stage were honoured with Athenian citizenship – Philemon certainly, probably Apollodorus of Carystus and Diodorus of Sinope (Webster, *SLGC* 225); nothing of this kind is recorded for Alexis.

(c) The anonymous tractate on comedy alleges that Menander spent much time with Alexis and was apparently trained by him (*test.* 2); although it is praised by modern scholars (e.g. A. Körte in *RE* s.v. *Menandros* 9, 710.6ff.), it has no claim to automatic credit when its statements differ from those in the *Suda*.

Two scenarios are possible. Alexis could have been Diopeithes' younger brother, born in Athens or Thurii. Since Thurii was founded only seventy years or so before Alexis' birth as a Panhellenic colony under the guidance of Pericles with Athenians among the new settlers, Diopeithes' family *might* have forged links with Thurii and Alexis *might* have been adopted and brought up by a kinsman of Diopeithes settled in the colony.

That is one possibility. An alternative appeals more to sober sceptics.[1] This has Alexis born in Thurii to a family unrelated to Diopeithes. Having come to Athens probably in his teens or early twenties and making a reputation there as a comic playwright, he taught his craft to the young Menander, just as the anonymous tractate says. The *Suda* would thus have corrupted a teaching relationship into one of blood. It can occasion no surprise that an aspirant comic poet from a family of wealth and standing should seek instruction from an experienced practitioner. The *Suda* often

---

[1] In addition to Kaibel and Körte in *RE* s.v. *Alexis* 9, 1468.29ff. and *Menandros* 9, 710.4ff. respectively, see e.g. Kirchner, *PA* 1.39 no. 549, Th. Williams, *Rh. Mus.* 105 (1962) 201, Gomme–Sandbach, *Comm.* p. 1, M. J. Osborne, *Naturalization in Athens* III/IV (Brussels 1983) 125.

confuses terms like μαθητής, συγγενής and φίλος to a ludicrous degree (A. Daub, *Studien zu den Biographika des Suidas* (Freiburg and Tübingen 1882) 21ff., 78ff.), turning Homer into Hesiod's second cousin, while 'some make Creophylus Homer's son-in-law, others only his friend', and Deinolochus was 'son of Epicharmus, or as some say, his pupil' (η 583, κ 2376, δ 338; cf. W. G. Arnott, *Studi Monaco* 1.337f.).

Yet is it enough just to reject the *Suda*'s allegation of a blood relationship between Alexis and Menander? Could not the master-and-pupil connection, which only the tractate mentions, also have been a fiction, invented with an aim of linking two generations of comic poet and perhaps additionally of explaining similarities in some of their works (cf. I.v.iii below)? When the tractate and *Suda* elsewhere conflict, the tractate too can be wrong. The *Suda* (α 2375) says that Antiphanes came originally from Cius, Rhodes or Smyrna; the tractate (13 p. 9 Kaibel, p. 10 Koster) calls Antiphanes Athenian, but adds 'some say he came from Larissa in Thessaly, but was illegally registered as an Athenian citizen by Demosthenes'. Modern scholarship is uncertain whether to accept or disbelieve the *Suda* here, but it unreservedly rejects the tractate's reference to false registration as a malicious fabrication or confusion with an otherwise unknown Antiphanes of Larissa (cf. Kaibel in *RE* s.v. *Antiphanes* 15, 2519.6ff.).

The figure of 245 plays attributed to Alexis by the *Suda* seems remarkably high for one playwright's output, but it may be accepted as the figure calculated by ancient scholarship from play texts bearing Alexis' name on the colophon and from didascalic evidence. How accurate that calculation was we cannot now say; it may have included (a) plays where Alexis was only the producer (ἐδίδαξε is what the *Suda* says) and not also the author, (b) plays by other dramatists like Antiphanes and Antidotus revamped and staged by Alexis under his own name (cf. introductions to Ὁμοία, Ὕπνος; 'False or Doubtful Attributions' I, II

Ἀλείπτρια, Ἄντεια; *Studi Monaco* 1.331f., and this introduction, 1.v below) and (c) plays falsely ascribed to Alexis (e.g. Ἀσωτοδιδάσκαλος, 'False or Doubtful Attributions' iii); it may have (d) counted twice some plays which (for various reasons: a second production, a wish by cataloguing scholars to distinguish like-named plays of different dramatists by adding a second title, or the popular ancient habit of renaming a play after its leading character or characters; see introduction to Ἀγωνίς) bore alternative titles. Probably therefore the *Suda's* figure is marginally too high. The known titles associated with Alexis number 146; of these 4 may be plagiarisms or false ascriptions, 1 appears to be a forgery, and 9 are alternative titles, leaving a total of 132 authentic, different comedies. If the *Suda's* 245 is an accurate count of all the titles associated with Alexis in antiquity, and if the proportion of titles to actual plays was the same for titles and plays known in antiquity as it is for those known today, we can guess that Alexis' output was about 220 comedies.

One question needs to be asked. How justified are we in accepting the *Suda* figure as an accurate compilation? A certain answer is impossible, but the high total fits in well with the known facts about Alexis and contemporary playwrights.

First, a figure such as 245 is no isolated phenomenon in Middle and New Comedy. The *Suda* gives alternative figures of 365 and (more plausibly[1]) 280 for Antiphanes, 108 for Menander, 104 for Eubulus and 97 for Philemon. The anonymous tractate on comedy (18 p.10 Kaibel, p. 10 Koster) assigns 100 plays to Diphilus.[2] Two conclusions may

---

[1] Cf. Meineke 1.310f. and Kaibel in *RE* s.v. *Antiphanes* 15, 2519.41ff. The anonymous tractate (13 p. 9 Kaibel, p. 10 Koster) gives a third figure (260).

[2] In all the cases mentioned here where no play has survived intact, the ratio of the number of titles known today to the number (given by the *Suda* or some other source) of plays composed by a playwright is fairly constant, between 47.86 and 61.86 to 100: Alexis 146:245, Antiphanes

be drawn from this evidence of high productivity: that playwrights like Alexis and Antiphanes must have worked fairly full time as writers and probably also as producers; and that a substantial proportion of their plays were not written for production at the two major Athenian dramatic festivals, the Lenaea and Dionysia. The latter conclusion has led to the suggestion that if Alexis hailed from Magna Graecia, some of his plays may have been composed for staging there[1]. The limited evidence that is available to us, however, does not support such a theory. The titles and fragments of Alexis are all Attic in dialect, and the many precise references to real persons, places, institutions and events in the fragments (not excepting 223(221K).15f., see comm. *ad loc.*) would make full sense only to an Attic audience. Those comedies of Alexis which were not produced at one of the major Athenian festivals are most likely to have been staged, if they were staged at all, in theatres outside Athens scattered throughout Attica.[2]

Secondly, a man alleged to have witten 245 plays must have had a long, active career. Plut. *Mor.* 420d (*test.* 4) claims that Alexis lived to be twice the age of Epicurus' friend Metrodorus of Lampsacus, who died in his fifty-third year according to Diog. Laert. 10.23. The mathematical accuracy of Plutarch and Diog. Laert. may be open to question, but other indications point to an active longevity. Plutarch elsewhere (*Mor.* 785b, *test.* 5) says that Alexis and Philemon both died while winning victors' garlands in dramatic competitions, while a witty anecdote recorded in Stob. 4.50b.83 and elsewhere (*test.* 15) describes Alexis

---

134:280 (or 260: see previous note), Diphilus 60:100, Eubulus 58:104, Philemon 60:97.

[1] So most recently H.-D. Blume, *Einführung in das antike Theaterwesen* (Darmstadt 1978) 109f.

[2] Cf. G. V. Vitucci, *Dioniso* 7 (1939) 210ff., 312ff., T. B. L. Webster, *CQ* 2 (1952) 23 n. 2, Pickard-Cambridge, *DFA*[2] 45ff. On the productivity of Greek comic poets see especially E. Mensching, *Mus. Helv.* 21 (1964) 15ff.

walking with difficulty in old age and explaining that he was dying 'step by step'. Even if the last two anecdotes are imaginative fictions, they are likely to have kept close to reality in order to achieve credibility.

Datable references in the extant fragments confirm the allegations of a long career. The philosopher Plato is mentioned as still alive in Ἀγκυλίων (fr. 1) and Παράσιτος (185(180K)), and so these two plays must have been written before 348/7. The musician Argas, who was invited to perform at Iphicrates' wedding-feast in or just before 386, is mentioned in Ἀποβάτης (19.3), but we do not know how long Argas' career extended and we cannot assume that he was still alive (and not a posthumous legend) at the time of a play which may not have been written before the 350s.[1] From the 340s on to the end of the century there is a string of references to contemporary celebrities in Athens (e.g. the politician Callimedon ὁ Κάραβος, the fish-merchant Chaerephilus and his sons, Eucrates ὁ Κορύδος, Misgolas, the cadaverous Philippides, Pythionice[2]) and to events that made news during the period (e.g. Demosthenes' quibble in the Halonnesus dispute of 343–342, Sophocles of Sunium's bill to control philosophers in 307, Demetrius Poliorcetes' naval victory off Cypriot Salamis in 306, the tiger sent by Seleucus to Athens at the turn of the century[3]). Finally in Ὑποβολιμαῖος (fr. 246(244K)) a toast is proposed to Ptolemy the king, his sister and ὁμόνοια. The only time when such a toast would be appropriate was during the marriage of Ptolemy Philadelphus and his sister Arsinoe (from between 279 and 273 to 268 BC[4]) when an *entente cordiale* flourished between Athens and Egypt.

A few further dates in Alexis' career are supplied by

---

[1] See also introductions to Ἀρχίλοχος, Γαλάτεια and Μίνως.

[2] See comm. on frs. 57(56K), 6, 48(47K), 3.2, 2.8, 143(139) respectively.

[3] See introductions to Ἀδελφοί, Ἱππεύς (and Appendix II), Κράτεια and Πύραυνος respectively

[4] See introduction to Ὑποβολιμαῖος.

inscriptions. In the list of victorious comic poets at the Lenaea (*IG* ii². 2325.150, *test.* 8) Alexis' name comes eight places after Anaxandrides, six after Eubulus, five after Antiphanes, fourteen before Menander. The poets seem to be listed here in the chronological order of their first victory at the festival; if the poets placed near Alexis were evenly spaced, Alexis' first victory would have come in the late 350s, although the possible limits could be stretched as far as 360–345. In one didascalic inscription (*IG* ii². 2318.278, *test.* 6) a victory at the Dionysia in 347 is recorded, in another (*IG* ii². 2322.92, *test.* 7) he came second, but festival and date are uncertain.

The various pieces of information about Alexis' career gleaned from all our sources – the *Suda*, Plutarch, Stobaeus, Attic inscriptions and the fragments of Alexis – fit together as snugly as the pieces of a jigsaw. They allow us to fix his earliest Attic comedies in the 350s, and to guess that he was born in the 370s[1] and died still producing, probably in the 270s. Even so, the available information yields two surprises. First, the number of victories won by Alexis at the Lenaea – between two and four (*test.* 8) – seems remarkably small for so productive a writer. There could have been several reasons for this: the quality of Alexis' material, political or personal prejudice against an incomer, the frequency or infrequency of his participation in the Lenaea competitions, but a stronger one is likely to have been the number and quality of his rivals. The same inscription records only three Lenaean victories for Anaxandrides, Diphilus, Eubulus and Philemon, and between two and four for Menander. Yet Antiphanes, the one playwright who matched Alexis in productivity, stands out on this list with eight victories.

The second oddity may be an *ignis fatuus*. A careful reading of the fragments reveals a host of precisely or loosely datable references down to around 300, and then nothing

---

[1] Cf. Kaibel 1468.22ff., E. Capps, *AJP* 21 (1900) 59f.

that *must* be dated later until the one and final allusion to Ptolemy Philadelphus and Arsinoe probably in the 270s (cf. i.ii above). One possibility is that Alexis retired from composition at some time around 300, when he had reached a reasonable age for closing a career after gargantuan productivity, but then returned to his craft one final time and produced his Ὑποβολιμαῖος victoriously just before he died. Possibly so: but more prosaic explanations of the thirty-year or so dearth of allusions are equally likely. Plays of the New-Comedy period seem to have been much less rich in allusions to contemporary persons and events. Or it might be a curious accident of preservation that all the datable references in the fragments (except one) belong to the period before *c*. 300.

(iv) Alexis and Comedy, Middle and New

In a career spanning the eighty years between the 350s and 270s, Alexis was a playwright of both Middle and New Comedy,[1] although Middle (like Old, unlike New) Comedy is more an indication of period (roughly 404–323 BC[2]) than of sporadically dominant types of plot. When Alexis came onto the scene, mythological travesty (parodying both the legends themselves and their treatments in 5th-century and contemporary tragedy) was beginning to lose the dominance it had exercised for half a century,[3] and embryonic traces were beginning to emerge of a new type of plot that

---

[1] Cf. Bergk 4.151, 154, Nesselrath, *MK* 332. Kroehnert's Byzantine *Canones* (*test.* 3), however, identify Alexis and Antiphanes as Middle-Comedy poets; cf. Nesselrath, *MK* 58f.

[2] Cf. Bergk 4.121, A. Körte in *RE* s.v. *Komödie (mittlere)* 1258.3ff., W. G. Arnott, *G and R* 19 (1972) 65ff., Hunter 4ff., 16ff., and especially Nesselrath's exhaustive discussions in *MK* 188ff.

[3] Cf. Platonius Περὶ διαφορᾶς κωμῳδιῶν Kaibel 1.11 p. 5 = Koster 1 p. 5 = F. Perusino, *Platonio* (Urbino 1989) 36. See also Bergk 4.129ff., Webster, *SLGC* 82ff., Hunter 22ff., Nesselrath, *MK* 188ff.

developed during the first thirty years of Alexis' career into
the standardised forms of New Comedy, with its five acts
separated by the performances of a chorus that took little or
no part in the action, a range of largely stereotyped characters belonging to or involved with two bourgeois families,
and plots in which love affairs surmount their various
obstacles to reach a successful conclusion.[1] The dates, titles
and extant fragments suggest that Alexis played a role in
these developments, but the nature of the evidence makes it
difficult to evaluate the importance or extent of his or any
other contemporary playwright's innovations.

Between thirteen and eighteen of Alexis' titles indicate
myth burlesque,[2] written presumably in the early part of
Alexis' career, although only Μίνως of these can on other
grounds be dated to before c.330. Extant fragments here
show that the figures of myth were presented as ordinary
Greeks transported anachronistically to the 4th century. In
Γαλάτεια a slave describes how his master (most probably
Polyphemus) studied as a youth under Aristippus of Cyrene
and acquired his master's wickedness (37(36K), see comm.
on vv. 8–9). In Λίνος the young Heracles is asked by Linus
to choose a book from a library of Greek classics including
Homer, tragedy and Epicharmus, and true to his tragic and
comic presentations elsewhere he picks out a (probably
4th-century) cookery-book. To Alexis' contemporaries myth
was part of their ancient history, and so it is not surprising to
see historical figures from the Athenian past treated exactly

---

[1] Cf. e.g. Webster, SLGC 74ff., W. G. Arnott, G and R 19 (1972) 75ff.
[2] The clearest titles are Ἀταλάντη, Γαλάτεια, Ἑλένης ἁρπαγή, Ἑλ.
μνηστῆρες and/or Τυνδάρεως, Ἑλένη (unless this is an abbreviated
form of one of the two Helen titles or an alternative to Τυνδάρεως),
Ἑπτὰ ἐπὶ Θήβας (or -αις), Ἡσιόνη, Κύκνος, Λίνος, Μίνως, Ὀδυσσεὺς
ἀπονιζόμενος and Ὀδ. ὑφαίνων, Ὀρέστης, Σκίρων. In addition,
perhaps Οἶνος (whether correctly transmitted so or corrupt for a name
such as Οἰνεύς, Οἰνόμαος or Οἰνοπίων) and Ὀπώρα (as separate plays
or alternative titles for the same play), and (Φρὺξ ἢ) Φρύγιος. See
introductions to these titles.

like Heracles, Linus and Polyphemus. In Αἴσωπος we see Solon defending to a non-Athenian (not necessarily Aesop) the practice of presumably 4th-century wine-sellers who illegally watered their wine before selling it (9.4ff.); the play cannot be dated, but like the (possibly parallel) Ἀρχίλοχος and the myth travesties it is most likely to have been an early production.

Körte[1] well noted that the boundaries between Middle and Old Comedy are not sharp. An echo of Old Comedy can be sensed in the undated Τροφώνιος, where apparently the chorus is addressed in Eupolidean metre by one of the characters and ordered γυμνοῦσθ᾽ αὐτούς (239(237K)), most probably at their first entrance.[2]

Although few innovations in metre and style are discernible in the remains of Middle Comedy, two features do stand out in its earlier period:[3] (i) One is a fondness for long passages in anapaestic dimeters spoken or chanted not by the chorus but by an individual actor. Many of those extant are descriptions of meals or lists of victuals (e.g. Anaxandrides 42(41K), Antiphanes 130(132K), 131(133K), Ephippus 12, 13), doubtless continuing a tradition of celebratory finales that goes back at least to Aristophanes (e.g. *Pax* 974ff.), but the one example that survives from Alexis' Ὀλυνθία (167(162K)) combines its list of poor men's victuals (vv.11–16) with a description of the speaker's family that suggests an expository function early in the play.

(ii) The second feature consists of sequences of iambic trimeters or trochaic tetrameters in strict tragic rhythm, employing a high-flown vocabulary that clearly owed much to serious poetry, although there is some doubt whether dithyramb or Euripidean tragedy was the major influence. These passages are marked too by asyndetic phrases rich in

---

[1] In *RE* s.v. *Komödie (mittlere)* 1258.40ff.
[2] On other possible echoes in frs. 42(41K) and 103(98K) see the introductions to Ἰσοστάσιον and Γυναικοκρατία.
[3] See especially Hunter 17ff., Nesselrath, *MK* 241ff.

adjectives, simple unsubordinated syntactical structures and images that range from the impressive to the absurd. The examples in Alexis are relatively few (5, 124(119K), 135(130K) vases; 83 food; 89(88K), cf. 88(85K), food and drinking; 153(149K) cook and hirer), but their subject matter of wining and dining is generally the one normal in the Middle-Comedy sequences that originated them and is maintained even in the iambic tetrameters of Menander's *Dyskolos* (932ff.). Here Alexis 153(149) provides an odd variant; the subject is still food, but the situation is a conversation between cook and hirer where both observe tragic rhythms religiously.

In the years after 350 the structure, characters and plots that typify New Comedy must have been developed, although comic titles and fragments securely dated to that period shed only fitful light on the details of that development and Alexis' part in it.

(I) Thus in Alexis' Κουρίς fr. 112(107K) announces the arrival of revellers in terms varying the formulas used by Menander to introduce his New-Comedy choruses at the end of the first act, and fr. 113(108K) seems to be part of a delayed prologue of a kind familiar in Menander and Plautus. The absence of convincing evidence to date Κουρίς, however, makes it uncertain whether Alexis here was a pre-Menandrean innovator or in the time of New Comedy following conventions already established.

(II) Several types of figure that enliven New Comedy – cooks, parasites, soldiers, *hetairai* in particular – already appear in plays that predate Menander, and here Alexis' role in developing paradigmatic characteristics is occasionally clear, more often just suspected.

(a) The regular appearance of cooks (μάγειροι) in later comedy was linked to the standardised feature of a celebratory meal often at the end of the play. All Alexis' cooks[1]

---

[1] Cooks appear in Ἀσκληπιοκλείδης fr. 24*, Δημήτριος 49(48K), cf. 51(50K), Ἐρετρικός 84, Θεοφόρητος 92(88K)*, Κράτεια 115(110K)*,

appear to conform to a general pattern of ἀλαζονεία combining arrogance, self-confidence, irritability and above all a claim to expertise in matters both culinary and extracurricular. Here priorities of innovation among contemporary comic poets are usually impossible to assign, but four important or unusual contributions may be singled out for Alexis. In fr. 129(124K) of Λέβης, which probably dates to before 324, his cook deliberately affects medical and scientific terminology; cf. perhaps fr. 177(173K) of the undated Παννυχίς. Secondly, the same fr. of Λέβης may contain (vv.6, 15) an embryonic example of linguistic characterisation, with the cook given an individualising pattern of everyday speech.[1] Thirdly, fr. 115(110K) of Κράτεια ἢ Φαρμακοπώλης, first performed between c.345 and 318, offers us the mystery of a cook who behaves in all the essentials like a standard μάγειρος (vv. 18–21) but claims not to be one; he is likely to have been either the φαρμακοπώλης of the alternative title or a bumptious ὀψοποιός. The final point covers a series of fragments (84, 129(124K), 138(133K), 191–3(186–8K) from several plays, of which only Λέβης can be dated to the period before Menander: the recipes which Alexis puts into the mouths of his μάγειροι have an authenticity which must have contributed to the realism of his portrayals.

(b) Most of Alexis' parasites too conform in the frs. to New-Comedy type,[2] with wit and edacity displayed in equal

---

Λέβης 129(124K)*, 132(127K), Λεύκη 138(133K)*, Μιλήσιοι 153(149K)*, Παννυχίς 177–80(173, 172, 174–5K)*, Πονήρα 191–4(186–9K), Συντρέχοντες 216(213K: two cooks), where an asterisk indicates the presence of bragging.

[1] Cf. here perhaps a different character's speech in fr. 222(219K) of Ταραντῖνοι (dating between c. 345 and c. 320, see introduction to that title), where the lack of logical tautness throughout may be an attempt to reproduce the thought processes of an average unintellectual, like Gorgias' sermon in Men. Dysk. 271ff.

[2] Parasites appear in Κυβερνήτης 121(116K), Ὁμοία 168(163K), Παράσιτος 183(178K), ? Πολύκλεια 190(185K), Πρωτόχορος 200(195K), Πύραυνος 205(201, 202 K), Τοκιστής 233–5(231–3K), fr. inc.

measure. Only one play in which the character appeared dates to the playwright's earliest years (347 or before), and that is significantly titled Παράσιτος. Fr. 183(178K) from it indicates that this was the parasite's nickname. Clearly at a time when κόλαξ was still the word in normal use for the profession, Alexis devised a nickname whose aptness quickly turned it into a common equivalent to κόλαξ.

(c) Soldiers, *hetairai*[1] and other staple characters of New Comedy can be identified in many of Alexis' plays, but there is little or no evidence in extant titles and frs. of innovatory language or techniques, with the possible exception of fr. 103(98K), where the use of trochaic tetrameters in a long and vivid description of the devices used by *hetairai* may be a Middle-Comedy attempt to replace the epirrhemata of Old-Comedy parabases (see introduction to 'Ισοστάσιον).

(d) A remarkable number of Alexis' titles, mostly undatable, feature occupations, interests or conditions: 'Αμπελουργός, 'Αποβάτης*, 'Εκπωματοποιός, Κιθαρῳδός*, Κονιατής, Κυβερνήτης (cf. -ῆται Menander), Κυβευταί, Μυλωθρός, Παγκρατιαστής*, Ποιητής* or -ταί, Σπονδοφόρος, Τοκιστής, Τραυματίας* male; Αὐλητρίς*, Κουρίς, 'Ορχηστρίς, Ποιήτρια female (asterisks denote titles found elsewhere in New Comedy). How far such titles reflect a real interest in unusual and everyday occupations, or how far they are gimmicks adding an unconventional character to a hackneyed plot, is unknown.

(III) The type of plot now associated with New Comedy

263(261K), perhaps also Δημήτριος 47–8(46–7K), Φρύξ 258(256K), Ψευδόμενος 262(260K).

[1] Three titles (Θράσων, 'Ιππεύς, Στρατιώτης) imply the presence of soldiers, as do fr. 120(115K) from Κράτεια and probably 63(62K) from Εἰσοικιζόμενος. Six plays at least seem to be named after *hetairai* ('Αγωνίς, Δορκίς, 'Ισοστάσιον, 'Οπώρα, Πεζονίκη, Πολύκλεια, perhaps too 'Ιασίς, Χορηγίς); Φιλοῦσα almost certainly involved *hetairai*, cf. fr. 255(253K), whether or no the title was the name of one, and Καρχηδόνιος must have included two, if that play was the original for Plautus' *Poenulus*.

is likely to have been developed in the period of Middle Comedy. According to the *Suda* s.v. Ἀναξανδρίδης it was this playwright who invented 'love affairs and the rapes of maidens'. Anaxandrides was of course thematically fore-stalled by fifth-century tragedies such as Euripides' *Aeolus*, *Antiope*, *Auge* and *Ion* and presumably by myth travesties-based on these legends (e.g. Αἴολος by Antiphanes, Eriphus; Ἀντιόπη by Eubulus, Αὔγη by Philyllius, Eubulus), but the *Suda*'s statement may garble a tradition that Anaxandrides was the first comic writer to incorporate such incidents into plays with non-mythical plots and characters some time between the early 370s and the 340s. Alexis' part in the further development of New-Comedy themes is impossible to assess, but in two at least of his early plays these themes can be identified. The characters of Ἀγωνίς (produced in the 340s or 330s) include a young man, the girl he loves (possibly the *hetaira* Agonis) and a 'fiery' ξένος (most probably a soldier and perhaps the young man's rival); the play's alternative title (Ἱππίσκος) is best interpreted as a recognition token; fr. 2 from it describes the preparations for a confidence trick. Στρατιώτης dates to the late 340s, and in its one fr. (212(209K)) two characters dispute the possession of a baby in a way that seems to anticipate either Men. *Epitr.* 218ff. or Plaut. *Truc.* 389ff.

(IV) Alexis' career extended into the first fifty years of New Comedy, and not surprisingly his frs. contain many things that can be paralleled in New Comedy or the Roman adaptations. They include

(a) formulas introducing the chorus 112(107K: cf. iv.(I) above), introducing a parasite's nickname 183(178K: cf. iv.(II).b), sanctioning a betrothal 79, perhaps praying for success at play end 166(161K);

(b) clichés like the talkative wife 96(92K), husbands in thrall to their wives 150(146K), 267(265K) the use of wealth, 283(281K) its impermanence;

(c) motifs and events such as the use of cups as recognition tokens 100–1(95–6K), a festival of Aphrodite (255(253K)), and those implied by the titles Μανδραγοριζομένη, Παννυχίς;

(d) character names like Chaireas 21, Demeas 205(202K).5, Tryphe
     232(230K).3 and the title figures of Κράτεια, Παμφίλη, Φαῖδρος,
     (Φαίδων ἢ) Φαιδρίας;
(e) even stale jokes, e.g. ἀθάνατος 164(159K).3, κόπτ' 177(173K).12. In
     most cases a dating of the Alexis passage or play is impossible. For full
     discussion of all those listed here see comm. *ad locc.*, and note also 1.vi
     below.

(v) Alexis and other Greek comic poets

(i) **Antiphanes**. See 'False or Doubtful Attributions' I, II,
and introduction to Ὕπνος. Athenaeus claims that the
authorship of three plays was disputed between Alexis and
Antiphanes. At 3.123b he cites fr. 26(25K) from the latter's
Ἀλείπτρια, adding φέρεται τὸ δρᾶμα καὶ ὡς Ἀλέξιδος. At
3.127c he cites fr. 36(34K) from Antiphanes' Ἄντεια,
adding this time τὸ δ' αὐτὸ τοῦτο δρᾶμα φέρεται καὶ ὡς
Ἀλέξιδος ἐν ὀλίγοις σφόδρα διαλλάττον. At 15.671d he
cites fr. 243(241K) ἐξ Ὕπνου (Schweighaeuser's correction
of A's ὑπονοίας: see introduction to Ὕπνος) Ἀλέξιδος,
adding τὰ αὐτὰ ἰαμβεῖα φέρεται καὶ παρὰ Ἀντιφάνει ἐν
Ὕπνῳ. Epit. of Ath. 2.66f introduces Alexis fr. 245(342K) =
Antiphanes 212(331K) with the words Σαμιακοῦ (so C:
σαμικοῦ E) ἐλαίου μνημονεύει Ἀντιφάνης ἢ Ἄλεξις, citing
in all probability a fr. from one of the three disputed plays
(see comm. directly after fr. 244(242K), and 'False or
Doubtful Attributions' VI on fr. 245(342K)). Ath.'s source or
sources in all these places presumably relied on information
provided by Hellenistic scholars, whose uncertainty would
have been caused by varied ascriptions on play texts or
didascalic records. One possibility is that Alexis (the
younger playwright) revamped one or more of Antiphanes'
plays (most plausibly Ἄντεια, in view of Ath.'s wording at
3.127c) after his death and produced them under his own
name (cf. e.g. Eusebius *Praep. Evang.* 10.3.12f. on Menander's alleged practice, *test.* 51 Körte). Another is that one of

the two playwrights acted as διδάσκαλος for the other, as commonly happened in comedy[1].

(ii) **Antidotus**. After citing the Ὁμοία of Alexis (168(163K)), Ath. 14.642d adds in terms closely similar to those cited just above τὸ δ' αὐτὸ δρᾶμα καὶ ὡς ᾿Αντιδότου φέρεται, taking his cue once again doubtless from Hellenistic scholarship. Possible explanations for the alternative ascription are doubtless the same as those discussed in i.v.(i). Antidotus' dates are unknown, so it is impossible to determine who is more likely to have plagiarised or produced the other's play. A second title (Πρωτόχορος) is shared by Alexis and Antidotus, but there is no allegation there of doubtful attribution.

(iii) **Eubulus**. After citing the three lines of Eubulus fr. 122(125K) (without play-title, as usual) Epit. of Ath. 1.25f adds τὸ αὐτὸ δὲ καὶ ῎Αλεξις σχεδὸν ἀπαραλλάκτως τοῦ 'σφόδρα' μόνου κειμένου ἀντὶ τοῦ 'ἀεί' (= Alexis fr. inc. 284(282K)). We do not know here who plagiarised whom, but such theft was not uncommon in later Greek comedy. See also comm. on 153(149K).16 and 284(282K).

(iv) **Menander**. Cf. *Wien. Stud.* 101 (1988) 184ff. The links of blood and/or tutelage (1.i *test.* 1, 2; 1.iii) alleged for Alexis and Menander are supported by, and may even have been fabricated because of, the presence of remarkable similarities between passages in their works. Four that seem most noteworthy are listed here; a possible fifth, linking Alexis' Λέβης and Men. *Dysk.* is discussed at 1.vi.iii.a below; a great many more, of varying degrees of closeness and cogency, are collected by Gil 311ff.

(a) Alexis 222(219K), Men. fr. 416.8ff. The similarities are discussed in detail in introduction to comm. on the Alexis fr. In Alexis' Ταραντῖνοι (dated between *c*.345 and *c*.320) an unidentified character reflects on human

---

[1] Instances are collected and discussed by Pickard-Cambridge, DFA² 84ff.

experience, comparing life on earth to an absence away from one's own city (ἀποδημία 10) or a visit to a festival (πανήγυρις 11, 17). This imaginative comparison is repeated also in Menander's Ὑποβολιμαῖος with similar terminology (πανήγυρις 8, ἐπιδημία 9; cf. also διατριβή in Alexis vv. 4, 13 and Menander v. 10, προσδιατρίβων Menander v. 13. G. Zuntz rightly concludes (*PBA* 42 (1956) 236) that 'the energetic but rather rambling model ... is outshone by the more classical concentration and nobility of Menander', but the meandering argumentation in the Alexis passage may have a definite purpose (see p. 22 n. 1).

(b) Alexis 35(34K), Ter. *Ad.* 739ff. In Alexis' Βρεττία a character compares life to dice (κύβοι): they don't always fall in the same way, nor does the pattern of life. In Terence's *Adelphoe*, adapted from Menander's second Ἀδελφοί, Micio tells Demea that human life is like playing at dice; you've got to use the skills you possess in order to deal with what chance sends you; it is likely that Terence here is following his original closely. The comparison between Alexis and Menander is again illuminating; Alexis expresses his idea elegantly but more superficially, while Menander develops in a less obvious way a simile that was by now becoming a commonplace.

Examples (c) and (d) require prior acceptance of two probable theories: that Plautus' *Poenulus* is adapted from Alexis' Καρχηδόνιος (see introduction to that play), and that in the Latin play those scenes which advance the plot derive their conception from the Greek original.

(c) Plaut. *Poen.* 1099ff., Men. *Sik.* 343ff. In the Plautine scene a shifty slave attempts to persuade an elderly Carthaginian, who has just arrived on the scene, to impersonate the father of two young ladies owned by a *leno*. That Carthaginian turns out to be the real father of the girls. This presumably Alexidean sequence is paralleled at the beginning of the last act of Men. *Sik.*, where Theron tries to persuade the newly arrived Kichesias to pretend to be the father of a particular girl, of whom by an identical irony he turns out to be the true parent.

(d) Plaut. *Poen.* 1296ff., Men. *Mis.* 210ff. In Plautus a soldier sees his girlfriend (one of the two aforementioned young ladies) embracing that same elderly Carthaginian, who has just discovered that the girl is his long-lost daughter, and the soldier immediately jumps to the wrong conclusion, accusing the old man of shameful behaviour. The sequence in Men. *Mis.* is very similar; here Demeas meets and embraces his newly found daughter, whereupon the slave of the girl's lover enters, sees them clasped together and concludes that this 'grey-haired old man of sixty' is misbehaving.

The most remarkable aspect of this pair of parallels is that neither of them involves a commonplace, stereotyped situation of a sort repeated in play after play; both are unusual developments of particularised plot-lines, confined so far to the passages discussed. It is tempting therefore to assume here two acts of deliberate imitation – but who is the imitator, who the model? We cannot be certain, even if *test.* 2 makes Alexis the instructor, Menander the student; the instructor long outlived his pupil.

(vi) Alexis and Roman Comedy

Aulus Gellius 2.23.1 (*test.* 11) names Alexis as one of the later Greek comic poets whose plays were 'taken and adapted' (*sumptas ac uersas*) for the Roman stage. Attempts have been made with varying degree of success to identify the titles of Alexis so used and their Roman users. The following list includes both accepted and implausible cases; fuller discussions of all of them (except those involving Plaut. *MG* and *Persa*) will be found in comm. under the relevant Alexidean titles.

(i) **Caecilius**. L. Spengel, *Caecilii Statii fragmenta* (Munich 1829) 6 suggests that Caecilius' *Epistula* and *Exul* may have been adapted from Alexis' Ἐπιστολή and Φυγάς, but there is no supporting evidence other than shared titles. The frs. of Caecilius' *Syracusii* seem compatible with those of Alexis' Συρακόσιος, but the difference in number between these two titles is disturbing.

(ii) **Naevius**. His *Commotria* was probably adapted from one of the three Κουρίς titles (by Alexis, Amphis, Antiphanes). J. Barsby, comm. on Plaut. *Bacch.* 912 (Warminster 1986) suggests that Naevius' *Demetrius* may have been taken from Alexis' Δημήτριος, but this is unlikely; Alexis' play was almost certainly adapted by Turpilius, and Roman playwrights did not make a habit of using Greek plays twice, see Δημήτριος p. 157 n. 2. Legrand, *NGC* 16 more plausibly links Naevius' *Glaucoma* with Alexis' Ἀπεγλαυκωμένος; the one remaining Roman fr. provides a tenable sequel to the dispute in Alexis 15. Naevius' *Paelex* was probably adapted from the Παλλακή of Alexis or Menander, or the Παλλακίς of Diphilus. Alexis' Ταραντῖνοι, however, is unlikely to have been the original of Naevius' *Tarentilla*; these two titles differ crucially in number and gender, and the Roman frs. have nothing in common with the Greek, see Ταραντῖνοι p. 625 n. 1.

(iii) **Plautus**.
(a) *Aulularia*. See *Wien. Stud.* 101 (1988) 181ff., *QUCC* 33 (1989) 27ff., introduction to Λέβης and Appendix III in this commentary, where I tentatively suggest that Alexis' Λέβης (dated to ?327–325) may be the Greek original of Plautus' *Aulularia*, and that the many similarities in structure, choice and presentation of characters, and details of plotting and dramatic technique between Menander's *Dyskolos* (produced 316) and the *Aulularia*[1] are most satisfactorily explained by an assumption that Menander's play was modelled on that of Alexis. This suggestion solves some but occasions other problems.

---

[1] These are listed and discussed in the papers cited in *Wien. Stud.* 187 (1988) 182 n. 6.

(b) *Menaechmi*. Webster, *SLGC* 67ff., 71ff. believes that this play could have been adapted from Alexis' Ἀδελφοί, but his arguments depend on a chain of possibilities that are largely incapable of proof or refutation, while δέδωκα ... ταύταις in Alexis 7.1 is hard to reconcile with the erring husband's gift in Plautus of the *palla* to Erotium alone.

(c) *Miles gloriosus*. L. Schaaf, *Der Miles Gloriosus des Plautus und sein griechisches Original* (Munich 1977) 362ff. points to structural similarities linking *MG* and *Poenulus*, both of whose plots are built out of apparently unconnected parts. Schaaf argues that Plautus modelled his *Poenulus* on Alexis' Καρχηδόνιος, and suggests that Alexis also provided the original for *MG* between 299 and 295 (cf. Schaaf 353ff.). Plautus, however, gives as the title of that original Ἀλαζών (*MG* 86), which is not recorded for Alexis, and there are no precise verbal ties between *MG* and extant frs. of the Greek dramatist, although Alexis 264(262K) could have followed directly on what Periplectomenus says at *MG* 672–81, fr. 291(302K) could have been incorporated into Acroteleutium's remarks in the scene beginning at *MG* 874, and 340(339K) – if Alexis – have come from Sceledrus' speech at *MG* 303–12. Schaaf's theory is plausible and attractively presented, but is short on hard evidence.

(d) *Persa*. After Wilamowitz, *De tribus carminibus latinis commentatio* (*Index scholarum* Göttingen 1893) 13ff. = *Kleine Schriften* 2 (Berlin 1941) 26off. had dated the Greek original to the period of Middle Comedy, F. Della Corte, *Da Sarsina a Roma* (Genoa 1952¹) 202ff., (Florence 1967²) 167ff. suggested Alexis as its author because of the importance in it of the parasite's role. Wilamowitz's initial dating of the model is stoutly but not incontestably (cf. e.g. H. D. Jocelyn, *CR* 33 (1983) 196f.) opposed by E. Woytek in his edition of *Persa* (Vienna 1982), who prefers a Greek model from late New Comedy. That question remains open, but there appear to be no verbal ties between *Persa* and any fr. of Alexis from a play known to involve a parasite.

(e) *Poenulus*. It is now generally agreed that this play was adapted from Alexis' Καρχήδονιος. Verbal ties link Alexis fr. 105(100K) from Καρχηδόνιος and *Poen.* 1318, Alexis fr. incert. 265(263K) and *Poen.* 522ff., while the papyrus frs. of Menander's Καρχηδόνιος are incompatible with the plot of *Poen.*

(f) *Pseudolus*. Th. Bergk, *Griechische Literaturgeschichte* 4 (Berlin 1887) 154f. n. 116 first suggested Alexis as the author of its Greek original. T. Mantero in *Miscellanea philologica* (Genoa 1960) 129ff. and *Maia* 18 (1966) 392ff., noting the similarity of the Plautine title to Alexis' Ψευδόμενος, attempted to link fr. 262(260K) with *Pseud.* 822 and 261(259K) with the scene in *Pseud.* beginning 790ff. The alleged ties, however, are unconvincing; see introduction to Ψευδόμενος.

(iv) **Turpilius**. J. J. Scaliger, *Coniectanea in Varronem* (Paris 1565) 197 = (1573) 170 first noted that fr. V of Turpilius' *Demetrius* was a close translation into the equivalent Latin metre of Alexis 47(46K).1–3; hence it may be assumed that Turpilius adapted his play from its Alexidean homonym. The Turpilius frs. are printed in Appendix I.

(vii) Style, humour, metres

Although the frs. of Alexis are not long enough to reveal his abilities at constructing plots or presenting characters, they do reveal something of his skill as a comic stylist. Such qualities as emerge are discussed in detail in the comm. *ad loc.*; here a summary list of features and passages is more appropriate.

(a) Lively dialogue: e.g. frs. 15, 140(135K), 177(173K). Note also 16.8–12 where a single speaker graphically quotes an altercation.

(b) Lively passages of description, e.g. 103(98K); narrative, e.g. 115(110K), 263(261K); and argument, e.g.

222(219K), 247(245K). Here Alexis shows an eye for the memorable observed detail (e.g. the examples listed in 103(98K).7–26 with the vivid image of vv. 23–25 towards the end; 115(110K).12–14) with its careful choice of rainbow-hued fish) and the imaginative idea (e.g. 19.3–4 ἡμέρας δρόμῳ κρείττων, 24.3–4 = 115(110K).21–3 teeth scrunching the plates, 47(46K).4–6 hurricane Phaÿllos, 63(62K) doves scattering perfume, 110(105K) and 248(246K) a wastrel making a ball of his patrimony, 178(172K).5 finger eating, 222(219K).4–6 life a ὑποκόρισμα for fate, 222(219K).10–14 life imaged as an ἀποδημία and a visit to a πανήγυρις, 230(228K) the evening of life, 237(235) life's final δίαυλος, 263(261K).5–10 the zodiac dish).

(c) This is combined with an Aristophanic talent for coining the telling phrase: cf. also 37(36K).9 the conjectured τὴν δ᾽ ἀτηρίαν συνήρπασεν, ὀφρῦς ... χιλιοταλάντους 121(116K).6–7, σῶμ᾽ ὑπόξυλον 197(192K), ? τῶν βαβαὶ βαβαί 209(206K) but see comm., διεσμιλευμέναι τε φροντίδες 223(221K).8.

(d) A flair for amusing conceits: 16.6–7 eyebrows crowning the head, 20 winged lovers, 35(34K) life like dice, 46(45K) man like wine, 76 fish are man's enemies, 91(87K) the sun as a torch, 115(110K).5–6 frightened fish, 128(123K).2 hare's milk, 149(145K).2 becoming an eel, 172(167K).4 toothless wine, 236(234K) what lovers must be, 242(240K) a conundrum about sleep, 247(245K) Ἔρως, 257(255K) hangovers should precede drinking, 263(261K).13–14 turning a plate into a sieve.

(e) The preceding section shows one way in which Alexis evokes a smile. His more conventional jokes are also funny. (i) Puns: ἔμψυχος 27.4–6, 223(220K), ποδαπός 94(90K).1, ὑπὸ μάλης 107(102K).2, κόραι 117(112K), ἀθάνατος 164(159K), κόπτω 177(173K).12, ψυχρός 184(179K).3. (ii) Building up to a climax: 131(126K).5–9 fishmongers seated, standing, suspended like gods from the μηχανή.

(iii) παρά προσδοκίαν: ἥδομ' 168(163K).7, the conjectured προσεῖτ' ἄν ‹ἄλλον› ἀποθανεῖν 198(193K).3 (see comm.).

(f) Other features of style. (i) Alexis shares with other comedians of Middle (and Old) Comedy a fondness for asyndetic lists of comestibles: 84.1–2, 115(110K).12–13, 15–16, 132(127K).4–8 (19 items), 167(162K).11–16 (12 items), 175(170K: partly syndetic), 178(172K).8–11, 179(174K).4–10 (21 items, not all food), 281(279K).1–2. Other lists: of nouns 96(92K), 111(106K), 113(108K).5–6), 140(135K).5–7, 173(168K).1–3, 201(197K).5–6, 207(204K).2–3, 252(250K).3–4; of adjectives 236(234K).2–6; of verbs 50(48K).2–3, 115(110K).25–6. (ii) Elaborate comparisons of A to B: 35(34K), 46(45K), 222(219K).4–6, 10–14, 280(278K), see also b and d above. (iii) Identifications of A as B: 47(46K).4, 57(56K).6, 77.2–4, 88(85K).4–5, 110(105K).2, 113(108K).5–6, 149(145K).2, 183(178K).3, 7, 207(204K), 258(256K), 292(290K). (iv) Irony: 9.4–10. (v) Climax (ἐποικοδόμησις): 160(156K). (vi) Passages in tragic rhythm: 5, 83*, 88(85K)*, 89(86K)*, 124(119K)*, 135(130K), 153(149K); an asterisk denotes that the fr. comes from a myth travesty.

(g) Metres. The frs. are predominantly iambic trimeters. Other metres that occur are (i) trochaic tetrameters catalectic 79, 103(98K), 120(115K), 122(117K), 160(156K), 169(164K), ? 170(165K), 215(212K); (ii) anapaestic dimeters 167(162K); (iii) dactylic hexameters 22, 262(260K); (iv) Choerilean (dactylo-epitrite) 137(132K); (v) Eupolideans 239(237K).

II SOURCES OF THE FRAGMENTS

(i) Athenaeus

Schweighaeuser's edition of Ath. 1.v ff., C. G. Cobet's *epistula ad Gaisfordium* (1845) published in B. Hemmerdinger, *Bolletino dei Classici* 10 (1989) 107ff., Kaibel's edition of Ath. 1.v ff., A. M. Desrousseaux's edition of Ath. 1 and 2 (Paris 1956) vii ff., Gow's edition of Machon pp. 25ff., Hunter 30ff., Hemmerdinger 106ff., J. Letrouit, *Maia* 43 (1991) 33ff. Of the 342 frs. of Alexis printed by Kassel–Austin, 212 (= 62 per cent) are cited in Athenaeus' Δειπνοσοφισταί, composed around AD 200.[1] The subject matter of this attempt to emulate Plato's *Symposium* (cf. 1.1f) inevitably leaves a biased and probably incorrect impression that the comic poet's gaze was also focused predominantly on food and drink, together with the people – cooks, parasites, fishmongers, *hetairai* – and objects that go with them. When Ath. cites extant prose authors such as Xenophon, Plato, Aristotle and Theophrastus, he shows himself careful and accurate. Errors that occur are usually the slips of copyists, whether in Ath.'s own sources or in the textual tradition of *Deipnosophistae*. Cases exist where a reading in Ath.'s citation is superior to that of the transmitted continuous text. Ath.'s readings, generally like those in papyri of extant writers, tend not to side with any one family of a cited author's MSS[2]. In his interpretation of cited material Ath. occa-

---

[1] Athenaeus lived at the end of the 2nd and beginning of the 3rd centuries AD; cf. e.g. J. Nicole in *Mélanges (Léon) Renier* (Paris 1887) 27ff., W. Dittenberger in *Apophoreton (XLVII. Versammlung deutscher Philologen und Schulmänner*, Berlin 1903) 1ff., B. Baldwin, *Acta Classica* 19 (1976) 21ff., Nesselrath, *MK* 65f. n. 3, B. Hemmerdinger, *Bolletino dei Classici* 10 (1989) 112f.

[2] Cf. especially K. Zepernick's careful study, *Philologus* 77 (1921) 311ff., and see also C. Collard, *RFIC* 97 (1969) 168ff., W. G. Arnott in Flores 355ff.

sionally deigns to correct an author (e.g. comm. on 22.3) or his source (e.g. on the attribution of Ἀσωτοδιδάσκαλος to Alexis: see 'False or Doubtful Attributions' III), occasionally misinterprets a passage (cf. Ὀδυσσεὺς ὑφαίνων p. 469 n. 1, comm. on 89(86K).1, perhaps 145(141K).10). One feature of his citations from comic poets such as Alexis is the frequency with which these begin and/or end in mid-sentence (see e.g. comm. on frs. 73, 83, 194(189K)); this practice, however, is by no means confined to Athenaeus (cf. e.g. comm. on fr. 136(131K: Pollux).

(a) Δειπνοσοφισταί survives today in two versions: a damaged copy of the original work, and an epitome taken mainly from that copy before it sustained its damage[1]. For the former we have the *codex Marcianus* = A (*Ven. Marc.* 447), written along with the Clarke MS of Plato and two of Aristides by John the Calligrapher probably between AD 895 and 917.[2] In it the first two books and the opening of the third (up to 3.73e in Casaubon's pagination), occupying probably between 40 and 55 folios, are lost; there are gaps of a few folios after 214 (11.466de) and of one after 239 (11.502b); and the final three folios (15.699f–702c) are badly mutilated. The surviving text occupies folios 3 to 372; each page has two columns normally of 43 lines, each line taking 15 to 26 (mainly 20 to 24) letters.[3] The large

---

[1] See particularly I. Düring, *De Athenaei Dipnosophistarum indole atque dispositione* in *Apophoreta Gotoburgensia Vilelmo Lundström oblata* (Göteborg 1936) 226ff., B. Hemmerdinger, *Bolletini dei Classici* 10 (1989) 113f. and J. Letrouit, *Maia* 43 (1991) 37ff. Letrouit shows that eleven uncial references in the margins of the *Marcianus* to τῶν εἰς λ' ('the version in 30') imply merely an earlier MS of Ath. where the work was copied on to thirty rolls. Kaibel's assumption from those references (his edition, 1.xxi ff.) that Ath. originally constructed his work in 30 books which were later abridged to the present 15 in the *Marcianus* must be rejected.

[2] See N. G. Wilson, *JHS* 82 (1962) 147f.

[3] These figures apply to filled lines of text. Gaps of a space of two or three letters, however, are often inserted to mark the end of a section, paragraph or citation, thus limiting the number of letters in a line to twelve.

minuscule hand is well described by Kaibel (1.viii) as *'planis-sima et nitidissima scriptura insignis'*; α is written with an iota-like tail, leading inevitably to confusion between α and αι (cf. introduction to Ἑπτὰ ἐπὶ Θήβαις and n. 2 on pp. 221f.). Citations are often (but not consistently) marked by the sign > affixed in the left-hand margin to each relevant line;[1] here verse is always written as if it were prose. Word-division, when attempted, is clumsy and careless, and there are many errors. Accents and breathings, however, are written consistently; a brief absence of both is often a sign of corruption in a passage (cf. e.g. comm. on 148(144K).1–3.iii).

Full stops and raised points are the usual method of punctuation, but occasionally an insertion of dicola (:) into passages of dramatic dialogue raises a problem: do these also indicate punctuation, or are they mechanically copied from earlier manuscripts which still used dicola to mark a change of speaker? The latter use of dicola has been noted in medieval MSS of Aristophanes,[2] and there are several dialogues cited from Alexis in the *Marcianus* where dicola may be similarly interpreted (cf. e.g. introductions to frs. 129(124K), 140(135K), 242(240K), 249(247K), comm. on 15.13, 177(173K).2).[3] In other places, however, the dicolon is used simply to mark the end of a section[4].

All other MSS of the unabridged version of Ath.[5] are

---

[1] Cf. Cobet's *epistula* (= Hemmerdinger 110). This letter contains by far the best and fullest description of the MS.

[2] See J. Andrieu, *Le Dialogue antique, structure et présentation* (Paris 1954) 210, J. C. B. Lowe, *BICS* 9 (1962) 27ff.

[3] For a possibly parallel dicolon in Epit. MSS (CE) see comm. on fr. 9.1–2.

[4] E.g. in dramatic frs. at line-end in Alexis 15.4, 47(46K).4, 124(119K).2 (mid-sentence!), 222(219K).9, Araros 8.2, 3, Epicharmus 35.8.

[5] E.g. B (*Laurentianus* 60, 1: second half of 15th century), D (*Parisinus gr.* 3056: books 1–9, copied in 1482 by Ermolao Barbaro from the *Marcianus* in Venice), P (*Palatinus Heidelbergensis gr.* 47: copied in 1505–6 by Paolo de Canale).

apographs of the *Marcianus*,[1] but from time to time they incorporate Renaissance conjectures which are often attributed to later scholars.

(b) The Epitome of Ath. survives complete, and thus provides a welcome if inferior substitute for the fuller version in those places where the *Marcianus* is lost or mutilated. The practice of its compiler was to omit some citations haphazardly and all titles of cited works (hence the number of *incertarum fabularum fragmenta* for Alexis and other dramatists), and to cut out or paraphrase sections of frs. Two MSS of Epit. are independent witnesses: E (*Laurentianus* LX, 2), copied by Jacob Questenberg around 1490 in Rome from a lost Vatican MS, and C (*Parisinus suppl. gr.* 841), copied by Demetrios Damilas between 1476 and 1506 from a text similar to, if not identical with, the exemplar of E.[2] Both E and C use abbreviations at word-end which at times are difficult to decipher.

The relationship between A and Epit. is still controversial. C. G. Cobet[3] was the first to claim that Epit. derives wholly from an undamaged *Marcianus*, and so is textually worthless except where it supplements the *Marcianus*' gaps and mutilations. Cobet pointed to Ath. 7.283a, where the error in the Epit. MSS (Κράτης) can be explained only as a misreading of A's correct παγ/Κράτης.[4] P. Maas noted that a scholion which Epit. mentions as being in his exemplar at 12.525c occurs there in the margin of A.[5] More recently

---

[1] This was first noted by Schweighaeuser, *praefatio* to his edition of Ath., p. ci. For the full arguments see R. Schöll, *Hermes* 4 (1869) 16off., W. Dindorf, *Philologus* 30 (1870) 73ff.

[2] See especially C. Aldick, *De Athenaei codicibus Erbacensi Laurentiano Parisino* (Diss. Münster 1928) and P. Canart, *Rivista di studi bizantini e neoellenici* 14–16 (1977–9) 281ff.

[3] In his *epistula* (Hemmerdinger 108), *Oratio de arte interpretandi* (Leiden 1847) 104ff., and elsewhere (cf. J. Letrouit, *Maia* 43 (1991) 33 n. 2).

[4] See Peppink, *Observ.* 19. Cf. also P. Maas, *BZ* 37 (1937) 186, Hemmerdinger 116, Letrouit 37.

[5] *The Year's Work in Classical Studies* 33 (1948) 6, *BZ* 45 (1952) 1f. = *Kleine Schriften* (Munich 1973) 521f., cf. *Textual Criticism* (Oxford 1958) 51f.

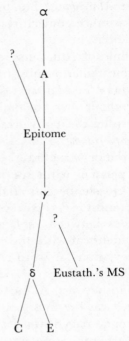

J. Letrouit has added two further pieces of evidence linking *Marcianus* and Epit.: a long list of errors in the Epit. MSS which are most satisfactorily explained as wild attempts to mend corruptions in A, and the fact that the pages containing Ath. 177a–82b, which are misplaced in A, are similarly misplaced in Epit.[1] The combined weight of this evidence seems overwhelming, and the Cobet claim has accordingly convinced good modern scholars.[2] It faces, however, one serious difficulty. If the *Marcianus* was Epit.'s only exemplar, those readings where Epit. is correct and A corrupt, or significantly different from A, must be interpreted as the

---

[1] *Maia* 43 (1991) 34ff.

[2] E.g. H. Erbse *Gnomon* 29 (1957) 290ff., cf. 25 (1953) 441 n. 1, , M. van der Valk, *Eustathii commentarii ad Homeri Iliadem pertinentes* 1 (Leiden 1971) lxxxii ff., Hemmerdinger 115f.

result of Byzantine conjecture. Yet Epit.'s corrections sometimes (cf. e.g. comm. on 115(110K).19 and 159(155K).1
with Ὀδυσσεὺς ὑφαίνων p. 467 n. 1) seem superior to those
made elsewhere by Byzantine scholars,[1] and so it may be
wiser to believe that the *Marcianus* was the main but not the
only source of Epit.

(c) The main source for Eustathius' citation of comic frs.
in his *Homeric Commentaries* was clearly Epit.,[2] but his text
appears in places to have differed from the tradition represented by C and E. How far this is to be explained by the
skill of his and other Byzantine conjectures, how far by
Eustath.'s use of better MS(S), remains uncertain.[3]

(d) The stemma printed on p. 38 may best indicate these
various relationships.

(e) I append a list of editions of Athenaeus, with a
selective bibliography.

Editio princeps: M. Musurus (Venice 1514). Its quality is
assessed by later editors of Ath. (Schweighaeuser 1.xxiv ff.,
Dindorf 1.xiii f., Kaibel 1.xiii f., Desrousseaux xliii f.), its
sources by J. Irigoin, *REG* 80 (1967) 418ff. On Musurus'
career see especially D. J. Geanakoplos, *Greek Scholars in
Venice* (Cambridge, Mass. 1962) 111ff. (155f. on the edition
of Ath.).

J. Bedrotus (Basle 1535). This edition added little new,
but did much to spread knowledge of Ath. north of the Alps.
See Schweighaeuser 1.xxix ff., Dindorf 1.xiv f., Desrousseaux xliv f.

I. Casaubon: edition, with Latin translation by J. Dalé-

---

[1] Cf. e.g. G. Zuntz, *An Enquiry into the Transmission of the Plays of Euripides*
(Cambridge 1965) 193ff., P. Easterling, *CQ* 17 (1957) 58ff., C. Collard,
RFIC 97 (1969) 158ff.

[2] M. van der Valk, *Eustathii commentarii* 1.lxxx ff. and *Mnemosyne* 39 (1986)
400 has effectively scotched the idea that Eustathius was the author of
Epit.

[3] Cf. H. Papenhoff, *Zum Problem der Abhängigkeit der Epitome von der
venezianischen Handschrift. des Athenaios* (Diss. Göttingen 1954) 56, M. van
der Valk 1.lxxix f., lxxxiv f.

champ (1597 Geneva, reprinted 1598 Heidelberg; 1612[2] and 1657[3] Paris); followed by *Animadversiones in Athenaeum* (Paris 1600[1], 1621[2]). See Schweighaeuser 1.xliii ff., Dindorf 1.xv f., Kaibel 1.xx f., Desrousseaux xlvii f. (also xlvi on Daléchamp). Casaubon's own diaries (ed. J. Russell, Oxford 1850) between April 1597 and August 1600 include some illuminating comments about his work on Ath.; cf. also M. Pattison's *Isaac Casaubon* (Oxford 1891[2]) 32, 35ff., 108ff.

G. H. Schäfer, Ath. 1–5 only (vols. 1–3, Leipzig 1796; text, L. de Villebrune's translation, Casaubon's *Animadv.*). See Desrousseaux xlix f. on Villebrune.

J. Schweighaeuser: edition, with Latin translation (vols. 1–5, Strasbourg 1801–5); concurrent with *Animadversiones . . . post Isaacum Casaubonum* (vols. 1–9, Strasbourg 1801–7; the final volume provides a still invaluable index). See especially P. Elmsley's unsigned review in *Ed. Rev.* 3 (1803) 181ff.; also Dindorf 1.xvi f., Desrousseaux l f.

W. Dindorf (3 vols., Leipzig 1827–8). See Desrousseaux li f. Fraenkel's comments (edition of A. *Ag.* 1.53f.) about Dindorf's editions of Aeschylus apply equally well to his edition of Ath.

A. Meineke: edition (3 vols., Leipzig 1858–9); followed by *Analecta critica* (1867). See Kaibel 1.xxi, Desrousseaux lii f.

G. Kaibel (3 vols., Leipzig 1887–90). His greatness as a scholar is rightly recognised (see e.g. Wilamowitz, *Erinnerungen*[2] (Leipzig 1929) 240ff., K. J. Dover in *Fifty Years (and Twelve) of Classical Scholarship* (Oxford 1962) 151 n. 3), but his edition of Ath. is somewhat marred by errors and omissions in his reports of A and Epit. MSS; see especially Peppink, *Observ.* 1ff., Desrousseaux liii, B. Hemmerdinger, *Bolletino dei Classici* 10 (1989) 116.

G. B. Gulick (7 vols., text with English translation in the Loeb series, London and New York 1927–41). See E. Harrison, *CR* 55 (1941) 78, G. Luck in *La filologia greca e latina nel secolo xx* 1 (Pisa 1989) 247.

S. P. Peppink: edition of epitome of Ath. from 3.74a to the

end (2 vols., Leiden 1937–9), preceded by *Observationes in Athenaei Deipnosophistas* (Leiden 1936). Still valuable, despite major flaws (it has no apparatus to record the readings of C and E, nor does it always transcribe accurately what is in the MSS). See P. Maas, *BZ* 37 (1937) 185f., 38 (1938) 201f., M. van der Valk, *Eustathii commentarii ad Homeri Iliadem pertinentes* 1 (Leiden 1971) lxxx.

A. M. Desrousseaux, with help of C. Astruc, Ath. 1–2 only (text and French translation in the Budé series, Paris 1956). An informative introduction, but see H. Erbse, *Gnomon* 29 (1957) 290ff.

G. Turturro, Ath. 1–2 only (text and Italian translation, Bari 1961). Of little critical value.

The lack of totally reliable collations of the *Marcianus* and Epit. MSS (C, E) has made it necessary for me in this commentary to check all readings against photographs kindly supplied by the relevant libraries.

(ii) Other sources

Three other sources account for a further 26 per cent of the frs. of Alexis: the lexicon of the Antiatticist (38 frs.), Pollux (26) and books 3 and 4 of Stobaeus' *Eclogae* (27).

(a) The Antiatticist

L. J. Sicking, *Annotationes*, J. de (von) Borries, *Phrynichi sophistae praeparatio sophistica* (Leipzig 1911) xxxvff., K. Latte, *Hermes* 20 (1915) 384ff. = *Kleine Schriften* (Munich 1968) 612ff., E. Fischer, *Die Ekloge des Phrynichos* (Berlin and New York 1974) 39ff. The so-called Antiatticist lexicon is 'the scanty excerpt of a lexicon of the second century AD, so abbreviated as to be often unintelligible'.[1] Most of its entries

---

[1] F. Jacoby, *CQ* 38 (1944) 65. On the origin of the name 'Antiatticist' see Sicking, *Annotationes* 2.

consist simply of a headword followed by the name of an author and his work where that word allegedly occurred. Even so, it is clear that the unknown author of the original lexicon was attempting to widen the acceptable range of Attic authors and vocabulary by admitting comic poets like Alexis into his magic circle. The precise relationship between this lexicon and those of much stricter Atticists like Phrynichus is disputed, but it seems very probable that sections of Phrynichus' *Eclogae* are composed as a direct attack on the Antiatticist.

The lexicon is preserved in one tenth-century MS (*Seguerianus* or *Coislinianus* 345, folios 156ʳ–165ᵛ) written in minuscule and titled simply ἄλλος ἀλφάβητος. It was published by I. Bekker in *Anecdota Graeca* I (Berlin 1814) 75–116, with critical notes in 3 (1821) 1074–7. In this commentary its readings have been checked against photographs of the MS supplied by the Bibliothèque Nationale, Paris.

(b) Pollux

Bethe in *RE* s.v. *Iulius* 398 (*Pollux*), 773.55ff. Julius Pollux came, like Athenaeus, from Naucratis, and was an opponent, like the Antiatticist, of the stricter school of Atticism represented by Phrynichus. Between AD 166 and 176 he wrote his *Onomasticon* as a thesaurus of Attic terms, arranged not alphabetically but by topics. The original work is now lost; what we possess is an abridgement, as a scholion prefixed to book 1 in A and other MSS shows. In citing comic poets such as Alexis Pollux sometimes names just the author, sometimes author and play-title.[1] The citations range in length from single words and phrases, as in the Antiatticist (e.g. 309(308K), 312–15(311–14K)), up to six iambic trimeters (132(127K).3–8).

---

[1] Cf. the index volume of E. Bethe's edition (Leipzig 1937) p. 1 s.v. Ἄλεξις.

42

All our MSS of Pollux seem to descend from a codex of the abridgement once owned by Arethas, Archbishop of Caesarea in the 10th century. They fall into four groups: (1) M (*Ambrosianus* D 34 *sup.*, 10th or 11th century: 1.21–2.78 only); (2) F (*Falcoburgianus* = *Parisinus gr.* 2646, 15th century like all the following MSS, except where otherwise indicated) and S (*Schottianus* = *Salmanticensis* 1.2.3); (3) A (*Parisinus gr.* 2670) and V (*Marcianus* 520: 1.1–151 only); and (4) C (*Palatinus Heidelbergensis* 375, 12th century), L (*Laurentianus* 56.1, 14th century: books 8–10 only) and B (*Tellerianus* = *Parisinus gr.* 2647, 13th century).

The *editio princeps* (Aldus, Venice 1502) was based on a lost MS of the second group and on a contaminated descendant of MSS linked to A and B. E. Bethe's edition (Leipzig: books 1–5 1900, 6–10 1931, index 1937) is palmary.

(c) Stobaeus

Hense in *RE* s.v. *Ioannes* 18 (*Stobaios*), *Nachtrag* 2549.3ff., S. Luria, *Rh. Mus.* 78 (1929) 81ff., 225ff., D. A. Campbell in D. E. Gerber (ed.), *Greek Poetry and Philosophy: Studies in Honour of Leonard Woodbury* (Chico Cal. 1984) 51ff., F. Hernández Muñoz, *Cuadernos de Filología Clásica* 23 (1989) 131ff. Stobaeus composed his anthology of poetry and prose probably in the early 5th century AD. The extracts from Alexis appear in books 3 and 4 of the anthology (the Ἐκλογαί section), which collect passages under a variety of ethical and social headings. As with Athenaeus, the principles of selectivity produce a limited and distorted picture of a cited writer's interests. It is clear that a good number of the extracts have been doctored in order to suit better the requirements of an anthology; words and phrases have been omitted or displaced, alterations of different kinds abound. Even so, in cases where checks can be made against surviving texts of Stobaeus' sources, the anthology sometimes preserves correct readings where the complete texts are corrupt.[1]

The MSS of books 3 and 4 fall into three groups: (1) S (*Vindobonensis Sambuci phil. gr.* 67, 11th century); (2) M (*Escurialensis Mendozae* 90, II.Σ.14, end of 11th or beginning of 12th century) and A (*Parisinus gr.* 1984, 14th century); and (3), containing selections only, L (*Laurentianus plut.* VIII.22, 14th century: see now A. L. de Lello-Finuoli, *QUCC* 4 (1967) 139ff.) and Br (*Bruxellensis cod. misc.* 11360, 14th or 15th century). The *editio princeps* (V. Trincavelli, Venice 1536, though the colophon is dated the year before) was based on *Marcianus class.* IV *cod.* XXIX, of the 15th or 16th century, a manuscript closely related to S but interpolated from other sources. O. Hense's edition (3 vols., Berlin 1894, 1909, 1912) is palmary.

---

[1] See e.g. the careful analyses of W. Görler, ΜΕΝΑΝΔΡΟΥ ΓΝωΜΑΙ (Diss. Berlin 1963) 106f., Barrett's edition of Eur. *Hipp.* pp. 82f. and E. W. Handley, comm. on Men. *Dysk.* 797–812.

COMMENTARY

Ἀγκυλίων

Meineke 1.359, Kock 2.164f., Breitenbach 74f., Hunter 85f., R. M. Rosen, *CQ* 39 (1989) 355ff., Nesselrath, *MK* 198f., 287 n. 10. In addition to being the title of 4th-century comedies by Alexis and Eubulus, Ἀγκυλίων appears as (1) the name of a monumental mason on an archaic inscription from the island of Anaphe (*IG* xii.3.255, cf. L. H. Jeffery, *The Local Scripts of Archaic Greece*[2] (Oxford 1990) 322 and pl. 62.26); (2) the name assigned by Aristophanes at *Vesp.* 1397 to the father of Myrtia the bread-seller for a reason now obscure (could it have been a joke on the nickname of some crooked contemporary? Cf. H. Müller-Strübing, *Aristophanes und die historische Kritik* (Leipzig 1873) 328n., H. Steiger, *Der Eigenname in der attischen Komödie, Acta Sem. Phil. Erlang.* 5 (1891) 8f.); and (3) the subject of an old μῦθος: Σ Ar. *Vesp.* 1178a Καρδοπίων· καὶ τοῦτο ἀρχὴ μύθου· Δίδυμος· ὁ Καρδοπίων ζητητέος· οὐδαμοῦ κωμῳδεῖται. ἀλλὰ Ἀγκυλίων, ἐπὶ τῷ τὴν μητέρα διατιθέναι. This scholiast is commenting on a cryptic line of Aristophanes, where Philocleon mentions the old story ὡς ὁ Καρδοπίων τὴν μητέρα ... (the speaker here suppresses the main verb, which in all probability would have been an obscenity such as ἐβίνησε rather than the feebler alternative suggested by the Σ at 1178b, ἔτυψεν or ἐτύπτησεν: cf. Hunter 85f., J. N. Adams, *Phoenix* 35 (1981) 121f.). The scholiast's own information is equally cryptic, for its κωμῳδεῖται is imprecise, and διατιθέναι obscure. The former word might imply (so Meineke, Breitenbach) that one comedy or more had been written about the adventures of this Ankylion, but it could as well refer to a passing taunt in a comedy on another subject, like the one at Ar. *Vesp.* 1397. τὴν μητέρα διατιθέναι is also difficult. Unless διατιθέναι is to be interpreted as a critic's euphemism for an obscenity such as βινεῖν (and I know of no parallel for such a usage), corruption must be presumed: thus <κακῶς> διατιθέναι Biset. Whatever the correct interpretation of διατιθέναι, however, information about the Ankylion μῦθος is today sadly deficient. The story was familiar enough to the ancients to have become proverbial (cf. Miller, *Mélanges* 374: ρμε΄· Ἀ<γ>κυλίωνος λεγομένην, sc. παροιμίαν; cf. Meineke, *Hermes* 3 (1869) 456)[1] but our ignorance about its origin

---

[1] Presumably the proverb derived from the folk-tale or caused the tale's invention in order to account for the proverb. There is a similar connection between the proverbial use of the name Ἔμβαρος (Men. *Phasm.* 80) and the folk-tale recounted in full by Pausanias the Atticist (Eustath. 331.26 = p. 177 Erbse; see Körte on Men. *Phasm.* 'fr. 2',

(traditional folk-tale? dimly remembered event?) and its subject matter (seduction of mother? – folk-tales with this theme still survive in southern Europe, cf. R. M. Dawkins, *More Greek Folk Tales* (Oxford 1955) 369ff. – or just general ill-treatment of her, such as beating?) is total. Nor can we be certain that the μῦθος had anything to do with either of the known Ἀγκυλίων titles, for although ancient comedy takes some part of its material from the world of folk lore (T. Zielinski, *Die Märchenkomödie in Athen* (St Petersburg 1885)), and is familiar with the motifs of mother-beating (Ar. *Nub.* 1443ff.; cf. Meineke 1.359) and maternal incest (Eubulus wrote an Οἰδίπους!), nothing that remains from Alexis' or Eubulus' Ἀγκυλίων supports the theory that either plot was based on the folk-tale. The surviving fr. of Alexis' play gives no tangible clue to the type of scene from which it comes; cooking, food and victory prizes are the main topics of the Eubulus frs., although his fr. 2(3K), with its references to all-night dancing and a baby's name-day celebration, seems (perhaps illusively) rather to belong to the world of intrigue that we associate with New Comedy, whatever the date of Eubulus' play may have been. And other interpretations of the title cannot be excluded. Thus the name would well suit a schemer, slave (so Nesselrath, *MK* 287 n. 10) or free; but whether in this connection an association with the Homeric ἀγκυλομήτης is involved (so Müller–Strübing), with compounds like ἀγκυλόκωλος, ἀγκυλοχήλης (so Bechtel, *Spitznamen* 34), or with deft manipulation of the wrist (ἀπ' ἀγκύλης) in the game of cottabus at symposia (so Rosen), is uncertain. Or again Ankylion could have been a prologue figure, introducing the plot in the garb of the folk-tale character; cf. Webster's idea (*SLGC* 83) that the earth-spirits Orthanes and Konisalos played similar roles in comedies with these titles by Eubulus and Timocles respectively.

Alexis' Ἀγκυλίων is probably to be dated before 347, since its one surviving fr. implies that the philosopher Plato was still alive (cf. Alexis' Παράσιτος, possibly also Μεροπίς). If consequently Alexis' play was written during Eubulus' lifetime (cf. Hunter 7ff.), Breitenbach's inference that it was not a διασκευή (on this term see the introduction to Δημήτριος) of Eubulus' play is plausible but not certain (for allegations of plagiarism during a victim's lifetime see Ar. *Nub.* 553f., cf. Σ *Av.* 750), and the relationship between the two plays must be considered doubtful.

I

Meineke 3.382, Kock 2.297, Edmonds 2.374, Kassel–Austin 2.24. The context is uncertain, but note that in Alexis fr. 129(124K).19f. a cook

---

Wilamowitz, *Schiedsg.* 141 n. 2, Escher in *RE* s.v. *Embaros* 2482.6ff., the Gomme–Sandbach comm. *ad loc.*

rebuffs a traducer of his professional skill in terms not too dissimilar, while at Ath. 4.161d one of the deipnosophists makes an accusation against philosophers that λαλεῖτε περὶ ὧν οὐκ οἴδατε. It would not be surprising if the man addressed here was an ἀλαζών, perhaps a cook who has just mentioned onions and carbonate of soda; the point in v. 2 would be clearer if these two things had already been referred to in the preceding conversation.

1 περὶ ὧν: hiatus after περί is admitted in comedy, as it is e.g. after τί (Alexis 27.6, etc.), ὅτι/ὅ τι (247(245K).15), possibly τι (27.8 and comm.), and in such phrases as οὐδὲ/μηδὲ εἷς (15.10, etc.), εὖ οἶδα (253(251K).2), μὴ ὥρασι (268(266K).1) and ἄχρι/μεχρὶ ἄν. See K. B. 1.197, Descroix 26ff., Gomme–Sandbach, *Comm.* on Men. *Sam.* 393.

συγγενοῦ: Cobet's certain correction (*NL* 284) of BFP's συγγενοῦς. The error (before τρέχων) possibly reflects the common confusion between minuscule τ and ligatured στ (e.g. ἑκατόν/ἕκαστον at Pl. *Resp.* 8.546c, διατάσεις corrupted to διαστάσεις 3.407c; G. Thomson, *The Oresteia of Aeschylus*[2], 2 (Amsterdam and Prague 1966) 238, E. W. Handley's edition of Men. *Dysk.* p. 51). The sequence συγγενοῦ (imperative) . . . καὶ γνώσῃ (future) is illustrated by Diggle, *Studies* 70, with numerous examples from drama (add Eur. *Alc.* 544, 1119). On the orthography γνώσῃ (? -σει) see comm. on fr. 182 (177K).

2 λίτρον: the MSS of Diog. Laert. 3.27 have λίτρον here, but the *Marcianus* at Ath. 6.230b and 11.502f has ἐκνενιτρωμένα twice in its two citations of Alexis fr. 2.4. λίτρον (carbonate of soda, used primarily in place of soap, but for other purposes as well: Schramm in *RE* s.v. *Nitrum* 776.6ff., Gow on Theoc. 15.16, W. K. Pritchett, *Hesperia* 25 (1956) 311f.) is the correct Attic orthography (*IG* i[3].422.150, Phrynichus, *Ecl.* p. 89 Fischer, Moeris and Photius s.v. λίτρον; cf. Chr. Theodoridis, *ZPE* 82 (1990) 44f., citing Phot. s.v. ἐκλελιτρωμένα· ἐκνενιτρωμένα), but is replaced by νίτρον in Hellenistic Greek (cf. Mayser–Schmoll, 1.1.10, 27). I support the MSS here mainly because they are less likely to corrupt a later (and contemporary) form into an earlier one than vice versa, but partly because of the date of Alexis' Ἀγκυλίων. At fr. 2.4 the decision is more difficult; there ἐκνενιτρωμένα might have ousted the Attic form ἐκλελι- from the MSS, or Alexis himself could have been inconsistent in his usage (note that the play from which 2.4 derives is slightly later than Ἀγκυλίων).

Sneers at Plato like that contained in fr. 1 seem to have been as fashionable in Attic comedy of the first sixty years or so of the 4th century as sneers against Socrates were in Old Comedy. Ten such attacks are collected by Diog. Laert. in the passage from which this fr. derives (3.26–8; also Alexis 151(147K), 163(158K), 185(180K)), but this does not exhaust even the extant material; Diog. Laert. fails to note, for instance,

COMMENTARY

Alexis 98(152K) and two celebrated frs. – Epicrates 10(11K) on Platonic analysis and Ephippus 14 ridiculing the clothes-consciousness of a member of the Academy – and he ignores the fact that Aristophon wrote a play entitled Πλάτων. The relevant frs. are listed by Meineke 5.845 s.v. Πλάτων; for general discussion see especially Meineke 1.287ff., R. Helm, *Lucian und Menipp* (Leipzig and Berlin 1906) 376ff., C. Ritter, *Platon: sein Leben, seine Schriften, seine Lehre* 1 (Munich 1910) 191ff., R. Fenk, *Adversarii Platonis quomodo de indole ac moribus eius iudicaverint* (Diss. Jena 1913) 39, A. Weiher, *Philosophen und Philosophenspott in der attischen Komödie* (Diss. Munich 1913), K. Lever, *CJ* 49 (1953) 176f., Webster, *SLGC* 50ff., G. J. de Vries, *Hermeneus* 27 (1955) 2ff., Gil 337f., Arnott, *G and R* 19 (1972) 70f., R. Stark, *Aristotelesstudien*[2] (Munich 1972) 73ff., K. Gaiser in U. Reinhardt and K. Sallmann (edd.), *Musa Iocosa: A. Thierfelder zum siebzigsten Geburtstag* (Hildesheim 1974) 62ff., R. Brock in E. M. Craik (ed.), *'Owls to Athens': Essays on Classical Subjects Presented to Sir Kenneth Dover* (Oxford 1990) 39ff. The jibes are based on superficial appearances, distortions, inaccurate or garbled rumour, prejudice of all kinds, and an anti-intellectual comic tradition that goes back at least as far as Aristophanes; naturally, Plato need not enter the dock to answer all the comic charges. The present fr., however, is particularly interesting for its bizarre collocation of onion and carbonate of soda. Why should a man in a comedy be told that he will learn about these two things from Plato? Part of the answer is doubtless that advanced implicitly by Meineke and elaborated by some of the scholars listed above: Alexis is pouring scorn on the Academy's interest in definition and classification during Plato's later years. This interest was pilloried by Epicrates in the fr. cited above, where the main target seems to be the triviality of the objects that the Academy selected for classification. In the same way Socrates' alleged practice was ridiculed by Aristophanes (*Nub.* 144ff.). But there may be more to Alexis' ridicule here than the triviality of λίτρον and κρόμμυον. Was the former word chosen to hint at the fastidious and elegant cleanliness that distinguished the Academy (at least in comic eyes: Ephippus 14, Antiphanes 35(33K)) from the scruffy ascetics (cf. the introduction to Πυθαγορί-ζουσα)? The implications of κρόμμυον are more difficult to see. We are not aware that Plato had a particular fondness for onions, as he is related to have had for olives (Anaxandrides 20(19K), Diog. Laert. 6.25) and figs (Ath. 7.276f citing Phanocritus, Plut. *Mor.* 668a);[1] but it is possible that to the comic poet onions symbolised the kind of existence idealised by Platonic philosophy. Onions were among the typical iron rations of

---

[1] J. Haussleiter sensibly notes (*Der Vegetarianismus in der Antike* (Berlin 1935) 184ff.) that this predilection did not necessarily make Plato a vegetarian.

soldiers on campaign (Ar. *Ach.* 1099ff., *Equ.* 600, *Pax* 1129), and they formed part of the simple lunch packet of the 5th-century ecclesiast according to the chorus of *Eccl.* 306ff. Such a diet of onions, olives and a scrap of bread might well be suggested to the comic poet's man in the street by (e.g.) the vegetarian diet proposed by Plato in *Resp.* 2.372a–d for the inhabitants of his πρώτη πόλις (even though onions are not specifically named there). This interpretation cannot of course be proved correct, but it is in keeping with the tone of the one fr. preserved from Aristophon's Πλάτων (8), where the speaker (most probably Plato or an assistant) threatens to make somebody thinner than the scarecrow Philippides (see comm. on Alexis 2.8) by his regimen.

Ἀγωνὶς ἢ Ἱππίσκος

Meineke 1.385ff., Breitenbach 135, N. Terzaghi, *Fabula* 1 (Milan 1912) 76f., W. G. Arnott, *PCPS* 196 (1970) 9ff., Nesselrath, *MK* 253 nn. 32, 34 and 319 n. 97, Kassel–Austin 2.24. The play is cited by Ath. twice with its alternative titles (8.339c, 15.678e), and at least three times just as Ἱππίσκος (3.120b, 6.230b, 11.502f; on 11.471c, where this title is conjecturally restored, see on fr. 5; on 13. 610e, see the introduction to Ἱππεύς and fr. 99(94K)). Alternative titles are recorded for eight or possibly nine of Alexis' other plays (Δημήτριος, Δορκίς, possibly one of the *Helen* plays, Κράτεια, Λευκαδία, Παννυχίς, Τοκιστής, probably Φαίδων (or Φείδων), Φιλόκαλος, qq.v.). In the cases of Δημήτριος and Κράτεια it seems highly likely that the second title was devised for a second production of the play in a revised version, but it is unwise to assume (as does B. W. Bender, *De graecae comoediae titulis duplicibus* (Diss. Marburg 1904) 51) that this explanation must be extended also to plays such as Ἀγωνὶς ἢ Ἱππίσκος, where there is no evidence for any restaging. Most probably Alexis called the play simply Ἱππίσκος – the title given in the majority of the citations, even though these may all have had a common source in Pamphilus' lexicon – while the alternative title Ἀγωνίς was added later from the name of a leading character, perhaps by some Alexandrian critic (cf. I. Capovilla, *SIFC* 19 (1912) 36off., Terzaghi 5–142, especially 76f.: still the most judicious full discussion of the question, R. Cantarella, *Rend. Ist. Lomb.* 93 (1959) 79f., Gomme–Sandbach, *Comm.* 129f., O. Taplin, *JHS* 95 (1975) 185, Hunter 146ff.), whose purpose can no longer be detected with certainty. If his aim was to avoid confusion with other titles of Greek comedy, why are alternative titles preserved for plays like Ἀγωνίς, where the chances of another play having existed with a similar title seem remote, and not for plays such as Alexis' Ἀδελφοί, which has at least seven comic namesakes, none with a recorded alternative title?

COMMENTARY

Here Ἀγωνίς clearly is a woman's name. It occurs again on a vase from Alexandria dated to 298 or 260 (F. Courby, *Les Vases grecs à reliefs* (Paris 1922) 216), and as the name of a freedwoman of Lilybaeum in Cicero's time (*Div. Caec.* 55f.) who had previously been a temple prostitute of Aphrodite of Eryx (cf. R. Schilling, *La religion romaine de Vénus* (Paris 1954) 237f.). An entry in the *Suda* runs (s.v.) Ἀγωνίς· ὄνομα ἑταίρας. The ultimate source of this entry is not likely to have been the passage of Cicero, but rather one of the lists of *hetairai* compiled by Hellenistic scholars; Ath. 13.583d names among their authors Aristophanes of Byzantium, Apollodorus and a Gorgias. There is no means of knowing whether the *Suda* reference was to a real-life *hetaira* or to Alexis' title. If the former, one possibility is that Alexis stole his heroine's name from a real-life courtesan of his own or a preceding generation. However, the extant frs. of Alexis' play suggest that it had for its plot a fictitious love intrigue (see below). Could Alexis have been pioneering a method used later by Menander in his Θαΐς and Diphilus in his Νέαιρα? This is not beyond the bounds of reason, but before we assign an inventor's role to Alexis here, we shall do well to remember the frequency with which 4th-century comedians named their plays after *hetairai*, both fictitious and historical. For the latter, note particularly Antiphanes' Μαλθάκη, Epicrates' Ἀντιλαΐς, Eubulus' Κλεψύδρα, Νάννιον and Πλαγγών, and Timocles' Νέαιρα, and cf. Körte in *RE* s.v. *Komödie* 1262.14ff., 1269.50ff. (after Breitenbach), H. Hauschild, *Die Gestalt der Hetäre in der griechischen Komödie* (Diss. Leipzig 1933) 14, Wehrli, *Motivstudien* 28, Webster, *SLGC* 22f., 63f.

The interpretation of ἱππίσκος is less certain. The word is used for a woman's garment and an article of jewellery.[1] Pollux 7.58 (citing Cratinus jun. 5, 4.340 Kassel–Austin) identifies it as a sort of χιτωνίσκος; Hesych. s.v. says it is ἐπίθεμα κεφαλῆς or γυναικεῖον κόσμιον. The latter definition might suggest a small brooch in the shape of a horse, as does the mid-4th-century inventory from the temple of Hera in Samos which lists a ἱππίσκος made of bronze (C. Michel, *Recueil d'inscriptions grecques* (Paris 1900) 832.41, D. Ohly, *Ath. Mitt.* 68 (1953) 47.41). But whether garment or jewellery, the ἱππίσκος in Alexis' play is most likely to have been used as a recognition token (Webster, *SM* 171 and *CQ* 2 (1952) 25); parallels would include Men. *Sik.* 280 (flap of χιτωνίσκος; cf. *Epitr.* 404); *Pk.* 768ff., 822, Longus 1.2, cf. 4.21 (small cloak); A. *Choeph.* 231f., Eur. *Ion* 1417ff. (ὕφασμα; cf. his *Alope*, with its *uestis scissa*: Hähnle 30ff.); *Ion* 1427ff., Men. *Epitr.* 384ff. (amulets, jewels, or toys in the form of animals, etc.; cf. also the 'winged horse' of *Pk.* 772, which Hähnle 82f., 87 inter-

---

[1] It also occurs in Attica as a proper name (Kirchner, *PA* 1.500, nos. 7607–8); but Breitenbach 108 is almost certainly right to discount this possibility here.

prets as a carved stone on a ring, but Gomme–Sandbach as a figure embroidered on or woven in cloth; and the *sucula* of Plaut. *Rud.* 1170, probably a jewel in the shape of a tiny pig). Yet other interpretations of the function of the ἱππίσκος in Alexis' play must not be excluded; note the very different use made of the *palla* motif in Plaut. *Men.* (W. Steidle, *Rh. Mus.* 114 (1971) 249ff.).

A little more may be learnt about the play's subject from the surviving frs. Fr. 2, despite corruption at a vital point in v. 2, gives most information. There are two speakers. One describes how he met a ξένος and showed him some curious silver plate.[1] The other says that this was a good idea – πρὸς ἀλαζονείαν. In introducing part of this fr. Ath. (6.230b) explains that here Alexis presents a young man in love who is showing off (ἐπιδεικνύμενον) his wealth to his beloved. But however high Ath.'s standards of care and accuracy may be in the transcription of citations (cf. K. Zepernick, *Philologus* 77 (1921) 311ff., C. Collard, *RFIC* 97 (1969) 157ff.), his interpretations of subject matter and dramatic context are frequently unsatisfactory (see on fr. 89(86K)). Here his remark about 'showing off' seems plausible only in a context where the young man was trying to impress his girl friend by describing the silver plate with which he had duped the ξένος.

On the analogy of other intrigue plays, it seems likely that ἡ ἐρωμένη (and therefore the second speaker of fr. 2) is the *hetaira* Agonis. The display of plate before the ξένος was probably aimed at forwarding the young man's affair with her; more than this we cannot say, in the absence of precise information about the identity of the ξένος (see on fr. 2.1–2). But young men in love with *hetairai* are normally poor by comic tradition; the hero of fr. 2 is perhaps unlikely to have owned the plate. If it belonged to his parents, a scene in which his mother inveighs against her son's dissolute passion might have provided an occasion for the son to retort with fr. 3. In the end the *hetaira* might have established free birth and rights of citizenship by means of recognition tokens, and married the young man; but this is only one of several possibilities.

How frs. 4 and 5 fit into such a scenario it is hard to say. In the former somebody (the young hero?) describes a dead man he appears to be seeing before him. As the description is in the present tense, the vision can hardly be a dream; more probably it is part of a 'mad scene' where the speaker pretends to see hallucinations (Webster, *SLGC* 76: see comm. on the fr.). Significantly, a parody in fr. 3 harks back to the mad scene of Eur. *Orestes*, which had a production at Athens in 340 (*IG* ii².2320.18f. = Pickard-

---

[1] On the implausible lightness of the silver plate, which may have had both a humorous and a dramatic purpose, see comm. on fr. 2.5–7.

COMMENTARY

Cambridge, *DFA*² 109, Mette III A 2 col. 2.21), perhaps just before Alexis' play was written (see below). Fr. 5 belongs to a large group of frs. and passages describing a meal and/or a drinking bout in elevated language (Alexis, especially 88(85K), 89(86K), 124(119K) and comm., 153(149K).15–19; cf. Meineke 1.291ff., W. Süss, *Rh. Mus.* 65 (1910) 450ff., Fraenkel, *MNC* 13ff., Webster, *SLGC* 22, 65f., Handley on Men. *Dysk.* 946–53, Hunter 19f., Nesselrath, *MK* 241ff.). Fraenkel points to 5th-century tragedy (e.g. Eur. *Alc.* 747ff., *Ion* 1122ff.) as the inspirational source, but contemporary influences certainly included dithyramb (cf. the introduction to fr. 124(119K).2–3). In Men. *Dysk.* 946ff. the context is a cook's account of the betrothal party closing the play. Though by analogy a slave or cook could have spoken fr. 5 here in a similar narrative at the end of Ἀγωνίς, the evidence is too slight to support such speculations.

The play may have been one of the earliest intrigue plays about which we have information. H. F. Clinton (*Fasti Hellenici* 2 (Oxford 1824) 127) dates it to *c.*344 because of the reference to Misgolas in fr. 3; he is followed by most scholars. 344 is the year following Aeschines' speech against Timarchus, in which Misgolas' homosexuality was attacked (see on fr. 3). But what reason is there to suppose that Misgolas' practices were any more notorious because of this one speech, or that he limited them to a few years in the middle 340s? Any date in the 340s or 330s must be considered in the absence of firmer evidence, though Webster's suggestion (*CQ* 2 (1952) 20f.), that the parody in fr. 3 would gain in point if Alexis' play came soon after the 340 production of Eur. *Orestes*, is attractive. The other historical figures mentioned in the frs., Philippides (2.8) and Phidippus (6), fit in with these dates without helping to achieve any greater precision.

Eculeus appears to have been one of Novius' Atellane titles (Ribbeck, *CRF*³ 311, Frassinetti 75), but it is impossible to say whether this had any connection with Alexis or not.

2

Meineke 3.383 (II), Kock 2.297, Edmonds 2.374, Kassel–Austin 2.24; cf. W. G. Arnott, *PCPS* 196 (1970) 9ff. The fr. is constructed from two overlapping citations in Ath.: 11.502f (beginning to v. 8 λεπτότερον) and 6.230b (v. 3 τοῖς παισί τ' to end of fr.). Differences of reading in the overlap cause trouble only at v. 7.

1–2 Interpretation of the two vv., and consequently knowledge about the events described in the fr. as a whole, are bedevilled by corruption in v. 2, where A has ησονην αἴθων ἀνήρ. Two lines of approach deserve mention. Either correct ησονην to ᾗ συνῆν, keeping αἴθων ἀνήρ as its subject, and take εἰς τὴν κατάλυσιν with ἀπήντων; basically this was the idea of Grotius, *Exc.* 557, 971. Alternatively, interpret the -ην part of A's gibberish as ἦν, construe αἴθων ἀνήρ as its predicate, and correct what remains to ἦγον (Meineke, *ed. min.* 689 and *Fragmenta comicorum graecorum* 5.87 after 3.384), ἦκον (R. Ellis, *AJP* 6 (1885) 288) or even ἦλθον (Blaydes, *Adv.* 1.104), taking εἰς τὴν κατάλυσιν with whichever of the conjectured verbs seems preferable. The latter approach has two advantages. The asyndetic piece of narrative thereby produced is of a type particularly favoured by comic poets[1] (E. Capps on Men. *Epitr.* '33'ff. = 250ff. Gomme–Sandbach, Handley on Men. *Dysk.* 19f.; cf. Fraenkel, *MNC* 23 and *passim*, J. D. Denniston, *Greek Prose Style* (Oxford 1952) 116ff.). Secondly, surprise words like αἴθων are logically and dramatically more effective in such contexts as part of the predicate than as part of the subject. ἦγον scores over the other verbs suggested because it keeps the ξένος (as its implied object) in the centre of the picture: an important point if the following ἦν is correctly interpreted as third person (see below). Although confusion between σ and γ is rather less common than might be expected from their similar appearance in some papyrus book hands, one may note instances in the transmission at A. *Ag.* 101, *Eum.* 221; *P.V.* 77; cf. D. L. Page on Eur. *Med.* 1296 and Jackson, *Marg. Scaen.* 238f.

On the provisional basis of this emendation, a guess may be hazarded at the dramatic implications of the two vv. The questions are three: what is the meaning and reference of αἴθων; who was the ξένος; how does the κατάλυσις relate to the actions mentioned in the fr.? First, ἦν αἴθων ἀνήρ. Well before Alexis' time αἴθων had passed from epic into general poetic currency, and sometimes it was used by 5th- and 4th-century writers as an epic cliché,[2] often in senses developed beyond Homeric usage. Its application to human temperament (= *feruidi ingenii*, Meineke) is an example of the latter kind of use, whose origin is perhaps to be explained as a misreading of contexts in earlier poetry where to later writers the word

---

[1] Thus Meineke's (3.384) conjectural additions of τε and δέ here (τ' ἦγον· ἦν δ' α. ἀ.) must be resisted.

[2] First, the imitation of Homer's αἴθωνι σιδήρῳ (*Il.* 4.485, *Od.* 1.184, cf. Hes. *Op.* 743) by Sophocles (*Aj.* 147) and Aristophanes (*Pax* 1328), and the brilliant allusion to this cliché in ? Hermippus 47(46K).7 (see Kassel–Austin 5.582f.), where Κλέωνι replaces σιδήρῳ for the joke. The comic poet here is playing on the secondary meaning of αἴθων, 'impetuous', with allusion to Cleon's well-known excitability (the idea that there may have been a reference to the colour of Cleon's hair is neatly squashed by R. A. Neil on Ar. *Equ.* 901). Secondly, the imitation of the epic phrase λιμὸν αἴθωνα (Hes. fr. 43a.5–7) by the author of the Herm

appeared to be ambiguously poised between the original visual ('glittering' or 'dull red-brown' like fire) and the later temperamental sense: e.g. Hom. *Il.* 16.487f. ταῦρον ... αἴθωνα μεγάθυμον, or Tyrtaeus fr. 13 West αἴθωνος δὲ λέοντος ἔχων ἐν στήθεσι θυμόν. Aeschylus is the first known writer to apply the adjective unequivocally to a fiery temper, *Sept.* 447f. ἀνὴρ δ' ... αἴθων τέτακται λῆμα; then generally in tragedy, S. *Aj.* 221 ἀνδρὸς αἴθονος, 1087f. αἴθων ὑβριστής, [Eur.(?)] *Rhes.* 122 αἴθων γὰρ ἀνήρ. When Plato used the word of animals in *Resp.* 8.559d αἴθωσι θηρσὶ καὶ δεινοῖς, clearly he meant the word to be taken in the temperamental sense (ὀξέσι τὴν ὁρμήν, Σ), but equally clearly he was influenced by the word's habitual application to animals in epic and other poetry in senses that he perhaps misunderstood. In comedy αἴθων is always an affected word, a choice jewel inserted into an everyday context to produce some unusual emphasis, often by way of parody.[1] Here in Alexis the suggestion of tragic language, if not of actual parody, is increased by the juxtaposition of ἀνήρ and by the absence of metrical resolution in the phrase, and the tragic elements underpin the meaning 'impetuous'. But who was impetuous? The speaker (i.e. ἦν 1st person: so Ellis)? If so, we should have an uninterrupted string of five 1st-person verbs in vv. 1–3, and the speaker's claim to impetuosity would harmonise well with the desire to make a display (which Ath. notes with partial accuracy) and with the ἀλαζονεία of v. 9. Yet the traditional view, which makes ἦν 3rd person and thus assigns the impetuosity to the ξένος, cannot be ruled out, if only because it focuses attention on the ξένος for a little longer.

The identity of the ξένος is also uncertain. He was apparently imposed on by the speaker, and if the impetuosity was his rather than the speaker's we should probably be justified in assuming that he was a soldier or his *cacula*. In later comedy soldiers are commonly ξένοι, whether by birth, adoption (e.g. Men. *Sik.*: E. W. Handley, *BICS* 12 (1965) 60 n. 3, R. Kassel, *Eranos* 43 (1965) 19), or simply the fact that they come from abroad to the scene of the play (e.g. Plaut. *Curc.*); they are often the victims of a trick; and they are characteristically impetuous (Ribbeck, *Alazon* 26ff., 8of., Wehrli, *Motivstudien* 101ff., J. A. Hanson in D. R. Dudley and T. A. Dorey (edd.), *Roman Drama* (London 1965) 51ff., W. T. MacCary, *AJP* 93 (1972) 279ff., W. Hofmann and G. Wartenberg, *Der Bramarbas in der antiken Komödie* (Berlin 1973); cf. also the introduction to Θράσων. Rival identifications of the ξένος, however, are not excluded; he

---

epigram quoted by Aeschines 3.184 (D. L. Page, *Further Greek Epigrams* (Cambridge 1981) 255ff.) and by Call. *H. Dem.* 66f.

[1] Eupolis fr. 349 Kassel–Austin may be only an apparent exception, but absence of context and presence of corruption make this an extremely difficult fr. to interpret; cf. Schmid–Stählin, 1.iv.119 n. 1.

could have been a *leno* (Webster, *SLGC* 76) or a banker. Pimps are often ξένοι (e.g. in Plaut. *Pers.*, *Poen.*, *Rud.*; cf. Herodas 2.33), and are tricked as frequently as soldiers.

Finally, to whose κατάλυσις was this ξένος brought? Hardly the lodgings of the ξένος, if ἦγον is correct, for then presumably the ξένος would would have 'taken' the young man to the lodgings, and not *vice versa*. Agonis' own lodgings are one possibility, if she was a *hetaira* working independently. The likeliest interpretation, however, is that the lodgings belonged to the speaker himself; this suits best the conventions of both Attic syntax and social comedy. In an expression like τὴν κατάλυσιν the article often marks the noun as belonging to the subject of the clause, where modern English would normally use a pronominal adjective (Gildersleeve, *Syntax* 2.227f., cf. K.G. 1.581d). The young speaker of the fr. would then be presented as having separate lodgings of his own where he could entertain friends, as well as a house shared with his family (cf. οἴκοθεν v. 3), like some other characters in Greco-Roman comedy (e.g. Charisios in Men. *Epitr.*; Chaerea in Ter. *Eun.*, cf. W. Ludwig, *Philologus* 103 (1959) 6f.). One might guess that the young man was trying to outbid a rival for the heroine's affections, partly perhaps by displaying the silver plate (but see on vv. 5–7). Further speculation is idle.

2 κατάλυσιν, 'lodging', may have been attacked by Atticists (cf. Antiatticist, 103.15 Bekker; Moeris s.v. καταγώγιον, p. 241 Pierson), but seems unexceptionable in Attic of its period (cf. Kock 2.16 on Antiphanes 16(15K)).

3 εἶπα: the first person singular of the weak aorist form is not uncommon in later comedy (Men. *Pk.* 318, Philemon 133(145K), Athenion 1.38, Evangelus 1.1); its rarity in other Attic writers (apparently only Solon fr. 34.6 West, Eur. *Cycl.* 101, Theodectes fr. 6.8 Snell, Xen. *Mem.*2.2.8, [Dem.] 47.41 if one accepts the reading of S, cf. trag. adesp. fr. 655.6 Kannicht–Snell; Veitch, *Greek Verbs*[4] 232f.) suggests that it may have been felt as a vulgarism.

4 ἐκλελιτρωμένα: see on fr. 1.2.

5 Kaibel deletes τἀκπώματα (after ἀργυροῦς) as a gloss at both 6.230c and 11.502f. He may well be right.[1] ἐκπώματα is the Attic word for 'cups' in general (D. A. Amyx, *Hesperia* 27 (1958) 206), and it is odd to find in a list of vessels the generic term cheek by jowl with the specific κύαθος, κυμβίον and ψυκτηρίδιον. Other arguments have been advanced in support of the deletion. Gulick's point that τἀκπώματα are together likely to have weighed more than two drachmas ought not to be pressed too

---

[1] In that case the unanimity of the two passages of Ath. probably implies that the error was already present in the text of the work which Ath. here used as his source.

hard, in view of comm. on vv. 5–7; more importantly, with A's text the last two items in the catalogue have their weights indicated, but the first one (κύαθος) has not. Kaibel's guess that the gloss may have driven out something like οὗτος μὲν οὖν (sc. the κύαθος) is plausible but can hardly be accepted as certain.[1]

5–7 To a thinking Athenian, the weights given by the speaker for the cups must have sounded ridiculously light. Silver to the weight of 2 drachmas (= 8.73g, just over $\frac{1}{4}$ oz.[2]) would provide less than 1cm^3 of working material (relative density of silver = 10.47), hardly enough for 'cups' or a ladle; extant metal ladles for pouring wine are very much larger (up to 50cm long, at least: E. Pottier in Dar.–Sag. s.v. *cyathus* 1675A ff., G. M. A. Richter, *Greek, Etruscan and Roman Bronzes* (New York 1915) 232ff., Richter–Milne, *Shapes* 30f.; the silver ladle published by M. Crosby, *AJA* 47 (1943) 209ff. weighed 174.18g = *c.* 40 drachmas); all that could have been produced from 2 drachmas of silver was a tiny miniature for e.g. dedication; cf. also Κράτεια p. 326 n. 1. The same goes, *mutatis mutandis*, for the κυμβίον of 4 drachmas (for its shape, see on fr.100(95K).1–2) and the ψυκτηρίδιον of 10 or 2 obols (= 7.28 or 1.46g).[3] The psykter was commonly used for cooling large quantities of wine (G. Karo in Dar.–Sag. s.v. 750Aff., Richter–Milne, *Shapes* 12f., B. A. Sparkes and L. Talcott, *Pots and Pans of Classical Athens* (Princeton 1958) fig. 20, and *Agora* XII 52 and fig. 2, pl. 2, nos. 35–44); a miniature of even 10 obols' weight could be only a toy or dedicated object, and here the diminutive ending clearly emphasises its ridiculous lightness. Alexis may

---

[1] T. G. Tucker's suggested replacement σταθμῷ τάχα (*CQ* 2 (1908) 191), for all its unnecessary palaeographic neatness, will not do; τάχα is out of place in a context where all the weights are precise, and the asyndeton before it is unduly harsh in an environment of connected clauses.

[2] Additional confirmation of the accuracy of the Polybian equation (1 drachma = 4.366g) is now substantially given by the Athenian agora discoveries: see M. Lang and M. Crosby, *Agora* X (*Weights, Measures and Tokens* (Princeton 1964)).

[3] The weights given for Seleucus' dedications of gold, silver and jewelled vessels at Didyma in 288–287 (*OGIS* 214.45, J. Pouilloux, *Choix d'inscriptions grecques* (Paris 1960) 37) contrast instructively with Alexis' derisory ones. The Didyma inscription records phialai of 113, 190, 198.5 and 247 drachmas, an oinochoe of 386, a jewelled psykter of 386, and a large silver psykter of 9,000. Of course such royal dedications would be far grander than the plate in an average rich Athenian household, but even when this is allowed for, the differences remain enormous. (The same point could be made just as well with reference to the Panagurište treasure: cf. D. A. Amyx, *Hesperia* 3 (1960) 206ff., H. A. Cahn, *Antike Kunst* 3 (1960) 26ff.).

have named these weights as a joke; whether additional reasons were involved – such as caricature of the speaker's ἀλαζονεία or poverty – we cannot now say.

6 ἦγεν (? or ἦγε¹) δύο δραχμάς: although the rhythm is not in itself objectionable (cf. Ar. *Ach.* 161 τοισδὶ δύο δραχμάς), it is hard to see why Alexis should not have written the smoother δρ. δύ' ἦγεν (J. Richter on Ar. *Vesp.* 691 (Berlin 1858)) or δύ' ἦγε δρ. If he wrote the latter (with its appropriate emphasis on the numeral), the corruption was presumably already present in Ath.'s source (cf. on v. 5); it would provide a classic example of *simplex ordo* error, in which a poet's interlaced order had been regularised into the one normal in prose (cf. G. Thomson, *CQ* 15 (1965) 161ff., Diggle, *Studies* 49f.).

ἦγεν here means 'weighed', but in v. 3 (and 2, if rightly conjectured there) ἦγον meant 'led'. Such repetitions of a common word in two or more different senses, however, are not uncommon: cf. e.g. S. *OR* 517, 519, 520 (φέρω = 'tend', 'bear', 'tend' in that order) and Jackson, *Marg. Scaen.* 243. Note that the Old-Comedy preference for scanning the initial syllable of δραχμή short (x 21 short, x 9 *anceps*, x 4 long: Ar. *Vesp.* 691 anapaests, *Pax* 1201, *Plut.* 1019, Plato com. 188(174K).17) is not maintained in later comedy (x 3 short, x 17 *anceps* including Alexis 15.16, 192(187K).2, x 6 long excluding the present passage: Antiphanes 145(147K).5, Philiscus fr. 215.11 Austin, Men. *Epitr.* 335, fr. 951.5, Philippides 9.7, com. adesp. fr. 262.7 Austin).

6–7 κυμβίον δὲ τέτταρας | ἴσως ἑτέρας: at Ath. 11.503a the citation omits ἴσως ἑτέρας. Kaibel (*Hermes* 19 (1884) 259), partly following the young Meineke (*Men. et Phil.* 130, retracted in *Anal. Crit.* 99) with his explanation of ἴσως ἑτέρας as a gloss or corrupt parallel reading, suggests that Alexis here wrote κυμβίον δὲ <δύ'> ἑτέρας, and that when δύ' had been omitted by a scribe, a marginal suggestion τέτταρας ἴσως was interpolated into the text. The weakness of this idea (cf. Kock) is that it requires one to posit further corruption: either a lacuna one metron long somewhere before πρὸς ἀλαζονείαν, or an assumption that the nine words after λεπτότερον are really Ath.'s prose, metricised by an errant scribe (but see below). A better course is to accept ἴσως ἑτέρας from Ath. 6.230c and to explain the omission of these words in 11.503a as a scribal *saut du même au même* (τέτταρας → ἑτέρας); for the idiom, cf. Ar. *Plut.* 1058, Damoxenus 3.2 (ἴσως qualifying a number); Nicostratus 26(25K).1f., [Dem.] 58.6 (ἕτεροι + number).

7 ψυκτηρίδιον occurs only here in verse. The attack on its short

---

¹ The presence of paragogic nu in A here (both citations) is no evidence that Alexis actually wrote ἦγεν: cf. W. J. W. Koster, *Autour d'un manuscrit d'Aristophane* (Groningen 1957) 218ff.

antepenult by Blaydes (*Adv.* 2.152) was characteristic of this scholar's niggling pedantry. Here it is enough to say that (1) Ath. 11.502f cites this part of the fr. just to illustrate the use of the form ψυκτηρίδιον; (2) both A and the Epit. MSS preserve this form; (3) the numerous examples of -ίδιον diminutives in comedy indicate clearly that the antepenult is often short in those diminutives which could have been created, like ψυκτηρίδιον, either from an already existing -ιον diminutive (ψυκτήριον) or directly from the primitive (ψυκτήρ), provided that the primitive stem has no final iota.[1] But since an important factor in the formation of each diminutive was the unscientific one of popular analogy, no absolute rule over the length of the antepenult can be formulated. Cf. especially W. Petersen, *Greek Diminutives in -ION* (Weimar 1910) 216f. (with criticism in *CQ* 7 (1957) 194 n. 3), A. Debrunner, *Griechische Wortbildungslehre* (Heidelberg 1917) 148, P. Chantraine, *La Formation des noms en grec ancien* (Paris 1933) 54ff., G. Dore, *RIFC* 92 (1964) 304ff. (with the reservations expressed in their commentaries by C. Dedoussi on Men. *Sam.* '18', '36' and Hunter on Eubulus 109(110K).2).

ψ. τε δύ' ὀβολούς, the reading of A and Epit. at 11.503a, seems to me slightly preferable to ψ. <δὲ> δέκ' ὀβ., Grotius' conjecture (*Exc.* 557, 971: printed by Kassel–Austin) based on A's unmetrical reading at 6.230c. Any permutation of δὲ/τε + δέκ'/δύ' would scan and produce tolerable sense; cases might be made for connective τε or adversative δέ, and where weights of two and ten obols are both ridiculously light, is it justifiable to assume that Alexis would choose the lighter and more absurd one? Further, δέ and τε are frequently confused by scribes (e.g. δέ right: Arist. *Poet.* 1455ᵇ21, Pl. *Resp.* 9.578a; τε right: Eur. *Med.* 487, *Or.* 880: see J. Diggle, *PCPS* 20 (1974) 3 n. 4 and *Studies* 59), while δύ' is as likely to be corrupted to δέκ' as the other way about, given the common confusion of κ and υ in minuscule. But the sequence A δὲ ..., B (or B μὲν οὖν) ..., C δὲ ..., D τε ... has an idiomatic, natural flavour (e.g. S. *Ant.* 1096f., *Trach.* 285f., Eur. *Ion* 1464ff., *Phoen.* 1625f., Thuc. 1.25.3, Pl. *Resp.* 2.367c, Xen. *Anab.* 5.5.8, Aeschines 3.80 *pace* Blass, Eubulus 108(109K), Epicrates 3.14ff., possibly Alexis 215(212K).2; cf. Denniston, *GP* 500, 513f.), unlikely perhaps to have been foisted upon Alexis by meddling scribes, while a progressive corruption εδυ → δευ → δέκ' is not unthinkable.

8 Φιλιππίδου λεπτότερον: all that is known about Philippides, the Athenian politician who favoured Macedon and was ridiculed by the comedians for his skinniness (Alexis also frs. 93(89K), 148(144K), Aristophon 8 ἰσχνότερον ... Φιλιππίδου, 10, Men. fr. 305 ὁ λιμὸς ὑμῖν τὸν καλὸν τοῦτον δακὼν | Φιλιππίδου λεπτότερον ἀποδείξει νεκρόν) is collected by Treves, *RE* s.v. 1, 2198.48ff.; cf. Webster, *SLGC* 45. Treves plausibly

---

[1] E.g. ἀσκίδιον (from ἀσκίον or ἀσκός), κροκωτίδιον (from κροκώτιον or κροκωτός).

suggests a life-span *c*.370–*c*.310, but his proposed dating of all the comic references to the period following Hyperides' speech against Philippides (i.e. after 336–335, § 4 of the speech) may not suit the present fr. of Alexis (see the introduction to Ἀγωνίς). λεπτός, when applied to human beings (cf. other victims of the λεπτότερος comparison, e.g. Leotrophides and Thumantis in Hermippus 36(35K)), usually has derogatory overtones (D. L. Page on Eur. *Med.* 1189).[1]

8–9 The words from ἀλλά to the end of the fr., rightly given by Schweighaeuser to a second speaker (Agonis herself?), could be an approving or sarcastically disparaging comment on the young man's trickery. The aberration of Dindorf (at Ath. 6.230, but note his apparatus) and the young Meineke (*Men. et Phil.* 130: retracted in his edition of Ath. and *Anal. Crit.* 99), that these words are Ath.'s prose, not Alexis' verse, may deserve mention but hardly detailed refutation; Cobet's brief words (*NL* 361) and an ability to distinguish the comic iambic trimeter from prose are enough. Ath. writes unintentional iambics as rarely as Plato (cf. J. Adam on *Resp.* 10.621b), and it would be odd if here a sequence of them not only began and ended with a full stop, but also hooked correctly on to the final words of a comic fr. ending in mid-verse. But see also on v. 9 and fr. 77. 2–4.

ὅλως: probably to be taken with οὐ κακῶς, 'not at all badly'. In this use ὅλως often precedes the negative, though rarely as here with any words intervening: e.g. Men. *Dysk.* 60, fr. 597, Xen. *Mem.* 1.2.35, Dem. 2.7, 3.35 (LSJ s.v. ὅλος, III.3). The idiom does not seem to have been popular in Athens before the 4th century.

Bothe's conjecture ὅμως (*PCGF* 519, followed by Ribbeck, *Alazon* 49) is no improvement on the transmitted text, although it could be justified palaeographically at least (cf. e.g. Eur. *Hipp.* 80: ὅμως some MSS, ολως *P.Sorbonne* 2252; cf. Barrett's edition of the play, p. 438).

9 νενοημέν' ἦν: Alexis' known use of periphrastic tenses, which accords with contemporary Athenian practice, seems to be limited to instances (a) of periphrases for the perfect or pluperfect (passive: here, 57(56K).1; active: 267(265K).8), (b) where the participle is adjectival or parallels an adjective (9.2, 37(36K).5, probably 100(95K).2, 129(124K).11, 145(141K).2, 172(167K).4, 236(234K).3, 247(245K).8–9, 272(270K).3–4). See Gildersleeve, *Syntax* 1.122ff., G. Björck, HN ΔΙΔΑΣΚΩΝ (Uppsala 1940), Schwyzer 1.811f., W. J. Aerts, *Periphrastica* (Amsterdam 1965); cf. J. Gonda, *Mnemosyne* 12 (1959) 97ff.

After νενοημέν' ἦν the text continues in Ath. 6.230cd οἶδα δὲ κἀγώ τινα πολίτην (so A: οἶδά τινα, φησὶν Ἄλεξις, πολίτην Epit.) ἡμέτερον πτωχ-

---

[1] Bechtel, *Spitznamen* 8 collects instances of people nicknamed from their thinness; of these the most interesting is perhaps Fronto's teacher, Dionysius ὁ λεπτός (Ath. 11.475f).

COMMENTARY

αλαζόνα, ὃς δραχμῆς ἔχων τὰ πάντα ἀργυρώματα ἐβόα καλῶν τὸν οἰκέτην ἕνα ὄντα καὶ μόνον, ὀνόμασι δὲ χρώμενον ψαμμακοσίοις "παῖ Στρομβιχίδη (so Epit.: –ιχίδης A), μὴ τῶν χειμερινῶν ἀργυρωμάτων ἡμῖν παραθῇς, ἀλλὰ τῶν θερινῶν". The Epit.'s comment φησὶν "Αλεξις has deceived many scholars into accepting these words as Alexis', either as a continuation of fr. 2 (so Musurus, Casaubon in his edition, and others) or as a separate new fr. (= 303b in Kock 3.744, Edmonds 2.516). In fact these words are clear prose, as Casaubon later realised (*Animadv.* 403f.: '*olim conati sumus in iambicos uersus omnia redigere. sed repugnat contumaciter uerborum modulus plerorumque*', cf. Porson, *Adv.* 78). I know of no comic citation in Ath. of corresponding length which has been so paraphrased into prose recalcitrant to metrification. The game is given away by the opening words οἶδα δὲ κἀγώ, a favourite transition formula among Ath.'s imaginary banqueters (Porson notes 12.541a; cf. also in one short passage 8.333b, 334a, 338b). This fact and the nature of the anecdote itself suggest that here Ath. was citing some gossip or gossip-writer (perhaps of his own time, if Porson is right in identifying the Strombichides of the tale as a slave of Pompeianus of Philadelphia: cf. Ath. 3.98a, where this Pompeianus is the originator of witticisms similar in some ways to the present anecdote). Peppink, *Observ.* 37 notes that in A the anecdote is marked off ostensibly as a citation by marginal signs > in such a way that a careless reader might assume the anecdote to be a continuation of the Alexis fr. (cf. my general introduction, II.i.a). The epitomist's error is thus explained; in his abridgement he quoted only the anecdote in the belief that this was the end of the Alexis fr. Similarly at 7.249a–b, where in A a quotation from Alexis is followed by one from Archedicus, the epitomist omits the former and cites the latter as by Alexis. See also the introduction to fr. 276(274K).

3

Meineke 3.383 (I), Kock 2.298, Edmonds 2.376, Kassel–Austin 2.25. The opening verse parodies Eur. *Or.* 255, with τὸν Μισγόλαν in v. 2 the surprise substitution for τὰς αἱματωποὺς καὶ δρακοντώδεις κόρας, the Furies of *Or.* 256. The comic effect may have been increased by the insertion of the parody into an everyday situation; there is no need to assume (with Webster, *SLGC* 73, 76) that fr. 3 (as well as fr. 4) came in a comic 'mad scene'. If the 'mother' of v. 1 was a character addressed on stage (one cannot be certain in this kind of parody), she may have been reproaching her son for his loose living (? with Agonis) and citing one or more contemporary debauchees as warning parallels; so Demeas illustrates his argument in Men. *Sam.* 601ff. by referring to Chaerephon and Androcles. The words of fr. 3 would then be the son's rejoinder. There is

62

an impressive number of examples of this sort of Euripidean parody in plays of the Middle-Comedy period, considering the scrappiness of the remains: e.g. Alexis 63(62K).7 (*Telephus* fr. 703 Nauck² = 109 Austin), 181(176K).2 (*Med.* 49), Anaxandrides 66(67K) (unless this is proverbial: Eur. fr. 920), Antiphanes 238(242K).3 (Eur. fr. 895), Eubulus 6(7K).2 (*Andr.* 369). If one added to these the examples from New Comedy, and quotations from Euripides for purposes other than parody, the total would not be far short of thirty; cf. A. Sehrt, *De Menandro Euripidis imitatore* (Diss. Giessen 1912), still useful although outdated by the more recent papyrus discoveries. It is no coincidence that Euripides was the most popular of the Attic tragedians in the 4th century and after (cf. e.g. W. N. Bates, *Euripides* (Philadelphia 1930) 17ff.), nor that the two plays most frequently parodied or pillaged by comedians after his death – the *Orestes* (Men. *Asp.* 424f., 432, *Sam.* 326, *Sik.* 176ff., 182, perhaps *Epitr.* 910; together with Alexis here) and *Medea* (Alexis 181(176K).2, Eubulus 26.1, Men. *Fab. Inc.* 13, Philemon 82(79K).1f., Theognetus 1.9; cf. B. M. W. Knox, *YCS* 25 (1977) 193 n. 2) – have produced (together with *Phoenissae*) the largest number of papyrus frs., while *Orestes* is known to have been produced at Athens in 340 (see the introduction to Ἀγωνίς). Nor again is Alexis' choice of parodic passage here surprising; these very lines of Euripides were singled out by [Longinus] 15.2 as a vivid example of φαντασία.

1 μὴ 'πίσειέ μοι is clearly read by Epit. MSS C and E (πείσειέ μοι A); Kaibel's apparatus (Ath.8.339c) and Peppink, *Observ.* 52 are misleading. ἐπισείω occurs in Alexis also in its literal sense, if its restoration at fr. 192(187K).6 (*pace* Kassel–Austin) is correct. The metaphorical sense here ('hold before as a bogey') is similar to that of ἀνασείω elsewhere in comedy: Ar. *Ach.* 347, Men. *Epitr.* 458 (cf. Gomme–Sandbach and Wilamowitz (his line '241') *ad loc.*).

2 Μισγόλαν: on him see M. N. Tod, *Ann. BSA* 8 (1901/2) 211ff. (Geyer in *RE* s.v. 2049.20ff. is unaware of the inscriptional evidence, *IG* ii².1554B, 2825). The Athenian citizen Misgolas, 44 or 45 years old at the time of Aeschines' action against Timarchus (345: Aeschines 1.49), was a καλὸς κἀγαθός (1.41) prominent enough to be selected as tribal representative of a decemviral board which made a dedication to Artemis about the middle of the century (*IG* ii².2825). It was presumably because of his prominence that contemporary comedians pilloried his alleged homosexual passion for young κιθαρῳδοί (on the precise meaning of this word, see Gow on Machon 6 and 141); cf. Aeschin. 1.41 ἀεί τινας ἔχειν εἰωθὼς περὶ αὐτὸν κιθαρῳδοὺς καὶ κιθαριστάς. Though gossip doubtless exaggerated the details, it seems unlikely that the charges were unfounded. Cf. K. J. Dover, *Greek Homosexuality* (London 1978) 19ff., 73f.

COMMENTARY

4

Meineke 3.384 (III), Kock 2.298, Edmonds 2.376, Kassel–Austin 2.26. Hirschig (confidently: *Diss.* 31, 57) and Meineke (tentatively: 3.385) interpret the fr. as dialogue, with change of speaker at ἀλλ' ἔχαιρε (v.2). The first speaker claims to see several people before him (τρίτος v. 1 is otherwise inexplicable), of whom one at least is known to be dead (2–3). He is not describing a dream (the tense of ἔχει excludes this), and he is unlikely to be a visitor to the underworld (the play's subject matter, so far as it is known, appears to exclude that). Meineke's suggestion that the speaker is looking at a picture or statue cannot be ruled out, but a vision in a fit of madness is perhaps more likely. On the Greco-Roman stage such madness, often presented as a parody of famous mad scenes in classical Greek tragedy (cf. J. Mattes, *Der Wahnsinn im griechischen Mythos und in der Dichtung bis zum Drama des fünften Jahrhunderts* (Heidelberg 1970) 74ff.), was either simulated in order to escape from a difficult position (Plaut. *Men.* 828ff.) or introduced as a device to heighten a lover's despair (*Cist.* 283ff., *Merc.* 930ff.). A situation of the latter sort could be imagined here, with the young lover speaking first and his slave (or some other βωμο-λόχος) commenting humorously on the vision, as in *Cist.* and *Merc.* Cf. Legrand, *NGC* 470, Webster, *SLGC* 49, 69.

1 **ὁ τρίτος οὗτος δ':** Meineke's correction (*Cur. Crit.* 74) of A's ὁ τρίτος δ' οὗτος restores the metre by postponing the particle. Postponed δέ frequently mystified copyists, who would restore it to its normal position as second word (also e.g. Alexis 78.6, 168(163K).2, 278(276K).3, Men. *Dysk.* 801 in Stob. 3.16.14, probably *Epitr.* 521, cf. *CQ* 18 (1968) 231), omit it (Eur. *Hipp.* 835, *Suppl.* 614, Theophilus 6.3) or corrupt it (Antiphanes 152(154K).4 διήψατο for δ' ἤψατ'). Postponement of particles such as δέ (in Alexis also 16.3 οὐ πάνυ τι θαυμάζω δέ, 78.6, 145(141K).6 τὰκ τῆς τροφῆς δέ, 255(253K).3 ταῖς ἡμέραις ταύταις δέ, 278(276K).3 ὃς ἂν εἰς ἑτέραν ληφθῇ δ', possibly also 123(118K).2), γάρ (see on fr. 37(36K).1), τε and τοίνυν (see on fr. 147(143K).1) from their customary position as second word is a phenomenon confined to no one period or type of writing, although the severer postponements occur mainly in post-Aristophanic comedy (e.g. 6th word: Alexis 278(276K).3; 7th word: *P.Didot* 1.33, probably Men. *Epitr.* 521). Often (but not always: Alexis 278(276K).3 and *P.Didot* 1.33 are exceptions) the words before the particle cohere (as they do in the present fr.) to form a syntactical unit. See T. W. Allen, *Rev. Phil.* 63 (1937) 280f., Denniston, *GP* 187ff., Handley on Men. *Dysk* 10, and K. J. Dover, *CQ* 35 (1985) 337ff., who subjects the material to a stringent linguistic analysis.

ἔχει: Meineke's tentative conjecture φέρει is unnecessary (στέφανον/-ους ἔχω is a regular phrase: e.g. Alexis 101(96K), Archippus 42(40K).2,

Xenarchus 13, Apollodorus Car. 5.22) but (as a synonymous substitution) not refutable.

2 κυλιστὸν στέφανον: it is for this term that Ath. 15.678e cites this fr. (along with Alexis 210(207K) ὥσπερ κ. στ. αἰωρούμενος, Eubulus 73 περιφοραῖς κυκλούμενος | ὥσπερ κ. στ., Antiphanes 53(51K), cf. also Alexis 274(272K).5). At 678f Ulpian asks τίς οὖν οὗτος ὁ στέφανος; ... καὶ τὸ εἶδος ὁποῖον ζητῶ, ὦ Κύνουλκε, καὶ μή μοι εἴπῃς ὅτι δεῖ τοὺς ἁδροὺς ἀκούειν (cf. Hesych. s.v. ἐκκύλιστοι[1]). The answer to this question provided by Casaubon ('*talem . . . ut rotari queat*': *Animadv.* 960, cf. 102) must be correct, in view of the term's use as an object of comparison in the whirling contexts of Eubulus 73 and Alexis 210(207K) (cf. comm. *ad loc.*); could such garlands have been whirled and rolled competitively in private games as cheap substitutes for the discus? The cited similes appear to rule out the otherwise attractive interpretation 'rolled/twisted in a circle' (LSJ s.v. κυλιστός, II).

On garlands in general see Ch. Saglio in Dar.–Sag. s.v. *Corona* 1520Bff., Ganszyniec in *RE* s.v. *Kranz* 1588.47ff., J. Köchling, *De coronarum apud antiquos ui atque usu* (Giessen 1914 = *RGVV* 14.2), L. Deubner, *ARW* 30 (1933) 70ff., M. Blech, *Studien zum Kranz bei den Griechen* (Berlin/New York 1982 = *RGVV* 38). According to Macrobius 1.7.25, fig garlands were worn in Cyrene in honour of Saturn, but here in Alexis the choice of plant is comic and satirical. The garland in the first speaker's vision indicated that its possessor was dead (on the corpse's στέφανος see Saglio 1526AB, Ganszyniec 1595.34ff., D. C. Kurtz and J. Boardman, *Greek Burial Customs* (London 1971) 144, C. Collard on Eur. *Suppl.* 973f., Blech 81ff.); its material, however, was specified only to provide a handle for the other speaker's comment, which Hirschig (*Diss.* 57) first interpreted as implying that the man with the fig garland was in life a συκοφάντης. The verbal connection between σῦκον and συκοφάντης was a comic commonplace, used both for direct moralising (Alexis 187(182K), q.v.) and for allusive comment as here (also Antiphanes 177(179K).3f., Eubulus 74.2, Ar. *Vesp.* 145, 897, *Plut.* 946, *Equ.* 529 = Cratinus 70(69K); cf. Alexis 122(117K), and see J. O. Lofberg, *Sycophancy in Athens* (Diss. Chicago 1917) 20). The allusion would be more mordant if ὁ τρίτος οὗτος were not an imaginary unnamed figure but some well-known recently dead Athenian συκοφάντης (cf. introduction to comm. on 187(182K)), but we can no more be sure that this was the case than in other such fragmentary listings (e.g. Eupolis 298(276K).

---

[1] ἐκκύλιστος *may* also be a technical term, perhaps interchangeable with κυλιστός (cf. Nicander of Thyateira in Ath. 678f = *FGrH* 343 F 7, Pollux 7.199), but from its use in Archippus 42(40K) (see Gulick on Ath. 678c)

COMMENTARY

It may be a pure coincidence that in the mad scene of Plaut. *Merc.* (see above, introduction to this fr.) the distraught lover similarly refers to figs (943 *hospes respondit, Zacynthi ficos fieri non malas*). **2–3 καὶ | ζῶν**. see comm. on 20.4–5. **3 τοιούτοις**: on the correption see comm. on 247(245K).1.

5

Meineke 3.385 (IV), Kock 2.299, Edmonds 2.376, Kassel–Austin 2.26. The *Marcianus* (Ath. 11.471e) gives the source of this fr. as Ἄλεξις ἐν ηπακωι; Casaubon's emendation (*Animadv.* 792) ἐν Ἱππίσκῳ is universally accepted and probably right. Although its distance from the *ductus* is uncomfortable, other known titles of Alexis (e.g. Ἱππεῖ, Ἡσιόνη) are even further away from A's nonsense. Presumably the corruption followed the route ιππισκωι → ιπακωι with an iotacistic detour. This brief fr.'s dramatic context is tentatively discussed in the introduction to Ἀγωνίς.

1 ἀκράτου: sc. οἴνου (so K.G. 1.265f.)? But ellipse of οἶνος is arguable only where ἄκρατος is unmistakably masculine (e.g. Men. *Sam.* 341, fr. 512, Sophilus 4(3K), com. adesp. fr. 375 Kock, Machon 276 Gow, Alciphron 4.8.2); and given the existence of a neuter by-form (e.g. Arist. *Poet.* 1461ᵃ15, cf. Antiphanes 25(24K).4 if punctuated after ἄκρατον), judgement is better suspended in ambiguous cases such as here, 9.4 (where ancient attitudes to drinking wine neat are discussed) and 246(244K).2. Over τοὺς ἀκράτους in 257(255K).5 see *ad loc.*

θηρίκλειον: in his chapter on Thericlean ware (11.470e–472e) Ath. alleges that Thericles was a Corinthian potter, γεγονὼς τοῖς χρόνοις κατὰ τὸν κωμικὸν Ἀριστοφάνη. This dating, which may be a shade too early,[1] indicates a *floruit* (not birth: on γεγονώς in such contexts, see

---

it is more likely to have been a purely comic coinage, misunderstood by grammarians.

[1] Ath. nowhere quotes a shred of evidence in support of his dating, and there is no reference to Thericles or his work in what we have of Aristophanes. He is first mentioned in Theopompus com. 33(32K), an Old-Comedy poet according to the ancient view, but not sufficiently important or well known to be included in the list of comic poets compiled by the anonymous author of περὶ κωμῳδίας (Kaibel, *CGF* 6ff., Koster III, 7ff.). Hence if a scholar (Ath. himself?) wished without too much trouble to elicit the facts still known about Theopompus, he would probably have consulted a dictionary containing such short biographical sketches of the comic poets as are today preserved in the *Suda*, where we find s.v. Θεόπομπος the note ἔστι δὲ τῆς ἀρχαίας κωμῳδίας κατὰ Ἀριστοφάνην. That scholar would then have felt himself able to say that Thericles lived during the time of the better-known

E. Rohde, *Rh. Mus.* 33 (1878) 161ff., 638f. and 34 (1879) 620ff. = *Kl. Schr.* 1 (Tübingen and Leipzig) 114ff.) at the end of the 5th and beginning of the 4th centuries. The enthusiastic tone of many of the writers, mainly 4th-century comedians, whom Ath. cites about Thericles' work, suggest that it made a great impression on contemporary Athens: note particularly Theopompus com. 33(32K), Aristophon 13(14K), Eubulus 42(43K: or Araros), 56. In fact the Athenian popularity, coupled with our knowledge of a decline in ceramic manufacture at Corinth in this period, has given rise to the generally accepted and probably correct supposition that Thericles, despite his Corinthian birth, set up or used a workshop in Athens as a metic (so E. Pottier in Dar.–Sag. s.v. *Thericlea Vasa* 212A ff., still the best discussion from both literary and archaeological viewpoints; cf. also Bentley's classic *Phalaris* 109ff. (London 1699) = 1.169ff. (Dyce, London 1836) and H. Nachod, *RE* s.v. *Therikles* 2, 2367.68ff.). The descriptions in the writers nearest to his own time indicate that he produced the black high-lustre ware (cf. Eubulus 56.4f., Alexis 124(119K).1) so popular in Athens during the 4th century, and did not confine himself to any one shape or size of pot. The different sizes included 2 and 3 *kotylai* (Dionysius 5), 4 and more than 7 (Theophilus 2, 10), a *metretes* (Dionysius 5); the shapes included δῖνος, κυμβίον, σκύφος, ῥυτόν (Dionysius 5), κρατήρ (Alexis 124(119K)) and ψυκτήρ (Dioxippus 5). Accordingly it is likely that the popularity of his wares was due not to the invention of basic new shapes, but rather to some attractive feature or features immediately recognisable as Thericles' own, whether of design, finish or decoration. In the course of time, however – after the present fr. of Alexis was written but possibly before the end of the 4th century – the term 'Thericlean' appears to have changed its meaning; it was applied less to vases of a particular workshop, more to ones of a particular shape and design; whether this design was invented in Thericles' own workshop, we cannot be sure. But the definition given by Ath. at 470e ἡ κύλιξ αὕτη ἐγκάθηται περὶ τὰς λαγόνας ἱκανῶς βαθυνομένη ὦτά τε ἔχει βραχέα ὡς ἂν κύλιξ οὖσα, with its precise definition of shape, is best referred to

---

Aristophanes, and by this substitution he erected a barrier against the identification of Thericlean ware by modern archaeologists. For it is known that between 380 and 370 new patterns of decoration and design in Athenian pottery came into vogue. But Aristophanes did not survive into the 370s, and a potter then working on new designs could hardly have been considered his contemporary. Theopompus on the other hand was still writing in the 370s: he refers in fr. 31(30K) to Callistratus as the founder of the naval confederacy of 377 (cf. Körte in *RE* s.v. *Theopompos* 6, 2174.59ff.).

COMMENTARY

this later application of the term.[1] Caution, however, over this and several other matters in Ath.'s treatment of θηρίκλειος is advisable; Ath. seems unaware of the way in which the word veered from identification of a workshop towards a description of shape, so that he confuses the two meanings in the arrangement he makes of his citations.

It is uncertain whether θηρίκλειον here is to be interpreted nominally, with ellipse of κύλικα (cf. Ath. 472b, citing as examples Men. fr. 275, *Theoph.* fr. 4, Dioxippus 4; he could have added Aristophon 13(14K), Dionysius 5, Eubulus 56, possibly Epigenes 5; note also τὴν μεγάλην and the note on this expression at 116(111K).1), or whether some such word as κύλικα was present in the immediate context of the fr.

ἔσπασεν: of wine-quaffing, also at Eur. *Cycl.* 417, 571, Men. *Theoph.* fr. 4; cf. Alexis 286(285K).2 (of ὄξος) and Diphilus 17.8 (where the words are so organised as to mislead the listener into believing that τὴν μεγάλην αὐτοῖς σπάσαι refers to wine-quaffing, until he reaches the fishy context of v. 9). Cf. the parallel use of ἕλκω, comm. on 88(85K).3.

2 κοίλην ὑπερθύουσαν: the heightened language (see introduction to Ἀγωνίς) is underlined by the lack of metrical resolution and the absence of any article, as well as by the choice of these two words, whose appropriateness has nevertheless not stayed the hand of the meddling emender. κοίλη is a regular if obvious attribute of κύλιξ and its concomitants, especially in comically elevated descriptions: Plato com. 205(189K).2, Eubulus 42(43K: or Araros).2, Men. *Dysk.* 947; cf. Antiphanes 47(45K).3. The compound ὑπερθύουσαν (= ὑπεραφρίζουσαν, Aristophon 13(14K).3, Eubulus 56.2) occurs only here in this form, but it provides the same kind of metaphor as Hom. *Il.* 21.234, where Scamander

---

[1] Cf. also Σ Clem. Alex. *Paed.* 2.3.35.2, pp. 325f. Stählin. Attempts to identify Thericlean vases in extant collections have not been successful. Nachod approves E. Pfuhl's suggestion (*Mahlerei und Zeichnung der Griechen* 1 (Munich 1923) 410) that these vases are recognisable in the splendid large 4th-century vessels which have a very bright gloss and are decorated with gold or coloured clay (cf. Alexis 101(96K)!), but Thericlean vases are alleged by the comedians to be often of a small size, while many of Pfuhl's examples date to the end of the 4th century, i.e. probably too late for Thericles to have manufactured them himself. S. S. Weinberg (*Hesperia* 23 (1954) 109ff.; cf. *AJA* 57 (1953) 111f.), assuming that Thericles' work was produced in Corinth, fails to account for its Athenian fame or to draw the necessary distinctions between the two different meanings that θηρίκλειος had at different periods. Cf. also G. Kopcke, *Ath. Mitt.* 79 (1964) 22ff. W. Miller's lengthy discussion (*Daedalus and Thespis* (New York or Columbia Mo. 1929–32) 2.544ff., 3.694ff.; cf. *TAPA* 52 (1921) 119ff.) amounts to little more than a naive and superficial survey of the literary evidence.

ΑΓΩΝΙΣ

ἐπέσσυτο οἴδματι θύων, cf. 21.324; see Korais in Schweighaeuser, *Animadv.* 6.103 and Meineke, *Anal. Crit.* 217. Herwerden's suggestion (*Coll. Crit.* 120) that we should substitute the form ὑπερθυίουσαν must be resisted; θυίω and its compounds may be accepted in dithyramb (Timoth. *Pers.* 65 ἅλμα στόματος ὑπερέθυιεν) and possibly epic (papyrus at Hes. *Theog.* 131, one or more MSS at *H. Herm.* 560, Nic. *Ther.* 129, Ap. Rhod. 3.755; see West on Hes. *Theog.* 109), but it is foreign to Attic usage (thus θύουσαν A. *Ag.* 1235).

6

Meineke 3.385 (v), Kock 2.299, Edmonds 2.376, Kassel–Austin 2.26. Ath.'s information here (3.120b) is ambiguous; we can interpret it either as indicating that the verse Φείδιππος ἕτερός τις ταριχηγὸς ξένος occurred in both Σώρακοι (fr. 221(218K)) and Ἱππίσκος, or (more probably) as implying merely that Alexis referred to Phidippus in the latter play. Elsewhere Ath. cites plays of Alexis and other poets where various personalities are 'mentioned' or 'ridiculed' without appending quotations: e.g. Alexis 218(215K) (Callimedon), 156(136K) (Menecrates), 109(104K) (Sinope), 155(151K), 161(157K) (Tithymallus). Elsewhere, too, we find the same line or lines repeated in more than one play of Alexis:24.2–4 = 115(110K).21–3, 49(48K) = 115(110K).9–11, 87(67K) = 249(247K), 256(254K).2 = 261(259K).1. The uncertainty here is all the more irritating because, if the Σώρακοι verse were repeated in fr. 6, it might provide a further (but doubtful) clue to the dating of Ἀγωνὶς ἤ Ἱππίσκος. Phidippus was one of two or three sons[1] of the salt-fish dealer Chaerephilus, who with his family was awarded Athenian citizenship at the instigation of Demosthenes (Dinarchus 1.43), possibly for services to Athens during the food shortages of *c.*330–*c.*326 (cf. J. McK. Camp in *Studies in Athenian Architecture, Sculpture and Topography Presented to Homer A. Thompson = Hesperia* suppl. 20 (1982) 12ff., and P. Garnsey, *Famine and*

---

[1] Ath. 3.120a (citing Alexis 77) and 8.339d mentions only two sons, Phidippus and Pamphilus. The Phidon named by Dinarchus 1.43 as another member of the family might have been Chaerephilus' father (so Raubitschek: cf. *IG* ii².1557.70), or alternatively, given the Greek custom of naming a male child after his grandfather, a third son, ignored by the comic poets because he took no part in Athenian public life (unlike Phidippus and Pamphilus, who performed a liturgy in the mid-320s, *IG* ii².417.14), or because he had died or left Athens at an early date (cf. Th. Bergk in K. Schiller's edition of Andocides (Leipzig 1835) 155ff., Lewis 230, M. J. Osborne, *Naturalization in Athens*, 3/4 (Brussels 1983) 75f.).

COMMENTARY

Food Supply in the Graeco-Roman World (Cambridge 1988) 144ff., 150ff., 154f.). In 323 Phidippus was trierarch (*IG* ii².1631.622). Yet if fr. 6 (like 221(218K)) called Phidippus a ξένος, it would be dangerous to assume too readily that this reference antedated his admission to Athenian citizenship, since even after admission a comic poet might still choose to call him a ξένος as a slur on Phidippus' origins (cf. D. Lewis, *Hesperia* 28 (1959) 230). For a judicious discussion of the sources, which include Alexis 77 (Chaerephilus' sons), probably 173(168K) ('Skombros') and 221(218K) (the other comic passages are listed by Webster, *SLGC* 39 n. 1), see A. Raubitschek, *RE* s.v. *Pheidippos* 2, 1937.21ff.

Ἀδελφοί

H. F. Clinton, *Fasti Hellenici* 2 (Oxford 1834) 142f., Meineke 1.387, Webster, *SLGC* 71ff., Nesselrath, *MK* 190f. This title is common in later Greek comedy. Alexis shares it with Apollodorus, Diphilus, Euphron, Hegesippus, Philemon and Menander, whose two plays so titled were adapted respectively by Plautus (*Stichus*) and Terence (*Adelphoe*). Pomponius wrote an Atellane *Adelphi* (Ribbeck, *CRF³* 269, Frassinetti 23); it is uncertain whether this is the play referred to by Festus p. 317 Müller, 418 Lindsay (cf. Ribbeck 131). But as the two extant Roman plays show, identity of title does not imply identity of subject; brothers might be identical twins (e.g. Plaut. *Men.*) or a contrasted pair (e.g. Ter. *Ad.*; see introduction to Κουρίς and fr. 113(108K)).

From Alexis' play only one small fr. survives, but this is doubly interesting. First, it dates the play with uncommon firmness. In 343 Philip offered the rocky islet of Halonnesus to Athens. Demosthenes replied to the offer with a speech now lost,[1] whose contents, however, were admirably summarised by Aeschines 3.83: ἀπηγόρευε μὴ λαμβάνειν, εἰ δίδωσιν ἀλλὰ μὴ ἀποδίδωσιν, περὶ συλλαβῶν διαφερόμενος. By this verbal distinction Demosthenes sought to show that Philip had no right to 'give' the islet to Athens, because it was *de jure* an Athenian possession; accordingly it could only be 'restored' to Athens. This quibble on δίδωμι ~ ἀποδίδωμι proved a godsend to the comedians of the day; most of the extant references to it are collected by Ath. 6.223d–224a (Alexis 7, 212(209K), Anaxilas 8(9K), Antiphanes 167(169K); cf. also Timocles 20(18K).4f.[2] Since the parody of political catchwords loses its amusing

---

[1] The extant speech attributed to Demosthenes (7) is spurious: see its hypothesis and W. Kroll, *RE* Suppl. iv s.v. *Hegesippos* 713.2ff., M. Croiset's edition of Demosthenes, *Harangues* 2 (Paris 1946) 38ff.

[2] Cf. also Jackson, *Marg. Scaen.* 233 on Theophr. *Char.* 15.5.

bite as soon as the incident to which the catchwords apply has ceased to be a live issue, it is safe to date all the plays in which the Halonnesus quibble was ridiculed to 342 or very shortly afterwards (so first Clinton, cf. Meineke, Nesselrath, Webster, *CQ* 2 (1952) 19 and my introduction to Στρατιώτης).

Secondly, Webster (*SLGC* 71ff.) claims tentatively that this fr. appears in Roman dress at Plaut. *Men.* 653ff.: MENAECHMUS I: *egon dedi?* MATRONA: *tu, tu istic, inquam.* PENICULUS: *uin adferri noctuam,* | *quae 'tu tu' usque dicat tibi? nam nos iam defessi sumus.* | MEN.: *per Iouem deosque omnis adiuro, uxor (satin hoc est tibi?),* | *non dedisse.* The subject of this dialogue is Menaechmus I's theft of his wife's *palla* and his gift of it to the courtesan Erotium. Mainly because of the alleged tie between this fr. of Alexis and the Plautine passage Webster suggests that Alexis' Ἀδελφοί *may* have been Plautus' Greek original. If Webster is right, it must be supposed that Plautus, while keeping at least two of the same speakers here (the husband speaking v. 1 of the Greek fr., the wife v. 2), replaced the Greek topical allusion by a Latin joke depending on the similarity of the Roman pronunciation of long *u* to a tawny owl's call. And it is not impossible that then Plautus added v. 657, MEN.: *sed ego illam non condonaui, sed sic utendam dedi,* in the attempt to preserve an echo of the original Greek antithesis. Webster's argument is ingenious, but it depends too much on a chain of possibilities that are largely incapable of individual proof or refutation. And there is one demonstrable weakness in the chain. In Plautus the *palla* was given to Erotium; in Alexis the 'something' (τι: see on v. 1) was given ταύταις. This plural would make better sense if it referred to (e.g.) a pair of courtesans working in a single establishment (cf. Plaut. *Bacch., Cist.*) than if to the household of one independent courtesan like Erotium. Webster's suggestion that ταύταις might be Erotium and a maid is not a convincing way out of the difficulty, since in Plautus the *palla* was a gift to the courtesan alone, and no other member of Erotium's household could be considered a joint recipient.[1]

7

Meineke 3.385, Kock 2.299, Edmonds 2.376, Kassel–Austin 2.27. If this fr. has no connection with Plaut. *Men.* 653ff., the attempt to guess at its

---

[1] This is no place to investigate the general question about the author of the Greek original of the *Menaechmi*; but see Schanz–Hosius I⁴.65, K. P. Abel, *Die Plautusprologe* (Diss. Frankfurt 1955) 69 and 135 nn. 402, 403, Dohm, *Mageiros* 265 n. 1, and P. Grimal, *Kokalos* 14/15 (1968/9) 231ff., supporting arguments in favour of Posidippus which are partly based on an untenable premise (see comm. on 134(129K) and Abel 134

COMMENTARY

dramatic context becomes uncommonly hazardous; calculation of the amount of sarcasm in the second speaker's words requires nice judgement, and some allowance must be made for incongruity whenever a topical reference is spatchcocked into a possibly alien context. The first speaker is male (λαβών v. 2), but we cannot be certain that ταύταις are courtesans and that the 'something' that they had received is money or valuables, although these are plausible interpretations. The second speaker who acts as censor could be the other's parent, friend, slave, wife (or brother, in view of the play's title); the implication of his or her remark is that the 'gift' of v. 1 was really part of a contract between the first speaker and the women: see below on ἐνέχυρον. The part-division first appeared in Daléchamp's Latin translation.

1 ἐγὼ δέδωκα γάρ τι: for the postponement of γάρ see comm. on 37(36K).1.

τι (A and Epit.) rather than τί (Dindorf, but Conti's translation *quid?* implies this reading or emendation already in 1556), for τί requires the answer οὐδέν not οὐκ.

2 οὐκ ἀλλ': 'not quite so, but . . .' (W. J. M. Starkie on Ar. *Vesp.* 946). ἀπέδωκας here and ἀπεδώκαμεν in the immediately preceding citation of Ath. (Alexis 212(209K).7) are corrupted to perfects (ἀποδέδωκας, – αμεν respectively: both corrected by Casaubon), under the influence of words in the previous verses (δέδωκα here, δεδώκαμεν 212(209K).6).

ἐνέχυρον: the transaction between the first speaker and ταύταις is viewed (? sarcastically) as a loan for which the borrowers (ταύταις) had deposited a security or pawn (ἐνέχυρον) with the lender (the speaker of v. 1). Thus the 'gift' in v. 1 is now transformed into the object or objects loaned to the woman, and the women's (? sexual) services to the man in return (if my interpretation is right) are viewed as the 'pawn' deposited by the women to secure the loan. The legal principles involved are discussed by J. H. Lipsius, *Das attische Recht und Rechtsverfahren* 2 (Leipzig 1908) 690ff., U. E. Paoli, *Studi di diritto attico* (Florence 1930) 141ff., E. Pringsheim, *The Greek Law of Sale* (Weimar 1950) 170f., A. R. W. Harrison, *The Law of Athens* (Oxford) 1 (1968) 253ff., 2 (1971) 244ff., D. M. MacDowell, *The Law in Classical Athens* (London 1978) 142ff.

Αἰπόλοι

Meineke 1.396. Cratinus wrote a Βουκόλοι (J. Th. M. F. Pieters, *Cratinus*

---

n. 399). Cf. also H. D. Jocelyn, *PLLS* 4 (1983) 3f., E. Lefèvre, *Gnomon* 57 (1985) 23ff., E. Stärk, *Die Menaechmi des Plautus und kein griechisches Original* (Tübingen 1989) 134ff. and A. S. Gratwick's edition of *Men.* (Cambridge 1993) 23ff. and n. 27.

ΑΙΠΟΛΟΙ

(Leiden 1946) 14f.) and Mnesimachus a Ἱπποτρόφος (Webster, *SLGC* 60, Nesselrath, *MK* 274ff.); but it is unlikely that Alexis' Αἰπόλοι, the only play known with this title, had anything materially in common with them.

In New Comedy and related genres, goatherds (along with other types of herdsmen) are traditionally finders of exposed babies. At Men. *Epitr.* 326ff. Syr(isk)os defends his claim to the trinkets found with the exposed baby by Daos (a shepherd, 243, 256, like the servant in S. *OR* and the baby's finder in Euripides' *Alope*) by alleging that in the myth a goatherd found Neleus and Pelias in similar circumstances and brought them up to be goatherds; this is a clear if inaccurate reference to Sophocles' *Tyro* (the finder was really a ἱπποτρόφος: cf. A. C. Pearson's edition of the fragments 2 (Cambridge 1918) 272f., Wilamowitz, *Schiedsg.* 65f., Gomme–Sandbach, *Comm.* on Men. *Epitr.* 326). In Longus' novel the goatherd Lamon discovered the infant Daphnis (1.2f.), while the shepherd Dryas found Chloe exposed (1.4).

8

Meineke 3.385, Kock 2.299, Edmonds 2.376, Kassel–Austin 2.27; cf. Fraenkel, *Kl. Beitr.* 1.465ff. Only by full quotation of the Zenobius and *Suda* entries s.v. τὰ τρία τῶν εἰς τὸν θάνατον (see Kassel–Austin) is it possible to gauge the extent of their confusion. Fortunately Miller's MS of Zenobius from Athos (cf. W. Bühler, *Zenobii Athoi proverbia* 1 (Göttingen 1987) 314ff.) removed one difficulty by confirming that Ἀλέξανδρος, the authorial ascription in the *recensio vulgata* of Zenobius (6.11 Leutsch–Schneidewin), was a corruption of Ἄλεξις: the error doubtless originated from an abbreviation of Alexis' name of the kind often found, for instance, in the MSS of Stobaeus (thus at 3.29.34 Hense = fr. 31(30K) S has ἀλέξιδ while M corrupts to ἀλεξίδου). The remaining difficulties in the entries are caused largely by the jumbling together of three different proverbs (εἴποις τὰ τρία, τὰ τρία τὰ παρὰ τῇ αὐλῇ, τὰ τρία τῶν εἰς (τὸν) θάνατον) and three different explanations (public hall, Delphic oracle, ways of dying). The 'public hall' explanation properly belongs to the proverbs τὰ τρία τὰ παρὰ τῇ αὐλῇ and εἴποις τὰ τρία; it has been transferred here from its rightful place under the lemma εἴποις τὰ τρία (*Suda* 2.531 Adler) by some old scholar misled by the superficial similarity between the wording of τὰ τρία τὰ παρὰ τῇ αὐλῇ and that of τὰ τρία τῶν εἰς (τὸν) θάνατον. The 'Delphic oracle' explanation, deriving from Aristides (presumably the Milesian, who wrote περὶ παροιμιῶν: Müller, *FHG* 4.327 fr. 33), also has nothing to do with τὰ τρία τῶν εἰς (τὸν) θάνατον, since its penalties are maimings, not death: cf. A. Persson, *Die Exegeten und Delphi* (Lund 1918) 70, P. Amandry, *La Mantique apollinienne à Delphes* (Paris 1950) 150.

73

COMMENTARY

Alexis' use of the proverb τὰ τρία τῶν εἰς (τὸν) θάνατον, whatever his precise wording (the presence or absence of definite articles before εἰς and before θάνατον is uncertain), whatever its application to the lost context, must be related to the explanation given correctly by the *Suda* with reference to Alexis and added at the end of the Zenobius note: that those condemned to death were given a choice of three methods of execution: sword, noose or hemlock. A muddled scholion on Pindar (*Ol.* 1.97e, f) drawn from several sources contains two lists of the 'three ways of dying' which differ from each other and from the *Suda*/Zenobius list: βρόχος κώνειον βάραθρον and ξίφος ἀγχόνη κρημνός. The first of this scholion's lists, with its strong Attic flavour, may well represent the 'three ways of dying' imagined by Athenian users of the proverb. Fraenkel sees the proverb reflected in Ar. *Ran* 117–35, where Heracles advises Dionysus to hang himself, drink hemlock or leap from a high tower (cf. 1504ff. and Jackson, *Marg. Scaen.* 56). He shows that the other fatal triads, too, are reproduced in literature. The *Suda*/Zenobius combination occurs in Diod. Sic. 19.11.6 and Lucian *Hist. Conscr.* 25. The Pindar scholion's sword, noose and cliff turn up in Hor. *Epod.* 17.70ff., with the cliff replaced (as in Ar.) by a tower; cf. Lucan 9.106f. Fraenkel fails to mention Eur. *Tro.* 1010ff., where Hecuba's taunt includes tower, rope and sword.

However, all these literary allusions refer to suicide and not to public execution. Is the *Suda*/Zenobius explanation inaccurate then, or were the literary references to suicide merely extensions from judicial practice? This is uncertain, but a possible hint to a partial solution, together with a final problem, is given by a further entry in the *Suda* s.v. τῶν τριῶν κακῶν ἕν (4.579 Adler; cf. Phot. s.v. and Hesych. s.v. τῶν τριῶν ἕν). This lemma may indicate a proverb entirely distinct from τὰ τρία τῶν εἰς (τὸν) θάνατον, or alternatively the two proverbs could be related, filling out a vaguer τὰ τρία (? κακά) formula in different terms. The *Suda* and Phot. entries go on to cite two snatches of Old Comedy (Ar. fr. 563(549K), Polyzelus 3) which refer to τὰ τρία Θηραμένους; the Polyzelus fr. defines the 'three things' as a choice of punishments which Theramenes proposed for one (or more) of his opponents, probably in 411 at the time of the four hundred.[1] An inaccurate memory of this incident, transferring it to the later oligarchy of the thirty, might account for the words ἐπὶ <τῶν> τριάκοντα in the Athos MS of Zenobius towards the end of 1.61 (omitted in the *recensio vulgata* 6.11).

---

[1] Kock 1.531 plausibly refers to Thuc. 8.70. The fr. of Aristophanes derives from the Τριφάλης, dated to 411 or shortly afterwards by its references to Aristarchus and the Iberian soldiers employed at Oenoe (Thuc. 8.98; see Kock, and Schmid–Stählin 1.iv.197f.). Cf. also R. Hirzel, *ARW* 11 (1908) 246 n. 5, A. C. Pearson on S. fr. 908.

ΑΙΣΩΠΟΣ

Αἴσωπος

Meineke 1.389f. This play (the only one so titled) cannot be dated, but Meineke's suggestion that it belongs to the Middle-Comedy period seems reasonable.[1] To the Greeks of Alexis' time Solon (a character in Αἴσωπος: fr. 9.1) and Aesop were figures of their remoter past, to be classed with the heroes of myth; myth burlesque throve in Athenian comedy at the beginning of Alexis' career but not later (Legrand, *NGC* 31f., Körte in *RE* s.v. *Komödie* 1262.33ff., Webster, *SLGC* 16ff., 82ff., Hunter 22f., Nesselrath, *MK* 188ff., 191 and n. 51).

Aesop is unknown elsewhere as a character in drama, but Solon appeared in at least two 5th-century comedies. Diog. Laert. 1.62 bears witness to his presence in Cratinus' Χείρωνες (fr. 246(228K); cf. J. Th. M. F. Pieters, *Cratinus* (Leiden 1946) 113ff.), and a plausible conjecture at Σ Aristides 3.672.4 Dindorf gives him a part in Eupolis' Δῆμοι (cf. fr. 99 Kassel–Austin = 92 Austin, *CGPF* v. 47; Kock 1.279, K. Plepelits, *Die Fragmente der Demen des Eupolis* (Vienna 1970) 106f.). The one fr. remaining from Alexis' play (9) tells us nothing about the plot. In it Solon is conversing with an unnamed character, whose words παρ' ὑμῖν, ὦ Σόλων, ἐν ταῖς 'Αθήναις (vv.1–2) indicate that their speaker was not Athenian. W. H. Grauert, *De Aesopo* (Diss. Bonn 1825) 28f., followed by many scholars, identified this non-Athenian as Aesop himself. Even though it would be wise to bear in mind the large number of non-Athenians in the legends associated with Aesop (Croesus, six of the seven sages, Cleobulina,[2] his Delphian murderers, for instance), Grauert's idea is attractive. In the tradition Solon and Aesop met at least twice: at the court of Croesus (Plut. *Solon* 28; Wilamowitz, *Hermes* 25 (1890) 218 suggests that the tradition goes back to Ephorus), and at Periander's banquet of the seven sages, which Plutarch sites at Lechaeum near Corinth (*Mor.* 146b–64d). Although one cannot be certain that words such as παρ' ὑμῖν, ὦ Σόλων, ἐν ταῖς 'Αθήναις were spoken in a non-

---

[1] Edmonds' suggestion (2.378 note b) that the Αἴσωπος may have been influenced by Demetrius of Phalerum's tract about Aesop, and so should be dated to *c.* 320, must be resisted. It ignores the almost total disappearance of myth burlesque and related types of plot by 320. It makes an unwarranted assumption that Alexis' play was influenced by Demetrius' work. Without any evidence it dates Demetrius' essay to *c.* 320. Finally it turns Demetrius' λόγων Αἰσωπείων συναγωγή (on which see E. Bayer, *Demetrios Phalereus der Athener* (Stuttgart and Berlin 1942) 145f.) into a 'tract about Aesop'.

[2] It is uncertain whether there was any relationship between Alexis' Κλεοβουλίνη (q.v.) and the Αἴσωπος.

75

COMMENTARY

Athenian setting (so Grauert: but Kock 2.300 prudently cites Ar. *Ach.* 729, 829, *Lys.* 170 to show that similar expressions are used also in Athens by non-Athenians to Athenians; see too the introduction to Alexis' Ταραντῖνοι and comm. on 224(222K).1–2), it still remains true that a non-Attic setting like Croesus' court (so A. Hausrath in *RE* s.v. *Fabel* 1709.58ff.) or Periander's banquet would have well suited Alexis' play. It is perhaps unlikely that Plutarch borrowed anything directly from Alexis for his own dialogue of the sages' banquet, even though he placed Aesop next to Solon in it (150a) and introduced the subject of drunkenness into the conversation (152d, 155e and following). A third possibility for the comedy's setting would be Delphi, the scene of the quarrel which led to Aesop's death, according to a tradition that goes back at least to the 5th century (Ar. *Vesp.* 1446ff., cf. Σ^{RV} *ad loc.*, Hdt. 2.134); and it was the place where the sages dedicated their two famous mottoes (Pl. *Protag.* 343ab, Paus. 10.24.1; cf. Plut. *Mor.* 116c, 385d, 511b). See G. Thiele, *Hermes* 41 (1906) 582, *RE* s.v. *Fabel* 1707.39ff. (A. Hausrath) and s.v. *Sieben Weise* 2242.37ff. (Barkowski), B. E. Perry, *Aesopica* 1 (Urbana 1952), especially 215ff. (collecting all the references to Aesop in ancient literature), A. Weichers, *Aesop in Delphi* (Meisenheim 1961), D. L. Clayman, *Callimachus' Iambi* (*Mnemosyne* Suppl. 59, Leiden 1981) 17f., W. Bühler on Zenobius 2.5 (p.76), M. Di Marco, *Timone di Fliunte, Silli* (Rome 1989) 160ff.

9

Meineke 3.386, Kock 2.299, Edmonds 2.378, Kassel–Austin 2.28. By a comic anachronism that has many parallels, especially in the mythological comedies of the mid-4th century (e.g. frs. 37(36K), 140(135K); Webster, *SLGC* 85, Nesselrath, *MK* 228f.), Solon is presented as excusing to his non-Athenian interlocutor the practice of 4th-century Athenian merchants who watered the wine before selling it. Alexis thus kills two birds with one stone: he ridicules the naivety of the wise Solon, and makes a veiled attack on fraudulent κάπηλοι. Directly before Ath. 10.431d cites this fr. of Alexis, he quotes Hegesander (Müller, *FHG* 4.417 fr. 22) for an example of a similar fraud in the camp of Lysander. Cf. also Nicostratus 22 ὁ κάπηλος γὰρ οὐκ τῶν γειτόνων, | ἄν τ' οἶνον ἄν τε φανὸν ἀποδῶταί τινι | ἄν τ' ὄξος, ἀπέπεμψ' ὁ κατάρατος δοὺς ὕδωρ, the αἰσχροκερδής in Theophr. *Char.* 30 οἰνοπωλῶν κεκραμένον τὸν οἶνον τῷ φίλῳ ἀποδόσθαι, Phrynichus' explanation of κάπηλον φρόνημα as deriving from τῶν καπήλων τῶν μὴ πιπρασκόντων εἰλικρινῆ καὶ ἀκέραια τὰ ὤνια (*Praep. Soph.* 84.15ff. de Borries), and LXX *Isaiah* 1.22.

1 κομψόν (*'fein, elegant, geistreich'* Wilamowitz, *Schiedsg.* 77) lends itself particularly well to malicious overtones: cf. Eur. *Suppl.* 426, fr. 16, Ar. *Equ.* 18, *Ran.* 967, LSJ s.v. κομψός 2.

1–2 παρ' ὑμῖν, ὦ Σόλων, ἐν ταῖς 'Αθήναις: the implications are discussed in the introduction to Αἴσωπος. In A and the Epit. MSS ὦ Σόλων is misplaced before τὸ ποῖον (v.3: transposed by Musurus); a reason for the error is not obvious. Perhaps at an earlier stage in the tradition when part-divisions were still indicated (are CE's dicola before and after τὸ ποῖον etiolated remains of the convention used in dramatic texts?[1]), Solon's name was written in the margin before τὸ ποῖον, and the vocative in v. 1 became confused with this.

2 ACE's εὑρημένον is printed in Kassel–Austin, but Herwerden's ηὑρημένον (*Coll. Crit.* 120) may be more acceptable at this play's conjectured date. The augmented form of the perfect and secondary tenses is Attic, and preserved in Attic inscriptions up to 300 (Meisterhans–Schwyzer 171f., Threatte 1.385; cf. K.B. 2.11, Schwyzer 1.709 n. 2). MSS of 4th-century Attic writers, however, vary between the augmented form (e.g. Pl. *Gorg.* 502a, *Leg.* 1.633a, 3.699b, etc., Dem. 55.31) and the Ionic and Hellenistic unaugmented form which replaced it (the orators generally, e.g. Dem. 19.17, 23.185, Aeschines 3.162; Ath.'s excerpts from comedy including Alexis 190(185K).2; the comic papyri, Men. *Dysk.* 489, *Epitr.* 534, 869, *Sam.* 615, com. adesp. frs. 285.8, 286.5, 129.30 Austin, the last probably from Men. 'Εγχειρίδιον); cf. O. Lautensach, *Grammatische Studien zu den griechischen Tragikern und Komikern* (Leipzig 1899) 47ff., opposed by D. J. Mastronarde, *Glotta* 67 (1989) 101ff. How far this divergence represents authorial intention, and how far modernisation of spelling by copyists, remains uncertain. Cf. also frs. 31(30K).3, 151(147K).3, 190(185K).2.

3 τὸ ποῖον: assigned to Solon first by Grotius, *Exc.* 559, 971. The presence of the article indicates that ποῖον is purely interrogative, without overtones of surprise, anger or doubt; cf. R. S. Bluck on Pl. *Men.* 95d, Handley on Men. *Dysk.* 753.

συμποσίοις: the συμποσίοισιν of the MSS (corr. Jacobs, *Spic.* 55) may have arisen when a scribe's eye leapt ahead to the ιν of πίνετε (or whatever form of that verb his MS, perhaps already corrupt, may have had: -εται A, -ετ' CE, corr. Musurus) and absorbed it into the longer form of the dative plural; cf. E. Maunde Thompson, *An Introduction to Greek and Latin Palaeography* (Oxford 1912) 156f., V. Coulon, *Essai sur la méthode de la critique conjecturale* (Paris 1933) 46. The apparently similar error in the lemma of fr. 180(175K) (q.v.) may have had a different cause.

3–4 ἄκρατος (or ἄκρατον: see comm. on fr. 5.1) was drunk in Attic symposia only for the toast ἀγαθοῦ δαίμονος and similar commemorations (cf. Alexis 246(244K); its consumption at other times was considered

---

[1] Cf. the general introduction, II.i.a.

COMMENTARY

barbaric (Σκυθικὴν πόσιν Anacreon fr. 356b.3 Page, Hdt. 6.84, Ar. *Ach.* 73ff., Pl. *Leg.* 1.637e; cf. Mau in *RE* s.v. *Comissatio* 610.49ff., D. L. Page, *Sappho and Alcaeus* (Oxford 1955) 308, R. G. Ussher on Ar. *Eccl.* 1123f.), and so the opposite of Ἑλληνικός or more precisely (in view of such complaints as the parasite's at Alciphron 3.15.3 about the ways of other Greek cities) Ἀττικὸς πότος: cf. also Philochorus in Ath. 2.38cd (*FGrH* 328 F 5b).

4–12 οὐ γὰρ ῥᾴδιον–κάδοις: first assigned to Solon by Schweighaeuser.

4–5 Meineke aptly compares Pollux 7.192 ἐπίπρασκον δ᾽ οὗτοι τὸ γλεῦκος, ἐφ᾽ ἁμαξῶν εἰς τὴν ἀγορὰν κομίζοντες.

7–8 τοῦ ... ἔχειν: Kock's explanation of this genitive ('προνοούμενοι *primum cum* τῶν ὠνουμένων *coniungitur, deinde per* ἐπεξήγησιν *additur* τοῦ – ἔχειν') is strictly correct, but does not go far enough. In the sense 'I take thought for' προνοοῦμαι takes a genitive either of the person (Men. *Sik.* 139) or of the thing (Thuc. 6.9) affected. Here τῶν ὠνουμένων (v.6) is an example of the former; the second genitive τοῦ ... ἔχειν is a colloquial afterthought, to be regarded partly as epexegetic with its case influenced by the particle προνοούμενοι (cf. Schwyzer 2.360f., §§ 3–4) but partly also as an instance of the genitive of purpose with an articular infinitive, a construction first known in Attic from Thucydides and Aristophanes but no stranger to later comedy (Men. *Epitr.* 524, *Pk.* 176, possibly Theophilus 11) or to Hellenistic Greek, where Thucydides' preference for its use with negatived infinitives is maintained. See especially K.G. 2.40ff., Schwyzer 2.132, Blass–Debrunner–Funk 206f., Dover on Ar. *Nub.* 22, and P. Burguière, *Histoire de l'infinitif en grec* (Paris 1961) 134ff. The closest parallels to Alexis' use here are S. *Phil.* 196ff. θεῶν του μελέτη, τοῦ μὴ πρότερον τόνδ᾽ ἐπὶ Τροίᾳ τεῖναι τὰ θεῶν ἀμάχητα βέλη (where Jebb's interpretation is unsatisfactory: see Burguière, *loc. cit.*) and Dem. 54.18 τραύματος πάλιν εἰσὶν γραφαὶ τοῦ μὴ τιτρωσκομένων τινῶν φόνους γίγνεσθαι.

8 ἐκ κραιπάλης: κραιπάλη includes both drinking-bout and the hangover it produces (LSJ s.v.; cf. J. André, *Ant. Class.* 33 (1964) 92ff.), and so ἐκ κραιπάλης may shade in meaning from 'after the bout' to 'as a result of the bout/hangover'. At Ar. *Ach.* 277, *Vesp.* 1255 both of the nuances of ἐκ can be felt; here the temporal one is dominant, although (since τὰς κεφαλὰς ὑγιεῖς ἔχειν is logically equivalent to 'not to feel the after-effects') the other nuance cannot be excluded.

ὁρᾷς: parenthetical, 'generally where there is a touch of malice' (Starkie on Ar. *Nub.* 355); in comedy also e.g. Ar. *Equ.* 92, *Thesm.* 496, 556, *Ran.* 1234, *Eccl.* 104, Amphis 38.1, Anaxandrides 18(17K).4, Men. *Pk.* 332, 511, *Sam.* 461, 595; cf. K.G. 2.353f.

8–11 τοῦτ᾽ ἔσθ᾽, ὁρᾷς, Ἑλληνικὸς ... πότος: for the idiom see on fr.

78

ΑΙΣΩΠΟΣ

99(94K).1. Repetitive sequences such as πότος ... ποτηρίοις (9) ... πότος (11) here in the space of nineteen words are an oddity of stylistic insensitivity to which ancient Greek authors were curiously prone (examples in Jackson, *Marg. Scaen.* 22off.; in Alexis, fr. 2.2–6 has ἦγον (probably: the most attractive conjecture) ... ἦγον ... ἦγεν in twenty-five words. Although the repetition of πότος in the present context adds a ranting emphasis in Solon's sermon on temperance, D. Bain (*LCM* 2 (1977) 87f.) may be right to argue that the first πότος here could be a scribal error induced by the ποτ- later in v. 9 and by the general subject matter of the fr., but in that event Naber's suggestion τρόπος (*Mnemosyne* 8 (1880) 254) is a more attractive replacement than Bain's own νόμος.

10 λαλεῖν τι καὶ ληρεῖν πρὸς αὐτοὺς ἡδέως: here λαλεῖν implies ordinary conversation (cf. P. Groeneboom on Herodas 4.32ff., Wilamowitz, *Schiedsg.* 60), ληρεῖν joking and frivolous nonsense; λαλεῖν τι as in Posidippus 28(26K).3 (Casaubon's certain conjecture), hence no need to conjecture τε. The idea itself is a commonplace reaching back at least to Theognis 1047 νῦν μὲν πίνοντες τερπώμεθα καλὰ λέγοντες, cf. 493–6.

αὐτούς with rough breathing (= ἀλλήλους) is clearly legible in C, and was printed already by G. Morel 133, Hertel 434 and Grotius, *Exc.* 559, before Meineke 3.387 independently resurrected it.

12 ψυκτῆρι πίνειν καὶ κάδοις: as one might do towards the end of a drinking-party, when the guests resorted to larger cups (Mau, *RE* s.v. *Comissatio* 615.15ff.); so Alcibiades in Pl. *Symp.* 213e, selecting a ψυκτήρ which held more than 8 kotylai. κάδος is briefly discussed by B. A. Sparkes, *JHS* 95 (1975) 127f. and pl. xii; cf. Sparkes and L. Talcott, *Agora* xii.201ff. and figs. 17, 20, 23, pls. 72, 99). ἐκ ποτηρίου πίνειν is the normal Attic construction when one drinks from a specified vessel (e.g. Ar. *Equ.* 1289 (said to be Eupolis), Xen. *Cyr.* 5.3.3, Pl. *Euthyd.* 299e, *Resp.* 3.417a, Antiphanes 161(163K).5); the use of the instrumental dative here adds a delicate emphasis to the size of cup named (i.e. not merely *from* the cup, but taking the whole cup ἀπνευστί). This subtlety of nuance was lost by Hellenistic and later writers, who use ἐκ + genitive, ἐν + dative, and simple instrumental dative indiscriminately.

θάνατος μὲν οὖν: μὲν οὖν indicates that these words belong to Solon's interlocutor (so first Hirschig, *Diss.* 35, 59), who, 'while agreeing with what the first has said, as far as it goes, shows that he regards it as inadequate by substituting a stronger form of expression' (Denniston, *GP* 475). For the hyperbolic use of θάνατος cf. e.g. S. *OC* 529 θάνατος μὲν τάδ' ἀκούειν, Cratinus 299(273K).1 πιεῖν δὲ θάνατος οἶνον ἦν ὕδωρ ἐπῇ, Alciphron 1.4.2 (to a fisherman) θάνατος ἡ γῆ.

79

COMMENTARY

Αἰχμάλωτος

About the play's subject nothing is known and little can be guessed. In 5th-century tragedy choruses of female prisoners are familiar (e.g. Eur. *Hec.*, *Tro.*, S. *Aichmalotides*). The mute captive women led on to the stage by Lichas in S. *Trach.*, though not a chorus, were doubtless just as moving for audiences who knew the effects of war from personal experience. Non-choral prisoners appear in at least three other plays of later comedy besides Alexis' Αἰχμάλωτος. Male captives are the heroes of Plautus' *Captiui*, and the ransoming of one and the identification of the other form its plot.[1] Menander's *Aspis* opens with a group of αἰχμάλωτοι accompanying Daos on to the stage (36), and we learn that Daos' master Kleostratos had become an αἰχμάλωτος of some Lycians (112). In the same dramatist's *Misoumenos* Krateia had been a free girl captured in war by the soldier Thrasonides, who fell in love with her; her description as αἰχμάλωτος (235 Sandbach) reminds us that Alexis' captive could also have been female; cf. LSJ s.v., citing other female examples (A. *Ag.* 1440, S. *Trach.* 417).

10

Meineke 3.387, Kock 2.300, Edmonds 2.378, Kassel–Austin 2.29. ἡμίκακον, the one word cited from the play, was a shuttlecock in the Atticist games of the second half of the 2nd century AD (cf. K. Latte, *Hermes* 50 (1915) 373ff.). It is supported as Attic by Pollux 6. 161, citing Euclides (?

---

[1] Date and authorship of the Greek original of *Captiui* are unknown, although many guesses have been made, the most plausible being *c.*314 or 280 for the date (see K. Abel, *Die Plautusprologe* (Diss. Frankfurt 1955) 125 n. 250) and Philemon's Αἰτωλός for the play (C. A. Dietze, *De Philemone comico* (Diss. Göttingen 1901) 15ff., Webster, *SLGC* 145ff., but see also W. Kraus in *Latinität und Kirche: Festschrift für Rudolf Hanslik = Wien. Stud.* Beiheft 8 (Vienna 1970) 169f.). Edmonds' suggestion (2.379 note c) that Alexis' Αἰχμάλωτος might have been Plautus' original cannot be discounted in view of our virtually total ignorance about Alexis' play and the uncertainty of rival claims, but it rests on the flimsiest of evidence. The one word of fr. 10 could have been translated at *Capt.* 272 *non multum ... molesta*, and Plautus could have altered a singular to a plural in the title. Again, *Capt.* 277f. appears at first sight to translate a fr. of Alexis' Θηβαῖοι (94(90K): see comm. *ad loc.*), but such a tie hardly strengthens the case for Αἰχμάλωτος; there is no evidence that Θηβαῖοι and Αἰχμάλωτος were alternative titles of the same play, and the subjects of Plautus' play were Aetolians and Eleans, not Thebans.

ΑΙΧΜΑΛΩΤΟΣ

of Megara: cf. R. Muller, *Les Mégariques* (Paris 1985) 23, fr. 22) and Sophocles fr. 1051 for the adjective, and Ar. *Thesm.* 449 for the adverb; the Antiatticist (98.13 Bekker) supplies this further instance of the adjective from Alexis. This view is firmly opposed by Phrynichus (ἡμίκακον· οὐχ οὕτως, ἀλλ᾽ ἡμιμόχθηρον φαθί, p. 93 Fischer), who could have quoted Pl. *Resp.* 1.352c in his favour. Both adjectives continued in use during the imperial period (-κακος Oenomaus in Euseb. *Praep. Evang.* 5.24.7, -μόχθηρος Philo 2.346, Galen 6.56 Kühn) and in Byzantine Greek (-κακος anon. in *Suda* s.v. Σπάδων, 4.414.9 Adler, -μόχθηρος Synesius *De Provid.* 7).

Ἀλαζών

See general introduction, 1.vi.iii.c.

Ἀλείπτρια

See 'False or Doubtful Attributions 1' (pp. 813ff.).

Ἀμπελουργός

Kann, *De iteratis* 73ff. The title is one of eleven or twelve shared with Amphis (the others are Γυναικοκρατία, Δακτύλιος, Ἑπτὰ ἐπὶ Θήβαις (? -βας), Ἔριθοι, Κονιατής, Κουρίς, Κυβευταί, Λευκαδία, Ὀδυσσεύς, Φιλέταιρος, possibly Ἀλείπτρια). How should one explain this *mira coniunctio*? In Kann's view Amphis might have been a plagiarist on the grand scale, but speculation is unprofitable in the absence of hard evidence.

Ἀμπελουργός is one of several agricultural titles in later Greek comedy (e.g. a Γεωργός by Menander and possibly also Timocles: see Clem. Alex. *Strom.* 4.7.1 introducing the latter's fr. 38(36K), Antiphanes' Κηπουρός, the 'Herdsmen' titles discussed in the introduction to Alexis' Αἰπόλοι), although it is uncertain whether this group of plays had anything in common other than their titles. Nothing is known about the subject of Alexis' play, but one of the two words preserved from it (ἀναδενδράς fr. 11) accords well with the title.

11

Meineke 3.388 (1), Kock 2.300, Edmonds 2.378, Kassel–Austin 2.29; cf. Sicking, *Annotationes* 39. Strict Atticists presumably opposed the use of

COMMENTARY

ἀναδενδράς, the normal word in post-classical Greek for 'tree-vine' (e.g. Theophr. *CP* 5.5.4, Plut. *Mor.* 290e, 342b, Σ Ar. *Vesp.* 326, *Et. Mag.* s.v.; cf. *TGL*, to whose references add Longus 2.1; the rhetorical lexicon in Bekker, *Anecd.* 1.203, 28f., however, gives ἀναδενδράδες· τὰ κλήματα τῆς ἀμπέλου τὰ ὑπερμήκη without supporting argument or citation). In place of this form Atticists must have supported ἀμάμαξυς, which *Et. Gen.* and *Et. Mag.* (1.372.16ff. Lasserre–Livadaras) define simply as ἀναδενδράς. The Antiatticist is right (p.82.4 Bekker) to defend ἀναδενδράς; he could have cited also Pherecrates 114(109K).1 and [Dem.] 53.15 in its favour, while in Attic ἀμάμαξυς appears only at Ar. *Vesp.* 326 (cf. Σ *ad loc.*). On the tree-vine itself see Hehn, *Kulturpflanzen* 73, Olck in *RE* s.v. *Arbustum* 421.19ff.; O. A. W. Dilke on Hor. *Epist.* 1.7.84. Cf. also V. Chapot in Dar.–Sag. s.v. *Vinum* 918 fig. 7512 and R. Strömberg, *Griechische Pflanzennamen* (Göteborg 1940) 111 and *Griechische Wortstudien* (Göteborg 1944) 39.

12

Meineke 3.388 (ii), Kock 2.300, Edmonds 2.378, Kassel–Austin 2.29; cf. R. Renehan, *Studies in Greek Texts* (Göttingen 1976) 110f. In correct Attic usage the aorist infinitive of ἀπολογοῦμαι is the middle form ἀπολογήσασθαι, not the passive ἀπολογηθῆναι; this was presumably the point that Atticist opponents of our Antiatticist had been making. In attempting to defend the aorist passive form as an allowable alternative in Attic Greek the Antiatticist (p.82.5 Bekker) is supporting a lost cause. Apart from Alexis here, the use of the aorist passive is certainly attested in only one Attic writer: the author of those tetralogies attributed to Antiphon (2.γ.1, δ.3, 3.γ.2, 4.γ.1) where the Greek displays many unattic features.[1] (I

---

[1] On the question of authorship scholars are still divided. Thalheim in *RE* s.v. *Antiphon* 14, 2528.19ff. lists the 19th-century contributions to the controversy; more recently K. J. Maidment, *Minor Attic Orators* 1 (Loeb edition: Cambridge, Mass. and London 1941) 36f., P. Von der Mühll, *Mus. Helv.* 5 (1948) 1ff., K. J. Dover, *CQ* 44 (1950) 56ff. and G. Pendrick, *Hermes* 115 (1987) 47ff. have opposed attribution of the tetralogies to Antiphon the orator and politician, while G. Zuntz, *Class. et Med.* 2 (1939) 121ff. and *Mus. Helv.* 5 (1948) 100ff., J. S. Morrison, *PCPS* 7 (1961) 49ff., F. Decleva Caizzi, *Antiphontis Tetralogiae* (Milan 1969) 11ff., 79ff. (tentatively) and H. C. Avery, *Hermes* 110 (1982) 145ff. have supported it; cf. also Lesky, *HGL* 353ff. But whether these works are genuine early Antiphon, or spurious and written in 5th-century Athens by a non-Athenian, the fact remains that their employment of the form ἀπολογηθῆναι contrasts notably with the use of the correct middle form ἀπολογήσασθαι in the genuine speeches of Antiphon (5.13, 60, 74 *bis*, 90, 6.8) and already seemed noteworthy to Pollux (2.119 ἀπολογήσασθαι· Ἀντιφῶν δὲ καὶ ἀπελογήθη ἔφη).

ignore Xen. *Hell.* 1.4.13, where ἀπελογήθη ὡς shows every sign of being a gloss, cf. Cobet, *NL* 307.) Its use by Alexis might well exemplify the encroachment of the *Koine* dialect on Attic comedy; it becomes the normal form in Hellenistic and later writers (*TGL* s.v.).

Ἀμφωτίς (or Ἄμφωτις?)

Meineke 1.396f., Kock 2.301, Kassel–Austin 2.30. This title poses problems of spelling, accent and meaning. Spelling: practically all the MSS, whatever the meaning or accent, give ἀμφωτις, the one exception being an entry that occurs in Hesych. and *Et. Mag.* (1.459.4 Lasserre–Livadaras) where the lemma offers ἄμφωξις, defined as a milk-pail. The spelling with xi may be a copyist's error, but other possibilities cannot be excluded: e.g. it may have been the spelling of an originally non-Greek word for 'milk-pail', later corrupted to ἀμφωτις by popular etymology from ἀμφί and οὖς, helped by the prior existence of a word ἀμφωτις correctly formed from these two stems in the sense of 'ear-pad'. Accent: ἄμφωξις is proparoxytone, ἀμφωτις varies between oxytone and proparoxytone, without any apparent attempt to distinguish meanings thereby. Meaning: 'wooden milk-pail (or cup)' is attested by the entries of Hesych. and *Et. Mag.* s.v. ἄμφωξις, Philitas (fr. 29 Kuchenmüller) in Ath. 11.783d, and Pollux 10.175 where the word is included in an agricultural list ἐκ τῶν σκευῶν; 'ear-pad' is indicated by Hesych. s.v. ἀμφωτίδες (cf. the lemma ἀμφωτίς directly following) and illustrated by passages such as Plut. *Mor.* 38b and 706c (pads worn by boxers and wrestlers to protect the ears). Both meanings are given by Eustath. 1324.39 (cf. Pausanias gram. fr. 108 Erbse), and Pollux 10.175 (after citing the word in his agricultural list) quotes a line of Aeschylus (fr. 102) where the meaning 'ear-pad' is apparent.

The frs. from Alexis' play are too scanty to afford help with the plot or the title's meaning. Yet the title is Ἀμφωτις, singular; if 'ear-pad(s)' had been intended, would the plural not have been more natural? Cf. Menippus' Ὄφεις (Meineke 1.494), where the reference is presumably to bracelets.[1]

---

[1] The play-title Ὦτις, attributed to the Middle-Comedy writer Nicostratus by the *Suda* (cf. Meineke 1.348), probably has nothing to do with ears, ear-rings or ear-covers. The word ὠτίς means 'bustard', and Ὦτις may well have been the nickname of a woman whose movements or build appeared as ungainly as the bird's; on the change of accent for a proper name, cf. Lobeck, *Paralipomena* 342f.

COMMENTARY

13

Meineke 3.387 (1), Kock 2.301, Edmonds 2.380, Kassel–Austin 2.30.

1 ὀνοκόπος: the man who cut in millstones the original striations which helped to crush the grain, and later renewed them when worn smooth: cf. the Latin *molicudus*. κόπτειν was the technical term for these operations: v. 2 of the present fr., Ar. *Vesp.* 648, Herodas 6.84. Pollux' introductory statement (7.20: cf. Blümner, *Technologie* 31 and n. 1) that in his day μυλοκόπος had replaced the older ὀνοκόπος is confirmed by papyri, e.g. *P. Tebt.* 278.12 (1st century AD), cf. Preisigke, *Wörterbuch* s.v. μυλοκόπος.

2 τῶν τοὺς ἀλετῶνας τῶνδε κοπτόντων ὄνους: when qualified by (1) ἀλετών as here, Alexis 207(204K).2 and in the Attic confiscation *stelai* (*IG* i³.422.24, 289, 290), or (2) ἀλέτης as in Xen. *Anab.* 1.5.5 and a 5th-century inscription from Gortyn (Collitz, *GDI* 4992.II.7), the word ὄνος means the upper, revolving millstone of the *mola trusatilis*. At fr. 207(204K) the phrase is a symbol for brutish insensitivity and/or stupidity. Cf. Blümner, *Technologie* 30 and n. 1, W. K. Pritchett, *Hesperia* 25 (1956) 298f., D. A. Amyx, *ibid.* 27 (1958) 282ff., L. A. Moritz, *Grain-Mills and Flour in Classical Antiquity* (Oxford 1958) 10ff., 218 note c, B. A. Sparkes, *JHS* 82 (1962) 125 and pl. IV.4 and (on this metaphorical use of ὄνος) Chantraine s.v. 2.804f.

τῶνδε: Meineke's τούσδε (3.387) *may* possibly be what Alexis originally wrote before an excerptor or scribe accommodated its case to that of the following word (a common error: examples are given by Coulon, *Essai* 45, J. Adam's edition of Pl. *Resp.* 2.522 s.v. 'accommodation', J. Diggle, *CQ* 34 (1984) 50f.), but in itself τῶνδε makes perfect sense ('the people here', whom the speaker indicates as present either physically or just in his imagination), and the demonstrative pronoun's position between the article and the participle κοπτόντων is perfectly correct when the noun or equivalent word which the demonstrative pronoun qualifies itself has an attribute: e.g. Pl. *Phaed.* 69c οἱ τὰς τελετὰς ἡμῖν οὗτοι καταστήσαντες, Dem. 6.21 αἱ πρὸς τοὺς τυράννους αὗται λίαν ὁμιλίαι, cf. K.G. 1.628.

14

Meineke 3.387 (II), Kock 2.301, Edmonds 2.380, Kassel–Austin 2.30, cf. P. T. Stevens, *Colloquial Expressions in Euripides* (*Hermes Einzelschr.* 38, Wiesbaden 1976) 63. This note of the Antiatticist's (108.10 Bekker), like his earlier one (81.12 ἀνάβα, κατάβα, διάβα, ἀπόστα· Μένανδρος Ἐπικλήρῳ· ὅρα σὺ καὶ φρόντιζε κἀπόστα βραχύ = Men. fr. 158; cf. also Oros s.v. ἀνάβηθι καὶ ἀνάβα, B 12 Alpers p. 199), defends by implication

ΑΜΦΩΤΙΣ

imperatival forms such as μετάβα in 'correct' Attic idiom. In continuous passages of Attic ἔμβα occurs at Eur. *El.* 113, fr. trag. adesp. 520, Ar. *Ran.* 378, *Eccl.* 478 (cf. *Lys.* 1303); κατάβα at Ar. *Vesp.* 979f., *Ran.* 35, Men. *Dysk.* 633, cf. Diog. Laert. 2.41, an anecdote about Plato; πρόβα at Eur. *Alc.* 872, Ar. *Ach.* 262; cf. ἐπίβα at Theognis 847. Such forms, which may be construed either as alternatives to the regular aorist imperative (-βαε → -βα, side by side with -βῆθι) of -βαίνω, or as the present imperative of the verb -βάω (cf. the participle προβῶντες at Cratinus 133(126K); see Veitch, *Greek Verbs*⁴ s.v. βαίνω, βάω, K.B. 2.380f.), belong in Attic more to the spoken than to the literary language. To some extent the grammarians who squabbled over these forms were asking the wrong questions.

Ἄντεια

See 'False or Doubtful Attributions II' (pp. 817ff.).

Ἀπεγλαυκωμένος

Meineke 1.397, Kock 2.301, Gil 330. In Greek medical writers γλαύκωμα is a cataract (LSJ s.v.) and ἀπογλαυκοῦμαι = 'I get (not 'have') a cataract'. The perfect participle of Alexis' title indicates a man already afflicted with this condition, but his role and the type of plot in which he was involved cannot now be determined from the extant frs. of the play, considerable as two of these are. In Aristophanes' *Plutus* the blind god of wealth recovers his sight at a shrine of Asclepius in a comedy where social values predominate over political ones. Could Alexis' title figure have been cured of his affliction by similar means in a play of the same type? Or could the blindness, whether simulated (so first Kock, cf. Gil) or real, have served some purpose in a conspiracy or confidence trick of New-Comedy pattern? In Plautus' *Miles Gloriosus* Pleusicles wears a woollen patch over one eye as part of his disguise as a ship's captain when he elopes with his lady-love (1177ff., 1284ff.). The title figure of the same author's *Curculio* suddenly becomes 'one–eyed' (392ff.) in order to impersonate a soldier's emissary and so gain money by a fraud; although Plautus leaves the details obscure, it is possible that Curculio's single eye was also part of a disguise (cf. Webster, *SLGC* 217ff., J. Collart's edition of the play (Paris 1962), comm. on 384).

The four extant frs. all deal with food, and it is likely that the context into which they fit is a δεῖπνον ἀπὸ συμβολῶν whose arrangements are touched on in fr. 15. Fr. 16 may be (? part of) an entrance monologue

COMMENTARY

spoken by the man who has just purchased provisions for the dinner, venting his anger on the fishmongers for their discourtesy. The other long fr. (15) seems to come from a scene after the meal, when the speaker of fr. 16 shares the stage with one (or more) of the friends who have agreed to split the costs. The shortness of the other two frs. makes them less easy to place. Fr. 18 may come from a scene during or before the dinner; its speaker may be the host asking a guest to eat, or a cook questioning the meal's organiser about any preference for particular dishes. Fr. 17 presumably comes from a description of the dinner by one of the participants, and consequently occurs later in the play than frs. 16 and 18. This interpretation is based on the hypothesis that there was only one dinner in the play, in accord with Roman and later Greek comic convention.

The Roman dramatist Naevius wrote a *Glaucoma*. This could have been an adaptation of Alexis' play (so Legrand, *NGC* 16); in that case its one remaining fr. (p. 17 Ribbeck: *quod de opsonio | stilo mihi in manum pupugit*) might be taken to describe an assault on the food-purchaser by the other speaker of Alexis 15 in a final fit of pique about the cost of the fish at the dinner.

15

Meineke 3.389 (1), Kock 2.301, Edmonds 2.380, Kassel–Austin 2.31, cf. Desrousseaux, *Obs.* 53ff. The situation implied by the fr. is briefly discussed in the introduction to Ἀπεγλαυκωμένος. Two people, one (A) certainly and the other (B) presumably male, are going over the accounts after a δεῖπνον ἀπὸ συμβολῶν for which A is now (in the words of the *Marcianus* at Ath. 3.117e, introducing a fr. which is omitted by Epit.) συμβολάς τις ἀπαιτούμενος. Here ἀπαιτούμενος must be passive, as Schweighaeuser first pointed out (*Animadv.* 2.319); the reference is to A, whose attitude throughout is that of a man under an obligation to pay his share for a dinner that has proved more costly than he had expected. The συμβολαί demanded from him (financial contributions to the expenses of a meal: LSJ s.v. συμβολή ɪv.a) are plural either because he is acting as spokesman for the other obligants, one or more of whom may (not must: see comm. on 7f., 18f. (ὑμῶν)) be mutely present with the two speakers during their accounting, or more simply because συμβολαί is often used in the plural by contemporary Attic writers of a single person's contribution (e.g. Antiphanes 27(26K).8, Dromon 1.5). B is clearly the man who was commissioned by the other participants to organise the dinner and purchase the victuals; he seems to be identical with the speaker of fr. 16. But he is not the *caupo*, as Casaubon (*Animadv.* 227, cf. 226) tentatively suggested, nor a cook (Meineke 3.390), nor a slave (G. A. Papavasileiou, *Athena* ɪ (1889) 213), though all three ideas have had their supporters.

ΑΠΕΓΛΑΥΚΩΜΕΝΟΣ

Ath. normally says when cooks are present in cited dialogues (cf. Alexis 129(124K), 153(149K), 178(172K)), and in vv. 18–19 of the fr. speaker B is shown to have done an action on his own initiative which would hardly have been possible for a huckster or hired cook, while the general impression given by the fr. of independent decision-making on the part of the buyer excludes a slave.

The frequent references to the δεῖπνον ἀπὸ συμβολῶν in comedy from the time of Aristophanes on (e.g. Eubulus 72, Timocles 8) and in other literature indicate that it was a form of entertainment especially popular among wealthier young Athenian bachelors. One of a group of friends undertook to organise a dinner and the wine for drinking afterwards, and the others engaged to pay their shares of the cost usually after the dinner (cf. Machon 315 and Gow ad loc.). Tokens such as rings were sometimes deposited with the organiser in advance as security. See Casaubon, *Animadv.* 224ff., *RE* s.vv. *Convivium* 1202.6ff. (Mau) and Συμβολή 1090.52ff. (Müri), Gow on Machon 44f., and below on Alexis 102(97K).

Scenes of accounting were probably not rare in later comedy and genres influenced by it; cf. especially Theophilus 8 (an athlete's food consumption reckoned up), Asclepiades 25 Gow–Page (preliminary audit of a slave by his master); Webster, *SM* 164 n. 1, G. Giangrande, *Entr. Hardt* 14 (1969) 142f., 175, A. D. Trendall, *Phlyax Vases*[2] (*BICS* Suppl. 19 (1967)) 33f. (no. 31, an early–4th-century Apulian bell-krater on which is depicted an old countryman whose accounts are being checked by a slave and a woman who could be the countryman's rich wife, cf. Webster, *CQ* 42 (1948) 26).

1–2 A's δ'ὡς, corrected to δῶς by Musurus, exemplifies one of this MS's most frequent types of error, faulty word-division; cf. in this fr. alone λέγεσθαι for (Musurus) λέγε. | ::ἔστ' vv. 3–4, ἐβόατ' εἶναι for (P. Elmsley,[1] *Ed. Rev.* 3 (1803/4) 190) ἐβοᾶτε; ::ναί v. 7. Translate 'If you don't give (i.e. tell) me all the items one by one, you won't receive (as your due) a brass farthing from me.' For this loose use of δίδωμι = 'I tell/explain/give an account of' (in the present fr. equivalent to λόγον δίδωμι), which is treated badly by lexica, cf. for example Pl. *Soph.* 263e δίδου μόνον 'only

---

[1] This correction and part-distribution appeared in Elmsley's review of Schweighaeuser's edition of Ath. eleven years before T. Kidd published the same idea above his own initials in his edition of *Porson's Tracts and Miscellaneous Criticisms* (London 1815) 236. At about the same time allegations were made that Elmsley's review of Schweighaeuser plagiarised some conjectures which Porson had previously communicated to him (cf. *Quarterly Review* 5 (1811) 207), but these charges were convincingly refuted by B. B. Rogers in an appendix to his edition of Ar. *Ach.* (London 1910) pp. 192ff.

COMMENTARY

give an explanation', after ἄν πρῶτον λάβῃς 'if you first understand' in the previous sentence. Alexis' δῷς here similarly gains some point from its contrast with ἀπολάβοις in the following verse (cf. Desrousseaux 54). For ἕκαστον in partitive apposition to πάντα cf. Pl. *Resp.* 1.346d αἱ ἄλλαι πᾶσαι (sc. τέχναι) τὸ αὑτῆς ἑκάστη ἔργον ἐργάζεται; K.G. 1.286ff. Failure to understand these idioms has led to a blight of vain conjectures.

2 χαλκοῦ μέρος δωδέκατον: an impossibly small coin, the χαλκοῦς itself being only one eighth of an obol. Bronze coinage was reintroduced in Athens some time after the middle of the 4th century, possibly because of the inconveniently small size of the equivalent silver coins (B. V. Head, *Historia Numorum*[2] (Oxford 1911) 374, A. R. Burns, *Money and Monetary Policy in Early Times* (London 1927) 262).

3 Distribution of parts is arbitrary. Schweighaeuser and the majority of modern editors (including Kassel–Austin) give ἀβάκιον, ψῆφον to speaker A; Kaibel, followed by Gulick and Desrousseaux, continue these words to B and then give λέγε to A. The second view is preferable. The person responsible for the original purchases is the one more likely to have initiated the accounting by ordering a slave to bring the abacus and its counters from a stage house (B's own?). On the abacus and ancient methods of calculation see Hultsch in *RE* s.v. *Abacus* 9, 5.43ff., E. Guillaume in Dar.–Sag. s.v. IA ff., A. Nagl, *Die Rechentafel der Griechen* (*SB Vienna* 177/5 (1914)), M. Lang, *Hesperia* 26 (1957) 271ff., *ibid.* 33 (1964) 146ff., *ibid.* 34 (1965) 224ff. Attic used both ψηφολόγιον (Ar. fr. 362(348K)) and ἀβάκιον (Lysias fr. 50 Thalheim) for the calculator.

ψῆφον (A) or ψήφους (Meineke 3.390)? ψῆφον would be a 'representative' singular, standing for an unspecified number of abacus counters (so Schweighaeuser, *Animadv.* 2.323 noting Daléchamp's translation *tabulam sume et calculos*, Desrousseaux; cf. K.G. 1.13f., Schwyzer 2.41f.); cf. e.g. the use of κάχληξ at Thuc. 4.26 and my note on the collective singular κέραμος at Alexis 259(257K).3. ψῆφος is basically a pebble, especially one employed (a) in abacus calculations, (b) for voting in the law-courts and elsewhere. Already in 5th-century Athens the use of ψῆφος had been extended from the pebble as a voting utensil to the verdict of the recorded votes, with a consequent blurring of distinctions between the literal and metaphorical meanings in phrases such as ψῆφον φέρειν, τίθεσθαι (*TGL* s.v. ψῆφος 1896c ff.), where ψῆφον in the singular is often both 'verdict' and collectively 'votes' (the English word 'vote' contains a similar ambiguity). It is possible that the frequent appearance of ψῆφον in such verbal phrases influenced its use as a 'representative' singular, both in the sense of 'vote(s)', e.g. Pl. *Leg.* 6.759d οἷς ἂν πλείστη γένηται ψῆφος (contrast 753d οἷς ἂν πλεῖσται γένωνται ψῆφοι), and in that of 'counter(s)', e.g. (?) Eur. *Rhes.* 309 ἐν ψήφου λόγῳ and here in Alexis – unless the processes of excerption and transmission have induced here the common error of assimilation of a word's ending to that of the preceding word. A's ψῆφον must be printed, but Meineke's conjecture could be right.

4 ὠμοτάριχος: σάρξ ἐστι θύννου τεταριχευμένου according to Dioscorides 2.31; masculine (-ος) here and in Dioscorides, etc., neuter (-ον) in Diphilus med. at Ath. 3.121b (saying that it is βαρὺ καὶ γλοιῶδες, προσέτι δὲ καὶ δύσπεπτον); uncertain in Nicostratus 1 and Matron, *SH* 534.17. LSJ's translation 'pickled flesh of the tunny's shoulder' (*sic*: after Xenocrates med. fr. 35 = Oribasius, *Coll. Med.* 2.58.144, cf. Pliny, *HN* 9.48) supports the derivation from ὦμος + τάριχος, but that from ὠμός + τ. is also possible (it is raw fish that is pickled/dried; cf. *Gloss. Lat.* 2.210, *CE* 84 *cetum crudum*, ὠμοτάριχος); cf. Thompson, *Fishes* 88, my comm. on 191(186K).5.

5 μῦς: mussels, *Mytilus edulus*; see Thompson, *Fishes* s.v., Strömberg, *Fischnamen* 109f., Saint-Denis, *Vocabulaire* s.v. *mys*. The form is probably nominative plural contracted (so Kock) as at Antiphanes 191(193K).1 (mussels), Herodas 3.76, Aelian *NA* 17.17 (mice), and not a 'representative' singular. Cf. Sandbach's note on Men. *Sam.* 98.

οὐδέν: this is the normal orthography in the *Marcianus*, and ought perhaps to be printed consistently in Alexis, but without total conviction that it was the form preferred by him. In Attic inscriptions οὐδείς/μηδείς is unchallenged before 378. From 378 to 320 examples of οὐδείς/μηδείς and οὐθείς/μηθείς are about equal. From 320 until the period of the Roman empire and the Atticists the -θείς form is unvaried (Threatte 1.472ff. updating Meisterhans–Schwyzer 258f.), although in papyri of the same period spellings with delta number between a fifth and a quarter of the whole (Mayser–Schmoll 1.1.148ff.). From the time of the empire on, when Atticists were encouraging the spelling with delta (Phrynichus, *Ecl.* s.v. οὐθείς διὰ τοῦ θ, p. 75 Fischer, Phot. s.v. οὐδείς), this orthography prevailed once more in Attic inscriptions. Those papyri of Menander which date from the 3rd and 5th centuries AD and contain the main body of his preserved work strongly favour the spelling with delta (e.g. 80 δ ~ 22 θ in the Cairo and Bodmer papyri: cf. C. Dedoussi's edition of *Sam.* (Athens 1965) p. 16, Durham, *Vocabulary* 83), either by assimilation to contemporary usage or by fidelity to authorial spelling. It may be more significant that the 3rd-century papyrus of Men. *Sik.* has two instances with θ, three with δ (if one includes οὐδέ[ν at 399); if popular and official usage overwhelmingly preferred orthography with θ at the time this papyrus was copied, two explanations of its variations are possible: (a) an authorial preference for δ was sometimes preserved by the copyist, sometimes corrupted to the form with θ preferred in the scribe's own time, or (b) Menander himself was inconsistent in his orthography. It is even harder to guess at the orthography of comic poets of the preceding generation; there are no early papyri with continuous passages of their work, and medieval MSS with systematised spelling are of no value here. All that can be aimed for is an unassertive consistency (Barrett on Eur. *Hipp.* 447–50).

5–6 οὐδὲν ἀσεβεῖς οὐδέπω ... ἀγνεύεις ἔτι: speaker A accepts the fairness of the prices for the mussels and sea-urchins in language whose precise frame of reference belongs to people's relationship with the gods (ἀσεβεῖν = to commit sacrilege by act or omission, ἀγνεύειν = to be ritually pure, particularly to be untainted by physical contact with anything or anybody polluted). Doubtless both verbs were used by contemporary Athenians in an extended sense covering a wide range of ethically approved and condemned activities, but retaining a strong emotive force from their religious associations (cf. here the use of ἀσεβής, ἱερόσυλος, etc. in secular contexts as words of violent abuse, e.g. Men. *Sam.* 322 with the comments of Sandbach and Dedoussi (v. 107 her numbering) *ad loc.*). Yet ἀσεβεῖς here retains more of its original associations than one might at first expect, since paying an unfair price = allowing oneself to be cheated and thus being party to an act of ἀσέβεια: cf. Pl. *Leg.* 11.917a–b. To the best of my knowledge ἀγνεύειν does not occur elsewhere in a commercial context, although the use of both verb and its cognates in extended senses is well attested, especially in later Greek, e.g. Plut. *Mor.* 464c ἀγνεύοντα καὶ λόγων πονηρῶν καὶ πράξεων ἀτόπων.

6 τῶν ἐχίνων ὀβολός (cf. v. 8 ταύτης δύ᾽ ὀβολούς) reverses the cases of μῦς ἑπτὰ χαλκῶν (cf. vv. 4, 9, 13, 15, 16, 19) by an idiom common to many languages (thus in English, fifty pence for the fish, fish for fifty pence), cf. K.G. 1.378. ἐχῖνοι are sea-urchins of various species, at least one of which (? *Paracentrotus lividus*:[1] Campbell, *Guide* 238f.) was a popular food in the ancient world: Arist. *HA* 4.530ª32ff., Ath. 3.91a–e, Apic. 9.8.1–5; André, *Alimentation* 106, Saint-Denis, *Vocabulaire* s.v. *echinus*, Thompson, *Fishes* s.v. ἐχῖνος, Palombi–Santorelli 284.

7–8 Elmsley's correction of the *Marcianus* and redistribution of parts (see above on vv. 1–2) are clearly correct. Desrousseaux' reapportionment (ἣν ἐβοᾶτε to A, ναί to B, v. 8 to A) necessitates a reversal of roles from v. 9 on, with A now listing and pricing, B commenting, which in the context is incongruous. Note also that with the traditional distribution A never addresses B in the second person plural, but B so addresses A at

---

[1] In the lands around the Mediterranean, according to Davidson (*Seafood* 217), only the five orange or rose ovaries ('corals') of this sea-urchin are now eaten: 'Tiny mouthfuls, but delicious. No cooking is needed, nor any accompaniment save a drop of lemon juice.' Colin Austin tells me that 'in Otranto the other day they were serving these live sea-urchins not with lemon but with fresh bread, and that's how it was offered to me at Antibes many years ago'.

ΑΠΕΓΛΑΥΚΩΜΕΝΟΣ

vv. 7 and 19: i.e. A is either attended by or standing proxy for one or more other diners: see on 18f.

7 ῥάφανος, the Attic word for cabbage, which other Greeks called κράμβη (cf. Apollodorus Car. 32(27K)) must be distinguished from ῥαφανίς, the classical Attic word for radish, which other Greeks (and the *Koine*) called ῥάφανος; the distinctions sometimes perplexed Alexandrian and post-Alexandrian scholars (the relevant passages are collected by Bethe at Pollux 1.247). Here Alexis clearly means cabbage; the guests had got drunk at the party (v.18), and boiled cabbage was a favoured prophylactic against drunkenness and remedy against hangovers (Ath. 1.34c–e citing Alexis 287(286K), Amphis 37, Anaxandrides 59(58K), Eubulus 124(127K), Nicochares 18(15K); [Arist.] *Probl.* 3.17, 873ᵃ37ff., Theophr. *HP* 4.16.6, Timaeus *FGrH* 3.566.F47, *Geoponica* 5.11.3 and J. N. Niclas' edition (Leipzig 1781) *ad loc.*, 7.33.1, Cato *Agr.* 176.1, Pliny *HN* 20.84; R. B. Onians, *The Origins of European Thought* (Cambridge 1951) 42f., and Hunter on Eubulus, *loc. cit.*).

ἐβοᾶτε: not *impense laudabatis* (so Meineke 3.390 and most subsequent editors, also LSJ s.v. βοάω II.4), since this secondary use of βοῶ appears to be confined to the passive voice (Hdt. 3.39, 6.131, Men. fr. 215.5, Theophr. *Char.* 8.7, Heliodorus 6.1, Libanius *Or.* 59.155, *Decl.* 5.53, 11.18, etc.); the implication here (as in v. 9) is rather that the guests 'kept shouting "Cabbage!"', i.e. they were calling for (more) helpings; cf. S. *Trach.* 772, Eur. *Phoen.* 1154, Xen. *Cyr.* 7.2.5, *Hell. Oxy.* 10.2, LSJ s.v. II.2.

8 For δύ' ὀβολούς Blaydes, *Adv.* 1.104 conjectured δύ' ὀβολώ. From a survey of relevant passages two points emerge: (a) in contexts where the phrase 'two obols' evokes a familiar association, the dual of the noun is obligatory, e.g. in reference to the soldier's pay (Ar. *Vesp.* 1189), certain official payments (*Ran.* 141 and Dover *ad loc.*), the cost of some theatre seats (Dem. 18.28); (b) while Old Comedy prefers δύ' ὀβολώ, later comic writers (on the admittedly uncertain evidence of the MSS) used the dual and plural forms of the noun interchangeably after δύο (thus plural at Philippides 9.5, Men. *Epitr.* 140). Here Alexis may reflect the general decline in use of the dual in 4th-century Athens; cf. Meisterhans–Schwyzer 199ff., A. Humpers, *Rev. Phil.* 46 (1922) 76ff., Schwyzer 2.46f.

9 τί γὰρ ἐβοῶμεν;: if γάρ is correctly transmitted, 'Yes, we shouted for it – why ever did we?' The question is rhetorical, equivalent to a statement which implies agreement with the previous speaker's words ('I gave two obols for the cabbage' = 'The cabbage was very expensive' – 'Yes, we were foolish to shout for it'), and the γάρ is accordingly assentient (Denniston, *GP* 86ff.). The idea comes in the end to the same thing as 'Why *then* did we shout for it?' (i.e. Alexis could alternatively have written τί οὖν or τί δῆτ'), without γάρ being inferential (Denniston, *GP* 57, cf.

COMMENTARY

Schwyzer 2.560); cf. the nuance in Men. *Epitr.* 365f. τί γὰρ ἐγὼ | ἐπέτρεψα τούτῳ? (= 'Yes, I was foolish to submit to his arbitration'). At the same time, it would be absurd in the case of a fr. like this to claim that Alexis *must* have written γάρ here; palaeographic considerations make τί οὖν and τί δῆτ' unlikely, and Herwerden's τί τἄρ' (*Coll. Crit.* 120) produces a collocation for which I know of no parallels in comedy; Sandbach suggested to me τί ἄρ', but this has the wrong tone ('Why, if one only knew ... ?': Denniston, *GP* 39) in a rhetorical question; possibly τί ποτ' ἄρ'.

κύβιον differs from ὠμοτάριχος, being applied specifically to pickled πηλαμύς (young tunny, or small species of tunny such as the albacore or bonito: Thompson, *Fishes* 197ff., cf. Strömberg, *Fischnamen* 79f., 128) cut into cubes (Hicesius in Ath. 3.118a–b, cited directly after the present fr. of Alexis). Galen 12.893 Kühn recommends it when burnt to ashes as a remedy for toothache. Cf. André, *Alimentation* 113.

10 †ονεῖλ|κε (*sic*: the fifth letter was first correctly identified as λ by Colin Austin) **χειρῶν γε†** **οὐκ ἐπράξατ' οὐδὲ ἕν**: the *Marcianus* here is gravely corrupt, and all that can be done is to delimit the damage and to establish roughly the drift of the dialogue. Before ονεῖλ|κε the MS has τριωβόλους (for -ωβόλου: corr. Musurus), where the added sigma probably originated in a scribal *saut des yeux* to the ὀβολούς ending the previous verse at a time when passages of verse were written not as prose (as they are in the *Marcianus*: cf. *PACA* 8 (1965) 43 on Machon 416f.) but κατὰ στίχον. In the second half of v. 10 οὐκ ἐπράξατ' οὐδὲ ἕν is probably sound, although it has often been assailed ineffectually. In v. 9 speaker B has given the price of the κύβιον as 3 obols; A's remark in v. 13 indicates that this was double the normal price (τὸ τάριχος there = the κύβιον, not the ὠμοτάριχος of v. 4 whose price passed without comment, being less than a quarter of that paid for the κύβιον). The speaker of v. 10 is likely to have been A, commenting as elsewhere on the cost of the purchase last mentioned. His comment was one of anger or amazement; this can be assumed partly from his later reference in v. 17 to the remission of an ague before its next attack, which symbolises his satisfied response to B's price at v. 15 after his irritated reaction to high prices in vv. 10 and 13 and before his next cry of pain at the end of v. 16, partly from the general tone of v. 13, and partly because A's remarks in v. 10 stimulate B into the exasperated riposte of vv. 11–12, 'It's all because the locusts have gobbled up the greens.' This sequence at first sight seems puzzling, but light is shed on it by Athenian gastronomic practice; pickled fish was often eaten with a garniture of, or a sauce made with, green herbs (Alexis 191(186K), q.v.; cf. the proverb σαπρὸς τάριχος τὴν ὀρίγανον φιλεῖ, Ath. 3.116e). To make sense in its context, therefore, v. 10 is likely to have begun with an expression of surprise or disapproval, and continued with a reference to the greens customarily served with κύβιον. οὐκ ἐπράξατ' οὐδὲ ἕν fits admirably into such a scenario, if rightly construed and punctuated. ἐπράξατ' cannot be second person plural active; A never so addresses B in this fr. (though B does use the second plural to A (see on vv. 7, 18f.)), and this combination of person and number is senseless anyway (not 'nihil comparauistis', Kaibel: οὐκ ἐπρ. οὐδὲ ἕν never meant that; and not 'you haven't charged', Gulick, since B never did any charging himself, but was charged by the provision merchants). Nor can ἐπράξατ' be the verb in a statement; A possesses no information about costs other than what B gives him. Thus ἐπράξατ' must be 3rd person singular middle, with ὁ κάπηλος the easily supplied subject, and the words from οὐκ to ἕν form part of a question: 'did he charge nothing for—?' The missing element is presumably (? a variety of) the greens covered by the λάχανα in v. 12 and expressed in the genitive. Kaibel's κιχορίων δ' (after Casaubon, Animadv. 227, whose κιχορείων may be the preferable orthography: see LSJ s.v. κιχόριον) gives the required sense, is near to the *ductus* and might even have deserved to be printed in the text,[1] but for one major difficulty. It prevents acceptance of an otherwise both simple and convincing restoration of the line's opening words to ὃ γ' εἷλκε· (Desrousseaux, Obs. 53ff.), which gives A a sarcastically pert reply to B's statement about the cost of the κύβιον: 'Yes – what it weighed!', with the implication that the price paid for it in silver obols (units of weight as well as of currency) was identical with its weight, and so absurdly excessive. Could then Alexis simply have written ὃ γ' εἷλκε· λαχάνων δ' . . .? The gallimaufry of inept conjectures which have been produced for this line is best ignored; often their Greek is eccentric, their sense irrelevant to the context and the *ductus* utterly disregarded. I mention here only Meineke's ὄλοιο· σίσαρον δ' οὐκ ἐπέθηκας οὐδὲ ἕν (Anal. Crit. 55), impossibly far from the transmitted letters but the first idea to recognise the required sense; Desrousseaux' continuation χεῖρόν γ' οὐκ ἐπράξατ' οὐδὲ ἕν, brilliantly close to the paradosis but rather limp in sense ('at least he didn't exact / [or less acceptably: see above] you didn't do anything worse'); and Capps' ὠνήν (= 'a bargain'), printed together with Kaibel's conjecture by Gulick and Edmonds, but unacceptable since there are no parallels for the use of ὠνήν as an adverbial accusative, and in any case the κύβιον was manifestly no bargain.

---

[1] In a handwritten note on his copy of Kaibel's edition of Ath., Headlam suggested σ' for Kaibel's δ' (cf. Casaubon), but a contrasting particle is here desirable. Otherwise, there would be nothing in it palaeographically: scribal confusion between γε and δέ, γε and σέ is too common to require extensive documentation. A brief list of instances from tragedy:

COMMENTARY

11 οἶσθας: this by-form of the Attic οἶσθα occurs several times in later Greek comedy (Men. *Epitr.* 481, fr. 286.5, com. adesp. fr. 257.65 Austin, probably also Men. *Mis.* 250, only Cratinus 112(105K) in earlier comedy) and occasionally elsewhere (e.g Herodas 2.55, the Ninos fr. A.II.21, III.25 Lavagnini, probably Babrius 95.14). Aelius Dionysius' claim (s.v., p. 131 Erbse) that οἶσθας was used for metrical reasons or to avoid a clash of vowels is largely borne out by the facts (cf. J.-M. Jacques on Men. *Dysk.* 798), but it is interesting to note that the metrically equivalent form οἶδας, which became standard in the *Koine*, occurs side by side with οἶσθας in later comedy (Phoenicides 3.2, possibly Philemon 45(44K).3). Cf. Schwyzer 1.662, P. T. Stevens, *Colloquial Expressions in Euripides* (Wiesbaden 1976) 59f.

ὦ μακάριε: this form of address, familiar in later comedy (Men. *Dysk.* 103, *Mis.* fr. 4 Sandbach, Diphilus 4.1, com. adesp. fr. 257.64 Austin) and Plato (e.g. *Alc.* 1.124a, *Crat.* 414c, *Phdr.* 236d, 241e, *Protag.* 309c, *Resp.* 4.432d), indicates here in Alexis and generally in Plato (the wording in *Crat.* is identical with that of Alexis, ὦ μακάριε, οὐκ οἶσθ' ὅτι ...) an amused, ironic or sarcastic exasperation at the failure of the person addressed to appreciate or understand something that seems obvious to the speaker. Cf. M. S. E. Brunius-Nilsson, ΔΑΙΜΟΝΙΕ (Diss. Uppsala 1955) 110ff., Stoessl on Men. *Dysk.* 103, Dover on Pl. *Symp.* 198b.

12 ⟨αἱ⟩ τρωξαλλίδες: the article (added by Erfurdt, *Obs.* 442 n. 12) was omitted in the *Marcianus* by one of its frequent *sauts du même au même*; cf. in this fr. alone vv. 13 (τό omitted after τοῦτο, added by Schweighaeuser) and 18 (ὄν omitted after οἶνον, added by Musurus).[1] By listing τρωξαλλίς along with ἀκρίς and πάρνοψ, Aelian, *NA* 6.19 implies that this creature is one (or more) species of the Saltatoria, and the present context points to a Mediterranean locust such as *Dociostaurus maroccanus* (cf. A. S. F. Gow, *CR* 6 (1956) 92 n. 6), M. Davies and J. Kathiri-thamby, *Greek Insects* (London 1986) 147f., I. C. Beavis, *Insects and other Invertebrates in Classical Antiquity* (Exeter 1988) 78ff.; cf. B. P. Uvarov, *Locusts and Grasshoppers* (London 1928) and *Grasshoppers and Locusts* 1 (Cambridge 1966) and 2 (London 1977), rather than to the house cricket (*Acheta domesticus*: so O. Keller, *Die antike Tierwelt* 2 (Leipzig 1913) 459f., cf. L. Gil Fernández, *Nombres de Insectos en Griego Antiguo* (Madrid 1959) 104) or one of the bush crickets (so Gossen in *RE Suppl.* viii. 180.10ff.). This interpretation takes Alexis' words at their face value; at the same time, however, the comic poet appears to be playing on the verbal

---

γε/δέ A. *Pers.* 719, *P.V.* 961, 969, Eur. *Med.* 512, *Andr.* 589; γε/σέ A. *Eum.* 221, *P.V.* 77, Eur. *IT* 1470.

[1] In the *Marcianus* the final alpha of the unelided λάχανα has the iota-like tail normal in early minuscule.

94

association κατεδηδόκασιν | τρώγω | τρωξαλλίδες (incorrect etymologising perhaps: τρωξαλλίς may derive from τρώζω = ψιθυρίζω, cf. Hesych. s.v., and Gil Fernández, Davies–Kathirithamby, *loc. cit.*), and so wordplay more than locust-like characteristics may have influenced the choice of τρωξαλλίδες here.

13 τέθεικας: so the *Marcianus* and Kassel–Austin, but τέθηκας (so Nauck, *MGR* 6 (1894) 96f.), the only spelling of this perfect in Attic inscriptions up to 69/62 BC (Meisterhans–Schwyzer 189), is more likely to have been the spelling used by Alexis (and his contemporaries:? including Hyperides, *Ath.* 13).

The dicola at the end of this verse in the *Marcianus* may be etiolated remains of the old system of part-division; see the general introduction, II.i.a.

14 ὁ ταριχοπώλης ἐστίν: 'It's the ταριχοπώλης (sc. who was responsible for doubling the price)'; ἐστίν here is copulative.

15 γόγγρος: see comm. on fr. 83.

16 τὸν ὀπτὸν ἰχθύν: cf. Philemon 83(80K) ἠγόρασα νῆστιν κεστρέ᾽ ὀπτὸν οὐ μέγαν. Baked ἠπάτιον also could be purchased in the market (Alexis 27.7). A letter dating from the mid-3rd century (*P.Cair.Zen.* 59066) mentions an official consignment of τὰ ὀπτά (sc. fish), but whether this was for sale or for the government kitchens in Ptolemaic Egypt, we are not told.

17 ὥσπερ πυρετὸς ἀνῆκεν, †εἶτ᾽ ἐνεπιτέλει writes the *Marcianus*; the extent and depth of the corruption are uncertain. In the preceding vv. speaker A has been first shocked by B's outlay (9–13), then placated by a more reasonable price (15), and now shocked again by the price of the baked fish (16). In v. 17 this sequence is compared, apparently in precise medical terminology, to the behaviour of a fever which alternates periods of remission with renewed attacks. The first three words of the line are unexceptionable. ὥσπερ, as often, apologises for the metaphor (LSJ s.v. II), and ἀνίημι, intransitive (cf. LSJ s.v. II.8, ignoring the medical use, however), is one of several terms (also λήγω, χαλῶ) applied by medical writers in Alexis' time to the abatement of a fever etc.: e.g. Hippocr. *Morb.* 2.40 ἐπὴν δὲ ἀνῇ ὁ πυρετός, cf. 41, *Int.* 40 ἡ νοῦσος ἀνῆκε, cf. 16. The context indicates that after ἀνῆκεν the speaker continues the metaphor by referring to the fever's next attack. In contemporary medical language the verbs commonly used in this signification were (1) ἐπιτείνω (the antonym of ἀνίημι: *TGL* under the latter verb, 799B: usually intransitive, cf. LSJ s.v. ἐπιτείνω 2d), e.g. Hippocr. *Epid.* 7.1 ἐπέτεινεν ὁ πυρετός, cf. 83, *Coac.* 114, cf. Heliodorus 4.5; and (2) ἐπιλαμβάνω (usually transitive), e.g. Men. *Georg.* 51f. θερμά τε | ἐπέλαβεν αὐτόν, cf. Aelian *Epist.* 2, but intransitive at Hippocr. *Int.* 16 ἔπειτα ἀνῆκεν ὁ πόνος καὶ αὖθις ἐπέλαβεν ὀξὺς δι᾽ ὀλίγου. Hence the *Marcianus*' εἶτ᾽ ἐνεπιτελει has been emended with nice impartiality to provide scope for both of these verbs, but *ductus* and the apparent absence of a direct object strongly favour Schweighaeuser's εἶτ' ἐπέτεινε(ν) (cf. his *Animadv.* 2.325). Yet if this is correct, it is not easy to see what originally followed it that could have given rise to the *ductus*: not αὖ (Dobree, *Adv.* 2.303), since in comedy αὖ does not mean 'in turn/again' on its own without the accompaniment of πάλιν or αὖθις; nor ἔτι (Emperius 346), which is hardly relevant after the second of two contrasting verbs; nor δή (Jacobs, *Addit.* 82), a particle whose presence would be welcome after εἶτα (Denniston, *GP* 207) but not after ἐπέτεινε (id. 214ff.: the tone of the phrase is neither paratragically pathetic nor ironic, and ἐπιτείνω does not belong to that class of *uerba sentiendi et dicendi* regularly emphasised by δή); perhaps then ἐπέτεινέ τι? Alternative conjectures may be largely ignored; some are based on false hypotheses (e.g. Kock's εἶτ' ἐπενετάθη, followed by G. A. Papavasileiou, *Athena* 1 (1889) 214 – but it is the patient, not the fever, that would be so described); others play too freely with the *ductus* (thus how could Meineke's suggested deletion of ὥσπερ, 3.380, cf. *ed. min.* 692, *Anal. Crit.* 55, be palaeographically justified?), and some produce nonsense (Edmonds' ἐν ἐπιτολῇ: feverish *stars?*). There remains the possibility that the *ductus* preserves the letters of Alexis' text correctly. Desrousseaux' idea that we should read εἶτ' ἐν ἐπιτελεῖ as an adverbial phrase introducing B's final words in the fr. has its attractions, but ἐν ἐπιτελεῖ in the sense of 'finally', though possible on the analogy of ἐν βραχεῖ, etc., is an unparalleled expression, and B's intervention in the dialogue at this point would reduce A's previous παπαῖ, | ὥσπερ πυρετὸς ἀνῆκεν to a pointless (because tailless: εἶτ' ἐπέτεινε or its equivalent is needed) exclamation. Desrousseaux did not think out his solution to its logical conclusion; otherwise he would have recognised the necessity of positing a lacuna. I suggest, *exempli gratia*,

> ... ἀνῆκεν, <εἶτ' ἐπέτεινέ τι.
> B. ὁ δ' αὖ κάπηλος ἐστίν·> εἶτ' ἐν ἐπιτελεῖ
> πρόσθες τὸν οἶνον ...

With something like that in his exemplar a scribe's eye might easily have jumped from ΕΙΤΕΠΕΤΕΙΝΕΤΙ to ΕΙΤΕΝΕΠΙΤΕΛΕΙ, especially in a script without word-division. Like Desrousseaux' conjecture, Headlam's brilliantly simple εἶτεν ἐπιτελεῖ (the Headlam–Knox edition of Herodas, p. 90 n. 1) preserves the letters of the *ductus* with different word-division and accentuation. But brilliance is not the same as plausibility; so long as εἶτεν and similar Ionicisms are foreign to later Attic comedy (cf. H. Usener, *Kleine Schriften* 1 (Leipzig and Berlin 1912) 239ff., Headlam on Herodas 2.52, Gow on Machon 370; Headlam's suggestion that here in Alexis it might be a quotation of Ionic medical language is ingenious but unlikely), and so long as the alleged 'medical' use of ἐπιτελεῖ (= *uehementer uexat*) is

confined to the late Byzantine historian Georgius Cedrenus (*Hist. Comp.*
1.234 *CSHB* = 129.269a Migne), this conjecture must be rejected.
18–19 μεθυόντων προσέλαβον ὑμῶν: i.e. 'I bought additionally when
you (speaker A and his friend(s): ὑμῶν must be so interpreted, but it does
not necessitate the presence of A's friend(s) now on stage with him) were
drunk'. Presumably the speaker had purchased extra wine during the
course of the party when the supply was running out. It is clear from the
present passage (cf. fr. 102(97K), Ath. 8.365de) that wine as well as food
was paid for ἀπὸ συμβολῶν.
λαμβάνω and its compounds in colloquial Attic often have the
meaning 'I take by purchase'; cf. Kock on Nicostratus 27(26K).4, Fraenkel on A. *Ag.* 275, LSJ s.v. λαμβάνω II.1.h, and note especially Sotades
com. 1, where λαμβάνω and προσλαμβάνω both appear in a shopping list
in parallel with ἀγοράζω and ἐπριαμήν.
19 The colloquial fluidity in the syntax (χοᾶς in apposition to οἶνον;
δέκ' ὀβολῶν ὁ χοῦς appended loosely with ellipse of ἐστι) has worried
formalistic scholars (hence Jacobs' conjecture <ἦν δὲ> δέκ', *Addit.* 82)
unnecessarily. Itemised accounting thrives on such ellipses: cf. here vv. 5,
6, 9, 15 (and contrast 4).
We do not know to what extent Alexis is deliberately exaggerating the
prices of the fish in this fr., and this prevents its use as a serious economic
document. The prices range from the allegedly reasonable $\frac{5}{8}$ obol for the
ὠμοτάριχος to a whole drachma for the baked fish; the latter figure is
probably grossly inflated for comic effect, although it would be difficult to
prove this, given on the one hand the vagueness of speaker B's words (no
quantity, no species named) and on the other a lack of reliable counter-
evidence. The price paid for the wine (10 obols a chous, which = 3240–
3300c[3], cf. F. Hultsch, *Griechische und römische Metrologie*[2] (Berlin 1882)
101f. 105ff., O. Viedebantt, *Abh. Leipzig* 34/3 (1917), 43, 60), Lang-
Crosby, *Agora* x.56ff., and my p. 326 n. 1 on Κράτεια), however, is clearly
on the high side; in comedy it is exceeded only by that paid in Men. *Epitr.*
130f. (1 obol a kotyle = $\frac{1}{12}$ of a chous), which Smikrines regards as
incredibly extravagant. The normal, real-life cost of wine in 4th-century
Athens seems to have been about 1$\frac{1}{2}$ obols a chous wholesale and from 2 to
4 obols a chous retail (com. adesp. fr. 1320 Kock, [Dem.] 35.10, 18, 42.20,
31; A. Körte, *Gnomon* 1 (1925) 21f., W. K. Pritchett, *Hesperia* 25 (1956)
199ff., Gomme–Sandbach on Men., *loc. cit.*). On ancient prices in general
see the sensible remarks of F. M. Heichelheim, *An Ancient Economic History*
2 (English translation, Leiden 1962) 168ff., with useful bibliography. In
one respect, however, this fr. does realistically reflect contemporary
Athens: the dinner consisted entirely of fish and other seafood, the staple
protein diet of Athenians; there was no meat, and it would be wrong to
assume that meat might have been mentioned in the unquoted context of

the fr., since v. 1 clearly opens the accounting, and v. 17 (whether ἐν ἐπιτελεῖ is right or not) just as clearly closes the list of solid foods. Meat was not normally eaten at a δεῖπνον ἀπὸ συμβολῶν (cf. Heichelheim 2.111), but reserved for special celebrations in the deme and family.

16

Meineke 3.391 (II), Kock 2.303, Edmonds 2.382, Kassel–Austin 2.32; cf. Nesselrath, *MK* 294 and n. 26. A lively fr., which reveals that Alexis had a talent for pithy cameos of everyday life. The speaker is probably to be identified as character B of fr. 15; his complaint about the arrogance of fishmongers suggests that he has just come back from the fish-market (the fr.'s opening words look like the beginning of an entrance monologue: see on v. 1), having bought the seafood for the δεῖπνον ἀπὸ συμβολῶν whose accounts form the subject matter of fr. 15 (which would thus come from a later stage in the play than fr. 16). Is there some irony, or at least an attempt at self-justification, in the speaker's verbal assault on fishmongers? To judge from fr. 15, these certainly rooked him over the κύβιον and the baked fish.

The fr. is cited by Ath. 6.224f (*Marcianus* and – omitting v. 3 θαυμάζω to end of 4 – Epit.) along with 17 others (224c–228b) to illustrate the attitude of Atic comedy to Attic fishmongers; this collection – and Ath. fails to cite Ar. fr. 402(387K) (from Νῆσοι, attributed by some ancient scholars to Archippus: *Vit. Ar.* p. 136 Koster) and Antiphanes 204(206K) – is drawn in the main from writers of the mid-4th century, although its antecedents went back to Old Comedy (Archippus 23(25K), Ar. (?) *loc. cit.*). It is possible that these comic assaults on fishmongers began, or at one period were associated, with a historical circumstance: a general food shortage, perhaps, like the one at Athens in the early 320s, when the demand for fish would have raised prices (see comm. on fr. 6). In the course of time, however, the theme would have become such a comic cliché that it can provide no reliable guide to the date of the plays in which these attacks appear.

In all commonplace themes particular details tend to be repeated, partly because some of them derive from the shared observation of daily life, and partly because one writer's good idea quickly becomes the stock property of all. The close similarity between the present fr. of Alexis and Amphis 30 has more than once been noticed. Both poets begin their criticism by comparing the arrogance of fishmongers with the more justifiable haughtiness of the generals, and both go on to illustrate their point by describing a single incident. The coincidence of theme and treatment led Kann (*De iteratis* 69f.) to argue that one passage was an imitation of the other, although the excellence of both hindered seeing

ΑΠΕΓΛΑΥΚΩΜΕΝΟΣ

who imitated whom. There is something slightly unreal in such a hypothesis, since with commonplace passages the criteria of piracy are inevitably ill-defined. Moreover, the similarities between Amphis and Alexis here (such as they are) can easily be explained without recourse to a theory of plagiarism. Greek writers are fond of introducing detailed descriptions with a general comparison, and allusion to the *hauteur* of στρατηγοί was a commonplace going back to the time of Archilochus (fr. 114 West). Similarities in phraseology between Alexis and Amphis are not impressive, while similarities in attitude and characterisation are stereotyped. And the point at the end of the detailed description is quite different in the two passages.

1 τοὺς μὲν στρατηγούς: the tenor of the opening statement suggests the beginning of an entrance monologue; this impression is reinforced by the fact that characters delivering such speeches often preface their remarks with a logically subordinate μέν clause before stating their main theme in the antithetic δέ clause: examples from 4th-century comedy include Ar. *Eccl.* 504ff., *Plut.* 322ff., Men. *Dysk.* 259ff. (the antithetical δέ clause 264f.), *Sam.* 616ff. The στρατηγοί whom Alexis has in mind, with their tiresome airs justified by prestige in the city, are military commanders such as Chares, Diopithes and Phocion, not the civil magistrates (as Bothe, *PCGF* 522 erroneously believed); in 4th-century Athens civil and military powers were distinct (Isoc. 8.54f.; see especially C. Mossé, *La Fin de la démocratie athénienne* (Paris 1962) 273ff.).

1–2 τὰς ὀφρῦς ... ἀνεσπακότας: a common phrase to describe an action which usually indicates arrogance or a feeling of self-importance. Sometimes this feeling is the only one expressed, or at least uppermost, as here; cf. Pollux 2.49 (the characteristic attitude of the ὑπερήφανος), Cratinus 348(355K) ἀνελκταῖς ὀφρύσι σεμνόν, the Phrynichus lemma ἀνωφρυασμένος ἄνθρωπος (*Praep. Soph.* 43.10 de Borries) with its explanation τὸν ἀποσεμνύνοντα ἑαυτόν, *Comp. Men. et Phil.* 1.219f. = 2.55f. = 3.23f. Jäkel. Other feelings may be intermingled with this arrogance: anger (Dem. 19.314, cf. Ar. *Equ.* 631, Men. *Sik.* 160), histrionic grief (Ar. *Ach.* 1069, Men. fr. 634), self-congratulation (Heliodorus 4.7) or deep thought (Plut. *Mor.* 68d, 657c; cf. ὀφρυανασπασίδαι applied to philosophers in the anonymous epigram quoted by Ath. 4.162a, = D. L. Page, *Further Hellenistic Epigrams* (Cambridge 1981) 475f. no. 155). Cf. J. Taillardat, *Les Images d'Aristophane* (Paris 1962) 173, Sittl, *Gebärden* 94, G. W. Williams, *Hermes* 91 (1963) 316, M. Di Marco, *Timone di Fliunte: Silloi* (Rome 1989), comm. on fr. 29.

2 δεινὸν μὲν ἡγοῦμαι ποεῖν: 'I think their action is dreadful'; τοὺς στρατηγούς is subject of ποεῖν, and δεινὸν ποεῖν means literally 'to do a dreadful thing', as in Ath. 10.441a citing Alcimus, *FGrH* 560 F 2 δεινὸν ἔφη ποιήσειν αὐτόν, εἰ ξένου χάριν τὸν πίθον τοῦτον ἀνοίξειεν. The translation 'I think that I ought to make a fuss/consider it dreadful' (implied by Edmonds' 'Nobody disapproves so much as I') is wrong: this requires δεινά in the plural (as at Thuc. 5.42, Pl. *Hipp. min.* 363c), and is partly tautologous (since in this idiom δεινὰ ποιῶ = δεινόν τι ἡγοῦμαι).

ποεῖν: the orthography preserved here, as well as in a fair number of other places in the *Marcianus* (e.g. Alexis 82, Machon 90, 343: Gow is in error on this point at his note on p. 71), may possibly represent the poet's own orthography. Attic inscriptions indicate that the iota of ποιῶ is always retained before O sounds, but can be (and in the 4th century regularly is) dropped before E sounds (Meisterhans–Schwyzer 57, Threatte 1.326ff.). Comic poets, however, are perhaps more likely to have followed a different rule, writing ποι- where the variable syllable scans long or *anceps,* and πο- where it scans short. Although papyri and medieval MSS of comic writers are generally inconsistent over this orthography (cf. Handley's edition of Men. *Dysk.* p. 43), there are a few notable exceptions that closely follow the rule linking spelling to scansion, e.g. R and V of Aristophanes (W. J. W. Koster, *Autour d'un manuscrit d'Aristophane* (Groningen and Jakarta 1957) 226ff.). Cf. also MacDowell on Ar. *Vesp.* 261 and my comm. on Alexis 247(245K).1.

3 On the postponement of δέ to so late a position in its clause, which here misled MSS and early editors into a nonsensical punctuation after τι instead of v. 2's ποεῖν, see on fr. 4.1. Note that the words preceding δέ cohere to form a single phrase unit. The placing of πάνυ is discussed by K. J. Dover, *CQ* 35 (1985) 332ff.

4 Wakefield's correction of A's μείζω to μεῖζόν τι (*Silv. Crit.* 2.71: Casaubon's curious μείζοτι here *may* anticipate the τι) satisfies the dictates of metre, idiom and palaeography. In the Attic idiom μέγα/μεῖζον/μέγιστον φρονεῖν (to have a high, etc., opinion of oneself: LSJ s.v. φρονέω II.2.b), the adjective was frequently corrupted by Byzantine scribes to the corresponding plural of their own contemporary usage, as Cobet, *NL* 268ff. demonstrates with an impressive list of examples, in which Eur. *Hcld.* 933 is rightly included. Once the corruption to μείζω had been made here in Alexis, the accompanying τι (which gives a slightly apologetic flavour to the statement: cf. K.G. 1.26f.) became unintelligible and consequentially was omitted.

6 κάτω βλέποντας: 'looking down' in order to avoid meeting the gaze of any other person(s) present – a mark here of arrogant or choleric disdain (cf. Pl. *Resp.* 6.500b, and the parallel expression κάτω κεκυφώς in Theophr. *Char.* 24.8), but elsewhere of brutishness (Pl. *Resp.* 9.586a, quoted later by [Longinus] 13.1), dejection (Eur. *Cycl.* 211, Plut. *Mor.* 528e, possibly Herodas 7.80, see I. C. Cunningham's note *ad loc.*), real or affected modesty (Nicarchus in *Anth. Pal.* 11.329, cf. [Lucian] *Am.* 44), or simply a desire to ignore attempts at contact (Plut. *Mor.* 532f).

ΑΠΕΓΛΑΥΚΩΜΕΝΟΣ

6–7 τὰς δ᾽ ὀφρῦς ἔχοντας ἐπάνω τῆς κορυφῆς exaggerates in comic, almost Wodehousian[1] fashion the idea of raised eyebrows prosaically expressed in vv. 1–2; if the hyperbole is original to Alexis, it certainly became a cliché later. Men. *Epitr.* 633f. (cf. *ZPE* 31 (1978) 12) used the same phrase as Alexis or one very similar. New Comedy may have provided the source for Alciphron 4.7 (= 1.34 Bergler, q.v.) τὰς ὀφρῦς ὑπὲρ τοὺς κροτάφους ἐπῆρας and similar phrases in Lucian *Dial. Mort.* 20(10).9 and [Lucian] *Am.* 54. *Comp. Men. et Phil.*, *loc. cit.* on vv. 1–2, introduces further fantasy, κἂν μέχρι <γε> νεφέων τὴν ὀφρῦν ἀνασπάσῃς (cf. Pollux 2.49); on Alexis 121(116K).6–7, see comm.

7 ἀποπνίγομαι: in the passive here with the extended sense 'I choke with fury', as at Lucian, *Navig.* 22, Ath. 9.396a (on its own), Dem. 19.199, Lucian *Gall.* 28 (with ἐπί + dative), but literally at Alexis 268(266K).4.

8 ἐὰν δ᾽ ἐρωτήσῃς: δ᾽ (*recc.*), not τ᾽ (A, Epit.), because (1) the particle introduces a new sentence, not a clause (but contrast Denniston, *GP* 499f. with 162 n. 3), (2) the anecdote of vv. 8–12 illustrates an aspect of fishmongers' arrogance one degree worse than that revealed by their gestures of vv. 5–7, and so the connection between these two passages must contain an element of contrast rather than of mere supplementation. As to the verb: Epit.'s ἐρωτήσῃς (but omitting the iota) must be right; the speaker is not talking about his own experiences as such (hence Dindorf's tentative ἐρωτήσω is out of court) but about what happens when *you* (= French *on*, German *man*, the ideal second person singular in Greek: Gildersleeve, *Syntax* 1.41) ask.

8–11 These lines sound so realistic that they might as well have been copied down word for word from a current market dispute. Apart from the crux in v. 11, two details deserve brief comment: (1) κεστρέας, grey mullets (probably any of the seven species of *Chelon/Mugil* and *Liza* found in the Mediterranean: cf. Thompson, *Fishes* s.v. κεστρεύς, Saint–Denis, *Vocabulaire* s.v. *Mugil*, Palombi–Santorelli 21ff., Campbell, *Guide* 282f., Davidson, *Seafood* 140f.) were a popular delicacy and a vehicle for a tedious pun (see on fr. 258(256K)); (2) in v. 10 τὸν ἕτερον is 'either of the two offered' (LSJ s.v. ἕτερος 1.1); the fishmonger is offering two mullets for 10 obols, one for 8.

11 ὦ τᾶν here indicates exasperated (and perhaps condescending) impatience; on the expression's use and etymology see especially Björck,

---

[1] The adjective is not idly chosen; in ch. 3 of *Stiff Upper Lip, Jeeves* (London 1963), for instance, 'My eyebrows rose till they nearly disarranged my front hair.' Cf. also Trollope's reference to 'penthouse brows' in ch. 1 of *Ayala's Angel* (London 1881).

COMMENTARY

Alpha Impurum 55, 275ff., G. J. de Vries, *Mnemosyne* 19 (1966) 225ff., O. J. L. Szemerényi, *Minos* 20–2 (1987) 569ff.; and cf. MacDowell on Ar. *Vesp.* 373, Dedoussi on Men. *Sam.* '202' (her numbering), Sandbach on Men. *Dysk.* 247. Then, after λαβὲ καὶ μὴ παῖζε, 'Take (or 'Buy': see on 15.18) them, and stop fooling about', the MSS write nonsense: τοῦσ ὀυδεῖ A, τοῦ, σοι δεῖ Epit. I discuss this crux at length in *CQ* 7 (1957) 190f.; the facts briefly are these. The slight differences between *Marcianus* and Epit. probably point to the existence of a reading ΤΟΥΣΟΥΔΕΙ in a common ancestor without word-division. Of the attempts to restore this to health, Dobree's τοσουδί (his edition of Ar. *Plut*, on v. 361), which is excellent sense ('At such a price as the one you are here offering?') and palaeographically neat (iotacistic and o/ου confusions are two a penny), has won the support of virtually every subsequent scholar (including Kassel–Austin), but it is unacceptable on metrical grounds. τοσουδί would split the anapaest after its first short in the second half of the second metron of the iambic trimeter, in a verse without penthemimeral caesura but with strong punctuation (full stop and change of quoted speaker) at the break in the anapaest. Exact and reliable parallels for such a break in these circumstances remain rare in comedy: Ar. *Vesp.* 1369 certainly, Men. *Dysk.* 230 possibly (on this and the unreliable other instances in *Dysk.*, see Handley's edition, pp. 64ff.); and while an example might be accepted on strong MSS evidence, it is hardly good textual criticism to invent one by conjecture. K. Bernhardi's τουσδί (*Acta Soc. Phil. Lipsiensis* 1 (1872) 256) is the equal of Dobree's τοσουδί in point of sense and palaeographic plausibility (translate 'These 8 obols that you're offering?'), and metrically more acceptable; I am convinced that it is what Alexis wrote.

17

Meineke 3.392 (III), Kock 2.303, Edmonds 2.382, Kassel–Austin 2.33.

1 ἐψητοί: small fish of various species (Ath. 7.301a, introducing Alexis 17 and 18 along with other comic citations; cf. Ath. 301c and Diphilus med. in Ath. 8.356c) for boiling. Terence translates the word by *pisciculi minuti* at *Andr.* 369 (= Men. *Perinth.* fr. 2 Sandbach).

2 δαιδάλεοί πως (so Epit. and Eustath. 1169.13, with correct accentuation: cf. Herodian 2.909 Lentz) is probably right; translate 'I suppose you might call them spangled.' For comic effect the speaker conjures up an unexpected adjective, a recherché synonym of ποικίλος (δαιδάλεον· ποικίλον Hesych., cf. *Et. Mag.* 251.2 Gaisford) that describes a pattern of spots on a different-coloured ground; cf. Nonnus *Dion.* 5.391 δαιδαλέης ἐλάφοιο; elsewhere fish are δαίδαλοι (Oppian *Cyn.* 1.58) or just ποικίλοι (e.g. Anaxippus 1.34, Lucian *Pisc.* 50, cf. Alexis 115(110K).20 and comm.). The πως serves merely to apologise for the daring adjective, as e.g. at Men. *Dysk.* 646.[1]

The *Marcianus*' reading δαιδαλαῖοί is probably just an etacistic corruption of a very common kind, and it seems foolhardy either to retain it here or to emend it to δαιδάλειοί[2] (so Schweighaeuser, proparoxytone, rather than δαιδαλεῖοί, Wilamowitz in Kaibel's apparatus, properispomenon: cf. H. W. Chandler, *A Practical Introduction to Greek Accentuation*[2] (Oxford 1891) 117f.); in classical literature the forms δαιδάλεος and δαιδάλειος seem to have been carefully differentiated, the latter (which LSJ fails to recognise) being confined in its application to objects associated with or reminiscent of the workshop of Daedalus, such as his moving statues (Eur. fr. 372, Cratinus 75(74K).4, cf. Herodian *Epim.* 19.3 Boissonade and Hesych. s.v. Δαιδαλεῖα with K. Latte *ad loc.*) or his wings (Lucian *Icar.* 2).

Meineke (*Cur. Crit.* 31f.) convincingly demonstrated that the words appearing in the MSS after δαιδάλεοί πως, τὰ γὰρ καλὰ πάντα Δαιδάλου καλοῦσιν ἔργα are explanatory comment by Ath., not a continuation of the fr. as was previously believed (but see Casaubon, *Animadv.* 527f.); yet the precise relevance of these words is no longer clear. They may simply reflect an ancient derivation of δαιδάλεος and all its congeners from Δαίδαλος (contrast Schulze, *Kl. Schr.* 118); alternatively, in Alexis immediately after the words cited in the present fr. there might have been a joke linking δαιδάλεος and Δαίδαλος, which was omitted by Ath. and/or his source.

18

Meineke 3.392 (IV), Kock 2.303, Edmonds 2.382, Kassel–Austin 2.34.

1 κορακίνων: under this name the ancient world recognised fish of several different species (πολλὰ γὰρ καὶ τούτων γένη Ath. 7.312a); these may have included the brown meagre (*Sciaena umbra* Linnaeus = *Corvina nigra* Cuvier) and the bast umber (*Imbrina cirrosa* Linnaeus), as well as pomacentrids and other sciaenids (so Thompson, *Fishes* s.v., but cf. Strömberg, *Fischnamen* 70, 78, 115, Saint-Denis, *Vocabulaire* s.v. *coracinus*; the two named species are described and illustrated in Palombi–Santorelli 46f., 50f. and Campbell, *Guide* 284f., cf. Davidson, *Seafood* 98f.). Their general culinary reputation is summed up in Amphis 22 ὅστις κορακῖνον

---

[1] Edmonds' suggestion that πως here is all that remains of an original πῶς < δοκεῖς; > qualifying the adjective ('quite remarkably spangled'; cf. Barrett on Eur. *Hipp.* 443–6) is ingenious, but it depends on acceptance of the unacceptable δαιδάλειοι.

[2] δαιδαλαῖος and δαιδάλειος are both admissible formations from Δαίδαλος (cf. Schwyzer 1.467f.), but the form in -ειος is here better attested.

COMMENTARY

ἐσθίει θαλάττιον | γλαύκου παρόντος, οὗτος οὐκ ἔχει φρένας; the joke in the present fr. of Alexis appears to be that the speaker is offering to the person addressed a real choice, but only from the cheapest kinds of fish.

2 τριχίδων: the term covers all the smaller clupeoids with hair-like bones, e.g. sardine/pilchard (*Sardina pilchardus*), sprat (*Sprattus sprattus*), sardinelle (*Sardinella aurita*), anchovy (*Engraulis encrasicolus*) and the twaite shads (*Alosa fallax, A. finta*); Thompson, *Fishes* 268ff., cf. H. R. Aubert and Fr. Wimmer, *Aristoteles Thierkunde* 1 (Leipzig 1868) 141, Palombi–Santorelli 6ff., Campbell, *Guide* 264ff., Davidson, *Seafood* 41ff. Again, fish of mean reputation in the kitchen: cf. Ar. *Equ.* 662, Ussher on *Eccl.* 54–6, Eupolis 156(154K).2, Alexis 159(155K).3.

οὐδ' οἷον: 'nor even'. The locution, which to the best of my knowledge occurs only here (contemporary ephemeral slang?), may be adapted from or closely related to οὐχ οἷον, but the two expressions differ radically in usage. οὐδ' οἷον apparently introduces the last item in a series where the previous item(s) is(are) negative, while οὐχ οἷον in the *Koine* has a range of meanings (see comm. on 205(201K).4) from 'not only (not)' (= οὐ μόνον (οὐ), commonly introducing the first of two contrasted clauses, the second being introduced by ἀλλὰ καί or ἀλλ' οὐδέ) to an unattic 'not just' (introducing the second of two contrasted clauses) at Alexis 205(201K).4. In several idioms οἷον is used adverbially without any strong relative function: e.g. with the participle (K.G. 2.97, LSJ s.v. οἷος v.3), and as a softening word ('so to speak/as it were', LSJ s.v. v.2d). The idioms with οὐχ and οὐδέ are no more than logical extensions of such usages.

Herwerden's attribution of the words οὐδ' οἷον ἐψητῶν τινων to a second speaker (*Coll. Crit.* 121) is possible but unlikely; κορακῖνοι, τριχίδες and ἐψητοί all belong to the same category of inexpensive fish, and there is no obvious reason why the host who offers a choice between the first two should be interrupted by someone else mentioning the third.

Ἀποβάτης

Meineke 1.380f., Kock 2.304; cf. E. N. Gardiner, *Greek Athletic Sports and Festivals* (London 1910) 237ff., W. W. Hyde, *Olympic Victor Monuments and Greek Art* (Washington 1921) 272ff., R. Clavaud, *Démosthène, Discours d'Apparat* (Paris 1974) 135ff. and figs. 1, 2. The ἀποβάτης engaged in a form of competitive acrobatics which is most clearly described in an ancient grammarian's note (Bekker, *Anecd.* 198.11; identical, apart from minor variants, with *Et. Mag.* 124.31 Gaisford): ἀποβατῶ· ἀγῶνος ὄνομα, ἐν ᾧ οἱ ἔμπειροι τοῦ ἐλαύνειν ἅρματα, ἅμα θεόντων τῶν ἵππων, ἀνέβαινον διὰ τοῦ τροχοῦ ('by means of the wheel': this translation is supported by the vase illustrations, see below) ἐπὶ τὸν δίφρον καὶ πάλιν κατέβαινον

ΑΠΟΒΑΤΗΣ

ἀπταίστως.[1] A similar account is to be found in Harpocration = Phot. (p.228 Theodoridis) = *Suda* s.v. ἀποβάτης = the anonymous '*Glossary of Useful Terms*' (Bachmann, *Anecd.* 122.20ff., cf. also 123.18ff. s.v. Ἀποβατῶν ἀγών; on this 5th-century compilation see H. Erbse, *Untersuchungen zu den attizistischen Lexica* (Berlin 1950) 22ff.). Harpocration, after citing Lycurgus fr. 20 and Dinarchus frs. 10, 64, adds the information that according to Theophrastus the contests were confined to Boeotia and Athens. This is to some extent borne out by information from other sources. While there is no mention of apobatic events in any of the great Panhellenic festivals, from Athens we possess plaques and vases of the early 4th century, including one dated to the 380s, which were presumably made to commemorate apobatic victories there (for a list and discussion, see H. Metzger, *Les Représentations dans la céramique attique du IVe siècle* (Paris 1951) 359, nos. 32–4). The most important festival at which this event was held was the Panathenaea;[2] since an anecdote recording Phocus' victory in it (Plut. *Phoc.* 20; a differently embellished version in Ath. 4.168f–9a) confirms that the event was already included in this festival by about the middle of the 4th century,[3] it seems reasonable to associate at least some of the extant plaques and vases with the Panathenaea and so push back the date of the event's introduction into it to the first half of the 4th century at the latest. An inscription (*IG* ii².2314.36) attests to its continued inclusion at the beginning of the 2nd century.

Kock conjectured that Phocus' victory was the subject of Alexis' play. This theory has little to commend it. It is true that the reference to Argas the musician (whose *floruit* was the 380s: see below) in the one extant fr. does not preclude a date for the play in the late 350s or early 340s, when Phocus achieved his victory; musicians sometimes live long and often are remembered after their deaths. But in the absence of any evidence positively linking Phocus and Alexis' Ἀποβάτης, those who try to explain Alexis' choice of title would do better to compare several other plays with athletic titles: Diphilus' Ἀποβάτης; Alexis', Theophilus' and Philemon's Παγκρατιαστής (one of these presumably the source of Ennius' *Pancratiastes*); Mnesimachus' Ἰσθμιονίκης; Eubulus' and Xenarchus' Πένταθλος. All these plays come from the 4th century, and it is probably no coincidence that this century saw the culminating developments of professionalism and

---

[1] The explanation in LSJ s.v. ἀποβάτης 'one who rode several horses leaping from one to the other' bears no relation to what grammarians record nor to what vase-painters illustrate.

[2] Cf. also the glossary note referred to above (123.18 Bachmann), οὗτος ὁ ἀγὼν ἤγετο τῇ Ἀθηνᾷ.

[3] Phocion, the father of Phocus, was born in 402; it is unlikely that his son could have gained his victory much before the late 350s, given the normal age of marriage of the Athenian male.

105

COMMENTARY

specialisation in Greek athletics (E. N. Gardiner, *Athletics of the Ancient World* (Oxford 1930) 102f., H. A. Harris, *Greek Athletes and Athletics* (London 1964) 42, M. I. Finley and H. W. Pleket, *The Olympic Games* (London 1976) 68ff.). Admittedly the specialist athlete was no new phenomenon, as the well-known attacks on him from 5th-century Athens testify (Eur. fr. 282, Achaeus fr. 4, cf. Xenophanes fr. B2 West); but it was in the 4th century more than any other that his uselessness for any important activity became generally recognised and faults such as gluttony (a weakness of wrestlers rather than gymnasts, admittedly) objects of ridicule. At a time when comedy, to judge from its remaining titles and frs., paid great attention to individual types of character and profession, especially to those that offered most scope for caricature by their florid exuberance – cooks, soldiers, parasites and the like – what type could have suited this purpose better than the athlete? How precisely he fitted into the scheme of plays named after him it is now idle to conjecture, yet in comedies with plots drawn from everyday life he was the obvious counterpart to roles like those of Heracles, Pelops the charioteer or Melanion the runner in myth travesty.

The date of Alexis' play has been the subject of speculation; the pegs on which it has been hung are Phocus' Panathenaic victory, discarded above as insecure, and the reference to Argas in fr. 19. Argas was evidently a popular and highly esteemed musician, or he would hardly have been invited to make music at Iphicrates' wedding feast (Anaxandrides 42(41K).17) in 386 or shortly before (*RE* s.v. *Iphikrates* 1, 2019.52ff. (Thalheim) and *Kotys* 2, 1552.32ff. (Kahrstedt)). This is the only date which can be attached to Argas; how long his career extended before and after this event is completely unknown. But it would be dangerous gratuitously to contract Argas' career into a shorter span of years than that e.g. of Cinesias, whose music interested Aristophanes from 414 (*Av.* 1372ff.) to the late 390s (*Eccl.* 330), or to assume from Alexis' words that Argas was still alive and not a posthumous legend at the time of the play. Thus Alexis' Ἀποβάτης could have been written in the late 360s (so Webster, *CQ* 2 (1952) 16 and n. 1) or even a decade or more later (cf. Kaibel in *RE* s.v. *Alexis* 9, 1468.45ff., Nesselrath, *MK* 198 n. 48). Nothing further than this can be established, since Choronicus, the other person mentioned in fr. 19, is a fiction of the poet, as Th. Bergk, *Griechische Literaturgeschichte* 4 (Berlin 1887) 154 n. 112) first realised; he was presumably one of the play's characters (see below on fr. 19.1).[1]

---

[1] Kaibel's idea (*loc. cit.*, cf. his note on Ath. 14.638c) that the name Choronicus conceals the identity of the real-life Telenicus, a 5th-century musician mentioned contemptuously by Phaenias alongside Argas in Ath., lacks supporting evidence.

19

Meineke 3.388, Kock 2.304, Edmonds 2.384, Kassel–Austin 2.34. A conversation between two unidentified characters on a subject whose relation to the plot is unknown. The fr. is cited by Ath. 14.638bc (A and Epit.); correct part-division and recognition that τίνων (v.2) and τί (v.3) were interrogatives are owed to Daléchamp (Latin translation of v.2) and Schweighaeuser (v.3).

1 Χορόνικος <ὁ> ποιητὴς ὁδί: see above, introduction to Ἀποβάτης. The name Choronicus does not occur elsewhere; it was presumably coined by Alexis to suit the character of a musician, just as in fr. 121(116K) the name Nausinicus has every appearance of being invented for the role of a seaman. The deictic ὁδί strongly suggests (though it does not confirm: see Sandbach on Men. *Dysk.* 125, 185, Hunter on Eubulus 14(15K).2: comedy; A. M. Dale, *JHS* 84 (1964) 166, O. Taplin, *The Stagecraft of Aeschylus* (Oxford 1977) 150f.: tragedy) that Choronicus was present on stage with the two speakers.

A's spelling ποιητής here is printed by Kassel–Austin; ποητής would be preferable (see on 16.2).

3 Ἀργᾶν: the facts about this musician of the first half of the 4th century are assembled by Meineke *ad loc.* and O. Crusius, *RE* s.v. *Argas* 687.36ff. Nothing is known for certain about his skill in performance or composition, but it is unlikely that a second-rate artist would have received the invitation for Iphicrates' wedding. When Phaenias of Eresus, writing towards the end of the 4th century, alleges that Argas and Telenicus were ποιηταὶ μοχθηρῶν ... νόμων (in Ath. 14.638b–c, fr. 10 Wehrli = 13 Müller, *FHG* 2.299), we may be sure that he is quoting at second hand a judgement gleaned from some earlier comic (this fr. of Alexis? hardly Anaxandrides 16(15K) or 42(41).17) or philosophical source that had no time for Argas' modernisms; it was presumably from that same source, if not from Phaenias himself, that Plutarch repeated the allegation (*Dem.* 4; cf. Hesych. s.v. Ἀργᾶς).

The name itself suggests non-Athenian birth; in Attic, formations of this kind in -ᾶς are normally contemptuous (cf. R. A. Neil on Ar. *Equ.* 534). We learn that Demosthenes acquired the nickname Ἀργᾶς at the beginning of his career (Aeschines 2.99, Plut. *Dem.* 4); the occasion for this may well have been, as L. Grasberger suggests (*Die griechischen Stichnamen*[2] (Würzburg 1883) 46f.), a witty comparison between Demosthenes' recitation of legal νόμοι and Argas' performance of their musical homonyms.

2 σεμνῶν πάνυ: K. J. Dover (*CQ* 35 (1985) 332ff.) well notes the metrically convenient placing of πάνυ at verse-end, after the adjective it qualifies.

3–4 ἡμέρας δρόμῳ κρείττων: a more vivid equivalent, literally applicable

COMMENTARY

to spatial differences, is substituted for πολλῷ; the locution probably originated in popular speech. Cf. Ar. *Nub.* 430 ἑκατὸν σταδίοισιν ἄριστον (Starkie *ad loc.* quotes ancient and modern derivatives), *Ran.* 91 πλεῖν ἢ σταδίῳ λαλίστερα, Eupolis 102(94K).3 ἐκ δέκα ποδῶν ᾕρει λέγων τοὺς ῥήτορας (here the metaphor is prepared for in v. 2 ὥσπερ ἀγαθοὶ δρομῆς; on the later imitations of Eupolis' image, see Nauck, *MGR* 6 (1894) 53ff., Kassel–Austin 5.353ff.), Synesius *Epist.* 135 πλεῖν ἢ παλαιστῇ καὶ δακτύλῳ σοφώτερος (possibly inspired by comedy: Blaydes, *Adv.* 1.250; cf. Kassel–Austin on Cratinus 137(133K)), Plaut. *Men.* 177 *mille passum commoratu's cantharum*, cf. *Truc.* 334.

ἡμέρας δρόμῳ is the standard expression for a day's journey: Hdt. 2.5, Dem. 19.273.

Ἀποκοπτόμενος (or -ομένη)

Kock 2.305. Two frs. are cited by Ath.; one (13.562d, fr. 20) is said to come from Alexis' Ἀποκοπτόμενος, and the other (10.431c, fr. 21) from his Ἀποκοπτομένη. It is unlikely that these citations come from different plays. Confusion about the endings of play titles is very common in Ath., Stobaeus and other excerptors; ten other titles of Alexis are similarly affected (Ἀρχίλοχος/-οι, Δίδυμοι/-αι, Ἱππεύς/-ος, Κύπριος/Κυπρίς, Λέβης/-ήτιον, Μιλησία/-οι, Ὀλύνθιος/-α/-οι, Ποιητής/-αί, Τίτθη/-αι, Φρύξ/Φρύγιος); the problems posed by this type of confusion are discussed fully and judiciously by N. Terzaghi, *Fabula* 1 (Milan 1912) 5ff., especially 21f., cf. also A. Blanchard and A. Bataille, *Rech. Pap.* 3 (1964) 162, A. M. Belardinelli, *Coroll. Lond.* 2 (1982) 15ff., Hunter 95. In practically all the cases, the divergence in the title's ending will be due to error: a scribe's careless copying, or the incorrect expansion of a title that was abbreviated either in the MSS (cf. the lemmata of Stobaeus) or in the didascalic inscriptions themselves (e.g. *IG* ii².2319.56 = III B 3 col. 4a, 5 Mette Ἀνασωιζομεν at a 3rd-century Lenaea, 2323a.49 = III B 2 col. 1, 24 Mette Παγκρατιασ at a 4th-century Dionysia). For Alexis here it is impossible to determine the correct form of the original title; both transmitted endings yield plausible interpretations, and we gain no help from the frs. themselves. Most scholars prefer the masculine Ἀποκοπτόμενος, interpreting the participle with reference to sexual mutilation (LSJ s.v. ἀποκόπτω 1, citing LXX *Deut.* 23.1 and Lucian *Eun.* 8 for comparable absolute uses in the passive, cf. O. Crusius, *Philologus* 46 (1888) 618); in this case Alexis' play would be about a man who was actually or pretended to be mutilated (cf. Chaerea in Ter. *Eun.*), or was threatened with mutilation, e.g. for adultery (cf. the ending of Plaut. *MG*). The alternative interpretation of the masculine ending proposed by Kock (Eros shorn of his wings by a *hetaira*; cf. also U. Reinhardt, *Mythologische Beispiele in der Neuen Komödie* (Diss. Mainz 1974) 96f.) is implausible; Ἔρως would then be required as part of the title, and in any case the idea depends on a careless misreading of fr. 20 (cf. F. Lasserre, *La Figure d'Éros dans la poésie grecque* (Paris 1946) 118 n. 1). The feminine Ἀποκοπτομένη would make the plot revolve around a lady shorn of her hair, either by brutal assault (cf. Glycera in Men. *Pk.*) or possibly as a sign of mourning (e.g. S. *El.* 449ff., Eur. *Hel.* 1224, *Or.* 128). There is no indication of the play's date. Webster (*CQ* 2 (1952) 22) argues for *c.* 345–320 because the conceit of 'wingless Eros' in fr. 20 occurs again in plays by Eubulus and Aristophon (see below, on fr. 20), the latter probably dating to that period; parallelism of motif, however, is no criterion of date.

20

Meineke 3.392 (1), Kock 2.305, Edmonds 3.384, Kassel–Austin 2.35; cf. Lasserre 111ff., U. Reinhardt, *Mythologische Beispiele in der Neuen Komödie* (Diss. Mainz 1974) 91ff., Hunter 131ff. The pretty conceit that Eros has lost his wings, or indeed has never possessed any, occurs three times in 4th-century comic poets: Eubulus 40(41K), Aristophon 11 and here; the similar motif of Eros moulting in Alciphron 4.16.5 and [Aristaen.] 2.1 may also derive from a comic source (cf. Kock 3.441, his adesp. fr. 172). Alexis and Eubulus contrast this idea of a wingless Eros with the conventional and allegedly false pictures of him drawn by artists of the time. These, carrying on a tradition perhaps originated by Anacreon (fr. 34 Page; Lasserre 6off.), perpetuated in literature by a host of writers (e.g. Eur. *Hipp.* 127off., Ar. *Av.* 574, 696f., 703f., 1737f., Timotheus com. fr. 2; Lasserre *passim* and especially 93f.), and maintained continuously throughout the 5th and 4th centuries in art (Waser in *RE* s.v. *Eros* 1, 497.48ff., Lasserre *passim*, H. Metzger, *Les Représentations dans la céramique attique du IVe siècle* (Paris 1951) 41ff., A. Greifenhagen, *Griechische Eroten* (Berlin 1957); cf. T. B. L. Webster, *Art and Literature in Fourth Century Athens* (London 1956) 103ff. and pl. 16 = Athenian oenochoe of *c.* 350–340), portrayed Eros with wings. The idea behind Alexis' formulation of the new conceit (that it was not Love but Lovers who were winged) presumably derives from current sophistic thought.[1] Investigation into the

---

[1] Alexis' words λέγεται ... λόγος ὑπὸ τῶν σοφιστῶν in vv. 1–2 of the fr. appear to be a clear acknowledgement of his sources; but our ignorance of the context, combined with our inability to identify the original sophist (the idea that here we may have an oblique reference to Plato, particularly to that passage in *Phdr.* 251–6 where the erotic sensation is compared to flight, is rightly rejected by Lasserre 119; while there may

COMMENTARY

nature of love was a popular subject for philosophers, sophists and essayists of the first half of the 4th century (Lasserre 110ff.; Pl. *Phdr.*, *Symp.*, Xen. *Symp.*, *Cyr.* 5.1.1–16, [Dem.] 61 are the sole survivors), and it is possible that a lost treatise on this theme lies behind Alexis' present argument, just as a passage of Pl. *Symp.* seems to lie behind the reasoning of fr. 247(245K). Lasserre suggests that the fr. derives from the play's prologue, with the general conceit preparing the way for factual exposition. The idea has its attractions, but any reflective monologue by or about a young man in love, whom we must suppose to have been a character in the play, would provide a suitable frame for the fr.

1–2 λέγεται γὰρ λόγος ὑπὸ τῶν σοφιστῶν: see above, introduction to this fr. On σοφιστής and its overtones in comedy see especially K. J. Dover's edition of Ar. *Nub.*, introduction liii ff. and comm. on 331; cf. also my note on fr. 27.1.

2 μὴ πέτεσθαι: in classical Attic the normal negative with the infinitive after *uerba dicendi et sentiendi* is οὐ, but in Hellenistic Greek the use of μή in its stead so increased that finally this use of οὐ fell into almost total abeyance (Mayser 2.2.55off., Schwyzer 2.594f.). In the present (undatable) passage, where there are no other signs of dialectal impurity, it would be foolish to stigmatise a usage that after all has several classical Attic parallels (LSJ s.v. μή B.5c, citing examples from Thuc., Xen., Pl.; cf. Fraenkel on A. *Ag.* 753f., Barrett on Eur. *Hipp.* 462ff., Schwyzer 2.595). Even so we cannot be sure here that μή is not a modernising corruption for οὐ introduced into the text by a copyist or even the excerptor himself.

3 τοὺς δ' ἐρῶντας: sc. πέτεσθαι, with a play on the verb's secondary meaning 'to be volatile/ all a-flutter' (LSJ s.v. II, cf. Ar. *Av.* 169f. ἄνθρωπος ὄρνις, ἀστάθμητος, πετόμενος,/ ἀτέκμαρτος, οὐδὲν οὐδέποτ' ἐν ταὐτῷ μένων). The symbolic connection between the wings of Eros and the flightiness of lovers is taken up by Heliodorus 4.2 οὐκ οἶσθα ὅτι καὶ τὸν Ἔρωτα πτεροῦσιν οἱ γράφοντες, τὸ εὐκίνητον τῶν ὑπ' αὐτοῦ κεκρατημένων αἰνιττόμενοι; cf. also Alciphron 4.16.5, [Aristaen.] 2.1, and the slightly different *jeu des mots* in Longus 2.7 θεός ἐστιν, ὦ παῖδες, ὁ Ἔρως, νέος καὶ καλὸς καὶ πετόμενος· διὰ τοῦτο . . . τὰς ψυχὰς ἀναπτεροῖ.

4 ἄλλως: i.e. otherwise than right, wrongly.

---

be some subtle interplay of reference between the two passages of Plato and Alexis, which would be easier to comprehend were more of the period's erotic literature extant, any connection between the two would be far more indirect than that of mere inaccurate interpretation), must inevitably make one hesitate even from pronouncing whether Alexis' words are to be taken at face value. Sometimes in comedy even a precise ascription of an idea to a named source must be taken with a pinch of salt: see on fr. 163(158K), and cf. Dover's introduction to his edition of Ar. *Nub.* xxxii ff.

4–5 ἠγνοηκότας... τοὺς γραφεῖς... αὐτὸν ζωγραφεῖν: the same point is made by Alexis himself at fr. 247(245K).3–4 and Eubulus 40(41K).1–3; cf. [Lucian] *Am.* 32 Ἔρως, οὐ κακὸν νήπιον ὁποῖον ζωγράφων παίζουσι χεῖρες (from a comic source? cf. Kock 3.609, fr. adesp. 1214). Menander similarly objects to the representations of Prometheus in art, fr. 718.

τοὺς | γραφεῖς: both tragedy (particularly Sophocles) and comedy (Menander and 4th-/3rd-century writers more than Aristophanes and Old Comedy) place prepositives at line end, presumably as part of an attempt to make the iambic trimeter less stichic and more flexible. Monosyllabic examples in Alexis are (1) the definite article (here, 24.2 = 115(110K).21, 257(255K).3; cf. e.g. S. *Ant.* 409, *El.* 879, *Phil.* 263, Ar. *Eccl.* 452, Antiphanes 85.4, Amphis 30.5, Men. *Asp.* 55, 144, *Georg.* 26, *Dysk.* 264, 407, fr. 333.9); (2) καί, both copulative (267(265K).5, probably 178(172K).17 but not 190(185K).2; cf. e.g. S. *Ant.* 171, *OR* 267, 1234, *Phil.* 312, Ar. *Vesp.* 1193, *Lys.* 1176, *Plut.* 752, Antiphanes 165(167K).2, Amphis 35.1, Eubulus 37(38K).1, Men. *Asp.* 338, 453, *Georg.* 70, *Dysk.* 106, 415, 671, *Epitr.* 283, 412, 527, *Pk.* 131, 160, *Sam.* 258, 393) and adverbial (4.2, cf. Ar. *Ach.* 143, Men. *Dysk.* 627); (3) ἤ, both = 'or' (113(108K).2; cf. Ar. *Ran.* 1296, Antiphanes 78(77K).1, Anaxandrides 34(33K).6, Amphis 30.5, Philemon 45(44K).1, Men. *Asp.* 341, *Dysk.* 88, *Sam.* 394, fr. 795.1) and = 'than' (cf. Timocles 12.1, Men. *Epitr.* 401); and (4) οὐ (96(92K).3, see comm.; cf. S. *Ant.* 5, *El.* 1466, 1491, Eur. *Hcld.* 1016, *Melanippe Desm.* 15 Page, fr. 492.4, Men. *Kol.* fr. 2.4 Sandbach). See (in addition to editors of cited texts) J. van Leeuwen, *Mnemosyne* 37 (1909) 164 n. 3 supplementing his comm. on Ar. *Plut.* 752 and Descroix 289ff., against the criticisms of Fraenkel on A. *Ag.* 1271 (p.588 n. 1), P. Maas, *Greek Metre* (English transl., Oxford 1962) 85, West, *Greek Metre* 83f.

21

Meineke 3.393 (II), Kock 2.305, Edmonds 2.384, Kassel–Austin 2.35. The fr. may be part of a narrative about a recent drinking-party.

1 γάρ postponed to fourth word: see on 37(36K).1.

δήμιος: sc. δοῦλος, the Attic euphemism for the public executioner (Ar. *Eccl.* 81 etc.); comparison with him of such people as the toastmaster here and the braggart soldier in Lucian *Dial. Meretr.* 13.4 was probably a feature of popular speech; cf. also Ach. Tat. 8.3.5, where the vulture is Prometheus' δήμιος. The reason for the comparison here is indicated by v. 2 κυάθους προπίνων εἴκοσιν; it was only in toasts that respectable drinkers took strong wine (i.e. neat wine in toasts to Ζεὺς Σωτήρ and one or two others, Xenarchus 2; wine mixed with an equal quantity of water in all the remaining toasts, Alexis 59(58K), 246(244K)), and the decision at a party about the number of toasts and the strength of the wine mixtures was

always taken by the συμποσίαρχος (Mau in *RE* s.v. *Comissatio* 612.62ff.,
P. Von der Mühll, *Ausgewählte kleine Schriften* (Basle 1976) 490ff., cf.
Dover's edition of Pl. *Symp.* p. 11). A similar accusation is made against a
toastmaster in Men. fr. 443.

2 ὁ Χαιρέας: either the name of a character in the play (cf. Men. *Asp.*,
Fab. Inc., anon. fr. 251 Austin, Ter. *Eun.*, where Χαιρέας/Chaerea is a
young man; Men. *Dysk.*, either young man or parasite, cf. Gomme–
Sandbach, *Comm.* p. 131; Men. *Kon.*, role uncertain), or alternatively a
persona ficta mentioned by the speaker here in order to give an air of
verisimilitude to his words (cf. Plaut. *Asin.* 865f., on which see Fraenkel,
MNC 28 n. 1).

Ἀρχίλοχος

Meineke 1.390. The title of this (as of the previous) play has a disputed
ending. Ath. 14.644b says that Ἄλεξις . . . ἐν τῷ ἐπιγραφομένῳ Ἀρχιλόχῳ is
the author of a quoted fr. (22); the Antiatticist (Bekker, *Anecdot.* 106.16)
gives Ἄλεξις Ἀρχιλόχοις as the source of a controversial form (fr. 23).
Meineke opts for the plural title, suspecting that Alexis' play imitated
Cratinus' Ἀρχίλοχοι. Here Meineke judges wrongly: not for reasons of
palaeography (the MSS of Ath. and the Antiatticist are equal villains in
faulty transmission of proper names and play titles), but of dramatic
history. Cratinus' Ἀρχίλοχοι owed its plural title in all probability to a
semi-chorus of Archilochus and his supporters battling against a semi-
chorus of epic poets in an Old-Comedy literary *agon* (J. Th. M. F.
Pieters, *Cratinus* (Leiden 1946) 32ff., 134f., cf Kassel–Austin 4.121); at the
time of Alexis' play, ninety years or more later, although vestigial remains
of a chorus active in the plot are observable in a handful of comedies (see
on Τροφώνιος and fr. 239(237K)), a play built on the Cratinus foundations would have been a pointless archaism; certainly no comic fr. or title
dating from the mid-4th century implies the existence of an *agon* of
Old-Comedy proportions. Since the only plausible explanation of a plural
title Ἀρχίλοχοι is the one that fits the conjectured Cratinus plot, it
follows that Alexis' play almost certainly had the singular title.

Of the two frs. surviving from the play, 22 alone has dramatic significance. It consists of an address couched in three dactylic hexameters
which (so H. Kleinknecht, *Die Gebetsparodie in der Antike* (Stuttgart 1937)
125) in structure, content and vocabulary may be intended to parody
formulas found at the opening of a formal prayer to the gods:

(i) the addressee is described as ὄλβιε: cf. A. *Suppl.* 526 ὄλβιε Ζεῦ,
Proclus *Hymn.* 1.33 ὅ. δαῖμον.

(ii) a participial phrase (here with ναίων) in apposition to the vocative identifies the place where the addressee may be found: cf. Hom. *Il.* 2.412 Ζεῦ ... αἰθέρι ναίων, 16.233, A. *Choeph.* 807f. τὸ δὲ καλῶς κτίμενον ὦ μέγα ναίων | στόμιον, Eur. *Hel.* 1584f. ὦ ναίων ἅλα, | πόντιε Πόσειδον, *Or.* 1225 ὦ δῶμα ναίων νυκτὸς ὀρφναίας πάτερ, *Phoen.* 84f. ὦ φαεννὰς οὐρανοῦ ναίων πτυχάς, | Ζεῦ.

(iii) a relative clause is then juxtaposed: cf. Hom. *Il.* 3.276ff., Ar. *Lys.* 1279ff., Orph. *Hymn.* 18.4, Proclus *Hymn.* 5.3ff.; see especially E. Norden, *Agnostos Theos* (Leipzig 1913) 168ff.

Alexis' addressee, τὴν ἠΰτυχῆ ναίων Πάρον, ὄλβιε πρέσβυ (v.1), is best identified as Archilochus himself, either in person on the stage or by apostrophe, but we cannot exclude some other aged denizen of the island such as Telesicles, Archilochus' father. The speaker appears to rank his addressee with the gods, and although his purpose cannot be identified, it is reasonable to suppose that some request followed, as normally in prayers. The use of dactylic hexameters may well have been influenced by the association of this metre with prayers; elsewhere in comedy they are used mainly for riddles (Antiphanes 192(194K), 194(196K), Eubulus 106(107K)), oracles (Ar. *Equ.* 197ff., 1015ff., *Av.* 967ff., Cratinus jun. 8[1]) and parodies of epic and other literature in that metre (Men. *Theoph.* fr. dub. 6–11, 20, 22, 26); cf. R. Pretagostini, *Dioniso* 57 (1987) 249ff.

The fr.'s context and the play's plot can only be guessed at, but the guess may have greater plausibility if we turn away from the literary battles of Old Comedy to such aspects of Archilochus lore as interested the 4th century. We are told that in Diphilus' Σαπφώ Archilochus appeared as Sappho's lover (fr. 71(70K)) in what must have been a historical travesty, chronology being ignored. Alexis' play could have been another such travesty; the apocryphal connection with Sappho might have featured in the plot, or any of the legendary incidents of Archilochus' career: his encounter with the Muses, for instance, or his rescue by a dolphin.[2] Stories about such events were already hallowed legend in 3rd-century Paros, as the Mnesiepes inscription testifies (*SEG* 15 (1958) 132ff., no. 516, printed also by Lasserre–Bonnard, M. Treu and G. Tarditi in their editions of Archilochus, cf. also M. Treu in *RE Suppl.* xi.138.36ff.), and might already have been familiar in Alexis' Athens; the 4th century witnessed the rehabilitation of Archilochus' memory, especially in Paros. We know that close and friendly relations flourished between the island and Athens in

---

[1] The Middle-Comedy examples (including Alexis 262(26oK)) are collected by Meineke 1.296ff. and A. Körte in *RE* s.v. *Komödie* 1265.36ff.

[2] It goes without saying that incidents of Archilochus' life treated in his poetry (e.g. the dealings with Lycambes and his family) would, suitably embroidered, have provided excellent comic material.

COMMENTARY

the sixteen years before Chaeronea (cf. O. Rubensohn in *RE* s.v. *Paros* 1819.63ff.); dare one date Alexis' play provisionally to the years between 354 and 338?

22

Meineke 3.393 (I), Kock 2.305, Edmonds 2.384, Kassel–Austin 2.36. On the fr.'s metre, dramatic context and probable parody of prayer formulas, see above.

1 ἠΰτυχῆ is my correction of A's εὐτυχῆ (*Hermes* 93 (1965) 298f.); I assume that this epicising form (cf. μακάρεσσι v. 3), coined on the analogy of ἠϋγένειος, ἠϋγενής, ἠΰκομος, etc., was corrupted to the prose spelling at metrical expense, just as ἠΰπυργον was at Pind. *Nem.* 4.12. Other conjectures seem less tolerable, either because they oust the idea of good fortune in which ἠΰτυχῆ and ὄλβιε complement each other and set the general tone for the exemplification of Parian good fortune that follows in vv. 2–3 (thus εὐτειχῆ Meineke after Dindorf, printed by Kassel–Austin, but Paros' walls were not remarkable, cf. Hdt. 6.133, O. Rubensohn in *RE* s.v. *Paros* 1806.59ff.; εὐαυγῆ Kock), or because they introduce Homeric licences a shade too subtle for comedy (Casaubon's εὐτυχέα, with lengthening of a short final alpha before following nu, but I have found no examples of such a licence in any comic dactylic hexameter).

3 κόσμον μὲν μακάρεσσι λίθον: Parian marble was recognised to be the whitest and brightest (Theoc. 6.38 and Gow ad loc., [Lucian] *Am.* 13, Fiehn in *RE* s.v. *Steinbruch* 2261.56ff.).

θνητοῖς δὲ πλακοῦντας: nothing is said elsewhere about the pre-eminence of flat-cakes from Paros, and so Ath.'s allegation that Alexis was (whether consciously or unconsciously) confusing Paros with Parium on the Hellespont, where according to Ath. the flat-cakes were famous, may be true. We find the same confusion in Polyaenus, *Strat.* 5.2.22, Macarius 6.22 and the scholia on Ar. *Vesp.* 1188–9.

23

Meineke 3.394 (II), Kock 2.306, Edmonds 2.384, Kassel–Austin 2.36. The Antiatticist's note claiming that Alexis used λαβόμενος ἀντὶ τοῦ λαβών is far too condensed for us in the absence of contextual quotation to divine clearly what the grammarians were battling about. Possibly there was an Atticist ban on the use of the middle of λαμβάνω with an object in the accusative expressed or implied (in Attic of the best period λαμβάνω in the middle either takes the genitive, LSJ s.v. B, or is used absolutely, Ar. *Pax* 508, *Ran.* 1379, 1390). If the Antiatticist is seeking to oppose the ban, Alexis 78.6–8 could have provided him with an apposite quotation ὃν ἂν

ΑΡΧΙΛΟΧΟΣ

δ' ἴδη ... ἀπάγειν λαβόμενον εἰς τὸ δεσμωτήριον. However, Meineke's suggestion that the Antiatticist here is referring to that passage of Alexis' Ἐπίκληρος, having misidentified his play source, ought not to be pressed; even if the idiom of 78.8 contains the solecism that the Antiatticist is trying to exonerate, was Alexis not capable of repeating it more than once in different plays?

Ἀσκληπιοκλείδης

Breitenbach 79f. As a personal name Ἀσκληπιοκλείδης is not recorded elsewhere, though the parallel formation Διοκλείδης does occur in Athens (Kirchner, *PA* 1.267, 2.455 = 3973–9, 3976a). This suggests that the present title was specially coined by Alexis, but his purpose is now partially at least mysterious. The first four syllables of the name may imply (so Breitenbach) that its bearer was a devotee of or otherwise connected with Asclepius, whose cult was widespread and influential enough in the 4th century (cf. Thraemer in *RE* s.v. *Asklepios*, particularly 1664.53ff., E. J. and L. Edelstein, *Asclepius* 2 (Baltimore 1945) 119ff.) to attract the interest of Attic comedy (in addition to Ar. *Plut.*, note the Ἀσκληπιός titles of Antiphanes and Philetaerus); dare one guess that Alexis' title figure claimed membership of the Asclepiadae? Such a conjecture would not tally badly with what little we know of the play. Its one fr. (24) appears to have been spoken by a μάγειρος who claimed to have been trained in Sicily, the home of *haute cuisine* in the ancient world (see on the fr.). According to Pl. *Gorg.* 464c–465b the contemporary cook sometimes claimed for his art undue qualities of usefulness and importance: προσποιεῖται τὰ βέλτιστα σιτία τῷ σώματι εἰδέναι. The Hippocratic writings lay great stress on dietetics, and doctors such as Diocles of Carystus wrote cookery books (M. Wellmann, *Fragmentsammlung der sikelischen Ärzte* (Berlin 1901) 174; cf. F. Bilabel, *SB Heidelberg* 23 (1920) 3ff.); doubtless the μάγειροι in return tried to profit from the medical interest in cookery and to gain for themselves some of the greater esteem in which the ancient medical profession was held. Fourth-century comedy was not slow to see opportunities for ridicule in cooks who aspired to medical and other sorts of scientific knowledge; their medical jargon is taken off by Alexis 129(124K), see comm. *ad loc.*, Damoxenus 2.16–41 (cf. Dohm, *Mageiros* 173ff.) and Anaxippus 1 vv. 16, 47. In the present play by Alexis it seems a reasonable possibility – no more – that the cook who spoke fr. 24 was the title figure, and that he claimed sufficient medical expertise to warrant a special relationship with Asclepius. But why in that case his name should have ended in -κλείδης is a question that baffles answer. It may be that Alexis was attacking under the guise of a medical cook some contemporary

COMMENTARY

Athenian whose name ended with those two syllables; the well-known 4th-century homosexual Autoclides (Aeschines 1.52, Harpocration s.v. Αὐτοκλείδης; in his Ὀρεσταυτοκλείδης Timocles seems to have represented him on stage in a travesty of the role of Orestes, cf. Meineke 1.432, V. Bevilacqua, *Dioniso* 7 (1939) 47, Webster, *SLGC* 59 and *CQ* 2 (1952) 21) would be an obvious candidate here, if only there were any evidence of medical or gastronomic interests on his part.[1] Yet if Alexis had wished to attack Autoclides by travestying him as Asclepius or a fanatically Asclepiad cook on the lines tentatively suggested above, it is difficult to understand why in that event Alexis should have suppressed the first syllable of Autoclides' name.[2]

24

Meineke 3.394, Kock 2.306, Edmonds 2.386, Kassel–Austin 2.37. The speaker's connection (if any) with the play title is discussed above in the introduction to Ἀσκληπιοκλείδης; he is clearly a μάγειρος of some kind. μάγειροι – men hired to butcher sacrificial victims such as sheep and cook them afterwards – were standardised in the period of Middle Comedy as garrulous and conceited boasters. We do not know the part played by Alexis in the development of the role, but it is likely to have been considerable; more frs. involving μάγειροι are extant from him than from any other comic writer (also frs. 49(48K), 84, 92(88K), 115(110K), 129(124K), 132(127K), 138(133K), 153(149K), 177–9(172–4K), 191–4(186–9K), 216(213K), possibly 83). The whole subject has achieved a daunting bibliography; I single out Ribbeck, *Alazon* 18ff., Rankin, ΜΑΓΕΙΡΟΙ, K. Latte in *RE* s.v. Μάγειρος 393.64ff., Webster, *SLGC* index s.v. cook, M. Treu, *Philologus* 102 (1958) 215ff., A. Giannini, *Acme* 13 (1960) 135ff., Fraenkel, *EP* 408ff., Dohm, *Mageiros*, Handley on Men. *Dysk.* 393, Gomme–Sandbach, *Comm.*, general index s.v. cooks, G. Berthiaume, *Les Rôles du mágeiros* (*Mnemosyne* suppl. 70, 1982), Hunter, index of subjects s.v. cooks, Nesselrath, *MK* 297ff. (on this fr. p. 303).

---

[1] The Autoclides who wrote esoterically on religious cult practice (*FGrH* 353) may well have been a priest, but it is hardly possible to identify him with the homosexual (Jacoby's tentative date for the exegete is the 3rd century), and there is nothing in his writings to suggest any particular connection with Asclepius.

[2] The titles of parallel travesties preserve all the significant elements of both names: Aristophanes' Αἰολοσίκων, Cratinus' Διονυσαλέξανδρος, Eubulus' Σφιγγοκαρίων, Menecrates' Μανέκτωρ, Polyzelus' Δημοτυνδάρεως, Timocles' Ὀρεσταυτοκλείδης. Can one rule out corruption of an original Ἀσκληπι<αυτο>κλείδης in the excerptors (Ath. 4.169d, Pollux 10.108)?

ΑΣΚΛΗΠΙΟΚΛΕΙΔΗΣ

1 ὀψοποιεῖν: the ὀψοποιός and the μάγειρος in comedy take pride in their own professions while denigrating each other's (see the introduction to Κράτεια), yet for some reason (presumably related to contemporary usage) the verb μαγειρεύω does not appear in comedy, and ὀψοποιῶ does double duty: 'I do the job of an ὀψοποιός/of a μάγειρος.' On the meaning of ὄψον in comedy see on fr. 47(46K).6.

2 περὶ <τὴν> Σικελίαν: the supremacy of Sicilian cooks and cookery (especially the Συρακοσία τράπεζα) was generally acknowledged (e.g. Ar. fr. 225(216K), Antiphanes 90, Cratinus jun. 1, Anaxippus 1, Pl. *Resp.* 3.404d, *Epist.* 7.326b, Ath. 12.518c, Lucian *Dial. Mort.* 19(9).2, Zenobius 5.94 and Leutsch *ad loc.*, Hor. *Od.* 3.1.18; cf. Ribbeck, *Alazon* 18f., Rankin, ΜΑΓΕΙΡΟΙ 40f., Göbel, *Ethnica* 122, M. Treu, *Philologus* 102 (1958) 219).

2–4 These verses (from ὥστε to the end of the fr.) are repeated, apparently with trivial alterations, in fr 115(110K).21–3 (spoken by a paradoxical μάγειρος). So also Alexis 49(48K) = 115(110K).9–11, 87(67K) = 249(247K), 110(105K).2 = 248(246K).3, 256(254K).2 = 261(259K).1 (cf. Meineke 1.377). Repetition of the same material in different plays need occasion no surprise when a playwright is as fertile as Alexis, who wrote an average of three plays a year during his long career (cf. E. Mensching, *Mus. Helv.* 21 (1964) 77; my general introduction, I.iii, pp. 13ff); but it is not always possible to say whether a particular instance represents the easy way out for a poet with an imminent deadline, a conscious or unconscious memory of a striking passage, or even an error in ascription by the citer (cf. Kann, *De iteratis* 52ff., Hunter on Eubulus 82(84K)).

3 βατάνι': Ath. 4.169d cites this fr. because it contains the word βατάνια spelled with initial β, but Pollux 10.108 says Ἄλεξις δὲ ἐν Ἀσκληπιοκλείδη πατάνια εἴρηκεν with initial π. Although it is possible that Alexis used both orthographies in the one play (? for comic effect: cf. Eubulus 37(38K) and Hunter *ad loc.*), the more likely assumption is that one of our sources is wrong, just as one of them (not necessarily the same one!) is at Antiphanes 95, which Pollux cites for initial π, Ath. for β. Which source is wrong here? The question is difficult.[1] Pollux's discussion of the π/βατάνιον orthography is generally well organised and scholarly, containing a definition of the word as τὸ ἐκπέταλον λοπάδιον (cf. Hesych. and Phot. s.v. πατάνια), with the correct comment that the spelling with β was κατὰ τὴν τῶν ἰδιωτῶν συνήθειαν εἰρημένον. The note in Ath., on the

---

[1] The Zavorda Photius entry s.v. βατάνια (1.329 Theodoridis), with its allegation that Alexis used the form βατάνια, is of doubtful relevance here. Apart from its failure to cite a play title, which makes it uncertain whether this entry refers to Ἀσκληπιοκλείδης or some other play (e.g. 178(172K).9, 18), it would be foolish to use a corrupt and abbreviated note of this kind in an orthographical dispute.

COMMENTARY

other hand, is less informative and poorly arranged as we have it now; it does not differentiate between instances of πατάνιον as a common noun and of the name Πατανίων derived from it, while the citation of Antiphanes 180(182K) in Ath. 4.169e–f is misplaced; it belongs to the section ending with the citation of Antiphanes 216(217K).1–4 shortly before. The evidence of usage also slightly favours Pollux. The diminutive π/βατάνιον is derived from πατάνη/α, a word clearly of Sicilian Greek origin (Sophron fr. 13 Kaibel, cf. Hesych. s.v. παντάνα, *sic*; and see below)[1] from which Latin borrowed *patina* (Photius s.v. πατάνια squashed ancient grammarians who got this the wrong way round). In later Attic comedy Ath. and Pollux between them cite Antiphanes 71(70K) and Eubulus 46(47K) for the form with π (cf. Πατανίων as a cook's name in Philetaerus 14(14 + 15K)), Hipparchus 5 for the form with β, and Eubulus 37(38K) for the presence of both orthographies. The word is spelled with initial β at Alexis 178(172K).9, 18 and Eubulus 130(132K) in passages cited by Ath. for other reasons. In the *Koine* only the form with β is found (*P.Oxy.* 739.9, Bilabel, *Ops.* ε.1, cf. the Antiatticist, 84.13 Bekker).[2] One possibility is that a more correct formation of the word with initial π was superseded by a vulgarised spelling/pronunciation with initial β probably before 300 (the rough date of a graffito on an Attic sherd which spells the word with β: M. Lang, *Agora* XXI.10 (B 12), B. A. Sparkes and L. Talcott, *Pots and Pans of Classical Athens* (Princeton 1958) fig. 23). Alexis Ἀσκληπιοκλείδης cannot be dated, but the balance of the evidence just favours (*pace* Kassel–Austin) the orthography with π here.

It is no coincidence that Attic comedians stress the word's Sicilian associations (περὶ τὴν Σικελίαν here, Σικελὰ πατανίων σωρεύματα Eubulus 46(47K), Σικελικὰ βατάνια id. 130(132K); to the Athenians of the time the word conjured up the exciting flavour of Sicilian *cuisine*. The absence of any such geographical reference in Alexis 115(110K) probably explains why this word is there replaced by λοπάδι', its metrically equivalent synonym; there is no need to think of a gloss ousting a more exotic counterpart. Vessels of the required shape (a flatter form of λοπάδιον, according to the Pollux definitions: see above) are illustrated in Sparkes and Talcott, *op. cit.* fig. 39 (left) and Sparkes, *JHS* 82 (1962) pl. VI.3 (centre), although their provenance probably makes them λοπάδια rather than πατάνια.

---

[1] The word's etymological relationships are discussed by Walde–Hofmann s.v. *patina*, with bibliography, and Frisk s.vv. βατάνη, πατάνη.

[2] For the Antiatticist's note here ὡς Ἀλεξανδρεῖς cf. 96.1 Bekker on ἐξαλλάξαι. This rules out a possibility that these two words are a corruption of <οὔτ>ως ʺΑλεξ<ις> Ἀντείᾳ. Cf. also Sicking, *Annotationes* 52f.

ΑΣΚΛΗΠΙΟΚΛΕΙΔΗΣ

ἐμβάλλειν: the MSS here (ἐκβαλεῖν A, ἐκβάλλειν CE) show the common error of confusion beteween ἐμ- and ἐκ- in compounds (cf. e.g. Hdt. 6.84, Eur. *Alc.* 1001; E. G. Turner, *BICS* 6 (1959) 63); the correct ἐμβάλλειν was imported here from the replication in Ath. 3.107d = Alexis fr. 115(110K).22 first to the best of my knowledge by the Hoeschel MS of the Epit. Up to the time of Kaibel, G. Morel's ἐμβαλεῖν (p.34) was generally printed at Ath. 4.169d (and in editions of comic fragments) because of the tense in A there, but the presence of ἐνίοτε makes the aorist infinitive less apposite.

3-4 The idea of the diners 'biting into the dishes for joy' is a variation on a popular comic theme. At Aristophon 9.9, Alexis 178(172K).5. Plaut. *Pseud.* 883f. and possibly Hermippus 23(24K) it is the fingers that are gnawed in ecstasy over the food; elsewhere gluttons are said to attack even the table (Mnesimachus 8, cf. Ar. *Equ.* 1298f.). Presumably it was the vigour of this image that led Alexis to use vv. 2–4 in two different plays.

Ἀσωτοδιδάσκαλος

See 'False or Doubtful Attributions' III (pp. 819ff.).

Ἀταλάντη

The large number of comedies from the 5th and 4th centuries with titles relating to the legends of Atalanta and Meleager (an Ἀταλάντη written also by Callias, Euthycles, Philetaerus, Strattis; Μελέαγρος by Antiphanes, Philetaerus; Μελανίων by Antiphanes) bears witness to the popularity of the saga on the comic stage. Unfortunately, these plays share one further feature: their remains are too scanty for any useful prediction about their plots.[1] The Calydonian boar hunt was a popular subject with

---

[1] About the plot of Alexis' play nothing ought to be said, although enough has been. A. Olivieri (*Dioniso* 7 (1939) 279) wildly suggests that Alexis' play was 'analogous' to Epicharmus' Ἀταλάνται, and that its subject was not mythical but drawn from the everyday world of spinners or weavers (ταλάσιοι). The extant frs. attributed to Epicharmus' Ἀταλάνται in fact derive from some other source; Kaibel, *CGF* 93f. notes the impossibility of fathering on to the Sicilian poet allusions to individuals attacked in Attic Old Comedy. This disposes of Olivieri's first point; the second needs no rebuttal. Even Meineke (3.396) falls short of his usually admirable standards in supposing that Turpilius' *Atalanta* may have been modelled on Alexis' play. No such title is recorded for Turpilius; Meineke presumably confuses Turpilius with

COMMENTARY

4th-century vase painters, whose attention may have been drawn to the myth by tragedy (H. Metzger, *Les Représentations dans la céramique attique du IVe siècle* (Paris 1951) 312ff., vases 21–6, A. D. Trendall and T. B. L. Webster, *Illustrations of Greek Drama* (London 1971) nos. III.3, 37–9, cf. III.3, 40 and 4, 1). Of these the most influential was Euripides' Μελέαγρος, and some of the comedies listed above may have parodied it (cf. T. B. L. Webster, *Hermes* 82 (1954) 296f.).

26

Meineke 3.396, Kock 2.307, Edmonds 2.386, Kassel–Austin 2.39. The critic who attacked the use or formation of the word μικρόφωνος, thus inducing the Antiatticist (108.3 Bekker) to cite Alexis in its defence, was a hypercritical pedant. Parallel compounds flourished in Attic: e.g. βαρύφωνος (Ar. fr. 793(753K)), cf. Men. fr. 209 and βαρυφωνία in Alexis 312(311K)), λεπτόφωνος (Ar. fr. 844(806K)), μεγαλόφωνος (Dem. 19.238), ὀξύφωνος (S. *Trach.* 963). Did the objector prefer Atticists to use λεπτόφωνος in place of μικρόφωνος, or did he feel that such compounds in general were too redolent of *Koine* usage? Perhaps the latter (cf. Bruhn, *Wortschatz* 39).

Ἀτθίς

Meineke 1.398, Breitenbach 164. Ἀτθίς occurs as a woman's name (a friend of Sappho: *Suda* s.v. Σαπφώ, Sappho frs. 49, 131, probably also 90.10a.15 Lobel–Page; a *hetaira*: Lucian epigram 49 Jacobitz = *Anth. Pal.* 6.17; cf. also *SEG* 15 (1958) no. 174, Attica, and 16 (1959) no. 583 A..ιδος, S. Italy), and Meineke so explained Alexis' title. But in view of the large number of titles in later Greek comedy that consist of adjectives denoting nationality, 'The Girl of Attica' seems a likelier interpretation (cf. Breitenbach; G. Kaibel, *RE* s.v. *Alexis* 9, 1469.48). Feminine titles of this type no doubt covered a large variety of subjects (e.g. Men. *Sam.*, Ter. *Andr.*), but on the evidence of those titles where we do know something about the plot, we should expect the scene of the play to be different from the title figure's origin. Plautus' *Rudens* (adapted from a still unidentified play by Diphilus; cf. Enk 2.2, 156f., W. A. Friedrich, *Euripides und Diphilos* (Munich 1953) 171ff.) is partly concerned, as Breitenbach notes, with the Athenian origin of at least one of two enslaved girls now in Cyrene

Pomponius, for whom an *Atalanta* is attested by Porphyrion (on Hor. *A.P.* 221); cf. Schanz–Hosius 1⁴.249 and Kurfess in *RE* s.v. *Pomponius* 101, 2355.23ff.

ΑΤΘΙΣ

(vv.35ff., 738ff.; cf. O. Skutsch, *CR* 16 (1966) 12ff.); Ἀτθίς or Ἀτθίδες would have been a suitable Greek title for such a plot. The frs. extant from Alexis' play provide no clues to its story-line. Fr. 27 looks like part of an entrance monologue by a man who has just come from the market after buying provisions for a meal. The speaker has a perky wit, but his status is uncertain; he could be parasite, free man (old or young), slave (so Edmonds, cf. Nesselrath, *MK* 294f.) or cook (M. Treu, *Philologus* 102 (1958) 218 n. 3, A. Giannini, *Acme* 30 (1960) 159). If he is a parasite or some other young man of idle habits, he might then be the addressee of fr. 28, with its admonition that one's daily bread ought to be earned. The context of fr. 29 is obscure; Meineke's conjecture (3.397) that somebody is comparing progressively increasing troubles to the accelerated gathering of clouds in the sky is as good as any.

The date of the play cannot be confidently established; the implicit allusion to Pythagorist vegetarianism in fr. 27.1–2 (see comm. *ad loc.*) does not necessarily point to a date between 345 and 320, during which some other plays with allusions to Pythagorists appear to have been written and the Pythagorist groups themselves to have particularly flourished (see introduction to Πυθαγορίζουσα; cf. Webster, *CQ* 2 (1952) 22). E. Capps (*AJA* 4 (1900) 87) vainly attempted to date Ἀτθίς to *c*. 270. When supplementing an Athenian didascalic inscription Ἄλεξις Ἀτ]θίσιν (*IG* ii².2323.249 = III B 3 col. 6, 4 Mette) and roughly dating this production by the identification of two actors mentioned in neighbouring productions with a Lysimachus and a Philon who occur in the Delphic Soteria lists about 270 (cf. G. M. Sifakis, *Studies in the History of Hellenistic Drama* (London 1967) 163) Capps made two errors. He dated the Athenian productions on this fragment of the inscription over a century too early (A. Wilhelm, *Urkunden dramatischer Aufführungen in Athen* (Vienna 1901) 8off., cf. E. Reisch, *Zeitschrift für die österreichischen Gymnasien* 58 (1907) 299, W. A. Dittmer, *The Fragments of the Athenian Comic Didascaliae found in Rome* (Diss. Princeton 1923) 25, C. A. P. Ruck, *IG ii².2323: The List of the Victors in Comedies at the Dionysia* (Leiden 1967) 52ff.), and he ignored the fact that three different sources quote Alexis' title in the singular. Even if the title of the play on this stone was Ἀτθίδες (but Ruck 54 supplements Τη]θίσιν), its author was not Alexis.

27

Meineke 3.396 (I), Kock 2.308, Edmonds 2.388, Kassel–Austin 2.40.

1–2 The speaker (on his status and situation see above) clearly alludes to Pythagorist vegetarianism, which was much ridiculed by comic poets and others in the second half of the 4th century (Alexis 201(196K).1–3, 223(220 + 221K), see comm. *ad loc.*, Antiphanes 133(135K).1–2,

COMMENTARY

Aristophon 9.8–10, 10, 12.7–8, Archestratus 154 *SH*, cf. J. Haussleiter, *Der Vegetarianismus in der Antike* (Berlin 1935) 97ff.). Here the Pythagorist is loosely termed σοφιστής (v.1) because he belongs to a class of nonconformist thinkers and livers, to any of whom this term might be applied in the 4th century and later by way of abuse (cf. e.g. Dem. 18.276, Aeschines 1.173, Lucian *Peregr.* 13), without a corollary that the person or group so described earned fees for teaching rhetoric (cf. also my note on fr. 20.1–2). Kock here objects to σοφιστής on the logical ground that not all sophists were vegetarians, and suggests that the text is corrupt. Comic poets, however, are not logicians, and it is unlikely that any audience would be mortified by the whole-and-part fallacy here; we shall therefore not tamper with the transmitted text (Ath. 9.386c: A, Epit.).

The speaker's opening phrase ὁ πρῶτος εἰπών (cf. com. adesp. fr. 115.1 Kock), its common variant ὁ πρῶτος εὑρών (Alexis 152(148K).1, 190(185K).1, Anaxandrides 31(30K).1, Eubulus 72.1, Men. fr. 14) and other 'first inventor' motifs in comedy (e.g. εὗρον ... πρῶτος Euphron 1.14, κατέδειξε πρῶτος Antiphanes 121(123K).1, Machon 464f., ἐμὸν εὕρημα Alexis 178(172K).4, εὕρηκα τέχνην Men. *Dysk.* 489; Latin equivalents in Plaut. *Men.* 451f., *Pseud.* 568ff., Plaut. or Aquilius *Boeotia* fr. 1, Naevius *Appella* fr. 2, Ter. *Eun.* 247) exemplify and at the same time parody that curiosity about the originators and inventors of everything, which began to burn in 5th-century Athens and raged violently the next century as a product of the sophistic spirit of enquiry. Historians and philosophers seriously investigated and catalogued inventions (A. Kleingünther, ΠΡΩΤΟΣ ΕΥΡΕΤΗΣ (*Philologus Suppl.* 26 (1933) 1ff.); that comedy made abundant humorous capital out of these studies is shown partly by the passages cited above, and partly by the derisive glorification of the cook-*alazon* as the inventor *par excellence* (Dohm, *Mageiros* 130 with further citations). Cf. also Bentley, *Phalaris* 1.lx–lxii, Leo, *Plaut. Forsch.*² 151ff., K. Thraede in *RAC* s.v. *Erfinder* 2.1191ff. and *Rh. Mus.* 105 (1962) 158ff., Barrett on Eur. *Hipp.* 407ff., A. Barigazzi, *La formazione spirituale di Menandro* (Turin 1965) 101ff., Hunter on Eubulus 72.1.

1, 3 οὐδὲ εἷς, οὐδὲ ἕν: the hiatus which is tolerated in comedy for this more emphatic form of οὐδείς (cf. my note on fr. 1.1) probably reflects popular pronunciation (cf. A. C. Moorhouse, *CQ* 12 (1962) 245ff.).

2, 4 ἔμψυχον: the joke, which depends on the word's ambiguity ('living' or 'connected with somebody or something which is alive or has once lived') is repeated at (or from) fr. 223(220K); cf. also *Anth. Pal.* 7.121 (Diog. Laert.). It has a special piquancy in contexts dealing with Pythagoreans and Pythagorists, because ἔμψυχος was the technical term used by the sects for the meat from which they were required to abstain (Diog. Laert. 8.13, 44, Iambl. *Protr.* 21, *Vit. Pyth.* 13.60, 16.68, 24.107, 108, etc., Porphyry *Vit. Pyth.* 7.23, 36, *Abst.* 1.26, etc.).

5 The spelling κρεᾴδι' (with subscript iota) is preferable to κρεάδι' (without it). The alpha of the antepenultimate is always long where its length may be reliably checked (Men. fr. 451.13, Machon 17, *P.Heidelberg* 184.11.11 (*c.* 280–240) = com. adesp. fr. 244.225 Austin; probably also Cephisodorus 8), and the presence of the iota in that very early papyrus may be a more reliable guide to correct orthography than its absence in medieval MSS (e.g. R at Ar. *Plut.* 227, the *Marcianus* here; on such neglected iotas see W. Petersen, *Greek Diminutives in -ION* (Weimar 1910) 214, Schulze, *QE* 48 n. 5). The diminutive would be coined by popular analogy with forms such as γρᾴδιον, ἐλᾴδιον, κερᾴδιον, where an iota was felt already to be present in the primitive (γραῖς, ἔλαιον, κεραία; cf. Schwyzer 1.471 n. 4, and my note on Alexis 2.7; on this word Petersen 213 and P. Chantraine, *La Formation des noms en grec ancien* (Paris 1933) 60 are wrong). After κρεᾴδι' the *Marcianus* and Epit. MSS have ἀρνὸς ἐσθίειν πίονος. Metre and sense localise the corruption to ἐσθίειν. Schweighaeuser's ἐστί may be too colourless and obvious a correction to have satisfied Kaibel (ἐφθά) or Headlam (ἔσθειν: MS note in his copy of Kaibel's edition of Ath.), but it is no less palmary for all that. Unlike other conjectures it provides exactly the word required, and its corruption to ἐσθίειν was presumably caused by conflation of the appearance or sound of ἐστί with ἐσθίει in v. 2, to which the eye – or more probably the mind[1] – of the copyist had wandered.

5–7 'There are chunks of fatty lamb – not living. For that's impossible (sc. to have living chunks of meat). What else? Oh yes, I also got grilled liver.' The text of the *Marcianus*, printed by Kassel–Austin with Casaubon's punctuation (cf. *Animadv.* 665), gives lively sense. ναί here, as often (e.g. after disjunctive questions: Pl. *Theaet.* 193a λέγω τι ἢ οὐδέν? :: ναί, ἀληθῆ γε), answers the idea implied by the preceding question rather than the question as formulated. The Epit. MSS omit from οὐχ to ναί in v. 6; the *recentiores* replace ναί with καί, either a corruption or a Byzantine conjecture; it is less vivid and merely duplicates the meaning of the prepositive (προσ-) in the verb that follows.

7 προσέλαβον: see on fr. 15.18–19.

7–8 The virtually unanimous reading of the *Marcianus* and Epit. MSS τούτων ἐὰν δείξῃ τις ἢ φωνήν τιν' (so A, -ὴν τίν' Epit.) ἢ ψυχὴν ἔχον produces an awkward, perhaps even impossible construction. Although

---

[1] I.e. the scribe wrote the word that the subject matter of the fr. subconsciously suggested, just as at Ath. 7.302f the squeamishness of the character there described led him to corrupt σηπίδια to σικχηπίδια (see comm. on fr. 159(155K).3 and *CQ* 7 (1957) 194). For a similar error in the MSS of Stobaeus see on fr. 46(45K).4. Cf. also Fraenkel's edition of A. *Ag.* 3.655 n. 1.

COMMENTARY

there are parallels for a substantival use of an unarticulated participle after *uerba dicendi et sentiendi* (e.g. Xen. *Anab.* 1.9.4 θεῶνται δ' οἱ παῖδες καὶ τιμωμένους ὑπὸ βασιλέως καὶ ἀκούουσι, καὶ ἄλλους ἀτιμαζομένους, *Cyr.* 5.1.12 ἀλλ' ἐγώ, ἔφη, ἑώρακα καὶ κλαίοντας ὑπὸ λύπης δι' ἔρωτα, καὶ δουλεύοντάς γε τοῖς ἐρωμένοις, K.G. 1.266, 2.47, J. M. Stahl, *Kritisch-historische Syntax des griechischen Verbums* (Heidelberg 1907) 696), here the participle would also have to be associated with the partitive genitive τούτων ('any of these things that has'), which is doubtful Greek. The one satisfactory conjecture is Grotius' φωνήν τι ἤ (*Exc.* 563, 972); this presupposes corruption prompted by a desire to remove the hiatus after indefinite τι. In comedy hiatus after ὅτι and interrogative τί is a frequent licence (P. C. Buttmann, *Ausführliche griechische Sprachlehre*[2] 1 (Berlin 1830) 112, K.B. 1.196f., Headlam on Herodas 5.10, Descroix 28f., cf. my comm. on Alexis 1.1); its extension to indefinite τι is sometimes rejected by modern scholarship (e.g. Fraenkel on A. *Ag.* 1115, cf. Handley on Men. *Dysk.* 247ff., 568), but a case can be made for it at least in Alexis, here and in frs. 129(124K).2 (with the identical *Marcianus* corruption), 183(178K).4 and possibly 123(118K).2 (where the postponed δ' after τι *may* have been inserted by a copyist). Yet doubts will always gnaw at an editor's mind, so long as possible instances are confined to fragmentary texts liable to corruption for a host of reasons supplementary to those of transcriptional error.[1]

9 ὁμολογῶ: again Grotius' emendation of A and Epit.'s unmetrical προσομολογῶ, where the added προσ- can be explained either as an untimely reminiscence of προσέλαβον in v. 7 or as an example of the habit so popular in *Koine* Greek of substituting compound for simple verbs (cf. K. Zepernick, *Philologus* 77 (1921) 340, citing seven further instances from Ath.). Other conjectures are founded on ignorance of these scribal practices: e.g. Kaibel's προσομολογῶ παραβαίνων, which postulates an

---

[1] It is not possible to bolster an admittedly insecure argument by adducing exact parallels from comic poets other than Alexis. A similarly rare licence of hiatus, however, seems to exist after vocatives of (usually) proper names in -ι. The list is not long: Ar. *Ach.* 749 Δικαιόπολι, ἤ, Men. *Pk.* 983 Δωρί. ἀλλά, perhaps *Sam.* 382 Χρυσί. ἐκ (but B's χρυσί' also makes good sense); cf. also Herodas 1.84 Γυλλί, ωνα[, 5.69 τατί, ἀλλά. Cf. V. Schmidt, *Sprachliche Untersuchungen zu Herondas* (Berlin 1968) 75 n. 6, 94, C. Austin, *Menandri Aspis et Samia: II, Subsidia interpretationis* (Berlin 1970) 75, Gomme–Sandbach, *Comm.* on Men. *Sam.* 381f. The hiatus at com. adesp. fr. 289a.4 Austin is easily remedied by transposition (to εἶπεν ἄρτι), cf. *BICS* 16 (1969) 68. Ezechiel *Exag.* 235 appears to have ὤφθη τι ἡμῖν, but this author's practices are no guide to what was acceptable on an Athenian stage.

inexplicable corruption in order to retain a προσ- that adds nothing to the sense (contrast e.g. Men. *Epitr.* 524).

28

Meineke 3.520 (XXXVI) and (= Jacobi) 5.cciii, Kock 2.308, Edmonds 2.388, Kassel–Austin 2.40. Probably a rebuke to a parasite or an idle son (see the introduction to Ἀτθίς and the final paragraph on this fr.).

1 γάρ: third word in its clause, see on fr. 37(36K).1.

1–2 Epicrates 3.1–3 describes the *hetaira* Lais as idle and a drunkard, τὸ καθ᾽ ἡμέραν ὁρῶσα πίνειν κἀσθίειν | μόνον.

3 μηδὲ περινοστεῖν: Porson's correction (*Adv.* 303) of μηδὲν π. δέ in S (the one MS citing the fr., Stob. *Anth.* 3.30.8) is as convincing as his δεῖ for S's ἀεὶ in v. 2. The error may have originated in a misreading of the accent of μηδὲ as the supralineal dash that represents, especially at the end of a word, the letter nu in MSS of all periods (cf. e.g. Eur. *Hipp.* 184, *Hyps.* fr. 60.117 Bond = 759.4 Nauck² οὐδέ corrupted to οὐδέν, Men. *Dysk.* 773 ὁρῶ to ορων, *Dysk.* 434 δεῖ to δεῖν in excerpted citations, cf. Pl. *Resp.* 6.485a; *Resp.* 6.511c οὖ to οὖν), and was then doubly aggravated by (1) the change of τι (before μηδέ) to τοι now that μηδέν provided an object for ποεῖν (cf. comm. on 16.2), and (2) the addition of δέ to connect μηδὲν περινοστεῖν to the previous clause. See also comm. on fr. 59(58K).2.

3–4 περινοστεῖν σχολὴν ἄγοντα, τῷ ζῆν πολεμιώτατον κακόν: to Phaedra in Eur. *Hipp.* 384 σχολή was a τερπνὸν κακόν (cf. D. L. Cairns, *Aidōs* (Oxford 1993) 322ff.), and the attitude of poor, hard-working countrymen to characters like the present addressee who can 'stroll around with time on his hands' is shown clearly by Gorgias' criticism of Sostratos in Men. *Dysk.* 293–5 οὐ δίκαιόν ἐστι γοῦν | τὴν σὴν σχολὴν τοῖς ἀσχολουμένοις κακὸν | ἡμῖν γενέσθαι. In Alexis here κακόν is accusative in apposition to the unexpressed internal object of the sentence: see K.G. 1.284, Wilamowitz on Eur. *Her.* 59, Fraenkel on A. *Ag.* 47, J. Diggle in R. D. Dawe and others, *Dionysiaca* (Cambridge 1978) 171f. and *PCPS* 28 (1982) 59f. τῷ ζῆν = τῷ εὖ ζῆν, here = 'live properly, i.e. as a man ought', as elsewhere in Alexis (frs. 177(173K).4, 236(234K).1, 237(235K).2), but in those three frs. the value system is hedonistic, in fr. 28 it appears to be puritanical. Cf. LSJ s.v. ζῶ II.

Views such as those expressed here can never be fully intelligible when detached from their original dramatic context. Their implications, moral basis and tone would be significantly different if they were addressed (1) by a penniless young lover to a parasite whose help he desperately needed in the management of a love-affair, (2) by an angry father to an idle, dissolute son. Even so, certain basic tenets of popular belief underlie the speaker's ideas: that excessive leisure is reprehensible, because too often it

COMMENTARY

leads to vile indulgence in the pleasures of sex, gambling, drunkenness or (as here) food; that the welfare of others should take precedence over a man's own enjoyments; and that the estimable things of life, such as a fine reputation and acclaim from one's fellows, can be achieved only by hard exertion. Sostratos in Men. *Dysk.* would have provided an excellent example for this speaker's sermon. Brought up as a wealthy idler, he nevertheless turned his back on frivolities, engaged in hard, physical toil, won the praise of Gorgias and Knemon, and so was able to achieve the end which seemed to him at the time most worth-while – marriage to Knemon's daughter (755ff., 764ff., 860ff.). Cf. here especially Dover, *GPM* especially 163f., 179f., and my own paper in *Philologus* 125 (1981) 215ff.

29

Meineke 3.397 (II), Kock 2.308, Edmonds 2.388, Kassel–Austin 2.41. '*Videtur poeta ingrauescens aliquod malum cum tempestate sensim sensimque ingruente comparasse*' (Meineke), cf. the introduction to Ἀτθίς.

1 πῶς: grammarians, most other excerptors (with the honourable exception of Ath.: cf. K. Zepernick, *Philologus* 77 (1921) 311ff., C. Collard, *RFIC* 97 (1969) 157ff.) and copyists are notorious for the wilful way in which they tamper with a quoted author's words in order that the citation may make sense independent of its original context (G. Kaibel, *Hermes* 30 (1895) 429ff., O. Hense in *RE* s.v. *Ioannes* 18 = *Stobaios* 2583.9ff., Handley on Men. *Dysk.* 797–812, cf. my remarks in Flores 365), and for this reason a fr.'s opening words, which frequently act as a link with the preceding context, are especially suspect. Here accordingly it is impossible to decide between three possibilities. (1) πῶς may be correct and exclamatory ('How the sky clouds over . . . !'); O. Lagerkrantz, *Eranos* 18 (1918) 27ff. has shown that this use of πῶς, so familiar in the *Koine* (e.g. *Ev. Marc.* 10.24, *Ev. Jo.* 11.36), has antecedents in 4th-century Attic[1] (e.g. Xen. *Anab.* 6.5.19 πῶς γὰρ δυσδιάβατον τὸ πεδίον, εἰ μὴ νικήσομεν τοὺς ἱππέας, where δυσδιάβατον is unexceptionable), cf. Schwyzer 2.626, Blass–Debrunner–Funk 225, 436. (2) Alexis may have written exclamatory ὡς, as at fr. 299(297K), perhaps also 279(277K) (the normal word in Attic: K.G. 2.439, Schwyzer *loc. cit.*; especially common in comedy, H. Thesleff, *Studies on Intensification in Early and Classical Greek* (Helsinki 1954) 191f.), and a modernising excerptor or scribe replaced it with πῶς

---

[1] The examples claimed by Lagerkrantz from 5th-century Attic (Eur. *El.* 570, Ar. *Ach.* 12 etc.), however, may be interpreted as questions rather than as exclamations; on Ar. *Ach.* 12 see also Fraenkel, *Beob.* 16ff.

(so Meineke). (3) πῶς may be correct, introducing an indirect question after some word like σκέψασθε in the unquoted preceding context (cf. Ar. *Equ.* 614); at Philemon 2.1 I suspect that the fr.'s opening words ὦ πῶς in the MSS are simply a corruption or wilful adjustment of ὅπως, with a governing *uerbum dicendi uel sentiendi* similarly to be posited in the lost preceding context.

ἐπινέφει (Grotius), not ἐπινεφεῖ (MSS); in classical Greek the compounds of νέφω (ἐπι-, συν-, ὑπο-) are consonant stems, although MSS habitually accent them as contracted -έω verbs.

ἡσυχῇ and not ἡσυχῆ appears to be the classical form; the iota is present in early papyri (LSJ s.v.), and parallel adverbial formations (ἁπλῇ, κοινῇ, πανταχῇ, ῥητῇ) have the iota on Attic inscriptions at all periods (Meisterhans–Schwyzer 145, cf. Threatte 1.353ff.).

2 μᾶλλον μᾶλλον: the emphatic repetition cited by Photius and the *Suda* here from Alexis is familiar in 5th-century Attic (Eur. *IT* 1406, Ar. *Ran.* 1001), and it seems likely that the present lexical entry, which cites also Alexis 186(181K) (cf. Antiatticist 108.5 Bekker) and Anaxilas 31(32K) (cf. also the adjacent Photius citation of Men. fr. 872) for the phrase, derives from the scholium to one of the 5th-century passages cited above. Similar locutions in comedy include πλέον πλέον Ar. *Nub.* 1288, μεῖζον μεῖζον and μικρὸν μικρόν Antiphanes 10; cf. *plus plusque* Plaut. *Aul.* 546. Doubtless this type of repetition was a feature of popular speech in Greek (cf. P. T. Stevens, *Colloquial Expressions in Euripides* (*Hermes Einzelschrift* 38, Wiesbaden 1976) 17), although the parallel Latin formation *magis magis* occurs also in serious poetry (e.g. Catullus 64.274, Verg. *Georg.* 4.311, cf. Austin on *Aen.* 2.299, van der Paardt on Apul. *Met.* 3.9).

Αὐλητρίς

This title, unknown for Alexis before the discovery of the Zavorda MS of Photius, is shared with Diodorus, Antiphanes (A. ἢ Δίδυμαι) and Menander (Ἀρρηφόρος ἢ Α.); Phoenicides wrote an Αὐλητρίδες, Titinius a *Tibicina* and Anaxandrides a Κιθαρίστρια. It is an oddity due doubtless to the lottery of survival that in play-titles the female pipers should outnumber the female harpists and citharists, yet in preserved passages of intrigue comedy it is string-players that predominate. Habrotonon in Men. *Epitr.* is a ψάλτρια (fr. 1, v. 589 etc.), the girl raped by Chaerea in Ter. *Eun.* a *fidicina* (457, 985), and Phaedria's beloved in *Phorm.* a *citharistria* (8off.), a *fidicina* appears in Plaut. *Epid.*; against these, the mute Habrotonon in Men. *Pk.* appears to be a piper (476 and Gomme–Sandbach, *Comm. ad loc.*)

COMMENTARY

30

Kassel–Austin 2.41. The Zavorda MS of Photius reports (s.v. ὡνέτης; K. Tsantsanoglou, *New Fragments of Greek Literature from the Lexicon of Photius* (Athens 1984) 79) that Alexis used (if he did not coin) ὡνέτης, a form hitherto unknown to the lexica, in place of the standard Attic form ὡνητής (ὀνήτης z), in comedy at Antiphanes 159(161K).7. The reason for Alexis' choice of an abnormality here is obscure: metrical convenience and humorous word-play are merely two possibilities. The formation itself is unobjectionable: ὡνέτης will relate to ὡνέομαι in the way that e.g. αἱρετής, γαμέτης, ἐπαινέτης, οἰκέτης relate to verbs in -έω; and although the economy of popular usage would normally act against the duplication of forms in both -ετης and -ητης from the same stem, we find (for instance) in Euripides both εὐνέτης (*Or.* 1392) and εὐνήτης (*Med.* 159, but see J. Diggle, *CQ* 33 (1983) 346f.); οἰκητής (S. *OR* 1450, Pl. *Phd.* 111b) occurs at the side of, but in a different sense from, οἰκέτης; and ἡγέτης (epigram 1035.13 Kaibel, [Orph.] *Hymn.* 52.7, Agathias in *Anth. Pal.* 6.167) is a metrically convenient alternative to ἡγητής (A. *Suppl.* 239). The fullest discussion of formations in -ετης and -ητης is still Ernst Fraenkel, *Geschichte der griechischen Nomina agentis* 2 (Strasbourg 1910) 124ff.; cf. also P. Chantraine, *La Formation des noms en grec ancien* (Paris 1933) 310ff., A. Debrunner, *Griechische Wortbildungslehre* (Heidelberg 1917) 170ff., Schwyzer 1.499ff., Buck–Petersen, *Reverse Index* 544ff.

Ἀχαΐς [1]

The play belongs to a (doubtless not homogeneous) class with titles indicating a woman's nationality (cf. the introduction to Ἀτθίς); the odds

---

[1] This spelling of the title is preferable to Ἀχαΐς, printed by Kassel–Austin. Kock's assertion (2.309) that *codices omnes* spell the title with two iotas was not true even at the time he wrote it; the Paris MS of Stob. 3.29.34 (citing Alexis 31(30K)) has ἀχλίδου (i.e. a corrupt expansion of ἀχαΐδ) with supralineal correction, and the Berlin and Zavorda MSS of Photius s.v. ἀγκύλη (p.18 Reitzenstein, 1.26 Theodoridis: citing fr. 32(31K)) have ἀχαΐδι. The form with one iota was already accepted in 4th-century Attic (cf. Schwyzer 1.265f.), in spite of the fact that the old Atticists supported forms in -αϊ- generally against those in -αϊ- (Phrynichus s.vv. Ἀλκαϊκόν ᾆσμα and ἀρχαϊκόν, pp. 62, 79 Fischer; the anon. 'Glossary of Useful Terms' in Bachmann, *Anecd.* 1.148.25ff.). But *nullus est fere locus in quo usus et consuetudo cum Grammaticorum praeceptis acrius contendat* (C. A. Lobeck's edition of Phrynichus (Leipzig 1820) 39); the inconsistent spellings that we find in medieval MSS (which may have

are that most of these dealt with the adventures of the titular heroine in another Greek city, which would often be Athens (cf. Körte in *RE* s.v. *Komödie* 1264.53ff.). The two frs. from Alexis' play tell us nothing about its plot, but the commonplace praise in 31(30K) of perseverance as the mother of invention would fit neatly into the monologue of a slave engaged in thinking out a clever scheme; in such a situation the Plautine Pseudolus meditates on the inventiveness of the poet (401ff.).

Ἀχαΐς has no firmly datable features, but E. Bignone (*RFIC* 2 (1924) 173f.; cf. Webster, *SLGC* 113, M. P. Paoletta, *AFLN* 26 (1983/84) 19ff.) detected a possibly Epicurean echo in the adjective συγγενικῶν at fr. 31(30K).7. The speaker there (see *ad loc.*) is cleverly applying (or *comically* misapplying) the language of contemporary philosophy to his own situation, but any link with Epicurus is far too tenuous for us to date this play on that account to the period after 306, when Epicurus was teaching in Athens.

Menander wrote an Ἀχαιοὶ ἢ Πελοποννήσιοι (see *P.Oxy.* 2462), of which one brief fr. – probably from a divine prologue commenting on the sad changes of fortune of a major character – survives (fr. 113 Austin, *CGFP* p. 129). A mosaic from Ulpia Oescus of the 3rd century AD portrays a scene from the play. Its single title Ἀχαιοί and the playwright's name can be read clearly, and three of its four figures can be identified as a soldier and two other young men; the fourth has been variously described as an old man and a *kore*. Nothing in the picture or the fr. conflicts with the hypothesis that Menander's play was a typical product of New Comedy with plot and characters drawn from the standard repertoire (cf. especially C. Corbato, *Studi menandrei* (Trieste 1965) 64ff., Webster, *MINC*[1,2] 167f. (XMI), Charitonidis and others, *Mosaïques* 98f. and plate 27.1).

31 (30K)

Meineke 3.397 (1), Kock 2.309. Edmonds 2.388, Kassel–Austin 2.41. The theme of the fr., that 'Nothing's so hard, but search (and hard work) will find it out', is a comic cliché; cf. Philemon 37 πάντ' ἔστιν ἐξευρεῖν, ἐὰν μὴ τὸν πόνον | φεύγῃ τις, ὃς πρόσεστι τοῖς ζητουμένοις, com. adesp. fr. 1264 Kock = Men. fr. 935 = trag. adesp. fr. 526 Kannicht–Snell (cited by Stob. *Anth.* 3.29.27 without lemma) ἅπανθ' ὁ τοῦ ζητοῦντος εὑρίσκει πόνος. Thus formulated the idea combines two strands of popular belief that can

---

been partly caused by confusion between α and αι in early minuscule: cf. the introduction to Ἑπτὰ ἐπὶ Θήβαις) were just as much a feature of Attic inscriptions at all periods (Meisterhans–Schwyzer 33, Threatte 1.287ff.).

COMMENTARY

be traced back to early Greek poetry: 'seek, and ye shall find' (cf. Xenophanes в 18 Diels–Kranz χρόνῳ ζητοῦντες ἐφευρίσκουσιν ἄμεινον and the (?) Theognidean aphorism πεῖρα δ' ἄριστον 571), and the praise of hard work rammed home in Hes. *Op.* The popularity of themes closely related to that of Alexis here can be judged from the number of excerpts that Stobaeus is able to include, more or less relevantly, in the section περὶ φιλοπονίας from which this fr. of Alexis derives; in comedy one may note Anaxandrides 64(63K), Damoxenus 2.9–11, Men. *Dysk.* 862f. (remodelling S. *OR* 110f.), fr. 526, Philemon 174(238K), com. adesp. fr. 532 Kock and Ter. *HT* 675 (the 'Plautine' verse cited by Herwerden, *Obs. Crit.* 68 and Kock); outside comedy e.g. Eur. *Ion* 575, Chaeremon fr. 21, trag. adesp. fr. 509 Kannicht–Snell and Gow on Theoc. 15.62.

1 At the beginning of this fr. ὅτι πάντα, the reading of all the MSS here (Stob. 3.29.34) except π (*Parisinius gr.* 3012, see D. Serruys, *Rev. Phil.* 35 (1911) 328), is likely to be correct. The excerptor doubtless snipped off introductory words such as λέγουσιν οἱ σοφώτατοι; cf. Plaut. *Capt.* 304, where the speaker introduces a platitude with *sed uiden? fortuna humana fingit artatque ut lubet.* In place of ὅτι πάντα the *Parisinus* has ἅπαντα, which was later conjectured by Meineke (3.398) and is now printed by Kassel–Austin; it represents exactly the sort of tidying up done by excerptors and scribes in order to make their quotations independent of an original context; cf. comm. on fr. 29.1.

2 προαποστῇς: i.e. 'you leave off too early'.

3–7 The speaker's *a fortiori* argument about human discoveries would be more illuminating if its context were known and the play precisely dated. The basis of the argument is the difference between τὰ θεῖα (sun and stars and their movements, vv. 4–6) and τὰ κοινωνικά (?: see below) καὶ συγγενικά (? shared things, things concerned with human relationships, vv. 6–7). An unsophisticated belief in the divinity of the heavenly bodies is traceable in popular Greek thought well back into the 5th century (M. P. Nilsson, *Harvard Theological Review* 33 (1940) 1ff., cf. Wilamowitz, *Glaube* 1.17), long before the dual impact on 4th-century Athens of the writings and teachings of Plato and Aristotle on the one hand, and the invasion of Babylonian astrology after Alexander's conquest of the east on the other (cf. A. Bouché-Leclercq, *L'Astrologie grecque* (Paris 1899) 35ff., F. V. M. Cumont in Dar.–Sag. s.v. *Zodiacus* 1046ff., H. Lloyd-Jones, *Myths of the Zodiac* (London 1978) 9ff.). In vv. 3–6, with the text as it now stands, Alexis' language, like that of Men. fr. 416 on a similar subject, is too general for profitable or convincing linkage with new philosophical ideas in Athens, although Bignone (*loc. cit.* in my introduction to 'Αχαΐς) drew attention to the way in which Aristotle similarly formulated the traditional concept of the dichotomy of substance between divine celestial bodies and mortal things of earth (*Metaph.* 12.8, 1074ᵃ38ff.,

ΑΧΑΪΣ

cf. *GA* 2.3, 736^b29ff.). Nor is there any overt reference here to matters
astrological, as there is e.g. in Alexis 263(261K) or Sosipater 1.25–29. But
in the last line of the fr. Alexis' use of the relatively uncommon word
συγγενικός may, as Bignone suggested, give us a small, tentative clue to
the fr.'s atmosphere of intellectual parody. In writers of the 5th and 4th
centuries, συγγενικός is used precisely and scientifically in senses closely
linked with those of the word from which it is derived, συγγενής: (1)
'congenital' (Hippocr. *Epid.* 3.1.6, cf. [Arist.] *Probl.* 4.18, 878^b27, Epicurus *Epist. Men.* 129 whence Diog. Laert. 10.129, Philodemus *Rhet.* 2.17 =
Nausiphanes fr. 2 Diels), (2) 'connected with the idea of kinship' (Arist.
Eth. Eud. 7.10, 1242^a1ff., *Magn. Mor.* 2.12, 1211^b19, cf. [Dem.] 25.89) and
(3) 'of the same γένος as something else' (Arist. *HA* 4.7, 531^b22 and 10.40,
623^b6). The present passage of Alexis *may* present us with a fourth sense,
roughly synonymous with that of κοινός to which the word is here
(corruptly, in my opinion: see on vv. 6–7) coupled in the MSS, 'general/
ordinary'. That sense would clearly be an extension of (3) above; that
which belongs in common with other things to one γένος is easily seen as a
common member of the γένος. Of writers earlier than or contemporary
with Alexis, Epicurus alone seems to use the word in this extended
meaning, *Epist. Hdt.* 72 αὐτὸ τὸ ἐνάργημα (sc. of time) ... συγγενικῶς
τοῦτο ἐπιφέροντας (so Bailey: ἐπιφέροντες Usener, περιφέροντες MSS)
ἀναλογιστέον. On the basis of this slender tie Bignone, Webster and
Paoletta (*locc. citt.* in introduction to Ἀχαΐς) argue that Alexis is here
parodying Epicurus' philosophical jargon; the idea is by no means
impossible, but it needs more than the available evidence to be persuasive.
Another possibility (that Alexis is using συγγενικός in sense (2) above,
'connected with kinship') is closely tied to my conjecture κοινωνικῶν in
v. 6 and so discussed at greater length below.

3 ηὑρήκασιν? See on fr. 9.2. Here, however, if Ἀχαΐς is a late play, the
orthography must be uncertain.

4–5 τοσούτῳ τῷ τόπῳ ἀπέχοντες: the MSS reading (with τῷ added
by A²), but unlikely Greek for two reasons. (1) The normal construction
would be τοσοῦτον τοῦ τόπου ἀπέχοντες (cf. Pl. *Parm.* 145b ἀλλὰ μὴν
τό γε μέσον ἴσον τῶν ἐσχάτων ἀπέχει; *TGL* s.v. ἀπέχω), and a dative such
as τοσούτῳ is found (as dative of the measure of difference) only in the
presence of a comparative or superlative adjective or adverb (K.G. 1.440f.,
Schwyzer 2.163f.). (2) τοσοῦτος normally takes attributive position in
both classical and *Koine* Greek (K.G. 1.630f., Gildersleeve, *Syntax* 2.269f.,
Schwyzer 2.210, Blass–Debrunner–Funk § 274; e.g. Pl. *Apol.* 25e, Dem.
18.305 with some doubt about the reading, N.T. *Apoc.* 18.17, *P.Oxy.*
532.8–9 2nd cent. AD, *BGU* 180.14–15 2nd/3rd cent. AD, *P.Leipzig* 64.42
4th cent. AD). The oft-quoted Thuc. 6.44.1 τοσαύτη ἡ πρώτη διασκευὴ
πρὸς τὸν πόλεμον διέπλει is only an apparent exception; here τοσαύτη is

131

COMMENTARY

predicative in a sentence that telescopes two clauses ('so great was the first force that ...'); yet a few instances of τοσοῦτος in predicative position without obvious predicative force do occur (e.g. Heliodorus 1.32, 2.8).[1] Hirschig's τοσοῦτον (or -οῦτο: so Herwerden, *Obs. Crit.* 68[2]) is one step towards a solution, but it leaves the dative τῷ τόπῳ still unexplained. Alexis might have written τοσοῦτον τοῦ τόπου ('being so far distant from the spot', sc. where the sun and stars are), and then corruption would originally have been caused by a confusion between ου and ω that is common at all periods, with subsequent assimilation of the ending of τοσοῦτον. But prudence demands here an obelised text.

5 ἄστρων ἐπιτολάς, δύσεις, τροπάς: ἐπιτολάς, the season of the year when various constellations first appear in the sky (e.g. Thuc. 2.78, Eur. *Phoen.* 1116, Sosipater 1.26–27); δύσεις, the season of their final disappearance from the sky (e.g. A. *Ag.* 826, *P.V.* 458); τροπάς, the time of the astral solstices (e.g. Pl. *Tim.* 39d, Arist. *HA* 5.9, 542[b]23, *Cael.* 2.14, 296[b]4). Cf. Damoxenus 2.16ff., a cook ridiculing the alleged relevance of astral phenomena to medicine (cf. Hippocr. *Aer.* 1f., Dohm, *Mageiros* 175f.).

6–7 The combined MSS tradition, τῶν κοινῶν | καὶ συγγενικῶν, omits a word (or part of a word) scanning ◡ ⊔ at the end of v. 6. There is no lacuna in the sense, however, and the supplements that have been proposed in modern times are colourless stopgaps, such as ποτε and ἔτι (Bücheler), ἅμα and βροτοῖς (Hense), <τε> καὶ | <τῶν> (Grotius, *Dict. Poet.* 129). Most editors of comedy print instead the κάτω that was added in A supralineally by a second hand, as if it represented part of the textual tradition; in fact it is either a Byzantine conjecture, rather better than most which disfigure this MS (cf. Hense's edition of Stob. *Anth.*3.p.xxxvi), or (more probably: cf. T. Dorandi in Flores 402) a scribe's indication that a correction or supplement had been written 'below' in the lower margin of that MS or one of its ancestors. Of the conjectures listed one is manifestly less probable than the others (βροτοῖς hardly fits a context where the word's poetical or self-pitying overtones are absent, and its idea is otiose given the presence of ἄνθρωπον in v. 7), but all share the same – admittedly not crucial – weakness: there is no obvious reason why any of

---

[1] On the similar rule for the position of τοιοῦτος see (in addition to the lexica and grammars) Handley on Men. *Dysk.* 164.

[2] Though the neuter form in -ον is normal in Attic (Schwyzer 1.406, Blass–Debrunner–Funk § 64.4), both forms appear in both classical and Hellenistic Greek. MSS evidence is very unreliable with prose authors (K.B. 1.606f.), but the Menander papyri, which give τοσοῦτον four times (*Asp.* 401, *Epitr.* 437, *Pk.* 543, 1004) and τοσοῦτο twice (*Asp.* 240, *Dysk* 402), are supported in all but one case (*Asp.* 240 *anceps*) by the metre.

these supplements should have been omitted by a copyist in the first place. I am tempted therefore (cf. my earlier cockshy in Flores 369f.) to try another explanation of the lacuna. Could Alexis have written not κοινῶν but κοινω<νικῶ>ν? Corruption would be easily explained as a further example (cf. comm. on 148(144K).1) of 'telescopic' error, where the scribe runs together the beginning of one and the ending of the same or next word; here too a psychological factor could have been involved, since a scribe might have expected to see κοινῶν written directly before a word (συγγενικῶν) that in meanings 3 and 4 discussed above was virtually synonymous with κοινῶν. If κοινωνικῶν is right, it would add to the parody of philosophical language already noted in συγγενικῶν. κοινωνικός also is a favourite word of the philosophers, ranging in sense almost imperceptibly from 'social' (because held or shared in common) to 'sociable' (Arist. *Eth. Nic.* 8.14, 1161^{b}14, *Eth. Eud.* 7.10, 1242^{a}25, *Pol.* 3.13, 1283^{a}38 etc., Epicurus fr. 525 Usener = Arrian *Epict.* 1.23.1). The speaker's point becomes slightly different, perhaps subtler. Alexis would be playing deliberately on the wide range of meaning possessed by both συγγενικός and κοινωνικός. Thus συγγενικῶν would be both 'ordinary' (to underline the contrast with the preceding five and a half lines) and '(things) affecting one's kin' (i.e. sense 2 in the discussion on vv. 3–7); and a mention of 'things shared in common and affecting one's kin' would fit the scenario (cf. introduction to Ἀχαΐς) most wittily if a cunning slave's scheme were designed (say) to help a blood-relation of his young master. Yet we are still unable to pin down the precise parodic reference. Is it merely to the fondness of philosophers from the late 5th century on down to Aristotle and Epicurus for the jargon of -ικός compounds (cf. the similar assaults by Aristophanes, *Nub.* 483, 728, 1172f., *Equ.* 1378ff., *Vesp.* 1209; C. W. Peppler, *AJP* 31 (1910) 428ff.)? Or is it to current philosophical concepts of συγγενικὴ καὶ κοινωνικὴ φιλία? One cannot be sure; but whatever the correct answers may have been, an apt comparison to Alexis' present techniques would be Men. *Epitr.* 1084ff., where Onesimos makes effective comic capital out of a farrago of philosophical ideas, Peripatetic and Epicurean perhaps included (Webster, *SM* 196f., A. Barigazzi, *La formazione spirituale di Menandro* (Turin 1965) 192ff.; more judiciously, Gomme–Sandbach *ad loc.*).

32 (31K)

Meineke 3.398 (II), Kock 2.309, Edmonds 2.390, Kassel–Austin 2.42. It is futile to try to make this fr. (whose context is unknown) scan by supplementing and emending the transmitted text or altering the word-order, as Meineke, Bothe (*PCGF* 525), Kock, Blaydes (*Adv.* 2.154), Edmonds and V. Schmidt (in Kassel–Austin) do in various ways and metres. The fr. is cited by Photius (s.v. ἀγκύλη, p. 18 Reitzenstein, 1.26 Theodoridis) and the *Lexicon Seguerianum* (1.23.10ff. Bachmann, 337.30ff. Bekker), whose lexicographical entries commonly preserve the key word or phrase of a citation accurately (here ἀγκύλην τῆς ἐμβάδος: not surprisingly, these words scan), but add from its context only those words which help to produce intelligible sense. Cf. my comm. on 194(189K).2–3.

ἀγκύλην τῆς ἐμβάδος: cf. A. A. Bryant, *HSCP* 10 (1899) 81, in *RE* Amelung s.v. 'Εμβάς 2482.27ff. and Hug s.v. *Schuh* 751.19ff., P. Paris in Dar.–Sag. s.v. *Embas* 593A ff., Ussher on Ar. *Eccl.* 47, Gomme–Sandbach, *Comm.* on Men. fr. 97. ἐμβάς is a general word for any boot or shoe as opposed to a sandal, but is applied particularly to one type of hard-wearing outdoor shoe, perhaps originating in Thrace (cf. M. Bieber, *Griechische Kleidung* (Berlin and Leipzig 1928) 28) and worn in classical Athens mainly by the poorer classes (Ar. *Vesp.* 1157, *Eccl.* 633, 850, Isaeus 5.11). It was usually made of leather, and a distinguishing feature was its fastening, which consisted as in some modern male shoes of a (leather) thong looped and knotted (Paris has useful illustrations). These thongs or laces were naturally called ἱμάντες (e.g. Men. fr. 97.3–4 ὑποδούμενος τὸν ἱμάντα . . . τῆς δεξιᾶς | ἐμβάδος ἀπέρρηξ'), and although Hesychius loosely identifies ἀγκύλαι (s.v.) as ἱμάντες ἐν κρηπῖσιν, the two words were not exact synonyms. In its various uses ἀγκύλη always means something bent or looped (LSJ s.v.: e.g. bend of arm or knee, loop of a javelin thong or dog leash, hook), and correspondingly with reference to boot or shoe fastenings ἀγκύλαι will have been ἱμάντες looped (as a fixture or temporarily) for fastening.

Βόστρυχος

The implication of the title is obscure. A lock of hair was a recognition token in A. *Choeph.* 168ff., 226ff. (cf. Eur. *El.* 91, 515ff., Ar. *Nub.* 534ff., Hähnle 19), and Glykera's haircut began the plot complications of Men. *Pk.* (172f.).

33 (32K)

Meineke 3.398, Kock 2.309, Edmonds 2.390, Kassel–Austin 2.42. The Antiatticist's note (115.12 Bekker) cites Alexis for the use of ὑποκροῦσαι simply in the sense of 'to hinder' (ἐμποδίσαι). What accounted for his entry and citation it is hard to say: hardly opposition to the views of stricter Atticists, for Phrynichus listed the word in *Praep. Soph.* 118.1 de Borries without any injunction against its use. Phrynichus there defines its meaning with greater precision than our text of the Antiatticist:

ΒΟΣΤΡΥΧΟΣ

ὑποκρούειν τοὺς ῥήτορας· τὸ μεταξὺ λεγόντων αὐτῶν ὑποφθεγγόμενον ἐμποδίζειν, i.e. 'to heckle'. This definition fits perfectly the known Attic usages of the word: Ar. *Ach.* 38 βοᾶν ὑποκρούειν λοιδορεῖν τοὺς ῥήτορας (clearly Phrynichus' source passage), *Eccl.* 256, 588, 596, Heniochus 5.4; cf. [Pl.] *Eryx.* 395e (= 'interject', intransitive). Alexis' use of what was probably a colloquialism is unlikely to have differed from these.

Βρεττία[1]

Meineke 1.398, cf. Kaibel in *RE* s.v. *Alexis* 9, 1470.20ff., P. Poccetti, ΑΙὼΝ 9 (1987) 227ff. 'The Bruttian Girl' carries on the series of titles indicating a woman's nationality. Here again the scanty frs. afford no valuable clues to the plot, although fr. 35(34K), a general comment on the mutability of fortune, leads one to expect a context in which the circumstances of one or more characters have changed for the worse. Kaibel's suggestion (cf. also Poccetti 237) that the choice of title may have been influenced by Alexis' South-Italian origins is interesting but sterile so long as information about the plot is virtually non-existent.

34 (33K)

Meineke 3.398 (I), Kock 2.309, Edmonds 2.390, Kassel–Austin 2.43. A conversation between two unidentified characters in an unknown context.

---

[1] Βρεττία appears to be the correct Greek orthography (so MSS MA of Stob. *Anth.* 4.41.4 citing Alexis 35(34K), Steph. Byz. s.v. Βρέττος (*sic*), Strabo 6.1.1–5 and *passim*, Appian *BC* 4.43, Diod. Sic. 12.22, the rhetorical lexicon in Bekker, *Anecd.* 1.223.18f., *Et. Mag.* 213.7 Gaisford). The orthography Βρούττιος, which occurs in authors of Roman imperial times (Ptol. *Geog.* 3.1.9, 74, Appian *BC* 5.19 most MSS but βρηττίων V), is clearly a transliteration of the Latin *Bruttius*. The spelling variations that commonly turn up in MSS are easily explained as corruptions from one of these two forms (βρετια H at Hesych. s.v. Βρεττία (Δ 1112), cf. PX at Diod. Sic. 16.15, Βρετίωνος *Et. Mag.* 213.8 Gaisford, βρεττaιων H at Hesych. *loc. cit.*, βρηττίων V at Appian *BC* 5.19; βρευτία A at Ath. 14.650c citing Alexis 34(33K), corrected by Daléchamp, cf. Casaubon, *Animadv.* 927), or as hybrids conceived illegitimately from a fusion of Βρέττιοι and Βρεντέσιον, the Greek form of *Brundisium* (Βρέντιοι Σ Ptol. *Geog.* 3.1.9, Hesych. s.v. (Δ 1105), Dionysius Periegeta 362). Kock invents a further illegitimate form at Antiphanes 47(45K).1: Βρυττικήν in place of A's βρυτικήν (Ath. 11.485b), which Meineke correctly interpreted as 'beery'. Kock's objection to the form βρυτικός is groundless: cf. the parallel formations οἰνικός and ὑδατικός (cf. LSJ s.v.).

COMMENTARY

2–3 Pears (ἀπίους here are cultivated pears: Hehn, *Kulturpflanzen* 626, 628, Olck in *RE* s.v. *Birnbaum* 492.34, Gow on Theoc. 7.120) were kept firm, clean and cool also in ancient times by being served in cold water. Pherecrates 8 refers to the practice: πρὶν ἀνακυκῆσαι τὰς ἀπίους ἁρπάζετε (sc. you are so greedy and uncouth that 'you snatch the pears before stirring' the water), the implication being that civilised Athenians, unlike the Ἄγριοι of Pherecrates' title, always stirred the water (presumably to wash the fruit around, as J. Toup, *Curae posteriores, sive Appendicula notarum atque emendationum in Theocritum* (London 1772) 7.15 suggested) before selecting a pear.

As corrections of A's πεινουσιν here (where a dot above the epsilon may indicate deletion: Ath. 14.650c), both Dobree's πίνουσιν (*Adv.* 2.137) and Casaubon's πεινῶσιν (cf. *Animadv.* 927) satisfy palaeographic canons; but at Athenian parties pears were not eaten at the beginning of a meal when the guests were still hungry and unwined, but as part of the δεύτεραι τράπεζαι at the end when serious drinking had begun (Mau in *RE* s.v. *Comissatio* 611.7ff., C. Morel in Dar.–Sag. s.v. *Coena* 1275B; note Matron in Ath. 4.137b = *SH* 534.111ff.).

3 ἐν ὕδατι; **(B.)** πολλὰ πολλάκις: Meineke's part-division and correction of A's undistributed ἐν ὕδατι πολλῷ· πολλάκις (the fr. is omitted in Epit.) is rightly printed by Kassel–Austin; cf. my discussion in *Hermes* 93 (1966) 299f., where the arguments in its favour are fully stated. The MS reading is objectionable on two counts. The point at issue is not the amount of water in which the pears are floating, but the frequency with which the custom described has been observed by the two speakers; secondly, the common idiom of juxtaposing for emphasis in one sentence two words of the same root, which has often been noticed in the case of πολύς and πολλ- stems (see Lobeck, *Paralipomena* 1.56 and LSJ s.v. πολύς II.6 for a list of examples), is an argument for taking πολλῷ (or whatever part of πολύς may have been corrupted into this) πολλάκις together. Hence Meineke's πολλὰ πολλάκις and Kock's πολλοῖς πολλάκις (both assigned to character B), which meet the two objections. Meineke's conjecture, however, is more likely to have been corrupted by a scribe unfamiliar with an Attic idiom that has escaped the notice of most commentators: the use of πολλὰ πολλάκις as a more emphatic substitute for πολλάκις. Doubtless this idiom originated with πολλά syntactically integrated into the sentence, but eventually the phrase came to be felt as an adverbial unit with the accusative force of πολλά virtually forgotten. Four Attic instances of the locution may be cited: Eur. *Med.* 1165f. δώροις ὑπερχαίρουσα, πολλὰ πολλάκις | τένοντ' ἐς ὀρθὸν ὄμμασι σκοπουμένη, where the sentence structure is similar to that of Alexis here; *Tro.* 1015 καίτοι σ' ἐνουθέτουν γε πολλὰ πολλάκις, where πολλά can (but perhaps ought not to) be explained as internal object of ἐνουθέτουν; Ar. *Eccl.* 1105 ὅμως δ' ἐάν τι πολλὰ πολλάκις πάθω; and *Thesm.* 287f. πολλὰ πολλάκις μέ σοι | θύειν ἔχουσαν, where a few commentators correctly interpret πολλὰ πολλάκις as purely adverbial. If this expression was felt to be colloquial, the analogous πολλὰ πολλαχῇ of S. *OC* 1626 was possibly a more poetical replacement. Cf. H. Thesleff, *Studies on Intensification in Early and Classical Greek* (Helsinki 1954) 174, B. Gygli-Wyss, *Das nominale Polyptoton im älteren Griechisch* (Göttingen 1966) 35f.

6 A's corruption δη ὄντι may have originated in a misreading of the minuscule compendium for δηλονότι (ΔΗᴸ); if the supralineal lambda was ill-written, smudged or damaged, a scribe might easily have misinterpreted its angled strokes with the following dash as abbreviations of ον (ᴸ) and τι (·|·) respectively; cf. Cobet, *NL* 38, and comm. on fr. 177(173K).14.

35 (34K)

Meineke 3.399 (II), Kock 2.310, Edmonds 2.390, Kassel–Austin 2.43; cf. M. Kokolakis, Μορφολογία τῆς κυβευτικῆς μεταφορᾶς (Athens 1965) 86ff., G. Vogt-Spira, *Dramaturgie des Zufalls* (Munich 1992) 54f. The speaker, contemplating presumably some recent or portended reversal of fortune, compares the experiences of human life to the fall of dice. The simile was a commonplace, developed by many writers with varied abilities and purposes. The closest counterpart to Alexis' simple equation is an anonymous imitator of Callimachus (*P.Oxy.* 1794; Powell, *Coll. Alex.* 78f., Page, *GLP* no. 122):

ἄλλοτε γὰρ ἄλλοις ὄλβου λάχος ἀνθρώποισιν·
οἵη τοι πεσσοῖο δίκη, τοίηδε καὶ ὄλβου·
πεσσὸς ἀμειβόμενος ποτὲ μὲν τοῖς, ἄλλοτε τοῖσιν
εἰς ἀγαθὸν πίπτει καὶ ἀφνεὸν αἶψα τίθησι
πρόσθεν ἀνολβείοντ', εὐηφενέοντα δ' ἄνολβον,

where πεσσός = κύβος; cf. [Aristaen.] *Epist.* 1.23. Rather different is Pl. *Resp.* 10.604c, arguing that in misfortune grief hinders reflection, τῷ βουλεύεσθαι ... περὶ τὸ γεγονὸς καὶ ὥσπερ ἐν πτώσει κύβων πρὸς τὰ πεπτωκότα τίθεσθαι τὰ αὑτοῦ πράγματα, ὅπῃ ὁ λόγος αἱρεῖ βέλτιστ' ἂν ἔχειν, where the spotlight is focused not simply on the comparison between life and the chance fall of dice (to that extent Plut. *Mor.* 467a κυβείᾳ ... ὁ Πλάτων τὸν βίον ἀπείκασεν is misleading), but rather on man's rational organisation of his affairs in the light of fortune's blows. In Ter. *Ad.* 739–41 (here almost certainly a faithful rendering of the Menandrean original: cf. O. Rieth, *Die Kunst Menanders in den 'Adelphen' des Terenz* (Hildesheim 1964) 95) Micio adopts the Platonic position: *ita uitast hominum quasi quom ludas tesseris:* | *si illud quod maxume opus est iactu non cadit,* | *illud quod cecidit forte, id*

COMMENTARY

arte ut corrigas. Here (as elsewhere: see the introduction to fr. 222(219K)) the contrast between Menander and Alexis is illuminating; Alexis points his theme elegantly without saying anything original or profound, but Menander operates at a less superficial level. Kokolakis discusses fully (55ff.) the origin and earlier treatments of these and related themes. The direct comparison between life and the hazards of dice play, as we find it in Alexis and the Hellenistic poet, does not occur in earlier authors now extant, although it would be surprising if Alexis were its πρῶτος εὑρετής; the Platonic and Menandrean formulation, however, is anticipated in a fr. of Sophocles (861 Nauck, 947 Pearson and Radt): στέργειν δὲ τἀκπεσόντα καὶ θέσθαι πρέπει | σοφὸν κυβευτήν, ἀλλὰ μὴ στένειν τύχην; cf. A. *Ag.* 32f. and Stob. *Anth.* 4.56.39 (a saying attributed to Socrates).

κύβοι are six-sided dice (cf. especially Lamer in *RE* s.v. *Lusoria tabula* 1935.34ff.), used sometimes by themselves and sometimes in association with board games.

1–3 Punctuate not after κύβοι (so traditionally up to and including Kassel–Austin), but with Wakefield (*Silv. Crit.* 4.141) after ἐστίν (cf. Nauck, *MGR* 5 (1884) 235f., Kock 3.741, Herwerden, *Coll. Crit.*122, Edmonds); thereby the flow of sense and syntax is much improved: 'That's what life is like; just as dice don't always fall in the same way, the same pattern doesn't last in our daily life either, it undergoes changes'. Thus τοιοῦτο as predicate refers to something in the lost preceding context, and ὥσπερ introduces the following clause asyndetically as elsewhere in good Attic writers (e.g. Pl. *Resp.* 8.557c, *Gorg.* 448e (the second ὥσπερ); K.G. 2.344f.).

Βωμός

In later comedy altars are generally a place of refuge for fugitive slaves, both male (Men. *Perinth.*, com. adesp. fr. 239 Austin = *P.Berlin* 11771 sometimes attributed to Alexis but see 'False or Doubtful Attributions' v, pp. 833ff. below, Plaut. *Most.* 1094ff.) and female (Plaut. *Rud.* 688ff. with H. Drexler, *Philologus Suppl.* 26 (1934) 46ff., probably Men. *Sik.*). Cf. also O. Crusius, *Philologus* 46 (1888) 610, F. Schmidt, *De supplicum ad aram confugientium partibus scenicis* (Diss. Königsberg 1911) 75ff., 83f., 95.

36 (35K)

Meineke 3.399, Kock 2.310, Edmonds 2.390, Kassel–Austin 2.44.

γυνὴ λινουργός: cf. Blümner, *Technologie* 191ff. She was probably a slave, like the women described as ταλασιουργοί in inscriptions (*IG* ii².1553–78, on which see M. N. Tod, *Epigraphica* 12 (1950) 5 and *passim*). What the woman 'lit upon and stole away' is uncertain: could it have been a young child from its parents or an attendant (cf. Men. *Sik.* 3ff. and Sandbach *ad loc.*, Plaut. *Capt.* 8ff., *Men.* 31ff., *Poen.* 64ff, *Rud.* 39ff., Ter. *Eun.* 519ff.)?

Γαλάτεια

Meineke 1.390 (cf. 1.254f.), Kock 2.310, G. Holland, *Leipziger Studien* 7 (1884) 218ff., Breitenbach 158f., F. Vierlinger, *Die Gestalt des Kyklopen Polyphemos in der griechischen und römischen Dichtung* (Diss. Vienna 1939) 90ff., G. Schiassi, *Rend. Ist. Lomb.* 88 (1955) 118f., Nesselrath, *MK* 295. Breitenbach's suggestion that Alexis' play treated the adventures of a (? fictitious) *hetaira* named Galatea (cf. Bechtel, *Frauennamen* 73) is inherently less likely than the more generally accepted theory of Meineke that it travestied the myth of Polyphemus and Galateia. This myth (cf. Holland 139–312: still the fullest judicious account of the literary sources; in *RE* Weicker s.v. *Galateia* 1, 517.34ff., Wüst s.v. *Odysseus* 1956.6ff., Scherling s.v. *Polyphemos* 2, 1812.26ff.; in Roscher Weizsäcker s.v. *Galateia* 1, 1586.51ff., Sauer s.v. *Polyphemos* 2, 2700.46ff.; Robert, *GH* 3.2.2.1351ff., J. Glenn, *G and R* 19 (1972) 47ff.) was apparently first set down in literary form when Philoxenus composed his dithyramb Κύκλωψ ἢ Γαλάτεια (so Duris, *FGrH* 76 F 58 = Σ Theoc. 6, introduction 'f' p. 189 Wendel) shortly before 388, when this poem was parodied by Aristophanes in the *Plutus*. The frs. of Philoxenus' dithyramb are scanty (Page, *PMG* 423ff.), and its treatment of the myth in several important details obscure (Holland 184ff., H. Schönewolf, *Der jungattische Dithyrambos* (Diss. Giessen 1938) 52ff., Holzinger on Ar. *Plut.* pp. 110f., 117ff., P. Maas in *RE* s.v. *Philoxenos* 23, 192.41ff., J. Mewaldt, *AAWW* 83 (1946) 279ff., Webster, *SLGC* 20f., Pickard-Cambridge, *DTC²* 47f.). Yet it is clear that in his poem Philoxenus combined the traditional story of Odysseus' imprisonment in the cave of the Cyclops with the new one of Polyphemus' infatuation for the nymph Galatea.

A tradition that can be traced back at least to the second half of the 4th century (Ath. 1.6f–7a citing Phaenias fr. 13 Müller and Wehrli; Σ Ar. *Plut.* 290, first Tzetzes recension, edited by L. M. Positano; cf. Hermesianax, *Leontion* fr. 7.69–74 Powell) alleges that Philoxenus' poem was a political allegory in which Polyphemus stood for the tyrant Dionysius I of Syracuse, the nymph Galatea for a human namesake who was an αὐλητρίς and Dionysius' mistress, and Odysseus for the poet himself, with the incidents of the myth so organised as to commemorate the poet's seduction of the real-life Galatea and his subsequent imprisonment by Dionysius in the quarries of Syracuse. Holland, followed by some later scholars, accepts this tradition as historical. Other ancient authorities (Diod. Sic. 15.6, Plut. *Mor.* 334c, Lucian *Indoct.* 15, Aristides 2.309 Dindorf = 2.236 Jebb, *Suda* s.vv. ἀπαγέ με and εἰς λατομίας; cf. the second Tzetzes recension of Σ Ar. *Plut.* 290), however, maintain that Philoxenus' imprisonment was due rather to Philoxenus' tactless criticism of Dionysius' own poetry. The problem with literary anecdotes is that plausible fictions often sound more authentic than tedious truth. Philoxenus lacks an extant Boswell, and we simply do not have the evidence to decide whether either of the two traditions is correct. Perhaps the likeliest interpretation of events is that sketched by Webster. This makes Philoxenus' dithyramb an unallegorical treatment of the myth[1] and explains the tradition presented in Phaenias as a Peripatetic aberration (cf. Robert, *loc. cit.*) which arose when its originator misconstrued as gospel truth some burlesque on the Athenian comic stage which parodied Philoxenus' poem by identifying the poet as Odysseus, inventing the story of Philoxenus' amour to suit the story in the dithyramb and travestying the short-sighted Dionysius as Polyphemus. Thus Philoxenus' imprisonment in the Syracusan quarries – if that ever was a historical fact – could have been burlesqued as Odysseus' confinement in the Cyclops' cave. To be effective such a burlesque would have had to be written when memories of the dithyramb were fresh and Dionysius an object of active scorn. Of the known Athenian comedies only Antiphanes' Κύκλωψ, Eubulus' Διονύσιος and Nicochares' Γαλάτεια could have filled this bill. Unfortunately the evidence provided by the frs. of these three plays is insufficient for any of them to be named with confidence as the source of the Peripatetic inaccuracy.

Alexis' Γαλάτεια, on the other hand, must have been written at a time when an attack on Dionysius I was pointless and a travesty of Philoxenus' dithyramb as stale as yesterday's beer. Philoxenus died in 380 or 379, and Dionysius I in 367. There is no compelling argument for dating the beginning of Alexis' dramatic career before the 350s (see the introduction

---

[1] In 388, when Aristophanes' *Plutus* was produced, Athens was fighting Sparta, and the Spartan fleet was reinforced by contingents from Syracuse. As Athens' enemy, Dionysius became a fit target for Attic comedians. At a slightly later date (so Webster, *SLGC* 28; contrast Hunter 116f.) Eubulus devoted his Διονύσιος to an attack on, or ridicule of, the tyrant. Ephippus 16 casts scorn on the literary abilities of Dionysius (cf. Diod. Sic. 15.6, Stephanus on Arist. *Rhet.* 3.2, p. 314.21ff. Rabe, Lucian *Indoct.* 15, Σ Ar. *Plut.* 290, second Tzetzes recension). In the *Plutus* itself Aristophanes refers to Dionysius in terms that imply condemnation. Is it then likely that if Philoxenus' dithyramb had been a political allegory against the tyrant, Aristophanes would have utterly ignored this aspect in his parody of it?

to this edition, I.iii). Even if the present play came early in Alexis' career,[1] references to Dionysius I and Philoxenus would already have become rather *passé*.

The extant frs. are easily interpreted (*pace* Breitenbach 159 and Nesselrath, *MK* 295) in terms of a non-political myth travesty, perhaps owing nothing more to Philoxenus than the general story. In fr. 37(36K) a slave (θεράπων: A in Ath. 12.544e so identifies the speaker) narrates the experiences of his master when young as a student of the Cyrenaic philosopher, the elder Aristippus. The fr.'s tone and its casual use of ἐνταῦθα in v. 3 together suggest that it derives from the prologue just after the play's scene had been revealed. This was probably Sicily, and the speaker's master Polyphemus (cf. Holland 219f., Schiassi 118). The anachronism by which a figure of myth is turned into the student of a recent philosopher accords well with the practice of Middle-Comedy burlesque, and is employed elsewhere by Alexis in his Λίνος (q.v.: cf. Webster, *SLGC* 16ff., 85, Nesselrath, *MK* 236, cf. 209ff., 218ff., 227ff.); here it contains an element of gross wit. Post-Homeric myths localise Polyphemus in the area of Sicily around Mt Etna; the elder Aristippus is known to have spent some considerable time in Syracuse (see on fr. 37(36K).4). What could be more natural for a comedian than to imagine a Polyphemus of his own time taking lessons from the famous visiting professor?

The remaining frs. of Alexis' play are negligible.

37 (36K)

Meineke 3.400 (1), Kock 2.311, Edmonds 2.392, Kassel–Austin 2.44; cf. Holland, *op. cit.* in introduction to Γαλάτεια, 218ff., R. Fenk, *Adversarii Platonis quomodo de indole ac moribus eius iudicaverint* (Diss. Jena 1913) 39, G. Giannantoni, *I Cirenaici* (Florence 1958) 34 n. 2, 193ff., E. Mannebach, *Aristippi et Cyrenaicorum fragmenta* (Leiden 1961) 2, Nesselrath, *LP* 377f., *MK* 295. The fr. is cited by Ath. 12.544e (all in A, vv. 1–8 δεσπότης abridged and paraphrased in Epit.); on its speaker and probable context, see the introduction to the play.

1 ὁ δεσπότης οὑμός: Polyphemus? – see introduction to Γαλάτεια. The postponement of γάρ to so late a position as seventh word or (what matters more) third phrase unit is a feature of comic (and also colloquial?) usage, although milder postponements, in which γάρ either remains second

---

[1] Alexis' Γαλάτεια cannot itself be dated more precisely than the period between the late 360s and the 340s, and even this dating is based on plausible but uncertain conclusions about Athenian responses to Aristippus of Cyrene (see on fr. 37(36K).3–4).

phrase unit (however many actual words precede) or occasionally is both third word and third phrase unit, occur in Attic tragedy and prose. In Alexis cf. also frs. 21.1, 28.1, 150(146K).6, 160(156K).4, 168(163K).3, 204(200K).4, 216(213K).3, 263(261K).8, 265(263K).4, 280(278K).4 and possibly also 140(135K).2 (but see comm. *ad loc*). K. J. Dover (*CQ* 35 (1985) 337f.) collects and usefully classifies the relevant passages; see also V. Coulon, *Quaestiones criticae in Aristophanis fabulas* (Diss. Strasbourg 1907) 154 on the Aristophanic instances and E. W. Handley at Men. *Dysk*. 66–68 (together with the Körte–Thierfelder *index verborum* appended to the Teubner edition of Menander, 2^2 (Leipzig 1959) 319) on the Menandrean. Cf. also Denniston, *GP* 95ff., Fraenkel on A. *Ag*. 222 and *Beob*. 49f., Jebb on S. *Phil*. 1451. On the similar (but perhaps slightly more restricted) postponement of δέ in comedy see comm. on fr. 4.1.

Blaydes' conjecture (*Adv.* 1.105) ὁ δεσπότης γὰρ περὶ λόγους οὑμός, with the aim of normalising the particle's position, *ought* to be an offence against palaeographical common law, since it replaces the abnormal but paralleled word order with one much more usual, in exactly the way that Byzantine and Renaissance scribes operate when corrupting a text (cf. W. Headlam, *CR* 16 (1902) 246f.). Yet the conjecture cannot be ignored; it eases the rhythm, its separation of ὁ δεσπότης from οὑμός affords a *raison d'être* for a *simplex ordo* corruption, and papyrus discoveries have at times confirmed similar, apparently unnecessary conjectures (cf. P. Maas, *Textual Criticism* (translated by B. Flower, Oxford 1958) 40, M. L. West, *Textual Criticism and Editorial Technique* (Stuttgart 1973) 55f.).

2 μειρακίσκος: the word (good Attic, despite the strictures of Thomas Magister: cf. Phrynichus *Ecl.* s.v. μείρακες καὶ μεῖραξ p. 78 Fischer, with the comments of Lobeck and Rutherford in their editions *ad loc.*, and Durham, *Vocabulary* 78) indicates an age older than that of a παῖς (cf. comm. on 167(162K).2) but before the bloom of youth has faded (cf. Pl. *Phdr*. 237b), i.e. the late teens. Cf. Gow on Machon 241, F. H. Sandbach, *PCPS* 193 (1967) 43 and *Comm. on Dysk*. 27, and L. Amundsen, *Symb. Osl.* 40 (1965) 7f.

2–3 φιλοσοφεῖν ἐπέθετο: for the construction cf. Isoc. 5.1, Pl. *Soph*. 242b (LSJ s.v. ἐπιτίθημι B.III). In this idiom the infinitive and the dative case are interchangeable (cf. Schwyzer 2.358ff.).

3 Κυρηναῖος here has the first syllable long, as Κυρήνη elsewhere in Attic (the town: Hermippus 63.4, a courtesan: Ar. *Thesm*. 98, *Ran*. 1328). At Alexis 241(239K).1 (q.v.) the same syllable appears to scan short, but the quoter there (Ath.12.510a) may have tampered with the word-order at the beginning of the fr. in order to introduce it more fancifully than usual. Outside Attic the length of the first syllable of Κυρήνη and its congeners is variable (short in Hesiod fr. 215.2 Merkelbach–West, Pind. *Pyth*. 4.2; long in Ap. Rhod. 2.500, Eratosthenes fr. 35.18 Powell, probably

ΓΑΛΑΤΕΙΑ

also Hermesianax fr. 7.95 Powell). One of the leading oscillators is Callimachus of Cyrene himself (short: *H.Ap.* 73, 94, *epigr.* 20.5, 21.2 Pfeiffer; long *H.Art.* 206, *epigr.* 13.2).[1]

3–4 The transposition of τις in the *Marcianus* (corrected by Schweighaeuser, cf. *Animadv.* 6.496) from after ἐνταῦθα to after Ἀρίστιππος is a typical *simplex ordo* corruption by a scribe who thought that τις qualified the name and not Κυρηναῖος; cf. W. Headlam, *CR* 16 (1902) 243ff., G. Thomson, *CQ* 15 (1965) 161ff. Jackson, *Marg. Scaen.* 228ff. cites Eur. *Phoen.* 885 (with Porson's correction) and *Rhes.* 460 for similar displacements of τις; the former is a possible, the latter a certain, instance. Translate 'There was in that place, as they say, a man of Cyrene, a brainy sophist.' The elder Aristippus (see, in addition to the works of Giannantoni and Mannebach cited at the head of comm. on this fr., also C. J. Classen, *Hermes* 86 (1958) 192ff., Nesselrath, *LP* 376ff.) is clearly the man referred to, the follower of Socrates who became a σοφιστής in the Platonic sense, a professional teacher of rhetoric and other subjects. Alexis here neatly inserts into his narrative allusions to the three things about Aristippus that seemed especially notable to his contemporaries: his quickness of mind (εὐφυής, v. 4: at this period a term applied particularly to those with a ready wit, cf. Isoc. 7.49 καὶ τοὺς εὐτραπέλους δὲ καὶ τοὺς σκώπτειν δυναμένους, οὓς νῦν εὐφυεῖς προσαγορεύουσιν, ἐκεῖνοι δυστυχεῖς ἐνόμιζον, 15.284, Theopompus in Ath. 6.260b–c = *FGrH* 115 F162; K. Wachsmuth, *Sillographorum Graecorum Reliquiae* (Leipzig 1885) 112), his fondness for a life ἐν πάσῃ τρυφῇ καὶ πολυτελείᾳ μύρων καὶ ἐσθήτων καὶ γυναικῶν (Ath. 12.544b: Alexis stigmatises this as incomparable licentiousness, v. 6), and the fact that πρῶτος τῶν Σωκρατικῶν μισθοὺς εἰσεπράξατο (Diog. Laert. 2.65, cf. 74; in v. 7 Alexis makes the student pay a comically exaggerated fee – but then all Athens presumably knew how expensive Aristippus' tastes were reputed to be!). Each of these features is noted, illustrated and epigrammatised by a host of ancient sources, now most conveniently arranged and docketed in Mannebach (3A–8B Aristippus' receipt of fees, 29–83B his cleverness and extravagance). Many of the anecdotes are localised in Syracuse at the court of 'Dionysius'; although their historicity may be individually dubious, the one problem that they collectively pose is whether Aristippus' residence in Sicily occurred during the reign of Dionysius I, Dionysius II, or both. Our sources here are vague or confused. A scholium on Lucian *Menippus* 13 (cf. Hegesander in Ath. 12.544c–d) identifies the tyrant as the elder Dionysius;

---

[1] But the published verse inscriptions from Cyrene have the first syllable long: G. Kaibel, *Epigrammata graeca ex lapidibus collecta* (Berlin 1878) 842a.1, *SEG* 9 (1944) 52 (190.3), G. Pugliese Carratelli and G. Morelli, *ASAA* 23/24 (1961/62) 257 (68.7).

Plut. *Dion.* 19 makes Aristippus meet Plato on his third visit to Sicily in 361 at the court of Dionysius II; and Lucian twice refers to Aristippus' visits to 'the tyrants' in the plural (*Vit. Auct.* 12, *Dial Mort.* 6(20).5); the question has been re-examined by Giannantoni 39ff., with a useful bibliography. It was suggested above (introduction to Γαλάτεια) that in v. 3 of this fr. ἐνταῦθα is probably Sicily, and that Alexis appears to be making comic capital out of Polyphemus' and Aristippus' Sicilian connections. Attempts to date the Γαλάτεια, however, on the basis of these references (e.g. Webster, *CQ* 2 (1952) 17, cf. *SLGC* 259, Edmonds 2.392 note b) face serious difficulties. Even if Alexis imagined Polyphemus to have been Aristippus' pupil during the latter's visit to Sicily in 361, we are still far from sure that Polyphemus was portrayed as a recent graduate and still young (indeed Holland's idea, 220, of an aged, lovesick Polyphemus in the play is attractively grotesque), or that Alexis intended to dress his mythical travesty in a cloak of historical verisimilitude. Nor can we assume from the fr. that Aristippus was still newsworthy, i.e. still active or recently dead (not that this would help much: the date of Aristippus' death is unknown, although he is unlikely to have survived long after 361), for the full, precise information that Alexis provided in this fr. could refer just as well to a celebrity dead some years before, about whom an audience would need to have its vague memories carefully jogged.[1] The only fair conclusion that may be drawn about the date of Γαλάτεια is that it was probably an early play written between (say) the late 360s and the 340s (cf. Holland 220).

4 ὣς φασ': 'as they (people in general) say', cf. also frs. 38(37K).1, 57(56K).2, 99(94K).4, 164(159K).2 and elsewhere in comedy Ar. *Lys.* 188, *Plut.* 11, fr. 596(580K).3, Eubulus 60.4 (after ἠκούσαμεν v. 1), probably Timocles 15(17K) (φασιν Musurus, φησιν A at Ath. 8.339d). In this and comparable idioms (e.g. (1) φασί in parenthesis, in comedy Antiphanes 173(175K).4, Philemon 103.5, Men. *Dysk.* 433, *Epitr.* 440, *Pk.* 291, perhaps fr. 447.2, cf. *Sam.* 503, R. Renehan, *HSCP* 75 (1971) 88f., 104f., and *Studies in Greek Texts* (Göttingen 1976) 146f; (2) the very common use of φασί with acc. and infinitive) the subject is normally vague and unspecified, but occasionally (i) implied by the context (e.g. Ar. *Eccl.* 555 ~ 550 ἠκκλησία, 774 ~ 770 τὸ πλῆθος), (ii) specified as 'everybody' (e.g. Alexis 94(90K).2, cf. 236(234K).1 τίς οὐχί φησι) or 'some people' (e.g. ὣς φασίν τινες Antiphanes 55(52K).16, Philemon 118(130K).2).

5–6 According to Holland (219) these verses are *uix integri* (faulty, that is, over and above the omission of τῶν in A by haplography after ἀπάντων

---

[1] The presence of τότε (rather than a scanning synonym of νῦν) at the end of v. 5 ought to be noted here. It is most straightforwardly taken as implying that Aristippus belonged to a past, not the current, generation.

in v. 5, where the correction was first made by G. Morel 134 in 1553, and the perhaps incorrect orthography ἀκολασίᾳ in v. 6). Holland argues that πρωτεύων needs a noun in the dative to balance ἀκολασίᾳ in v. 6 (which is constructed with διαφέρων), and he posits a lacuna of a whole verse on the lines of τῶν τότε | <ἀσωτίᾳ, τῶν δ' ἐσομένων δ' ἀπληστίᾳ,> | ἀκολασίᾳ τε.... This is ingenious, but stems from misinterpretation of a healthy text with a sly joke in it. By a common comic technique Aristippus is first praised in reasonable terms (σοφιστὴς εὐφυής, 'a brainy professor'); this praise is then extravagantly magnified ('no, rather the leading man of his own generation': on τῶν τότε see also footnote 1 on vv. 3–4), where the lack of precision about the area of his primacy is intentional; finally the climax – the point of the joke – extends the previous verse's praise in order to twist it into ridicule ('and excelling men now alive in *debauchery*'). This slur on Aristippus' character clearly derives from his well-remembered fondness for the good things of life (above, comm. on vv. 3–4).

6 ἀκολασίᾳ, the classical form, is the reading here of both A and Epit. MSS; but Photius s.v. ἀκολασία (p.62 Reitzenstein, 1.84 Theodoridis) and the Seguerian *Glossary of Useful Terms* (1.57.11 Bachmann, 367.24 Bekker) have the entry ἀκολασία Θουκυδίδης (3.37, 6.89) ἔφη, ἀκολαστία δὲ Ἄλεξις (fr. 345 Kock). In consequence Meineke (*ed. min.* 697, cf. *FCG* 3.400, 5. p. cciii), followed now by Kassel–Austin, elected to print ἀκολαστίᾳ here. He *may* be right; in minuscule MSS the confusion between σ and ligatured στ is far too common for confidence to be placed in the MSS of Ath. here on palaeographic grounds alone. But the lexical notes neither identify the play nor quote the context where Alexis is alleged to have used the orthography with στ. They do not affirm that Alexis invariably spelled the word thus. And I find it hard to believe that this present fr. was the only passage in the 245 plays of Alexis where the word occurred. A judicious editor would do well not to follow the example of Meineke here. – On the formation of ἀκολαστία see comm. on fr. 345 Kock (p. 812 below).

7 γίγνεται: here, at 76.3 and 280(278K).2 Kassel–Austin print G. Morel's restoration (pp. 134, 129, 137 respectively) of the classical Attic orthography while the MSS of Ath. (A at 12.544f, 6.226f, CE at 2.36f) give the Ionic, post-Aristotelian Attic and *Koine* γίνεται; cf. also 47(46K).7 (Ath. 8.338e: γίγνεται A, γίν- C), 153(149K).17 (Ath. 9.379c: γίνεσθαι A, γιγν- Casaubon, *Animadv.* 655), 167(162K).9 (Ath. 2.55a: γίνεται CE, γίγν- R. Walpole, *Comicorum graecorum fragmenta quaedam* (Cambridge 1805) 10), 178(172K).15 (Ath. 12.516f: γίνεται A, γίγν- Dindorf). Similarly at 70.2 (see comm.) Kassel–Austin print Dindorf's Atticisation γιγνώσκει while A at Ath. 13.563d has γινώσκει. In both verbs the γιγν- spelling was retained at Athens for official purposes until 306/5 (Threatte 1.652ff., cf. Meisterhans–Schwyzer 177ff. and nn. 1478, 1479),

COMMENTARY

but how far the state lagged behind popular usage in its adoption thereafter of the γιν- form is an unanswerable question. The earlier comic papyri (all later than 306/5) are, not surprisingly, inconsistent: thus γίνομαι com. adesp. fr. 258.24 Austin, γίγνεται Men. *Sik.* 27. We may be wrong to demand any greater consistency from comic authors whose careers began in the first half of the 4th century. Cf. also Wilamowitz, *Schiedsg.* 61, Schwyzer 1.214f., Mayser–Schmoll 1.1.156, M. Lejeune, *Phonétique historique du mycénien et du grec ancien* (Paris 1972) 78f.

8–9 The speaker's master 'didn't at all get a thorough grounding in the art' he had paid Aristippus to teach him (sc. rhetoric and philosophy: cf. vv. 1–3 of the fr.); instead τὴν ἀρτηρίαν συνήρπασεν. Thus the *Marcianus* and Epit. MSS; they conspire to produce a problem of interpretation that I discussed in detail at *Hermes* 93 (1965) 300f. In extant texts ἀρτηρία is used solely of certain tubular parts of the human anatomy: the wind-pipe (in the plural, bronchial tubes), an artery or (again in the plural) ureters (LSJ s.v.). How Aristippus' pupil 'picked up' one of the above-named organs in our context remains a mystery, in whatever way we interpret συνήρπασεν: whether literally 'he snatched up and removed', or metaphorically 'he learnt' (LSJ s.v. συναρπάζω 3, citing S. *Aj.* 16, Ar. *Nub.* 775, Simylus in Stob. *Flor.* 4.18.4 = Meineke, *FCG* 1.p.xiii). The only way that one might defend the MSS reading is by an assumption that Alexis was alluding to some well-known incident that connected Aristippus with an ἀρτηρία: perhaps the theft of one by or from Aristippus, or its employment by him in a catchword, vivid example or image that caught the popular imagination. But this is guesswork. It may be preferable to posit corruption in the MSS tradition, as scholars have done since the 16th century. Korais (in Schweighaeuser: cf. *Animadv.* 6.497) conjectured τὴν δ' ἀρτηρίαν συνέσπασεν, arguing that a choked wind-pipe was so described by ancient medicine and recognised as a symptom of pleurisy and other lung diseases (Hipp. *Morb.* 1.28 πήγνυται δὲ τὸ πλεῦρον καὶ τὰ ἐν αὐτῷ τῷ πλευρῷ φλέβια, καὶ ξυσπᾶται; cf. 1.26 which alleges the cause of such disease to be πόσιες ἀλέες τε καὶ ἰσχυραί, and *Int.* 2; at Plaut. *Curc.* 237 the sick *leno* complains that *pulmones distrahuntur*. Korais' idea is clever but unconvincing. Medical symptoms of the kind here adduced tend to be expressed in the passive voice (English too says 'his lungs were congested', not 'he congested his lungs'). Again, the δ' clause in v. 9 is intended as the comic climax to the sentence; even accepting Korais' diagnosis of the textual malady, we should still expect a simpler, more direct statement like 'he caught pleurisy as a result of his potations', not a pedantic description of one of the disease's internal symptoms. More support has been given to the conjecture ἀρτυσίαν for ἀρτηρίαν first proposed by G. Morel (p.134; see *PCPS* 196 (1970) 4), but there are palaeographical difficulties in explaining a corruption of υσ to ηρ, and the word ἀρτυσία, coined on the analogy of ὀψαρτυσία, is not recorded in Greek. These facts militate against the conjecture, despite the excellent sense it would yield: Aristippus was an expert on cookery (Diog. Laert. 2.75, Lucian *Vit. Auct.* 12, *Par.* 33, Σ on *Menipp.* 13, Michael Italicus in Cramer, *Anecdota Graeca* 3.168.3 = *epist.* 18 in P. Gautier's edition (Paris 1972) p. 157.1). T. G. Tucker, *CQ* 2 (1908) 191 conjectured something equally apposite, palaeographically more plausible and excellent sense (anticipating me in my *Hermes* paper): τὴν δ' ἀτηρίαν συνήρπασεν, 'he picked up (= learnt) his *wickedness* (i.e. Aristippus' passion for high living, discussed on vv. 3–4 above). ἀτηρία is a rare but well-attested Attic word: e.g. Plato com. fr. 198(182K), Xen. *Mem.* 3.5.17 (where C corrupts to ἀπειρία).

38 (37K)

Meineke 3.401 (II), Kock 2.311, Edmonds 2.392, Kassel–Austin 2.45; cf. Holland, *op. cit.* in introduction to Γαλάτεια, 221. The fr. as quoted has lost its main verb, originally expressed (one presumes) in the preceding or following context. That verb is unlikely to have been Meineke's δεῖ, for the reason shrewdly given by Holland: such a supplement would suggest that the speaker was some sort of cook, and comic cooks are not normally so humble as to qualify their culinary assertions with remarks like ὡς φασιν (v.1: cf. especially my introduction to Λέβης). Holland himself proposes that the slave who spoke fr. 37(36K) should continue here '*haud ita magno interuallo*' (could it even be immediately?) with the explanation that his master Polyphemus has learnt (with μεμάθηκε supplemented as main verb) cookery from Aristippus, an expert in that art (see on fr. 37(36K).8–9). This is a shot in the dark, since fr. 38(37K) could easily belong to a different part of the play; yet it has a plausible ingenuity.[1] Whatever solution we accept for the textual crux of fr. 37(36K).9, the slave speaker might well have said that instead of learning philosophy and rhetoric, his master had specialised in follies such as cookery.

1–2 If Tucker's ἀτηρίαν is adopted at 37(36K).9, and if 38(37K) does follow shortly or directly after 37(36K) (two very big ifs), μὲν οὖν would be

---

[1] Note that the same character would then be presented as using the qualificatory phrase ὡς φασιν twice in a short space of lines (frs. 37(36K).4, 38(37K).1): perhaps an embryonic example of that type of linguistic characterisation most familiar today from Menander's plays (see F. H. Sandbach, *Entretiens Hardt* 16 (1970) 111ff., D. Del Corno, *Stud. Class. e Orient.* 24 (1975) 13ff., and my own discussions in *G and R* 17 (1970) 32ff., 22 (1975) 146ff., the introduction to my Loeb edition of Menander, 1 (Cambridge, Mass. and London 1979) xxxv f., and in F. de Martino and A. H. Sommerstein (editors), *Lo spettacolo delle voci* 2 (Bari 1995) 147ff.

used here in its emphatic sense, where the speaker replaces an inadequate form of words by one comically stronger (Denniston, *GP* 478f.): 'he picked up Aristippus' wickedness. [Wickedness, do I say? No, far worse than that.] He has learnt, so they say, how to bake a whole stuffed ray.' νάρκη is the electric ray (*Torpedo marmorata* and two similar species, *T. torpedo* and *T. nobilana*: Thompson, *Fishes* s.v. νάρκη, Palombi–Santorelli 245ff., Campbell, *Guide* 26of.), here stuffed with spices or force-meat and then baked. Alexis 84 describes the preparations for stuffing a τευθίς (cf. Sotades 1.15), and Apicius 9.4.2 lists boiled skinned brains, pepper, raw egg and force-meat as ingredients for stuffing a cuttlefish; cf. Alexis 275(273K), Athenion 1.28. Elsewhere, as Holland observes, νάρκη is described as boiled (ἐφθή), not baked (Plato com. (or Cantharus) 164(150K), Archestratus in Ath. 7.314d = fr. 179 *SH*), yet Ephippus 22 maintains that baking is the Sicilian method of cooking fish such as the skate, πότερον ἐγώ | τὴν βατίδα τεμάχη κατατεμὼν ἕψω... | ἢ Σικελικῶς ὀπτὴν ποήσω; :: Σικελικῶς.). Thus the hypothesis of Γαλάτεια's Sicilian setting may be delicately reinforced.

39 (38+316K)

Meineke 3.401 (III), Kock 2.311 and 405, Edmonds 2.392 and 518, Kassel–Austin 2.45. The Antiatticist (93.1 Bekker) claims that Alexis used εὐοψίαν in his Γαλάτεια in the sense 'good looks', i.e. as a derivative of ὄψις. Pollux 6.38, on the other hand, writes Ἄλεξις δ' εὐοψίαν[1] εἶπεν (without specifying the play but almost certainly referring to the same passage as the Antiatticist[2]) at the end of a section which lists ὄψον derivatives. This clash of interpretations is easily resolved. One of the two may have been guilty of a careless error, but more probably each has stated half of the truth. In 4th-century Greek and later, εὐοψία (together with its congeners εὐοψῶ and εὔοψος) normally refers to an abundance of ὄψον, i.e. fish normally (see comm. on 47(46K).6): Alciphron 1.1.4 φεῦ τῆς εὐοψίας· ὅσον ἰχθύων ἐξειλκύσαμεν, 1.13.1 εὐοψία μὲν ἦν καὶ πλῆθος ἰχθύων. Doubtless Alexis used the word primarily in this sense, but played at the same time with a fanciful etymology from ὄψις, ' *ioci causa quaesita ambiguitate*' (Herwerden, *Mnemosyne* 6 (1878) 68f.; cf. Kock, Sicking,

---

[1] εὐοψωνίαν in MSS AB here (εὐοψίαν FSC) is merely a corruption induced by the presence of five ὀψων- compounds in the lines immediately preceding. The word accordingly needs to be expunged from lexica such as LSJ.

[2] There can be little doubt about this. εὐοψία is not a common word, and both citers quote Alexis for its use in the accusative singular. There is no real case for turning the Pollux reference (with either reading) into a separate fragment *incertae sedis*, as Kock and Edmonds do (their fr. 316).

Annotationes 94, Holland 221f. adding inappropriate speculation); cf. the similar pun in Ach. Tat. 5.13.5 ποῖον γὰρ ὄψον ... μοι πολυτελὲς ἢ ποῖος οἶνος τιμιώτερος τῆς σῆς ὄψεως;.[1] Many contexts for such a pun would offer themselves in a play where the heroine was an attractive nymph of the sea.

Why the Antiatticist felt obliged to support the word here, it is hard to determine. He may have been prosaically opposing an Atticist fiat that linked the word only with ὄψον, or more probably defending the actual existence of the abstract compound against a general charge of impure Atticism.

40 (39K)

Meineke 3.401 (IV), Kock 2.311, Edmonds 2.392, Kassel–Austin 2.46. In a play about the pastoral Polyphemus who may have played and sung either to win his love or (cf. Theoc. 11) to console his disappointment, a possible explanation of the grammarians' definition of νομικόν here as τὸν ἐπιστήμονα τῶν νόμων (Photius s.v., Antiatticist 109.11 Bekker) would be that these νόμοι were 'melodies' or (accented oxytone) 'pastures'.[2] The normal meaning of νομικός, however, is 'connected with the law' (e.g. Pl. *Leg.* 1.625a; LSJ s.v.), and Alexis could have diverged from this significance only for a facetious pun.

Γραφή

Meineke 3.402. The one fr. preserved from the comedy, in which a tale is told about a man who fell in love with a statue, led Meineke to suggest that Alexis' plot dealt with a man's infatuation with the picture of the title. The idea is attractive but unverifiable. Alexis' hero could have been an artist in love with the portrait of a pretty girl he had painted (cf. [Aristaen.] 2.10, which in Meineke's view might derive some of its material from Alexis[3]). Alternatively, the object of the man's passion could have been not a portrait, but the girl herself seen in circumstances which deluded her

---

[1] In Ath. 8.338b–c Chamaeleon records Lasus' humorous definition of some raw fish as ὀπτόν because it was *visible*; cf. also Ath. 3.98a, Lucian *Lex.* 9.

[2] Holland's suggestion (222 n. 1) that these νόμοι may have been τὸ νόμισμα, οὓς οἱ Ἰταλικοὶ νούμ<μ>ους καλοῦσιν (Antiatticist 109.24) is better ignored.

[3] The idea is quite tenable. This epistolographer often borrows both subject matter and phraseology from later Greek comedy (cf. *GRBS* 14 (1973) 202ff., *YCS* 27 (1982) 306ff.).

viewer into a belief that he had been looking at a picture (cf. Men. *Phasm.*, where the heroine was first believed by the young man who saw her to be the apparition of the title; see E. G. Turner, *GRBS* 10 (1969) 307ff. and Gomme–Sandbach, *Comm.* 673ff.). G. Norwood's theory (*Greek Comedy* (London 1931) 45) that the girl might have come magically to life like Pygmalion's statue would be more persuasive if the play belonged to the period of Middle Comedy.

A tolerable frame for fr. 41(40K) would be an expository prologue which terminated or interrupted an account of the plot antecedents with a reference to a contemporary parallel (cf. τοιοῦθ' ἕτερον v. 2).

41 (40K)

Meineke 3.401, Kock 2.312, Edmonds 2.392, Kassel–Austin 2.46. Ath. 13.605f–606a cites this fr. together with Philemon 127(139K) as references to the behaviour of a certain Cleisophus of Selymbria, who fell in love with a marble statue in a Samos temple, locked himself in there in order to enjoy its favours, but being frustrated by the stone's resistance substituted for it some obscure alternative.[1] Similar incidents were recorded about a statue in one of the treasuries at Delphi (Ath. *ibid.*), Praxiteles' Cnidian Aphrodite (Clem. Alex. *Protr.* 4.57.3 citing Posidippus, *FGrH* 447 F 2, [Lucian] *Am.* 13–16, Philostratus *Vit. Apoll.* 6.40, Pliny *HN* 36.21), and an Agathe Tyche in Athens (Aelian *VH* 9.39). They became a topic for second-sophistic declamation (Philostratus *Vit. Soph.* 2.18, Libanius *Eth.* 27; cf. also A. Lesky's German translation of [Aristaenetus] (Zürich 1951) 174f., A. Garzya, *Dioniso* 35 (1961) 75ff., B. Lavagnini, *Maia* 15 (1963) 322ff.).

2 τοιοῦθ' ἕτερον: see the introduction to the play.

2–3 λιθίνης ἐπεθύμησεν κόρης ἄνθρωπος: Alexis begins the anecdote in the pithy, unadorned style of a traditional αἶνος (cf. Fraenkel on A. *Ag.* 719). Note accordingly (1) the asyndetic opening (partly explicable too because the story elucidates the preceding τοιοῦθ' ἕτερον: cf. Alexis 63(62K).7f., 183(178K).7; K.G. 2.344f., Denniston, *GP* xliii f., Fraenkel on A. *Ag.* 1284), for fables and suchlike tales normally dispense with the introductory γάρ *narrantis*; (2) ἄνθρωπος = 'a certain man' (for the absence of τις cf., in addition to the examples collected by Fraenkel on A. *Ag.* 719, the opening of two Aesopic fables, ἄνθρωπος πένης ἀκρίδας

---

[1] The obscurity is textual. Ath. 13.605f writes προβαλλόμενος τὸ σαρκίον ἐπλησίασεν, where τὸ σαρκίον probably ought to be retained (*pace* T. W. Lumb, *CR* 37 (1923) 115) and interpreted as the clitoris (Soranus *Gynaec.* 1.18 = Oribasius *Coll. Med.* 24.31.41–43). It is possible that some words here, identifying whose clitoris it was, have been omitted, perhaps out of prudery, by a scribe or Ath. himself.

θηρεύων ..., ἄνθρωπος ἀπερχόμενος ..., 298 and 300 Hausrath; yet in such accounts ἄνθρωπός τις is no less common, e.g. [Aesop] 32 II, 33 II, 34 II, etc. In telling the same story as Alexis here Philemon 127(139K).2 writes ἄνθρωπος ... τις).

3 ἐγκατέκλεισέ θ' αὐτόν: this correction of A's ἐγκατέκλεισέν θ' ἑαυτόν is partly Casaubon's (printing -έκλεισεθ' αὐτόν), partly Schweighaeuser's (separating -έκλεισέ θ').

Γυναικοκρατία

C. A. Boettiger, *Kleine Schriften* (Dresden and Leipzig 1837) 1.300f., Meineke 1.398f., Schmid–Stählin 1.iv.372f. Boettiger and Meineke persuaded earlier scholars (e.g. Th. Bergk, *Griechische Literaturgeschichte* 4 (Berlin 1887) 154, Kann, *De iteratis* 78f., Kock 2.238) that the plays of Amphis and Alexis with this title were Middle-Comedy adaptations (or at least imitations) of Aristophanes' *Ecclesiazusae*. A title Γυναικοκρατία may suggest *prima facie* some thematic affinities with *Eccl.* (cf. for instance 105ff., 210ff., 229ff., 427ff. etc. of that play), but coincidence of theme does not necessarily carry with it similarities of plot or treatment. In Alexis fr. 42(41K) a speaker of unidentified sex tells two or more women (characters on stage or possibly the chorus, cf. R. L. Hunter, *ZPE* 36 (1979) 37) 'You (plural) must sit there in the theatre (presumably the Athenian theatre of Dionysus) in the block of seats right at the back and watch just like foreign women.' Schmid–Stählin compares this instruction with *Eccl.* 86f., where the female conspirators are told to take their seats in the Athenian assembly; Kann refers to *Eccl.* 296ff., where the chorus confirms its intention to obey this command. In Aristophanes, however, the women disguise themselves as men (96ff.) in order to seize power ostensibly by legal means at a meeting of the assembly in the Pnyx. But if Alexis' women in fr. 42(41K) are being given parallel instructions before a seizure of power, it is hard to see how the transference could have used legal forms. The location of the theatre of Dionysus and Alexis' reference to 'the block of seats right at the back' may rather imply that his women were being ordered to wait until the men of Athens were firmly ensconced in their seats for a performance in the theatre, and then by occupying the seats near the north-western exit to block the way out to the Acropolis and so allow another group of women to storm it (cf. Ar. *Lys.*) while their menfolk were detained below in the theatre. All this, however, is surmise; it is safer to acknowledge that nothing certain is known about the date, plot and purpose of either Alexis' or Amphis' Γυναικοκρατία. On the motif of gynaecocracy in Greek literature, cult and myth see especially R. F. Willetts, *Hermes* 87 (1959) 495ff., J. Vogt, *Von der Gleichwertigkeit der*

COMMENTARY

Geschlechter in der bürgerlichen Gesellschaft der Griechen (*Abh. Mainz* 1960, 2), S. G. Pembroke, *JWCI* 30 (1967) 1ff., P. Vidal-Naquet in C. Nicolet (ed.), *Recherches sur les structures sociales dans l'antiquité classique* (Paris 1970) 63ff., W. B. Tyrrell, *ASNP* 12 (1982) 1213ff.

42 (41K)

Meineke 3.402 (I), Kock 2.312, Edmonds 2.392, Kassel–Austin 2.46. The relevance of this fr. to the title is discussed immediately above.

1 ἐνταῦθα: Kock's observation, *theatrum in theatro repraesentatum fuisse Meinekius arbitratur. at tum* ἐνθάδε *dicendum erat, non* ἐνταῦθα, reveals a double blindness: to Attic idiom and to dramatic convention. The use of both ἐνταῦθα and ἐνθάδε in the senses of either 'here' or 'there' (i.e. *in mea uel tua uicinia*) is too common in Athenian writers to need illustration (Schwyzer 2.157f.; Zoilists might compare Ar. *Ran.* 82 with Arist. *Metaph.* 1.9, 990ᵇ34f.); no purely spatial distinction between the words can safely be drawn. And in any case an actor, pointing to a block of seats in the auditorium, might designate it as either 'here' (ἐνθάδε, ἐνταῦθα) or 'there' (ἐνθάδε, ἐνταῦθα, ἐκεῖ), depending partly on his point of view at that precise moment, and partly on whether the dramatist wished to preserve or to shatter the dramatic illusion. In this fr. a sure interpretation of what Alexis intended is unattainable without the preceding context.

1–2 Although it is dangerous to draw general conclusions from short contextless passages, these lines appear to offer evidence that foreign[1] women were permitted to attend some theatrical performances in the 4th century, and that they (? normally) sat in the rear blocks at one or both sides of the auditorium (cf. Pickard-Cambridge, *DFA²* 269). Did these women (and ξένοι generally) make their own reservations, or were they permitted to attend only as guests of citizens? The combined evidence of Dem. 18.28, [Dem.] 44.37 and Theophr. *Char.* 9 (cf. Ussher *ad loc.*) suggests the latter. κερκίς is the technical term for one of the wedge-shaped blocks of seats in the auditorium (Pickard-Cambridge, *TDA* 139).

43 (42K)

Meineke 3.402 (II), Kock 2.312, Edmonds 2.394, Kassel–Austin 2.47. Of Hippocles the actor nothing is known (cf. J. B. O'Connor, *Chapters in the History of Actors and Acting in Ancient Greece* (Diss. Chicago 1908) p. 105

---

[1] This is not the place to enter into the controversy whether Athenian women formed part of the audiences in the theatre of Dionysus. The general view is that they were allowed into the theatre (cf. e.g. Pickard-Cambridge, *DFA²* 264f., 269), but this has once more been strongly challenged by N. G. Wilson, *GRBS* 23 (1982) 158f.

no.259, Bonaria in *RE* Suppl. iv s.v. *Hippokles* 4, 324.50ff., I. E. Stefanis, Διονυσιακοὶ Τεχνῖται (Heraklion 1988) p. 232 no. 1281); was he a real person, or possibly only a character in the play? The name itself and profession suggest Athenian or at least civilised Greek origins; the adjective Κίλιξ is accordingly best interpreted as stock comic abuse. It implies that in the view of the speaker Hippocles was not Athenian *comme il faut* (cf. the similar attacks on Cleophon in Old Comedy: Ar. *Ran.* 678, 1532 and Σ *ad loc.*), either because of unattic appearance or habits in general (cf. e.g. the similar uses of Τριβαλλός, Φρύξ: comm. on fr. 243(241K).1, introduction to Φρύξ), or because of a vicious cruelty allegedly characteristic of Cilicians in particular (Theopompus hist. *FGrH* 115 F 314, LSJ s.v. Κιλικίζω; this is presumably the point of Demodocus' imitation of Phocylides, *Anth. Pal.* 11.236; cf. also K. Schmidt, *Hermes* 37 (1902) 184).

2 ὁ ζωμοτάριχος: so the *Marcianus* correctly, 'pickled/dried-fish soup' as a nickname. Nauck's conjecture ὀζωμοτάριχος (*Philologus* 6 (1851) 419) is ingenious, correctly formed (Herwerden, *Coll. Crit.* 122, against Kock; cf. ὀζόστομος) and certainly wrong. The definite article is required before nicknames, professional designations and the like when these are added as distinguishing features in apposition to proper names (K.G. 1.600f.; in Alexis Ἀριστογείτονα τὸν ῥήτορα 211(208K), Διόδωρος οὑπίτριπτος 110(105K).1, Ἐπιχαρίδης ὁ μικρός 248(246K).2, Καλλιμέδων ὁ Κάραβος 118(113K), etc.). Furthermore, the lemma of Ath. here (3.125b) cites the fr. to illustrate the word ζωμοτάριχος. Elsewhere ζωμός and τάριχος are applied separately to people in pejorative descriptions, ζωμός (cf. comm. on fr. 145(141K).8) in the sense of 'fat and greasy' (Anaxandrides 35(34K).5, Aristophon 5(4K).3), τάριχος (cf. comm. on 191(186K).5) with the idea of 'smelly' (Ar. fr. 207(200K), cf. Diphilus of Siphnos in Ath. 3.121c; Casaubon, *Animadv.* 229).[1]

ὑποκριτής: see on fr. 140(135K).16.

Δακτύλιος

Hähnle 65 n. 2. The title is common in later Greek comedy (it was used by Amphis, Menander, Philemon, Timocles and an unknown dramatist of

---

[1] In the text of this fr. it is better to end the incomplete first line at Ἱπποκλῆς with Meineke and the other editors of the comic frs., rather than at Κίλιξ with Casaubon and all the editors of Ath. except Meineke. Either arrangement is possible, but Meineke's produces a penthemimeral caesura in the second verse. Of the first 100 iambic trimeters in Alexis (frs. 1–31), 56 have penthemimeral caesura, 30 hephthemimeral without penthemimeral and 14 neither, at a rough count; the state of

COMMENTARY

the 2nd century, IG ii^2.2323.133 = III B 3 col. 2b.22 Mette; cf. Pomponius' *Anulus posterior*, whose title is explained by F. Ritschl, *Parerga zu Plautus und Terenz*, I (Berlin 1845) 134f.). Rings and the imprints of their seals are most frequently used in ancient comedy as instruments of recognition (Men. *Epitr.*, *Pk.*, *P.Antinoopolis* 15 = com. adesp. fr. 240 Austin, probably from a play by Menander, cf. Gomme–Sandbach, *Comm.* 722f.; Plaut. *Curc.*, *Vidularia*, Ter. *HT*, *Hec.*), but their other comic uses should not be forgotten. Rings may be used as warrants, sometimes fraudulently, for identification of their bearers (Plaut. *Bacch.* 327ff., cf. the tricks in *Curc.*, *MG*, *Pseud.*; Fraenkel, *EP* 420f.), and as betrothal gifts (Ter. *Ad.* 347 and R. H. Martin *ad loc.*).[1] The frs. of the present play offer no clue about the function of its ring.

44 (43K)

Meineke 3.403 (1), Kock 2.312, Edmonds 2.394, Kassel–Austin 2.47. A platitude on the evils of drunkenness (cf. frs. 82, 160(156K), 257(255K)) is likely to have been spoken by a puritanical moralist – *paedagogus*, father, father-in-law (cf. Men. *Epitr.* 127ff.), for instance – while the opposite view (e.g. Alexis 285(283, 284K) suits parasites, free but not necessarily young revellers, and amoral slaves.

1 The common use of εἶτ' οὐ to introduce an irritated or sarcastic question at the beginning of a speech (in comedy also Alexis 145(141K).1, Amphis 1.1, 17.1, Antiphanes 157(159K).1, Aristophon 11.1, Men. *Dysk.* 153, *Her.* 7, fr. 718.1, cf. Pl. *Apol.* 28b; LSJ s.v. εἶτα II, Handley on Men. *Dysk.* 153ff., U. Reinhardt, *Mythologische Beispiele in der Neuen Komödie* (Diss. Mainz 1974) 88ff.; contrast in mid-speech Alexis 264(262K).3) suggests that here too we may have the beginning of an angry tirade.

κακὸν: this, the reading of A (Ath. 10.443e–f), is to be preferred to κακῶν, Valckenaer's conjecture (Peppink, *Observ.* 62). In locutions where something is said to be the worst, best, etc. thing of all, normally a noun in the predicate agrees in case with the superlative adjective, and not with the word 'all' in the genitive: e.g. Philemon 92(88K).1f. πολύ γ' ἐστὶ πάντων ζῷον ἀθλιώτατον | ἄνθρωπος, Hipparchus com. 2 πολύ γ' ἐστὶ πάντων κτῆμα τιμιώτατον | ἅπασιν ἀνθρώποισιν εἰς τὸ ζῆν τέχνη, cf. Eur. *Ion* 836 καὶ τῶνδ' ἁπάντων ἔσχατον πείσῃ κακόν. But when there is no predication and no copulative verb, the noun described as worst, best etc. thing of all more commonly agrees with the word 'all' in the genitive

---

the text and incompleteness of some verses prevent exact computation. Cf. also comm. on 77.2–4.

[1] A ring is mentioned also at Men. *Mis.* 146, but in a context so tattered and lacunose that its connection with the plot is wholly uncertain (cf. Sandbach *ad loc.*).

ΔΑΚΤΥΛΙΟΣ

(Ar. *Av.* 366, *Ran.* 722, *Plut.* 1112, Plato com. 105(98K).2, Eubulus 115(117K).8, com. adesp. fr. 44 Kock, etc.), and less commonly with the superlative adjective (Eupolis 316(290K), Antiphanes 212(331K) = Alexis 245(342K)). Very occasionally the noun is repeated to agree with both (Ar. *Plut.* 445f.).

45 (44K)

Meineke 3.403 (II), Kock 2.313, Edmonds 2.394, Kassel–Austin 2.47. ἐκκόπτειν in the sense 'to defeat at dice' was presumably a slang expression (cf. the English 'lick') which found its way into comic usage in both the active (here and Menecrates com. 1 Kassel–Austin) and the passive (Hesych. s.v. ἐκκεκομμένος· ὁ διὰ τοῦ κυβεύειν τὰ ἑαυτοῦ ἀπολέσας, most probably from a comic source, cf. Blaydes, *Adv.* 1.239). A colloquialism of this kind would readily be attacked by strict Atticists.

Δημήτριος ἢ Φιλέταιρος

Meineke 1.388f., Fritzsche in J. Töppel, *De fragmentis comicorum graecorum quaestiones criticae, spec. tert.* (Progr. Neubrandenburg 1867) 9ff., Kock 2.313, Breitenbach 67ff., 103f., G. Capovilla, *SIFC* 19 (1912) 372ff., N. Terzaghi, *Fabula* 1 (Milan 1912) 77f., Webster, *SLGC* 75, A. M. Desrousseaux, edition of Ath. I–II (Paris 1956) 91f. n. 1; cf. J. J. Scaliger, *Coniectanea in Varronem* (Paris 1565) 197 = (1573) 170, Casaubon, *Animadv.* 589, Ribbeck, *CRF³* 100ff., L. Rychlewska, *Turpilii comici fragmenta* (Wrocław 1962) 12, 19f., 61ff., and *Turpilius: Fragmenta* (Leipzig 1971) IX, 7ff. From this play Ath. 6.241b cites fr. 48(47K) with the double title Ἄλεξις Δημητρίῳ ἢ Φιλεταίρῳ; elsewhere the title is given as Δημήτριος alone, both by Ath. (3.108a, 7.314d, 8.338d, 14.663c, citing frs. 51, 49, 47, 50 (50, 48, 46, 49K) respectively) and by Stobaeus (*Anth.* 4.50a.5 Hense, citing part of fr. 46(45K)), although at 14.663c Ath. notes that his citation comes ἐκ τοῦ διεσκευασμένου δράματος, ὃ ἐπιγράφεται Δημήτριος.[1] In consequence Meineke argued that Alexis' play was first produced with the title Φιλέταιρος, a common comic title (namesakes by Amphis, Antiphanes, Heniochus, Philemon; a Φιλέταιροι by Hegesippus[2]), but was restyled Δημήτριος for a later production. This argument has won general agreement (see e.g. W. Bender, *De graecae comoediae titulis duplicibus* (Diss.

---

[1] To the frs. from this play may possibly be added the single word φιλεταιρία (= fr. 335(334K), see comm. *ad loc.*).
[2] So Ath. 7.279d (*Marcianus*); the *Suda* s.v. Ἡγήσιππος corruptly reports the title in the singular (see Meineke 1.475ff.).

Marburg 1904) 40, Breitenbach 67 n. 175, Terzaghi 77f., Pickard-Cambridge, *DFA*² 101) and is probably right, even if the reason why this particular play received its second performance is today unknown.[1] Of the six extant frs., 50(49K) certainly, and all the others probably, derive from the second version, since the title Δημήτριος appears first or alone in all the citations where the play is named; it seems likely enough that this version was the only one preserved in the Hellenistic libraries where Ath. or his source (cf. Bender 32ff.) wrote out his citations. In that case it would be this second production[2] that is roughly dated by the reference in fr. 48(47K) to the parasite Eucrates nicknamed Κόρυδος, whose notoriety was commented upon by Machon and the comic poets in the years between *c.* 345 and 305 (cf. Breitenbach 70 n. 182, Webster, *CQ* 2 (1952) 21f., Gow's edition of Machon pp. 10, 59, Gow–Page on Posidippus epigram 16.1).

However, the title of the play poses other problems besides those of recension and date. Φιλέταιρος, for instance, could have been a proper name, either a *nomen fictum* or with allusion to a contemporary celebrity such as the playwright son of Aristophanes; but it is much more likely to have been a descriptive adjective, since the word occurs in the plural as the title of Hegesippus' play, and in the singular it appears too often as a comic title at different periods for it consistently to designate a historical figure (cf. Kock 2.104, Breitenbach 103f., in *RE* Kaibel s.v. *Amphis* 2, 1954.11f., Körte s.v. *Philonides* 3, 62.32ff.). It would accordingly be analogous to such titles as Φιλάδελφοι (Menander and others) or Φιλοδέσποτος (Sosigenes, Theognetus, Timostratus), and imply that one of the play's characters was a loyal comrade (Breitenbach 103f., Terzaghi 78), perhaps like Nikeratos in an un-

---

[1] The first production, for instance, might have won great acclaim, like Ar. *Ran.*; or Alexis, when asked for the script of a new play at too short a notice, could have taken the easy way out by retouching an old play of his. The great demand for fresh comedies made by Athenian and other dramatic festivals doubtless taxed the creative energy of playwrights even in that fertile age (cf. E. Mensching, *Mus. Helv.* 21 (1964) 45ff.), and it is not surprising that signs of haste, such as the repetition of passages from other plays, may be detected in the frs. of plays given a second production. Or is it mere coincidence that frs. 49(48K) and probably 51(50K) (Δημήτριος) = fr. 115(110K).9–13 (Κράτεια, also produced twice)? Cf. also comm. on fr. 24.2–4. On second productions in general see the discussions of Kann, *De iteratis* and Pickard-Cambridge, *DFA*² 100f.; and on the problems provided by alternative titles, the introduction to Ἀγωνὶς ἢ Ἱππίσκος and the works cited there.

[2] Not the first, as Meineke 1.388f. (cf. Breitenbach 70) suggests, basing his argument on the false premise that Δημήτριος was Demetrius Poliorcetes.

identified comedy (fr. 257.20ff., 67ff. Austin) and several young and old men in the Roman adaptations of Plautus.[1] Capovilla's idea that this title should be accented properispomenon and referred to a man's passion for *hetairai* is less plausible; the adjective is not to my knowledge elsewhere used with this shade of meaning, even if that description could be applied – albeit by a prejudiced observer ignorant of the dénouement – to New-Comedy characters like Charisios in Men. *Epitr.* or Aeschinus in Ter. *Ad.*

The relation between the two versions of Alexis' play is unknown; one possibility is that in the second version the loyal comrade was now (if not before) named Demetrios. Clearly this Demetrios was a fictitious character. Attempts to see behind the name a caricature of D. Phalereus (Edmonds 2.394 note d) or Poliorcetes (Meineke 1.388) are misguided, as scholars have pointed out (W. Fielitz, *De Atticorum comoedia dipartita* (Diss. Bonn 1866) 10 n. 2, Breitenbach 68). Alexis' Δημήτριος was a revision of an earlier play, and political satire lends itself less easily to revival than the conventional intrigue patterns of New Comedy. It is also less likely to have been adapted 200 years later for the Roman stage.

The adapter in this case was Turpilius with his *Demetrius* (Ribbeck 100ff., Rychlewska (1962) 61ff., (1971) 7ff.).[2] First Scaliger, then Casaubon pointed out that fr. v of Turpilius' *Demetrius*,

> antehac si flabat aquilo aut auster, inopia
> tum erat piscati

was a close translation into the equivalent Latin metre of Alexis 47(46K).1–3. The frs. of Turpilius' *Demetrius*[3] are numerous, but individually too short for a sure reconstruction of its plot. The elements of an apparently typical New-Comedy intrigue, however, are glimmeringly discernible from ambiguous hints thrown out by some of them. Thus there is evidence of the presence in Turpilius' cast of a *meretrix* (xiv, cf. xi), a *iuuenis* who was doubtless in love with her (xiv, cf. ii, xi, xvi), and a father

---

[1] E.g. Pistoclerus in *Bacch.* 385ff., 405ff., 475, 625ff. (= Moschos in *Dis Ex.*, the Menandrean original), Eutychus in *Merc.*, Lysiteles in *Trin.*, all these being young men like Nikeratos. The best example of a Plautine γέρων φιλέταιρος is probably Callicles in *Trin.* (cf. especially 1110ff., 1128ff.).

[2] Naevius also wrote a *Demetrius* (Ribbeck 16), from which one word survives. Conjecture about its Greek original is futile, but it is unlikely to have been Alexis' play, *pace* J. Barsby, comm. (Warminster 1986) on Plaut. *Bacch.* 912; cf. F. Klingner, *Hermes* 64 (1929) 139, W. Beare, *CR* 51 (1937) 106f., W. R. Chalmers, *CR* 7 (1957) 13.

[3] For the convenience of users of this commentary a full text of the frs. of Turpilius' *Demetrius*, with brief interpretative comment, is given in Appendix 1 (pp. 851 ff.).

who has been cheated by his son (probably but not necessarily this same *iuuenis*) of a talent (XVI). Standard Greco-Roman comic themes are detectable, though their permutation in the plot is uncertain: false accusation (VII), estrangement of friends (IV), a woman's use of tears to persuade a reluctant man (XI), probably also a slave's mockery of an older master (VIII), and an orphaned (?) child's discovery of her (or his) true parentage (XIII). It is not recorded how faithful or free Turpilius was in his adaptation of Greek models;[1] yet we have no evidence that he wilfully altered the outline of his plots, and it seems likely that the characters and motifs traceable in the Turpilius frs. appeared also in Alexis' play.

Unfortunately, the Greek frs. add little of value to our picture of the plot. The elegant generalities of fr. 46(45K) derive from a monologue by an unspecified character, presumably after a scene in which an old man had simmered down from fierce anger to comparative affability;[2] it is (perhaps misleadingly) tempting to guess that this old man and his wrath were the subject of the scene described in Turpilius fr. XVI. Most of the remaining Alexidean frs. appear to describe the antecedents of a luncheon (?: cf. συναριστᾶν fr. 48(47K).2) party. Fr. 47(46K) is a monologue about a market locust called Phayllos. Although an Athenian of this name held office as trierarch in the 330s and 320s (Kirchner, *PA* 2.346, no. 14129, Davies, *APF* 533f.), when at least one version of Alexis' play could have been produced, there is no evidence that this or any other historical Phayllos was attacked on the Athenian stage or elsewhere as a scourge of the Athenian fish-market. More probably Alexis' Phayllos was the *nomen fictum* of a parasite in the play. And, as Breitenbach notes (70f.), although the Turpilian translation of Alexis 47(46K).1–3 breaks off before Phayllos is named, the organisation of ideas in the Alexidean context requires the Roman adapter also to have mentioned Phayllos or a renamed equivalent. Turpilius *might* just have translated here in parrot fashion a topical allusion that neither he nor his audience understood, as Plautus appears occasionally to have done (e.g. *Aul.* 394ff., 504 (but see Fraenkel, *EP* 131, 413), *Pers.* 824, 826; cf. also *Bacch.* 911f., discussed in the next paragraph); it is much more reasonable to suppose, however, that a parasite called Phayllos by Alexis appeared in the Turpilian version as well. We cannot identify the speaker of Alexis 47(46K), but most probably he is returning from market with provisions for a meal. Of the other placeable

---

[1] On at least one occasion, however, Turpilius (like Terence in the *Andria*) turned a Menandrean expository monologue (fr. 152 Körte–Thierfelder) into a dialogue scene (Ribbeck 106 fr. 1); cf. also Bigott in *RE* s.v. *Turpilius* 7, 1429.18ff., and Rychlewska (1962) 13ff., (1971) XIIf.

[2] Desrousseaux' suggestion that the *senex iratus* spoke the fr. (cf. Webster) is attractive but unverifiable.

ΔΗΜΗΤΡΙΟΣ

frs., 50(49K) may be spoken by the marketeer or an associate as he hands over his purchases to two or more women of the household where the meal is to be held (? that of the *meretrix*: cf. Webster, *SLGC* 75), while 49(48K), cf. 51(50K), contains the typical braggadocio of the cook who has been hired for the occasion. It is particularly unfortunate that none of the Greek and Latin frs. (with the possible exception of Turpilius fr. iv) sheds light on the role of Alexis' titular φιλέταιρος.

One final point. Plautus' *Bacchides*, adapted from Menander's Δὶς ἐξαπατῶν, contains the following pair of lines (911f.):

> *satin est si plura ex me audiet hodie mala*
> *quam audiuit umquam Clinia ex Demetrio?*

From the time of Lambinus the editors of Plautus have interpreted this as a reference to a scene in some lost ancient comedy. In that event Plautus must have either reproduced from his Menandrean exemplar or independently introduced an allusion to some currently famous (Athenian? Roman?) comic scene in which there was a fierce quarrel between two characters named Clinia/Kleinias and Demetrius/-ios; for a possibly self-referential parallel cf. Men. *Epitr.* 341f., if there the author has his own *Pk.* in mind (but contrast E. Sehrt, *De Menandro Euripidis imitatore* (Diss. Giessen 1912) 64, Webster, *SM* 155 n. 2). Fritzsche (*loc. cit.*) conjectured that the scene to which *Bacch.* 911f. refers came in Alexis' Δημήτριος, without fully realising the circumstantial evidence in his favour. The alternative title of Alexis' play and the frs. remaining from its Turpilian adaptation imply that two friends played a major role in it, while Turpilius fr. iv may come from a quarrel between them. Yet Fritzsche's case must not be pressed too hard. Kleinias is a standard name for a comic youth (Men. *Mis.*, *Theoph.*; Clinia in Ter. *HT*, cf. *Andr.* 86), and it may be accidental that the name Demetrios (-ius) is confined to the titles of the plays by Alexis, Turpilius and Naevius. The Plautine couplet could possibly refer to a scene in a comedy other than Alexis' Δημήτριος (so K. Gaiser, *Philologus* 114 (1970) 81f.; contrast Bain, *Actors* 211 n. 3). Nor can one sensibly exclude a third possibility. F. Leo (*Hermes* 18 (1883) 559 = *Ausgewählte kleine Schriften* i (Rome 1960) 4) argued that the Plautine Demetrios and Kleinias might have been historical figures, e.g. rhetors contemporary with his Menandrean source who had won a brief celebrity from a slanging match. In that event Demetrios might plausibly be identified with the Phalerean (Leo; cf. B. Prehn, *Quaestiones Plautinae* (Diss. Breslau 1916) 69f., Webster, *SM* 104f., F. Della Corte, *Da Sarsina a Roma* (¹ Genoa 1952) 113 = (² Florence 1967) 98f.) rather than with Poliorcetes (J. Mette, *Lustrum* 10 (1965) 53 n. 1); cf. also F. A. Hüffner, *De Plauti comoediarum exemplis Atticis* (Diss. Göttingen 1894) 37f.

COMMENTARY

46 (45K)

Meineke 3.405 (VI), Kock 2.313, Edmonds 2.394, Kassel–Austin 2.48. The theme of this monologue, whose contextual reference is discussed in the introduction to Δημήτριος, is the similar way in which man and wine mellow with maturity. The fr. owes its charm not to any novelty in the concept (a parallel theme is handled by Antiphanes 250(240.1–2K) more bluntly and with a different point; cf. also Plaut. *Curc.* 98, Cic. *Sen.* 65, L. Holford-Strevens, *Aulus Gellius* (London 1988) 159 n. 86 on 13.2.5 of his author; in modern times N. Kazantzakis, *The Last Temptation* (tr. P. A. Bien, London 1961) 173, has Zebedee say '*Youth, bless it, is like wine, but we sober up soon enough and slide under the yoke without any more kicking*') but to the imaginative ambivalence of its vocabulary.

Alexis has couched his comparison in the form of an εἰκών. εἰκόνες and other αἰνίγματα[1] appear early in Greek literature (Hes. *Op.* 533ff., Sappho fr. 115 Lobel–Page), originating probably in folklore and popular speech.[2] Their frequent use in comedy is doubtless explained by their popularity as a form of symposial wit in 5th- and 4th-century Athens; in the theatre an audience might be expected to applaud any well-turned or imaginative example, and the comic poet's anger would seethe against any rival who stole a good one from him (Ar. *Nub.* 559ff., referring to *Equ.* 864ff.; H.-J. Newiger, *Metapher und Allegorie* (Munich 1957) 132f.). It may have been Aristophanes' elaborate εἰκόνες in which statesmanship was compared to spinning (*Lys.* 574ff.) and citizenship to coinage (*Ran.* 718ff.), where the vocabulary was carefully chosen with ambiguous overtones equally applicable to the subject of the εἰκών and the object to which it was compared, that set the pattern for the elaborate examples of later comedy, like Alexis here and 280(278K), Plaut. *Asin.* 178ff., *Aul.*

---

[1] The εἰκών or εἴκασμα is an (often elaborate) comparison of one thing with another, a σκῶμμα καθ᾽ ὁμοιότητα, or τὸ λέγειν 'ὅμοιος εἶ τῷδε' (Hesych. s.v. εἰκάζειν). An αἴνιγμα, on the other hand, is basically any word puzzle (i.e. any γρῖφος), and so the genus of which εἰκών is one species. In common use, however, αἴνιγμα is applied mostly to one particular type, the riddle or conundrum (cf. comm. on Alexis 242(240K).6). Thus Aristotle defines αἴνιγμα generally as τὸ λέγοντα ὑπάρχοντα ἀδύνατα συνάψαι (*Poet.* 1458ᵃ26ff.), a definition which embraces most word puzzles, but he exemplifies his definition by a conundrum.

[2] Cf. Fraenkel on A. *Ag.* 1629ff. and *EP* 162ff., 421f., N. Zagagi, *Tradition and Originality in Plautus* (Göttingen 1980) 21ff. A useful collection of material is provided by G. Monaco, *Paragoni burleschi degli antichi* (Palermo 1963), but see A. Schäfer, *Gnomon* 37 (1965) 620f.

ΔΗΜΗΤΡΙΟΣ

595ff., *Most.* 84ff., *Poen.* 210ff., 240ff.,[1] *Truc.* 35ff. In Athenian social intercourse one εἰκών was commonly capped by another (hence the verb ἀντεικάζειν; cf. Fraenkel, *EP* 421; Pl. *Meno* 80a–c, Dio Chrys. *Or.* 8.2f.), and this procedure was imitated on the comic stage (Ar. *Vesp.* 1308ff., cf. Plaut. *Poen.* 210ff., 240ff.). One must therefore allow for the possibility that the εἰκών in Alexis 46(45K) was immediately capped by another, developing or rebutting the comparison of man with wine. Directly after citing fr. 46(45K), Ath. 2.36e–f cites just such an oppositional εἰκών from an unnamed play of Alexis (280(278K)) with the words ἀλλαχοῦ δὲ τοὐναντίον φησὶν Ἄλεξις, leaving one to wonder (cf. A. M. Desrousseaux in his edition of Ath. I–II (Paris 1956) pp. 91f. n. 1) whether the epitomist's ἀλλαχοῦ might have replaced a word such as προσελθών in A's version of Ath., with fr. 280(278K) then following fr. 46(45K) either immediately or at a short interval in the same scene of the Δημήτριος.

The fr. is cited by Stob. 4.50a.5 (ἐκ Δημητρίου MA) and Ath. 2.36ef (= Epit., omitting the title, as usual).

1 ὁμοιότατος (Ath.) or -ότατον (Stob.)? It is true that in some parallel formulations (e.g. Ar. *Vesp.* 187ff., Pl. *Meno* 80a) a predicative ὁμοιότατος is found, agreeing with a masculine singular subject; yet Stob.'s neuter is equally idiomatic (K.G. 1.58ff.) and more likely to be corrupted to Ath.'s -ότατος than the other way round (cf. for instance Men. *Dysk.* 449).

2 τὸν γάρ, not καὶ γάρ, which some editors like Meineke and Kock adopt on the false assumption that this is the reading of the Paris MS of Stobaeus. In fact this MS has καὶ γὰρ τὸν, a corruption clearly induced by a scribal *saut des yeux* to the καὶ τὸν at the same metrical position in the following verse.

3 πολλή 'στ' ἀνάγκη (E Ath.) is clearly right, and π. γ' ἀν. (Stob., editors of Ath. before Dindorf) wrong. A restrictive or confirmatory γε is inapposite in the middle of this sentence (cf. G. Hermann on S. *Trach.* 295,

---

[1] These examples from *Poen.* come in a scene (1.2) whose original source is much disputed. Even if the play as a whole was adapted by Plautus from Alexis' Καρχηδόνιος (see my introduction to that play), Fraenkel's theory that scene 1.2 of *Poen.* has a different pedigree from the rest (*EP* 253ff.) is supported by arguments which still seem strong to me, despite the battering they have sustained from subsequent scholarship: B. Krysiniel, *Eos* 34 (1932/3) 27ff., H. Hauschild, *Die Gestalt der Hetäre in der griechischen Komödie* (Diss. Leipzig 1933) 64ff., W. Theiler, *Hermes* 73 (1938) 292f., W. Friedrich, *Euripides und Diphilos* (Munich 1953) 242f., P. J. Enk, *Rostock WZ* 12 (1963) 211, G. Maurach, *Philologus* 108 (1964) 256 n. 1 and 259f. (but contrast now the palinode in his second (Heidelberg 1975) edition of the play, pp. 47f., 53, 192f., 229f.), J. C. B. Lowe, *BICS* 35 (1988) 101ff., O. Zwierlein, *Zur Kritik und Exegese des Plautus, I: Poenulus und Curculio* (Mainz 1990) 142ff.

COMMENTARY

Denniston, *GP* 114f.). And copyists are more likely to have corrupted an elided and prodelided 'στ' to γ' or (so C Ath.) τ' than an original γ' to 'στ'; cf. especially S. *El.* 309 (πολλῆστ' L, π. γ' or τ' *recentiores*), *OC* 293 ('στ' L, τ' or γ' *rec.*), where in both cases the structure of the sentence resembles that of Alexis here; and contrast Eur. *Alc.* 378 (see Dale *ad loc.*), *Hec.* 396, where πολλή γ' ἀνάγκη at the beginning of a clause is the apposite reading of most MSS.

3–4 ἀποζέσαι ... ἀφυβρίσαι τ': the two verbs are selected to balance and complement each other. In contemporary Greek usage ἀποζεῖν is commonly transitive, 'to boil thoroughly'[1] (ἀπο- intensive: Schwyzer 2.431f., 445; Diphilus 17.9, Euphron 10(11K).9 (fish), *IG* xii(7).515.78 (Amorgos, meat), Hippocr. *Acut.* (*Sp.*) 30 (onions)); but at Hippocr. *Flat.* 14 the verb is intransitive, 'to stop bubbling' (ἀπο- cessative: Schwyzer 2.432, 445): ἀποζέσαντος τοῦ ἀφροῦ (sc. after an attack of epilepsy). In the present passage of Alexis also the verb is intransitive, but the context requires more emphasis to be placed on the intensive than on the cessative function of the prefix; translate 'to ferment thoroughly (? and then stop effervescing)'. The verb suits particularly the vinous half of the comparison; the addition of τὸν ἄνδρα, however, as its second subject is no zeugma, since ζεῖν both simple and compounded is often applied metaphorically to the raging of human passions (e.g. intransitively ζεῖν S. *OC* 434, Pl. *Resp.* 4.440c, ἐπιζεῖν Ar. *Thesm.* 468; transitively ἐπαναζεῖν *P.V.* 370). It is probably accidental that no other similar application of ἀποζεῖν is preserved, but cf. Ter. *Ad.* 152 *sperabam iam deferuisse adulescentiam*.

ἀποζέσαι is here counterbalanced by ἀφυβρίσαι, likewise intransitive and admirably defined by the Seguerian *Glossary of Useful Terms* (1.173.27ff. Bachmann, 1.473.3f. Bekker; cf. introduction to Ἀποβάτης) as τὸ ἀκολάστως ὑβρίσαι ... εἰς κόρον καὶ ὥστε ἀποπληρωθῆναι, which fits every recorded use (e.g. Men. fr. 319, Plut. *Demetr.* 19, Pollux 1.217, Agathias hist. 4.9, 19; cf. Durham, *Vocabulary* 48). ἀφυβρίσαι thus properly belongs to the human half of the comparison, yet the simple ὑβρίζειν is often metaphorically applied to inanimate objects running wild, such as a river in spate (Hdt. 1.189) or a luxuriant tree (Theophr. *HP* 2.7.6). Accordingly there is no essential difficulty in applying the compound not only to man, but also to wine that is allowed to bubble over during fermentation.

4 ἀπανθήσαντα δέ: so Valckenaer (comm. on Hdt. 9.31, in P. Wesseling's edition (Amsterdam 1763) p. 706.51). Epit. of Ath. seems to have ἀπανθῆσαι (but C's final compendium is badly written, E's fifth letter strangely formed) πάλιν, which introduces an awkward asyndeton into Alexis' flowing sentence; doubtless -ήσαντα had been assimilated into the

---

[1] The LSJ entries for ἀποζέω and ἀφυβρίζω are badly classified and inaccurately defined.

162

infinitive under the influence of the three neighbouring verbs, with πάλιν subsequently ousting δέ for metrical reasons. Stob.'s ἀποινήσαντα (a legitimately formed but otherwise unrecorded compound) δέ is explicable only as a psychological error: the scribe or excerptor had combined the correct prefix and ending with the word that was uppermost in his mind as he surveyed the whole fr.: οἶνος (cf. also Alexis frs. 27.5, 159(155K).3 and comm.).

ἀπανθεῖν here is neatly ambivalent. It is applied to human beings losing the flower of their youth (e.g. Pl. Symp. 196a, Arist. Rhet. 3.4, 1406^{b}37); and since one technical meaning of ἄνθος is the surface scum that forms on wine during fermentation (LSJ s.v. I.2, Galen, De San. Tuenda 1.22, Geoponica 6.3.9, 7.15.6, 17, 7.25; cf. W. B. Stanford, G and R 5 (1935/6) 156f.), the verb also implies a picture of wine losing that scum after fermentation.

5 σκληρόν: 'harsh' or 'sour', elsewhere applied commonly to people (Ar. Pax 350 etc., LSJ s.v. σκληρός II.2), sometimes also to wine (Ath. 1.30c, Dioscorides Alex. Praef., cf. Theophr. CP 6.14.12 οἴνου ... σκληρότης, Ar. fr. 688(579K).

5–8 The first step towards a correct interpretation of these lines is Kock's punctuation (with a comma before ὧν λέγω, but none after ἁπάντων), the second is achieved by awareness of Alexis' employment in this fr. of complementary pairs of words. Here, as in vv. 3–4, two verbs are chosen, one (παρακμάσαντα) basically applicable to anything animate or inanimate that has a transitory ἀκμή, but usually employed with reference to the fading of human beauty and strength (Xen. Symp. 4.17, 8.14, Mem. 4.4.23, Arist. Pol. 3.1275^{a}17, Rhet. 2.1389^{b}13), and the other (ἀπαρυθέντα) applicable primarily to liquids like wine that get a surface skin that has to be skimmed off (cf. Hdt. 4.2). To force the parallelism of his εἰκών Alexis is willing to strain syntax and word order. Although παρακμάζω is strictly intransitive, it is here made to balance ἀπαρυθέντα, which retains a direct object in the passive by analogy with other verbs of deprivation that govern two direct objects in the active (K.G. 1.324ff.); translate 'having passed his/its prime and been skimmed of this exterior layer of folly which consists of all those things I'm mentioning'. ὧν λέγω τούτων ἁπάντων defines τὴν ἄνοιαν, as Kock points out; it is deliberately placed directly after παρακμάσαντα δ', however, in order to hint delicately that men too are liberated from the follies of youth when they pass their prime. The words ὧν λέγω τ. ἁ. refer to ἀποζέσαι ... ἀφυβρίσαι τ' (3–4) and σκληρὸν γενέσθαι (5). – The MSS of Stob. (SMA) omit the words after γενέσθαι (5) up to γενέσθαι (8) by a saut des yeux du même au même.

6–7 τὴν ἄνω ταύτην ἄνοιαν ἐπιπολάζουσαν: parallel imagery again, playing on the double meaning of ἐπιπολάζω, whose basic sense 'I float on the surface' (LSJ s.v. 1) eminently suits the 'top' (ἄνω) scum that floats on fermenting wine (cf. *Geoponica* 7.15.6 τὸ δὲ μελανὸν ἢ ξανθὸν ἄνθος ἐπιπολάζον τῷ οἴνῳ), while the transferred sense 'I am prevalent' fits the folly of men. As there is no noun in Greek which unites the meaning of 'folly' and 'wine scum', Alexis underlines the parallelism by the echoing assonance of ἄνω (suggesting the scum) and ἄνοιαν.

7 It is only *after* the floating film has been skimmed off that man and wine become mellow; Boissonade's τότε (in Schweighaeuser, *Animadv.* 8.398) for the MSS ποτ(ὲ) is inescapable. Confusion between these two words is endemic in MSS over a wide range of centuries (e.g. Eur. *Andr.* 52, *El.* 42, Isaeus 5.8, Pl. *Resp.* 5.451b, Men. *Dysk.* 16, 531); here presumably the initial syllable of the following word (πότιμον) was the springboard for the error.

8 πότιμον: literally 'drinkable' (Heraclitus fr. 61 Diels–Kranz = 35 Marcovich, Hdt. 8.22, etc.) and in a transferred sense applied to those who are good company at drinking-parties, i.e. 'sociable' (Theoc. 29.31 and the passages collected by Gow *ad loc.*). The *double entendre* here is obvious, providing firm evidence for the existence of the secondary sense half a century or more before Theocritus. For the pun cf. also Heliodorus 3.10 ποτιμώτερον τὸ συμπόσιον ἀπεργαζόμενος, and perhaps Xen. Eph. 1.9.3.

καταστῆναι: of wine, 'to settle' after fermentation (*Geoponica* 7.14.9); of people, 'to become composed' (Arist. *Pol.* 8.1342ᵃ10, LSJ s.v. καθίστημι B.4), and especially 'to gain the composure of maturity', so that οἱ καθεστηκότες = 'those of mature years' (Hippocr. *Aph.* 1.13, cf. Thuc. 2.36, [Pl.] *Epist.* 3.316c).

9 ἡδύν: of wine, 'pleasant to the taste', already in Homer (*Od.* 3.51, 9.197, etc., cf. Xen. *Anab.* 6.4.6 ἀμπέλους ἡδυοίνους); of people, 'agreeable', first apparently in Alcman (fr. 59b.1 Page), but not attested in Athens until the second half of the 5th century (S. *Aj.* 105, *OT* 82, etc.).

47 (46K)

Meineke 3.403 (1), Kock 2.314, Edmonds 2.394, Kassel–Austin 2.48. The fr. is (? part, perhaps the opening lines, of) a monologue delivered on entry by an unidentified character who has just been to market (see the introduction to Δημήτριος).

1–3 The implications of the tie between these vv. (as far as οὐδενὶ φαγεῖν) and Turpilus, *Demetrius* fr. v are fully examined in the introduction to Δημήτριος.

2 λαμπρός: of winds, 'fresh' (LSJ s.v. 5).

ἰχθῦς οὐκ ἐνῆν: 'there was no fish in (sc. the city or the market)'. ἐνῆν here is correctly transmitted by the MSS (A, Epit. of Ath. 8.338d); the construction (imperfect indicative without ἄν) is the one normal in the apodosis of a frequentative in historic sequence (K.G. 2.450f., Goodwin, *MT* 170f., 204f.). Efforts to interpret the sentence otherwise as an example of a mixed condition and to insert ἄν in the apodosis (οὐκ ἄν ἦν Porson, *Adv.* 102, οὐκέτ' ἦν ... φαγεῖν ἄν with ἄν awkwardly placed Meineke, *Anal. Crit.* 150) wilfully disregard the signal of past time posted by the fr.'s first word.

3 Schweighaeuser's metrically rectifying νυνὶ δὲ for ACE's νῦν δὲ is an almost certain correction, in view of the frequency of this particular corruption in MSS written when the deictic form νυνί was obsolete; cf. Ar. *Equ.* 531, *Ran.* 419, Men. *Epitr.* 1121, *Kol.* 51, fr. 740.17, Ath. citing Anaxilas 22.15, Clearchus 3.4 (cf. Porson, *Adv.* 50, *pace* Kassel–Austin 4.80).

4 Φάϋλλος: probably a character in the play (a parasite?), see the introduction to Δημήτριος.

προσγέγονε χειμὼν τρίτος: comparison or identification of violent or voracious men with storms and the like is a comic commonplace that probably draws its inspiration from popular language. At Alexis 183(178K).4–7 (see comm. *ad loc.*) a host prays for a parasite λῆξαι πνέοντα καὶ γαληνίσαι ποτέ· | χειμὼν ὁ μειρακίσκος ἐστὶ τοῖς φίλοις. In Aristophanes Cleon is vituperated as τυφώς and ἐριώλη (*Equ.* 511, cf. 430f.), with the voice of a χαράδρα (*Vesp.* 1034, cf. *Equ.* 137, *Ach.* 381) and the throat of a Χάρυβδις (*Equ.* 248), and Dikaiopolis says to the Boeotian ὡσπερεὶ χειμὼν ἄρα | ὀρνιθίας εἰς τὴν ἀγορὰν ἐλήλυθας (*Ach.* 876f.). Similarly the verbal fluency of the regenerated Cratinus is compared to the torrent Ilissus (Cratinus 198(186K), and a woman's tirade to a χαράδρα (Pherecrates 56(51K)). In Menander Nikeratos is described as στρόβιλος ἢ σκηπτός (*Sam.* 555f.); cf. also *Asp.* 402f. σκηπτός τις εἰς τὴν οἰκίαν | ῥαγδαῖος ἐμπέπτωκε, monost. 823 χειμὼν κατ' οἴκους ἀνδράσιν κακὴ γυνή. Closely parallel is Horace's description of Maenius as *pernicies et tempestas barathrumque macelli* (*Epist.* 1.15.31).

5 ἐκνεφίας, continuing the identification, is in apposition to the subject (K.G. 2.495f.). It would be wrong, in a discussion of this idiom, to talk about any 'omission of ὥσπερ': in fact the thing compared is identified with the object of comparison, and we have an example of what Fraenkel terms (on A. *Ag.* 1178ff., 3.542) the 'mutual penetration' of things and their objects of comparison, which is a special feature of dramatic language. Cf. e.g. Ar. *Vesp.* 144 καπνὸς ἔγωγ' ἐξέρχομαι and Starkie *ad loc.*, Men. *Mis.* 168 ἀγαθὸν ἄκουσμ' ἥκεις πρὸς ἡμᾶς, Alexis 183(178K).3 and comm. *ad loc.*, Herodas 6.13f. κἠγὼ ἐπιβρύχουσ' ἡμέρην τε καὶ νύκτα | κύων ὑλακτέω τῆ[ς] ἀνωνύμοις ταύτης and Headlam *ad loc.*; Kock on Cratinus 56(52K), P. Shorey, *CPhil.* 4 (1909) 433ff., Handley on Men. *Dysk.* 444f. and especially Fraenkel, *EP* 47ff.

ἐκνεφίας (in Greek comedy only here and Teleclides 48, cf. M. Grone-

COMMENTARY

wald, *ZPE* 42 (1981) 9) is a violent, roughly north to north-westerly (cf. D'A. W. Thompson, *CR* 22 (1918) 49ff.) wind blowing in spring and (particularly) autumn (Arist. *Meteor.* 2.6, 365ᵃ1ff.), taking its name κατὰ ῥῆξιν νέφους ... καὶ ἀνάλυσιν τοῦ πάχους ([Arist.] *Mund.* 4, 394ᵇ16ff., cf. also *Meteor.* 2.8, 366ᵇ31ff., [Arist.] *Probl.* 26.6, 940ᵇ30ff., Theophr. *Sign.* 36, Diod. Sic. 20.88.7, Pliny *HN* 2.131, Seneca *Quaest. Nat.* 15.12, and F. Marx on Lucilius xvi, 527 (2.198ff.)). καταιγίζειν is properly applied to such strong winds (καταιγίσαι· καταπνεῦσαι σφοδρῶς Σ A. *Sept.* 63, cf. Hesych. s.v. καταιγίς, Erotian s.v. πόνος καταιγίζων, Strabo 16.4.5, Josephus *AJ* 3.5.2), but the meaning was extended metaphorically as early as Aeschylus (*Sept.* 63, fr. 195); cf. Alexis 249(247K).3, com. adesp. fr. 1227 Kock. Demosthenes' attack on Meidias (21.72) was said by [Longinus] 20.3 to be ὡς αἱ καταιγίδες, and the verbal congener suits here with equal felicity Phayllus' onslaught on the fish-market.

6 τοὖψον: 'fish being the preferred ὄψον, that word is often employed ... to mean *fish* as a comestible' (Gow on Machon 28); cf. Plut. *Mor.* 667f, Ath. 7.276e–f, LSJ s.v. ὄψον 3, *RE* s.v. Ὄψον 789.18ff. (Hug) and *Kochkunst* 950.41ff. (Orth), O. Longo, *Materiali e Discussioni per l'analisi dei testi classici* 18 (1987) 9ff.

7 γίγνεται: see comm. on 37(36K).7.

8 ἐν τοῖς λαχάνοις: i.e. that part of the market where vegetables were on sale (cf. Ar. *Lys.* 557, Diphilus 31(32K).22, *Suda* s.v. λαχάνοις), by the vivid Attic idiom which called the place in the market where a commodity was sold by the name of that commodity (Pollux 9.47, Σ Aeschines 1.65). Similarly ἐν τοῖς ἰχθύσιν (Ar. *Vesp.* 789 and Starkie *ad loc.*, Alexis 57(56K).3, 78.5, Antiphanes 123(125K).1, cf. Ar. *Ran.* 1068), εἰς τοὖψον (Pollux and Aeschines, *locc. citt.*, Ar. fr. 258(247K), Alexis 249(247K).2, Antiphanes 201(203K), cf. Ar. fr. 557(545K).1, πρὸς τοὖλαιον (Men. fr. 700), εὐθὺ τῶν ἀρωμάτων Eupolis 327(304K).3, εἰς τὸν χλωρὸν τυρόν (Lysias 23.6), etc., with a few interesting extensions to non-comestible, non-domestic products, e.g. ἐν τοῖν δυοῖν ὀβολοῖν (the two-obol seats in the theatre, Dem. 18.28), παρὰ ταῖς πόρναις (the red-light district, Ar. *Pax* 165). Cf. Hermann–Blümner, *Privatalterthümer* 135 n. 1, Durham, *Vocabulary* 57.

48 (47K)

Meineke 3.404 (ii), Kock. 2.314, Edmonds 2.396, Kassel–Austin 2.49. This fr. is quoted by Ath. 6.241b for its mention of the parasite usually known as Κόρυδος[1] – his real name apparently was Eucrates (Lynceus in

---

[1] Ribbeck, *Kolax* 8of. collects the extant information about him, deriving mainly from Ath. 6.241a–242d, 245d–246a, whose source throughout in

ΔΗΜΗΤΡΙΟΣ

Ath. 241d, Machon 1)[1] – who was active in the city of Athens during the years c. 345–305. (cf. introduction to Δημήτριος). This dating is secured by his association with several better-known Athenians at the time such as Callimedon ὁ Κάραβος (see introduction to Δορκίς and comm. on fr. 57(56K), who all belonged together with Eucrates to a famous Athenian dining-club which met in the shrine of Heracles at Melite (see introduction to Ἰσοστάσιον). Of Eucrates himself little is known; according to contemporary comic poets he was poor (Timocles 11), fond of his food (Alexis here, Cratinus jun. 8, Timocles 10, 11, Euphanes 1.6) and always ready with a joke (Alexis 188(183K), 229(227K); Lynceus cites specimens, some lively, some flat). These characteristics were typical of the stage parasite, who was doubtless modelled on men like him. The reason for his nickname is obscure. The 5th-century tragedian Philocles also was nicknamed Κόρυδος (Ar. Av. 1295), and we are told that he was ugly (Thesm. 168 and Σ ad loc.); Bechtel, Spitznamen 39f. suggests that the ugliness might partly have consisted of untidy hair which stuck up like the crest of the bird κόρυδος (crested lark, Galerida cristata; cf. Thompson, Birds s.w. κορύδαλος). However, no ridicule is directed at Eucrates' hair, so possibly one must look elsewhere (pace Gow on Machon 1) for an explanation of the nickname. It could have been given because Eucrates was particularly fond of eating small birds like larks (cf. Anaxandrides 42(41K).65); alternatively, it might have stigmatised an unpleasantly shrill voice. The crested lark's call involves a shrill repetition of two notes, and its song is far less distinguished than a skylark's. Ancient writers called the bird unmusical (Dioscorides, Anth. Pal. 11.195 = 36 Gow–Page 5f. ἐν γὰρ ἀμούσοις | καὶ κόρυδος κύκνου φθέγγετ' ἀοιδότερον, cf. Eustath. 1072.40, J. T. Allen, CR 42 (1928) 5). Thus Ribbeck's suggestion (Kolax 71) that the nickname was attached to Eucrates 'vom Lacheln und seiner hellen Stimme' stems from an ornithological misidentification.

The speaker of this fr. seems to be accepting an invitation to luncheon (ἄριστον), not without a show of reluctance. More than this dare not be said.

1–2 ἀλλ' αἰσχύνομαι . . . εἰ δόξω: for the construction cf. Eur. Ion 1074f. αἰσχύνομαι τὸν πολύυμνον θεόν, εἰ . . . ὄψεται, Hyps. fr. 60 Bond = 60.i Cockle 58f. αἰσχύνομαι δὲ Φοῖβον . . . ψεῦδος εἴ τ]ι λέξομεν, Xen. Oec. 21.4, Lysias 3.3, [Dem.] 25.63.

4 Dindorf's substitution of the Attic form ἄν for ACE's ἐάν removes a split anapaest rare at this sedes (CQ 7 (1957) 189), cf. also frs. 103(98K).22,

---

all probability was Lynceus of Samos, a contemporary of Theophrastus. Cf. also Breitenbach, Webster, Gow, and Gow–Page, locc. citt. in the introduction to Δημήτριος.

[1] A common Athenian name: Kirchner lists some fourteen examples from the 4th century alone (PA 1.372f., 2.460, among 5746b–66).

COMMENTARY

145(141K).11, 234(232K).4; 'nempe in codd. antiquissimis sexcenties EAN pro AN scribi solet uitiosissime' (Cobet, NL 551, cf. Mayser 2.1.263ff., 2.3.58, Handley's edition of Men. Dysk. p. 64).¹

At the end of the verse Nauck's supplement <ἄν τε μή> (MGR 2 (1866) 733, after Bothe's ἄν δὲ μή, PCGF 528) is virtually certain: not merely does it complete the verse with an appropriate sense-perfect idiom (cf. e.g. Ar. Eccl. 981, 1097, Plut. 638, Alexis 103(98K).26), it also provides the most plausible punch line for a joke about Eucrates; the gate-crashing parasite was a standard comic theme (cf. comm. on Alexis 213(210K).2, and also Plaut. Trin. 474f.).

49 (48K)

Meineke 3.404 (III), Kock 2.314, Edmonds 2.396, Kassel–Austin 2.50. The fr. is part of a conventional cook's monologue describing his food purchases in pretentious terms. Virtually the same three verses reappear in the middle of another such speech, extensively preserved, from the Κράτεια (115(110K).9–11). Did Alexis in one of these two plays repeat with or without modification a whole ῥῆσις from the earlier play? The transfer would not have been difficult; scenes involving cooks often appear to be episodic additives of humorous content with only minimal integration into the plot. The sole pretext a 4th- or 3rd-century comic poet needed for the introduction of a cook into his gallery of characters was a luncheon or dinner-party at some point in his plot. Either on entry or later the cook would be expected by the audience to deliver a long, arrogant and pretentious encomium of the mageiric art. Of the two fully developed examples in complete comedies, the cook's big scene in Plautus' Pseudolus (790ff.), which seems to preserve the main features of its unknown Greek original, presents with its farrago of Munchausen-like braggadocio, lists of real and imaginary seasonings, and grotesquely inflated language, some typical features of the genre. A great number of the contextless frs. preserved in Ath. would fit like a glove into parallel scenes; from Alexis alone one might cite along with 49(48K) frs. 24, 84, 92(88K), 115(110K), 129(124K), 132–3(127–8K), 138(133K), 153(149K), 177–80(172–5K), 191–4(186–9K).²

---

¹ Accordingly, at [Men.] P.Didot 1.27 the text needs to be corrected to φέρ' ἄν.

² See especially Dohm, Mageiros 84ff., whose useful analysis of the relevant material is slightly marred by an errant attempt to force the various motifs and formal patterns into a chronological straitjacket (cf. JHS 85 (1965) 183). For further discussion of the material see the bibliography in the first paragraph of comm. on fr. 24; on the cook scene

ΔΗΜΗΤΡΙΟΣ

In favour of the theory that Alexis partly or substantially used the same cook's monologue in both Κράτεια and Δημήτριος is a point first noted by Meineke (3.430). Ath. 3.108a asserts that in Δημήτριος Alexis mentions ταγηνιστοὶ ἰχθύες (= fr. 51(50K), 'just as' (καθάπερ) in the fr. of Κράτεια (115(110K)) which Ath. had quoted immediately before. The reference to ταγηνιστοὶ ἰχθύες in fr. 115(110K).12–14 comes directly after the three verses shared with Δημήτριος fr. 49(48K). It is highly probable that the cook's speech in Δημήτριος continued after the end of fr. 49(48K) with vv. 12–14 of fr. 115(110K) perhaps completely unaltered.

The cook who makes this speech would have been hired to cook the luncheon mentioned in fr. 48(47K).2 (see the introduction to Δημήτριος).

1 ἔλαβον: 'I bought': see comm. on 15.18.

2–4 ἐνθυμούμενος ... παθεῖν: an engaging example of cook's ἀλα-ζονεία. The speaker imagines fallaciously that the electric organs of the νάρκη (electric ray: see comm. on 38(37K)) might still endanger a lady's delicate fingers even when the fish is dead and being either prepared for the table or eaten. The live ray's numbing discharge was familiar to 4th-century Athenians (e.g. Pl. *Men.* 80a καὶ γὰρ αὕτη τὸν ἀεὶ πλησιά-ζοντα καὶ ἁπτόμενον ναρκᾶν ποιεῖ, Arist. *HA* 9.37, 620ᵇ19ff., cf. Ath. 7.314a–e; Thompson, *Fishes* s.v. νάρκη); they may have been unable to explain the phenomenon with scientific accuracy, but they knew that it was physical contact with the fish (or any conductor attached to the fish) that caused the shock. Oppian *Hal.* 2.63 names the electrical organs κερκίδες, a word that suits perfectly the vertical hexagonal columns (between the head and pectoral fins) which discharge the electricity. Was Alexis – or his cook – aware of the location of these electric organs? In this fr. the source of the danger is given as the ἄκανθα (v.3), a term normally applied to the backbone of such creatures (LSJ s.v. 6, citing A. fr. 275, Ar. *Vesp.* 969 and these words of Alexis as they appear in fr. 115(110K).11). But ἄκανθα is used of other fish bones (e.g. the hair bones of ἀφυαί and similar species, Ath. 8.357e) and even (in the plural) spiny parts of a fish's exterior (see comm. on 138(133K).2–3), so that the word *may* here have been intended to signify the ray's columnar organs. Alternatively, the cook's ignorance might have extended beyond his assumption that dead rays could sting; he may have been intended to suppose that their mysterious discharges emanated from the backbone.

3 τούτους: sc. the women's fingers. At fr. 115(110K).11 this is corrup-ted by the *Marcianus* (Ath. 3.107c) to a pointless τούτων (see comm. *ad loc.*)

---

in Plaut. *Pseud.* see also J. C. B. Lowe, *Class. Ant.* 4 (1985) 89f., *CQ* 35 (1985) 411ff.

COMMENTARY

50 (49K)

Meineke 3.404 (v), Kock 2.315, Edmonds 2.396, Kassel–Austin 2.50. The speaker is most probably a parasite, cook or slave, to judge from his present function and indecent language in v. 3. He is delivering some fish (ὄψον v. 1, see on fr. 47(46K).6), which presumably he or an associate had bought in the market (the purchaser spoke fr. 47(46K)), to two or more women (cf. λαβοῦσαι v. 1), probably the household of the courtesan whose part in the plot is attested by the Turpilian fragments; cf. a similar scene in Plaut. *Truc.* 551ff. The women here addressed were perhaps not on stage, but imagined to be somewhere behind the half-open door of a stage-house.

1 τἀπεσταλμένον (apograph P of the *Marcianus* at Ath. 14.663d, Musurus, Kassel–Austin) makes less good sense dramatically as an emendation of A's ταπεταλμενον than Hirschig's τοὐπεσταλμένον (*Annot.* 10); the fish is presumably 'sent to' (? and extorted from her lover by) the *hetaira* at whose house it is now being delivered.

3 λέπεσθε, ματτυάζετε: the sequence of second-person plurals (here probably all imperatives, but Alexis may be playing on the ambiguity of form between indicative and imperative: cf. e.g. Men. *Dysk.* 623f. and my note in *Gnomon* 39 (1967) 346) reaches its climax with these two indelicate expressions. For the women there is first the meal to be prepared, secondly sumptuous feasting, thirdly the drinking of toasts. After the toasts, when the participants in the revelry have become tipsy or drunk, comes λέπεσθε. The LSJ entry for λέπω is wrong in its range of meanings and grouping of examples. The comic occurrences need reclassifying as follows:

(1) 'peel': Eupolis 275(255K).2 (λέποντα Meineke's correction of a nonsensical βλέποντα in ACE at Ath. 4.170d), Antiphanes 133(135K).3 (λέπει = 'takes the crust off' a loaf; the mistranslation 'eats', which goes back to Daléchamp,[1] is alien to the word's normal usages and misses the point of Antiphanes' joke. The man described is so mean or poor that he not only abstains from eating meat but even after buying a piece only of the cheapest bread he doesn't eat it all but first removes the crust; if we possessed more of the fr. we should probably learn that he put the crust away for another meal).

(2) By a natural (probably colloquial) metaphorical extension, 'flay': Plato com. 12, Apollodorus Car. 5.10, Timocles 31(29K).3.

---

[1] The only evidence that has ever been adduced in support of this mistranslation is a corrupt note in Photius: †λέπτει†· κατεσθίει· οὕτως Εὔπολις (465(427K)), where Meineke (2.575) conjectured λέπει for λέπτει. Even if Meineke's conjecture is correct (to me Schleusner's λάπτει seems preferable), the likeliest source of the Photian definition would be a misinterpretation of a passage such as Eupolis 275(255K).

ΔΗΜΗΤΡΙΟΣ

(3) Ath. 12.663c–d cites the grammarian Artemidorus for a third meaning which the latter illustrates by citing the present fr. of Alexis and defines as follows: τῷ δὲ λέπεσθαι χρῶνται οἱ Ἀθηναῖοι ἐπὶ ἀσελγοῦς καὶ φορτικῆς δι' ἀφροδισίων ἡδονῆς. Artemidorus appears to have been influenced by a more illustrious predecessor, Aristophanes of Byzantium (the facts about the relationship are confused: see Wentzel in *RE* s.v. *Artemidoros* 31, 1331.30ff.); one example of this influence may have been the interest in Greek comedy which led Artemidorus to compile a λέξεων συναγωγή, the source doubtless of the passage citing Alexis and cited by Ath. Artemidorus' interpretation of λέπεσθαι here has the ring of truth. In this third meaning λέπεσθαι (middle rather than passive: cf. LSJ) has developed (from peeling and flaying) sexual overtones which Artemidorus (in the passage quoted by Ath.) does not specify, but Eustathius 1752.2ff. (after copying out Artemidorus' words) exemplifies with ἡδονῆς ὁποία τοῦ δέφεσθαι. Although δέφεσθαι is always applied to male masturbation, the basic ideas of peeling and flaying in λέπεσθαι would make an extension of meaning to female masturbation no less appropriate in the present passage of Alexis (cf. J. Henderson, *The Maculate Muse* (New Haven and London 1975) 220ff.).

(4) Mnesimachus 4.18f.: πρόποσις χωρεῖ, λέπεται (Porson in Dobree, *Adv.* 2.323: λείπεται ACE at Ath. 9.403a) κόρδαξ, | ἀκολασταίνει νοῦς μειρακίων, where the context is remarkably similar to that of the Alexis passage, seems to present a stage in the development of the meaning of λέπεσθαι half-way between (2) and (3) above. Its κόρδαξ 'is thrashed out', presumably with the provocative and indecent limb movements of a dance whose lewdness was notorious.

The final word in Alexis' chain is ματτυάζετε. It would be astonishing if the speaker chose as the last in his series of increasingly forceful and vulgar expressions a verb which meant simply 'make (or eat) the rich, spiced dish called ματτύη', as all the lexicographers, editors and translators (following Ath. 663c τὸ δὲ ματτυάζειν τὸ παρασκευάζειν αὐτά, sc. ματτύας) assume when dealing with this passage, the only one in Attic authors where the verb is known to occur. Admittedly the noun ματτύη is often used in a purely culinary sense, but its associations with heavy drinking and the more debauched activities at parties (cf. Pollux 6.70, where ματύλλη is synonymous with ματτύη, and Photius s.v. ματτύης) gave the word insalubrious overtones, and there is one passage (Alexis 208(205K): see comm. *ad loc.*, discussing also culinary aspects) where an indelicate significance may be uppermost. It is accordingly likely that the verb at times bore the same indecent overtones, becoming a vulgar but picturesque synonym of ἀσελγαίνω. Artemidorus, despite his interest in the culinary aspects of ματτύη, goes out of his way to emphasise τὴν ἀκολασίαν τῆς παρασκευῆς when introducing the present fr. of Alexis (in Ath. 663c).

COMMENTARY

51 (50K)

Meineke 3.404 (IV), Kock 2.315, Edmonds 2.396, Kassel–Austin 2.50.
Ath.'s words (3.108a) ταγηνιστῶν δ' ἰχθύων μνημονεύει Ἄλεξις ἐν
Δημητρίῳ καθάπερ κἀν τῷ προκειμένῳ δράματι (sc. the Κράτεια, fr.
115(110K).12–13) imply (as Meineke 3.430 first observed: cf. my introduction to fr. 49(48K)) that the text of 115(110K).12–13 was repeated,
perhaps verbatim, in Δημήτριος; fr. 51(50) would then be a continuation
of fr. 49(48K). Ath.'s phrase ταγηνιστῶν ἰχθύων would thus be paraphrasing Alexis' different words; it is almost superfluous to add that this
passage of Ath. has accordingly no title to be cited as evidence that Alexis
ever used the adjective ταγηνιστός.[1]

Διαπλέουσαι

'Women sailing across the sea (or? through the straits)' is a unique title. In
view of the play's negligible remains there is no point in speculating about
the relation of voyage to plot. Worth noting, however, are the small but
necessary roles played by voyages of the Andrian women and the Bacchis
twins before the beginning of Ter. *Andr.* (69ff.) and Plaut. *Bacch.*
respectively, the more important impact of Palaestra's and Ampelisca's
voyage and shipwreck in the first act of Plaut. *Rud.*, and the voyage across
from Ephesus that two women seem to have made just before the action of
Men. *Kith.* begins (cf. *ZPE* 31 (1978) 28f.). Such parallels may be illusory;
they will at least discourage scholars from altering Alexis' title to Δὶς
πλέουσαι, as Meineke 3.406 suggested.

52 (51K)

Meineke 3.406, Kock 2.315, Edmonds 2.396, Kassel–Austin 2.51. The
context is unknown.

ἐπιχαιρέκακος, whose use is tolerated by Atticist and Antiatticist alike,[2]
is a compound adjective first appearing in 4th-century comedy (cf. also
Anaxandrides 60(59K).2 and Timocles' title). Arist. *Eth. Nic.* 2.7,

---

[1] Yet LSJ s.v. ταγηνιστός fall into this trap. With more care they would
have noticed the difference between e.g. the actual words of Alexis in fr.
54(52K) and the introductory lemma in Ath. 15.686a–b.

[2] The Antiatticist (91.21 Bekker) cites the present line of Alexis, Pollux
3.101 allows the word to be ἀνεκτόν and Phrynichus admits it with
definition but no further comment into his *Praep. Soph.* (71.1 de Borries).
Cf. G. Kaibel, *De Phrynicho sophista* (Göttingen 1899) 18.

172

ΔΙΑΠΛΕΟΥΣΑΙ

1108[b]1ff. places ἐπιχαιρεκακία as the vice opposite to φθόνος, where νέμεσις is the mean (cf. M. Tierney, *PRIA* 43c (1936) 252f., A. Barigazzi, *La formazione spirituale di Menandro* (Turin 1965) 224ff.).

Δίδυμοι (and/or Δίδυμαι)

In quoting frs. 55(53K) and 54(52K) Ath. 10.446f and 15.686a reports the title twice as Alexis' Δίδυμοι, but in quoting fr. 53(54K) Pollux 9.153 identifies its source as ἐν Διδύμαις (so FSC: L however has -ύμοις[1]). Probably all three references are to the same play, as editors have generally assumed, with the gender difference due to a corruption at some stage of excerption or transmission; errors of this kind involving title endings are unhappily frequent (cf. the introduction to Ἀποκοπτόμενος). At the same time, since identical twins both male and female appear so often as title figures or heroes and heroines in Greco-Roman comedy,[2] the possibility that Alexis composed both a Δίδυμοι and a Δίδυμαι cannot be ruled out. No help is given by the frs. for the elucidation of title, date or plot; the context of frs. 54(52K) and 55(53K), however, seems to be a drinking party, as frequently in frs. cited by Ath. On the attribution of Kock's fr. 278b to this play, see below on fr. 53(54 + 278b K).

53 (54 + 278bK)

Meineke 3.406 (III), 407; Kock 2.316, 3.744; Edmonds 2.398, 510; Kassel–Austin 2.51.

(a) 53(54K + 278bK). Pollux 9.153 cites Alexis' Δίδυμαι (see above) for use of the phrase ὡς ἐπὶ τὸ πλῆθος (54K), and Stob. *Anth.* 4.19.40 cites from Alexis without play title four iambic trimeters beginning ἀλλ' ἐπὶ τὸ

---

[1] L's date and ancestry (see Bethe's edition of Pollux, 1 (Leipzig 1900), *praef.* p. x) seem to indicate that this reading is less likely to represent correct tradition than to be a corruption or even an adjustment of the Pollux text in the light of the Athenaeus parallels.

[2] Plays entitled Δίδυμοι were written by Anaxandrides, Antiphanes the younger (for fr. 81 could not have been written by the elder Antiphanes: cf. Webster, *SLGC* 108, 240), Aristophon, Euphron and Xenarchus; Δίδυμαι titles are ascribed to Menander and the elder Antiphanes (Αὐλητρὶς ἢ Δίδυμαι, dated roughly to the middle of the 4th century by the references to Phoenicides and Taureas in fr. 50(48K): cf. Webster, *SLGC.* 68). Titinius wrote a *togata* entitled *Gemina*, Novius an Atellane farce *Gemini*, and Laberius a mime *Gemelli*. Extant Roman comedy provides natural pairs of identical twins in Plautus' male *Menaechmi* and female *Bacchides*.

COMMENTARY

πλῆθος (278b Kock, 3.744). Meineke's suggestion (3.407) that the Stob. fr. '*integrum locum, quem respexit Pollux, fortasse seruauit*' persuaded Kassel–Austin to print it under the Δίδυμοι title, injudiciously on two accounts. (1) The formula ὡς ἐπὶ τὸ πλῆθος, which is well attested in Attic and later writers (e.g. Pl. *Phdr.* 275b, *Resp.* 2.364a, Musonius fr. 18 Hense p. 104.8f., Hierocles in Stob. *Anth.*4.28.21 Hense p. 698.6f.; a variant reading in Arist. *GA* 5.6, 786ᵃ35), is likely (as a metrically convenient variation of the commoner ὡς ἐπὶ τὸ πολύ) to have occurred more than once in Alexis' vast output. (2) The Stob. fr. begins with ἀλλ' ἐπὶ τὸ πλῆθος not ὡς ἐπὶ τὸ πλ.; the lack of exact correspondence with Pollux is an extra inducement to caution, however ready we may be to admit the proneness of excerptors to error at the beginning of citations (cf. comm. on 29.1).

(b) 53(278bK). The four verses are an unidentified character's comment about a slave's recent (possibly good, possibly bad) behaviour. Although in Alexis' time a popular belief existed that perpetual war was waged between slaves and their masters (cf. Dover, *GPM* 92f., 114f., 285), the idea that shared habitation could also produce similar behaviour was evidently a commonplace at least in later comedy, expressed by e.g. the (pretended) master in Plaut. *Amph.* 959ff.:

> *atque ita seruom par uidetur frugi sese instituere:*
> *proinde eri ut sint, ipse item sit; uoltum e uoltu comparet:*
> *tristis sit, si eri sint tristes; hilaris sit, si gaudeant...*

and by the slave in *Most.* 872f.:

> *nam, ut serui uolunt esse erum, ita solet.*
> *boni sunt, <bonust>* (Th. Bergk: *bonis sum* MSS); *improbi sunt, malus fit.*

The passages suggest possible contexts for the Alexis fr. Cf. also Petronius 58.3 *plane qualis dominus, talis et seruus.*

1–2 For the wording cf. e.g. Ar. *Vesp.* 1102f. πολλαχοῦ σκοποῦντες ἡμᾶς εἰς ἅπανθ' εὑρήσετε | τοὺς τρόπους καὶ τὴν δίαιταν σφηξὶν ἐμφερεστάτους.

3 οἷς ὑπηρετοῦσ' ἀεί: Valckenaer's palmary correction (in Gaisford's edition of Stob., 2 (Oxford 1822) 449.40 note b; cf. *praef.* 1.x) of SMA's τοῖς ὑπηρετοῦσα καὶ. The grammatical antecedent of οἷς here is τοῖς ἤθεσιν, but 'the characteristics which they serve' is clearly colloquial shorthand for 'the characteristics of those whom they serve'.

4 τούτοις ἡ φύσις κεράννυται: cf. e.g. Pl. *Epist.* 7.326c οὐχ οὕτω θαυμαστῇ φύσει κραθήσεται;, Philo 2.64.10 Wendland τὴν δὲ φύσιν ἀπένειμε τοῖς φυτοῖς κερασάμενος αὐτὴν ἐκ πλείστων δυνάμεων; κεράννυμι + ἤθη Pl. *Legg.* 12.949e, cf. *Phdr.* 279a; + νοῦς *Legg.* 12.961d; + σύνεσις Men. fr. 531.

54 (52K)

Meineke 3.406 (II), Kock 2.315, Edmonds 2.396, Kassel–Austin 2.52. The occasion for the garlands here mentioned may have been a drinking party (cf. fr. 55(53K)) which ended the play (cf. my note in *Hermes* 93 (1965) 254f., and Sandbach on Men. *Dysk.* 964). Our main literary source on ancient garlands (for a brief modern bibliography see on fr. 4.2) is Ath. 14.671d–686c, from where the present fr. derives. The value of Ath.'s lavish information, however, is slightly impaired by shaky organisation and an inability to distinguish correctly those passages in which garlands are given specific or technical names (e.g. names of places or plants) from others in which garlands are just casually described, as here. Alexis is not identifying a particular kind of wreath by an appellative χυδαῖοι, as Ath. implies, but simply describing garlands that had been 'plaited higgledy-piggledy'. There is a similar error at 679e–f in Ath.'s categorisation of ἑλικτοὶ στέφανοι as a separate group.

τούτων <τῶν> χύδην πεπλεγμένων: τῶν, omitted in A by haplography, was conjectured by Bergk (see Meineke 5.cciii) nine years before Meineke himself made the same suggestion (*Anal. Crit.* 335).

55 (53K)

Meineke 3.406 (I), Kock 2.315, Edmonds 2.398, Kassel–Austin 2.52. Translate 'Drink this man's health, so that he himself too (may drink) another's.' These words are probably part only of a complete sentence, but it is futile to speculate on the number or identity of the words lost in transition from Alexis' original text to excerptor's tag. Yet the context is clear. The scene is a drinking-party, similar perhaps to the one that closes Plautus' *Stichus* (where cf. especially vv. 708, 710). The speaker is proposing a toast. In Attic symposia one drank the health of all the participants in succession, passing on the loving-cup (φιλοτησία: see on fr. 59(58K)) anti-clockwise (cf. e.g. Pl. *Symp.* 214, Ath. 10.432d–e, 11.463f, Heliodorus 3.11.2, 7.27; Navarre in Dar.–Sag. s.v. *Symposium* 1580a, Mau in *RE* s.v. *Comissatio* 613.61ff.).

Δὶς πενθῶν

Meineke 1.399. The title, of a form familiar in Greek comedy (Kock 2.316 compares Menander's Δὶς ἐξαπατῶν, Heniochus' Δὶς ἐξαπατώμενος and Augeas' Δὶς κατηγορούμενος; the Roman stage supplies an anonymous *Bis compressa*, Aul. Gell. 3.3.9), is self-explanatory to anyone familiar with comic motifs (double mourning in Men. *Asp.* 1ff., 343ff., single in Ter.

COMMENTARY

Andr. 105ff., *Phorm.* 95ff.). The one surviving fr., however, tells us nothing about its own or the title's relevance to the plot. One would like to know whether the two deaths implied by the title were simulated (like that of Chairestratos in Men. *Asp.*; cf. my introductions to Μανδραγοριζομένη, Συναποθνῄσκοντες), falsely reported (like that of Kleostratos in *Asp.*) or real (like those in Ter. *Andr.*, *Phorm.*).

56 (55K)

Meineke 3.407, Kock 2.316, Edmonds 2.398, Kassel–Austin 2.52. The absence of any verb in the citation prevents our knowing whether this Zopyra is being abusively called a 'wine-pot' (for a discussion of both predication and image see comm. on fr. 88(85K).4), or whether she is described in comically inflated language as e.g. picking a pot up, with the verb in the unquoted context. Either way it is likely that Zopyra was pilloried for her love of wine, a failing associated with women in general and especially the old, according to ancient comic convention (cf. fr. 172(167K) and comm. *ad loc.*). Zopyra's identity is a further mystery. She could have been a character in the play (? wet-nurse, midwife, old female slave) or a contemporary Athenian woman of whom all knowledge is now lost. The name is well attested in Athens, occurring there on a large number of gravestones of women who came originally from many different parts of the Greek world (*IG* ii-iii².7756 (Athens), 7902 (Ancyra), 8669–72 (Heraclea, probably the one near Miletus), 9114 (Cythnos), 9312–13 (Megara), 9624–6 (Miletus), 11531–53); cf. Bechtel, *Frauennamen* 112f.). Equally common in Athens is the male counterpart Zopyrus (cf. Kirchner, *PA* 1.407f., 2.462, nos. 6255–72, 6256a–b).

Δορκίς (or 'Ρόδιον or -ιος) ἢ Ποππύζουσα

Schweighaeuser, *Animadv.* 9.23, Meineke 1.387, W. Bender, *De graecae comoediae titulis duplicibus* (Diss. Marburg 1904) 52, Breitenbach 135. Ath. 3.104d (fr. 57(56K)) and 10.431a (fr. 59(58K)) introduces two citations from this play with the words Ἄλεξις ἐν Δορκίδι ἢ Ποππυζούσῃ, but at 9.395b (fr. 58(57K)) his text runs Ἄλεξις ἐν 'Ροδίῳ ἢ Ποππυζούσῃ. The unusual second title Ποππύζουσα, 'The girl who pops her lips', is common to all three citations, which probably therefore derive from the same play; but it is uncertain whether the variants Δορκίδι and 'Ροδίῳ imply a play produced at different times in different versions with two different titles (so first Schweighaeuser: cf. my introduction to Δημήτριος), or represent a textual corruption of a sort only too frequent in the transmission of titles and proper names (so Meineke tentatively, Kaibel more firmly: see the latter's edition of Ath., vol. 3, p. ix, and *RE* s.v. *Alexis* 9, 1469.56f.). Perhaps the fact that Ath. does not allude in his three citations to a δρᾶμα διεσκευασμένον will be a slight inducement to believe that 'Ροδίῳ is corrupted from Δορκίδι, and that the existence of alternative titles Δορκίς ἢ Ποππύζουσα is due to an ancient scholarly practice of sometimes replacing a comedy's didascalic title with one taken from the name of a leading character in the play (cf. the introduction to Ἀγωνίς). Whatever the correct solution to that series of problems, the play titled Δορκίς can be dated roughly within the limits *c.* 345–318,[1] the period when Callimedon, mentioned in fr. 57(56K), was active in Athenian politics.

Little information about the play may be gleaned from either title or fragments. If Ath.'s 'Ροδίῳ at 9.395b is not a corruption, it could be either masculine, 'The man from Rhodes', and so belong to Greek comedy's crop of geographical titles, or interpreted in the neuter as a girl's name. Both Rhodion and Dorkis would be apt names for servants or *hetairai*;[2] since

---

[1] It is safer to admit the possibility of so high a top date for Callimedon's entry on to the political scene (so T. B. L. Webster, *CQ* 2 (1952) 22 and *SLGC* 45f.), even though he does not appear to have been a front-ranker much before 324 (see especially Swoboda in *RE* s.v. *Kallimedon* 1, 1647.41ff., Davies, *APF* 279, Hunter 95f.). The bottom date of 318 is firm because he was then condemned to death in absence (Plut. *Phocion* 35, cf. also introduction to Κράτεια). On his nickname ὁ Κάραβος see below, comm. on fr. 57(56K).

[2] No Dorkis is known elsewhere from comedy, but Breitenbach notes a *hetaira*'s servant called Dorkas in Lucian *Dial. Meretr.* 9 (cf. K. Mras, *Wien. Stud.* 38 (1916) 335) and a *hetaira* named Dorkion in Asclepiades *Anth. Pal.* 12.161 = 20 Gow–Page. A Dorkion appears in a papyrus fr. of New Comedy (? Menander, *P.Hamburg* 656 = fr. 951 Körte–Thierfelder); she is young but of uncertain status (cf. Gomme–Sandbach, *Comm.* 738f.). One Dorcium is mentioned as a 'married' servant in Ter. *Phorm.* 152, and another played an uncertain part in Turpilius' *Leucadia* fr. xvi. The name Rhodion is also unknown elsewhere in comedy, but its cognate Rhode occurs three times (cf. Breitenbach). One is mentioned as a great drinker in Philemon 87(84K).1, the second addressed in Menander's Ἱέρεια (fr. 210), the third similarly addressed in Men. fr. 592 from an unnamed play which may or may not have been Ἱέρεια (Webster, *SM* 149f., Gomme–Sandbach, *Comm.* 715); the roles of all three are uncertain. On Attic tombstones I have found no instance of a Dorkis, but Dorkion and Rhodion both occur, mainly as names of women of non-Athenian origin (e.g. *IG* ii–iii².8906, 9524, 11216, Dorkion; 8544, 8773–4, 8922, 10310 Rhodion). In the present context it will be appropriate to add that the names Dorkion and Rhodion appear again in the Athenian Asclepius inscription of the early 3rd century (*IG* ii–iii². 1534.282, 294) as beneficiaries and benefactors, and that one of

COMMENTARY

many comedies are named after *hetairai* but none (so far as I know) after servant girls, Alexis' titular heroine is likely to have been a *hetaira*. Whether it was she or some other female character who popped her lips, is uncertain. So is the purpose of the popping; we know only that Athenians normally ἐπόππυζον in ὂrder to attract the attention of children and domestic animals (Ar. *Plut.* 732 and Σ, Xen. *Equ.* 9.10, cf. Timocles 23(21K).7), or as an apotropaic response to a flash of lightning (Ar. *Vesp.* 625 and Σ, cf. Pliny *HN* 28.25); Sittl, *Gebärden* 61, 185.

The frs. from the play give little help. 59(58K) comes from a drinking bout, where *hetairai* would not be out of place; 57(56K) may be part of a character's entrance monologue on arriving from the fish market with provisions for a meal (cf. frs. 16, 47(46K) and comm. *ad loc.*); 58(57K) could belong to a variety of contexts.

57 (56K)

Meineke 3.407 (1), Kock 2.316, Edmonds 2.398, Kassel–Austin 2.53. The subject of the excerpt quoted here by Ath. 3.104d–e is the relationship between Attic fishmongers and Callimedon ὁ Κάραβος. Callimedon's *floruit* is discussed in the introduction to Δορκίς (n.1). About his early career nothing is known. His wealth depended partly at least on mining interests (*IG* ii².1587). As an orator and politician he supported Macedon in opposition to Demosthenes (Ath. 3.100c, Lucian *Demosth. Enc.* 46, 48), engaging in a series of stormy intrigues that led to his downfall in 318.

Like other contemporary comedians, Alexis found him a convenient object of ridicule (cf. also frs. 102, 117–18, 149, 173, 218, 249 (= 97, 112–13, 145, 168, 215, 247 Kock); here as elsewhere (e.g. Alexis 249(247K), Antiphanes 77(76K), Eubulus 8(9K)) the point of the jibe is Callimedon's passion for eating fish; his particular favourite seems to have been eels (Alexis 149(145K), Men. fr. 264.13f.). For a fish-lover who was also a member of the famous dining club of sixty (see introduction to Ἰσοστάσιον) the nickname Κάραβος, 'Crayfish' or 'Spiny Lobster' (*Palinurus elephas*: not 'Crab', as Webster, *SLGC* 45 and others mistranslate it: see Thompson, *Fishes* s.v., Gossen and Steier in *RE* s.v. *Krebs* 1678.33ff., O. Keller, *Die antike Tierwelt* 2 (Leipzig 1913) 191ff.; cf. Palombi–Santorelli 369f., Campbell, *Guide* 204f., Davidson, *Seafood* 180) was obviously appropriate; but it is unlikely (*pace* Ath. 3.104d, followed by Swoboda) that his passion for fish was the original reason for his nickname. Bechtel, *Spitznamen* 23f. is probably right in suggesting that Callimedon

---

their close neighbours on the stone is a Gnathaena – perhaps the celebrated *hetaira* of that time (cf. Gow's edition of Machon (Cambridge 1965) pp. 8ff.); cf. also inscription 1298.

was called Κάραβος for another reason: because he squinted badly. Large scleroid eyes that move and focus independently of each other are a conspicuous feature of κάραβοι (cf. Arist. *HA* 4.2, 526ᵃ8ff.), and Callimedon's own strabismus is well attested (Timocles 29(27K), Alexis 117(112K), cf. comm. *ad loc.* and A. Olivieri, *Atti Accad. Napoli* 9 (1926) 47off.). It is personal appearance (of which most free males in a city like Athens would be aware as soon as a man spoke in the assembly) which accounts for sobriquets more frequently than personal food preferences, which would not be public knowledge until a man like Callimedon had secured an established fame. Naturally once this passion for fish had become known, comic poets would kill two birds with the one stone. Thus according to Alexis here Callimedon's love of fish has led the fishmongers to consider him their saviour and to put forward the proposal that a bronze statue of him should be erected in the fish-market. Whether this is just a piece of comic fancy, or based at however great a remove on some historical fact, we cannot now say, but Alexis' words would gain in satirical point if a recent or projected honorific decree lay behind them. Is it possible that Callimedon was named σωτὴρ τῆς πόλεως in such a decree and voted a bronze statue like so many Athenian benefactors? Cf. comm. on vv. 2–3, 5–6 and fr. 249(247K).5.

1 ἐστὶν ἐψηφισμένον: see on fr. 2.9.

2–3 χαλκῆν Καλλιμέδοντος εἰκόνα στῆσαι Παναθηναίοισιν ἐν τοῖς ἰχθύσιν: the words mimic the technical terminology of contemporary honorific decrees: cf. for instance *IG* ii².682 = *SIG*³ 409.66ff., *c.* 275–274) ἀγαθεῖ τύχει δεδόχθαι τεῖ βουλεῖ ... ἐπαινέσαι Φαῖδρον Θυμοχάρου Σφήττιον καὶ στεφανῶσαι αὐτὸν χρυσῶι στεφάνωι κατὰ τὸν νόμον ἀρετῆς ἔνεκ[α] καὶ εὐνοίας ἣν ἔχων διατελεῖ περὶ τὸν δῆμον τὸν Ἀθηναίων· καὶ ἀναγορεῦσαι τὸν στέφανον Διονυσίων τῶν μεγάλων τῶι ἀγῶνι τῶι καινῶι, καὶ Παναθηναίων τῶν μεγάλων τῶι γυμνικῶι ἀγῶνι· ... στῆσαι δὲ αὐτοῦ τὸν δῆμον καὶ εἰκόνα χαλκῆν ἐν ἀγορᾶι, together with other examples cited by Kassel–Austin *ad loc.* The erection of a bronze statue was a common method of honouring benefactors of Athens (W. Larfeld, *Griechische Epigraphik*³ (Munich 1914) 390ff., H. A. Thompson and R. E. Wycherley, *The Agora of Athens* (Princeton 1972: = *Agora* xiv) 158ff., *IG* ii–iii².4.1 p. 49 s.v. εἰκὼν χαλκῆ, A. S. Henry, *Honours and Privileges in Athenian Decrees* (Hildesheim 1983) 294ff.), and comedy naturally burlesqued the custom (e.g. Plaut. *Curc.* 140f. (with Fraenkel, *EP* 54), 439ff., cf. Alciphron 4.3.3).

στῆσαι correctly A, not στήσειν CE (cf. Diod. Sic. 12.72.8 ἐψηφίσαντο ... ἀποσφάξαι correctly P, other MSS -σφάξειν): aorist and present infinitives are the normal construction after ψηφίζομαι and other verbs expressing resolution both in Attic decrees (e.g. the example cited on vv. 2–3 above) and in drama (e.g. Eur. *Hcld.* 141f., Ar. *Vesp.* 591, *Av.*

COMMENTARY

1626); LSJ s.v. ψηφίζω II.3, H. W. Smyth, *Greek Grammar*[2] (Cambridge, Mass. 1926) p. 444).

3 Παναθηναίοισιν: so also e.g. Lysias 21.1 Παναθηναίοις τοῖς μεγάλοις, decree in Dem. 18.116; the locative dative of time is regularly used alone without any preposition for the Attic festivals (K.G. 1.445). Inscriptional evidence indicates that during the festival the Athenians publicly proclaimed (ἀναγορεῦσαι: see above on vv. 2–3) and implemented awards such as golden crowns, but it does not endorse Alexis' suggestion that bronze statues were also erected on the same occasion. These honours are curiously neglected in discussions of the Panathenaea (e.g. L. R. Farnell, *The Cults of the Greek States* 1 (Oxford 1896) 293ff., L. Deubner, *Attische Feste* (Berlin 1932) 22ff., H. W. Parke, *Festivals of the Athenians* (London 1977) 33ff.).

ἐν τοῖς ἰχθύσιν: see on fr. 47(46K).8.

4 κάραβον ἐν τῇ δεξιᾷ: I discuss the metrical anomaly of the split anapaest at *CQ* 7 (1957) 192f. Here the break occurs after the second short of an anapaest in the second half of the second metron of a verse with penthemimeral caesura, and the words between which the anapaest is split do not form such a cohesive unit as would make the anomaly more tolerable. Although at least seven exact parallels for this particular anomaly can be cited in Greek comedy (Ar. *Ach.* 107, *Pax* 233, *Av.* 1226, Cratinus 269(250K).2, Eubulus 6(7K).9, Men. fr. 397.3 and an *adespoton* printed by Kock as Philemon 228.2), and although the MSS tradition (ACE) is unanimous and the sense unexceptionable, it is hard to resist a suspicion that Alexis wrote κάραβον ἔχουσαν ὀπτόν (so Blaydes, *Adv.* 1.106, 2.155, anticipating my suggestion, *op. cit.* 193), and that the split anapaest was introduced by a Byzantine scribe who wished to transpose κάραβον to a more normal prose position next to its adjective ὀπτόν (cf. Jackson, *Marg. Scaen.*, especially 228ff., G. Thomson, *CQ* 15 (1965) 161ff., Hunter on Eubulus 6(7K).9).

5 ὡς αὐτὸν ὄντ᾽ . . .: the accusative absolute with a personal subject is not uncommon in clauses introduced by ὡς (K.G. 2.95f.).

5–6 These lines have been attacked by itching emenders (V. Slothouwer, *Acta literaria societatis rheno-trajectinae* 3 (1801) 117, Kock, inevitably Blaydes, *Adv.* 1.106, 2.155; the voice of sanity is Herwerden, *Mnemosyne* 14 (1886) 184) who have failed to notice that the transmission preserves Alexis' pithy antithesis. Callimedon's love of fish has made him the fishmongers' best customer, 'the one and only saviour of their craft' by Alexis' witty exaggeration. Is the poet here ridiculing some recent speech or decree that honoured Callimedon as σωτὴρ τῆς πόλεως? That phrase is a cliché of the orators (e.g. Andoc. 1.45, Aeschines 3.250, Isoc. 7.84); cf. the formula in honorific decrees by which a man was praised for services ἐφ᾽ ὑγιείᾳ καὶ σωτηρίᾳ τῆς βουλῆς καὶ τοῦ δήμου (examples collected in *IG*

ΔΟΡΚΙΣ

ii–iii².4.1 p. 64 s.v. σωτηρία). By contrast with Callimedon 'all the other' Athenians are a 'dead loss' to the trade, since none of them buys anything worth mentioning in comparison. This use of ζημία (= 'a bad bargain' LSJ s.v. III) in predication is probably colloquial; cf. Xen. *Mem.* 2.3.2 εἴ τις τοὺς μὲν ἀδελφοὺς ζημίαν ἡγεῖται, Alciphron 2.5.2 ζημίαν ἡγούμενος τὴν προσηγορίαν, Ar. *Ach.* 737 (φανερὰ ζ.), Alciphron 2.18.1 (ζ. καθαρά), 36.2 (μάλα λαμπρὰ ζ.).

58 (57K)

Meineke 3.408 (ii), Kock 2.316, Edmonds 2.398, Kassel–Austin 2.53. Ath. 9.395b quotes the fr. in order to make two points: that Alexis uses the feminine form περιστερά as the word for 'pigeon', the feral and domesticated descendants of the rock dove, *Columba livia* (this is in fact the normal Attic form, cf. LSJ s.v.; the masculine form περιστερός which Alexis uses at 217(214K).1 for a special purpose is a solecism), and secondly that Sicilian pigeons are διαφοροί, 'superior'. This opinion is endorsed by a fr. of Nicander (73 Schneider, Gow–Scholfield) quoted by Ath. in the same section, by a gloss which has insinuated itself into the text of the *Marcianus* at Ath. 14.658b (a citation of Philemon 79(76K), where the words τυρὸς Σικελικὸς ὅτι κράτιστος ἦν αἵ τε περιστεραὶ Σικελικαί were first recognised as a gloss by Bentley, *Emend. Men. et Phil.* 118, reprinted in Meineke, *Men. et Phil.* 543), and by the ἄρεοκος of Theophr. *Char.* 5.9, who kept only Sicilian pigeons. To plume oneself on rearing these birds marks the speaker in Alexis here as a petty snob – but whether a pampered youth, boastful soldier or some other ἀλαζών, it is impossible to say. – An alternative line-structure for the fr., with περιστερός and τούτων beginning successive trimeters, is less satisfactory (because of its split anapaest: πάνυ κομψ-) than the one printed by Kassel–Austin.

59 (58K)

Meineke 3.408 (iii), Kock 2.317, Edmonds 3.398, Kassel–Austin 2.54. The speaker is proposing a toast at a party. As cited the fr. is probably part only of a longer sentence, and the lack of context blurs (and perhaps distorts) the facts on which textual decisions about two readings in the *Marcianus* (Ath. 10.431a; Epit. has only a reference to ἴσον ἴσῳ v. 2) must be based.

1 Here A writes τῆς φιλοτησίας: correct or corrupt? The problem has seemed more complicated since Meineke adduced in A's favour the following grammarian's note included in the excerpts from Phrynichus *Praep. Soph.* (121.18ff. de Borries, 70.8ff. Bekker): φιλοτησίας προπίνειν· διττόν ἐστι τὸ δηλούμενον. καὶ ποτὲ μὲν κατὰ γενικὴν λέγεται, ἄλλοτε δὲ κατ' ὀρθὴν {καὶ εὐθεῖαν} (del. W. Dindorf, *TGL* s.v. φιλοτήσιος 893d) ἢ

COMMENTARY

αἰτιατικὴν ἢ κλητικήν. ἂν μὲν οὖν κατὰ γενικήν, σημαίνει αὐτὴν τὴν πρόποσιν, αὐτὸ τοὖργον καὶ τὴν δεξίωσιν τὴν ἐν τῷ πίνειν. ἐκλήθη γοῦν ἀπὸ τῆς φιάλης. τὸ δὲ κατ᾽ ὀρθὴν ἢ αἰτιατικὴν ἢ κλητικὴν μόνως τάττεται ἐπὶ τῆς κύλικος. Δημοσθένης· φιλοτησίας προὔπινεν (19.128). τοῦτο τῆς κατὰ γενικὴν συντάξεώς ἐστι (συντάξεως καὶ διὰ MS: corr. de Borries) παράδειγμα. οὐ γάρ, ὡς οἴονταί τινες, φιλοτησίας τὰς κύλικας λέγει (λέγειν MS: corr. Bekker), ἀλλὰ τῆς φιλοτησίας λέγει. καὶ ἔστιν ἐλλειπτικὸς ὁ τρόπος, οἷον χάριν ἢ ἕνεκα, ἵν᾽ ᾖ τὸ ἐντελές, φιλοτησίας ἕνεκά σοι προπίνω, οἷον φιλίας. Λουκιανός.[1]

It is surprising that so stupid and clumsy a gloss should have deceived anybody. Apart from its more palpable errors (the misinterpretation of the passage cited from Demosthenes, the explanation of the genitival idiom as due to an ellipse), it maintains that τῆς φιλοτησίας is acceptable Greek as an example of the (possessive) 'genitive of the toast', sc. the genitive of the deity or person in whose honour a toast is drunk (cf. Neil on Ar. *Equ.* 85, Hunter on Eubulus 56.7, K.G. 1.376). This genitive, most common when the toaster invokes a convivial god or hero (e.g. ἀγαθοῦ δαίμονος: Ar. *Equ.* 85, 106, Nicostratus 19(20K).1–3; Διὸς σωτῆρος: Alexis 234(232K).2, 272(270K).5, Eubulus 56.7; Dionysus: Ar. *Equ.* 107; Heracles: Lucian *Symp.* 16), a contemporary and sometimes deified celebrity (e.g. Alexis 116(111K).4–6, 246(244K).1–2, Antiphanes 81.5), or an ordinary person (e.g. Callimachus epigr. 29 Pfeiffer = *Anth. Pal.* 12.51, Theoc. 14.18f., Meleager epigr. 42, 43 Gow–Page = *Anth. Pal.* 5.136, 137), is sometimes extended to abstract expressions like φιλίας (Alexis 116(111K).2, Clearchus 1.3), ὑγιείας (Antiphanes 147(149K), Eubulus 93(94K).2, Callias 9(6K), Nicostratus 3, 18(19K).2–3, Philetaerus 1.2), ὁμονοίας (Alexis 246(244K).5, where it is impossible to draw a meaningful distinction between the abstract expression and its personification as a deity (cf. T. B. L. Webster, *Art and Literature in Fourth Century Athens* (London 1956)

---

[1] This subscription is a puzzle. In the extant excerpts from *Praep. Soph.* there is no other reference to a Λουκιανός, and no other entry bearing a signature of a grammarian or Atticist. And there is no evidence that Lucian of Samosata composed a glossary with entries like this. Dindorf (*loc. cit.*) and de Borries rightly argue that the whole gloss is spurious. It probably dates from the Byzantine period when Lucian was admired, studied and imitated (cf. Helm in *RE* s.v. *Lukianos* 1774.4ff., C. Robinson, *Lucian and his Influence* (London 1979) 68ff.); its author would have either forged Lucian's name to give greater authority to his stupidities, or have garbled a lost scholium on one of the passages (*Herm.* 11, *Gall.* 12, *Pseudol.* 31) where Lucian used the phrase φιλοτησίας προπίνειν (so Dindorf).

ΔΟΡΚΙΣ

38ff.). But how could τῆς φιλοτησίας be analogous to such partial abstracts? ἡ φιλοτησία occurs substantivally only with the ellipse of κύλιξ (cf. comm. on Alexis 116(111K).1); it is concrete, the loving-cup passed round from guest to guest as toasts were drunk (comm. on fr. 55(53K)). There is no abstract ἡ φιλοτησία, nor any need to spawn such a monster merely to defend a doubtful reading here. Drinkers who wished to toast the spirit of friendship as embodied in the loving-cup invoked not φιλοτησία but φιλία. Support for the view that φιλοτησίας here is not genitive singular but accusative plural governed by some part of προπίνω[1] is provided by the existence of parallel phrases with φιλοτησίαν in the singular (with and without κύλικα): e.g. Theopompus com. 33(32K).9, Alexis 293(291K) and comm. on 202(198K), cf. Ar. *Ach.* 985. μεστάς and κεκραμένας will then be attributes of φιλοτησίας, and A's τῆς a corruption. For τῆς Jacobs (*Spic.* 54f., *Addit.* 234) conjectured τρεῖς (printed by Kassel–Austin), and Blaydes (*Adv.* 1.106, 2.155) τάς; both are possible, but τῆς could also be the truncated remains of an original <ταύ>της, <'Αφροδί>της or something similar.

Without the context one cannot decide whether φιλοτησίας is adjectival (? in agreement with an unquoted κύλικας) or substantival.

2 A's προπίνω ἴσον produces an intolerable hiatus (cf. comm. on 1.1, 27.8). Of the attempts to remove it, Blaydes' προπίομ' is too violent a change, and Jacobs's addition of γ' after προπίνω emphasises the wrong word. Dindorf suggested προπίνων or προπίνω δ'; one of these is likely to be right. A scribe's failure to notice a supralineal dash that sometimes does duty for a final nu (cf. comm. on 28.3, Cobet, *NL* 530ff.) could account for corruption of προπίνων; δ' on the other hand might have been omitted by a scribe unaware that postponement of δέ to sixth word or later in its clause is a feature of later Greek comedy (cf. comm. on Alexis 4.1).

ἴσον ἴσῳ κεκραμένας: the parent phrase is οἶνος ἴσον ἴσῳ κεκραμένος (cf. Strattis 64(61K)), where ἴσον is internal accusative, ἴσῳ instrumental dative. ἴσον ἴσῳ, however, soon developed into a fossilised unit with little reference to its original syntactical organisation, used either adverbially (as here and at fr. 246(244K).4) or even virtually as a noun (e.g. Cratinus 196(184K), Alexis 232(230K).2). The expression signifies a mixture of equal parts of water and wine, considered excessively strong in ancient Athens (μανίαν ποεῖ com. adesp. fr. 106.12 Kock, cf. Ar *Plut.* 1132 and Σ)

---

[1] A possible support to this interpretation is provided by Photius = Harpocration = *Suda* s.v. φιλοτησία, attesting that Alexis used φιλοτησία

183

and confined almost exclusively to toasts (cf. Mau in *RE* s.v. *Comissatio* 613.21ff., O. Navarre in Dar.–Sag. s.v. *Symposium* 1579b, Starkie on Ar. *Ach.* 355).

Δρωπίδης

Meineke 1.399, Kock 2.317, Breitenbach 47, A. Körte in *RE* s.v. *Komödie* (*mittlere*) 1261.6off. Three of the six Athenians known to Kirchner (*PA* 1.305f. nos. 4572–77) with the name Dropides were figures of some interest. One was a relation and friend of Solon (*PA* 4573, Davies, *APF* 322ff.), a second was grandfather of the tyrant Critias, with a house renowned for κάλλος, ἀρετή and εὐδαιμονία (Pl. *Charm.* 157e; *PA* 4574, Davies 326), and the third was an Athenian emissary to Darius who was captured by Alexander in 322 at Hyrcania and held under guard by him (Q. Curtius 3.13.15, Arrian *Anab.* 3.24.4; Kirchner in *RE* s.v. 4, 1720.67ff. = *PA* 4575). Yet it is unlikely that Alexis' Δρωπίδης was concerned with any of this trio. Solon's relation and Critias' grandfather were not names of sufficient celebrity in Alexis' day to have been chosen as the heroes of comedies, even if Alexis' interest in the coterie of the former is shown by his Αἴσωπος, in which Solon was a character. Breitenbach, Kock, Körte and Edmonds (2.398) all subscribe to the view that the third of these Dropidae, Alexis' contemporary, was the subject of his play, which would have been *ex hypothesi* a political satire after the manner of Old Comedy. This seems implausible; so far as we know, this Dropides was a relatively insignificant figure when matched against the leading Athenians of his time, and although he may have gained some spectacular and short-lived notoriety from an escapade or characteristics unknown to us, that would have provided material for a derisive reference, hardly for a whole plot.

If Alexis' Dropides was not a historical figure, he is most likely to have been a *persona ficta* in some conventional New-Comedy intrigue, wealthy perhaps and socially important, like his real-life namesakes. The frs. that remain from the play, scanty as they are, give some slight support to this interpretation. Fr. 60(59K) describes an opulently stylish wine-party,

---

of the cup itself. But whether they are referring to the present fr., 202(198K), 293(291K), some lost passage or Alexis' general usage, is uncertain.

with a *hetaira* in attendance; 62(61K) provides a word connected with the preliminaries for such a party.[1]

60 (59K)

Meineke 3.408 (1), Kock 2.317, Edmonds 2.400, Kassel–Austin 2.54, cf. Fraenkel, *MNC* 24f. The speaker could have been host, guest, cook or slave at the entertainment here described. Such entertainments and their descriptions commonly (but not exclusively: contrast e.g. Men. *Epitr.* 412ff., 430ff., Ter. *Eun.* 419ff., 615ff.) occur towards the end of the plays that contain them (e.g. Men. *Dysk.* 935ff. and Handley on 946–53, Plaut. *Pers.* 753ff, *Pseud.* 1246ff., *Stich.* 641ff.). Here it is noticeable that neither rhythm nor style appear to deviate from the comic norm, as they do in the Menandrean passage cited and some parallel frs. of Alexis (5, 88(85K), 89(88K), 124(119K): see the introduction to Ἀγωνίς). The identity of the *hetaira* who entered with the drink is as uncertain as her role in the plot; it seems likely, however, that the party took place in her house (would she otherwise have been the person to bring in the *vin nouveau*?), like similar entertainments elsewhere in comedy and related literature (e.g. Plaut. *Bacch.* 79ff., 1117ff., *Men.* 173ff., 208ff., Ter. *Andr.* 86ff., Machon 258ff., Lucian *Dial. Meretr.* 15, Alciphron 4.14; O. Navarre in Dar.–Sag. s.v. *Meretrices* 1828B f., Schneider in *RE* s.v. *Hetairai* 1347.55ff., H. Herter, *JAC* 3 (1960) 101).

1 εἰσῆλθεν ἡταίρα . . .: there is no means of knowing whether the sentence began thus asyndetically or whether a connecting particle was omitted by excerptor or copyist (e.g. εἰσῆλθε δ' or <εἶτα δὲ> | εἰσῆλθεν could have been Alexis' original words).

τὸν γλυκύν: sc. οἶνον. ὁ γλυκύς and τὸ γλυκύ occur frequently with and without the article in this nominal use (e.g. masculine: Alexis 178(172K).14, [Arist.] *Probl.* 3.28, 875^{b}2, Herodas 6.77; neuter: Nicander *Alex.* 386; ambiguous: popular recipes and prescriptions such as *P.Oxy.*

---

[1] The imaginary addressee of Aelian *Epist.* 2 is a Dropides, but it would be dangerous to assume too readily that this author here had quarried material from Alexis' Δρωπίδης. Aelian's sources include Menander (*Epist.* 2, 13–16; cf. I. Thyresson, *Eranos* 62 (1964) 7ff.) and probably Alexis (7–8: see my introduction to Ὀπώρα), but they are not confined to later Greek comedy; thus *Epist.* 4 is modelled on Ar. *Ach.* 995–8, 6 on Dem. 55 (cf. *YCS* 27 (1982) 302). The first sixteen words of *Epist.* 2 draw on Men. *Georg.* 48–52; the provenance of the letter's remaining material is unknown. That, together with the names in the letter (Hemeron, Komarchides, Mania as well as Dropides), may come from Alexis' play, or it may not.

COMMENTARY

234.ii.6, 1088.51 and Bilabel, *Ops.* ζ 25) to denote the pressed juice of the grape before fermentation (must, new wine); there appears to be no discernible distinction in meaning from the commoner τὸ γλεῦκος (cf. especially K. Kerényi, *Symb. Osl.* 36 (1960) 5ff.).

2–4 Careful description of vases seems to be a characteristic of Alexis (cf. frs. 100(95K), 101(96K), 272(270K); Fraenkel, *loc. cit.*), and here the poet highlights his account not by elevating the style or tragically stiffening the metre but by including three small but significant details. First, the vase is silver; this adds to an occasion that touch of opulence which delights less wealthy members of certain audiences,[1] as Greek comic dramatists were not slow to observe (cf. Fraenkel; the relevant passages, which include Alexis 2, are conveniently collected by W. Miller, *Daedalus and Thespis* 2 (New York and Columbia, Mo. 1929–32) 558ff.). Secondly, the vase itself is an unusual one, a πέταχνον. This word is sufficiently rare in extant texts to have extended or defeated the spelling powers of copyists (πετάχμωι A here at Ath. 3.125f, corr. Casaubon *ad loc.* and *Animadv.* 239f.; πένταχνον Epit. at Ath. 11.496a; lemmata such as πέδαχνα and πέτακνον in Hesych.; the correct orthography is preserved in A at Ath. 11.496a, Phot. s.v. πέταχνον, and possibly also a sherd of the 1st or 2nd century AD in J. G. Tait, *Greek Ostraca in the Bodleian Library at Oxford* 1 (Oxford 1930) 52 no. 318.5 with πεταχ (νον) τι).[2] This rarity in our texts may have been matched by a corresponding rarity in Athens of the object itself; if his audience had been completely familiar with expression and vase, would Alexis have devoted so much care to the definition of its shape: half-way between two differently shaped bowls, τρύβλιον (see on 146(142K).2) and φιάλη (see on 111(106K))? Ath. 11.496a, Hesychius and Photius jointly describe the vase as ποτήριον ἐκπέταλον, perhaps relying on the Alexis passage and an easy etymology. It is hardly surprising that the shape has not been certainly identified by modern experts, but Alexis' description does at least suit (as Professor B. B. Shefton informs me) a luxurious and rare class of silverware that appeared in Athens during the earlier part of Alexis' career, the so-called 'Achaemenid phiale' (D. E. Strong, *Greek and Roman Silver Plate* (London 1966) 99, cf. 76f., 82f., plates 16a, 25a, fig. 20b).

---

[1] And which, incidentally, would well suit the household of a prosperous *hetaira* perhaps connected in some way with a wealthy Athenian family (cf. the introduction to this play).

[2] Similarly with the verb πεταχνοῦμαι, apparently coined from the noun by Aristophanes (fr. 301(288K)); the correct spelling, which occurs only in Phot. s.v. πεταχνοῦνται, is corrupted to πεδαχνοῦται in Hesych. s.v. and to πενταχνευται in A. and the Epit. MSS at Ath. 11.496a.

ΔΡΩΠΙΔΗΣ

For Alexis' third detail, see on v. 4.

4 ῥυθμοῖν: 'shapes'. The basic meaning of ῥυθμός (see E. Wolf, *Wien. Stud.* 68 (1955) 99ff.) is 'controlled movement to and fro'; an extension to 'shape' is particularly favoured by the Ionian atomists Leucippus and Democritus (Wolf 112ff., LSJ s.v. v; Diels, *Vorsokr.* 67A.6, 28, 68A.38, 125); cf. Philoponus *in de An.* 68.3 ῥυσμὸς λέξις ἐστὶν Ἀβδηρική, σημαίνει δὲ τὸ σχῆμα. But the usage did not originate with the atomists, as Philoponus, Kock (on v. 4 here) and Wolf imply. Hdt. 5.58 τὸν ῥυθμὸν τῶν γραμμάτων and the Hippocratic author of *Art.* 62 (2.214.2 Kühlewein) ὑποδημάτιον ... οἷον αἱ Χῖαι ῥυθμὸν ἔχον may perhaps have been influenced by atomist terminology, but Aeschylus fr. 78, describing a moulding ἐν τριγώνοις ... ῥυθμοῖς, was not.[1] If this extension of usage did come from Ionia, it antedated the atomists. Its naturalisation in Athens was early but precarious. There is no record of this meaning there between Aeschylus and Xen. *Mem.* 3.10.10, where the author plays on the word's ambiguity in the early 4th century by making his Socrates wilfully misinterpret Pistias' use of its Ionian meaning. Aristotle's adoption of the usage (*Metaph.* 1.4, 985^{b}16, 8.2, 1042^{b}14) is clearly influenced by the Ionians (note his retention of the dialect spelling). To a 4th-century Athenian the usage doubtless still sounded a novelty, rich in exotic or philosophical overtones; hence presumably its choice by Alexis in the present context for his third striking detail.

61 (60K)

Meineke 3.409 (II), Kock 2.317, Edmonds 2.400, Kassel–Austin 2.55. The context is unknown.

1 τὴν σπάθην: Pollux 10.120–1 appears to be claiming that the forms σπάθη (cited from Alexis here) and σπαθίς (cited from Ar. fr. 210(205K) and Eubulus 98(100K)) were both used in Attic to denote the spatula which extracted μύρον (the general word for unguent or perfume: Hug in *RE* s.v. *Salben* 1851.48ff., Gow on Theoc. 15.114) from the λήκυθος. Elsewhere this use of σπάθη is, so far as I know, confined to medical writers (Galen 13.378, 812 Kühn: the latter passage a citation from Heraclides of Tarentum). At the time of Alexis the word was applied to a variety of implements with a flat blade (see LSJ s.v.), but particularly to the long sword (instances collected by Bruhn, *Wortschatz* 41f.: add to his list Men. *Mis.* 178, 276, *Sam.* 687, 720, com. adesp. fr. 260.25 Austin) which may have been introduced by Iphicrates (Diod. Sic. 15.40).

---

[1] Nor was Pindar, who may provide another non-Ionian, pre-atomist example of this usage in *Pae.* 8.67 Snell; cf. R. Renehan, *Glotta* 48 (1970) 104.

2 The text is uncertain. Editors of Pollux and the comic frs. generally adopt the reading of CL ἐν τῷ μύρῳ καθῆκεν. Alexis could certainly have written this. ἐν + dative is occasionally found in 4th-century Attic after verbs of motion with the idea of movement towards and rest in a place (e.g. Pl. *Leg.* 10.905a–b; cf. K.G. 1.540ff.). And how can one be sure that in the original context καθῆκεν was not followed by something like εἰς τὸν πύνδακα? Yet if Alexis did write ἐν τῷ μύρῳ καθῆκεν, it becomes difficult to account for the variant reading in FS ἐν τὸ μύρον ἐγκαθῆκεν. Herwerden's conjecture (*Coll. Crit.* 122) ἐς (εἰς would be preferable) τὸ μύρον ἐγκαθῆκεν is alluring, since it restores a pure Attic idiom (the emender aptly compares Ar. *Lys.* 308 τῆς ἀμπέλου δ᾽ εἰς τὴν χύτραν τὸν φανὸν ἐγκαθέντες) and at the same time helps to account for the postulated double corruption in the MSS. Byzantine writers were wretchedly confused about the uses of εἰς and ἐν, often substituting the latter for the former after verbs of motion (J. Humbert, *La Disparition du datif en grec* (Paris 1930) 54ff., with abundant exemplification). If Herwerden is right, FS would present an earlier stage and CL the final version of such a substitutional corruption.

62 (61K)

Meineke 3.409 (iii), Kock 2.318, Edmonds 2.400, Kassel–Austin 2.55. Ath. 4.171b cites Cratinus 99(92K) for παροψωνεῖν and Alexis here for παραγοράζειν, both verbs in the sense 'to buy (dainties) over and above (the ordinary comestibles)'. For παροψωνεῖν cf. also Ar. *Eccl.* 226; παραγοράζειν has been supplied conjecturally at Men. *Pk.* 350, but with little plausibility.

Εἰσοικιζόμενος

Kock 2.318, Nesselrath, *MK* 327f. A man εἰσοικίζεται when he moves into a new house or part of it as tenant or lodger (Ar. *Pax* 260, Aeschines 1.124). Could the title figure of Alexis' play have delivered fr. 63(62K)? The speaker there is a Munchausen figure (even the pedantic citer, Ath. 15.691e, recognises that these lines are λῆρος), bragging about his entertainment in a sybaritic household. The exaggeration of the language, the fantastic unreality of the events described and the supercilious tone of vv. 1–2 collectively indicate that this character was a *miles gloriosus* (cf. Kock, Nesselrath). New-Comedy soldiers are inveterate travellers, and they make a habit of acquiring new houses or lodgings just before the incidents of the plot get under way (Men. *Pk.* 145f., cf. *Mis.*, Plaut. *MG*, Ter. *Eun.*). But whether the soldier of 63(62K) is the new tenant or not, we can neither reconstruct the plot of the play nor put a date to it.[1] Apart from 63(62K), which may have been part of a long monologue and/or scene in which the soldier related his imaginary adventures, the remains of the play are scanty. In 64(63K) somebody did something while drunk; this could be a reference to a young man's nocturnal rape of a maiden (the comic occurrences of this motif are listed by H.-D. Blume, *Menanders Samia: Eine Interpretation* (Darmstadt 1974) 16 n. 31), although there are many other possibilities. The wine-cooler of 65(64K) may or may not indicate a party. All told, these frs. suggest a set of conventional New-Comedy motifs, but a few pieces of a jigsaw are not the same as the finished picture.

63 (62K)

Meineke 3.410 (1), Kock 2.318, Edmonds 2.400, Kassel–Austin 2.55, cf. Fraenkel, *MNC* 28f. An imaginative description of a shower-bath from perfumed flying pigeons. The speaker is identified above as a *miles gloriosus*; in his boasts he has more in common with (the originally Menandrean) Thraso of Ter. *Eun.* 397ff., whose fabrications also aspired to social glory, than with the coarser captains of Pl. *MG* 1ff. and (? originally Alexidean, see introduction to Καρχηδόνιος) *Poen.* 470ff., whose bombast is stuffed with slaughter and (in *MG*) sex.

1 ἀλαβάστου: here (Ath. 15.691e), at Alexis 147(143K).3 (Ath. 8.365d) and elsewhere (cf. R. Schöll, *Hermes* 4 (1870) 166) the *Marcianus* preserves the older Attic spelling of this word and its congeners (without

---

[1] Webster (*CQ* 2 (1952) 15f.) suggests that Alexis 63(62K) is a variant of (and so possibly contemporary with) Antiphanes 200(202K), in which a similar braggart soldier describes how a king was fanned by doves in Cyprian Paphos (cf. *SLGC* 39). Webster goes on to identify this king with Nicocles of Salamis (which the dramatist has allegedly altered to the 'better-known' Paphos), and provisionally dates the play of Antiphanes which contains the fr. (and with it Alexis' Εἰσοικιζόμενος) to a period shortly after Nicocles' Cyprian campaigns (the late 360s). All this is much too speculative. There were other kings in Cyprus long after Nicocles (cf. Men. *Mis.* fr. 5 Sandbach, where somebody, possibly a soldier, has been 'faring quite gloriously' under 'one of the kings' there; E. G. Turner, *BICS Suppl.* 17 (1965) 17f.), and how is Paphos in Cyprus better known than Salamis? If we cannot securely date Antiphanes' play, which actually mentions Cyprus and one of its kings, how can we attempt to date Alexis', where neither place nor plutocrat is identified? Even the alleged link between the two frs. is not certain; one (not necessarily Antiphanes 200(202K)) may have influenced the other after an unspecifiable interval of time – or it may not have.

the intrusive rho) which was supported by the Atticists and allegedly preferred by Menander (fr. 307). The form with rho (-αστρο-) first appears in Attic inscriptions of the 330s (*IG* ii².1501.17, cf. Threatte 1.482). MSS of Attic authors vary disconcertingly over the spelling. Cf. J. Tischler, *Glotta* 56 (1978) 50ff., Hunter on Eubulus 98(100K).1, Kassel–Austin on Ar. fr. 561(548K).

ἀλάβαστος denotes the familiar narrow-necked, elongated vase of 'alabastron' shape (Richter–Milne, *Shapes* 17 and figs. 109–11, cf. Hermann–Blümner, *Privatalterthümer* 164 and n. 8, D. A. Amyx, *Hesperia* 27 (1958) 213ff.).

2 γιγνόμενον ἀεί: 'normal and everyday/common or garden'. In 4th-century Attic the participle γι(γ)νόμενος (on the orthography see comm. on fr. 37(36K).7) begins to acquire this meaning, which later became widespread (LSJ s.v. γίγνομαι 1.2, b); e.g. Dem. 24.82 τὸ γιγνόμενον (τίμημα) 'the normal penalty', 38.25 γιγνομένην χάριν 'normal gratitude', perhaps also Xen. *Cyr.* 5.4.51 ἐν ταῖς γιγνομέναις ἡμέραις 'in the usual number of days'.

κρονικόν: Κρόνος was the superannuated god of long ago (Ar. *Vesp.* 1480, Pl. *Euthyd.* 287b, Anaxippus 1.8; cf. Phrynichus *Praep. Soph.* s.vv. κρονοθήκη, κρονοδαίμων 79.13, 80.16 de Borries and Pollux 2.16), and so the adjective κρονικός came to mean 'ancient/old-fashioned/out of date' in a pejorative sense: e.g. Ar. *Plut.* 581, Pl. *Lys.* 205c, com. adesp. fr. 253.12 Austin. Cf. A. W. Bulloch on Call. *Lav. Pall.* 100.

3 περιστεράς: see comm. on 58(57K).1.

4–5 A's text here (from εἰς to ἑκάστην) has come under heavy fire from an army of scholars beginning with Dobree (*Adv.* 2.353),[1] but the sense given by it (as I tried to show in *Hermes* 93 (1965) 301f.) is perfect and almost certainly reproduces Alexis' own words. Three features of elegant Attic idiom must be noted: (i) the locution by which ὁ αὐτός in one case and gender is repeated in the same clause in another case and gender (in English one of the ὁ αὐτός phrases is normally translated 'each/every'): e.g. Thuc. 1.22 οὐ ταὐτὰ περὶ τῶν αὐτῶν ἔλεγον 'would not tell *the same* story about *each* matter', Antiphon 5.14, 50, Pl. *Gorg.* 490e; (ii) the juxtaposition of cognate words against normal rules of word order (K.G. 2.602); and (iii) the principle of variation in the second half of an

---

[1] Much of the resultant misapplied ingenuity is recorded in Kock and the apparatus of Kaibel's edition of Ath. *ad loc.*; cf. also Bothe, *PCGF* 532, R. Ellis, *AJP* 6 (1885) 288f., Richards, *AO* 84. Kock and Kaibel attribute to Hirschig Meineke's τὰς πάσας (his edition of Ath., cf. *Anal. Crit.* 338). Edmonds prints τὴν ἀγέλην, a conjecture which Headlam scribbled in the margin of his copy of Kaibel's Ath. but wisely never published.

antithesis. In this passage of Alexis, the person described dipped 'not *every* bird into *the same* perfume, but each into its own'. The interlacing of τὴν αὐτήν inside ταὐτὸν μύρον recalls a large number of passages in 4th-century Attic (e.g. Pl. *Phdr.* 277c ποικίλη μὲν ποικίλους ψυχῇ), and in the antithesis between v. 4 and the first part of v. 5, τὴν αὐτήν is exactly balanced by ἑκάστην, but εἰς ταὐτὸν μύρον is varied to ἰδίῳ. This variation places no strain on the syntax; ἀποβάπτω (see LSJ s.v.) occurs both with an instrumental dative and with εἰς + accusative to indicate the vessel into which something is dipped. For ἰδίῳ the Epit. MSS have the variant ἰδία(ι), which is sound Greek (cf. e.g. Thuc. 8.1, Pl. *Leg.* 12.946d) but weakens the antithesis (in the passage of Pl. cited, ἰδίᾳ is balanced by a corresponding *adverb*: κοινῇ); it was doubtless conjectured by a Byzantine scholar who failed to see the precise point of ἰδίῳ.

On μύρον see comm. on fr. 61(60K).1.

5 μὰ Δία: the oath emphasises, although here it is not placed next to, the preceding negative οὐχί: for the idiom see comm. on 233(231K).1–2, for the word-order Dover, *CQ* 35 (1985) 331.

6 Dindorf's emendation of the MSS θαιματια τα στρώματα to θαἰμάτια καὶ στρώματα. is elegant and correct. Scribes tended to panic when confronted by the idiom in which one article is common to a pair of related or contrasted substantives (on it see especially Gildersleeve, *Syntax* 2.277, 278 with many examples); in verse passages they would add (as here) the second article whose omission had perplexed them. Cf. e.g. Ar. *Equ.* 320 τοῖς δημόταισι καὶ {τοῖς} φίλοις AV (δημόταις A), S. *El.* 991 καὶ τῷ λέγοντι καὶ {τῷ} κλύοντι L¹A and *rec.*

7 In *Theocriti decem Eidyllia ... eiusdemque Adoniazusae* (Leiden 1773) p. 414 Valckenaer first noted that this verse accurately quotes a line of Euripides' *Telephus* (fr. 703 Nauck²; cf. E. W. Handley and J. Rea, *BICS Suppl.* 5 (1957) 42) which was parodied also in Ar. *Ach.* 496, where the tragic line fits more smoothly into its comic context. It is possible that Alexis' parody was triggered off by a recent production of the *Telephus*; more probably the line of Euripides had by now become proverbial as a request to be taken seriously in unprepossessing circumstances. The contrast between the original tragic context (where the speaker was dressed in rags as a beggar) and that of Alexis (where extravagant luxury is being described) is striking, but may be accidental. In Euripides the ἄνδρες Ἑλλήνων ἄκροι whom the speaker (Telephus) addressed were stage characters (individual actors or more probably the chorus: cf. Handley–Rea 32); in Alexis' parody these ἄνδρες are more likely to have been the audience addressed in a monologue (cf. F. Leo, *Der Monolog im Drama* (*Abh.* Göttingen 10, 1908) 79ff., Fraenkel, *MNC* 28f., Wilamowitz, *Schiedsg.* 97, Handley on Men. *Dysk.* 194, Dedoussi on Men. *Sam.* '54' in her numeration), Bain, *Actors* 190ff.), just as in Aristophanes' specially adapted quotation of Euripides' words. On the asyndeton in an explanatory clause cf. Alexis frs. 41(40K).2 and comm., 183(178K).7.

8 Behind θυόμενος in the *Marcianus* must lurk ὑόμενος, as Meineke saw; no other word fits the context so well. But whence the intrusive θ? It is unlikely to have been a product of crasis between τοι and the participle (so Bothe, *PCGF* 532), for which there would be no relevant parallel; in comedy τοι combines only with ἄν, ἄρα (LSJ s.v. τοι, Denniston, *GP* 555) and (probably by prodelision) ἐγώ (Ar. *Ran.* 971, Crates 17(15K).1). The original villain of the piece may have been an article-adding scribe, with θυόμενος a later misreading or wilful alteration of ὁ ὑόμενος; Ο and Θ are often confused (Cobet, *NL* 179). But more probably the theta represents an elided τε (so Emperius 352); in that case it must be assumed that this fr., like so many others, is cut off in mid-sentence, before a continuing clause introduced by καί. Cf. also my general introduction, II.i.

ἱρίνῳ[1] μύρῳ: perfume manufactured from the root of the orris, *Iris florentina* (Theophr. *HP* 9.7.3f., 9.9.2, Dioscorides 1.1, 56). Cf. Hug in *RE* s.vv. *Salben* 1863.61ff. and *Gartenbau* 825.46ff., R. L. Beaumont, *JHS* 56 (1936) 184, H. L. Lorimer, *Homer and the Monuments* (London 1950) 74 n. 6, S. Lilja, *The Treatment of Odours in Classical Antiquity* (Helsinki 1972) 229, A. Huxley and W. Taylor, *Flowers of Greece and the Aegean* (London 1977) 156 and pl. 403.

64 (63K)

Meineke 3.411 (III), Kock 2.318, Edmonds 2.400, Kassel–Austin 2.56. Ath. 14.613c describes an unnamed guest at his dinner-party who was asked by Ulpian where in literary Greek the adjective ἔξοινος occurred, and replied παρ' Ἀλέξιδι ἐν Εἰσοικιζομένῳ, ἔξοινος ἐποίει (so A: but see comm. on 16.2) ταῦτά γε (so Kaibel for A's ταῦτατ': a likely conjecture in view of the inveterate scribal confusion between τε and γε, although one cannot exclude the possibility that a correctly transmitted ταῦτά τ' represented the beginning of Alexis' next clause or sentence, crudely mangled by excerptor or copyist). The guest's answer indicates that the Alexis citation consists of just the four words ἔξ. ἐ. τ. γε (or τε),[2] but Ath.'s

---

[1] This correction of A's ηρινω is often attributed to Canter, *Nov. Lect.* 3. 164, but *irino* appears already in de' Conti's translation published in Venice eight years before. It was doubtless the idea of an unknown Italian humanist.

[2] Porson, *Adv.* 146 curiously argued that ἔξοινος ἐποίει ταῦτα here was not a citation from Alexis but a comment by Ath.'s Ulpian claiming that Alexis was drunk when he wrote. Such an interpretation is totally at variance with the meaning of the words in the passage and ignores

accuracy in so brief a fr. and the context of Alexis' words are equally indeterminate (cf. the introduction to Εἰσοικιζόμενος).

ἔξοινος, where the prefix expresses completeness ('*utterly* drunk'), is not known to occur elsewhere in Greek of this or earlier periods (but in the *Koine* cf. e.g. Machon 114 and Gow *ad loc.*, Alciphron 4.14.7), although Pollux sets the Atticist seal of approval on it and (more tentatively) on ἐξοινῶ (Hegesander fr. 21 Müller, *FHG* 4.417, cited by Ath. 11.477e, is the first recorded occurrence of this verb with ἐξ- completive). Euripides used ἐξῳνωμένος (from ἐξοινό- ομαι: *Bacch.* 814). Alexis' contemporaries seem to have preferred the weaker synonyms πάροινος and παροινῶ.

65 (64K)

Meineke 3.411 (II), Kock 2.319, Edmonds 2.400, Kassel–Austin 2.56. The *Marcianus* introduces this fr. with the reference Ἄλεξις ἐν οἰκιζομένῳ; Schweighaeuser's emendation Ἄλ. Εἰσοικιζομένῳ (*Animadv.* 8.504, cf. 9.22) seems preferable to Dindorf's Ἄλ. ἐν Εἰσοικιζομένῳ; a scribe will have divided the title into the two words εἰς Οἰκιζομένῳ, and then altered the preposition to the ἐν which his misinterpretation required and which in Byzantine times was frequently confused with εἰς (see comm. on fr. 61(60K).2).

Ath. cites Alexis for the use of the phrase τρικότυλον ψυγέα, but there is no need to assume that this phrase was necessarily written in the accusative case or with adjective and noun juxtaposed in this order. Yet even if these two forms did so appear side by side, Meineke's suggestion (1.295) that the final syllable of ψυγέα here probably suffered correption is unjustified; the phrase could have (e.g.) straddled the end of one and the beginning of the next iambic trimeter without any necessity of assuming a metrical licence.

ψυγέα: it is not clear why Alexis chose to use (instead of the normal Attic forms ψυκτήρ, ψυκτήριον, ψυκτηρίδιον) a congener which appears to have sounded non-Attic to 4th-century Athenian ears (cf. Euphron 3). See also on fr. 2.5–7.

66 (344K)

Meineke 3.517 (xxix), Kock 2.408, Kassel–Austin 2.56, omitted inadvertently by Edmonds; G. Kaibel, *Observationes criticae in Athenaeum* (*Index lectionum*, Rostock 16.4.1883) 8ff. This fr. is almost entirely lost. In the

---

the fact that Ath. habitually introduces dramatic citations by naming playwright and title. Cf. Meineke, *ed. min.* 704 and *FCG* 5.88.

Marcianus (Ath. 15.700e) it was written on folio 371ʳ, column b, lines 6 to 8 or 9. The right-hand side of this column is now torn off, leaving only the first one to eight letters of each line. The partial and tentative reconstruction by Meineke and Kaibel (*loc. cit.* and in his apparatus to Ath. 700e) of the missing text, as printed in Kassel–Austin, takes scholarship as far as it can go without the serendipity of new discoveries. Epit.'s laconic ξυλο-λυχνούχου δὲ μέμνηται "Αλεξις at this point (cf. also Eustath. 1571.20) identifies as Alexis the user of ξυλολυχνοῦχος who was named in the *Marcianus* in the missing part of f.371ʳb.4. The *Marcianus*' next line (b.5) preserves the first eight letters (Εἰσοικιζ) of the play-title from which this fr. derives, making its supplementation easy and sure. The length of the original quotation may be computed within limits. It began with ὁ δὲ λυχνοῦχος in b.6, and it was already ended five *Marcianus* lines later when a quotation begins from Theopompus com. 8(7K) to exemplify the use of the word ὀβελισκολύχνιον; that quotation is preserved elsewhere by Pollux 10.118. Before citing Theopompus Ath. must have introduced and probably defined the use of ὀβελισκολύχνιον (cf. Epit. *ad loc.*). That introduction, which doubtless followed the Alexis quotation directly, at its longest could have reached back to b.9 (cf. Kaibel's conjectural restoration, *locc. citt.*), and at its briefest to b.10 (e.g. ἔστι δὲ καὶ τὸ] | ὁ[βελισκολύχνιον, ὅ ἐστι] | κ[αὶ στρατιωτικόν. μνημο]|νε[ύει κ.τ.λ.; cf. Pollux 10.118). The length of the Alexis fr. must accordingly have been between 2½ and 3½ lines of the *Marcianus*, i.e. *c.* 50 to 70 letters (its lines hereabouts average 19 to 22 letters) = *c.* two iambic trimeters.

ὁ δὲ ξυλο[λυχνοῦχος: sc. a λυχνοῦχος (see comm. on fr. 107(102K).1) made of wood; this particular compound is not elsewhere attested, but cf. Cicero *Ad Q. Fr.* 3.5.9 *lychnuchum ligneolum*.

If this fr. is written in iambic trimeters, its opening words ὁ δὲ ξ. would form either the first metron and half the second, or the second metron and half the third, with (?) πυρός following 4 to 7 letters (i.e. half a metron) later. In this context mention of a fire seems natural enough, but can one be sure that Alexis wrote (e.g.) τοῦ] πυρός and not]πυρ' or] πῦρ οσ[?

Εἰς τὸ φρέαρ and Ἐκκηρυττόμενος

See below, Ἡ εἰς τὸ φρέαρ (frs. 85–7(65–7K)) and Κηρυττόμενος (fr. 107(102K).

Ἐκπωματοποιός

The title, which is recorded for Alexis (in addition to the quoters of the three frs. see also Pollux 7.190 Ἐκπωματοποιὸς δὲ δρᾶμα Ἀλέξιδος) and

ΕΚΠΩΜΑΤΟΠΟΙΟΣ

probably also Philippides (E. Livrea, *ZPE* 58 (1985) 15, 16f.; Kassel–Austin 7.340), is self-explanatory; it presumably denotes a character in the play. Nothing is known about its date, and no clues to its plot are yielded by the three frs., although the comment in 68 (= Antiphanes 270 Kock) about the pains brought by ill-gotten gains could be fitted to situations as varied as Smikrines' plan to marry for money in Men. *Asp.* (cf. 329ff.), Lyconides' slave's theft of Euclio's gold-filled pot (Plaut. *Aul.* 808ff.), or Gripus' claim to keep Labrax's trunk (*Rud.* 953ff., 1045ff.).

67 (68K)

Meineke 3.411 (1), Kock 2.320, Edmonds 2.402, Kassel–Austin 2.57. Generalised, gnomic statements that characterise a particular γένος ('class', 'section' or – as here – 'race') as inclined to a particular vice, virtue or habit (usually expressed by an adjective with a φιλο- prefix) are familiar clichés of Greek literature, with roots probably in popular speech. Such predications burgeoned in the plays of Sophocles and Euripides:[1] S. *Ant.* 1055 τὸ μαντικὸν γὰρ πᾶν φιλάργυρον γένος, fr. 587 Pearson, Radt φιλάργυρον μὲν πᾶν τὸ βάρβαρον γένος, Eur. *Phoen.* 356 καὶ φιλότεκνόν πως πᾶν γυναικεῖον γένος, *Her.* 636 πᾶν δὲ φιλότεκνον γένος, *IT* 1061 γυναῖκές ἐσμεν, φιλόφρον ἀλλήλαις γένος, cf. *IA* 520. Thereafter examples of these formulations are legion; a brief list might include Xenarchus 7.4f. τῶν δ᾽ ἰχθυοπωλῶν φιλοσοφώτερον γένος | οὐκ ἔστιν οὐδὲν οὐδὲ μᾶλλον ἀνόσιον, Ach. Tat. 5.5.1 φιλόμυθον γάρ πως τὸ τῶν γυναικῶν γένος, Heliodorus 2.17 ἄπιστον τὸ τῶν βουκόλων γένος, 5.12 *bis*, 6.13, Aelian *NA* 3.16, Ath. 7.290b.

Lydian perfume in general, and particularly that variety of it styled βάκκαρις, enjoyed a high reputation in antiquity (Ath. 15.690a–691d citing Ion fr. 24 Snell βακκάρεις τε καὶ μύρα | καὶ Σαρδιανὸν κόσμον, Σ A. *Pers.* 41). Cf. G. Radet, *La Lydie et le monde grec* (Paris 1893) 46, G. M. A. Hanfmann, *Sardis und Lydien* (*Abh.* Mainz (1960) 514ff., S. Lilja, *The Treatment of Odours in Classical Antiquity* (Helsinki 1972) 49, 62f. Its celebrity chimed in well with the general Greek attitude to Lydian ἡδυπάθεια.

Σάρδεων: correctly proparoxytone (*pace* Canter, *Nov. Lect.* 164, with Kaibel's tentative support) in A and Epit. here and MSS of other Attic authors (e.g. S. *Ant.* 1037, Eur. *Bacch.* 463, Xen. *Anab.* 1.2.5, *Cyr.* 7.2.1,

---

[1] Blaydes, *Adv.* 2.155 (cf. Herwerden, *Coll. Crit.* 122), with his usual eye for the half-truth, turns the relation between the line of Alexis and the cited passages of Sophocles into one of direct imitation. Imitators and parodists, however, seize on the picturesque words in their sources, not on colourless expressions like πᾶν, γένος or the φιλο- prefix.

COMMENTARY

4.12, 5.57, *Hell.* 1.1.10), because it belongs to the πόλις class of nouns (Choerob. *in Theod.* 195.18ff. Hilgard).

68 (= Antiphanes 270K)

Meineke 3.148 (xl), Kock 2.123, Edmonds 2.298, Kassel–Austin 2.57; E. Livrea,[1] *ZPE* 58 (1985) 11ff. and in I. Andorlini and others, *The Rendel Harris Papyri* 2 (Zutphen 1985) = *P. Harris* 170). These two lines are quoted by Stobaeus 3.10.22 Hense with an attribution to Antiphanes but no play title. *P. Harris* 171 (a mutilated portion of an anonymous glossary, 2nd century AD), however, attributes the same two lines more precisely to Ἀλέξ[ι]δος Ἐκπωματο[ποιῶι (corr. Livrea: -ωπμ- pap.). It appears likely that the papyrus identifies the source correctly, and that Stobaeus or a copyist corrupted Alexis' name to that of Antiphanes (for a long list of similar corruptions in Stob. see S. Luria, *Rh. Mus.* 78 (1929) 86), although a possibility that the same commonplace couplet occurred in plays by both Antiphanes and Alexis cannot be ruled out.

The idea that ill-gotten gains bring more pain than pleasure accords well with 4th-century attitudes in Athens about the acquisition of wealth and its insecurity when acquired (cf. Dover, *GPM* 109ff., 170ff., W. G. Arnott, *Philologus* 125 (1981) 220ff.), although in this fr. of Alexis and elsewhere the wish may be father of the thought. Cf. Democritus B 220 κακὰ κέρδεα ζημίαν ἀρετῆς φέρει and 221 Diels–Kranz 2.189, Eur. *Cycl.* 311f. πολλοῖσι γὰρ | κέρδη πονηρὰ ζημίαν ἠμείψατο, fr. 459 Nauck[2] = 77 Austin κέρδη τοιαῦτα χρή τινα κτᾶσθαι βροτῶν, | ἐφ' οἷσι μέλλει μήποθ' ὕστερον στένειν and Alexis 297(295K) φεῦγ' ἡδονὴν φέρουσαν ὕστερον βλαβήν with comm. *ad loc.*

1–2 τὰς μὲν ἡδονὰς ἔχει μικράς: sc. 'the pleasures that (wicked gains) bring are small'. The expression ἡδονὴν (-ὰς) ἔχει occurs in Attic comedy (but not in extant Aristophanes) with two characteristic constructions: (1) its subject a non-personal noun, as here and Men. fr. 559.1 ὁ τῶν γεωργῶν ἡ. ἔ. βίος; (2) its subject an infinitive or infinitival phrase (Pherecrates 155(145K).2, Antiphanes 267(269K), Crobylus 3.1), or implied from e.g. a temporal clause (Anaxandrides 55(54K).1).

2 ἔπειτα δ' ὕστερον: Gesner's correction of the unmetrical εἶτα δ' ὕστερον τὰς in the Stob. MSS (SMA) is partly supported by the new papyrus, which rightly has no article after ὕστερον, although its traces of the word before δ' are uncertain (possibly]πειτα with a very doubtful π and a hint above of a superscript letter which may be θ: see Livrea). Here,

---

[1] I should like to express my gratitude to Professor Livrea for his kindness in making available to me the text of his edition of the papyrus fr. before publication.

however, Alexis must have written ἔπειτα not εἶτα; although both adverbs are found in classical and later Attic side by side with ὕστερον (ἔπειτα + ὔ. Pl. *Resp.* 3.406b, *Symp.* 187b; εἶτα + ὔ. Eur. *Andr.* 756, Antiphanes 54(53K).4, Arist. *Pol.* 5.4, 1304ᵇ11), it is difficult to see what monosyllable or elided disyllable could have appropriately preceded εἶτα in the present context. For a possible further instance of scribal confusion between εἶτα and ἔπειτα see R. Kassel, *ZPE* 14 (1974) 124 (Straton fr. 1.50 Kassel–Austin = 219.50 Austin, *CGFP*).

λύπας μακράς: here probably 'substantial' rather than 'long-lasting pains' (cf. LSJ s.v. μακρός 1.4). This adjective is not infrequently thus attached to non-quantifiable nouns like ὄλβος (Pind. *Pyth.* 2.26), πλοῦτος, γέρας (S. *Aj.* 130, 825), χάρις (*Trach.* 1217) and ἀρετή (Pind. *Isthm.* 3/4.31). For its use here in this antithetical contrast cf. especially Thuc. 3.39 ἐλπίσαντες μακρότερα μὲν τῆς δυνάμεως, ἐλάσσω δὲ τῆς βουλήσεως.

69

Meineke 3.411 (II), Kock 2.320, Edmonds 2.402, Kassel–Austin 2.58; cf. Sicking, *Annotationes* 39f. The use of ἄσημος as an adjective (= 'unstamped', of gold and silver plate)[1] was too well established in classical Athens (e.g. Thuc. 2.13, 6.8, *IG* ii².1388.72 early 4th-century) for it to have required Antiatticist defence. The alleged anomaly, therefore, must have been Alexis' use of ἄσημον (note that this is the form quoted in the Antiatticist's lemma, 82.7 Bekker; cf. also Photius s.v. ἀσήμαντα· ... καὶ ἄσημον τὸ ἀργύριον τὸ ἀχάρακτον, 1.273 Theodoridis) as a neuter noun (= 'unstamped plate'); as such a usage cannot be paralleled before the *Koine* (e.g. LXX *Job* 42.11, Palladas in *Anth. Pal.* 11.371), it may well have fallen foul of Atticist rigour.

THE *HELEN* TITLES

J. A. Fabricius, *Bibliotheca Graeca* I (Hamburg 1705) 702, Schweighaeuser, *Animadv.* 9.19 s.v. Ἑλένη and 23 s.v. Τυνδάρεως, Meineke 1.391, J. O. Schmidt, *JCP Suppl.* 16 (1888) 399f., G. Schiassi, *Rend. Ist. Lomb.* 88 (1955) 112 n. 1, Nesselrath, *MK* 199 n. 51. It will be convenient to discuss under this one heading the plays of Alexis which apparently have the myth of Helen as their common theme. The relevant titles, as given by their citers, are:

---

[1] Hesych. s.v. ἄσημος· ἄργυρος, implying use of the masculine form too as a noun, is not supported by extant texts.

COMMENTARY

(1) Ἑλένη: Ath. 13.563d (fr. 70);

(2) Ἑλένης ἁρπαγή: Priscian *Inst.* 18.211 (71) and Antiatticist 106.23 Bekker (72);

(3) Ἑλένης μνηστῆρες: Antiatticist 96.10 (74) and 99.20 (75);

(4) Μνηστῆρες: Ath. 14.650f (73);

(5) Τυνδάρεως: Ath. 12.510a (241(239K)).

The vagaries of citers, especially when quoting from plays and other works with cumbrous or alternative titles,[1] and the brevity of the frs. themselves contribute to the difficulty of gauging the precise number and specifying the correct form of the *Helen* titles attested for Alexis. Of the five recorded variants only two can be considered certain and mututally exclusive: Ἑλένης ἁρπαγή and Ἑλ. μνηστῆρες. Both indicate by use either as a title elsewhere (a Ἑλ. ἁρπαγή is recorded for Sophocles[2]) or as a set phrase (Thuc. 1.9 already refers to the Ἑλ. μνηστῆρες) the customary Greek way of referring to different parts of the Helen myth.

The Ἑλ. ἁρπαγή presumably burlesqued the story of Helen's abduction by Paris; her previous adventure with Theseus cannot be excluded as an alternative subject but seems less likely. Alexis' treatment of the theme is unknown. Did he guy an existing tragedy, such as Sophocles' Ἑλ. ἁρπαγή or Ἑλ. ἀπαίτησις? Or was Alexis' play a free fantasy, a 4th-century counterpart to Cratinus' Διονυσαλέξανδρος with (or more probably without) political overtones? The two frs. firmly wedded to the play provide no clues for answering such questions. Fr. 71 is a complaint: somebody 'is immoral, and doesn't respect (another's) grey hairs'. The sex of the person attacked is uncertain; Paris and Helen are the likeliest identifications, if Alexis' plot followed the familiar story. But whose were the grey hairs? They could have belonged to Leda, Tyndareos or even (given the known exaggerations in Middle-Comedy myth burlesque: cf. Webster, *SLGC* 18f., 85, Hunter 24ff., Nesselrath, *MK* 204ff.) Menelaus. And who spoke fr. 71? The owner of the grey hairs, or an involved third party? The other fr. (72) implies that the land of Laconia and/or a

---

[1] For instance Ath. will sometimes quote a long title in full (ἐν τῷ Ὡλιεὺς τὸν ἀγροιώταν 3.86a, 7.288a, ἐν τῷ Περὶ τῶν Ἀθήνησιν ἑταιρίδων 13.586a), and sometimes abbreviate it (ἐν τῷ Ἀγροιώτᾳ 7.309c, ἐν τῷ Περὶ ἑταιρῶν 13.591c). On his similar inconsistencies when citing plays with alternative titles see my introductions to Ἀγωνίς, Δημήτριος, Δορκίς, Κράτεια and the other plays of Alexis with two titles.

[2] It is mentioned only once for Sophocles, in the hypothesis prefixed to *Ajax*; no frs. survive. This led Nauck (Nauck[2] 171) to the view that Ἑλ. ἁρπαγή may be an error, perhaps induced by the existence of Alexis' title, for the more frequently cited Ἑλ. ἀπαίτησις; cf. the editions of the Sophocles frs. by Pearson (1.123) and Radt (180f.).

Laconian girl were mentioned in the play – hardly surprising when Helen was born and raised in Sparta.

The title Ἑλ. μνηστῆρες also defines a story line, although the frs. cited specifically from it are insignificant. It is, however, likely that two further frs. (73, 241(239K)), both quoted by Ath. (14.650f, 12.510a) and of considerable interest, derive from the same play. Fr. 73 is cited from Alexis' Μνηστῆρες, but Ath.'s habit of abbreviating titles has already been noted (n. 1 on p. 198), and the pages of the *Marcianus* in which this fr. is embedded contain lacunae and other evidence of damage and disturbance (see comm. on the fr.). In any case Μνηστῆρες is unlikely to have stood on its own as an Attic play-title.[1] μνηστήρ/-ῆρες was not applied in 4th-century Athens to everyday suitors, and so is unlikely to have been selected as the title of a conventional New-Comedy intrigue. In prose usage it was confined to a few sets of celebrated suitors in myth, such as those who wooed Helen and Penelope.[2] Alexis' Μνηστῆρες most probably therefore is to be identified with the Ἑλ. μνηστῆρες (so first Meineke 1.391), even if one other interpretation is just conceivable – that those unspecified suitors formed an alternative title to Alexis' Ὀδυσσεὺς ἀπονιζόμενος and were courting Penelope.

Fr. 241(239K) is introduced by Ath. with the words κατὰ τὸν Ἀλέξιδος Τυνδάρεων. This formula, not uncommon in Ath., implies that Τυνδάρεως was the title of the play from which his extract was taken, not necessarily that the title figure also spoke the words quoted.[3] Yet if Tyndareos did

---

[1] A list of plays that the *Suda* gives s.v. Τιμησίθεος includes a bald Μνηστῆρες without attributive genitive. Here it is likely that Ἑλένης has slipped out in the transmission (so Meineke 1.391; cf. *TGrF* 1² p. 324f.); the title Ἑλένης ἀπαίτησις comes shortly afterwards in the list.

[2] The one exception to this rule is more apparent than real: Sopater's title Βακχίδος μνηστῆρες (Kaibel, *CGF* p. 192). Several of Sopater's titles suggest tragic or mythological burlesque (Ἱππόλυτος, Νέκυια, Ὀρέστης). Βακχίδος μνηστῆρες is likely to have taken the theme of a courtesan's wooing and given it a mythical or tragic ambience. Sopater seems also to have written a Βακχίδος γάμος and Βακχίς, if these are not inaccurate, alternative or abbreviated titles of one and the same play.

[3] In Ath. this formula appears invariably to denote the title of a cited work, not to name a character speaking in an unidentified play. Obviously the formula is particularly apt when the speaker's name coincides with the play title, as it does certainly at 8.347c–d (*P.V.* 816ff.), probably at 8.358d (Antiphanes 182(184K)) and 14.623f (Theophilus 5; Meineke 1.435 here judges wrongly). Unfortunately in many cases (as here and at fr. 98(152K)) it is uncertain whether title and speaker coincide or not.

COMMENTARY

utter this fr., its most plausible context would be a conversation with a man who had just arrived uninvited as a suitor for Helen's hand (so first J. O. Schmidt).[1] In that case the Τυνδάρεως would have dealt with the courtship of Helen, and since perhaps Alexis is unlikely to have written two unrelated plays on an identical subject, the most probable explanation of the twin titles ʽΕλ. μνηστῆρες and Τυνδάρεως would be that they were alternative names for the same play (so first Schweighaeuser), with the second title added for one of several possible reasons – a further production of the play conceivably in a revised version, the ancient custom of naming some plays after both subject and leading character, or an Alexandrian critic's whim (cf. the introduction to Ἀγωνίς). Did Alexis' play travesty an existing tragedy, or was it free fantasy? We cannot say; but we do know that the earlier adventures of Helen's life were as popular a subject on the Athenian stage as her experiences during and after the Trojan War. Sophocles wrote a Τυνδάρεως, whose subject is unknown (2.268ff. Pearson, 461f. Radt), and a ʽΕλ. γάμος, a satyr play which probably celebrated the union of Paris and Helen on the island of Cranae (1.126ff. Pearson, 181ff. Radt). Comedies titled ʽΕλένη were written by Philyllius, Anaxandrides and Alexander (if the last playwright's name at his title's sole occurrence in the Antiatticist 96.33 Bekker is not an error for Alexis, cf. Kassel–Austin 2.19 and my comm. on Alexis 8), a Τυνδάρεως ἢ Λήδα by Sophilus, a Λάκωνες ἢ Λήδα by Eubulus; their respective subjects, however, are as problematical as their relationships to earlier or contemporary tragedy.[2]

The final fr. for discussion under this group of titles is 70, assigned by Ath. 13.563d to a ʽΕλένη *tout court*. There is no way of deciding whether ʽΕλένη here is an abridgement (see n. 1 on p. 198) of ʽΕλένης ἁρπαγή (so Fabricius, Meineke) or ʽΕλ. μνηστῆρες (so Schweighaeuser, cf. L. B. Ghali-Kahil, *Les Enlèvements et la retour d'Hélène dans les textes et les documents*

---

[1] Schiassi advances an alternative interpretation of the fr., suggesting that it was addressed not by, but to, Tyndareos, and that the occasion was Helen's wedding-feast, gatecrashed by a crowd of disappointed suitors with their hangers-on. This is implausible; the exaggerated comments in the fr. on the size of a guest's entourage suit only a disgruntled host's mouth. It is tempting to add two questions: was Tyndareos portrayed by Alexis as a skinflint like Euclio, were the μνηστῆρες a Middle-Comedy chorus?

[2] Theodectas (on this spelling see Snell, *TGrF* I[2] p. 228 T 3, Mette V A I col. 3.11) wrote a ʽΕλένη (p.231 Snell) in which the heroine seems to have been presented as a captive soon after the fall of Troy (cf. Eur. *Tro.*; G. Xanthakis-Karamanos, *Studies in Fourth-Century Tragedy* (Athens 1980) 67ff.), possibly between *c.* 370 and 350 (T. B. L. Webster, *Hermes* 82 (1954) 479f.).

200

figurés (Paris 1955) 143), or whether it indicates the existence of a third play by Alexis on some other part of the Helen story. The fr. itself is an attack on the hedonistic association of ἔρως with the physical beauty of youth alone. It could be interpreted as a comment about Helen's preference for a younger Paris over a more mature Menelaus, but it seems unprofitable to speculate about the speaker (Hera or Athena, Schiassi; Odysseus, Schmidt).

A strass gem of the 1st century now in Würzburg (see E. Zwierlein–Diehl, *Glaspasten im Martin-von-Wagner-Museum der Universität Würzburg* 1 (Munich 1986) 223 no. 604 and pl.) contains relief pictures of masks of a slave, cook and (twice: one in reverse) *hetaira* with the inscription *HELENA*. It seems likely that the portrayed masks ultimately come from a comedy with Ἑλένη as (? part of) its title, but there is no way of deciding whether that play was by Alexis or some other comic poet (? Alexander, Anaxandrides, Philyllius).

Ἑλένη

70

Meineke 3.411, Kock 2.320, Edmonds 2.402, Kassel–Austin 2.58. The ideas expressed in this fr., which is cited by Ath. 13.563d (complete in A, vv. 2 from τὸν and 4–5 omitted in Epit.), criticise in tragic rhythm and style the lover whose infatuation is induced only by physical beauty in its youthful perfection. A modern reader is inevitably reminded of some of Pausanias' remarks in Pl. *Symp.* 183de: πονηρὸς δ' ἐστὶν ἐκεῖνος ὁ ἐραστὴς ὁ πάνδημος, ὁ τοῦ σώματος μᾶλλον ἢ τῆς ψυχῆς ἐρῶν· καὶ γὰρ οὐδὲ μόνιμός ἐστιν, ἅτε οὐδὲ μονίμου ἐρῶν πράγματος. ἅμα γὰρ τῷ τοῦ σώματος ἄνθει λήγοντι, οὗπερ ἤρα, "οἴχεται ἀποπτάμενος, " πολλοὺς λόγους καὶ ὑποσχέσεις καταισχύνας; cf. also 181c–182a. A. Weiher, *BBG* 65 (1929) 27f. thinks that Alexis may have intended a direct allusion to this passage of Plato,[1] but the suggestion is almost certainly wrong for two reasons. Pausanias' point is basically very different from that of Alexis' speaker; Pausanias is contrasting lust and spiritual love in a pederastic context (cf. K. J. Dover, *Greek Homosexuality* (London 1978) 82f.), while the comic character seems to be pleading on behalf of the older man for the affections of a beautiful woman (see above, introduction to the *Helen* titles). More importantly, it is short-sighted to view this fr. merely against the

---

[1] A. Olivieri, *Dioniso* 7 (1939) 291 prefers to see in fr. 70 a *parodia platonica* of the ideas put foward at the beginning of the pseudo-Platonic *Alcibiades* 1, but his argument fails for substantially the same reasons as Weiher's does.

COMMENTARY

background of Plato's discussions of ἔρως, rather than in the light of the massive general interest in ἔρως as a speculative concept which flourished from the time of Gorgias' *Helen* until at least the mid-4th century, and embraced a whole series of ἐρωτικοὶ λόγοι which have virtually all perished (see on fr. 20). Alexis' theme is an erotic cliché, refurbished by every interested generation (e.g. Pl. *Leg.* 8.837bc ὁ μὲν γὰρ τοῦ σώματος ἐρῶν, καὶ τῆς ὥρας καθάπερ ὀπώρας πεινῶν, ἐμπλησθῆναι παρακελεύεται ἑαυτῷ, τιμὴν οὐδεμίαν ἀπονέμων τῷ τῆς ψυχῆς ἤθει τοῦ ἐρωμένου, varying Pausanias' statement; [Aristaen.] *Epist.* 2.1 οἱ δὲ τῶν καλῶν σωμάτων ἐρασταὶ τῇ τοῦ φαινομένου κάλλους ἀκμῇ παραμετροῦσι τὸν ἔρωτα). For the contrary view cf. Amphis 15, cited by Ath. directly before Alexis 70, τί φῇς; σὺ ταυτὶ προσδοκᾷς πείσειν ἐμέ, | ὡς ἔστ' ἐραστής, ὅστις ὡραῖον φιλῶν | τρόπων ἐραστής ἐστι, τὴν ὄψιν παρείς; | ἄφρων γ' ἀληθῶς.

1 Without the preceding context the function of ὡς is uncertain. There are four possibilities: (1) the use which is explained sometimes as elliptical (= ἴσθι ὡς, LSJ s.v. F.2), sometimes as a special case of exclamatory ὡς (LSJ s.v. D, cf. Fraenkel, *Beob.* 96, Dover on Ar. *Nub.* 209, Diggle, *Studies* 88), but very familiar in Greek drama (examples listed in LSJ s.v. F.2, e.g. Ar. *Ach.* 333, *Lys.* 499); (2) the general exclamatory use, normally followed by adjective, adverb or verb; (3) the causal use (= *nam*; LSJ s.v. D.4); and (4), after some such phrase as an interrogative οὐκ οἶσθα γάρ in the preceding context.

2 τὸν ἄλλον δ' οὐδὲ γινώσκει χρόνον ('but doesn't even recognise (sc. the existence of) the remaining part of a person's life') is the reading of the *Marcianus*. Here χρόνον worried Musurus, who printed the conjecture λόγον after rejecting an earlier idea τρόπον (cf. Kaibel's edition of Ath., 1 *praef.* xiii f. and apparatus at 13.563d). Subsequent editors (with the exception of Edmonds) have preferred λόγον, which, in addition to being palaeographically unjustifiable, both misses and changes the point, to the MS reading, which alone provides the sense demanded by the context. In v. 1 the speaker lambasts the ordinary lover's concentration on αὐτῆς τῆς ἀκμῆς τῶν σωμάτων, 'physical beauty just at its prime', where ἀκμῆς by the common metaphor (cf. K. Jax, *Die weibliche Schönheit in der griechischen Dichtung* (Innsbruck 1933) 68f.) refers to the one brief period in human life when beauty's bloom can be fresh and flawless. The rest of life by contrast may be termed τὸν ἄλλον χρόνον; χρόνος is applied to the span of human life as a whole (e.g. Eur. *Alc.* 650 βιώσιμος χρόνος) or to any part of that span (e.g. Pl. *Resp.* 5.460e μέτριος χρόνος ἀκμῆς), and comes close at times to being synonymous with βίος (e.g. S. *Phil.* 306, *OC* 112, 374, [Pl.] *Ax.* 365b).

γινώσκει is the spelling of the *Marcianus* here, as it is generally of the comic papyri. Although Athenian inscriptions preserve the older Attic orthography γιγν- to about 325 (Meisterhans–Schwyzer 178, Threatte 1.562), the change to the Ionic and *Koine* spelling γιν- doubtless came much earlier in the vernacular. In such circumstances the question of Alexis' own practice, if indeed he had a consistent one, is unanswerable. See also comm. on 37(36K).7.

5 ἄπιστον ... πᾶσι τοῖς ἄλλοις: i.e. the man who amorously pursues only the paragons of youthful beauty gives Eros a bad name (ἄπιστον, 'untrustworthy') with everybody else, not presumably for any Platonically moral reasons but because such conduct lessens the erotic chances of all those not in the bloom of youth. Meineke's conjecture π. τ. καλοῖς (*Anal. Crit.* 261) is palaeographically neat, but the conceit which it introduces is alien to the context. The speaker here is concerned not with the effect of Eros on the young and beautiful, but rather with the unfairness of his neglect of those who are no longer so young.

Ἑλένης ἁρπαγή

71

Meineke 3.412 (1), Kock 2.320, Edmonds 2.402, Kassel–Austin 2.59. This fr., cited by the Latin grammarian Priscian (*Inst. gramm.* 18.211) has clearly – the scansion indicates it – suffered the sort of violence, be it here abridgement, wilful alteration or careless corruption, that often befalls comic citations in the hands of grammarians (cf. comm. on 194(189K).2–3). Priscian's purpose here was to illustrate the construction of ἐντρέπομαι (in the sense of 'I pay heed to/regard') with the accusative (a *Koine* usage, unparalleled before Alexis: cf. LSJ s.v. ἐντρέπω II.3, citing Polyb. 3.10.3, *Ev. Marc.* 12.6) instead of with the genitive (the normal construction in Attic and earlier Greek, LSJ s.v. II.2). Presumably therefore those parts of the citation directly relevant to Priscian's purpose, viz. the verb ἐντρέπεται and its object (of which τὴν πολιάν forms the whole or part: see below), reproduce with reasonable accuracy but uncertain order some words that Alexis wrote. Attempts to reconstruct Alexis' original verses (Grotius, *Exc.* 597 resurrected by Edmonds, Meineke, Blaydes, *Adv.* 2.155) are accordingly futile.

τὴν ... πολιάν: is this all or only part of the grammatical object? If all, πολιάν must be a noun (= 'grey hairs'), and Alexis be fathering a usage alien to pure Attic (which always employs for this meaning the plural αἱ πολιαί, sc. τρίχες: cf. Kock *ad loc.*, Neil on Ar. *Equ.* 520, and Hopkinson on Call. *H. Dem.* 96) but current in the *Koine* (LSJ s.v. πολιά, F. Williams

COMMENTARY

on Call. *H. Ap.* 14).[1] There is, however, no reliable prallel for this use in later Greek comedy; the two alleged instances ([Philemon] fr. 179 Kock = *Men. et Phil. Comp.* 3.52, monost. 661) in the Meineke–Jacobi *comicae dictionis index* (5.861) are of doubtful authenticity.[2] Thus it is far likelier that Priscian or his copyists have mangled Alexis' original words by the omission of a noun to which πολιάν was adjectivally attached. Kock's τὴν δε πολιὰν <μητέρα> deserves mention as an *exempli gratia* supplement, restoring both metre and appropriate sense (*'mater uidetur esse Leda'* Kock).

72

Meineke 3.412 (II), Kock 2.320, Edmonds 2.402, Kassel–Austin 2.59; Rutherford, *NP* 427f. The rule reported here by the Antiatticist (106.22 Bekker), Λάκαιναν τὴν παρθένον φασὶ δεῖν καλεῖν, τὴν δὲ χώραν Λακωνικήν, corresponds to strict Attic usage and is endorsed by Phryn. *Ecl.* s.v. Λάκαιναν, p. 94 Fischer. In view of the general pattern of disagreement between Phrynichus and the Antiatticist on points of usage, it is possible that the latter in his original, unabbreviated text here reported this rule only to express his disagreement with it, citing Alexis as evidence of an alleged failure to cover every example of Attic idiom. If Alexis did apply Λάκαινα to the country and Λακωνική to one of its girls, he would have had precedents. The former use was permitted, at least adjectivally, in Attic poetry (to the examples cited by LSJ add Eur. *Andr.* 194, 209, fr. 1083.9 Nauck[2]), as Phrynichus acknowledges, but its particular association with Ionic (e.g. Hdt. 7.235) and *Koine* writers was likely to arouse Atticist suspicions. Λακωνικός was occasionally used of persons in Attic (e.g. Ar. *Lys.* 628). Cf. also W. Dittenberger, *Hermes* 42 (1907) 164ff., Bölte in *RE* s.v. *Sparta* 1279.36ff. In a play about Paris' elopement with Helen there must have been ample opportunity for Alexis to exploit both words, perhaps even either word in both senses.

---

[1] Two passages of Aristotle (*GA* 5.4, 784[b]13, fr. 235 Rose; cf. [Arist.] *Probl.* 10.34, 894[b]9), where ἡ πολιά = the disease of premature greying, may help to explain how ἡ πολιά came to duplicate αἱ πολιαί in later Greek. If the use of ἡ πολιά as a noun in the singular originated as a technical term of medicine, it could have been extended in the vernacular to normal as well as abnormal greying.

[2] Cf. Körte–Thierfelder, *Menandri quae supersunt* 2[2] (Leipzig 1959) ix f., W. Görler, ΜΕΝΑΝΔΡΟΥ ΓΝΩΜΑΙ (Diss. Berlin 1963) 102ff., S. Jäkel, *Menandri Sententiae* (Leipzig 1964) xvii ff.

? ΕΛΕΝΗΣ ΜΝΗΣΤΗΡΕΣ

<?'Ἑλένης> Μνηστῆρες

73

Meineke 3.412 (III), Kock 2.321, Edmonds 2.402, Kassel–Austin 2.59; cf.
E. L. von Leutsch, *Philologus* 1 (1846) 159. The *Marcianus*[1] text of Ath.'s
brief chapter on pomegranates (14.650e–651b), which includes the
present fr., is in a parlous state: '*haec omnia turbata et mutilata*' notes Kaibel
ad loc. Some lemmata and citations have apparently been omitted and
others disarranged. A Menander citation is misplaced at the end. It is then
no surprise that when Alexis 73 is quoted in the middle of the section the
play-title has almost certainly (see above, introduction to the *Helen* titles)
been abridged or corrupted to Μνηστῆρσιν, or that the text of the fr. (ῥόαν
γὰρ ἐκ τῆς χειρὸς αὐτῶν A) is probably mutilated and corrupt. Leutsch
suggested that a fuller and more accurate version of Alexis' words may be
preserved in the collection of proverbs made by Michael Apostolius
(13.16b), or rather added to that collection by his son Arsenius (*Viol.*
40.69).[2] The paroemiographic version runs οὐδὲ ῥοιὰν γλυκεῖαν ἐκ τῆς
δεξιᾶς | δέξαιτ' ἄν. No identification of source is attached, but dialect and
iambic metre point to Attic drama. The accidents that frequently happen
to small frs. in transmission would readily account for the differences
between the two versions. Non-key words are often omitted or mutilated,
especially at the beginning and ending of citations; this could explain the
omissions of οὐδέ in Ath. and αὐτῶν in Apostolius/Arsenius, possibly also
the mutilation of γλυκεῖαν in Ath. to γάρ. In the Ath. version δέξαιτ' ἄν
could have disappeared by virtual haplography after δεξιᾶς, and δεξιᾶς
itself have been replaced by the obvious gloss χειρός. We cannot be
certain that Leutsch's suggestion is correct, but it is strongly supported by
the circumstantial evidence and deserves at least provisional acceptance.

Even so, the fr. remains puzzling. After citing his proverb the paroemiographer explains its meaning with παρὰ πονηρῶν οὐδὲ χρηστὰ λαμβάνειν.
But is the text a genuine Attic proverb? It is not cited elsewhere in classical

---

[1] The Epit. here is so abbreviated that it provides no supplementary help;
its version of the chapter suggests that its abridgement was made from a
text of Ath. no fuller than A's.

[2] E. L. von Leutsch and F. G. Schneidewin, *Corpus paroemiographorum
graecorum* 2 (Göttingen 1851) 578; cf. the former's preface 2.xv, Rupprecht in *RE* s.v. *Michael* 2, 1520.11ff., and W. Bühler, *Zenobii Athoi
proverbia* 1 (Göttingen 1987) 293ff. The proverb appears also in a
collection attributed to Diogenian (*codd. Barocc.* 219, *Vatican.* 1458; cf.
L. Cohn and O. Crusius, *Philologus Suppl.* 6 (1891) 233 no. 100), and it
may be, as Professor Bühler has suggested to me by letter, that Arsenius
gained his knowledge of the proverb from that latter collection.

literature, and this fact alone arouses suspicion, in view of the known selection procedures of Apostolius and his son (cf. Crusius in *RE* s.v. *Apostolios* 182.46ff.). If the text is not a proverb, it must presumably be taken at face value, and the paroemiographer's interpretation, which fails to match its text in either syntactical structure or emblematic plausibility, must be dismissed as nonsense. Even with a literal reading of the text, however, problems remain; who 'wouldn't receive even a sweet pomegranate' from whom? Helen or Tyndareos from one or more of the less acceptable suitors?

1 The opening words of the paroemiographic version need correction only to οὐδὲ ῥοάν (Meineke (*ed. min.* xviii), since in Attic drama initial rho 'may always count as a double consonant' and thus lengthen a preceding syllable ending in a short open vowel (P. Maas, *Greek Metre* (tr. H. Lloyd-Jones, Oxford 1962) 8of.; cf. Descroix 19f., Dodds on Eur. *Bacch.* 59, West, *Greek Metre* 16, and my comm. on Alexis 115(110K).15). Hence Leutsch's earlier emendation to οὐδ' ἂν ῥοάν is strictly unnecessary, although its duplication of ἂν introduces a favourite Attic idiom (cf. J. Wackernagel, *Indog. Forsch.* 1 (1892) 392ff. = *Kleine Schriften* 1 (Göttingen 1954) 6off., Barrett on Eur. *Hipp.* 270, my own note in *BICS* 15 (1968) 121).

ῥοάν (A's orthography at Ath. 14.650e) is the classical Attic spelling (cf. Björck, *Alpha Impurum* 43), which was ousted by the allegedly Ionic form ῥοιά (cf. Photius s.v. ῥοιάς) in the second half of the 4th century (cf. the spellings βοηθῶ, ὀγδοίη etc., which creep into Attic inscriptions about the same time: Meisterhans–Schwyzer 58, Threatte 1.333f.). If Attic dramatists varied according to scansion their spelling of such *anceps* syllables, as some of the evidence seems to suggest (cf. comm. on fr. 16.2), the *Marcianus* here may preserve Alexis' own orthography.

γλυκεῖαν is no idle ornament, but a recognised specific for one kind of pomegranate (*Punica granatum*), a cultivar presumably with a relatively acid-free fruit: cf. Theophr. *HP* 2.2.5, *CP* 1.9.2, Dioscorides 1.110.1; Hehn, *Kulturpflanzen* 240ff.

Ἑλένης μνηστῆρες

74

Meineke 3.412 (1), Kock 2.321, Edmonds 2.402, Kassel–Austin 2.60. The idiom εἷς ἕκαστος, where εἷς intensifies ἕκαστος (not to be confused with καθ' ἓν ἕκαστον, which construes differently, cf. fr. 15.1), is the purest of pure Attic (Meineke 2.88; 11 instances in Thuc., at least 12 in Xen., 13 in Pl., 5 in Isoc.; in comedy, Cratinus 135(128K), Ar. fr. 67(68K), Men.

fr. 477). The Antiatticist's citation of Alexis here (96.10 Bekker), taken at face value, presupposes an Atticist attack on the idiom, but it is difficult to see what the point of criticism could have been.

75

Meineke 3.412 (II), Kock 2.321, Edmonds 2.402, Kassel–Austin 2.60. It is hard to define precisely the dialectal issues that lie behind the Antiatticist's citation of Alexis here (99.20 Bekker) for the use of the compound θερμολουτεῖν. Meineke tentatively suggested that some Atticist may have insisted on a spelling -λουτρεῖν as correct Attic. If the postulated Atticist did so, he was in error. So far as one can judge from the treacherous evidence of our MSS, in compounds of -λουτ(ρ)εῖν the spelling without rho is good Attic (θερμολουτεῖν also Hermippus 68(76K), ψυχρολουτεῖν Ar. fr. 247(237K)), while the Ionic medical writers (the prevalent employers of these compounds) and *Koine* authors vary in their usage from compound to compound and sometimes even in the same compound (thus always ἀλουτεῖν, Hippocr. *Salubr.* 4, *Morb. Mul.* 1.11, Arrian *Epict.* 3.22.73 etc.; but θερμολουτεῖν Herodotus. med. in Orib. 10.39.6, θερμολουτρεῖν [Arist.] *Probl.* 1.29, 863ᵃ4; ψυχρολουτεῖν Hippocr. *Morb.* 2.66, Hdt. med. in Orib. 10.39.6, Agathinus, *ibid.* 10.7.6, Plut. *Alc.* 23, ψυχρολουτρεῖν [Arist.] *Probl.* 1.29, 862ᵇ36, Arrian *Epict.* 1.1.29 (where S has -λουτρεῖν with ρ erased), Strabo 3.3.6; *hapax legomena* include φιλολουτρεῖν Hippocr. *Acut.* 68, σκαφολουτρεῖν Alex. Trall. *Febr.* 2, and ξηρολουτρεῖν Hesych. s.v., where H gives ξηραλουτρειν and Latte corrects unnecessarily to -λουτεῖν). It was the presence, not the absence, of an intrusive rho after tau in such words as θερμολουτ(ρ)εῖν, ἀλάβαστ(ρ)ος and παλαιστ(ρ)ικός that indicated to strict Atticists a decline from pure Atticism and therefore encouraged their invective (cf. my comm. on frs. 63(62K).1 and 326(325K); C. A. Lobeck's edition of Phrynichus (Leipzig 1820) 594).

A dramatic context cannot be conjured from the single word θερμολουτεῖν, but the average Athenian considered warm baths a mark of dissipation or effeminacy (cf. the passages collected by V. Ehrenberg, *The People of Aristophanes*² (Oxford 1951) 104f.; R. Ginouvès, *Balaneutikè* (Paris 1962) 216f.).

Τυνδάρεως and fr. 241 (239K)

See below, pp. 676 ff.

COMMENTARY

Ἑλληνίς

Breitenbach 164. Although Ἑλληνίς does once occur in its Doric form as a proper name (Agathias in *Anth. Pal.* 7.614),[1] Breitenbach and others are probably right to interpret this title simply as 'Greek girl'. This has interesting implications; the title figure must have been so described in order to contrast her with a group of non-Greeks. Does this further involve a non-Greek setting[2] and a number of non-Greek characters?[3] The subject of the one surviving fr. (a complaint about the high price of fish) is a commonplace of later Greek comedy, but the transfer of Athenian topicalities to a non-Greek setting would in itself be a potential source of humour.

76

Meineke 3.413, Kock 2.321, Edmonds 2.404, Kassel–Austin 2.60; cf. Nesselrath, *MK* 294f. n. 26. The fr., probably spoken by a customer on his way to or from the fish-market, is cited by Ath. 6.224c–228b along with seventeen others to illustrate the attitude of later Greek comic poets to the arrogant ways and preposterous prices of Athenian fishmongers (cf. introduction to fr. 16). The hyperbolic allegation that these prices reduce purchasers to penury is repeated elsewhere in Alexis (frs. 78, 204(200K)).

1 ἀεί: so first G. Morel 129. Both A and the Epit. MSS here (Ath. 6.226f) have αἰεί in a position where the first syllable is *anceps* (cf. Alexis 88(85K).4; the same MSS often write αἰεί also in places where the first syllable must scan long (e.g. Machon 236, 261, 284 Gow). Is it possible

---

1 As does rarely the congeneric Ἕλλην (Kirchner, *PA* 1.311 no. 4667). Cf. also the introduction to Ἀτθίς.

2 Timocles' Αἰγύπτιοι, Philemon's Πανηγυρίς and the play from which com. adesp. fr. 286 Austin (with its reference to an Egyptian official) derives may have been set in Egypt, and Philemon's comedy even been written there (Webster, *SLGC* 125f.). In Menander's Ἐγχειρίδιον, however, references to Sarapis (fr. 139 Körte–Thierfelder = 4 Arnott) and to Egyptian men or things (*PSI* 109.6, cf. D. Del Corno, *PP* 23 (1968) 306ff.) seem not to imply an Egyptian setting (see *ZPE* 31 (1978) 4).

3 Characters, not character in the singular. Such evidence as we possess indicates that it is plays with one major character non-Greek and most of the others Greek that take their title from the non-Greek's nationality: e.g. Αἰγύπτιος, Καρχηδόνιος and Plautus' *Poenulus* (see below on Alexis' K.), Περσίς, perhaps Σικελικός. The converse might be expected to apply to a title such as Ἑλληνίς.

ΕΛΛΗΝΙΣ

that some Byzantine scholar's edict imposed for comic and related texts[1] this adoption of a long obsolete orthography in those *sedes* where the word's first syllable scanned long or *anceps*, since the same convention appears to obtain in certain MSS of Aristophanes also (cf. W. J. W. Koster, *Autour d'un manuscrit d'Aristophane* (Groningen and Jakarta 1957) 235)? If so, the edict was ill-advised and imperfectly obeyed. Ill-advised, because later comic poets and Hellenistic writers like Machon (*pace* Gow at v. 443) are unlikely to have used a form that disappeared from Attic inscriptions after 350 (Threatte 1.275) and from less formal usage even earlier, in all probability; imperfectly obeyed, since medieval scribes import the spelling αἰεί into places where its first syllable must scan short (e.g. Alexis 145(141K).15, 177(173K).1, 219(216K).4, 222(219K).10, Men. fr. 537, Machon 443).[2] The comic papyri normally write ἀεί in every *sedes* of the iambic trimeter; exceptions are few (for Men. *Dysk.* 31 and 904 see Handley on 902ff.).

2 Jacobs' τἀν (*Addit.* 133) is a highly plausible, if not a wholly certain,[3] conjecture for the transmitted ἐν: 'nimirum excidit τά post τεθνηκότα' (Meineke 3.413).

3 ὡς γίγνεται: 'as happens', a use otherwise confined to the *Koine* Greek of Alexander of Aphrodisias' commentaries on [Arist.] *Probl.* 2.1, 46.32f., *Top.* 2.2, 33.9ff., *Meteor.* 3.2, 24.22ff.; but cf. οἷα γίγνεται, Plato com. 102(95K).1, and *ut fit* commonly in Latin (e.g. Ter. *Eun.* 98, Cic. *Verr.* 2.2.56). Cf. also comm. on 37(36K).7.

4 νέων τις: 'one swimming'.

καταπεπώκασ' εὐθέως: 'they (sc. the fish) swallow him up before he knows what has happened'; the perfect tense emphasises the action's immediacy (K.G. 1.150, Goodwin, *MT* 15).

5–6 These verses *add* the second way in which fish ruin men; the connective τ' is therefore here (and also, as it happens, in v. 8) rightly transmitted in the MSS, and must not be altered to either δ' (Bothe, *PCGF* 533, Blaydes, *Adv.* 2.155) or γ' (*recentiores*, and editions before Schweighaeuser).

7 Editors have been slow to adopt Grotius' conjecture ἡμῖν (*Exc.* 567: two and a half centuries before its resurrection by Kock) for the transmitted ἡμῶν, although the balance of the arguments tilts in favour of ἡμῖν.

[1] On the transmission of this word in Attic comedy see Björck, *Alpha Impurum* 97, 151, 230, 235.
[2] For a possible but partial explanation of this (confusion between α and αι in early minuscule) see the introduction to Ἑπτὰ ἐπὶ Θήβας.
[3] The preceding context might have contained a neuter plural such as τὰ ὄψα or τὰ ἰχθύδια, whose presence would have eliminated the necessity for an expressed subject in vv. 1–2 of the fr.

COMMENTARY

With the dative the sense is slightly improved ('on sale to us at the price of one's total assets'), and the position of the pronoun more acceptable (with ἡμῶν one might rather have expected τῆς οὐσίας ἡμῶν γὰρ εἰ. ὤ., which admittedly *could* have been corrupted to the MSS text by a scribe worried about the postponed γάρ: cf. on frs. 4.1, 37(36K).1). Corruption of ἡμῖν to ἡμῶν would have been induced by assimilation to the opening syllable of the following ὤνιοι; for parallel instances see Fraenkel on A. *Ag.* 119 (and the works there cited) and Jackson, *Marg. Scaen.* 186ff.

εἰσὶν ὤνιοι is commonly used in Attic as the passive of πωλοῦσι, whose regular passive forms are rare there apart from the participle πωλούμενος (Neil on Ar. *Equ.* 1247, cf. Rutherford, *NP* 213).

Ἐπιδαύριος

Meineke 1.389. The one citation from this play is introduced by the *Marcianus* at Ath. 3.119f with the lemma Ἄλεξις ἐν Ἐπιδαύρωι. Meineke's correction of the play title to Ἐπιδαυρίῳ is palaeographically convincing and dramatically necessary. In later Greek comedy over a hundred titles consist of substantivally used adjectives denoting nationality (cf. the introduction to Ἀτθίς), but none solidly attested[1] is merely the name of a city, island or state. The palaeographic argument is reinforced by information about the transmission of the two identically named comedies by Theophilus and Antiphanes. The Theophilus lemma, like that of Alexis, is corrupted to ἐν Ἐπιδαύρωι by the *Marcianus* at Ath. 10.417a on the one occasion when its title is cited; there again Meineke (1.435) provided the requisite correction. Antiphanes' title is preserved twice: correctly in the MS of the anonymous *Glossary of Useful Terms* (154.20 Bachmann), but corrupted to Ἐπιδαύρωι in the Antiatticist (98.28 Bekker). A production of one of these plays seems to be mentioned on *IG*

---

[1] Four other titles at first sight might give one pause: Antiphanes' Βυζάν-τιος or -ιον, Alexis' Λεύκη and Μεροπίς, and Timocles' "Δῆλος". However, the lemma at Pollux 7.170 Ἀντιφάνης ἐν Βυζαντίῳ, introduc-ing its one fr. (70(69K)), leads one to expect Βυζάντιος rather than -ιον as the title in view of normal practice. If Alexis' Λεύκη denotes the island of ghosts, that place is as mythical and unreal as his Μεροπίς (see the introductions to those plays). A single lemma in the *Marcianus* at Ath. 8.341e cites Τιμοκλῆς ἐν Δήλωι, where Meineke's correction to Δηλίῳ (1.429, 3.591n.) has surprisingly won less acceptance than his Ἐπιδαυρίῳ corrections, although the same hypothesis underlies them all. A Δῆλος is attested elsewhere for Philostephanus, a Δηλία for Antiphanes and Sophilus.

ΕΠΙΔΑΥΡΙΟΣ

Urb. Rom. 222 p. 192 Moretti, Ἐ]πιδαυρ[ίωι, see general introduction 1.i
(*testimonium* *9). About the plots and any possible interrelation of the three
plays sharing the title we know nothing, but the fr. extant from Alexis'
comedy (77), with its reference to the enfranchisement of Chaerephilus'
sons, enables us to date the play within narrow limits. The enfranchisement was engineered by Demosthenes *c.* 328 (cf. comm. on fr. 6), and
a comic sneer at it would hardly have retained topicality and point after
321, when the issues of Athenian citizenship were differently orientated.

77

Meineke 3.413, Kock 2.322, Edmonds 2.404, Kassel–Austin 2.61; cf.
Hirschig, *Annot.* 10f.

1 τοὺς Χαιρεφίλου δ' υἱεῖς Ἀθηναίους: presumably these accusatives
were originally governed by some part of ποιῶ (or another verb of similar
meaning), whose absence in the extant fr. may be variously explained: (i)
a parallel or contrasted (? μέν) clause may have preceded v. 1 containing
the required verb, which was then to be supplied in the preserved δέ
clause; (ii) alternatively, the verb may have dropped out directly before
τούς or have been corrupted into the transmitted δ' υἱεῖς (hence ποιεῖς
Kock, the neatest of such conjectures, to be interpreted as an apostrophe to
the Athenian δῆμος or to Demosthenes, the sponsor of the enfranchisement).

2 εἰσήγαγεν: its subject is the father, Chaerephilus. εἰσάγω is the
technical term for '(I) import' (LSJ s.v. 1.3), and in this sense its object is
normally expressed without the article, as here (τάριχος), Thuc. 2.6, Isoc.
18.61 (σῖτον), [Dem.] 35.35 (οἶνον); cf. Hdt. 3.6, Thuc. 4.26, Andoc. 2.11,
Ar. *Ach.* 916, *Av.* 1524. At Alexis 278(276K).2 τὸν οἶνον εἰσάγουσιν, the
article is added to give a discriminatory emphasis (the wine of Lesbos as
distinct from other sorts).

2–4 οὓς καὶ Τιμοκλῆς ... ἐν τοῖς σατύροις: the 16th-century editors of
Ath. printed these words as part of the Alexis quotation (cf. Meineke, *Cur.
Crit.* 32f.), but Schweighaeuser ended the fr. at τάριχος (v.2) and
interpreted what followed as a scholarly comment by Ath. More recently
scholars have been fairly evenly divided; supporters of the earlier view
include Meineke, Kaibel, Gulick, Edmonds and Kassel–Austin, while
Hirschig, Kock, and V. Bevilacqua (*Dioniso* 7 (1939) 27) side with
Schweighaeuser. In a question that seems capable of final decision it is odd
that attempts at reasoned argument have been so rare.

The case for the elimination of these words from a comic source was
stated with great force by Hirschig: '*Pulchri sane uersiculi, quos uncis inclusi!
isto modo paucis mutatis bonam Athenaei Deipn. partem in senarios redigere
licet. scripserat Athenaeus* οὓς καὶ Τιμοκλῆς ἰδὼν ἐπὶ τῶν ἵππων ἐν τοῖς

211

COMMENTARY

ΣΑΤΥΡΟΙΣ ἔφη δύο σκόμβρους εἶναι. *Timoclis fabula huius nominis memoratur Athen. VIII p. 339d . . . saepius Athenaei uerba, paucis mutatis, deletis uel additis a librariis pro poetae uerbis uenditata obseruauerunt uiri docti.*' The passage of Ath. 8 to which Hirschig refers runs Πυθιονίκην δέ φασι (so A, Epit.: φησι Musurus) φιληδεῖν ταρίχῳ, ἐπεὶ ἐραστὰς εἶχε τοὺς Χαιρεφίλου τοῦ ταριχο-πώλου υἱούς, ὡς Τιμοκλῆς ἐν Ἰκαρίοις (so Casaubon: νικοκλῆς ἐν ἀκαρίοις A) φησιν (fr. 15(17K))· Ἄνυτος ὁ παχὺς πρὸς Πυθιονίκην ὅταν ἐλθὼν φάγῃ τι· καλεῖ γὰρ αὐτόν, ὥς φησιν (so A), ὁπόταν Χαιρεφίλου τοὺς δύο σκόμβρους ξενίσῃ μεγάλους ἡδομένη. Hirschig believed that this passage quoted in fuller detail (although not accurately enough for the original verses to be confidently reconstituted) a fr. of Timocles' Ἰκάριοι σάτυροι[1] to which Ath. 3.120a was allegedly referring; accordingly Hirschig (unwittingly following a suggestion made fourteen years earlier by Th. Bergk in C. Schiller's edition of Andocides (Leipzig 1835) p. 156) printed σατύροις in capital letters at Ath. 3.120a, thus identifying those satyrs as the genre-defining part of the play title from which Timocles' quip derived, and not as part of the quip itself.

Hirschig's argument is attractive but wrong. First, his sarcastic refer-ence to *pulchri uersiculi* is clearly inspired by the absence of penthemimeral or hephthemimeral caesura in vv. 3 and 4 (they are absent too in v. 1!) of the fr. But Alexis' metrical practice, so far as we can judge it, differed little from that of Aristophanes and Menander in the use of caesurae (cf. e.g. J. W. White, *The Verse of Greek Comedy* (London 1912) 51ff., Handley's edition of Men. *Dysk.* p. 57, West, *Greek Metre* 88); while verses with penthemimeral or hephthemimeral caesurae predominate, single and indeed successive verses may be instanced where these normal caesurae do not occur or the break comes in the middle of the second metron as in vv. 1, 3 and 4 here: e.g. frs. 37(36K).1, 4, 5; 140(135K).2, 3, 4, 11, 12 (cf. also comm. on Γυναικοκρατία, p. 153 n. 1). Secondly, if Ath. 3.120a

---

[1] There is no certain solution to a number of problems that beset the interpretation of this puzzling title. Did it denote a comedy or a satyr play? If a satyr play, was its author still Timocles ὁ κωμικός? Was it produced once or twice, and when? The most useful discussions of these questions are found in G. Coppola, *RFIC* 55 (1927) 454ff., who argues convincingly for a production date in 330/29 (cf. also T. B. L. Webster, *CQ* 2 (1952) 20 and *SLGC* 46f.); V. Bevilacqua, *Dioniso* 7 (1939) 50ff., who makes up for some implausible conclusions by a good analysis of his predecessors' attempts to confront the problems; and E. Constantinides, *TAPA* 100 (1969) 49ff., who concludes that Timocles' play was a comedy. This seems to me right; the extant frs. (15–19 Kassel–Austin = 14–17 Kock + 222b Austin), with a series of references to at least eleven contemporary personalities, are wholly comic in spirit (cf. Körte in *RE* s.v. *Timokles* 3, 1260.50ff., W. Steffen, *Eos* 63 (1975) 233ff.).

originally contained the lemma Τιμοκλῆς ἐν Σατύροις followed by a direct quotation, it is difficult to see why any scribe or Byzantine scholar should select just this one out of several thousand citations for an exercise of misapplied ingenuity, separating author's name from title, turning a direct quotation into indirect speech and still managing to keep the whole passage metrical. Thirdly, the phrase ἰδὼν ἐπὶ τῶν ἵππων would be out of place as an adjunct to a lemma; Ath. does not qualify his source quotations with such descriptive material. Finally and most decisively, unless the words ἐν τοῖς σατύροις are themselves part of the quip, that quip becomes pointless. This Timocles (see on v. 2 below), we are told here, observed the sons of the fish-importer Chaerephilus riding on horseback. It was the contrast between the genteel activity of riding and the riders' alien origins combined with their trading connections that sparked off the witticism. Upstart foreigners aping Athenian aristocrats were as inappropriate as mackerel in the midst of satyrs. The choice of symbol was not haphazard. Mackerel suggested the trade on which the family fortunes had been built (see below on v. 3), and Chaerephilus' sons may indeed already have been nicknamed after this type of fish, either by the Athenian public at large or by the comic poets (cf. Timocles 15(17K)). Satyrs were chosen because they indicated somewhat derisively the idea of equitation, but partly also perhaps for the sigmatic alliteration with σκόμβρους. I doubt whether there is more to the joke than this; side allusions to the licentiousness of satyrs (and of rich young Athenians? Cf. S. Petit, *Miscellanea* 2 (Paris 1630) 94, and my own discussion of Men. *Dysk.* 259ff. in *Philologus* 125 (1981) 223ff.), to the distinctive name of a squadron of cavalry in which Chaerephilus' sons may have enrolled if they were classed as ἱππεῖς (cf. Meineke 3.414), or even to Timocles' 'Ικάριοι (which was probably produced only shortly before Alexis' play), are totally unnecessary. But Timocles' quip was pithy, and Alexis doubtless felt that it deserved to be broadcast to a wider audience which would appreciate its malicious chauvinism.

2 This Timocles (contrast Alexis 113(108K).3 and comm. *ad loc.*) is almost certainly the comic poet, if it was he who patented the nickname 'Mackerel' for the sons of Chaerephilus in his recent 'Ικάριοι (fr. 15(17K)). There is no evidence, however, that Alexis lifted his quip from that play (plagiarists do not normally name their sources), and its origin is more likely to have been an impromptu witticism outside the theatre.

From the plays of Timocles, who was writing between the late 340s and the regime of Demetrius of Phalerum, a bare forty or so frs. remain, but several of them reveal the same lively and felicitous wit as the quip attributed to him here. Cf. the works cited in p. 212 n. 1.

3 ἐπὶ τῶν ἵππων: 'on their horses' simply. Athenian writers differentiated precisely between ἐφ' ἵππου ('on horseback', of individuals, very

COMMENTARY

common), ἐφ' ἵππων ('on horseback', referring to *either* two or more riders, e.g. Xen. *Cyr.* 1.4.25, 8.3.15, *or* one rider on two or more occasions, e.g. Xen. *Ages.* 2.25) and ἐπὶ τῶν ἵππων ('on his/her/their horses', e.g. Xen. *Cyr.* 4.5.54, 58, *Anab.* 7.4.4, *Hell.* 6.4.11, Pl. *Meno* 93d, *Resp.* 7.537a). The presence of the article here implies solely that the sons of Chaerephilus owned the horses they were riding, not that they were necessarily members of the Athenian class of ἱππεῖς as some modern scholars assume on the evidence of this fr. alone, following Casaubon's misinterpretation, '*intelligo de equitum transuectione*' (*Animadv.* 231).

σκόμβρους: common mackerel (*Scomber scombrus* Linn., cf. Thompson, *Fishes* s.v., Palombi–Santorelli 105f., Campbell, *Guide* 302f.), a pertly malicious nickname for enfranchised sons of a non-Athenian ταριχο-πώλης. In the ancient world as until recently mackerel were common and cheap, so the choice of this species as a sobriquet would stigmatise the alleged vulgarity of parvenus. At the same time mackerel were regularly caught in the Hellespont, Bosporus and the Black Sea, and imported from there to Athens after pickling (Hermippus 63.5 ἐκ δ' Ἑλλησπόντου σκόμβρους καὶ πάντα ταρίχη, cf. Euthydemus in Ath. 3.116bc = *SH* 455.7ff.; M. Besnier in Dar.–Sag. s.v. *Salsamentum* 1022B ff., Neil on Ar. *Equ.* 1005–10, cf. André, *Alimentation* 113), and may well have been one of Chaerephilus' specialities. Because the fish was often pickled, the nickname σκόμβρος may also have acquired an innuendo of that graceless stolidity which appears to have been conveyed by nicknames like τάριχος (e.g. Timocles 16(14K).5 with probable reference to these same sons of Chaerephilus, possibly also Ar. fr. 207(200K) unless the words there are intended literally; cf. Plaut. *Poen.* 240ff.). See further comm. on 43(42K).2, 173(168K).3.

Ἐπίκληρος

The term ἐπίκληρος, usually translated 'heiress', designated more strictly in Athenian law a girl or woman who was the daughter of a citizen who had died without leaving a son by issue or adoption. To preserve the estate within the dead man's family an ἐπίκληρος was required under certain conditions to marry her nearest male relative outside the forbidden degrees of consanguinity. The legal questions are fully discussed in A. R. W. Harrison, *The Law of Athens, 1: The Family and Property* (Oxford 1968) 10ff., 132ff., cf. D. M. MacDowell, *The Law in Classical Athens* (London 1978) 95ff., J. Gould, *JHS* 100 (1980) 43ff.; their complications afforded a rich source of material for subterfuge in later Greek comedy. In Menander's *Aspis*, for instance, the stratagem of Chairestratos' feigned death is devised in order to prevent the marriage of one ἐπίκληρος to

ΕΠΙΚΛΗΡΟΣ

Smikrines, an uncle who now had the legal right to her hand (cf. E. Karabelias, *Rev. hist. de droit français et étranger* 48 (1970) 357ff., D. M. MacDowell, *G and R* 29 (1982) 42ff., P. G. McC. Brown, *CQ* 23 (1983) 412ff.), while the titular hero of Terence's *Phormio* (an adaptation of Apollodorus' Ἐπιδικαζόμενος: ἐπιδικασία was the name given to the procedure by which the permitted next-of-kin established his claim to the ἐπίκληρος) engineered Antipho's marriage to the orphaned and brotherless Phanium by a fraudulent claim that Antipho was her next-of-kin (cf. my paper in *G and R* 17 (1970) 34f., E. Lefèvre, *Der Phormio des Terenz und der Epidikazomenos des Apollodor von Karystos* (Munich 1978) 5ff.). Similar artifices may have been employed in some at least of the plays entitled Ἐπίκληρος (their authors were, in addition to Alexis: Antiphanes, Diodorus, Diphilus, Heniochus and Menander, the last-named writing two plays with this title, cf. Körte–Thierfelder 2.63f., Webster, *IM* 136f.; one of the Menander titles was adapted by Turpilius, and probably another of the seven plays by Caecilius Statius), although it must always be remembered that identity of title does not guarantee identity of theme. Cf. also Handley on Men. *Dysk.* 729–39 and *P.Oxy.* 3972, Gomme–Sandbach, *Comm.* 29 n. 1.

Little[1] now survives from Alexis' Ἐπίκληρος, but enough to shed a flicker of dim light on two of its scenes. Fr. 78, another complaint about the high cost of fish, most likely derives from a monologue spoken by a disgruntled customer on the way home from market after making (or failing to make: cf. Plaut. *Aul.* 371ff.) purchases for a celebratory meal (cf. the introductions to Ἀπεγλαυκωμένος and fr. 16). That meal might have been planned in honour of the event which is under way in the trochaic tetrameters of 79, where, according to the Antiatticist (81.17ff. Bekker), some man is giving away a daughter in marriage (ἐκδιδόντος τινὸς θυγατέρα). The speaker there addresses a παῖς, utters a formula of betrothal and promises to do all that a third man asks. The language in later Greek comedy on such occasions is wholly stereotyped (Men. *Asp.* 540ff., *Dysk.* 761ff., 842ff., *Mis.* 444ff., *Pk.* 1013ff., *Sam.* 726ff., *Fab. Inc.* 29f., fr. 682, com. adesp. frs. 250.8ff., 251.4ff., 266.10ff., 292.4ff. Austin; cf. H.-D. Blume, *Menanders "Samia": Eine Interpretation* (Darmstadt 1974) 281), and it enables us to identify the speaker as the κύριος of the girl being

---

[1] The early (3rd-century) papyrus frs. of a comedy (*P.Berlin* 11771 = com. adesp. fr. 239 Austin), first published by Wilamowitz (*SB Berlin* (1918) 743ff.) and tentatively attributed by him to an unknown play by Alexis, were re-examined by A. Körte (*Ber. Leipzig* 71/6 (1919) 36ff.) and even more tentatively assigned to Alexis' Ἐπίκληρος. The text of these frs. is published below at '*False or Doubtful Attributions*', v (pp. 833ff.), with commentary and full discussion of dramatic context and authorship.

COMMENTARY

betrothed, and the third person as the prospective bridegroom. Two
problems, however, remain unsolved. The first is the identity of the παῖς.
The likeliest option is a family slave who had dedicated himself to the
coming union (in Menander the vocative παῖ is most commonly addressed
to slaves). The girl herself can safely be excluded; in comic betrothal scenes
her consent is taken for granted, and she is never addressed. The other
problem arises from the introductory words of the Antiatticist (cited
above) to fr. 79. If these correctly identify the fr.'s speaker as the girl's
father, that girl cannot be the ἐπίκληρος of the play title, unless Alexis
devised a plot which reunited the ἐπίκληρος with a father previously
believed dead.

78

Meineke 3.414 (i), Kock 2.322, Edmonds 2.405, Kassel–Austin 2.62. The
fr., cited by Ath. 6.227d (A, Epit. MSS), is a further attack on the high
prices extorted by fishmongers (cf. the introduction to fr. 16), here varied
by the conceit that a poor man can afford current prices only by going out
at night to mug victims. The idea is repeated by (or from) Diphilus
31(32K).12ff., where less crispness and imagination are revealed.

1 ὄψον: 'fish', see on fr. 47(46K).6.

2 ἀπορούμενος ... εὐπορεῖ: cf. fr. 236(234K).5–6 εὐπόρους | ἐν τοῖς
ἀπόροις and comm. ad loc.

3–4 I.e. he is a λωποδύτης (cf. Gow, comm. on Machon 100f.),
stripping his victims of their outer clothing and any valuables concealed
about the person. Even in a context like this, γυμνός need not mean 'stark
naked', but only 'without their cloaks'; cf. Dover on Ar. Nub. 498, Ussher
on Eccl. 408–10, and my comm. on Alexis 239 (237K).5.

4–8 From εἶτ'[1] to the end of the fr. 'omnia Graeco planissima', claimed
Casaubon, Animadv. 402; although he misunderstood εἶτα, this pithy
comment and his general interpretation here remain valid. εἶτα is purely
temporal ('next'); the infinitives τηρεῖν and ἀπάγειν, with subject accusative (in agreement with λαβόμενον v. 8, but unexpressed and to be
supplied from the τις in v. 4: sc. the victim of the mugging), are used in
imperatival sense (cf. Grotius, Exc. 566f., K.G. 2.22f.) with an obvious
intent to parody official legislative style. The speaker accuses poor young
men who buy expensive fish in large quantities of being the type of
criminals who in contemporary Athens were characteristically arrested by
ἀπαγωγή; cf. Dem. 24.113 εἰ δέ τις νύκτωρ ὁτιοῦν κλέπτοι, (sc. ὁ Σόλων

---

[1] Attempts to emend εἶτ' (so A, Epit.) to δεῖ τ' (Meineke 3.415), δεῖ δ'
(Hirschig, Annot. 11, cf. Cobet in Peppink, Observ. 36f.) or ὥστ' (Bothe,
PCGF 534) are misguided.

216

ΕΠΙΚΛΗΡΟΣ

νόμον εἰσήνεγκεν) τοῦτον ἐξεῖναι καὶ ἀποκτεῖναι καὶ τρῶσαι διώκοντα καὶ ἀπαγαγεῖν τοῖς ἔνδεκα, εἰ βούλοιτο, cf. 54.1. See J. H. Lipsius, *Das attische Recht und Rechtsverfahren* (Leipzig 1905–15) 77ff., 320ff., A. R. W. Harrison, *The Law of Athens, 2: Procedure* (Oxford 1971) 221ff., M. H. Hansen, *Apagoge, Endeixis and Ephegesis against Kakourgoi, Atimoi and Pheugontes* (Odense 1976) 36ff., D. M. MacDowell, *The Law in Classical Athens* (London 1978) 148f.

5 ἐν τοῖς ἰχθύσιν: see comm. on fr. 47(46K).8.

6 ὃν ἂν δ' ἴδῃ: see comm. on fr. 4.1.

πένητα καὶ νέον: 'poor' because, without stealing, such a person would be unable to afford more than one eel (cf. Oder in *RE* s.v. *Aal*, 3.14ff., Thompson, *Fishes* s.v. ἔγχελυς, Starkie on Ar. *Vesp.* 510); and 'young' because only then would he be likely to have strength enough for his style of robbery.

7 Μικίωνος: Ath. 6.227b calls him simply ἰχθυοπώλου τινός. He is otherwise unknown. Herodas' τὰ Μικίωνος κηρί' (7.43) are obscure, but apparently have nothing to do with Alexis' fishmonger (cf. O. Crusius, *Untersuchungen zu den Mimiamben des Herondas* (Leipzig 1892) 135, Headlam–Knox, comm. *ad loc.*); and it seems unlikely that the Athenian family which included a syntrierarch in the mid-4th century (Kirchner, *PA* 2.885 no. 10190, Davies, *APF* p. 392) and distinguished itself further at the end of the 3rd (Modrze in *RE* s.v. *Mikion* 2, 1554.40ff.) was related by blood to him. The name is given also to milder old men in later comedy (*P.Oxy.* 3970.19, cf. Micio in Ter. *Ad.*).

ἐγχέλεις (so A), not ἐγχέλυς (Epit. MSS); the former form is Attic and universal in comedy, Ar. *Equ.* 864, *Lys.* 36, Antiphanes 104(105K).3, Timocles 11.6, Men. fr. 264.5; cf. Ath. 7.299a–d, Aelius Dionysius s.v. ἔγχελυς, p. 116 Erbse, LSJ s.v. Cf. also introduction to 149(145K) and comm. on 159(155K).5.

8 λαβόμενον: see on fr. 23.

79

Meineke 3.415 (II), Kock 2.322, Edmonds 2.406, Kassel–Austin 2.62. The dramatic context of this fr., cited by the Antiatticist (81.17ff. Bekker), and the identities of its οὗτος (presumably on stage along with the speaker) and παῖς are discussed in the introduction to Ἐπίκληρος.

1 ἐγώ‹γ', ὦ› παῖ: Dobree's correction (*R. Porsoni notae in Aristophanem* (Cambridge 1820), add. p. 130 on *Ach.* 254) of the MS's unmetrical haplography ἐγὼ παῖ.

δίδωμι: sc. in marriage. Although the compound ἐκδίδωμι is the technical term for this action by the father or guardian of the prospective bride (LSJ s.v. 1.2.a, A. R. W. Harrison, *The Law of Athens, 1: The Family*

217

and Property (Oxford 1968) 2), the simple verb is often used in the same sense (LSJ s.v. II.2), e.g. Men. *Dysk.* 762, and especially with the betrothal formula παίδων ἐπ' ἀρότῳ γνησίων, *Mis.* 444f., *Pk.* 1013f., *Sam.* 726f., fr. 682, com. adesp. fr. 250.8f. Austin.

1–2 καὶ ποιήσω [? better ποήσω: see comm. on 16.2] . . . **παρ' ἡμῶν**: this *may* refer to the dowry, but our ignorance of the dramatic antecedents prevents a more definite statement.

2 αἰτεῖται: Bekker's correction of αἰτεῖ παῖ in the MS, where the copyist's mind was doubtless influenced by what he had written in the previous verse.

The Antiatticist's note here, which seeks to differentiate between the active αἰτεῖν (allegedly 'to ask for as a gift') and the middle αἰτεῖσθαι ('to ask for as a loan') is repeated in substantially the same terms, but without the Alexis citation, in other lexica: Ammonius *Diff.* p. 4 Nickau, Harpocration 94.5ff. Bekker = 125 Keaney (н18), Photius s.vv. αἰτούμενος, αἰτήσασθαι = 1.76, 78 Theodoridis, *Suda* s.vv. αἰτήσασθαι, αἰτούμενος = 2.185, 186 Adler, the anon. *Glossary of Useful Terms* 1.48.1ff. Bachmann. We do not know the identity of the grammarian originally responsible for making this distinction in meaning between αἰτεῖν and αἰτεῖσθαι, but a survey of the passages cited by LSJ and Passow–Crönert quickly reveals that the alleged distinction is largely chimerical. In Attic of the classical period the meanings of this verb's active and middle are often indistinguishable; preference for one voice or the other seems partly to depend on the period when an author wrote.[1] And yet perhaps we ought not to dismiss the Antiatticist's canon altogether as pedantic poppycock. It would be unnatural if in the course of time the active and middle of αἰτεῖν did not come to be separately associated with particular phrases where the employment of one voice became by usage correct, of the other incorrect. The Antiatticist's canon may have resulted from unwise generalisation about some of these phrases. For instance, the middle is often used in the sense 'to ask for' certain sorts of object whose return would naturally be expected, like pots (e.g. [Dem.] 49.24, Theophr. *Char.* 18.7, Men. *Dysk.* 472, 505, 914; cf. Men. fr. 410, cited by the Antiatticist here as well as by other grammarians and lexicographers) and clothes (e.g. Ar. *Ach.* 423); when the active is used with reference to such objects, any notion of 'borrowing' is usually absent (e.g. Ar. *Lys.* 444, *Thesm.* 633). Again, αἰτεῖν

---

[1] Cf. J. U. Powell in *CR* 28 (1914) 191ff., noting that 'in Aeschylus the middle predominates over the active, and to some extent in Sophocles; in Herodotus, Thucydides and Euripides the instances are about equal; in Aristophanes in the more dignified passages the middle predominates; in Lysias and Andocides the middle, but in the later Attic of Plato and Demosthenes, the active; in Xenophon they are about equal'.

is commonly used in the active in idioms where the middle does not occur and there is apparently no element of 'borrowing', e.g. with the nouns δωρεάν (Dem. 22.8, [Dem.] 58.47, Pl. *Criti.* 108a, Din. 1.17), ἀργύριον (Ar. *Plut.* 156, [Dem.] 35.41) and μισθόν (Pl. *Apol.* 31c, *Resp.* 1.345e). Of the two passages cited by the Antiatticist here in illustration of his canon, Men. fr. 410 appears to be in harmony with it, but the present fr. of Alexis will be only an uncertain support so long as we do not know whether the prospective bridegroom is asking for a (returnable) dowry or for something else.

80

Meineke 3.415 (III), Kock 2.323, Edmonds 2.406, Kassel–Austin 2.63. Good Attic writers appear to have distinguished between κακουχία (active sense, 'maltreatment') and καχεξία (passive sense, 'bad condition/disposition'); see LSJ s.vv. This distinction, however, was not always drawn by *Koine* writers, who sometimes used κακουχία in the passive sense proper to καχεξία, e.g. Polyb. 3.64.8 (Hannibal's forces weak and useless διὰ τὴν κακουχίαν), Diod. Sic. 19.16.3, [Plut.] *Mor.* 112c. If Alexis too used κακουχία in this passive sense, it would be easy to account for an Atticist attack on, and our Antiatticist's defence here (104.24 Bekker) of, such an anomaly.

Ἐπιστολή

As a comic title Ἐπιστολή appears at widely different periods; instances are known also from Euthycles and Machon, while Timocles wrote an Ἐπιστολαί. In extant Greco-Roman comedy letters play an important role, often in furtherance of confidence tricks (Plaut. *Bacch.*, *Curc.*, *Pers.*, *Pseud.*, *Trin.*). Only one word survives from Alexis' Ἐπιστολή, however, and it would be foolish to speculate about the function of its letter in the plot. Equally futile, in the total absence of corroborative evidence, is the suggestion (made by L. Spengel, *Caecilii Statii fragmenta* (Munich 1829) 6, cf. Ribbeck 47) that Caecilius' *Epistula* may have been modelled on Alexis' play.

81

Meineke 3.415, Kock 2.323, Edmonds 2.406, Kassel–Austin 2.63. The Antiatticist's point here (112.9 Bekker = Phot. and *Suda* *s.v.* προσέκοψεν, both omitting the play title), when he supports Alexis' use of προσκόπτω in the sense of προσπταίω, is not precisely clear. These two verbs share

COMMENTARY

several usages and meanings (LSJ s.vv.): transitive 'I hurt (e.g. a limb) by striking it against an obstacle (προσκόπτω: Ar. *Vesp. 275, Koine* ; προσπταίω: Hdt. 6.134, *Koine*), and intransitive, both literally 'I stumble (against)' (προσκόπτω: not before the *Koine*;[1] προσπταίω: Ar. *Plut.* 121, Men. *Dysk.* 92 and commonly), and metaphorically 'I offend' (προσκόπτω: Posidippus 39(36K), *Koine*; προσπταίω: *Koine*). If the Antiatticist was attempting to defend a usage which stricter Atticists stigmatised as non-Attic, Alexis is perhaps most likely to have been using προσκόπτω intransitively in the sense 'I stumble', given the evidence of usage summarised above.

Ἐπίτροπος

Nothing is known, and little can safely be guessed, about Alexis' Ἐπίτροπος, the only play known with this title[2]. The title figure would probably have been the guardian of a male ward (cf. A. R. W. Harrison, *The Law of Athens, 1: The Family and Property* (Oxford 1968) 98, 108f.) in a New-Comedy plot of intrigue.

82

Meineke 3.416, Kock 2.323, Edmonds 2.406, Kassel–Austin 2.63. The evil of excessive wine-bibbing is a cliché that appears first in Greek literature as a generalisation in the Theognidean corpus (509 οἶνος πινόμενος πουλὺς κακόν, cf. 479ff.), and it is repeated times without number in comedy and elsewhere (e.g. Men. *Sam.* 340f. πολλὰ δ' ἐξεργάζεται | ἀνόητ' ἄκρατος καὶ νεότης, fr. 512, Philemon 162(193K)).In the conventional story-lines of New Comedy the rape of a free-born girl was typically excused by a plea of drunkenness (e.g. Men. *Sam.* 340f. above, Plaut. *Aul.* 744ff., 791ff., *Truc.* 826ff., Ter. *Ad.* 470f.; cf. Men. *Epitr.* 472f., Ter. *Hec.* 822ff., *Phorm.* 1017f.), and it is at least possible that the ἁμαρτία implied by Alexis 82 was such a rape. A. Nauck (*MGR* 6 (1894) 97, cf. Blaydes, *Adv.* 1.107) compares the wording of monost. 774 τὸ πολλὰ τολμᾶν πόλλ' ἁμαρτάνειν ποεῖ (cf. also

---

[1] LSJ s.v. προσκόπτω 1.1.b wrongly cite Xen. *Equ. 7.6* σκληρὸν μὲν γὰρ ἔχων τὸ σκέλος εἰ προσκόψειέ τῳ, προσκεκλασμένος ἂν εἴη as an example of this intransitive use before the *Koine*. In fact the verb there is transitive, with τὸ σκέλος the object ἀπὸ κοινοῦ of both it and ἔχων.

[2] Diphilus' Ἐπιτροπή is rightly transmitted, and needs no alteration to Ἐπίτροπος or Ἐπιτροπεύς (so Meineke 1.454f.); see F. Marx's edition of Plaut. *Rud.* (Leipzig 1928) pp. 273f.

ΕΠΙΤΡΟΠΟΣ

Eur. fr. 576 and Nauck *ad loc.*), but this coincidence of wording is probably fortuitous.

Ἑπτὰ ἐπὶ Θήβας (or Θήβαις)

The *Marcianus* at Ath. 7.294a introduces the one quotation from this play with the words Ἄλεξις ἐν Ἑπτὰ ἐπὶ Θήβαις, and shortly afterwards (295e) the sole fr. of Amphis' homonym similarly, with Θήβαις in the dative. Aeschylus' tragedy, on the other hand, is normally referred to as Ἑπτὰ ἐπὶ Θήβας (even by the Epit. MSS at Ath. 1.22a; cf. Ar. *Ran.* 1021, [Longin.] *Subl.* 15.5, Plut. *Mor.* 715e, the hypothesis to Aeschylus' play and the didascalic notice attributed to Aristophanes of Byzantium, Zenobius 5.43 (MSS BP), Eustath. 146.12, 1596.26), and general references to the myth itself were almost invariably couched in the same terms, with Θήβας in the accusative (e.g. Lys. 2.10, [Dem.] 60.8, Arist. *Metaph.* 14.6, 1093ᵃ15f., Diod. Sic. 4.66.1, Eustath. 489.8, 809.17, Σ Eur. *Phoen.* 1377, Σ Aristid. p. 323 Dindorf; cf. com. adesp. fr. 109.9 Kock).[1]

It is not easy to see why Alexis' and Amphis' titles should be transmitted with Thebes in a case different from the mythical and Aeschylean norm. The difference in meaning ('at Thebes' as opposed to 'against Thebes') is unlikely to have had major dramatic significance, although the loss of the two comedies will naturally stifle dogmatic assertions about that. It may be that the *Marcianus* at Ath. 7.294a and 295e is corrupt (α with its vertical tail is often confused with αι in early minuscule[2]), or that Ath. himself

---

[1] The facts are incorrectly stated by some earlier editors of Aeschylus (e.g. in the editions of C. J. Blomfield (⁶London 1833) p. 5 and G. Hermann (²Leipzig 1852) 2.266, from which the judgements of T. G. Tucker in his edition of *Sept.* (Cambridge 1908) p. 3 n. 2 and Kock at 2.323 derive). The vast majority of references to Aeschylus' play and the myth in general have the city in the accusative; the exceptions known to me are Σ Eur. *Phoen.* 751 (MTB) and *Or.* 87 (MT), Σ Ar. *Lys.* 188, Σ S. *OC* 1375, one MS (M) in the hypothesis to Eur. *Phoen.* (line 26 in Murray), all MSS except R of the Ar. Byz. hypothesis to the same play (four in Murray), the hypothesis to A. *Sept.* in *P.Oxy.* 2256 (suprascript), and one MS (H) of Zenobius 5.43, all referring to Aeschylus' title; Apollon. Dysc. *Pron.* 119b p. 93 Schneider citing Corinna fr. 6 Page; and Clem. Al. *Strom.* 1.21.137, referring to the myth. Cf. now G. O. Hutchinson's edition of *Sept.* (Oxford 1985), p. xvii.

[2] A long list of instances can be produced from the *Marcianus* alone. Here is a sample: (1) α miscopied as αι: 6.247e γαίμων, 7.318e and 323f ποτ' αἰναί for ποταναί, 10.419b = Alexis 219(216K).4 αἰεί at line-end

221

COMMENTARY

made a mistake in his reporting of the comic titles. But another explanation is possible. The two comedies could have been burlesquing a recently produced tragedy. That tragedy, if the *Marcianus* and Ath. are both correct, would not have been Aeschylus' play (which was still remembered at the time of Ar. *Ran.* and could have been one of the old tragedies restaged in 4th-century Athens, although we have no positive information on that score). Nor would it have been Euripides' *Phoenissae*, even though the present condition of that tragedy's text is best explained by the assumption that it was popular among actors and frequently performed (D. L. Page, *Actors' Interpolations in Greek Tragedy* (Oxford 1934) 20ff., E. Fraenkel, *Zu den Phoenissen des Euripides (SB Munich* 1963) 4 and *passim*; M. D. Reeve, *GRBS* 13 (1972) 451ff.). The travestied tragedy would have been rather a 4th-century drama on the Theban subject, its author choosing Ἑπτὰ ἐπὶ Θήβαις for a title with that craving for banal originality which seems to have been a mark of later tragedy. A papyrus fr. (*PSI* 1303) has been attributed by some scholars (Page, *GLP* 172ff. no. 33, T. B. L. Webster, *Hermes* 82 (1954) 297f.) to just such a 4th-century tragedy, but its pedestrian quality smacks more of an imperial schoolroom (cf. now R. Kannicht, *TrGF* 2 F 665).

83

Meineke 3.416, Kock 2.323, Edmonds 2.406, Kassel–Austin 2.64; cf. W. G. Arnott, *PCPS* 196 (1970) 1f. The *Marcianus* here (Ath. 7.294b; Epit. omits the fr.) gives an unmetrical citation: γόγγρου δ᾽ ὁμοῦ μέλη σωρευτὰ πιμελῆς ὑπογέμοντα. Porson's restoration (*Adv.* 96) of metre and more commonplace sense, by transposing σωρευτὰ πιμελῆς before μέλη and altering ὑπογέμοντα to ὑπεργέμοντα (ὑπεργ. also Jacobs, *Addit.* 173), has been accepted by all editors of Ath. and the comic frs. since Dindorf. The restoration cannot be proved wrong, but its automatic adoption is unwise; there are too many other possible explanations of the transmitted text. The violent disturbances and mutilations suffered by short, syntactically incomplete quotations in Ath. and elsewhere have already been abundantly discussed (comm. on frs. 29, 55(53K), 71, 73; cf. also 98(152K), 128(123K), 194(189K)); it is usually impossible to restore the

for ἀεί, 10.421e = Alexis 183(178K).6 γαιληνισαι for γαληνίσαι; (2) αι miscopied as α: 6.230b = Alexis 2.3 πᾶσι for παισί, 7.283d πομπεύσας, 295c βοιωτια, 313b εὐνά. This confusion in early minuscule needs to be borne in mind when the evidence in related questions of ancient orthography (e.g. ἀεί or αἰεί, cf. comm. on Alexis 76.1; Ἀχαΐς or -αΐς, cf. the introduction to that title) is evaluated.

original text of such frs., and wasted labour to make the attempt. The unmetricality of the present fr. may be due to omission or corruption of one or more words, change in word-order, or a combination of these faults. Yet in all probability much of Alexis' original diction may be preserved in the transmitted words, which contain four peculiarities:

(1) σωρευτός (though correctly formed) does not occur elsewhere in Greek; this may be an accident of preservation, but in this context we are more likely to be dealing with a nonce coinage,'up-piled'.[1]

(2) ὑπογέμοντα likewise, if correctly transmitted, is a *hapax* whose most remarkable feature is the clash between the ideas conveyed by the prepositional prefix ('to some extent') and the verbal stem ('being brimful'). In colloquial speech such an implicit contradiction is readily explained by the habitual inclination to qualify absolutes and universals; the language of this fr., however, lacks any colloquial element.

(3) The use of μέλη is strange. In comparable passages of comedy this word is applied by grandiloquent cooks to the legs of geese (Eubulus 14(15K).3 and Hunter *ad loc.*) or goats (Antiphanes 1.4, cf. Ar. *Plut.* 294, where a slave is burlesquing Philoxenus); but the conger eel (*Conger conger* Linn.; cf. Thompson, *Fishes* s.v. γόγγρος, Palombi–Santorelli 200f., Campbell, *Guide* 264f.), which is given μέλη here, totally lacks protruding members, and μέλη is never used as a synonym for τέμαχη.

(4) A possible fourth incongruity is the association of conger eel and πιμελή. The fr. implies that this fish is naturally πιμελώδης, but in fact πιμελή is basically the layer of fat that comes between the skin and flesh of land animals like pigs and horses (Arist. *HA* 3.17, 520ª6ff.); fishes such as the conger eel lack πιμελή.

Some of these four oddities are easily removed by conjecture, but their presence together in the short space of seven words suggests rather that the nonsensical grotesquerie is intentional, deriving perhaps from a wish by Alexis to characterise the ἀλαζονεία of a pretentious μάγειρος, speaking (like the cooks of Antiphanes and Eubulus cited above) with affected, perhaps even tragic or dithyrambic, diction (note the absence of a definite article with πιμελῆς and μέλη, and a rhythm which remains striking even when one allows for the possibility of corrupt transmission); cf. the μάγειροι in frs. 129(124K), 153(149K), and Nesselrath, *MK* 252ff. and 254 n. 37. But what was a cook doing in *The Seven at Thebes*? Could he have served one or more of the generals?

---

[1] Chr. Theodoridis, *ZPE* 67 (1987) 7 suggests that an entry in Photius (ε 1638) ἐπίμεστα λέγουσιν, οὐχὶ σωρευτά, τὰ μὴ ἀπεψημένα, with the adjectives cited in the nom./acc. neuter plural, may possibly derive from an Atticist grammarian's condemnation of Alexis here.

COMMENTARY

Ἐρετρικός

W. Dittenberg, *Hermes* 42 (1907) 25. When applied to a man, an ethnic in -ικός less commonly indicates birthplace or family origins (but see the introduction to Ποντικός, and cf. those to e.g. Ἀτθίς, Ἐπιδαύριος) than some other connection with a city or area (W. Dittenberger, *Hermes* 41 (1906) 78ff., 161ff, 42 (1907) 1ff., cf. Schwyzer 1.497). One possibility is that Alexis' title figure was portrayed as a follower of the philosopher Menedemus of Eretria (? *c.* 339–*c.* 265: cf. von Fritz in *RE* s.v. *Menedemos* 9, 789.26ff.), whose students were regularly called Ἐρετρικοί (e.g. Diog. Laert. 1.17 τῶν δὲ φιλοσόφων οἱ μὲν ἀπὸ πόλεων προσηγορεύθησαν, ὡς οἱ ... Ἐρετρικοί, 2.61, 126, Strabo 9.1.8).[1] Nothing is known about the play's plot or characters, except that a cook delivered its one fr. (84: so Ath. 7.326d).

84

Meineke 3.416, Kock 2.323, Edmonds 2.406, Kassel–Austin 2.64. This fr. of a cook's speech contains two popular features of 4th-century comedy: a food-list and a recipe. Catalogues of one sort or another are a hardy perennial in Greek literature, from the slaughter rolls and troop lists of the *Iliad* down to (e.g.) the inventories of *hetairai* in Hellenistic cataloguers (Ath. 13.583d–e, cf. Alciphron 4.14.2; L. Radermacher, *Mythos und Sage bei den Griechen*[2] (Brno 1943) 137f., 158, 247f.). Comic poets – and presumably their audiences – were particularly attracted by lists of comestibles and kitchen utensils. The Old-Comedy examples are collected by Dohm, *Mageiros* 59ff.; from Middle and New Comedy note especially the following frs.: Alexis 115(110K).12f.†, 132(127K), 167(162K)11ff.*, 179(174K), 281(279K), Anaxandrides 28(27K)†*, 42(41K).37ff.†*, Anaxippus 6, Antiphanes 71(70K), 130(132K)†*, 131(133K)†*, 140(142K), 177(179K), 191(193K)†, 223(224K), 233(236K), 243(249K), 273(275K), 295(302K)*, Axionicus 7, Dionysius 5, Ephippus 12†*, 13*, 24, Epigenes 5, Eubulus 18(19K), 37(38K), 63*, Heniochus 3†, Mnesimachus 4.29ff.†*, Posidippus 15(14K)†. Daggers denote that the cited list includes or consists of fish, and asterisks that it is composed in anapaestic dimeters. The large number of lists in that metre, even when we

---

[1] Cf. Edmonds 2.407 note f, whose attempt to identify the title figure as Menedemus himself is not supported by evidence. Since he was born in Eretria, the philosopher is regularly described as (ὁ) Ἐρετριεύς (e.g Diog. Laert. 1.19, 2.60, 105), although his headship of the school makes descriptions such as Μενεδήμου τοῦ Ἐρετρικοῦ (Diog. Laert. 6.91) also feasible.

allow for the vagaries of preservation and the interests of the excerptors, suggests that such long catalogues were delivered in a standardised way, perhaps at the high speed of the patter songs in Gilbert and Sullivan (cf. Hunter on Eubulus 63). These comic lists are not confined to food or kitchenware; the same authors catalogue the constituents of ἔρως (Alexis 247(245K).10ff.), Mediterranean islands (Alexis 270(268K)), dice throws (Eubulus 57), drinks on the way to drunkenness (Eubulus 93(94K)), and *hetairai* (Timocles 27(25K)). Plautus (but not Terence) took over this pleasure in lists for the Roman stage: e.g. *Aul.* 167f., 508ff., *Bacch.* 892ff., *Curc.* 100ff., *Epid.* 230ff., *Pseud.* 814ff. (a cook's speech, probably derived with expansions from the Greek original: cf. Dohm, *Mageiros* 140ff., J. C. B. Lowe, *CQ* 35 (1985) 411ff., and contrast O. Zwierlein, *Zur Kritik und Exegese des Plautus III: Pseudolus* (Stuttgart 1991) 157ff.), *Trin.* 251ff., *Truc.* 902ff. Cf. also Headlam–Knox on Herodas 7.57–61.

Alexis' present fish-list is followed by precise instructions for the preparation of τευθίς (squid: see below), the first fish named in the list. The recipe, like all the others preserved in the frs. of Alexis (129(124K), 138(133K), 178(172K), 191–3(186–8K)), is neither extravagant nor impractical. Squid was commonly served stuffed in the ancient world (Antiphanes 130(132K).3, Sotades 1.15, Ath. 1.4b; cf. Dohm, *Mageiros* 116ff., Thompson, *Fishes* 261), just as today (Davidson, *Seafood* 211 'Squid are ideal for stuffing. Most stuffings incorporate the chopped up tentacles', cf. 264, 295, 338, 350f.), and Apicius' recipe (9.3.2 = 407 André) mentions herbs (*coliandrum, ligusticum*) as ingredients for the sauce served with it, while Alexis here specifies them as seasonings (cf. on vv. 4–5). Detailed recipes, like lists, were a popular motif in Greek literature throughout its history, and a good number are preserved in the frs. of later Greek comedy (cf. Dohm, *Mageiros* 104ff., M. Treu, *Philologus* 102 (1958) 215ff., Handley on Men. *Dysk.* 546–51, Nesselrath, *MK* 302f.). Their popularity was doubtless due partly to the fact that they enabled the audience to enjoy their favourite courses by proxy.

1–2 The list of comestibles with which this fr. opens (τευθίδες· σπιναι· βατίς· δῆμος· ἀφύαι· κρεάδι'· ἐντερίδια in the *Marcianus* at Ath.7.326d–e; Epit. does not begin its citation until v. 3) has sustained corruption more serious perhaps than is usual even at the beginning of excerpts (cf. comm. on 83). Problems are posed (i) generally, by the scansion, and (ii) particularly, by three items in the list: σπιναι (*sic*, unaccented in A), δῆμος and ἐντερίδια.

(i) As it stands the list is unmetrical. The most satisfactory starting-point for investigation is τευθίδες, σπιναι, βατίς, which looks like the end of a trimeter. Then δῆμος, ἀφύαι might form a metrically tolerable opening to the following verse, which would be closed by ἐντερίδια with long antepenult (unobjectionable: cf. *CQ* 7 (1957) 194 n. 3), and a lacuna of

COMMENTARY

five elements ($1\frac{1}{4}$ metra) would have to be posited between ἐντερίδια and ἀλλὰ τὰς μὲν τευθίδας in v. 2 Kassel–Austin (so basically Bothe, *PCGF* 534, Edmonds). Alternatively, all the metrical and two of the verbal difficulties would disappear if δῆμος and ἐντερίδια were deleted as glosses; the second verse would then open with ἀφύαι, κρεᾳδι'. It is difficult, however, to see what δῆμος and ἐντερίδια could have glossed in the present list. A third possibility is that δῆμος, ἀφύαι (or whatever words of Alexis lie behind this puzzling juxtaposition) have been transposed from an original position before τευθίδες by a scribe or excerptor who preferred his citation to begin with the head-word τευθίδες. In this medley of possibilities one thing alone is certain: δῆμος, ἀφύαι, with the divided resolution in its first three syllables, cannot have ended a comic trimeter (cf. Handley's edition of Men. *Dysk.* p. 68).

(ii) σπίναι and δῆμος are foreign bodies. Food lists in later Greek comedy normally have their items arranged in homogeneous groups (see the frs. cited in the introductory note to this fr.). σπίνα is explained by Hesych. s.v. as another form of σπίνος, a small bird that (like Aristotle's σπίζα) is today generally identified as the chaffinch (*Fringilla coelebs*; cf. Thompson, *Birds* s.v. σπίνος). In fact this identification is far from certain (cf. F. Capponi, *Ornithologia Latina* (Genoa 1979) 234ff.), but any species of bird is out of place in a short list of fishes. A's σπίναι is almost certainly a corruption (by dittography after the preceding -ες) of πίναι,[1] the correct 4th-century orthography (see LSJ s.v. πίνη) for a bivalve (see below) that Attic comedians frequently mention as a food: Cratinus 8, Philyllius 12(13K).2, Antiphanes 192(194K).15, Anaxandrides 42(41K).61, Alexis 281(279K).1, Posidippus 15(14K).3 (where A at Ath. 3.87f preserves the correct orthography). δῆμος is also a problem in this company of fishes. If Meineke rightly alleges that behind it '*latet piscis nomen*', nobody has yet enticed it out from its lurking-place. Meineke's own χῆμος (*Anal. Crit.* 144) invents a form not attested in Greek (it would have to relate to χήμη as χάννος to χάννη); Kock's πρημνάς and Bothe's σῖμος would make the corruption hard to explain. The best idea has been curiously neglected: Daléchamp's δῆμος ἀφυῶν, 'a commonwealth of whitebait' (cf. Casaubon, *Animadv.* 565). If these words were brought forward to open Alexis' list (? preceded by <ἦν>), the first item in the catalogue would be tricked out with a facetious metaphor appropriate to the multitude of whitebait and the

---

[1] So Meineke first (*Anal. Crit.* 144), although an apograph of the *Marcianus* (B) appears to have πίναι (*sic*) here, and C. Gesner, *Historiae Animalium* 4 (Zürich 1558) 1062 had previously suggested the vulgate form of the word πίνναι. However, Strömberg, *Fischnamen* 112ff., 117 lists fourteen fish which in Greek have names identical with those of birds, and he defends σπίναι here as a fish name by analogy with these.

character of the speaker (cf. especially comm. on 129(124K)). For this figurative use of δῆμος cf. Alciphron 2.27.1 δῆμον ὅλον ὀρνέων, Philostratus *VA* 3.4 πιθήκων δῆμος. Finally, the form ἐντερίδια occurs only here, and it is not easy to find a reason (other than a cook's facetiousness) for the choice of this diminutive at the end of a basically straightforward list. If κρεᾴδι' began a verse which ended with τὰς μὲν τευθίδας, verbal and metrical normality would be achieved by acceptance of Jacobs' ἔντερ(α) (*Addit.* 180, thus anticipating Janson in Kaibel's edition of Ath.); corruption would be due to homoeoteleuton after the appropriate diminutive κρεᾴδι'.

The fish and other seafood listed are most conveniently described and illustrated in Campbell's *Guide*: 180f. τευθίδες (= squid, both the long-finned *Loligo vulgaris* and the sagittal *Ptodarodes sagittatus*); 160f. πῖναι (= fan-mussel, of which there are at least three species in the Mediterranean, *Pinna nobilis*, *P. rudis*, *P. squamosa*); and 262f. βατίς (= common skate, *Raja batis* and up to sixteen similar species). Cf. also Thompson, *Fishes* s.vv., Steier in *RE* s.v. *Muscheln* 787.15ff., Saint-Denis, *Vocabulaire* s.vv. *lolligo, pina, raia*; for τευθίς, H. Aubert and Fr. Wimmer, *Aristoteles, Thierkunde* I (Leipzig 1868) 150, Palombi–Santorelli 295ff., Dohm, *Mageiros* 111f. and Neil on Ar. *Equ.* 927; for βατίς, Strömberg, *Fischnamen* 47, Palombi–Santorelli 250ff. ἀφύαι (always in the plural in good Attic: 'whitebait') is not a species name but rather the popular/commercial one for the fry of many kinds of fish; cf. Thompson s.v. ἀφύη, Starkie on Ar. *Vesp.* 496, Dohm 115ff.

2 κρεᾴδι': see comm. on 27.5.

ἀλλά here is wrongly attacked by Dindorf and Edmonds; it indicates (cf. Denniston, *GP* 8) simply that the catalogue is ended and the speaker will now turn to a more important theme, the recipe.

3 τὰ πτερύγι': see comm. on 192(187K).2–3.

3–4 στεατίου μικρὸν παραμείξας: cf. Ar. *Vesp.* 878 μέλιτος μικρόν, Eubulus 41(42K).4 ἑκάστου μικρόν. παραμείξας (not -μίξας) is the contemporary Attic spelling: see A. Nauck, *MGR* 6 (1894) 66f., Meisterhans–Schwyzer 181, LSJ s.v. μείγνυμι.

4–5 περιπάσας ἡδύσμασι λεπτοῖσι χλωροῖς ὠνθύλευσα: 'having sprinkled (the squid) with finely chopped green seasonings, I stuff it . . .'. Erotian (46.6 Nachmanson) defines ἡδύσμασι as the Attic word for τοῖς χλωροῖς καὶ ξηροῖς ἀρτύμασιν: i.e. herbs like the horn-onion and coriander (Ar. *Equ.* 676ff.) or the nineteen items Alexis includes in his κατάλογος ἡδυσμάτων (so Ath. 4.170a) at fr. 132(127K). λεπτοῖσι = 'chopped fine', as elsewhere in culinary contexts (e.g. Alcaeus com. 17.1, Sotades 1.32); χλωροῖς here similarly qualifies ἡδύσμασι, although τὰ χλωρά can stand on its own = ἡ χλόη (e.g. Bilabel, *Ops.* 3ff., ζ 18–19).

5 ὠνθύλευσα: see on fr. 38(37K).1. It is possible (but not necessary) that Alexis' sentence continued after ὠνθύλευσα with some indication of the ingredients for the stuffing. The aorist here and elsewhere in cooking instructions (cf. particularly Ar. *Av.* 532–6, Alexis 153(149K).9–13, 191(186K).9–10, Sotades 1 *passim*) is interpreted by Dohm, *Mageiros* 105 n. 2 as 'gnomic'. It is in fact a small part of the cook's armoury of conceit; 'this is how I've done it in the past,' he implies, 'and how I always do it'.

Ἔριθοι

See below, Παννυχὶς ἢ Ἔριθοι (frs. 177–82(172–7K)).

Ἡ εἰς τὸ φρέαρ

Schweighaeuser, *Animadv.* 2.249 and 9.24 s.v. Φρέαρ, Meineke 1.399f., Kock 2.319. Athenaeus cites three frs. from this play, two of them introduced with the words ἐν τῇ εἰς τὸ φρέαρ (3.109b, 8.364f, frs. 86(66K), 85(65K) respectively), and the other with ἐν τῇ ἐπιγραφομένῃ εἰς τὸ φρέαρ (8.340c, fr. 87(67K)). Ath.'s formulas for expressing titles are conventional but illuminating:

(i) When Ath. quotes a play title in the nominative case, the introductory formula is rigid: ἐν τῷ ἐπιγραφομένῳ δράματι or just ἐν τῷ ἐπιγραφομένῳ (e.g. 4.134c ἐν τῷ ἐ. Ἰσοστάσιον, 13.568a ἐν τῷ ἐ. δράματι Ἰσοστάσιον, 13.606a ἐν τῷ ἐ. δράματι Γραφή, where Kaibel's text needs correction, see Gulick *ad loc.*); cf. Gildersleeve, *Syntax* 1.2f. Never to my knowledge does Ath. replace this formula by an equivalent ἐν τῇ ἐπιγραφομένῃ κωμῳδίᾳ/τραγῳδίᾳ, with the relevant noun expressed or implied.

(ii) When the title itself is assimilated to the dative case of an introductory formula such as ἐν τῷ ἐπιγραφομένῳ or even a plain ἐν τῷ, the gender and number of article and participle are attracted to the gender and number of any substantival element in the title, whether expressed or implied (e.g. 14.644b ἐν τῷ ἐπιγραφομένῳ Ἀρχιλόχῳ, 15.685b ἐν τοῖς ἐ. Ἀγαθοῖς, 15.686a ἐν ταῖς ἐ. Κηρσίν, 10.446e ἐν Ταῖς ἀφ᾽ ἱερῶν).

Accordingly, the gender of the article in the formulas at Ath. 8.364f and 3.109b, and of the article + participle at Ath. 8.340c, can be satisfactorily explained only if the feminine article was an integral or implicit part of Alexis' title here,[1] as Grotius (*Exc.* 590–1) was the first to realise. And as

---

[1] Of course, the presence or absence of an introductory definite article makes little difference to the vast majority of play titles, which are predominantly substantival in form and unambiguous in gender. In

part of the title, the article sheds light upon an element in Alexis' lost plot. It was a girl or woman who for some reason went into the well.

Comedies which featured a well were not uncommon on the Attic stage, to judge from extant texts and titles. Knemon's well in Menander's *Dyskolos* is the plot's major catalyst; it was not, however, visible to the audience, and the events which occurred in and around it are all reported at second hand (190f., 576ff., 620ff.). In Old Comedy, Lysippus' Βάκχαι (fr. 1) seems to have contained a scene between two characters in a well, Plato's Ἑλλάς (fr. 19(21K)) may have included the rescue on stage of an unidentified person from a well or subterranean pit,[1] and Aristophanes' Ἀνάγυρος apparently burlesqued a legend in which the hero's concubine threw herself into a well (Phot. and *Suda* s.v. Ἀναγυράσιος δαίμων, cf. Kassel–Austin 3.2.51f.). Later comedy provides a fr. (1) from Apollodorus of Gela's Ἀπολείπουσα in which a woman's actions at a well are described, while Anaxippus and Diphilus both wrote plays apparently (but see Kassel–Austin 2.65) with the title Φρέαρ. Plautus' *Commorientes*, adapted from Diphilus' Συναποθνήσκοντες, contained the words *saliam in puteum praecipes*, but the context of this remark is unknown.

The frs. remaining from Alexis' Ἡ εἰς τὸ φρέαρ in no way elucidate the title,[2] but are not without interest. Fr. 85(65K) comes from a dialogue in which a slave explains to an old woman, who was probably a servant in one of the stage houses, that he has been sent to fetch extra wine from her. Here presumably we have to deal with the antecedents or prolongation of an off-stage party involving the slave's master.

According to Ath. 8.340c, fr. 87(67K) is identical with fr. 249(247K) from Alexis' Φαίδων (if that is the correct form of the title: see the introduction to that play); it contains a satirical reference to Callimedon which might easily be transferred from one play to another so long as the quip remained topical. This quip dates the play to the period of Callimedon's political activity, which may have begun as early as the 340s but ended in 318 (see the introduction to Δορκίς, especially p. 177 n. 1).

---

such cases, naturally enough, Ath.'s use of the article when he cites a title briefly can be inconsistent (e.g. ἐν τῷ Παρασίτῳ 10.421d but ἐν Παρασίτῳ 3.123e: the same play). But there is no parallel inconsistency over the citation of exceptional titles like the present one of Alexis or the Αἱ ἀφ' ἱερῶν of Plato com., where the article plays an informative as well as a defining role. No Greek play-title began simply with a preposition. Cf. Wilamowitz, *Analecta Euripidea* (Berlin 1875) 60.

[1] In Ar. *Pax* the title figure is hauled up from her prison in a subterranean cavern (223ff.), not a well as such.

[2] Cf. R. Cantarella, *Rend. Ist. Lomb.* 93 (1959) 77 n. 1. The speculations of Edmonds (2.408 note a) are implausible.

COMMENTARY

85 (65K)

Meineke 3.409 (I), Kock 2.319, Edmonds 2.408, Kassel–Austin 2.65.

1 νυνὶ τέ μοι is the reading of the *Marcianus* here (Ath. 8.364f; Epit. omits the fr.), but Greek says not μοι but με ... προΰπεμψε(ν) ... κομιοῦντα. Schweighaeuser's τέ με ... προΰπεμψεν obviously, and Meineke's γε τοι ... προΰπεμψε μ' more cleverly (3.409, cf. *Anal. Crit.* 161), restore the required sense, but neither conjecture makes its corruption readily explicable. Blaydes (*Adv.* 1.106) suggested τέ σοι, and this (preferably with Meineke's προΰπεμψέ μ') is rather more plausible; once the μ' had been lost or corrupted to ν (a letter often confused with μ at all periods: cf. F. W. Hall, *A Companion to Classical Texts* (Oxford 1913) 159, Diggle, *Studies* 66), a scribe or excerptor was likely to foist the needed first-person pronoun into the beginning of the fr., even at the expense of an incorrect case.

2–3 In this context ἔνδοθεν clearly refers to the same place as ἐκεῖθεν, and Kaibel's part-division ... οἴνου κεράμιον | τῶν ἔνδοθεν κομιοῦντ'. :: ἐκεῖθεν; μανθάνω (for the structure of the response cf. Ar. *Pax* 663 ταῦτ' ἐπικαλεῖς; μανθάνω) creates a lively and pointed exchange, far preferable to the tautological dullness of Casaubon's division after κομιοῦντ' ἐκεῖθεν (correcting A's -οῦντες κεῖθεν), which other editors (including Kassel–Austin) print. For the general idea, cf. Ar. fr. 310(299K).1f., τρέχ' ἐς τὸν οἶνον, ἀμφορέα κενὸν λαβὼν | τῶν ἔνδοθεν; Plaut. *Stich.* 647, *cadum modo hinc a me huc cum uino transferam.*

4 ἐπιδόσιμον: Ath. 8.364f cites this fr. and Crobylus 5 in support of his claim that classical writers used the term ἐπιδόσιμα δεῖπνα in the same sense as an expression current in Alexandria, δ. ἐξ ἐπιδομάτων (i.e. contribution dinners, in Attic normally δ. ἀπὸ συμβολῶν: see the introduction to fr. 15). However, in the two cited passages (and elsewhere: e.g. Dicaearchus in Ath. 4.141b = fr. 72 Wehrli) ἐπιδόσιμος appears rather to mean what its etymology would indicate, 'contributed additionally', and there is as little warrant on the evidence available for accepting Ath.'s claim as there is for assuming with Gulick (*ad loc.*, p. 151 note c; cf. also LSJ s.v. 1) that the contribution was a special and unexpected luxury.

5 αἰσθητικὴν: so correctly A; Kock's conjecture μαθητικήν ('*ne iocus pereat*') misses the point. The slave's final remark (assigned to him first by Meineke) is not intended as verbal mockery of the old woman's μανθάνω, but rather as a sarcastic comment attributing shrewd insight to her statement of the obvious in vv. 3–4. αἰσθητικήν (only here to my knowledge in this extended sense: '*non simpliciter Quae est facultate sentiendi praedita, sed Quae ui et acrimonia pollet in sentiendo*' TGL s.v.; was it current slang in this use?) appropriately fits a woman judging subjectively and empirically from her own faculties, while μαθητικήν would more correctly

230

suit an objective, scientific assessment (cf. Arist. *Anal. Post.* 1.13, 79ᵃ2ff.).

The fr. provides us with a pert male slave of one family, and an elderly female slave of another living in a stage-house with a wine store; what were the connections between the two families and with the girl who went into the well?

86 (84K)

Meineke 3.409 (II), Kock 2.319, Edmonds 2.408, Kassel–Austin 2.66. In Ath. 3.109b Cynulcus is made to greet the appearance of the bread by quoting this fr. of Alexis, and Kock makes the ingenious suggestion that Cynulcus may have substituted the word ἄρτοις in the fr. for an original 'πτηνοῖς *uel tale aliquid*'. Ingenious, but unnecessary; in its context (either a complete sentence with ὅσας exclamatory: cf. Ar. *Plut.* 748, Xen. *Cyr.* 1.3.4, K.G. 2.439, Schwyzer 2.626; or a subordinate relative clause with the main clause unquoted, e.g. <θαυμαστόν ἐστι – ∪ >) τοῖς ἄρτοις makes admirable comic sense. The unknown speaker apes the language of tragedy, as the rhythm of the whole fr. and in particular the choice of the phrase οἱ ταλαίπωροι βροτοί show (cf. Sophocles fr. 555.1, Eur. *Bacch.* 280); locutions with the pattern article + ταλαίπωρός + disyllabic noun regularly fill the post-caesural portion of a tragic trimeter, e.g. S. *OC* 91, Eur. *Hec.* 1170, *Tro.* 1276, *Or.* 662, *IA* 491, Critias fr. 19.30 Snell, cf. also Eur. *Suppl.* 949 ὦ ταλαίπωροι βροτῶν, but are rare in comedy – elsewhere only Alexis 148(144K).3 (? paratragic) and Men. *Asp.* 91 (the solemn euphemisms of bereavement). The heightened tone increases the comic effect of a splendidly absurd metaphor of men setting traps to catch their daily bread. παγίς is the wooden (*Batrachom.* 116) spring trap that was commonly baited to catch mice (Call. fr. 177.17) and birds; ἱστάναι παγίδα is the normal expression for setting it (cf. Ar. *Av.* 527). The noun is sometimes used metaphorically, especially of *hetairai* setting traps for the possessions of their lovers (e.g. Amphis 23.4 παγίσι τοῦ βίου, Lucian *Dial. Meretr.* 11.2, cf. Ar. fr. 869(666K), Dioscorides 1 Gow–Page = *Anth. Pal.* 5.56); see F. Marx, comm. on Lucilius 990.

87 (67K)

Meineke 3.410 (III), Kock 2.319, Edmonds 2.408, Kassel–Austin 2.66. This fr. is identical in wording with 249(247K), where a commentary will be found.

COMMENTARY

Ἡσιόνη

Meineke 1.391, H. Jacobi in Meineke 5. p. ccxv, Fraenkel, *MNC* 24, O. Weinreich, *SB Vienna* 220/4 (1942) 15ff., 123ff., Nesselrath, *MK* 235. Extant from this play are two frs. cited by Ath. (9.367f, 11.470e: frs. 89(86K), 88(85K)), and some scraps of a quotation in a grievously mutilated papyrus fragment of a glossary of rare words (*P.Oxy.* 1801: fr. 90). The three frs. are all tragic in rhythm and elevated in style (e.g. 88(85K).3 the asyndetic ἕλκει καταντλεῖ, 89(86K).3 βρύουσαν + genitive, 90 κομπάσματα; cf. Fraenkel, *loc. cit.*); clearly in at least part of the play Alexis was guying the conventional tragic treatment of a myth, probably in the earlier years of his career, when myth travesty was a popular comic form. The remains of Greek tragedy do not include a Ἡσιόνη or Λαομέδων title, but this may be fortuitous. According to a commonly accepted interpretation of the Pronomos vase (Naples, Nat. Mus. 3240; Beazley, *ARV*² 2.1336 and *Hesperia* 24 (1955) 313 n. 24, P. E. Arias, M. Hirmer, B. B. Shefton, *History of Greek Vase Painting* (London 1962) 377ff., plates 218–19, T. B. L. Webster, *Monuments illustrating Tragedy and Satyr-play*² (*BICS Suppl.* 20, London 1967) 47ff., Pickard-Cambridge, *DFA*² 186f., A. D. Trendall and T. B. L. Webster, *Illustrations of Greek Drama* (London 1971) 29, B. Snell, *TrGF* 1. p. 189), Demetrius produced a satyr-play titled Ἡσιόνη shortly before 400, in which Heracles, Hesione and Laomedon were the leading roles.[1] This or another play may have provided the Greek original for an anonymous Roman composition, possibly a tragedy, with the title *Laomedon* (Σ Veron. on V. *Aen.* 2.81; Ribbeck, *TRF*³ 270).

The frs. of Alexis' Ἡσιόνη are tantalising but informative. Frs. 88(85K) certainly (see introduction to fr. below) and 89(86K) in all probability describe Heracles, Hesione's rescuer from the sea-monster, conventionally as a drunkard and guzzler (see comm. on 88(85K).3–5); but before the drinking begins in fr. 88(85K) Heracles is described as 'having barely regained his right mind', if that is the correct interpretation of γενόμενος δ' ἔννους μόλις (v. 1). Had Heracles previously suffered an attack of madness in Alexis' play? There is no mention of any such fit in the existing Hesione saga (cf. Drexler in Roscher s.v. *Hesione* 3, 2592.20ff., Robert, *GH* 2.553ff., Weinreich, *loc. cit.*); Alexis must either have invented some comic occasion for the attack, or have imported into his plots elements extraneous to the

---

[1] This interpretation is now challenged by E. Simon, *Arch. Anz.* (1971) 199ff. and *The Ancient Theatre* (tr. C. E. Vafopoulou-Richardson, London and New York 1982) 17ff. She prefers to identify the title and the female figure on the vase as Omphale, and the male figure clothed in oriental luxury as her father, the Lydian king Iardanus. Cf. also *TrGF* 1². p. 351.

main Hesione story. Mad scenes were a popular feature of 4th-century drama (cf. introduction to fr. 4), and madness a traditional feature of Heracles myths going back to the *Cypria* (Proclus *Chrest.* in T. W. Allen's edition of Homer, vol. 5 (Oxford 1912) p. 103.22f.; cf. Bond's edition of Eur. *Her.* pp. xxviii ff.). In fr. 89(86K), which may derive from the same scene and even the same speech as 88(85K) (so Fraenkel, *MNC* 24, sensibly placing the food of 89(86K) before the drink of 88(85K)), the speaker claims that some person (presumably Heracles) no longer had eyes 'for me' after seeing the food. If the speaker was Hesione, the remark *may* imply that Heracles had fallen in love with her. In the normal tradition, however, Hesione was not Heracles' inamorata; after Heracles had sacked Laomedon's Troy she became the prize and mistress of Telamon. Yet there are some ambiguous traces of an alternative version in which Hesione was promised to (Callimachus fr. 698) or herself chose (Diod. Sic. 4.42) Heracles as her mate; a love interlude is suggested also on the Pronomos vase by its depiction of a kneeling Eros with hands held out towards the heroine. Fr. 90 likewise poses unsolved problems. Its mention of κομπάσματα and implied reference to Antiphanes of Berga together indicate that a character in the play was denying the truth of a narrative or claim; but both character and incident remain stubbornly obscure.[1]

88 (85K)

Meineke 3.417 (1), Kock 2.324, Edmonds 2.408, Kassel–Austin 2.66.
When citing this fr., Ath. 11.470e identifies τὸν Ἡρακλέα πίνοντα[2] as its

---

[1] Weinreich's interpretation of the fr. (16ff., 126) as a negative response to a messenger's speech about Heracles' battle with the sea monster is one only of many possibilities. Edmonds' fantasies (2.409 note c), on the other hand, which turn a Middle-Comedy myth travesty into a political allegory where Hesione represents Perinthus and Heracles the hungry Athenian people, have neither evidence nor reason to commend them. Jacobi suggests that Alexis fr. 263(261K) may derive from the Ἡσιόνη; this fr. is also spoken by a guzzler, whose identity could be any of Alexis' parasites (e.g. in Κυβερνήτης, Παράσιτος, Πύραυνος, Ψευδόμενος), portrayals of Heracles (e.g. in Λίνος), or other bon viveurs. Fr. 263(261K) cannot be tacked on to the end of fr. 89(86K) (so Kock, misinterpreting Jacobi); the main verb presupposed by the end of fr. 89(86K) would be third person singular, but fr. 263(261K) begins and continues as a first-person narrative.

[2] Ath. adds μήποτε . . . θηρικλείῳ, but there is no evidence in the words of the fr. that Heracles' cup was an anachronistic 'Thericlean' (on this term see comm. on fr. 5). Ath.'s guess either derived from something in the fr.'s unquoted context or was a laboured device to introduce a

COMMENTARY

subject, either from his own (or a previous excerptor's) knowledge of the
dramatic context, or by intelligent inference from the play title and the
words of the fr. The description of Heracles' drinking evidently comes
from the burlesque of a tragic messenger's speech, but its location in the
plot is uncertain (cf. the introduction to Ἡσιόνη and comm. on vv. 1, 3
below).

1 γενόμενος δ' ἔννους μόλις: elsewhere in relevant contexts ἔννους
γίγνεσθαι implies the recovery of mental equilibrium after a fit of madness
or other psychological disturbance (e.g. with reference to Agave in Eur.
Bacch. 1270, Onetor in Dem. 31.2, Aristotimus in Plut. *Mor.* 252e; in Men.
Sam. 619 Moschion's use of the phrase indicates that his previous recon-
ciliation with Demeas was an act of lunacy; cf. *Suda* s.v. ἔννους· ... ταῦτα
δράσας ὕστερον ἔννους ἐγένετο, καὶ ἐσωφρόνησεν).[1] Although extant
versions of the Hesione saga say nothing of any Heraclean brainstorm, it
seems likely that Alexis imported one into the story for comic effect (see
above, introduction to Ἡσιόνη).

2 ᾔτησε κύλικα: the use here could be reconciled with the grammarian's
rule discussed above on fr. 79, only if the cup were assumed to stand loosely
for its 'non-returnable' contents. κύλικα, preserved (or conjectured) in the
Epit. MSS, must be right; A has the curious error κυλην, which can be
partly explained as a product of haplography (ΚΥΛΙΚΑΙ) and etacism.
Other attempts to account for κυλην (e.g. Bothe's conjecture κωλῆν, *PCGF*
535: but the context is bibulous, not gluttonous; κοίλην Scaliger in Canter,
Paris MS 35ᵛ; or ? κάλπην), or even to defend it (e.g. H. Stephanus in *TLG*
4 (1572) p. 1313; F. G. Welcker, *Rh. Mus.* 6 (1839) 412, countered by
Meineke), are wasted efforts. Cf. also Bentley, *Phalaris* 123 (London 1699)
= 1.82 (Dyce, London 1836).

πυκνάς: sc. κύλικας (in the sense of 'cupfuls': see Hunter on Eubulus
148(150K).8). and my comm. on Alexis 116(111K).1, Cf. πυκνάς also at
Eubulus 48(49K).1, μεστάς Antiphanes 205(207K).1, τὴν μεγάλην Alexis
116(111K). 1, τὴν μείζον' Sophilus 4(3K); on φιλοτησίαν see comm. on
59(58K).1. Other examples are collected by Gow on Machon 447.

3 ἕλκει καταντλεῖ: asyndetic juxtaposition of virtually synonymous
verbs in this part of the trimeter is so favourite a feature of tragic style (e.g.

---

quotation that Ath. saw no other way of incorporating. Cf. Bentley,
Phalaris 1.181f.
[1] These parallels indicate that alternative explanations of the phrase by
Fraenkel (*MNC* 24 *e grauissima crapula uix suscitatum compotem factum ...
audimus*) and Nesselrath (*MK* 235 *scheint ... Herakles durch die Rettung der
Hesiones vor dem Seeungeheuer so entkräftet zu sein, daß ihm erst einmal schwarz
vor der Augen wird*) are misguided. Cf. also K. Klaus, *Die Adjektiva bei
Menander* (Leipzig 1936) 57.

234

ΗΣΙΟΝΗ

A. *Sept.* 60, 186, *Choeph.* 289, S. *Trach.* 787, *Phil.* 11, Eur. *Hec.* 1175, *Her.* 602 and Bond *ad loc.*) that comedy could hardly fail to ridicule it (cf. Ar. *Ran.* 1173ff.). ἕλκει = 'drinks in long draughts' (LSJ s.v. ἕλκω II.4; cf. the parallel use of σπάω, comm. on fr. 5.1), most commonly with an accusative denoting the drink (e.g. Eur. *Ion* 1200, *Cycl.* 417, Ar. *Equ.* 107 and Neil *ad loc.*, Teleclides 27(24K), Rufinus 2 Page = *Anth. Pal.* 5.12.2) or its container (here and e.g. Antiphanes 205(207K).1f., 234(237K), Eubulus 56.7). καταντλεῖ = 'pours down (the throat)', only here of drinking (yet similarly the simple ἤντλουν at Pherecrates 113(108K).31), but elsewhere of pouring e.g. water (*PSI* 3.168 2nd century AD, cf. Epicharmus fr. 85.252f. Austin, *CGFP*).

3–5 κατά τε τὴν παροιμίαν ἀεί ποτ' εὖ μὲν ἀσκὸς εὖ δὲ θύλακος ἄνθρωπός ἐστι: the proverb occurs only here in Greek (cf. O. Crusius, *Philologus* 46 (1888) 619, Strömberg, *Greek Proverbs* 17), but its meaning is unambiguous: Heracles is both wineskin and mealsack, i.e. *bibax et edax* Daléchamp. *Annot.* 775. The characterisation of Heracles as glutton and drinker permeates Greek literature from early epic (*Od.* 11.603) to Alexandrian poetry (Theoc. 17.22, Call. *H. Art.* 146ff.), and becomes a cliché of drama (tragedy: S. *Trach.* 268, Eur. *Alc.* 747ff.; satyr play: e.g. Eur. *Syleus* p. 575 Nauck², B. Seidensticker in G. A. Seeck (ed.), *Das griechische Drama* (Darmstadt 1979) 225, 241; Attic comedy: Ar. *Av.* 1565ff., *Ran.* 60ff., cf. *Vesp.* 60, *Pax* 741 and Σ *ad loc.*, probably also Δράματα ἢ Κένταυρος (cf. Kassel–Austin III.2.158ff.), Alexis 140(135K), Mnesimachus 2, G. K. Galinsky, *The Heracles Theme* (Oxford 1972) 81ff., cf. B. Effe, *Poetica* 12 (1980) 160f.; on Heracles in Epicharmus and Doric comedy see especially E. Wüst, *Rh. Mus.* 93 (1950) 353ff., cf. Kaibel, *CGF* 185). Vases and figurines of the 4th century frequently portray the gorging Heracles, and it seems likely that the artists' main source was contemporary comedy (H. Metzger, *Les Représentations dans la céramique attique du IVe siècle* (Paris 1951) 405 no. 37 etc., Webster, *SLGC* 85f.). Cf. Ath. 10.411a–412b.

Identification of a person with the object of comparison is a feature of colloquial Greek, and there are several standard types of phraseology: (i) 'a/the person is X' (e.g. here and fr. 217(214K).1, Men. *Sam.* 555f.), (ii) 'he/she is X, and no man/woman' (e.g. Crobylus 8.4), (iii) he/she, an X, does ...' (e.g. Alexis 183(178K).3 and comm.); cf. Fraenkel, *EP* 47ff., 402 with bibliography, Headlam–Knox on Herodas 6.4, Groeneboom on Herodas 6.13f. ἀσκός is elsewhere applied to tipplers of Falstaffian girth (Antiphanes 20(19K) τοῦτον οὖν | δι' οἰνοφλυγίαν καὶ πάχος τοῦ σώματος | ἀσκὸν καλοῦσι πάντες οὑπιχώριοι, cf. Ar. *Ach.* 1002, Σ Eur. *Med.* 679), and also to those with an inflated sense of their own importance (the Doric saying αὖτα φύσις ἀνθρώπων, ἀσκοὶ πεφυσαμένοι = fr. 246 Kaibel, *CGF* p. 136, Timon the sillographer fr. 11 Di Marco, Iamblichus

235

COMMENTARY

in Stob. 1.49.43, 1.384.13 Wachsmuth; cf. Petronius 42 *utres inflati*). The Athenians similarly were called μολγοί by Aristophanes (fr. 308(694K)), and a drunkard χώνη (Aelian *VH* 2.41, Polemon in Ath. 10.436e = fr. 79 Preller); cf. also comm. on Alexis 56(55K). Although θύλακος is not on its own applied analogously to people, its coupling with ἀσκός in the proverb is easily explained. ἀσκός and θύλακος are the standard terms (cf. F. G. Sturz's lexicon to Xenophon (Leipzig 1801–4), s.v. ἀσκός) respectively for containers of liquids (particularly wine, water) and dry goods (particularly comestibles like barley-meal). The two nouns are complementary, so much so that a joint food-and-drink haversack was styled an ἀσκοθύλακος (Ar. fr. 180(174K), Archippus 4, Diocles 3).

ἄνθρωπος (Meineke) is a certain correction of ἄνθρωπος (A, Epit.); the article is required with the subject, and when it undergoes synaloephe or 'grammatical contraction' (Schwyzer 1.402) with its noun (cf. also 140(135K).17, 177(173K).4, ἀρχιτέκτων in 153(149K).2), the rough breathing that it introduces is often corrupted to smooth in medieval MSS (cf. e.g. Dover on Ar. *Nub.* 492; papyri often omit breathings); cf. also comm. on 113(108K).6, 140(135K).17, 145(141K).1, 249(247K).5.

ἀεὶ (Epit. MSS, Eustath. 1646.19 ~ ἀιει (*sic*) A): see comm. on 76.1.

89 (86K)

Meineke 3.418 (II), Kock 2.324, Edmonds 2.410, Kassel–Austin 2.67. On the fr.'s dramatic context see introduction to Ἡσιόνη.

1 εἶδε: Valckenaer's correction (see Peppink, *Observ.* 55, pointing out that Natale de' Conti's Latin translation (Venice 1556) already had *uidit*) of A's ἴδε at Ath. 9.367f (the fr. is omitted by Epit.), anticipating Schweighaeuser (cf. *Animadv.* 5.13).

ποικίλων παροψίδων: in the section from which this citation comes (9.367b–368c) Ath. tries to establish three classical uses of παροψίς: (i) basically and commonly ἐπὶ ... ὄψου παρεσκευασμένου ποικίλου καὶ εἴδους τινὸς τοιούτου, (ii) by metaphorical extension an 'accessory delight', (iii) the plate on which a παροψίς in sense (i) was served. Ath. cites five passages (Antiphanes 61(60K), Alexis here, Magnes 1(2K), Achaeus fr. 7 Snell, Sotades com. 3) under heading (iii), but all of them fit satisfactorily under the other two headings: e.g. Alexis' ποικίλων παροψίδων here (cf. 263(261K).5) are clearly food courses, and Antiphanes' ἐν παροψίδι (cf. Pollux 10.88, quoting the fr. at greater length in a discussion of the same point) comes under heading (ii). In fact no recorded use of παροψίς in Attic comedy and related literature (e.g. Archestratus fr. 6 Brandt = 137 Lloyd-Jones–Parsons, *SH*) need be classified under Ath.'s third heading (the LSJ entry s.v. accordingly needs correction). The desire of Ath. and Pollux to secure classical precedents for the use of παροψίς in the sense of 'plate' is easy to explain; this third use was so prevalent in *Koine* Greek (cf. Rutherford, *NP* 265) that any attempt to prove classical ancestry seemed better than none. Strict Atticists rightly stigmatised the use as unattic (Phryn. *Ecl.* s.v. p. 74 Fischer, *Praep. Soph.* 103.10f. de Borries, Moeris, Photius, Thomas Magister s.v.); in trying to defend it, Pollux and Ath. betray once again the fallibility of their judgements in the interpretation of comic passages.[1]

3 κόσμου βρύουσαν: a comic incursion into the diction of high poetry. In classical Greek βρύειν itself ranks as a 'poetical' word (LSJ s.v., Starkie on Ar. *Nub.* 45), and here its construction (in the sense 'teem with') + the genitive, rather than the more normal dative, heightens that poetical effect. Cf. A. *Choeph.* 69f. †παναρκέτας† νόσου βρύειν, S. *OC* 16f. βρύων | δάφνης, ἐλαίας, ἀμπέλου (see Jebb *ad loc.*), [Pl.] *Ax.* 371c ἄφθονοι μὲν ὧραι παγκάρπου γονῆς βρύουσιν ('evidently pieced together from some poet' Jebb. *loc. cit.*).

After οὐκέτ' εἰς ἐμὲ the *Marcianus* has βλέπον, which could be accepted only on the unlikely supposition that the lost or omitted subject was μειράκιον or some other appropriate neuter (but cf. e.g. Ar. *Vesp.* 687, Eupolis 104(100K).2, Nicostratus 31(32K).1f.). As a correction βλέπων (P = P. Degan's apograph of A, copied in 1505–6 under the aegis of Musurus, cf. Kaibel's edition of Ath. 1.xiii f.) seems superior to (ἔμ') ἔβλεπεν (Schweighaeuser, cf. *Animadv.* 5.13, printed by Kassel–Austin), partly because of the frequency of confusion between O and ω in MSS of all periods from papyri uncial to medieval minuscule, but partly too because a citation ending in mid-sentence (as it would with βλέπων, not uncharacteristically in Ath.: cf. Alexis 128(123K), 194(189K), and my discussion in *PCPS* 196 (1970) 2f.) might prove more troublesome to a copyist.

Lengthening of a syllable containing a short vowel before βλ and γλ is normal in comedy even when the double consonant begins a new word (Descroix 19); many of the examples are to be found (as here, but not at Alexis 229(227K).3) at the end of the first half of the third metron in the iambic trimeter (cf. I. Hilberg, *Das Princip der Silbenwägung* (Vienna 1879) 218ff., Fraenkel on A. *Ag.* 627, Barrett on Eur. *Hipp.* 760 and p. 435). In comedy cf. especially (in the third metron) Ar. *Lys.* 426 σὺ βλέπεις, *Eccl.* 1142 ἑτέρωσε βλέπει, *Plut.* 99 ὁ βλέπων, 968 and 1173 ἤρξατο βλέπειν,

---

[1] Cf. the introduction to Ἀγωνίς and comm. on frs. 147(143K) and 286(285K). Two further instances of similar misinterpretations: Ath. 9.373c–d (ὄρνιθα φοινικόπτερον in Cratinus 121(114K) does not prove a masculine use of ὄρνις, since φοινικόπτερος is of two terminations); Pollux 10.62 (citing Diphilus 51(52K) for the use of ξυστίς in the sense of στλεγγίς, but the grammarian has missed the point of the joke, see Kock *ad loc.*).

COMMENTARY

Men. *Karch.* 36 τί βλέπεις, *Sik.* 212 γενόμενος ἔβλεπεν. Cf. also comm. on 91(87K).4.

90 (= *P.Oxy.* 1801.50ff.)

B. P. Grenfell and A. Hunt, *The Oxyrhynchus Papyri* 15 (London 1922) 150ff., W. Crönert, *Lit. Zentr.* 73 (1922) 425, A. Körte, *Arch. Pap.* 7 (1924) 246, O. Weinreich, *SB Heidelberg* 220 (1942) 15ff., 123ff., W. Luppe, *Philologus* 111 (1967) 86ff. (with a photograph, and citing material from S. Kurz, *Die neuen Fragmente der attischen Alten Komödie* (Diss. Tübingen 1947, unpublished)), Austin, *CGFP* 340ff. (fr. 343.50ff.). *P.Oxy.* 1801 (1st century AD) contains a glossary of rare words, compiled perhaps by an Alexandrian grammarian between the periods of Lycophron and Didymus (so Crönert); extant are badly mutilated portions of two columns, containing entries that begin with βα, βε or βη and illustrations derived almost completely from satyric drama and earlier Attic comedy. The Ἡσιόνη fr. is cited to illustrate the gloss Βεργαῖος, 'relating to (Antiphanes of) Berga'; its interpretation is seriously handicapped by abscission. Only the left-hand portion – a width of from 17 to 24 letters – of the column containing the Alexis citation is preserved. This citation was written out as prose; scholars who wish to supplement parts of the missing text must first establish the metrical position of the extant words. Even the width of the original papyrus column poses a problem. By a series of ingenious arguments Luppe (90ff.) seeks to establish that normal lines in the column (as opposed to those beginning with a lemma, which extend an additional 2–3 letters into the left-hand margin) contain 66–7 letters, but this would be an unparalleled width in such a glossary, and Grenfell and Hunt's assumption of 30–7 letters seems more plausible.[1]

A further difficulty: where does the Alexis citation end? Crönert, Weinreich (126f.) and (tentatively) Kassel–Austin assume that it stretches from line 50 of the papyrus, which opens with the Βεργαῖος lemma and the reference to Alexis' Ἡσιόνη, right up to the lost end of line 54; certainly the preserved portion of this span consists entirely of iambic verses, with the

---

[1] Comparable papyrus texts provide no column widths to match this. One Oxyrhynchus glossary (*P.Oxy.* 1802, 2nd/3rd century AD) has lines of up to 54 letters, and the Didymus commentary on Demosthenes (*Berliner Klassiker Texte* 1, 1904) of up to 42; the majority average fewer than 30 letters to the line (*P.Oxy.* 1803, glossary, 6th century AD, 18–22 letters; 1804, rhetorical glossary, 3rd century AD, 26–30 letters; 2087, glossary, 2nd century AD, 25–8 letters for normal lines, 28–33 for lines with lemmata; *P.Rylands* 532, Harpocration, 2nd/3rd century AD, 21–33 letters).

return of explanatory prose at 55 (ἔστιν δ' ἡ Βέργη ...) signalled by the customary paragraphus above that line. But this assumption is unacceptable for two reasons. It would give for the Alexis citation a length of at least four iambic trimeters, but glossarists do not cite their sources so extensively (Luppe 99). It also compels its adherents to explain the further paragraphus appearing beneath line 52 as an indication of change of speaker (for which there would be no parallel in glossarial citations on papyrus), rather than of the end of the Ἡσιόνη fr. in line 52, most probably after the word ὕθλο[ν,[1] and the beginning of a different citation (cf. Luppe 101). In that event the total length of the Alexis citation would most probably be two iambic trimeters, and the extant portions in lines 51 and 52 would be the last $1\frac{3}{4}$ of the first and the last two metra of the second.

1 (?)]εστι καὶ κομπάσματα: although the preceding context is uncertain (but Ar. *Ran.* 21, 92 support Luppe's ταῦτ'] ἐστὶ), something of the speaker's tone is revealed by κομπάσματα, a word favoured by old tragedy (A. *Sept.* 551, 794, *P.V.* 361; cf. Ar. *Ran.* 940; Sophocles and Euripides prefer κόμποι, which is equally rare in comedy and classical prose, cf. comm. on fr. 25.8–9). How accidental is it that all three surviving frs. of Ἡσιόνη are tinted with tragic colour?

2 (?) Βεργαῖον ἀποδείξειν ὕθλο[ν: ἀποδείκνυμι elsewhere in Alexis (110(105K).2, 263(261K).14) and commonly in Greek (LSJ s.v. I.6, II) is factitive in meaning and construction; here therefore most probably 'to be about to show (X to be) Bergaean twaddle'. The fr. is cited for its use of Βεργαῖος, presumably (although no definition appears in the preserved portion of the papyrus) in the sense of ψευδής (cf. Steph. Byz. 163.14ff. Βέργη· πόλις Θράκης πρὸς τῇ Χερσονήσῳ ... ἐξ ἧς Ἀντιφάνης ὁ κωμικός (probably an error: see Kassel–Austin 2.574). ἄπιστα δὲ οὗτος συνέγραψεν, ὥς φασιν· ἀφ' οὗ καὶ παροιμία βεργαΐζειν ἀντὶ τοῦ μηδὲν ἀληθὲς λέγειν, Strabo 2.3.5 Βεργαῖον διήγημα, 4.2). Antiphanes of Berga (Schmid in *RE* s.v. 19, 2521.62ff., cf. E. Rohde, *Der griechische Roman*[3] (Leipzig 1914) 238 n. 2, Göbel, *Ethnica* 99, Weinreich, *loc. cit.*) was the Munchausen of antiquity, and his tall stories must have been sufficiently familiar to an Athenian audience already in Alexis' time for an allusive use of Βεργαῖος to be comprehensible. Before this papyrus scrap was published, it was known only that Antiphanes of Berga predated Eratosthenes (cf. Polyb. 34.6.15); now that his *floruit* has been put back at least to the 4th century, it becomes uncertain whether he is to be identified with any other known

---

[1] Luppe (p.100) surprisingly interprets Βεργαῖον ἀποδείξειν ὕθλο[ν as '*nicht Dichtung, sondern vielmehr erklärende Prosa*'. But ought one to attribute so imaginative an expression (and one furthermore that scans as the second and third metra of an iambic trimeter) to a mere glossarist?

239

COMMENTARY

Antiphanes of Alexis' time or earlier: hardly the Middle-Comedy poet (so Schmid, Göbel), more plausibly the Bergaean mentioned on a mid-4th-century inscription (*IG* iv².94.I.b, 19 : so Weinreich).

Θεοφόρητος

Meineke 1.400. The title implies that one of the characters, probably but not certainly male,[1] was or appeared to be 'divinely possessed' during the course of the play or in its antecedents. The περιοχή of Menander's Ἱέρεια (text: Körte I³.146f., Sandbach 305f.; discussion: most recently Webster, *SM* 149f., *IM* 149ff., Gomme–Sandbach, *Comm.* 694f., A. Barigazzi, *Prometheus* 6 (1980) 97ff.) reveals that during the play a male slave feigned divine possession in order to become a patient of the priestess of the title, and so uncovered a secret. The papyrus frs. of the same poet's Θεοφορουμένη (see especially E. W. Handley, *BICS* 16 (1969) 88ff.; cf. Sandbach, *Comm.* 400ff., Webster, *IM* 189ff.) may contain part of a scene in which the title figure behaved as if sent into a trance by the pipes and cymbals of Cybele's votaries, and then sang or chanted divinely inspired lyric dactyls. In all probability this possession too was spurious, as were the votaries (cf. Handley 95). The frs. of Alexis' Θεοφόρητος give no clue to the way in which the theme of possession was handled, nor is it possible to date the play within narrow limits. In fr. 92(88K) a Ptolemy is mentioned; he is more likely to have been Soter, the son of Lagus, whose tenure of power in Egypt extended from 323 until his death in 283 or 282, than his son Philadelphus, whose reign began in 285. This fr. was spoken by a μάγειρος, and 91(87K) by a daylight reveller; both seem to involve situations familiar in later Greek comedy (see below), but unfortunately neither of them contains any material relevant to the most interesting question posed

---

[1] Θεοφόρητος is of two terminations, but Alexis would perhaps have chosen Θεοφορουμένη or some other unambiguously feminine form if he had intended his title figure to be a girl. No help is given here by the words of Ath. 15.700a and 9.369e introducing frs. 91(87K) and 92(88K); he says simply ἐν Θεοφορήτῳ. The idea of 'divine possession', which Alexis and Menander probably used as an interesting ingredient of otherwise typical intrigue plots, is fully discussed by E. Rohde, *Psyche*⁸ (English translation by W. B. Hillis, London 1925) 255f. and E. R. Dodds, *The Greeks and the Irrational* (Berkeley 1951) 64ff. The use of Θεοφόρητος and Θεόφορος with reference to such possession is as old as Aeschylus (*Ag.* 1140 -ητος of a woman, 1150), although Fraenkel (*ad loc.*) notes that Θεοφόρητος is 'a rare word in old Greek'. Cf. also Strabo 12.2.3, Jo. Philopon. *De aeternitate mundi* 6.29 p. 241.14 Rabe.

by Alexis' title: was there any relationship between this play and either of the two undated Menandrean comedies discussed above (particularly Ἱέρεια, in view of the sex of its supposed demoniac)?

91 (87K)

Meineke 3.418 (1), Kock 2.325, Edmonds 2.410, Kassel–Austin 2.68. This fr. seems to be part (but not the opening, if οἶμαι δ' is rightly conjectured in v. 1) of an entrance monologue by a reveller whose party has either lasted until sunrise or anticipated sunset. Drunk scenes and monologues are a favourite ingredient in later Greek comedy and the Roman adaptations (Legrand, *NGC* 470ff., Webster, *SLGC* 134 and n. 3, 215 and n. 1); in extant plays the drinkers include free young men (e.g. Callidamates in Plaut. *Most.* 313ff., Chremes in Ter. *Eun.* 727ff.) and household slaves (e.g. the title figure in Plaut. *Pseud.* 1246ff., Stichus and Sangarinus in *Stich.* 683ff., Syrus in Ter. *Ad.* 763ff.), but the absence of other categories (e.g. parasites) from the list is probably an accident of transmission.

1 In the *Marcianus* (Ath. 15.700a) the citation opens with οἶμαι γὰρ ἐπιτιμᾶν before the penthemimeral caesura, giving the verse a syllable too many. Unless there is a concealed lacuna here, caused by the excerptor omitting what to him were non-significant words, the point of the corruption must be γάρ, which incidentally is omitted in Epit.'s version of the fr. (a paraphrase, with several omissions and τηνικάδε for τηνικαῦτα in v. 2). All editors from Dindorf to Kassel–Austin print Jacobs' οἶμαί γ' ἐ. (*Addit.* 368), but γε here would add a touch of irony (cf. e.g. Ar. *Nub.* 1391 and Starkie *ad loc.*, possibly also Alexis 274(272K).1) inappropriate to the context (τηνικαῦτα is the only word in vv. 1–2 meriting a limitative γε). Sentences in drama structured with οἶμαι/οἴομαι (as opening word) + infinitive most commonly link on to the preceding sentence with either γάρ (e.g. S. *OR* 1227, *Phil.* 536, Ar. *Nub.* 1311, *Eccl.* 164, 1036, cf. Men. *Sam.* 140) or δέ (e.g. S. *OC* 28, Eur. *Or.* 288, *Bacch.* 1151, Ar. *Nub.* 1114, *Vesp.* 295, *Plut.* 267, Men. *Sik.* 249). Here accordingly Alexis is most likely to have written οἶμαι δ' ἐ.; δέ and γάρ are frequently confused in MSS of continuous texts (cf. Fraenkel on A. *Ag.* 560), but at the beginning of this citation, carelessness or faulty anticipation of v. 3 is a more probable source of error (cf. Ath. 14.626a citing Polyb. 4.20).

2 ἡμῖν, ὅτι τηνικαῦτα μεθύων περιπατῶ: the switch from first person plural (ἡμῖν = 'men in my state', sc. of drunkenness, ἀπὸ κοινοῦ with ἐπιτιμᾶν and ἀπαντώντων) to first person singular ('I in particular') is not uncommon in dramatic texts and elsewhere, usually without any discrimination in meaning or tone (a good list of examples in K.G. 1.83f.), but for the distinction drawn in Alexis here cf. Pl. *Symp.* 186b ἄρξομαι (=

241

COMMENTARY

Eryximachus personally) δὲ ἀπὸ τῆς ἰατρικῆς λέγων, ἵνα καὶ πρεσβεύωμεν (= Eryximachus speaking in the name of all physicians) τὴν τέχνην.

τηνικαῦτα: *lucente etiamnum sole*, Schweighaeuser, *Animadv.* 8.349. The situation may have been a comic cliché; cf. Simo's remark to the drunken slave in Plaut. *Pseud.* 1298f. *quae istaec audaciast te sic interdius | cum corolla ebrium incedere?*

περιπατῶ: on the use of this verb by Alexis (also 151(147K).2, 152(148K).1, 182(177K), 207(204K).2) and elsewhere in later Greek comedy see R. F. Thomas, *HSCP* 83 (1979) 182ff.

3-4 The sequence of thought (indicated by the γάρ) is 'they blame us wrongly, for the sun by day is far better than any torch at night to guide the reveller home'. This amusingly absurd idea is agreeably paralleled by Claud Halcro's words in Sir Walter Scott's *The Pirate*, 'The sun, my boy, is every wretched labourer's day-lantern' (ch. 16).

3 φανός, 'torch', is carefully distinguished by ancient grammarians (Phrynichus *Ecl.* s.v. φανός, p. 63 Fischer, but see especially Rutherford, *NP* 131f., and Phryn. *Praep. Soph.* 87.1ff. de Borries; cf. Pollux 10.116, Ath. 15.699d–700e, Photius s.v. πανός, Σ Ar. *Lys.* 308) from λύχνος 'lamp' and λυχνοῦχος 'lantern'. These distinctions in Attic usage are well brought out by passages like Anaxandrides 49(48K) (a φανός employed to light the λύχνος) and Alexis 107(102K).[1] As torches were a *sine qua non* for nocturnal travellers (not merely to light their way home: contrast Alexis 152(148K) with Men. *Dysk.* 60, Plaut. *Pers.* 569), their appearance on stage was normally a hint to the audience that the dramatic time had reached dusk (cf. P. Arnott, *Greek Scenic Conventions in the Fifth Century* (Oxford 1962) 120f., J. Dingel, *Das Requisit in der griechischen Tragödie* (Diss. Tübingen 1967) 74).

ὦ πρὸς τῶν θεῶν; the oath comically underlines the urgency of the question; cf. Barrett on Eur. *Hipp.* 219.

4 ὁ γλυκύτατος ἥλιος: 'the darling sun'; cf. R. Bultmann, *Philologus* 97 (1948) 1ff., D. Bain, *Antichthon* 18 (1984) 36f. From the time of Aristophanes (e.g. *Ach.* 462, 467, *Eccl.* 124, 241) on, ὦ γλυκύτατε (-άτη) appears

---

[1] φανός, which the MSS of Ath. and Epit. correctly preserve here, is the 'later Attic' (Photius s.v. πανός, but naming Aristophanes!) orthography; allegedly it replaced the form πανός, which grammarians attest for classical tragedy (A. *Ag.* 284, S. fr. 184 Pearson/Radt, Eur. *Ion* 195, fr. 90). There are, however, enough exceptions to this distinction (e.g. Men. fr. 55, Diphilus 6 are cited for the orthography with π) to make one hesitate about unconditional acceptance of it, or the MSS (e.g. at A. *Ag.* the direct transmission has φανός), or both. Cf. also Bruhn, *Wortschatz* 28, Björck, *Alpha Impurum* 147, W. Bühler, *Quaderni Cagliari* 2 (1967) 93f.

in Attic and elsewhere as a standard gushingly or cajolingly affectionate style of greeting, and the emotional overtones deriving from that use clearly carry over to places where γλυκύτατος as merely an attributive qualifier lacks its basic reference to taste or smell. Here the effect seems precious or facetious; at Antiphanes 81.5 (τοῦ γ. βασιλέως) the tone is enthusiastically complimentary, but later (e.g. in some private letters such as *P.Oxy.* 531.21) the idiom apparently has withered into a conventional formula applied to one's nearest and dearest.

On the lengthening of ὁ before γλυ-, see comm. on 89(86K).3; similarly, after penthemimeral caesura, ὁ γλάμων at Ar. *Eccl.* 254, 398 (cf. *Ran.* 588).

92 (88K)

Meineke 3.419 (II), Kock 2.325, Edmonds 2.410. Kassel–Austin 2.69. A plausible context for this line, which the *Marcianus* (Ath. 9.369e) quotes accurately (*pace* Meineke and some followers[1]), is readily supplied. Comic μάγειροι are frequently accused of talkativeness (e.g. Men. *Sam.* 283ff., *Dysk.* 504, 512, Eubulus 106(107K).6, Strato 1.31f. = Kassel–Austin 7.622, cf. Alexis 177(173K).15, Nicomachus 1.29, A. Giannini, *Acme* 13 (1960) 159), and the cited line is most probably a cook's riposte to such an accusation: 'Who are you to tell me to shut up – me, who habitually talk when cooking for people far more important than you – for example, Ptolemy?' Name-dropping is a characteristic of the stage ἀλαζών; a cook in Demetrius II 1.4ff. boasts of his services to Seleucus and Agathocles, and the soldier Pyrgopolinices (Plaut. *MG* 75ff.) brags about his personal aid to Seleucus. On the identity of this particular Ptolemy see introduction to Θεοφόρητος.

γογγυλίδος ὀπτῶν τόμους: 'roasting the slices of a turnip'. Turnips are so cooked elsewhere (Eubulus 3(4K)), and their slices are correctly termed τόμοι (cf. Phryn. *Ecl.* s.v. τέμαχος, p. 61 Fischer).

Θεσπρωτοί

Meineke 3.419. A reference to the notorious beanpole Philippides in the one extant fr. (93(89K)) would have been unlikely in a comedy produced after *c.*310 (see the introduction to Ἀγωνίς and comm. on fr. 2.8; cf.

---

[1] Th. Bergk, *Griechische Literaturgeschichte* 4 (Berlin 1887) 153 n. 108, Bothe, *PCGF* 525, and Kock. Epit.'s ὀπτῆς, which Meineke (cf. also Kock) preferred to A's ὀπτῶν, is simply an instance of an ending attracted into the case of the preceding word (γογγυλίδος); cf. Jackson, *Marg. Scaen.* 186.

T. B. L. Webster, *CQ* 2 (1952) 21, 25), but this does not help us to identify the play's subject. Was it a typical New-Comedy plot of love and intrigue, with the Thesprotians a pair of friends in an alien community (cf. the introduction to Ἀτθίς)? Was it alternatively a Middle-Comedy burlesque, ridiculing Thesprotian idiosyncrasies and especially an oracle of the dead which flourished in that region (Hdt. 5.92, Pausanias 9.30.6; cf. Hesych. s.v. θεοὶ Μολοττικοί)?[1] As Meineke first noted, the words of the fr. – an invocation to Hermes προπομπός and to Night in mock-tragic (not dithyrambic, as Nesselrath, *MK* 253 n. 32 suggests) rhythm and diction – would fit in well with the latter interpretation. Or could the play have combined Middle-Comedy burlesque with New-Comedy intrigue? In Alexis' Τροφώνιος, where the oracle at Lebadeia must have played some part (see introduction to that play), there was an active chorus that may still have had specially composed lyrics for it to sing; Webster's suggestion (*op. cit.* 25) that Alexis' Thesprotians may have been a similar chorus is worth consideration.[2]

93 (89K)

Meineke 3.419, Kock 2.325, Edmonds 2.410, Kassel–Austin 2.69; cf. W. Frantz, *De comoediae Atticae prologis* (Diss. Strasbourg 1891) 36. If the Thesprotian νεκυομαντεῖον has rightly been connected with Alexis' present title and this fr. (see above), the fr. may open a speech or even a scene in which one or more prophetic ghosts were conjured up. Such a scene, with its opportunities for theatrical display and tragic parody (cf. in particular the ghost-raising scene in A. *Pers.*, where also Hermes is one of the gods invoked, v. 629; H. D. Broadhead's edition (Cambridge 1960) xxxvi ff. and pp. 305ff., Pickard-Cambridge, *TDA* 35f., O. Taplin, *The Stagecraft of Aeschylus* (Oxford 1977) 114ff.), would have been most effective at a climactic point in the plot. Alternatively, could these two lines have begun the play, as Frantz suggests? Invocations to deities are a standard opening in Greek drama: A. *Suppl.*, *Choeph.* (Hermes!), Eur. *Suppl.*, *Phoen.*, *Cycl.*, cf. Men. *Mis.* (Night!), com. adesp. fr. 240 Austin

---

[1] The site of the oracle is directly east of the modern village of Mesopotamo, about 800 metres from where the Kokytos flows into the Acheron; see especially D. Müller, *Topographischer Bildkommentar zu den Historien Herodots: Griechenland* (Tübingen 1987) 909ff. and figs. 1–6.

[2] Edmonds' speculations (2.410 note c) about the play, introducing Philip and Olympias into the play under the guise of Orpheus and Eurydice, cannot be taken seriously; they lack not only evidence but also internal logic: how could a living Olympias be transformed into the dead Eurydice?

(Night! – probably by Menander: cf. Sandbach, *Comm.* 722f.), and the parody of a tragic invocation at the beginning of Ar. *Eccl.*, ὦ λαμπρὸν ὄμμα.

1 Ἑρμῆ θεῶν προπομπὲ: the *Marcianus* reading here (Ath. 12.552d: Epit. omits the fr.) gives rise to suspicion. Hermes does appear in myth as an escort of divinities (e.g. he conducted Persephone back from the underworld, he ushered the three goddesses for their contest before Paris, he conveyed the infant Dionysus to Athamas, he is associated with the Graces, he is sometimes portrayed attending Athena's chariot: cf. S. Eitrem in *RE* s.v. *Hermes* 785.3ff.), but that is hardly to the point in a context which plays on his psychagogic function and couples him with Night's Eye. For this reason Casaubon (*Animadv.* 858, cf. Cobet, *NL* 119f.) proposed Ἑ. νεκρῶν πρ., which has won much support. The main argument in its favour is that νεκρῶν would neatly prepare the way for the joke about Philippides' cadaverousness. But the conjecture has an insecure palaeographical foundation. This would matter less if it produced the *mot juste*; however, in normal Greek usage from Homer onwards the creatures whom Hermes escorts to Hades are termed ψυχαί rather than νεκροί, and references to Hermes in this function as νεκροπομπός (Lucian *Dial. Deor.* 4(24).1), νεκυαγωγός (a 3rd-century AD magic tablet from Carthage, fr. 242.10 Audollent, *Defix.* p. 325) or νεκυηγός (a verse inscription from Avdjilar in Asia Minor, E. Fabricius, *SB Berlin* (1894) 908) are rare, late and unattic.[1] Possibly Ath. or his source was misquoting the original words of Alexis; in that case the palaeographical argument against Casaubon's νεκρῶν would disappear. Possibly Alexis was himself guilty of a slipshod expression, and intended by θεῶν πρ. no more than 'Divine Guide (of Souls)', with θεῶν partitive and not objective genitive (cf. Meineke, *ad loc.*); in that event, however, θεῶν would contrast awkwardly against the apparently matched following genitive Φιλιππίδου.[2]

In tragedy Hermes is given the epithets πομπός (A. *Pers.* 626, S. *OC* 1548) and πομπαῖος (A. *Eum.* 91, S. *Aj.* 832, Eur. *Med.* 759).

1–2 Φιλιππίδου κληροῦχε: the point here is unequivocal and not complicated by the problem of the preceding phrase. The living Philip-

---

[1] In Lucian *Cont.* 2 νεκραγωγοῦντα refers to Charon, not Hermes; LSJ s.v. is in error here. On the function of Hermes as 'Guide of Souls' see especially P. Raingeard, *Hermès psychagogue* (Diss. Paris 1934, 1935), K. Kerényi, *Hermes der Seelenführer* (Zurich 1944), M. P. Nilsson, *Geschichte der griechischen Religion* 1³ (Munich 1967) 508f.

[2] Nauck² 843, on his trag. adesp. fr. 19 (= Alexis fr. 93(89K)!), attempts to solve the problem by emendation and transposition, θεῶν κληδοῦχε καὶ Φιλιππίδου προπομπέ; but Hermes is never styled κληδοῦχος, and even if he were, the epithet would be irrelevant in the present context.

pides so resembled a corpse (see comm. on fr. 2.8) that Hermes Guide of Souls already had a claim on him. Philippides is likened to a corpse also by Menander fr. 305; other cadaverous beanpoles are compared to skeletons (Cinesias in Plato com. 200(184K), cf. Ar. fr. 885(851K)) or sculptors' moulding frames (Sannyrion in Strattis 21(20K)).

κληροῦχος is a bold metaphor ('holder by allotment', usually with reference to land distributed to new settlers in previously alien territory), here doubtless inspired by tragedy (cf. S. *Aj.* 508 μητέρα πολλῶν ἐτῶν κληροῦχον).

2 νυκτός τ' ὄμμα τῆς μελαμπέπλου combines two tragic clichés: (i) μελάμπεπλος νύξ (Eur. *Ion* 1150; L. Bergson, *L'épithète ornementale dans Eschyle, Sophocle et Euripide* (Lund 1956) 131; Shakespeare has 'night's black mantle', *3 Henry VI* iv.2.22, cf. *Romeo and Juliet* iii.2.15, and Milton 'Sable-vested Night', *Paradise Lost* 2.962), and (ii) ὄμμα νυκτός (A. *Pers.* 428, Eur. *IT* 110, cf. νυκτὸς ὀφθαλμός A. *Sept.* 390). In these tragic passages Night's Eye is simply the moon; whether Alexis implied anything more than that here is uncertain.

Frantz (*loc. cit.*) may be right to argue from the words of this fr. that the action of the scene took place at night. This adds a slight support to two theories: (1) that the scene guyed Thesprotian necromantic rites, for consultation of such oracles normally took place at night (cf. J. G. Frazer, *Pausanias' Description of Greece* 3 (London 1898) p. 347); and (2) that the fr. came at or near the beginning of the play, for in later Greek comedy the action often opens in the darkness just before dawn of the plot's staged day (e.g. Ar. *Eccl.*, Men. *Mis.*, com. adesp. fr. 240 Austin, cf. Plaut. *Amph.*, *Curc.*, and my discussion, *PLLS* 2 (1979) 346ff.).

Θηβαῖοι

Both Alexis and Philemon wrote plays with this title, and there is little more that can be said about either play. The one fr. from Alexis' play in no way illuminates title (but cf. here the introduction to 'Ἀτθίς), date of production, or plot, despite one misguided attempt (see below, on the fr.) to identify this play as the Greek original of Plautus' *Captiui*.

94 (90K)

Meineke 3.419, Kock 3.326, Edmonds 2.410, Kassel–Austin 2.70; cf. F. Groh, *Listy Filolog.* 19 (1892) 15f. The fr. contains a joke which recurs twice in ancient literature: in an anecdote from a lost treatise by Chrysippus (fr. XVII.2 von Arnim, *Stoicorum veterum fragmenta* 3 (Leipzig 1903) 196) which Ath. 4.159d prefixes to his citation of the Alexis fr.,

ΘΗΒΑΙΟΙ

Χρύσιππος δ' ... νεανίσκον φησί τινα ἐκ τῆς Ἰωνίας σφόδρα πλούσιον ἐπιδημῆσαι ταῖς Ἀθήναις πορφυρίδα ἠμφιεσμένον ἔχουσαν χρυσᾶ κράσπεδα. πυνθανομένου δέ τινος αὐτοῦ ποδαπός ἐστιν ἀποκρίνασθαι ὅτι πλούσιος, and in two lines of Plaut. *Capt.* (277f.):

> Hegio: *quo de genere natus illic Philocrates?* Philocr. *Polyplusio,*
> *quod genus illi est unum pollens atque honoratissimum.*

This joke may have sprung independently from Plautus' brain or been taken from the Greek original. Unfortunately, date and identity of that original are unknown, although many attempts have been made to discover them (cf. introduction to Αἰχμαλωτός, n. 1). Using as his sole evidence the similarity between Plaut. *Capt.* 277f. and Alexis 94(90K), Groh suggested that Alexis' Θηβαῖοι was the Plautine model. This theory founders on the fact that there are no Thebans in the Roman play, which turns on the experiences of men from Elis and Aetolia after a war between those two states. A likelier explanation of the verbal similarity between the two passages (and the Chrysippus anecdote) is given below, comm. on v. 1.

1 **ποδαπὸς τὸ γένος ... πλούσιος**: the joke plays on the two meanings of ποδαπός, (i) 'from what country', as commonly and correctly in Attic (LSJ s.v. 1; e.g. Ar. *Ach.* 768, *Pax* 186, Men. *Asp.* 241, Amphis 36, Alexis 177(173K).3, 232(230K).3), and (ii) 'of what kind', = ποῖος (LSJ s.v. 2). It is essential for the joke that both uses should have been understood in Athens at the time of the play, but the second use need not yet have been naturalised into colloquial Attic. In fact the use of ποδαπός as a synonym for ποῖος seems to have been condemned by Phrynichus in an obscurely worded note (*Ecl.* s.v. ποταπός, p. 63 Fischer; cf. Apollonius Dysc. *Synt.* 1.33 Uhlig = 1.3.26 Bekker), which Rutherford, *NP* 128ff. has convincingly explained. This use became common only in the 3rd century; before that time (with the possible exception of this fr., an undated special case) there is no certain instance of it in any Attic writer.[1] Rutherford's suggestion that this use originated in Ionia is plausible; an Ionian is the subject of the Chrysippus anecdote, and if his answer to the Athenian questioner resulted from a dialectal confusion, the story gains extra point. In that event Chrysippus could have been retelling a well-known story about an earlier incident which Attic comedy had already exploited for its own purposes.

Here the *Marcianus* (along with Epit. MSS) spells the adjective

---

[1] Four earlier Attic instances are sometimes alleged: Ar. *Pax* 186, *Av.* 906, S. fr. 453 Pearson/Radt and [Dem.] 25.40. In all these passages the normal Athenian use ('from what country') can be defended (cf. Rutherford, *NP.* 130 and Pearson on the Sophocles fr.).

ποδαπός, but at Alexis 232(230K).3 (Ath. 10.431b; cf. also 177(173K).3, Ath. 9.386a) it gives ποταπός. ποδαπός is the correct Attic orthography for the correct Attic usage, generally preserved in MSS of classical Athenian authors (e.g. A. *Choeph.* 575, Ar. *Pax* 186, Pl. *Apol.* 20b), but replaced by the ποταπός variant (in both senses of the word) during the time of the *Koine*. Inevitably there will be doubt over the spelling preferred by later Greek comedians; it cannot safely be assumed that they were always consistent with themselves or each other. Cf. also A. N. Jannaris, *An Historical Greek Grammar* (London 1897) 164 § 591, Rutherford, *loc. cit.*, Schwyzer 1.256.

Part-division at πλούσιος was first indicated by Schweighaeuser.

2 τούτους δὲ πάντες: δέ is just possible here, introducing an explanation (i.e. in place of γάρ, cf. Denniston, *GP* 169f.), but Alexis is perhaps more likely to have written τούτους γε (cf. Denniston 121ff.).

Bothe's conjecture πάντας (*Griech. Kom.* 51) in place of πάντες (so A, Epit.) is palaeographically implausible (scribes habitually assimilate rather than dissimilate juxtaposed endings), but not impossible.

2–3 The MSS (*Marcianus* and Epit.) have εὐγενεστάτους, | πένητας δ' εὐπατρίδας οὐδὲ εἷς ὁρᾷ, admirable in sense but defective in metre. Most of the suggested remedies heal the latter at the expense of the former (e.g. <ἐπεὶ> πένητας εὐπατρίδας οὐδεὶς ὁρᾷ Meineke, *Anal. Crit.* 76 and <ἀλλ' οὖν> π. εὐπ. οὐδεὶς ὁ. Heimsoeth, *Comm. Crit.* xiv, but v. 3 is stronger as a contrast to the preceding clause than as an explanation of it. Wilamowitz's πένητα δ' εὐπάτριδ' οὐδὲ εἷς ὁρᾷ ⏑ ⏓ , which has received spurious authority from its acceptance by Kaibel in his text of Ath., offends against metrical and linguistic usages. The split anapaest that it introduces into the first half of the second metron may perhaps be condoned by the position of the break (after the second short) and the elision across it (cf. *CQ* 7 (1957) 189); εὐπάτριδα, however, can hardly be tolerated as accusative singular of masculine εὐπατρίδης (cf. LSJ s.vv. εὐπατρίδης, εὔπατρις, J. Wackernagel, *Kleine Schriften* 2 (Göttingen 1954) 858f. = *Glotta* 14 (1925) 50f.). One conjecture neither weakens sense nor mangles metre: Dindorf's εὐγενεστάτους | <εἶναι>· πένητας δ' εὐπατρίδας οὐδεὶς ὁρᾷ, which editors of the comic frs. (including Kassel–Austin) have accepted, perhaps too readily. The loss of εἶναι in the MSS (? by virtual haplography before (π)ένη-) may be explicable, but replacement of a transmitted οὐδὲ εἷς by the more prosaic οὐδείς, which Meineke and Heimsoeth also were forced by metre to incorporate in their conjectures, gives one pause. The verse is better obelised; could Alexis have written εὐγ., | πένητας εὐπατρίδας δὲ, <δέσποτ',> οὐδέ εἷς | ὁρᾷ?

The speaker's equation of Eupatrid status with wealth (cf. Dover, *GPM* 110ff.) would have been more illuminating if anything was known about his/her identity and character, the context of the remark and the play's date. Here εὐπατρίδαι is a general term for the old Athenian aristocracy, which largely maintained its wealth during the period when Alexis was active (cf. H. T. Wade-Gery, *CQ* 25 (1931) 1ff., 77ff., Barrett on Eur. *Hipp.* 151–4, P. L. MacKendrick, *The Athenian Aristocracy 399 to 31 B.C.* (Cambridge, Mass. 1969) 16ff., Davies, *APF* 10ff.).

Θητεύοντες

Θητεύοντες are hired labourers, often on a farm (e.g. the murderer in Pl. *Euthyphr.* 4c, Gyges in *Resp.* 2.359d, probably the reapers in Theoc. 10). Their number and role in Alexis' play are unknown.

95 (91K)

Meineke 3.420, Kock 2.326, Edmonds 2.412, Kassel–Austin 2.70. The unidentified speaker appears to be parodying, at least indirectly, the words and attitude of Zeus in Hom. *Il.* 1.526f. οὐ γὰρ ἐμὸν παλινάγρετον οὐδ᾿ ἀπατηλὸν | οὐδ᾿ ἀτελεύτητον, ὅ τί κεν κεφαλῇ κατανεύσω.

Θράσων

Kock 2.326, Breitenbach 59f. Thrason was a common name in ancient Greece,[1] and Kock's suggestion (taken up by Edmonds 2.412 note b) that Alexis' play took its title from the most celebrated bearer of this name in 4th-century Athens, Thrason of Erchia, cannot be totally discounted. Yet this man's career (he was Theban πρόξενος in Athens and a supporter of Philip: Dem. 18.137, Aeschines 3.138, Dinarchus 1.38; Schwahn in *RE* s.v. *Thrason* 1, 562.54ff., Davies, *APF* 239f.) was hardly distinguished or notorious enough to have sustained a whole comedy. Hence Breitenbach's far more plausible idea that Alexis used this name episematically for a (more or less) bold soldier in an intrigue plot of New-Comedy type. Significant names on the θρασ- stem were regularly given to soldiers in later Greek comedy and its imitators (Ribbeck, *Alazon* 26ff., 34f., F. Poland, *Neue Jahrb.* 33 (1914) 588, K. Mras, *Wien. Stud.* 38 (1916) 312). Thraso is Terence's name for the *miles* in *Eunuchus* (in Men. *Kol.*, the Greek

---

[1] Kirchner, *PA* 1.484f. (7375–95), 2.465 (7374a, b) already listed twenty-three instances from Athens alone (Th. of Erchia = 7384), and that number is increased by more recent discoveries (*SEG* 12 (1955) no. 101.7, 42; 17 (1960) 44.16, 19 (1963) 149.308; 21 (1965) 527.35, unless that Thrason = Kirchner no. 7387, and 927).

COMMENTARY

original from which some of the military material derives, he was called Bias; if there was a soldier also in Terence's other model, Menander's *Eunouchos*, we do not know his Greek name; cf. now H. Marti, *Lustrum* 8 (1963) 63ff., W. Steidle, *Rh. Mus.* 116 (1975) 327, 340, 342ff.). Menander's *Thrasyleon*, which Turpilius probably adapted for the Roman stage, was named after a soldier (Körte–Thierfelder 2.79f., cf. Aelian *Epist.* 9); the same author's *Misoumenos* was alternatively titled *Thrasonides*, after its soldier (cf. E. G. Turner, *BICS Suppl.* 17 (1965) 5), whose name in all probability inspired Alciphron 2.13; a character in the unidentified (? Menandrean) comedy on *P.Antinoopolis* 55 (com. adesp. fr. 242 Austin) has a name beginning Θρασ- (v. 55, margin).

A soldier called Hermaiskos appears to have been a character in Alexis' Κράτεια (see introduction to fr. 120(115K), and others with unknown names appeared in his Λευκαδία, Στρατιώτης, Τραυματίας, possibly also Ἀγωνίς (see introductions to these titles); cf. also Nesselrath, *MK* 327ff. The postulated soldier does not appear in the one remaining fr. of Θράσων, where an (? elderly) husband accuses his wife of talkativeness.

96 (92K)

Meineke 3.420, Kock 2.326, Edmonds 2.412, Kassel–Austin 2.71. Husbands who attack wives' garrulity are as much a commonplace of ancient drama (e.g. Antiphanes 247(253K), Xenarchus 14, Men. fr. 60, Philemon 154(208K), Plaut. *Rud.* 905; cf. also Eur. *Phoen.* 198ff., Ar. *Eccl.* 120, Plaut. *Aul.* 124ff., *Poen.* 32ff., *Rud.* 1114; Libanius *Declam.* 26.34, which is a conglomerate of comic motifs gleaned doubtless from this fr., ἡ γυνὴ ... τρυγόνος λαλιστέρα, κίττης, ἀηδόνος, κερκώπης; Legrand, *NGC* 230, H. G. Oeri, *Der Typ der komischen Alten* (Basle 1948) 38f.) as are their scolding wives (e.g. Plaut. *Asin.*, *Men.*, Ter. *Phorm.*). Here Alexis' list of objects of comparison develops the theme amusingly, but we cannot penetrate into its context.

2–4 The text of this catalogue of negatives, as transmitted by the united testimony of A and Epit. (Ath. 4.133b–c), has been attacked on three fronts by scholars who maintain that (1) the sequence οὔτε ... οὐ ... οὐ etc. is not tolerable in Attic comedy; (2) the nightingale is out of place in a list of continual chatterers (so e.g. Meineke, *Anal. Crit.* 61 and on Moschus 3.38 in his final edition of Theoc., Bion and Moschus (Berlin 1856) pp. 439f. and n., S. A. Naber, *Mnemosyne* 8 (1880) 255f.); and (3) the minor corruption in v. 3, which is revealed by the failure of the transmitted ἀηδόνα οὐ τρυγόνα to scan, can be remedied only on the assumption that a further item in the list has dropped out (Meineke, *loc. cit.*, Cobet, *NL* 33). The criticisms are best examined separately.

(1) Denniston, *GP* 510f. has a long list of examples of οὔτε followed by

οὐ *n* times and other similar sequences, commenting that 'the writer intends to express the addition formally, but, for emotional effect, breaks off with an asyndeton'. But neither Denniston nor other discussions (e.g. Elmsley on Eur. *Med.* 1316, K.G. 2.289; cf. Naber, *loc. cit.*, Gomme–Sandbach, *Comm.* on Men. *Sam.* 510) isolate clearly enough those lists (like the present fr.) which consist of single-word items individually negatived. Relevant parallels to Alexis here include Hdt. 8.98.1 τοὺς οὔτε νιφετός, οὐκ ὄμβρος, οὐ καῦμα, οὐ νὺξ εἴργει, Men. *Dysk.* 724ff. οὐκ ἐῶντά τ' ... οὐ βοηθήσαντά τ' ... οὐ προσειπόντ', οὐ λαλήσανθ' ἡδέως, S. *Ant.* 953f. οὔτ' ἄν νιν ὄλβος οὔτ' Ἄρης, | οὐ πύργος, οὐχ ἁλίκτυποι | κελαιναὶ νᾶες ἐκφύγοιεν, Eur. *Hec.* 1234f. οὔτ' εὐσεβῆ γὰρ οὔτε πιστὸν ... οὐχ ὅσιον, οὐ δίκαιον: a sample that gives the lie to Denniston's claim that this use is 'almost entirely confined to serious poetry'.[1]

(2) The attack on the ἀηδών (basically = nightingale, *Luscinia megarhynchos*, but in antiquity never distinguished from the thrush nightingale, *Luscinia luscinia*, a regular passage migrant in Greece) is easily repelled. ἀηδόνα seems already to have been part of this citation in the 4th century AD, when Libanius made his paraphrase (see above); if the word is corrupt, corruption must have set in early, perhaps caused by misquotation on the part of Ath. or his source. Yet why should corruption be posited? Those who object to the inclusion of the nightingale in this list have been seduced by the bird's melodious tones into forgetting that its song continues loudly and persistently day and night in the more wooded parts of Greece from the end of April into June (cf. Arist. *HA* 9.49B, 632ᵇ20ff. ᾄδει μὲν συνεχῶς ἡμέρας καὶ νύκτας δεκαπέντε (an understatement in fact, but see *JHS* 99 (1979) 193), ὅταν τὸ ὄρος δασύνηται. μετὰ δὲ ταῦτα ᾄδει μέν, συνεχῶς δ' οὐκέτι); cf. Thompson, *Birds* s.v. ἀηδών. Poets accordingly called it πολυκώτιλος (Simonides fr. 81 Page) and ἀκόρετος βοᾶς (A. *Ag.* 1143); cf. Alciphron 4.13. And other writers than Alexis saw a similarity between the nightingale's endless serenading and the prattle of human ranters: e.g. the anonymous Hellenistic epigrammatist who wrote ὄρνιθες ψίθυροι, τί κεκράγατε; μή μ' ἀνιᾶτε, | τὸν τρυφερῆ

---

[1] Is this usage perhaps an anomaly of colloquial asyndetic speech? In comedy the standard sequences appear to be (a) οὐ *n* times (e.g. Ar. *Av.* 141f., fr. 380(363 + 364K), Alexis 179(174K), Men. fr. 267, cf. Alciphron 2.6.1; the list is sometimes introduced by οὐδείς Ar. *Av.* 1133f., *Plut.* 1114f., or by οὐδεπώποτε Ar. *Ach.* 34f.); (b) [οὐ ...] οὔτε *n* times (e.g. Men. *Dysk.* 505ff.); (c) οὐ ... οὐδέ *n* times (Ar. *Ran.* 1043, fr. 333(318K).4ff., Alexis 263(261K); in this sequence οὐ may be substituted for one or more occurrences of οὐδέ, e.g. Ar. *Eccl.* 452, fr. 334(317K), Ameipsias 24(25K); at Ar. *Av.* 979 and Eupolis fr. 175(162K) the text is doubtful).

COMMENTARY

παιδὸς σαρκὶ χλιαινόμενον,· | ἑζόμεναι πετάλοισιν ἀηδόνες· εἰ δὲ λάληθρον | θηλὺ γένος (the ancient world believed that it was the hen bird that sang, not the cock), δέομαι, μείνατ' ἐφ' ἡσυχίας (*Anth. Pal.* 12.136 = 10 Gow–Page). Cf. the proverb ἀηδόνες λέσχαις ἐγκαθήμεναι· ἐπὶ τῶν ἀδολεσχούντων Diogenian 2.48 and Leutsch *ad loc.*, Dio Chrys. *Or.* 47.16.[1]

(3) The corruption in v. 3 could have arisen in any of three ways. An item in Alexis' list could have been omitted by Ath. or a later copyist here (just as e.g. at 9.372b, citing Ar. fr. 581(569K).2); hence Cobet, *NL* 33 unconsciously improving on an earlier suggestion of Meineke's (*Anal. Crit.* 61), proposed οὐκ ἀηδόν', <οὐ χελιδόνα>, | οὐ τρ. ('*non potuit poeta* τὴν κωτίλην χελιδόνα *in hoc grege avium loquacium omittere*');[2] this supplement is printed by Kassel–Austin. Secondly, one of the items in Alexis' list could have been replaced by a gloss or similar item: cf. e.g. Alexis 132(127K).8 (σέσελι Ath. 4.170b, πέπερι Pollux 6.66), Ar. fr. 332(320K).4 (μύρον Pollux 7.95, νίτρον Clem. Al. *Paed.* 2.124), Men. *Dysk.* 507 (ἀλλ' οὐδέν B, ὀρίγανον Choeroboscus *In Theodos.* 1.259.16 Hilgard). This is the least likely explanation of the present error, in view of the fact that Libanius' paraphrase includes four of Alexis' five items, and the fifth (τέττιγα) is outside the area of corruption. Thirdly, the οὐ before τρυγόνα might have supplanted another form of the negative: not οὔτε (Porson, *Adv.* 69), which produces a sequence of negative forms anomalous in comic lists (see above and p. 251 n. 1; yet outside comedy e.g. Theoc. 15.137ff.), but rather οὐχὶ (Blaydes, *Adv.* 1.107; cf. my comm. on Alexis 304(301K).1). This last conjecture has a plausible simplicity that ought to gain it the verdict over Cobet's homoeoteleuton supplement.

Alexis' list of chatterers is imaginatively assembled. In classical Greece κίττα is the jay (*Glandarius glandarius*),[3] notorious alike for its garrulity

---

[1] And in more recent times (i) the poem of Anne, Countess of Winchelsea, *To the Nightingale*: 'Cease then, prithee, cease thy tune; | Trifler, wilt thou sing till June'; (ii) David Niven on the Normandy landings in June 1944, ch. 12 of *The Moon's a Balloon* (London 1971): 'lying in a ditch that first night in Normandy, my most vivid recollection was the sound of the nightingales. Before the war, eminent lady cellists were employed by the B.B.C. to sit in remote black woods to try and coax these timid little birds into song. The nightingales of Normandy were made of sterner stuff – they all but drowned out the gunfire with their racket.'

[2] Cf. also Schweighaeuser, *Animadv.* 2.419, here anticipating largely Naber's conjecture, *loc. cit.*

[3] Cf. O. Keller, *Die antike Tierwelt* 2 (Leipzig 1913) 112ff., Thompson, *Birds*[2] s.v. κίσσα, André, *Oiseaux* s.v. *pica*, F. Capponi, *Ornithologia Latina* (Genoa 1979) 414ff. Ancient Greek descriptions of the κίσσα fit the jay rather than the magpie (*Pica pica*), which from Byzantine times onward shared the same name. Pliny *HN* 10.78 claims that the magpie had only

(λάληθρος Lycophron *Alex*. 1319, in an obscure reference to the Argo; cf. Ar. *Av*. 1297 and Σ, citing Eupolis 220(207K); Antip. Sid. 28 Gow–Page = *Anth. Pal*. 7.423, Martial 14.76) and its raucousness (Theoc. 5.136; cf. Ovid, *Met*. 5.678 *raucaque garrulitas*). The monotonous croon of the τρυγών, the turtle dove (*Streptopelia turtur*), caused the expression τρυγόνος λαλιστέρα, which Alexis here expands, to become proverbial (Zenob. 1.55 Bühler; cf. Men. fr. 346, Alciphron 2.26; Meineke, *Men. et Phil*. 148, D. S. Tsirimbas, *Sprichwörter und sprichwörtliche Redensarten bei den Epistolographen* (Diss. Munich 1936) 51); cf. also Theoc. 15.87f., where the Syracusan matrons are abused as τρυγόνες and asked to stop their chatter. To the cicada the attitude of Greek writers was as ambivalent as it was to the nightingale; they praised the melodiousness of its chirring (e.g. Hes. *Op*. 582f. and West *ad loc*., Pl. *Phdr*. 259c, Theoc. 1.148, Apollonides or Philippus in *Anth. Pal*. 9.264 = 18 Gow–Page, *Anacreont*. 34 Preisendanz and West, Longus 1.23, the proverb τέττιγος εὐφωνότερος Apostolius 16.37; LSJ s.v. τέττιξ, Benner–Fobes on Philostratus *Epist*. 71), but condemned its relentless persistence (e.g. Aristophon 10.6f., Novius 25f. Ribbeck *totum diem | argutatur quasi cicada*; Steier in *RE* s.v. *Tettix* 3, 1113.68ff., Dohm, *Mageiros* 16).

Ath. precedes his citation of this fr. with the comment ἔστιν δ᾽ ἡ κερκώπη ζῷον ὅμοιον τέττιγι καὶ τιτιγονίῳ; in fact τέττιξ is a generic term for all the larger Greek cicadas (including *Cicada orni*, probably the commonest species in Greece today), while τιτιγόνιον applies to the smaller species (e.g. *Cicadetta montana*) and κερκώπη, as its name suggests, to those species whose abdomens taper to a tail-like point (e.g. the very large *Lyristes plebejus*: cf. Aelian *NA* 6.19). There was, however, an alternative ancient interpretation of the κερκώπη as the name given to the female τέττιξ (Σ Ar. *Av*. 1095, Hesych. s.v. κερκώπη, Eustathius 396.1), but this is unlikely to have been Alexis' intention here, for a straightforward biological reason. Only the male τέττιξ drums,[1] as Alexis' contemporaries knew (Xenarchus 14, cf. Hesych. s.v. ἀχέτης). See, in addition to the works already cited, C. J. Sundevall, *Die Thierarten des Aristoteles* 2 (Stockholm 1863) 200f., Keller, *op. cit*. at p. 253 n. 3, 2.401ff., A. S. F. Gow, *CR* 6 (1956)

---

recently been observed in Rome, and even then not commonly; to previous generations *pica* was always the jay.

[1] The noise is not made by stridulation (as in grasshoppers, locusts, field crickets, etc.) but by the vibration of two membranes ('tymbals'), one on each side of the abdomen, under the action of tiny muscles. Some knowledge of the mechanism is shown in Aristotle's biological writing (e.g. *HA* 4.9, 535^{b}6ff., 5.30, 556^{a}14ff., *Resp*. 9, 474^{b}36ff.). See especially J. G. Myers, *Insect Singers* (London 1929); F. Ossiannilsson, *Insect Drummers* (*Opuscula Entomologica, Suppl*. 10, Lund 1949).

COMMENTARY

93 n. 4, L. Gil Fernández, *Nombres de insectos en griego antiguo* (Madrid 1959) 121f., M. Davies and J. Kathirithamby, *Greek Insects* (London 1986) 113ff., 131f., I. C. Beavis, *Greek Insects and other Invertebrates in Classical Antiquity* (Exeter 1988) 91ff.

Ἰασίς

A. F. Naeke, *Choerili Samii quae supersunt* (Leipzig 1817) 42, Meineke 1.391 (cf. also *Quaest. Scen.* 35), Nauck, *MGR* 3 (1869–74) 82, Kock 2.327, Breitenbach 170. Just a single word is preserved under this title, which the corrupt MS of the Antiatticist (83.15 Bekker) records dativally as Ἰάσιδι, proparoxytone. A corruption here for Ἰάσονι (Meineke: a tragedy of that name is mentioned once – by the Antiatticist! – and attributed to Antiphon, cf. Meineke 1.316, Nauck² 792, Snell, *TrGF* 1.195), or less plausibly for Ἰάσῳ (Nauck: presumably Demeter's lover, otherwise Iasion) or even Ἰασοῖ (Kock, comparing Ar. *Plut.* 701, fr. 21, Hermippus fr. iamb. 1 West) cannot be ruled out; but if the transmitted title is correct, Ἰασίς may be interpreted in three ways. (1) As a nymph of a healing spring in Elis (Paus. 6.22.7) she could have appeared appropriately as the prologue of a play that included some sick character; the nymph Kalligeneia appeared as prologue in Aristophanes' second Θεσμοφοριάζουσαι (fr. 331(335K)), and a few other titles such as Eubulus' Ἠχώ, Eubulus' and Alexis' Παννυχίς (q.v.), and Timocles' Λήθη ought perhaps to be interpreted in a similar way (cf. Webster, *SLGC* 17). Alternatively, this Iasis might have been introduced during the play in the role of a healing divinity, comparable to Diallage in Ar. *Lys.* or Peace in Ar. *Pax*. (2) Iasis could have been the name of a human character (*hetaira*? visitor from abroad?) in an intrigue play of New-Comedy type. Although no Athenian (male or female) is known to have borne this name (cf. Breitenbach 170 n. 1), inscriptional evidence reveals that Iasis was a fairly common name in at least one part of the Greek world, Cyrenaica, where (curiously enough) it seems to have been confined to males (e.g. *SEG* 9 (1944) nos. 20.4, 77; 16 (1959) 870a; 20 (1964) nos. 735b.1.73, d.9, 10, 741a.1.23). (3) The possibility, that Ἰασίς (oxytone: cf. Meineke, *Quaest. Scen.*; Dindorf in *TGL* s.v. Ἴασος 494c) should be interpreted as a female ethnic (from the city of Iasos in Caria: so Naeke; cf. W. Bluemel, *Die Inschriften von Iasos* 2 (Vienna 1985) 168, T 60.1, 8, Threatte 1.523f.), perhaps deserves most favour, in view of New Comedy's fondness for such titles (those certainly attested for Alexis are listed e.g. in the introduction to Λευκαδία).

97 (93K)

Meineke 3.421, Kock 2.327, Edmonds 2.412, Kassel–Austin 2.72; cf.

W. K. Pritchett, *Hesperia* 25 (1956) 244ff. There can be no dispute over the Antiatticist's implied claim (83.15 Bekker) that the form ἀμφιτάπης was as Attic as the object it denotes; not only does it appear elsewhere in later comedy (Diphilus 50(51K)), but it has been identified on the Athenian inscriptions of 415/14 recording the confiscations of property of those who allegedly desecrated the mysteries (W. K. Pritchett, *Hesperia* 22 (1953) 243 = *SEG* 13 (1956) no. 12 = *IG* i³.421.164–72), where B. D. Meritt's supplementation of this word (eight times) is the only one possible, given the space and the ending. Other forms of this hybrid compound (ἀμφίτα-πις and -ταπος: on the stem's etymology see Frisk 2.854 s.v. τάπης) are not preserved before the *Koine* (LSJ, Passow-Crönert s.v.). ἀμφιτάπης is defined by the grammarians as a χιτών (Hesych. s.v.), or more correctly a rug or coverlet, with wool on both sides: i.e. reversible (*Suda* s.v., Pollux 6.9, Eustath. 746.39 (citing Ael. Dionys. fr. 112 and Paus. Gr. fr. 103 Erbse) and 1057.8; cf. Blümner, *Technologie* 182). White, crimson and 'Orchomenian' ἀμφιτάπητες are attested; their primary function was apparently to cover a person reclining or resting on a κλίνη; but perhaps more relevant to Alexis' use of the word is the fact that these rugs are usually mentioned as objects of luxury in the houses of the wealthy (cf. also Pollux 10.38, Ath. 5.197b, 6.255e).

Ἰμίλκων[1]

Meineke 1.381, Edmonds 2.414 and notes 1 and a, W. G. Arnott in Flores 367f. The one fr. from this play is introduced by Ath. 8.354d with the

---

[1] Edmonds and Kassel–Austin spell the name with a rough breathing, perhaps rightly. Initial laryngal consonants in Punic were represented in Latin by *h* (cf. J. Friedrich, *Phönizisch–punische Grammatik*, *Analecta Orientalia* 32 (Rome 1951) §§ 32, 34), but apparently in Greek by a smooth breathing, at least when the initial vowel is alpha (thus Ἀμίλκας, Ἀννίβας, Ἄννων, Ἀσδρούβας). Admittedly the evidence for Greek practice is neither wholly reliable (Byzantine MSS of *Koine* authors) nor consistent (MSS generally give Ἰ- as against Ἀ-), but there is no philological reason for an assumption that Attic writers would represent the initial Punic h differently in (e.g.) Ἀννίβας and Ἰμίλκων. Language, however, does not always develop on logical lines, and it is conceivable that Athenians of Alexis' and other times assimilated these strange-sounding Punic names incorrectly to the more familiar patterns associated with existing Greek initial syllables, where ἱμ- (ἱμάς, ἱμάτιον, ἱμείρω, ἵμερος and derivatives) was normal, ἰμ- (Ἴμβρος; ἴμεν, ἴμεναι in epic with their spelling variants) and ἀνν- (ἀννησον, ἀννέφελος in epic) relatively rare, and ἀνν- non-existent. It is unfortunate that the pre-

COMMENTARY

words κατὰ τὸν Ἀλέξιδος τοῦ κωμῳδιοποιοῦ Μίλκωνα (so A), which imply[1] that Μίλκων is its title or a corruption of it. If the title is correctly transmitted, Milkon will presumably be the play's male hero bearing an otherwise unattested name – a less likely but not impossible hypothesis in view of parallels such as Alexis' (and Antiphanes') Μίδων (q.v.). Edmonds' suggestion, however, that A's Μίλκωνα is corrupt for <Ἰ>μίλκωνα, is very attractive; the change is slight and its consequences fruitful.[2] Ἰμίλκων, the Greek form of a common Carthaginian name (ḥī-Milkōt = brother of Milkot), would be a stage portrayal not of some contemporary Carthaginian in the news (so Edmonds tentatively, refer-ring *exempli gratia* to the general who fought Agathocles in 307: Diod. Sic. 20.60.4–61.4), but rather of an imaginary Carthaginian in a play of New-Comedy style. In that case could Ἰμίλκων be an alternative title for Alexis' Καρχηδόνιος? So Edmonds, equally tentatively; his suggestion deserves serious consideration. Alexis' Καρχηδόνιος (see its introduction) is the putative main source for Plautus' *Poenulus*. Although the Carthaginian in Plautus' play is called Hanno, not Himilco, this is no argument against Edmonds; Plautus elsewhere changes character names from his originals (cf. E. W. Handley, *Menander and Plautus: A Study in Comparison* (London 1968) 8f., 19 n. 4 = E. Lefèvre (ed.), *Die römische Komödie: Plautus und Terenz* (Darmstadt 1973) 257f. and n. 4).

The Ἰμίλκων fr. (see below) appears to belong to a context in which one or more speakers discuss the relative merits of hot and cold food. It is hardly surprising that no passage of the *Poenulus* directly translates it, for the fr.'s reference to 'Plato's Good' (1f.) would lack relevant point to a Roman audience just after the end of the Second Punic War. Yet several passages of *Poen.* provide a conceivable setting for the Greek fr.: 240–9 (Milphio's *coqua est haec quidem . . . scit muriatica ut maceret* might substitute a typical Plautine formulation for the specifically Greek reference), 699–703 (note Lycus' *ibi ego te repplebo*), 1422 (*nos curemus* might perhaps replace a

---

Euclidean inscription of 407/6, recording an alliance between Athens and Carthage (*IG*i³.123, R. Meiggs and D. Lewis, *A Selection of Greek Historical Inscriptions to the End of the Fifth Century B.C.* (Oxford 1969) 280f. no. 92), is broken or illegible at the crucial point where a real-life Imilkon is named (16]ιλκο). R. Herzog, *Philologus* 56 (1897) 33ff., especially 44ff., is particularly useful on the Greek transcription of Punic names, but does not touch on this point.

[1] See above, introduction to the *Helen* titles, p. 199 n. 3. Meineke 3.454 corrects his earlier mistake on this point perpetrated at 1.381.

[2] For the corruption of Ἰμίλκωνα cf. Appian *Pun.* 97 (Ἰμίλκωνος C, καὶ μίλκ- V), where V's error may have influenced that in Eunapius fr. 82, which Edmonds cites.

conventional Greek closing scene of feasting and celebration), less probably 759–60:

> Lycus. *calidum pransisti prandium hodie? dic mihi.*
> Agorastocles. *quid iam?* Ly. *quia os nunc frigefactas, quom rogas.*

Here the superficial similarity of language (*calidum pr. prandium* ~ παραθῶσι θερμά) ought not to blind readers to the underlying difference between the Latin context (with its typically Plautine 'conundrum' joke) and any dramatic situation implied by the Greek fragment.

The 'Ιμίλκων, whether identical with Καρχηδόνιος or not, cannot be dated. The reference in its fr. to 'Plato's Good' is of no help in this respect, since this phrase continued in popular use for several decades after Plato's death, at least up to the time of the New-Comedy poet Philippides (his fr. 6: see below). On the inadequacy of attempts to date the Καρχηδόνιος see the introduction to that play.

98 (152K)

Meineke 3.453, Kock 2.353, Edmonds 2.414, Kassel–Austin 2.72; cf. K. Gaiser, *Phronesis* 25 (1980) 11f. What character (or characters) spoke these words, and in what kind of context? To such questions the answers are speculative even when the excerptor or phrases in a fr. provide unambiguous clues. Here, whether or not there be any relationship between Plaut. *Poen.* and this fr., the clues are uncertain and the difficulties increased by the fr.'s incoherent opening, due perhaps to a lacunose text (on citations beginning in mid-sentence see my general introduction, II.i, and comm. on frs. 29, 55(53K), 71, 73, 83, etc.), but more probably to the circumstances in which Ath. 8.354d makes Cynulcus quote the fr. The deipnosophists' cooks have been warned not to serve their dishes cold, 'for nobody can eat cold food'.[1] Cynulcus then interposes the Alexis fr.: 'In the words of Alexis' 'Ιμίλκων,' he says, 'I (sc. can eat cold food: cf. Schweighaeuser, *Animadv.* 4.627), if they (the μάγειροι) don't serve it hot ...' It seems likely that the Alexis fr. opens with this unconnected ἐγώ, but what preceded it in the play? The fr.'s interpretation, punctuation, even part-assignments depend on uncertain guesses about this. Two possibilities are:

(i)   <φαγεῖν θέλοιμ' ἂν ψύχρ'> ἐγὼ
    ἂν μὴ παραθῶσι θερμά. τἀγαθὸν Πλάτων ...

---

[1] οὐδεὶς γὰρ ἂν φάγοι ψυχρῶν. With transposition of φάγοι and ψυχρῶν (cf. Kaibel *ad loc.*) this forms two iambic metra and may come from a comic source.

257

COMMENTARY

Here the whole fr. would belong to one speaker (? a parasite), expressing his willingness to eat any food, hot or cold.

(ii)   <(B.) ψύχρ' ὄψα δὴ
θέλεις φαγεῖν, ἂν μὴ παραθῶσι θέρμ';> (A.) ἐγώ;
ἂν μὴ παραθῶσι θερμά; (B.) τἀγαθὸν Πλάτων ...

Here B. (? a μάγειρος: yet there is no μάγειρος nor hirer nor parasite in *Poen.*!) would be asking whether A. (? his hirer or hirer's slave) would tolerate a cold meal; A. would be flabbergasted by such a request (cold ὄψα were unpopular in Athens: see comm. on fr. 145(141K).11), and B. would interrupt, supporting his suggestion with an absurd appeal to Plato (? typical of mageiric arrogance). Kock already suggested the part-division before τἀγαθόν.

Other possibilities abound, but the two suggested have the advantage of accepting the transmitted text;[1] they require neither the postulate of a lacuna after ἐγώ (with Kaibel) nor the replacement of ἂν by κἂν (with Kassel–Austin: so first Schweighaeuser *ad loc.* and *Animadv.* 4.627, with orthographical adjustment by Meineke 3.453).

2 παραθῶσι: the standard term (going back in comedy at least to the time of Epicharmus, fr. 159.4 Kaibel) for 'set on the table/serve', with particular reference to the main course of a meal (meat, fish); cf. 129(124K).14–15, 178(172K).2, 5, 10, 177(173K).5, 216(213K).6, 260(258K).1, 263(261K).5; by contrast παραφέρω = 'I hand round/serve' with special reference to τραγήματα (Alexis 176(171K).1 and comm., cf. Neil on Ar. *Equ.* 1215, Hunter on Eubulus 13(14K).1, Dohm, *Mageiros* 24).

2–3 τἀγαθὸν Πλάτων ...: the speaker's argument is that (i) Plato says the Good is always good and the Pleasant always pleasant in all circumstances; hence (ii) good food must always be good in all its states – hot, cold or lukewarm. 'Plato's Good' is here a slogan whose popular application in the sense of 'that which is best and unchanging' gains its effect from the weakness of the logic that the reference is intended to bolster. It is notoriously difficult to pinpoint the origin of such slogans, but here the main stimulus may have been Plato's celebrated lecture 'On the Good', delivered probably towards the end of his life and chronicled by Aristotle's

---

[1] A's ἐάν (amended by Dindorf to the metrically necessary ἄν) hardly deserves the name of error. Confusion between the two was so common in papyri (e.g. *P.Bodmer* of Men. has four examples of the same error as the *Marcianus* here: *Dysk.* 176, 205 (see Handley's edition p. 64), *Sam.* 440, 471) and medieval MSS that ἐάν was frequently written in mistake for ἄν even in subordinate relative clauses (Cobet, *NL* 551, Mayser–Schmoll 1.1.128).

pupil Aristoxenus in his *Harmonica* 2.30–1 (cf. especially W. D. Ross, *Plato's Theory of Ideas* (Oxford 1951) 147ff., K. Gaiser, *Platons ungeschriebene Lehre* (Stuttgart 1963) 451ff. and *Phronesis* 25 (1980) 5ff., W. K. C. Guthrie, *A History of Greek Philosophy* 5 (Cambridge 1978) 424ff.). This lecture could have familiarised Athens with the expression itself, while certain passages in the published works such as *Symp.* 210e–211b (the vision in Diotima's narrative):[1]

τι ... καλόν, ... πρῶτον μὲν ἀεὶ ὂν καὶ οὔτε γιγνόμενον οὔτε ἀπολλύμενον, οὔτε αὐξανόμενον οὔτε φθίνον, ἔπειτα οὐ τῇ μὲν καλόν, τῇ δ᾿ αἰσχρόν, οὐδὲ τοτὲ μέν, τοτὲ δ᾿ οὔ, οὐδὲ πρὸς μὲν τὸ καλόν, πρὸς δὲ τὸ αἰσχρόν, οὐδ᾿ ἔνθα μὲν καλόν, ἔνθα δὲ αἰσχρόν, ὡς τισὶ μὲν ὂν καλόν, τισὶ δὲ αἰσχρον ... ἀλλ᾿ αὐτὸ καθ᾿ αὑτὸ μεθ᾿ αὑτοῦ μονοειδὲς ἀεὶ ὄν,

Resp. 5.478e–479a or *Phd.* 78d, would provide fuel to fan the flames of vulgarisation. In comedy the slogan is applied also by Amphis 6 and Philippides 6 to contexts mockingly irrelevant; Philemon 74(71K) wryly discusses philosophers' ineffectual attempts to identify the Good. Cf. also R. Helm, *Lucian und Menipp* (Leipzig and Berlin 1906) 377, R. Fenk, *Adversarii Platonis quomodo de indole ac moribus eius iudicaverint* (Diss. Jena 1913) 48, A. Weiher, *BBG* 65 (1929) 26f., G. J. de Vries, *Hermeneus* 27 (1955) 7f., Gil 337.

3 μανθάνεις: see on fr. 129(124K).15.

4 A's θ᾿ (the reports of Kock, Kaibel and other editors before Kassel–Austin here are inaccurate) is perfectly acceptable; the function is purely additive.

κἀκεῖ κἀνθάδε: the 'there' and 'here' could just possibly be two specific places defined in the lost context with reference to the dramatic scene, but far more probably ἐκεῖ = the underworld, ἐνθάδε = 'the world where we live', by the common idiom (LSJ s.vv.; S. *Ant.* 75f., Eur. *Hel.* 1422, Ar. *Ran.* 82, Pl. *Resp.* 1.330d contrast the two adverbs likewise euphemistically). The phrase thus becomes a vigorous endorsement of v. 3's ἀπανταχοῦ (Grotius, *Exc.* 581, 973: A wrongly divides with πλάτωνα πανταχοῦ).

Ἱππεύς

Schweighaeuser, *Animadv.* 7.312, Meineke 1.387, 393f., 3.421f., 511, *Anal. Crit.* 355, Th. Bergk, *Griechische Literaturgeschichte* 4 (Berlin 1887) 4.151 and n. 97. Ath. quotes two frs. certainly from Ἱππεύς (11.481f–482a =

---

[1] See my introduction to Alexis' Φαῖδρος and comm. on fr. 247(245K) for discussion of alleged references there to this same Diotima narrative.

COMMENTARY

100(95K), 11.471e = 101(96K)), and one which, according to the *Marcianus*, appears ἐν ἵππωι (13.610e = 99(94K)). Ἵππος is nowhere else attested as a comic title, and indeed known plays which take their titles from animals in the singular (e.g. Leucon's Ὄνος ἀσκηφόρος) belong to Old Comedy and even there are exceptional. In the earlier part of Alexis' career Ἵππος might conceivably have been chosen as the title of a burlesque on the myth of the Trojan horse, but fr. 99(94K) comes from a play written in the last decade of the 4th century (see below), when mythological travesty had gone out of fashion (Webster, *SLGC* 85, 115, Nesselrath, *MK* 189ff., 201ff.). In that case, could such a title refer to a small figurine of a horse, used perhaps as a recognition token in a typical New-Comedy plot? Just possibly, although ἱππίσκος rather than ἵππος is the word normally used in this sense (cf. the introduction to Ἀγωνίς). All things considered, it seems best to follow Schweighaeuser's suggestion that A's ἵππωι at 13.610e is corrupted from Ἱππεῖ and that frs. 99–101(94–6K) all derive from the same play.[1]

If this hypothesis be accepted, Ἱππεύς is one of the few plays of Alexis that can be precisely dated. Fr. 99(94K) refers to a law of 'Demetrius and the νομοθέται, ... expelling' from Athens those who instructed the young in 'τὰς τῶν λόγων ... δυνάμεις'. Directly after Demetrius Poliorcetes had overthrown the regime of his Phalerean namesake at Athens in 307, Sophocles of Sunium proposed a bill requiring all philosophers to be registered by the state. The bill was passed, and in high dudgeon the philosophers immediately withdrew from the city. The speaker of Alexis' fr., who applauds the measure in terms that imply it was still in force, must have pronounced these words at the Lenaea, Dionysia or some local performance early in 306, since before the next dramatic festivals in Athens came along, Sophocles' bill had been repealed and the situation reversed.[2]

A comedy written at such a time would most likely have conformed to the conventions of New-Comedy plots and characters. The three frs. extant and the title adequately fit such a hypothesis. In the fr. discussed above the speaker is most plausibly identified as either a father who believes that his son has been corrupted by the philosophers (so first

---

[1] Schweighaeuser alternatively suggested that ἵππωι might have been a corruption of Ἱππ<ίσκ>ῳ, the alternative title of Alexis' Ἀγωνίς. Although this conjecture is palaeographically as neat as the other, it is ruled out by the chronology, as Meineke (1.387) showed. Fr. 99(94K) dates to 306, and Alexis' Ἀγωνίς to the 340s or 330s.

[2] See Appendix II. The play was first correctly dated by Bergk, *loc. cit.*; cf. E. Bignone, *L'Aristotele perduto* 2 (Florence 1936) 243, Edmonds 2.405 note d.

Meineke 3.421) or the *paedagogus* of that son. Although one obvious parallel for such a situation would be Strepsiades' disillusion at the end of Ar. *Nub.* (cf. 1338ff.), in a play of New-Comedy date the reason for paternal or pedagogic rage would doubtless have been different: an amatory scrape perhaps, like those of Aeschinus and Ctesipho in Ter. *Ad.* (cf. Demea's words, 757ff.), or of Pistoclerus in Plaut. *Bacch.* (cf. Lydus' words, 163f.) – a scrape which expensive education at the hands of the day's leading teachers had not prevented. The other two frs. (100(95K), 101(96K)) may well derive from a single scene (cf. Meineke 3.422, Fraenkel, *MNC* 25).[1] In it a woman is conversing with a person who has knowledge of some curious cups which apparently touches a sad chord in the woman's memory. Unfortunately the part played in the plot by these cups and the woman is completely unknown, and speculation is hardly rewarding so long as the medley of possibilities is so varied. Were the cups recognition tokens? Could they have been stolen or cozened from the woman (cf. the use of cups for a trick in Alexis' Ἀγωνίς: so Meineke, *Anal. Crit.* 355)? And what role did the knight of the title play in the action? We do not know whether he was a *miles gloriosus* or a wealthy young Athenian on ephebe service.

99 (94K)

Meineke 3.421 (1), Kock 2.327, Edmonds 2.414, Kassel–Austin 2.73; cf. M. Isnardi Parenti, *Senocrate-Ermodoro* (Naples 1982) 71. This fr., whose importance for the dating of the play has been established above, can be interpreted correctly[2] only if the reader is alive to the fact that it represents the views of a definite character in a definite context. A speaker who attacks philosophy's corruption of the young (τοῖς νέοις v. 4) will most probably be a father or *paedagogus* (see above, introduction to Ἱππεύς)

---

[1] On the unattributed fr. 272(270K), which Meineke 3.511 (his fr. *fab. inc.* XII) tentatively places in the same scene of Ἱππεύς, see below, commentary *ad loc.*

[2] Wilamowitz, *Antigonos von Karystos* (Berlin 1881) 195f. strangely mis-interprets the fr.'s five verses. Punctuating v. 1 as a statement, he assumes that it is meant to contrast against the other four verses, the virtuous Academy being thus differentiated from a corrupt Peripatos. Such a reading requires one first to posit that a malicious or careless excerptor has torn v. 1 from a preceding context of words in praise of the Academy, and secondly to accept a grammatical implausibility – that Alexis would point the alleged contrast between Peripatos and Academy without the aid of particles like μέν and δέ. Wilamowitz's interpretation also fails to account for the careful wording of the periphrasis in vv. 3–4 of the fr.

COMMENTARY

who seems to have grounds for believing that his son or tutee's education in rhetoric at the Academy has proved morally disastrous. Whether or not in real life the Academy taught rhetoric (Ephippus 14 earlier made a similar allegation: cf. Webster, *SLGC* 51f., *Art and Literature in Fourth Century Athens* (London 1956) 47) is immaterial; its stage counterpart could do so, just as in Epicrates 10(11K) it could teach the classification of gourds. Alexis was as well aware as other comedians (cf. here Dover's edition of Ar. *Nub.* pp. xxxii ff.) that nice distinctions about philosophic curricula would not be drawn by an audience disposed to label all philosophers with imprecise tags and to ridicule them as fools, charlatans, or both. Alexis' speaker reacts against the Academy's teaching with amusing sophistry. He begins by raging at the alleged moral decline of the present-day Academy – a decline which Alexis, for all we know, may himself have fabricated for the purpose of his plot. In pained surprise the speaker asks 'Is *this* the Academy, *this* Xenocrates?' Xenocrates, the head of the Academy from 339 to 314, had now been dead for eight years, but in his lifetime he revealed such an impressive personality and enjoyed such a reputation for incorruptible integrity (Diog. Laert. 4.6ff.; cf. Dörrie in *RE* s.v. *Xenokrates* 4, especially 1513.53ff., with good bibliography) that the speaker can hardly believe how his Academy had sunk to such depravity in so short a time. An audience would remember the past reality and watch the present fiction without necessarily realising that Alexis was not fairly comparing like with like. The speaker then goes on to congratulate Demetrius and the lawgivers for improving the position by a measure which had got rid of 'those transmitting the power of argument' to the young. This cant phrase (see on vv. 3–4) has been carefully chosen. It enables the attack to be shifted from the Academy proper to all the contemporary schools of rhetoric, thus blurring any precise distinction between the Academy and its existing or potential rivals.

1 τοῦτ' ἔστιν Ἀκαδήμεια, τοῦτο Ξενοκράτης;: The line must be punctuated as a question, not as a statement, because the logic of the argument requires a contrast between the unimpeachable austerity of Xenocrates' reputation (see above) and the alleged present-day corruption of rhetorical teaching.

In predications of the type τοῦτ' ἔστι τὸ ἔργον, the demonstrative pronoun is most commonly attracted into the gender and number of the predicate, but it may sometimes remain neuter (singular or plural) when a special effect is intended: e.g. (i) in definitions (e.g. Lysias 3.28 τοῦτο ἔστιν ἡ πρόνοια, Pl. *Gorg.* 478c οὐ γὰρ τοῦτ' ἦν εὐδαιμονία, ὡς ἔοικε, κακοῦ ἀπαλλαγή), or (ii) where an emotion such as scorn, anger or amazement is involved (as here; also e.g. Men. *Epitr.* 319 οὐχ εὕρεσις τοῦτ' ἔστιν, ἀλλ' ἀφαίρεσις, perhaps *Mis.* 398, Heliodorus 4.7 τοῦτο σοφία, τοῦτο φιλία, συνεχῶς ἀναβοῶν); occasionally, however, it is hard to see any significant reason for the choice of the neuter (e.g. at Alexis 9.8). Cf. LSJ s.v. οὗτος B.II, Gildersleeve, *Syntax* 1.58f.

On the orthography of Ἀκαδήμεια, see comm. on 25.2.

2 πόλλ' ἀγαθὰ δοῖεν οἱ θεοί: the two conventional prayers for πόλλ' ἀγαθά are this (cf. Ar. *Thesm.* 351*, Antiphanes 161(163K).6–7*), in which the blessings are invoked on a third party, and the commoner wish in favour of the addressee or speaker πόλλ' ἀγαθά σοι (μοι) γένοιτο (Ar. *Eccl.* 1067, Men. *Epitr.* 358, *Sik.* 266*, Alciphron 4.3.2, etc.). Cf. Fraenkel on A. *Ag.* 350, Headlam–Knox on Herodas 7.25. In formulas such as πόλλ' ἀγαθά, the καί which normally links parts of πολύς to qualitative attributes like ἀγαθός is omitted rather more frequently than standard studies of Greek syntax (e.g. K.G. 2.252, Denniston, *GP* 290) admit (e.g., in addition to the unasterisked references above, also Eupolis 85(75K), Ar. *Eccl.* 435, Men. *Kol.* fr. 1.6, Lys. 12.64, *IG* i³.78.45 πόλλ' ἀγαθά; Eur. *Med.* 871, *Suppl.* 634 πολλὰ φίλα), although the variant form πολλὰ κἀγαθά does occur sporadically in the wish formulas discussed above (the three passages asterisked, Xen. *Anab.* 5.6.4).

2–3 Δημητρίῳ καὶ τοῖς νομοθέταις: the Demetrius is Poliorcetes (see introduction to Ἱππεύς and Appendix II), but who are the νομοθέται? Meineke (and Kock) assume that Alexis refers loosely to Sophocles of Sunium (promulgator of the bill against philosophers) and his supporters, but the reference may be more specific. One of the first acts of the restored democracy was the reinstitution of the board of νομοθέται, with the avowed aim of revising the Phalerean's legislation (W. S. Ferguson, *Hellenistic Athens* (London 1911) 103f., cf. S. Dow and A. H. Travis, *Hesperia* 12 (1943) 157; on revision of Athenian law in general, C. Hignett, *A History of the Athenian Constitution* (Oxford 1952) 299ff., D. M. Mac-Dowell, *JHS* 95 (1975) 62ff.), and it is possibly they whom Alexis has (at least partly) in mind. Sophocles may or may not have been a member of this board; his own law, however, would have needed its approval, and a reference to it would be perfectly in place here. At the same time it would be unreasonable to expect a comic poet to draw precise distinctions between this board of νομοθέται in its supervisory capacity and Sophocles as νομοθέτης in his legislative function.

3–4 τοὺς τὰς τῶν λόγων, ὥς φασι, δυνάμεις παραδιδόντας: the phrasing is significant (see the introduction to this fr.). In this deliberate periphrasis, by which Alexis avoids naming any particular school of rhetoric or philosophy, the words ὥς φασι (cf. comm. on 37(36K).4) suggest that he is adopting a cant phrase, coined probably by 4th-century rhetoricians and now generally familiar in Athens. Towards the beginning of his *Rhet.* Aristotle uses a very similar expression to describe his subject (τῇ τοιαύτῃ δυνάμει τῶν λόγων 1.1, 1355ᵇ3f., cf. 1.6, 1362ᵇ22), and this philosopher's habit of employing δύναμις as a rough synonym for τέχνη or

COMMENTARY

ἐπιστήμη is well known (H. Bonitz, *Index Aristotelicus* (Berlin 1870) s.v. 1 *fin.*; e.g. *Top.* 1.3, 101ᵇ6, *Metaph.* 5.12, 1019ᵃ17, *EN.* 1.2, 1094ᵇ2–3, *Rhet.* 1.2, 1355ᵇ26). Parallel expressions, however, occur too frequently in the works of the rival establishments (ἡ τῶν λ. δύναμις: e.g. Pl. *Tim.* 48d, Isoc. 5.21, 13.14, 15.5, 54, cf. 206; δύναμις developing in the direction of τέχνη: e.g. Pl. *Gorg.* 455d, 456a, Isoc. 3.9) for the phrase or usage to be a slogan peculiar to any one rhetorical school at the time of Alexis' play. Cf. also in comedy Plato 52(53K), Men. fr. 546.2.

The juxtaposition of three articles here (τοὺς τὰς τῶν) is an accidental consequence of the rules of Attic word order (article + noun in genitive splitting article + noun to which they relate, article + participle/infinitive splitting their article + noun object); cf. e.g. Isoc. 15.2 τὸν τὸ τῆς Ἀθηνᾶς ἕδος ἐργασάμενον, Dem. 3.11 τὴν τοῦ τὰ βέλτιστα λέγειν ὁδόν, and Rehdantz–Blass, *Index* p. 3.

5 Dobree's ἐρρίφασιν (*Adv.* 2.347) is a palmary emendation of A's ἔρρειν φασιν, which (*pace* Kassel–Austin) can be legitimately construed only as an indirect statement ('they say that those transmitting . . . are going to hell . . .': tolerable Greek but in this context rather feeble writing). Some defenders of A's text here have tried to strengthen the sense by assuming a syntactical anomaly: φημί + accusative and infinitive in the sense and construction of κελεύω, which would be unparalleled in Attic (cf. Herwerden, *NAC* 31; φημί in this sense takes dative and infinitive on the analogy of λέγω, φράζω, etc.: e.g. Lys. 16.13)). Corruption of ἐρρίφασιν to the *ductus* would have been easy; a scribe, still remembering ὡς φασι from the previous verse, would naturally but wrongly divide ἐρρίφασιν into ἐρρί φασιν (Herwerden, *Coll. Crit.* 123), and then misinterpret the accent on the first iota as a suprascript lineal nu (see above on frs. 28.3, 59(58K).2); familiarity with the curse ἔρρ' ἐς κόρακας might well have contributed to the error. It is no argument against Dobree's conjecture to claim that there are no parallels in Attic comedy for the phrase ἐς κόρακας ῥίπτειν. Although the imprecation ἐς κόρακας (on whose orthography see Wilamowitz, *Schiedsg.* 53, Jackson, *Marg. Scaen.* 82, W. J. W. Koster, *Autour d'un manuscrit d'Aristophane* (Groningen and Jakarta 1957) 240f. with some inaccurate reporting of MSS) frequently forms part of a limited number of standard phrases (after ἄπαγ', βάλλ', ἔρρ', οὐκ; in οὐκ ἐ. κ. ἀποφθερεῖ), its use is by no means confined to these, and there are several examples in Greek comedy of unparalleled phrases incorporating the imprecation (e.g. Ar. *Nub.* 123 ἐξελῶ σ' ἐ. κ. ἐκ τῆς οἰκίας, *Pax* 1221 ἀπόφερ' ἀπόφερ' ἐ. κ. ἀπὸ τῆς οἰκίας, fr. 601(584K) οὐκ εἶ λαβὼν θύραζε τὰ ψηφίσματα | καὶ τὴν ἀνάγκην ἐ. κ. ἐντευθενί;, Men. *Sam.* 352ff. ἐκ τῆς οἰκίας | ἐπὶ τὴν κεφαλὴν ἐ. κ. ὦσον τὴν καλὴν | Σαμίαν).

Sophocles' law did not in fact prescribe exile, but merely registration, for the philosophic schools (see introduction to this fr. and Appendix II).

Its enactment, however, angered the Peripatetics sufficiently for them to prefer voluntary exile to compliance with it, and Alexis, presumably writing directly after their departure, takes a comic poet's licence of blurring together prescribed and accessary effects.

100 (95K)

Meineke 3.422 (III), Kock 2.328, Edmonds 2.414, Kassel–Austin 2.73; cf. Nesselrath, *MK* 76f. Context and speakers of this and the next fr. are discussed in the introduction to Ἱππεύς. Fr. 100(95K) is cited by Ath. 11.481f–482a (only A: omitted in Epit.); Dobree's (*Adv.* 2.333) minor restorations of text (<ἆρ'> ἦν v. 2, ἐγὼ 3) and part-division (νὴ τὸν Δί', ἦν γάρ v. 3 assigned to speaker B) are generally superior (but see below on v. 3) to the alternatives suggested by Jacobs (*Spic.* 67, *Addit.* 260) and Bothe (*PCGF* 537); they provide livelier sense, a more natural flow of dialogue and smoother rhythm (Jacobs' placing of τά τε κυμβία at the end of a trochaic tetrameter gives a less acceptable split resolution: cf. P. Maas, *Greek Metre* (tr. H. Lloyd-Jones, Oxford 1966) 71 § 118, Handley's edition of Men. *Dysk.* pp. 60, 306, West, *Greek Metre* 92).

1–2 τά τε κυμβία ... πρόσωπ' ἔχοντα χρυσᾶ παρθένων: the citations collected by Ath. 11.481d–482e to illustrate the term κυμβίον (which incidentally omit Alexis 2.6, q.v.) describe it as a deep upright cup without base (so Dorotheus; a scholiast on Lucian *Lexiph.* 7–10 p. 197.30 Rabe calls it 'round but deep'), without handles (Dorotheus, Nicander of Thyateira *FGrH* 343 F 14 citing Theopompus com. 32(31K)), but with a brim curved like a boat (Didymus fr. 40 p. 75 M. Schmidt, who is copied by Macrobius 5.21.9, cf. Σ Lucian *Dial. Mort.* 22.2, p. 263.3f.). Even if these details are correct and complementary, they are not precise enough to allow confident identification with any known 4th-century vase shape.[1] But how many of those details are correct? If all κυμβία, for instance, lacked handles, there would be a real difficulty over the interpretation of Alexis' words here about κυμβία 'with golden faces of girls'. These golden faces can hardly have been painted flat as a surface decoration, since gold paint is not known to have been so used in pottery of the period; and they are unlikely to have been embossed inside the cups, since all existing embossed heads in that position (e.g. the famous Syracusan coin-type heads) are neither coloured nor gilded. Accordingly, only two interpretations of Alexis' words are feasible. Either the vases themselves were modelled in the shapes of girls' heads and gilded; or the heads were

---

[1] Cf. E. Pottier in Dar.–Sag. s.v. *Cymbé* 1698B ff.; Richter–Milne, *Shapes* perhaps wisely omit all consideration of the word and shape.

moulded in clay (or just possibly engraved in metal, if the vases were metal ones) on the handles of the cups, and then gilded. The former alternative is much less probable; such plastic cups would hardly fit the descriptions of κυμβία that Ath. and others cite, and Alexis' words imply rather that the heads were part of, and not the whole, design of the vases.[1] It may be justifiable to assume, therefore, that the heads were attached to the top or bottom of the vases' handles, in a way known to have been used about the time of Alexis' play (e.g. Berta Segall, *Katalog der Goldschmidarbeiten, Benaki Museum*, no. 38 tab. 5, lists and pictures a silver hydria of the beginning of the 3rd century with a girl's head engraved in full relief on the lower attachment of the handles; this head bears traces of gilding), and that the vases in question had a deep belly, being possibly a type of *kantharos* or *skyphos*. Yet with this assumption the testimony of Dorotheus and Nicander that κυμβία lacked handles must be rejected or at least qualified to the extent that the presence or absence of handles was not a diagnostic feature at the time of this play.[2]

2 ἦν...ἔχοντα: periphrastically for εἶχε, see comm. on fr. 2.9.

3 ὦ τάλαιν' ἐγὼ κακῶν: Dobree's correction (ἐγὼ for A's ἔγωγε), which turns this exclamation into an (? unconscious) echo of Eur. *Hel.* 139, is plausible but not certain; the alternative conjecture ἔγωγε <τῶν> | κακῶν (cf. Jacobs, *locc. citt.*), with its legitimate line-end division between article and attribute (cf. e.g. Alexis 20.4f., 24.2f. = 115(110K).21f., 257(255K).3f., Men. *Asp.* 55f., 144f., *Dysk.* 264f., 859f., *Pk.* 493f., my comm. on fr. 20.4) cannot be ruled out. This use of τάλαινα in self-apostrophe, which is characteristic of female speakers in comedy, seems always to contain an element of tragic parody (cf. C. Dedoussi on Men. *Sam.* '30' (her numbering) and *Hellenica* 18 (1964) 1ff., Barrett on Eur. *Hipp.* 366f., D. Bain, *Antichthon* 18 (1984) 35); the phrases of which the adjective forms part always preserve strict tragic rhythm and avoid specifically untragic vocabulary (e.g. τάλαιν' ἐγώ, ὦ τ. ἐγώ, ὦ τ. ἔγωγε, οἴμοι τάλαινα with exclamatory genitive).

---

[1] There is an additional argument against this interpretation of Alexis' words here: plastic vases in the shape of female heads had gone out of fashion in Athens by 306. On Attic figurine vases see especially M. Trumpf-Lyritzaki, *Griechische Figurenvasen* (Bonn 1969) and E. R. Williams, *Hesperia* 41 (1978) 356ff.

[2] The information about vases in this discussion and those of fr. 101(96K) owes a great deal to the generous help of Professor P. E. Corbett, whose expertise I hope I have not too grossly misrepresented.

101 (96K)

Meineke 3.421 (II), Kock 2.328, Edmonds 2.414, Kassel–Austin 2.74.

1–2 The fr.'s description of a Thericlean cup affords no valid clue to the identification of this puzzling type of pottery (see comm. on fr. 5.1). In the 4th century many different shapes and sizes of vase had a gilded wreath, generally of *appliqué* clay, as part of their decoration. A few examples are figured in *CVA Brussels* fasc. 3, III L and N, pl. 3; cf. H. B. Walters, *History of Ancient Pottery* 1 (London 1905) 410 (black glazed ware), 498 (Gnathia ware), F. Courby, *Les Vases grecs à reliefs* (Paris 1922) 182ff., 189ff., 348, 381, 405, 419f. (Hellenistic Egypt). The difficulty of ascertaining what Alexis had in mind here is increased by the textual problem in v. 2 (q.v.).

2 The *Marcianus* here (Ath. 11.471f) gives χρυσοῦν οὐ γὰρ ἐπίκτητόν τινα with no punctuation. ἐπίκτητον itself provides a (? tolerable) metrical anomaly (anapaest split after the first short, in the second half of the second metron after penthemimeral caesura; cf. *CQ* 7 (1957) 189, 196, and Handley's edition of Men. *Dysk.* pp. 63ff.), and sits implausibly in its context even when taken in its most appropriate sense ('imported', cf. Philostratus *Epist.* 8). In its place ἐπίτηκτον, independently advanced by Porson (*Misc.* 242) and Korais (in Schweighaeuser *ad loc.* and *Animadv.* 6.103), has been universally accepted, because it appears to restore the *mot juste*: 'with gilding etc. soldered/fused/put on by heat' (cf. LSJ s.v., with examples from inscriptions). Yet with the standard punctuation of this verse (colon after χρυσοῦν) this conjecture produces doubtful sense: how could a gold or gilded wreath be attached as an integral part to the Thericlean cup without having been subjected to some form of heating process? Unless Alexis intended here something very unusual (e.g. a separable gold or gilt wreath that might be used in ceremonies of 'crowning' the cup: see comm. on 124(119K).6), acceptance of ἐπίτηκτον must be accompanied by recognition that the adjective ought to complement, not contrast with, χρυσοῦν. F. H. Sandbach's solution to the problem, proposed by letter, is ingeniously simple: ... χρυσοῦν, οὐ γάρ; ἐπίτηκτόν τινα, with οὐ γάρ interpreted as a parenthetic interjection in the sense of 'is that not so?' (Denniston, *GP* 86; the usage is particularly characteristic of 4th-century Attic; in comedy e.g. Ar. *Eccl.* 765, Men. *Dysk.* 782, *Pk.* 524). This suggestion deserves tentative acceptance (other possibilities exist: οὐ γάρ might itself be a seat of corruption, supplanting an address to an interlocutor such as ὦ Σύρ'), but in the absence of further context it is impossible to decide (a) whether v. 2 was spoken all by one character or divided between two (ἐ. χ., οὐ γάρ; (B.) ἐπ. τ., or ἐ. χ. (B.) οὐ γάρ; ἐπ. τ.), and (b) whether Alexis' sentence continued after τινα or not.

267

COMMENTARY

Ἱππίσκος

See above, Ἀγωνὶς ἢ Ἱππίσκος (frs. 2–6).

Ἰσοστάσιον

Jacobs, *VS* 4.373 n.29, Meineke 3.422 n., Bechtel, *Frauennamen* 118f., Breitenbach 135f., Fraenkel, *MNC* 87f., 73ff., L. Radermacher, *SB Vienna* 202.1 (1924) 39, T. B. L. Webster, *CQ* 2 (1952) 21f., *SM* 165, 167 n. 2, *SLGC* 63, Edmonds 2.417 note b, W. G. Arnott, *G and R* 19 (1972) 78ff., Bain, *Actors* 215 n. 4. A noun ἰσοστάσιον is not elsewhere attested, but would probably need to be interpreted as an ellipsis of ἰσοστάσιον μύρον (literally 'perfume of equal weight/value'), which Hesych. s.v. defines as a name for oil of myrrh. In this play it is most likely to have been, as Jacobs first suggested, the name of a *hetaira*. The real-life *hetaira* Stagonion took her name from the field of cosmetic adornment (Ath. 13.586b), and names such as Μυρώ and Στακτή were not uncommon for women (Bechtel, cf. Breitenbach). The long, critical description of whorish stratagems in fr. 103(98K) gains dramatic relevance if the titular figure was herself a member of the profession.[1]

Fr. 103(98K) is of exceptional interest. The longest extant fr. that is positively assigned to Alexis, it consists of an uninterrupted harangue of twenty-six trochaic tetrameters (and possibly also one iambic trimeter: see comm. after v. 26) whose function and place in the unknown plot can only be surmised. One suggestion (Webster, *SM*, *SLGC*) is that the speaker was a *paedagogus* or father, warning an errant son about the dangers of falling into the clutches of *hetairai*. If that is correct (there is, however, at least one plausible alternative suggestion: see below), the young man is likely to have fallen in love already with one such girl, perhaps Isostasion herself, on the analogy of known intrigue plots in Greco-Roman comedy. The fr.'s form and content – that of an undramatic rhesis in trochaic tetrameters on a subject of general interest – has striking parallels in both Old and New Comedy (cf. Fraenkel 87f.). Aristophanes uses the same metre for the epirrhemata of his parabases, where subjects of topical concern (sometimes related, sometimes unrelated to the immediate plot) are often introduced. In Menander's time the Old-Comedy parabasis was defunct, but monologues in which current (not necessarily the poet's own) views on

---

[1] Edmonds (2.417 note b) puts forward an alternative suggestion that ἰσοστάσιον could also have been a slang term for a *hetaira* (someone 'equal to' a wife, as it were). The idea is ingenious, but fails for lack of evidence.

a variety of general issues are expressed may still be found, although now fully integrated into the plot and accommodated to the speaker's outlook. Knemon's speech of self-justification in the fourth act of *Dysk.* (? 708ff.) is the most memorable example, and its use of trochaic tetrameters tempts the question whether the form, content and metre of that speech owe anything to Old-Comedy traditions. If they do, as I incline to believe (cf. my paper cited above, following Fraenkel, cf. Handley's edition of Men. *Dysk.* pp. 252f.), the connecting link between Aristophanic choral epirrhemata and Knemon's monologue may have been topical passages in trochaic tetrameters like the present fr., Anaxilas 22 (also on *hetairai*) and Aristophon 5(4K) (a parasite on his ways). If Alexis 103(98K) was spoken by an individual character and integrated into the plot, the affinities with Knemon's speech would be close. Another possibility, however, cannot be discounted. In a play which may have been written as much as a quarter of a century before the *Dyskolos* (but see below), a passage like the present fr. might still have been delivered extra-dramatically, perhaps as an entr'acte, by the leader of the chorus. An arguably similar passage in Plaut. *Curc.* (462ff.: the famous guide to ancient Rome), written in the corresponding metre of trochaic septenarii, is interposed by the Plautine stage-manager as an unusual sort of link between two dramatic scenes (cf. A. Freté, *REL* 8 (1930) 53). If this replaced a comparable speech in the Greek original, as Fraenkel argued most cogently (*MNC* 98ff.; cf. also H. Bosscher, *De Plauti Curculione disputatio* (Diss. Leiden 1903) 102, G. Monaco's edition of the play (Palermo 1969) 193ff.; opposing but mutually incompatible views in O. Zwierlein, *Zur Kritik und Exegese des Plautus I: Poenulus und Curculio* (Stuttgart 1990) 253ff., and E. Lefèvre, *Plautus barbarus* (edited by him and others, Tübingen 1991) 79 and 100f.), the Plautine property-man may have replaced an Athenian coryphaeus in the original. In that event the source of the *Curculio* speech, together with Alexis 103(98K), would occupy a position logically (but not perhaps historically[1]) midway between the 5th-century epirrhemata and Knemon's great apology.

The other fr. of ᾽Ισοστάσιον (102(97K)) uses iambic trimeters to

---

[1] The Greek original of the *Curculio* can be neither identified nor dated, although it is most likely to have been a play of the New-Comedy period. See e.g. Wilamowitz, *Isyllos von Epidauros* (Berlin 1886) 39, G. W. Elderkin, *AJA* 38 (1934) 35f., Webster *SLGC* [1]196ff. = [2]217ff., P. Grimal in R. Chevallier (ed.), *Mélanges d'archéologie et d'histoire offerts à André Piganiol* 3 (Paris 1966) 1731ff., S. Settis, *PP* 23 (1968) 55ff., G. Monaco's edition of the play (Palermo 1969) 8ff. E. Lefèvre's theory (*op. cit.* 89ff.) that *Curc.* has no Greek original is ingeniously argued but ultimately unconvincing, cf. J. C. B. Lowe, *JRS* 83 (1993) 197.

describe the presence of several men, all bearing names or nicknames drawn from foodstuffs, at a drinking-bout. Whether the party was an off-stage adjunct to the plot (i.e. imagined to have occurred in the house of one of the characters), or an extra-dramatic allusion with or without reference to some recent notoriety, can no longer be established. In either event at least two of the people mentioned were well-known Athenians of the time. (1) Cobius (a real name) appears elsewhere as one of the lovers of Pythionice (Ath. 8.339a citing Antiphanes 27(26K).19ff., cf. 339e), a courtesan who left Athens in 330/29 (see comm. on fr. 143(139K)). Antiphanes calls Cobius ἀνδρῶν ἄριστον, which implies either noble Athenian lineage (in that case he could have been the grandson of Cobius of Salamis mentioned shortly after 403 by Archippus 27) or (by comic antiphrasis) very low birth. In Alexis' parallel list of names at fr. 173(168K) (where Κάραβος and 'Semidalis' also recur) his name appears under the form Κωβίων; if the text there (Ath. 6.242d) is correctly transmitted by the *Marcianus*, the spelling in -ων is probably to be taken as a nickname variant of a familiar kind (see comm. there). (2) Better known than Cobius is Callimedon, nicknamed ὁ Κάραβος (see the introduction to fr. 57(56K)), who was a member of the celebrated Athenian dining club of sixty (Ath. 6.260a–b, 14.614d–e citing Hegesander and Telephanes = Müller, *FHG* 4.413 fr. 3, 507 respectively; cf. A. D. Schaefer, *Demosthenes und seine Zeit* 3² (Leipzig 1887) 32 n. 1, A. Dieterich, *Pulcinella* (Leipzig 1897) 42 n. 4, Webster, *SLGC* 45f., A. Scobie, *Rh. Mus.* 122 (1979) 235f.). The story that Philip of Macedon paid a talent for a copy of the club's jokes implies that it won its reputation before Chaeronea; how long it may have survived after 338 we have no means of knowing. It would be wrong to assume, however, that because Philip enjoyed the club's wit in the late 340s, Alexis' Ἰσοστάσιον must accordingly be dated to that brief period (so Webster, *CQ* 2 (1952) 21f.). For one thing, the dining club could have continued to function at least until Callimedon left Athens in 318; for another, it is by no means certain that fr. 102(97K) contains a reference to the club. None of the other drinkers mentioned here is known to have belonged to it, and Alexis might have invented a meeting of socially disparate people with nothing in common but their (nick)names (see comm. on vv. 2–4) for purely comic reasons, as he could also have done in fr. 173(168K). There is thus no hard evidence for dating Ἰσοστάσιον between any closer confines than those of Callimedon's career, which extended in Athens from *c.* 345 to 318 (cf. Bain, *Actors* 215 n. 4). (3) On 'Semidalis' see comm. on 102(97K).3–4.

102 (97K)

Meineke 3.425 (II), Kock 2.328, Edmonds 2.416, Kassel–Austin 2.74; cf. Th. Bergk, *Commentationum de reliquiis comoediae Atticae antiquae libri duo*

(Leipzig 1838) 379f., W. G. Arnott, *LCM* 10 (1985) 98f. The value of this fr. for dating the play is discussed in the introduction to 'Ισοστάσιον. Interpretation is hampered by our ignorance of its context (see on vv. 2–4).

1 ἀπὸ συμβολῶν ἔπινον: see the introduction to fr. 15. This is the only reference known to me of a drinking bout (as opposed to a meal with drinks to follow) organised ἀπὸ συμβολῶν, but it would be unwise to draw any conclusions from that without more context.

1–2 ὀρχεῖσθαι μόνον βλέποντες, ἄλλο δ' οὐδέν: 'looking only to dance, and nothing else'. Cf. Ar. *Ach.* 376 οὐδὲν βλέπουσιν ἄλλο πλὴν ψηφηδακεῖν, *Vesp.* 847 τιμᾶν βλέπω, Men. *Epitr.* 398 ὁ προσελθὼν εὐθὺς ἁρπάζειν βλέπει. The construction here (with ὀρχεῖσθαι balanced by ἄλλο . . . οὐδέν as at Ar. *Ach.* 376) suggests that this use of the infinitive with βλέπω (possibly a colloquial idiom, confined as it is to comedy) is closely analogous to that of the internal accusative of nouns and adjectives with the same verb (κάρδαμον βλέπω, ὀξὺ βλέπω etc.; cf. K.G. 1.309 and comm. on Alexis 236(234K).6).

As Ath. 4.134a–d cites this and three other comic frs. (Alexis 224(222K), Antiphanes 111(113K), Eriphus 1) to illustrate the Athenian custom of dancing at symposia, it seems extraordinary that ὀρχεῖσθαι here should have been oppugned by Herwerden (*Mnemosyne* 3 (1875) 300, 21 (1893) 161) and Kock. This custom is abundantly attested in literature (in addition to the frs. already cited, e.g. Hdt. 6.129 (the story of Hippoclides), Ar. *Vesp.* 1476ff., Xen. *Hier.* 6.2, an anon. hexameter cited by Ath. 10.428a and perhaps inspiring Eriphus 1 (see A. Nauck, *MGR* 6 (1894) 98), Theophr. *Char.* 6 and 12; cf. Men. *Dysk.* 950ff., 957, Plaut. *MG* 668, *Stich.* 381f., 754ff.) and art (e.g. a plate by Psiax now in a private collection, G. M. A. Richter, *Attic Red-figured Vases* (New York 1946) 47 and fig. 36; an amphora by Euthymedes now in Munich, P. E. Arias, M. Hirmer, B. B. Shefton, *History of Greek Vase Painting* (London 1962) 327 and pl. 117). A refusal to dance on such occasions was considered a mark of αὐθαδία (Theophr. *Char.* 15), but the tactful guest would not take the floor until he was decently drunk (Theophr. *Char.* 12; cf. Cicero, *Pr. Mur.* 6.13 *nemo . . . fere saltat sobrius, nisi forte insanit*). Cf. Mau in *RE* s.v. *Comissatio* 617.42ff.

2–4 The text of the *Marcianus* here (the fr. is omitted by Epit.) poses three problems. Is its ὄψων (v.3) to be regarded as genitive plural of ὄψον (so Daléchamp, translating with *obsoniorum*) or as a proper name in the nominative (so Bergk and Meineke)? In v. 4 the reading καὶ κωβιὸς καὶ σεμίδαλις is unmetrical; should the second καί be deleted (so Dindorf; the scribal habit of adding καί gratuitously in lists is well exemplified by Fraenkel in his edition of A. *Ag.* 2.76 n.2), or should one rather posit a lacuna between it and σεμίδαλις? Is the fr. continuous speech by one

COMMENTARY

speaker, or part of a dialogue? The lack of further context prevents certain answers to these questions, and two alternative texts can be constituted:
(a) Bergk and editors of Ath. and the comic frs. subsequently:

> (A.) ... ὄψων ὀνόματα
> καὶ σιτίων ἔχοντες, Ὄψων, Κάραβος
> καὶ Κωβιός, Σεμίδαλις ...

(b) Arnott, *LCM* 10 (1985) 98f.:

> (A.) ... ὄψων ὀνόματα
> καὶ σιτίων ἔχοντες. (B.) ὄψων; (A.) Κάραβος
> καὶ Κωβιός. (B.) καὶ <σιτίων>; (A.) Σεμίδαλις ...

Bergk's text is less lively, and creates two difficulties. It requires the acceptance of the sequence A, B καί C, D in a list of four names, unusual but not perhaps impossible if Κάραβος and Κωβιός were conceived as a linked pair (Denniston, *GP* 289f.). Secondly, it postulates the existence of an otherwise unknown figure called Ὄψων. The name's formation is acceptable (the -ων suffix, in sobriquets at least, tends to indicate 'qualities that meet with disapproval', Buck–Petersen, *Reverse Index* 247), but it may be significant that the name Ὄψων does not recur in the list at Alexis 173(168K), while the other three names in 102(97K) do. Accordingly, with some hesitation (but cf. the passages collected by Diggle, *Studies* 50ff.), I opt for text (b).

3–4 Κάραβος and Κωβιός are names derived from ὄψα (cf. comm. on fr. 47(46K).6), Σεμίδαλις a name drawn from a σιτίον. On Κάραβος, the nickname of the politician Callimedon, see the introductions to fr. 57(56K) and Ἰσοστάσιον; on Cobius the man, introduction to Ἰσοστάσιον. Σεμίδαλις appears as a nickname only here and in fr. 173(168K) (on Strattis 2 see Meineke 2.764). The double mention in different plays implies that 'Semidalis' was a real person, who took his nickname ('his', not 'her': other males with nicknames drawn from feminine nouns include Philoxenus ἡ Πτερνοκοπίς Ath. 6.242b–c, Axionicus 6.2, and Glaucetes ἡ Ψῆττα Plato com. 114(106K).2) from one of the finest wheaten flours of antiquity, ground apparently from a variety of *Triticum durum* (N. Jasny, *The Wheats of Classical Antiquity* (Baltimore 1944) 18f., 57ff., 89ff.). Cf. also Blümner, *Technologie* 53, 75ff., Björck, *Alpha Impurum* 64.

At 3.127c Ath. notes that in his Ἰσοστάσιον Alexis σεμιδάλεως μέμνηται. In all likelihood this is a loose reference to the mention of the name Σεμίδαλις in this verse of 102(97K), although the possibility cannot be excluded that (e.g.) the list of names here was followed in the play by a comment involving the word σεμίδαλις as a common noun.

ΙΣΟΣΤΑΣΙΟΝ

103 (98K)

Meineke 3.422 (1), Kock 2.329, Edmonds 2.416, Kassel–Austin 2.75; among the many textual and interpretative discussions devoted to all or part of this fr., see especially Grotius, *Exc.* 57off., 972, Dobree, *Adv.* 2.343, Meineke, *Cur. Crit.* 63, Jacobs, *VS.* 4.326ff. and 371ff., R. Argenio, *Vichiana* 5 (1968) 131ff.; cf. also Legrand, *NGC* 79ff., K. Jax, *Die weibliche Schönheit in der griechischen Dichtung* (Innsbruck 1933), H. Herter, *JAC* 3 (1960) 70ff., P. Domenicucci, *A and R* 26 (1981) 175ff. The theme of this long rhesis is the cunning of *hetairai*, whose greed leads them to adopt a series of subterfuges in order to reach accepted standards of beauty. Long speeches of a similar sort, each with its own viewpoint or particular conceit, seem to have been conventional features of those comedies where the courtesan plays a significant role: e.g. the closely parallel Anaxilas 22 (from another play named after a *hetaira*, Νεοττίς: see Meineke 1.409), in which the speaker develops the idea that *hetairai* resemble fabulous monsters; also Plaut. *Poen.* 210ff., where the courtesan herself embellishes the conceit that a woman (sc. of her profession) is like a ship, requiring a large expenditure of money and labour to keep her in trim (the core idea here doubtless derives from Greek comedy, but possibly not Plautus' main source, Alexis' Καρχηδόνιος, cf. Fraenkel, *EP* 161ff., 260ff., G. Maurach's edition of Plaut. *Poen.* ([1] Heidelberg 1975) pp. 53, 192f., 229ff.; dissentient voices include P. W. Harsh, *Studies in Dramatic "Preparation" in Roman Comedy* (Chicago 1935) 50 n. 25 and 71f., A. Gratwick, *Cambridge History of Classical Literature* 2 (1982) 110 and n. 2, and J. C. B. Lowe, *BICS* 35 (1988) 101ff.), *Bacch.* 368ff., *Truc.* 22ff.

The various motifs that Alexis introduces in this fr. come largely from a common stock: (a) the calculated greed of *hetairai* (vv. 1–3), cf. Men. fr. 185, Machon 333ff., Lucian *Dial. Meretr.* 7, 15, Alciphron 4.9, 15, Plaut. *Asin.* 521ff., *Truc.* 22ff., 533ff., 901ff., Legrand 79ff., Herter 80ff.; (b) the old *hetaira* trains her young successors (3–6), cf. Lucian *Dial. Meretr.* 3, 6, 7, Ter. *Eun.* 116ff., H. Oeri, *Der Typ der komischen Alten in der griechischen Komödie* (Basle 1948) 61ff., Herter 95; (c) the use of cosmetics, amongst other things, to remedy natural deficiencies (7–18), cf. Ar. *Eccl.* 878ff., [Lucian] *Am.* 39ff., Philostr. *Epist.* 22, Plaut. *Poen.* 210ff., *Truc.* 272ff., and contrast the antithetical arguments of Ar. *Eccl.* 900ff., Eubulus 97(98K) with Hunter *ad loc.*, Philostr. *Epist.* 27, Plaut. *Most.* 272ff., Herter 91ff. Even so, Alexis selects and presents his examples in fr. 103(98K) with an observant and lively immediacy which suggests that

273

he was holding up his mirror as much to human nature itself as to literary traditions.[1]

The function of the speech and its use of troch. tetr. have already been discussed (introduction to 'Ισοστάσιον); metrically, however, its combination of strictness with regard to caesurae (median diaeresis in all 26 troch. tetr.) and freedom in its admission of resolution (15 examples, three in v. 9) is a notable feature, putting Alexis here closer to Menander in his practice than to Old Comedy (cf. Gil 334f., West, *Greek Metre* 92).

The fr. is unusual in having two citing sources for most of its length: Ath. 13.568a–d (complete in the *Marcianus*, but only vv. 2 ῥάπτουσι–3 ἐπιβουλάς, 7–12 ἰδόντας, 16–26 in Epit.; Eustath. 1522.10 derives his quotation of parts of vv. 7–8 from Ath.), and Clem. Alex. *Paed.* 3.2.8. Ath. appears to be the more accurate source; Clem. omits portions of the text (2 ῥάπτουσι–6, 23–4 κρανία, 27), and the *codex Parisinus* of *Paed.* (the archetype of the other extant MSS containing the work: cf. O. Stählin's edition (² Leipzig 1936, ³ Berlin 1972) xvi ff.) is bedevilled by a series of corruptions that might be blamed with equal plausibility on the carelessness of excerptor or copyist: explanatory addition (v.2), substitution of synonyms (ἐς 1, βλαύτησιν *p.c.* 7, ταῦτα 14), omission of single words (τε 9, ὀρθὸν 25), and other instances of negligence (ἐνεγκάττεται (ατ erased) 8, καταβάλλουσα 9, συμβέβηκεν 17, πετεύρων δ' 18, probably δεικνύει 19, ἐὰν 22). This plethora of errors, however, ought not to blind us to the value of having a second witness. In v. 14 the *Parisinus*, though itself corrupt, sheds light where the *Marcianus* provides total obscurity; in v. 12 it supplies the word that the *Marcianus* has left out; and there are four other places where P is right and A is wrong (πρῶτα 1, θεωρῶσιν 21, διατελεῖ 22, ἔχουσα 25). Clearly the texts of Ath. and Clem. here are uncontaminated by and unrelated in any other way to each other.

1 τὸ συλᾶν τοὺς πέλας: this idea of a *hetaira*'s primary function may be a commonplace (see above), but its expression is imaginatively varied by the comic poets. Thus the *hetaira* is an assassin, a Charybdis (Anaxilas

---

[1] P. Domenicucci, *A and R* 26 (1981) 175ff. suggests that this fr. was the major Greek source for Lucretius in his catalogue of women at 4.1160–70. That there are similarities between the two passages is indisputable: *nigra* 4.1160 ∼ 103(98K).17, *parua* 1162 ∼ v. 7, *magna atque immanis* 1163 ∼ v. 8, *prae macie* 1167 ∼ v. 18, *tumida et mammosa* 1168 ∼ v. 12), but the looseness of at least one of the parallels (1167), the divergences in other parts of the two lists and in their general arrangement, the fact that many of the motifs in both passages derived from popular overused stock, and finally a clear disparity in purpose between Alexis and Lucretius make a direct dependence of the latter upon the former unlikely.

ΙΣΟΣΤΑΣΙΟΝ

22.16, 18f.), a bloodsucker (Plaut. *Bacch.* 372), an expert angler (*Truc.* 35ff.).

2 γίγνεται: see comm. on fr. 37(36K).7.

2–3 ῥάπτουσι δὲ πᾶσιν ἐπιβουλάς: the metaphor goes back to Homer *Il.* 18.367, *Od.* 16.379, 421f. Cf. Festus 406.25 Lindsay = 310.27 Müller <*sutelae dolosae*> *astutiae, a simili<tudine suentium di>ctae sunt*, H. Fränkel, *Glotta* 14 (1925) 3f., Fraenkel on A. *Ag.* 1603.

3 εὐπορήσωσιν: i.e. the concentration on profits leads to the accumulation of capital, which is then ploughed back into the business by acquisition of new girls as trainees; cf. Wehrli, *Motivstudien* 26. Kock's conjecture ἐκκορηθῶσιν (= *scortando exhaustae erunt*) is difficult to justify in terms of palaeography or relevance; it is the *hetaira*'s success, not her retirement after an exhausting career (contrast Plaut. *Cist.* 40f.), that causes her to take in apprentices.

4 ἀνέλαβον: 'they take into their houses' (gnomic aorist, with primary sequence: see comm. on fr. 153(149K).9), sc. as boarders. The word is regularly used of installing in one's home a mistress (Machon 458, Ath. 13.586f, 590c, 592d, in the last passage citing Hermippus of Smyrna, *FHG* 3.49 fr. 55) or catamite (Aeschines. 1.52–8 *passim*, Ath. 13.593a), and may possibly carry unsavoury overtones from its use in such contexts.

καινάς: Musurus' correction of A's κενάς, where the ε is dotted by a scribe to signify an error but no amendment has been made. Confusion between the two words, which were pronounced alike from the 2nd century onwards, is notoriously common (e.g. Eur. *Ion* 641, Thuc. 3.30.3, Cobet, *NL* 330, cf. Mayser–Schmoll 1.1.83ff., Threatte 1.294ff.).

πρωτοπείρους τῆς τέχνης: 'novitiates in the trade', cf. Polyb. 1.61.4 τὰ δ' ἐπιβατικὰ ... πρωτόπειρα πάσης κακοπαθείας καὶ παντὸς δεινοῦ, anon. in *Suda* s.v. πρωτόπειρος· ... πρ. τῶν κατὰ πόλεμον ἔργων, Theopompus com. fr. 95(94K).

5 ταύτας: the demonstrative carries an appropriate degree of emphasis; Hirschig's -ν αὐτάς (*Annot.* 12) and Kock's τ' αὐτάς are unnecessary changes.

7–13, 16–20 The use of parataxis (τυγχάνει μικρά τις οὖσα· φέλλος ἐν ταῖς βαυκίσιν ἐγκεκάττυται, etc.), where the dullness of logic would prescribe a general conditional clause (ἐὰν τυγχάνη ... ἐγκαττύεται), is particularly common in comedy: e.g. Ar. *Eccl.* 179, Anaxandrides 35(34K).5ff., Anaxippus 1.31ff., Timocles 6.13ff., Men. *Dysk.* 58ff., 64ff., Machon 2.7f. Kassel–Austin and Kock = 473f. Gow, Plaut. *MG* 663f., Ter. *Ad.* 117ff. As Handley notes (on Men. *Dysk.* 57ff.), punctuation in these sentences is problematical: should the protatic clauses be interpreted as statements or questions? Cf. also R. Horton-Smith, *The Theory of Conditional Sentences in Greek and Latin* (London 1894) 113ff., K.G. 2.233f.

7 βαυκίσιν: expensive yellow shoes (Pollux 7.94), apparently of Ionian

275

COMMENTARY

origin (anon. commentator on Arist. *EN.* 4.13, 20.200.10 Heylbut, citing Ar. fr. 355(342K), and luxurious also, if its root βαυκός = τρυφερός (*Et. Mag.* s.v., cf. on Alexis 224(222K).9). They were worn by women (Herodas 7.58 and Headlam *ad loc.*, anon. commentator on Arist. above). Cf. Mau, *RE* s.v. βαυκίδες 153.27ff., A. A. Bryant, *HSCP* 10 (1899) 89. The practice of thickening a shoe's foundations in order to appear taller, as well as the use of ψιμύθιον to lighten a dark complexion (v.17) and of other cosmetics to add colour to a pale skin (v.18), was not confined to *hetairai*; the Athenian Ischomachus once found his wife ἐντετριμμένην πολλῷ μὲν ψιμυθίῳ, ὅπως λευκοτέρα ἔτι δοκοίη εἶναι ἢ ἦν, πολλῇ δ᾿ ἐγχούσῃ, ὅπως ἐρυθροτέρα φαίνοιτο τῆς ἀληθείας, ὑποδήματα δ᾿ ἔχουσαν ὑψηλά, ὅπως μείζων δοκοίη εἶναι ἢ ἐπεφύκει (Xen. *Oec.* 10.2). Tallness was considered a necessary part of female beauty (cf. Jax 68f., G. Giangrande, *CQ* 13 (1963) 73 n. 1), but vv. 8–10 imply that even so there were limits to what was acceptable.

8 ἐγκεκάττυται: i.e. the cork is stitched inside the shoe to form a hidden sole (κάττυμα); cf. Neil on Ar. *Equ.* 314, Bryant 96. The use here of the perfect tense, which gives the impression that a consequential action has already been completed (K.G. 1.150), side by side with presents and gnomic aorists, is a feature of such paratactical schemata as this (cf. Timocles 6.13ff., Anaxandrides 35(34K).5ff.), and contributes to the lively effect.

διάβαθρον: a type of sandal associated mainly with women (Hesych. s.v.; cf. Herodas 7.61), but worn also by effeminate men (a parasite in Alciphron 3.10.3, possibly Bacchus in Naevius fr. trag. inc. IV Ribbeck[3], Klotz); Pollux 7.90 is thus to some extent justified in saying that these sandals were common to both sexes. Cf. E. Saglio in Dar.–Sag. s.v *Diabathrum* 119B, Mau in *RE* s.v. Διάβαθρον 301.54ff.

φορεῖ: the normal verb for what 'one has constantly about one (clothes, bodily and mental features and qualities)', Barrett on Eur. *Hipp.* 316. Cf. v. 21.

10 τοῦτο τοῦ μήκους ἀφεῖλεν: 'this makes a reduction in (literally 'from') the height'. For this intransitive use of the verb with a genitive of separation, cf. Solon 5.2 West τιμῆς οὔτ᾿ ἀφελὼν οὔτ᾿ ἐπορεξάμενος, Xen. *Vect.* 4.4 οὐδεὶς τοῦ πλήθους ἀφαιρεῖ, Dem. 20.66 ἥρμοττεν ... τῶν ἀτυχημάτων ἀφαιρεῖν; A. Wifstrand, *Eikota* 1.7f. (= *Kunglinga Humanistika Vetenskapssamfundet, Arsberättelse* (Lund 1930/1) 135f.

11 ὑπενέδυσ᾿ ἐρραμμένα αὐτὴν is the joint reading of Ath. (Epit.: -μενα A without accent) and Clem. If this is what Alexis wrote, it can mean only 'she (sc. the older *hetaira*) dresses her (the novitiate with flat buttocks) underneath with sewn-on (sc. artificial) haunches' (so Schweighaeuser, *Animadv.* 7.63); the first aorist form (-)ενέδυσα is always used of one person dressing another (K.G. 1.326, LSJ s.v. ἐνδύω II; e.g. Ar. *Lys.* 1021, *Thesm.* 1044). There may be a slight awkwardness in the unannounced change of

276

subject from young to old *hetaira* again, but it would cause no difficulty to a listener who still had vv. 1–6 fresh in his mind, and the switch is no greater than that from singular *hetaira* to plural in vv. 12–13. To avoid this change of subject several scholars (first Herwerden, *Mnemosyne* 14 (1886) 185, and J. B. Mayor in a letter to O. Stählin, see the latter's edition of Clem. *Protr.* and *Paed.* p. lxxxii) have suggested that αὐτὴν may be a corruption for the reflexive αὑτὴν. The alteration is minimal, and the corruption common, but ὑπενέδυσ᾽ αὑτήν would be a strangely unidiomatic alternative for the normal Attic ὑπενέδυ. LSJ (s.v. ῥάπτω) wrongly take ἐρραμμέν᾽ here as a participial noun ('stitched work, a cushion or pad'); it is clearly adjectival, with ἰσχία to be supplied from v. 10.

11–12 τὴν εὐπυγίαν ἀναβοᾶν need mean no more here than 'shout aloud that the girl has fine buttocks'; on this use of the accusative with βοᾶν and some of its compounds see Fraenkel on A. *Ag.* 48ff., Gow on Machon 205, and my note on Alexis 15.7. The ancient criteria of εὐπυγία are clearly stated in Alciphron 4.14.4–6 and Rufinus 11 Page = *Anth. Pal.* 5.35, cf. Ath. 12.554c–e, Lloyd-Jones, *Females of the Species: Semonides on Women* (London 1975) 83.

12 εἰσιδόντας: F. Sylburg's correction (edition of Clem., Heidelberg 1592) neatly incorporates elements of both the Clem. and Ath. readings, and alone makes credible the two corruptions.

12–15 The sentence from κοιλίαν to (?) ἀπήγαγον contains several difficulties of text and interpretation, but a reasonable (if not always certain) solution to all the problems can be achieved without recourse to the drastic rewritings proposed by (e.g.) Th. Bergk, *Zeitsch. f. d. Alterthumsw.* 7 (1840) 1079 or Emperius, *Rh. Mus.* 1 (1842) 460f. The problems are best tackled in the order that they arise.

(1) τιτθί᾽ (v.13) lies behind the *Parisinus* of Clem., as Jacobs first saw (*Addit.* 301), and στηθί᾽ behind the *Marcianus* of Ath., as Dindorf noted. Choice between synonyms is not always easy, but here (*pace* Kassel–Austin) τιτθί᾽ is to be preferred. In Attic Greek τιτθός and its congeners denote the female breast (LSJ s.v., Pollux 2.163, cf. Ar. *Thesm.* 640, Antiphanes 105(106K).4, Men. *Sam.* 266, 536, 540), while στῆθος and its congeners = 'breast' generally, with no sexual distinction. Since in *Koine* and Byzantine Greek στῆθος became very much the dominant form, it seems clear that the *Marcianus* reading represents an assimilation to current usage on the part of Ath. or a later copyist.

(2) αὐταῖσι (13) refers to the *hetairai* themselves, not to their elderly instructors, as E. Harrison (*CR* 52 (1938) 197) supposes; from v. 12 on the differentiation between superannuated and young *hetairai* becomes irrelevant to the argument, and so is ignored.

(3) οἱ κωμικοί (13) are comic actors, as Jacobs (*VS.* 374) first explained, and the reference here is evidently to the false bosoms (προστερνίδια,

Lucian *Salt.* 27) worn by male actors when playing female roles. How far such a reference breaks the realistic illusion cannot now be estimated in our ignorance of the scenic context; cf. M. Treu, *Philologus* 108 (1958) 230ff., Bain, *Actors* 208ff. (215f. on this fr.).

(4) ὀρθὰ προσθεῖσαι τοιαῦτα (14): 'having put attachments *just like this* on straight (i.e. not askew)'. The expression is unexceptionable. τοιαῦτα was attacked by Kock (who proposed τε ταῦτα, after the reading of the *Parisinus*) and Jacobs (*Addit.* 301, ξυλάρια!), neither of whom realised the comic appropriateness of τοιαῦτα. A competent actor (even one playing a male role) could raise a laugh as he said this word, by drawing with his hands the shape of a large female bosom.

Up to this point the text can be corrected and interpreted with some confidence. The eleven words following τοιαῦτα, however, are much more puzzling; even so, it is perhaps still possible to restore what Alexis originally wrote and to interpret satisfactorily what he had in mind.

(5) The *Marcianus*' γ'οὖν αὐτῶν and the *Parisinus*' ου τον τυνδυτον are likely to be corruptions of τοὐνδυτόν,[1] as Sylburg[2] (1592 edition of Clem. Alex., cf. his *Annotationes* p. 363) first saw. τοὐνδυτόν[3] τῆς κοιλίας is presumably that portion of the *hetaira*'s πέπλος which covered her stomach, and we must assume that this dress was imagined by Alexis to be worn without a waist-belt, so that it hung freely over the false breasts and dropped clear from there to the ground (so Edmonds in his translation and note e, p. 417, cf. Argenio 131ff.). With this interpretation full justice can be given to every word in the Greek text; the fall of the dress over the bosom would bring it 'away (from the stomach) in front' (εἰς τὸ πρόσθ'

---

[1] Two other conjectures here deserve honourable mention, although palaeographically they are hard to justify: Grotius' τοὐξέχον (*Exc.* 571: before Blaydes, *Adv.* 2.157) and Kaibel's τοὐκλυτόν. Both ideas require the object of ἀπήγαγον to be the slack flesh of the paunch, but how would the flabbiness be concealed by bringing it 'away to the front' (εἰς τὸ πρόσθ' ἀπ-)? Kaibel realised that his conjecture necessitated three further alterations (in themselves highly improbable: κοντοῖσιν εἰς τοὔπισθε τοῖσδ' ἀνήγαγον) to the transmitted text.

[2] Or rather Sylburg corrected (so far as the accent was concerned) by Dindorf. In both MSS the error doubtless originated from a failure to understand the crasis of τὸ ἐνδυτόν to τοὐν-. In the *Marcianus* this was associated, as so often in this MS, with a misreading of uncial characters (Τ/Γ, Δ/Λ); the *Parisinus* corruption probably involves the
incorporation of interlinear readings (τυνδυτον with ου above) into its text.

[3] Oxytone according to Arcadius 123.26 Barker = 142.19 M. Schmidt, but Lobeck, *Paralipomena* 491 argues for proparoxytone.

278

ἀπ-), and so, by hanging loose, conceal the fleshiness of the paunch; and the false breasts could thereby be described as operating 'like poles' because the effect of the dress dropping vertically from the bosom would resemble that of a piece of material (e.g. in a tent) being held flat and upright by means of poles.

Dr Edna Jenkinson has drawn my attention to a curious modern parallel to this stratagem of artificially amplifying the bust as a counter to corpulence below. The Baroness von Trapp, whose life-story was popularised in the musical and film *The Sound of Music*, after her marriage toured with the choir formed by her stepchildren and her own increasing family. During her pregnancies she is said to have continued on stage up to the final month on each occasion, and to have worn large 'falsies' because she believed that nobody would suspect her condition if her bosom protruded well beyond her abdomen when seen in profile.[1]

13 τούτων ὧν: sc. false breasts 'belonging to the class of those which . . .'; τούτων is a partitive genitive (K.G. 1.337f.) and ὧν attracted into the case of its antecedent (K.G. 2.406ff.).

15 κοντοῖσι: κοντός is always a long straight wooden pole, used (e.g.) on board ship to avoid contact with another ship or land (Hom. *Od.* 9.487, Eur. *Alc.* 254, Thuc. 2.84; cf. Epicrates 9(10K).4, where the obscene sense of an erect penis is one of a series of nautical/sexual puns *à double entente*), on land to poke the muddy bottom of a lake or stream (Hdt. 2.136, 4.195), to fend off wild cattle (*P.Cair.Zen.* 59362ʳ.34, a letter of 242), to wound an opponent (sharpened at one end presumably, or with a spear head affixed, Lucian *Tox.* 55), or as a crutch to help a disabled person walk (Galen *UP* 3.5, p. 137.25 Helmreich).

16–18 On the use of these various cosmetics by *hetairai* and other women, see my introduction to this fr. and on v. 7; in addition to the works cited there, V. Chapot in Dar.–Sag. s.v. *Unguentum* 593B, E. B. Abrahams, *Greek Dress* (London 1908), 122f., H. Blümner, *Die römischen Privatalter-tümer*[3] (Munich 1911) 437.

Indirectly at least v. 16 appears to reflect contemporary Athenian prejudices. Red hair was regularly assumed to be a sign of servile and indeed barbarian origins (especially Thracian: Xenophanes fr. 14.2 Diehl, cf. Ar. *Ran.* 730 and Σ *ad loc.*; V. Ehrenberg, *The People of Aristophanes*[2] (Oxford 1951) 172f.), sometimes also of bad character (Adamantius, *Physiogn.* p. 394 Förster, cf. L. Radermacher, *Philologus*, 57 (1898) 224f. and on Ar. *Ran.* 730). In such circumstances a young *hetaira* who wanted to give an impression of impeccable Greek origins and honourable behaviour might well paint red eyebrows with soot or lamp-black (ἄσβολος, feminine

---

[1] I no longer subscribe to the views expressed in *LCM* 10 (1985) 99ff.

COMMENTARY

in Attic, but said to have been used as a masc. by Hipponax fr. 138 West; the by-form ἀσβόλη occurs in Ionic and *Koine* Greek, cf. Phryn. *Praep. Soph.* 28.1 de Borries). Lamp-black is employed to darken eyebrows also in Juvenal 2.93 (men dressing up as women, cf. E. Courtney's commentary (London 1980) *ad loc.*); cf. Clem. Alex. *Paed.* 3.2.7.3, Pollux 5.102, P. Wilpert and S. Zenker, *RAC* s.v. *Auge* 957ff.

17–18 Context (especially the contrast of λευκόχρως) shows that μέλαιναν here refers to complexion, as commonly elsewhere (e.g. Diphilus 91.3, Asclepiades 5.3 and Philodemus 8.1 Gow–Page = *Anth. Pal.* 5.210 and 121, almost certainly Alexis 170(165K), q.v., all female; Dem. 21.71, Pl. *Resp.* 5.474e, male). In a girl swarthiness was apparently often regarded with disfavour (cf. Asclepiades *loc. cit.*, Theoc. 10.26f. and Gow *ad loc.*).

17 κατέπλασε ψιμυθίῳ: so correctly Ath. (the *Marcianus* adds a parago-gic nu to the verb, unnecessarily: the lengthening by position of an open vowel at the end of a word is permitted when that word is polysyllabic and penultimate in its verse: I. Hilberg, *Das Princip der Silbenwägung* (Vienna 1879) 218; cf. here also v. 24, κρανίᾱ ξυλήφιον). καταπλάσσω ψιμυθίῳ is the standard phrase for the operation (e.g. Ar. *Eccl* 878 and R. G. Ussher *ad loc.*, Alciphron 4.12.2, Lucian in *Anth. Pal.* 11.408.3; cf. Eubulus 97(98K).1, περιπελασμέναι ψιμυθίοις and Hunter *ad loc.*). ψιμύθιον is white lead, obtained by placing a piece of lead over a bowl of vinegar, scraping off the white rust that forms, and grinding it in a mortar (Theophr. *Lap.* 56, Dioscorides 5.88, Aetius 2.82). It was the universal pigment for lightening a dark complexion (in addition to the passages just cited cf. also Xen. *Oec.* 10.2 quoted above on v. 7, Lysias 1.14, Ar. *Eccl.* 929, 1072, *Plut.* 1064, fr. 332(320K).3, Macedonius in *Anth. Pal.* 11.374, Pollux 5.102, Plaut. *Most.* 258ff.). See especially E. C. Caley and J. F. C. Richards, *Theophrastus on Stones* (Columbus, Oh. 1956) 187ff.

18 λευκόχρως: in comedy also at Eubulus 34(35K).2 (an eel, in a 'dithyrambic passage': cf. Hunter *ad loc.*, Nesselrath, *MK* 253 and n. 31), Men. *Sik.* 200 (a man: cf. Sandbach *ad loc.*). In a young woman a pale complexion was usually the desideratum (Himerius *Or.* 9.19 Colonna; K. Jax, *Die weibliche Schönheit in der griechischen Dichtung* (Innsbruck 1933) 82f., 186ff., P. Fedeli, *Il carme 61 di Catullo* (Fribourg 1972) 101f., Hunter *loc. cit.*).

παιδέρωτ' ἐντρίβεται: 'she rubs rouge in (her cheeks)'. LSJ s.v. ἐντρίβω II incorrectly calls this use of the middle 'metaphorical'. παιδέρως (only here in comedy with this sense; elsewhere Ath. 12.542d quoting Duris *FGrH* 76 F 10, Alciphr. 2.8.3, 4.6.4, cf. K. F. Hermann and H. Blümner, *Lehrbuch der griechischen Privatalterthümer* (Freiburg and Tübingen 1882) 26 n. 4) is one of several ancient cosmetics (others include ἄγχουσα = Attic ἔγχουσα, made from alkanet, *Anchusa tinctoria*; συκάμινον, mulberry [juice]; φῦκος, orchil, deriving from the lichen *Roccella tinctoria*) applied like the modern rouge to give colour to pale cheeks; its source, according to Dioscorides 3.17, was the ἄκανθος (*Acanthus spinosus*; A. Huxley and W. Taylor, *Flowers of Greece and the Aegean* (London 1977) 131 and pl. 269), with its red roots.

19 δείκνυται (A Ath.) or δεικνύει (P Clem.)? Both forms can be supported with arguments; decision between them is uncertain. In Old Comedy, wherever possible, athematic endings are chosen (x13 in Ar., including ἀναδείκνυται *Nub.* 304), but later comedians vary when there is a choice (athematic: Antiphanes 234(237K).5, Men. *Dysk.* 768 and fr. 383 (both δείκνυται), fr. 471; thematic: Alexis 115(110K).25, Men. frs. 77, 745, com. adesp. fr. 240.13 Austin, probably Phoenicides 4.6; the optative form δεικνύοι at Men. *Epitr.* 456, would be obligatory in Attic at all periods: Schwyzer, 1.699). The -υται form in A here *could* be a corrupt assimilation to the ending of the last word in the line above; -ύει in P *could* be a later modernising adoption of the thematic form, cf. Schwyzer, 1.688. Here -υται is preferable, if only because Ath. seems the more careful excerptor and A the more accurate MS. But then a further question: is δείκνυται passive (cf. ἐγκεκάττυται v. 8) or middle (cf. ἐντρίβεται 18)? If middle, there would be no change of subject from 17 to 20, and an extra nuance of meaning is added ('displays for herself' = 'flaunts').

20–1 Cf. Catullus 39.1f. *Egnatius, quod candidos habet dentes,* | *renidet usque quaque.*

20 ἔσχεν: the aorist is gnomic (cf. comm. on v. 8 above), and θεωρῶσ' was probably corrupted to θεωροῖεν (so A, Epit. of Ath.) by scribes unaware of the classical rule that primary sequence is required after such an aorist (Goodwin, *MT* 58, § 171).

21 τὸ στόμ' ὡς κομψὸν φορεῖ: Blaydes (*Anal.* 325, *Misc. Crit.* 183) aptly compares S. fr. 930.2 Pearson σιγᾶν ἀνάγκη, κἂν καλὸν φορῇ στόμα (so Cobet for φέρῃ, MSS SMA at Stob. *Flor.* 3.24.4).

22–5 Alexis' point is clear, but his syntax is colloquially loose. The antecedent of ἅ (v. 23) is probably neither κρανία (so Meineke) nor ξυλήφιον (Blaydes, *Adv.* 2.157), but rather an unexpressed indefinite demonstrative, 'the things (which)', as commonly when the relative clause precedes the leading clause (cf. K.G. 2.402f.).

τοῖς μαγείροις here are butchers (cf. e.g. Ar. *Equ.* 418, Machon 18 Gow; Rankin, ΜΑΓΕΙΡΟΙ 64ff., Latte in *RE* s.v. Μάγειρος 393.64ff., Fraenkel, *EP* 408ff., L. Robert, *Opera Minora Selecta* 1 (Amsterdam 1969) 289f. n. 4, G. Berthiaume, *Les Rôles du mágeiros (Mnemosyne Suppl.* 70, 1982) 62ff. and 117ff., nn. 7, 15, 29), displaying on their market stalls the heads of carcases with wooden pegs in the mouths to keep them open. A similar custom (but with live pigs) is mentioned also by Ar. *Equ.* 375ff.: καὶ νὴ Δί' ἐμβαλόντες αὐ-|τῷ πάτταλον μαγειρικῶς | εἰς τὸ στόμ', εἶτα δ' ἔνδοθεν | τὴν

COMMENTARY

γλῶτταν ἐξείραντες αὐ-|τοῦ σκεψόμεσθ' εὖ κἀνδρικῶς | κεχηνότος | τὸν πρωκτὸν (!), εἰ χαλαζᾷ (where the joke barely masks the real function of the plug: it enables prospective customers to form an opinion about the health of the beast at slaughter by examining the tongue); possibly also *Thesm.* 222. An Attic red-figure lekythos (*c.* 480–70) in a private collection shows a young μάγειρος with a haunch in one hand and his μάχαιρα in the other standing before a table, on which a goat's head is placed (R. Lullies, *Eine Sammlung griechischer Kleinkunst* (Munich 1955) 28f. and fig. 62).

26 τῷ χρόνῳ: 'in course of time', cf. e.g. Ar. *Nub.* 66, 865, 1242, *Vesp.* 460, Wilamowitz on Eur. *Her.* 740.

σεσηρέν' (so implicitly A, Epit. of Ath., with *scriptio plena*; S. A. Naber, *Mnemosyne* 8 (1880) 258 proposes it as if it were an independent conjecture) is more likely to have been corrupted to σέσηρεν (P of Clem., printed here by Kassel–Austin) than vice versa. A further point: elsewhere in this fr. clauses introduced by ὥστε to express the consequences of the *hetairai*'s schemes have their verbs in the infinitive, not the indicative (5–6, 11–12). For a perfect infinitive in a consecutive clause cf. e.g. Thuc. 6.12 (ηὐξῆσθαι), Dem. 18.257 (ἐστεφανῶσθαι), Xen. *Anab.* 1.5.13 (ἐκπεπλῆχθαι); it emphasises the 'completion and decisiveness of the action' (Goodwin, *MT* 226 §590). σέσηρα exists only as a perfect (LSJ s.v. σαίρω [A], K.G. 1.149); 'when used of laughter, commonly implies malice, contempt or mockery' (Gow on Theoc. 7.19), denoting precisely the kind of grin that bares the teeth (cf. Ar. *Vesp.* 901).

ἄν τε βούλητ' ἄν τε μή: cf. e.g. Ar. *Lys.* 939, 1036, *Eccl.* 981, 1097 (all with βούλη), Eur. *Cycl.* 332, *Hec.* 566, *IA* 1271 (θέλη, -ων, -ω respectively); A. Otto, *Die Sprichwörter und sprichwörtlichen Redensarten der Römer* (Leipzig 1890) 362, H. Friis Johansen and E. W. Whittle, comm. (Copenhagen 1980) on A. *Suppl.* 862.

βούλητ': here Schweighaeuser (*Animadv.* 7.67) is more accurate than Kaibel. Of the two main Epit. MSS of Ath., C clearly has βούληται (*sic:* ται by compendium); whether this was copied from the lost Vatican ancestor of C and E, or represents a Byzantine conjecture (by Damilas? Cf. P. Canart, *Riv. Stud. Biz.* 14–16 (1977–9) 287ff.), is uncertain.

After the 26 tetrameters of fr. 103(98K) the *Marcianus* of Ath. has ὄψεις διὰ τούτων σκευοποιοῦσι τῶν τεχνῶν, a sequence which scans as an iambic trimeter but is omitted by Epit. MSS and by Clem. The words are *not* likely to be (1) the defective remains of a 27th troch. tetr. (so several scholars, including Dobree, *Adv.* 2.343, and Cobet in Peppink, *Observ.* 77: but without extensive rewriting, the rhythm of these words is far rougher than that of the 26 tetrameters, which have a virtually Euripidean metrical elegance (cf. Gil 334f.); or (2) a comment by Ath. about the preceding fr., either accidentally scanning or made to scan by a mischievous or undiscerning copyist (so tentatively E. Harrison, *CR* 52 (1938) 198:

but it is not Ath.'s custom so to comment on a preceding citation). Of the two possibilities that remain, perhaps the less probable is that the words are a comic trimeter originally quoted in the margin of a MS of Ath. as a parallel to the Alexis passage, and later incorporated by mistake into the text (so implicitly Dindorf, Kaibel). The words relate so well to the preceding tetrameters, however, that I am inclined to read them (with Meineke, *Cur. Crit.* 63) as a continuation of the troch. tetr. speech in another metre. Parallels for such a rhythmical switch in comedy without change of speaker include Ar. *Equ.* 242ff. (introducing the chorus); *Nub.* 1415, probably *Pax* 733, possibly Cratinus 203(199K) (for parodic purposes: cf. A. T. Murray, *CPhil.* 5 (1910) 489f.); Men. *Dysk.* 88off. (beginning with an address to the piper); Ar. *Equ.* 610ff., *Lys.* 706f. (transition from troch. tetr. of the parabasis to the iambic trimeters of the ensuing dialogue). The last two passages would be the most significant parallels, if fr. 103(98K) were after all an entr'acte speech delivered by the coryphaeus (see above, introduction to 'Ισοστάσιον); in that case v. 27 might be the first verse of a new scene.

ὄψεις ... σκευοποιοῦσι: 'they make masks of their appearances'; sc. their use of make-up, false breasts, etc., disguises reality just like an actor's mask (LSJ s.v. σκευοποιέω ΙΙ fails to note the metaphor here).

Καλάσιρις

The one brief fr.[1] in no way helps to elucidate the title. Kalasiris could be the name (cf. *Suda* s.v. καλάσιρις) of a character in the play; in Heliodorus' *Aethiopica* an elderly wandering sage originally from Egypt is so called and plays an important role (cf. J. R. Morgan, *Class. Ant.* 1 (1982) 247). Alternatively καλάσιρις might signify a garment also apparently of Egyptian origin (cf. Hdt. 2.81 ἐνδεδύκασι δὲ (sc. the Egyptians) κιθῶνας λινέους περὶ τὰ σκέλεα θυσανωτούς, τοὺς καλέουσι καλασίρις; Σ Ar. *Av.* 1294; Hesych., Photius, *Suda* s.v.), but in classical times manufactured in Corinth and Persia as well as Egypt (Ath. 12.525d, citing Democritus of Ephesus, *FHG* 4.383f.; cf. A. B. Büchsenschütz, *Die Hauptstätten des Gewerbfleisses im klassischen Alterthume* (Leipzig 1869) 72); it was known in Athens already before the end of the 5th century (Cratinus 32(30K), Ar. fr. 332(320K).6). In a play of later Greek comedy such a garment could perhaps have functioned as a recognition token (cf. the introduction to 'Αγωνίς and my paper in Flores 367).

---

[1] See also comm. on fr. 286(285K).

COMMENTARY

104 (99K)

Meineke 3.426, Kock 2.331, Edmonds 2.418, Kassel–Austin 2.78. Punctuation and part-assignments are uncertain. There are three possibilities: (a) one question by one speaker as he or she is taken to some destination (so most editors, including Kassel–Austin: simplest and best, 'where are you taking me to via the κύκλοι?'); (b) two questions (ποῖ δή μ' ἄγεις; διὰ τῶν κύκλων;), one speaker (so Edmonds); (c) question by one speaker, answer by a second (so Bentley in a letter to Hemsterhuys, cxiii in *The Correspondence* I (London 1842) 273: with πῇ for ποῖ[1]).

διὰ τῶν κύκλων: so CL (Pollux 10.18: ἐν τῷ κύκλῳ FS). οἱ κύκλοι originally = the place in the market where slaves were sold (Pollux 7.11 citing New Comedy, Harpocration s.v. κύκλοι citing Men. fr. 171, Dinarchus fr. XI.3 explaining the use with the statement that slaves for sale stood around in a circle). Pollux 10.18, however, quotes the present fr. and Diphilus 55 as evidence that the area in the market where σκεύη were sold was also termed κύκλοι. As the last claim may be based on a hasty misreading of the Diphilus fr. (where κύκλος appears in the singular shortly after a list of σκεύη), it may be safer to confine the market meaning of κύκλοι to slave rings. See also Ath. 10.452f Ἰσχόμαχος ὁ κῆρυξ . . . ἐν τοῖς κύκλοις ἐποιεῖτο τὰς μιμήσεις, where κύκλοι may still have the same significance. Cf. Bruhn, *Wortschatz* 23, Jacoby's comm. on Demon 327 F 8 (*FGrH* 3B Suppl. 2 p. 327).

Καρχηδόνιος

Th. Bergk, *Griechische Literaturgeschichte* 4 (Berlin 1887) 154 n. 116, C. A. Dietze, *De Philemone comico* (Diss. Göttingen 1901) 82, G. Zuntz, *Mnemosyne* 5 (1937) 61 n. 1, H. Lucas, *Rh. Mus.* 58 (1939) 189f., W. G. Arnott, *Rh. Mus.* 102 (1959) 252ff. and *Dioniso* 43 (1969) 355ff., H. J. Mette, *Lustrum* 10 (1965) 143f., C. Questa, *Entr. Hardt* 16 (1970) 187ff., G. Maurach's editions of Plaut. *Poen.* (Heidelberg 1975[1], pp. 58ff. and 1988[2], 33f.). In later Greek comedy, plays with the title Καρχηδόνιος are attested only for Alexis (fr. 105(100K)) and Menander (frs. 226–8, 230–3, *P.Oxy.* 2654, where vv. 7–8 = Men. fr. 228; cf. *P.Oxy.* 866, *P.Cologne* 5031). One of these

---

[1] Here Bentley was anticipated by Manutius, the ed. princ. of Pollux (Venice 1502, at 10.18), but although ποῖ and πῇ are frequently confused by scholars in both their interrogative and indefinite forms (e.g. Theognis 586, Eur. *Hec.* 163, Ar. *Equ.* 35), there is no reason here to question the paradosis, as my translation shows.

is likely to have been the primary source of Plautus' *Poenulus*; the case for Alexis and against Menander rests on three pieces of evidence.

(1) No portion of Plautus' play translates any of the papyri or book frs. of Menander's Καρχηδόνιος, and the dramatic foundations of those two plays appear to have been different. The scene of Menander's comedy was probably Athens (cf. Gomme–Sandbach, *Comm.* p. 408), where the Carthaginian pursues a girl who claims to be a citizeness (38f.), and he himself talks about being registered as a member of an Attic deme (39). Plautus' *Poenulus*, on the other hand, was set in the Aetolian city of Calydon, and the Carthaginian of its title is an old man searching for his lost daughters who now live in the house of the pimp who had bought them from their kidnappers.[1]

(2) The two words (βάκηλος εἶ) of the only fr. (105(100K)) cited specifically from Alexis' Καρχηδόνιος appear to be translated at *Poen.* 1318 *te cinaedum esse arbitror*, as Dietze first noted.

(3) A further fr. of Alexis (265(263K)), whose play source is not named by its citer (Epit., Ath. 1.21c–d) may well be adapted (with typical Plautine freedom) at *Poen.* 522ff. The opening two lines or so of the Greek fr. (ἐν γὰρ νομίζω τοῦτο τῶν ἀνελευθέρων | εἶναι, τὸ βαδίζειν ἀρρύθμως ἐν ταῖς ὁδοῖς, | ἐξὸν καλῶς) are translated fairly closely, although Alexis' iambic trimeters are turned into trochaic septenarii (*liberos homines per urbem modico magis par est gradu | ire, seruile esse duco festinantem currere*). The Alexis fr., however, then continues with more than five verses of social comment on the advantages of an orderly gait, which is replaced in the Plautine passage by a brief topical comment on the restoration of peace

---

[1] Admittedly at *Poen.* 372 the slave Milphio claims that one of those daughters will be transformed into *ciuis Attica atque libera*. This reference to Athenian citizenship, however, makes no coherent sense in the context of the Plautine plot as a whole, and is perhaps best explained by Fraenkel's hypothesis (*EP* 161ff., 26off.) that the scene in which it occurs (I.2) was adapted by Plautus from a second Greek source different from his primary model. Cf. also Maurach's editions of Plaut. *Poen.* (1975), pp. 53, 192f., 229ff.; (1988), pp. 100f., and my discussions in *Dioniso* 43 (1969) 359f. and the introduction to fr. 103(98K) above. For divergent views on (1) the scene as a whole see e.g. P. W. Harsh, *Studies in Dramatic 'Preparation' in Roman Comedy* (Chicago 1935) 50 n. 25 and 71f., A. S. Gratwick, *Cambridge History of Classical Literature* 2 (ed. E. J. Kenney and W. V. Clausen, 1982) 110 and n. 2, J. C. B. Lowe, *BICS* 35 (1988) 101ff., O. Zwierlein, *Zur Kritik und Exegese des Plautus I: Poenulus und Curculio* (Stuttgart 1990) 138ff.; and (2) on *Poen.* 372 see W. Friedrich, *Euripides und Diphilos* (Munich 1953) 243f., Zwierlein 168f.

after the despatch of unspecified enemies[1] (*praesertim in re populi placida atque interfectis hostibus | non decet tumultuari*). Such changes of metre, together with the alternation of close translation and original composition in his adaptation of Greek models, are wholly characteristic of Plautus' method, as Fraenkel had already demonstrated (cf. *EP* 339ff.) before the confirmatory evidence of the *Dis Exapaton* papyrus was discovered. At least one further particularity links the passages of Alexis and Plautus. Although the idea that a disorderly gait was unbecoming to a free man formed an article of general belief in classical Athens (see comm. on fr. 265(263K)), its formulation in these precise terms (with the personal expression of belief, νομίζω/*duco*; the use of the infinitive as a verbal noun; and the yardstick of ἐλευθερία | ἀνελευθερία rather than e.g. εὐταξία) is confined in Greco-Roman comedy to the two passages of Alexis and Plautus. Ar. *Nub.* 964f. and Philemon 4(5K) demonstrate that singularity very clearly; they make similar points about a seemly gait, but their expression and perspectives (the εὐταξία of children, and εὐκοσμία to the exclusion of other qualities, respectively) are rather different. Hence I confidently assign the Alexis fr. to Καρχηδόνιος, although commentary on it is postponed to pp. 740 ff., since Kassel–Austin prefer to print the fragment as 265(263K) among the *incertarum fabularum fragmenta*.

The identification of Alexis' Καρχηδόνιος as Plautus' main model in *Poen.* and the assignment of fr. 265(263K) to the Greek play have some important corollaries. Although the detailed relationship of the two plays remains a mystery which we lack the evidence to dispel, it would nevertheless appear that at least two passages of the Roman comedy reflect more or less closely its Greek original: the scenes where (a) the *aduocati* (who may – or may not!)[2] – have been a chorus in Alexis' play, led on to the stage for an entr'acte performance like Karion's farmers in Ar. *Plut.*) enter with Agorastocles (504ff.) and (b) the soldier enters to find the old Carthaginian embracing Adelphasium (1280ff.). The latter scene goes

---

[1] The production date (? dates) of *Poen.* is (are) uncertain; arguments have been advanced in favour of the mid–190s (with those enemies despatched at Cynoscephalae, 197) and the early 180s (with the victory won at Magnesia, 190 or 189). Cf. most recently K. H. E. Schutter, *Quibus annis comoediae Plautinae primum actae sint quaeritur* (Diss. Groningen 1952) 119ff., K. Abel, *Die Plautusprologe* (Diss. Frankfurt 1955) 89f.; and Maurach's editions of *Poen.* (1975) 41ff. and (1988) 32f.

[2] Cf. J. C. B. Lowe, *Rh. Mus.* 133 (1990) 274ff., whose arguments against their having been a chorus in the ancient sense seem to me far more convincing than his attempt to show that the link between Alexis 265(263K) and Plaut. *Poen.* 522ff. may be fortuitous (cf. here also Zwierlein (*op. cit.* in n. 1) 280 n. 576).

well with Alexis' title, but the earlier one prompts an awkward question: how much (if any) of the Collybiscus intrigue in Plaut. *Poen.* was derived from the Greek model? Although this question has been much discussed for over a century (see most recently Maurach's 1975 edition, pp. 43ff., with a survey of some previous studies; A. S. Gratwick, *Cambridge History of Classical Literature* 2 (ed. E. J. Kenney and W. V. Clausen, Cambridge 1982) 98ff.), the only safe answer with the evidence at present available is *non liquet*.

The date of Alexis' play is unknown. G. Zuntz (*Ant. Class.* 23 (1954) 199 n. 3) suggested that Athenian interest in Carthage might have been stimulated by the visit of an embassy from that city between *c.* 330 and 310 (*IG* ii².418, Dittenberger, *SIG*³ no. 321). Gratwick (*Hermes* 99 (1971) 27 n. 2) argued that the two pirate raids which led to the kidnapping of Agorastocles and Hanno's daughters (*Poen.* 64ff., 83ff., 896ff., 1058, 1346) would have been historically feasible only at a time when Carthage's defences were under attack: e.g. during the invasion of Agathocles in 310–307 (Diod. Sic. 20.38–42). The pirate raids in *Poen.* occurred at least ten years before the play's scenic date, which Gratwick then fixed too precisely as 300–299 (a more plausible span would be 300–294). This is an argument of some ingenuity, but it rests on the unverifiable hypothesis that Alexis intended the background events of his plot to reflect recent history with scrupulous fidelity, and that Plautus then reproduced the relevant details without any modification.

On the possible identity of Καρχηδόνιος with Alexis' Ἰμίλκων, see the introduction to the latter play.

105 (100K)

Kock 2.331, Edmonds 2.418, Kassel–Austin 2.78. In Attic and *Koine* Greek βάκηλος was used in both a precise and a wider sense, as the careful notes of Phryn. *Ecl.* 238 (formerly 240; p. 272 Lobeck, 339 Rutherford, 85 Fischer) and Zenobius 2.70 (Miller, *Mélanges* 365) indicate: (1) properly 'castrated', especially with reference to the priests of Cybele; e.g. Lucian *Sat.* 12, cf. *Eun.* 8. Hesychius (in an ill-organised note) and Phryn. here define βάκηλος as Γαλλός, while an anon. rhetorical lexicon (Bekker, *Anecd.* 1.222.4) explains it as ὁ κατὰ θεοῦ μῆνιν ἀπόκοπος; (2) secondarily, and by a natural extension of meaning, βάκηλος is used κατὰ τῶν ἐκλύτων καὶ ἀνάνδρων (Phryn., Zenobius; cf. Phot. s.v.) as a general sexual pejorative; e.g. Antiphanes 111(113K).2, Men. fr. 412, cf. Durham, *Vocabulary* 49. Here Alexis would have used the word in the latter sense, if the Plautine choice of *cinaedus* to translate it (*Poen.* 1318: see above, introduction to Καρχηδόνιος) is anything to go by.

COMMENTARY

Καταψευδόμενος

See below, Τοκιστὴς ἢ Καταψευδόμενος (frs. 232–5(230–3K)).

Καύνιοι

Kock 2.332, cf. Nesselrath, *MK* 199 n. 51. A play with this title was written also by Timocles (on which V. Bevilacqua, *Dioniso* 7 (1939) 40 has ingenious but unverifiable speculations), but the plot and titular implications of both plays are unknown. If Alexis' Καύνιοι was a typical product of the New Comedy, it could have featured the adventures of two or more men of Caunus away from home (cf. the introduction to Θεσπρωτοί). Kock, however, suggests that the play burlesqued the myth of Caunus' and Byblis' incestuous love-affair (cf. Parthenius 11 citing Nicaenetus fr. 1 Powell, Ovid *Met.* 9.450ff. with H. Tränkle, *Hermes* 91 (1963) 46off.; *RE* and Roscher s.vv. *Byblis* (Hoefer (4) 1098.31ff., Schirmer 839.66ff. respectively) and *Kaunos* (Weicker (3) 88.42ff., Stoll 1006.27ff. respectively), E. Rohde, *Der griechische Roman*[3] (Leipzig 1914) 101, Gow, comm. on Theoc. 7.115; hence the proverb Καύνιος ἔρως, Arist. *Rhet.* 2.25, 1402[b]3, Hesych. and *Suda* s.v., cf. διακαυνιάζειν Ar. *Pax* 1081 and Σ *ad loc.*; Göbel, *Ethnica* 115f.), but if such a travesty had been Alexis' main intention, a title incorporating the name(s) of Caunus and/or Byblis would have been more apposite.

The one surviving fr. from Alexis' play offers no clues to the plot, but its reference to a closed or non-functioning bath-house perhaps gives us a glimpse of the author's dramatic technique, if the speaker was explaining thereby an unexpectedly early return to the stage after an intended visit to the baths. Unachieved aims provide the reason for early returns to the stage at e.g. Men. *Dysk.* 259ff., Plaut. *Aul.* 371ff., Ter. *Eun.* 629ff., 84off.

106 (101K)

Meineke 3.426, Kock 2.332, Edmonds 2.418, Kassel–Austin 2.78. Here as elsewhere (cf. comm. on frs. 71, 83, etc.) a grammarian (Pollux: 7.166) appears to have quoted carefully only those words in his citation (ταῖς ἐσχάραις, τἀλειπτήριον) which illustrate his theme (terms associated with bath-houses). When the errors of copyists are added to a quoter's carelessness, restoration of the original text is often impossible and always speculative. Here there are four textual problems.

(i) μήτε πῦρ FS, μήτε τὸ πῦρ A. Bethe and the editors of the comic frs. adopt the reading without the article; the rhythm of the verse is in their favour, although split anapaests do occur in the second half of the

288

second metron of an iambic trimeter after hephthemimeral caesura (see *CQ* 7 (1957) 189, Handley's edition of Men. *Dysk.* pp. 63ff.). Scribal practice here offers no guide; copyists add superfluous and omit correct articles with equal abandon. Without further context it is impossible to say whether the sense is better here with or without τό.

(ii) μήτε... ἐνόν is read by all the MSS. What construction can explain the presence of μήτε... τε sandwiching two participles? There are several possibilities. Kock suggested *[quid igitur facerem, si] neque ignis in focis erat?*' (better would have been '*si neque ignem in focis [esse repperi]*', otherwise Meineke's ἐνῆν would be demanded, 5.88). One might alternatively assume that an angry exclamation such as ἰδεῖν ἐμέ preceded ('To think that I saw ...'; for this use of the accusative and infinitive cf. e.g. Ar. *Vesp.* 835, *Nub.* 819, Dem. 21.209, K.G. 2.23f.), accounting thus for the form of the negative and the presence of the participles. On the sequence μήτε... τε, where the second clause cancels the negative of the first, see Denniston, *GP* 508.

(iii) All the MSS write ἐνὸν καὶ κεκλ-, but the particle is meaningless, ruins the scansion, and probably arose from dittography and the common confusion between ε and αι; it was deleted by W. Seber (edition of Pollux (Frankfurt 1608), cf. his *Notae* p. 109).

(iv) κεκλεισμένον A, -ημένον F, -υμένον S. Herwerden (*Coll. Crit.* 123) here argues for the orthography κεκλειμένον, which was standard in Attic Greek from about the mid-4th century, replacing there the older spelling in -ημένον which Kassel–Austin oddly print (LSJ s.v. κλείω (A), Schwyzer 1.727, Threatte 1.370). The -εισμένον form in AM, however, cannot simply be dismissed as a *vox nihili*. This form occurs several times in good MSS of comic authors: Ar. *Vesp.* 198 (RV), *Lys.* 423 (B: -κλισμαι R), *Plut.* 206 (RU); cf. also Men. fr. 452.3 (MSS DE of Harpocration s.v. Κτησίου Διός: but the *Cairensis* has κεκλειμενη at *Epitr.* 1076), Xen. *Cyr.* 7.5.27. The combined evidence of the quoted MSS shows that the -εισμ- spelling was a variant known and accepted by Byzantine copyists (presumably by popular analogy with forms like σέσεισμαι, πέπεισμαι, ἔσπεισμαι, πεφεισμένος), but whether the variant was admissible also as an Athenian colloquialism remains uncertain.

2 τἀλειπτήριον: in both public baths and gymnasia the room for anointing clients with oil often doubled as the steam bath (πυριατήριον), as several ancient texts indicate (e.g. Theophr. *Sud.* 28, Plut. *Cimon* 1.7, cf. Philostr. *Gymn.* 58; Reisch in *RE* s.v. Ἀλειπτήριον 1362.15ff., J. Delorme, *Gymnasion* (Paris 1960) 301ff., R. Ginouvès, *Balaneutikè* (Paris 1962) 138f., C. Foss, *GRBS* 16 (1975) 217ff.). Doubtless the ἐσχάραι mentioned in v. 1 of the fr. (at this period portable braziers: cf. D. A. Amyx, *Hesperia* 27 (1958) 229ff., Sparkes–Talcott, *Agora* XII.234f. and fig. 19, pl. 98, nos. 2028–40) heated the ἀλειπτήριον. Cf. also my introduction to Ἀλείπτρια

289

COMMENTARY

and comm. on Antiphanes 26(25K).2–4 below ('False or Doubtful Attributions' I, pp. 815f.).

Κηρυττόμενος (? or better ᾽Εκκηρυττόμενος)

Meineke 1.400. The one fr. from the play (107(102K)) is cited by Ath. 15 p. 550 Kaibel. At this point (folio 370) the *Marcianus* suffered damage before or during the early Renaissance. Epitome, Renaissance apographs of A and editions of Ath. before Schweighaeuser all omit the fr. It is still possible to read most of the fr. in A, although with difficulty, but its lemma and v. 1 up to and including ἐκ τοῦ have now disappeared into a hole removing virtually all of lines 27 to 29 and the first half of 30 in the left-hand column of f.370ᵛ. The last reader to decipher the lemma and opening of v. 1 of the fr. was Jean Schweighaeuser's son Geoffroi, who collated the *Marcianus* for his father; he read the fr.'s source as ῎Αλεξις δ᾽ ἐν Κηρυττομένωι, but even to his eyes the ἐν was already *euanida* (Schweighaeuser, *Animadv.* 8.345, cf. R. Schöll, *Hermes* 4 (1870) 16off., 167). This led the elder Schweighaeuser to doubt the accuracy of his son's decipherment of the ἐν (cf. Meineke 1.400) and to suggest that what was really written in the MS was ῎Αλεξις δ᾽ ᾽Εκκηρυττομένωι. In A κ and ν are sufficiently similar to be confused when a page is difficult to read, but according to his father (*praef.* of edition 1.ciii ff.) the younger Schweighaeuser was a competent palaeographer.

If ᾽Εκκηρυττόμενος is correct, as I believe, the title figure would be deprived by proclamation of some right or position, probably that of domicile in a particular city (cf. Lysias 12.35, 95, Aeschines 3.258), but possibly that of inclusion in a γένος (Pl. *Leg.* 11.929b) or of a commission in the army (Lysias 3.45). Κηρυττόμενος is a vaguer title, but not impossible; it would denote a man 'named in a proclamation', for either praise (Lysias 19.63) or condemnation (Dem. 25.56, Arist. *Ath. Pol.* 61[1]).

107 (102K)

Meineke 3.426, Kock 2.332, Edmonds 2.400, Kassel–Austin 2.79. There is nothing in the fr.'s description of a person moving about at night which helps to relate it to the title or any sort of plot.

1 One *Marcianus* error (λυχνου | τον χου τον λυχνον for λυχνούχου τὸν λύχνον, corrected by Elmsley, comm. on Ar. *Ach.* 938) is easily

---

[1] Yet even here Blass conjectured <ἐκ>κ[η]ρῦξαι in the sense 'to cashier' (as in Lysias 3.45: cf. now P. J. Rhodes's *Commentary* (Oxford 1981) *ad loc.*

explained; a scribe thought that he saw τοῦ λύχνου followed by τὸν λύχνον, and having written as far as τον he realised his error, but failed to delete the misplaced τον after adding the correct χου.

This and other comic frs. (e.g. Ar. fr. 290(279, 280K), Pherecrates 44(40K)) confirm the grammarians' claim (Phryn. *Praep. Soph.* 87.1 de Borries, cf. *Ecl.* s.v. φανός p. 63.77 Fischer, Photius s.v. λυχνοῦχον) that in correct Attic usage λυχνοῦχος is the lantern into which the terracotta lamp (λύχνος) was placed for outdoor use. See s.v. *Lanterna* Hug in *RE* 693.13ff., J. Toutain in Dar.–Sag. 924B ff., Rutherford, *NP* 131ff., R. Zahn, *Jahrbuch der Königlich-preussischen Kunstsammlungen* 37 (1916) 14ff., Forbes, *Technology* 6.147ff.[1] = 151ff.[2], R. H. Howland, *Agora IV: Greek Lamps and their Survivals* (Princeton 1958) 78, 133f., 149f., Kassel–Austin on Ar. fr. 8.

2 μικροῦ here with the aorist indicative (cf. K.G. 1.204, 387, Schwyzer 2.135) = 'almost'; like Menander (cf. Handley on Men. *Dysk*.437ff.) Alexis uses μικροῦ in this sense rather than the generally more common ὀλίγου. See also comm. on 232(230K).2.

The *Marcianus* reading ἔλαθεν εαυτον could be a corruption of either ἔλαθεν αὐτὸν (Bothe, *PCGF* 539) or ἔλαθ' ἑαυτὸν (Elmsley). Decision between them is impossible; elsewhere Alexis has αὐτ- twice, frs. 9.10, 239(237K).5, ἑαυτ- never, but Menander has some fifty-nine instances of ἑαυτ against thirty of αὐτ-.

ὑπὸ μάλης has troubled those scholars unable to see the joke; their gratuitous conjectures are listed in *Hermes* 93 (1965) 302. By holding his lamp too near his *stomach*, the speaker burnt himself ὑπὸ μάλης. Logically this ὑπὸ μάλης adds little or nothing to μικροῦ and the main verb ('he almost . . . didn't realise it, furtively'); for a rare use of ὑπὸ μάλης without apparent local significance cf. Dem. 29.12. But Alexis chose this expression because he wanted to emphasise the local overtones; ὑπὸ μάλης, literally 'under the armpit', takes its secondary meaning 'furtively' just because small weapons and the like may conveniently be concealed underneath the armpit; cf. e.g. Xen. *Hell.* 2.3.23, Pl. *Gorg.* 469d, Alciphron 3.10.3. Thus ὑπὸ μάλης has a delightful comic incongruity when juxtaposed with a different part of the body, τῇ γαστρί. Ar. *Lys.* 985 also makes a joke out of the phrase's local overtones by having a δόρυ there/so concealed.

Κιθαρῳδός

As a title in later Greek comedy Κιθαρῳδός[1] occurs nine times (its other

---

[1] On the word's precise meaning see Gow on Machon 6 and 141, and my comm. on Alexis 3.2.

authors are Antiphanes, Sophilus, Theophilus, Clearchus, Diphilus, Apollodorus, Anaxippus, Nicon), Κιθαριστής twice and Αὐλητής three times. The reason for this vogue in musical male heroes is unknown; the remains from all of these plays are too scanty to justify any theory that (e.g.) the musical element in them might have been greater than normal. Something admittedly is known about the plot of Menander's Κιθαριστής,[1] in which the title figure was the rich father of a girl involved in a love intrigue, but its surviving frs. do not reveal whether his lyre-playing had any relevance to the plot or dramatic action.

108 (103K)

Meineke 3.427, Kock 2.332, Edmonds 2.420, Kassel–Austin 2.79. The Antiatticist (96.9 Bekker) quotes four words (ἐξέβη ἡμῖν τὸ ἐνύπνιον) from Alexis' play without comment. As transmitted they do not scan; a copyist could have meddled with their order (hence Meineke conjectured ἐξέβη | τοὐν. ἡμῖν; Sicking, *Annotationes* 108 τοὐν. ἡμῖν ἐξέβη), or the excerptor could have picked out from a fuller context just the words that suited his purpose. Analogous citations from Menander (e.g. *Dysk.* 50ff., *Pk.* 533f.) suggest that the two possibilities are not mutually exclusive.

Although no lexical explanation for the Antiatticist's citation now survives, it is probable that the use of ἐκβαίνειν in the sense of 'to be fulfilled/come true' was being defended as good Attic. ἀποβαίνειν is more normal in this meaning (LSJ s.v. ii, Jackson, *Marg. Scaen.* 237f.; e.g. Pl. *Symp.* 181a τοιοῦτον ἀπέβη, Ach. Tat. 2.12.3 ἀπέβη τοῦ τέρατος τὸ ἔργον; with reference to dreams, Arist. *Div. Somn.* 1, 463ᵇ9f. πολλὰ τῶν ἐνυπνίων οὐκ ἀποβαίνει), but the parallel use of ἐκβαίνειν is well established in Attic (e.g. Dem. 19.28 εἰ μὲν ἐκβέβηκεν ὅσ' ἀπήγγειλε, S. *Trach.* 672 τοιοῦτον ἐκβέβηκεν), even though I cannot trace a second application of the verb to dreams.

The function of the dream[2] in Alexis' play is unknown, but see comm. on fr. 274(272K).

---

[1] The text of fr. 1 of this play must be reconsidered in the light of the evidence now provided by *P. Turner* 5 published by E. W. Handley in *Papyri Greek and Egyptian edited by various hands, in honour of Eric Gardner Turner* (London 1981) 25ff.

[2] Artemidorus' attempt (1.1; proem of 4, 238.20ff. Pack) to draw a semantic distinction between ὄνειρος (allegedly a prophetic dream) and ἐνύπνιον (one without such a significance) may have reflected the practice of second-sophistic oneiromancers, but it never accorded with classical Greek usage, where the two nouns were synonymous and ambivalent (cf. LSJ s.v. ἐνύπνιον).

ΚΛΕΟΒΟΥΛΙΝΗ

Κλεοβουλίνη

Meineke 1.390, Wilamowitz, *Hermes* 34 (1899) 219ff. = *Kleine Schriften* 4 (Berlin 1962) 60ff.; cf. Th. Zieliński, *Die Märchenkomödie in Athen* (St Petersburg 1885) 19, Kaibel in Kassel–Austin 4.168, J. Th. M. F. Pieters, *Cratinus* (Leiden 1946) 144ff. Wilamowitz shows that in the 3rd century there existed in Alexandria a book of riddles in hexameter verse ascribed to Eumetis *alias* Cleobulina, the alleged daughter of Cleobulus, mother of Thales and companion to the seven sages. It is probably from this book that the riddles quoted by Plutarch in his *Banquet of the Seven Sages* (*Mor.* 150e, 154b; Diog. Laert. 1.89 calls her αἰνιγμάτων ἑξαμέτρων ποιήτριαν; the known riddles associated with her are collected by Th. Bergk, *Poetae lyrici graeci*[4] 62f.) derive. Did Cleobulina really exist, or was she a literary invention? If the latter, the likeliest source must be Cratinus' Κλεοβουλ-ῖναι. Wilamowitz suggests that the comic poet may have created her as a riddling foil to her father Cleobulus, but there is no evidence to support this theory in that play's frs. or elsewhere. The most convincing explanation of Cratinus' plural title is provided by Pieters, arguing that the Κλεοβουλῖναι were a chorus of women supporting Cleobulus' daughter, just as the same poet's Ὀδυσσεῖς seems to have been named after a chorus of Odysseus' followers. In Κλεοβουλῖναι Cleobulina presumably propounded riddles; fr. 94(87K) has the appearance of one, and frs. 95(88K) and 96(89K) are couched in allusive language.

The one fr. surviving from Alexis' Κλεοβουλίνη is a reference to Sinope the *hetaira* (see below, comm. on fr. 109(104K)), which probably dates the play to the first half of Alexis' career, before *c.* 320.[1] Could Alexis' play have been influenced by Cratinus' as Meineke thinks? Only within certain limits: a play written a hundred years or so before Alexis'[2] and dependent in all likelihood upon a lively chorus and the structural features of Old Comedy can have provided only sketchy guidelines for a composition of Middle Comedy, even though a fondness for riddles[3]

---

[1] T. B. L. Webster (*CQ* 2 (1952) 21) works out Sinope's *floruit* as *c.* 360–330 by an ingenious set of combinations, but a *hetaira* of her notoriety is unlikely to have been immediately forgotten by the Athenian populace.

[2] Wilamowitz dates Cratinus' Κλεοβουλῖναι to *c.* 450, Pieters to 439–437.

[3] Cf. Alexis 242(240K) and comm. *ad loc.* At least three 4th-century comedies (Antiphanes' Πρόβλημα and Σαπφώ, Eubulus' Σφιγγοκαρίων) appear to have made extensive use of riddles. See Meineke 1.277f., Schultz in *RE* s.v. *Rätsel* 99.22ff., Webster, *SLGC* 82, Hunter 200ff.

and mythological burlesque[1] seems to have been common to the two periods.

109 (104K)

Meineke 3.427, Kock 2.333, Edmonds 2.420, Kassel–Austin 2.80. The *hetaira* Sinope came to Athens from her native Thrace by way of Aegina (Theopompus 115 F 253 Jacoby in Ath. 13.595a), and practised her profession successfully until she was quite old (Herodicus in Ath. 13.586a). She was a favourite butt of contemporary comedians; Ath. 586a collects references to her in seven plays (including Alexis here) but omits Amphis 23.3 and Anaxilas 22.12f. Dem. 22.56 called her and Phanostrata ἀνθρώπους πόρνους, cf. [Dem.] 59.116.

Ath. 586a says simply that Alexis 'mentions' (μνημονεύει: see comm. on 156(136K)) Sinope in the Κλεοβουλίνη. A lexicographical entry under the heading σινωπίσαι shared by Photius (-ῆσαι MS, corr. Naber, cf. A. Nauck, *Philologus* 6 (1851) 119) and the *Suda* s.v. Σινώπη (cf. also Hesych. s.v. σινωπίσαι, Apostolius 15.50, *App. Prov.* 4.72 = *Prov. Bodl.* 840) claims the *hetaira* was attacked in comedy ἐπὶ τῷ κατασχημονῆσαι (ἀσχημονεῖν Hesych., cf. *App. Prov.*), καθάπερ Ἄλεξις ἔφη. This presumably means that Alexis (a) used (or coined) the verb σινωπίζω (cf. πεφιλιππίδωσαι fr. 148(144K).2), or (b) attacked Sinope's indecency, or (c) perhaps did both (but not necessarily in Κλεοβουλίνη). See also Göbel, *Ethnica* 104.

Κνιδία

It is the only comedy known with this title (Menander's Κνιδία is a spurious invention of modern scholarship: cf. Austin, *CGFP* 171, Gomme–Sandbach, *Comm.* 539f.), but the type of title – 'The girl/woman from X', where X = the name of a city, state or island – is widespread in later Greek comedy (cf. the introductions to Ἀτθίς, Ἀχαΐς, Βρεττία, etc.). The one fr. cited from Alexis' play describes a familiar character in the plots of this genre – the young man who has squandered his father's fortune.

---

[1] In the age of Attic comedy Cleobulina seems to have been more a figure of legend than of historical reality. Several of the stories involving the seven sages would have offered scope for Middle-Comedy burlesque: particularly their banquet (which is particularly associated with Cleobulina's riddles) and the contest for the tripod. Cf. *RE* s.v. *Sieben Weise* 2252.54ff., 2248.65ff. (Barkowski) and *Andron* 15, 2160.61ff. (Wellmann), W. Wiersma, *Mnemosyne* 1 (1934) 150ff., and my introduction to Αἴσωπος.

110 (105K)

Meineke 3.427, Kock 2.333, Edmonds 2.420, Kassel–Austin 2.80. The fr. (cited by Ath. 4.165d, A and Epit.) can be interpreted in two ways. It may be part of a narrative (? in an expository prologue) describing the actions of a character in the play who had squandered money presumably in the conduct of a love affair with a *hetaira*. Alternatively the man named in the fr. could have been a real Athenian of the time whose notorious extravagance was being cited as a warning example to a young stage wastrel by a relative, servant or friend. Plautus' *Mostellaria* opens with a scene in which one slave reproaches another for the way in which the latter has helped the young master to squander the family fortune in the absence of the master's father (especially 20ff.). Cf. Alciphron 4.11.8.

1 Διόδωρος οὐπίτριπτος: the fact that Diodoros occurs nowhere else as a character name in comedy is no bar to its use as such here: many other names of free males are known to occur in only one play (e.g. the title figure of Alexis' Δημήτριος q.v., Δημύλος Sosipater 1.2, Ἱππόνικος Antiphanes 177(179K).2, Κλέων Philemon 178(213K).1, Κνήμων Men. *Dysk.*, Ναυσίνικος Alexis' Κυβερνήτης q.v., Πάταικος Men. *Pk.*). If on the other hand the reference is to a living contemporary, it is impossible to pin him down, for the name is common in Athens (Kirchner, *PA* 1.263–6 nos. 3915–69, 2.455 nos. 3920a–3935a), and several of its bearers belonged to propertied families (Davies, *APF* 155f.). οὐπίτριπτος marks the speaker's reaction to Diodorus' dissipations very clearly; the adjective is applied to 'persons to whom one says ἐπιτριβείης' (LSJ s.v. ἐπίτριπτος).

ἐν ἔτεσιν δύο: indeclinable δύο is universal in Homer but totally foreign to the formal Attic of inscriptions until the Roman period (Meisterhans–Schwyzer 157f.). When it does appear in the MSS of Attic prose authors (e.g. Thuc. 3.89, Xen. *Anab.* 3.4.9, *Mem.* 2.5.2) and comedy (here, Damoxenus 2.3), the question arises whether it may sometimes be an error by copyists, but metre confirms its correctness in the Damoxenus passage (ἐν δύ' ἔτεσιν opening a trimeter), and perhaps it should be considered an Ionicism or rare colloquialism.

2 σφαῖραν ἀπέδειξε τὴν πατρῴαν οὐσίαν: 'made a ball of his patrimony' (and let it roll away). This vivid metaphor for 'squandered' (only here and in the similarly phrased Alexis 248(246K).3 σφ. ἐποίησε τὴν π. οὐσ.) and the analogous use of συστρογγύλλω (Alexis 248(246K).4, Nicomachus 3.2) may have been contemporary slang. The idea of squandering riches spawned a rich brood of lively metaphors:[1] κατεσθίω (Alexis

---

[1] 'Metaphor' is not the most appropriate term for the κατεσθίω/βρύκω/ καταμασῶμαι/ *comedo*/ *abligurrio*/ *ablingo* cluster of examples, since from the time of the *Odyssey* (e.g. 1.375 = 2.140, 3.315f. = 15.12f., 14.41f.)

COMMENTARY

128(123K).1f., Anaxandrides 46(45K).2, Anaxippus 1.31f., Antiphanes 236(239K).1, Hegesippus 1.30, Men. *Epitr.* 1065, frs. 287.3f., 326; cf. Aeschines 1.42, Machon 425) and other verbs of 'eating' (βρύκω Diphilus 42(43K).27, καταμασῶμαι Alexis 110(105K).3, cf. *comedo* Plaut. *Trin.* 417, *abligurrio* Ter. *Eun.* 235, ? *ablingo* com. adesp. fr. cited by Donatus on Ter. *Phorm.* 339, cf. *G and R* 17 (1970) 37 n. 2); ἀνακυλίω (Alexis 121(116K).7), ἀποβάλλω (*P.Didot* 1.30, cf. Alciphron 3.25.3), ἐκκοκκίζω (Nicomachus 3.2), ἐξαλίνδω (Ar. *Nub.* 33 with play on its literal sense), ἐξαντλῶ (Alciphron 3.38.1), ἐπιτρίβω (Aelian *Epist.* 10), καταλούομαι (Ar. *Nub.* 838, cf. *elauo* Plaut. *Asin.* 135), the mundane οὐσίαν μικρὰν ποῶ (Men. *Kith.* 60), ῥυμβονῶ (Aelian fr. 146), σπαθῶ (Ar. *Nub.* 55 with play on its literal meaning, Diphilus 42(43K).27, Alciphron 2.32.1, 3.29.2; κατασπαθῶ similarly in Alciphron 3.14.1), *dilapido* (Ter. *Phorm.* 897, com. adesp. fr. 38 Ribbeck), *distimulo* (Plaut. *Bacch.* 64). Cf. Fraenkel, *EP* 24.

3 ἰταμῶς: the word's normal sense ('hastily/rashly': LSJ s.v. -μός) is foremost in later comedy at Men. *Pk.* 713, but after the ball metaphor here and at Alexis 248(246K).4* (οὕτω συνέστρογγυλεν ἰταμῶς καὶ ταχύ sc. τὴν πατρῴαν οὐσίαν, cf. Euphron 1.25*), there is presumably also a witty consciousness of the adverb's derivation (ἰέναι → ἴτης, ἰταμός; cf. A. Bulloch, comm. (Cambridge 1985) on Call. *Lav. Pall.* 25). Cf. the similar word plays in Pl. *Protag.* 349e καὶ ἴτας γε, ἔφη, ἐφ' ἃ οἱ πολλοὶ φοβοῦνται ἰέναι, Men. *Dysk.* 393ff. τουτὶ τὸ πρόβατον ... οὐ προέρχεται (see L. A. Post, *AJP* 80 (1959) 404, W. G. Arnott, *Phoenix* 18 (1964) 123); possibly also Heliodorus 1.9.3 ἐπεὶ δὲ ἰταμώτερον προσῄει. Sense and the comic parallels asterisked prove the correctness here of A's ἰταμῶς, which Epit. MSS trivialise to ἱκανῶς.

κατεμασήσατο: see above on v. 2. The simple verb and all its compounds (ἀνα-, δια-, κατα-) are confined in Attic to comedy (LSJ s.v. μασάομαι) and thus presumably to popular speech.

Κονιατής

Both Amphis and Alexis wrote plays titled Κονιατής ('Plasterer', a craftsman working mainly with unslaked lime on walls: cf. Pollux 7.124, Hesych. and *Suda* s.v. κονιαταί). Of Amphis' play no fr. survives, of Alexis' just a four-word list of wine-vessels that may – or may not – come from a description of a party.

---

onwards 'eating up' one's patrimony was a literally true method of squandering it; cf. B. Vickers, *Towards Greek Tragedy* (London 1973) 232f., Hopkinson, comm. on Call. *H. Dem.* 113.

111 (106K)

Meineke 3.427, Kock 2.333, Edmonds 2.420, Kassel–Austin 2.81.

1 κυμβία: see comm. on fr. 100(95K).1–2.

2 φιάλαι: shallow bowls without handles and generally with a central boss, used especially for libations (Richter–Milne, *Shapes* 29f. and fig. 181, H. Luschey, *Die Phiale* (Bleicherode am Harz 1939), Sparkes–Talcott, *Agora* XII.105f. and fig. 6, pls. 23, 52, nos. 518–26).

τραγέλαφοι: Ath. 11.500d–f quotes the present fr. of Alexis with three others (Antiphanes 223(224K), Eubulus 47(48K), Men. fr. 24) to illustrate this word, which he defines simply as τινὰ ... ποτήρια; neither the frs. cited nor Diphilus 81(80K).1 supplement this meagre information. LSJ s.v. are probably right, however, to suggest that these vessels took their name from representations of the fabulous 'goat-stag' either worked in relief on them or forming a major part of the shape. Ceramic rhyta in the form of goat and deer heads survive in some number from Athens in the late 5th century and South Italy from the last quarter of the 4th (H. Hoffmann, *AJA* 64 (1960) 276ff. and pl. 78, cf. his *Attic Red-figured Rhyta* (Mainz 1962) and K. Tuchelt, *Tiergefässe in Kopf- und Protomengestalt* (Berlin 1962) 69ff.). Among the gold rhyta probably dating from *c.* 300 in the Panagyurishté treasure are two shaped as a stag's head and another with the foreparts of a goat (*Thracian Treasures from Bulgaria*, British Museum Catalogue of the 1976 exhibition, 362, 363, 364 and colour pl., D. E. Strong, *Greek and Roman Gold and Silver Plate* (London 1966) 101f. and pl. 23B).

Κουρίς

Meineke 1.389, W. Frantz, *De comoediae atticae prologis* (Diss. Strasbourg 1891) 44, F. Leo, *Hermes* 43 (1908) 308ff., cf. *Der Monolog im Drama* (Berlin 1908) 44f., Webster, *SLGC* 60, 69, Bain, *Actors* 104 n. 3. According to the grammarian Helladius (in Photius *Bibliotheca* 530a, 8.171.12ff. Henry, cf. Moeris s.v. κομμώτριαν, Pollux 7.165; Kock 2.62, Bruhn, *Wortschatz* 63, Durham, *Vocabulary* 72) κουρίς replaced κομμώτρια in the sense of 'lady's maid' in later Attic and the *Koine*; presumably cutting the mistress's hair and dressing her were jobs done by the same female servant. It seems likely, however, that a woman working independently as a hairdresser would also be called a κουρίς. Three writers of later Greek comedy – Antiphanes, Amphis, Alexis – composed plays with this title, and one of the trio in all probability was the model for Naevius' *Commotria* (Ribbeck,

CRF^3 13).[1] None of the extant frs. from any of these plays give a clue to the role of the title figure, but in Plautus' *Truculentus* a *tonstrix* who plied her trade in several households acted as a go-between, tracking down an illegitimate baby boy and handing him over to a *meretrix* for a trick on a soldier (389ff.).

Fr. 113(108K) of Alexis' Κουρίς refers to a certain Timocles in terms which suggest he was a contemporary Athenian with a reputation for drunkenness. Although this Timocles could have been the comic poet, whose career extended from the 340s till after 317 (so Webster), there is no evidence that the comic poet was a notorious toper, and too many other Athenians bore the same name during Alexis' lifetime (cf. Kirchner, *PA* 2.319f., 484) for this identification to be sustained (cf. Meineke 1.389, V. Bevilacqua, *Dioniso* 7 (1939) 26f., Bain, *Actors* 104 n. 3, and my comm. on 113(108K).2–3).

The impossibility of dating Alexis' play even roughly is especially frustrating, since two of its three frs. appear to derive from identifiable sections of the play, and as the placing of these frs. is based on a comparison with similar passages in plays of Menander, it would have been helpful to know whether Alexis' play preceded, coincided with or came after the period of Menander's career. Fr. 112(107K), as Leo first noted (*Hermes* 43 (1908) 308ff.), announces the arrival of some male revellers in terms which remind us of the formula inserted by Menander at the end of each first act to introduce a chorus usually of comasts, whose sole function apparently was to entertain the audience in the four intervals between the acts. In Menander this formula is part sometimes of a monologue (*Dysk.* 230ff., probably *Pk.* 261ff., cf. Gomme–Sandbach, *Comm. ad loc.*), sometimes of dialogue (*Asp.* 245ff., *Epitr.* 169ff., cf. Plaut. *Bacch.* 105ff., A. Primmer, *Handlungsgliederung in Nea und Palliata* (Vienna 1984) 57f.).[2] The formula looks like a tired cliché in the Menandrean passages, but Alexis invests it with a fresh and lively imagination that may indicate either the writer's mode of dealing with established conventions or novelty in a device not yet devitalised by overuse. The speaker of fr.

---

[1] Κομμώτρια is nowhere attested as a Greek comic title.

[2] Cf. also (1) Antiphanes 91, which resembles the four Menander passages and Alexis 112(107K) in import, although its use of dithyrambic diction and anapaestic dimeters (cf. Nesselrath, *MK* 253 n. 31, 270 and n. 79) may possibly point to a time when the formula was still being developed, well before ossification into a cliché (cf. Webster, *SLGC* 60); and (2) com. adesp. fr. 256.25ff. Austin, where the traditional comasts may have been replaced by a chorus of night guards, according to a plausible interpretation of a badly mutilated passage (cf. K. Latte, *Gnomon* 27 (1955) 497 = *Kleine Schriften* (Munich 1968) 794f.).

112(107K) was male (vv. 3, 6) and probably alone on stage at the time (vv.3–6, where the approaching revellers are apostrophised, leave an impression of soliloquy), like Daos at the end of the first act in *Dysk*. If he habitually wore a ἱμάτιον, as is implied by v. 6, he will have been free rather than a slave, but we have no further clues to his identity.[1]

In the plays of Menander this chorus of comasts is always attached to a New-Comedy plot of love and intrigue, and the combination of Alexis' title here and the subject matter of the play's other sizable fr. (113(108K)) makes it likely that Κουρίς also conformed to the same pattern. Frantz argued persuasively that fr. 113(108K) comes from a delayed prologue speech, in which the father of two sons, one a country yokel and the other a city wastrel, contrasts their characters in terms which indicate that the latter son has already been seen on stage. Similar references to an earlier appearance occur in Menander's delayed prologues and those of Roman adaptations (*Asp.* 122, *Pk.* 127f., Plaut. *Cist.* 149ff., cf. *MG* 88f.; T. Williams, *Rh. Mus.* 105 (1962) 203f.), although the Menandrean examples come from divine prologues, while the speakers in Alexis and *MG* are human.

If Alexis' play emphasised a contrast between the boorish ignorance of a rustic and the dissipated sophistication of a townsman, it would have been developing a motif that can be traced back on the Athenian comic stage at least as far as Aristophanes, in whose first play (Δαιταλῆς) a comparable pair of sons appeared, as Frantz noted (Ar. *Nub.* 528ff. and Σ *ad loc.* = *testimonia* c, d in A. C. Cassio's edition (Pisa 1977) of the frs.). A parallel contrast was featured in Menander's Ὑποβολιμαῖος (Körte–Thierfelder 2.146ff., Webster, *SM* 100f., G. Zuntz, *PBA* 42 (1956) 236f.), and is perhaps implied also by a difficult fr. of Antiphanes (127(129K)), where a character is described as ὁ μὲν ἀγρῷ τρεφόμενος (v.1). That fr. breaks off before the antithetical clause is reached, and so the identity of the person contrasted with this rustic is a mystery:[2] unfortunately so, for the fr.

---

[1] Webster's suggestion (*SLGC* 60, cf. 69) that he was a parasite was based, as he once told me, on the facts that he wore a ἱμάτιον and was alone, while a wealthy man would have been accompanied by a slave. Stage behaviour, however, did not always mimic real life, and men as wealthy as Kallippides could be introduced entering by the πάροδος without escort (Men. *Dysk.* 776).

[2] This person need not have been either male or sibling. Contrast between unrelated rustics and townsmen is a familiar motif in Greco-Roman comedy: e.g. Men. *Dysk.*, Plaut. *Truc.*, probably also Men. *Georg.*, *Heros*. Cf. my paper in *Phoenix* 18 (1964) 114f., citing earlier discussions (especially Wehrli, *Motivstudien* 49), K. Gaiser in O. Rieth, *Die Kunst Menanders in den 'Adelphen' des Terenz* (Hildesheim 1964) 147

derives from Antiphanes' Κουρίς. Is the presence of a country-bred male in the two like-named plays of Alexis and Antiphanes a coincidence, or was there some significant link (e.g. Alexis adapting or plagiarising the other's plot: cf. the introductions to Ἀλείπτρια, Ἄντεια)? There is not enough evidence to decide.

Although with the above interpretations fr. 113(108K) must come before 112(107K) in the play, Kassel–Austin print the latter fr. first, as do earlier editors of the comic fragments. The third fr. from Alexis' Κουρίς (114(109K)) cannot be securely placed.

112 (107K)

Meineke 3.428 (1), Kock 2.333, Edmonds 2.420, Kassel–Austin 2.81; cf. F. Leo, *Hermes* 43 (1908) 308f., J. Taillardat, *Rev. Phil.* 37 (1963) 100. Despite the fresh and witty presentation in this fr. of the formula used in New Comedy for introducing the chorus at the end of the first act (see above, introduction to Κουρίς, where the speaker's identity and situation are discussed), four stereotyped motifs are clearly recognisable:

(1) The approach of a group of men is signalled (also Men. *Asp.* 246ff., *Dysk.* 230f., *Epitr.* 169f., *Pk.* 261f., cf. Antiphanes fr. 91).

(2) This approach is offered as an explanation (here and at *Asp.* 245f., *Dysk.* 230 introduced by καὶ γάρ, cf. Denniston, *GP* 108ff.; at *Epitr.* 169 by ὡς καί); in the Menander passages it explains the speaker's decision to leave the stage or to instruct others to do so, and we may confidently guess that some such decision was expressed in the lost context of the Alexis fr.

(3) The approaching men are tipsy revellers (*Asp.* 248, *Dysk.* 231, *Epitr.* 170, *Pk.* 261), i.e. comasts usually (but devotees of Pan in *Dysk.*, ? night-guards in com. adesp. fr. 256.25ff. Austin, see above, p. 298 n. 2).

(4) It would be inadvisable to get in the revellers' way (*Dysk.* 232, *Epitr.* 171).

The formula and the type of chorus it introduces were doubtless developed into stereotyped form during the period of Middle Comedy, although embryonic parallels can be found in late Aristophanes (*Eccl.* 279ff.) and in Euripides (*Hipp.* 51ff., *Phoen.* 193ff., *Cycl.* 36ff., possibly fr. 105); cf. Fraenkel, *MNC* 71, *Beob.* 23 n. 1, Wilamowitz, *Schiedsg.* 54f., Handley, comm. on Men. *Dysk.* 230–2, W. G. Arnott, *ZPE* 31 (1978) 18f.

The history and function of the comic chorus in the 4th century have

n. 13, E. S. Ramage, *Philologus* 110 (1966) 194ff., D. Del Corno, *Dioniso* 43 (1969) 85ff., G. Bodei Giglioni, *SCO* 22 (1982) 85ff., D. Wiles, *The Masks of Menander* (Cambridge 1991) 175f., 185f.

been extensively discussed; the more recent discussions include K. J. Maidment, *CQ* 29 (1935) 1ff., Pickard-Cambridge, *TDA* 160ff., Webster, *SLGC* 58ff. and *The Greek Chorus* (London 1970) 191ff., K. J. Dover in *Fifty Years (and Twelve) of Classical Scholarship* (Oxford 1968) 116ff., G. M. Sifakis, *Studies in the History of Hellenistic Drama* (London 1967) 113ff. and *AJP* 92 (1971) 416ff., E. Pöhlmann, *WJA* 3 (1977) 68ff., and R. L. Hunter, *ZPE* 36 (1979) 23ff.

1 ἐπικώμων: Musurus' conjecture for A's meaningless ἐπὶ κώμων (Ath. 8.362c: citation omitted in Epit.) is probably correct (cf. Alciphron 4.10 ἐπίκωμός ποτε πρὸς ἡμᾶς ... ἐφοίτα), but neither Casaubon's ἐπὶ κῶμον (-μον corrupted to -μων by assimilation to the ending of the following word; cf. Xen. *Symp.* 2.1 ἔρχεται ... ἐπὶ κῶμον Συρακόσιός τις ἄνθρωπος) nor my own ἐπικωμάζον (cf. Chariton 1.3.2) can be ruled out. A further uncertainty over the transmission, however, hinders an assured solution here; if ἐπικώμων or ἐπὶ κῶμον is accepted, it must be assumed that A has a lacuna of half a metron in the opening trimeter. The formulaic parallels in Menander (*Asp.* 245f., *Dysk.* 230: see my introduction to fr. 112(107K)) suggest that in this motif καί and γάρ are not separated but open verse and sentence together; in that case the gap must come either (with both ἐπικώμων and ἐπὶ κῶμον) between the penthemimeral caesura and ἀνθρώπων (the best supplements here are Naber's <πλεῖστον>, *Mnemosyne* 8 (1880) 258 and Blaydes' <ἄφατον>, *Adv.* 1.108, cf. πάμπολλ' in the parallel Men. *Pk.* 262; but Richards' <ἐγγύς>, *AO* 84 and (e.g.) <μέθυσον> are also possible); or (with ἐπὶ κῶμον) between γάρ and ἐπί (hence Leo's <μεθύσων>, *Hermes* 43 (1908) 308, corresponding to the Menandrean μεθυόντων *Asp.* 248, cf. *Pk.* 261, and ὑποβεβρεγμένων *Epitr.* 170, cf. *Dysk.* 231).[1] With ἐπικωμάζον one needs either to assume a brief lacuna (thus <τόδ'> ἐπικωμάζον or ἐπ. <τόδε> Diggle, noting that some form of ὅδε is regular with such announcements in Greek drama, cf. *ZPE* 24 (1977) 292; alternatively καί and γάρ might be split by e.g. <νῦν>), or to suppose (less plausibly) that the opening sentence of the citation began in the second quarter of the first metron.

κῶμον: this feature of Athenian life, in which young men, usually after an evening's carousal, roamed through the streets with garlands on their heads and torches in their hands, endangering any luckless passer-by as they rampaged irresponsibly on to the house of some lady-love or handsome boy whom they wished at least to serenade, is richly illustrated from ancient literature by Headlam–Knox, comm. on Herodas 2.34–7; cf. also Starkie on Ar. *Ach.* 981, *RE* s.vv. *Comissatio* (Rau, especially 618.50ff.)

---

[1] The conjectures of Jacobs, *Addit.* 196, Bothe, *PCGF* 539, Blaydes, *Adv.* 2.158, T. G. Tucker, *CQ* 2 (1908) 197, Peppink, *Observ.* 54f. and Edmonds range from implausibility to impossibility.

COMMENTARY

and *Komos* (Lamer, esp. 1289.29ff.), Gow's introductory note on Theoc. 3, and F. R. Adrados, *Emerita* 35 (1963) 249ff.

2–3 ὡς τῶν καλῶν τε κἀγαθῶν ἐνθάδε συνόντων: so A correctly. The speaker comments on the social class of the approaching comasts: 'I see a lot of men approaching, it looks as if the gentry are here together'. Here ὡς qualifies a genitive absolute construction (see LSJ s.v. c.1.3); for σύνειμι in this sense with indication of place cf. e.g. Ar. *Vesp.* 236 ἡνίκ' ἐν Βυζαντίῳ ξυνῆμεν. One may admire the ingenuity of conjectures such as προσιόντων, ὡς καλῶν (Meineke, *ed. min.* 714, after Casaubon, but the definite article adds a welcome defining touch) and προσίον. ὦ τῶν καλῶν (Leo, supported by Taillardat: but the genitive of exclamation is normally limited to nouns alone or nouns with adjectives; I have found no instance with a participial phrase attached), but they are totally unnecessary. Blaydes' συνιόντων (*Adv.* 1.108) is objectionable less for its graceless repetition προσίον ... συνιόντων (classical Greek is less sensitive to such duplications: cf. Jackson, *Marg. Scaen.* 22off., Barrett on Eur. *Hipp.* 29–32) than for its introduction of a proceleusmatic sequence (cf. J. W. White, *The Verse of Greek Comedy* (London 1912) 49f.).

τῶν καλῶν τε κἀγαθῶν: in comic trimeters the metrical equivalent of Attic prose's normal τῶν καλῶν κἀγαθῶν, here clearly with the class significance ('the gentry') uppermost. Menander's use of this expression is tinged with irony (*Asp.* 311 and Sandbach *ad loc.*, *Dis Ex.* 91); it is uncertain whether similar irony is intended here, or whether real criticism is directed against the class with wealth and leisure enough to engage in comastic rampage. See V. Ehrenberg, *The People of Aristophanes²* (Oxford 1951) 95ff., H. Wankel, Καλὸς καὶ ἀγαθός (Diss. Würzburg 1961) 54 n. 2, 85ff., Dover, comm. on Ar. *Nub.* 101 and *GPM* 41ff., G. E. M. de Ste. Croix, *The Origins of the Peloponnesian War* (London 1972) 371ff., W. Donlan, *AJP* 94 (1973) 365ff.

3–4 μὴ γένοιτό μοι (or rather -οιτ' ἐμοί: see below) **μόνῳ νύκτωρ ἀπαντῆσαι:** LSJ (s.v. γίγνομαι 1 *fin.*) quote no examples of this impersonal use of γίγνεται μοι/ἐμοί + infinitive (= 'I chance to') before Epictetus; the construction is in fact good (? colloquial) Attic, e.g. Ar. fr. 111(109K), Alexis 233(231K).5, Xenarchus 5; cf. K.G. 2.12f. Here γένοιτ' ἐμοί (so Diggle, in a handwritten note to me) must be printed, and not A's -τό μοι (so Kassel–Austin and previous editors), because both in this idiom and on other occasions when the personal pronoun is linked with μόνῳ, μόνῃ, μόνον, etc. (e.g. Eur. *Hipp.* 84, fr. 454, Ar. *Ach.* 51f. = 130f., Men. fr. 334.5; probably also Eur. *Cycl.* 187, Hegesippus 1.5; similarly σοὶ μόνῳ/μόνη with the pronoun first word in its clause at S. *El.* 289, Ar. *Eccl.* 7), the emphatic form of the pronoun is normal. Cf. also comm. on fr. 233(231K).5.

4–5 καλῶς πεπραγόσιν ὑμῖν περὶ τὸν βαλλισμόν: Ath. 8.362a–d cites this and three other frs. (Epicharmus fr. 79, Sophron frs. 11, 12) to illustrate the use of βαλλισμός and βαλλίζω. Tone (vulgar? colloquial?), geographical range and precise meaning of the two words were disputed in antiquity, and the debate still continues (F. Leo, *Hermes* 43 (1908) 309, L. Radermacher, *Mélanges Émile Boisacq* 2 (Brussels 1938) 206ff. and *Rh. Mus.* 91 (1942) 52ff., H. Paessens, *Rh. Mus.* 90 (1941) 146ff., J. Taillardat, *Rev. Phil.* 37 (1963) 100f.; cf. Frisk 1.215, 3.48 and Chantraine 161). Ath.'s Ulpian claims that a correct (i.e. Attic or Atticising) speaker should not say βαλλισμός but κωμάζουσιν ἢ χορεύουσιν ἤ τι ἄλλο τῶν εἰρημένων, and this ruling from Rome in the 2nd century AD seems to have been influential in persuading Leo that here too in Alexis βαλλισμός means 'dancing'. Although Leo's paper convinced some editors (e.g. Gulick, Edmonds) and LSJ s.vv., it does not take sufficient account of four facts: (1) βαλλίζω and βαλλισμός are derived from βάλλω 'I throw (at)', basically with reference to missiles; (2) up to Alexis' time the context sometimes confirms the meaning 'I throw' for βαλλίζω (e.g. Sophron fr. 12 βαλλίζοντες τὸν θάλαμον σκάτους ἐνέπλησαν, cf. 32) but never 'I dance'; (3) throwing stones etc. at people was a well-known habit among drunken comasts (e.g. Ar. *Vesp.* 1253ff., Eubulus 93(94K).10, cf. Lysias 3.7–8, 12, 15–19); (4) in the present fr. of Alexis the speaker's alarm at the approach of comasts makes more sense if these have 'had a great time' with their 'hooligan assaults' than if with 'dancing' merely. Most of these facts were clarified by Radermacher, Paessens and Taillardat, but they sought in turn to oversimplify their final definitions by aiming for a too precise, one-track translation. 'Pelting' is certainly the core meaning of βαλλισμός in this passage, but the word has a penumbra of associations evoked by the behaviour of a rampaging κῶμος, associations which include the music of cymbal, drum and pipes, singing and doubtless also drunken dancing.[1] καλῶς πεπραγόσιν is ironic here only in so far as it presents the action from the viewpoint of the comasts and not from that of their potential victims; Meineke's κακῶς for καλῶς (5.89) is thus unwarranted.

5–6 Cloaks (ἱμάτια) were stolen from undefended Athenians in the streets at night by footpads who specialised in this type of theft (λωπο-δύται), to judge from numerous references in comedy and elsewhere (Ehrenberg 244 and n. 9, R. G. Ussher, comm. (Oxford 1973) on Ar. *Eccl.* 544–6), and it is clear from Dem. 54.8 that comasts sometimes imitated these footpads: there Ariston claims to have been attacked and stripped of his cloak by Conon and a band of drunken revellers. However, the victim of such an assault might himself remove and jettison his cloak in order to

---

[1] There is, however, no firm evidence that either βαλλίζω or βαλλισμός ever meant 'dance' *tout court* before the imperial period, when this new meaning was first attested in Magna Graecia. See especially Paessens' thorough discussion, *loc. cit.*

COMMENTARY

make a speedier escape, as did the boyfriend in Lys. 3.12 ὁ δὲ ῥίψας τὸ ἱμάτιον ᾤχετο φεύγων.

6 μὴ φύσας πτερά: 'without growing wings', a favourite idea of Eur. in comparable contexts: e.g. *Or.* 1593 ἤν γε μὴ φύγῃς πτεροῖς, *Phoen.* 1216, *Hel.* 618f., and cf. Ar. *Av.* 785ff., 1418ff.

113 (108K)

Meineke 3.428 (ii), Kock 2.334, Edmonds 2.422, Kassel–Austin 2.82; cf. W. Frantz, *De comediae atticae prologis* (Diss. Strasbourg 1891) 44, F. Leo, *Der Monolog im Drama* (Berlin 1908) 45, Bain, *Actors* 186ff. Part of a deferred prologue, delivered after a scene in which the speaker's drunken son had already appeared. The other son, described as a stupid yokel, was clearly intended to contrast with him in a pairing paralleled elsewhere in ancient comedy (see above, introduction to Κουρίς).

1 ὁ μὲν οὖν ἐμὸς υἱός: on the rhythm see *CQ* 7 (1957) 193. What is unusual here is that divided resolutions occur in two successive anapaests.

1–2 οἷον ὑμεῖς ἀρτίως εἴδετε: cf. the prologue of Men. *Pk.* 127f. τῆς παιδός, ἥν νῦν εἴδετε | ὑμεῖς. Speakers normally address the audience directly (in the second person plural) only in the prologue and at the end of the play (also Men. *Asp.* 113, *Dysk.* 1, 46, *Phasm.* 19, *Pk.* 170f., *Sam.* 5, Philemon 95(91K).8, com. adesp. fr. 252.12 Austin; these and other passages are collected by Bain 186f.). The words of Alexis (οἷον ... τοιοῦτος) suggest that this son had actually been presented as drunk on his initial stage appearance.

τοιοῦτος (with correption: cf. MacDowell's edition of Ar. *Vesp.* p. 22, West, *Greek Metre* 11) preceded by οἷος; at fr. 91(87K).3–4 ποῖος ... τοιοῦτος οἷος. In the extant frs. of Alexis the οι of ποῖος is always *anceps* (×3), of οἷος sometimes long (×5) and sometimes *anceps* (×2), of τοιοῦτος sometimes long (×2), more often short (×5) or *anceps* (×7).

2–3 In this list of 'drunkards' the MSS (A, Epit.[1]) of Ath. 10.443e omit a syllable between κάπηλος ἤ and Τιμοκλῆς. Porson, *Adv.* 120 supplied τις to fill the gap, but this word more commonly follows the word to which it is attached (cf. K.G. 1.665 n. 6; in Alexis it follows 34 times, including the two instances in 113(108K).2–3, and precedes 6 times, among which only frs. 152(148K).2 and 247(245K).15–16 would be directly comparable here). Dindorf's καί is preferable; it gives extra emphasis to the last name in the list ('or even – Timocles!'), with particular appropriateness since Timocles was the only real (and presumably still living) figure named. Cf.

---

[1] Peppink's text of Epit., which prints τις between ἤ and Τιμοκλῆς, is incorrect here, misleading W. Vollgraff, *REG* 53 (1940) 176; CE have the same lacuna as A.

304

Denniston, *GP* 306, and (on the easy confusion between ἤ and abbreviated καί, which might help to explain the corruption as quasi-haplography) Diggle, *Studies* 27, 120. Bergk's ἤτοι (in Meineke 5.ccvi) is most unlikely; this particle rarely introduces a second or later item in a series of disjunctives (Denniston, *GP* 553).

Oenopion (Keyssner in *RE* s.v. *Oinopion* 1, 2272.5ff., Wörner in Roscher s.v. 1, 791.18ff., B. Gentili, *Helikon* 1 (1961) 493ff, A. Veneri, *QUCC* 26 (1977) 91ff.), the legendary king of Chios and son of Ariadne and either Dionysus or Theseus, heads Alexis' list not just because of his legendary associations with the wine god (on Attic vases he seems to be portrayed as a youth at Dionysus' side: Beazley, *ARV*² 1159, 1341) and the vine, but more perhaps because his name suggests an etymology from οἶνον πιών.[1] A comedy by Philetaerus is named after him; its frs. reveal only that a cook was worked into the plot; the same title (perhaps the same play or a revised version: cf. Meineke 1.348) may well have been attributed also to his brother Nicostratus, if a plausible emendation is accepted (cf. Kassel–Austin 7.83).[2] Oenopion is the *nom parlant* of a young cupbearer in Lucian *Pseudol.* 21 and the addressee of Alciphron 2.11.

Maron (Kruse in *RE* s.v. 2, 1911.16ff., Schirmer in Roscher s.v., 2382.44ff.; cf. Preller–Robert, *GM* 1.731, Headlam–Knox on Herodas 3.24–5, Seaford, comm. on Eur. *Cycl.* 141) is a son or more probably grandson of Oenopion, according to Hes. fr. 238 Merkelbach–West; his father is named Euanthes by Homer *Od.* 9.197, Dionysus by Eur. *Cycl.* 141 (cf. also R. G. Ussher, comm. (Rome 1978) *ad loc.*) and Silenus by Nonnus 14.99. The exceptional strength of the red wine he gave to Odysseus (*Od.* 9.209f., cf. Clearchus fr. 5; the scene is portrayed on a mid-4th-century Sicilian vase in Lipari, inv. 2297, possibly inspired by drama, cf. A. D. Trendall and T. B. L. Webster, *Illustrations of Greek Drama* (London 1971) 114 and fig. III.6.2) doubtless explains his presence in Alexis' list.

Next after Oenopion and Maron in the MSS comes Κά- or κάπηλος. No such proper name is attested from myth or Athenian real life (*pace* V. Bevilacqua, *Dioniso* 7 (1939) 27 and Kassel–Austin); accordingly, two

---

[1] Probably an incorrect popular derivation; the link with οἶνοψ seems more plausible, as F. G. Welcker, *Die Aeschylische Trilogie Prometheus* (Darmstadt 1824) 549 n. 848 first suggested.

[2] The MSS of the *Suda* s.v. ἀμφίας cite for that word Νικόστρατος οἰνοποιῶ, corrected to Οἰνοπίωνι by J. Meursius (in J. Gronovius (ed.), *Thesaurus Graecarum antiquitatum* 10 (Leiden 1701) 1585A); this is the only citation from the Nicostratus title (fr. 17(18K)). Philetaerus and Nicostratus were both sons of Aristophanes, and the authorship of a second play (Ἄντυλλος: cf. Meineke 1.347f.) was already disputed between the two in antiquity (Ath. 3.108c, 118e, cf. 2.65d).

solutions are open. Either we posit textual corruption and assume that behind the *ductus* a third (? mythical) figure is lurking – e.g. καὶ Στάφυλος. Staphylus (Gebhard in *RE* s.v. *Staphylos* 1, 2145.19ff., Ostern in Roscher s.v. 1414.62ff.), like Oenopion, is a son of Ariadne and either Dionysus or Theseus (the sources, given by Gebhard, oscillate between the two), and the significant name would make him an appropriate member of Alexis' list. Or – and I am inclined to favour this alternative – we keep the MSS reading and interpret κάπηλος as a common noun. In comic (= ? popular) usage, when this noun appears without any qualification (genitival or otherwise), it normally has the specific meaning of 'innkeeper' or 'wine-seller' (LSJ s.v. 2, e.g. Ar. *Lys.* 466, *Thesm.* 347, 737, Plato com. 188(174K).4, Antiphanes 25(24K).2, Eubulus 80.4, Diphilus 3.5; cf. Nicostratus 22, where the κάπηλος sells wine, vinegar and torches, and com. adesp. fr. 245.35 Austin, badly mutilated but with wine mentioned in the two following lines);[1] κάπηλος consequently would fit very well into any list of wine-bibbers.

Finally, ἢ <καὶ> Τιμοκλῆς, presumably a contemporary Athenian in the climactic final place after two mythical and probably one generic figures. The audience would immediately have identified the man pilloried by Alexis as a toper; we cannot do so. Timocles was a common name in Athens (see introduction to Κουρίς), and at least six men in Kirchner's now incomplete catalogue (cf. Davies, *APF* 505f. no. 13675) are possible contenders for the identification here: *PA* nos. 13725 (ἀρχιτέκτων in the naval records, 342 and later, *IG* ii².1622.170, 1623.124, etc.), 13726 (the comic poet), 13726a, 13729, 13737 and 13739.

4 μεθύει γάρ, οὐδὲν ἕτερον: Kassel–Austin print the transmitted ἕτερον, which can be given a defence of sorts if (i) a comma or colon is placed after γάρ (so Kaibel: 'you see, he's drunk – nothing but that'), and (ii) comparison is made with some passages in Attic comedy and later Greek where οὐδεὶς (or οὐχ) ἕτερος is used loosely in place of οὐδεὶς (or οὐχ) ἄλλος: e.g. Antiphanes 318(324K).4, cited by Stob. 4.20.12 with καταλείπετ' οὐδὲν ἕτερον ἢ τεθνηκέναι (but the same passage is attributed by Ath. 13.563a to Theophilus 12.4 with ἄλλο πλὴν replacing ἕτερον ἢ, Plut. *Mor.* 671b τὸν δ' Ἄδωνιν οὐχ ἕτερον ἀλλὰ Διόνυσον εἶναι νομίζουσιν; cf. Alexis 177(173K).7, Men. *Epitr.* 609, LSJ s.v. ἕτερος II). There are no parallels, however, for the kind of paratactic use required by the paradosis here, and Porson's μεθ. γὰρ οὐδὲν ἧττον (*Adv.* 120) provides a welcome comparative link with the list of examples in the preceding

---

[1] Possibly also Ar. *Av.* 1292, *Eccl.* 49 (see Ussher *ad loc.*), fr. 285(274K) and Hermippus fr. 61, but in these four passages the context is either unspecific or inadequate.

clause. It could easily have been corrupted by assimilation to the following ὁ δ' ἕτερος.

4–6 For the wording of the question cf. A. *Ag.* 1232f. τί νιν καλοῦσα . . . τύχοιμ' ἄν; and Eur. *IT* 1321 πῶς σε . . . ὀνομάσας τύχω; (with the comments of Diggle, *Studies* 89ff.); for a parallel question-and-answer sequence inside a single speech cf. Heliodorus 2.4 ἀλλ' ὦ – τί ἄν σέ τις ὀνομάσειε; νύμφην; . . . γαμετήν;. More often, however, such questions are purely rhetorical and receive no answer: e.g. Ar. *Nub.* 1378 ὦ – τί σ' εἴπω;, Dem. 18.22 εἶτ' ὦ – τί ἄν εἰπών σέ τις ὀρθῶς προσείποι;, and the examples collected by Fraenkel on A. *Ag.* 1232f.; cf. also Barrett on Eur. *Hipp.* 826f.

5–6 βῶλος, ἄροτρον, γηγενὴς ἄνθρωπος: Alexis has a parallel list of insensitive things at fr. 207(204K); the present selection indicates that the son described was a rustic dunderhead. ἄροτρον and βῶλος are not applied elsewhere to human beings (but cf. the use of πηλός at com. adesp. fr. 890 Kock; *lutum* as a pejorative in Latin implies villainy rather than stupidity, e.g. Plaut. *Pers.* 406, 414, Catullus 42.13, Cic. *Pis.* 62); γηγενής follows them here with clear emphasis on its derivation ἐκ γῆς γενόμενος, 'born from the soil' and so 'cloddish' like a βῶλος, cf. Xenarchus 1.5 γηγενὴς βολβός. Elsewhere in comedy the adjective is used of the Giants (Ar. *Av.* 824) and their various attributes, especially great size (Ar. *Ran.* 825, Antiphanes 180(182K).3) and impiety (Ar. *Nub.* 853 and Σ, with Dover *ad loc.*). Cf. A. Josephson, *Eranos* 54 (1956) 246ff.[1]

Without the following context it is hard to decide whether Alexis wrote ἄνθρωπος (so MSS: cf. Blaydes, *Adv.* 1.108 suggesting that it should be followed by a question mark, 2.337) as part of the third item in the predicate, or ἄνθρωπος (so first one of the Dindorfs, *TGL* s.v. ἄροτρον; later also Meineke 3.428f., Barrett in his edition of Eur. *Hipp.* pp. 322, 439) as subject of the clause. The same problem recurs at Men. *Dysk.* 88f. (see Sandbach *ad loc.*). Cf. also Alexis 145(141K).1 with comm., and contrast 88(85K).3–5, 140(135K).17.

114 (109K)

Meineke 3.429 (III), Kock 2.334, Edmonds 2.422, Kassel–Austin 2.82.

δεδείπναμεν (here and Eubulus 90(91K)), δεδειπνέναι (Ar. frs. 260(249K), 480(464K), Plato com. 157(144K), Antiphanes 141(143K), Eubulus 91(92K), Epicrates 1), ἠρίσταμεν (Ar. fr. 513(496K), Theopompus com. 23(22K)) and ἠριστάναι (Hermippus 60) are 'second' perfect forms found

---

[1] In Latin the equivalent expression *terrae filius* seems to have a more restricted social implication: 'a man without antecedents' (*OLD* s.v. *terra* 4b, citing Cic. *Att.* 1.13.4, *Fam.* 7.9.3, Petronius 43.5).

in Attic comedy (and presumably popular speech) towards the end of the 5th and throughout the 4th centuries. Possibly coined on the analogy of such established forms as ἕσταμεν and ἑστάναι, they were distinctive enough for the cited instances to be collected by ancient grammarians (Ath. 10.422e citing Alexis here, Antiatticist 89.26 Bekker, Photius s.v. ἠριστάναι, cf. Eustath. 1900.9). Side by side with them occur 'first' perfect forms in -ηκ-: δεδείπνηκας (Ar. *Eccl.* 1133, possibly also Men. fr. 838, but see Körte *ad loc.*), ἠριστήκατε (Men. *Dysk.* 779), ἠριστηκώς (Alexis 123(118K), Antiphanes 216(217K).25, Diphilus 45(46K), Dromon 2). Cf. H. Osthoff, *Zur Geschichte des Perfekts im Indogermanischen* (Strasbourg 1884) 361ff., Veitch, *Greek Verbs*[4] 99, 174, K.B. 2.373f., 397, O. Szemerényi, *Syncope in Greek and Indo-European* (Naples 1964) 25ff.

Κράτεια ἢ Φαρμακοπώλης

Meineke 1.395f., Th. Bergk, *Rh. Mus.* 35 (1880) 259ff., K. Zacher, *BPW* 6 (1886) 714 (under 'Eubulus 110.18' by error), G. Kaibel, edition of Ath. 1 p. xl, III p. vii, *Hermes* 25 (1890) 98f. and *RE* s.v. *Alexis* 9, 1469.31ff., O. Crusius, *Philologus* 46 (1888) 619, W. Headlam, *CR* 13 (1899) 6f., Breitenbach 159f., W. S. Ferguson, *Hellenistic Athens* (London 1911) 114f. n. 7, A. Olivieri, *Atti Accad. Napoli* 9 (1926) 463ff., Wilamowitz, *Glaube* 2.176 n. 2, Edmonds 2.422f. note b, Webster, *SLGC* 105, A. Giannini, *Acme* 13 (1960) 159, W. G. Arnott in Flores 367, Nesselrath, *MK* 305 n. 54, 324 n. 114, 328 n. 127. Six frs. are preserved from this play, all in Ath. The *Marcianus*[1] records the title (always in the dative with iotas adscript) as follows:

Κρατίαι ἢ Φαρμακοπώληι: 3.95a = fr. 115(110K).15, 8.340a = 117(112K).
Κρατίαι ἢ Φαρμακοπώλη: 15.678c = 119(114K).
Κρατίαι: 8.340c = 118(113K), 11.473d = 120(115K).
Κρατείαι ἢ Φαρμακοπώληι: 3.107a = 115(110K).
Φαρμακοπώληι ἢ Κρατείαι: 6.254a = 116(111K), wrongly reported by Kaibel *ad loc.* as Κρατεύᾳ, but see III *praef.* p. vii.

Kaibel in 1890 first recognised that (1) Κρατία was an iotacistic misspelling of Κρατεία (same error, same name in *P.Oxy.* 2656 at Men. *Mis.* 305 and in the Vienna MS of a collection of apophthegms, 181 Wachsmuth, published as part of *Festschrift zur XXXVI. Philologenversammlung* (Freiburg 1881): see also below, p. 311 n. 2), and that (2) in Hellenistic catalogues

---

[1] The only relevant MS: Epit. of Ath. omits the title (as usually) at 107a, 340a and 678c, and the whole citation in the other four places.

the title was usually given as Κράτεια (not -τείας[1]) ἢ Φαρμακοπώλης. Alternative titles were added to comedies for a variety of reasons (cf. introduction to Ἀγωνίς); here the explanation is less likely to have been an Alexandrian pedant's wish to distinguish Alexis' play from others featuring (but not necessarily named after) a heroine called Krateia (e.g. Men. *Mis.*), more probably Φαρμακοπώλης was substituted as title for a second production of the play in a revised version while Alexis was still alive (cf. introduction to Δημήτριος). Such a hypothesis best explains the presence in the extant frs. of references to people and events several years apart.

The original production of Alexis' play (presumably with the title Κράτεια) would be dated to the period *c.* 345–318 because frs 117(112K) and 118(113K) mention the pro-Macedonian politician Callimedon (fr. 117(112K) in terms which imply that he was alive and active; but he had left Athens by 318,[2] cf. introductions to Δορκίς, Ἰσοστάσιον). Fr. 116(111K), however, toasts an event in the last decade of the century: a victory associated with the names of Antigonus τοῦ βασιλέως, Demetrius τοῦ νεανίσκου and Φίλας Ἀφροδίτης. Meineke correctly identified the first two as A. Monophthalmus and his son D. Poliorcetes, but the third (Phila deified as Aphrodite) was not D.'s mother (as Meineke claimed) but his wife (or perhaps ex-wife: cf. Kaibel in *RE* s.v. *Alexis* 9, 1469.31ff. and Ferguson 114f. n. 7). Meineke also recognised that the victory celebrated by Alexis here was the one gained at sea by Demetrius over the Ptolemaic fleet off Cyprian Salamis in spring or early summer 306,[3] when D. was still

---

[1] Κρατείας (which never occurs as a character name in comedy) was once suggested as the nominative form of this part of the title by Kaibel (his Ath., I p. xl) but quickly forgotten. Before Kaibel's day editors generally assumed (following Casaubon, *Animadv.* 181) that Alexis' title was rather Κρατεύας and its subject the great pharmacologist of this name (cf. the play's alternative title). This Crateuas, however, flourished *c.* 100 as the court physician to Mithridates VI (cf. M. Wellmann, *Abh. Göttingen* 2/1 (1897) 3ff.), and no other pharmacist with this name is known to have existed (the letter from Hippocrates to Crateuas, no. 16 in the Hippocratic corpus, is spurious; and the 4th-century supporter of Cassander was a general, not a physician (Diod. Sic. 19.50.7ff.).

[2] Here we lose track of him; he is not mentioned again in our sources and probably died in exile. Edmonds' theory (2.425 note b) that Callimedon survived the period of the Phalerean's regime and returned to Athens in 306 (thus making it possible that Alexis' Κράτεια was produced only once, in 305) is backed by no evidence and seems inherently unlikely for a politician who had already surfaced in the 340s.

[3] Cf. A. E. Samuel, *Ptolemaic Chronology* (Munich 1962) 6, K. Buraselis, *Das hellenistische Makedonien und die Ägäis* (Munich 1982) 52f. and G. A. Lehmann, *ZPE* 72 (1988) 1 and n. 2.

COMMENTARY

νεανίσκος (29/30 in Diod. Sic. 19.69.1, 27/8 in Plut. *Demetr.* 5.2); after this battle A. openly assumed the status of βασιλεύς (Diod. Sic. 20.53.2, Plut. *Demetr.* 18), and Phila's deification was confirmed in 305 by the erection of a temple in Athens (Dionysius son of Tryphon in Ath. 6.255c names Adeimantus of Lampsacus and his friends as her sponsors; cf. Ferguson 114f. n. 7).[1]

This interpretation of fr. 116(111K) presupposes that a second production of Alexis' play was mounted in Athens shortly after the victory at Salamis (? Lenaea or Dionysia 305, if the occasion was a major state festival), with these commemorative lines specially written for the new performance and a new title (Φαρμακοπώλης: see above) replacing the original one. Significantly, fr. 116(111K) is the only fr. cited from the play by Ath. with Φαρμακοπώλης presented as its first and not alternative title.

One apparent difficulty, however, with this interpretation of the references in fr. 116(111K) was indicated by Bergk. At the time of Salamis Demetrius was divorced from Phila and married[2] to an Athenian aristocrat, Euthydice, a descendant of Miltiades and widow of Ophellas. Could Alexis have tactfully toasted the Macedonian ex-wife when the star of the new Athenian bride was in the ascendant? The answer is, probably yes; it would be wrong to assume modern susceptibilities anachronistically for 4th-century Athens. After all, Phila's temple was built after the divorce, and the ex-wife enjoyed great esteem as daughter of Antipater and widow of Craterus, one of Alexander's leading generals.[3] Such prestige would not have been substantially diminished by divorce, which was entered into on the flimsiest grounds in 4th-century Athens (W. Erdmann, *Die Ehe im alten*

---

[1] On this and other deifications at this period (e.g. Lamia, Leaena) see especially K. Scott, *AJP* 49 (1928) 137ff., M. P. Nilsson, *Geschichte der griechischen Religion* 2 (Munich 1950) 142f. and C. Habicht, *Gottmenschentum und griechische Städte* (Munich 1956) 63 n. 22. Many extravagant honours were showered upon Antigonus and Demetrius by the Athenians as liberators of their city (see especially W. B. Dinsmoor, *The Archons of Athens in the Hellenistic Age* (Cambridge Mass. 1931) 13f., cf. also K. J. Beloch, *Griechische Geschichte* 4.1² (Berlin and Leipzig 1925) 150ff., H. Bengtson, *Griechische Geschichte* (Munich 1950) 354 and G. Glotz, P. Roussel, R. Cohen, *Histoire grecque* 4.1² (Paris 1945) 320f., 329f.

[2] Diod. Sic. 20.40.5, Plut. *Demetr.* 14; cf. Ferguson 111, Glotz–Roussel–Cohen, *Histoire grecque* 4.1² 320f.

[3] Plutarch (*Demetr.* 14.1) indeed suggests that D. never actually divorced her, but was married to both Phila and Euthydice at the same time. On Phila's later career see Ferguson 114f. n. 7; she did not die before 306, as Kaibel erroneously thought (*RE* s.v. *Alexis* 9, 1469.31ff.), but lived on until 288.

Griechenland (Munich 1934) 90, 96f., 358f. and *passim*). Accordingly the reference to Phila in 116(111K).5 need have implied no slur on the new Athenian wife, whether any laudatory mention of Euthydice appeared in the fr.'s lost context (or in the gap at v. 6: see comm. *ad loc.*) or not.

Bergk's difficulty thus proves illusory, and does not call for an alternative interpretation or dating of fr. 116(111K). Bergk himself was driven to propose[1] that the fr. was inserted into the play for a revival after Alexis' death, commemorating a victory gained by Antigonus Gonatas (the husband of a Phila and father of a Demetrius!) over the Molossi in 264. This suggestion is untenable for several reasons (cf. Ferguson 114f. n. 7), but most particularly because in 264 Gonatas was Athens' enemy in the Chremonidean War (cf. W. W. Tarn, *JHS* 40 (1920) 143ff. and *Cambridge Ancient History* 7[1] (1928) 705ff., C. Habicht, *Untersuchungen zur politischen Geschichte Athens im 3. Jahrhundert v. Chr.* (Munich 1979) 108ff., F. W. Walbank, *Cambridge Ancient History* 7.1[2] (1984) 236ff.), and thus unlikely to have had a success commemorated there in such fulsome terms.

The play's titles imply that two of its characters were a drugseller and a woman called Krateia. In real life Krateia occurs as the name of (1) both free and slave women in and outside Attica,[2] (2) a divinity associated with the Cabiri (see below). On the comic stage, however, this name is carried by only one identifiable character: the heroine of Men. *Mis.*, who was captured by a soldier during a campaign (probably in Cyprus), became his slave and mistress, but eventually regained her status as the daughter of a free citizen (cf. E. G. Turner, *BICS* Suppl. 17 (1965) 11, Gomme–Sandbach, *Comm.* 438). We have no means of knowing whether Alexis' Krateia played a comparable role, although the limited evidence from

---

[1] Bergk also offered (as a δεύτερος πλοῦς) a further explanation of the references in the fr., suggesting that the victory mentioned in v. 4 might have been gained before Phila's divorce at the overthrow of the Phalerean's regime, after Poliorcetes sailed with his fleet into the Piraeus in June 307 (cf. also P. S. Dunkin, *Post-Aristophanic Comedy* (Urbana 1946) 156 n. 12). Even if that revolution could have been termed a 'victory' by its supporters, Bergk himself realised the weak point in this interpretation of the references: at the time of the revolution Antigonus had not yet assumed the title of 'king'.

[2] Attic inscriptions give Krateia as the name of a priestess in 211/10, a married woman of the 3rd or 2nd century, and a freedwoman of the 4th century AD (respectively *IG* ii².1315.5, 4030 = 8733, 8734 Kirchner, *IG* ii/5.775b, III 16); cf. Bechtel, *Frauennamen* 23. The name was also borne by a female slave from Celaetha liberated in 170 (Collitz, *GDI* 1756; cf. M. Lambertz, *Die griechischen Sklavennamen* (Vienna 1907) 20), Periander's mother (Diog. Laert. 1.96), and the alleged authoress of an apophthegm in a Vienna MS (*loc. cit.* on p. 308).

dates, identifiable characters and subject matter in the frs., as we shall see, tends to support the hypothesis that Alexis' Κράτεια had a typical New-Comedy plot.[1]

At least two other characters in the play can be identified. In fr. 120(115K) a man named Hermaïskos is described as drinking 'with blanket and haversack' by his side. The accoutrements show that he was a soldier, and the definite article before Hermaïskos' name in v. 1 suggests that he was already familiar to the audience (see respectively comm. on v. 3, introduction to the fr.). As the description is neutral in tone without obvious satirical point, it seems unlikely that Alexis here refers to an otherwise unknown contemporary soldier; we shall best assume that Hermaïskos was a character in the play.

Mnesimachus also wrote a Φαρμακοπώλης, but nothing is known about that play's plot or the role of its drugseller. In real life a φαρμακοπώλης sold not only remedial drugs but charms too and other wares with allegedly magical uses or effects (e.g. burning glasses, precious stones,

---

[1] Attempts have been made to interpret Alexis' play as political fantasy or religious travesty. Little space need be wasted on the unlikely and unevidenced speculations of A. Olivieri (*Atti Accad. Napoli* 9 (1926) 463ff.) and Edmonds (2.422f. note b). The former saw the play as an Old-Comedy extravaganza with the politician Callimedon caricatured in the role of physician-cum-cook. Edmonds suggested that Krateia and the drugseller burlesqued respectively Polyperchon's daughter-in-law Cratesipolis and the botanist Theophrastus. More impressive and transiently persuasive was G. Kaibel's idea (*Hermes* 25 (1890) 98f., cf. Kern in *RE* s.v. *Kabeiros und Kabeiroi* 1441.2ff.) that the play travestied Cabiric ritual and myth. Kaibel supported this theory by pointing out that (1) Krateia is portrayed side by side with Cabiric divinities on a 4th-century vase fragment from the Cabiric sanctuary at Thebes (H. Winnefeld, *Ath. Mitt.* 13 (1888) 420ff. and pl. 9, O. Kern, *Hermes* 25 (1890) 7ff., I. M. Linforth, *The Arts of Orpheus* (New York 1973) 140ff., B. Hemberg, *Die Kabeiren* (Uppsala 1950) 192f., 203f., W. K. C. Guthrie, *Orpheus and Greek Religion*[2] (London 1952) 123ff.), and (2) in two frs. of Κράτεια Alexis mentions Melampus (117(112K): a mythical founder of Bacchic rites, cf. Hdt. 2.49) and Orpheus (118(113K)). It may be true that elements of Cabiric, Dionysiac and Orphic myth and practice were assimilated or confused with each other both elsewhere and in Athens (cf. e.g. Kern, Linforth, Guthrie), but Kaibel's case in the end rests on a tendentious combination of shaky interpretations (cf. Wilamowitz, *Glaube* 2.176 n. 2). Krateia has no Cabiric associations in Men. *Mis.*, so far as we can see, and the references to Melampus and Orpheus in the Alexis frs. can safely be understood as casual jokes (see comm. *ad loc.*) without any need to import either figure as a character into the play.

snakes: Ar. *Nub.* 766ff. and Σ, Arist. *HA* 8.4, 594ᵃ23f., Aelian *NA* 9.62), and this association with amulets and quackery earned them much less respect than an ἰατρός proper (Plut. *Mor.* 80a, Sext. Emp. *Math.* 2.41; cf. S. Reinach in Dar.–Sag. s.v. *Medicus* 1679b, Hermann–Blümner, *Privatalterthümer* 355, W. Morel in *RE* s.v. *Pharmakopoles* 1840.24ff.). Alexis' drugseller is probably (cf. Meineke 3.431) one of the two speakers in fr. 117(112K), bragging about his medical practice in terms reminiscent of an ἰατρὸς ἀλαζών.[1]

Soldier and drugseller make two ἀλαζόνες in Alexis' play. Could there have been a third? The speaker of fr. 115(110K)'s twenty-six trimeters describes his purchase of various fish and meats, and his intention to cook them, with a conceited panache that would normally label him as a typical comic μάγειρος, but for his explicit statement in vv. 18–21 that 'a μάγειρος will not come near these (victuals), will not even set eyes upon them – he'll suffer for it, by Zeus, if he does. No – I myself will organise them, skilfully and elegantly and with subtle variations in such a way – you see, I'm cooking the fish (πῶ γὰρ τοὖψον) myself.' Who is this paradoxical cook whose antagonism to μάγειροι implies that he is not one of their number? There are two plausible answers, neither of which requires any postulate of a corrupt transmission (*pace* Kock 2.336, 3.742). One derives from the existence of catering hierarchies in 4th-century Attica, on and off[2] the comic stage. The μάγειρος, who was normally hired to butcher and then cook an animal for some special festivity (see on fr. 24), apparently claimed the leading position, but other catering jobs were performed by the δημιουργός (primarily a confectioner: Alexander com. fr. 3, Antiphanes 224(225K); female in Men. fr. 451.12), ὀψοποιός (the man who prepared ὄψα = particularly fish, see comm. on fr. 47(46K).7: Alexis 153(149K).6, Dionysius com. 2.9; G. Berthiaume, *Les Rôles du mágeiros* (Leiden 1982) 77), and τραπεζοποιός (butler, waiter and general dogsbody: Antiphanes 150(152K), Men. *Asp.* 232ff., *Dysk.* 647, *Sam.* 290, Philemon 64(61K); W. K. Pritchett, *Hesperia* 25 (1956) 279, Ch. Dedoussi's edition of Men. *Sam* (Athens 1965), comm. on v. '75' in her numeration, Sandbach, *Comm.* on *Dysk.* 647). All these categories guarded their own prerogatives while trespassing on those of their competitors (at

---

[1] See comm. on fr. 146(142K). L. Gil and I. R. Alfageme, *Cuadernos di Filología Clásica* 3 (1972) 35ff. provide an exhaustive survey of the role of the ἰατρός in Attic comedy that outdates all previous work.

[2] Pl. *Resp.* 2.373c seems to distinguish between μάγειρος and ὀψοποιός, but doubtless in ordinary life the demarcations were not strictly drawn by either the practitioners themselves or non-professional observers. At *Theaet.* 178d Plato has an ὀψοποιός in charge of a banquet, while in Theophr. *Char.* 20 a μάγειρος cooks ὄψα.

least on the comic stage), and offensive remarks by μάγειροι against the other categories are commonplace (μ. on ὀψ. Alexis 153(149K).6ff., Dionysius 2.9; μ. on τρ. Men. *Asp.* 232ff., *Dysk.* 646f.; cf. Men. fr. 451, a householder on μ. ~ δ.; cf. Handley on Men. *Dysk.* 646, Dohm, *Mageiros* 81f., 235ff.). The provisions bought by the speaker of fr. 115(110K) are mainly fish (= ὄψα, vv. 1–14), and in v. 21 he says ποῶ . . . τοὔψον αὐτός. Is he an ὀψοποιός? If so, Alexis' Κράτεια includes three ἀλαζόνες in its cast-list.[1]

Zacher first proposed, and Crusius and Headlam independently reiterated, a more economical, but not necessarily more persuasive, identification of the speaker of fr. 115(110K) as the φαρμακοπώλης himself, who would thus be arrogating as part of his ἀλαζονεία an expertise in cooking. Physicians stressed the role of diet in health (e.g. Hippocr. *Acut.* 28, Diocles fr. 141 Wellmann; cf. W. Jaeger, *Paideia* 3 (tr. G. Highet, Oxford 1945) 30ff., J. Schumacher, *Antike Medizin²* (Berlin 1963) 58ff., Hunter on Eubulus 6(7K).7), and some even wrote cookery books (Dohm has a useful list, 180; cf. also C. Fredrich, *Hippokratische Untersuchungen* (Berlin 1899) 172ff., Rankin, ΜΑΓΕΙΡΟΙ 2ff., Bilabel, *Ops.* and *RE* s.v. *Kochbücher*, 984.3ff., M. Treu, *Philologus* 102 (1958) 220f.). In fr. 129(124K) Alexis presents a μάγειρος with medical pretensions; the reverse situation here, with a drugseller fusing the roles of medical man and cook, would merely have stretched everyday realities in the customary manner of comic caricature.[2]

Although several characters in the play can thus be pinpointed, virtually nothing is known about its plot. Fr. 115(110K) tells us only that its speaker has bought provisions, presumably for a banquet at some stage in the play. The topical toast in fr. 116(111K) may have been part of the staged action spilling over from that banquet. A minimum of three

---

[1] If one accepts Ribbeck's categories of ἀλαζών (*Alazon* 1ff.), which include soldiers, cooks and doctors but leave out other characters whose occasional braggadocio is only a subsidiary feature (*lenones*, bankers, etc.), it is easy to find plays of later comedy with two ἀλαζόνες in the cast (e.g. Men. *Kol.*, Plaut. *Curc.*, *Men.*, *MG* , *Pseud.*), but none so far with three.

[2] These are the two credible (as opposed to wildly implausible: see p. 312 n. 1) identifications of the speaker of this fr. One other (advanced by Nesselrath, *MK* 305 n. 54; cf. A. Giannini, *Acme* 13 (1960) 159) has an outside chance: a household slave who could cook as well as shop. Such slaves existed in real life (cf. e.g. Xen. *Cyr.* 8.2.6; V. Ehrenberg, *The People of Aristophanes²* (Oxford 1951) 130 n. 6, Dohm, *Mageiros* 67), but none so far have been recognised as characters in later Greek comedy, where their duties are confined to marketing and assisting the μάγειρος (e.g. Mnesimachus 4.52ff., Men. *Dysk.* 456ff., 546).

revellers must have been present, for the speaker in v. 7 addresses ἄνδρες συμπόται; whether the παῖς addressed in v. 1 of the fr. was one of them or just a mute servant, we do not know. The garlands mentioned in 119(114K) could have been associated with this revelry or perhaps with the drugseller's medical function. The other three frs. (117, 118, 120 (112, 113, 115K)) cannot safely be assigned to a dramatic context.

115 (110K)

Meineke 3.429 (1), Kock 2.335, Edmonds 2.422, Kassel–Austin 2.83; cf. K. Zacher *BPW* 6 (1886) 714 (under 'Eubulus 110.18' by error), O. Crusius, *Philologus* 46 (1888) 619, W. Headlam, *CR* 13 (1899) 6f., A. Giannini, *Acme* 13 (1960) 159, Nesselrath, *MK* 305 n. 54, W. G. Arnott in R. Pretagostini (ed.), *Miscellanea di Studi in onore di Bruno Gentili* 3 (Rome 1993) 719ff. Although the precise identity of the speaker poses a problem (ὀψοποιός? the φαρμακοπώλης? some other non-μάγειρος? See introduction to the play), the structure and contents of this witty and imaginative long monologue link it very closely with one common type of rhesis, in which a cook/μάγειρος, on returning from market, lists the purchases that he has made, describes how he will prepare them for a banquet and brags fantastically about his skill (here vv. 18–26). Cf. particularly Alexis 84, 191–4(186–9K), Archedicus 2, 3, Philemon 82(79K), Sotades com. 1, which illustrate how much humour can be squeezed out of a limited number of formulas repeated with little real variation (Dohm, *Mageiros* 104ff., Handley on Men. *Dysk.* 393f.).

Sections of the fr. are attributed also to other plays of Alexis: vv. 9–11 to Δημήτριος (fr. 49(48K)),[1] and vv. 21(from ὥστε)–23 to Ἀσκληπιοκλείδης (fr. 24), where the consecutive clause is tagged on to a different leading idea. The most plausible explanation for these shared attributions derives from Alexis' productivity. A playwright credited with over 200 plays, in which situations like a cook's arrival with his food purchases must have recurred many times, would be likely to use the same material – consciously or unconsciously – more than once, especially if it contained an image as vivid as that in vv. 21–23 here. Cf. Kann, *De iteratis* 56 and my comm. on frs. 24, 49(48K).

1–2 The *Marcianus* here (Ath. 3.107b; Epit. omits vv. 1–5 ἀπολυθείς) gives an unmetrical text: πρῶτον μὲν ὄστρεα παρὰ Νηρεῖ τινι | ... φυκίοις ἠμφιεσμένωι. There are three problems.

(i) The opening of v. 1 is easily restored. P. Elmsley (*Ed. Rev.* 3 (1803)

---

[1] The Δημήτριος speech may well have included vv. 12–14 too: see comm. on fr. 49(48K).

190) introduced the correct Attic form ὄστρεια (ὄστρεια ... μόνως οὕτως ἔλεγον οἱ ἀρχαῖοι Ath. 3.92e citing Cratinus 8, Epicharmus fr. 42;[1] cf. A. fr. 34, Anaxandrides 42(41K).61 = Ath. 4.131e; the orthography in -ει- is required by metre in all the verse passages as in Alexis here. Moeris s.v. ὀστρία (*sic*!: p. 285 Pierson) recommends the spelling ὄστριον with long ι (cf. Photius s.v. ὄστρεα), which never occurs in MSS of Attic authors), and the syllable missing before it is most likely to have been οὖν (so Elmsley), a particle omitted with curious frequency by scribes (in dramatic texts e.g. Eur. *Or.* 1091, Ar. *Lys.* 113, Cratinus 304(282K), Epicrates 10(11K).20).

(ii) παρὰ Νηρεῖ τινι is interpreted by Meineke as a reference to a celebrated cook from Chios (Euphron 1.6), possibly burlesqued in comedies entitled Νηρεύς by Anaxandrides and Anaxilas (cf. Webster, *SLGC* 66). Alexis' Nereus, however, is no cook but a fishmonger, and the presence of τινι (which Meineke was forced to alter to τινα) after the name suggests rather that Schweighaeuser (*Animadv.* 2.235) was right to explain the phrase as a facetious designation of an aged fisherman who had brought his catch to market. The sea-god Nereus (Preller–Robert, *GM* 1. 554ff., Herzog-Hauser in *RE* s.v. 24.28ff., A. Lesky, *Thalatta* (Vienna 1947) 123ff.) is still an unnamed ἅλιος γέρων in Homer (*Il.* 18.141, *Od.* 24.58), which is close to the idea of an old fisherman (ἁλιεὺς γέρων Men. fr. 696), and in the elevated language of cooks and dinner narratives fish are styled Νηρείων τέκνων (Euphanes 1.2 = 'Euphron' 8.2 Kock) and *Neptuni pecudes* (Plaut. *Pseud.* 834); cf. Liv. Andr. *Aegisthus* fr. II Ribbeck = fr. 5 Warmington, Pacuvius fr. inc. XLV Ribbeck = fr. 352 Warmington; a cuttlefish is Νηρῆος θυγάτηρ in Matron 534.33f. Lloyd-Jones–Parsons, an eel Δαναὸς ποτάμιος in com. adesp. fr. 262.11 Austin, a (?) sheatfish Ἄδωνις ... ποτάμιος in v. 7 of the *comoedia Dukiana* (W. H. Willis, *GRBS* 32 (1991) 331ff.).

(iii) A's unmetrical φυκίοις is best explained as a scribal error for Elmsley's φυκί'; could the apostrophe indicating elision have been misread as the tachygraphic sign for -οις?[2] Translate 'dressed in seaweed', with the noun's case explained as either a retained object accusative with a

---

[1] The actual readings in the *Marcianus* and Epit. MSS show confusion over the spelling; in the statement at 92c (with CE) and citation at 131e (om. CE) A corrupts -ει- to -ε-, but has -ει- correctly in the citations of Cratinus (with CE) and Epicharmus (om. CE).

[2] Cf. F. G. Bast, *Commentatio palaeographica* (printed as a postscript to G. H. Schaefer, *Gregorii Corinthii libri de dialectis linguae graecae*, Leipzig 1811) 770, '*haec etiam nota, quando in membranis semiuanida esset aut oculos minus feriret, nonnumquam pro apostropho habita cum eaque confusa est*'. A parallel confusion between the elision mark and the contraction for -ος is exemplified by Jackson, *Marg. Scaen.* 181f.

passive verb (so LSJ s.v. ἀμφιέννυμι) or (less plausibly) direct object with a middle (so K.G. 1.327). Cf. e.g. Ar. *Vesp.* 1172 δοθιῆνι σκόροδον ἡμφιεσμένῳ, *Thesm.* 92, *Eccl.* 879, Eupolis 299(277K) and 357(328K), Alexis 211(208K), Anaxilas 34(35K). The diminutive form φυκίον (or φύ-: the accent is uncertain, cf. LSJ s.v.) is far commoner in the plural (Pl. *Resp.* 10.611d, Arist. *HA* 7(8).2, 590ᵇ11, Theoc. 7.58, anon. in *Anth. Pal.* 6.24, Plut. *Mor.* 980d, Julian *Epist.* 46 Hertlein = 4 Bidez–Cumont 427b) than in the singular (? only Arist. *HA* 6.13, 568ᵃ6).

With A's ἡμφιεσμένωι it is not the oysters but the old fishmonger who is swathed in seaweed – an image perfectly compatible with his designation as an old Nereus (cf. the description of Glaucus in Pl. *Resp.* 10.611d). Accordingly there is no necessity to accept Korais' ἡμφιεσμένα (in Schweighaeuser, *Animadv.* 2.235), which gives the oysters their natural clothing, although the conjecture is palaeographically admissible (error from case-ending assimilated to that of the nearest noun) and just possibly right. On *Ostrea edulis* see especially A. Marx in *RE* s.v. *Austern* 2589.11ff., O. Keller, *Die antike Tierwelt* 2 (Leipzig 1913) 562ff., Thompson, *Fishes* s.v. ὄστρεον, Palombi–Santorelli 322f., Campbell, *Guide* 164f., Davidson, *Seafood* 197.

3 ἔλαβον: see comm. on 15.18; ἐχίνους: see comm. on 15.6.

3–4 ἔστι γὰρ προοίμιον δείπνου ... ταῦτα: cf. comm. on 99(94K).1, and Sophilus 7(6K).1f. γαστρισμὸς ἔσται δαψιλής· τὰ προοίμια | ὁρῶ.

4 πεπρυτανευμένου: πρυτανεύω, literally 'I am president of the πρυτάνεις' (in the Athenian Boule, LSJ s.v.), is found as a political metaphor in the sense of 'I organise/manage' first in Demosthenes (5.6, 9.60), and its transfer from government to the kitchen is either a happy invention by Alexis (but cf. Ion fr. eleg. 26.14 West (Διόνυσε) ... εὐθύμων συμποσίων πρύτανι) or a contemporary colloquialism.

5 ἰχθυδίων: the υ of the diminutive is always long in comedy where the text is sound and the vowel's length can be checked (also Ar. fr. 402(387K).8, Theopompus 63(62K).3, Anaxilas 19.2 twice, Cratinus jun. 13, Xenarchus 8.3, Men. fr. 397.4; *anceps* at Sotades 1.23; at Mnesimachus 3.6, cited by Ath. 8.359d, CE's ἰχθύδι' with long υ makes better sense than A's -ύδιον with υ *anceps*. Cf. also comm. on 178(172K).13.

6 τρεμόντων τῷ δέει τί πείσεται: 'trembling with fear as to what they are going to suffer'. The indirect question depends on the verbal phrase τρεμόντων τῷ δέει = δεδοικότων. The nouns δέος and φόβος occur regularly in constructions of this kind, introducing relative clauses (e.g. S. *OC* 223 δέος ἴσχετε μηδὲν ὅσ' αὐδῶ), governing direct objects (e.g. Dem. 4.45, 19.81, cf. K.G. 1.299, Fraenkel on A. *Ag.* 1316) and infinitives (e.g. Eur. *IT* 1342). Cf. also K.G. 2.417, H. W. Smyth, *Greek Grammar* (Cambridge, Mass. 1920) 503 § 2234.

7 θαρρεῖν ἕνεκ' ἐμοῦ: cf. e.g. Pl. *Leg.* 1.642d θαρρῶν δὴ ἐμοῦ γε ἕνεκα,

COMMENTARY

Crat. 428a, *Soph.* 242b, S. *Phil.* 774, Ar. *Nub.* 422, Herodas 2.77 and Headlam *ad loc.* Thereafter A's wrong word-division (ταὐτοῦ δὲ ἐν) is corrected by Epit. (οὐδὲ ἕν is clearly legible in both C and E, *pace* Peppink).

8 φήσας: the aorist form is not uncommon in Attic; to the passages instanced in Veitch, *Greek Verbs*[4] 675 and K.B. 2.212 n. 4, add now com. adesp. fr. 244.265 Austin.

γλαῦκον μέγαν: two very different (? groups of) fish were called γλαῦκος, presumably from their greenish-grey colour: (1) one with pyloric caeca (Arist. *HA* 2.17, 508b[b]20), perhaps one of the corbs (*Umbrina cirrosa* suits the colour perfectly, cf. Campbell, *Guide* 284f.), and (2) a viviparous fish, probably therefore one or more species of shark or dogfish. If μέγαν here indicates size, Alexis' γλαῦκος will belong to the second group, but precise identification of species is impossible. The group is a very large one; even today several different species of shark and dogfish around the Mediterranean share the same name in popular or commercial usage, and at least seven species satisfy the criteria of size, colour, geographic distribution and edibility: *Galeorhynus galeus* (tope), *Isurus oxyrinchus* (mako), *Mustelus mustelus* (smooth hound), *M. asterias* (stellate smouth hound), *Prionace glauca* (blue shark), *Sphyrna zygaena* (hammerhead shark) and *Squatina squatina* (monkfish or angelshark). Cf. Thompson, *Fishes* 48, Dohm, *Mageiros* 107f., Palombi–Santorelli 216ff., Campbell, *Guide* 256ff., Davidson, *Seafood* 26ff. According to various comic poets the γλαῦκος was a delicacy (Amphis 22) best boiled in brine (Antiphanes 221(222K)), but requiring skill for its preparation (Cratinus 336(303K)); its head was particularly prized (Baton 5.16ff., cf. Amphis 16, 35, Antiphanes 77(76K), Sotades com. 1.5). Archestratus fr. 20 Brandt = 151 Lloyd-Jones–Parsons implies that its habitat included coastal shoals near Olynthus and Megara, cf. Antiphanes 191(193K).2, where (*pace* Kassel–Austin 2.420f.) γλαῦκοι Μεγαρικοί (so CE suprascript at Ath. 7.295c) seems the preferable reading. In these passages, however, the poets are sometimes describing the corb (e.g. Archestratus *loc. cit.*, cf. Campbell, *Guide* 284, '*Umbrina cirrosa* ... Habitat in shallow water over sand and mud, often near estuaries'), sometimes the larger fishes, and it is not always easy to be sure which.

9–11 These vv. reappear in Δημήτριος: see above, introduction to this fr. and comm. on fr. 49(48K). In citing v. 11 here, however, the *Marcianus* writes μηδὲ ἓν τούτων, but at Ath. 7.314d in citing fr. 49(48K) A (along there with CE, which omit the pronoun here) has μ. ἓ. τούτους. Only τούτους makes sense (= δακτύλους, as subject of παθεῖν); it was presumably inserted by the poet in order to make the transition clearer from δ. as object of ἐπιφερούσης to δ. as subject of παθεῖν. τούτων on the other hand lacks point; the context does not say what 'these things' are, of which a lady must suffer none.

318

12 ἐπὶ τὸ τάγηνον φυκίδας: so correctly A, but Epit. implies the existence of a variant reading ἐπὶ τήγανόν τε φ. by (1) adding an otiose τε (asyndeton at clause linkages adds liveliness to a bald narrative incorporating lists, cf. v. 15; J. D. Denniston, *Greek Prose Style* (Oxford 1952) 116ff.), and (2) by using suprascript dots to indicate that τάγηνον is a conjecture, correction or alternative reading (cf. Peppink, *Observ.* 25 and 4f.). The two forms τάγηνον and τήγανον are used indiscriminately by Attic writers of the 5th and 4th centuries (in Alexis τάγη- also 192(187K).6, τήγα- 179(174K).8). τήγανον seems to be originally the Ionic, τάγηνον the native Attic spelling (cf. Photius s.v. τάγηνον; Schwyzer 1.268) of an oriental loan-word. The thing itself was probably a shallow pan mainly used for grilling (B. A. Sparkes, *JHS* 82 (1962) 129 and pl. V.5, Sparkes–Talcott, *Agora* XII.228f. and fig. 17, pl. 96, no. 1983).

12–13 The text of the fish list in both A and Epit. agrees, scans and makes sense, but it has been challenged in two places. Meineke, *ed. min.* 715 suspected that τινάς might have replaced a further fish name (κτένας, scallops, cf. Alexis 175(170K).2), but note that v. 15 of our fr. (another list) ends ῥύγχη τινά. In v. 13 φύκην seems odd after φυκίδας in the line before (cf. Blaydes, *Adv.* 2.158, more on target than 1.108). φύκης is the male, and φυκίς the female, wrasse (Arist. *HA* 6.13, 567ᵇ19f., cf. Diphilus of Siphnos in Ath. 8.355b, Thompson, *Fishes* 276f.). About twenty species of wrasse are native to the Mediterranean (descriptions and illustrations of several in Palombi–Santorelli 61ff. and Campbell, *Guide* 286ff.), with a remarkable range of gaudy colours and patterning not only between different species (e.g. *Labrus bergylta* green, red or brown with red-brown reticulations; *L. turdus* reddish or light green, sometimes with a horizontal white stripe; most spectacularly of all *Thalassoma pavo*, its head pink with blue reticulations, body green with blue and pink vertical stripes, fins and tail-edges blue), but also between male and female of the same species (e.g. *Labrus mixtus*, male with head, flanks and tail-edge blue, the rest orange; female orange with black patches; the differences are so pronounced that male and female were long considered different species, cf. Thompson 277). Yet despite such sexual variation a more probable explanation of the transmitted text here is scribal error (cf. *BICS* 16 (1969) 67), with φύκην simply transposing two letters (under the influence of φυκίδας just before) of a correct κυφήν, an epithet so commonly attached to the word that directly precedes it here (καρῖδα) that it became almost part of that creature's name ('hump-backed prawn': on the species so labelled, see below): e.g. Eubulus 110(111K), Matron 534.63f. Lloyd-Jones–Parsons, Asclepiades 26 Gow–Page, Arist. *HA* 4.2, 525ᵇ1, cf. 5.17, 549ᵇ12.

ψήττας: apparently the name of smaller species of dextral flatfish in the seas around Greece, especially the flounder (*Platichthys flesus*) and the

319

various soles (*Solea solea* etc.). Those near Eleusis were celebrated (Pollux 6.63, cf. Clem. Alex. *Paed.* 2.1.3). Cf. Thompson, *Fishes* 294f., Palombi–Santorelli 158ff., Campbell, *Guide* 304f., Davidson, *Seafood* 160ff. (hereafter in the immediately succeeding notes abbreviated to Th., P.–S., C. and D. respectively).

καρῖδα κυφήν: prawns such as *Palaemon serratus* and *P. elegans* (= *Leander squilla*) especially, but not excluding other decapods, of which there are about thirty species in the Mediterranean. Cf. Th. 103f., P.–S. 361ff., C. 200ff., D. 173; O. Keller, *Die antike Tierwelt* 2 (Leipzig 1913) 494ff., Gossen and Steier in *RE* s.v. *Krebs* 1684.3ff., Dohm, *Mageiros* 106. In Old Comedy and other verse up to the end of the 5th century καρίς declines with the iota short, but thereafter it is always long with the accent modified to circumflex where necessary; cf. LSJ s.v., and to the examples there cited add (a) -ῐ-: Ar. fr. 333(318K).2, cf. Epicharmus fr. 44.3 (κουρῖδες), probably also 44.1; (b) -ῑ-: Alexis 115(110K).13, Cratinus jun. 13, Sotades 1.1, 1.25, probably also Eubulus 110(111K), Ophelion 1; outside comedy also Asclepiades 26 Gow–Page, Matron 534.63 Lloyd-Jones–Parsons, Marcellus Sid. fr. 1.32 Heitsch. The alpha is always long, cf. Björck, *Alpha Impurum* 253f.

κωβιόν: 'goby', i.e. any member of a large group of cheap small fish with large heads, prominent eyes and pouting cheeks, abundant in the Mediterranean. Cf. Th. 137ff., P.–S. 125ff., C. 296ff., D. 135; Gossen in *RE* s.v. *Schwarzgrundel* 794.8ff., Dohm, *Mageiros* 114, Gow, comm. on Machon 31.

πέρκην: in a context exclusively of seafood this is the comber (or sea perch), of which three species (*Serranus cabrilla, S. hepatus, S. scriba*) are common in the Mediterranean. Epicharmus calls the fish αἰόλη (frs. 47, 48), and Matron 534.51 ἀνθεσίχρως, with reference presumably to the contrast of dark vertical stripes on the upper back and the bluish horizontal striping or patch on the lower abdomen of the first and third species named. Cf. Th. 195f., P.–S. 41ff., C. 274, D. 73; Wellmann in *RE* s.v. *Barsch* 27.32ff.

σπάρον: probably one or more of the smaller species of sea-bream, of which there are more than twenty in the Mediterranean. The majority have sharp teeth, hence the description in Marcellus Sid. fr. 11.24 of one as ὀξυόδους is not diagnostic. In modern Greek the name is given particularly to *Diplodus annularis* and *D. vulgaris*, annular and two-banded bream respectively. Cf. Th. 248f., P.–S. 78ff., C. 278ff., D. 74ff.

14 αὐτὸ: sc. τὸ τάγηνον (so Epit. MSS correctly; A's αὐτὸν is presumably an assimilation to the ending of the last-mentioned noun σπάρον). With this carefully chosen list of seafood the speaker's pan has indeed become ποικιλώτερον ταῶ, 'more gaily speckled than a peacock' (cf. V. Slothouwer, *Acta Literaria Societatis Rheno-Trajectinae* 3 (1801)

117f.), including as it does ἐρυθραὶ καρῖδες (cf. Anaxandrides 23(22K)), comber with brown and blue patches, green or brown flatfish, bream with black markings, and – deliberately placed at the head of the list – wrasses with their remarkable patterns and a coloration including peacock blue, green and orange. Cf. O. Crusius, *Untersuchungen zu den Mimiamben des Herondas* (Leipzig 1892) 76f., Headlam–Knox on Herodas 3.89, 5.67, Gow on Machon 28, W. G. Arnott in R. Pretagostini (ed.), *Miscellanea di Studi in onore di Bruno Gentili* 3 (Rome 1993) 719ff. and a modern parallel in P. Gray, *Honey from a Weed* (London 1986) 58.

ποικιλώτερον ταῶ: the peacock's spread tail, with its varicoloured eyes set in a green field, was the acme of ποικιλία; cf. Antiphon fr. 57 Thalheim, Arist. *HA* 6.9, 564ᵃ25ff. The bird became a relatively common possession of wealthy Athenians in the 4th century (Antiphanes 203(205K), Anaxandrides 29(28K); cf. Thompson, *Birds*[2] 277ff., Steier in *RE* s.v. *Pfau* 1414.52ff., F. Capponi, *Ornithologia Latina* (Genoa 1979) 389ff., Hunter on Eubulus 113(114K)). On the bird's use as food see comm. on Alexis 128(123K).3. On the orthography of ταῶς with an internal aspirate (replacing a lost digamma in an originally non-Greek word) see K.B. 1.113 and LSJ s.v.[1]

15 The text of this verse is defective in the MSS: κρεάδια· ποδάρια· ῥύγχη τινὰ A, just the first three words CE. A paraphrasing cross-reference in Ath. 3.95a to part of vv. 15–16 ποδῶν ... καὶ ὡτίων, ἔτι δὲ ῥύγχους ᾿Άλεξις ἐν Κρατείᾳ ἢ Φαρμακοπώλῃ (sc. μνημονεύει) gives some support to ποδάρια and ῥύγχη here, but provides no help with the missing half-metron in v. 15. The speaker is listing his various purchases in vv. 8–9, 12–13 (fish) and 15–16 (meat) in the accusative (as objects of ἐπριάμην and ἔλαβον, 8f.: ἔλαβον is easily supplied in 12–13, perhaps less easily remembered in 15–16), and adds a humorous comment after each section of the list (9–11, 14, 17). Several supplements have been suggested in 15, but none is compelling. Thus κρεάδια <καὶ> ποδάρια <καὶ> ῥ. τ. Elmsley, *Ed. Rev.* 3 (1803) 190, but in parallel comic lists (note also vv. 12–13, 16 of this fr.) the nouns tend to be strung together asyndetically, while the double omission of καί is hard to justify palaeographically.[2] Or κρεᾴδι' <ἄττ>α, π., ῥ. τ. Dobree, comm. on Ar. *Plut.* 227, printed by Kassel–Austin: palaeographically neat (ΑΤΤ omitted by quasi-

---

[1] LSJ reflect the variable practice of medieval MSS when they say that the noun is declined sometimes oxytone, sometimes perispomenon. Ancient grammarians (Tryphon in Ath. 8.397e = fr. 5 Velsen, Seleucus in 398a, Herodian 2.722.33ff. Lentz), however, plump for perispomenon. Cf. K.B. 1.407.

[2] The split anapaest in κρεᾴδῐᾰ καὶ is not in itself objectionable: cf. *CQ* 7 (1957) 189, 194f.

haplography before ΑΠ), and tolerable in sense; the last syllable of ποδάρια would now be lengthened before the initial rho of ῥύγχη: an acceptable licence at this and other *sedes* in the iambic trimeter when the open vowel ends a disyllable (e.g. Ar. *Plut.* 51, Alexis 73 and comm. *ad loc.*, probably Nicochares 18(15K).1), but less frequent when it ends a quadrisyllable as here except before the final word in a verse;[1] however, cf. S. fr. 958.1 Radt ἐδέξατο ῥαγεῖσα (opening of trimeter), Eur. fr. 360.15 Nauck[2] πατρίδα τε ῥυώμεθα (same *sedes* as here). Other supplements are possible: e.g. κρεᾴδι' <ἔλαβον>, with the same metrical licence as Dobree's suggestion; the verbs in vv. 8–9 are now far enough away for a reminder to be welcome.

κρεᾴδι': see comm. on 27.5.

16 ἡπάτιον ἐγκεκαλυμμένον: Ath. 3.107e goes on to comment that liver was served in intestinal casings and cites Hegesander of Delphi (*FHG* 4.419 fr. 29) for a reference to τὰ κεκαλυμμένα ἡπάτια, presumably the culinary term for the dish. A recipe in Apicius 7.7.2 tells the cook to wrap pork liver *in omento* before grilling it. Here Alexis either uses ἐγκεκαλυμμένον as an alternative technical term or (more probably) introduces the compound solely to prepare the way for the joke in v. 17: the liver is 'wrapped up' to conceal its shame at 'blushing'. ἐγκαλύπτω is particularly associated in the middle voice with the gesture of covering the face for shame (LSJ s.v. ΙΙ, e.g. Pl. *Phd.* 117c, Aeschines 2.107). The same joke appears in Crobylus 7, but there is no reason to suspect direct imitation there of what was doubtless a familiar witticism.

17 πελιδνόν: ACE's unmetrical (cf. West, *Greek Metre* 16f. § 4) *Koine* spelling is printed by Kassel–Austin, but the classical Attic form πελιτνόν (Moeris s.v., Aelius Dionysius fr. 278 Schwabe = p. 135 Erbse) was restored here by Porson, *Adv.* 65. Clem. Alex. *Paed.* 2.2.26 applies the adjective to the colour of men's faces when they spend their times indoors drinking to excess.

18, 21 The significance of these lines for the identity of the speaker is discussed in the introduction to Κράτεια.

---

[1] I. Hilberg (*Das Princip der Silbenwägung* (Vienna 1879) 206ff., 218ff.; cf. A. Nauck, *MGR* 6 (1894) 97) attempts to codify the instances into a law which totally confines the lengthening to the final open vowel of disyllables, except when the word affected takes penultimate position. Hilberg's legislation, however, is faulty; it is based on statistically insufficient instances, and ignores – or is forced to reject with an allegation of corrupt transmission – one polysyllable (S. fr. 958.1) and several monosyllables (e.g. Chaeremon fr. 14.9, trag. adesp. fr. 394.1 Nauck[2] = Diog. Sinop. 5.1 Snell, *TrGF* 1.257).

18 οὐδ' ὄψεται: Bothe's correction (*PCGF* 541)[1] of οὐκ ὄψ. in the MSS is likely but not certain; with its climactic effect ('nor even will see'; cf. Denniston, *GP* 193) it makes v. 18 less jerky and perhaps links more fluently with οἰμώξεται γάρ in v. 19 ('for [if he should try,] he'll pay for it', cf. *GP* 6of.)

19 νὴ Δί'. ἀλλ' ἐγὼ σοφῶς: so correctly Epit. (νὴ δία λέγω σαφῶς A with wrong word-division, haplography of λ, and the common confusion between σαφῶς and σοφῶς: cf. e.g. Eur. *Bacch.* 1271, *Hipp.* 1076). In vv. 5–20, where both A and CE preserve the text, CE are correct five times where A is corrupt (also v. 7 wrong word-division, 10 δὴ for δεῖ, 14 ἐποιήσατ' αὐτόν, 17 ὂν omitted by haplography); A is correct three times where CE go wrong (11 μηδέν, 12 τε added, 15 τινα omitted); A and CE are corrupt together probably five times (11 τούτων A, omitted CE, 13 φύκην, 15 lacuna, 16 ὑιηπάτιον A, ὕειον ἠπ. CE, 18 οὐκ). The passage (cf. my general introduction, II.i.b) provides some evidence for a limited independence of the Epit. tradition.

19–20 σοφῶς ... καὶ γλαφυρῶς καὶ ποικίλως: cf. Ar. *Av.* 1272 ὦ σοφώτατ', ὦ γλαφυρώτατε, Dionysius com. 3.1f., Arist. *HA* 9.39, 623ᵃ8. γλαφυρῶς implies that the speaker will implement his skill with polish and style. ποικίλως probably combines both 'with subtle variations' and 'colourfully', reminding us of the boast at v. 14.

21–3 The clause from ὥστε to ἡδονῆς turns up also in Ἀσκληπιοκλείδης (fr. 24.3–4, cited by Ath. 4.169d) with a different main clause to introduce it and βατάνι' replacing λοπάδι' (Casaubon's correction of A's λοιπὰ δι-, cf. *Animadv.* 205). A here and CE at Ath. 169d give -βάλλειν, A at 169d -βαλεῖν; the presence of ἐνίοτε two words later confirms the correctness of the present infinitive in both places. The speaker of fr. 24 (see comm. *ad loc.*) claims to have learnt cookery in Sicily, and so uses βατάνια, the Sicilian word for 'casserole'; the speaker of 115(110K) appears to have no such connections (see introduction to Κράτεια), and uses the Athenian word. The diminutive λοπάδιον occurs in Attic comedy (also Ar. *Plut.* 812, Alexis 191(186K).7, Axionicus 7.1, Eubulus 8(9K).3, 37(38K).2, Men . fr. 397.9) as a metrically convenient alternative to λοπάς without any apparent distinction in size. The utensil was a shallow earthenware dish, often with a lid, used almost exclusively for stewing or boiling fish (D. A. Amyx, *Hesperia* 27 (1958) 210 n. 76, B. A. Sparkes, *JHS* 88 (1962) 130 and pl. VI, cf. B. A. Sparkes and L. Talcott, *Pots and Pans of Classical Athens* (Princeton 1958) fig. 44 and Sparkes–Talcott, *Agora* XII.227f. and fig. 18,

---

[1] Anticipating S. A. Naber, *Mnemosyne* 8 (1880) 258, whose further change ἄψεται for ὄψεται destroys the climax, for the second verb needs to convey an idea of greater, not less, remoteness from the items of food.

pl. 95, nos. 1959–82, M. Lang, *Agora* XXI.10 (B12), Gomme–Sandbach, *Comm.* on Men. *Dysk.* 520).

24 The Marcianus has τὰς σκευασίας . . . καὶ τὰς σκευάσεις, where the tautology is more likely a product of scribal miscopying than of authorial carelessness. σκευασία (= 'preparation', especially of food; in the plural almost 'recipes': LSJ s.v.) is standard Attic in comedy (also Axionicus 4.7, Men. *Phasm.* 74 Sandbach, com. adesp. fr. 1330 Kock) and elsewhere (e.g. Pl. *Lys.* 209e, *Alc.* 1.117c, *Min.* 316e, cf. Durham, *Vocabulary* 91), while σκεύασις occurs elsewhere only as a doubtful reading in LXX *Eccl.* 10.1. The *Marcianus* here may provide a clue to the origin of its error; σκευασίας is the first word in one line of the MS, σκευάσεις first word in the next. The scribe probably copied the correct ending of the second word (-σεις) but conflated it by ocular or mental aberration with the stem of the noun directly above it. Certain restoration of the original noun is impossible, but the suggestions offered up to now either duplicate the meaning of σκευασίας (διαθέσεις Meineke, συστάσεις Kaibel) or introduce irrelevances (εὑρέσεις Kock, but the speaker has made no claim of inventing new dishes). Perhaps something about serving the dishes would be better: ? παραθέσεις.

25 δεικνύειν, λέγειν: cf. e.g. Phoenicides 4.5f. οὗτος τὰς μάχας | ἔλεγεν, ἐδείκνυ' ἅμα λέγων τὰ τραύματα.

26 θέλη: Alexis' preference for the aphetic form θέλω both generally (here and 198(193K).1) and in set phrases like ἂν θεὸς θέλη (233(231K).4, 249(247K).1) accords with the usage of other contemporary comic poets, who unlike their 5th-century predecessors reserve the ἐθέλω form for rare occasions of heightened formality (e.g. Men. *Dysk.* 269, where the poor but polite Gorgias addresses a social superior, cf. Sandbach *ad loc.* and my discussion in *Phoenix* 18 (1964) 117). See also Rutherford, *NP* 415f., Wilamowitz on Eur. *Her.* 18, K.B. 1.187f., Meisterhans–Schwyzer 178 and n. 1481, Threatte 1.426f. Porson's suggested change to ἂν θέλη (*Adv.* 232) is unnecessary.

116 (111K)

Meineke 3.432 (III), Kock 2.336, Edmonds 2.424, Kassel–Austin 2.85; cf. Meineke 1.395f., Th. Bergk, *Rh. Mus.* 35 (1880) 259ff., G. Kaibel in *RE* s.v. *Alexis* 9, 1469.31ff., W. S. Ferguson, *Hellenistic Athens* (London 1911) 114f. n.7. This fr., preserved by Ath. 6.254a–b (*Marcianus* only) is unusually corrupt. There are three lacunae (of one syllable in vv. 2 and 4, of two metra in 6–7) and at least two other errors (vv. 3, 8). Two details of staging are uncertain. (1) Does the fr. have one or two speakers? See below on v. 4. (2) How many characters are present? The person proposing the toasts addresses a παῖς in v. 1 and ἄνδρες συμπόται in v. 7. Is the παῖς a

324

reveller or a (mute) servant? Are the men addressed in v. 7 two or more characters with roles in the plot (cf. introduction to Κράτεια), or – less probably – members of a chorus of comasts (cf. introduction to Κουρίς)?

Despite these obscurities the scene is clearly a drinking-party, a sequel possibly to the meal for which the provisioning is described in fr. 115(110K), but whether the bout came at the end of the play (cf. e.g. Men. *Dysk.*, Plaut. *Asin.*, *Pers.*, *Stich.*) or earlier in the plot (cf. e.g. Plaut. *Most.*) we have no means of knowing. Staged parties, to judge from the Greek comic frs., regularly included a toasting sequence (in Alexis also frs. 21, 55(53K), 59(58K) and comm., 202(198K), 228(226K), 234(232K), 293(291K)); Plaut. *Stich.* 708, 710 indicates the type of context into which they would fit.

This fr., with its references to a victory by Antigonus the king, young Demetrius and Phila Aphrodite, provides one foundation for the theory that this play was produced a second time more than twelve years after its original staging (see introduction to Κράτεια). It is noteworthy that these references are blocked together (vv.4–7) in such a way that they could have been inserted into an existing text with a minimum of rewriting.

1 τὴν μεγάλην δός: it is easy to assume either an ellipse of κύλικα with this and similar expressions (e.g. ἑτέραν, μεστήν, φιλοτησίαν, cf. comm. on 59(58K): so for instance K.G. 1.266f., Starkie on Ar. *Vesp.* 106, Headlam–Knox on Herodas 1.81) or mention of this word in the lost preceding context, but the use of the feminine adjective on its own nominally or adverbially is so widespread in ancient Greek that at times all consciousness of ellipse seems to have been lost (cf. C. A. Lobeck, *Paralipomena* (Leipzig 1837) 363, Wilamowitz on Eur. *Her.* 681, Fraenkel on A. *Ag.* 916). Cf. Men. fr. 443.2 "ἄκρατον" ἐβόων, "τὴν μεγάλην", Diphilus 17.8, and Meineke *ad loc.* (4.382), Machon 447 and Gow *ad loc.*, [Arist.] *Probl.* 3.25, 874^{b}11, and the variation in Sophilus 4(3K) τὴν μείζον'.

Although temperate Athenians prided themselves on the small size of their drinking cups (cf. Alexis 9.8–9), on those occasions when a dinner was followed by a bout of heavy drinking, the call for big(ger) cups marked the point of transition. Cf. (in addition to the passages of comedy and Machon already cited) Eur. *Ion* 1177ff., Epicrates 9(10K), Dioxippus 4, Machon 108f. and Gow *ad loc.*, Pl. *Symp.* 223c, Ath. 11.504b, Cic. *Verr.* 2.1.66; Fraenkel, *MNC* 19, Mau in *RE* s.v. *Comissatio* 615.15ff.

ὑποχέας: at this period (but apparently not in more archaic times, Ath. 11.782a–b, cf. Hes. *Op.* 595f., Xenophanes fr. 5 Diels–Kranz, West) wine was poured first (and so 'underneath') into the mixing-bowl, and the water with which it was mixed then added on top. Cf. Antiphanes 81.2, Sophilus 5(4K), Diphilus 5, 107, Men. *Dysk.* 946f. and fr. 2, Xen. *Oec.* 17.9, Herodas 1.8of., Ath. 4.129e–f), and the proverbial ἀπώλεσας τὸν οἶνον ἐπιχέας ὕδωρ (Aristeas fr. 4); cf. Cobet, *NL* 601.

325

COMMENTARY

2 The *Marcianus* text contains a brief lacuna but still makes perfect sense. The servant must first pour in 'four ladles¹ of wine to friendship, in honour of present company', and this command is balanced by a second: to add (vv. 3–7) 'later the three ladles to Love: one in honour of a victory by Antigonus the king', and the other two in honour of Antigonus' son and wife or ex-wife. In vv. 2 and 3–7 two different applications of the so-called (possessive) 'genitive of the toast' (see comm. on 59(58K)) are combined: (a) that which names an abstraction or its personification as a deity (Φιλίας v. 2, Ἔρωτος v. 3²) whose blessing or achievement the toaster seeks, and (b) that which names the humans celebrated in the toasts (the drinkers themselves v. 2, contemporary royalty vv. 4–7). Normally the two applications are not associated in a single toast (but note Alexis 246(244K) Πτολεμαίου τοῦ βασιλέως ... τῆς τ᾽ ἀδελφῆς ... καὶ τῆς Ὁμονοίας, Hor. *Carm.* 3.19.10 *da noctis mediae, da ... auguris Murenae*), but their combination causes no difficulty of comprehension or syntax.

Several supplements for the gap have been suggested: before τῶν παρόντων, <τοὺς> Schweighaeuser (cf. *Animadv.* 3.507), <μὲν> Meineke 3.432, <μοι> Blaydes, *Adv.* 1.199, <τῆς> Cobet (in Peppink, *Observ.* 41); also <γε> κυάθους Bothe, *PCGF* 542, <συμ>παρόντων Meineke (in his edition of Ath., cf. *Anal. Crit.* 111). Choice is not easy, but Schweighaeuser's idea has the double advantage of balancing τοὺς τρεῖς in v. 3 and of being easiest to justify palaeographically (haplography after κυάθους).

προσαποδώσεις: the text is sound, despite the qualms of Cobet, *NL* 61of. and Kaibel. Translate 'you (sc. the παῖς of v. 1) will provide as an additional obligation'; for the use cf. Dem. 41.27, Diphilus 67(66K).13. Provision of wine for the three toasts to Love in honour of Antigonus, Demetrius and Phila is imaged as payment owed for their services to Athens (primarily liberation of the city from the Phalerean's regime and restoration of democracy, one presumes, although the only event actually mentioned is 'victory', v. 4). It is difficult to gauge the seriousness of this apparent praise. Webster, *SLGC* 105 wishes to identify here a genuine

---

¹ The κύαθος here is both implement (cf. comm. on fr. 2.5–7) and measure (= ⅙ of a κοτύλη). The volumetric figures given by Galen and other ancient literary sources (κύαθος = 45.6 cm³, κοτύλη = 273.6 cm³; cf. F. Hultsch, *Griechische und römische Metrologie²* (Berlin 1882) 101f. 105ff., O. Viedebantt, *Abh. Leipzig* 34/3 (1917), 43, 60), have been substantially confirmed by archaeological finds (cf. Lang–Crosby, *Agora* x.56ff.).

² Since it is impossible to draw a significant distinction between abstract expression and its personification as a deity (cf. comm. on fr. 59(58K)), there is uncertainty whether the initial letters of these two nouns should be upper or lower case.

pro-democratic enthusiasm in this flattery of the liberators, but such an interpretation may well misread remarks made for a strictly theatrical purpose (see below on v. 4), and it ignores a possible ironic undertone. The toast honouring the royal trio is not to φιλία, health or freedom (as one would expect in real flattery), but to Ἔρως, as with toasts drunk to one's beloved (cf. Eubulus 93(94K).3f., Theoc. 2.151f.). Demetrius Poliorcetes was a sexually attractive womaniser and pederast (cf. Ferguson 110f., 118f.) still in his early manhood, and Phila's cult-title of Aphrodite made her the mother of Eros.

Here A writes ἔρωτας, with the ending assimilated in case and number to that of the preceding τοὺς τρεῖς; correction to -ωτος is correctly attributed to Daléchamp, who first translated the word as a genitive (*Amoris tres alios mihi tu dabis postea*) but made no mention of his conjecture in *Annot.* 742; cf. Schweighaeuser, *Animadv.* 3.507.

4 The line has two textual problems. (i) To supplement the brief lacuna at its beginning Casaubon's <ἕν'> (sc. κύαθον, cf. *Animadv.* 449) is widely accepted, but Headlam's <τῆς> (scribbled in the margin of his copy of Kaibel's edition of Ath.) ought not to be discounted (it makes the reference in νίκης more specific, while scribal omission of τῆς immediately before masculine Ἀντιγόνου is easily understood). (ii) In the *Marcianus* the verse ends νίκης καλῶς, which barely construes as part of a continuous text, but makes admirable sense if καλῶς is interpreted as a one-word interjection of approval by a second speaker (presumably one of the συμπόται addressed in v. 7): so tentatively Dobree, *Adv.* 2.312. This colloquial use of καλῶς is common in Greek drama; it has a wide range of tones, from the supportive 'Fine!' here (also e.g. Eur. *Her.* 599, *Ion* 417, *Or.* 1216, cf. Dem. 39.15), through a polite 'Thank you' (Men. *Epitr.* 293, 354) or even 'No, thank you' (Ar. *Ran.* 888) to a grudging 'All right' (*Ran.* 532). See LSJ s.v. καλός c.ii.6, J. H. Quincey, *JHS* 86 (1966) 136f., 139ff., P. T. Stevens, *Colloquial Expressions in Euripides* (*Hermes Einzelschrift* 38, Wiesbaden 1976) 54f., and cf. comm. on 232(230K).2. Such an interjection here would show command of theatrical psychology; an audience in a mood of euphoric adulation towards its liberators would empathise with the second speaker's καλῶς, which would then provide a suitable opportunity for applause.

Dobree's proposal, especially if taken in conjunction with Headlam's <τῆς> at line beginning, eliminates all necessity to alter A's text; other conjectures combine various amounts of rewriting with implausible idiom, syntax or palaeography: e.g. νίκης καλῆς Casaubon, but an article is required with καλῆς in attributive position; νικηφόρου Herwerden, *Coll. Crit.* 124, but such an adjective would have to come between τοῦ and βασιλέως; <ἕν'> ... κύαθον (or <ἕν> ... σκύφος or δέπας) καλῷ W. Morel, *Rh. Mus.* 77 (1928) 166f., comparing Phylarchus in Ath. 6.255a = *FGrH* 81

COMMENTARY

F 29 καὶ τὸν ἐπιχεόμενον κύαθον ἐν ταῖς συνουσίαις Σελεύκου Σωτῆρος καλοῦσι ('they name the measure of wine ... in honour of Seleucus the Saviour'): ingenious, but unreasonably far from the *ductus*, and δέπας at least with its highly poetic flavour stylistically inappropriate.

Ἀντιγόνου τοῦ βασιλέως νίκης: Antigonus Monophthalmus assumed the title of king after the naval victory off Cyprian Salamis in 306: see introduction to Κράτεια.

5 τοῦ νεανίσκου ... Δημητρίου: D. Poliorcetes, Antigonus' son, aged between 27 and 30 at the time of the victory: see introduction to Κράτεια.

6 At least two metra are missing here (plus perhaps one or more lines), after τρίτον (especially if φέρε here *'non "affer" significat, sed deliberantis est, cuius in nomen tertium cyathum infundi iubeat: "age uero, cui tertium libabo cyathum? Philae Veneri"'* Meineke, cf. LSJ s.v. φέρω ιx) or Δημητρίου or Ἀφροδίτης (now with φέρε in its primary sense 'bring', cf. e.g. Alexis 136(131K); could Alexis have written φέρε τὸν τρ. Φ. Ἀφροδίτης. <χαίρετε> | x – ∪ – x, χαιρετ᾽, ἄνδρες συμπόται, with the lacuna explained as a scribal *saut du même au même?*). There is no obvious gap in sense; attempts at supplementation (Herwerden, *Anal. Crit.* 47, Kock, W. Morel, *Rh. Mus.* 77 (1928) 166f., Edmonds) are shots in the dark.

τὸν τρίτον: in enumerations the ordinal is occasionally attached to only one member of a series, as here (if one reads <τῆς> in v. 4, q.v.); cf. Asclepiades, *Anth. Pal.* 5.167 = 14 Gow–Page ὑετὸς ἦν καὶ νὺξ καὶ τὸ τρίτον ἄλγος ἔρωτι, | οἶνος (on the text, wrongly suspected by Gow of irremediable corruption, see G. Giangrande, *Entr. Hardt* 14 (1969) 122ff.; cf. F. Lasserre, *La Figure d'Éros dans la poésie grecque* (Paris 1946) 163) or Oppian *Hal.* 1.254ff.

7 Φίλας Ἀφροδίτης: Phila, daughter of Antipater and wife or ex-wife of Demetrius; her deification as Aphrodite was backed by the erection of an Athenian temple in 305 (see introduction to Κράτεια). The *Marcianus* here first writes φιλας but corrects to -ης with a suprascript eta, but elsewhere in this MS the name always retains alpha in its declension (this Phila, -ας twice in Ath. 6.255c quoting Dionysius son of Tryphon; Demetrius' daughter, -αν 13.577e; the 4th-century *hetaira*, -α 13.587e citing Philetaerus 9.5, -αν 13.590d, -ας 593f; the sister of Derdas and wife of Philip, -αν 13.557c). Athenian inscriptions sometimes atticise, sometimes preserve the original dialectal spelling of such names (cf. Threatte 1.136); Attic and *Koine* writers betray similar inconsistency, but the *alpha impurum* is favoured in first-declension nouns, perhaps inspired by tragic practice (Ἀθάνα, Ἀνδρομέδα, Λήδα etc.); cf. Björck, *Alpha Impurum* 133f., 352ff. Cobet has a long list of real-life examples, *VL²* 202ff.

ἄνδρες συμπόται: see introductions to this fr. and to Κράτεια, and cf. Pl. *Symp.* 216d, fr. adesp. eleg. 27.1 West.

ΚΡΑΤΕΙΑ

8 ὅσων: Casaubon's correction (cf. *Animadv.* 449) of A's ὅσην (assimilated to the other two -ην endings in the verse).

117 (112K)

Meineke 3.431 (II), Kock 2.337, Edmonds 2.424, Kassel–Austin 2.86. Here in all probability the φαρμακοπώλης exhibits his talent at bragging in a scene with an unidentified companion. Treating Callimedon's squint might well have been only one in a series of parallel boasts (perhaps a τόπος of doctor scenes, cf. Plaut. *Men.* 885f.). This and any other passage whose topical point had been blunted after Callimedon left Athens in 318 (cf. also fr. 118(113K)) could have been excised for the play's second production in 305.

In extant scenes of Greco-Roman comedy doctors – real and impersonated – appear in only Men. *Asp.* (cf. S. Goldberg, *The Making of Menander's Comedy* (London 1980) 32, 128 n. 5) and Plaut. *Men.*, but the history of what clearly became a popular character in the genre goes back to Attic Old Comedy and possibly Epicharmus: cf. especially the full survey by L. Gil and I. R. Alfageme, *Cuadernos de Filología Clásica* 3 (1972) 35ff., and E. G. Turner, *Wien. Stud.* 89 (1976) 48ff., with a postscript by E. W. Handley. Cf. also comm. on 146(142K).

Part-division in the fr., cited by Ath. 8.340a, was first correctly established by Daléchamp in his Latin translation.

1–2 Callimedon's squint (cf. Timocles 29(27K) εἶθ' ὁ Καλλιμέδων ἄφνω | ὁ Κάραβος προσῆλθεν, ἐμβλέπων δ' ἐμοί, | ὡς γοῦν ἐδόκει, πρὸς ἕτερον ἄνθρωπόν τινα | ἐλάλει· συνιεὶς δ' οὐδὲν εἰκότως ἐγώ | ὧν ἔλεγεν ἐπένευον διὰ κενῆς. τῷ δ' ἄρα | βλέπουσι χωρὶς καὶ δοκοῦσιν αἱ κόραι) seems to have been the original name for his nickname ὁ Κάραβος: see comm. on fr. 57(56K).

τὰς κόρας: the joke on this word's ambiguity (girl/pupil of the eye) was a commonplace. It forms the point of an anecdote about the cynic Diogenes (Diog. Laert. 6.68), and is instanced as an illustration of ψυχρότης by [Longinus] *Subl.* 4.4–5, quoting Xen. *Resp. Lac.* 3.5 (where the MSS of Xen. corrupt the key-word ὀφθαλμοῖς to θαλάμοις) and Timaeus (= *FGrH* 566 F 122); cf. also Prudentius *Hamartigenia* 308ff.

2–3 'Does that mean he has daughters?' ἦσαν here is correct (*pace* Jacobi in Meineke 5.ccvi); the imperfect implies that the words of the previous speaker, which have prompted the surprised question, are considered as already past; cf. Goodwin, *MT* 13, K.G. 1.145f.

κόραι θυγατέρες: a composite noun, cf. e.g. παῖς υἱός Alexis 167(162K).2, παῖς κόρη Ar. *Lys.* 595, Theophilus 12.6, Men. *Epitr.* 477. Dem. 21.79 (MSS), υἱεῖς ἄνδρες [Dem.] 25.88, ἀδελφὴ κόρη Thuc. 6.56, γέρων πατήρ Hom. *Il.* 1.358, Eur. *Alc.* 820.

4–5 The daughters of Proetus king of Tiryns were driven mad either by Hera for an insult to her or by Dionysus because they opposed the institution of his rites. Melampus, the prophet and missionary of Dionysus, healed them, receiving in payment a third of Proetus' kingdom for himself and his brother Bias. There are the usual problems of alternative versions (the cause of the madness) and contamination (a different tale has Dionysus driving the women of Argos mad at the time of king Anaxagoras), which the publication of papyrus frs. from Hesiod's version(s) of the myth (*PSI* 1301, *P.Oxy.* 2487 fr. 1 = frs. 37, 129 Merkelbach–West) has done little to resolve. The new papyri, however, have outdated some otherwise excellent discussions (Pley in *RE* s.v. *Melampus* 1, 395.61ff., O. Wolff in Roscher s.v. *Melampus* 2570.48ff., J. A. E. Bethe, *Thebanische Heldenlieder* (Leipzig 1891) 46f., 173f., P. Friedländer, *Argolica* (Diss. Berlin 1905) 31ff., Robert, *GH* 1.245ff.). See now especially I. Löffler, *Die Melampodie-Sage* (Meisenheim am Glan 1963) 37ff., F. Vian, *REA* 67 (1965) 25ff., A. Henrichs, *ZPE* 15 (1974) 300f. and M. L. West, *The Hesiodic Catalogue of Women* (Oxford 1985) 78ff. Theophilus' Προιτίδες presumably burlesqued the story. The cure of Proetus' daughters is also mentioned by Diphilus 125(126K) as an example of medical skill in a hexameter passage ridiculing quack doctors.

5 καταστήσειεν ἄν: 'would set right/restore to their previous situation', the term used by doctors in their professional writing, with the disease, the diseased part or the patient as the verb's object: e.g. Hippocr. *Mul.* 2.133 τὸ σῶμα, Dioscorides 4.1.4 ἰκτεριῶντας, cf. *TGL* s.v. καθίστημι col. 789BC.

118 (113K)

Meineke 3.433 (v), Kock 2.337, Edmonds 2.426, Kassel–Austin 2.87. This association of Callimedon and Orpheus was used by G. Kaibel, *Hermes* 25 (1890) 98f. as evidence to support his theory that Alexis' comedy burlesqued Cabiric rites with Orpheus in the role of φαρμακοπώλης. The lack of any context for the present fr. is one reason why total demolition of Kaibel's theory is impossible (cf. introduction to Κράτεια p. 312 n. 1), yet more plausible explanations of Orpheus' association with Callimedon here may be advanced. If this fr. (cited by Ath. 8.340c) came from the same scene as fr. 117(112K) (cited by Ath. just previously at 340a), the drug-seller might have been boasting that in addition to Callimedon he had also treated the legendary Orpheus (? for grief after the loss of his wife, or even – since an ἀλαζών is not limited to practical possibilities – for his fatal dismemberment).[1] Alternatively the main reason for the juxtaposition of

---

[1] Cf. also the introduction to fr. 140(135K).

names could have been a joke linking their fishy connections: Callimedon with his nickname ὁ Κάραβος ('Crayfish', see on fr. 57(56K)), Orpheus and the fish ὀρφώς.[1] Kock notes the parallel word play at Archippus 17 ἱερεὺς γὰρ ἦλθ' αὐτοῖσιν ὀρφὼς τοῦ θεοῦ, from a play (the Ἰχθύες!) loaded with fishy puns (cf. frs. 15, 16(19K), 18, 25(23K), 27). ὀρφώς is normally the grouper or dusky perch (*Epinephelus guaza* Linnaeus = *Serranus gigas*), a delicious fish which grows to a length of 1.4 metres and is still called ὀρφός or ροφός in modern Greek (Campbell, *Guide* 276f., Davidson, *Seafood* 70). Thompson, *Fishes* 187f. suggests that ὀρφώς also covered the wreckfish (*Polyprion americanus* = *P. cernium*), which is similar in appearance and size to the grouper. It is conceivable that ancient authors and fishermen did not distinguish between the two fish, but wreckfish has always been relatively uncommon as a food fish (it is sought by rod and line at a depth of 150 metres), and is not found in the East Mediterranean (cf. Davidson 69). Cf. also Strömberg, *Fischnamen* 21, Palombi–Santorelli 39f.

119 (114K)

Meineke 3.433 (VI), Kock 2.337, Edmonds 2.427, Kassel–Austin 2.87. The context is uncertain, but the garlands here (cf. also comm. on fr. 4.2) are perhaps most likely to have been described as 'hanging' (κρεμαμένους) in a place associated either with their use at the party implied by fr. 116(111K) (e.g. the manufacturer's shop, a stand in or near the dining-room, even a beloved's door) or with the drugseller of the play's title. The plant μελίλωτος is traditionally and correctly identified as 'melilot', i.e. the various and in most cases superficially similar species of the genus *Melilotus*: T. G. Tutin and others, *Flora Europea* 2 (Cambridge 1968) 148ff., cf. Steier in *RE* s.v. *Lotos* 1531.3ff., R. Strömberg, *Griechische Pflanzennamen* (Göteborg 1940) 62, André, *Lexique* 204, W. G. Arnott, *BICS* 39 (1985) 79ff.[2]. The sweetish scent of these plants, which becomes stronger and very

---

[1] Or ὀρφῶς: the accentuation is disputed. Ancient authorities (Ath. 7.315a, Pollux 6.50, Herodian 1.224.21, 245.2 Lentz) agree that the form ὀρφός is *Koine*, -ῶς Attic, but Ath. and Pollux allege that the Attic form is oxytone, Herodian perispomenon. MSS do not help; they sometimes impose the *Koine* form on Attic authors, but when the Attic spelling is correctly presented, the *Marcianus* of Ath. naturally favours its prescribed oxytone (e.g. Archippus 17, Cratinus 154(147K), 171.50(161K), Ephippus 12.7, Plato com. 175(160K).1, while at Ar. *Vesp.* 493 the MSS divide. Cf. K.B. 1.407.

[2] British scholars (e.g. LSJ s.v., Gow–Scholfield on Nicander *Ther.* 897, D. L. Page, *Sappho and Alcaeus* (Oxford 1955) 91) have tended to accept uncritically Sir Arthur Hort's dogmatic misidentification (Loeb edition

COMMENTARY

agreeable when they are dried (Theophr. *CP* 6.14.8, Pliny *HN* 21.39) doubtless accounts for their popular inclusion in garlands (e.g. Cratinus 105(98K).7, Philochorus in Σ Eur. *Hipp.* 73 = *FGrH* 328 F 188a, cf. Pliny *HN* 21.53), while their important role in herbal medicine from antiquity on (e.g. Hippocr. *Mul.* 2.210, *Ulc.* 19, Dioscorides 3.40, Galen 12.70, 13.183, 186, 977 Kühn, Scribon. Larg. 258, Pliny *HN* 21.151, 22.123, 23.85, 29.37; cf. John Gerard, *The Herball* (London 1597), book 2 chapter 488) would explain their presence in any drugseller's stock. Cf. also A. Olivieri, *Atti Accad. Napoli* 9 (1926) 469f.

120 (115K)

Meineke 3.433 (IV), Kock 2.338, Edmonds 2.427, Kassel–Austin 2.87. In a trochaic tetrameter scene an unidentified speaker here is talking περί τινος ἐν καπηλείῳ πίνοντος (so Ath. 11.473d introducing the fr.). The accoutrements described as lying by the drinker's side (vv. 2–3) indicate that he was a soldier. His name is given as τὸν Ἑρμαΐσκον (v.1), where the presence of the article implies that he was somebody already familiar to the audience (cf. K.G. 1.598ff., Gildersleeve, *Syntax* 2.229ff.), almost certainly (in a descriptive context like the present one) as a play character already seen or at least mentioned in the stage action. This is the commonest significance of the article before proper names in extant scenes of Menander: (i) characters previously on stage: e.g. Daos in *Asp.* 163, 274, 497; Gorgias in *Dysk.* 536, 670, 683, 820, 900; Daos in *Dysk.* 541, 594: Doris in *Pk.* 751; (ii) characters before first entry but previously named: e.g. Kleostratos in *Asp.* 110 ~ 14, Tibeios in *Her.* 28 ~ 21.[1]

---

of Theophr. *HP*, vol. 2 (London and New York 1916) p. 463) as *Trigonella graeca*.

[1] In Menander, however, there are a few practices which perhaps merit more detailed study. Slaves are occasionally identified with article + name by their masters shortly before initial entry and without previous reference to them (Getas in *Dysk.* 182, 259, possibly Pyrrhias in *Dysk.* 71 if the references at 42 and 48 are not to him: see Gomme–Sandbach, *Comm.* on v. 42 and my discussion in the Loeb edition, vol. 1 (Cambridge, Mass. and London 1979) 193 n. 1). At *Sam.* 56 ἡ Χρυσίς is thus named for the first time in our extant text, but (i) this is preceded by two references to an innominate Σαμία ἑταίρα 21, 25; (ii) about twenty-three lines of text have been lost between 29 and 31. At *Her.* 24f. both Plangon and Gorgias are given articles by a deferential speaker when first named. Some characters never have the article before their names (e.g. Demeas, Nikeratos in *Sam.*). When characters refer to themselves in the third person, the names are anarthrous (e.g. *Dysk.* 693, *Mis.* 263, *Sam.* 512, 647f., 652, *Sik.* 188 if Βλέπης is rightly conjectured there as a

ΚΡΑΤΕΙΑ

Soldiers appear as characters also in Alexis' Θράσων, Λευκαδία, Στρατιώτης and possibly Ἀγωνίς (cf. comm. on fr. 2.1–2).

1 Ἑρμαΐσκον: the name does not appear elsewhere in comedy, but is generally so spelled on inscriptions (x 6 -μαϊσ-, ~ x 2 -μαιισ-: on this variation see the introduction to Ἀχαΐς, p. 128 n. 1) with reference to historical Athenians (Kirchner, *PA* 1.335 nos. 5090–91, W. Pape and G. E. Benseler, *Wörterbuch der griechischen Eigennamen*[4] 1 (Brunswick 1911) 381, Threatte 1.289). The form Ἑρμεῖσκον, which Blaydes (*Adv.* 1.109, 2.158) gratuitously conjectures here, never occurs, although names derived from Ἑρμῆς show forms with -ε- (e.g. Ἑρμεῖνος, Ἑρμεῖον) as well as with -α- (e.g. also Ἑρμάδιον, Ἑρμαῖον).

1–2 τῶν ἀδρῶν τούτων τινὰ κάνθαρον: J. G. J. Hermann's correction (*De metris poetarum Graecorum et Romanorum* (Leipzig 1796) 118f.) of A's ἀνδρῶν to ἀδρῶν is certain. The confusion occurs elsewhere in the same MS (in its two citations of Diphilus 5, at Ath. 11.497a A has ἀδρότερον correctly, at 496f it corrupts to ἄνδρ᾽ ἕτερον); cf. also Pl. *Resp.* 6.498b, ἀνδροῦται E (*Venetus* 184) correctly, ἀδροῦται[1] all other MSS.

The κάνθαρος, a two-handled drinking-cup of various shapes but always with a deep belly (Richter–Milne, *Shapes* 25f. and figs. 167–9, B. A. Sparkes and L. Talcott, *Pots and Pans of Classical Athens* (Princeton 1958) fig. 9, and *Agora* XII.113ff. and figs. 6, 7, 27 and pls. 27–9, 47, 56, nos. 624–723), is aptly called ἀδρός, 'bulky', cf. Epigenes 4 τοὺς κανθάρους ... ἐκείνους τοὺς ἀδρούς (so also the μάνης cup, Nicon 1; cf. also Headlam on Herodas 1.81, Aelian *Epist.* 4, Alciphron 2.34.3) and suited deep drinkers (Xenarchus 10). Alexis' phrase here (noun in singular, here agreeing with τις; article and adjective at genitive plural, denoting the class to which the noun belongs) follows normal Attic idiom (K.G. 1.337f.), e.g. Ar. *Nub.* 348f. κομήτην | ἄγριόν τινα τῶν λασίων τούτων, where the τούτων adds a slight touch of contempt.

2 καταστρέφοντα: '*invertentem, i.e. funditus educentem et siccantem*'

---

proper name, 344, 346). How far these patterns reflect niceties of (i) contemporary speech, (ii) social differentiations, (iii) character individualisation, and how far they (or some of them) are delusive consequences of chance in the preservation of texts (Charisios in *Epitr.* is always anarthrous in the Cairo papyrus, but see now *P.Oxy.* 3532.18 = *Epitr.* 829 in the second edition of Sandbach's Oxford Text (1990) p. 350) – these are questions unanswered and possibly unanswerable.

[1] There is also the still unresolved controversy about the variants ἀνδροτῆτα and ἀδροτῆτα (or ἀδρο-) in the Homeric formula (*Il.* 16.857, 24.6, etc.), where the confusion is not merely palaeographic (J. Latacz, *Glotta* 43 (1965) 62ff.; contrast G. C. Horrocks, *PCPS* 206 (1980) 10).

Meineke. Cf. Sotades com. fr. 1.33 κἂν ᾖ δικότυλος λήκυθος, καταστρέφω, Sophron fr. 105 Kaibel κατάστρεψον, τέκνον, τὰν ἡμίναν.[1]

3 A's στρωμάτεα (sic) τε καὶ γυλιον (sic) αὐτοῦ poses two problems more serious than missing or wrong accents.

(1) At the beginning of a trochaic tetrameter in comedy στρωματέα may be scanned (a) with each syllable given its normal length, thus producing a dactyl in the first half of the first metron (– ∪ ∪ –), (b) with synizesis of -εα (– ∪ –), (c) with shortening of the final alpha (– ∪ ∪ ∪). Although (a) is a rare but acceptable licence in this and parallel metrical positions (troch. tetr., 1st metr. Ar. *Equ.* 319, 3rd m. *Ach.* 318, *Vesp.* 496, Men. *Dysk.* 774, *Pk.* 340; troch. dim., 1st m. Ar. *Av.* 396; cf. Hephaestion p. 35.5f. Consbruch, Wilamowitz, *Isyllos von Epidauros* (Berlin 1886) 7ff., J. W. White, *The Verse of Greek Comedy* (London 1912) 100f., F. Perusino, *RCCM* 4 (1962) 51, Handley's edition of Men. *Dysk.* p. 60, W. Strzelecki in F. Zucker (ed.), *Menanders Dyskolos als Zeugnis seiner Epoche* (Berlin 1965) 61ff., West, *Greek Metre* 92),[2] the evidence provided by occurrences elsewhere in Attic tragedy and comedy of accusative singulars in -έα from nouns in -εύς indicates that (c) is the most probable scansion here: cf. J. Pierson's edition of Moeris (Leiden 1759) 192, Meineke 1.295f., Rutherford, *NP* 234 n. 1, K.B. 1.448, J. La Roche, *Wien. Stud.* 19 (1897) 1ff., Descroix 25, 34 n. 1. I cite only the significant passages: Eur. *El.* 599, 763, *Hec.* 882 φονέα, Theophilus 1.3 τροφέα, Euphron 3.1 ψυγέα (on Alexis 65(64K) see comm.), all after penthemimeral caesura in iambic trimeters, where only -έᾰ is possible; Philemon 83(80K) κεστρέ', Machon 171 Gow βασιλέ', where -έ' + elision of a short syllable must be presumed.

(2) στρ. τε καὶ γύλιον αὐτοῦ would produce a line scanned – ∪ ∪∪ ∪/– ∪ ∪∪ –/– without median diaeresis, unparalleled elsewhere in Alexis' 50 troch. tetr. and rare in Menander (see comm. on fr. 291(302K).1–2). Dindorf secured diaeresis by deleting τε (? dittography after -τέα, or scribal addition of clarificatory particle, see Fraenkel on A. *Ag* 124 and cf. my comm. on 115(110K).12); other suggestions are less beguiling (στρώματά τε Musurus, cf. Casaubon, *Animadv.* 793, but this requires the further change of κείμενον to -να, and replaces a rarer by a

---

[1] In view of the parallels cited here and in the preceding note conjectures such as Kaibel's κανθάρων and Blaydes' κάτω στρέφοντα (*Adv.* 1.109, 2.158) are unnecessary.

[2] Modern scholarship does not always draw the necessary distinction between anomalous dactyls (in the first half of a trochaic metron) and those where the two shorts resolve a possible *anceps* (in the second half). Two of the cited anomalies (Ar. *Equ.* 319, Men. *Dysk.* 774) feature the same phrase (νὴ Δία) and may be special cases (with the iota consonantalised: cf. Sandbach, *loc. cit.*, West 14).

commoner noun; ? possibly *exempli gratia* στρωματέα τε <καὶ σπάθην> καὶ γ. αὐ. with the omission explained as a *saut du même au même*, although this produces median diaeresis after a postpositive, unparalleled in the Alexis frs., but see Handley's edition of Men. *Dysk.* p. 60).

στρωματεύς occurs also at Apollodorus Gel. 5 in a list of soldier's equipment. In Attic Greek it is a blanket or coverlet, but in the *Koine* apparently it took on the meaning of στρωματόδεσμος (or -ον), the bag into which bedding was packed (Pollux 7.17, Phrynichus *Ecl.* 380(379) p. 102 Fischer = p. 487 Rutherford). Either meaning would be appropriate here, although in existing comic lists of military equipment (e.g. Men. *Kol.* 30f., fr. 282, Diphilus 55) bedding of various sorts is mentioned (στρώματα Diph., κῴδιον Men. *Kol.*), but no specific container for it. γύλιος (but oxytone accent is vouched for by *Et. Mag.* 244.22ff. and the rhetorical lexicon in Bekker, *Anecd.* 228.29ff.) is the long, tapering bag (Σ Ar. *Pax* 788) in which soldiers carried their provisions (Σ *Pax* 527, Hesych. s.v., *Et. Mag.* and rhet. lex.; cf. also Ar. *Ach* 1097 and Σ, Ath. 11.483b citing Critias fr. 34 Diels–Kranz).

Κυβερνήτης

Nesselrath, *MK* 314. Two frs. are cited from this play. Fr. 121(116K), a piquant but puzzling vignette of two types of parasite, comes from a lecture delivered by an unnamed parasite to a character named Nausinikos (vv. 1, 14). Fr. 122(117K), which describes in trochaic tetrameters how dessert was served, may derive from a report of a celebratory party towards the close of the play. Both frs. suggest situations characteristic in New Comedy, but neither the date (*pace* Nesselrath: see below, introduction to fr. 121(116K)) nor the subject of the play is known.

Menander wrote a Κυβερνῆται, Eudoxus a Ναύκληρος and Nausicrates a Ναύκληροι, but the remains from these plays are too scanty for profitable guesswork about the roles of their respective seamen. In Menander's Ναύκληρος (? the original of Caecilius' *Nauclerus*, pp. 63ff. Ribbeck) a young man returns safely from a sea voyage (cf. frs. 286, 287). The steersman Blepharo has a small part in Plaut. *Amph.* 1035ff., being called upon to adjudicate between the true and false Amphitruos. In the same playwright's *Miles gloriosus* young Pleusicles impersonates a steersman as part of the trick against the soldier,[1] and the naval costume he must wear is fully described by the scheming slave (1177ff.):

---

[1] Comedies occasionally take their titles from the roles impersonated by characters: e.g. Plaut. *Pers.*, Ter. *Eun.*

> *facito uti uenias ornatu huc ad nos nauclerico:*
> *causeam habeas ferrugineam, et scutulam ob oculos laneam,*
> *palliolum habeas ferrugineum, nam is colos thalassicust,*
> 1180 *id conexum in umero laeuo, exfafillato bracchio,*
> *praecinctus aliqui: adsimulato quasi gubernator sies.*

This passage clearly shows that a particular style of dress made steersmen immediately recognisable on the comic stage (cf. S. Brandt, *Rh. Mus.* 34 (1879) 587f.). It may also imply that a precise distinction between ναύκληρος (technically the man whose command of the ship followed from ownership or at least some financial stake in it) and the κυβερνήτης (the officer in charge of the poop) was not always drawn; doubtless there were occasions when one man was both *v.* and κ. at the same time (cf. especially J. Vélissaropoulos, *Les Nauclères grecs* (Geneva and Paris 1980) 52f., 77ff.).

It is highly probable that Nausinikos, the man on stage with the parasite in fr. 121(116K), was himself the κυβερνήτης. The names given to several types of character in Greco-Roman comedy reflect their occupation or qualities associated with it (cf. F. Poland, *Neue Jahrb.* 17 (1914) 585ff. and my introduction to Θράσων), and a more appropriate name for a steersman than Nausinikos (borne in real-life by several Athenians: Kirchner, *PA* 2.113, nos. 10581–4) could hardly be devised.

121 (116K)

Meineke 3.433 (1), Kock 2.338, Edmonds 2.426, Kassel–Austin 88; cf. Webster, *SLGC* 48, 65, W. G. Arnott, *Hermes* 93 (1965) 303ff., Bain, *Actors* 213ff., Nesselrath, *LP* 20 n. 16, 104, *MK* 314. The fr. has a parasite talking to Nausinikos, who is probably (see above) the play's title figure and also perhaps the parasite's patron. Vv. 14f. of the fr., in which Nausinikos gives qualified approval to the parasite's remarks (cf. Sostratos in Men. *Dysk.* 68f.) while forestalling a possible request for sustenance, may well imply this relationship (so Bain 214 n. 1), but the evidence is not conclusive. The sermon which the parasite preaches here is of a type familiar in Greco-Roman comedy, where the speaker, normally just after his first entrance, analyses or elaborates upon the techniques or burdens of his profession without specific relevance to the individual plot (e.g. Men. *Dysk.* 57ff., Plaut. *Capt.* 69ff., Men. 77ff., *Pers.* 53ff., *Stich.* 155ff., Ter. *Eun.* 232ff.; contextless frs. include Antiphanes 142(144K) and Aristophon 5(4K); cf. Fraenkel, *MNC* 73ff., Handley on Men. *Dysk.* 57ff.).[1]

---

[1] On the role of the parasite see also Ribbeck, *Kolax* 21ff., W. Süss, *De personarum antiquae comoediae atticae usu atque origine* (Diss. Giessen 1905) 48ff., Legrand, *NGC* 228f., 467ff., E. Wüst and A. Hug in *RE* s.v.

In the world of his time, says the first speaker, there are two classes of parasite. One is 'the ordinary kind you see in comedy' (v.2), the impoverished but witty satellite of a wealthy patron like the speaker himself. Identification of the second class would be easier if the text of vv. 3–7 were less corrupt, if we knew the date of the play, and if we had more information about the social conditions and popular attitudes prevalent in Athens at the time. This other class is described as 'acting the part of (ὑποκρινόμενον, 6) satraps ... and distinguished generals' with arrogant extravagance. However one interprets and seeks to correct the MSS tradition hereabouts (see below on vv. 3–7), Alexis' language is ambiguous and allows for alternative identifications of this grander type of parasite: either (especially with V. Schmidt's conjecture παρασιτοῦν in v. 4) the men who sponge on generals or satraps (Ath. 6.248d–252f lists real-life examples), or (with ACE's παρασίτους in 4) the generals and satraps themselves, whose services to foreign rulers as mercenary captains and administrators would then be boldly imaged as analogous to (even if on a grander scale than) those performed by parasites in comedy. The latter interpretation is favoured by (e.g.) Webster, Bain and Nesselrath, *MK* 314: rightly so, because there would be little point and less wit in making a distinction between ordinary parasites on the comic stage and the sponging satellites of famous generals, especially since several parasites in comedy are presented as the satellites of military officers: e.g. Strouthias in Men. *Kol.*, Artotrogus in Plaut. *MG*, Gnatho in Ter. *Eun.* If this grander class of spongers is then correctly identified as including successful generals and statesmen,[1] Alexis may have had in mind military adventurers like Chabrias, who served foreign potentates in Egypt and Cyprus, where the luxury of life at court was notorious (cf. Antiphanes 200(202K), possibly Alexis 63(62K) and comm.), and statesmen like Nicostratus of Argos, who was alleged by Theopompus (in Ath. 6.252a–b = *FGrH* 115 F 124) to have acted as κόλαξ to the king of Persia during the Egyptian expedition of 351.

Parasitos 2, 1381.4ff., Webster, *SLGC* 64f. and *Greek Theatre Production* (London 1956) 82, M. Bieber, *History of the Greek and Roman Theater*² (Princeton 1961) 98ff., 150f., W. G. Arnott, *GRBS* 9 (1968) 161ff., Nesselrath, *LP* 15ff. (especially 20 n. 16, 104).

[1] Alexis' description of generals and satraps as large-scale parasites and the definition of their activities as a 'contest in flattery' (κολακείας ἀγών v. 10) led Webster (*SLGC* 55) to suspect a deliberate allusion to the ideas and language of Pl. *Gorg.* 464b–465a. Although Alexis can be shown to have parodied or rehashed Plato's theories elsewhere in his plays (cf. especially comm. on frs. 98(152K) and 247(245K)), I fail to detect any significant echo of Platonic diction or thought in fr. 121(116K).

It would be unwise, however, to see these real-life instances as even tentative or loose pointers to the date of Alexis' Κυβερνήτης. This *may* have been one of his earliest plays, but the breed of military adventurer did not disappear with Chabrias' death in 357, and Nicostratus' conduct was no isolated example of political sycophancy in the 4th century.[1]

1 Ναυσίνικε: see introduction to Κυβερνήτης.

2–3 The speaker plays with the dramatic illusion here without quite breaking it (Bain 213ff., cf. A. Thierfelder, *Hermes* 71 (1936) 321f.) when he refers first to the class of parasites to which he himself belongs as 'the ordinary kind you see in comedy (see above, introduction to the fr.) – we darkies', while later (v. 6) he describes the grander class as 'acting the role of' satraps and generals. Bain (214 n. 1, cf. 199 and n. 1) rightly identifies the plural in οἱ μέλανες ἡμεῖς as 'professional' (= 'I and my fellow-practitioners': e.g. Men. *Asp.* 445, *Dysk.* 646, Antiphanes 121(123K).6, 142(144K).7, Nicomachus 1.3, com. adesp. fr. 244.221ff. Austin, cf. K.G. 1.83f., Gildersleeve, *Syntax* 1.27). The reference in μέλανες may be to the colour of the parasite's (1) dress (so first Schweighaeuser, *Animadv.* 3.391, citing Pollux 4.119 καὶ πορφυρᾷ δ' ἐσθῆτι χρῶνται οἱ νεανίσκοι, οἱ δὲ παράσιτοι μελαίνῃ ἢ φαιᾷ, sc. on the comic stage), (2) hair (on the mask: so C. Robert, *Die Masken der neueren attischen Komödie* (Halle 1913) 59 and Wüst in *RE* s.v. *Parasitos* 2, 1395.10ff.), or (3) complexion (on the mask: so Pickard-Cambridge, *DFA* 205f.[1] = 225²; cf. Pollux 4.120 τοῖς δὲ παρασίτοις πρόσεστι καὶ στλεγγὶς καὶ λήκυθος, 148 κόλαξ καὶ παράσιτος μέλανες, οὐ μὴν ἔξω παλαίστρας, clear allusions to the outdoor life and consequent suntan of those stage parasites portrayed as haunting the palaestra: cf. Robert, *loc. cit.*). The third of these ties in best with Alexis' use of μέλας elsewhere in comparable contexts (see on frs. 103(98K).17, 170(165K)), and is to be preferred here; in any case an actor's gesture as he said μέλανες would easily remove any doubt about the word's intended application. There is a similar ambiguity in Cicero's description (*Caecin.* 27) of the Terentian parasite Phormio as *niger*.

3–6 The *Marcianus* text here (Ath. 6.237b)[2] poses problems; ὑποκρινόμενον (v. 6) lacks the object needed to complete its sense, ζητῶ (3) and ἐκ μέσου (5) fit awkwardly into their contexts, and the triple occurrence of

---

[1] The existence of such historical examples in the early part of Alexis' career gives the lie to Nesselrath's suggestion (*MK* 314) that the references in 121(116K).4 would not be comprehensible before Alexander's invasion of Persia in 334.

[2] Epit. cites only portions of vv. 1–5 of the fr., omitting the vocative in v. 1 and the final three words of v. 3, turning v. 1 into *oratio obliqua*, and ending the quotation with the words στρατηγοὺς ἐπιφανεῖς, οὓς καὶ σεμνοπαρασίτους φησί.

(-)παράσιτος in the space of twenty words (vv. 1, 4, 5) seems a carelessness of style excessive even for the hurried pen of a productive dramatist. Although these points of suspicion are interrelated, separate discussion of each reveals more clearly the extent of corruption and feasibility of correction.

(i) The participle ὑποκρινόμενον (v. 6, dependent on γένος v. 3) requires as its object a word or phrase indicating the role that the superior class of parasites acts (cf. LSJ s.v. ὑποκρίνω B.II), and σατράπας (with or without παρασίτους as next word, see (iii) below) καὶ στρατηγοὺς ἐπιφανεῖς (v. 4) is the one group of accusatives that aptly supplies this object. In its transmitted position, however, v. 5 effectively erects a syntactical barrier between participle and object; hence Grotius (*Exc.* 573, 972) transposed v. 5 after v. 8, turning it into an amplification of Nausinikos' καὶ μάλα, while Dobree (*Adv.* 2.310) placed the line between vv. 3 and 4 as an embellishment to θάτερον ... γένος (3). Dobree's suggestion is better than Grotius' (with 5 after 8 we should expect καλεῖται or an equivalent verb in the indicative, rather than a participle), but not necessarily the correct solution; it does not remove a major difficulty in the transmitted text of v. 5. To this we now turn.

(ii) According to v. 5, the superior type of sponger is called σεμνοπαράσιτον ('high-parasitic', a hapax) ἐκ μέσου. The last two words are difficult in their context, whether or not the line is transposed. In Attic usage ἐκ μέσου/ ἐκ τοῦ μέσου most commonly = 'away' (with a verb implying removal: e.g. Dem. 18.294, the spurious 10.36, Euphanes 1.5 ('Euphron' 8.5 Kock), com. adesp. fr. 289b.8 and probably also 244.227 Austin, possibly Men. fr. 216), but occasionally appears in less expected senses and contexts (= either 'half', with an ordinal, Thuc. 4.133; or 'openly/in the midst', like ἐν μέσῳ, but qualifying a verb which implies movement or a source, Eur. *IA* 342, possibly *El.* 797 (unless Keene's conjecture ἐς μέσον is accepted); LSJ s.v. μέσος III.c is inadequate). None of these usages can easily be accommodated here, and R. Ellis' attempt (*AJP* 6 (1885) 289) to invent a new one 'apart from the mass/special/extraordinary' fails for lack of a single parallel, cf. Kock 3.742. Conjectures replacing ἐκ μέσου are numerous but unconvincing: e.g. ἐνδίκως (Blaydes, *Adv.* 1.109: good sense but palaeographically inexplicable), ἐν μέσῳ (Kock: near to the *ductus*, but 'publicly' is not one of the meanings of this expression, cf. LSJ s.v. μέσος III.a). Either the correct emendation has not yet been divined, or perhaps (*pace* Nesselrath, *LP* 20 n. 16) v. 5 as a whole should be deleted as an interpolation. Could some reader of the fr. have cited this line in the margin as a parallel? If so, ἐκ μέσου could be the botched Greek typical when interpolations are forced into alien contexts (cf. Fraenkel, *Beob.* 40).

(iii) If v. 5 does not belong to this fr., one repetition of the παράσιτος stem is eliminated and the presence of παρασίτους in 4 is less of an irritation (its sense and syntactical structure with σατράπας was always acceptable, cf. K.G. 1.271ff.). If on the other hand v. 5 is a genuine but misplaced line of the fr., the idea that παρασίτους in 4 has corruptly telescoped the -ους ending of some appropriate attribute to σατράπας with the stem of (σεμνο)παράσιτ(ον) miscopied from its corresponding position in the adjacent verse becomes attractive, although the nature of the postulated error makes correction impracticable. Conjectures like Dobree's μεγίστους (*Adv.* 2.310) and E. Harrison's πολυχρύσους (*PCPS* 148 (1931) 4) are neither more nor less likely than W. Headlam's ἀπροσίτους (*CR* 15 (1901) 98f.: ingenious, but needlessly close to the *ductus*). V. Schmidt's παρασιτοῦν, which Kassel–Austin print, ingeniously approaches the problem from a different angle, but is unacceptable for three reasons. Elsewhere in Attic comedy παρασιτεῖν (i) is intransitive (Alexis 200(195K).3, Antidotus 2.3, Axionicus 6.1, Diodorus 2.5, Diphilus 63, Nicolaus 1.18, 22, cf. e.g. Lucian *Par.* 25, 30, Alciphron 3.11.4), or (ii) governs a dative (Alexis 205(201K).1, cf. Pl. *Lach.* 179b–c, Ath. 13.591d–e, Lucian *Par.* 4, 33, Plut. *Mor.* 220c); the only instance cited for παρασιτεῖν + accusative is doubtful, καὶ τοὺς ἐμοὺς παρεσίτει (παρασ- before correction) παρ' ἀλκινο[in the papyrus scrap of Philodemus fr. 223/3 (*Herculanensium voluminum collectio altera* 8 (Naples 1873) p. 139). Secondly, ὑποκρινόμενον now becomes intransitive and thereby less pointed: 'playing a (false) part/being an actor': cf. e.g. Arist. *EN* 7.3, 1147ᵃ23, Chares of Mytilene in Ath. 12.538f = *FGrH* 125 F 4, LSJ s.v. ὑποκρίνω Β.II.4 (on A's following εὖ τοῖς βίοις see below). Thirdly, παρασιτοῦν turns this grander parasitic group into satellites merely of great men, too similar to their counterparts in Greco-Roman comedy for Alexis' distinction of two classes here to be effective (see introduction to this fr.).

(iv) the final problem is ζητῶ (v. 3): a surprising word to introduce the second category of parasites. Earlier scholars (from Daléchamp to Meineke 3.433) tackled the difficulty by giving the last three words of v. 3 to Nausinikos, but 'I'm looking for/investigating the other class' makes an unnatural interruption if v. 1 of the fr. is (as seems likely) a first reference to the theme of the two classes, while vv. 4–7 connect better with what precedes if they are taken as a continuation and expansion of the same speaker's words. On the parasite's lips, however, ζητῶ is not the *mot juste*; he is not conducting a physical search, and even if vv. 4–14 can be interpreted as burlesque of a philosophical investigation, the verb introduces what follows rather jerkily and abruptly. Yet if ζητῶ is corrupt, none of its conjectural replacements has won or deserved universal support. Herwerden (*Coll. Crit.*124) claims that δέ is required after θάτερον in responsion to the μέν of v. 2; a string of conjectures includes the particle (e.g. δ' ἐστὶν Blaydes, *Adv.* 2.158, δ' ἥκει Richards, *AO* 84f. with εἰς μέσον in v. 5, δ' ἐγώ Peppink, *Obs.* 39 with καλῶ ⏑ – for καλούμενον in 5: all palaeographically difficult; ? perhaps δέ τοι, cf. Ar. *Eccl.* 1150, Denniston, *GP* 552). After words like θάτερον, however, a responding δέ is not obligatory (*GP* 376f.); hence a second group of conjectures which keep very close to the *ductus* (ζηλῶ Bothe, *Griech. Kom.* 52, and ζήτω 'long live (the other class)', cf. LXX *Reg.* 1.10.24, 4.11.12, W. G. Arnott, *Hermes* 93 (1965) 303ff., but the speaker's tone is critical, not envious or laudatory; ζῇ τοι A. Lumb in Gulick's edition of Ath., but τοι ζῇ would be the normal order).

No definitive solution to this nexus of interrelated problems seems possible. Tentatively I should retain v. 5, follow Dobree in transposing it before v. 4, keep A's παρασίτους in v. 4, and obelise ζητῶ (3) and ἐκ μέσου (5).

4 σατράπας: still in Menander's time familiar examples of mighty leaders (*Kol.* 41, 91f.: in the latter passage coupled as here with στρατηγός), who expected blandishments (cf. Men. fr. 668). See also introduction to this fr. and p. 338 n. 1.

6 εὖ τοῖς βίοις: so the *Marcianus*, but Kock's emendation ἐν τ. β. is very attractive. The point at issue is not the excellence but the simple fact of the acting, and in this idiom ἐν is normal with article and noun, e.g. Dem. 19.250 ἃ δ' οὐδεπώποτ' ἐν τῷ βίῳ ὑπεκρίνω.

6–7 Herwerden (*Obs. Crit.* 69, cf. later Blaydes, *Adv.* 2.158) suggests moving τ' from its position in A after ἀνακυλῖον to immediately before it, in order that χιλιοταλάντους may agree with οὐσίας and not ὀφρῦς. This must (*pace* Kassel–Austin) be right. Without either definite article or adjectival attribute οὐσίας would be baldly unidiomatic; and although the phrase (τὰς) ὀφρῦς ἔχειν is often strengthened in the comic poets and related literature by a qualifying adjective or adverbial phrase that lends vigour to this image of haughtiness (cf. Alexis 16.1–2, 6–7 and comm. *ad locc.*), noun and verb do occasionally appear without such qualification, e.g. Ar. *Ran.* 924f. (on Aeschylus' diction) ῥήματ' ... ὀφρῦς ἔχοντα καὶ λόφους.

6 ἔχον: Grotius' correction (*Exc.* 573, 972) of A's unmetrical ἔχοντα, where the error was presumably introduced by a scribe who had forgotten that the accusative singular participles in vv. 2–7 are all neuter (agreeing with γένος v. 3). The same scribe may have intended ἀνακυλίοντ' in the next verse, thus causing or at least compounding the transpositional error with τ' there.

7 ἀνακυλῖον: ἀνακυλίω occurs elsewhere in its literal sense 'I overturn' (e.g. ἁμάξας Plut. *Mor.* 304f); the metaphorical extension of meaning to 'I run through/squander' (sc. the enormous fortunes that generals and satraps had amassed) is found only here and may have been a contemporary colloquialism.

COMMENTARY

Of this compound only the form ἀνακυλίω is recorded; for the simple verb and most compounds the standard Attic forms are κυλινδέω/-ίνδω (-ίνδω also epic, hence more poetical in tone with Athenian writers), which began to be replaced by κυλίω from the second half of the 4th century on (cf. Cobet, *VL* ² 133f., Veitch, *Greek Verbs* ⁴ 400f., K.B. 2.453, LSJ s.v. κυλίνδω). In the Aristotelian corpus -ίω occurs seven times, -ίνδω three (one a Homeric citation). Other writers of Alexis' time or the following generation preferring the form in -ίω include com. adesp. fr. 294.2 (all MSS of Diog. Laert. 2.108), Theoc. 24.18 and an anonymous epigram = *SH* 980.3 (? by an older contemporary of Callimachus, cf. Wilamowitz, *SB Berlin* (1912) 547ff.).[1]

8 The *Marcianus* text makes excellent sense but is a syllable short (either in the second half of the first metron or the first half of the second). Choice appears to rest between three haplographies: τό <τε> γένος Porson, *Suppl. ad praef.*, edition of Eur. *Hec.* (Cambridge 1808) xvii, νοεῖς <σύ> Reisig, *Conjectaneorum in Aristophanem* 1 (Leipzig 1816) 179, and γένος <σύ> Jacobs, *Spic.* 30 and *Addit.* 142.

καὶ μάλα: Daléchamp in his translation (*B: novi probe*) and Grotius, *Exc.* 573 were the first to see that these words were Nausinikos's endorsement (cf. e.g. Ar. *Nub.* 1326, *Ran.* 890, Men. *Dysk.* 754, *Epitr.* 479, *Pk.* 294, 349, Philemon 67(64K)2) of the parasite's question; the *Marcianus* does not record part-divisions. In this idiom καί is emphatic ('very well in fact'), not additive; cf. Denniston, *GP* 317f., H. Thesleff, *Studies on Intensification in Early and Classical Greek* (Helsinki 1954) 46f.

9 τούτων ἑκατέρου: so A correctly, with no connecting particle.[2] Here as elsewhere (frs. 9.8, 27.7, 37(36K).7, 115(110K).18) Alexis follows the common Attic practice of asyndeton when a sentence opens with a demonstrative pronoun, cf. K.G. 2.343f., γ.

10 κολακείας ἀγών: the occupations of the two classes of parasite are claimed to be identical, a 'contest in flattery', because both superior and ordinary parasites secure patronage by the kinds of service clearly described in Epicharmus fr. 35 and Eupolis 172(159K): complimenting the patron, making him laugh and doing menial services. These actions

---

[1] When the κυλίω form appears (occasionally) in the MSS of 5th-century Attic authors (e.g. RVJ at Ar. *Vesp.* 202), it is best regarded as a 'modernising' corruption from the Hellenistic period or later (note that a scholiast at *Nub.* 375 glosses κυλινδόμεναι with κυλιόμεναι).

[2] Kaibel's edition of Ath. gives a false impression that τούτων δ' ἑκατέρου is the reading of A. The particle was first added by the earliest editors of Ath. (τούτου δ' Musurus, τούτων δ' Casaubon), conjectured presumably by Musurus himself or by some unknown scholar whose idea found its way into the MS used as the basis for the Aldine edition.

involve a 'contest' (LSJ s.v. ἀγών II) because each parasite maintains his position only by outdoing potential rivals; ἀγών may at the same time include a subsidiary reference to the 'struggle' (LSJ s.v. III) and torments to which parasites (in comedy at least) were often subjected: facial injuries including crushed ears and loss of an eye; blows from fists, sticks and whips; pots smashed in the face; boiling water or animal's blood poured over the head; the head smeared with pitch; attacks by guard dogs; even arrest and gaol (Plaut. *Capt.* 88f., 472, *Curc.* 394ff., *MG* 33, *Stich.* 215f., Ter. *Eun.* 244f., Pollux 4.148, Alciphron 3.2, 3, 7, 9–12, 15, 18, 32, 34–6, deriving much of his material from comedy, see W. Volkmann, *Studia Alciphronea, I: De Alciphrone comoediae imitatore* (Diss. Breslau 1886) and cf. Legrand, *NGC* 74.

On the use of κολακεία to describe the activity of παράσιτοι see comm. on 262(260K).2.

11 ὥσπερ ἐπὶ τῶν βίων δέ: for the postponement of δέ see on fr. 4.1. The meaning of vv. 11–12 is clear, despite telescoped expression in the comparison. The goddess Tyche assigns some parasites to grand patrons and others to inferior ones, just as in the case of (cf. LSJ s.v. ἐπί A.III.3) human lives (or, more precisely, livelihoods) she makes some persons prosperous and others less so. This idea, along with many others about the arbitrary and irrational operations of Tyche, the goddess who (particularly in the 4th and 3rd centuries) was popularly regarded as responsible for those actions not controlled by or explained in terms of human will (cf. Alexis 288(287K); see especially G. Vogt-Spira, *Die Dramaturgie des Zufalls* (Munich 1992), and cf. L. Gernet, *Recherches sur le développement de la pensée juridique et morale en Grèce* (Paris 1917) 336ff., Wilamowitz, *Glaube* 2.298ff., M. P. Nilsson, *Geschichte der griechischen Religion* 2 (Munich 1940) 190ff. and *Greek Piety* (tr. H. J. Rose, Oxford 1948) 86f., Gomme–Sandbach, *Comm.* on Men. *Asp.* 147–8, Dover, *GPM* 138ff., W. G. Arnott, *Philologus* 125 (1981) 219f., J. D. Mikalson, *Athenian Popular Religion* (Chapel Hill and London 1983) 59ff.), was a cliché in contemporary comedy; cf. the parasite's words in Alciphron 3.37 (? from a comic source: see above on v. 10) ἀλλ' ὦ μοιραῖοι θεοὶ καὶ μοιραγέται δαίμονες, δοίητε παρατροπὴν τῆς ἀδίκου ταύτης τύχης καὶ μὴ τοὺς μὲν διηνεκῶς φυλάττετε ἐν εὐτυχίᾳ, τοῖς δὲ τὸν Λιμὸν συνοικίζετε, cf. also 3.8.

The *Marcianus* text here needs one or two minimal corrections (v.12 Musurus' μεγάλοις for -αις, probably also his ἐλάττοσι<ν>), but otherwise preserves Alexis' piquant and racy phraseology, by which Tyche assigns parasites to patrons, and not patrons to parasites. Blaydes' major rewriting to produce the latter sense (τοῖς μὲν ... μεγάλους ... τοῖς δ' ἐλάττονας, *Adv.* 2.158), which once found favour (Herwerden, *Coll. Crit.* 124, Richards, *AO* 85), does nothing for either sense or syntax.

13 The strict rhythm (with hephthemimeral caesura and no resolutions), succinctly pointed antithesis and probably also the use of ἀλύομεν mark the line as paratragic and possibly even a direct quotation from tragedy.

ἀλύομεν: in Attic drama the υ is always long, but in epic it is short except when ἀλύων or ἀλύει appears at line-end (Hom. *Od.* 9.398, Ap. Rhod. 3.866, Oppian *Hal.* 4.195); cf. LSJ s.v. ἀλύω *fin.*, Schulze, *QE* 311 n. 2.[1] In a range of senses linked by the disconcerting effect of strong emotion, frenzy and pain ('I am excited/frenzied/in despair, 'I roam/thresh about in frenzy'; LSJ s.v. 1.1–6) ἀλύω occurs in Ionic prose (e.g. Hippocr. *Epid.* 5.64, *Morb.* 2.16, *Virg.* 1) and epic, Ionic and Attic poetry, where it was a favourite word of the tragedians (A. *Sept.* 391, S. *OR* 695, *El.* 135, *Phil.* 174, 1194, Eur. *Hipp.* 1182, *Or.* 277, fr. 665, cf. *Cycl.* 434 and the tragic parodies in Ar. *Vesp.* 111[2] and here, where the meaning is 'we are at our wits' end'). In prose of the imperial period, however, a weaker set of extended meanings ('I am idle/roam about': e.g. Chariton 1.4.3, 3.6.3, Longus 1.28, Heliod. 1.14, 2.22, LSJ s.v. II) co-exists side by side with the traditional range of senses (e.g. Xen. Ephes. 5.10.5, Chariton 2.1.1, 4.2.8, Heliod. 3.7, 10.30). Photius (p.83.2ff. Reitzenstein = A 1060 p. 113 Theodoridis; cf.Eustath. 1636.25) wishes to push back this weakened use to the early *Koine* and Menander; however, neither *Epitr.* fr. 3, which Photius adduces, nor *Epitr.* 559 incontrovertibly supports Photius' claim, for both passages of Menander make good sense with ἀλύω understood in its stronger sense (contrast the commentaries of E. Capps (Boston 1910) p. 100 and Gomme–Sandbach p. 293). See especially Bruhn, *Wortschatz* 30f., Durham, *Vocabulary* 40f. and F. Sisti, *SIFC* 3 (1985) 239f.

On the difficulties of the poor parasite's life (a comic commonplace from the time of Epicharmus fr. 35.9ff. onwards) see comm. on v. 10.

14 ἆρά γε διδάσκω, Ναυσίνικ': Musurus' correction of A's διδάσκων (? dittography of ν, or misreading of a supralineal dash which indicated that Ναυσίνικ' was a proper name as if it were a sign for ν: cf. Cobet, *NL* 530f.) is certain. Here διδάσκω is used absolutely, as often in conversational exchanges (e.g. A. *Eum.* 431, S. *Ant.* 992, Ar. *Eccl.* 662, Alexis 138(133K).2). On ἆρά γε, where the second particle 'adds liveliness and emphasis to the question', see Denniston, *GP* 50.

14–15 The correct part-division, with everything from οὐκ ἀστόχως to

---

[1] Empedocles 145 (ἀλύοντες with υ lengthened at the beginning of the fourth foot) is exceptional.

[2] Cf. E. W. Hope, *The Language of Parody* (Diss. Baltimore 1906) 12. The verb is not found elsewhere in Aristophanes; at *Ach.* 690 ἀλύει must be rejected as an inferior variant reading (cf. Rutherford, *NP* 41), and at *Thesm.* 2 the transmitted ἀλοῶν is supported by the testimony of Photius p. 80.23f. Reitzenstein = A 1029 p. 110 Theodoridis.

the end of the fr. assigned to Nausinikos, was first divined by either
Meineke or F. J. de La Porte Du Theil.[1] οὐκ ἀστόχως = 'right on target',
perhaps a contemporary idiom, cf. Arist. *HA* 7.10, 587ᵃ9 οὐκ ἀστόχου
διανοίας. At the end of the fr. the *Marcianus* has μέτι, which is correctly
interpreted as μέ τι, not μ' ἔτι: cf. Du Theil in Schweighaeuser, *Animadv.*
3.393, Wilamowitz, *Schiedsg.* 86f., and Diggle, *Studies* 83f.

122 (117K)

Meineke 3.435 (II), Kock 2.339, Edmonds 2.428, Kassel–Austin 2.89.
Despite an uncertainty over the interpretation of θύμου in v. 2, this brief
fr., which describes in trochaic tetrameters a serving of dessert, derives
most probably from an account (? near the end of the play: cf. Handley,
comm. on Men. *Dysk.* 946–53) of the later stages of a festive meal. The
language and rhythm, however, seem not to deviate from comic norms;
there is no trace here of paratragic or dithyrambic diction such as we find
in (e.g.) frs. 89(86K) or 124(119K).

1 εἰσέβαινον: in the meal descriptions of later Greek comedy the
various courses are often said to 'come in' rather than 'be served': e.g.
Ephippus 8.1, Diphilus 31(32K).24, Crobylus 6.1. Cf. Hunter on Eubulus
fr. 36(37K).1, listing some of the more extravagant synonyms (ἐπεχόρευσε
Diphilus 43(44K).1, 64.4; ἐπεδόνει Antiphanes 183(185K).3; ἐπιβακχευ-
σάτω Nicostratus 5(4K).1, ἐπεισέπλει Eubulus 36(37K).1).

1–2 ἰσχάδες, τὸ παράσημον τῶν Ἀθηνῶν:[2] Alexis calls dried figs 'the
emblem of Athens' (for the expression cf. Nicostratus fr. 28(27K), Plut.
Mor. 399f, LSJ s.v. παράσημον II) primarily because in antiquity Attic figs
both fresh and dried enjoyed the highest of reputations (Ath. 14.652b–
653b citing Dinon = *FGrH* 690 F 12, Lynceus, Philemon the grammarian
and Phoenicides fr. 2; Antiphanes 177(179K), Clem. Alex. *Paed.* 2.1.3

---

[1] Meineke 3.434 was the first scholar to print the correct part-assignment,
attributing it to Du Theil. In Schweighaeuser, *Animadv.* 3.391–3,
however, where Du Theil's other suggestions are reported from
unpublished notes, there is no reference to this part-division. It is
impossible to know whether Meineke had access to material not printed
in Schweighaeuser, or whether with uncharacteristic carelessness he
was attributing one of his own ideas to Du Theil.

[2] So the *Marcianus* correctly at Ath. 14.652d. The Epit. MSS (CE)
corrupt this to the unmetrical gloss τῶν Ἀττικῶν, an error which is
repeated by Eustathius when he copies out this fr. in his Homer
commentaries (955.8, 1411.35), thus clearly indicating his dependence
on the Epit. of Ath. Cf. Bentley, *Phalaris* 1.189, L. Cohn in *RE* s.v.
Eustathios 1482.1ff., P. Maas, *BZ* 35 (1935) 299ff.

COMMENTARY

(where 'Chelidonian' = Attic: cf. Pollux 6.81), Σ Theoc. 1.147). Figs were a favourite dessert (τράγημα, see comm. on 168(163K).2, served with other titbits at the end of dinner in order to stimulate thirst for drinking wine (e.g. Pl. *Resp.* 2.372c, Ath. 652c, cf. Ch. Morel in Dar.–Sag. s.v. *Coena*, especially 1275f., Olck in *RE* s.v. *Feige* especially 2138.45ff., H. Michell, *The Economics of Ancient Greece* (Cambridge 1940) 77f.). Webster, *SLGC* 49 n. 1 suggests that Alexis might also have intended here an ironic reference to the equally high Athenian reputation for συκοφαν-τία, which flourished throughout the 4th century (e.g. [Dem.] 25.49ff., Theophr. *Char.* 26, Diog. Laert. 5.9; in comedy Alexis 187(182K) and comm., Plaut. *Trin.* 843ff., where the character and scene clearly derive from the Philemon original, cf. F. Muecke, *TAPA* 115 (1985) 167ff., Ter. *Andr.* 814f., probably also Antiphanes 177(179K) and Axionicus 4.15ff., where see Ath.'s accompanying comment, 8.342c), but there is nothing in Alexis' wording to require such an interpretation. Cf. also Alexis 311(310K) and comm.

2 θύμου δέσμαι τινές: doubtless also a part of the dessert, but the precise identity of θύμον (? -ος) here as elsewhere (cf. A. C. Andrews, *Osiris* 13 (1958) 150ff., Hunter on Eubulus 18(19K).4) poses a problem which LSJ treat inadequately. In Attic usage θύμον covers at least two different types of native plant: (i) the aromatic shrublet *Thymus capitatus* (sometimes less correctly classified as a *Corydothymus*, *Satureja* or *Thymbra*), Cretan thyme or headed/summer savory (Theophr. *HP* 1.12.2, 3.1.3, 6.2.3–4[1]), and (ii) edible bulbs, probably including *Allium neopolitanum* (Naples garlic), *A. roseum* (rose garlic) and *Muscari comosum* (tassel hyacinth), cf. Hesych. s.v. θύμον· τὸ σκόροδον. Here it is impossible to determine which type of plant is meant by the speaker; cloves of garlic were often nibbled both as dessert and at other times (e.g. Ar. *Plut.* 253, Antiphanes 166(168K).7f., 225(226K).7, Ath. 4.130d), while various herbs seasoned with salt were a common stimulator of post-prandial thirst (Antiphanes 132(134K), Ephippus 8, Ath. 9.366b, Pollux 6.71).

---

[1] At 6.2.3 Theophrastus mentions the existence of 'white' and 'black' (τὸ μὲν λευκόν, τὸ δὲ μέλαν) forms of the plant. This is probably not to be explained as confusion between two different species (so e.g. C. Fraas, *Synopsis plantarum florae classicae*[2] (Leipzig 1870) 174, 176, K. H. E. Koch, *Die Bäume und Sträucher des alten Griechenlands*[2] (Berlin 1884) 93, J. Berendes, comm. (Stuttgart 1902) on Dioscorides 3.38 = 3.36 Wellmann), nor by the assumption of lighter and darker varieties in *Thymus capitatus* (so Andrews, *loc. cit.*), but rather by Theophrastus' failure to remark that the calyx of this plant, which has spreading white hairs during the spring flowering period, turns black in summer (cf.

Κυβευταί

Meineke 1.364f., Hunter 142. Κυβευταί (this noun and congeners like κυβεύω, κυβευτικός etc. cover gaming with both κύβοι, six-sided dice, and ἀστράγαλοι, knucklebones with only four effective surfaces; cf. Lamer in *RE* s.v. *Lusoria tabula* 1933.28ff., still the best general account, although needing to be updated from more recent archaeological discussions (e.g. R. Hampe, *Die Stele aus Pharsalos im Louvre* (Berlin 1951), G. R. Davidson, *Corinth XII: The Minor Objects* (Cambridge, Mass. 1952) 217ff.), is a familiar title in plays of the Middle-Comedy period (homonyms by Amphis, Antiphanes and Eubulus; Pomponius' *Aleones* may in part have been influenced by one or more of these, p. 270 Ribbeck). Gambling was an Athenian passion with an unsavoury reputation (cf. Eupolis 99.85 Kassel–Austin ὦ πανοῦργε καὶ κυβευτὰ σύ, Ar. *Vesp.* 74ff., Aeschines 1.59, Ath. 8.342b (citing Philetaerus 2) and 10.444d, and the passages cited by Hunter 142); but whether shared titles implied shared outlooks, with violent denunciations (and long descriptions) of the *aleatorum insania* (so Meineke 1.364), or whether some at least of these titles reflect merely characters and incidents in an intrigue plot of a type familiar in New Comedy (cf. Men. *Epitr.* 504f. and Alciphron 3.18, possibly inspired by comedy), we cannot now say.

123 (118K)

Meineke 3.435, Kock 2.339, Edmonds 2.428, Kassel–Austin 2.89; cf. Desrousseaux, *Obs.* 29. Ath. 3.96a (only A) cites a brief fr. of narrative, torn from an unknown context and impossible to interpret with assurance.

1 ἠριστηκότων: cf. comm. on 114(109K).

2 σχεδόν τι δ' ἡμῶν: postponement of δέ to fourth word (or even later, if ἠριστηκότων was not the first word in Alexis' original sentence) is no matter for concern in a passage of later Attic comedy (see comm. on fr. 4.1), but the possibility that δ' here may have been gratuitously added by a scribe in order to remove a possibly defensible hiatus after τι (see on fr. 27.7–8) cannot be ruled out (so Blaydes, *Adv.* 2.158).

ἐξ ἀκροκωλίου: Meineke and Desrousseaux object to the preposition, the regular construction with ἀριστᾶν and δειπνεῖν being object accusative or partitive genitive (K.G. 1.355f.); Meineke conjectured δ' ἡμῶν ἔξ (*FCG* 3.435) and even τι, Δήμων, ἔξ (*ed. min.* 718), and Desrousseaux with

---

O. Polunin and A. Huxley, *Flowers of the Mediterranean* (London 1965) 162 and pl. 157).

implausible[1] brilliance δήμων ἔξ. No change in fact is needed; ἀριστᾶν ἐκ + genitive may be defended by analogy with τρέφειν ἐκ (e.g. Isoc. 15.152 δυνάμενος ἐκ τῶν ἰδίων τρέφειν ἐμαυτόν),[2] ζῆν ἐκ (e.g. Xen. *Hell.* 3.2.11 ζῶντας ἐκ τούτου, sc. their plunder), perhaps also πίνειν ἐκ (cf. Headlam–Knox on Herodas 1.25); and we cannot in any case be sure that in Alexis' original sentence ἐξ ἀκρ. τινός was intended to construe with ἠριστηκότων.

Κύκνος

Meineke 1.391, G. Schiassi, *Rend. Ist. Lomb.* 88 (1955) 107 n. 3, Hunter 183. This title and Eubulus' Προσουσία ἢ Κύκνος most probably indicate plays burlesquing myths associated with Cycnus – but which Cycnus? The stories of at least two legendary figures with this name yield material suitable for comic treatment:

(1) the son of Ares (Adler in *RE* s.v. *Kyknos* 2, 2435.20ff., Engelmann in Roscher 1690.66ff., Robert, *GH* 2.508ff., F. Vian, *REA* 47 (1945) 5ff., H. A. Shapiro, *AJA* 88 (1984) 523ff., R. Janko, *CQ* 36 (1986) 48ff.), a brigand who waylaid travellers on the road between Tempe and Thermopylae and was killed by Heracles.

(2) Poseidon's son (Adler s.v. *Kyknos* 3, 2438.59ff., Engelmann 1695.10ff., Robert *GH* 1.81f., W. R. Halliday, *CQ* 21 (1927) 37ff., J. Diggle's edition of Eur. *Phaeth.* (Cambridge 1970) pp. 8, 195, 213), about whom two different but not irreconcilable[3] stories were told: (a) an ally of the Trojans, he was slain by Achilles at the beginning of the war (*Cypria* according to Proclus' summary, *Epicorum Graecorum Fragmenta* p. 32 M. Davies (Göttingen 1988) = p. 19 G. Kinkel (Leipzig 1877), Pind. *Ol.* 2.82, *Isthm.* 5.39) and metamorphosed into a swan; (b) king of Colonae to

---

[1] The idea of six demes lunching on a single pig's trotter goes beyond the claims of any ἀλαζών even in the fantasy world of Old Comedy; Desrousseaux concedes that with his conjecture the trotter would have to be magical. For Alexis and later Greek comedy, however, the skinny little ox and single deme of Men. *Sik.* 183ff. appear to provide a more acceptable yardstick of imaginative tolerability.

[2] LSJ s.v. τρέφω III.1 cite for this construction also Pl. *Resp.* 2.372b, θρέψονται δὲ ἐκ μὲν τῶν κριθῶν ἄλφιτα σκευαζόμενοι, where ἐκ ... κριθῶν depends not on θρέψονται but on σκευαζόμενοι.

[3] Modern scholarship (e.g. Adler 2441.41, cf. Engelmann 1695.10ff.) generally assumes that the same Cycnus is the subject of both Trojan sagas, but Hunter sounds here a wiser note of caution.

the north-east of Troy, he had two children, Tennes and Hemithea, by his first wife, but his second wife fell in love with Tennes, was rejected by her stepson and brought a false accusation against him by the perjury of an αὐλητής; Cycnus then imprisoned his children in a chest which was cast into the sea and floated ashore at Tenedos, which got its name from Tennes.

The one surviving fr. of Alexis' Κύκνος, which describes in elevated language and tragic rhythms (see below, introduction to fr. 124(119K)) a mixing bowl full of wine, offers no decisive evidence for identification of titular hero or plot. Admittedly Heracles is elsewhere a character in at least two of Alexis' plays ('Ησιόνη, Λίνος: q.v.), while the theme of hero defeating brigand presumably featured in his Σκίρων, but it is unsafe to conclude from these facts alone that Alexis' Cycnus was Ares' son, or that the context of fr. 124(119K) was Heracles' victory carousal after despatching the bandit (so Schiassi). In Attic tragedy the Troad sagas can twice be distinguished. The warrior Cycnus was apparently a hero in a lost play by Aeschylus, to judge from a passing comment in Ar. *Ran.* 963 (cf. Nauck[2] p. 39, H. J. Mette, *Der verlorene Aischylos* (Berlin 1963) 99ff., S. Radt, *TrGF* 3.250); Euripides' *Tennes* dealt with the infatuation of Tennes' stepmother and its consequences (the play's hypothesis is partially preserved in *P.Oxy.* 2455 fr. 14 = Austin, *NFEP* p. 97). The subject of a third play, Achaeus' *Kyknos* (*TrGF* 1.122 Snell) is indeterminable. Alexis' play may have guyed any or none of these tragedies; the beaching of a mysterious chest is handled in satyr drama (Aeschylus' *Diktyoulkoi*) and New Comedy (Plaut. *Rud.*, from an unidentified play by Diphilus; see most recently E. Lefèvre, *Diphilos und Plautus* (*Abh. Mainz* 1984/10) 18); such analogies, however, are no less inadequate guides to the subject of a comic Κύκνος than Alexis' aforementioned use elsewhere of Heracles as hero, and a bandit as villain.[1]

124 (119K)

Meineke 3.435, Kock 2.339, Edmonds 2.429, Kassel–Austin 2.90; cf. Meineke 1.290ff., Fraenkel, *MNC* 13ff., Handley, comm. on Men. *Dysk.* 946–53, Hunter 19f., 166f., Nesselrath, *MK* 241ff., 253 n. 32, 255. This fr., cited by Ath. 11.472a–b (complete in A, only vv. 1–3 ἀφρίζων in Epit.), seems to be part of a narrative describing the preparations for a party and spoken probably by a household slave (cf. Plaut. *Stich.* 676ff.; Nesselrath

---

[1] Edmonds' suggestion (2.429 note c) that the play might rather have treated the story of Leda is less absurd than his speculation about the theme of Eubulus' Κύκνος (2.122f. note e), but its credentials are weak so long as Alexis' recorded title is Κύκνος and not Λήδα ἢ Κύκνος.

COMMENTARY

255); its relation to the play's subject, however, is as uncertain as that subject itself. The five or so iambic trimeters preserved are notable for their severely tragic rhythm (no resolutions, penthemimeral or hephthemimeral caesura in every line, strict observance of Porson's law) and elevated poetic diction. In comedy this type of writing, aping tragedy for several verses without discernible parody of a particular passage or any insertion of bubble-pricking vulgarity, can be identified as early as Ar. *Av.* 1706–19, and lingers on to Menander's time (e.g. *Dysk.* 946–53), but it is especially associated with Middle Comedy (cf. Meineke 1.290ff., collecting a plethora of passages but omitting Ar. *Eccl.* 1–18). Some of the extant passages (e.g. Alexis 124(119K).2, 153(149K).15–19, Antiphanes 216(217K), Eubulus 75) additionally contain features more at home in late 5th-century dithyramb (e.g. grotesque or riddling metaphors, extravagant compound adjectives: cf. R. A. S. Seaford, *Maia* 29/30 (1977/8) 88f., Nesselrath 244 n. 10), but it is impossible to determine how far such features indicate direct influence from contemporary dithyramb, or how far they were filtered through those late 5th-century tragedies which had adopted the same ornaments in their lyrics (cf. Hunter 166f., Nesselrath 241ff.). Fr. 124(119K), like several other – but not all – passages in this style (e.g. Alexis 88(85K), 89(86K), cf. introduction to Ἡσιόνη, Antiphanes 104(105K), 174(176K), Eubulus 9(10K), 14(15K)), comes from a play whose title suggests myth travesty. More notably the present fr. shares with a large group of comic fellows (cf. especially Fraenkel and Handley, *locc. citt.*, and the introduction to Ἀγωνίς) a connection with food and/or drink, where the mention of Thericlean vases (cf. e.g. Alexis 5, Eubulus 56 (iamb. trim.), Aristophon 13(14K) (troch. tetr.), Antiphanes 172(174K) (troch. tetr. mingled with dactylic vv.)) often seems to stimulate the poet (as here) to dizzier heights of poetic – or parodic – expression.

1 φαιδρὸς δὲ κρατὴρ θηρίκλειος: on Thericlean vases see comm. on fr. 5. The adjective φαιδρός, in its primary meaning 'bright/shining' (LSJ s.v., cf. M. Treu, *Studium Generale* 18 (1965) 89 *Das nachhomerische, auch nachhesiodische Glanzadjektiv* φαιδρός ... *verknüpft vom Anfang an Glanz mit dem Gemütswert des Stillen, Rühig-heiteren*),[1] is confined to serious poetry and comic parodies of it (also Ar. *Pax* 156, Cratinus 334(301K)). Here it happily (cf. F. W. Schmidt, *Kritische Studien zu den griechischen Dramatikern* 3 (Berlin 1887) 59f.) describes the brilliant black glaze of Thericlean vases (cf. v. 4 ποήσας λαμπρόν, Eubulus 56.1–6 ἄρτι μὲν μάλ' ἀνδρικὴν | τῶν θηρικλείων ὑπεραφρίζουσαν ... | μέλαιναν, εὐκύκλωτον,

---

[1] In its secondary, metaphorical sense 'beaming with pleasure' (with special reference to facial expression), however, the adjective is part of everyday Attic speech (LSJ s.v. 2, e.g. Ar. *Equ.* 550, Xen. *Anab.* 2.6.11, *Apol.* 27, *Cyn.* 4.2, Dem. 18.323).

ὀξυπύνδακα, | στίλβουσαν, ἀνταυγοῦσαν, ἐκνενιμμένην, | κισσῷ κάρα βρύουσαν).

1–2 ἐν μέσῳ ἕστηκε: sc. the bowl now stands (after it is cleaned, polished and filled with wine, vv. 3–6) surrounded by the other preparations for the forthcoming party. Cf. Eur. *Ion* 1165f. χρυσέους τ᾽ ἐν μέσῳ συσσιτίῳ | κρατῆρας ἔστησ᾽.

2–3 λευκοῦ νέκταρος παλαιγενοῦς πλήρης, ἀφρίζων: a brief emergence of riddling language in dithyrambic style (see above, introduction to the fr.). Both expression and ideas can be paralleled in 4th-century comedy: e.g. Alexis 5 μεστὴν ἀκράτου θηρίκλειον ... | ... ὑπερθύουσαν, Antiphanes 172(174K).2–4 ἦλθε θηρίκλειον ὄργανον, | τῆς τρυφερᾶς ἀπὸ Λέσβου σεμνοπότου στάγονος | πλῆρες, ἀφρίζον, 234(237Κ).1–3 βακχίου παλαιγενοῦς | ἀφρῷ σκιασθὲν (so L. C. Valckenaer, *Callimachi elegiarum fragmenta* (Leiden 1799) 258: σκιὰ καί CE at Ath. 11.781e in a passage where the *Marcianus* is defective, 3 p. 17 in Kaibel's edition) χρυσοκόλλητον δέπας | μεστόν, Aristophon 13(14K).2–3 τῶν θηρικλείων εὐκύκλωτον ἀσπίδα, | ὑπεραφρίζουσαν, Eubulus 56 (cited above, introduction to the fr.), 121(124K) Θάσιον ἢ Χῖον λαβὼν | ἢ Λέσβιον γέροντα νεκταροσταγῆ, Men. *Dysk.* 946 Εὔιον γέροντα πολιόν.

The first three words in the lemma are an arabesque for 'of old white wine'. λευκός was already the technical term for pale wine made by separating the grape juice from the crushed pulp straight after pressing: cf. comm. on frs. 191(186K).8, 245(342K).2. The use of νέκταρ (and its derivatives) as a poetical metaphor for οἶνος was doubtless originally inspired by Homeric passages such as *Il.* 4.2f. Ἥβη νέκταρ᾽ ἐῳνοχόει and *Od.* 9.359 τόδ᾽ (sc. drink of wine) ἀμβροσίης καὶ νέκταρός ἐστιν ἀπόρρηξ; it occurs sporadically in Pindaric lyric (*Isthm.* 6.37) and Attic comedy (in its elevated and parodic styles: also Ar. fr. 688(579K), Hermippus 77(82K).10, Eubulus 121(124K); cf. Alciphron 3.2.2 στάμνια τοῦ Μενδησίου νέκταρος ... πεπληρωμένα, probably influenced by comedy); in Hellenistic poetry it has become a cliché (e.g. Theoc. 7.153 and Gow *ad loc.*, Callimachus fr. 399, Nicander *Alex.* 44, *Ther.* 667, Eudemus and Pancratis, *SH* 412A.10 and 602.2).

4 τρίψας, ποήσας λαμπρόν: cf. Eubulus 95(96K) Ἑρμῆς ὁ Μαίας λίθινος, ὃν ... | ... λαμπρόν, ἐκτετριμμένον, Herodas 1.79 τὴν μελαινίδ᾽ ἔκτριψον and Headlam *ad loc.*, 6.9 νῦν αὐτὸν (sc. a stool) ἐκμάσσεις τε καὶ ποεῖς λαμπρόν.

4–5 ἀσφαλῆ βάσιν στήσας, συνάψας: βάσις here is a poeticism replacing the normal Attic terms ὑπόστατον (*IG* ii².1421.19f. ὑπόστα-[τον] | [κρα]τῆρος ὑπόχαλκ[ον], cf. 1388.43, i³.405.6, Pollux 10.79) and ὑπόσταθμον (*IG* i³.342.12, 422.32ff.; Ionic Greek preferred ὑποκρητήριον and -ηρίδιον), the stand on which the mixing bowl rested (illustrated in Richter–Milne, *Shapes* fig. 54, cf. p. 7 and E. Pottier in

COMMENTARY

Dar.–Sag. s.v. *Crater* 1553b). συνάψας construes with the preceding, not the following, context: 'having set the stand down to be secure and fitted bowl and stand together'. Editors of Ath. and the comic frs. (including Kassel–Austin) prefer to link the participle less appropriately with καρπίμοις κισσοῦ κλάδοις, but in that case we should have expected either ἀνάψας rather than συν- (cf. Meineke, *Anal. Crit.* 217 conjecturing that participle) or καρπίμους ... κλάδους (Bothe's conjecture, *PCGF* 543).

5–6 καρπίμοις κισσοῦ κλάδοις ἔστεψα: note the alliteration. At Eubulus 56.6 (cited by Ath. 11.471d) the Thericlean cup is similarly κισσῷ κάρα βρύουσαν. In both these passages of parodically elevated style the *Marcianus* correctly preserves (as Meineke first noted) the orthography with -σσ-, which in Attic was confined to poetic diction from the earliest times (cf. Meisterhans–Schwyzer 101f., Threatte 1.537ff.). Comedy seems to be remarkably consistent over the spelling of this word and its compounds. The form in -σσ- is used in choral and solo lyric (Ar. *Av.* 238, *Thesm.* 988, 999, Ecphantides 4(3K) cited by Cratinus 361(324K), Eubulus 102(104K).5) and in passages of tragic or dithyrambic parody (also Antiphanes 207(209K).7), but where there are no reasons to heighten the style the everyday form κιττός is employed (Ar. *Pax* 535, Eupolis 13(14K).4, Men. *Georg.* 36); cf. F. Selvers, *De mediae comoediae sermone* (Diss. Münster 1909) 36. The practice of garlanding vases and especially mixing bowls at parties is often mentioned in ancient literature (e.g. Ar. fr. 395(380K), Eubulus 56.6, Phanodemus in Ath. 10.437c–d = *FGrH* 325 F 11, V. *Georg.* 2.528, *Aen.* 1.724, 3.525f.,Tib. 2.5.98, Sid. Apoll. *Epist.* 9.13 vv. 6of. of anacreontics) and pictured on Athenian pottery (e.g. a red-figure vase in Basle illustrated in *Ath. Mitt.* 86 (1971) pls. 38, 39; also Beazley, *ARV²* 359.19, 467.118); cf. E. Saglio in Dar.–Sag. s.v. *Corona* 1526b, Ganszyniec in *RE* s.v. *Kranz* 1588.46ff., K. Baus, *Der Kranz in Antike und Christentum* (Bonn 1940) 77 and M. Blech, *Studien zum Kranz bei den Griechen* (Berlin 1982) 64. The choice of ivy for symposiac wreaths is clearly dictated by its traditional association with Dionysus and his worship (e.g. *H. Hom.* 7.40f., 26.1, S. *Trach.* 220f., *OC* 674ff., Eur. *Bacch.* 81f. and Dodds *ad loc.*, Ath. 15.675a–f citing the physician Philonides and an Apollodorus, Plut. *Mor.* 647a).

Κύπριος

Meineke 1.400. Two frs. are quoted from the play by Ath. (125(120K) at 3.114d, 126(121K) at 110e), and one word is cited by the Antiatticist (127(122K) at 89.6 Bekker) with the lemma Ἄλεξις Κύπριδι (so the MS). Κύπρις, which could be interpreted only as one of Aphrodite's names,

352

ΚΥΠΡΙΟΣ

seems an unlikely title for Alexis;[1] as play titles – and particularly their endings – are as prone to corruption in the MS of the Antiatticist (e.g. Alexis 10, 226(224K) not recorded in Kassel–Austin, 231(229K)*, Eubulus 50(51K)*, 51(52K)*: asterisks indicate terminal error) as elsewhere (cf. introduction to Ἀποκοπτόμενος), Meineke's correction of Κύπριδι to Κυπρίῳ has much to recommend it, and is slightly preferable to his alternative suggestion Κουρίδι.

The title, which is unique in comedy (Dicaeogenes wrote a tragedy Κύπριοι of uncertain subject, see *TrGF* 1 p. 291), may imply that the Cypriot hero is now staying in or visiting some other Greek city, chosen as the scene of the play (cf. introduction to Ἀτθίς). In Men. *Mis.* Demeas has just returned from Cyprus (231ff.) and the soldier Thrasonides had served there 'under one of the kings' (fr. 5 Sandbach). The title figure of Antiphanes' Στρατιώτης also claims to have been a mercenary soldier under a Cypriot king 'all the time the war lasted' (fr. 200(202K).2). Turpilius' *Paedium*, adapted presumably from a like-named original by Menander, Apollodorus or Posidippus (cf. L. Rychlewska's editions (Wroclaw 1962) p. 12, (Leipzig 1971) p. ix) was probably set in Cyprus (fr. 1, cf. *Gnomon* 40 (1968) 34). The frs. of Alexis' Κύπριος, however, yield no clues to either subject or date, although it may be more than a coincidence that in a play with this title two frs. (125(120K), 126(121K)) deal with bread; during Alexis' lifetime Cyprian bread seems to have had an excellent reputation (Ath. 3.112e citing Eubulus 77, cf. Hipponax fr. 125 West).

125 (120K)

Meineke 3.436 (1), Kock 2.340, Edmonds 2.428, Kassel–Austin 2.91; cf. Dobree, *Adv* 2.303. In citing this fr. the scribe of the *Marcianus* (Ath. 3.114d; not in Epit.) as usual neither prints the lines as verse nor indicates part-divisions; the former was first done correctly by Dobree, the latter by Daléchamp in his Latin translation. Their combined efforts provide nearly four trimeters of lively dialogue in which a character newly arrived on stage from some bakery discusses the purchase of bread with another character. Their identities are unknown.

---

[1] Why should Alexis have chosen Κύπρις rather than Ἀφροδίτη? In later Greek comedy divine titles are sometimes given to myth burlesques, but then a descriptive word is normally added to the deity's name in order to make the dramatic intention clearer (e.g. Ζεὺς κακούμενος, Ἀφροδίτης γοναί). When gods or goddesses appear as prologues in plays of intrigue, their names feature comparatively rarely as titles (Menander's

353

COMMENTARY

1 The loss of preceding context makes the implications of the opening question uncertain.

1–2 μόλις ὀπτωμένους κατέλαβον: 'I found them (sc. the loaves) only just being baked'. In comedy μόλις normally qualifies a verb, often in participial form (e.g. Ar. *Ach.* 890, *Vesp.* 1110, *Lys.* 328, *Thesm.* 1024, Alexis 88(85K).1, Men. *Dysk.* 537, *Her.* fr. 5 Sandbach, fr. 23.) – a circumstance which makes Edmonds' punctuation with a colon after μόλις less likely.

2 ἀτάρ: cf. Hunter on Eubulus 69.2. Correction of A's wrongly divided ἀταρπος οὕς το ἀτὰρ πόσους is normally attributed to Casaubon, but he was anticipated by Daléchamp's translation *sed quot*.

3 οἶσε: Dobree's correction of A's οισο appears certain; corruption was clearly due to assimilation to the ending of the next word. The imperatives οἶσε, οἰσέτω, οἴσετε and οἰσόντων, which are explained either as irregular formations from the future οἴσω or (more plausibly) as sigmatic aorists (cf. Veitch, *Greek Verbs*[4] 671, K.B. 2.560, Schwyzer 1.788, P. Chantraine, *Grammaire homérique* 2 (Paris 1953) 195f., C. L. Prince, *Glotta* 48 (1970) 155ff.) occur in (i) epic (Hom. *Il.* 3.103, 19.173, *Od.* 8.255, 22.106, 481, Antim. Col. fr. 19 Wyss), (ii) Hellenistic poetry (under Homeric influence: Theoc. 24.48, Call. *Lav. Pall.* 17 with Bulloch, comm. *ad loc.*, 31, 48, *H. Dem.* 136, fr. 283.3 Lloyd-Jones–Parsons, *SH* p. 123, possibly fr. adesp. 961.11 p. 464), and (iii) Attic comedy (also Ar. *Ach.* 1099, 1101, 1122, *Ran.* 482, probably Anaxippus 6.1). The spread of comic passages indicates that οἶσε at least was a colloquialism in 5th- and 4th-century Athens, interchangeable with φέρε and ἔνεγκε without discernible distinction in meaning and tone (*pace* Starkie on Ar. *Ach.* 1099). Although the three instances in *Ach.* all come from the mouth of a bombastic Lamachus, the other passages show no sign of parodic or elevated style. Cf. also Moeris s.v. οἶσε, Ἀττικῶς· φέρε, Ἑλληνικῶς καὶ κοινῶς.

The verse lacks its final one or (with δεῦρ') two syllables. Dobree supplied μοι, Meineke (edition of Ath. and *Anal. Crit.* 52) δή and Peppink (*Observ.* 26) ἰδού as the opening word of (B.)'s response. One of these is probably right, but I know of no rational means for its selection. In Menander and the unidentified papyri of later Greek comedy δεῦρο δή occurs twice as a complete sentence (*Sam.* 476, 722), δεῦρο δή + imperative once (*Pk.* 334), imperative + δεῦρό μοι two or three times (*Dysk.* 889, *Epitr.* 861, possibly *Sam.* 725), imperative + δὴ δεῦρό μοι once (com. adesp. fr. 244.187 Austin), imperative + δεῦρο answered by ἰδού twice (*Dysk.* 406, *Sam.* 312).

Ἥρως is a certain example; possibly also his Μέθη and Ὀργή, cf. Webster, *IM* 162, 168).

4 λευκούς: so A correctly. Dobree's conjecture λευκῶν was misguided (τῶν λευκῶν would have been required, to match τῶν φαιῶν in the balancing phrase, cf. Herwerden, *Coll. Crit.* 124); the varied construction presented by A conforms more closely to the spontaneity of everyday speech. The 'white' and 'grey' (φαιούς is crudely but not inaccurately interpreted by Ath. when introducing the fr. as ῥυπαρούς, 'dirty', whence Hesych. s.v. φαιούς) loaves were all baked in Athens from flour (σεμίδαλις, cf. comm. on 102(97K).3–4) ground apparently from a variety of durum wheat (*Triticum durum*), but the flour of the 'grey' bread had fewer impurities removed in the milling. Cf. N. Jasny, *The Wheats of Classical Antiquity* (Baltimore 1944) 89ff. and *Osiris* 9 (1950) 227ff., pointing out that even the purest (ἄρτος καθαρός, see on fr. 223(221K).10) and whitest (cf. Matron 534.4f. Lloyd-Jones–Parsons, *SH* p. 259 καλλίστους ἄρτους . . . λευκοτέρους χιόνος) bread in antiquity was very impure by modern standards, and now 'even in only moderately civilised countries, would be considered good enough only for swine' (Jasny (1950) 244); Blümner, *Technologie* 76.

126 (121K)

Meineke 3.436 (II), Kock 2.340, Edmonds 2.428, Kassel–Austin 2.91. Possibly from the same scene as fr. 125(120K).

αὐτόπυρον: 'made of wheat and nothing but wheat'; on the meaning and formation see G. C. Richards, *CR* 37 (1923) 23f. and W. J. Verdenius, *Mnemosyne* 21 (1968) 137, 148f. On the kind of wheat see comm. on 125(120K).4. The adjective is not known before Alexis (to the later occurrences cited by LSJ s.v. add the market-price inscription from Ephesus, 1st or 2nd century AD: J. Keil, *JÖAI* 23 (1926) cols. 280f., with T. R. S. Broughton in T. Frank (ed.), *An Economic Survey of Ancient Rome* 4 (Baltimore 1938) 879f.), but αὐτοπυρίτης ἄρτος appears in Phrynichus com. fr. 40(38K) and the Hippocratic corpus (*Int.* 20, 22).

ἄρτον ἀρτίως: such jingles, in which syllables of juxtaposed words are echoed with no connection of root or meaning, are so common a feature of ancient comedy at all periods (e.g. Ar. *Ran.* 136 ὁ πλοῦς πολύς, 184 χαῖρ', ὦ Χάρων quoted from Achaeus' satyr play *Aithon* 1 F 11 Snell, 735 χρῆσθε τοῖς χρηστοῖσιν, 740 πίνειν . . . καὶ βινεῖν, 1478 τὸ πνεῖν δὲ δειπνεῖν, Men. *Dysk.* 746 ἔστ' ἀρεστά, Plaut. *Men.* 610 *palla pallorem incutit*, *Rud.* 305 *Venerem hanc ueneremur*, *Truc.* 2 *amoenis moenibus*) that a humorous intention must be assumed for at least the majority of these passages, from which I have excluded instances of what appear to be purely adventitious echoes (e.g. Ar. *Ran.* 55 πόθος; πόσος τις) and patterns produced solely by inflectional agreements (e.g. Alexis 145(141K).9–13, where see comm.).

COMMENTARY

Cf. J. D. Denniston in *OCD*[2] s.v. *Assonance, Greek* and *Greek Prose Style* (Oxford 1952) 124ff., J. Defradas, *REA* 60 (1958) 36ff. and Handley on Men. *Dysk.* 735f.

127 (122K)

Meineke 3.436 (III), Kock 2.340, Edmonds 2.430, Kassel–Austin 2.91. The Antiatticist here (89.6 Bekker) rightly supports the transitive use of διπλάζω, presumably against an opponent's claim that this was not good Attic. In Athenian writers διπλάζω is transitive also at Eur. *Suppl.* 781 and Men. fr. 264.10,[1] intransitive at S. *Aj.* 268 (cf. Lobeck's discussion *ad loc.* (2nd edition, Leipzig 1835), showing that no rigid rules can be formulated for the government of verbs in -άζω; some are always transitive, some always intransitive and some (like διπλάζω) can be both). Cf. also Sicking, *Annotationes* 80.

Λαμπάς

Meineke 1.400, cf. 313, Breitenbach 128. The title, which is shared with Antiphanes, is of uncertain significance in both plays. In everyday Athenian usage the common noun λαμπάς was (i) a torch, (ii) a torch-race (cf. LSJ s.v.). Neither meaning can be excluded here, though neither is plausible. Admittedly torches were so regular a feature of the processions and revels which formed a standard ending of Greek comedy from Aristophanes (*Pax* 1317, *Ran.* 1525, *Eccl.* 1150, *Plut.* 1194) to Menander (*Dysk.* 964, *Mis.* 459, *Sam.* 731, *Sik.* 418)[2] that expressions like ὥσπερ λαμπάδιον δράματος (Heliod. 10.39.2) and ἐπὶ τὴν δᾶδα ... προελθεῖν (Plut. *Mor.* 789a) became clichés for '(to reach) the finish' (cf. *Hermes* 93 (1965) 253ff.), yet such a torch hardly seems distinctive enough for a play title. When comedies in the 4th century and later took their titles from

---

[1] Perhaps also at [Andocides] 4.11 εἰ ... τὸν φόρον ... διπλάσειεν (so A: διπλασιάσειεν Q). In Hesychius (δ 1942 Latte) the MS corrupts a lemma to διπλα πασαι, which has been variously corrected to διπλάσαι (M. Schmidt) and διπλασιάσαι (Salmasius) in the light of its explanatory gloss διπλᾶ ποιῆσαι. In both places the form from διπλάζω is preferable; διπλασιάζω (cf. LSJ s.v.) and διπλάζω co-exist with similar meanings and a similar preponderance of transitive over intransitive uses, but διπλάζω seems much less common at all periods and so more likely to be corrupted.

[2] Cf. also Antiphanes frs. 197(199K), 269(272K) and 'Chrysippus' fr. 1 (see Kassel–Austin 4 p. 78).

common utensils, the objects either tended to be recognition tokens (cf. introductions to Alexis' Δακτύλιος, (Ἀγωνὶς ἤ) Ἱππίσκος, Καλάσιρις; Webster, *SM* 99 on Menander's Πλόκιον and Κεκρύφαλος, *SLGC* 127 on four Philemon titles, *IM* 135f. on Menander's Ἐγχειρίδιον), or fell into well-defined groups like cooking implements and drinking-cups (e.g. Alexis' Λέβης q.v., Antiphanes' or Menander's Ὑδρία, Antiphanes' Βομβυλιός, cf. Plautus' *Aulularia*). Comic practice also makes an interpretation of λαμπάς as 'torch-race' unlikely; plays with athletic subjects commonly took their titles from the competitor (e.g. Alexis' Ἀποβάτης, Παγκρατιαστής, Mnesimachus' Ἰσθμιονίκης, Xenarchus' Πένταθλος), not the event.

There is, however, one other explanation of the play title more attractive than the two dismissed above. Tentatively advanced first by Meineke and then developed by Breitenbach, it makes Lampas the name of a character in the comedy, most probably a *hetaira*. In his chapter on *hetairai* Ath. mentions one with this name (13.583e, cf. Bechtel, *Frauennamen* 122), but gives no information about her city or date; was she a real person or just a character in a play, perhaps Alexis' or Antiphanes' Λαμπάς? We have no means of knowing. Other *hetairai* in Ath.'s list have related names (Lychnos and Thryallis, also 583e), and Menander's Φάνιον (or -νίον) was named after a *hetaira* (Ath. 567c).[1] If such a character were the heroine of Alexis' play, the one surviving fr. (see introduction to 128(123K)) could be explained with reference to her impoverishment of a young man in love with her.[2]

128 (123K)

Meineke 3.436, cf. 5.89, Kock 2.340, Edmonds 2.430, Kassel–Austin 2.92. Interpretation of the fr., cited by Ath. 14.654f (both A and Epit.), is hampered by syntactical incompleteness (the opening sentence is certainly

---

[1] In Roman comedy Lampadio occurs as the name of a male slave (Plaut. *Cist.*, fr. pall. inc. LXXIX Ribbeck, possibly from Naevius' *Lampadio*). Cf. K. Schmidt, *Hermes* 37 (1902) 192.

[2] Meineke 1.400 alleges, on the authority of '*Scaliger ad Varr. VI p. 248 Bip.*' (*M. Terentii Varronis de lingua Latina libri qui supersunt, cum fragmentis eiusdem. Accedunt notae Antonii Augustini, Andriani Turnebi, Josephi Scaligeri et Ausomi Popmae* (Zweibrücken 1788) = J. Scaliger, *Coniectanea in M. Terentium Varronem de lingua Latina* (Paris 1565) 197), that Turpilius adapted Alexis' Λαμπάς for the Roman stage. J. J. Scaliger's notes on Varro, however, do not contain anywhere (here I have the valued support of Mr T. Tarver) the suggestion asserted by Meineke. No fr. of Turpilius translates, adapts or ties in any way with Alexis 128(123K); no title *Lampas* (or any possible Latin translation of λαμπάς) is attested for Turpilius. Meineke's allegation must be an aberration.

COMMENTARY

defective, the last line and a half possibly so) and corruption in vv. 2–3. Even so a plausible context is easily imagined. The fr. implies an accusation that a great deal of money has been squandered. In plays where young men lavish gifts on *hetairai* with whom they are infatuated such accusations are commonplace (e.g. in Ter. *Eun.* 79 the slave Parmeno describes Thais as *nostri fundi calamitas*; cf. Smikrines at Men. *Epitr.* 127ff., 749ff.), and spendthrift lovers sometimes acknowledge their validity (e.g. Diniarchus in Plaut. *Truc.* 43ff. *si semel amoris poculum accepit meri | eaque intra pectus se penetrauit potio, | extemplo et ipse periit et res et fides*, cf. *Most.* 144ff.). The present fr. could be spoken by an angry father (or *paedagogus* or friend) claiming that he himself would never have been so extravagant, or by the infatuated lover picking up his accuser's words and trying to refute them.

1–2 καταφαγεῖν αὐτὸς τοσοῦτ' ἀργύριον: Meineke's interpretation of καταφαγεῖν as an '*infinitivus indignantis*' is misguided; such infinitives in Attic, even when not articulated, are governed by an accusative, not a nominative, subject (e.g. A. *Eum.* 837ff. = 870ff. ἐμὲ παθεῖν τάδε, | φεῦ, | ἐμὲ ταλαιόφρονα κατά τε γᾶν οἰκεῖν, | ἀτίετον μύσος, Ar. *Nub.* 819 τὸν Δία νομίζειν ὄντα τηλικουτονί and Dover *ad loc.*; cf. also Goodwin, *MT* 314 §787, K.G. 2.23, P. T. Stevens, *CQ* 31 (1937) 187 = *Colloquial Expressions in Euripides* (*Hermes Einzelschrift* 38, Wiesbaden 1976) 61, Fraenkel on A. *Ag.* 1662f.). It is far more likely that here Ath.'s citation begins in mid-sentence or with its syntax to be explained from the preceding context; if <οὐκ ἂν δυναίμην> or something similar[1] were supplied before καταφαγεῖν, the fr. could be construed as the remains of one sentence containing a mixed conditional construction of a fairly common type (Goodwin, *MT* 190 §503; K.G. 2.471f. are strangely sceptical about the Attic examples); translate '<I couldn't> gobble up so much money – not even if I'd got hare's milk and been eating peacocks.'

καταφαγεῖν: see on fr. 110(105K).2.

2–3 γάλα λαγὼ² εἶχον: Schweighaeuser's correction (cf. *Animadv.*

---

[1] Blaydes, *Adv.* 1.110 suggested <ἂν δυναίμην> (oddly without any negative or punctuation as a question), but in cases where the verb in the apodosis of an unfulfilled condition indicates necessity, obligation or possibility, ἄν is regularly (but not invariably: cf. Xen. *Cyr.* 1.2.16) omitted; cf. Goodwin, *MT* 151f. §415, K.G. 1.216.

[2] The accentuation of the Attic form has been disputed since antiquity. Tryphon, *loc. cit.* maintains that it is declined oxytone throughout, but Herodian (1.245.2, 2.198.26, 629.20, 714.18 Lentz) has the genitive singular always and the nominative singular virtually always (λαγώς at 2.198.26 may be a printer's or editor's error) perispomenon. Cf. LSJ s.v. λαγώς, Schwyzer 1.557.

7.622) of the MSS reading (A, Epit.) γάλα εἶχον λαγοῦ, which is unmetrical and introduces the alien form λαγοῦ (which oddly Kassel–Austin print) into Athenian comedy. Ancient grammarians (Tryphon in Ath. 9.400a–d = fr. 19 Velsen, Phryn. *Ecl.* p. 75 Fischer, Philetaerus in L. Cohn, *Rhein. Mus.* 43 (1888) 414) firmly maintain that λαγώς is Attic, λαγός Ionic, although the Ionic form is admitted by Tryphon into serious Athenian poetry (S. fr. 107 Nauck² = 111 Radt), and by Philetaerus into general Attic usage for the secondary meaning of 'sea-hare', a gastropod (*Aplysia depilans*; Thompson, *Fishes* 142f., Campbell, *Guide* 148f.). Attic comedy almost invariably (*pace* Fraenkel on A. *Ag* 119) uses the Attic form; λαγός is correctly transmitted only at Ameipsias 17(18K), possibly an Ionic doctor (or somebody ridiculing him) prescribing a concoction of sea-hare to a patient.[1] Scholars (with the exception of Bothe, *PCGF* 544) have been reluctant to accept Schweighaeuser's correction *in toto* despite its palaeographic plausibility (simple transposition, replacement of an original form[2]), partly at least because it preserves a reference to 'hare's milk' that is unique in ancient Greek literature. Yet it would be surprising if a precise parallel could be cited, since the phrase is almost certainly a nonce coinage by Alexis. The context here demands an expression denoting the costliest and most extravagant of luxuries. Hare's meat was considered a delicacy in Athens (cf. Ar. *Equ.* 1192), and the phrase ἐν πᾶσι λαγῴοῖς (*Vesp.* 709) was proverbial in the sense ἐν ἀγαθοῖς πᾶσι... ἀντὶ τοῦ ἐν τρυφῇ (Σ *ad loc.*). Another expression for a prized dainty was ὀρνίθων γάλα (e.g. Ar. *Vesp.* 508, *Av.* 734, 1673, Eupolis 411(379K), Mnesimachus 9, Men. fr. 892). Alexis here presumably conflated the two ideas for comic effect, placing λαγώ deliberately after γάλα in order to increase the surprise. A parallel witticism occurs at Ar. *Vesp.* 724, where κωλακρέτου γάλα is the unexpected substitute for ὀρνίθων γάλα.

---

[1] Although the sea-hare was believed in antiquity to be lethally poisonous (Nicander *Alex.* 465ff. and Σ citing Hipponax fr. 157 (cf. 26a.1) West, Plut. *Mor.* 983f, Aelian *NA* 2.45, 9.51, 16.19, Pliny *HN* 9.155, 32.8f.), it was used in medicine for ointments and depilatories (Pliny *HN* 32.70, 104, 110, 135). Cf. Meineke 2.708, Thompson, *Fishes* 142f.; the note of Kaibel's cited by Kassel–Austin 2.205f. is misleading.

[2] The Ionic form prevailed also in *Koine* Greek (cf. Ath. 9.400a τὸ καθ' ἡμᾶς ἐστι λαγός). Confusion between the Attic and Ionic/Koine forms doubtless led to similar corruptions of λαγῴ at Philemon 93(89K).5 (*pace* Kassel–Austin) in Stob. 3.2.26 (λαγοί M, λαγῳοί A Br Mac., cf. Hense 3.xxxx ff., xxxxviii f., corr. Meineke) and λαγώς at Euangelus 1.6 in Ath. 14.644e (λαγωοὺς A similarly conflating the two forms, corr. Schweighaeuser).

COMMENTARY

3 μὰ τὴν γῆν: in comedy this oath (also Ar. *Pax* 188*, 1117*, Anaxilas 8(9K).1, Ephippus 11*, Theophilus 2.4*, Men. *Dysk.* 908*, Strato 1.41* and perhaps[1] v. 47*, com. adesp. fr. 232.10 Austin) and μὰ γῆν (Ar. *Av.* 194*, Antiphanes 288(296K) = Timocles 41(38K)) is used, on the evidence of passages (here asterisked) where the speaker's sex is identifiable, only by males. Cf. F. W. Wright, *Studies in Menander* (Baltimore 1911) 23ff., noting that 'it is not always easy to tell ... whether the goddess as a person is clearly distinguished from the element'; accordingly γῆν is better printed with lower-case γ. On the position of the oath in its sentence, several words after the negative which it reinforces, see K. J. Dover, *CQ* 35 (1985) 328ff., especially 331.

καὶ ταῶς κατήσθιον: eating (not merely possessing) peafowl is the speaker's climactic example of wasteful extravagance. The bird's relative familiarity in the Athens of Alexis' time (along with the accentuation and internal aspirate of ταῶς) is discussed in comm. on fr. 115(110K).14. According to Aelian *NA* 3.42 dining on peafowl was a mark of ἀσωτία. Our main evidence for the practice comes from Rome (Hortensius, presumably the orator and consul of 69 BC, was allegedly the first Roman to have sacrificed and dined off the bird, Aelian *NA* 5.21; cf. Cic. *Fam.* 9.20.2, Varro *Rust.* 3.6.6, Hor. *Sat.* 1.2.115f., 2.2.23ff., Petron. 55 (cf. 33), Pliny *HN* 10.45, Juv. 1.143, Apic. 2.2.6; André, *Alimentation* 134f.), but Clem. Alex. *Paed.* 2.1.3 is talking about Greeks when he says that gourmands share the cost when buying peafowl; anecdotes in Aelian *NA* 11.33, 5.21 imply that in Egypt the birds were fattened for the table and in India Alexander the Great forbade their slaughter, presumably for the kitchen. In the Middle Ages peafowl had pride of place at state banquets (cf. P. Montagné, *Larousse gastronomique* (English translation, London 1961) 719); the brass to Robert Braunche in St Margaret's Church, King's Lynn, portrays such a feast in the mid–14th century, and a lively memory of these occasions is preserved three centuries later in paintings like Jan Steen's *The Wrath of Ahasuerus* (the Birmingham version, Barber Institute of Fine Arts).

This interpretation of the fr., based on Schweighaeuser's conjectures in vv. 2–3 and Musurus' punctuation of v. 3, scores over its rivals because it yields the wittiest and most appropriate contextual sense with the fewest and palaeographically most acceptable changes to the transmission. It is not necessary to discuss in detail the various textual assaults on the fr. by scholars who have largely failed to appreciate its wit and language:

---

[1] So the version preserved in Ath. 9.383b, but the papyrus text (*P.Cairo* 65445) replaces μὰ τὴν γῆν with παραστᾶσ'. On the relationship between the two versions see R. Kassel, *ZPE* 14 (1974) 124ff.

Dobree, *Adv.* 2.349, wholesale rewriting in order to get rid of 'hare's milk'; Herwerden, *Anal. Crit.* 33, κατῆσθον ἄν at the end of v. 3, under the influence of Schweighaeuser's mispunctuation with a comma after ταῶς, which turns 'peacocks' into a second object of εἶχον and leaves κατῆσθον without ἄν as an apodotic verb; J. N. Madvig, *Adversaria Critica* 3 (Copenhagen 1884) 73f., εἷλκον for εἶχον, gratuitously ingenious; Blaydes, *Adv.* 2.159, implausible rewriting; O. Kaehler, *Annotationes ad comicos Graecos* (Weimar 1901) 11, οὐδ' ἄν γ. λ. | ἔχων, assuming that the ἄν goes with an apodotic κατῆσθιον; Edmonds, οὐδ' <ἄν> εἰ γάλα | λαγώ... καὶ τ. κ., but one doesn't eat milk. However, although Schweighaeuser's mispunctuation of v. 3 is now rightly rejected, two other pointings of the fr. must be acknowledged as possible variants: (1) Kaibel's interpretation of the first four words as a question (this would make the speaker reprobate himself, echoing indignantly an attacker's accusation: e.g. '<How could I> myself <have> squandered so much money?'); and (2) with or without the assumption involved in (1), the possibility that the fr. ends in mid-sentence, with an apodosis to follow.

Λέβης

Meineke 1.400f., Webster, *SLGC* 46, 66, W. G. Arnott, *Wien. Stud.* 101 (1988) 181ff., *QUCC* 33 (1989) 27ff., and cf. in this commentary Appendix III (pp. 859 ff.), D. Bain, *LCM* 17 (1992) 68ff.; cf. Meineke, *Anal. Crit.* 97, W. A. Becker, *Charikles*[3] 2 (revised by H. Göll, Berlin 1878) 205, E. Bayer, *Demetrios Phalereus der Athener* (Stuttgart and Berlin 1942) 41ff., E. Fraenkel, *Horace* (Oxford 1957) 127 n. 2, Dohm, *Mageiros* 90 and n. 5, Nesselrath, *MK* 302 n. 44, 304. The play's title is cited correctly five times: four times by Ath. (*Marcianus* at 9.383c, 6.226a, 4.170a, 3.76d, introducing frs. 129, 130, 132, 133 Kassel–Austin = 124, 125, 127, 128 Kock respectively), once by Pollux 6.66 (quoting fr. 132(127K).3–8), but the *Marcianus* at Ath. 14.661d refers to Ἄλεξις ... ἐν Λεβητίωι (fr. 134(129K)) when describing that play's cook. Corruption of inflected title-endings in the MSS of Ath. and other excerptors is so common (at least nine other plays by Alexis are so affected: cf. introduction to Ἀποκοπτόμενος) that it seems safe to reject the possibility that the dramatist wrote both a Λέβης and a Λεβήτιον, and to assume with Meineke 1.400f. that at 661d A's reading is an error for Λέβητι. Accordingly the cook mentioned there will be identified with the main speaker of frs. 129(124K) and 133(128K).

This μάγειρος is the one character in the play of whom the extant frs. give a clear impression. If textual corruption at Ath. 14.661d is confined to the title ending, the cook is there called πολίτης ... τις οὐκ ἀπινής, 'a scruffy citizen' (cf. comm. on the fr.). Such a description looks more like a paraphrase or quotation of an isolated, prejudiced remark made by a character in the comedy than a critic's considered judgement founded upon knowledge of the play as a whole. In frs. 129(124K) and 132(127K) this same cook takes a lead in two conventional exchanges which may derive from different scenes or different parts of the same scene. The former fr. has him explaining to a παῖς (v.14: this could be (i) his own slave or a free pupil, cf. e.g. Men. *Asp.* 222, Euphron 9(10K), perhaps Antiphanes 216(217K), so Kock, A. Giannini, *Acme* 13 (1960) 160, Nesselrath, *MK* 302 n. 44; (ii) his hirer's slave, cf. e.g. Men. *Dysk.*, *Epitr.* fr. 1, Plaut. *Aul.* 28off., so Dohm, *Mageiros* 90 and n. 5; or (iii) a hired τραπεζοποιός, cf. e.g. Diphilus 42(43K); cook and attendant are frequently portrayed on vases, e.g. a red-figure pelike at Erlangen University, Inv. 486, R. Lullies, *Ath. Mitt.* 65 (1940) pl. 2/2, cf. B. Schweitzer, *JDAI* 44 (1929) 117ff. and Fraenkel, *EP* 412f.) a method for disguising the taste of some pork which an unidentified character had previously burnt, perhaps (but not necessarily) in an earlier scene of the play; the cook's exposition is embellished with scientific and medical jargon as the particular token of his ἀλαζονεία (see comm. *ad loc.*). In fr. 132(127K) the cook converses with his hirer or hirer's slave, and lists some of the ingredients he will need for the meal he has presumably been asked to prepare. The relevance of this meal to the plot of the play is uncertain, but the first item in the cook's list is sesame, a spice especially associated with wedding-cakes (see on 132(127K).3).

If this cook has been hired for a wedding, the play's title may perhaps take on extra significance. A λέβης was a large, round-bottomed, metal or earthenware cauldron in everyday use for boiling water (cf. comm. on Antiphanes 26(25K).2–4 in 'False or Doubtful Attributions' I, p. 815f.) and stewing meat (A. de Ridder in Dar.–Sag. s.v. *Lébès* 1000a ff, F. von Lorentz in *RE Suppl. VI* s.v. Λέβης 218.55ff., D. A. Amyx, *Hesperia* 27 (1958) 199f., Handley on Men. *Dysk.* 472f., Sparkes–Talcott, *Agora* XII.57 and pl. 4, nos. 85–7). Its pertinence to scenes involving a cook was obvious even before discovery of the *Dyskolos*; but could it possibly have had a different function in Alexis' plot, e.g. as a container for treasure? Could Alexis' Λέβης have been the Greek original of Plautus' *Aulularia*? This question is examined more fully in Appendix III and by the papers of Bain and myself cited at the head of this introduction; although the evidence for *any* identification of Plautus' source is inadequate, a tentative[1] case can be

---

[1] Even more tentative is the suggestion that Alexis' Λέβης may have been alternatively titled Ὑπόνοια, with fr. 243(241K) deriving from a scene comparable to or inspiring Plaut. *Aul.* 296ff. Cf. the introductions to Ὕπνος (p. 679 n. 1) and Appendix III.

made for the Λέβης based on (1) the identity of the two titles, (2) the presence of cooks in both plays, hired for a wedding certainly in Plautus, arguably in Alexis, (3) the existence of situations in *Aul.* into which all the Λέβης frs. can be fitted:

Alexis fr.		Plaut. *Aul.*
129(124K)	~	II.iv
130(125K), 131(126K)	~	III.v or II.viii
132(127K)	~	II.v or vi, cf. vv. 336, 341
133(128K)	~	II.viii or III.v
134(129K)	~	III.ii, cf. 415ff.

There are, however, no strong verbal ties of the sort that link Alexis' Καρχηδόνιος and Plautus' *Poenulus*, and one impediment was acutely noted by Bain: the brilliant cross-purposes of *Aul.* 731–63, which require the gender of the treasure-pot (*aula* in Latin) to be feminine, would have been impossible in a Greek scene using the masculine noun λέβης. If my linking of Λέβης and *Aul.* is wrongly based, a variety of other uses for Alexis' cauldron might be suggested – as a container of recognition tokens, a cinerary urn, a gift or prize in a contest, or for the rituals of a wedding-ceremony.

Frs. 130(125K), 131(126K), and 133(128K) all deal with marketing and presumably the preliminaries to the meal for which the cook has been hired. Fr. 133(128K), where fig-sellers are assailed, may be (? part of) a monologue or speech by a character (? the organiser of the meal and hirer of the cook) returning from market (cf. e.g. Men. *Sam.* 399ff., Plaut. *Aul.* 371ff. or 475ff., *Pseud.* 790ff.). Frs. 130(125)K and 131(126K) attack fishmongers (cf. comm. on fr. 16); in both frs. a speaker (not necessarily one and the same person, not necessarily identical with the speaker of fr. 133(128K)) couples his abuse with praise of the lawgiver Aristonicus (in 130(125K).1–2 Ar. 'the wealthy') for passing or proposing laws to curb the excesses of fishmongers. Although no inscriptional or other literary evidence about any such decree now survives, we have no reason to doubt here an allusion to contemporary history, and the identification of Alexis' lawgiver with the politician Aristonicus of Marathon (Thalheim in *RE* s.v. *Aristonikos* 1, 960.57ff., Kirchner, *PA* 1.137 no. 2033), rather than with any other Athenian of this name in Alexis' time (e.g. the man who in 340 proposed the award of a golden crown to Demosthenes, Dem. 18.83, 223,

312, Plut. *Mor.* 846a, 848d: = 2025[1] Kirchner; cf. also 2024, 2030) is highly probable for two reasons. The Marathonian's political activity is known to have extended from 334 to 322, thus straddling the period of food shortages in Athens (330–326: cf. comm. on fr. 6, introduction to fr. 16) when laws controlling the prices of basic foodstuffs would be most likely. Secondly, in fr. 129(124K) the cook's cure for burnt pork is saluted by the παῖς with the words Ἄπολλον, ὡς ἰατρικῶς. ὦ Γλαυκία, ταυτὶ ποιήσω (vv.13f.). Glaukias here is often taken to be the name of the cook (e.g. by Kock, Kaibel, Rankin, ΜΑΓΕΙΡΟΙ 32, Gulick, Fraenkel, *Beob.* 81, Nesselrath, *MK* 304, Kassel–Austin). This cannot be proved wrong, but no other cook in later Greek comedy is so called; the standard names are Karion (Men. *Epitr.* and Gomme–Sandbach, *Comm.* p. 290, Euphron 9(10).1 and 5, cf. Themist. *Or.* 21.262d) and Sikon (Men. *Dysk.*, cf. Sosipater 1.13f., [Alexis] 25.4 and comm.), and Webster's alternative interpretation of fr. 129(124K).13f. (*SLGC* 66) is attractive. Noting the cook's elaborately scientific language in vv. 5–12 of the fr. and the response that it evokes ('Apollo! How like a doctor!'), he suggests that ὦ Γλαυκία facetiously dignifies the cook not with his own name but with that of a celebrated contemporary physician, who attended Alexander the Great's general Hephaestion and was crucified shortly after his patient's death in 324

---

[1] This identification is canvassed by Kock 3.742. Two others deserve mention. W. A. Becker, *Charikles*[3] 2 (revised by H. Göll, Berlin 1878) 205 suggested that Alexis' 'Aristonicus' was a *nom de guerre* for the philosopher Plato, who was the son of an Ariston and drafted legislation in *Leg.* 11.917b similar to that fathered on Aristonicus in Alexis 130(125K); but why should Alexis mask Plato's identity under a pseudonym when praising him, if elsewhere he names him openly several times (frs. 1, 98(152K), 151(147K), 163(158K), 185(180K) in non-laudatory contexts? E. Bayer, *op. cit.* at the head of the introduction, 41ff. identifies 'Aristonicus' as Demetrius of Phalerum and dates the Λέβης to the period of his regime (317–307), but the evidence he adduces in support is flimsy. A statement of Demochares (*FGrH* 75 F 4, cited in Polyb. 12.13.9), which Bayer uses to document his claim that Demetrius passed legislation on the lines suggested by Alexis 130(125K), makes no reference to any commercial enactment (cf. K. J. Beloch, *Griechische Geschichte* 4.1[2] (Berlin and Leipzig 1925) 147). Bayer also alleges that certain expressions in the two comic frs. (νομοθέτης 130(125K).1, 131(126).2, καινὸν νόμον 131(126K).4, the reference to Solon 131(126K).1) are slogans associated with Demetrius; even if that were true, the Phalerean could hardly claim a monopoly on such commonplace phraseology. And again: why should Alexis have hidden Demetrius' glory under a pseudonym?

because he failed to save him (Arr. *Anab.* 7.14.4, Plut. *Alex.* 72; Gossen in *RE* s.v. *Glaukias* 9, 1399.64ff., H. Berve, *Das Alexanderreich* 2 (Munich 1926) 112 no. 228). If Webster is correct here, he provides an argument for narrowing down the dating of Alexis' Λέβης to the years immediately preceding 324.

After quoting fr. 130(125K), Ath. 6.226b goes on directly to introduce fr. 131(126K) with the words καὶ προελθών δέ φησιν. This is Ath.'s regular formula for citing a second extract from a later scene or later in the same scene of the play from which he has just quoted one fr. (e.g. 2.60c = Antiphanes 225(226+227K), 4.161b = Alexis 223(220+221K), 13.559b = Eubulus 115(116+117K) and Hunter *ad loc.*, cf. Fraenkel, *Horace* (Oxford 1957) 179 n. 2). The difficulty of gauging the length of the gap between the end of 130(125K) and the start of 131(126K) is compounded by the fact that 131 neither follows on naturally from 130 nor introduces a fresh topic, but repeats the opening idea of 130 with a varied development. This similarity between the two frs. led Meineke (*Anal. Crit.* 97) to assume that they could not both derive from the same play, and he suggested that another fr. of Alexis with its play title had originally stood in the text of Ath. before καὶ προελθών and been carelessly omitted (by abridger or copyist). The theory is tenable, but it rests on the false premise that no scenario could be envisaged for the sequence of frs. 130(125K) and 131(126K) in a single drama. Precise study of the two frs. reveals two striking points. First, the praise of Aristonicus is more fulsome in 131, with its emphatic οὐ ... οὐδὲ εἷς and the comparison with Solon (vv.1–2). Secondly, the law fathered on Aristonicus in 130 has an authentic ring about it; Alexis may well be quoting or paraphrasing the terms of a recent enactment (cf. comm. *ad loc.*). The bill described in 131, on the other hand, clearly has no basis in historical reality, but is a fantastic extravaganza foisted on Aristonicus solely for comic effect. If 130(125K) were delivered as a topical and essentially serious comment in support of a recent law, 131(126K) could then follow immediately or shortly afterwards as a ludicrously parallel addition by a βωμολόχος. Such parallelism of speech and scene was a familiar device throughout Athenian comedy: e.g. Ar. *Ach.* 1078ff., 1190ff., *Ran.* 464ff., Men. *Dysk.* 456ff., 910ff.; cf. A. G. Katsouris, *LCM* 6 (1981) 73ff. and my introduction to Alexis 46(45K).

129 (124K)

Meineke 3.439 (v), Kock 2.341, Edmonds 2.430, Kassel–Austin 2.92; cf. Rankin, ΜΑΓΕΙΡΟΙ 84f., W. G. Arnott, *PCPS* 196 (1970) 5ff., Nesselrath, *MK* 304. The identity of the speakers in this imaginative dialogue is discussed in the introduction to Λέβης. Ath. 9.383c–e's citation of the fr. is found only in A, whose dicola at the ends of vv. 2, 4, 12 and after ὀνειδίζεις in v. 20 may be vestiges of the original indications for part-division in unexcerpted play texts (cf. my general introduction, II.i.a and the introduction to fr. 140(135K)); the remaining assignments were first made by Grotius, *Exc.* 574ff., 973 (vv.1–17), Daléchamp's translation (18–19 μάγειρος) and Hirschig, *Diss.* 11, 39 (19 ὃ λέγεις to the end).

A typically pretentious and canting μάγειρος (cf. the introduction to fr. 24) describes with arrogant assurance (vv.3–4, cf. 14–15) the way to conceal the taste of burnt pork by soaking it in wine-vinegar. The ingenuity of cooks when faced by such calamities is a τόπος in later Greek comedy (cf. Rankin, *loc. cit.*: e.g. Euphron 10(11K), a cook explaining how mock anchovies can be created from turnips when the fish is not available; Archedicus 2, one who is late with his cooking can remedy the situation by pouring olive oil on to the fire to make it blaze). The subterfuge of Alexis' present μάγειρος has a double claim on our attention. First, it is not a piece of humbug but actually seems to work. Pork rind is easily charred when cooked on an open fire, and 19th-century kitchen girls were advised to rub on 'a little sweet oil' as soon as the meat became warm to safeguard against scorching (Esther Copley, *The Housekeeper's Guide* (London 1834) 126). Soaking charred pork in vinegar helps both to tenderise any part that has been hardened and toughened, and to disguise the burnt taste. In fact the deipnosophist in Ath. here is made to introduce this fr. with the claim that he had himself profited from the stratagem. Secondly, Alexis' cook dresses up his remedy in scientific (and especially medical) language throughout (cf. *PCPS* 196 (1970) 5ff.). He prefaces his recipe with ἰάσιμον . . . τὸ πάθος ἐστί (v.4), goes on repeatedly to mimic the jargon of Ionic science and medicine (5–12, see comm. *ad loc.*), and does it all with a bravura that finally elicits from his partner an outburst of sarcastic admiration for the cook's medical skill (13–14). Alexis' μάγειρος is not unique in his arrogation of medical expertise; cf. also Anaxippus 1 vv. 16 and 45–7, Damoxenus 2.25–33, Nicomachus 1.30–5 (Dohm, *Mageiros* 70, 161ff., 173ff.). Such pretensions, however exaggerated for the comic stage, would nevertheless have appeared less grotesque in a society where the prestige of cooks was low and that of physicians high, and where a professional interest in dietetics had led physicians to write cookery books from the second half of the 4th century onwards (see introduction to Κράτεια).

The cook's predilection for medical jargon is one important element in his presentation. A second may be discernible. In a fr. of under 20 vv. the cook twice introduces a parenthetic 'Do you understand?' (συνιεῖς; v. 6, see comm. *ad loc.*, μανθάνεις; 15). Is this an attempt at characterisation through idiosyncratic speech patterns, using a technique most familiar today in Menander (see F. H. Sandbach, *Entr. Hardt* 16 (1970) 111ff., W. G. Arnott, *G and R* 17 (1970) 32ff., 22 (1975) 146ff. and D. Del Corno, *Studi Classici e Orientali* 24 (1975) 13ff.; cf. also my general introduction here, I.v.iii)?

1 ἦψέ μοι δοκεῖ: so A (but with δοκει unaccented), 'he was boiling, I believe'. Here ἦψε = imperfect of ἕψω, not aorist of ἅπτω (a strange hallucination of LSJ s.v. B.III, who compound the error by assuming that ἅπτω can mean 'I cook'[1]). Most editors (including Kassel–Austin) accept the *Marcianus* reading, with its two final words interpreted as a parenthesis; for the idiom (which breaks a norm of Greek word order by placing a postpositive at the beginning of a separable clause; cf. K. J. Dover, *Greek Word Order* (Cambridge 1960) 12f.) note in Attic e.g. Ar. *Pax* 1266f. ἵνα | ἅττ' ᾄσεται προαναβάληταί μοι δοκεῖ and Dem. 19.197 ταύτην ... πίνειν ἡσυχῇ καὶ τρώγειν ἠνάγκαζον οὗτοί μοι δοκεῖ.[2] Even so, we cannot be certain that Alexis did not write either ἦψ', ἐμοὶ δοκεῖ (cf. Ar. *Av.* 1225ff. δεινότατα γάρ τοι πεισόμεσθ', ἐμοὶ δοκεῖ, / εἰ τῶν μὲν ἄλλων ἄρχομεν, ὑμεῖς δ' οἱ θεοὶ / ἀκολαστανεῖτε), or ἦψ', ἐμοὶ δοκεῖν (with limiting infinitive: the commonest of these parallel idioms, e.g. A. *Pers.* 246, S. *El.* 410, Thuc. 7.87, 8.64, Pl. *Men.* 81a, *Euthyd.* 273a, 274b, Lysippus fr. 1.2; K.G. 2.19, Goodwin, *MT* 311; hence Meineke's suggestion (3.439) that ἐμοὶ δοκεῖν should be restored here is as tempting as Cobet's identical idea (*Mnemosyne* 2 (1853) 105) for Ar. *Av.* 1225. A similar problem is provided by Men. *Asp.* 73f. συντετριμμένην †διεμοι† (so B: δέ μοι Sandbach, δ' ἐμοὶ Handley, διό μοι Kassel) δοκεῖ | οὐκ ἔλαβεν αὐτὴν οὐδὲ εἷς τῶν βαρβάρων; cf. C. Austin, *Menandri Aspis et Samia II: Subsidia interpretationis* (Berlin 1970) 9, 11 on vv. 49, 73 respectively.

2 I should prefer to print πνικτόν τι ὄψον δελφάκειον, Dindorf's correction of A's π. τιν' ὄψον δελφάκιον, on the assumption that (i) hiatus after τι is legitimate in comedy, and (ii) the corruption was probably

---

[1] In this context ἦψε (from ἅπτω) could mean only 'he set on fire', but this is ruled out by the cook's response ἡδύ γε (v.2) and his companion's continuation ἔπειτα προσκέκαυκε (3), which is dramatically more effective if it introduces a new idea of 'burning', not one already prefigured.

[2] With μοι δοκεῖ parenthetic to a main verb in the imperfect, as in Alexis, thus making Kaibel's suggestion ἦ. μοὐδόκει here otiose. A further conjecture, ἕψειν μοὐδόκει, is attributed by Meineke, *Anal. Crit.* 168 (cf. *ed. min.* xviii) and Kock to Hirschig, *Diss.* 39, but in my copy of that dissertation the only emendation advanced for the opening vv. is προσκέκαυκε (3); the idea is best disregarded, so long as we do not know the contextual basis for this statement by the παῖς. He could have been referring to an earlier incident in the play of indeterminate importance, or been describing something altogether unrelated to the plot.

introduced by a scribe unaware of the metrical licence (cf. fr. 27.7 and comm. *ad loc.*). Other conjectures which avoid the hiatus (e.g. ὄψον τι πνικτόν Kock, πνικτόν τι δελφάκειον ὄψον Bailey according to Blaydes, *Adv.* 1.110, but it does not appear in J. Bailey, *Comicorum Graecorum Fragmenta* (Cambridge 1811), so far as I see) cannot be ruled out, but they produce a less attractive word order (by removing πνικτόν from its emphatic position at the head, or δελφάκειον at the end, of the phrase unit), and make the corruption less easy to explain.

Although by Alexis' time ὄψον was coming in Athens to be restricted more and more to the preferred delicacy of fish (see comm. on fr. 47(46K).6), the word still carried enough of its basic meaning: any cooked or prepared food – fish, meat (e.g. the finches and thrushes of Ar. (?) fr. 402(387K).7, a passage which answers the objections of Herwerden, *Coll. Crit.* 125 to its use here in Alexis), vegetables or fruit – that was eaten as a snack with bread and wine. The man described here was evidently reheating previously stewed leftovers.

4 ἰάσιμον γὰρ τὸ πάθος ἐστί: the noun has a wide range of meanings (based on 'that which happens/is done to one', LSJ s.v. πάθος), but in the Hippocratic corpus it is the standard term for a patient's medical condition (e.g. *Epid.* 5.81, 7.86 τὸ Νικάνορος πάθος, *Epist. Dem. Hipp.* 1.18 ἰητρεύειν τὸ πάθος). ἰάσιμος is predominantly a medical term (cf. N. van Brock, *Recherches sur le vocabulaire médical du grec ancien* (Paris 1961) 65), but in Attic can be used metaphorically of (e.g.) ἁμαρτήματα and general κακά (Pl. *Gorg.* 525b, *Leg.* 5.731c–d). The cook's interpretation of the accident therefore has its essentially medical taste (cf. introduction to this fr.) seasoned with a touch of (perhaps designed) ambivalence, to whet the audience's appetite.

τῷ τρόπῳ;: 'In what way?', a complete question interposed at line end as in Ar. *Ran.* 1404; with identical meaning, function and *sedes* τίνι τρόπῳ Ar. *Ach.* 919, τίνα τρόπον Men. *Dysk.* 362; cf. also τρόπῳ τίνι at line end in Ar. *Pax* 689, Men. *Sam.* 175.

5 ὄξος: see comm. on fr. 286(285K).3.

ἤν: so A (but without accent or breathing), but elsewhere in the frs. of Alexis this conditional particle is always in the form ἐάν (x 7: e.g. 16.8, 178(172K).5) or ἄν (x 21: e.g. 31(30K).2, 259(257K).8, sometimes corrupted to ἐάν, cf. comm. on fr. 48(47K).4; also κἄν x 4: e.g. 289(288K).1, corrupted to ἐάν at 98(152K).2). ἤν is standard in Ionic (e.g. Hdt., Hippocr., where the Maloney–Frohn concordance shows 3086 instances against 49 for ἐάν, 2 for ἄν in MSS) and common in 5th-century Attic, but increasingly rare in later Attic, although Isoc. seems to prefer ἤν (x *c.* 167) to both ἄν (x 57: κἄν x 12) and ἐάν (x 20). In later comedy ἤν is attested by MSS also at Antiphanes 194(196K).14, Anaxandrides 53(52K).6, Timocles 6.1, Cratinus jun. 8.2, Apollodorus 6.1, Nicomachus 1.7, Men. fr.

ΛΕΒΗΣ

665.1 Körte, possibly 163.148 (= *Kol.*) in Austin, *CGFP*; emendation to ἄν should be considered in most of these places (cf. Meineke 3.592, 4.451f., 584), but here in Alexis it is conceivable that ἥν is a deliberate Ionicism flavouring the contextual medical language. Cf. K.B. 1.223, 642.

λεκάνην: one of several derivatives of λέκος (cf. λεκάνιον, -νίς, -νίσκη, λεκάριον) used particularly in Attic and the *Koine* for a series of relatively large, broad and shallow bowls of pottery, metal and even wood, to which (like the similarly shaped English 'basin') a remarkable variety of uses is assigned: holding meat and other food (Ar. *Ach.* 1110, Teleclides 1.11, Theopompus com. 83(80K), Xen. *Cyr.* 1.3.4, Machon 448, Pollux 6.85–6, Ath. 4.149f), liquid for cleaning shoes (Ar. *Vesp.* 600), water for washing (Pollux 10.77, Ath. 5.197b, Σ Ar. *Plut.* 1061), feminine cosmetics and trinkets (Lucian *Amor.* 39), medicine or medical equipment (Pollux 10.149), collecting juice from pressed grapes (Ar. (?) fr. 402(387K).6), carrying mud for building (Ar. *Av.* 840, 1143, 1146). playing κότταβος (Pollux 6.110), and receiving vomit (Ar. *Nub.* 907, Polyzelus 4, Cratinus 271(251K), cf. Theopompus com. 41(40K).1, Pollux 10.76, Plut. *Mor.* 801b). Alexis' λεκάνη here was big enough for a χύτρα (see on v. 6) to stand inside it, but neither the above references nor the brief descriptions in lexica, etc. (e.g. Pollux 6.85–86, Σ Ar. *Ach.* 1110, Photius s.v. λεκάνη, *Suda* s.v. λεκάνια) indicate unambiguously an identifiable shape (cf. L. Couve in Dar.–Sag. s.v. *Lekane* 1099a, F. von Lorentz in *RE Supp.* vi s.v. Λεκάνη 221.24ff., Richter–Milne, *Shapes* 23f. and fig. 149, D. A. Amyx, *Hesperia* 27 (1958) 204f., B. A. Sparkes and L. Talcott, *Pots and Pans of Classical Athens* (Princeton 1958) figs. 13, 20, 22 and *Agora*, XII.164ff., 211ff. and figs. 11, 15, 17, 19–21, 23 and pls. 40–2, 81–7, nos. 1206–84, 1739–1843, cf. B. A. Sparkes, *JHS* 82 (1962) 128f.

6 συνιεῖς: A has ξυνιεὶς, with incorrect accent (cf. e.g. the same MS at Ath. 15.666f citing Antiphanes 57(55K).1, and the MSS of Stob. 3.35.6 citing Philonides II 3(18K)) and suspect orthography. Already by the 390s in Athens συν- had totally displaced ξυν- in public inscriptions except for the one phrase γνώμην δὲ ξυμβάλλεσθαι τῆς βουλῆς (Meisterhans–Schwyzer 220f., Threatte 1.553f., and so there is no call (*pace* Kassel–Austin, who print ξυν- here) to retain the older form in those relatively few passages of colloquial Attic in later comedy where the MSS give it.[1] The verb's ending poses a more difficult problem. Should one

---

[1] These are Antiphanes 17(16K) (ξυνακόλουθος all MSS of Pollux 10.62, against sense and metre; both are restored as well by ἀσυνακόλουθος as by the usually accepted ἀξυν- of Salmasius), 75(74K).3 and 6 (ξύνοισθα, -οιδα A at Ath. 10.459a; read συν- in both places), Men. fr. 381.1 (σύνοιδεν M^dBr, ξυν- A at Stob. *Ecl.* 3.4.7, 'sed forma ξυν apud Menandrum non exstat' Körte *ad loc.*). At Eubulus 106(107K).3 the

correct it to the athematic -ίης regular in Attic (so Dindorf, cf. [Herodian] 2.830.20 Lentz, Porson on Eur. *Or.* 141, A. Nauck, *MGR* 6 (1894) 90), or accept -ιεῖς (cf. Canter, Paris ms., 40ᵛ; ? or -ίεις) as an example of the intrusion into later Attic and the *Koine* of thematic forms (e.g. LXX *1 Kings* 18.15, Castorion in Ath. 10.455a = *SH* 310.5; cf. Eustath. 1500.52)?[1] ξυνιεῖς (συν-, -ίεις) appears from time to time in respectable MSS of Attic dramatists (e.g. L of S. *Ant.* 403, *OR* 628, *El.* 1347, cf. *El.* 596; R and V at Ar. *Plut.* 45, where the scholia appear to support -ίης; cf. A at Ath. 15.666f and 6.228a, citing Antiphanes 57(55K).1 and Diphilus 31(32K).13), although these are no guarantors of the playwrights' own spellings (cf. K.B. 2.193, 213, Schwyzer 1.687f.). Attic inscriptions record no instance of the second-person singular of this verb, but the thematic form of the third-person imperfect indicative active occurs there as early as 287 (Meisterhans–Schwyzer 188). If Λέβης was written shortly before 324 (see introduction to the play), Alexis could have written either form, but perhaps -ιεῖς is the more likely.

For συνιεῖς here as a parenthetical question cf. Diphilus 31(32K).13; similarly μανθάνεις v. 15 below and the references cited there; ὁρᾷς and δοκεῖς Ar. *Nub.* 355 and *Ach.* 12, δοκεῖτε and οἴεσθε Chariton 8.8.7, 1.10.3.

θερμὴν τὴν χύτραν: the predicative position of the adjective emphasises that the χύτρα (a pot usually with two handles, used for boiling or stewing meat: cf. S. Weinberg, *Hesperia* 18 (1949) 152 and pl. 16.15 and 16 right, D. A. Amyx, *Hesperia* 27 (1958) 211f. and pl. 48h, B. A. Sparkes and L. Talcott, *Pots and Pans of Classical Athens* (Princeton 1958) figs. 40, 42, 44 and *Agora* xii.224ff. and figs. 18, 20, pls. 93–4, nos. 1922–58, B. A. Sparkes, *JHS* 82 (1962) 130, 136, pls. v.4, 6, vi.1) must still be hot when placed in the ὄξος.

7 ἐνθῇς: the *Marcianus* has ἐνθεὶς here and ἐγχέας in v. 5, thus failing to provide the necessary subjunctive in the protasis of vv. 5–7. Dobree, *Adv.*

---

archaic forms ἀξυνετὰ ξυνετοῖσι are appropriate in hexameter riddles and required by the metre (Ath. 10.449e). At Athenion 1.45f. (Ath. 14.661d) and Nicolaus 1.19 (Stob. 3.14.7), where conjectures involving forms in ξυν- have sometimes been accepted, read respectively <νῦν> συνείσιθι | ἐμοί (Kaibel, after Dobree, *Adv.* 2.351 and Cobet, *NL* 25: A συνέσθιέ μοι) and ηὔξηκας (anon. in margin of *cod. Parisinus* 1985: νὐξηκας S, νὐξ ἧκας MᵈA). In comic papyri it is noticeable that forms in ξυν- are confined to 5th-century plays (Cratinus 171.5, Eupolis 192.185 and 268.26 Kassel–Austin = Austin, *CGFP* 73.5, 95.185, 98.26 respectively, and anon. 220.165 Austin).

[1] Similar difficulties arise with other -μι verbs, particularly τίθημι (LSJ s.v., *init.*), where the evidence also rests mainly on a series of disputed MSS readings (Fraenkel on A. *Ag.* 1317 begs the question when he claims that τιθεῖς is 'a legitimate form of the indicative for tragedy').

2.322 suggested changing either ἐνθεὶς to -θῆς or ἐγχέας to -χέης; the former is preferable for three reasons: a scribe's eye could have wandered to the ending of ξυνιεὶς (*sic*: see on v. 6) in the previous line; confusion of H or HI with EI is particularly common in MSS, whether by iotacism or by misreading of similar uncials; and the sequence of participle first, climaxing verb introduced by εἶτα second, accords with the regular idiom (e.g. S. *El.* 51ff. ἡμεῖς δὲ πατρὸς τύμβον . . . | στέψαντες, εἶτ' ἄψορρον ἥξομεν πάλιν, *Aj.* 1091f., 1094, Antiphanes 152(154K).1–3, Philemon 28.5–7 χοὶ μὲν πλέοντες ἐνίοθ' ἡμέραν μίαν | ἢ νύκτα χειμασθέντες εἶτ' ἐκ τοῦ κακοῦ | σωτηρίας ἐπέτυχον, cf. LSJ s.v. εἶτα 1.2).

7–12 The passage bristles with jargon appropriate to the claim (v.4) that the accident with the pork was ἰάσιμον and to the riposte (v.13) ὡς ἰατρικῶς about the remedy. The cook's phrases ἕλξει δι' αὐτῆς νοτίδα (8), λήψεται διεξόδους σομφάς (9f.), τὴν ὑγρασίαν ἐκδέξεται (10) and δροσώδη τὴν σχέσιν (12) parody medical and other scientific writing of the period. The technical and more unusual word or form is preferred: ἀτρεμεῖ not ἀτρέμα, δροσώδης not ὑγρός (12), ζυμούμενος not ζέων (8), ὑγρασία not ὑγρότης (10). Six words – ἔγχυλος, ζυμόω, νοτίς, σομφός, σχέσις and ὑγρασία – do not occur elsewhere in comedy. The whole passage, with its blend of exoticism and pseudo-science, bears useful testimony to the comic imagination of Alexis. Cf. *PCPS* 196 (1970) 5ff.

7 διάπυρος: elsewhere in comedy only in the metaphorical sense ('inventive' as well as LSJ's 'ardent': Timocles 18(16K).4, Men. *Dysk.* 183), but not uncommon in scientific and particularly medical writers (x 11 in the Hippocratic corpus) in the literal meaning it has here, 'red-hot', cf. Eur. *Cycl.* 631. The medical associations, rather than (e.g.) an attempt to avoid using its synonym θερμός twice in successive lines, may account for its selection here.

8 ἕλξει δι' αὐτῆς νοτίδα: sc. the heat of the χύτρα will increase its porosity and thus enable more moisture (from the ὄξος) to pass through into the burnt pork. The idea could reflect either the deep interest in physiological and physical πόροι shown by Theophrastus (e.g. *CP* 5.6.1 ἡ χύτρα . . . τὴν ἐκ τῆς γῆς ἕλκει νοτίδα) and other followers of Aristotle (e.g. *Meteor.* 4, wrongly ascribed to Aristotle: H. B. Gottschalk, *CQ* 11 (1961) 67ff.), or the stress placed on physical passages by contemporary medicine (cf. I. M. Lonie, *Mnemosyne* 18 (1968) 128, 'in a sense, all Greek medical theories are theories about πόροι; the human body is simply a system of πόροι'), which also used language very similar to Alexis' here (e.g. Hippocr. *Morb.* 1.20 a damaged blood-vessel διαθερμαίνεται καὶ ἕλκει ἐς ἑωυτὸ νοτίδα τινὰ ὑγρήν). In science and medicine from the 5th century on, the favoured verb to indicate the attraction, absorption, etc. of moisture is ἕλκω: e.g. Diogenes of Apollonia A33 Diels–Kranz τοῦτο γὰρ πάσχειν (sc. lodestones rusting after an application of ὄξος or olive-oil)

371

COMMENTARY

διὰ τὸ ἕλκειν ἐξ αὐτῶν τὴν ἰκμάδα τὸ ὄξος, Arist. *PA* 3.11, 673^b7 ὁ δ᾽ ὑμὴν
... ἄσαρκος ... ὥστε μὴ ἕλκειν μηδὲ ἔχειν ἰκμάδα, *Meteor.* 1.6, 343^a8ff.).
Unlike ἕλκω, νοτίς seems not to have been in Athens a word of everyday
speech. It is more likely to have reached technical prose there (first in Pl.
Tim. x 6, Arist. x 8) from Ionian science and medicine (x 9 in the Hippocr.
corpus) than from e.g. Attic tragedy (Eur. *IT* 107, *Bacch.* 705 and four
other places, trag. adesp. F 261 Kannicht–Snell).[1]

ζυμουμένη: the hot χύτρα and its contents 'bubbling and hissing' as
they come into contact with the cold dish of vinegar. In this transferred
sense the passive of ζυμόω (cf. LSJ s.v. 2) is little more than a colourful
synonym of ζέω, perhaps but not necessarily with some medical resonance
(cf. Hippocr. *Vet. Med.* 11 ζέουσάν τε καὶ ἐζυμωμένην). The word occurs
only here in comedy, unless ζυμήσασθαι at Ar. fr. 398(383K) is a
corruption for ζυμώσασθαι (first G. Dindorf in *TLG* s.v. ζυμόω, col. 50B).

9–10 λήψεται διεξόδους σομφάς: 'will form porous outlets'. διέξοδος is
the standard scientific and medical term for 'through-passage' (x 27 in the
Hippocratic corpus; also e.g. Pl. *Tim.* 67e, 84d, 91c, Arist. *PA* 4.9, 684^b26:
all physiological; cf. K. Gaiser in *Synusia: Festgabe für Wolfgang Schadewaldt*
(ed. Gaiser and H. Flashar, Pfullingen 1965) 173ff.). Elsewhere in
4th-century comedy it occurs twice in paratragic contexts (Antiphanes
174(176K).4, Heniochus 4.5), possibly as a skit on Euripides' fondness for
technical jargon.

10 δι᾽ ὧν τὴν ὑγρασίαν ἐκδέξεται: Meineke's conjecture εἰσδέξεται
(*Anal. Crit.* 168) is palaeographically neat and has received support (S. A.
Naber and H. van Herwerden, *Mnemosyne* 8 (1880) 260 and 21 (1893) 161
respectively, Blaydes, *Adv.* 2.159), but it is wrong and the paradosis
correct. δι᾽ ὧν and ἐκδέξεται pick up exactly the prefixes of διεξόδους. Cf.
also Hippocratic *Gland.* 3 αἱ δὲ (sc. ἀδένες) ... τὴν αὖθις γινομένην ὑπὸ τῶν
πόνων ὑγρασίην ἐκδεχόμεναι, and 5 τὰ δὲ ἔντερα ... ἐκδέχεται καὶ καθίησι
τὴν ὑγρασίην. The Ionic form ὑγρασίη is familiar from the Hippocratic
corpus, as are other terms with the same ending (e.g. θερμασίη, φλεγμασίη),
and it would be tempting to assume that its medical resonance led Alexis
to choose ὑγρασία in this context rather than the common Attic form
ὑγρότης (e.g. Eur. *Phoen.* 1256, Lycurgus 33, Crobylus 4.3; also Pl., Arist.,
Theophr.). That temptation, however, is dangerous; the Hippocratic

---

[1] When the Aristophanic Socrates nearly a century earlier was made to
ridicule the theories and language of Diogenes of Apollonia (*Nub.*
227ff., cf. Dover on 230–3), in a passage (A33, cited above on v. 8 ἕλξει
δι᾽ αὑτῆς νοτίδα) with some verbal similarity to that of Alexis here
(cf. Blaydes, *Adv.* 1.110), it is noticeable that the word for 'moisture'
used by Diogenes and guyed by the comic poet was a different one:
ἰκμάς.

corpus uses ὑγρότης (x 41 times) even more than ὑγρασίη (x 38), sometimes in the identical meaning of 'moisture' (e.g. *Vet. Med.* 22 ἑλκύσαι ἐφ'
ἑωυτὸ καὶ ἐπισπάσασθαι ὑγρότητα). Alexis' choice could have been
dictated partly by metrical convenience or the intrusion of Ionicisms into
Attic during the development of the *Koine* (cf. especially Schwyzer 1.128).

10–11 ἐκδέξεται τὰ κρεᾳδι', ἔσται τ': this punctuation and correction
of A's unmetrical and overparticled ἐκδέξεται· τὰ κρέα δ' εσται τ' is owed to
the successive efforts of Casaubon (*ad loc.* and *Animadv.* 661f.), who saw
that κρέα δ' in the MS was the result of a faultily divided κρεᾳδι' (better
κρεᾳδι': see comm. on 27.5) and Bothe (*PCGF* 545), who was the first to
realise that κρεᾳδι' was the subject of ἐκδέξεται and so required a comma
after, not A's colon before, it. This punctuation (*pace* Kassel–Austin)
improves the sense (the meat rather than the pot now receives the desired
moisture), normalises the position of τ' as second word in its clause
(postponements to 4th word, after article, substantive and verb are very
rare: see Denniston, *GP* 517f., Sandbach on Men. *Pk.* 128), and secures an
effective arrangement of ideas with the key one (the meat's reconstituted
juiciness) held back to the climactic end. Some other conjectures (e.g. τὰ
κρέ' ἠδέ' ἔσται κοὐκ Jacobs, *Addit.* 204, τὰ κρέ' ἁπάλ' ἔσται Peppink,
Observ. 56) have their merits (ἡδύς of meat at Antiphanes 219(220K).3,
Athenion 1.12, ἁπαλός similarly at Ar. *Lys.* 1062, Diphilus 14.3), but they
depart further from the *ductus*, and weaken the impact of v. 12 by
anticipating its ideas more mundanely in v. 11.

11 ἀπεξηραμμένα: so A, but this form of the perfect passive of
(-)ξηραίνω is not recorded before Alexis (elsewhere first in Theoph. *CP*
5.14.6), becoming standard only in the *Koine*, where it ousts the Ionic
(Hdt., Hippocratic corpus) and Attic (only Antiphanes 216(217K).13)
form in -ασμαι. Arguably, in this particular context the form used by
medical writers might be more appropriate, with the *Koine* form intruding
later into the paradosis. Cf. Veitch, *Greek Verbs*[4] 472, K.B. 2.495.

12 ἔγχυλα δ' ἀτρεμεί: 'rather succulent'. The use of ἀτρέμα(ς) and its
by-form ἀτρεμεί to qualify an adjective or adverb in the sense 'slightly/
rather',[1] which K. Zacher (*BPW* 6 (1886) 712) correctly identified here, is
inadequately handled by *TGL* and LSJ (cf. W. F. R. Shilleto, A. W. Mair
and especially W. Headlam in *CR* 16 (1902) 284 and 319, W. G. Arnott,
BICS 15 (1968) 121f., V. Schmidt, *Gnomon* 45 (1973) 15). The idiom first

---

[1] At Men. *Dysk.* 534 (ἀπεξυλούμην ἀτρέμα δ', cf. Handley's comm.
ad loc.) and [Aristaen.] 1.25 (στίλψασα τὰς παρειὰς ἀτρέμα, cf. *BICS* 18
(1968) 121f.) ἀτρέμα qualifies a verb in what has sometimes been
interpreted as a similar sense, but Sandbach (*Comm.* on the Men.
passage) argues strongly for the word's root meaning 'quietly' in such
contexts.

appears in the Hippocratic corpus (*Morb.* 3.16 ἡ κόπρος ... ἀτρέμα χολώδης, *Dieb. Judic.* 2, *Hebd.* 46 ἀτρέμα βραδύτερον; also Diocles med. fr. 141 p. 183.21 Wellmann οἰνάριον λεπτὸν ἀτρέμα μαλακόν), cf. also Lycophron fr. 2.8 Kannicht–Snell κυλίκιον ... ἀτρέμα παρεξεστηκός (satyric), Plut. *Mor.* 1062c τῶν ἀτρέμα ... λευκῶν. In discussing this and parallel usages (ἠρέμα, ἡσυχῇ: LSJ s.vv. 2 and 3 respectively), Headlam concluded that they seemed 'properly to belong to the language of scientific discovery, that is, Ionic'; this may be true, although the evidence is neither contextually homogeneous (e.g. the Lycophron extract lacks any scientific flavour) nor extensive enough for convinced agreement. It may be coincidental too that the by-form ἀτρεμεί in literature elsewhere (I ignore grammarians such as Theognostus and anon. in Cramer, *Anecdota Graeca* 2.165.12, 313.13f.) occurs only once (Ar. *Nub.* 261, where RV have the *falsche Schreibung* ἀτρεμί, cf. K.B. 2.303; the other MSS trivialise to ἀτρέμας), and in a context where the speaker 'Socrates' spouts intellectual jargon (e.g. 225, 233) in a way similar to Alexis' cook here. On adverbial formations in -εί see Jebb on S. *OC* 1251, Dover on Ar. *Nub* 261, Schwyzer 1.623.

δροσώδη τὴν σχέσιν: while the accusative of respect may (or may not) be intended to emphasise the speaker's pedantic finicality, the choice of τὴν σχέσιν (rather than the normal Attic τὸ σχῆμα, here admittedly unmetrical) clearly adds pseudo-medical flavour to the phraseology. Medical writers stressed and perhaps originated the contrast between ἕξις (permanent condition) and σχέσις (temporary and alterable state) with regard to the human body (e.g. Hippocr. *Art.* 8, *Mochl.* 41, cf. LSJ s.v. σχέσις). The adjective δροσώδης on the other hand never occurs in the Hippocr. corpus (but 2,759 instances of 318 other adjectives in -ώδης do: D. op de Hipt, *Adjektive auf -ώδης im Corpus Hippocraticum* (Hamburg 1972) 7); elsewhere in Attic it belongs to the vocabulary of serious poetry (Eur. *Bacch.* 705, lyrics in Pherecrates 114(109K).2, paratragedy in Antiphanes 55(52K).13). Juxtaposition of medical and poetical diction produces an effect highly characteristic of the cook ἀλαζών (Ribbeck, *Alazon* 7ff.).

13 ὡς ἰατρικῶς: see the introductory notes to Λέβης and this fr., and comm. on vv. 7–12.

ὦ Γλαυκία: the cook is addressed probably not by his own name but (? sarcastically) by that of a celebrated contemporary physician (see introduction to Λέβης).

14 ταυτὶ ποιήσω: the normal formula to express compliance with an order, cf. Fraenkel, *Beob.* 77ff. with examples. On Kassel–Austin's spelling ποι- see comm. on fr. 16.2.

14–15 παρατίθει ... ὅταν παρατιθῇς: see comm. on 98(152K).2.

15 μανθάνεις;: parenthetically, as at e.g. fr. 98(152K).3, Ar. *Av.* 1003, Crates 22(20K), Pherecrates 74(68K).2, Men. *Pk.* 338, *Sam.* 378,

Damoxenus 2.23, 53, possibly also Eubulus 101 (103K) with Hunter's note *ad loc.*. See also the introduction to 129(124K) and comm. on ξυνιεῖς v. 6.

ἐψυγμένα: presumably the pot containing the meat is plunged into a vessel of cold water, in order to achieve the effect described in vv. 16–17.
16–17 The cook briefly returns to a more picturesque style. The idea of steam and the delicious odours arising from food in preparation regularly evokes inflated language from the later comic poets to emphasise the transports of delight into which the recipients (and audiences too possibly) are sent: e.g. Eubulus 75.9f. ὀσμὴ δὲ πρὸς μυκτῆρας ἠρεθισμένη | ᾄσσει, Ephippus 3.3 οὐ κνῖσα κρούει ῥινὸς ὑπεροχὰς ἄκρας, Nicostratus 13(15K).3ff. ὀσμὴ δὲ ... | ἄνω 'βάδιζε καὶ μέλιτι μεμιγμένη | ἀτμίς τις εἰς τὰς ῥινάς; cf. Plaut. *Pseud.* 841 *is odos demissis pedibus in caelum uolat.* Their elevated style may in general be influenced by 'the high poetry of ritual and cult', as Hunter suggests (comm. on Eubulus 75.9 with references) and/or by other types of lyric (e.g. *P.V.* 115 τίς ἀχώ, τίς ὀδμὰ προσέπτα μ' ἀφέγγης;), but it would be interesting to know whether here specifically (as in vv. 7–12) Alexis echoes the phraseology of medicine (e.g. Hippocr. *Morb.* 2.26 ἐπὴν ... ἡ ἀτμὶς ἀνίῃ, cf. *Mul.* 2.133, *Flat.* 8 ὥσπερ ... ἀπὸ τῶν λεβήτων ἀτμὸς ἀνέρχεται πολὺς ἑψομένου τοῦ ὕδατος).

Unfortunately the text of vv. 16–17 is too insecure at crucial points for certainty on this and other matters. At the beginning of 16 the *Marcianus* has ἀτμὶς, which occurs in 4th-century Attic (e.g. Nicostratus 13(15K).5, Pl. *Tim.* 87a, Aristotle) as a more recherché (and thus here palaeographically preferable) by-form of ἀτμός with no obvious distinction in meaning (Olympiodorus' claim (*In Arist. Meteor.* 165.25) that ἀτμίς is moist, ἀτμός dry, steam, is not borne out by usage, e.g. Hippocr. *Flat.* 8). Yet if A's καταφαγών in v. 17 is corrupted from another masculine participle in agreement with the noun, ἀτμὶς will have to be replaced by ἀτμὸς (so first Schweighaeuser, cf. *Animadv.* 5.108). In v. 17 A's unmetrical nonsense ἀνωμαλίσει καταφαγών was restored to ἄνω μάλ' εἶσι καταφυγών by Scaliger (in Canter, Paris MS 40ᵛ; cf. Grotius, *Exc.* 973). The conjecture is palaeographically attractive (faulty word-division in ἄ. μ. ε. and transposition or confusion of ι and ει; καταφαγών a psychological error induced by the culinary context, cf. Fraenkel on A. *Ag.* 1391), and produces relevant sense in generally appropriate diction. Yet the restoration does not wholly convince. It requires ἄνω μάλ' to be taken together ('right up'), but I have not come across μάλα elsewhere thus qualifying a directional adverb (cf. Cobet, *NL* 21), and καταφυγών necessitates the further change of ἀτμὶς to ἀτμὸς in v. 16. Other suggestions diverge too far from the paradosis: e.g. ἄνω βαδιεῖται (S. A. Naber, *Mnemosyne* 8 (1880) 260), or διαλήσει (Arnott, cf. Isoc. 3.16 διαλήσει χρηστὸς ὤν, with ΔΙΑΛΗ → ΜΑΛΙ) with καταφυγών; in place of the participle Kaibel's κατ' ὀροφήν and Edmonds' κατ' ἀφανές allow retention of ἀτμίς. Prudence here demands obeli, around ἀνωμαλίσει as well as καταφαγών.

18 πολλῷ γ': Casaubon's correction (*Animadv.* 662) of A's πολλῶν τ' restores the emphatic exclamatory particle appropriate at the beginning of a dismissive response (cf. Denniston, *GP* 126f.).

ἦσθ' ἄρα: 'the imperfect ἦν (generally with ἄρα) may express a *fact* which is just recognised as such by the speaker or writer, having previously been denied, overlooked, or not understood' (Goodwin, *MT* § 39, citing e.g. Ar. *Av.* 280 οὐ σὺ μόνος ἄρ' ἦσθ' ἔποψ;); cf. also L. F. Heindorf, *Platonis dialogi selecti* (Berlin 1810) on *Phd.* 68b, K.G. 1.145f., Denniston, *GP* 36f., Dover on Ar. *Nub.* 1028. On γε + ἄρα see J. C. B. Lowe, *Glotta* 51 (1973) 33ff., especially 36 n. 3.

18–19 The form of this riposte ('you are a better X than Y/ you are an X not a Y', sometimes followed by '<because> your behaviour has more/much in common with that of an X') and of a few others related to it in later Greek comedy (e.g. Ar. *Eccl.* 1021f., Antiphanes 250(240aK), 255, Aristophon 1, Alexis 148(144K).1–2, Timocles 19.3ff., Diphilus 84(83K)) foreshadows a favourite type of Plautine joke (e.g. *Men.* 160f. *ne tu, ut ego opinor, esses agitator probus.* | *:: quidum? :: ne te uxor sequatur respectas identidem, Poen.* 248f. *coqua est haec quidem, Agorastocles, ut opinor:* | *scit muriatica ut maceret*); Fraenkel, *EP* 35ff. It is the cook's clever way with words in vv. 4–12 and 16–17 that induces the παῖς here to call him a λογογράφος, a professional writer of speeches for use by litigants in Athenian courts, who was evidently despised in the 4th century (cf. Aeschines 2.180, 3.173, Dem. 19.246, 250, Hyperides 3.3, Pl. *Phdr.* 257c) because he was paid for being a τεχνίτης λόγων (Aeschines 1.170, 3.200) just like a σοφιστής; cf. Jebb on Theophr. *Char.* 17 (his 22), K. J. Dover, *Lysias and the Corpus Lysiacum* (Berkeley and Los Angeles 1968) 155ff.

ὃ λέγεις οὐ λέγεις: 'you don't *mean* what you *say*'. In thus correctly interpreting what was presumably a popular idiom, Richards, *AO* 85[1] aptly compares Arist. *Rhet.* 3.11, 1412ᵃ33 τὰ δὲ παρὰ γράμμα (i.e. verbal witticisms, puns) ποιεῖ οὐχ ὃ λέγει λέγειν, and ᵃ22 τὰ ἀστεῖά ἐστιν ἐκ τοῦ μὴ ὃ φησι λέγειν. The idiom thus inverts the common colloquial expression λέγ' ὅ τι (or ὃ) λέγεις, ' *Say* what you *mean*', e.g. Eupolis 99.80, Men. *Epitr.* 515, *Karch.* 14. Cf. also S. *Ant.* 403 λέγεις ὀρθῶς ἃ φής, and Ar. *Av.* 1381 ἀλλ' ὅ τι λέγεις εἰπέ μοι where λέγεις = 'you mean' (and εἰπέ = 'say'), as in the second passage of Arist. *Rhet.* cited.

These words and the closing phrase of the fr. are spoken by the cook in rejoinder to the preceding insult by the παῖς, as Hirschig rightly noted (*loc.*

---

[1] Cobet, *NL* 21 gets the meaning the wrong way round (*quod dicere vis, non dicis*); cf. Pickard-Cambridge, *GCP* 190. All other scholars who have discussed the passage (e.g. Dobree, *Adv.* 2.322) are way off target.

cit. in introduction to fr. 129(124K)). The clue to the speaker's identity lies in τέχνην δ' ὀνειδίζεις, 'It's an art that you're reviling.' It is comic cooks, not their revilers, who make a fetish of their τέχνη: e.g. Dionysius com. 2.33ff., Men. *Dysk.* 646 and Handley *ad loc.*, Athenion 1.1 and Dohm, *Mageiros* 169ff., Nicomachus 1.3; cf. Dohm 203ff. and Rankin, ΜΑΓΕΙΡΟΙ 9off.

130 (125K)

Meineke 3.438 (III), Kock 2.342, Edmonds 2.432, Kassel–Austin 2.94. The historical background and dramatic relevance of frs. 130(125K) and 131(126K) are fully discussed in the introduction to Λέβης. In both frs. legislation about the sale of fish is ascribed to 'Aristonicus the wealthy' (130.1–2), the politician whose political activity extended from 334 to 322 (introduction to Λέβης). The law described in fr. 130, which threatens with summary arrest any fishmonger who sells a fish below the stated price, is not attested for the city elsewhere in literature or inscriptions, but its terms are more in line with the kind of enactment that one might have expected in Athens during (e.g.) the food shortages of 330–326 than with purely comic fantasy (*pace* J. H. Lipsius, *Das attische Recht und Rechts-verfahren* I (Leipzig 1905) 79 n. 106), although Alexis may well have added here and there a touch of parody, exaggeration or unreality. The basic idea that the seller should stick to the price he has stipulated and not subsequently *lower* it is perhaps one such touch, a sarcastic παρὰ προσ-δοκίαν where an audience could have expected (especially in times of shortage) a ban rather on *raising* prices. Even so, selling for less than (as well as for more than) a stated figure contravened a fixed principle of ancient practice: viz. that in sales for cash the stipulated price should always be binding. Cf. for example (i) Pl. *Leg.* 11.917b–c εἰ δ' οὖν μὴ πείθοιτο (sc. the erring shopkeeper), ὅδε νόμος· ὁ πωλῶν ὁτιοῦν ἐν ἀγορᾷ μηδέποτε δύο εἴπῃ τιμὰς ὧν ἂν πωλῇ, ἁπλῆν δὲ εἰπών, ἂν μὴ τυγχάνῃ ταύτης, ἀποφέρων ὀρθῶς ἂν ἀποφέροι πάλιν, καὶ ταύτης τῆς ἡμέρας μὴ τιμήσῃ πλέονος μηδὲ ἐλάττονος ... ἐὰν δέ τις ἀπειθῇ τούτοις, ὁ παρα-τυγχάνων τῶν ἀστῶν ... ἀνατὶ τυπτέτω τις, (ii) the Delian law on a 3rd-century inscription (E. Schulhof and P. Huvelin, *BCH* 31 (1907) 46ff., lines 8ff.) μηδὲ ἐξέστω πωλεῖν ἀλλ' αὐτοῖς τοῖς | εἰσάγουσιν, μηδὲ πλείονος πωλεῖν ἢ ὅσου ἂν | ἀπογράψωνται πρὸς τοὺς πεντηκοστολό|γους μηδὲ ἐλάσσονος, (iii) Cicero *Off.* 3.15.61–2; F. Pringsheim, *The Greek Law of Sale* (Weimar 1950) 97ff., 126ff. The similarity between the Greek passages and Alexis 130 is best explained by assumption of a common source in Athenian law.

1–2 On the identity of Aristonicus see introduction to Λέβης; his wealth is not mentioned elsewhere. Alexis' repeated description of him as ὁ

COMMENTARY

νομοθέτης (130(125K).1, 131(126K).2, cf. 3) may indicate that Aristonicus proposed his law not as an independent citizen (cf. LSJ s.v. νομοθέτης) but as a member of a special board of νομοθέται set up in the Lycurgan period to carry through a heavy programme of legislative revision (cf. W. S. Ferguson, *Hellenistic Athens* (London 1911) 8ff.). See also Woltke in *RE Supp.* vii s.v. Νομοθέται 578.3ff., C. Hignett, *A History of the Athenian Constitution* (Oxford 1952) 299ff., D. M. MacDowell, *JHS* 99 (1975) 62ff., P. J. Rhodes, comm. on [Arist.] *Ath. Pol.* (Oxford 1981) 512f.

2 The *Marcianus* at Ath. 6.226a quotes this verse as Ἀριστονίκου· τίθησι γάρ νυνὶ νόμον¹, giving it an unmetrical extra syllable after the penthemimeral caesura. Dindorf (followed by Kaibel) postulated a lacuna of a least 2¾ metra between Ἀριστονίκου and τίθησι, but it is difficult to see what could have stood in the gap; the sense of the paradosis runs on with perfect smoothness. Of other attempts to heal the scansion only two merit mention: Wakefield's νῦν τίθησι γάρ (*Silv. Crit.* 2.131, before P. Elmsley, *Ed. Rev.* 3 (1803/4) 192 and Bothe, *Griech. Kom.* 52:? corruption by a scribe ignorantly restoring a postponed γάρ to its normal position, cf. comm. on frs. 37(36K).1, 4.1), and Emperius' Ἀριστονίκου· ᾽θηκε γὰρ νυνὶ (347:? a scribe either mystified by the prodelision, which is a comic as well as a tragic licence, e.g. Ar. *Ach.* 10, *Nub.* 65 ('τιθέμην), *Thesm.* 481 (after μου), Men. *Dysk.* 511, but doubtful perhaps at the beginning of a clause, or objecting to the use of an aorist with νυνί, but with aorist or imperfect νυνί and νῦν mean 'just now', e.g. Alexis 85(65K).1, Men. *Dysk.* 238f. (aorist), *Asp.* 176f. (imp.), cf. LSJ s.vv.). Wakefield's conjecture wins my vote.

In Athens the legislator νόμον τίθησι, the people or the legislature νόμον τίθεται (middle), cf. LSJ s.v. τίθημι v.1, Dover on Pl. *Symp.* 182c.

3–4 πωλῶν ... ἀποδῶτ': the passage illustrates the difference between πωλεῖν ('to offer for sale') and ἀποδίδοσθαι ('to sell' = 'to hand over' goods in return for a cash payment); see especially Neil on Ar. *Equ.* 160f.

The *Marcianus* has πωλῶν τὸν | ἰχθὺν, where the article (omitted in Epit.) is nonsensical (no fish has previously been specified) and unmetrical (for ∪ ⊔). In its place Porson's τινι (*Adv.* 50) gives sound sense and makes the error explicable (TINI → TIN before IXΘYN by haplography → TON in a misguided attempt at correction), but the possibility that Alexis wrote τινα (so Kaibel) cannot be ruled out.

4 ὑποτιμήσας: 'having set a price on' it. This use of ὑποτιμᾶν in the active is unexceptionable, if unparalleled; cf. the derivative ὑποτίμησις used as a technical term = 'estimate of one's liability' to pay a tax or legal penalty (e.g. hypothesis to Dem. 21, LSJ s.v.). Wakefield, *Silv. Crit.* 2.131f.

---

¹ Epit.'s version of the fr. is only a paraphrase up to ὅστις in v. 3, but it still writes τίθησι here.

378

and Korais in Schweighaeuser, *Animadv.* 3.300 wrongly proposed ἐπιτιμήσας in its place;[1] in the context this could mean only 'having raised the price' of the fish (LSJ s.v. ἐπιτιμάω, citing Diphilus 31(32K).27, Dem. 34.39, [Dem.] 50.6), which would be an unexpected, perhaps intrusive, but not pointless idea here.

5 ἧς εἶπε τιμῆς: the subject of εἶπε is the fishmonger. Had Alexis intended anyone else (e.g. the νομοθέτης, as E. Bayer, *Demetrios Phalereus der Athener* (Stuttgart and Berlin 1942) 41ff. mistakenly thinks), he would have been obliged to express it.

6 ἀπάγεσθαι τοῦτον: accusative and infinitive of indirect command after τίθησι (or 'θηκε) νόμον in v. 2, as commonly in Attic (e.g. Eur. *Tro.* 1031f., fr. 228.7f., Ar. *Nub.* 1423f., Pl. *Protag.* 322d, cf. K.G. 2.544 n. 1). Similarly after νόμον + τίθεμαι (e.g. Aeschines 3.158), + ἐξευρίσκω (S. *Trach.* 1177), + εἰσφέρω (Alexis 131(126K).4ff., the construction introduced by τό), + διατάσσω (Hes. *Op.* 276); after νομοθετῶ (Isoc. 11.26), νόμος ἐστί (Ar. *Ran.* 761ff., Pl. *Phd.* 58b, *Phdr.* 256d, *Crat.* 400e, Alexis 255(253K).3f.), νόμος without ἐστί (A. *Choeph.* 400, *Eum.* 448, Alexis 201(196K).2f., Anaxandrides 40(39K).10f.).

6–7 ἵνα δεδοικότες τῆς ἀξίας ἀγαπῶσιν is the reading of both A and Epit.; to defend it, one of three unlikely assumptions must be made. (i) ἀγαπῶσιν governs the genitive τῆς ἀξίας in the sense 'put up with the price' (so LSJ s.v. ἀγαπάω III.5), a usage without parallel (elsewhere the verb takes accusative or dative in this meaning) but perhaps just possible by analogy with the similar construction after ἀνέχομαι (LSJ s.v. ἀνέχω c.II.3). Or (ii) τῆς ἀξίας must be construed as genitive of price or value, but such genitives occur only where there is a verb of buying, selling, exchanging and the like in the immediate neighbourhood, or where both genitive and verb belong to a small range of expressions (ποιεῖσθαι/τιμᾶσθαί τι πολλοῦ/ὀλίγου etc.) which do not include τῆς ἀξίας ἀγαπᾶν (cf. K.G. 1.377f.). Or finally (iii) πωλοῦντες or ἀποδιδόμενοι is to be supplied from vv. 4–5, so that τῆς ἀξίας may after all be interpreted as genitive of price (so Jacobi in Meineke 5.ccvii, Pickard-Cambridge, *GCP* 190, Richards, *AO* 85), but it is doubtful whether an audience could be expected to retain the supplied verb in their memory after the intervening references to prison, arrest and fear. In the circumstances corruption seems a safer postulate, and it is possible to localise, if not to cure, it. E. Tournier, *Exercices critiques de la Conférence de Philologie Grecque* (Paris 1875) 3.34 no. 85 (cf. A. M. Desrousseaux, *Mélanges offerts à M. Octave Navarre* (Toulouse 1935) 139 n. 1) and Kaibel impugn δεδοικότες and

---

[1] Wakefield also added after this participle a τ' which is unnecessary but may be right.

379

conjecture δεδωκότες, thus replacing an apt with a senseless word. Fishmongers would fear arrest, but hardly be content with having given their wares away; and we cannot interpret δεδωκότες as if it were ἀποδεδομένοι. Meineke suggested τὰς ἀξίας for τῆς ἀξίας, but this noun is almost invariably used in the singular, not only by the comic poets (Ar. *Av.* 1223, fr. adesp. 1326 Kock) but throughout 4th-century literature (Xen. *Mem.* 2.5.2 provides two exceptions). These conjectures, however, may misplace the corruption; the faulty word is more likely to be ἀγαπῶσιν, and a glance at the previous verse will perhaps help to reveal how the error – one of a type fruitfully analysed by Fraenkel in his edition of A. *Ag.*, vol. 3 p. 655 n. 1 – could have arisen. The scribe's eye strayed to ἀπάγεσθαι in v. 6, and his mind conflated the stem of that word with the ending of the original verb in v. 7; at the same time he unconsciously amended the conflation ἀπάγωσιν, which would be nonsensical in the context, to ἀγαπῶσιν, which produced sense enough for the scribe to have imagined that this was what he had read. A corruption of this kind can rarely be corrected with certainty; Alexis might have written πωλῶσιν (Hirschig, *Annot.* 12), ἀποδῶσιν (Kock: = ἀποδῶνται, 'sell', if this use of the active survived into the 4th century; earlier Eur. *Cycl.* 239, Ar. *Ran.* 1235 and Σ^RV ἀπόδος· ... ἀντὶ τοῦ πωλῆσον, Thuc. 6.62.4 and Gomme– (Andrewes)–Dover *ad loc.*, LSJ s.v. ἀποδίδωμι III, D. L. Page, *Wien. Stud.* 69 (1956) 123) or another verb of similar meaning, with τῆς ἀξίας now an acceptable genitive of price.

8 ἅπαντας: Grotius' correction (*Exc.* 575) of ἅπαντες (A, Epit.); had the copyist's eye strayed to v. 10?

10 A and Epit. here write πεμφθείς, but although the idea of a servant 'sent' to buy fish is appropriate in this context (Korais in Schweighaeuser, *Animadv.* 3.302 cites Theophr. *Char.* 18 ἀποστείλας τὸν παῖδα ὀψωνήσοντα), its expression here (with nom. masc. sing. participle placed between and referring to neut. sing. παιδίον and masc. plur. ἅπαντες) is grammatically harsh. Conjectures in place of πεμφθείς are numerous and unconvincing. Nearest to the *ductus* are W. Morel's πεντετές (*Rh. Mus.* 77 (1928) 166), but the buyer's age is irrelevant and in any case too young, especially since in marketing contexts παιδίον is more likely to be 'slave' than 'child'), and A. Lumb's πεμπτῆς (in Gulick's edition of Ath.: translated there incorrectly as 'at a fifth of the price', which would rather require ἐπὶ τῷ πεμπτῷ μέρει; πεμπτῆς = only 'at a fifth of a stater', cf. LSJ s.v. ἕκτη, an implausible price for a city which did its sums at the fish-stall in obols and drachmas). Blaydes' ἀπαξάπαντες (*Adv* 2.159) could be justi-fied only by the unsupported assumption that πεμφθείς was a stopgap inserted by a scribe to fill a lacuna between παιδίον and ἅπαντες (cf. Antiphanes 63.2(62.3K), Herwerden, *NAC* 19, *Coll. Crit.* 125). More satisfying are conjectures that provide a relevant object for ἀγοράσουσι (in later comedy transitive or passive twenty times, intransitive only five): viz. ἰχθῦς (H. van Herwerden, *Mnemosyne* 19 (1891) 207) or some commonly eaten species, e.g. μεμβράδας (Kaehler, *Annot.* 17) or τευθίδας; unfortunately no appropriate fish name is close enough to the *ductus* to warrant unqualified acceptance.

131 (126K)

Meineke 3.438 (IV), Kock 2.342, Edmonds 2.432, Kassel–Austin 2.95. The relationship between this fr. and 130(125K) and their dramatic relevance are discussed in the introduction to Λέβης, cf. also introduction to 130(125K). Both frs. describe laws attributed to Aristonicus. That of 130 sounds reasonable, conforms to the practices of Attic law, and may be genuine; that of 131 is a grotesque and extravagant fancy of the comic poet's, preparing the way for a παρὰ προσδοκίαν joke in v. 9.

1 Solon's codification of Athenian law in the early 6th century led to a popular conviction in the city that he was the paragon of legislators (e.g. Ar. *Nub.* 1187ff. and Dover *ad loc.*, *Av.* 166off., Philemon 3(4).1–4; Lysias 30.2, 28, Dem. 18.6, 22.25, Isoc. 15.231f.; Rhodes on [Arist.] *Ath. Pol.* p. 110). On his appearance as a character in Alexis' Αἴσωπος, see the introduction to that play.

Ἀριστονίκου: see introduction to Λέβης and comm. on 130(125K).1–2.

2–3 An unknown comic poet (fr. adesp. 110.1–2 Kock) introduces a law attributed to Charondas in similar terms, τὸν νομοθέτην φασὶν Χαρώνδαν ἔν τινι | νομοθεσίᾳ τά τ' ἄλλα καὶ ταυτὶ λέγειν.

3 νενομοθέτηκε: so A and Epit. (Ath. 6.226b: Epit. cites the fr. (complete apart from the last three words of v. 3) directly before 130). H. van Herwerden, *Mnemosyne* 4 (1876) 303 conjectured -θέτηκ' εὖ, on the ground that Alexis was stressing the quality rather than the quantity of Aristonicus' laws; in this idiom, however, where a speaker singles out from the general facts of a situation one that is most relevant to the argument, those general facts are normally mentioned first in a clause introduced by ἄλλοι/ἄλλα (cf. LSJ s.v. ἄλλος II.6) τε, ἀεί τε, etc., sometimes with (e.g. S. *Ant.* 506ff., Eur. *Bacch.* 770ff.) and sometimes without (e.g. Pl. *Theaet.* 142c, Alexis 259(257K).1–2) evaluative qualification of the kind that Herwerden's conjecture would impose here.

On the position of γάρ see comm. on 37(36K).1.

4–5 καινὸν εἰσφέρει νόμον τινὰ χρυσοῦν: even if E. Bayer (*loc. cit.* in comm. on fr. 130(125K).5, following C. Ostermann, *De Demetrii Phalerei vita* I (Progr. Hersfeld 1847) 42) is right in identifying one καινὸς νόμος (? or two: on the regulation of dinners and μάγειροι) mentioned by Timocles 34(32K).4 and Men. fr. 238.3 as part of the legislative programme of Demetrius of Phalerum, this does not limit use of this term to that

COMMENTARY

programme (cf. e.g. Ar. *Nub.* 1423f.; introduction to Λέβης, p. 364 n. 1, and J. Triantaphyllopoulos, *Das Rechtsdenken der Griechen* (Munich 1985) 111 n. 104). The position of χρυσοῦν here, last word in its clause and held over to the beginning of a new verse, is important. In its metaphorical sense (= 'splendid') the adjective is sometimes used seriously in later comedy (apparently Antiphanes 173(175K).4, 210(212K).5, Amphis 17.1, cf. elsewhere e.g. Pl. *Phdr.* 235e), sometimes ironically (Men. *Dysk.* 675 and Sandbach *ad loc.*; cf. Aelian *Epist.* 19, Alciphron 2.14, 3.33, Lucian *Laps.* 1), and sometimes with a designed ambiguity that is especially appropriate here at the very moment when the speaker turns from ostensible praise of a real person to absurd fantasy. Cf. also E. Degani, *RCCM* 5 (1963) 291f.

5 τὸ μὴ πωλεῖν: cf. comm. on 130(125K).6, and A. Oguse, *Rev. Phil.* 92 (1966) 63.

καθημένους ἔτι: Jacobs' transposition (*Addit.* 132) of an unmetrical ἔτι καθ. in A and Epit., where doubtless a scribe wished to write the words in their normal prose order (cf. W. Headlam, *CR* 16 (1902) 243ff., G. Thomson, *Humboldt-Universität Berlin, Wissenschaftliche Zeitschrift, Geschaftl.-Sprachwiss. Reihe* 12 (1963) 54f.; most of the examples in Jackson, *Marg. Scaen.* 228ff. are of similar provenance). In the Athenian agora retailers normally sold their wares sitting. When Dikaiopolis sets up his stall, he will make his profit ἐν ἀγορᾷ καθήμενος, Ar. *Ach.* 837f.; cf. Pherecrates 70(64K) (perfume), Men. *Pk.* 284 (cheese), Pl. *Resp.* 2.371c.

7 εἰς νέωτα: 'next year', cf. K.G. 1.538ff., Gow on Theoc. 15.143. Alexis then adds κεκραμένους as a teasing introduction to his fantasy. The audience is intended to wonder about the form of suspension (cf. Gomme-Sandbach, *Comm.* on Men. *Dysk.* 249) the speaker has in mind, until the explanation comes in v. 9.

9 Fishmongers are to dangle, like the gods in tragedy, from a μηχανή. This was 'a kind of crane for swinging personages, human or divine, through the air, so as to give the illusion of flying' (Pickard-Cambridge, *TDA* 127; cf. also O. Crusius, *Philologus* 48 (1889) 697ff., P. Arnott, *Greek Scenic Conventions* (Oxford 1962) 72ff., who warns 'exactly how it worked cannot be known', Barrett on Eur. *Hipp.* 1283, N. C. Hourmouziades, *Production and Imagination in Euripides* (Athens 1965) 146ff., S. Melchinger, *Das Theater der Tragödie* (Munich 1974) 194ff., C. W. Dearden, *The Stage of Aristophanes* (London 1977) 75ff., O. Taplin, *The Stagecraft of Aeschylus* (Oxford 1977) 443ff., H.-J. Newiger in G. A. Seeck (ed.), *Das griechische Drama* (Darmstadt 1979) 451f. and *Dioniso* 59 (1989) 173ff.). In the 4th century references to its continued use are found in comedy (also Antiphanes 189(191K).15) and elsewhere (Pl. *Crat.* 425d, *Clit.* 407a, Arist. *Poet.* 15, 1454^{b}1f.), and by the time of Demosthenes the phrase ἀπὸ μηχανῆς θεός (with or without ἐπεφάνης) was being used for the unexpected but timely appearance of a benefactor to resolve a crisis (Dem. 40.59, cf. e.g. Men. *Theoph.* fr. 5, frs. 243 and 951.12 Körte, Alciphron 3.4.1).

132 (127K)

Meineke 3.437 (II), Kock. 2.343, Edmonds, 2.432, Kassel–Austin 2.96; cf. Nesselrath, *MK* 304. The cook asks the man who has hired him (cf. introduction to Λέβης) for the condiments with which he is going to garnish the meal. His list of these (vv.3–8), containing twenty items, is likely to amuse an audience in various ways: by its delivery as patter (like many other such lists in comedy: cf. introduction to fr. 84), by the obvious contrast between the banality of practically all the items demanded, which would be found in any reasonably stocked store-cupboard, and the imperious arrogance of the cook's opening remark, which would lead a listener to expect a catalogue of exotic and expensive luxuries, and perhaps finally by a faint medical flavour in the list (cf. comm. on v. 8), which would chime in well with the cook's arrogation of medical terminology in fr. 129(124K). The fr. is cited (as a whole) by Ath. 4.170a–b as a ἡδυσμάτων κατάλογος and (vv. 3–8) by Pollux 6.66 as a πλῆθος ἡδυσμάτων including πέπερι. Their differences and corruptions (vv. 2, 3, 5, 7, 8) produce a series of problems which shed as much light perhaps on the imperfections of the texts available to excerptors as on the errors of subsequent copyists. Correct part-division was first worked out by Korais (cf. Schweighaeuser, *Animadv.* 2.603), after an unsuccessful earlier attempt by Daléchamp.

1 The line is one *anceps* short at or near the beginning in A of Ath. (Epit. gives an abridged version of only vv. 4–8 of the fr., listing seven items in a different order). There are two possible explanations: either (i) the excerptor ignored an initial word belonging to a previous sentence or speech; (ii) excerptor or copyist carelessly omitted a word from the quoted initial sentence. In the latter case Meineke's μὴ <μὴ> (cf. e.g. Ar. *Vesp.* 1418, *Lys.* 740) or my own μὴ <δὴ> (cf. Denniston, *GP* 223) would be palaeographically preferable to the often printed <καὶ> δὴ of Musurus. At the beginning of citations, however, textual criticism is particularly hazardous.[1]

μὴ προφάσεις ἐνταῦθά μοι: in whatever way the line originally opened, ellipse of a governing verb (here πάρεχε or πρότεινε) must probably be

---

[1] But one suggestion, Desrousseaux' <δός> μή, *Obs.* 103, may be totally discounted. A verb would not precede its negative thus unless the negative idea were being contrasted with another (μή A ἀλλά B), and in any case the aorist imperative is extremely rare in Attic for negative commands (Goodwin, *MT* 89, K.G. 1.237f.).

COMMENTARY

assumed, as commonly in comedy with angry expostulations of the type 'don't <make> excuses' or 'don't <mention> X': e.g. Ar. *Ach.* 345 ἀλλὰ μή μοι πρόφασιν, ἀλλά..., *Nub.* 84ff. μή μοί γε τοῦτον... ἀλλά..., *Vesp.* 1179, 1400, *Lys.* 922, Pherecrates 73(67K).4, Alexis 177(173K).14, Ephippus 21.3; the proverb cited in Zenobius 5.3 μήτε μοι Λυδῶν καρύκας, μήτε μαστίγων ψόφους may also come from a comic source. The standard formula for introducing these remarks is μή μοι or μή μοί γε; the transmission in Alexis here, with unemphatic μοι, is evidence supporting that spelling of the pronoun (and not 'μοί) in the formula. Cf. K.G. 2.571f., Schwyzer 2.707f., Gow–Page on Dioscorides 3.4 (*Hellenistic Epigrams* 2 (Cambridge 1965) 239), Dover on Ar. *Nub.* 433.

προφάσεις here = simply 'excuses' without overt implication of their truth or falsity (LSJ s.v. 1.1; in later comedy e.g. Men. *Dysk.* 135f., 322). The word's various meanings and overtones have spawned a large bibliography (e.g. H. R. Rawlings, *A Semantic Study of Prophasis to 400 BC* (*Hermes Einzelschrift* 33, Wiesbaden 1975), L. Pearson, *TAPA* 83 (1952) 205ff. and 103 (1972) 381ff., M. Chambers in W. M. Calder (ed.), *The Cambridge Ritualists Reconsidered* (Atlanta 1991) 74ff.); for drama contrast the brief comments of Neil on Ar. *Equ.* 465f., Handley on Men. *Dys.* 135f., Gomme–Sandbach, *Comm.* on *Kon.* 20, W. Stockert on Eur. *IA* 1434 (Vienna 1992).

μηδ' "οὐκ ἔχω": elsewhere such brief quotations are often introduced by the neuter article: e.g. Ar. *Nub.* 1174 τὸ "τί λέγεις σύ;", *Equ.* 24f.*, Men. *Pk.* 1006 πάνυ σοῦ φιλῶ τὸ "νῦν διαλλαχθήσομαι", Dem. 18.88*. Usually when the article is omitted, and sometimes even when it is not (the asterisked references above), a verb of saying governs the quotation: e.g. S. *Ant.* 567 ἀλλ' "ἥδε" μέντοι μὴ λέγ', Ar. *Equ.* 21, Men. frs. 395.2, 634.3. Cf. also comm. on 209(206K).

2 ἀλλὰ λέγ' ὅτου δεῖ is Dobree's correction (*Adv.* 2.307: improving on Musurus' ἀλλά γε λέγ' οὗ δεῖ and Casaubon's ἀλλ' ἄγε, λέγ' οὗ δεῖ, cf. *Animadv.* 303) of A's ἀλλὰ λέγοντα· οὐ δει, where the corruption stems from faulty word-division (ΛΕΓ'ΟΤΟΥ → ΛΕΓΟΤ'ΟΥ) and a subsequent attempt to create a word, if not sense, from the ensuing jumble. Cf. Ar. *Av.* 1419. Cobet's ἀλλὰ λέγ' ὃ βούλει (in Peppink, *Observ.* 31) gives equally good sense, but then the error is harder to explain.

2–3 λήψομαι ... λάβ': '(I shall) buy', cf. comm. on fr. 15.18–19.

3 A of Ath. gives ὀρθῶς τὸ πρῶτον μὲν, the MSS of Pollux (FSA) ὀρθῶς γε· πρῶτον (omitting μὲν), with no indication of part-division (cf. introduction to this fr.). In conversational response both ὀρθῶς (e.g. Eur. *Ion* 1025, *Bacch.* 838, Men. *Dysk.* 581, *Sik.* 257 *bis*) and ὀρθῶς γε (Eur. *Hipp.* 94, Ar. *Lys.* 1228, *Plut.* 1033, Men. *Sik.* 245, Diphilus 31(32K).18) are common abridgements for ὀρθῶς λέγεις, while πρῶτον and τὸ πρῶτον are used without apparent distinction of nuance to introduce the

384

ΛΕΒΗΣ

first item in a list (Blaydes, *Adv.* 2.159 is simply wrong to claim that τὸ πρῶτον is never so used: cf. e.g. Dem. 1.12 τὸ πρῶτον Ἀμφίπολιν λαβών, μετὰ ταῦτα Πύδναν, πάλιν Ποτείδαιαν, Μεθώνην αὖθις, εἶτα Θετταλίας ἐπέβη). By the narrowest of margins I prefer the Pollux version (with Ath.'s μὲν), if only because in a response γε adds a touch of liveliness (Denniston, *GP* 136f.).

σήσαμα: the fruit and particularly the seeds of the sesame (*Sesamum orientale* is the correct binomial: cf. L. S. Cobley, *Introduction to the Botany of Tropical Crops* (London 1956) 103ff.). The plant seems to have reached Greece from the Orient (like its name – ? Semitic: H. Lewy, *Die asiatischen Fremdwörter im Griechischen* (Berlin 1895) 28f., cf. I. Przyluski and M. Régamey, *Bull. Sch. Or. Stud.* 8 (1935–7) 706ff., Frisk 2.698 and Chantraine 2.999f., s.v.). It was an important ingredient of wedding-cakes (e.g. Ar. *Pax* 869 and Σ (διὰ τὸ πολύγονον), *Av.* 159ff., Men. *Sam.* 74, 125, 190, Steier in *RE* s.v. *Sesamon* 1851.54ff., W. Erdmann, *Die Ehe im alten Griechenland* (Munich 1934) 260), and may owe its position at the head of this list of required comestibles to a possibility that the cook had been hired to prepare a wedding-feast in a New-Comedy plot.[1] Cf. also D. A. Amyx, *Hesperia* 25 (1956) 189f., André, *Alimentation* 40f.

4 ἀσταφίδα κεκομμένην: larger varieties of dried grapes (our muscatels, sultanas) would then as now need to be chopped before use as ingredients in breads and cakes.

5 μάραθον: so correctly the MSS of Ath. (A, Epit.: the MSS of Pollux corrupt to -αθα either by homoeoteleuton with σήσαμα or by miscopying the first letter of the following word. The noun's orthography is mishandled by LSJ s.vv. μάραθον, μάραθρον. μάραθον is supported for Attic by Hermippus 75(81K) (pun on Μαραθών) and good MSS (e.g. Dem. 18.260, A also at Ath. 4.131e, 13.596a citing Anaxandrides 42(41K).59 and Python's *Agen* of 324, *TrGF* 1 F 1.13); also in Doric (Epicharmus 159, 161) and in a 3rd-century AD papyrus of a cookery book (Bilabel, *Ops.* ζ 27). μάραθρον is Ionic (e.g. Hippocr. *Acut.* 54, *Nat. Mul.* 8, 32: 34 times in the corpus, with the MSS favouring this spelling, *pace* the Mahoney–Frohn concordance), but is not attested for the *Koine* vernacular until the 2nd century (*UPZ* I.89.9). Cf. comm. on 63(62K).1 (ἀλάβαστ(ρ)ος). μάραθον is fennel, *Foeniculum vulgare*; its uses in the ancient kitchen seem little different from those today, cf. Olck in *RE* s.v. *Fenchel* 2172.42ff., André, *Alimentation* 203, Dohm, *Mageiros* 144ff.

---

[1] Perhaps the plot of the Greek original of Plaut. *Aul.*: cf. introduction to Λέβης and Appendix III. Of course sesame cakes were not confined to weddings (e.g. Ar. *Ach.* 1092, *Thesm.* 570, Lucian *Symp.* 27, 38, Alciphron 3.12.2, Pollux 6.108), nor sesame seeds to sesame cakes only (Steier, André, *locc. citt.*).

COMMENTARY

ἄνηθον: the alpha is short in Hellenistic literary Doric (Theoc. 7.63, 15.119 → V. *Ecl.* 2.48, [Mosch.] 3.100) and in Lesbian Aeolic (Sappho 81b.2, Alcaeus 362), but in Attic (apart from here) *anceps* (Alexis 179(174K).4, Eubulus 35(36K).3) or long (Ar. *Nub.* 982, *Thesm.* 486). In the last two passages Dindorf overrules the MSS orthography in ἄνη- and substitutes ἄννηθον, relying on the evidence of the anon. *Glossary of Useful Terms* 1.96.23 Bachmann which defends the spelling ἄννηττον, and of later writers like Theophr. *HP* 9.7.3 ἄννητον ∼ 1.11.2 ἄνηθον (cf. the cookery-book in Bilabel, *Ops.* ε 20 ἄννη- ∼ ζ 8 ἄνη-), although the majority of MSS of authors from all periods agree in ἄνη- (x 9 in Hippocr. corpus, e.g. *Morb.* 2.50, *Vict.* 2.54, Galen 9.832 Kühn, N.T. *Ev. Matt.* 23.23). Confusion over the word's ending (-θον, -τον, –ττον) in *Koine* Greek may stem originally from dialectal variation (note -τον in Sappho, Alcaeus, Anacreon 151; ἀνήτινος Theoc. 7.63), but the spelling with double nu may be influenced by analogy and muddle with another herb: ἄννησον (anise), whose similarity to ἄνηθον (dill) in name, appearance and culinary use as a seasoning has helped to perpetuate this confusion in more modern times;[1] Dover's comm. on Ar. *Nub.* 982 sheds useful light on this confusion. On the ancient use of dill (now *Peucedanum graveolens*, cf. Cobley, *op. cit.* on v. 3, 217) see Olck in *RE* s.v. *Dill* 639.41ff., André, *Alimentation* 203. On ἄννησον see on v. 7.

νᾶπυ: Alexis' use here also of a correct Attic form (cf. Phrynichus *Ecl.* 252 p. 118 Fischer σίνηπι οὐ λεκτέον, ἀλλὰ νᾶπυ, with the editions of C. A. Lobeck (Leipzig 1820) 288 and Rutherford, *NP* 349f.; see also A. Carnoy, *Dictionnaire étymologique des noms grecs de plantes* (Louvain 1959) 185, 245, H. von Staden in W. M. Calder (ed.), *Werner Jaeger Reconsidered* (Atlanta 1992) 26off.) is attested by all the MSS (Ath., Pollux) and demanded by the metre; cf. also in comedy Ar. *Equ.* 631 (with Neil *ad loc.*), Eubulus 18(19K).1, fr. adesp. 289(b).14 Austin. σίναπι is attested at Anaxippus 1.45, σιναπίζειν probably at Xenarchus 12.2. On the word's etymology (? non-Greek) and variant forms, see also Przyluski and Régamey, *op. cit.* in comm. on v. 3, 703ff., Björck, *Alpha Impurum* 64, Frisk 2.288f. s.v. νᾶπυ. On the plant itself, Hehn, *Kulturpflanzen* 211f., Steier in *RE Supp.* vi s.v. *Senf* 812.45ff., André, *Alimentation* 32, 203f.

καυλόν, σίλφιον: the united reading of the MSS (Ath., Pollux), most reasonably interpreted as '(silphium) stalk, silphium (seed)'. Theophr. *HP* 6.3.1–6 (cf. 4.3.1) gives a full account of the silphium plant of Cyrene, which despite allegations that it became extinct by the middle of the 1st century AD was commercially available at least until the beginning of the

---

[1] In *Ev. Matt.* 23.23 ἄνηθον is translated 'anise' in *AV* but corrected to 'dill' in *RV*; and Gow's edition of Theocritus rightly comments on ἀνήτινον at 7.63 as 'dill' but mistranslates it as 'anise'.

5th century AD (cf. e.g. the edict of Diocletian in AD 301: 36.132 in the Aphrodisias copy published in S. Lauffer, *Diokletians Preisedikt* (Berlin 1971) pp. 200, 290f., 34.66 in that from Aezani, M. H. Crawford and J. M. Reynolds, *ZPE* 34 (1979) 183, 207; Synesius *epist.* 106, 134 A. Garzya (Rome 1979); Sulpicius Severus *Dialogus* 1.4.4 p. 156 Halm (*CSEL* 1 (Vienna 1866)); see D. Roques, *REG* 97 (1984) 218ff., 106 (1993) 380ff.). Its botanical identity has never been satisfactorily established, although it seems to have belonged to the asafoetida group. See especially Neil on Ar. *Equ.* 894f., Steier in *RE* s.v. *Silphion* 103.7ff. and – in response to the detailed scientific study by E. Stranz, *Zur Silphionfrage* (Berlin 1909) – *RE Supp.* v. 972.45ff., G. Nencioni, *SIFC* 16 (1939) 30ff., A. C. Andrews, *Isis* 33 (1941) 232ff., F. Chamoux, *Cyrène sous la monarchie des Battiades* (Paris 1953) 246ff., Gow–Scholfield on Nicander *Ther.* 85, André, *Alimentation* 207ff., J. I. Miller, *The Spice Trade of the Roman Empire* (Oxford 1969) 100, 118. Although καυλός strictly = 'stalk' without reference to a specific plant (LSJ s.v.), it is used on its own elsewhere in contexts where its identification as silphium stalk is certain (e.g. Hermippus 63.4 καυλός from Cyrene; cf. also the comic citations asterisked below). σίλφιον on the other hand is frequently mentioned in lists along with parts of itself (e.g. Eubulus 18(19K).3–4* καὶ καυλὸν ἐκ Καρχηδόνος | καὶ σίλφιον, where the reference to Carthage confirms the interpretation of καυλός, 6(7K).3* οὐ καυλοῖσιν οὐδὲ σιλφίῳ, Antiphanes 88.3–4* ἵπποις, σιλφίῳ, συνωρίσιν, | καυλῷ, κέλησι, μασπετοῖς, πυρετοῖς, ὀπῷ, where in a list of Cyrenaic products silphium and its parts – stalk, leaves and juice – alternate with horses and fevers), but never with the one other part of the plant that has culinary and medical uses – its seed; accordingly it appears reasonable to assume that in such collocations σίλφιον refers primarily to the seed.[1]

6 κορίαννον αὗον: in this fr. Alexis repeatedly employs correct Attic forms (μάραθον, ἄνηθον, νᾶπυ, κορίαννον: the last replaced by κόριον in the *Koine*, cf. Galen 12.36 Kühn); thus he is more likely (*pace* Kassel–Austin) to have written αὗον (confirmed as Attic by e.g. Ar. *Ran.* 1089 ἐπαφηυάνθην) than the unaspirated form of the *Koine* and our MSS here; cf. S. Srebny, *Eos* 43 (1949) 48 n. 1, Schwyzer 1.220, 304. κορίαννον is coriander, *Coriandrum sativum*; cf. Hehn, *Kulturpflanzen* 209, W. K. Pritchett, *Hesperia* 25 (1956) 185, André, *Alimentation* 203. Its fruit is dried to produce the 'seeds' familiar in our kitchens; although no other reference to its drying is known to me, there is no call to suspect αὗον here of being a corruption for e.g. ᾠόν (so Herwerden, *Coll. Crit.* 125).

---

[1] Whatever the merits of this assumption, the parallels cited from Eubulus and Antiphanes show that there is no need to alter the joint reading of Ath. and Pollux here to καυλὸν σιλφίου (so Hirschig, *Diss.*).

ῥοῦν, κύμινον, κάππαριν: respectively sumach (*Rhus coriaria*; Hehn 427f., André 210f.), cummin (*Cuminum cyminum*; Gossen in *RE Supp.* viii s.v. *Kümmel* 255.39ff., Hehn 208ff., André 203) and caper (*Capparis spinosa*; André 202). The fruits of sumach and caper and the seeds of cummin were used then as now for flavourings; there is no evidence that caper buds were ever pickled for this purpose in ancient Athens (Theophr. *HP* 3.2.1 limits his discussion to the fruit).

7 ὀρίγανον: the word's gender varies in comedy, as elsewhere[1] (LSJ s.v.): fem. Ar. *Eccl.* 1030, Plato com. 169(154K), Alexis 193(188K).1 and probably 138(133K).6 (see comm.); masc. Anaxandrides 51(50K), cf. a hexameter by Ion fr. 28 West; neut. Epicharmus 17, Ameipsias 36(35K); masc. or neut. Eubulus 18(19K).5; indeterminate in other passages of comedy (including here and Alexis 179(174K).4); cf. Ath. 2.68b, *Et. Mag.* 630.46 = *Et. Gen.* in Miller, *Mélanges* 227 s.v. ὀρίγανον. It is the general name for several species of *Origanum*, including *O. vulgare* (marjoram), *O. heracleoticum* (winter m.) and *O. onites* (pot m.); the leaves were used, probably both fresh and dried, for seasoning. Cf. Steier in *RE Supp.* vii s.v. *Origanum* 813.4ff., André, *Lexique* 230f. and *Alimentation* 205, A. C. Andrews, *Economic Botany* 56 (1961) 73ff.

After ὀρίγανον the MSS of Pollux have γήτιον ἄνοιττον (γίτιον FS, ἄν. om. A), A of Ath. has γήτειον σκόροδον (om. Epit.). Alexis clearly wrote γήτειον (a now unidentifiable and possibly lost variety of onion that either did not bulb or was pulled before bulbing.[2] ἄνοιττον in the Pollux MSS is most likely to be a misspelling (so first Olck in *RE* s.v. *Anis* 2215.68f.) of

---

57), although the conjectured phrase, which does occur at Ar. *Equ.* 894f., requires only a minimal change.

[1] Without any apparent distinction of meaning. Feminine at Ar. *Eccl.* 1030 refers to the whole plant, masculine at Anaxandrides 51(50K) to the seed, but in *HP* Theophrastus uses feminine (6.2.3, 7.6.1) and neuter (1.9.4, 7.1.6) indifferently for the plant.

[2] Theophr. *HP* 7.4.10 describes the γήτειον as an onion which does not form a bulb (ἀκέφαλον), with a long neck; it is cut, like the leek, and raised from seed. *Et. Mag.* s.v. calls it a χλωρὸν κρόμμυον. The best discussion is Stadler's in *RE* s.v. *Lauch* 987.8ff., ruling out some attempted identifications on geographical (*Allium fistulosum*, the Welsh onion, originating in Siberia) or historical (the shallot variety of *Allium cepa*, not cultivated before the 16th century AD) grounds. A. Hort's translation of it as 'horn-onion' (index to his edition of *HP* 2 (London and New York 1916) 444, influenced by W. Thiselton-Dyer and accepted by LSJ: cf. *BICS* 32 (1985) 79) would have been more helpful if he had explained what he meant by a term unknown to dictionaries and horticulturists. Cf. also G. D. McCollum in N. W. Simmonds (ed.), *Evolution of Crop Plants* (London and New York 1976) 186ff.

ἄννησον, the form most commonly in use for 'anise' (*Pimpinella anisum*: cf. Olck 2215.6off., André, *Alimentation* 203) up to the end of the 4th century (x 52 in Hippocr. corpus, twice with variant spelling ἄνη-, *Reg. Acut.* 23 Jones, *Mul.* 1.26; Hdt. 4.71, Theophr. *HP* 1.11.2, 12.1, Phaenias in Ath. 9.371d = fr. 39 Wehrli; cf. also Bilabel, *Ops.* ζ 9), and corrupted in FS partly by iotacism, partly under the influence of the *Koine* spelling ἄν(ν)ισον (which was conjectured here for Pollux in S. Grynaeus' Basel edition of 1536, and for Alexis by Dobree, *Adv.* 2.239), and partly by confusion with ἄνηθον in its *Koine* spelling (ἄν(ν)ηττον:[1] see above on v. 5). The non-metrical reading of A in Ath. could be explained as a corruption of e.g. σκορόδια γήτειον (so Dobree, *Adv.* 2.308), with Ath.'s source in that case differing (as also in v. 8) from Pollux's; it is, however, far more likely that σκόροδον replaced ἄννησον as a gloss on the previous word γήτειον. Already by the time of Lucian (*Lex.* 3: see A. M. Harmon's edition, 5 (London and Cambridge, Mass. 1936) p. 291, Neil on Ar. *Equ.* 677, B. Baldwin, *Studies in Lucian* (Toronto 1973) 41ff.) γήτειον was obsolete and generally unintelligible, and it is easy to conceive of its being glossed by another species of *Allium* with which it had a close affinity (cf. Ar. fr. 5, roots of the γήθυα have a σκοροδομίμητον φύσιν, where γήθυα = γήτεια, cf. *Et. Mag.* 230.23ff. s.v. γήτειον, Hesych. s.v. γήτεια, [Herodian] 2.486.16f. Lentz, and comm. on fr. 179(174K).6–7).

θύμον: see on 122(117K).2.

8 σφάκον: various species of sage (doubtless including *Salvia cretica*, *pomifera* and *triloba*), whose leaves have been used for flavouring since antiquity. Cf. A. C. Andrews, *Economic Botany* 10/3 (1956) 263ff., André, *Alimentation* 205.

σίραιον: a decoction of new wine (γλεῦκος etc.: see on fr. 60(59K).1), originally slightly bitter, but sweetened with honey to taste (Σ^V Ar. *Vesp.* 878, cf. Pollux 6.16, Pliny *HN* 14.9). The next item in Alexis' list is uncertain: σέσελι in Ath. (A, Epit.), πέπερι in Pollux (A: FS have the unmetrical variant πέπεριν). Dindorf (in his edition of Ath. *ad loc.*) was the first to point out that Pollux 6.65–6 quoted this fr. in order to exemplify the use of πέπερι, but this does not prove that Alexis wrote πέπερι here, only that in the 2nd century AD Pollux had a source text of the passage with this reading. πέπερι (and πέπερις: pepper, *Piper nigrum*, cf. Orth and Steier in *RE* s.vv. *Kochkunst* 952.53ff. and *Pfeffer* 1421.11ff. respectively, André, *Alimentation* 209) was already known as a condiment in 4th-century Athens (e.g. Antiphanes 274(277K).1, Eubulus 125(128K).1). σέσελι (and σέσελις: an umbellifer generally identified as *Tordylium officinale*, but

---

[1] Kassel–Austin print here their own conjecture ἄννηττον; if this is a variant spelling of the *Koine* ἄνηττον (cf. my comm. on v. 5), it would make Alexis unaccountably name the same plant (dill) twice.

COMMENTARY

probably including other species of *T.* as well as species of the genus *Seseli*: cf. André, *Lexique* s.v. *seselis*) is mentioned frequently in antiquity (x 27 in Hippocr. corpus, e.g. *Mul.* 1.78; Arist. *HA* 9.5, 611ᵃ18, Theophr. *HP* 9.15.5, cf. Pliny *HN* 8.112) as a medicinal herb, but nowhere (? else) as a food. If Alexis wrote σέσελι here, the evidence for its use in the kitchen may have been lost, or just possibly its inclusion in the cook's list may have been inspired by the claim to medical expertise which he made in fr. 129(124K). Or is it a pure coincidence that when σέσελι occurs in the Hippocr. corpus, it is associated fifteen times with ἄννησον (x 12 in juxtaposition), six times with κύμινον, and once with ἀσταφίς, πήγανον and the juice of πράσον? However that may be, σέσελι seems to me preferable here as the more imaginative word and *difficilior lectio*, and (*pace* Kassel–Austin) I should reject πέπερι as a trivialising variant – but with an uncomfortable feeling that the common association of ἄννησον and σέσελι in medicine could also have induced a scribe to expect and then wrongly write the second of these words here after he had correctly copied the first.

πήγανον, πράσον: respectively rue (*Ruta graveolens*, favoured particularly by the Romans as a condiment, despite the unpleasant smell of leaves and fruit; cf. Hehn, *Kulturpflanzen* 202, Stadler in *RE* s.v. *Raute* 296.42ff., A. C. Andrews, *CJ* 43 (1948) 371ff., André, *Alimentation* 205f.) and leek (*Allium porrum*; cf. Hehn 193ff., 206f., Stadler in *RE* s.v. *Lauch* 986.61ff., André 32f., 201f.).

133 (128K)

Meineke 3.437 (1), Kock 2.343, Edmonds 2.434, Kassel–Austin 2.97. The fr. opens with the question 'And why should we mention further/ additionally (ἔθ' v. 2) the men who always sell figs in their baskets?' The presence of ἔτι here indicates that the fr. is part of a longer tirade made by some disillusioned speaker, whether householder or slave, against the practices of various tradesmen. It would have been a reasonable guess that the attacks on fishmongers in frs. 130(125K) and 131(126K) came earlier in the same scene, even if there had been no grounds for supposing that Plautus' *Aulularia*, with just such a lengthy tirade by Megadorus in III.v, could have been adapted from Alexis' Λέβης (cf. introduction to the play and Appendix III). – On the theme of dishonest tradesmen, cf. introduction to fr. 9.

3 συρίχοις: baskets in which figs were harvested (cf. Hesych. s.v. συρίσκος, Theognost. *Can.* 2.23.20 Cramer on ὑρισσός, Pollux 10.129 with σύρισσος). In place of συρίχοις here (so A at Ath. 3.76d: Epit. omits the fr.) Dindorf tentatively suggested ὑρίχοις (? assuming dittography after τοῖς), a form nowhere transmitted (LSJ wrongly cite Ar. fr. 581(569K).5, cited by A at Ath. 9.372c with the spelling ὑρίσους, which scans, is recognised by Phot. s.v. ὑρισοί, and may be explained as a metrically convenient by-form of ὑρισσός (Hesych. s.v., Theognost. *loc. cit.*); ὑρίχοις there is an unnecessary conjecture by Porson, *Adv.* 109). The wide variety of forms and spellings attested for the one object (also e.g. ἀρίσκος Hesych. s.v., ἀρριχίς Ath. 4.139c, ἄρριχος Ar. *Av.* 1309 etc., ἄρσιχος Diod. Sic. 20.41 etc., ὕρισχος Phryn. *Praep. Soph.* 116.4 de Borries, ὑρρίς Zonaras s.v., ὑρράδα Theognost. *loc. cit.*) may perhaps be partly due to faults in transmission, but is also likely to reflect the word's subliterary ambience (Frisk 2.822 and Chantraine 2.1071 s.v.; cf. also Lobeck, *Prol. Path.* 337, K. Latte, *De saltationibus graecorum capita quinque* (Giessen 1913) 106 n. 2); on the co-existence of forms with aspirates and initial sigma, see especially R. Hiersche, *Untersuchungen zur Frage der Tenues Aspiratae im Indogermanischen* (Wiesbaden 1964) 222, Schwyzer 1.217, 303.

κάτωθε: Musurus' correction of A's unmetrical κάτωθεν, which was either a slip of the pen (assimilation to the ending of the following word) or a pedantic attempt to restore the common form with final nu. ἄνωθε, ἐπάνωθε, ἔσωθε, κάτωθε, etc., arising perhaps by analogy with πρόσθε, occur as metrically convenient variants in Euripides (*Alc.* 463 but -θεν BVP, *Hcld.* 42), Aristophanes (*Eccl.* 698, a reading at *Pax* 313 acknowledged by Σ) and 4th-century comedy (also Eubulus 15(16K),1, cited by Ath. 15.666c with κάτω θέμενοι A, κ. θέμενος Epit., corrected to κάτωθέ μοι by Musurus), but also in 4th-century inscriptions (καθύπερθε Meisterhans–Schwyzer 146). Cf. also F. Selvers, *De mediae comoediae graecae sermone* (Diss. Münster 1909) 14, M. Lejeune, *Les Adverbes grecs en -θεν* (Paris 1939) 304, 325f., Schwyzer 1.628, Hunter on Eubulus *loc. cit.*

3–5 Cf. Francis Bacon's report of a remark made by Queen Elizabeth I (*Apophthegmes New and Old*, in J. Spedding and others, *The Works of Francis Bacon* 7 (London 1879) 133 no. 54), that the great officers of state were accustomed to treat her 'like strawberry wives, that laid two or three great strawberries at the mouth of their pot, and all the rest were little ones'.

4 τὰ σκληρὰ καὶ μοχθηρά: Musurus deleted A's second τὰ, added unmetrically before μοχθηρά by a scribe perhaps unaware of shared articles in such collocations (cf. Gildersleeve, *Syntax* 2.277f., Jebb on S. *OC* 606, Fraenkel on A. *Ag.* 314).

6, 8 ἔδωκεν ... ἀπέδοτο: presumably gnomic aorists.

7 The custom of carrying small change in one's mouth, which is often mentioned in Attic comedy (Ar. *Vesp.* 791 and Σ, *Av.* 502f., *Eccl.* 818, frs. 3, 48, 625(614K); cf. Theophr. *Char.* 6), arose doubtless because of the absence of pockets in ancient dress and the minuscule size of low–value coins (silver obols were no bigger than fish scales, Ar. *Vesp.* 791; an eighth of an obol was the size of a pin-head). Cf. H. Michell, *The Economics of Ancient Greece* (Cambridge 1940) 328.

COMMENTARY

8 ἐρίν': Ath. 3.76d–e cites this fr. in a section which identifies ἐρινός as the wild fig tree and ἐρινόν as its fruit. This is generally true, but Ath. (as also LSJ) fails to note a further use of ἐρινά as the immature fruit of the cultivated fig (*Ficus carica*) which drop after May showers from the trees before ripening (so here probably, cf. Pickard-Cambridge, *GCP* 190; Theophr. *HP* 3.3.8 and 7.3, 4.14.5, *CP* 2.9.5ff., 5.9.12; Olck in *RE* s.v. *Feige* 2105.26ff., Pearson on S. fr. 181).

ἀπέδοτο ... πωλεῖν: see comm. on 130(125K).4.

ὀμνύων: the thematic form of the present participle prevails in later comedy (also Antiphanes 237(241K).1, Amphis 42.1, Alexis 165(160K), Men. fr. 524, cf. e.g. Dem. 54.40, 57.56 (but -ύντας A) ~ ὀμνύς Ar. *Nub.* 1135, cf. 1241, but -μειγνύων *Plut.* 719, see van Leeuwen and Holzinger *ad loc.*). Cf. also Schwyzer 1.642ff., 698f., my comm. on Alexis 103(98K).19.

134 (129K)

Meineke 1.400, 3.440 (introduction to his comm. on fr. v), Kock 2.343, Edmonds 2.434, Kassel–Austin 2.97; cf. Rankin, ΜΑΓΕΙΡΟΙ 17ff., Körte in *RE* s.v. *Poseidippos* 1, 427.25ff., Webster, *SLGC* 71, A. Giannini, *Acme* 13 (1960) 138 and 159 n. 220, Dohm, *Mageiros* 19ff., 67f., J. C. B. Lowe, *Class. Ant.* 4 (1985) 71ff. Ath. 14.661d claims that in this play (if Meineke's correction of A's Λεβητίωι to Λέβητι here is accepted, 1.400: see introduction to Λέβης) we have evidence that ἡ μαγειρικὴ τέχνη ἐπιτήδευμα ἦν ἐλευθέρων, because Alexis' cook is presented there as πολίτης ... τις οὐκ ἀπινής. These words are usually interpreted as an objective, unemotional assessment, based on knowledge of the play, but I prefer to read them as a paraphrase or loose quotation of words actually spoken by one or two characters in one of its scenes, and so tied to subjective and perhaps impassioned views expressed in a particular dramatic situation. The argument for this lies partly in the rhythm of the Greek phrases cited above (they would slip easily into the comic trimeter), and partly in their form and content.

(i) ἀπινής ('spotless') is a ἅπαξ λεγόμενον, but correctly formed (cf. e.g. δυσπινής, εὐπινής, κακοπινής, πολυπινής in Attic; Schweighaeuser, *Animadv.* 7.680), and conjectures which remove either it (e.g. ταπεινός Gulick, ἀπηνής Valckenaer and ἀγεννής Cobet in Peppink, *Observ.* 89, ἀγενής Kaibel citing and dismissing Schoenemann's κακοπινής) or the negative οὐκ (despite the textual confusion caused elsewhere by double negatives, cf. Gomme–(Andrewes)–Dover on Thuc. 7.75.4) are unnecessary, stemming from an incorrect assumption that the words in Ath. here are an objective description of the cook. More probably they come from a scene in Λέβης where the cook had called attention to his status as a free man directly after or before another character claimed that he wasn't a

ΛΕΒΗΣ

spotless example of citizenship. The confrontation between an enraged Euclio and the cook Congrio in Plaut. *Aul.* III.ii would provide the right sort of background for such an exchange (a cook under assault might well protest his citizenship), even if there were no grounds for believing that *Aul.* could have been adapted from Alexis' Λέβης (see introduction to the play and Appendix III).

(ii) Cooks in later Greek comedy frequently make protestations about their τέχνη and its status (e.g. Men. *Dysk.* 646 ἱεροπρεπής πώς ἐστιν ἡμῶν ἡ τέχνη, Demetrius II 1.3 καπνιζομένη τυραννὶς αὕτη 'σθ' ἡ τέχνη, cf. Alexis 153(149K).1ff., Dionysius 2.30ff., 3.4, Nicomachus 1.11ff., Sotades 1.34, Rankin 90ff.), and some such remark by the Λέβης cook might have been the source for Ath.'s remark that ἡ μαγειρικὴ τέχνη was a profession of free men.

In 4th-century comedy the μάγειρος was normally a free man hired in the agora to butcher and cook for a particular occasion (cf., in addition to the works cited at the head of comm. for this fr., G. Berthiaume, *Les Rôles du mágeiros* (Leiden 1982)), but he was typically presented as associating with slaves (e.g. Men. *Asp.*, *Dysk.*), and despite the self-aggrandising claims which he makes on stage (and are made occasionally for him elsewhere, e.g. by Heraclides of Syracuse and Glaucus of Locris in Ath. 14.661e), his status was low (cf. especially Theophr. *Char.* 6).

According to Ath. 14.658f slave μάγειροι (sc. hired professionals, as opposed to those household slaves who helped to prepare all kinds of meal, cf. Men. *Sam.* 221ff.; Rankin 13, Lowe 76 and n. 28) were featured in later Greek comedy only by Posidippus (frs. 2, 25(23K)). Such evidence as we have by and large endorses Ath.'s statement (cf. especially Rankin 17ff., Dohm 19ff., Lowe 75), although Karion in Men. *Epitr.*, whose status is not made clear in the extant frs., has a name bestowed elsewhere in comedy on slaves (certainly Ar. *Plut.*, probably also Euphron 9(10K), where Karion is apprentice to a (? free) cook). Posidippus may have been reflecting a change in social conditions, due perhaps (as Ath. himself suggests) to the Macedonian conquests; it is notable that names of slave μάγειροι first appear on Athenian manumission inscriptions c. 330 (*IG* ii².1555.21f., 1570.36, 90, cf. M. N. Tod, *Ann. BSA* 8 (1901/2) 208 and *Epigraphica* 12 (1950) 8).[1]

---

[1] The status of cooks in Roman comedy is not strictly relevant to the present discussion (an up-to-date, full and judicious account is provided by Lowe 71ff.), but in view of my suggestion that Λέβης may have been the model for Plaut. *Aul.*, a word about the cooks in the latter play is in place. Their status is not consistently presented; at 309f. Anthrax says that he and Congrio are both slaves, but at 456ff. Congrio threatens Euclio with legal action as if he were a free man. The two cooks were

COMMENTARY

Λευκαδία ἢ Δραπέται

Three[1] brief frs. are cited: 135(130K) and 136(131K) with the lemma Ἄλεξις ἐν Λευκαδίᾳ (Ath. 11.498e, Pollux 10.144 respectively), 137(132K) with Ἄλεξις ἐν Λευκαδίᾳ (λυκ- A: corr. Musurus) ἢ Δραπέταις (Ath. 3.95a: on the possible implications of alternative titles, see introduction to Ἀγωνὶς ἢ Ἱππίσκος). Frs. 137(132K) and 135(130K), with their mentions of food service and a cup, may perhaps come from the same speech (see introduction to 137); 136(131K) is an order (presumably to his slave) by a soldier or some other young man of military or hunting inclinations (cf. Moschion in Men. *Sam.* 659f.); but the relation of these frs. and their speakers to the girl from Leucas and the runaways (presumably slaves: cf. Nesselrath, *MK* 287 n. 10) of the title is unclear. The play is perhaps most likely to have been a New-Comedy type of intrigue in which the girl had some role (not necessarily major or amatory: cf. Körte in *RE* s.v. *Komödie (mittlere)* 1264.53ff.) more or less analogous to that of one or other of those numerous women in Alexis whose place of origin forms the title of their plays (Ἀτθίς, Ἀχαῖς, Βρεττία, Κνιδία, Λημνία, perhaps Ὀλυνθία: q.v.). Diphilus and Menander each wrote a Λευκαδία, Antiphanes a Λευκάδιος,

---

hired in a typically Athenian way (280, 448, 452, 455, 457) to prepare the wedding-feast for Megadorus and Euclio's daughter; they enter, again like their Greek counterparts (e.g. Men. *Dysk.* 393ff., cf. *Sam.* 399ff.) with lambs to sacrifice and cook; and their scenes contain motifs characteristic in later Greek comedy (the complaint about cooking for a niggard 335ff., pilfering 342ff., orders given to assistants 398f., references to borrowing 390f., 400f.; Lowe 87). The presence of Congrio is essential to the plot, since it leads to Euclio's decision to remove the pot of gold from his house and hide it elsewhere. It seems certain that the role of Congrio at least was taken from the Greek original; Lowe's suggestion (p. 88) that Plautus altered his status (albeit incompletely) from free hireling to slave, in order to accommodate it to a situation normal in contemporary Rome, is persuasive. Whether both cooks featured in the Greek original as professional equals, however, is uncertain. Plautus could have added the second one to increase his opportunities for humour, or substituted him for a cook's assistant (? the παῖς of Alexis 129(124K).14), or (most probably) for a household slave working in tandem with the μάγειρος (like Getas with Sikon in Men. *Dysk.*).

[1] Ath. 7.322c cites also Ἄλεξις ἐν Λεύκῃ (fr. 138(133K)), where the title might be a transcriptional error induced by an abbreviation of Λευκαδίᾳ in the parent MS (cf. p. 395 n. 1 and introductions to Ἀποκοπτόμενος, Δίδυμοι, Κύπριος); but because Λεύκη is comprehensible as a title in its own right, it is foolish to assume corruption without further evidence.

Amphis either a Λευκάδιος or a Λευκαδία.[1] Menander's play was adapted by Turpilius in his *Leucadia* (pp. 113ff. Ribbeck, 29ff. Rychlewska (Leipzig 1971): Servius Danielis on V. *Aen.* 3.279 couples the names of the two playwrights in a comment perhaps influenced by Men. fr. 258, and *P.Oxyrhynchus* 4024, plausibly identified as Men. Λευκαδία by its first editor, P. J. Parsons, *The Oxyrhynchus Papyri* 60 (London 1994) 42ff., clearly at vv.2f. preserves the Greek original of Turpilius, *Leucadia* fr. XI)[2]; its scene was Leucas (fr. 258 from the prologue may have followed a statement about its location, cf. *Dysk.* 1ff.), and its subject almost certainly the adventures of ordinary people (cf. Wilamowitz, *Sappho und Simonides* (Berlin 1913) 25f., Webster, *SM* 57 n. 2, *IM* 161f.), not a parody of the myth of Phaon and Sappho (so first O. Ribbeck, *JCP* 69 (1884) 34ff., followed by Edmonds 2.435 note a and Rychlewska; but such travesties are avoided by Menander, cf. Körte in *RE* s.v. *Menandros* 9, 720.44ff. and *Komödie (neue)* 1270.13ff., W. G. Arnott, *Gnomon* 40 (1968) 33, Nesselrath, *MK* 202), although Wilamowitz's suggestion that Menander may have transformed incidents of the myth into experiences of ordinary folk is appealing.

135 (130K)

Meineke 3.442 (II), Kock 2.344, Edmonds 2.434, Kassel–Austin 2.97. Tragic rhythm and high poetic diction are characteristic features of comic descriptions of feasts and drinking-bouts (cf. introduction to 124(119K)).

γεραιοῖς χείλεσιν: whose 'aged lips': the cup's, or the drinker's? In the absence of any governing verb (such as προσφέρω) we have no means of telling. γεραιός is normally used only of people or their animate parts (A. *Ag.* 710 Πριάμου πόλις γεραιά is clearly no exception, *pace* LSJ s.v.), but such a restriction hardly holds for comic flights of pseudo-dithyrambic fancy, where e.g. γέρων is applied adjectivally to wine (Alexis 172(167K).5, Epinicus 1.6, Eubulus 121(124K).2, Men. *Dysk.* 946; hence Th. Bergk's conjecture γεραιοῦ here, see Meineke 5.ccviii).

---

[1] Ath. 7.277c quotes the one fr. (26) with the lemma Ἄμφις ἐν Λευκάδι. At Alexis 136(131K) Λευκαδία and at Antiphanes 140(142K) Λευκαδίῳ are identically abbreviated or corrupted in Pollux by BL at 10.144 and AF at 6.66 respectively. One of these two titles is more likely for Amphis than the transmitted Λευκάς, in view of the rarity of place names and the frequency of ethnics as titles in later Greek comedy.

[2] This evidence is persuasive, but is ignored by – or was unavailable to – those who prefer to link Turpilius' play with the Λευκαδία of either Diphilus (G. Coppola, *Atene e Roma* 5 (1924) 185ff.) or even – with no

μέγα σκύφος: Ath. 11.498e cites σκύφος here as a third-declension neuter form, along with (in Attic) Ion trag. fr. 26, Archippus 7 and Epigenes 3. At 498a he rightly observes (cf. LSJ s.v. σκύφος) that ὁ σκύφος (2nd declension) occurs side by side with it in Athenian authors (e.g. Eur. *Cycl.* masc. 256, 556, neut. 390, 411, cf. Seaford's edition on 390); how then can we be sure that Ath. or his source text was not corrupted by haplography from μέγας σκύφος?

The σκύφος is identified as a deep cup, frequently with two horizontally set handles; cf. Richter–Milne, *Shapes* 26f. and figs. 170–7, B. A. Sparkes and L. Talcott, *Pots and Pans of Classical Athens* (Princeton 1958) fig. 6, and *Agora* XII.81ff. and figs. 4, 20 and pls.14–17, nos. 303–77.

136 (131K)

Meineke 3.442 (III), Kock 2.344, Edmonds 2.434, Kassel–Austin 2.98. Pollux 10.144 cites the fr. in a section on στρατιωτοῦ... σκεύη; on possible dramatic implications see introduction to Λευκαδία.

The MSS read φέρε τὴν (ABL: τὸν S) σιβύνην. The meaning is clear ('bring my spear': σ. is most commonly a hunting spear, used e.g. against wild boar: Hesych. s.v. συ μ βίνης, corr. M. Schmidt, but carried by a guard in Diod. Sic. 20.33; a non-Greek word, perhaps of Thracian or Phrygian origin, so Frisk 2.700 s.v. σιβύνη, but Illyrian, according to Paulus in Festus p. 453 Lindsay s.v. *sybinam*), but (a) gender, (b) spelling and (c) – if, as I believe, the transmision is correct here – scansion vary. (a) ἡ σιβύνη also Ephippus Olynth. in Ath. 12.537e = *FGrH* 126 F 5, Hesych. and *Suda* s.v., cf. the references for ζυβίνη below; ὁ σιβύνης (Doric -νας) Antipater (Thess.) 32, Meleager 5 Gow–Page = *Anth. Pal.* 6.93, 7.421 respectively. (b) σιβύνη(ς) generally (the passages cited above except Hesych.; also Callixenus in Ath. 5.201b = *FGrH* 627 F 2, Diod. Sic. 18.27, 20.33), but also συβίνη (with metathesis: *P.Cair. Zen.* 362.34, 242 BC, for protection against wild cattle), ζιβύνη (e.g. LXX *Is.* 2.4, Philo mech. *Excerpta* 92.44 Diels–Schramm, Hesych. s.v.) and ? ζηβήνη (so Hesych. s.v., but this may be an etacistic error for ζιβύνη). (c) The υ scans short in *Anth. Pol.* 6.93, 7.421, but would be long here in Alexis (unless the copyist omitted τά before πλατύλογχα, cf. Blaydes, *Adv.* 2.160). This metrical anomaly persuaded Kassel here to conjecture (and Kassel–Austin to print) σιγύνην, which (in its various forms) always[1] scans with the υ long (Ap. Rhod. 2.99,

---

evidence apart from the existence of *Leucadia* and *Fugitiui* as uncoupled titles in Turpilius – Alexis (Casaubon, *Animadv.* 181).

[1] The *Suda* s.v. σιγύνη cites Antipater Thess. 32.2 Gow–Page = *Anth. Pal.* 6.93.2 with σιγύνην at the end of a pentameter, but this is an error for σιβύνην (so P in *Anth. Pal.*: see Gow *ad loc.*).

Lycophron 556, Macedonius and Agathias in *Anth. Pol.* 6.176.1 and 7.578.5 respectively, Oppian *Cyn.* 1.152). σιγύνης is also primarily a hunting spear (so the cited passages apart from Ap. Rhod., where it is used in battle; note Hesych. s.v. σίγυνοι· τὰ ξυστὰ δόρατα ἢ τοὺς ὁλοσιδήρους ἄκοντας, similarly Σ [Pl.] *Amat.* 135e p. 111 Greene), a foreign word (Cyprian according to Hdt. 5.9 and Arist. *Poet.* 21, 1457^{b}6, but associated with the Sigynnae tribe of Scythia according to Σ Ap. Rhod. 4.320, cf. Frisk 2.702 s.v. σιγύν(ν)ης) which varies in gender and spelling (-ύνης masc. Hdt. 5.9, Oppian; -υνος masc. Macedonius; -υννος Ap. Rhod., *Suda* s.v. σιγύνη; -υνον neut. Arist., Agathias, -υμνον Lycophron), but the absence of strong evidence for a feminine form (only in *Suda* s.v. σιγύνη, where the two examples cited in support have τὸν σιγύνην and σίγυνον respectively, = *Anth. Pal.* 6.93.2 and 176.1) militates against Kassel's conjecture here. Still less convincingly Herwerden, *Coll. Crit.* 125 conjectured συβήνην ('quiver', e.g. Ar. *Thesm.* 1197, 1215, cf. Threatte 1.167); σιβύνην and συβήνην might easily be confused by scribes, but in later Greek and Roman comedy real and would-be soldiers carry spears (Men. *Kol.* 31, *Pk.* 527, fr. 282, Apollodorus Gel. 5) and swords (Men. *Mis.* 178, 276, fr. 6 Sandbach, *Sam.* 659f., 687, 720, fr. 793 Körte, Philemon 73(70K), Apollodorus Gel. 5, Plaut. *MG* 1423), not bows and arrows.

πλατύλογχα: by closing the citation here Pollux prevents our knowing (cf. *IG*ii².1487.98, end of 4th century) whether πλατύλογχα is used as a noun ('broad-pointed javelins') or as an adjective with its noun (? ἀκόντια: so J. Toup, *Emendationes in Suidam et Hesychium et alios lexicographos Graecos* 4 (ed. R. Porson, Oxford 1790) 243, cf. Ar. frs. 492(476K), 493(477K), possibly variant quotations of the same fr.: so Dindorf, but see Kassel–Austin *ad loc.*) coming in the unquoted context.

137 (132K)

Meineke 3.442 (1), Kock 2.344, Edmonds 2.434, Kassel–Austin 2.98. The line as Ath. 3.95a cites it is a Choerilean (D — D: Wilamowitz, *Griechische Verskunst* (Berlin 1921) 71f. n. 1, 431, cf. J. W. White, *The Verse of Greek Comedy* (London 1912) 220, R. Pretagostini, *Dioniso* 57 (1987) 254f.), which occurs elsewhere in comedy at Ar. *Nub.* 474–5 (choral lyrics, close of dactylo-epitrite system) and Antiphanes 172.3,4,6(174.2,5,6K) (alternating with troch. tetr. cat.). As the Antiphanes fr. (i) describes a feast in elaborately poetic diction (cf. Nesselrath, *MK* 244 n. 12, 253f., 262 n. 56) and (ii) consistently has word end after the bridge (D —// D) just like Alexis here, it seems reasonable to suppose that the Alexis Choerilean is not an adventitious result of corruptly cited, much resolved iambics (so Casaubon, *Animadv.* 181 ... ἧκε καὶ περίκομμά τι, Blaydes, *Adv.* 1.110 ... ἧκε καὶ | περικομμάτιον), but intended, and that the original contexts of the two frs. were similar. If Alexis 137(132K) was part of an actor's lyrical narrative in a form similar to that of Antiphanes 172(174K), Alexis 135(130) could also have belonged to it (? as part of a troch. tetr.).

χορδαρίου τόμος: comic poets strictly follow the Attic rule (Phryn. *Ecl.* s.v. τέμαχος p. 61 Fischer, cf. Rutherford, *NP* 72ff. and my comm. on Alexis 92(88K)) that τόμοι are slices of meat or cakes, τεμάχη only of fish (cf. Alexis 191(186K).8). χορδῆς τόμοι are sausages made (just as now) by encasing tubes of mince in intestinal skin and drawing the ends together (cf. com. adesp. fr. 289b.7f. Austin), e.g. Cratinus 205(192K), Axionicus 8.4, Mnesimachus 4.14f., com. adesp. fr. 244.226 Austin, cf. Antiphanes 73(72K); also ἀλλᾶντος τόμος Pherecrates 113(108K).8, Eubulus 14(15K).7, Mnesimachus 4.14, πυοῦ τ. Pherecrates 113(108K).19, γαστρὸς τ. Ar. *Equ.* 1179. Cf. also M. Treu, *Philologus* 102 (1958) 217.

περικομματίων, A's reading here (Ath. 3.95a: Epit. cites only the first word of the fr.), should be retained and not altered to -άτιον (so first Meineke, printed by Kassel–Austin); at the end of so brief a fr., the genitive could well have depended on a word in the unquoted following context. περίκομμα (sing.: Alexis 180(175K), Damoxenus 2.48, Dionysius 3.14, possibly also Ar. fr. 128(130K).2 where it is the reading of A in Pollux 6.69; plur.: Ar. *Equ.* 372, Metagenes 6.7, Men. *Sam.* 293) and its diminutive in -άτιον (sing.: Athenion 1.31; plur.: also Ar. *Equ.* 770) denote chopped up scraps of meat which were often cooked with the main joint or whole animal (cf. Σ Ar. *Equ.* 770). See also Dohm, *Mageiros* 33.

Λεύκη

Breitenbach 167. Ath. 7.322c introduces fr. 138(133K) with Ἄλεξις ἐν Λεύκῃ. If the title is not a corruption for Λευκαδία (see introduction to that play, p. 394 n. 1: the cook who speaks most of fr. 138 would fit easily into a play that apparently included an elaborate description of food and possibly drink), it can be interpreted as (i) an ordinary girl's name (in Athens *IG* ii².1469.165 320/319, 2934 mid–4th century; cf. Breitenbach), (ii) the name of a nymph abducted to the underworld by Pluto and metamorphosed after her death into a white poplar from which Heracles took his garland (Servius on V. *Ecl.* 7.61; cf. Stoll in Roscher s.v. *Leuke* 1, 1986.65ff.), (iii) an Ionian town on the north side of the gulf of Smyrna (Bürchner in *RE* s.v. Λεύκη 6, 2209.18ff.) or (iv) the island to which Achilles and other mythical figures were transported as shades (cf. Σ Pind. *Nem.* 4.79, Eur. *Andr.* 1262, *IT* 435; Escher in *RE* s.v. *Achilleus* 240.19ff., Stoll in Roscher s.v. *Leuke* 2, 1987.6ff., Robert, *GH* 3.2.1.1194ff., Breitenbach). The first three of these are the least likely; Leuke does not occur elsewhere as a character name in comedy or related literature; we

ΛΕΥΚΗ

have no evidence that the myth of the nymph was pre-Hellenistic; and in later Greek comedy ethnics, not town names, are standard in titles. If Leuke were the island of ghosts, at least two possibilities (not mutually exclusive) open up: myth travesty (? Achilles' amatory links with Helen, Iphigeneia, Medea) and utopian fantasy of a type still popular in the first half of the 4th century (cf. H. C. Baldry, *G and R* 22 (1953) 49ff., Dohm, *Mageiros* 61ff., W. Fauth, *Wien. Stud.* 86 (1973) 39ff., Hunter on Eubulus 74).

In the one fr. a μάγειρος (so identified by Ath.) describes the way to prepare scad for the table. Although in later comedy cooks are typically associated with the adventures of ordinary families, such characters were no strangers in myth burlesque: e.g. Aeolus may have been presented as a cook in Aristophanes' Αἰολοσίκων, Oedipus as a parasite in Eubulus' Οἰδίπους (contrast Webster, *SLGC* 18f., 85, Hunter's introduction to the latter play pp. 161f., Nesselrath, *MK* 235 n. 155, 311).

138 (133K)

Meineke 3.442, Kock 2.344, Edmonds 2.434, Kassel–Austin 2.98. Ath. 7.322c cites a dialogue (the opening of v. 2 first given to a second speaker in Daléchamp's Latin version) between a cook and an assistant (Dohm, *Mageiros* 89f., 102, 125, A. Giannini, *Acme* 13 (1960) 160), house slave or his hirer (cf. Nesselrath, *MK* 300f. n. 40, 302 n. 44), in which the cook expounds with confident authority a recipe which has every appearance of authenticity (see on v. 1). Recipes were a standard feature of cook scenes in Alexis' time (e.g. his frs. 84, 129(124K), 191(186K), 192(187K), Antiphanes 216(217K), 221(222K), Philemon 82(79K), Sotades 1; Rankin, ΜΑΓΕΙΡΟΙ 86ff., Dohm, *Mageiros* 125f.); no other comic fr., however, preserves so well the spare directness of style (with its repeated participles and imperatives) of contemporary cookery-books (cf. e.g. Artemidorus' recipe for ματτύη in Ath. 14.663d–e, Bilabel, *Ops.* 6ff.).

1 τὸν σαῦρον: scad or horse-mackerel (*Caranx* or *Trachurus trachurus*) and other visually similar species (e.g. *T. mediterraneus*); cf. Thompson, *Fishes* 230, Strömberg, *Fischnamen* 121, Palombi–Santorelli 116ff., Campbell, *Guide* 276f., Davidson, *Seafood* 101). Their flesh is coarser than generally similar fish like mackerel, which themselves 'tend to be dry, and need stuffing' (B. Worsley-Gough, *Cooking Ahead* (London 1957) 48). The stuffing prescribed by Alexis' cook differs significantly from those in modern cookery-books only by its inclusion of cheese, but cf. Philemon 82(79K).5f. (a fish) οὐ πεφαρμακευμένον | τύροισιν, and Mithaecus' recipe for *cépole rougeâtre* in Ath. 7.325f.

2 ἀλλ' ἂν διδάσκῃς: the response is typically elliptic, '(No,) but if you act as instructor, (then I'll know)', where ἀλλά introduces (as commonly) an answer which qualifies or opposes the previous speaker's question or statement. Cf. e.g. Eur. *Alc.* 43f. καὶ νοσφιεῖς με τοῦδε δευτέρου νεκροῦ; | :: ἀλλ' οὐδ' ἐκεῖνον πρὸς βίαν σ' ἀφειλόμην, S. *Ant.* 1251ff., *Trach.* 978ff., Pl. *Resp.* 3.396b. Curiously Denniston fails to insert this passage of Alexis in its proper section (*GP* 7, §3 (i)), but misinterprets it as an isolated freak (19 §6 (ii, b)).

2–3 The first three tasks are to remove the βράγχια (not 'fins' but 'gills', the word's only acceptable biological meaning, *pace* LSJ and Gow on Theoc. 11.54;[1] note here that the cook advises 'taking off' the βράγχια, which is possible with the bare hands if these are gills, but 'fins' have to be cut or chopped away with knife or chopper, cf. v. 3), wash the fish and cut off τὰς ἀκάνθας τὰς κύκλῳ. The scad has a spiny ridge of plate-like scales extending laterally over the whole length of the body, along with a full complement of fins, some of which (and particularly the first dorsal) are hard and prickly. These together are presumably meant by τὰς ἀκάνθας τὰς κύκλῳ here, but partly because they go all round the fish, and partly because ἄκανθα on its own might seem ambiguous (see LSJ s.v. 5, 6: in such a context ἄκανθαι might be either external prickles or – especially in the singular – internal backbone, cf. comm. on fr. 49(48K).3), Alexis has added τὰς κύκλῳ to make his meaning clear to those members of the audience who had failed to observe that so far the cook had not split the fish open to reach the backbone. Cf. also Aelian *NA* 16.13.

The same preliminaries appear as orders in e.g. Plaut. *Aul.* 398f. *Dromo, desquama piscis. tu, Machaerio,* | *congrum, murenam exdorsa quantum potest, Stich.* 359, Ter. *Ad.* 378.

περικόψας... κύκλῳ: this dative, used adverbially (= 'round'), often (as here and fr. 179(174K).1 κύκλῳ ... περιτρέχειν) but not invariably (cf. 63(62K).5, 101(96K).1) occurs alongside a verb compounded with περι- (LSJ s.v. κύκλος 2).

4 παράσχισον: 'split lengthwise': the method used for filleting fish (also Epicharmus fr. 164) and embalming corpses (Hdt. 2.86, Diod. Sic. 1.91).

4–5 διαπτύξας θ' ὅλον τῷ σιλφίῳ μάστιξον: 'having filleted it completely, beat it with the silphium'. Opening the fish so that it can be spread out flat (= διαπτύξας) obviously involves removing the backbone. The

---

[1] This secondary meaning 'fins' is alleged on the sole evidence of 'Arion' 1.4 Bergk = fr. lyr. adesp. 21.4 Page (a second-rate piece of verse dated by Page to the 4th century), which attaches βράγχια to dolphins. Dolphins have fins but (as mammals) no gills. This fact, however, does not entitle a lexicographer to assume that βρ. elsewhere and in other contexts may mean 'fins'; all it proves is that one poet misidentified as gills a dolphin's flippers (which emerge from the side of the body roughly in the same place).

second operation, elsewhere in comedy described as σιλφίῳ σφενδονῶν
(Axionicus 8.3f.) and σ. πυκνῷ πατάξας (Alexis 193(188K).4f., see comm.),
requires the cook to rub the fish vigorously with the stalk or root (presumably: but see comm. on 132(127K).5) of the silphium plant, in order to
impregnate the fish with its pungent juice, just as the modern cook rubs
toasted bread with garlic when making *croûtons* for soup. μάστιξον displeased
some 19th-century scholars (Kock *ad loc.* and 3.742, G. A. Papavasileiou,
Athena 1 (1889) 214f., Blaydes, *Adv.* 1.110, 2.160, H. van Herwerden,
Mnemosyne 14 (1886) 188 and *Coll. Crit.* 125) as an alleged epicism out of
place in such a context, but (side by side with the regular Attic μαστιγῶ)
forms of μαστίζω occur in both Attic comedy (also Eupolis 83(72K) ὦ
ῥύμβε μαστίξας (or -μβ' ἐμάστ.) ἐμέ, so not lyrics) and *Koine* prose (e.g.
Lucian *Tim.* 23, *Pro Imag.* 24, N.T. *Act. Ap.* 22.25, Plut. *Alex.* 42, *Sull.* 29);
thus μάστιξον is acceptable here (cf. W. G. Rutherford, *JCP Supp.* 13
(1847) 365f. and *NP* 10f., Herwerden, *Obs. Crit.* 70f., and O. Kaehler, *Woch.
Klass. Phil.* 2 (1885) 901f., Kassel–Austin on the Eupolis fr. cited), to be
explained as either a colloquial by-form or just possibly an example of the
idiosyncratic vocabulary affected by real-life Athenian cooks already in
the 5th century (ῥηματίοις μαγειρικοῖς Ar. *Equ.* 216) and then exploited so
often in later comedy that it became a typical feature of their presentation:
e.g. Antiphanes 216(217K) (tragic language), Epinicus 1 (dithyrambic),
Damoxenus 2, Posidippus 1 and (if one of the speakers is a cook)
Antiphanes 169(171K). Sikon in Men. *Dysk.* (e.g. 505 χυτρόγαυλον, 515
βεβωλοκόπηκεν, 517 σφαιρομαχοῦσ') shows an equal if less blatantly
underlined fondness for unusual words (A. Giannini, *Acme* 13 (1960) 190,
W. G. Arnott, *G and R* 15 (1968) 24f. and 17 (1970) 56, F. H. Sandbach,
Entr. Hardt 16 (1970) 119f.). Cf. also comm. on 129(124K) (introduction),
153(149K).16ff., Dohm, *Mageiros* 195ff. with special reference to Sosipater
1. I leave till last fr. 1 of Straton (preserved in two versions: Kassel–Austin
7.618ff., cf. Kassel, *ZPE* 14 (1974) 121ff.); in it complaints are made at
great length about a particular cook's obsession with Homeric vocabulary
(cf. Giannini 164f., Dohm 198ff.). Here the influence of contemporary
gastronomic poems like the Ἡδυπάθεια by Archestratus of Gela (*SH*
pp. 46ff.: written in mock-epic style) has plausibly been suggested (cf.
Ribbeck, *Alazon* 21f.).

5 εὖ τε καὶ καλῶς is Dindorf's correction of the transmitted εὖ γε κ. κ.
(A, Epit.). In this context εὖ γε could be interpreted only as an interruption by the second speaker (cf. e.g. Men. *Dysk.* 300f., *Epitr.* 528, *Her.* 72; see
'False or doubtful attributions' V: *P.Berlin* 11771, comm. on v. 26),
ironically applauding the cook's graphic previous phrase; cf. Denniston,
GP 127 on the particle's 'exclamatory force'. Yet although εὖ γε frequently
on its own and occasionally with emphatic expansions (e.g. εὖ γε ... εὖ
σφόδρ' Nicostratus 7(8K).1, εὖ γ' εὖ γε Ar. *Equ.* 470, ὑπέρευγε Men. *Epitr.*

COMMENTARY

525) is found in comedy and prose dialogues, the expression εὖ γε καὶ καλῶς is unparalleled, while εὖ (τε) καὶ καλῶς (e.g. Pl. *Lach.* 188a, *Resp.* 6.503d with τε, Ar. *Eccl.* 253 without) and καλῶς (τε) καὶ εὖ (e.g. Pl. *Euthyd.* 276c, *Parm.* 128b with τε, *Charm.* 172a, *Protag.* 319e without) are standard formulas in such literature. Cf. Lobeck, *Paralipomena* 65, D. Tarrant, *CQ* 40 (1946) 109, H. Thesleff, *Studies on Intensification in Early and Classical Greek* (Helsinki 1954) 186f.

6 ἁλσί τ᾽ ἠδ᾽ ὀριγάνῳ is the united reading of A and Epit. (ἠδοριγάνῳ C), where τ᾽ ἠδέ (if correctly transmitted) will possibly be a second instance of this cook's use of Homeric words. τ᾽ ἠδέ (τε ... ἠδέ) is a collocation common to Homer (*Il.* 2.206, 262, 9.99, 12.61, 17.335), 5th-century elegy (Ion fr. 30.1 West) and lyric (Pind. *Ol.* 13.43f., fr. 168.5 Snell–Maehler), Attic tragedy (e.g. A. *Sept.* 862, *Pers.* 26, *Eum.* 188, S. frs. 386, 549 Pearson, perhaps *Ant.* 673) and Old Comedy (once only: anapaests, Eupolis 13(14K).3), but ἠδέ is never found in Attic prose on its own or in any sequence of particles (Denniston, *GP* 287f.). As an example of cook's Homeromania, however, τ᾽ ἠδέ seems insipid and not specifically Homeric after the vitality of μάστιξον, and its transmission here has been suspected, and not only by those critics who demand from Alexis slavish adhesion to the norms of Attic prose. Hence a spate of unsatisfactory conjectures: e.g. τ᾽ εἶτ᾽ Meineke (but the corresponsion τε (...) εἶτα does not occur, cf. Denniston, *GP* 513f.), κᾆτ᾽ Blaydes, *Adv.* 2.160 (but the sequence A τε B κᾆτ᾽ Γ is not Greek), ἀλφίτοις Kock for ἁλσί τ᾽ ἠδ᾽ (ingenious but unrealistic – fish stuffing needs salt – and too far from the *ductus*). To this group might be added my own former suggestion (*PCPS* 196 (1970) 3) ἁλσί· τῇ δ᾽ ὀριγάνῳ, which legitimately assumes (i) faulty word-division in the MSS, (ii) a fr. ending in mid-sentence (cf. Alexis frs. 89(86K), 128(123K), 193(188K), 194(189K) – all in Ath. – and comm. *ad locc.*) and (iii) ὀρίγανος as a feminine noun (see on fr. 132(127K).7), but it faces two serious objections. It leaves ἁλσί without any particle linking it to τυρῷ (a problem solved by the further change of ἁλσί to ἁλί τε, cf. Axionicus 8.3, but for the sense 'salt' the plural is normal in later comedy and used elsewhere by Alexis, 179(174K).7, 192(187K).5), and it removes the marjoram from the place where it is wanted, in the stuffing. Hesitantly I accept the paradosis, printed here by Kassel–Austin.

For the use of instrumental dative rather than genitive with σάττω cf. e.g. Hdt. 3.7, 7.86, Theoc. 17.94, Cercidas fr. 3 Powell, Lucian *Hermot.* 65, *Peregr.* 30, *Syr. D.* 48; at Theopompus com. 46(45K), cited by Pollux 10.41, the MSS fluctuate between genitive and dative. Cf. K.G. 1.355 n. 1.

ΛΗΜΝΙΑ

Λημνία

A further title taken from a female ethnic in the singular (cf. the introductions to Ἀτθίς, Ἀχαΐς, Βρεττία, Κνιδία, Λευκαδία and Ὀλυνθία), whose significance in the plot is unknown. Terence's *Phormio* (modelled on Apollodorus' Ἐπιδικαζόμενος) is partly about the adventures of a Lemnian girl who marries Antipho and turns out to be Chremes' bigamously conceived daughter. Plautus' *Cistellaria* (from Menander's Συναριστῶσαι) treats the imagined rivalry for Alcesimarchus' affections between Selenium and 'the Lemnian relation' (cf. 98ff.). The one surviving fr. from Alexis' play, in which a character mentions a pot of beans, tells us nothing about speaker or context.

E. Capps' suggestion (*AJA* 10 (1905) 391) that Alexis' play could have been a revision of Aristophanes' Λήμνιαι is best forgotten; no evidence supports it, and the difference in number between the two titles stands in the way. Comedies entitled Λήμνιαι were written also by Nicochares, Antiphanes and Diphilus. The myth of Hypsipyle and her countrywomen formed the subject certainly of Aristophanes' play (cf. Euripides' like-named tragedy), possibly too of Nicochares' (cf. fr. 15(12K); the subjects of those by Antiphanes and Diphilus are uncertain, although the latter's is most likely to have had a New-Comedy type of plot and been the model for Turpilius' *Lemniae* (Ribbeck pp. 111ff., Rychlewska pp. 27ff., cf. p. ix).

On G. A. Gerhard's tentative but mistaken attribution of *P.Heidelberg* 175 to Alexis' Λημνία see 'False or doubtful attributions' IV, pp. 830ff.

139 (134K)

Meineke 3.443, Kock 2.345, Edmonds 2.436, Kassel–Austin 2.99. The whole fr., along with author and title, is cited by Pollux 10.100 to illustrate the use of ἀνθράκιον, a diminutive of ἄνθραξ which Pollux links with βοῦνος (a brazier) and defines as a χυτρόπους (a stand for a χύτρα); the *Glossary of Useful Terms* (98.3 Bachmann), and various Byzantine lexica (Phot. s.v. ἀνθράκιον α 1969 Theodoridis 1 p. 191 = p. 140.1 Reitzenstein, Hesych. s.v. ἀνθράκιον, *Suda* s.vv. ἀνθράκιον and τρίπος) define it as a small three-legged stand and cite (all except Hesych.) Alexis for the word. There can be little doubt (*pace* D. A. Amyx, *Hesperia* 27 (1958) 230 n. 97) that the three-legged, shallow, earthenware pots with one or two handles that have been found in Athens from Mycenaean (O. Broneer, *Hesperia* 8 (1939) 398f. and fig. 81b) to Hellenistic (B. A. Sparkes, *JHS* 82 (1962) 130 and n. 82, pl. v 3, middle) times match the grammarians' definitions admirably. Charcoal is placed in the bowls and a cooking pot or grill placed on top.

COMMENTARY

2 σείσων τε κυάμων μεστός: the MSS (FSCL) here are plagued with trivial errors (τε καὶ SL ται C, μεστόν FSL, παρῆν μὲν F in v. 1). After citing the fr. Pollux goes on to define σείσων (cf. also Hesych. s.v.) as an (earthenware, Hesych.) pot in which beans etc. were roasted; while cooking these would need to be shaken about repeatedly in it (hence the name: LSJ s.v., Frisk 2.689 s.v. σείω 5) to avoid sticking to it and being burnt. Sparkes–Talcott, *Agora* xii.228f. and fig. 17, pl. 96 (no. 1987) tentatively identify a round-bottomed shallow bowl with a single looped strap handle (end of 5th or 4th century) as just such a bean-roaster; cf. B. A. Sparkes, *JHS* 82 (1962) 128 and pl. iv.6. Axionicus 7 includes σείσων in a list of earthenware vessels.

κυάμων: see comm. on 167(162K).11. Lemnian beans had a reputation for excellence (Ar. fr. 372(356K) from his Λήμνιαι), but whether Alexis referred to this here we have no means of knowing.

Λίνος

Meineke 1.391f., Greve in Roscher s.v. *Linos* 2057.42ff., Pickard-Cambridge, *GCP* 190, Gruppe in *RE Supp.* iii s.v. *Herakles* 1018.8ff., Kroll in *RE* s.v. *Linos* 1, 716.4ff., Robert, *GH* 2.621ff., R. Pfeiffer on Callimachus fr. 23.6, Webster, *SLGC* 85, G. Schiassi, *Rend. Ist. Lomb.* 88 (1955) 103ff., K. Schauenburg, *JDAI* 94 (1979) 49ff., Nesselrath, *MK* 227ff.; cf. also F. Ostermayer, *De historia fabulae in comoediis Plautinis* (Diss. Greifswald 1884) 23, T. B. L. Webster, *CQ* 2 (1952) 18, Bain, *Actors* 217. Ath. 4.164a–c discusses and cites from this undatable myth burlesque the one fr. certainly preserved (140(135K)), in which Linus vainly attempts to introduce Heracles to masterpieces of Greek literature. Although Hesiod fr. 306 Merkelbach–West had already described Linus as a citharist παντοίης σοφίης δεδαηκότα, the story of his tuition of Heracles and other heroic pupils (Thamyras, Orpheus: Diod. Sic. 3.67 but [Apollodorus] 2.4.9 and Nicomachus *Exc.* p. 266 Jan make Orpheus Linus' brother and teacher respectively; Iphicles: skyphos by Pistoxenus painter, Beazley, *ARV²* 863.30, illustrated in F. A. G. Beck, *Album of Greek Education* (Sydney 1975) fig. 31; Musaeus: cup by Eretria painter, Beazley, *ARV²* 1254.80, fig. 30 Beck), and of his murder by Heracles after the master struck his pupil because of his slowness and the pupil angrily retaliated by hitting Linus with a cithara (Diod. Sic. *loc. cit.*, [Apollodorus], Tzetzes *Chil.* 2.213), its plectrum (Aelian *VH* 3.32), a stone (*Suda* s.v. ἐμβαλόντα) or a stool leg/stool (cups by Duris and Stieglitz painter (Beazley, *ARV²* 437.128 and 829.45, figs. 26 and 29 Beck) seems to have begun its development in the first half of the 5th century (the earliest Athenian vases featuring Linus date to *c.* 470) and may well have derived many details from dramatic versions of the legend on the Athenian stage in that century and the one following (cf. Gruppe, Schiassi).

The only other drama known to have been entitled Λίνος is a satyr play by Achaeus (fr. 26), but further dramatisations of the subject may be surmised even from the limited evidence available. If a play of the 470s inspired any of the vases painted about that time (in addition to Beazley, *ARV*[2] 437.128, 829.45 and 863.30 also a stamnos by the Tyszkwiéwicz painter, *ARV* 291.18 = fig. 27 Beck; cf. E. Buschor in A. Furtwängler and K. Reichhold, *Griechische Vasenmalerei* 3 (Munich 1932) 272f., E. Paribeni, *EAA* s.v. *Lino*), it would have antedated Achaeus' Λίνος by over twenty years (*Suda* s.v. Ἀχαιός dates this playwright's first production to 447). K. Schenkl, *Commentationes Woelfflinianae* (Leipzig 1891) 327 plausibly suggested that the speaker in Anaxandrides 16(15K) (from a Ἡρακλῆς) was Linus addressing a pupil.[1] Hardly anything is known about the plots of any of these plays, and so an attempt to assign details and variants in the myth tradition to innovations by individual authors is better not made. Alexis was not the first to portray Linus as a teacher of letters (rather than, or in addition to, music), although he stands at the head of the known literary tradition (cf. Theoc. 24.105; Diod. Sic. 3.67 has Linus adapting to the Greek language the alphabet brought from the east by Cadmus, cf. the variant in Zenobius 4.45 and O. Crusius, *Analecta critica ad paroemiographos graecos* (Leipzig 1883) 94f. n. 3, *Suda* s.v. Λίνος); on the cup by the Eretria painter (*c.* 430) mentioned above Linus already holds a papyrus roll and his pupil Musaeus writing-tablets.

In Plaut. *Bacch.* 155 Pistoclerus makes a veiled reference to the murder of Linus when he tells his own tutor Linus *fiam, ut ego opinor, Hercules, tu autem Linus*, after Lydus has complained of his pupil's violent behaviour. Whether this verse was adapted from Men. *Dis Ex.*, the Greek model (see J. Barsby's judicious discussion *ad loc.* in his edition of Plautus *Bacchides* (Warminster 1986)), it implies that the murder story was well enough known for an oblique reference to be comprehensible. In such circumstances it is unlikely that Alexis would have omitted so central an incident

---

[1] A corrupt note in Σ[LT] Hom. *Il.* 11.515 refers to a comedy or satyr play by Dionysius (? of Syracuse: so Nauck p. 794, cf. Snell, *TrGF* I p. 243) which presented Heracles apparently sick (νοσῶν, cf. Eustath. 859.49: corrupted in the scholia to a meaningless τῶν νόσων) and Silenus attempting to give him an enema. The scholia's indication of title (ἐν Λιμῷ) was unjustifiably changed by Meineke 1.420, 3.554 to ἐν Λίνῳ. There is no trace of a sick Heracles in the Linus myth, while Λιμός is an appropriate title for a play about a hero obsessed with eating (cf. Schiassi 103 n. 4, Snell *ad loc.*, my comm. on Alexis 88(85K).3–5 and 140(135K).17–18).

from his version. Could he also have included after the murder a trial scene such as the one described in [Apollodorus] 2.4.9, where Heracles was acquitted after citing a law of Rhadamanthys, ὃς ἂν ἀμύνηται τὸν χειρῶν ἀδίκων ἄρξαντα, ἀθῷον εἶναι? Here the combination of fantasy (in the idea of Heracles as a legalist) and of Athenian legal jargon (in the law's formulation, cf. e.g. Antiphon 4.2.1 ἄρχων ...χειρῶν ἀδίκων, Lysias 4.11) suggests that the mythographer's source was a scene of Attic comedy (cf. Robert 622) or satyr drama.

Alexis frs. 156(136K) and 300(298K) were conjecturally assigned to the Λίνος, the former by Meineke with an unnecessary conjecture (3.445; see my introduction to Μίνως and Bain 217 n. 2), the latter more plausibly by Dobree (*Adv.* 1.606, cf. Meineke 3.524 fr. LXII), since this otherwise unattributed (or corruptly attributed) fr. looks like an order for someone to play a musical instrument (see comm. on fr. 300(298K)).

140 (135K)

Meineke 3.443 (I), Kock 2.345, Edmonds 3.436, Kassel–Austin 2.100.Ath. 4.164b introduces the fr. with an unusually full description of the scenic action ('Alexis presents Heracles being educated in Linus' house. Heracles has been told to read out his choice from a large number of papyrus rolls (or books) that lie before him. He took a cookery-book and held on to it very keenly with both hands'[1]), although everything in this account can be deduced or guessed from the words of the fr. alone and requires no knowledge of the play beyond that. Preserved is a portion of dialogue between Heracles and Linus (correct part-division, except perhaps for two words in v. 3, was first worked out by Daléchamp in his Latin translation, although A's dicolon in v. 8 may echo (? uncomprehendingly) the original indication of speech-division in an unexcerpted play text: see my general introduction (II.i.a) and introduction to fr. 129(124K)). Heracles is presented – though still presumably a boy (cf. e.g. Paus. 9.29.9, Aelian *VH* 3.32, *Suda* s.v. ἐμβαλόντα, Tzetzes *Chil.* 2.213) – in his characteristic role of

---

[1] The Greek text here is clear and transmitted without corruption, but its idioms have caused some scholars needless trouble (Kaibel *ad loc.*, Cobet in Peppink, *Observ.* 30, Desrousseaux, *Obs.* 95). ἐντυχεῖν has its common *Koine* sense of 'read' (LSJ s.v. ἐντυγχάνω III), ἐκράτει = '(he) held in the hands' (also *Koine*: LSJ s.v. κρατέω IV.5) and ἀπὸ βιβλίων ...λαβόντα = 'taking (one/some) of the books', where ἀπό + genitive has partitive force (cf. K.G. 1.457, 3b, LSJ s.v. ἀπό 1.6) and a direct object need not be expressed *usitatissima ellipsi* (Schweighaeuser, *Animadv.* 2.571); thus the conjecture advanced by Cobet to supply such an object (λαβόντα <ἒν> ἐντυχεῖν) is palaeographically neat but unnecessary.

ΛΙΝΟΣ

one who prefers food to literature (Ar. *Ran.* 52ff. provides a close parallel; cf. comm. on fr. 88(85K).3–5), and Linus as a contemporary schoolmaster (γραμματιστής: cf. F. A. G. Beck, *Greek Education 450–350 BC* (London 1964) 111ff., 117ff.) with his collection of book-rolls (cf. comm. on 140(135K).5–7). Alexis transports characters and ambience from the heroic past to the Athens of his own day, and this involves him, like other Greek writers of mythical comedy from Epicharmus onwards, in amusing anachronisms (Heracles *might* have selected, for instance, a copy of Sophocles' *Trachiniae*). Cf. e.g. Epicharmus 100 (Odysseus or an associate at the Eleusinian mysteries), Antiphanes 170(172K) (a character in his Οἰνόμαος ἢ Πέλοψ criticises the tiny portions of Athenian meals), Anaxandrides 16(15K) (the musician Argas, cf. comm. on Alexis 19.3, is mentioned in the Ἡρακλῆς, 41(40K) (other 4th-century figures named in Πρωτεσίλαος), Eubulus 72 (δεῖπνα ἀπὸ συμβολῶν in the Οἰδίπους); cf. comm. on fr. 9, Bentley, *Phalaris* 124f. (London 1699) = 1.183f. (Dyce, London 1836), Webster, *SLGC* 85, Nesselrath, *MK* 227ff.

1 A here has βυβλίον (in Epit. vv. 1–4 of the fr. are omitted, 5–15 ὀψοποιός summarised, 15 ὡς δοκεῖ to end cited in full), but Musurus, followed by all editors of Ath. and the comic frs. except Kock, prints βιβλίον, and indeed A and Epit. MSS themselves write βιβλί- twice in Ath.'s introduction to the fragment. Alexis could have used either spelling. The facts are complex and confused; LSJ's summary s.v. βυβλός is oversimplified. As a diminutive of βυβλός[1] βυβλίον became βιβλίον by assimilation, and this in its turn induced the same vowel change in the stem noun and other derivatives without any iota in their original formation. At many periods βυ- and βι- spellings seem to have co-existed, although at least two sources of error clearly affect the transmission: a similarity in classical Attic (cf. comm. on fr. 146(142K).2) and subsequently (from the *Koine* on) identity of pronunciation between υ and ι, and the close resemblance of βυβ- and βιβ- in 10th-century AD minuscule. The assimilated spelling occurs in Athenian inscriptions of 403/2 (a decree: *IG* ii².1.61) and AD 395/6 (an edict: 1121.29), but between these dates we find only βυ-, although nothing is preserved from Alexis' own lifetime (Threatte 1.263). βυ- prevails also in papyri of the Ptolemaic period, with βι- common only from the 2nd century on (Mayser–Schmoll 1.1.80). The best MSS of 4th-century Attic authors generally have βι-: e.g. Plato (M. Schanz, preface to edition of *Euthydemus* (Würzburg 1872) vi), Demosthenes (S. L. Sternbach, *Meletemata Graeca* 1 (Vienna 1888) 103),

---

[1] On the disputed etymology see, in addition to Frisk 1.235 and Chantraine 1.200f. s.vv. βίβλος and βύβλος respectively, E. Masson, *Recherches sur les plus anciens emprunts sémitiques en grec* (Paris 1967) 101ff. and N. Lewis, *Papyrus in Classical Antiquity* (Oxford 1974) 7f. n.7.

COMMENTARY

Aristotle (W. Crönert, *Memoria Graeca Herculanensis* (Leipzig 1903) 21f.); in the MSS of Isocrates (as of Aristophanes), however, there is no clear preference (C. Haeberlin, *Centralblatt für Bibliothekswesen* 7 (1890) 275ff.). The evidence of the grammarians is partly helpful, partly absurd (cf. Sternbach 102f., Haeberlin 276). Pollux 7.211 cites βι- from Middle Comedy (Antiphanes 160(162), 195(197K), Cratinus jun. 11) but without supporting argument. Moeris s.v. βιβλία 192.23 Bekker = 95 Pierson claims that βι- is the Attic spelling as in Plato, and βυ- *Koine* as in Demosthenes. Although the Roman imperial period saw a general reversion to the βυ- spelling, Moeris' claim about Demosthenes is contradicted by the evidence of the MSS. Even more ridiculous is *Et. Mag.* s.v. βυβλίον (216.39ff.) with its claim that βυ- indicates τὸ ἄγραφον, βι- τὸ γεγραμμένον. Here in Alexis I support βιβλίον with little confidence.

βιβλίον here means both 'papyrus roll' and the writing contained in it (so 'book'), but whether the word still retained in Alexis' time any of that pejoratively dismissive tone with which it is tinged in the anti-intellectual Aristophanes (cf. J. D. Denniston, *CQ* 21 (1927) 117f., V. Ehrenberg, *The People of Aristophanes*[2] (Oxford 1951) 287) is uncertain. On books and papyrus see especially E. G. Turner, *Athenian Books in the Fifth and Fourth Centuries BC* (London 1952), and Lewis, *op. cit.* at p. 407 n. 1.

2 προσελθὼν γὰρ λαβέ: postponement of γάρ to seventh word and fifth phrase unit in the sentence would in itself be an acceptable licence in comedy (see comm. on 37(36K).1: parallels include Antiphanes 210(212K).7, Men. fr. 13 = 8th word; Men. *Epitr.* 1071, *Pk.*. 360, *Perinth.* 14, fr. 8, Athenion 1.5 = 7th), but here acceptance rests on two unverifiable assumptions: (i) that Ath.'s citation opens at the beginning of a sentence (but the first five words of the fr. could belong to an incompletely quoted previous sentence: cf. e.g. frs. 77, 128(123K) and comm.); and (ii) that a speaker said something in the immediately preceding context that would make an order (λαβέ) introduced by γάρ (a particle normally associated with reasons and explanations, not commanded action) less of a logical inconsistency than it appears. In place of γὰρ λαβέ several conjectures have been advanced, of which two deserve mention: Scaliger's παράλαβε (in Canter, Paris MS, 41ᵛ; cf. Erfurdt, *Obs.* 451, W. Luppe, *Philologus* 123 (1979) 324 n. 2: palaeographically neat, but παρά- would imply that Linus was holding the rolls, ἐντεῦθεν that he wasn't, and note λαμβάνω v. 8, ἔλαβες v. 12), and Jacobs' attractive παῖ, λαβέ (*Addit.* 103; cf. e.g. Pl. *Theaet.* 143c ἀλλά, παῖ, λαβὲ τὸ βιβλίον).

2–3 λαβέ, ἔπειτ' ἀναγνώσει: in such implied conditions, where an imperative replaces the protasis, the verb in the apodosis is more regularly introduced with καί (e.g. Pl. *Theaet.* 154c σμικρὸν λαβὲ παράδειγμα καὶ πάντα εἴσει ἃ βούλομαι, cf. K.G. 1.237).

3 πάνυ γε: if these words form part of Linus' speech, as has always been assumed, they must qualify either διασκοπῶν (so H. Thesleff, *Studies on Intensification in Early and Classical Greek* (Helsinki 1954) 60, citing parallels for the association of the adverb with verbs of '*perception, observation, understanding*, and the like') or (more probably) ἀτρέμα (so K. J. Dover, *CQ* 35 (1985) 334, citing parallels for the separation of πάνυ from the qualified adverb; Thesleff admits this as an alternative possibility). On the confirmatory/intensive function of γε in this idiom see Thesleff 72 and Denniston, *GP* 120f. Even so, I am strongly tempted to suggest that πάνυ γε here was not spoken by Linus but interjected by Heracles as a formula of assent to Linus' command (e.g. Ar. *Vesp.* 519ff. δίδαξον ἡμᾶς ... :: πάνυ γε; Denniston, *GP* 134f., Thesleff 73ff., Fraenkel, *Kl. Beitr.* 1.439). In that case Linus would continue speaking at διασκοπῶν.

4 ἐπιγραμμάτων: first here (and v. 10), 'titles', at this period probably written on the back of the opening columns of rolls rather than as later attached on a parchment tag (Th. Birt, *Die Buchrolle in der Kunst* (Leipzig 1907) 237ff., C. Wendel, *Die griechisch–römische Buchbeschreibung verglichen mit der des vorderen Orients* (Halle 1949) 24ff., Turner, *op. cit.* on v. 1, p. 15 and *Greek Manuscripts of the Ancient World*[2] (*BICS Supp.* 46 (1987) 13f., C. W. Müller, *Gnomon* 50 (1978) 635f., W. Luppe, *ZPE* 27 (1977) 89ff. discussing five known examples on early papyri).

ἀτρέμα: here in its literal sense, 'quietly/gently'; contrast fr. 129(124K).12 and comm.

5 τραγῳδίαι: so correctly A (omitted in Epit.). In the sense of the plays themselves this plural occurs as early as Aristophanes (*Av.* 101, *Lys.* 138, *Thesm.* 450 with the article, *Ran.* 90 as here without); its use embedded in a list primarily of named authors may be explained as a convenient shorthand for the great triad, whose separate naming would have made the list cumbersome (although Εὐριπίδης could have been entered here as a metrically equivalent substitute). Tj. Halbertsma's suggestion (*Adversaria critica* (Leiden 1896) 66f.) that A's reading or Musurus' τραγῳδία (based presumably on an error in his apograph) was a misreading of a gloss such as τραγῳδιοποιός, originally written in the margin to explain Χοιρίλος and later finding its way into the text in place of another proper name, is gratuitously ingenious.

5–7 Linus' words present us with a randomly arranged and selected list of authors and texts (*pace* A. F. Naeke, *Choerili Samii quae supersunt* (Leipzig 1817) 5: see *CQ* 7 (1957) 194) available in Alexis' time. We may imagine a collection of papyrus rolls in either a book-case (βιβλιοθήκη, already in Cratinus jun. 11) or a basket such as that pictured on a 5th-century bronze mirror in the Tyszkwiéwicz collection (figured in W. K. C. Guthrie, *Orpheus and Greek Religion* (London 1935) 66), with Linus reading out some of the titles without necessarily having to open the rolls (see above on v. 4). F. G. Kenyon, *Books and Readers in Ancient Greece and Rome*[2] (Oxford 1951)

COMMENTARY

24 puts such 'small, private collections of books, amounting at most to a few score rolls', into their cultural and historical perspectives; cf. also Nesselrath, *MK* 228 n. 138. Of the authors mentioned 'Orpheus' is to be interpreted as the jumble of Orphic poetry frequently mentioned by writers from the second half of the 5th century onwards (e.g. Eur. *Hipp.* 952ff. with Barrett's admirable note, Pl. *Resp.* 2.364e, Arist. *de An.* 410^{b}28; cf. O. Kern, *Orphicorum fragmenta* (Berlin 1922) 63ff., 80ff., I. M. Linforth, *The Arts of Orpheus* (Berkeley and Los Angeles 1941) 104ff., Guthrie 11f. and 23 n. 2, M. L. West, *The Orphic Poems* (Oxford 1983) 7ff.), although the attribution of some of these works to Orpheus (e.g. the *Descent to Hades* and the *Robe*, frs. 293–6 and 314 Kern) had already been discounted in Alexis' time by such men as Epigenes (? the follower of Socrates: cf. Linforth 114ff.; Clem. Alex. *Strom.* 1.131). References to 'Epicharmus' are not infrequent in 4th-century literature: e.g. Pl. *Theaet.* 152e, Arist. *Rhet.* 1.7, 1365^{a}16 (cf. introduction to comm. on Alexis 160(156K)), *Poet.* 3, 1448^{a}33, *GA* 1.18, 724^{a}28, Men. fr. 614.1, although it is uncertain how many of these references are based upon extensive familiarity with Epicharmus' works, whether dramatic and genuine[1] or non-dramatic and spurious (e.g. the *carmen physicum* referred to by Menander: cf. Kaibel, *CGF* 133ff.).[2] The Sicilian's name was presumably included in Alexis' list partly because works ascribed to him were then in vogue at Athens, but mainly because the inclusion of a celebrated comic poet was desirable. 'Choerilus' finally may seems a surprising entry, We cannot be certain whether Alexis has in mind (i) the 5th-century-BC epic poet of Samos (*testimonia* in *FGrH* 696 F 33/34, fragments in G. Kinkel, *Epicorum graecorum fragmenta* i (Leipzig 1877) 265–72, where 8 and 11 need to be deleted), whose celebrated *Persika* was still being read in the 3rd century AD (cf. *P.Oxyrhynchus* 1399), or (ii) the early Athenian tragic poet, of whose dramas little is now known, and only one title ('Aλόπη) and two meagre frs. from unknown plays survive (Snell, *TGrF* 1.66ff.). However, if the *Suda* is correct to credit the latter poet with 160 plays produced from 523 on with thirteen victories, a reference to him in Alexis might imply that some texts still survived in the 4th century.

---

[1] Kaibel's edition of the then known frs., genuine and spurious, is still the most acceptable, although it needs to be supplemented from Austin, *CGFP* frs. 81–91 and E. G. Turner, *Wien. Stud.* 89 (1976) 48ff.

[2] Pickard-Cambridge's suggestion (*DTC*[1] 364f. = [2] 240f.), that Alexis here may have been thinking of Epicharmus as the alleged author of the Χείρων, a work which may in part have been an ὀψαρτυσία (cf. F. Susemihl, *Philologus* 53 (1894) 564; Kaibel on Epicharmus fr. 290), is ingenious but unnecessary. Linus' collection specifically included one

6 Scaliger's conjecture Ἐπίχαρμος, Ὅμηρος, Χοιρίλος (in Canter, Paris MS, p. 41ᵛ, long before Jacobs, *Addit.* 103f.) for A's unmetrical Χοιριλος (*sic*), Ὅμηρος, Ἐπίχαρμος (Epit.'s paraphrase has the equally unmetrical order Χ., Ἐ., unaccented Ὀ., cf. Peppink, *Observ.* 4) by a simple transposition is by far the simplest and soundest solution[1] to the textual problem (cf. Blaydes, *Adv.* 2.160, W. G. Arnott, *CQ* 7 (1957) 193f.); other attempts (e.g. Erfurdt, *loc. cit.* on v. 2 Αἰσχύλος for Ἐπίχαρμος, but tragedy already has a double mention; G. Hermann's ἔστ᾽ Ἐπίχαρμος, γράμματα in Dindorf's edition of Ath., cf. Cobet's εἶτ᾽ Ἐπ., γρ. in Peppink, *Observ.* 30 and V. Schmidt's οὑπίχαρμος, γρ. in Kassel–Austin; see also Meineke *ad loc.* and Bothe, *PCGF* 547) are harder to justify palaeographically.

συγγράμματα: 'prose works', cf. Isoc. 2.7 τῶν μετὰ μέτρου ποιημάτων καὶ τῶν καταλογάδην συγγραμμάτων, also 42, Pl. *Leg.* 7.810b. The works listed before this in vv. 5–6 are all verse.

8 ὥρμησε, the reading of A and Epit., may safely be defended. In Attic tragedy and comedy the aorist is used idiomatically of an action now occurring or about to occur which the speaker views as if it had just taken place; translate here 'by this means you'll show what in particular your natural taste is/was', sc. at the moment when Heracles selects/selected a book. Cf. Goodwin, *MT* 18 §60 (wrongly claiming that the usage is colloquial), K.G. 1.163ff., J. D. Denniston on Eur. *El.* 215. Conjectures which introduce another tense (ὥρμηκε Meineke, printed by Kassel–Austin, ὁρμᾷ σε W. Luppe, *Philologus* 123 (1979) 324) are therefore not needed, although in palaeographical plausibility both stand high. Yet Luppe's introduction of σε does not improve idiom or meaning, since in 4th-century Greek ὁρμάω (cf. LSJ s.v.) is more commonly intransitive in its secondary sense 'I turn/incline to', e.g. vv. 13f., Pl. *Resp.* 4.439b ἡ ψυχὴ ... ἐπὶ τοῦτο ὁρμᾷ, Isoc. 15.10 τοῖς ἐπὶ τὰ μαθήματα καὶ τὴν παιδείαν ὁρμῶσιν, Arist. *Eth. Nic.* 7.5, 1149ᵃ31 ὁ θυμὸς ... ὁρμᾷ πρὸς τὴν τιμωρίαν, cf. *VV* 2, 4 and 5, 1250ᵃ11, 41, 1250ᵇ13, contrasting with transitive instances such as Pl. *Leg.* 9.875b ἐπὶ πλεονεξίαν ... ἡ θνητὴ φύσις αὐτὸν ὁρμήσει ἀεί, cf. *Ion* 534c.

---

cookery-book by Simus, and it would weaken the joke if Heracles had had two such works to choose from.

[1] Metrically sound also. The transposition produces a trimeter opening with two anapaests, the second with word ending after the first short. Descroix 202 noted 126 instances of comic trimeters opening with two anapaests long before the accretions of new papyri, and the split ∪/∪ – in the second half of the first metron was always permissible in e.g. lists with penthemimeral caesura as here (e.g. Ar. *Nub.* 684 Λύσιλλα, Φίλιννα opening a verse; cf. *CQ* 7 (1957) 188ff.).

COMMENTARY

9 δεῖξον τί ἐστι πρῶτον: Kock's ὅ τι for A's τί (a section omitted in Epit.) is perverse, less for metrical reasons (word-end after the first short of a dactyl in the first metron is admissible, cf. Handley's edition of Men. *Dysk*. p. 67 with examples) than after comparison with the parallel construction (ἐπὶ τί v. 8) in Linus' previous remark.

ὀψαρτυσία: Heracles reveals his true propensities by his choice of book. The first reference to an ὀψαρτυσία comes in Plato com. 189(173K).4 (from the Φάων, produced 391, cf. Σ Ar. *Plut*. 179), referring to the new ὀψαρτυσία of a Philoxenus whose precise identity remains uncertain, cf. e.g. Ribbeck, *Alazon* 78f., Webster, *SLGC* 21f.: more probably Philoxenus of Leucas than the poet from Cythera, cf. Bilabel in *RE* s.v. *Kochbücher* 941.10ff. Some twenty-five other names of authors of such cookery-books are known, seventeen listed in Ath. 12.516c, two in 7.308f, six in Pollux 6.70–1; works of this kind are frequently mentioned by cooks in later Greek comedy, sometimes with contempt (Dionysius 2.24ff., Sotades 1.34f.), once with praise (Baton 4), once with emulative intent (Anaxippus 1.1ff., 21f.). In Alexis' time these books were often in verse (Ath. preserves over 300 mock-epic hexameters from Archestratus of Gela's Ἡδυπάθεια (*SH* 46ff. frs. 132–92; cf. A. Olivieri, *Dioniso* 7 (1939) 110ff., M. Bettini, *Studi e note su Ennio* (Pisa 1979) 58ff.), but later compilations seem to have been in prose (e.g. the papyrus fr. published by Bilabel, *Ops*.). Cf. especially Bilabel's introduction and *RE* s.v. *Kochbücher* 932.38ff., Rankin, ΜΑΓΕΙΡΟΙ 2ff., W. Fauth, *Wien. Stud*. 86 (1973) 39ff.

10 φιλόσοφος: Alexis hits off perfectly the pedantic sarcasm of Linus' profession.

11 εὔδηλον: elsewhere in comedy at Ar. *Ach*. 1130, Men. *Dysk*. 94, *Her*. 3, *Mis*. 282, but parenthetically (cf. Meineke 5.89) only here, where the placing of the adjective at the end of the clause is significant; cf. the similar use and placing of δῆλον in S. *Aj*. 906, fr. 585.1, Theoc. 10.13.

τοσαῦτα: probably implying both quantity ('so many') and quality ('so great'). Hirschig's suggestion τοιαῦτα (*Annot*. 12) here is inferior, even if he can point to a parallel error in A and Epit. MSS at Ath. 10.449e (Alexis fr. 242(240K).8).

12 The joke in vv. 13–16 makes sense only if a real-life Simus (by name or nickname) doubled as tragic actor and cook in Alexis' Athens, but he is otherwise unknown (= no. 438 O'Connor, 2275 Stefanis, p. 356 Ghiron-Bistagne; cf. Bain, *Actors* 217). Identification with the dedicator of a mask in Callimachus *epigr*. 26 Gow–Page = 48 Pfeiffer is made unlikely by the poem's date. If Simus was a nickname, it could have derived from its possessor's snub nose or reputation for acting satyric characters (cf. Gunning in *RE* s.v. *Simos* 2, 199.54ff.), or from abbreviation of a longer name. Two such are known for actors in 4th-century Athens: Simmycas (?: Theophr. fr. 130 Wimmer in Ath. 8.348a, σιμμύκαν accusative in A; = no.

412

439 O'Connor, 2276 Stefanis, p. 356 Ghiron-Bistagne), and Simylus (*Vita Aeschinis* 2 §7 Blass, Harpocration s.v. Σιμύλος citing Dem. 18.262, where the MSS divide between Σιμύλῳ and Σιμ(μ)ύκᾳ; Simylus = no. 440 O'Connor, 2277 Stefanis, p. 356 Ghiron-Bistagne). Cf. also Ghiron-Bistagne pp. 92, 108, 154, 158, 161.

On the position of τίς here see G. Thomson, *CQ* 33 (1939) 147ff.

13–16 Linus opens his speech with a further instance of characterising sarcasm (cf. comm. on v. 10). The witticism that follows is the first appearance known to me[1] of what has subsequently become an over-worked formula: e.g. Cicero *De or.* 1.180 *Q. Scaeuola ... iuris peritorum eloquentissimus, eloquentium iuris peritissimus*, cf. *Brutus* 145 (cited by H. van Herwerden, *Mnemosyne* 14 (1886) 185) and 148 *Crassus erat elegantium parcissimus, Scaeuola parcorum elegantissimus*; Samuel Johnson in Boswell's *Life* (1.266 of the Hill–Powell edition, Oxford 1934), 'This man [sc. Lord Chesterfield] ... I thought had been a Lord among wits; but, I find, he is only a wit among Lords!'; Thomas De Quincey, *Tait's Edinburgh Magazine*, August 1839, 514 = *Recollections of the Lakes and the Lake Poets* (Penguin edition, 1970) 239, 'He [Southey] was the most accomplished litterateur among the erudite scholars of his time, and the most of an erudite scholar amongst the accomplished litterateurs.' The rhetorical figure structuring these *bons mots* was termed ἀντιμεταβολή (Quintilian 9.3.85) or *commutatio* (*Rhet. Herenn.* 4.39).

13 εὐφυής: see comm. on 37(36K).3–4.

14–16 ὑποκριτής: cf. also 43(42K).2. In the sense of 'actor' the word is first attested at Ar. *Vesp.* 1279 (but Pickard-Cambridge, *DFA*[1] 127ff. = [2] 126ff. argues forcefully that this use of the noun goes back at least to the time of Aeschylus), and ὑπόκρισις = 'acting' first probably in Pind. fr. 125 Bowra = 140b Snell, v. 69 (but see D. L. Page, *CR* 6 (1956) 191f.). Whether these terms came into use because the first actor 'answered' the chorus-leader (so e.g. A. Lesky, *Studi in onore di U. E. Paoli* (Florence 1955) 427ff., cf. T. V. Buttrey, *GRBS* 18 (1977) 5ff.), or because he 'expounded/interpreted' a situation to chorus and audience (so e.g. B. Zucchelli, ΥΠΟΚΡΙΤΗΣ: *Origine e storia del termine* (Brescia 1962)), remains fiercely disputed. Cf. also e.g. G. Curtius, *Rh. Mus.* 23 (1868) 255ff., D. W. Lucas on Arist. *Poet.* 4, 1449[a]16, A. H. M. Kessels, *Studies on the Dream in Greek Literature* (Utrecht 1978) 63ff. n. 16, cf. 97.

15–16 ὀψοποιός: Simus was therefore allegedly not a μάγειρος hired to butcher and cook meat, but one of the other categories of professional cook whose responsibilities were defined as σκευάσαι χρηστῶς μόνον ... τοὔψον

---

[1] Before Alexis the nearest approach to the formula comes in Ameipsias 9.1 Σώκρατες, ἀνδρῶν βέλτιστ' ὀλίγων, πολλῶν δε ματαιόταθ', ἥκεις, but this lacks the verbal transpositions.

(i.e. particularly fish) Alexis 153(149K).6f., where the speaker is a pre-judiced and self-important μάγειρος. Cf. introduction to Κράτεια.

16 τοῖς χρωμένοις: supply αὐτῷ or Σίμῳ, 'his associates/contacts/employers'. This use of the participial phrase without expressed instru-mental dative is common in Euripides (*Hipp.* 999, *Bacch.* 1152, frs. 19, 257.2) and 4th-century comedy (also Alexis 153(149K).3, 265(263K).5, Diodorus 2.41, anon. fr. 106/107.2 and 4 Kock). In individual passages different shades of meaning can be detected, but they are all rooted in 'those who have experience' (of a thing or person), and so 'associates' rather than either generally 'friends' (*pace* LSJ s.v. χράω c.iv.b) or specifically here 'connoisseurs' (so Pickard-Cambridge. *GCP* 190, after Kock, but this would require εὖ or καλῶς).

17–18 The witticism about Simus is complete at the end of v. 16 (Gulick's attempt to continue it into a following verse allegedly omitted by Ath. or scribe weakens the epigrammatic effect, cf. E. Harrison, *CR* 44 (1930) 84); thereafter an immediate transition to Heracles (for βούλιμός ἐσθ' ἄνθρωπος at the beginning of v. 17 is most naturally interpreted as a reference to Heracles' insatiable appetite) seems unacceptably harsh in the absence of any textual indication that such a transition is being made.[1] Two ways out of the difficulty are possible. Either (i) Linus intends βούλιμός ἐσθ' ἄνθρωπος as a final verdict on Simus, but Heracles wrongly interprets these words as criticism of himself and responds accordingly; such misconstructions are a standard humorous device in ancient comedy (e.g. Plaut. *Aul.* 727ff., *Bacch.* 842ff., *Men. passim*; cf. W. Theiler, *Hermes* 73 (1938) 270), but would be comprehensible here to an audience only if Heracles had already been presented as a character prone to misunderstanding what was said to him. Or (ii) a remark by Heracles protesting his hunger has been lost in a lacuna of one or more verses between 16 and 17 (so Jacobs, *Addit.* 104, followed by most editors including Kassel–Austin).[2]

---

[1] Non-textual indications (e.g. visual stage-business by Heracles, reveal-ing a desire for food) should normally be ruled out for ancient drama unless they are endorsed by the text; O. Taplin's claim for Greek tragedy, that 'the *significant* stage action ... is recoverable from the words' (*Greek Tragedy in Action* (London 1978) 175, cf. *The Stagecraft of Aeschylus* (Oxford 1977) 28ff., 75ff., 159), applies also to comedy.

[2] A third suggestion, made by A. F. Naeke (*op. cit.* above on vv. 5–7) 5f., would have been forgotten but for its endorsement by Meineke. This gives vv. 17–18 entirely to Heracles, with βούλιμός ἐσθ' ἄνθρωπος spoken in praise of Simus. βούλιμος, however, is not a word that conveys approval (see comm.), and the last four words of v. 17 are a rejoinder to, not a continuation of, the words that precede.

ΛΙΝΟΣ

17 βούλιμος: 'ravenous hunger'. In Alexis' time the noun[1] and its congeners (-μία, -μιάω, -μιώδης) were applied to both the hunger induced by starvation and the disease of bulimia (e.g. Ar. *Plut.* 873 and Σ, βουλιμιᾳ̈ ... πεινᾳ̈ λίαν, τινὲς δὲ εἶδος νόσου φασὶν ἐν ᾗ πολλὰ ἐσθίοντες οὐ πληροῦνται; disease at Timocles 13.3, hunger at Xen. *Anab.* 4.5.8, *Cyr.* 8.1.44, although the distinction between the two meanings is not always clear; it may be significant that no word of this stem occurs in the Hippocratic corpus, and that the earliest known analysis of the morbid condition comes at the end of the 4th or beginning of the 3rd century: Erasistratus in Aul. Gell. 16.3.9, possibly [Arist.] *Probl.* 8.9, 887[b]38ff., cf. Plut. *Mor.* 693f–695e; the disease divinely inflicted on Erysichthon in Call. *H. Dem.* is described with symptoms appropriate to bulimia, but characteristically the poet disdains the obvious labels and uses instead imaginative paraphrases, vv. 66ff., 102).[2] Words prefixed with βου- (implying prodigious size: from βοῦς, cf. Schwyzer 1.434, 577; note the similar use of ἱππο- in compounds) occur regularly in comedy (e.g. βουβαυκαλόσαυλος Anaxandrides 42(41K).5 by a plausible conjecture, βούγλωττος Xenarchus 8.4 with a pun on the flatfish so named, βουκόρυζα Men. fr. 834, βούπαις Ar. *Vesp.* 1206, Eupolis 437(402K)) but are not exclusive to it (e.g. βούβρωστις Hom. *Il.* 24.532, Call. *H. Dem.* 102, βούπαις Ap. Rhod. 1.760). Cf. also Schulze, *Kl. Schr.* 399f., Durham, *Vocabulary* 50.

On the structure of this predication, see comm. on 88(85K).3–5. Comedy favours it particularly when the predicate involves a striking metaphor, as here: cf. fr. 88(85K).4f., perhaps 113(108K).5f., Ar. *Vesp.* 495, *Av.* 1009, Men. *Dysk.* 88f., 480, *Sam.* 348, 555f. ἄνθρωπος here was restored by Jacobs (*Addit.* 104: ἄνθ- A and Epit. MSS, cf. comm. on 88(85K).3–5, contrast 113(108K).6, 145(141K).1).

Λοκροί

One of several titles in Alexis taken from male ethnics in the plural (cf. Θεσπρωτοί, Θηβαῖοι, Καύνιοι, Ταραντῖνοι), but since such titles occur at

---

[1] In medical writers βούλιμος is always a noun (cf. LSJ s.v.), and there is no evidence to support E. Risch's suggestion (*Kleine Schriften* (Berlin and New York 1981) 59 n. 2) that the use here in Alexis may be adjectival.

[2] Cf. also the witty metaphor in a phrase cited by Phryn. *Praep. Soph.* 53.11 de Borries, βουλιμιᾳ̈ τὰ βαλλάντια; if this derives from Attic comedy, as seems possible (hence com. adesp. fr. 660 Kock), the metre is restored better by deletion of τά than by a return to the orthography βαλάντια (so MS: corr. Meineke 4.664).

COMMENTARY

all periods of Attic comedy from Old (e.g. Cratinus' Λάκωνες, Σερίφιοι,
Ar. *Ach.*, Βαβυλώνιοι, Crates' Σάμιοι) to New (e.g. Menander's Λοκροί,
Philemon's Θηβαῖοι, Criton's Ἐφέσιοι), they were not limited to any single
type of plot. Of Alexis' Λοκροί (as indeed of Menander's, the only other
play with this title) too little survives for any guess at its subject.

141 (137K)

Meineke 3.445 (1), Kock 2.347, Edmonds 2.438, Kassel–Austin 2.101. The
slave girls described here were presumably preparing someone's bath (cf.
Hippocr. *Acut.* §65 Jones = 18 Littré (2.366), Plaut. *Bacch.* 105, *Rud.* 411,
Ter. *Eun.* 582, 592ff.; R. Ginouvès, *Balaneutikè* (Paris 1962) 204 n. 5).

2 The transmitted text here (A, Epit. at Ath. 3.123e) ἡ δ' ἑτέρα
μετάκερας is one syllable short. Choice almost certainly lies between (i)
R. Bentley's ⟨τὸ⟩ μετάκερας (*Emendationes in Menandrum et Philemonem*
(Utrecht 1710, published Cambridge 1714 under the pseudonym 'Phileleutherus Lipsiensis') 113, reprinted in Meineke, *Men. et Phil.* 538, mistakenly attributing the fr. to Philemon; omission of the article is one of the
commonest faults in MSS, and its addition here provides a neat but not
essential balance to τὸ θερμόν preceding), and (ii) Dindorf's ἀτέρα δέ
(better ἠτέ-; this conjecture assumes that a scribe had restored normal
prose order after *scriptio plena* was substituted for the crasis). ἠτέρα (either
crasis, ἡ + ἑ → ἡ, or prodelision, ἡ 'τέρα) is the correct Attic orthography,
supported by the grammarian Pausanias (θ 2 = 185.28ff. Erbse), attested
in inscriptions of Alexis' time (*IG* ii².1615.14, 87 after 358/7 BC, 1498.76 of
340–333, cf. Threatte 1.426, 431), and commonly found in good MSS (e.g.
S. *OC* 497, R in Ar. *Av.* 1365, *Lys.* 85 and J. Henderson *ad loc.* (Oxford
1987), 90).

μετάκερας: hot and cold water 'mixed', and so varying from warm to
tepid. Ath. calls it χλιαρόν, citing also Amphis 7, Philemon 40 and
Sophilus 1. Photius s.v. explains it as τὸ εὔκρατον ἢ τὸ ψυχρόν citing
Philyllius 32. Tepid water is warm when contrasted with cold, cold when
contrasted with hot. The word is quoted only from Attic comedy, but τὸ
μετακέρασμα occurs in Hippocr. (*loc. cit.*) in the same sense.

142 (138K)

Meineke 3.446 (11), Kock 2.347, Edmonds 2.438, Kassel–Austin 2.101.
Entries on the use of (i) ναύκληρος = 'manager of a tenement house (and
collector of its rents)' are to be found in Harpocration s.v. p. 180 N 3
Keaney (the fullest and most accurate note, citing Sannyrion 6, Diphilus
36(37K), Hyperides fr. 37 Kenyon), the anon. collection of λέξεις
ῥητορικαί 1.282.10 Bekker, Hesych. s.v. and Pollux 1.74–5; of (ii) ναυκλη-

ΛΟΚΡΟΙ

ρεῖν defined as οἰκίας δεσπόζειν in the Antiatticist 109.10 Bekker (citing ῎Αλεξις Λοκροῖς) and Phot. s.v. (citing ῎Αλεξις but no title). Hyperides' use of the noun and Isaeus' of the verb (6.19 ἀπελευθέρα ἦν αὐτοῦ ... ἣ ἐναυκλήρει συνοικίαν) indicate that both were accepted in Attic as normal terminology, and did not deserve censure from the Antiatticist's putative opponent(s), who presumably wished to restrict such words to their original meanings, by which ναύκληρος = the man who charters a merchant ship, loads it with cargo and sometimes sails on it himself as captain (cf. L. Casson, *Ships and Seamanship in the Ancient World* (Princeton 1971) 315f. and nn. 67, 69). The graphic extension of the two words to the world of the συνοικία probably took in its wake ναῦλος, originally 'fare for a voyage', but later 'rent in a tenement' (Pollux 1.75).

Λυκίσκος

Breitenbach 59 was probably right in suggesting that Alexis' play took its title from the leading character. Λυκίσκος (formed originally as a diminutive of Λύκος: cf. Hunter p. 177) was in common use as a personal name in Athens (Kirchner, *PA* 2.21 and 472 lists fifteen instances (nos. 9212–25, 9215a), including the archon of 344/3 (no. 9214), but none of them appears to have been celebrated or notorious enough to form the subject of a comedy. In an unidentified comedy by Plautus (fr. inc. xxix Leo, Lindsay) a mute Lyciscus was one of five slaves ordered to bring out cudgels, Lykos a thieving cook's thieving assistant in Euphron 1.1 and 21, Lycus a *leno* in Plaut. *Poen.*, and Lyco a banker in *Curc.*, where the names reflect the predatory wolfishness of the characters concerned. Such names, however, were not confined to villains; Lyconides in *Aulularia* was a young lover (cf. Lykon in [Aristaen.] 2.20) whose honesty led him to return the pot of gold stolen by his slave. In plays like Alexis' Λυκίσκος and Antiphanes' Λύκων, where so little survives, it would be foolhardy to guess the title-figure's role or status (*pace* Nesselrath, *MK* 287 n. 10).

A play mentioning Pythionice (fr. 143(139K)) must have been written when she was newsworthy, certainly within the limits *c.* 340–315, most probably 335–320, see comm. below.

143 (139K)

Meineke 3.446 (1), Kock 2.347, Edmonds 2.440, Kassel–Austin 2.102; cf. H. Berve, *Das Alexanderreich* 2 (Munich 1926) 338 no. 676, Ziegler in *RE* s.v. *Pythionike* 564.34ff. Ath.'s claim (13.595d) that Alexis 'mentions' (μνημονεύει: cf. comm. on 156(136K)) Pythionice comes in a section (594d–595e) devoted to this woman's career, where he cites Dicaearchus

417

COMMENTARY

(fr. 72 Müller, *FHG* 2.266f., fr. 21 Wehrli), Posidonius and Theopompus (*FGrH* 87 F 14, 115 F 253), Python or Alexander's satyr play Ἀγήν produced soon after Pythionice's death (p.810 Nauck², *TGrF* 1.259) and Philemon 15(16K); cf. also 586c, 8.339d, Diod. Sic. 17.108.4–6, Plut. *Phoc.* 22, Paus. 1.37.5, Antiphanes 27(26K).19–22, Timocles 16(14K), 15(17K), 27(25K). Diodorus Siculus and Plutarch call her Πυθονίκη, relying presumably on independent traditions of doubtful reliability (cf. Ziegler). Pythionice is said originally to have been a slave of a (presumably freed) αὐλητρίς of the *hetaira* Sinope (fl *c.* 360–330: cf. T. B. L. Webster, *CQ* 2 (1952) 22 and my introduction to Κλεοβουλίνη). She practised as a *hetaira* herself in both Corinth and Athens (associating in the latter place with Chaerephilus' sons and Cobius: Antiphanes 27(26K).19–22 and Timocles 15(17K); cf. my comm. on fr. 6 and introduction to Ἰσοστάσιον). In 330–329 she left Athens to become the mistress (Pausanias says wife) of Harpalus in Babylon, where she died after bearing him a daughter and was buried some time before Harpalus fled from Babylon in 325. A huge cenotaph was erected in her memory shortly afterwards just outside Athens on the road to Eleusis; in her case death did not mean an end to her notoriety.

144 (140K)

Meineke 3.446 (ii), Kock 2.347, Edmonds 2.440, Kassel–Austin 2.102. The Antiatticist here (98.2 Bekker) cites Alexis for the use of ζῳδάριον without comment or quotation; cf. 108.32 Bekker, where he cites Diphilus 21 for μναδάρια with the comment ὑποκοριστικῶς τὰς μνᾶς. This may imply a blanket condemnation by strict Atticists of all -δάριον diminutives (formed as they were not directly from the parent stem but from already existing diminutives in -διον: see especially W. Petersen, *Greek Diminutives in* -ION (Weimar 1910) 26off., Schwyzer 1.470f.), which were formed and used extensively in the *Koine*, often without distinction in meaning from their parent stems. Even so, they have a good Attic pedigree going back to the 5th century (e.g. βιβλιδάριον Ar. fr. 795(756K), κῳδάριον *Ran.* 1203, παιδάριον *Thesm.* 447; in his edition of *Ach.* Starkie lists examples in Ar. at pp. lv f., in other comic poets on *Ach.* 517; cf. also my comm. on 159(155K).2). What Alexis intended ζῳδάριον to mean is uncertain. In Arist. (*HA* 5.32, 557^{b}1, 9.34, 619^{b}22 etc.) it is a general term for any minute creature such as a grub or insect; on a late 4th-century Athenian inscription (*IG* ii².1491.4) it is a tiny figurine (so also Ath. 5.210c alongside ζωύφιον; cf. also ζῴδιον in Men. fr. 683.5, of ivory or emerald; also the Delos inventory, *IG* xi[ii].161 b 74). Small figurines might be employed as recognition tokens (e.g. a cock, Men. *Epitr.* 384f.; a pig, Plaut. *Rud.* 1170; Hähnle 66ff., 110f.).

418

MANΔΡΑΓΟΡΙΖΟΜΕΝΗ

Μανδραγοριζομένη

Kock 2.347, 349, Webster, *SLGC* 76 and *CQ* 2 (1952) 25, Gil 328f.; cf. also G. Schiassi, *Dioniso* 19 (1956) 26off., still useful despite misidentification of the play now known to be Men. *Asp.* In this title the participle could be passive (the heroine drugged by someone else) or middle (drugging herself), but the parallel Menandrean title Κωνειαζόμεναι seems to be interpreted correctly as a middle by Photius (s.v. -ομέναις· θανάσιμον φάρμακον πινούσαις; cf. Durham, *Vocabulary* 73, A. Körte's edition of Menander, 1[3] (Leipzig 1938) l, Webster, *SM* 53f.). The Greek species of μανδραγόρας (mandrake) is *Mandragora autumnalis*, a perennial herb with violet flowers (A. Huxley and W. Taylor, *Flowers of Greece and the Aegean* (London 1977) pls. 255–6), whose fleshy root, fruit and leaves yield a juice of great importance in ancient medicine, where it was prescribed as an emetic, purge and analgesic for a wide range of painful complaints (e.g. gout, snake-bites, wounds: Hippocr. *Loc. Hom.* 39, *Fist.* 9, *Morb.* 2.43, *Mul.* 1.74, 80, 2.199, Theophr. *HP* 9.9.1, Pliny *HN* 25.147ff., Dioscorides 4.75), alleged to be an aphrodisiac (Theophr. *HP* 9.8.8, 9.9.1, Diosc.), but above all used as an effective narcotic (which could prove fatal if taken in overdose) and anaesthetic for surgery (Xen. *Symp.* 2.24, Pl. *Resp.* 6.488c, [Dem.] 10.6, Arist. *Somn.* 3, 456[b]30, Theophr. *HP.* 9.9.1, *CP* 6.4.5, Lucian *Tim.* 2, Pliny and Dioscorides *locc. citt.*, Phot., Hesych. and *Suda* s.v., *Lex. Rhet.* 1.280.20f. Bekker). Frontinus *Strateg.* 2.5.12 describes a ruse in which troops were drugged with mandrake and lay around *in modum defunctorum*. Cf. especially Steier in *RE* s.v. *Mandragoras* 1028.20ff., although his statements about taxonomy and distribution are inaccurate.[1]

If Alexis' heroine drugged herself with mandrake in order to become unconscious, her aim must have been the prosecution of some intrigue

---

[1] Taxonomy of the *Mandragora* genus is difficult largely because of the range of variation within individual species, but botanists now generally recognise two species: *M. officinarum* with whitish-green flowers, native to north Italy and the west of what used to be Yugoslavia, and *M. autumnalis* with violet flowers, native to Greece and Turkey; cf. J. E. Hawkes, *Journal of the Linnean Society of London (Botany)* 65 (1972) 356f., T. G. Tutin and others, *Flora Europaea* 3 (Cambridge 1972) 199f. Greek medicine and science up to Roman times appear to have been familiar only with the pale-flowered form; the first reference to the existence of a form with dark flowers comes in Pliny *HN* 25.147ff., cf. Dioscorides 4.75, describing the former as 'male', the latter as 'female'. Such a differentiation is more likely to have been due to false inferences drawn from variations in appearance and time of flowering within one species than to any awareness of distinctions between the Greek and Italian species.

whose details are now obscure, although a few clues are provided by (i) the five frs. from the play, all preserved by Ath. (145–9(141–5K): 3.123f–124b, 14.621d–e, 8.365d, 12.552e, 8.340c respectively), and (ii) a series of thematic parallels from New Comedy and elsewhere which indicate some of the options open to Alexis for plot-construction.

(i) In fr. 147(143K) a younger woman tells an old one that she will be there with 'ribbons and perfume jars'; in referring to these objects she uses an unusual term which she explains as being local to Chalcis. The implications are that the younger woman hails from Chalcis, now lives elsewhere, and is either planning to be at a funeral or visit a grave. In fr. 148(144K) two characters (of unspecified sex) are present; one is described as very thin and says 'I'm almost dead.' If we combine the information from these two frs. with the implications of the title, possible scenarios begin to emerge: e.g. two girls from Chalcis, now living in another city (not necessarily Athens) under duress, plan to trick their way out of an undesirable situation for at least one of them (? forced marriage or liaison, a future as a *hetaira*) by having her take mandrake and feign death in the resultant stupor. The near corpse of 148(144K) would be the title figure, speaking most probably (so Schiassi) just after waking from her drugged sleep; and the younger woman of 147(143K) the other girl from Chalcis, playing her role in the charade by going to the heroine's mock funeral or grave. The other three frs. would fit smoothly into such a scenario. Frs. 145(141K) and 146(142K) both dilate on the contrariness of human nature. They could be part of one speech (so Meineke 3.448), but would fit the proposed scenario better if 146(142K), with its comments about the illogical preference for doctors who speak in Doric dialect, were prompted by the recent or prospective visit of such a doctor as part of the charade after the heroine had taken the drug, and then 145(141K) followed on, perhaps directly but more plausibly from a different speaker, with its more general remarks on contrariness. Finally fr. 149(145K) expresses love for some ξένοι with a wit and choice of image which suggest that the speaker is more likely to be a parasite with beneficent patrons (cf. comm. *ad loc.*) than e.g. a now happy title figure (so Schiassi). The relation of such a parasite to Alexis' plot is uncertain, but if the ξένοι were 'foreigners' rather than or as well as 'hosts', they too might have arrived from Chalcis and been associated with the two girls by ties of blood or affection.

(ii) Thematic parallels:

(a) Drugs producing death or sleep. Antheia, the heroine of Xenophon of Ephesus' novel, loves her husband but after being violently separated from him is wooed by Perilaus. To avoid marriage with the latter she plans suicide, but is tricked by her doctor into taking θανάσιμον μὲν οὐχὶ φάρμακον, ὑπνωτικὸν δέ (3.5.11); after taking it, she falls into a deep sleep (3.6.5), Perilaus believes her dead and lays her body in a burial vault

(3.7.4). On recovering consciousness she is carried off by brigands and further adventures intervene before she is finally reunited with her husband. A similar mechanism is employed, as Kock notes (2.347), with tragic results in the fourth act of Shakespeare's *Romeo and Juliet*, where Friar Lawrence helps the heroine to avoid an unwelcome marriage to Count Paris by supplying her with a draft that produces a deathlike sleep. A further example from comedy may be provided by Menander's Κωνεια-ζόμεναι, although its remains are too fragmentary for us to know the relationships and the reasons of the women who there took – or threatened to take – hemlock (cf. Gomme–Sandbach, *Comm.* p. 434, whose scepticism is wiser than the speculations of Körte, *loc. cit.*, or Webster, *SM* 53, *IM* 161).

(b) Linked pairs of girls, where one (at least) in each case was taken from her home city in infancy and raised elsewhere in the house of a pimp or bawd, are a standard motif in New Comedy: e.g. Selenium and Gymnasium in Plaut. *Cist.* (= Plangon and Pythias in the Greek original, Menander's Συναριστῶσαι), where Selenium was exposed as a baby and passed into the hands of a *lena*, whose daughter Gymnasium befriended her, 156ff.; Adelphasium and Anterastilis in *Poen.* (very probably adapted from Alexis' Καρχηδόνιος, q.v.), sisters kidnapped in Carthage and sold to a *leno* who took them to Calydon, 83ff.; Palaestra and Ampelisca in *Rud.* (from Diphilus), where Palaestra was kidnapped as a baby and sold to a *leno* who brought her and Ampelisca to Cyrene, 39ff.

(c) Death feigned as part of a trick. *Romeo and Juliet* belongs here too, but Men. *Asp.* is the clearest example from ancient comedy. Here the slave Daos devises the stratagem: Chairestratos feigns death in order to make his daughter a wealthy heiress and so divert his brother's marriage plans towards her and away from a niece who had previously been promised to another man. A bogus doctor speaking Doric adds circumstantial credibility to the ruse, but in this plot Chairestratos takes no drugs to make him look like a corpse; a muffled dummy is used instead (345f.).

These parallels suggest several lines on which Alexis could have constructed his plot; Webster's suggestion that the title figure took mandrake to escape from a *leno* or rival lover merely selects two of the more obvious possibilities.

One final point. Frs. 148(144K) and 149(145K) mention two contemporary Athenians, Philippides ὁ λεπτός (possibly *c.* 370–310: see comm. on fr. 2.8) and Callimedon (*fl. c.* 345–318: see introduction to Δορκίς). These references enable us to date Alexis' Μανδραγοριζομένη to the period of Callimedon's prominence, almost certainly before Menander wrote *Asp.* or *Kon.* It would be interesting to know whether either or both these plays borrowed motifs directly from Μανδραγοριζομένη and so revealed further evidence of indebtedness to Alexis (cf. Gil 328f.).

COMMENTARY

145 (141K)

Meineke 3.446 (1), Kock 2.348, Edmonds 2.440, Kassel–Austin 2.102. A long speech illustrating the contrarieties in everyday life is likely to have been prompted by some appropriate incident, situation or remark in the preceding context (one such possibility, together with the relationship of this fr. to 146(142K), is discussed in the introduction to Μανδραγοριζομένη). Cf. Plaut. *Trin.* 669ff., where Lysiteles claims that inconsistencies of this kind are caused by love, Antiphanes 94 and 235(238K) (the latter fr. alternatively assigned to Crates).

Alexis presents his illustrations with some wit and style. After a general introduction (vv. 1–2) the earlier instances succeed each other asyndetically (3–5), giving the impression of ideas tumbling out too quickly for elaborate rhetorical structuring. The remaining illustrations come in balanced μέν/δέ clauses (6–13; on vv. 14–16, see *ad loc.*), with each example occupying a single verse and the last five (9–13) ending with rhyming verb-forms in -ομεν (cf. also 146(142K).4–6, possibly from the same scene, see introduction to Μανδραγοριζομένη; Webster, *SM* 195). Rhyming assonance, introduced to Greek rhetoric apparently by Gorgias as a means of emphasising antitheses (cf. E. Norden, *Die antike Kunstprosa* 1 (Leipzig 1898) 30ff.) is used effectively (intention, however, is not always provable in an inflected language) but more sparingly in Attic comedy: e.g. Ar. *Nub.* 494–6, 711–15 with Dover *ad loc.*, Hermippus 48(47K).1–3, Nicophon 10(19K), Anaxandrides 28(27K).2–4, Men. *Dysk.* 571–3, 743f. with Handley on 735f.

The fr. is cited by Ath. 3.123f–124b (complete in A, vv. 1–4 ἔχοντες, 7–11, 14–16 in Epit.).

1 εἶτ' οὐ: see comm. on 44(43K).1.

περίεργον: here in its primary sense (cf. LSJ s.v. -ος) 'taking needless trouble'. Before specifying the area of man's absurdity about which he proposes to talk, the speaker chooses a vaguer word in order to puzzle his audience and so engage their attention.

ἄνθρωπος, the reading of A and the Epit. MSS, is correct, and Hirschig's conjecture ἄνθρ- (*Diss.* 18, cf. Cobet in Peppink, *Observ.* 27; see also 113(108K).6, and contrast 88(85K).3–5 with comm., 140(135K).17) is wrong. The speaker is discussing mankind in general, not one particular person now or recently on stage; otherwise his transition to the first-person plural in v. 3, thereby identifying himself and his audience with the objects of his remarks, would be harsh. Besides, in predications of this type (X is a Y φυτόν) the subject is normally general, not particularised. In this idiom φυτόν has poetic, and especially tragic, overtones (e.g. Eur. *Med.* 231, Theodectes 1 Nauck² = 1a Snell; similarly Pl. *Tim.* 90a in a poetic context, [Men.] monost. 398 Jäkel; cf. also A. *Suppl.* 281, Eur. *Hipp.* 630),

422

highlighting the weakness of, rather than contempt for (so Page on *Med.*, Barrett on *Hipp.*), the group so indicated.

2 'Engaging in the largest number of actions that are pre-eminently inconsistent with each other.'

3 ἀλλοτρίων balances συγγενεῖς and is masculine; its meaning is ambiguous, either 'other people's (wives/husbands)' or 'foreigners/ strangers' (= non-Athenians, banned from marriage with Athenians, cf. W. Erdmann, *Die Ehe im alten Griechenland* (Munich 1934) 236, A. R. W. Harrison, *The Law of Athens* 1 (Oxford 1968) 24ff.). By falling in love with them we disregard/neglect our families both generally and in at least two ways particularly relevant to Alexis' Athens: the expense of supporting a non-Athenian *hetaira* or concubine diminished the family estate, and a love-affair of that kind might make a man less likely to marry a girl in his own γένος.

4 A and the Epit. MSS have a raised point after instead of before ἔχοντες, and this odd punctuation was printed by Musurus and defended by Schweighaeuser (cf. *Animadv.* 2.366). Yet common experience tells us that our neighbours tend to believe us richer (not poorer) than we in fact are, and a better contrast is achieved between vv. 4 (perverse consequences of poverty) and 5 (perverse consequences of having money enough to help those in need) if we punctuate after οὐδέν (so first Bedrotus in the 1535 Basel edition of Ath. and de' Conti in his 1556 Latin translation published in Venice).

5 ἐράνους φέροντες: in the 4th century ἔρανος is primarily[1] (1) an interest-free loan raised by contributions from several friends for the benefit of one in need, and then by extension (2) any favour or service done without an eye for profit (in Alexis cf. 222(219K).16, 282(280K)). See Th. Reinach in Dar.–Sag. s.v. *Eranos* 805A ff., Ziebarth in *RE* s.v. Ἔρανος 328.21ff., M. I. Finley, *Studies in Land and Credit in Ancient Athens* (New Brunswick 1952) 100ff., J. Vondeling, *Eranos* (Groningen 1961), P. Benvenuti, *ERANOS* (Diss. Padua 1980), O. Longo in *Mélanges Edouard Delebecque* (Aix-en-Provence 1983) 247ff., P. C. Millett in P. Cartledge and others, *Nomos: Essays in Athenian Law, Politics and Society* (Cambridge 1990) 183f., 187, and *Lending and Borrowing in Ancient Athens* (Cambridge 1991) 153ff. and 294f. n. 33). The usual phrases for making these loans or doing these favours are ἔρανον φέρειν (as here; also e.g. Antiphanes 260, Dem. 21.101, 184, [Dem.] 25.58) and εἰσφέρειν (e.g. Philemon

---

[1] The Homeric use (a meal to which guests brought their individual contributions: *Od.* 1.226, cf. 11.415) is not found in Attic (LSJ s.v. wrongly interpret Pl. *Symp.* 177c as a metaphorical extension; it should be classified under the 'loan' heading), which replaces it with δεῖπνον ἀπὸ συμβολῶν (cf. comm. on fr. 102(97K).1).

COMMENTARY

178(213K).14, Pl. *Symp.* 177c, *Leg.* 11.927c, Isoc. 11.1, [Dem.] 53.8, 61.54, Theophr. *Char.* 15, cf. Diog. Laert. 1.37). Alexis' point here is that when we try to help people, we succeed only in doing it 'badly', i.e. the help is insufficient, clumsily offered or accepted with bad grace. The Greek makes such relevant sense that it is hard to see why Grotius (*Exc.* 577, 973, cf. also I. G. Patakis, *Philologus* 8 (1853) 523f.) wanted to replace κακῶς with a less appropriate κακοῖς. On the idiom οὐ (φέρομεν) ἀλλ᾽ ἤ (κακῶς) see Denniston, *GP* 25 (ii), and add to his list of examples Xen. *Anab.* 7.7.53 ἀργύριον μὲν οὐκ ἔχω ἀλλ᾽ ἤ μικρόν τι.

6–7 The speaker now turns to a new area of contrarieties: that of food. After an introductory verse announcing the new field (6: omitted in Epit.) he goes on to give seven examples (7–13). The text in vv. 6–7 presents problems of transmission, interpretation and punctuation which are inadequately reported and faultily analysed in editions of Ath. and the comic frs.

(i) At the beginning of 6 A has τἀκτῆς τροφῆς. Meineke interpreted this as τακτῆς τροφῆς, '(our daily) ration of food'. Such a genitive could perhaps be justified as a harsh example of categorising partitive, but the expression itself, although relevant to discussions of prison and army regimes (e.g. Pl. *Leg.* 10.909c, cf. Thuc. 4.16), hardly suits a context where attention is focused on the variety in Athenian eating habits and seven different items (including dainties like ἀβυρτάκη) are listed. A's breathing and accents point the way rather to τἀκ τῆς τροφῆς, which Kassel–Austin correctly print (after Casaubon, cf. *Animadv.* 237; Pickard-Cambridge, *GCP* 190f.), but they fail to punctuate with a necessary colon at the end of v. 6. Translate 'Next, matters arising from our daily food', and interpret τά as a pendent nominative or accusative, both cases being used in headings; see especially K.G. 1.47 §6 (nom.: e.g. Xen. *Oec.* 1.14 οἱ δὲ φίλοι· ἄν τις ἐπίστηται αὐτοῖς χρῆσθαι ὥστε ὠφελεῖσθαι ἀπ᾽ αὐτῶν, τί φήσομεν αὐτοὺς εἶναι;, Pl. *Crat.* 403a ὁ δὲ Ἅιδης· οἱ πολλοὶ μέν μοι δοκοῦσιν ὑπολαμβάνειν τὸ ἀϊδὲς προσειρῆσθαι τῷ ὀνόματι τούτῳ) and 1.330f. (acc.: e.g. Xen. *Hipparch.* 2.4 τούς γε μὴν ἐν μέσῳ τῶν πρώτων καὶ τῶν τελευταίων· εἰ οἱ δεκάδαρχοι ἐπιστάτας ἕλοιντο καὶ οἱ ἄλλοι ἐφέλοιντο, οὕτως εἰκὸς ἑκάστῳ πιστότατον τὸν ἐπιστάτην εἶναι, Isoc. 12.99 ἀλλὰ μὴν καὶ τὰς στάσεις καὶ τὰς σφαγὰς καὶ τὰς τῶν πολιτειῶν μεταβολάς ... ἐκεῖνοι μὲν ἂν φανεῖεν ἁπάσας τὰς πόλεις πλὴν ὀλίγων μεστὰς πεποιηκότες τῶν τοιούτων συμφορῶν καὶ νοσημάτων). The neuter plural or singular article is more commonly followed by a simple genitive in expressions of this type (τὰ τῆς ὀργῆς, τὰ τῆς πόλεως, etc., cf. K.G. 1.269; hence Meineke's alternative conjecture τὰ τῆς τροφῆς, cf. Dem. 1.22), but the existence of e.g. τὰ ἀπὸ τῆς τύχης (Thuc. 2.87) by the side of τὸ τῆς τύχης (4.18, 7.61) provides supporting evidence (cf. also Diggle, *Studies* 79) for τἀκ τῆς τροφῆς here.

(ii) In v. 7, A and the Epit. MSS read γλιχόμεθα μὲν τὴν μᾶζαν ἵνα λευκὴ παρῇ, which is feeble sense (a statement that we do certain things to our μᾶζα to make it white, e.g. add milk to it, cf. Σ Ar. *Pax* 1 = *Suda* s.v. μᾶζα· ἡ τροφὴ ἡ ἀπὸ γάλακτος καὶ σίτου, would perhaps be more effective in this context of actions and means) and doubtful syntax (in Attic γλίχομαι is normally constructed with genitive and/or infinitive; with accusative elsewhere only for certain at [Pl.] *Hipparch.* 226e, for at Hippocr. *Epist.* 17 (= 9.364 Littré, 302 Hercher) and Philo 36.37 the genitive is better attested; with a true final clause nowhere else, but with ὡς and future indicative at Hdt. 7.161; cf. Kock *ad loc.*). Yet if γλιχόμεθα is corrupt, it is hard to know what it could have supplanted; neither Kock's δεχόμεθα (with ἄν for ἵνα) nor Blaydes' εὐχόμεθα (*Adv.* 2.160) is an improvement, and Kaibel's repunctuation of vv. 6–8 with the one major stop after γλιχόμεθα requires one to accept τακτῆς τροφῆς in v. 6 as the price for taking the genitives there with γλιχόμεθα, to transpose μέν and τήν in v. 7 (so first Grotius, *Exc.* 973, cf. Meineke 5.89, W. Headlam, *CR* 16 (1902) 246), and to take τὴν μᾶζαν with μηχανώμεθα in v. 8, a triad of implausibilities. Since neither λευκούμεθα μέν nor λευκαίνομεν (for γλιχόμεθα μέν) is tolerable with λευκή later in the same verse, it would be preferable to obelise γλιχόμεθα.

6 τῆς τροφῆς ... τῆς καθ' ἡμέραν: a standard phrase (e.g. Thuc. 1.2, [Dem.] 49.15, Philemon 92(88K).6, Heliodorus 6.10.2) along with – and sometimes interlaced with – ἡ ἀναγκαία τροφή; cf. E. W. Whittle, *CPhil.* 56 (1961) 179 n. 4.

7 τὴν μᾶζαν: barley was the staple cereal grown in Greece, and its grits were kneaded (μάττειν → μᾶζα) into a cake with water, milk or olive-oil (cf. also Ath. 3.114e–115b, Hesych. s.v.) to form a basic food; one modern counterpart is the tsampa of Tibet, made in the same way (although chang or butter-tea is sometimes the liquid agent, cf. Rinjing Dorje, *Food in Tibetan Life* (London 1985) 62). Cf. Hermann–Blümner, *Privatalthertümer* 217ff., Orth in *RE* s.v. *Kochkunst* 948.28ff., N. Jasny, *Osiris* 6 (1950) 244, 247, L. A. Moritz, *Grain-Mills and Flour in Classical Antiquity* (Oxford 1958) 150, West on Hes. *Op.* 590, M.-C. Amouretti, *Le Pain et l'huile dans la Grèce antique* (Paris 1986) 124ff., 278f., 281. The whitest barley-cake, made from the finest flour (termed 'Achillean', Pherecrates 137(130K).4, Theophr. *HP* 8.4.2, Ath. 3.114f, Σ Ar. *Equ.* 819) was evidently highly praised; cf. Pherecrates 137(130K).8 and Meineke 2.317, Philoxenus' Δεῖπνον fr. 836(b).6 Page (*PMG* p. 434).

8 'With this barley-cake we make black soup'; here μᾶζα is the thickening agent (Edmonds' wild conjecture δ' ἐπ' αὐτῇ for δὲ ταύτῃ reveals that he was no cook). μέλας ζωμός, highly esteemed in both Sparta (Plut. *Lyc.* 12.6, cf. P. Leigh Fermor, *Mani* (London 1958) 153f.) and Athens (Pherecrates 113(108K).3, 137(130K).3f., Nicostratus 16(17K), Euphron

COMMENTARY

1.8, Matron *Conv.* 534.94 Lloyd-Jones–Parsons), was a thick, meatless soup that owed its colour presumably to ingredients such as the black variety of ἐρέβινθος (chick-pea or Bengal gram, see comm. on 167(162K).13). Gypsies still served the dish at fairs in northern England up to the 1940s.

9 A and the Epit. MSS write τὸ καλὸν δὲ χρῶμα, which can be defended as a rare, quasi-inferential use of the particle (= οὕτω δέ, cf. Denniston, *GP* 170); but it is far more probable that Alexis here wrote τε (so Meineke, *Anal. Crit.* 57), which idiomatically introduces the last item in a series (where previous items have been linked by δέ or καί), and so sums up or clinches what precedes (Denniston, *GP* 500). The transmissional error would doubtless have resulted from a scribe's memory of, or glance at, the δέ similarly positioned in the previous verse.

δευσοποιῷ: supply χρώματι, 'with a non-removable (dye from the ζωμός)'. δευσοποιός (= 'fast' of colours: cf. Harpocration δ 24 pp. 70f. Keaney and Timaeus, *Lex. Plat.* in K. F. Hermann's edition of Plato, 6 (Leipzig 1902) 400, both s.v.) was presumably a technical term of the dyeing trade; e.g. Pl. *Resp.* 4.429e, Diphilus 73(72K).2, trag. adesp. fr. 441 (p.924 Nauck², 2.128 Kannicht–Snell); H. Blümner, *Technologie und Terminologie der Gewerbe und Künste bei Griechen und Römern* I² (Leipzig and Berlin 1912) 230f.; cf. LSJ s.v. The intrusive article in A and Epit. before δευσιποιῷ, which mars the scansion, was deleted first by Hertel 440 (cf. Grotius, *Exc.* 577, 973, Porson, *Adv.* 68, Peppink, *Observ.* 27).

For the point in vv. 7–9 cf. B. Worsley-Gough, *Cooking Ahead* (London 1957) 48, 'How odd that the English, who choose brown paint and mud-coloured carpets and porridge-coloured upholstery, insist on having the heart bleached out of their linen and their bread, and even demand chalk-white fish.'

10 Ath. cites the whole fr. in support of his claim that οἱ ἀρχαῖοι ... καὶ χιόνα (so Meineke 3.447, cf. C. Ohlert, *Neue Jahrb.* 29 (1883) 753: χιόνας A, Epit.) ἔπινον. What Alexis says, however, is something less precise: 'we prepare snow for drinking' (παρασκευάζω with accusative + epexegetic infinitive, a regular construction in Attic, cf. LSJ s.v. A.4, e.g. Pl. *Resp.* 3.405c ἀγνοῶν ὅσῳ κάλλιον καὶ ἄμεινον τὸ παρασκευάζειν τὸν βίον αὑτῷ μηδὲν δεῖσθαι νυστάζοντος δικαστοῦ). Alexis' words can be taken to cover not only the drinking of snow (a practice confirmed by e.g. Dexicrates fr. 1, Asclepiades 1 Gow–Page = *Anth. Pal.* 5.169, condemned by Aristotle fr. 214 Rose, cf. Oribasius v.1.10ff. = *CMG* vi.1.1 pp. 112f.), but also using it to cool water and wine by admixture or stuffing it into surrounding vessels (e.g. Strattis fr. 60(57K).3, Xen. *Mem.* 2.1.30, Machon 276 and Gow on 259 and 270, Seneca *Epist. Mor.* 78.23, Martial 5.64.2, 6.86.1, 12.17.6; cf. Mau in *RE* s.v. *Comissatio* 612.24ff. and F. Lissarague, *The Aesthetics of the Greek Banquet* (tr. A. Szegedy-Maszak, Princeton 1990) 96f.).

11 τὸ δ᾽ ὄψον: Casaubon claims (*Animadv.* 237) that this correction of τὸ δ' ὅλον in the MSS (A, Epit.) was taken *ex membranis*, i.e. from an anonymous jotting in either a lost apograph or even a printed book (cf. Schweighaeuser, *Animadv.* 2.367f. and Kaibel *ad loc.*; on the employment of such terms by scholars of Casaubon's time see W. S. Watt, *Hermes* 93 (1965) 244ff.). By ὄψον here Alexis presumably means, above all, fish (cf. comm. on fr. 47(46K).6); a cook in fr. 177(173K).3ff. is correspondingly astonished by his hirer's reluctance to have this food served hot.

διασύρομεν: see comm. on 239(237K).2.

12 ἐκπυτίζομεν: only here in Greek, but ἀποπυτίζω Ar. *Lys.* 205, Hippocr. *Epid.* 7.25, Arist. *HA* 4.3, 527^{b}22, διαπ- Archedicus 3.12; the simple verb only in *Et. Mag.* 697.58 s.v., but *pytisso* in Ter. *HT* 457. Wilamowitz's otherwise excellent note on Ar. *Lys.* 205 in his edition (Berlin 1927) fails to recognise, however, that the word is derived by dissimilation from the onomatopoeic πτύω (cf. Frisk 2.617f. and Chantraine 2.951 s.v. πτύω).

13 ἀβυρτάκαισι: the point of the remark is made clear by an entry common to several lexica s.v. (Phot. 1.14, α 66 Theodoridis, 8.7ff. Reitzenstein = Paus. p. 152.7f. Erbse = the anon. *Glossary of Useful Terms* 1.6.12ff. Bachmann) ἀβυρτάκη· ὑπότριμμα (cf. comm. on 193(188K).3) ἐκ δριμέων σκευαζόμενον, ἐκ καρδάμων καὶ σκορόδων καὶ σινάπεως καὶ σταφίδων, ᾧ πρὸς κοιλιολυσίαν ἐχρῶντο. Other writers list the ingredients differently: cress, leeks, pomegranate seeds in Aelius Dionysius s.v. p. 97.3f. Erbse = *Suda* s.v., cf. Eustath. 1858.18, cress and leeks in Theopompus com. 18(17K), greens (χλόη) in Antiphanes 140(142K).3.

ἐκβακχεύομεν: metaphorically, 'we absolutely rave' (with ἐπί + dative, 'over', like μαίνομαι in a similar – and doubtless equally colloquial – sense, cf. comm. on 225(223K)), intransitive only here and Philodemus *Ir.* p. 35 Wilke; in Attic normally transitive with the meaning 'rouse to Bacchic frenzy' (Eur. *Tro.* 408, Pl. *Phdr.* 245a; passive Eur. *Bacch.* 1295, Pl. *Resp.* 8.561a). βακχεύω and its compounds oscillate between transitive and intransitive uses; in Attic intr. βακχεύω A. fr. 58, S. *Ant.* 136, Eur. *Ion* 1204, *IT* 1243, *Bacch.* 343, etc., ἀνα- Eur. *Bacch.* 864, ἐπι- Nicostratus 5(4K).1, συμ- Eur. *Bacch.* 726, Pl. *Phdr.* 234d. Choice of so evocative a verb here may be due partly to its climactic position at the end of five rhyming lines (see introduction to this fr.), partly to the jingle it creates after ἀβυρτάκαισι.

14–16 These three vv., cited in Epit. as well as A, would give to the speaker's argument an oddly pessimistic conclusion: that if our daily life is so full of largely trivial contrarieties, then, in the words of the old saw, not to be born – or failing that, to die as quickly as possible – is best. The lack of balanced judgement in the logic here can be explained plausibly in several different ways, with the correct one impossible to determine securely so long as we lack information about the dramatic context and the character (or characters) present on stage.

(a) Kock reacted to the strained logic by claiming that these vv. '*manifeste aliunde excerpti sunt*'. Although this scholar's inability at times to comprehend the rules for the dialectics of absurdity is notorious (e.g. K. J. Dover in M. Platnauer (ed.), *Fifty Years of Classical Scholarship*[1] (Oxford 1954) 98 = *(and Twelve)*[2] (1968) 125, W. G. Arnott, *PCPS* 196 (1970) 1), the case for removing these vv. from their position at the end of the fr. does not rest on a subjective sense of inappropriateness alone. 'It is well known', writes Fraenkel (comm. on A. *Ag.*, 2.408 n. 4), '... that not infrequently maxims which do not belong to the original have been jotted down beside lines with which they have a rough (often quite superficial) similarity'; cf. L. K. Valckenaer on Eur. *Phoen.* 558, Wilamowitz, *Hermes* 40 (1905) 133ff. = *Kl. Schr.* 4 (Berlin 1962) 187ff., G. Jachmann, *Nachr. Gött.* (1936) 140, Fraenkel on A. *Ag.* 834–7, 899–902 and *Eranos* 44 (1946) 81ff. Such parallels, which were wrongly incorporated into the continuous text by subsequent copyists, were commonly citations of Euripides. It is notable that the three vv. discussed here are wholly tragic in style and rhythm (on the penthemimeral caesura before μέν in v. 15 see Descroix 284ff., M. L. West, *Greek Metre* (Oxford 1982) 83), and that the traditional saying contained in them is one that Euripides three times reproduces elsewhere with varied wording (frs. 285.1–2, 449, 908 Nauck[2]). Could vv. 14–16 therefore be a fourth exploitation from a lost Euripidean play? '*Amat prouerbia paullum mutare Euripides*' notes Porson (comm. on *Or.* 68–9).

(b) A second possibility – but the least likely, it seems to me, of the ones scouted here – is that a passage of unknown length has been omitted between vv. 13 and 14 by excerptor or scribe. Although lacunae undoubtedly occur in our texts of Ath.'s citations (K. Zepernick, *Philologus* 77 (1921) 335ff.; in Alexis, frs. 116(111K).6, 140(135) 17–18*, 178(172K).7, 9, 17, 18, 216(213K).5, 268(266K).7), they normally (apart from one possible exception, asterisked) cover only part of a line and are due to carelessness by copyist or excerptor. When longer and deliberate omissions are made by Ath., he usually signals the fact with προελθὼν δέ φησιν, μετ' ὀλίγα or similar expressions (cf. in Alexis frs. 18, 131(126K), 201(197K), 205(202K), 223(221K)).

(c) It would be foolish to demand from Alexis, whose career began midway between the death of Aristophanes and the first production of Menander, the same criteria of comic logic that is observable in the latter poet. If exploitation of humour can take precedence over consistent presentation of character and situation in Aristophanes, a similar licence might perhaps be granted to Alexis. In that event vv. 16–18 may follow on directly after v. 15 of the fr., and the logical hiccup be explained as a concession to παρὰ προσδοκίαν humour. Thus either (1) a single speaker may have delivered vv. 1–18 in the role of βωμολόχος, i.e. a character whose function in the plot was subordinated or at least closely linked to that of comic entertainer (e.g. if he was the parasite postulated as the speaker of 149(145K), he could have been given speeches similar to those of e.g. Gelasimus in Plaut. *Stich.*, where a series of witty remarks leads up to an outrageous final absurdity, 193ff., 503f., 639f., cf. *BICS* 19 (1972) 64ff.; here the Latin poet's methods have more in common with Aristophanes than with his Menandrean model). Or (2) vv. 14–16 could have been delivered by a second character in the βωμολόχος role, adding the lines as an amusing but inconsequential comment of a sort familiar from e.g. Dionysus' remarks in the *agon* of Ar. *Ran.*, e.g. 1195f., 1242.

In the end I favour interpretation (c.1) (with Webster, *SM* 195, Edmonds 2.442 note a, Gil 339, whose further suggestion that vv. 14–16 reflect Alexis' personal philosophy lacks any evidence), but only by the smallest of margins over (a).

14 οὐκοῦν: so A and Epit. MSS, but see Barrett on Eur. *Hipp.* 331–2.

πολλοῖς τῶν σοφῶν: among the passages cited below (on vv. 15–16) the *Certamen* ascribes the maxim to Homer, and the folk-tale recounted by Aristotle has Silenus preaching it to Midas; the author of vv. 14–16 here may have such attributions in mind, but more probably an imprecise reference to the wisdom of preceding generations is intended.

15–16 The maxim rephrased in these trimeters appears to have begun its literary life as two hexameters, ἀρχὴν μὲν μὴ φῦναι ἐπιχθόνιοισιν ἄριστον, | φύντα δ' ὅπως ὤκιστα πύλας Ἀΐδαο περῆσαι, of unknown authorship and date according to Aristotle's *Eudemus* (fr. 44 Rose = 6 Walzer, Ross) but familiar already to Bacchylides (5.160f.) and labelled πανταχοῦ θρυλούμενον by Euripides fr. 285.1 (from *Bellerophon*, before 425). If these lines came originally from an early lost epic (? telling the story of Silenus' capture by Midas: see below), their incorporation in the *Certamen Homeri et Hesiodi* (78–9 Allen), a compilation which has been ascribed to Alcidamas in the 4th century (with the otherwise incorrect reference to him in Stob. *Flor.* 4.52.22 as author of the two hexameters thus accounted for), and certainly goes back in one version (*P.Petrie* 25) to the 3rd century, would be plausibly explained; cf. F. Nietzsche, *Rh. Mus.* 25 (1870) 528ff., Wilamowitz, *Die Ilias und Homer*[2] (Berlin 1920) 396ff., G. S. Kirk, *CQ* 44 (1950) 149f., R. Renehan, *HSCP* 75 (1971) 85ff. The *Theognidea* pad out the lines with pentameters (425–8). Later citers vary between direct (and sometimes inaccurate) quotation of (1) the two hexameters (also Procopius *Epist.* 47, Diogenian 3.4, Apostolius 3.85; Epicurus *Epist.* 3.126 quotes part of the first, and all the second, line, cf. E. Bignone, *RFIC* 52 (1924) 152ff.; Diog. Laert. 10.126 and Plut. *Mor.* 611f quote line two), and (2) the elegiac quatrain (with or without naming 'Theognis': all four vv., Sext. Emp. *Pyr.* 3.231, Stob. *Flor.* 4.52.30;

COMMENTARY

vv. 425–7, Clem. Alex. *Strom.* 3.3.15.1, Macarius 2.45, *Suda* s.v. ἀρχήν). Other writers paraphrase (1) the two hexameters, like our author here (S. *OC* 1224ff., Posidippus epigram 22.9–10 Gow–Page countered by Metrodorus 1 Page, *Further Greek Epigrams* (Cambridge 1981) = *Anth. Pal.* 9.359–60; (2) only line 1 ([A.] fr. 401 Nauck² = 466 Radt, Eur. frs. 285.1–2, 908.1, cf. the looser version in 449; an indirect allusion in Lysias 2.81; Bacchyl. 5.160f. rephrases *Theognid.* 425–6); (3) just line 2 (Men. fr. 416). Aristotle's *Eudemus* (*loc. cit.*) included an amusing version of the story of Midas' capture of Silenus, who utters a paraphrase of the two hexameters, cf. Cic. *Tusc.* 1.48.114–15, Lactantius *Div. Inst.* 3.19.13–14; references to the tale also in Hdt. 8.138 and Theopompus in Aelian *VH* 3.18 = *FGrH* 115 F 75c) but without the maxim; cf. E. Rohde, *Der griechische Roman*³ (Leipzig 1914) 218ff., W. Jaeger, *Aristotle*² (tr. R. Robinson, Oxford 1948) 48f., M. P. Nilsson, *Greek Piety* (tr. H. J. Rose, Oxford 1948) 58, G. Zuntz, *PBA* 42 (1957) 218 n. 6. Cf. also Ausonius 7.2.49f.

The popularity of such a maxim, with its message of total pessimism, doubtless owed something to its striking paradoxy; at the same time its background was a world dominated by disease, food shortage, natural disasters, war and human violence, where in the 5th and 4th centuries both belief in and rejection of the Greek gods brought little consolation. Zuntz 217ff. has a detailed discussion of the maxim; cf. also A. Nauck, *MGR* 6 (1892) 97f., W. C. Greene, *HSCP* 46 (1935) 31.

15 ἀεί: so Epit. (CE but with grave accent, αἰεί A). Whether the reading of the Epit. MSS comes from the paradosis or a medieval conjecture, it is right and A (*pace* Kaibel) is wrong. See comm. on fr. 76.1.

16 ἔχειν τέλος: a euphemistic periphrasis for 'to die', first recorded in 4th-century Attic (e.g. Xen. *Cyr.* 7.3.11 οὗτος . . . ἔχει τὸ κάλλιστον τέλος· νικῶν γὰρ τετελεύτηκε, Pl. *Leg.* 6.772b ζῶντος μέν . . . τέλος δὲ σχόντος, cf. 4.717e and (with τοῦ βίου) 7.801e; LSJ s.v. τέλος II.3;[1] F. M. J. Waanders, *The History of* ΤΕΛΟΣ *and* ΤΕΛΕΩ *in Ancient Greek* (Amsterdam 1983) 131f.).

146 (142K)

Meineke 3.448 (II), Kock 2.348, Edmonds 2.442, Kassel–Austin 2.104; cf. Ribbeck, *Alazon* 15ff., W. Süss, *De personarum antiquae comoediae atticae usu atque origine* (Diss. Giessen 1905) 29ff., A. Tresp, *Die Fragmente der griechischen Kultschriftsteller* (Giessen 1914) 134f., Legrand, *NGC* 100,

---

[1] However, LSJ's statement that Hesych. s.v. ἔχει τέλος calls the expression Laconian should be disregarded; M. Schmidt already saw that the οἱ Λάκωνες attached to this entry in the MS was misplaced from the previous gloss, cf. Latte *ad loc.*

ΜΑΝΔΡΑΓΟΡΙΖΟΜΕΝΗ

Pickard-Cambridge, *DTC*[1] 228ff. = [2] 134ff., Webster, *SLGC* 54, 68 n. 2, M. Gigante, *PP* 127 (1969) 302ff., Gil 328f., L. Gil and I. R. Alfageme, *Cuadernos de Filología Clásica* 3 (1972) 63ff., Gomme–Sandbach, *Comm.* on Men. *Asp.* 374, Hunter on Eubulus 81 (83K). Fr. 146(142K), like 145(141K), illustrates incongruities in human nature. A possible scenario (with 146 prompted by the recent or expected appearance of a Doric-speaking doctor or a character pretending to be one, and 145 an elaborate response to 146) is discussed in the introduction to Μανδραγοριζομένη. Yet it must be stressed that fr. 146(142K), taken by itself, merely describes an Athenian preference for Doric-speaking doctors, at least on the comic stage; it does not actually say that Alexis used one in his plot.

Ath. 14.621d–e introduces the fr. (complete in A, a few words omitted in Epit.: ἔωθεν 3, καὶ τρούβλιον 4, πάλιν 5; whence also Eustath. 884.24ff.) with a quotation from Sosibius (probably his περὶ τῶν μιμηλῶν (?) ἐν Λακωνικῇ: *FGrH* 595 F *7) which alleges that fruit thieves and the ξενικὸς ἰατρός were characters in early Doric farce. In Sicilian comedy Deinolochus wrote an Ἰατρός (*P.Oxy.* 2659 = fr. 78 Austin), and E. G. Turner published a scrap of papyrus which may come from a doctor's speech in a play by Epicharmus (*Wien. Stud.* 89 (1976) 48ff.; but see also E. W. Handley, *ibid.* 57ff., L. E. Rossi *A & R* 22 (1977) 81ff., H. Thesleff, *Arctos* 12 (1978) 153ff.). Crates is the first comic poet known to have presented a Doric-speaking doctor on the Athenian stage (fr. 46(41K)). A series of plays in later Attic comedy with titles such as Ἰατρός (by Antiphanes, Aristophon, Philemon, Theophilus), Φαρμακοπώλης (Mnesimachus, Alexis: see the introduction to Κράτεια) and Φαρμακόμαντις (Anaxandrides) bears witness to the continuing popularity of medical roles, although no dialectal evidence there survives. In Men. *Asp.* a friend of Chaireas is persuaded to equip himself with cloak and staff, emblems presumably of an itinerant ξενικὸς ἰατρός (374, 379), and in his imperso-nation of a doctor speaks medical technicalities in mock Doric (431ff.) as part of a ruse to outwit Smikrines. A genuine doctor appears in Plaut. *Men.* (v. 4, 5), summoned to treat the bogus insanity of one of the Menaechmus twins, and he utters his technicalities with the same arrogant confidence as his spurious counterpart in Men. *Asp.*, but in a Latin dialectally identical with that of the other characters.[1] Not every doctor in Attic comedy can be

---

[1] The question whether Plautus took this scene from his main Greek original or from a secondary source (perhaps even his own imagination) is still disputed; see e.g. Th. Ladewig, *Philologus* 1 (1846) 289f. (second-ary source or invented by Plaut.), W. Steidle, *Rh. Mus.* 114 (1971) 247ff. (secondary source), E. Stärk, *Die Menaechmi des Plautus und kein griechisches Original* (Tübingen 1989) 115f. (whole play invented by Plaut.), E. Woytek, *Wien. Stud.* 16 (1982) 161ff. (Greek original), A. S. Gratwick,

guaranteed to have spoken stage Doric (if Ameipsias 17(18K), Diphilus 98 and anon. fr. 344 Kock were spoken by doctors, the first used Ionic and the other two Attic), but allusions to their Doricisms here, in Epicrates 10(11K).27–9 (in Plato's Academy the very mention of a Sicilian doctor involves a switch to stage Doric) and probably Euphron 3 (where a doctor seems to be described in terms similar to the present fr.) imply its prevalence in Greek comedy.

Although the origins of the ξενικὸς ἰατρός have been identified in Doric farce, his continuing stage popularity in Athens may have owed something to the realities of life, however fossilised by convention and exaggerated by caricature. Many of the medical schools were in Doric-speaking areas (e.g. Sicily, Croton and Locri, Cnidos, even Cos – despite the use of Ionic by its medical writers, cf. Gil 328f.), their pupils after training came to mainland Greece (Sandbach notes Agesilaus' employment of a Syracusan surgeon, Xen. *Hell.* 5.4.58) and demands from patients for τὸ ξενοπρεπὲς καὶ τὸ ἄδηλον (in treatment at least) were recognised in antiquity too (Hippocr. *Praecept.* 5, 9.256 Littré).

2 ἰατρός: on the scansion (with ι optionally long or short in comedy) see Schulze, *QE* 382, Barrett on Eur. *Hipp.* 296.

2–3 τρύβλιον τούτῳ δότε πτισάνης ἔωθεν: both prescription and phraseology are modelled on contemporary medical practice, as the Hippocratic corpus abundantly shows: e.g. *Intern.* 13 πτισάνης δύο τρύβλια ῥοφεέτω μέλι παραχέας, 27 τοῦτο ἔωθεν πινέτω, cf. 51, *Morb.* 2.40 ἔωθεν μὲν διδόναι μελίκρητον ὕδατος; a similar echo in Ar. *Ach.* 278 ἔωθεν εἰρήνης ῥοφήσει τρύβλιον, cf. Fraenkel, *Beob.* 27f.

πτισάνη is the gruel made from ground peeled barley, flavoured with salt, and consumed either cold or warm (Hippocr. *Acut.* 40 Jones = 11 Littré, Ath. 10.455e, *Geoponica* 3.9); its use in the sick room was highly commended (*Acut.* 10, 11 Jones = 4 Littré) because it neither caused constipation nor swelled up in the stomach. Cf. E. Fournier in Dar.–Sag. s.v. *Cibaria* 1143, Gomme–Sandbach, *Comm.* on Men. *Epitr.* 140, M.-C. Amouretti, *op. cit.* in comm. on fr. 145(141K).7, p. 123.

τρύβλιον: in everyday use (cf. Alexis 60(59K).3) a small, flattish, multi-purpose bowl of various shapes (B. A. Sparkes and L. Talcott, *Agora*, xii.132ff., nos. 843–89, pl. 33 and fig. 9, cf. H. van Effenterre, *Rev. Phil.* 37 (1963) 41ff., Ussher on Ar. *Eccl.* 252f.), but particularly in medical prescriptions employed as a unit of liquid measure, explained in the ancient metrological tables most commonly (LSJ here needs correction) as equivalent to one κοτύλη or 9 liquid ounces (i.e. *c.* 273 cm³; e.g. Galen

comm. (Cambridge 1993) on *Men.* 889ff. (Greek original; cf. also p. 23f. n. 27, countering Stärk). See also F. Muecke, *Plautus Menaechmi: A Companion to the Penguin Translation* (Bristol 1987) 72f.

19.752, 763 Kühn, metrolog. 1.208 Hultsch), but occasionally as $\frac{1}{4}$ κοτύλη (1.236 Hultsch, Hesych. s.v.) or 4 liquid ounces (1.277 Hultsch).

4 ἂν δὲ 'πτισάνας' καὶ 'τρούβλιον': Alexis' intention (to repeat two key words of his prescription in Doric dress) is clear, but what he actually wrote is not.

(a) πτισάνας Epit. MSS and (with -ισσά-) Eustath., πτισάναν A. Both readings substitute Doric long α for Attic η in the singular of a first-declension -η stem (cf. F. H. L. Ahrens, *De dialecto dorica* (Göttingen 1843) 124ff., Thumb–Kieckers 70f., Björck, *Alpha Impurum* passim, C. D. Buck, *The Greek Dialects* (Chicago 1955) 21) in a way that would have been familiar to Athenian audiences from choral lyric in drama and elsewhere. Both readings can be defended; when Greek writers quote inflected nouns etc., they may write them either in the original case (thus here -άνας) or with the case adjusted to that required by its new context (here -άναν after εἴπῃ supplied from v. 2: e.g. Ar. *Nub.* 63f. and Dover *ad loc.*, 1240 ἥσθην θεοῖς = 'I enjoyed your use of the word θεούς, *Av.* 58 ἀντὶ τοῦ παιδός referring to the exclamation παῖ παῖ).

(b) τρύβλιον A (the word is omitted by Epit. and Eustathius), which is how the word would be written at this time in both Doric and Attic, but blurs the difference between the two dialects then in the pronunciation of υ: similar to French *u* or German *ü* in Attic, similar to Latin *u* or the English *oo* (of e.g. boot) in Doric (cf. Thumb–Kieckers 82, E. Bourguet, *Le Dialecte laconien* (Paris 1927) 5f., 97ff.), Buck 28. This latter sound was expressed in Attic by ου, and we should have expected writers like Alexis to have represented the Doric pronunciation with that combination. Some glossographers do precisely this (e.g. Hesych. s.vv. κάρουα, οὐδραίνει, τούνη; cf. Pamphilus in Ath. 2.53b), but the MSS of Attic comedy tend to spell the Doric sound as υ (e.g. τύ Ar. *Ach.* 775, 777, μύσιδδε *Lys.* 94, cf. 981, 1076, ὑσπλαγίδος 1000, φυσατήρια (R) 1242, ὀνυμάζειν Men. *Asp.* 445). It would be possible to argue, however, that this spelling convention was imposed on our MSS by Alexandrian scholarship, in order to bring them into line with the practice of poets like Callimachus and Theocritus in literary Doric. At all events we might reasonably suppose that in the present passage Alexis would have wished in writing as well as in sound to distinguish the Doric and Attic pronunciations of τρ(ο)ύβλιον, hence Kassel–Austin are surely right to print Herwerden's τρού- (*Obs. Crit.* 71f.) here.

5–6 'τευτλίον' ... 'σεῦτλον': Meineke's correction of a nonsensical paradosis (A, CE, Eustathius), σευτλίον ... τευτλίον. The various spellings and forms all denote the common beet (*Beta vulgaris*), mentioned here not as usually in its gastronomic role (e.g. eels in beet, cf. Hunter on Eubulus 34(35K).1) but because (i) it too was often a constituent of medical prescriptions (e.g. Hippocr. *Intern.* 30, 41, 42, 51: all in association with τρύβλιον), and (ii) the Attic and Doric spellings were different: τεῦτλον, -τλίον Attic (Moeris 362.1 Pierson, 210.11 Bekker τευτλίον Ἀττικοί, σεῦτλον Ἕλληνες, cf. Eustath. 813.4f.; e.g. Ar. *Pax* 1014, *Ran.* 942, fr. 128(130K).1, Crates 16(14K).8, Pherecrates 113(108K).12, Anaxandrides 42(41K).40, Eubulus 34(35K).1, 36(37K).4, 92(93K).1, possibly Diphilus 46(47K)[1]), σεῦτλον, -τλίον non-Attic (cf. Schwyzer 1.319, Mayser–Schmoll 1.1.198, Mayser 1.3.48; LSJ s.v. τεῦτλον misinterprets the Alexis passage as a reference to Ionic, not Doric, usage). Logic demands that Alexis wrote Attic τευτλίον in v. 5, non-Attic σεῦτλον (this rather than σευτλίον; cf. the back-reference in v. 7, while σευτλίον would provide a split anapaest in the first half of the second metron in v. 6, cf. *CQ* 7 (1957) 189); the error in the MSS here (and in the passages cited in n. 1 below) was influenced doubtless by the prevalence of the sigma form in later Greek.

παρείδομεν . . . ἠκούσαμεν: gnomic aorists.

7 Tresp's suggestion (p.135) that this verse, which Eustathius omits, is not part of the comic fr. but a grammarian's explanation of vv. 5–6, is wrong. The v. scans too well, and adds a telling reinforcement to tne speaker's argument. In these circumstances Eustathius' failure to cite it is of little account, even if he may have had access to a better text of Epit. than we possess (cf. H. Papenhoff, *Zum Problem der Abhängigkeit der Epitome von der venezianischen Handschrift des Athenaios* (Diss. Göttingen 1954) 4, Hunter's edition of Eubulus p. 32, my general introduction, II.i.c).

For the construction (accusative absolute introduced by ὡς) see comm. on 57(56K).5.

147 (143K)

Meineke 3.449 (IV), Kock 2.349, Edmonds 2.442, Kassel–Austin 2.104; cf. H. G. Oeri, *Der Typ der komischen Alten in der griechischen Komödie* (Basle 1948) 49. The fr., cited by Ath. 8.365d, is a dialogue between two women, one of whom (B.) is old; the other states her intention of bringing 'ribbons and perfume vases', for which she uses a Chalcidian word. The obvious implications are that she comes from Chalcis, and is going to a funeral or visiting a grave (see introduction to Μανδραγοριζομένη and comm. on

---

[1] This weight of evidence suggests that when the *Marcianus* attributes a spelling with initial sigma to Attic comedians – also Antiphanes 71(70K).1 at 4.169e, cf. Euphron 3.2 (making a point similar to Alexis' here) at 11.503a – it is simply wrong. σευτλίον occurs also in a 3rd-century comic papyrus (*P.Tebt.* 693 = anon. fr. 292.22 Austin), but whether this is a parallel error or evidence of non-Attic composition (so A. Körte, *Arch. Pap.* 11 (1935) 265f.) cannot be determined.

vv. 1–3). The alternative interpretation of her words advanced by Oeri (that she does not mean literally what she says, but is sneering rather at B.'s extreme age as if the latter were already a corpse, cf. Ar. *Eccl.* 1030ff.) cannot be ruled out in the absence of context but seems inherently less likely. Correct assignment of parts was first established by Schweighaeuser *ad loc.*

1–3 Ath. quotes this fr. in order to explain the use of συμβολαί (i.e. 'contributions') in a δεῖπνον ἀπὸ συμβολῶν (on this expression see introduction to fr. 15). This misled some scholars (e.g. Casaubon, *Animadv.* 634f., Meineke; cf. Gow on Machon 267) into believing that the ribbons and pots of perfume mentioned here were intended for a banquet. It is true that perfume and beribboned garlands had their place in Athenian parties (Machon *loc. cit.* mentions them together with wine, τραγήματα, meat and ὄψον; cf. Ganszyniec in *RE* s.v. *Kranz* 1589.31ff., M. Blech, *Studien zum Kranz bei den Griechen* (Berlin and New York 1982) 63ff.), and this fact presumably led Ath. to a by no means unique (cf. comm. on 89(86K).2) misinterpretation of the Alexis fr. Kock was the first to observe that ἀλάβαστοι and ταινίαι were most commonly associated in the decoration of funeral stelae, as the pictures on Attic white-ground lekythoi demonstrate (e.g. London, British Museum D.70, 71 = Beazley, *ARV²* 1371, 1384, illustrated in H. B. Walters, *History of Ancient Pottery* (London 1905) pl. 55.2 and A. Fairbanks, *Attic Lekythoi with Outline Drawing in Matt Colour on a White Ground* (New York 1914) pl. 28.2; cf. Ch. Lecrivain in Dar.–Sag. s.v. *Funus* 1372f., A. Fairbanks, *Attic Lekythoi with Outline Drawing on Glaze Varnish on a White Ground* (New York 1907) 342, R. S. Young, *Hesperia* 20 (1951) 111f., D. C. Kurtz and J. Boardman, *Greek Burial Customs* (London 1971) 100ff., 142ff., Blech 81ff.; literary references include Ar. *Eccl.* 1030ff., see Ussher *ad loc.*). The present passage appears to imply that συμβολαί meant 'grave offerings' in Euboean Ionic. No inscriptional or other literary evidence survives to explain how the use originated or how far it spread: ? perhaps just a local extension of the word's general meaning, 'contributions' made to the dead.

1 φέρουσα: so A correctly (the fr. is omitted in Epit.). Jacobi's conjecture φέρων σοι (in Meineke 5.ccviii) clashes with Greek custom; the decoration of funeral stelae was undertaken predominantly by women (see on vv. 1–3).

τοίνυν: Denniston, *GP* 579f. explains most postponements of this particle (here fourth word in its clause, cf. Men. *Asp.* 238, *Dysk.* 783; fifth word in (?) Chionides 6 (but attributed to Menander by Bergk in Meineke 2.1193)), which seems commoner in Plato than in comedy, to 'a desire to avoid separating words which form a logical unity', but here metrical considerations may be paramount. Cf. also comm. on 4.1 (postponement of δέ), 37(36K).1 (of γάρ).

435

COMMENTARY

2 πῶς συμβολάς: when a word is repeated in an angry or incredulous question, it has the same case or form as that of its previous occurrence. Cf. e.g. Eur. *IA* 460 τὴν δ' αὖ τάλαιναν παρθένον. :: τί παρθένον;, Men. *Dysk*. 320f. καὶ χρήσιμός γ' εἶ . . . :: τί χρήσιμος;, and Diggle, *Studies* 50f.

3 ἀλαβάστους: see on fr. 63(62K).1.

A similar routine (where somebody uses a word unintelligible to an Athenian, and then explains it as a dialectal usage) occurs in Xenarchus 11 . . . καπάνας . . . | :: τί λέγεις; <καπάνας; πῶς;>[1] :: καπάνας Θετταλοὶ | πάντες καλοῦσι τὰς ἀπήνας. :: μανθάνω. Cf. also Theoc. 2.156 and Gow *ad loc.*

148 (144K)

Meineke 3.449 (v), Kock 2.349, Edmonds 2.442, Kassel–Austin 2.105. The passage of Ath. (12.552d–f) in which this fr. is embedded deals with the politician Philippides, whose skinny frame was a byword in contemporary comedy (cf. comm. on frs. 2.8, 93(89K).1–2). Its reference to Alexis' coinage of the verb φιλιππιδόω (cf. comm. on v. 2) appears also in Ath.'s contemporary Aelian *VH* 10.6 τὸ πάνυ κατισχνῶσθαι τὸ σῶμα πεφιλιππιδῶσθαι, φασίν, ἔλεγον· μάρτυς Ἄλεξις, with the word corrupted to πεφιλιππῶσθαι in the MSS of both authors; this suggests that the extract from Alexis was already thus corrupted in a common source (? Pamphilus). Not surprisingly, when the passage of Ath. was later quarried by the lexicographers (*Suda* = Photius = epit. of Harpocration = *Et. Gen.* in Miller, *Mélanges* p. 301, all s.v. Φιλιππίδης) and Eustath. 1646.17, the error was either faithfully repeated (Eustath. defended it as syncopation) or made worse (πεφιππῶσθαι MSS B of *Et. Gen.* and E of Harp. epit., πεφιππφαι Phot.).

The three lines of the Alexis fr. are bedevilled by a series of petty corruptions over and above the one already cited, but all fortunately remediable; with the errors removed and the parts correctly (so first in Schweighaeuser) assigned to their speakers, they yield a vivid, witty exchange between two characters, of whom one is emaciated and 'almost dead' (v.3). A possible link with the plot is suggested in the introduction to Μανδραγοριζομένη.

1–3 The five corruptions in the *Marcianus* (Epit. abridges the lemma and omits the fr.) are to some extent interlinked and best discussed together.

(i) A has κακῶς ἔχει 1, τέθνηκε 3 (the latter missed by Kaibel). These

---

[1] Cobet's supplement (*NL* 16), printed by Kassel–Austin; but G. Hermann's <καπάνας; :: ναί·> καπάνας (in Erfurdt, *Obs.* 465) is equally attractive.

436

readings imply that a third person, not one of the two speakers, was in a bad way, but that conflicts with the second person εἶ (A omits the accent) in v. 1 and πεφιλιππίδωσαι (when corrected) in v. 2. The likeliest explanation is that a copyist omitted the sigma of ἔχεις by haplography before στρου-, and afterwards the ending of τέθνηκα was changed to a corresponding third person. The corrections here were first made by Casaubon (margin to his text and *Animadv.* 858).

(ii) Connected with this is the error πεφιλιππῶσθαι in both v. 2 (A) and the headnote (A, Epit.), emended in the former place to -ιππίδωσαι by Casaubon and in the latter to -ιππιδῶσθαι first by H. Stephanus in the index to *TGL* (1572) p. 1657. Ath. is here quoting and commenting on a verb coined from Philippides' name. Parallel formations most commonly add -ίζω to the name's stem, whatever its original declension (e.g. διευριπιδίζω, εὐριπιδαριστοφανίζω, ὁμηρίζω, σισυφίζω, σωκρατίζω, φιλιππίζω), but examples in -όω | -όομαι include ἐγκεκοισυρωμένην (Ar. *Nub.* 48, from Coesyra), ἐγκεχοιριλωμένη (Hesych. s.v., = λεπρά, probably coined by a comic poet after some now unknown leprous Choerilus) and πριαμωθήσομαι (Hesych. s.v., = ξυρήσομαι, see com. adesp. fr. 1123 Kock). The choice of ending in φιλιππιδόω here (and also the retention of the -ιδ- component, which is occasionally dropped in comic formations, e.g. κομψευριπικῶς Ar. *Equ.* 18) may be influenced by the need to avoid any confusion with the already existing φιλιππίζω (Dem. 18.176, Aeschines 3.130).

(iii) The second and third metra of v. 1 run in A στρουθις ακαρης νὴ Δί᾽ εἶ (with no accents on στρ., ακ. and εἶ, sometimes in this MS an indication of scribal awareness that all is not well), with the line a syllable short. No noun στρουθίς is known from ancient Greek (Eustathius' employment of the word at *Opuscula* 312.1 Tafel is presumably explained by his acceptance of the corrupt text of Alexis here); it is best rejected as a *vox nihili* (*pace* LSJ s.v.), in all probability truncating an original στροῦθ<ός τ>ις, Blaydes' palmary emendation (*Adv.* 2.161), which restores known vocabulary, heals the metre and produces exactly the sense required by the context (on the meaning of στροῦθος see below). I have discussed this type of corruption ('telescopic assimilation') more fully in Flores 368ff; cf. also comm. on fr. 31(30K).6.[1]

---

[1] Other conjectures are legion. Most accept στρουθίς without a word of justification (e.g. στρουθὶς <γάρ> Dindorf, νὴ <τὸν> Δί᾽ Casaubon, <παρ᾽> ἀκαρές Meineke; Kaibel printed νὴ Δί᾽ ἐγένου, too far from the paradosis, cf. Fraenkel, *EP* 49 and n. 3). Of those that remove στρουθίς Meineke's <ὦ> Στρούθι᾽, ἀκαρής (4.600 n., cf. 5.89) deserves an honourable mention; it turns the half-dead creature into a male (thus conflicting with my provisional plot scenario in the introduction

COMMENTARY

(iv) A's οσομου (without accent or breathings) at the beginning of v. 3 was convincingly remedied by J. Toup (*Emendationes ad Suidam* 2 (London 1766) 345f.) to ὅσον οὐ, the exact sense required, '(I'm) almost (dead)', cf. K.G. 2.412 n. 7, LSJ s.v. ὅσος iv.5a; μ and ν are easily confused in both papyrus uncial and early minuscule.

1 To an Athenian στροῦθ<ός τ>ις (see (iii) above) would denote either (i) any small dun-coloured, sparrow-like bird, but primarily the three species of sparrow native to Greece (*Passer domesticus*, house sparrow; *P. hispaniolensis*, Spanish sparrow; *P. montanus*, tree sparrow), or (ii) the ostrich (*Struthio camelus*), sometimes (but not always: e.g. Ar. *Ach.* 1105, Theophr. *HP* 4.3.5) differentiated by the addition of μέγας/μεγάλη, ἄγριος, Λιβυκός, etc. At Ar. *Av.* 877 Cleocritus is called the son of an ostrich (ὡς στρουθόποδα, τούτεστι μεγαλόπουν, Σ); but here, unless my interpretation of frs. 145–9(141–5K) in relation to the play-title is totally wrong, a reference to the addressee's sparrow-like attenuation is demanded by the context; cf. Bechtel, *Spitznamen* 8f., 17, Thompson, *Birds*[2] 268ff.

Herodian (1.xix Lentz = Σ Ar. *Av.* 877) cites Chares as his authority for the accentuation of στροῦθος as properispomenon in Attic, oxytone in Hellenistic Greek; cf. Steier in *RE* s.v. *Sperling* 1628.34f., Schwyzer 1.383.

ἀκαρής: cf. Ammonius *Diff.* § 35 Nickau ἀκαρής σὺν τῷ σ̄ (sc. as an adjective in apposition to the subject) . . . σημαίνει τὸ παρὰ βραχὺ ὄν ('within a hair's breadth' LSJ s.v. II). This quasi-adverbial usage, in Attic apparently confined to later comedy (also Men. *Asp.* 307, *Dysk.* 695, com. adesp. fr. 581 Kock; cf. Hierocles in Stob. *Flor.* 39.36, Alciphron 3.4), may at the time have been colloquial.

νὴ Δί': on the placing of the oath see K. J. Dover, *CQ* 35 (1985) 331.

2 πεφιλιππίδωσαι: cf. also the introduction to this fr. and comm. on vv. 1–3. That the verb is a nonce coinage by Alexis is implied by the response μὴ σὺ καινῶς μοι λάλει (cf. Antiphanes 169(171K) ἡ σταθμοῦχος δ' ἐστὶ τίς; / . . . ἀποπνίξεις με καινὴν πρός με διάλεκτον λαλῶν, Straton 1.3f., Pl. *Resp.* 3.405d, R. Kassel, *ZPE* 14 (1974) 122). The implication is that the person so described is not merely sparrow-tiny but also Philippides-thin. Cf. also Plaut. *Trin.* 977 (the hired agent addressing Charmides) *proin tu te, itidem ut charmidatus es, rursum recharmida.*

3 τοῦ ταλαιπώρου πάθους: almost certainly a genitive of exclamation (K.G. 1.388f.) and colloquial in tone (P. T. Stevens, *Colloquial Expressions in Euripides* (*Hermes Einzelschr.* 38, Wiesbaden 1976) 61f.), although the

---

to Μανδραγοριζομένη), but cf. the names Strouthias (parasite in Men. *Kol.*, cf. Sandbach, *Comm.* 419, 420f.), Strouthion (parasite, Alciphron 3.7) and ? Struthus (Leo's conjecture at Plaut. *Trin.* 1020, a passing mention of an unsavoury character).

possibility that the case might originally have depended on words in the lost following context (cf. e.g. Men. *Sik.* 357f.) cannot entirely be excluded. Cf. Men. *Mis.* 258 ὧ τοῦ παραδόξου καὶ ταλαιπ[ώρ]ου [∪ ⊔], where the missing noun is likely to have been either πάθους (C. Austin, *CR* 16 (1966) 296) or βίου (E. W. Handley, *BICS Suppl.* 17 (1965) 45, cf. Men. fr. 335.6, S. *OC* 91).

149 (145K)

Meineke 3.449 (III), Kock 2.350, Edmonds 2.442, Kassel–Austin 2.106. Parasites are the characters in ancient comedy most given to protesting their love for the patrons who provide them with free meals (e.g. Alexis 205.5ff.(202.1ff.K), Plaut. *Capt.* 142ff., 148ff., *Stich.* 372, 465f., 583f.; Handley on Men. *Dysk.* 57ff. well identifies them as 'the class who make friendship a profession'), and to making jokes about food which involve self-disparagement (e.g. Epicharmus 34.4, Nicolaus 1.26 and the patter speeches of the Plautine parasites: Ergasilus in *Capt.*, Curculio, Peniculus in *Men.*, Saturio in *Pers.*, Stichus in *Stich.*); hence one such is the likeliest speaker of this fr. (cf. introductions to Μανδραγοριζομένη and to fr. 121(116K) with its bibliography in p. 336 n. 1). For the semantic structure of the fr. ('if I don't love/hate X most of all, may I suffer a hateful/desirable transformation into a Y') the closest parallel is Ar. *Equ.* 399f. εἴ σε μὴ μισῶ, γενοίμην ἐν Κρατίνου κῳδίον, | καὶ διδασκοίμην προσᾴδειν Μορσίμου τραγῳδίᾳ (cf. also 767–72), as Herwerden, *Coll. Crit.* 125 first noted.[1] In both Aristophanes and Alexis the awful transformation would result in the speaker becoming the property of a contemporary celebrity: here Callimedon, the politician whose passion for eating fish (see introductions to Δορκίς and fr. 57(56K)) would make him likely to buy an ἔγχελυς (*Anguilla anguilla*, the common eel; Thompson, *Fishes* 58ff.,[2] Palombi–Santorelli 198f., Campbell, *Guide* 264f.) for his table.

---

[1] Fraenkel, *EP* 21ff., 401f. discusses the transformation aspect of this motif authoritatively from the primary standpoint of Plautine comedy, where the examples are sown more thickly than in Attic, but always with a sensitivity to the existence of Greek precursors (e.g. A. *Suppl.* 787ff., S. fr. 476, *carmina conuiualia* 17 and 18 Page, *PMG* p. 476). The closest parallel in Roman drama to vv. 2–3 of Alexis here is Plaut. *Most.* 218f., *in anginam ego nunc me uelim uorti, ut ueneficae illi | fauces prehendam atque enicem scelestam stimulatricem.*

[2] In an ill-considered *envoi* (p.61) Thompson suggests that in this fr. Alexis may be alluding to 'the struggle between the κάραβος and the eel'. Callimedon was admittedly nicknamed ὁ Κάραβος, but Thompson here is firstly confused over the then alleged biological facts (Arist. *HA*

2 ξένους ἑτέρους ὑμῶν: the identity of the ξένοι is unknown (see introduction to Μανδραγοριζομένη), but if the speaker is a parasite, they are likely to have been or become his patrons. ἑτέρους is Musurus' correction of A's ἑταίρους (Ath. 8.340c: the Epit. MSS begin their citation only at γενοίμην); confusion between the two words, resulting from an assimilation of αι and ε in pronunciation which was finalised by the 2nd century AD but occasionally leaves its trace in MSS much earlier (e.g. παλεομισημ', the 4th-century papyrus of Timotheus 15.79 Page), is very common in MSS of all periods (cf. Cobet, *NL* 517, *VL²* 121): e.g. Ar. *Lys.* 1153 (ἑταίρους *Suda* κ 1114 Adler correctly ~ ἑτέρους R), Eubulus 8(9K).1 (ἕτεροι Musurus ~ ἕταιροι A at Ath. 8.340d), Men. *Sam.* 393 (ετεραι Bᵖᶜ, εταιραι Bᵃᶜ), *Pk.* 1024, Eur. *Or.* 804, Pl. *Symp.* 183c, *Resp.* 8.568e, Ath. 13.567c (ἑταιρῶν Musurus ~ ἑτέρων A); at Men. *Dysk.* 516 ἑτέραν is corrupted to αιτεραν in B.

3 ἵνα Καλλιμέδων ὁ Κάραβος πρίαιτό με: see introduction to fr. and on v. 1. After a future wish expressed by an optative the sequence in a subordinate final clause may be either primary or (by assimilation of mood) secondary, as here; cf. e.g. A. *Eum.* 297f. ἔλθοι ... | ὅπως γένοιτο τῶνδ' ἐμοὶ λυτήριος, S. *Trach.* 953ff. εἴθ' ἀνεμόεσσά τις | γένοιτ' ἔπουρος ... αὔρα | ... ὅπως | θάνοιμι; Goodwin, *MT* 61 § 181, K.G. 1.255f.

Μάντεις

W. G. Arnott, *LCM* 14 (1989) 31ff. Several plays in Greek and Roman comedy take their titles from soothsayers and clairvoyants in the singular (Antiphanes' Οἰωνιστής and Μητρ- or Μηναγύρτης, Menander's Μηναγύρτης, Philemon's Ἀγύρτης; Naevius' *Ariolus*, Afranius' and Pomponius' *Augur*, which is also the title of a mime by Laberius), but Alexis' title is the only one with prophets in the plural. These could have been a pair (or more) of interesting characters in a New-Comedy intrigue, a chorus or a succession of ἀλαζόνες in an early play designed to ridicule their pronouncements (cf. the scenes with the χρησμολόγος and ἱερεύς in Ar. *Av.*),

---

7(8).2, 590ᵇ16f. states that crayfish prey on the conger, not the common, eel). However, apart from the fact that Alexis is not writing for an audience of fishermen and amateur naturalists, any such adjunct reference would distract attention from the main target: Callimedon and his ὀψοφαγία. Successful satirists introduce into their barbs only such material as will sharpen their main point. If any subsidiary idea is intended here, it is likely to be that Callimedon's unpopularity with the anti-Macedonian party would make the fate of becoming his dinner all the worse for a patriotic democrat.

or perhaps more probably a group of seers (? as chorus) in a travesty of the myth about the seer Polyidus and his success in elucidating an oracle and restoring Glaucus, the son of Minos, to life after the local seers had failed (cf. Höfer in Roscher s.v. *Polyeidos* 2, 2646.13ff., Robert, *GH* 1.197ff., Bernert in *RE* s.v. *Polyidos* 1, 1647.7ff.). This myth was the subject of several tragedies: probably Aeschylus' Κρῆσσαι, certainly Euripides' Πολύιδος and Sophocles' Μάντεις ἢ Πολύιδος (cf. my introduction to Alexis' Μίνως, pp. 459f. n. 1). Sophocles' play is the only one to share Alexis' title; could Alexis have intended a large-scale parody? We cannot know, but several details in the story (e.g. Glaucus chasing a mouse and drowning in a jar of honey, the mysterious calf that changed colour, the snake's resurrection: cf. [Apollodorus] 3.3, Hyginus *Fab.* 49, *Poet. Astr.* 2.14) would lend themselves to comic treatment.

If Alexis' Μάντεις burlesqued the Polyidus myth, the possibility that it and Μίνως were alternative titles of the same play must be considered; when two different titles are recorded in antiquity for one play, one title is often the name of a leading character (cf. the introduction to Ἀγωνὶς ἢ Ἱππίσκος). Μίνως can be dated roughly to the earlier part of Alexis' career.

The one extant fr. of Μάντεις (150(146K)) presents a husband attacking dowried wives. Although the theme is particularly associated with New Comedy (cf. the introduction to the fr.), it is found already in Aristophanes (e.g. *Nub.* 41ff.) and is conceivable in the Mid-Comedy world of myth travesty, where heroes of myth can be redrawn as unglamorous inhabitants of contemporary Greece (cf. the introductions to Γαλάτεια and fr. 140(135K)). If Minos (e.g.) spoke 150(146K), Alexis would be presenting the king's marriage to Pasiphae, daughter of the Sun, as a subjection to a dowried harridan.

150 (146K)

Meineke 3.450, Kock 2.350, Edmonds 2.344, Kassel–Austin 2.106. A husband (cf. introduction to Μάντεις) deplores in general terms the consequences of marrying women with dowries. Attacks on marriage (e.g. Ar. *Eccl.* 323f., Alexis 264(262K), Amphis 1, Antiphanes 220(221K), 285(292K), Aristophon 6(5K) ~ Eubulus 115(116K), Menander frs. 59, 142, 251, 573–6, 578, 718, Philemon 167(198K), monost. 160, 282 Jäkel, cf. Plaut. *Men.* 114ff.) and in particular dowried wives (e.g. Anaxandrides 53(52K), Antiphanes 270(329K), Diodorus 3, Menander frs. 333–5 (the Πλόκιον), 579, 582, 593, monost. 154 Jäkel; cf. Plaut. *Asin.* 87, *Aul.* 478ff., 532ff., *MG* 678ff.) are a commonplace of Middle and New Comedy, with the accusations that the speaker of Alexis 150(146K) makes (the loss of male freedom, petticoat tyranny) repeated in play after play. The

COMMENTARY

misogynistic bias is a recurrent feature throughout male-dominated ancient Greek literature (cf. K. J. Reckford, *TAPA* 99 (1968) 336f., H. Lloyd-Jones, *Female of the Species: Semonides on Women* (London 1975) 25ff., Hunter on Eubulus 115(116K)), yet underneath the layers of caricature, badinage and convention (cf. Legrand, *NGC* 116ff., 230f., 458) a core of truth (at least about dowries) may be detected; in *Leg.* 5.742c Plato wants a total ban on dowries, and at *Eth. Nic.* 8.10.5, 1161ᵃ1 Aristotle observes that ἐνίοτε ... ἄρχουσιν αἱ γυναῖκες ἐπίκληροι οὖσαι.

1 In the MSS here (Ath. 13.558e, where A cites the whole fr., Epit. only vv. 1–3) the opening line is metrically defective, with the gap (most probably ∪ — or its equivalent, although a longer gap cannot be ruled out) immediately preceding or following πεπρακότες; there is, however, no obvious impairment in sense. A majority of the supplements suggested can be eliminated after consideration of the normal patterns of expression in later Greek comedy after exclamations of the type ὦ δυστυχεῖς ἡμεῖς | ὦ τάλαιν' ἐγώ. These are (i) not accompanied by particles (hence not μὲν οἱ Grotius, *Exc.* 579, 973, μὲν εἰ and μὲν οἱ Bailey, *CGF* 35, ἄρ' οἱ or οἱ Meineke, γε παραπεπρακότες Edmonds); (ii) sometimes independent, sometimes closely linked with what follows, which may be (a) a main clause whose subject is the same as that of the exclamation (statement: *Men. Sam.* 245ff.; question: *Dysk.* 189f., *Sam.* 568, fr. 68), (b) main clause with different subject (statement: *Dysk.* 177f.; question: *Dysk.* 203f., 620f., *Mis.* A20f. (p. 26 Sisti, p. 352 Sandbach²), 177), (c) appositional phrase (*Men.* fr. 251.1), (d) relative (sometimes exclamatory relative) clause introduced by οἷον (*Sam.* 532ff.), ὅσοι (Antiphanes 244(250K)), ὅσον (com. adesp. fr. 257.48f. Austin) or ὅστις (*Men.* frs. 335, 511), (e) exclamatory clause introduced by ὡς (*Men. Mis.* 247ff.), and (f) conditional protasis (*Men. Her.* fr. 8 Sandbach = 7 Körte); it is doubtless an accident of preservation that some other patterns (e.g. ὅταν + temporal clause, cf. Ach. Tat. 4.9.6) do not occur. After ἡμεῖς Alexis is most likely to have written something of form (a), (d), or a limiting subordinate clause. If (a), possible supplements are legion (e.g. γάμῳ, before or after πεπρακότες; hardly Gulick's γαμεταί = 'husbands', for masc. γαμετής is not used by Attic comic poets, cf. LSJ s.v., although fem. γαμετή occurs x 9). If (d), Hirschig's ὅσοι (*Annot.* 12f., cf. Cobet in Peppink, *Observ.* 76) stands out. One further supplement perhaps deserves consideration, if only because its omission by the MSS can be neatly explained. Directly before quoting the fr. the *Marcianus* writes ὁ Λεωνίδης ... τὰ ἐκ τῶν Μάντεων Ἀλέξιδος προσηνέγκατο ταυτὶ τῶν ἐπῶν (Epit. abridges to Ἄλεξις φησί που), where τῶν ἐπῶν was rightly deleted by Kaibel. These words are nonsensical in their context; could they have originated in a misreading or adjustment of a misplaced (marginal? suprascript?) ἐπάν originally in the fr. before πεπρακότες?

442

1–3 The lines combine two metaphors. Men on marriage to dowried wives have 'sold' (πεπρακότες: wittily appropriate, since dowries turn marriage into a commercial transaction) their independence and become 'slaves' (so also Anaxandrides 53(52K).5ff., the husband of such a wife ἔχει δέσποιναν ... | ἧς ἐστι δοῦλος, Plaut. *Men.* 766ff., 795ff., *MG* 683, 701f.; cf. Eur. fr. 502.3f., a woman's rule in the house δουλοῖ τὸν ἄνδρα, κοὐκέτ᾽ ἔστ᾽ ἐλεύθερος). The lost freedom is exemplified by παρρησία (to Athenians the indispensable complement of ἐλευθερία, e.g. Eur. *Hipp.* 422, *Ion* 674f., Pl. *Resp.* 8.557b) and τρυφή (high living, often with connotations of drunken parties and sexual indulgence: in the world of comedy sometimes condoned for young bachelors but generally condemned for husbands, e.g. Men. *Epitr.* 1062ff., the endings of Plaut. *Asin.*, *Cas.*, Ter. *Phorm.*, where the denunciations, whoever originally penned them, have more in common with the popular views of 2nd-century Rome than with the far more complaisant male attitudes in 4th/3rd-century Athens; cf. V. Ehrenberg, *The People of Aristophanes*[2] (Oxford 1951) 194ff., W. K. Lacey, *The Family in Ancient Greece* (London 1968) 114, Dover, *GPM* 179f.

4 A's reading ἔπειτ᾽ ἔχειν προῖκ᾽ οὐχὶ τιμὴν πάσχομεν is accepted by Kock, Kaibel and Kassel–Austin, but its Greek is intolerable; πάσχω never takes an infinitive, and normally in Attic does not govern nouns like προῖξ and τιμή in the accusative but only neuter adjectives and (very rarely: Dem. 21.17) πράγματα (cf. LSJ s.v. III). Auratus' φάσκομεν (in Canter, *Nov. Lect.* 184f., anticipating Nicolaus Sturio in Casaubon, *Animadv.* 861f.: corrupted to πάσχ- presumably by a spooneristic transposition of the aspirate, φκ → πχ, cf. Jackson, *Marg. Scaen.* 208 n. 1), printed by Meineke and Edmonds, restores perfect sense when punctuated as a question: 'and then do we really claim that we possess a dowry, not a τιμή?' In Attic ἔπειτα commonly introduces emphatic, sneeringly consequential questions (LSJ s.v. II.3; on the similar use of εἶτα see comm. on 44(43K).1). τιμήν here is carefully chosen and positioned because of its ambiguity (honour/esteem? reward/honorific payment? penalty imposed by law?); by a familiar comic technique the speaker pauses on a word intended to puzzle his audience and so retain their attention before he goes on directly to resolve that ambiguity: 'yes, one that is bitter and full of female gall' – and so a penalty. A large dowry may at first seem to confer honour and financial advantage on a husband, but in this speaker's view it brings the penalty of an irritable wife. Cf. also Mithridates' words at Chariton 5.7.5, γάμον ὀνόμαζε τὴν πρᾶσιν καὶ προῖκα τὴν τιμήν.

6–7 A's unaccented gibberish (cf. comm. on 148(144K).1–3 iii) προσκεινην μεν λιοι μεν γε was corrected by (i) Dindorf, πρὸς ἐκείνην (cf. Meineke 2.583, κεῖνος *'forma plane inusitata est poetis comicis'* except when prodelided after a vowel, e.g. Ar. *Equ.* 1012, *Nub.* 195, or in quotation from/parody of tragedy), and (ii) Musurus, μέλι· | οἱ μέν γε (ΜΕΛΙ → ΜΕΝΛΙ by combination presumably of virtual dittography, cf. Cobet, *VL²* 4, 141, 364, and anticipation of the following μέν). Honey is the universal metaphor and object of comparison for sweetness, as gall (e.g. Alexis 16.12) is for bitterness; in comedy Ar. *Thesm.* 1192, fr. 598(581K) (language), probably fr. 633(622K) (with Meineke's correction, 5.cli: behaviour). Cf. also Plaut. *Truc.* 178ff. *in melle sunt linguae sitae uostrae atque orationes,* | *facta atque corde in felle sunt sita atque acerbo aceto,* | *eo dicta lingua dulcia dati', corde amara facitis, Cas.* 223, *Cist.* 69.

6 ἡ τῶν γὰρ ἀνδρῶν: cf. comm. on 37(36K).1.

7–8 A's text has come under attack (for γε συγγνώμην Meineke suggests γὰρ οὐ γνώμην, for ἀδικοῦσαι Dobree in Bailey, *CGF* 35 and Hirschig, *Annot.* 13 suggest ἀδικοῦσι), but yields perfect sense: men are willing to forgive (see LSJ s.v. συγγνώμη 1.a) when they are wronged, but their dowried wives, when they are doing wrong themselves, even (καί) go on the offensive and make accusations in addition to (προσ-: but see S. Schröder, comm. on Pl. *De Pyth. Orac.* 15, 401b (Stuttgart 1990), correcting LSJ s.v. προσεγκαλέω) committing the wrong; cf. also Headlam on Herodas 7.35 (p.339 n. 2).

9–10 ὧν ... ὧν δ': the two genitives are not personal, as Herwerden (*Coll. Crit.* 125) interprets, but general and all-embracing. What the women should be in charge of = 'the three duties of raising children, producing clothes with their maidservants' help, protecting the house' (W. K. Lacey, *OCD²* 1139, cf. *The Family in Ancient Greece* (London 1968) 167ff.; so Xen. *Oec.* 7.17–37); what they should not control are their husbands and activities outside the women's quarters in the house (cf. Ar. *Lys.* 507ff.). A similar complaint is made by the husband in Men. fr. 334 ἔχω δ' ἐπίκληρον Λάμιαν ... | ... κυρίαν τῆς οἰκίας | καὶ τῶν ἀγρῶν καὶ <τῶν ἁ>πάντων ἀντικρυς | ἔχομεν, cf. fr. 251.5f. ἐπὰν δ' ἀνοίξῃ τὰς θύρας, τρισάθλιος, | γυνὴ κρατεῖ πάντων, ἐπιτάττει, μάχετ' ἀεί.

10–11 F. W. Schmidt's conjecture οὐδὲν ἢ κακὸν ἔρδουσι (*Kritische Studien zu den griechischen Dramatikern* 3 (Berlin 1887) 53), like those he makes and I have ignored on vv. 1, 4–5 of the fr., are wholesale rewritings of basically healthy text; here his ἔρδουσιν would introduce a word alien to comedy (only Ar. *Vesp.* 1431 quoting a proverb: Σ *ad loc.*), but it at least demonstrates the need to interpret the transmitted text correctly: 'they don't have anything wrong with them (κακὸν ἔχουσι in the sense 'they are unwell', cf. Men. *Phasm.* 50f. εἰ μὲν τὸ κακὸν ἀληθὲς εἶχες, Φειδία, | ζητεῖν ἀληθὲς φάρμακον τούτου σ' ἔδει, and 39: an idiom not noticed by LSJ s.vv. ἔχω, κακός), and they say every time that they're ill' (LSJ s.v. κάμνω II.3).

Μεροπίς

E. Rohde, *Der griechische Roman und seine Vorläufer*[1] (Leipzig 1876) 207 n. 3 = (1900², 1914³) 222f. n. 3; Kock 2.351 and 3.742, Kaibel in *RE* s.v. *Alexis* 9, 1469.58, Breitenbach 165; cf. Gisinger in *RE* s.v. *Meropis* 1, 1056.67ff. The significance of the title is uncertain. Μεροπίς could just possibly have been (1) a *hetaira* (so Kaibel, but the word is never recorded, at least in Attica, as a personal name, cf. Breitenbach), (2) a poetical name for the island of Cos (e.g. Strabo 15.33, Aristides 7.43 Dindorf, Ant. Lib. xv, Steph. Byz. s.v. Κῶς; cf. Lloyd-Jones–Parsons, *SH* 405ff. no. 903A, the title of an anonymous poem about Cos; cf. Kock 3.742, Kruse in *RE* s.v. *Merops* 1, 1066.5ff., H. Koller, *Glotta* 46 (1968) 24f., B. Kramer, *Kölner Papyri* 3 (1980) 24f., 29ff., but comedies tend to avoid titles taken from the names of real islands or cities, cf. the introduction to Λεύκη), (3) the title figure in a myth travesty localised in Cos, where Meropis was one of Eumelus' three headstrong children who refused to pay due respect to the gods and were punished by transformation into birds (Ant. Lib. xv from Boio(s), whose Ὀρνιθογονία was known to Philochorus, *FGrH* 328 F 214, cf. Knaack in *RE* s.v. *Boio* 633.32ff., but there is no evidence linking the Boio(s) version, which seems to derive from a local legend, with the Athenian stage). Rather more plausible is a suggestion first advanced by Rohde (1876¹, 207 n. 3) that Alexis' play was designed to ridicule τὴν παρὰ Θεοπόμπῳ Μεροπίδα γῆν (Strabo 7.3.6), a utopia probably inspired by Plato's Atlantis and described at length in Theopompus' *Philippica* (*FGrH* 115 F 74, 75; main source Aelian *VH* 3.18; cf. also Rohde, *Kleine Schriften* 2 (Tübingen and Leipzig 1901) 11ff., Wilamowitz, *Platon* 1² (Berlin 1920) 594ff.). This Meropis was a country where crops grew without human toil, and such wonderlands were still a favourite theme in Middle Comedy (cf. introduction to Λεύκη). Theopompus' description came in the 7th book of a 58-book work centred on the career of Philip, who ruled Macedon from 359 till 336; if the historian began writing early in Philip's career, digressions such as that on Meropis could have been circulating independently in Athens already by the 350s or 340s. The one fr. extant from Alexis' Μεροπίς (151(147K)) refers to Plato in terms which imply that he was still alive or had died so recently that his practices were yet vividly remembered (cf. the introduction to Ἀγκυλίων and T. B. L. Webster, *CQ* 2 (1952) 17f.).

151 (147K)

Meineke 3.451, Kock 2.351, Edmonds 2.444, Kassel–Austin 2.107. The speaker is a woman who has apparently been on stage some time, walking up and down as she vainly ponders some problem. Now she greets a newly

COMMENTARY

arriving character (of unspecified sex) whom she has presumably arranged to see. Scenes with one woman waiting for one or more others open Ar. *Lys.* (cf. 4ff.) and *Eccl.* (cf. 19ff.), and Men. *Mis.* begins with its male hero walking about anxiously (A6ff.) before he is joined by his slave (A15 p. 26 Sisti, p. 351 Sandbach²), but parallel situations occur frequently at later points in comedies (woman speaking: Ter. *Eun.* 743ff. and W. Ludwig, *Philologus* 103 (1959) 14ff.; man speaking: e.g. Men. *Sam.* 639f.*, Plaut. *Amph.* 957*, *Bacch.* 842ff., *Curc.* 301ff., *Epid.* 202f., *Men.* 139*, *Merc.* 964*, *Most.* 574, *Pers.* 101*, Ter. *Andr.* 533, 783, 974, *HT* 179). On the stars see comm. on v. 1.

1 εἰς καιρὸν ἥκεις: here the new arrival appears to have been expected by the speaker, but elsewhere in comedy these and similar words (*opportune/-nus/optato/optume aduenis*) are sometimes employed simply as a formula to cover a dramatically convenient but unexplained entry (e.g. the passages starred above). Cf. also comm. on 177(173K).9–10 and introduction to fr. 153(149K).

1–3 The comparison with Plato presumably involves both the speaker's ἀπορία in v. 1 (which has not found a typically 'clever' Platonic resolution) and her anxious pacing up and down while she ponders. This passage is the only contemporary reference, so far as I know, to Plato's indulgence in the latter habit (but later cf. Aelian *VH* 3.19 ἐνόσει δὲ τότε Σπεύσιππος, καὶ διὰ ταῦτα ἀδύνατος ἦν συμβαδίζειν τῷ Πλάτωνι ... καὶ διὰ ταῦτα ἀποστὰς ὁ Πλάτων τοῦ ἔξω περιπάτου ἔνδον ἐβάδιζε σὺν τοῖς ἑταίροις; also Epicurus fr. 171 Usener, Ammonius on Arist. *Categ.*, *CIAG* IV.4 p. 3.8; Plato himself describes it of Socrates (*Phd.* 96a–b), Protagoras (*Protag.* 314e–315b) and 'the stranger' (*Soph.* 242a–b). On the reference(s) of περίπατος/περιπατεῖν in Aristotle see I. Düring, *Aristotle in the Ancient Biographical Tradition* (Göteborg 1957) 404ff.; in other philosophers [Alexis] 25.1ff., Epicurus fr. 423, Diog. Laert. 7.5, Lucian *Jup. Trag.* 1 ~ Men. fr. 722, Dicaearchus fr. 29 Wehrli in Plut. *Mor.* 796d. Cf. also C. Ritter, *Platon* 1 (Munich 1910) 193 n. 1, R. Fenk, *Adversarii Platonis quomodo de indole ac moribus eius iudicaverint* (Diss. Jena 1913) 40, A. Weiher, *Philosophen und Philosophenspott in der attischen Komödie* (Diss. Munich 1913) 26, G. J. de Vries, *Hermeneus* 27 (1955) 6, and also my comm. on Alexis 91(87K).2. Characters in comedy who so behave are either perplexed (also *P.Didot.* II.11, p. 330 Sandbach and *Comm.* 728f., cf. Men. *Phasm.* 35f.) or depressed (Ar. *Lys.* 709, Men. *Mis.* A7). P. T. Stevens, *Colloquial Expressions in Euripides* (*Hermes Einzelschr.* 38, Wiesbaden 1976) 10f. collects the instances of ἄνω κάτω (τε) in Attic, suggesting that the use here may be colloquial.

3 εὕρηκ': cf. comm. on fr. 9.2.

κοπιῶ τὰ σκέλη: cf. Men. *Phasm.* 35f. περιπατεῖς [— ∪ ⊔], | εἰσῆλθες εὐθύς, ἂν κοπιάσῃς τ[ὰ σκέλη]. In the restricted sense of 'I am tired' κοπιάω is widespread in Attic comedy (also Ar. *Av.* 735, *Thesm.* 795, frs. 333(318K).8, 618(602K), Men. fr. 416.13), but not found in tragedy or good Attic (~ Ionic, *Koine*) prose: ? perhaps a colloquialism imported from Ionic; cf. Bruhn, *Wortschatz* 30. After κοπιῶ the MSS (Diog. Laert. 3.27) split between τὼ σκέλη (F, omitting accents, but this combination of dual article + plural noun is doubtful) and τὰ σκέλη (the rest). In 5th-century Attic τὼ σκέλει is normal for human legs (Ar. *Pax* 241, 325, 820 τὼ RV ~ τὰ Γ, 825, 889, *Av.* 1254 R, *Thesm.* 24, 256, Eur. *Cycl.* 183 with article; Ar. *Lys.* 1172 without), but later the plural replaces the dual in all applications (also Antiphanes 105(106K).3, Anaxilas 22.21, Men. *Perinth.* 18 where the proverbial expression of Ar. *Pax* 241 is transferred to the plural, com. adesp. fr. 208 Kock, Pl. *Phd.* 61c, 117a, e; possibly also Ar. *Eccl.* 265 τὼ σκέλη RAΓ ~ τὰ σκέλη. B Ald.) where the duality is not specifically emphasised.

Μίδων

Meineke 1.401, Breitenbach 53, Legrand, *NGC* 28f., Kann, *De iteratis* 70 n. 2. Μίδων is a rare name borne by nonentities in Attica (father or teacher of the poet Lamprocles, Σ Ar. *Nub.* 967; title figure of a spurious Platonic dialogue, Diog. Laert. 3.62)[1] and elsewhere (a gardener in *Anth. Pal.* 16.255) unlikely (*pace* Meineke, Legrand) to have provided subjects for extended satire. As the title of plays attributed to both Antiphanes and Alexis it probably indicates a fictitious character with a prominent but unknown role. Only one word survives from Antiphanes' play (fr. 155(157K)), two trimeters from Alexis' (fr. 152(148K)); there is no evidence to decide whether one of the two ascriptions is a textual corruption of the other, or whether one play (? Alexis') plagiarised the other (cf. the introductions to Ἀλείπτρια, Ἄντεια in 'False or Doubtful Attributions' I, II).

152 (148K)

Meineke 3.451, Kock 2.351, Edmonds 2.444, Kassel–Austin 2.108; cf. also W. Frantz, *De comoediae atticae prologis* (Diss. Strasbourg 1891) 36. The speaker carries a lamp to light the way in the dark. Night scenes in ancient drama – comedy as well as tragedy – come regularly at the beginning (e.g. A. *Ag.* 1ff., Eur. *El.* 54ff., Ar. *Nub.* 3ff., *Vesp.* 244ff., *Lys.* 72, *Eccl.* 1ff., Men.

---

[1] Kirchner's entry at *PA* 2.86 no. 10165, however, needs to be deleted, being based on an implausible supplement in *IG* ii².4331 (better [Φε]ίδων Michel than [Μ]ίδων Koehler).

COMMENTARY

Mis. A1ff., com. adesp. fr. 240.4ff. Austin, Plaut. *Amph.* 153ff., *Curc.* 1ff.) and/or ending (e.g. A. *Eum.* 1022ff., 1041f., Ar. *Pax.* 1316f., *Ran.* 1524ff., *Eccl.* 1149f., *Plut.* 1194ff., Antiphanes fr. 269(272K) and Ath. 15.686c commenting on it, Men. *Dysk.* 963f., *Mis.* 459f., *Sam.* 731f., *Sik.* 418ff., Plaut. *Bacch.* 1203ff.; cf. *Hermes* 93 (1965) 253ff.), functioning as chronological markers for those plays whose time-scales extend beyond the norm of dawn to dusk into the darkness before and/or after daylight; cf. *PLLS* 2 (1979) 343ff. and *ZPE* 70 (1987) 19ff. Although there are occasional exceptions to this general procedure (the action of *Rhesus* occupies a night; a night intervenes between Acts II and III of Ter. *HT*), it is probable that Alexis 152(148K) comes from a speech very early or very late in the plot. Frantz's suggestion that the two verses open the play is unverifiable speculation; generalities like those in 152 typically begin or end entrance monologues at any stage in the action (cf. e.g. Fraenkel, *EP* 150ff., 422ff., J. Blundell, *Menander and the Monologue* (Göttingen 1980) 50, 58f., 61).

The speaker's identity is uncertain. Possibilities include a woman out before daybreak (cf. openings of Ar. *Lys.*, *Eccl.*), a slave (cf. Plaut. *Amph.* 153ff.) or particularly a parasite (cf. Epicharmus 35.7ff. κἤπειτα πολλὰ καταφαγὼν, πόλλ' ἐμπιών, | ἄπειμι· λύχνον δ' οὐχ ὁ παῖς μοι συμφέρει, | ἕρπω δ' ὀλισθράζων τε καὶ κατὰ σκότος | ἔρημος) out early or late; less likely would be a prosperous free man, for he would expect to have with him a slave carrying lamp or torch (cf. Plaut. *Curc.* 1ff.).

1 ὁ πρῶτος εὑρών: cf. also 190(185).1, comm. on 27.1–2.

περιπατεῖν: sc. '(having discovered) how to walk about'. εὑρίσκω and its compounds may take the same infinitival construction as other verbs of learning/teaching/knowing (cf. K.G. 2.68ff.), although LSJ s.v. (a badly arranged entry, wrongly separating uses 1.4 and 11.2, but see also IV) and Goodwin, *MT* p. 365 mistakenly claim that the construction occurs only with εὑρίσκομαι in the middle (e.g. Eur. *Med.* 196 ηὕρετο ... παύειν), but note also S. *OR* 120 ἓν γὰρ πόλλ' ἂν ἐξεύροι μαθεῖν with Jebb's comm. *ad loc.*

2 κηδεμὼν τῶν δακτύλων: 'guardian of the fingers'. κηδεμών (technically one's legal protector: cf. Ar. *Vesp.* 242 and Starkie *ad loc.*) adds an amusingly pompous touch. Kock here interprets δακτύλων as toes, on the ground that they (not fingers) would be injured if one walked about at night on the uneven surfaces of Athenian streets *sine lucerna*. But λυχνοῦχος is not a lamp, but the holder in which the lamp is placed, as Schweighaeuser (*Animadv.* 8.348 on Ath. 15.700a citing the fr.) accurately observed; the fingers are protected by the holder from being burnt by the lamp (cf. Alexis 107(102K).1f. ἐξελὼν <ἐκ> τοῦ λυχνούχου τὸν λύχνον | μικροῦ κατακαύσας ἔλαθ' ἑαυτόν, and comm. *ad loc.*).

448

ΜΙΛΗΣΙΟΙ

Μιλήσιοι (or -ησία)

Meineke 1.388 ~ title at 3.451ff.; cf. T. B. L. Webster, *CQ* 2 (1952) 22, Bain, *Actors* 103 n. 4, Nesselrath, *MK* 253 n. 34. Ath. 9.379a (fr. 153(149K)) and Stob. *Anth.* 4.48a.5 (fr.154(150K)) cite from Alexis' Μιλήσιοι,[1] Ath. 6.240c (fr. 155(151K)) refers to his Μιλησία. Alexis could have written both a Μιλησία (also the title of plays by (i) Philemon III in Athens 183 BC, *IG* ii².2323.159 = Pickard–Cambridge, *DFA*² 111 = Mette III B 3 col. 3b, 13, cf. Kock 3.357, and (ii) Agathenor in Magnesia, first half of 1st century, O. Kern, *Die Inschriften von Magnesia am Maeander* (Berlin 1900) 88 d 4f. = Mette II B 2cd 9f: no frs. of either play survive) and a Μιλήσιοι, but more probably one of the endings is a corruption of the other (cf. especially introduction to Ἀποκοπτόμενος or -ομένη). Titles denoting one girl or two or more men from a city other than Athens seem equally common in later Greek comedy;[2] if here -ήσιοι is preferred, it is mainly because two citations allege this ending, against one with -ησία; confusion with the Philemon (but hardly the Agathenor) title may possibly have played a part.

Such titles are regularly associated with the adventures of natives of the named city in another part of the Greek world, often Athens (cf. the introductions to Ἀτθίς and the other titles cited below in n. 2). Frs. 153(149K) and 154(150K) could easily be accommodated in plots like those of Men. *Sam.* or Ter. *Andr.*; in 153 a μάγειρος talks about his craft probably to his hirer and one or more others (see introduction to the fr. and comm. on vv. 1, 5, 15) with a combination of cocksureness, elevated language and sound sense; in 154 a man apparently intends to help a relation or friend.

The third citation (155(151K)) merely claims that Alexis mentioned the parasite Tithymallus, whose name is linked elsewhere with personalities of the second half of the 4th century like Eucrates ὁ Κόρυδος (Timocles 10: *fl. c.* 350–320, see introduction to Alexis 48(47K)) and Philippides (Aristophon 10: lived *c.* 370–310, see on Alexis 2.8) and mentioned in Timocles fr. 18 which probably ridicules Demosthenes' famous quibble in the Halonnesus dispute of 343 (cf. introduction to Alexis' Ἀδελφοί and frs. 7, 212(209K); V. Bevilacqua, *Dioniso* 7 (1939) 40f.). Yet we know neither how old Tithymallus was in the late 340s nor how long he survived afterwards; the floruit assigned to him by Webster (*c.* 345–320, to which

---

[1] Meineke 3.453 misreports the Stobaeus lemma.

[2] In Alexis, singular girl: Ἀχαΐς, Βρεττία, Κνιδία, Λευκαδία, Λημνία; plural men: Θεσπρωτοί, Θηβαῖοι, Λοκροί, Ταραντῖνοι. Cf. Ὀλύνθιοι or -ιος or -ία (presenting the same problem as here), Ἀτθίς, Ἑλληνίς.

plays referring to this parasite would then be dated: cf. Nesselrath) is no more than an intelligent shot in the dark (cf. Bain).

153 (149K)

Meineke 3.451 (1), Kock 2.351, Edmonds 2.446, Kassel–Austin 2.108; cf. Wilamowitz, *Nachr. Gött.* (1895) 226ff. = *Kleine Schriften* 5.2 (Berlin 1937) 15ff., Kann, *De iteratis* 64, Nesselrath, *MK* 261f. and n. 55, 302f. A cook, introduced here apparently with an unidentified hirer (cf. Dohm, *Mageiros* 103, 154ff.) and one or more others (see comm. on vv. 1, 15) for an unknown celebration (but see comm. on v. 5), proves no less garrulous than his fellows in frs. 115(110K), 129(124K) and 177–9(173,172,174K) (cf. A. Giannini, *Acme* 13 (1960) 160f.), but two aspects of his presentation deserve special notice. First, he speaks throughout (as does his interlocutor in vv. 5, 14: v. 5 was first assigned to the latter by Daléchamp in his translation, v. 14 by Bothe, *PCGF* 551, following a hint by Dobree, *Adv.* 2.322) in elevated language with the strictest of tragic rhythms (no resolutions, Porson's law always observed, always penthemimeral or hephthemimeral caesura), rising in his last five vv. to those heights of riddling imagery which are associated in the late 5th and early 4th centuries particularly with the dithyramb. The style is well analysed by Hunter on Eubulus 75 and Nesselrath, *MK* 241ff.; cf. also my introduction to Alexis 124(119K). Secondly, the main lesson that Alexis' cook teaches – the importance of καιρός (here and at 151(147K).1 'appropriate time'; contrast 177(173K).9–10 and comm.) to cook and guests alike (cf. later the μάγειροι in Dionysius 2.33ff. ἐὰν δ' | εὖ μὲν σὺ χρήσῃ τῇ τέχνῃ, τὸν τῆς τέχνης | καιρὸν δ' ἀπολέσῃς, παραπόλωλεν ἡ τέχνη, and Sosipater 1.48ff. τὸ γὰρ παραθεῖναι κἀφελεῖν τεταγμένως | ἕκαστα καὶ τὸν καιρὸν ἐπὶ τούτοις ἰδεῖν | ... ταῦτα πάντα <δὴ> (suppl. Musurus) | ἐν τοῖς στρατηγικοῖσιν ἐξετάζεται | μαθήμασιν) – is neither foolish nor comic in itself but fundamental to all successful cookery; cf. e.g. A. Brillat Savarin, *Physiologie du goût* (Paris 1846), *aphorisme* 16 ' *La qualité la plus indispensable du cuisinier est l'exactitude: elle doit être aussi cette du convié.*' Alexis' cook here as elsewhere (e.g. 129(124K), 138(133K)) knows his business.

1 ἴστε: the second-person plurals here and in v. 15 (ἐστήκαθ') presumably imply that more than one character is being addressed, although very occasionally in later Greek comedy this plural is directed (with specifically dramatic purpose) to an audience of one (e.g. Knemon to Sostratos, Men. *Dysk.* 173–6, cf. *G and R* 22 (1975) 147).

τῶν τεχνῶν: of which ἡ μαγειρική in this speaker's view is naturally one; cf. comm. on 129(124K).18–19 and Dohm, *Mageiros* 203ff.

2 οὐχ ἀρχιτέκτων: so independently in 1855 Bothe, *PCGF* 550f. and Herwerden, *Obs. Crit.* 73 (but note that Grotius, *Exc.* 579 already printed

ΜΙΛΗΣΙΟΙ

οὐχ ἀρχι-), a certain correction of A's οὐ κάρχι- (*sic* at Ath. 9.379a; Epit. cites only vv. 7 ἂν μέν–16 κύνες of the fr.); see comm. on 88(85K).3–5. In Attic ἀρχιτέκτων = literally 'master-builder/director of works', both generally and in relation to specific state functions (e.g. ἐπὶ τὰς ναῦς [Arist.] *Ath. Pol.* 46.1 with Rhodes' comm. *ad loc.*; ἐπὶ τὰ ἱερ[ά] *IG* ii.².840.13f.; manager of the Theatre of Dionysus, Dem. 18.28, *IG* ii².792.8); the secondary sense of 'organiser' (so here, doubtless with designed pomposity) may have originated as a poetical metaphor (first in Eur. *Cycl.* 477), but became established in 4th-century prose (e.g. [Dem.] 40.32, 56.11 τούτῳ τῷ ἀρχιτέκτονι τῆς ὅλης ἐπιβουλῆς, Arist. *Pol.* 7.3.5, 1325ᵇ23 τοὺς ταῖς διανοίαις ἀρχιτέκτονας, *Eth. Nic.* 7.11.1, 1152ᵇ2). The noun appears only here in Attic comedy, but passages such as Plaut. *MG* 901f. *hic noster architectust.* :: *salue, architecte* may translate or be inspired by a similar use of ἀρχιτέκτων in the Greek original (on *architectus, -tecton* in Plautus see G. P. Shipp, *Glotta* 34 (1955) 151f.). The verb ἀρχιτεκτονῶ appears in its literal sense 'I act as master-builder/director of works' at Ar. *Pax* 305 (sc. with reference to rescuing Peace from the pit; cf. Hdt. 3.60, an ἀρχιτέκτων in charge of building a tunnel) and Sosipater 1.16 (used by a cook; cf. ἡ ἀρχιτεκτονική sc. τέχνη literally at v. 36); also Ar. fr. 201(195K), context unknown.

3–4 ἀλλὰ κἀκ τῶν χρωμένων συμβάλλεταί τις, ἂν καλῶς χρῶνται, μερίς: 'but some contribution is made by his employers too, if they employ him well'. As a cook-ἀλαζών the speaker is deliberately cryptic, but the transmitted text makes perfect sense after the one minor correction of A's καί to κἀκ (so Richards, *AO* 61f.: without this correction τῶν χρωμένων would have to depend on τις μερίς, with inappropriate sense if the genitive were taken as partitive, 'some part of his employers', since the cook's success is achieved by the punctuality of all – not some – of the diners,[1] and with unnatural phraseology if the genitive were construed as subjective, 'some contribution made by his employers'). συμβάλλεταί τις ... μερίς here turns into the passive the common idiom συμβάλλομαι (middle) μέρος εἰς/πρός τι, cf. LSJ s.v. συμβάλλω 1.9, with μερίς substituted for μέρος presumably in order to make it clear that the noun is in the nominative. On τῶν χρωμένων and χρῶνται see comm. on 140(135K).16.

The general theme of vv. 1–4, that art, for its success, requires the collaboration of artist and appreciator, is repeated by (?) Philemon 196(72.4–5K).

5 ποῖόν τι: ποῖον is Porson's correction (*Adv.* 111) of A's οἶον, without breathing (cf. comm. on 148(144K).1–3, iii and iv). The corruption may

---

[1] A similar argument rules out Blaydes' conjecture μέρος (*Adv.* 2.164) as object of a middle συμβάλλεται, 'one of the employers (sc. diners) makes a contribution'.

451

have been due to a copyist's failure to understand the syntax (ποῖόν τι is one of a series of expressions, e.g. (τὸ) ποῖον (δή), (τὰ) ποῖα (δή), used frequently in conversation with reference to a nominative or accusative neuter singular or plural expressed in the words directly preceding,[1] but here picking up exceptionally the feminine μερίς in v. 4 as if it were conceptually neuter; cf. Xen. *Mem.* 4.6.2 ποῖόν τι νομίζεις εὐσέβειαν εἶναι; Pl. *Gorg.* 462d τίς τέχνη ὀψοποιΐα; ... ἀλλὰ τί, φάθι; K.G. 1.58ff.) and substitution of an exclamatory (but here inappropriate) οἷον.

τὸν ξένον: the precise meaning (or range of meanings) is uncertain as long as we do not know the identity of the speaker and the relation of the cook scene to the plot. In an Athenian culinary context normally ξένος = 'guest', ξενοδόκος 'host' (LSJ s.vv.), but occasionally ξένος occurs in the sense of 'host' (e.g. Hom. *Il.* 15.532, Ap. Rhod. 1.208); if the word does bear this meaning here, its choice may possibly have been dictated by a desire to play additionally with one or two further meanings of ξένος: (i) 'ignorant' (LSJ s.v. B.II, normally with the genitive; cf. Kock *ad loc.*, noting the possibility of neither pun nor sarcasm), (ii) 'foreigner' (LSJ s.v. A.III, cf. Herwerden, *Obs. Crit.* 72; in Men. *Mis.* Demeas, who comes ἐκ Κύπρου v. 231, is habitually so labelled, cf. Gomme–Sandbach, *Comm.* pp. 438f.). The speaker of this line was probably accompanied by at least one person who keeps silent throughout the fr. (see on v. 1); could the two have been the Milesians of the likelier title, foreigners in Athens? Cf. also comm. on 149(145K).2.

6–7 On the ὀψοποιός and this definition of his role see introduction to Κράτεια and cf. comm. on fr. 140(135K).15–16. **τοὖψον** (Pierson's correction of A's τοῦτον in his edition of Moeris (Leiden 1759) p. 274: confusion between Τ and Ψ in MSS is common, e.g. Men. fr. 486, τύχην corrupted to ψυχήν; cf. Porson on Eur. *Med.* 553, Cobet, *NL* 74) at this period primarily means fish (see on fr. 47(46K).6). In the absence of dramatic context it is impossible to say why the μάγειρος (his identity is confirmed at v. 14) makes a provocative and prejudiced (but probably accurate: cf. G. Berthiaume, *Les Rôles du mágeiros* (Leiden 1982) 77) statement about a rival at this point in his argument; we do not know whether (e.g.) an ὀψοποιός was playing a minor role in the play at his side (? like the τραπεζοποιός in Men. *Asp.* 232ff.).

σκευάσαι χρηστῶς ... τοὖψον: cf. Archestratus in Ath. 7.311b, fr. 176.12 Lloyd-Jones–Parsons (*SH* p. 67) χρηστῶς σκευαζέμεν ἰχθῦς.

---

[1] E.g. ποῖον Ar. *Lys.* 1163, *Ran.* 1021, Antiphanes 200(202K).5; ποῖόν τι Ar. *Thesm.* 76; τὸ ποῖον Pl. *Phd.* 89c, Lucian *Cat.* 9, *Herm.* 31; τὸ ποῖον δή Pl. *Phdr.* 279a, *Theaet.* 187d; τὰ ποῖα Xen. *Oec.* 10.1, Lucian *Tim.* 28; τὰ ποῖα δή Pl. *Soph.* 217a. Cf. also τὸ ποῖον δὴ λέγεις Pl.

8 Epit. here has ὁ μέλλων ἐσθίειν καὶ κρίνειν (CE: A κρινειν without accent), thus imposing an impossible spondee in the second half of the last metron. Alexis is more likely to have coupled together two present or two future infinitives after μέλλων than to have varied the tenses (thus Dindorf's κρινεῖν alongside ἐσθίειν, printed by Kassel–Austin, and Heimsoeth's κρινῶν alongside μέλλων, *Comm. Alt.* xiii, do not convince). ἐσθίειν is clearly the *mot juste* (*pace* Blaydes, *Adv.* 1.111) in a dining context (for the precise import of the present infinitive with μέλλω, 'the man who will presumably be eating', see O. Szemerényi, *AJP* 72 (1951) 346ff.), and καὶ κρίνειν will then corruptly displace a parallel present infinitive, either a less usual word of comparable meaning supplanted by a gloss (I cannot think of one), or more probably Meineke's (κ)εὐκρινεῖν (*Anal. Crit.* 167; for the postulated corruption, cf. comm. on vv. 3–4 above). εὐκρινεῖν occurs first = 'select/arrange (troops) carefully' in Xen. *Hell.* 4.2.6 (cf. διευκρινεῖν in *Oec.* 8.6), then = 'judge well' in *P.Cair.Zen.* 59150.22 (266 BC, yet σὺ | εὖ κρίνεις are alternative readings; but cf. here διευκρινεῖν in Polyb. 31.8.1); here appropriately 'discern well', i.e. as a connoisseur. The 4th century saw a great expansion in εὐ- compounds, with comedy naturally in the forefront with new coinages or early uses: e.g. εὐδοκεῖν Men. *Asp.* 4, εὐδρομεῖν Men. fr. 934, εὐειματεῖν Antiphanes 56(54K), εὐκερματεῖν Eubulus 142(144K), εὐκυβεῖν Amphis 11; striking nouns/adjectives include in Alexis Εὐημερία personified fr.166(161K), εὐοψία 39(38K), εὐπυγία 103(98K).11, in Men. εὐῆλιξ *Dysk.* 950, εὐόφθαλμος *Sik.* 399, εὐπάτειρα *Dysk.* 968, *Mis.* 465, *Sik.* 422; not surprisingly some of these formations fell foul of stricter Atticists (εὐοψία, cf. Antiatticist 93.1 Bekker and my comm. on Alexis 39(38K); εὐκερματεῖν Phryn. *Ecl.* p. 97 Fischer).

9 εἰς καιρὸν ἐλθών: now for the first time, after seven vv. of highsounding generalisations and diversions (which tease the audience by their delaying tactics: a common technique in e.g. Ar. and Plaut.), the cook explains precisely how the guest can help: by being punctual. Cf. also introduction to this fr.

ὠφέλησε: gnomic aorist (like ἀπεστέρησε in v. 13), which counts as a primary tense, and so the subordinate clause in v. 10 (an indefinite condition) is constructed with ἄν + subjunctive, not εἰ + optative; cf. Goodwin, *MT* 58 § 171, 205f. § 533, and K.G. 1.16of.

10–13 The unanimous text of A and Epit. here makes perfect sense: 'but if a guest comes after (ὑστερίζῃ, with a genitive as at Men. *Sam.* 670, cf. LSJ s.v.) the agreed moment, with the result that (the cook) must either warm up the food again if he has roasted/grilled it in advance, or else complete

---

Phdr. 265a, *Theaet.* 187c; τὰ ποῖα δὴ (ταῦτα) λέγεις Pl. *Phlb.* 13d, *Phd.* 81e.

the cooking in a rush if he hasn't, then he (the guest) removes the pleasure from the craft.' Even so, objections have been registered. (i) Herwerden (*Obs. Crit.* 72f.) finds the unspecified change of subject in the ὥστε clauses (11–12) unacceptable and proposes a lacuna after v. 10, where he supplies a verse beginning <ἢ πρότερος ἔλθῃ> (cf. Kock, completing the verse). This is absurd; a guest's *early* arrival would not create difficulties in the kitchen, and the change of subject from guest to cook is clearly signalled by the use of *accusative* and infinitive in the consecutive clauses. The identity of the new subject does not need to be expressed; in comedy only cooks cook, and the absence of τὸν μάγειρον in vv. 11–12 can be compared to the normal omission of expressed subjects with 'professional' verbs such as σαλπίζει, κηρύττει, etc. (K.G. 1.32f., § b). (ii) With more acuteness Blaydes (*Adv.* 1.112, 2.164) observes that ἀποστερεῖν is commonly constructed with an accusative of the victim and genitive of the object removed (LSJ s.v. 1.1) and so conjectures in v. 13 τὴν τέχνην τῆς ἡδονῆς (cf. e.g. Ar. *Nub.* 1072). This verb, however, often also takes an accusative of the object removed (e.g. Ar. *Nub.* 1305f., 1463f., *Eccl.* 449, LSJ s.v. I.4), and the genitive in v. 13 may be construed, notwithstanding its position, as possessive, not separative.

10 τῆς τεταγμένης ἀκμῆς: ἀκμή, like καιρός, is the critical point in a period of time (LSJ s.v. III); the cook's expression here is precisely targeted and not merely a pretentious variant for the standard phrase ὁ τεταγμένος χρόνος (e.g. singular Hdt. 2.41, Isoc. 6.8; plural Pl. *Tim.* 89b, Aeschines 3.126, Dem. 24.26, Arist. *Meteor.* 2.2, 355ᵃ28).

11–12 προοπτήσαντα: the compound verb occurs twice here but nowhere else in Greek literature.

χλιαίνω and χλιαρός in Attic comedy normally scan the first syllable long (verb: also Ar. *Lys.* 386, *anceps* Antiphanes 216(217K).4; adjective: Magnes 2(1K).2, Cratinus 130(125), 150(143K).4, Ar. *Ach.* 976, fr. 520.8(506.6K), probably Cratinus 154(147K) but could be *anceps* if that brief fr. does not end a trimeter). In other genres and/or dialects the first syllable may be shortened by correption (e.g. verb: epigram in Ath. 13.604f = Page, *FGE* 303f., Meleager 91.4 Gow–Page = *Anth. Pal.* 12.63; adjective: Epicharmus fr. 290).[1]

14 This interjection by the second speaker (cf. introduction to this fr.), which (like that in v. 5) breaks up an otherwise long as well as high-flown speech by the cook (cf. Bain, *Actors* 102), is inspired by the elaborately periodic construction of the single sentence in vv. 7 ἂν μέν –13, with an example of parisosis (10 ∼ 11) encapsulated in an antithesis (7–9 ∼ 10–13),

---

[1] At Ar. *Eccl.* 64 the major MSS (RΑΓ) unite with ἐχλιαινόμην, but this reading raises grave doubts (better ἐχραινόμην Boissonade: see C. Austin, *Dodone* 10 (1987) 90).

features here designed to parody the 'sophistic' (on the term σοφιστής in Alexis see comm. on 20.1–2, 27.1) style introduced to Athens by Gorgias. ἐγγράφω is the technical term in Athens for registering a person (accusative) in a particular group (εἰς + accusative): especially the deme (εἰς τοὺς δημότας e.g. Dem. 18.261, [Arist.] *Ath. Pol.* 42, Men. *Karch.* 39, cf. 33f.; or εἰς τοὺς ἐφήβους e.g. [Pl.] *Axioch.* 366e, Heliodorus 1.13), but also e.g. the phratry (Dem. 39.4) and military levies (Ar. *Equ.* 1369ff.); thence metaphorically with the same construction (as here) = 'I include': e.g. Ar. *Equ.* 925f., Men. fr. 199.2.

15–19 At this point the stylistic level rises even higher (cf. introduction to this fr.), as the cook adds an ingenious conceit (17–19) and the wild imagery of kenning (16–17) to his tragic rhythms and diction. After this extravagant climax the cook doubtless made his exit, to pursue his tasks in one of the stage-houses. There is an engaging irony in the fact that he blames the other people now present on stage for the waste of valuable time which he himself has caused by his speech on the importance of time for a cook. In all probability it was partly a failure to appreciate the appropriateness of this irony and the style in which it is expressed, partly ignorance of the correct part-assignments in vv. 14–19, that led to two misgotten theories that these vv. (i) formed part of a separate speech (Hirschig, *Annot.* 10) or (ii) were separated from what preceded in the MSS by a lacuna (Meineke, *Anal. Crit.* 167).

15 ἐστήκαθ': sc. 'stand *idle*' (LSJ s.v. ἵστημι B.II.1, cf. Headlam on Herodas 5.40). Over the plural see comm. on v. 1.

15–16 Eustath. 1151.40 cites the passage from κάεται to Ἡφαίστου κύνες, punctuating after ἤδη. This is preferable to punctuation before ἤδη adopted by most editors of Ath. and the comic frs. (apart from Edmonds); it attaches the adverb more fittingly to the general statement about the fire and normalises the position of δέ in 16.

κάεται: the normal Attic orthography in the 4th century (by which 'in pre-vocalic position αι was frequently simplified to α through loss of iota' Threatte 1.268) is preserved in A and Epit. here, as generally in comic papyri with κάω (Men. *Perinth.* 20) and κλάω (x 14 α ~ x 3 αι + *Asp.* 76 where B's κλαιειν is probably an error for κάειν (R. Kassel), and Eupolis 268.40 where the reading κλαιειν is uncertain). Cf. also introduction to Ἀχαΐς n. 1, K.B. 2.452, MacDowell on Ar. *Vesp.* 584.

16 Ἡφαίστου κύνες: sc. 'sparks'. Right from the beginning of Greek literature the name of Hephaestus (as those of other divinities: e.g. Aphrodite (cf. 222(219K).15 and comm., 273(271K).4), Demeter, Dionysus = Bromius (cf. 225(223K).2, 232(230K).3, 278(276K).1), Achelous, Nereus) was attached to an associated element or other object in two striking ways: (1) by simple metonymy (Hephaestus = 'fire'), e.g. Hom. *Il.* 2.426, Archilochus fr. 9.11 West, S. *Ant.* 123, 1006f.; and (2) by a

COMMENTARY

development perhaps related to that metonymy, wherein objects like flame or lava are described as properties of the god, and Hephaestus can be interpreted as both god and fire, e.g. φλὸξ Ἡφαίστοιο Hom. *Od.* 24.71, *Il.* 17.88, σέλας Ἀφ. Pind. *Pyth.* 3.39, Ἀφ. κρουνούς = 'lava' *Pyth.* 1.25; fuller lists in Wilamowitz, *loc. cit.* in introduction to this fr., Malten in *RE* s.v. *Hephaistos* 330.31ff., Fraenkel on A. *Ag.* 281. Comedy in its turn exploits or parodies both uses: (1) metonymy e.g. Plaut. *Amph.* 341 *quo ambulas tu, qui Volcanum in cornu conclusum geris?* spoken by Mercury with tragic grandiosity to a slave, *Men.* 330 *haec appono ad Volcani uiolentiam* spoken by a slave cook but see J. C. B. Lowe, *Class. Ant.* 4 (1985) 90ff., *Aul.* 359, *Rud.* 761; (2) Hephaestus' property, e.g. Ἡφαίστου φλογά (-γί) Ar. *Plut.* 661, Men. *Sam.* 674. The present passage, which develops the second of these uses as part of a γρῖφος, raises two problems which we do not have enough evidence to solve. (1) Eubulus fr. 75 (from the Ὀρθάννης, an undatable play), possibly also spoken by a cook, describes the preparations for a meal in the same tragic rhythms and tragico-dithyrambic, riddling style as Alexis here, and vv. 7–8 in Eubulus run ῥιπὶς δ' ἐγείρει φύλακας Ἡφαίστου κύνας | θερμῇ παροξύνασα τηγάνου πνοῇ. Kann 64 (cf. Wilamowitz, *Nachr. Gött.* (1895) 227 n. 7 = *Kl. Schr.* 5.2.16 n. 7, Nesselrath 262) suggests that Alexis was copying Eubulus; the reverse is equally possible, as is a common borrowing from a tragic (cf. Wilamowitz, *Glaube* 1.20 n. 1) or a dithyrambic source (cf. Hunter, comm. on Eubulus *ad loc.*). (2) Hesych. s.v. κύων (κ 4764) gives as his first definition ὁ ἐλαυνομένου τοῦ σιδήρου τοῦ ἀργοῦ (sc. unwrought) ἐξαλλόμενος σπινθήρ. If this correctly reports a usage by smiths which goes back to the 4th century, and is not an over-ingenious grammarian's attempt to explain without evidence passages like those of Alexis and Eubulus, the two comic poets may be playing on this and/or a further metaphorical meaning of κύων in poetry, 'companion/servant' (usually of the gods; LSJ s.v. III, e.g. A. *Ag.* 135f., *Choeph.* 924, 1054, *P.V.* 1022, Pindar fr. 86 Bowra = 96* Snell, Arist. fr. 196 Rose, cf. Wilamowitz on Eur. *Her.* 420, Fraenkel on A. *Ag.* 136).

17 αἴθραν: a rare word of high poetry, confined mainly to the epic hexameter (Hom. *Il.* 17.646, *Od.* 6.44, 12.75, Archias in *Anth. Pal.* 6.179.5) and Lycophron (700, 822), and replaced in Ionic and some Attic (Xen., Arist.) by αἰθρία. Neither form occurs in tragedy, probably through the accidents of preservation, but note αἴθρα in lyrics at Ar. *Av.* 778 and tragico-dithyrambic parody at Antiphanes 55(52K).14, Anaxilas 22.30 (both trochaic tetrameter), and αἰθρία in anapaests at Ar. *Nub.* 371, Cratinus 58(53K).2. The elaborately poetic context here (16 ἄττουσιν chiefly poetic, Ἡφαίστον κύνες; 17–19 a conceit in the style of Euripides) guarantees its correctness (*pace* Casaubon, cf. *Animadv.* 655, weakly conjecturing αἰθέρ'). The picture of red-hot (or white-hot) sparks

rising into a clear blue sky is graphic and imaginative, but not sufficiently precise to be used as evidence for its author's sensitivity to colour.
γίγνεσθαι: see comm. on 37(36K).7.
17–19 Translate: 'for whom alone an unseen law of inevitability has linked together (i.e. synchronised) both birth and the end of life'. A's text, apart from one instance of faulty word-division at the beginning (ὅϊσθὅ, corrected to οἷς τὸ first by Petavius in his edition of Themistius (Paris 1618) pp. 670f.), accurately[1] preserves Alexis' clever parody of a Euripidean 'scientific' conceit (cf. e.g. T. B. L. Webster, *The Tragedies of Euripides* (London 1967) 20ff., Kannicht on Eur. *Hel.* 138, 1137–43, Bond on *Her.* 104) in impeccable tragic diction. τὴν τελευτὴν τοῦ βίου: cf. S. *Trach.* 79, *OC* 1473 (a standard expression: cf. Men. *Dysk.* 715f. and Stoessl *ad loc.*; βιότοιο τελευτή in Hom. *Il.* 7.104, 16.787; Eur. has only θανάτου τελευτή, fr. 916.7, cf. *Med.* 153). συνῆψε: a favourite word of Eur. (x 59, + 1 in *Rhes.*). ἀνάγκης θεσμός: so too Aristarchus fr. 2 (cf. Eur. *Hec.* 847 τῆς ἀνάγκης οἱ νόμοι, but also Pind. *Nem.* 10.28 ἐν Ἀδραστείῳ νόμῳ, Pl. *Phdr.* 248c θεσμός τε Ἀδραστείας ὅδε). οὐχ ὁρώμενος: cf. A. *Choeph.* 293f. οὐχ ὁρωμένην πατρὸς μῆνιν, Eur. fr. 29.3 Austin ἡ δ' (sc. Δίκη) οὐχ ὁρωμένη trag. adesp. fr. 493 Δίκην ἄναυδον οὐχ ὁρωμένην and 492, A. *Ag.* 683.

154 (150K)

Meineke 3.453 (II), Kock 2.352, Edmonds 2.446, Kassel–Austin 2.109. The speaker, who is presumably about to help some friend or relative (cf. introduction to Μιλήσιοι) in an unknown situation (Sostratos at Men. *Dysk.* 797ff. uses a related argument in support of his plan to help Gorgias), defends himself in tragic rhythm and diction (Blaydes, *Misc. Crit.* 183 compares Eur. fr. 282.7f. οὐδ' αὖ πένεσθαι κἀξυπηρετεῖν τύχαις | οἷοί τ'). Here with ὢν ἄνθρωπος Alexis stresses a person's humanity in relation to the fortunes of others (cf. Plaut. *Trin.* 447, Ter. *HT* 77, Gil 344), elsewhere more frequently his fallibility (e.g. Baton 1, cf. Herodas 5.27f. and Headlam *ad loc.*), mortality (e.g. Chariton 4.4.8), limitations (e.g. Men. *Epitr.* 912, *Phasm.* 31ff.; cf. the similar implications of θνητὸς ὢν) or the unreliability of fortune (e.g. Simonides fr. 16.1 Page, Xen. *Anab.* 7.6.11, Men. frs. 46, 395, Polyb. 3.31.3). On the precept about behaviour that underlies the speaker's words see Dover, *GPM* 180ff., 273, 276ff. (although the implications of this fr. are misinterpreted at p. 271).

---

[1] Even so Kock prints his own conjecture νόμοις for A's μόνοις in v. 19, on the ground that sparks are not unique: lightning and thunder also die immediately after birth. True; but Alexis is a comic poet not a pedantic schoolmaster, and νόμοις would be tautologous by the side of θεσμός.

COMMENTARY

ποῦ: Porson's correction (comm. on Eur. *Or.* 792 (802) and *Adv.* 282) of εἶτ' οὐ in the MSS (SMA at Stob. 4.48a.5: an error due to the common confusion between Π and ΙΤ/ΤΙ in uncials, e.g. Pl. *Resp.* 9.581d ποιώμεθα MSS for τί οἰώμεθα). In questions ποῦ is often a livelier substitute for πῶς; for its introduction of a conditional apodosis cf. e.g. Dem. 23.58 καὶ μὴν εἴ τις ἐκεῖν' ὑπολαμβάνει, ποῦ δὲ γένοιτ' ἂν ταῦτα;

φρονῶν: 'in my right mind' (LSJ s.v. φρονέω IV). Naber's conjecture φρενῶν (*Mnemosyne* 8 (1880) 261) is unnecessary.

155 (151K)

Meineke 3.453 (III), Kock 2.352, Edmonds 2.446, Kassel–Austin 2.110; cf. Bechtel, *Spitznamen* 41. Ath. 6.238c and 240c–f tells us all we know about Tithymallus the parasite (240c is the source of the references here and at frs. 161(157K) and 164(159K)). His associates and possible dates are discussed in the introduction to Μιλήσιοι. According to Dromon 1.4 he was ruddier than a κόκκος (the female kermes scale insect, *Lecanium ilicis*, misidentified in antiquity as the berry of the kermes oak, *Quercus coccifera*, Theophr. *HP* 3.16, Pliny *HN* 16.32, and the source of a red dye; cf. S. C. Atchley, *Wild Flowers of Attica* (Oxford 1938) 40, H. Michell, *The Economics of Ancient Greece* (Cambridge 1940) 190 n. 1). Parasites were often known by nicknames both in real life and on the comic stage, and so Tithymallus would have been so called from the similarity of his complexion to the colour of the τιθύμαλλος plant (so Bechtel), whose features and properties are described by [Theophr.] 9.11.7–9, Dioscorides 4.164 and Pliny *HN* 20.209, 26.62–71 with such precise details that all seven of the 'kinds' distinguished in antiquity can be identified as individual species of the genus *Euphorbia* (= 'spurge'); cf. Steier's excellent entry in *RE* s.v. *Tithymalos* 1524.62ff.[1] Several of the spurges native to Greece have reddish stalks, leaves and/or involucres: e.g. *Euphorbia characias, cyparissias, heliosco-pia, paralias* (all identified in antiquity), *nicaeensis, palustris, peplis* (cf. especially T. G. Tutin and others, *Flora Europaea* 2 (Cambridge 1968) 2.213ff.; also E. von Halácsy, *Conspectus Florae Graecae* 3 (Leipzig 1904) 94ff., Atchley 38ff.[2]

---

[1] One of Steier's binomials needs correcting; *Euphorbia sibthorpii* is now *Euphorbia characias* subsp. *wulfenii* (Tutin 2.226 no. 105).

[2] Over forty species of *Euphorbia* are native to Greece today; it must be assumed that in antiquity a good number of these would have been included in or confused with some of the seven 'kinds' described in Dioscorides and Pliny.

458

ΜΙΛΚΩΝ

Μίλκων (and fr. 152K)

See above, Ἰμίλκων (and fr. 98 Kassel–Austin).

Μίνως

Meineke 1.392 ~ 3.445 (cf. *Quaest. Scen.* 35), Helbig in Roscher s.v. *Minos* 2993.1ff., Poland in *RE* s.v. *Minos* 1890.2ff., Robert, *GH* 1.352ff., O. Weinreich, *Menekrates Zeus und Salmoneus* (Stuttgart 1933), G. Pugliese Carratelli, *Studi sul mondo antico* (Naples 1976) 225ff., Bain, *Actors* 216f. and 217 n. 2 ~ T. B. L. Webster, *CQ* 2 (1952) 18, W. G. Arnott, *LCM* 14 (1989) 31ff.; cf. Nesselrath, *MK* 199 n. 51. Ath. 7.289f alleges that Alexis 'mentions Menecrates' (see below) ἐν Μίνῳ. The various myths involving Minos (cf. Helbig, Poland, Robert, Pugliese Carratelli) are a favourite subject of both tragedy and comedy over a long period,[1] and so it

---

[1] The tragedies may be listed according to subject. (i) The Minotaur: Euripides' Θησεύς (p. 477 Nauck[2]); source material for the plot in Σ Ar. *Vesp.* 313, *Ran.* 467, cf. also Tzetzes *Chil.* 11.552ff., implying that the subject pleased others beside Euripides. This or another tragedy may have been a model for Accius' *Minos* or *Minotaurus* (Ribbeck, *TRF*[3] p. 226). (ii) Pasiphae: Euripides' Κρῆτες (p. 505 Nauck[2] + Austin, *NFEP* p. 49), in which Minos was a character. (iii) Daedalus: Sophocles' Δαίδαλος (1.110 A. C. Pearson (Cambridge 1917), 171 S. Radt (*TrGF* 4 (Göttingen 1977)). (iv) Polyidus the seer: Aeschylus' Κρῆσσαι (228 Radt) possibly, Sophocles' Μάντεις ἢ Πολύιδος (2.56 Pearson, 338 Radt), Euripides' Πολύιδος (558 Nauck[2]). (v) Cocalus: Sophocles' Καμικοί (2.3 Pearson, 310 Radt). Clem. Alex. *Strom.* 6.2.10.7 (= 2.430.1 Stählin) cites also a Sophoclean Μίνως; this may have been identical with Καμικοί or Δαίδαλος (2.69 Pearson, cf. 1.xviii, 2.4,; 348 Radt) or Μάντεις.
Comedies about Minos also abounded until the middle of the 4th century; we do not know how many simply burlesqued a myth, how many parodied specific tragedies. Titles known (or suspected) include Aristophanes' Δαίδαλος (in fr. 193(185K) a big egg has been hatched; in 192(188K) a character ascends into the sky; the *Suda* s.v. Εὐρύβατος says that Zeus changed into several shapes in the play. Kock suggests that Aristophanes introduced an inventive Daedalus into the story of Zeus' seduction of Leda, cf. Kassel–Austin, iii.2.116), Κώκαλος (Aristophanes' last play, incorporating a rape and recognition according to the ancient *Vita* = *testimonium* 1, line 50 in Kassel–Austin iii.2 p. 3, cf. 201 and Kock 1.482; in fr. 359(345K) someone has blisters on his feet: Daedalus after his journey to Crete, or Minos after his pursuit of Daedalus?), and Πολύιδος; Plato's Δαίδαλος; Alcaeus' Πασιφάη pro-

seems wiser to accept the transmitted text on the one occasion when the title is cited for Alexis (so Meineke 1.392, cf. Weinreich 98f., Bain, Nesselrath) than to endorse an earlier idea of Meineke's (*Quaest. Scen.*) that Μίνῳ in the *Marcianus* of Ath. was a corruption (however easy to justify on palaeographical grounds) for Λίνῳ. Alexis' plot could have dealt with any or several of the legends associated with Minos, but if the comic poet's Μάντεις (see introduction to that play, and my *LCM* paper cited above), like the Sophoclean tragedy with this title, treated (with or without tragic parody) the legend of Polyidus' visit to Minos, the possibility that Μάντεις and Μίνως were alternative titles of the same play cannot be ruled out.

Ath. 7.289a–f is our major source of information about Menecrates (cf. also Aelian *VH* 11.51, Clem. Alex. *Protr.* 4.84, Plut. *Ages.* 21, *Mor.* 191a, 213a, *Suda* s.v. Μενεκράτης; Weinreich collects, compares and discusses the material usefully, but with a tendency to make bricks from insufficient straw; cf. also Ribbeck, *Alazon* 17f., Raeder and Göbel in *RE* s.v. *Menekrates* 29, 802.1ff., H. Bengtson, *Griechische Geschichte*[5] (Munich 1977) 297). He was a physician from Syracuse who claimed, possibly under paranoid delusion, to be Zeus, and went round with an entourage of former patients accoutred as Olympian deities. He is said to have written letters to Agesilaus (Plut. *locc. citt.*: Agesilaus was king of Sparta from 399 until his death in 360/59), Agesilaus' son Archidamus (Ath.: active from *c.* 371 to 338) and Philip (Aelian, Ath.: king of Macedon from 359 to 336).[1] If the period of Menecrates' notoriety extended from (say) *c.* 370 to *c.* 335 (Webster's estimate of *c.* 360–340 may be too confined, cf. Bain), Alexis' Μίνως might appropriately (for a myth travesty) be dated to the first twenty or twenty-five years of Alexis' career.[2]

156 (136K)

Meineke 3.445 (II), Kock 2.346, Edmonds 2.438, Kassel–Austin 2.110; cf. Weinreich (*op. cit.* in introduction to Μίνως) 98. Ath.'s statement (7.289f)

---

duced in 388; Antiphanes' Μίνως; Eubulus' and Philippus' Δαίδαλος, and possibly Alexis' Μάντεις (see above). A man called Daedalus has the role of hired μάγειρος in Philostephanus' Δήλιος, but whether he was the legendary figure in a myth travesty or a conventional cook (so named because of his virtuosity?) in an intrigue plot is quite uncertain.

[1] The terms of the letters to (and replies from) Agesilaus and Philip are identical, and although both exchanges *could* have been authentic, it is more likely that one of the stories is a spurious duplicate of the other, or even that both are anecdotal fabrications. Cf. Schmid–Stählin[6] 2.1.433.

[2] Alexis must have begun writing some time in the 350s (see my general introduction, 1.iii, and cf. *Rh. Mus.* 102 (1959) 256 n. 11 and *Studi di filologia classica in onore di Giusto Monaco* 1 (Palermo 1991) 333ff.).

that Alexis 'mentions' (μνημονεύει) Menecrates implies an extra-dramatic quip or passing reference, as in Ephippus 17 (cf. Men. *Sam.* 603ff. in its context), not an active dramatic role in the play for Menecrates (as Weinreich thinks, misinterpreting Ath.'s formula, cf. L. Gil and I. R. Alfageme, *Cuadernos de Filología Clásica* 3 (1972) 6of.).

Μνηστῆρες

See above, the *Helen* titles (and fr. 73).

Μυλωθρός

A collection of proverbs attributed to <Zeno>bius on its Athos MS[1] and first published by Miller, *Mélanges* 341ff. cites Ἄλεξις ἐν Μυλωθρῷ (Miller's correction of MS -οθρῷ, = 2.46 p. 363). It is the only comedy known from ancient Greece with this title, but Eubulus wrote a Μυλωθρίς (the female counterpart), Antiphanes a Μυλών and Pomponius a *Pistor*. Μυλωθρός can mean either manager of a mill or simply a person employed in grinding there (cf. H. Lloyd-Jones, *ZPE* 15 (1974) 210 n. 2). The fr. cited from Alexis' play (157(153K)) reveals nothing about plot or date, but references to slaves being sent to the mill for punishment and working there in fetters are common in later comedy (e.g. Men. *Her.* 2f., *Pk.* 277f., Plaut. *Bacch.* 781 and J. Barsby's comm. (Warminster 1986) *ad loc.*, *Asin.* 31ff., *Men.* 974f., *Most.* 15ff., Ter. *Andr.* 199, *Phorm.* 249), and this probably explains why Harpocration s.v. μυλωθρός (pp. 177f. in J. J. Keaney's edition, Amsterdam 1991) is able to say ἔστι ... καὶ παρὰ τοῖς κωμικοῖς πολὺ τοὔνομα, even though in extant plays and fragments Alexis' title is the word's only occurrence, but μυλωθρεῖν occurs in Men. *Pk.* 277.

157 (153K)

Kock 2.353, Edmonds 2.446, Kassel–Austin 2.110; cf. O. Crusius, *Analecta critica ad paroemiographos graecos* (Leipzig 1883) 150f., S. Radt in *TrGF* 4.191, F *201h, Kassel–Austin 7.368 (Philonides fr. 11). E. Miller's paroemiographer (see introduction to Μυλωθρός) and the anonymous *Appendix Proverbiorum* 3.35 (1.423 Leutsch–Schneidewin) allege that in an unnamed play by Sophocles (presumably either Ἐπίγονοι or Ἐριφύλη, if these are not alternative titles for the same play: so first F. G. Welcker, *Die*

---

[1] The MS has Βίου, plausibly supplemented by Miller to <Ζηνο>βίου.

COMMENTARY

griechischen Tragödien I (Bonn 1839) 269ff.; cf. in their editions of the fragments Pearson 1.129ff. and Radt 183ff., 189ff.) Eriphyle addressed Alcmaeon with the words καὶ γὰρ Ἀργείους ὁρῶ. The paroemiographers do not say what prompted Eriphyle's remark, but it seems quickly to have achieved proverbial status (cf. Hesych. s.v. Ἀργείους ὁρῶ) ἐπὶ τῶν ἐκτενῶς πρὸς ὁτιοῦν βλεπόντων καὶ καταπληκτικόν τι δοκούντων ὁρᾶν (*App. Prov.* 3.35; cf. Macarius 2.38 and *Suda* s.v. Ἀργείους ὁρᾷς with slightly varied wording), perhaps as a result of comic parody. The Argives whom Eriphyle saw – or thought she saw – may have astounded or terrified her because they arrived (with Alcmaeon?) intending to kill her (cf. Pearson on S. fr. 198), but we have no means of guessing what horrific sight greeted the speakers in the two comedies where the phrase is recorded (besides Alexis also Philonides fr. 11, cited in the Zavorda MS of Photius, 1.255 Chr. Theodoridis, Berlin 1982 = 143f. K. Tsantsanoglou, Athens 1984), nor do we know whether the phrase still retained tragic associations for either comedian, or whether it had become just a saying. *App. Prov.* 3.35 and Macarius 2.38 complicate the picture by quoting the proverb with ὁρᾷς and offering an alternative explanation (ἐπὶ τῶν εἰς κλοπὴν ὑπονοουμένων· κωμῳδοῦνται γὰρ Ἀργεῖοι ἐπὶ κλοπῇ, ὥσπερ καὶ Σοφοκλῆς (!) ἐχρήσατο *App. Prov.*; Macarius varies the phrasing and omits the last four words). Crusius suggests that Σοφοκλῆς may be an error for Ἄλεξις, induced presumably by an inapposite memory of the proverb's source, and that Alexis may have sought to combine or juxtapose for comic purposes the Ἀργείους ὁρῶ proverb with another about the same folk, Ἀργεῖοι φῶρες (cf. *Suda* s.vv. citing Ar. fr. 60(57K) = Macarius 2.28 without the citation, ἐπὶ τῶν προδήλως πονηρῶν· οἱ γὰρ Ἀργεῖοι ἐπὶ κλοπῇ κωμῳδοῦνται). Crusius' idea would help to account for the double explanation of Ἀργείους ὁρᾷς and for the odd final reference to Sophocles in a comic context at *App. Prov.* 3.35, but all that he says can now be shown to apply just as much to Philonides as to Alexis, and in any case his theory rests on a foundation of doubtful assumptions. The double explanation in *App. prov.* could with equal plausibility be put down to a grammarian's muddle or stupidity; if it did originate as an elucidation of some comic word-play, as Crusius supposes, Aristophanes too must be considered a possible progenitor in view of the *Suda* citation just referred to (cf. Radt p. 191). There is additionally one positive argument against Crusius; *App. Prov.* links its comments to the lemma Ἀργείους ὁρᾷς, while both Alexis and Philonides are cited for Ἀργείους ὁρῶ.

The Sophoclean phrase may perhaps be exploited also by Aristophon 5(4K).3f. (a parasite boasting about his skills and playing also on the reputation of Argive wrestlers) δεῖ τιν' ἄρασθαι μέσον | τῶν παροινούντων, παλαιστὴν νόμισον Ἀργεῖόν μ' ὁρᾶν (cf. O. Crusius, *Philologus* 46 (1888) 616), but the further use of Ἀργείους ὁρᾷς at Lucian *Charon* 24 looks more like an unintended echo (*pace* Göbel, *Ethnica* 41). It is hard to say why these words caught on; perhaps a comic poet seized on the opportunity for a pun on Ἀργεῖος ~ Ἄργος the sharp-eyed herdsman who guarded the bovine Ἰο, πυκνοῖς | ὄσσοις δεδορκώς *P.V.* 678f., cf. e.g. 569, Eur. fr. 1063.14, Plaut. *Aul.* 555, Wernicke in *RE* s.v. *Argos* 19, 791.9ff. Aristophanes plays on Ἀργεῖοι ~ ἀργοί = 'idle' at *Pax* 475, 493; Crusius, *Anal. Crit.* 55 n. 1 collects further examples of such ethnic puns.

Ὀδυσσεὺς ἀπονιζόμενος

Meineke 1.392, J. O. Schmidt, *JCP Suppl.* 16 (1888) 392, G. Schiassi, *Rend. Ist. Lomb.* 88 (1955) 112f. Odysseus was a popular character in Old and Middle Comedy (titles listed and discussed by Schmidt 373ff.), and he is the title figure in two of Alexis' comedies (also Ὀδ. ὑφαίνων); whether he appeared in Γαλάτεια is unknown. From the present play only one word (and that probably corrupt: see comm. on 158(154K)) survives, cited in the MS of the Antiatticist (98.17 Bekker) with the title spelled Ὀδ. ἀπονιπτομένῳ. The Attic form of this verb in the present paradigm was always (-)νίζω (in comedy e.g. Ar. *Vesp.* 608, Crates 16(14K).7, Pherecrates 45(41), Dromon 2.3, Men. *Georg.* 60, Damoxenus 2.44; if monost. 832 Jäkel is Menander, νίπτει needs correction to the Attic spelling), and (-)νίπτω (as a back-formation from future νίψω, aorist ἔνιψα) did not come into widespread use until the 2nd century AD; hence S. A. Naber (*Mnemosyne* 8 (1880) 261) was right (*pace* Kassel–Austin 2.111) to restore Alexis' title to -νιζόμενος; cf. K. Kondou, ΛΟΓΙΟΣ ΕΡΜΗΣ 1 (1866) 366ff., Veitch, *Greek Verbs*[4] 465ff., K.B. 2.493. We have no means of dating Ὀδ. ἀπονιζόμενος (but myth travesties are very rare in the period of New Comedy, cf. Webster, *SLGC* 85f., 115, Nesselrath, *MK* 189ff.), nor of identifying which of Odysseus' two[1] celebrated ablutions accounted for the title (after *Od.* met Nausicaa, Hom. *Od.* 6.210ff., so Schiassi; or when he was recognised by Euryclea, *Od.* 19.386ff., so with more plausibility Meineke, Edmonds; cf. also Wörner in Roscher s.v. *Nausikaa* 35.11ff., Schmidt 392 n. 1). The stories of (i) Nausicaa and (ii) Odysseus' return to Ithaca were featured in several Attic tragedies (i Sophocles' Ναυσικάα ἢ Πλύντριαι; ii Sophocles' Νίπτρα, cf. Radt *ad loc.*, Aeschylus' and Philocles'

---

[1] A memorable third ablution in the lost *Telegonia* of Eugammon has been generally assumed (e.g. Schmidt 392 n. 1, A. C. Pearson's edition of the frs. of Sophocles 2 (Cambridge 1917) 108) ever since Brunck suggested that Νίπτρα and Ὀδυσσεὺς ἀκανθόπληξ were alternative titles of the same play, but Brunck's theory is both unnecessary and implausible; see now S. Radt in *TrGF* 4 p. 373.

Πηνελόπη), and comedies (travesties with or without parody of like-named tragedies: i Philyllius' and Eubulus' Ναυσικάα; ii Polyzelus' Νίπτρα, Theopompus' 'Οδυσσεύς (cf. fr. 34(33K)) and Πηνελόπη, if these are not alternative titles of one play, cf. Robert, *GH* 3.2.2.1428 n. 2, perhaps Amphis' 'Οδυσσεύς (cf. fr. 27)). Cf. also my introduction to the *Helen* titles.

158 (154K)

Meineke 3.454, Kock 2.354, Edmonds 2.448, Kassel–Austin 2.111; cf. S. A. Naber, *Mnemosyne* 8 (1880) 261, W. G. Arnott, *Hermes* 117 (1989) 374ff. If the MS reading here (Bekker, *Anecd.* 98.17) is correct, the Antiatticist would be defending as Attic the form, orthography or use of ἥδιον against attack from allegedly overstrict Atticists. ἥδιον (as comparative of ἡδύς, adjectival or adverbial), however, is unexceptionable (Kock's suggestion that a possible shortening of the penultimate as a metrical licence (cf. my comm. on fr. 25.6, 'False or Doubtful Attributions' III, p. 827), could have aroused controversy is unlikely; the Atticists were not concerned with prosody). Hence Naber is probably right to suspect here an itacistic corruption of ἴδιον (a common type of error in this MS: e.g. 86.9 βόλβητον for -ιτον, 98.21 ἥδι for ἥδη, cf. 87.27, 100.32, 33, 102.21),[1] but wrong to interpret his emendation as imperfect of ἰδίω (far less common in Attic[2] than its synonym ἰδρόω, but well enough established there to have made Atticist opposition to its use unlikely: e.g. anapaests Ar. *Pax* 85, iambic dimeters *Ran.* 237, ἐξιδίω trochaic tetrameter *Av.* 791, ἀνιδίω probably Pl. *Tim.* 74c). Strict Atticists were angered rather by the use which had developed in the *Koine* of ἴδιος on its own as a reflexive possessive adjective; thus Phryn. *Ecl.* 409 (p.107 Fischer) τὰ ἴδια πράττω καὶ τὰ ἴδια πράττει οἱ πολλοὶ λέγουσιν εἰκῆ, δέον τὰ ἐμαυτοῦ πράττω καὶ τὰ σαυτοῦ πράττεις λέγειν ὡς οἱ παλαιοί; cf. A. N. Jannaris, *An Historical Greek Grammar* (London 1897) § 1416, Meisterhans–Schwyzer 235, Mayser II/2, 73.23ff., Schwyzer 2.205, J. H. Moulton and N. Turner, *A Grammar of New Testament Greek* 3 (Edinburgh 1963) 191f., Blass–Debrunner–Funk 149f. § 286. The use stigmatised by Phrynichus is foreign to good Attic, but clearly developed from the frequent employment of ἴδιος as an intensifier alongside possessive pronouns/adjectives ('my/your own' etc.) in Attic (cf.

---

[1] The *Marcianus* makes the same error at Ath. 12.521c (ἥδιον, but ἴδιον correctly Epit.).

[2] And in other dialects too: e.g. in the epic dialect of Homer ἰδίω occurs only at *Od.* 20.204, Hesiod fr. 165.4 Merkelbach–West ~ ἰδρόω x 8 Hom.; in the Ionic prose of the Hippocratic corpus, ἰδίω x 6 ~ ἰδρόω x 80, according to the *Concordance* edited by G. Maloney and W. Frohn (Hildesheim 1986–9).

ΟΔΥΣΣΕΥΣ ΑΠΟΝΙΖΟΜΕΝΟΣ

LSJ s.v. 1.3, e.g. Antiphon 5.61, Andoc. 2.2, 3.36, Dem. 19.307, 50.66, Isoc. 6.8, 8.127); the *Koine* use occurs already in Men. fr. 532.3 (ὁ δ' ἴδιος ... τρόπος = 'my character'), and a parallel (? earlier) use in Alexis might well have inspired the Antiatticist to cite it as a counter to his Atticist opponents.

Ὀδυσσεὺς ὑφαίνων

J. O. Schmidt, *JCP Suppl.* 16 (1888) 399, Robert, *GH* 3.2.2.1360 n. 5, W. Crönert, *Symb. Osl.* 14 (1935) 129 n. 1, T. B. L. Webster, *CQ* 43 (1948) 23 and *SLGC* 57, G. Schiassi, *Rend. Ist. Lomb.* 88 (1955) 113; cf. also my introduction to Ὀδυσσεὺς ἀπονιζόμενος. The title Ὀδυσσεὺς ὑφαίνων is a puzzle to which the three extant frs. provide clues but not solutions. In 159(155K) one character attacks the practices of fishermen (with an anachronistic transfer of the mythical situation to contemporary Athens, as elsewhere in Alexis and other comic poets who wrote such travesties: see the introduction to fr. 140(135K)), while a second speaker informs the audience that the first character once ate much poorer food than he does now. Fr. 160(156K) is a spirited description in trochaic tetrameters of the steps by which a dinner may deteriorate into a brawl; a second person (see introduction to the fr.), after commenting on the normality of this sequence, asks καὶ τί μάντεως ἔδει; (v.7: sc. to express such obvious facts). References to food, dinners and brawling in a play whose title figure was Odysseus would most appropriately embellish a plot about the suitors in Ithaca and the hero's return (so Crönert, Schiassi). The two speakers of 159(155K) would then most probably be a *nouveau-riche* suitor and one of his critics (? a rival suitor, Odysseus or one of the hero's supporters). The roles in 160(156K) are harder to assign, but Schiassi suggests that if the second speaker's reference to a μάντις is taken literally, the first speaker might be identified as Theoclymenus, the seer with the suitors in Ithaca (Hom. *Od.* 15.256ff. etc.); unfortunately τί μάντεως ἔδει; appears to be a proverb or trope simply stressing the triteness of the previous comment (*vide ad loc.*), and thus no clue to the identity of the character addressed. Fr. 161(157K) merely refers to the parasite Tithymallus (see introduction to Μιλήσιοι and comm. on 155(151K)), dating the play roughly to the second half of the 4th century.

If the plot involved Odysseus with the suitors, what was he weaving? Plots and guile about the future of his kingdom, says Crönert; but although ὑφαίνω is metaphorically so used several times in *Il.* and *Od.* with nouns like δόλον (*Il.* 6.187, *Od.* 5.356, 9.422*), μῆτιν (*Il.* 7.324, 9.93, *Od.* 4.678, 739, 9.422*, 13.303*, 386) and μήδεα (*Il.* 3.212), sometimes with Odysseus himself as the weaver of guile (the passages asterisked), never-

465

theless in play-titles brevity and clarity go hand in hand, and for Crönert's theory to win credence we should need δόλον or μῆτιν to be expressed as part of the title, since ὑφαίνω on its own carries no metaphorical implication. Schmidt, followed by Robert, believed that Odysseus might have been compelled by Calypso or Circe (cf. *Od.* 5.61f., 10.221ff.) to become a weaver, but such a theory chimes ill with the apparently Ithacan ambience of the frs. Webster's explanation of the title raises fewer difficulties. Pointing to several 4th-century Athenian comedies in which the traditional version of a myth appears to have been turned upside down (e.g. Arist. *Poet.* 13, 1453ᵃ36, Orestes and Aegisthus ending as friends, cf. my introduction to 'Ορέστης; Phaon becoming a male prostitute in Plato's Φάων, cf. fr. 188(174K) and Servius on V. *Aen.* 3.279), Webster suggests something parallel in 'Οδυσσεὺς ὑφαίνων, with Odysseus replacing Penelope as the weaver of Laertes' shroud (*Od.* 2.94ff., 15.517, 19.137ff., 24.128ff.).[1]

159 (155K)

Meineke 3.455 (II), Kock 2.354, Edmonds 2.448, Kassel–Austin 2.111. The identity of the man who attacks Athenian fishermen (vv.1–3; normally it is the fishmongers who are assailed, cf. introduction to fr. 16, although the two employments were not always kept distinct, cf. Plato com. 28(29K) and V. Ehrenberg, *The People of Aristophanes*[2] (Oxford 1951) 130ff.) is discussed in introduction to 'Οδυσσεὺς ὑφαίνων. Whatever reading is preferred at the beginning of this fr. (see on v. 1), vv. 1–3 appear to be part only of a longer tirade begun earlier, in a scene perhaps constructed like Plaut. *Capt.* 790ff., where a parasite inveighs against (1) people who get in his way, (2) pig-raising millers, (3) fishermen as here (introduced by *tum piscatores* 813) and (4) butchers. There after each section Hegio comments in an aside, like the second speaker here at

---

[1] Similar inversions are portrayed on South Italian vases roughly contemporary (*c.* 350–325) with Athenian comedies like 'Οδ. ὑφαίνων: e.g. Ajax being seized by Cassandra as he takes refuge at the Palladion, on a fragment of a kalyx-krater painted by Assteas (A. D. Trendall, *Phlyax Vases*[2] (*BICS Suppl.* 19, 1967) 54f. no. 86, Trendall and Webster, *Illustrations of Greek Drama* (London 1971) IV.30 with photograph, T. B. L. Webster and J. R. Green, *MIOMC*[3] 135, O. Taplin, *Comic Angels* (Oxford 1993) 81f. and pl. 17.17). These vases are commonly assumed to derive their inspiration from local Italian drama, but they are linked by Webster (especially *CQ* 43 (1948) 17ff.) and Taplin more plausibly with Athenian Middle Comedy, although Taplin has reservations over a dramatic source for the Assteas vase.

vv. 4–5 (this part-division was first noted by Schweighaeuser, cf. *Animadv.* 4.240). Cf. also Plaut. *Aul.* 475ff. and see Bain, *Actors* 102.

1 καὶ τοὺς ἁλιέας δ': the *Marcianus* (Ath. 7.303a) has καί . . . δὲ, Epit. omits both particles. Even though καί . . . δέ becomes such a cliché in post-classical Greek that the δέ could have been added by Ath. or a copyist almost without thinking, this combination of particles is not uncommon in comedy (e.g. Ar. *Equ.* 711, *Pax* 250, 523, 632, *Plut.* 764, 838, Plato com. 71(69K).3) and Attic generally, where in one characteristic use – that of introducing a new item in a series, as probably here (see introduction to fr.), cf. e.g. Pl. *Clit.* 409b, *Alc.* 118d, 126b, Xen. *Oec.* 8.8 – the two particles retain their individual functions (δέ connects, καί = 'also/even') and only one phrase unit separates them; see especially Denniston, *GP* 200ff., Mayser 2.3.131f.

εἰς τὸ βάραθρον ἐμβαλῶ: so Epit. MSS correctly[1] (A clearly has ἐμβάλ| λω). This imprecatory formula (e.g. Ar. *Equ.* 1362 also ἐμβαλῶ, *Ran.* 574 ἐμβάλοιμι, *Nub.* 1448f. and *Plut.* 1109 ἐμβαλεῖν, cf. com. adesp. fr. 253.10 Austin), which, alongside several variants (ἄπαγ' . . . Men. *Dysk.* 394, 575, . . . ἐμπέσοις com. adesp. fr. 233.1 Austin, εἰς τὸ β. on its own *P.Cologne* 203 c.1.2; cf. also Plaut. *Bacch.* 149, *Curc.* 121, *Rud.* 570), occurs frequently in comedy, originates from the Athenian practice of executing certain types of criminal (e.g. 'enemies of the people') by throwing them into the βάραθρον (e.g. Xen. *Hell.* 1.7.20. Pl. *Gorg.* 516d–e, Alciphron 3.16.3, Heliodorus 1.13–14; R. J. Bonner and G. E. Smith, *The Administration of Justice from Homer to Aristotle* 2 (Chicago 1938) 278f.), which was situated north of the angle between the northerly long wall and the city wall (cf. Pl. *Resp.* 4.439e), probably below the rocky bluff on the west side of the Hill of the Nymphs (see Neil on Ar. *Equ.* 1362, Thalheim in *RE* s.v. Βάραθρον 2853.21ff., W. Judeich, *Die Topographie der Athen*² (Munich 1931) 140).

2 ἀπελευθέρων ὀψάρια: *Ganz gewöhnlich ist das Asyndeton, wenn der zweite Satz ein Erklärungssatz ist, der sonst durch* γάρ *oder auch durch* ἄρα . . . *angereiht wird* (K.G. 2.344); in Alexis cf. frs. 140(135K).5, 148(144K).3. Translate 'miserable little fish, fit only for freedmen'; see comm. on 47(46K).6 (the meaning of ὀψ.) and 144(140K) (the form of the diminutive, from which ψάρι in modern Greek derives, cf. J. E. Kalitsunakis in *Festschrift für Paul Kretschmer* (Vienna 1926) 96ff.). The diminutive here, like those in v. 3, indicates contempt for cheaper kinds of seafood.

3 A's corruption of σηπίδια to σικχηπίδια is an amusing example of a

---

[1] They are correct again with σηπίδια (and A wrong) in v. 3, wrong in v. 4 with λάβη (λάβοι correctly A), probably wrong in omitting δέ (which A has) in v. 1. At v. 5 A has θύννας, Epit. θύννους, both possibly wrong. On the relationship between Epit. and A see the introduction, ii.i.b.

scribe's conflation of the word he is copying with one suggested by the contextual description of a fastidious (σικχός) buyer; see *CQ* 7 (1957) 194 and Fraenkel on A. *Ag.* pp. 655 n. 1, 683 n. 3. Elsewhere in comedy σηπίδιον always scans with antepenult long (Ar. frs. 258(247K), 333(318K).1, Ephippus 3.9 ≏ Eubulus 148(150K).6, Ephippus 15.4 ≏ Eubulus 109(110K).2 and Hunter *ad loc.*; on -ίδιον diminutives and their prosody see comm. on Alexis 2.7); here such a scansion produces an anapaest split after its second short in the second half of the second metron of a verse with no penthemimeral caesura, a licence rarer than when there is penthem. caesura (cf. comm. on 57(56K).4), but one for which several sound parallels exist in Attic comedy (e.g. Men. *Sam.* 312, where elision at the end of the first metron may be a substitute for penthemimeral caesura, fr. 397.3, Baton 2.1; fuller discussion in *CQ* 7 (1957) 194f.). σηπία and σηπίδιον cover the sepia or cuttlefish (*Sepia officinalis*, up to 30 cm long) and a few other cephalopods such as the little cuttle (*Sepiola rondeleti*, up to 5 cm). The larger sepia was considered rather an expensive purchase (Ar. *Eccl.* 554 and Σ, Eriphus 3.3, Anaxippus 1.33ff.; three a drachma, Alexis 192(187K), adding a recipe); accordingly it seems reasonable to guess that when the diminutive form appears in a passage decrying the mollusc's cheapness (as e.g. here and Ephippus 15.4 ≏ Eubulus 109(110K).2), it refers primarily to undifferentiated baby sepias and adult little cuttles. Cf. Thompson, *Fishes* 231ff., Palombi–Santorelli 290ff., Dohm, *Mageiros* 110f., Campbell, *Guide* 180f., Davidson, *Seafood* 208ff.

τριχίδια: diminutive of τριχίς, see on fr. 18.2. They were cheap and sold by the hundred (Ar. *Equ.* 662).

φρυκτούς: whitebait for broiling over charcoal, elsewhere called (ἐπ-) ἀνθρακίδες (Ar. *Ach.* 670, *Vesp.* 1127, Philyllius 12(13K).3); cf. Thompson, *Fishes* 64. They remain today a staple part of the menu in a Greek seaside taverna. Contrast ἑψητοί, small fish for boiling, comm. on fr. 17.1.

4–5 The text of A and the Epit. MSS (CE) in v. 4 has a spondee in the second half of the third metron (λάβοι θύννου A, λάβῃ θύννου. CE), and is a syllable short before that; in v. 5 A has θύννας, CE θύννους. Certain restoration is impossible, but the margins of error may be identified and some steps taken towards a solution.

(a) The general sense is not destroyed nor even blurred by the corruption. The two lines are a comment by a second character (see introduction to the fr.) on what he has heard: 'If ever this fellow (sc. the speaker of vv. 1–3) bought (λάβοι: see comm. on 15.18) a tunny's head in former times, he would think he'd got eel and (θύννας/-ους/some other delicacy).' Clearly the man who now sneers at cheap food was once poor and then considered tunny's head a great luxury, cf. Dobree, *Adv.* 2.315. If θύννας (or -ους) is correctly transmitted here, which I gravely doubt (see (d) below), we are obliged to contrast a pauper's 'tunny's head' with

468

(whole) tunnies (whether male or female, very large fish – *Thunnus thynnus*, the blue-fin tunny or tuna, grows up to three metres in length – and for the gourmet's cuts expensive). The parodist Matron in his Ἀττικὸν δεῖπνον (second half of 4th century) says οἴη δ' αὖ θύννου (so correctly CE at Ath. 4.135e, *pace* Lloyd-Jones–Parsons) κεφαλὴ θαλαμηδιάδαο ... τὸ δὲ πῆμα θεοὶ θέσαν ἀνθρώποισι (*SH* 534.53ff.); cf. Xenocrates in Oribasius 2.58.7 κεφαλαὶ δὲ πάντων (sc. fish) διὰ τὸ ἁλμυρὸν καὶ λιπῶδες ἄτροφοι καὶ δυσδιοίκητοι), but the tunny's body was prized as highly as the eel by ancient gastronomes and comic poets alike (Ath. 7.301e–304e collects many of the paeans of praise; cf. Steier in *RE* s.v. *Thynnos* 731.17ff., Thompson, *Fishes* 88ff., Strömberg, *Fischnamen* 79f., 126ff.), and the choicest cuts from the shoulders (κλεῖδες) and especially the underbelly (ὑπογαστρίδια, ὑπήτρια, ἠτριαῖα) cost too much for a poor man's budget (Eriphus 3, cf. Eubulus 36(37K).1).

(b) With the basic sense established, we can examine the textual details. Transposition to θύννον λάβοι (Casaubon, cf. *Animadv.* 531) heals the end of v. 4; what Alexis wrote in the first two metra remains unsure. Possibilities include οὗτος πρότερον κεφάλαιον εἰ (first Meineke 5.90, cf. Cobet in Peppink, *Observ.* 48: the error to be explained by a copyist's belief that Alexis' words exactly corresponded to those of Ath. introducing the fr. καὶ τὴν κεφαλὴν τοῦ θύννου ἐπαινῶν;[1] but cf. Callias 6(3K).1 θύννου τε κεφάλαιον τοδί, Amphis 35.2, Sotades 1.5), οὗτ. πρ. κεφαλήν <τιν'> εἰ (Dobree, *Adv.* 315), οὗτός <γε> πρ. εἰ κεφαλὴν θύννου λάβοι (W. G. Arnott after Edmonds' οὗτ. πρ. θ. <γε> κ. εἰ λ., cf. Denniston, *GP* 121ff., and οὗτος <δὲ> πρ. εἰ κεφαλὴν θ. λ. (Erfurdt, *Obs.* 463 after Casaubon's (i) οὗτ. <δὲ> πρ. in the margin of his text of Ath. and (ii) οὗτ. <δὲ> κεφαλὴν πρ. εἰ, *Animadv.* 531).

(c) We may safely eliminate conjectures in v. 4 which either misinterpret the relation of vv. 4–5 to the preceding remark (<γὰρ> εἰ R. Ellis, *AJP* 6 (1885) 289: but these lines are not an explanation of, but an antithesis to, vv. 1–3), or remove θύννου, for which Ath. cites the fr. (θύμου Dobree and κυνός Kock after λάβοι, γλαύκου λάβοι Blaydes, *Adv.* 2.161).

(d) In v. 5 A's θύννας (rather than Epit.'s θύννους, which looks like substitution of a common for a less common form) could be defended; the contrast here between a tunny's head and (whole) female tunnies is not absurd (see (a) above), and different forms of this noun (θύννος, -α, -ίς)

---

[1] Ath.'s ἐπαινῶν (which can only mean 'praising': '*at non laudat*' Kaibel, after Schweighaeuser, *Animadv.* 4.239f.) suggests that he may not have fully understood the fr. of Alexis; had it already sustained corruption, and its part-division at the end of v. 3 been obliterated, before it reached Ath.'s hands?

appear elsewhere in proximity to each other in similar contexts (e.g. Cratinus 171.49–50(161K) ἐγὼ γάρ εἰμι θυννὶς ἡ μέλαινά σοι | καὶ θύννος, Mnesimachus 4.31 θύννου τεμάχη ~ 35 θυννίς, cf. Epicharmus 74). θύννα (this form of the nominative, rather than -η, is attested by A's θύνναν at Ath. 7.304b citing Hipponax 26.2 West; other cases in e.g.Antiphanes 127(129K).4, Archestratus 168.1 Lloyd-Jones–Parsons, Opp. *Hal.* 1.756, 4.505) and θυννίς both = 'female tunny', with no apparent distinction in meaning.[1] Yet why should Alexis have wished to single out the *female* fish here? No superiority in taste was ever alleged or can indeed be sustained. Could θύννας then be a corruption, arising from conflation of the ending (-ας) of some other word and the stem of θύννου in the previous verse, to which the scribe's eye had unluckily wandered (note that in A here θύν|νου and θύν|νας straddle the ends of successive lines)? If so, the nature of the error makes sure restoration impossible: ? something like βατίδας (skate and its relatives, cf. comm. on 84.1; a gourmet's dish at Ar. *Vesp.* 510, there too linked with eels; cf. the coinage βατιδοσκόποι *Pax* 810).[2]

In addition to the blue-fin tunny, θύννος seems to have included smaller relatives like the bonito (*Euthynnus alletteratus*) and the albacore (*Thunnus alalunga*). See Steier and Thompson, *locc. cit.* in (a) above, P. Rhode, *Thynnorum captura quanti fuerit apud veteres momenti* (Leipzig 1890–1), O. Keller, *Die antike Tierwelt* 2 (Leipzig 1913) 382ff., Palombi–Santorelli 109ff., Campbell, *Guide* 302ff., Davidson, *Seafood* 125ff.

5 ἐγχέλεια: pieces of eel cooked or ready for cooking. Neil on Ar. *Equ.* 354 coins the term 'menu word' for this nominal use of the neuter of adjectives in -ειος, formed from nouns which are the names of edible creatures. Cf. e.g. λαγῷα 168(163K).5, and the original but continuing adjectival use of ὕειος 115(110K).16, δελφάκειος 129(124K).2.

On ἔγχελυς = common eel see on 149(145K).2.

160 (156K)

Meineke 3.454 (1), Kock 2.354, Edmonds 2.448, Kassel–Austin 2.112; cf. Wilamowitz, *Hermes* 8 (1873) 147f., A. Olivieri, *Dioniso* 7 (1939) 279f.,

---

[1] LSJ s.v. θυννίς (cf. Thompson, *Fishes* 79) wrongly translates 'young female tunny'; this is based on a misreading of Arist. *HA* 6.17, 571^{a}19, but here and elsewhere in *HA* (e.g. 5.9, 543^{a}9) the word simply denotes the female. An immature tunny of either sex is πηλαμύς.

[2] I have some doubts, however, over the metrical acceptability of a conjecture which would introduce a one-word tribrach into the first half of the third metron. Although parallels can be cited for this licence (e.g. S. *Aj.* 459, *OR* 719, 1496, with a proclitic preceding; Ar. *Vesp.* 43,

G. Schiassi, *Rend. Ist. Lomb.* 88 (1955) 113. The fr., cited by Ath. 10.421a (complete in A, only vv. 1–6 in Epit.; Eustath. 1312.38 cites vv. 3 ἡ σκῶψις – 6 τύπτεσθαι), was correctly (*pace* Kassel–Austin) divided by Wilamowitz before ταῦτα (v.6) between two speakers whose identities are uncertain (on Schiassi's suggestion that one was Theoclymenus see introduction to 'Οδ. ὑφαίνων and comm. on vv. 6–7), but their attitudes call to mind confrontations of strict and lenient fathers in New Comedy (cf. Kock, Legrand, *NGC* 231).

The description of a banquet's transformation into a brawl is couched in the rhetorical form of an ἐποικοδόμησις or 'climax' (cf. Arist. *Rhet.* 1.7, 1365ᵃ16 and the edition of E. M. Cope and J. E. Sandys (Cambridge 1877) *ad loc.*), and its similarity in form, content and even metre (trochaic tetrameter) to Epicharmus fr. 148 Kaibel[1] is striking:

(A.) †ἐκ μὲν θυσίας θοίνα†,
ἐκ δὲ θοίνας πόσις ἐγένετο. (B.) χαρίεν, ὥς γ' ἐμοὶ <δοκεῖ>.
ἐκ δ' ὑανίας <δίκα ⏖, ἐκ δίκας δὲ κατα>δίκα,
ἐκ δὲ καταδίκας πέδαι τε καὶ σφαλὸς καὶ ζαμία.

Yet we cannot be sure that the similarity of Alexis 160(156K) to this passage is a result of deliberate mimicry, or that even if it were, Alexis was influenced by Epicharmus on other occasions. Olivieri tried to bolster his theory that Sicilian Doric comedy frequently inspired Alexis by pointing to a few titles and trivial words shared between them, but the idea lacks evidence and credibility. Alexis may have been born in Magna Graecia (Thurii according to *Suda* s.v. Ἄλεξις, *testimonium* 1 Kassel–Austin; cf. my general introduction, 1.iii), but Thurii was over 300 km distant from Syracuse, and there is no evidence linking Alexis with Sicily. Indeed all his known career from the 350s onwards seems to have been focused on Attic comedy, where the influence of Epicharmus has been shown to be minimal or even doubtful (Pickard-Cambridge, *DTC* ¹410ff., ²285ff., E. Wüst, *Rh. Mus.* 93 (1950) 337ff., cf. Dohm, *Mageiros* 29f.). No other passage in Alexis can be linked inextricably with Epicharmus, and no detailed knowledge of the Sicilian's comedies would have been needed for a remodelling of Epicharmus 148, which was so well known in Athens during

---

45, followed by ἔχων; cf. Descroix 163), I can trace no certain instance in the frs. of Alexis, while noting that at fr. 110(105K).1 (Ath. 4.165e) the verse ends ἐν ἔτεσιν δύο in A, ἐν ἔτεσι δύο in Epit.

[1] The fr. is cited by Epit. of Ath. 2.36c–d in a text that is both corrupt (owing to the scribe's ignorance of Doric) and defective (Epit. commonly omits words – such as connectives – and phrases in its citations). My text is based on Kaibel's in his edition of Ath.; a fuller apparatus but inferior text can be found in Desrousseaux's (Paris 1956).

COMMENTARY

the second half of the 4th century as a standard example of ἐποικοδόμησις that Aristotle could refer to it (in the *Rhet.* passage cited above) and paraphrase it (*GA* 1.18, 724ᵃ28ff.) without exact citation.

It must also be noted that the similarities between the Epicharmus and Alexis passages are not reinforced by verbal echoes. Both may have been founded on independent observation of life (cf. vv. 6–7 in Alexis ταῦτα γὰρ | κατὰ φύσιν πέφυκεν οὕτως), on traditional motifs from sympotic literature (cf. Theogn. 479–83, 501f., 507f., 841f.; G. Giangrande, *Entr. Hardt* 14 (1967) 98ff., Hunter on Eubulus 93(94K)), or on a mixture of both. There is no sign of Sicilian influence when the motif is exploited elsewhere in Attic comedy (e.g. Ar. *Ach.* 551, *Vesp.* 1253–5, *Eccl.* 663f., Eubulus 93(94K), or with equal imagination in contexts as widely different as Heliodorus 5.29 (description of a banquet which turned into a bloody brawl, φιλεῖ γὰρ εὐημερία παραλόγως ὕβρεως ἔργα προκαλεῖσθαι) and Stob. *Ecl.* 3.18.25 (Ἀνάχαρσις ἔφη, κιρναμένου κρατῆρος ἐφεστίου, τὸν μὲν πρῶτον ὑγιείας πίνεσθαι, τὸν δὲ δεύτερον ἡδονῆς, τὸν δὲ τρίτον ὕβρεως, τὸν δὲ τελευταῖον μανίας, fr. 6 Mullach 1.292); cf. also Panyassis fr. 13 Kinkel, Eur. *Cycl.* 534.

1–2 ἡ μακρὰ συνουσία καὶ τὰ συμπόσια τὰ πολλὰ καὶ καθ' ἡμέραν: 'hours of socialising and many parties every day'. By Alexis' time in such contexts συνουσία became virtually synonymous with συμπόσιον (e.g. Xen. *Mem.* 1.5.4, Pl. *Symp.* 176e, Isoc. 1.32, LSJ s.v. II) but still retained something of its original sense of 'being with' people at the party (s.v. 1.4). I have not found it linked elsewhere with μακρά, but cf. e.g. μακροτέρας σχολᾶς Pind. *Nem.* 10.46, μ. ὁμιλίαν Eur. *Hipp.* 1441, μ. ἀπουσία *IA* 651, 1172, *Rhes.* 467, μ. συνήθεια Plut. *Mor.* 611e. In τὰ πολλὰ καὶ καθ' ἡμέραν the article goes equally with καθ' ἡμέραν, cf. Alexis 145(141K).6, 223.9(221.3K).

2 ποιεῖν: so ACE here, but see comm. on fr. 16.2.

3 πλεῖον ... πολύ: to be taken together, 'much more'. πλεῖον is Grotius' conjecture (*Exc.* 581, 973, cf. Peppink, *Observ.* 60) for the transmitted (A and Epit.) πλέον, which does not scan here but is nevertheless the generally accepted spelling in Attic throughout the classical period (πλεῖον does not appear in inscriptions until 131/30, *IG* ii².1227.16, cf. Threatte 1.321f.; the epigraphical evidence is overwhelmingly endorsed by the best MSS of 4th-century Athenian prose and by comic papyri). This led some stricter modern Atticists (e.g. A. Nauck, *MGR* 6 (1894) 117, Körte on Men. frs. 485.3, 612.6) to oppose the acceptance of πλεῖον anywhere in Attic comedy. They are wrong. πλεῖον, formed by analogy with πλείων, is attested there as a metrically convenient licence from the early 4th century on (Ar. *Eccl.* 1132 all MSS, Men. frs. 485.3, 543.5 MSS of Stob. *Ecl.* 3.3.23, 4.1.30, Athenion 1.16 and 26 MSS ACE and A of Ath. 14.661a–b, adesp. fr. 231.7 Austin from Old Comedy, cf. also adesp. fr.

244.100 Austin from New Comedy in a *sedes* where the first syllable scans *anceps*; on Alexis 257(255K).3 (πλέον Α ~ πλείω Epit. at Ath. 10.429e) see comm. *ad loc.*), and so is legitimately conjectured where πλέον is transmitted unmetrically (also Philemon 106.5 SMA at Stob. 4.35.1, πλεῖον Gesner).[1] Comedy also provides several examples of the form πλεῖν, which can be explained only as a contraction from πλεῖον (K.B. 1.216, Schwyzer 1.127, 249): e.g. Ar. *Av.* 1305, *Ran.* 90, *Plut.* 1184, Men. *Epitr.* 419. Cf also Th. Kock, *Rh. Mus.* 48 (1893) 214f., A. Thierfelder in Körte's edition of Men. 2² (Leipzig 1959) 297 on frs. 485, 612, Kassel–Austin 7.285 on Philemon 106.5.

4–5 ἂν δ' εἴπῃς ἅπαξ, εὐθὺς ἀντήκουσας: Kassel–Austin accept the transmitted text (ἂν Epit., ἀν unaccented A), but L. K. Valckenaer's conjecture ἂν (in his edition of Eur. *Phoen.* (Franeker 1755) on v. 1651, p. 556) is to be preferred; it is palaeographically neat (the error is common: cf. e.g. Eur. *Suppl.* 180, *Ion* 378, Ar. *Nub.* 89, *Lys.* 1057, Alexis 279(277K).3, Pl. *Gorg.* 486e, *Resp.* 10.606c) and adds precision to the sense, but surprisingly has been adopted only by Bothe, *PCGF* 552 and Edmonds.

γίγνετ': comm. on 37(36K).7.

5–6 λοιδορεῖσθαι λείπεται … τύπτεσθαι δέδεικται καὶ παροινεῖν: the reality of common experience confirms the correct transmission of the infinitives in this sequence, but both main verbs have been attacked. F. W. Schmidt, *Kritische Studien zu den griechischen Dramatikern* 3 (Berlin 1887) 53f.) took exception to λείπεται because λοιδορεῖσθαι is not the final item in the series. The objection might be valid in a dialectical sorites, but hardly in the looser logic of comedy, where λείπεται means little more than '(abuse) comes next'. For the impersonal use of λείπεται with the infinitive cf. Pl. *Phdr.* 235c λείπεται δὴ … διὰ τῆς ἀκοῆς πεπληρῶσθαί με δίκην ἀγγείου. Schmidt goes on to claim that τύπτεσθαι δέδεικται καὶ παροινεῖν is not acceptable Greek (cf. Blaydes, *Adv.* 1.112, 2.162, Herwerden, *Coll. Crit.* 126); it would have been more accurate to say that no exact parallel for this construction of δέδεικται + infinitive with the apparent sense '*uerbera et conuicia apparent*' (*TGL* s.v. δείκνυμι) has been found. Similar constructions, however, do occur with other unexpected verbs (e.g. S. *Ant.* 233 ἐνίκησεν μολεῖν, Xen. *Resp. Lac.* 9.2 ἕπεται τῇ ἀρετῇ σῴζεσθαι εἰς τὸν πλείω χρόνον, where Morus' conjecture <τὸ> σῴζεσθαι is unnecessary); here the infinitives have been interpreted as subjects without the article (K.G. 2.3f.) or object clauses with an impersonal verb (Jebb on S. *Ant.* 233, plausibly where the main verb is active), and the passive use of δείκνυται, δέδεικται, etc. in passages like Men. *Dysk.* 767f. ἐν δὲ τούτῳ τῷ μέρει μάλιστ' ἀνὴρ | δείκνυται, Libanius *Epist.* 278.3 δέδεικται δὲ ἐν μεγάλοις καιροῖς ὁ

---

[1] I omit from the discussion Men. *Dysk.* 528 and fr. 612.6 (Stob. *Ecl.* 4.29.6a), where the paradosis is gravely corrupt.

τρόπος is not too dissimilar. Even so, one other possibility must be considered; an intransitive use of δέχομαι with the meaning 'succeed/ come next' is recorded, at least in epic dialect (LSJ s.v. iv: e.g. Hom. *Il.* 19.290, Hes. *Theog.* 800); could Alexis have written δέδεκται here (so A. Palmer, according to Blaydes, *Adv.* 1.112, cf. 2.162, Herwerden, *Coll. Crit.* 126) with infinitival subject? For confusion of δέδεκται and δέδεικται in MSS cf. e.g Hippocr. *De Arte* 10. Either form would be a gnomic perfect; cf. in comedy Ar. *Equ.* 718, *Vesp.* 494, 561, 591, *Lys.* 595, 1234, *Ran.* 970, Antiphanes 202(204K).3, 7, 8 and the other passages cited there by Kock, Alexis 259(257K).8; outside comedy e.g. Pind. *Ol.* 1.53, S. *OC* 1235; cf. Goodwin, *MT* § 155.

6–7 ταῦτα γάρ: the second speaker (see above, introduction to this fr.) agrees (γάρ = 'Yes, for', cf. Denniston, *GP* 73f.), but points out that this sequence of events is natural. κατὰ φύσιν πέφυκεν may appear tautologous, but κατὰ φύσιν is added to πέφυκεν because by the end of the 5th century 'the force of the latter had become weakened by usage' (Jebb on S. *Phil.* 79 φύσει πεφυκότα), so that it was little more than a synonym for ἐστί. Cf. also Eur. *Bacch.* 896, Pl. *Crat.* 389c, Philemon 94(90K).2 πέφυκε τῇ φύσει, Baton 2.8.

καὶ τί μάντεως ἔδει;: the second and third words are Canter's correction (*Nov. Lect.* 184) of A's wrongly divided τιμᾶν τέως. Wilamowitz's suggestion that this phrase may have been proverbial is supported by the occurrence of similar expressions elsewhere in Attic, e.g. S. *OR* 393f. τό γ' αἴνιγμα . . . μαντείας ἔδει, Eur. *Hipp.* 236 τάδε μαντείας ἄξια πολλῆς, *Rhes.* 952 οὐδὲν μάντεως ἔδει, Pl. *Symp.* 206b μαντείας . . . δεῖταί ὅ τι ποτε λέγεις. The imperfect ἔδει in *Rhes.* and Alexis indicates a 'sudden appreciation of the real state of affairs' (Gildersleeve, *Syntax* 1.96f., cf. Starkie on Ar. *Vesp.* 183, K.G. 1.145f.). In all the passages quoted the references to μάντις and μαντεία approach the metaphorical (cf. LSJ s.v. μάντις 1.2, cf. S. *OC* 1080 a chorus singing μάντις εἴμ' ἐσθλῶν ἀγώνων), and no professional seer is present or involved.

161 (157K)

Meineke 3.455 (iii), Kock 2.355, Edmonds 2.448, Kassel–Austin 2.112. See the introductions to Ὀδυσσεὺς ὑφαίνων and Μιλήσιοι and comm. on fr. 155(151K).

Οἶνος

Meineke 1.393; cf. G. W. Elderkin, *AJA* 40 (1936) 348ff. and the introduction to Ὀπώρα. The Antiatticist (95.15 Bekker) cites Ἄλεξις Οἴνῳ for

the use of the adverb ἐμπειρικῶς (fr. 162(243K)). At first sight Οἶνος seems
an unlikely title for later Greek comedy, and the MS of the Antiatticist
often corrupts cited titles (in Alexis alone cf. introductions to Αἰχμάλωτος,
Κύπριος, Ταραντῖνοι); hence Meineke's suggestion that Οἴνῳ was an error
for Ὕπνῳ was supported by Kock and Edmonds. Yet this seems a harsh
change; palaeographically easier would have been Οἴνει (title of tragedies
by Philocles, Chaeremon, perhaps Sophocles,[1] satyr play by Euripides,
comedy by Dinolochus), Οἰν<ομά>ῳ (tragedies by Euripides and Sophocles,
the latter's being given a new production at the Rural Dionysia in the
mid–4th century with Aeschines in the title role, Dem. 18.180, Hesych. s.v.
ἀρουραῖος Οἰνόμαος, comedies by Antiphanes, Eubulus) and Οἰνο<πίων>ι
(comedies by Philetaerus and possibly Nicostratus; see comm. on
113(108K).2–3). Yet Οἶνος itself can be defended in two different but not
irreconcilable ways: (i) as a personification of wine (? cf. Menander's
Μέθη, see Webster, *IM* 162) speaking the prologue in a play whose plot
dealt with e.g. the consequences of a drunken rape; and/or (ii) as the name
of a leading character. In art a Silenus-like figure is twice labelled Οἶνος:
on a bell-krater of the Pothos painter (*CVA Providence RI* III.1e, fasc. 1
pl. 23, Beazley, *ARV*[2] pp. 1188 no. 1, 1686), and on a 3rd-century AD
mosaic from Antioch (W. A. Campbell, *AJA* 40 (1936) 4f. and fig. 7, D.
Levi, *Antioch Mosaic Pavements* (Princeton 1947) 1.186ff. and 2.pl.XLII a, b),
where he holds a wine-cup. A woman labelled Ὀπώρα also appears on the
mosaic; if Elderkin is right to interpret this mosaic as inspired by a scene
from a comedy such as Alexis' Ὀπώρα (the idea is possible but unlikely,
see introduction to that play), the two figures would have been characters
in the same play, and we should be obliged to consider a possibility that
Οἶνος and Ὀπώρα were alternative titles for it.

162 (243K)

Meineke 3.494 (IV), Kock 2.386, Edmonds 2.490, Kassel–Austin 2.113.
The attempt of the Antiatticist here (95.15 Bekker) to defend ἐμπειρικῶς
(as an Attic synonym for the standard ἐμπείρως: Dem. 59.18 etc., cf. LSJ
s.v. ἔμπειρος II) by citing Alexis cannot be judged successful. No instance of
either the adjective ἐμπειρικός or its adverb -ικῶς, apart from this undated
fr. of Alexis, is known before Aristotle (adjective *HA* 4.7, 532[b]21 where PD
have ἐμπορικῶν; adverb *GA* 2.6, 742[a]17, also e.g. Diod. Sic. 26.1), and
even in post-classical writers these forms are rare outside of their appellative function for the Empiric school of medicine from the middle of the 3rd
century on.

---

[1] But see A. C. Pearson's edition of the frs., 2 (Cambridge 1917) 120f. and
Kannicht–Snell, *TrGF* 2 on anon. F 625.

COMMENTARY

Ὀλυμπιόδωρος

Meineke 1.381, O. Crusius, *Philologus* 46 (1888) 620, Breitenbach 51, R. Fenk, *Adversarii Platonis quomodo de indole ac moribus eius iudicaverint* (Diss. Jena 1913) 50, Edmonds 2.449 note i, 450f., Gil 337. In the one fr. preserved from this play (163(158K)) a character hears a description of a deadly experience and then asks (v. 3) ταῦτ᾽ οὐ σχολὴ Πλάτωνος; Although philosophic and scientific theories lose neither validity nor influence with the deaths of their originators, the particular reference here to Plato's σχολή (either 'teaching' or 'group': see comm. *ad loc.*) suggests that Plato was still alive or only recently dead, with his 'group/teaching' still associated with him and not with his immediate successors at the head of the Academy. It is likely therefore that Alexis wrote Ὀλυμπιόδωρος before (say) 340.

Such a dating would exclude a play focused on that Olympiodorus whose successes as a general between 305 and 286 earned him statues in Athens and Delphi and a portrait in Eleusis (Paus. 1.25.2, 26.3; Kirchner, *PA* 2.167 no. 11388 and in *RE* s.v. *Olympiodoros* 1, 199.40ff., Wilamowitz, *Antigonos von Karystos* (Berlin 1881) 206 n. 31, W. S. Ferguson, *Hellenistic Athens* (London 1911) chs. 3, 4), and no other of the many Athenians who bore this name (Kirchner, *PA* 2.167–9 and 478 lists 34; cf. also Davies, *APF* 419f.) seems to have been celebrated or notorious enough (not even the man attacked as a blackguard in 341 by [Dem.] 48 = 11386 Kirchner, cf. Kroll in *RE* s.v. 4, 200.13ff.) to merit a play named after him. Alexis' title figure is accordingly most likely to have been a *persona ficta* of unidentifiable status (but note Olympio, slave bailiff in Plaut. *Cas.*) in an unidentifiable type of plot.

Lack of context and textual problems in 163(158K).1–2 (see comm.) make the deadly experience there described something of an enigma, but the possibilities are limited. Somebody says that his/her or someone else's body had become 'dry' and life either had departed or was departing. Crusius (followed by Fenk, Edmonds, Gil and – to judge from their text – Kassel–Austin) suggest that the speaker here is a ghost, because in his view vv. 1–2 make him/her refer to his/her own death in the past tense. This theory cannot be rejected out of hand, but it rests on one false and one questionable premise: respectively that ἐμοῦ is the correct reading in v. 1, and that Alexis wrote an aorist (ἐξῆρε) and not an imperfect (ἐξῆρε) in v. 2. An imperfect here would probably imply an alternative situation where the person described in vv. 1–2 either (i) *was* dying, but something happened to produce a recovery; or (ii), by a typically comic hyperbole, was experiencing a moment of sheer terror (such as e.g. Moschion faced with Nikeratos' threats in Men. *Sam.* 515, or Pheidias after seeing what he thought was a ghost in *Phasm.*, when *primo aspectu ... perculsus exhorruit*: Donatus on Ter. *Eun.* prol. 9.3).

476

163 (158K)

Meineke 3.455, Kock 2.355, Edmonds 2.448, Kassel–Austin 2.113; cf. also
(among the works cited at the end of comm. on fr. 1) especially Fenk, *loc.
cit.* at head of introduction to 'Ολυμπιόδωρος, A. Weiher, *Philosophen und
Philosophenspott in der attischen Komödie* (Diss. Munich 1913) 28f., G. J. de
Vries, *Hermeneus* 27 (1955) 6. The fr., cited by Diog. Laert. 3.28, was first
divided by Meineke (3.455, cf. 5.90) between two speakers, with the
second contributing v. 3. The other character's claim (1f.) that his/her/
someone else's mortal body had become dry, while the immortal element
had set out or was setting out on its journey into the air, is rooted in
popular ideas about death that are at least as old as Homer. There, at life's
end the ψυχή leaves the body and flies away on its journey to Hades (*Il.*
9.408f., 16.855f., 23.100, *Od.* 11.65; E. Bickel, *Homerischer Seelenglaube*
(Berlin 1926) 78f., W. Jaeger, *The Theology of the Early Greek Philosophers*
(Oxford 1947) 74f., R. B. Onians, *The Origins of Greek Thought*[1] (Cambridge 1951) 93ff., 261f.). The Presocratics developed this idea in various
ways; thus for Anaximenes the ψυχή floated upward from the body at
death to rejoin the atmosphere (fr. 2 Diels–Kranz, *Vorsokr.*[6] 1.95), for
Empedocles the ψ. was a vital warmth which was absorbed at death by the
fiery element from which it came (fr. 85 Diels–Kranz 1.301, cf. E. R.
Dodds, *The Greeks and the Irrational* (Berkeley 1951) 153), for Diogenes of
Apollonia the ψ. departed to rejoin the αἰθήρ (fr. 4 Diels–Kranz 2.6of., cf.
E. Rohde, *Psyche*[8] (translated by W. B. Hillis, London 1925) 436ff. and
nn. on 46off.). These intellectualisations co-existed alongside – and doubtless by ordinary Athenians were confused with – folk beliefs in a home of
the dead above the αἰθήρ, to which there are many references in
5th-century writers (e.g. frs. 245, 265 ascribed to Epicharmus, Eur. *Suppl.*
531ff., 1139f., *Or.* 1086f., fr. 971, the Potidaea epitaph of 432, *IG* i[2].945 =
Kaibel, *Epigr. Gr.* 21; Rohde, *loc. cit.*, J. G. Griffith, *JHS* 73 (1953) 4of.,
A. Pippin Burnett, *CPhil.* 55 (1960) 159ff.).

Although Plato himself rejected these folk beliefs as childish (*Phd.* 77de
~ 70a), it is easy to see how the lay imagination could have muddled them
with Plato's own views of the immortality of the ψυχή and its liberation
from the body at death (e.g. *Phdr.* 245c, *Phd.* 64c; cf. C. Lehrs, *Populäre
Aufsätze aus dem Alterthum*[2] (Leipzig 1856) 339), especially when these were
expressed in images as memorable as that in the *Phaedrus* myth of the ψ. as
a heavenly charioteer (cf. e.g. 246b ψυχὴ πᾶσα παντὸς ἐπιμελεῖται τοῦ
ἀψύχου, πάντα δὲ οὐρανὸν περιπολεῖ, 246c ἐπτερωμένη μετεωροπορεῖ τε
καὶ πάντα τὸν κόσμον διοικεῖ). Plato's stress on the immortality of the
ψυχή may well lie behind Alexis' substitution of τὸ ἀθάνατον for it in v. 2
of the fr. Whether Alexis himself misunderstood or disregarded the
differentiae between Plato's real views and those ascribed to him (if only
interrogatively) in the fr., or whether he made his speaker do so simply for

a laugh, we have no means of knowing; cf. also comm. on fr. 1 and (on the whole question of comedy's relation to contemporary philosophy) Dover's edition of Ar. *Nub.* pp. xxxii ff.

1–2 Here Alexis almost certainly wrote σῶμα μὲν ὁμοῦ τὸ θνητὸν . . . τὸ δ' ἀθάνατον. ὁμοῦ, the reading of B (*'longe optimus est codex'* H. Breitenbach and others, *Juvenes dum sumus* (Basle 1907), introduction to their edition of Diog. Laert. 3, p. iii) and also perhaps of P originally, stresses the antithesis; cf. e.g. S. *OR* 4f. πόλις δ' ὁμοῦ μὲν θυμιαμάτων γέμει, | ὁμοῦ δὲ παιάνων τε καὶ στεναγμάτων, Heliodorus 2.25 ὁμοῦ μὲν εἴκων ταῖς μοιρῶν ἀνάγκαις . . . ὁμοῦ δὲ τὴν ἀποτρόπαιον Ῥοδῶπιν ἀποφεύγων; the idiom may be a poetic or rhetorical variant of the very common locutions ὁμοῦ A (τε) καὶ B, A τε ὁμοῦ καὶ B, ὁμοῦ καὶ A καὶ B. Most of the other MSS (including P after alteration) have ἐμοῦ without accent or breathing; it is printed by virtually all editors from Grotius, *Exc.* 583 to H. S. Long and Kassel–Austin, even though this form of the genitive of the first-person singular pronoun is avoided as an attribute (Attic says (τὸ) ἐμὸν σῶμα and (τὸ) σῶμά μου, not (τὸ) σῶμα ἐμοῦ, cf. K.G. 1.559f., Björck, *Alpha Impurum* 99), and any other interpretation of ἐμοῦ here (e.g. as a partitive) would be forced. For the confusion between ὁμοῦ and ἐμοῦ in MSS see Eur. *Andr.* 1257, cf. *Hel.* 1447 and R. Kannicht's apparatus at 641. W. Headlam allegedly (Herwerden, *Coll. Crit.* 126, but this does not concur with *CR* 13 (1899) 7) conjectured ἐμὸν σῶμα, without realising that this was the reading of V (a MS *'misere corruptus'*, Breitenbach xi); its sense is better than its palaeographical base (a sequence ὁμοῦ → ἐμοῦ → ἐμὸν is intelligible, but the opposite route less so).

αὖον: on the breathing see comm. on 132(127K).6. The word can be applied to corpses (e.g. Σ Ar. *Ran.* 194 παρὰ τὸ αὖους τοὺς νεκροὺς εἶναι, cf. Onians, *op. cit.* in introduction to this fr., 254ff.) and to live bodies petrified with fear (e.g. Ar. *Lys.* 385, Men. *Epitr.* 901, *Pk.* 352f., *Sam.* 515); cf. introduction to Ὀλυμπιόδωρος.

2 ἀθάνατον: see above, introduction to this fr. and (on the initial long alpha) comm. on 164(159K).3; τὸ θνητόν in v. 1 was clearly inserted to prepare the way for it. Directly afterwards it is uncertain whether Alexis wrote ἐξῆρε (so the MSS at Diog. Laert. 3.28, cf. Kassel–Austin 4.viii) or ἐξῇρε; see the introduction to Ὀλυμπιόδωρος. An intransitive use of ἐξαίρω is not found elsewhere before the *Koine* (with two different senses, *pace* LSJ s.v. 1.1b: (i) 'I rise' (into the air), here and Diod. Sic. 2.50.5 citing Posidippus, *FGrH* 87 F 114, an ostrich διὰ . . . τὸ βάρος οὐ δυνάμενον ἐξᾶραι καὶ πέτεσθαι) and (ii) 'I march out', Polyb. 2.23.4, 18.19.3, etc., LXX *Gen.* 35.5, *Num.* 2.9), but this may be an accident of preservation; the simple verb αἴρω and several other compounds (e.g. ἀπ-, ἐπ- Evangelus 1.10, κατ-) are common intransitively in Attic writers. Accordingly emendations replacing this verb (e.g. ἐξῆξε K. F. Hermann,

ΟΛΥΜΠΙΟΔΩΡΟΣ

Allgemeine Schulzeitung (Darmstadt 17 April 1829) 373) seem uncalled for.

πρὸς τὸν ἀέρα: in the context of folk belief the region to which the ψυχή normally ascends at the body's death is αἰθήρ (e.g. Eur. *Suppl.* 533, 1139, fr. 971, the Potidaea epitaph cited in the introduction to this fr.; so also Diogenes of Apollonia fr. 4 Diels–Kranz; cf. Rohde, *Psyche*[8] (tr. Hillis) 436), and it is possible that careless quotation or copying corrupted a correct α<ἰθ>έρα here. Yet ἀήρ and αἰθήρ were not always carefully distinguished from each other (Rohde 460, cf. West on Hes. *Theog.* 697), and in any case the departing ψυχή must pass through ἀήρ in its ascent to αἰθήρ.

3 ταῦτ' οὐ σχολὴ Πλάτωνος;: a comically pedantic question by the second speaker (see introduction to 'Ολυμπιόδωρος); on its structure see comm. on 99(94K).1. Here σχολή most probably = 'teaching' (apparently for the first time in extant Greek), cf. especially Arist. *Pol.* 7.2, 1323[b]39 ἑτέρας γάρ ἐστιν ἔργον σχολῆς ταῦτα, LSJ s.v. II.1), although the related meaning which flourished particularly in later *Koine* and the Roman empire, 'school' (i.e. group of students and teacher involved in their teaching) was already developing in the 4th century (cf. Arist. *Pol.* 5.9, 1313[b]3 μήτε σχολὰς μήτε ἄλλους συλλόγους ἐπιτρέπειν γίνεσθαι σχολαστικούς and W. L. Newman, comm. *ad loc.* (Oxford 1902, 4.452), LSJ s.v. II.2).

'Ολυνθία (or -ιοι or -ιος)

Grotius, *Exc.* 975, Meineke 1.388f., 3.456, K. Mras, *Anz. Alt.* 3 (1950) 103f., Webster, *SLGC* 77, A. M. Desrousseaux, edition of Ath. 1–2 (Paris 1956) p. 135 n. 1, Edmonds 2.450 note a. Alexis is credited with an 'Ολύνθιοι by Ath. 6.240c (fr. 164(159K)) and Stob. *Anth.* 3.27.9 (165(160K): so SMA, but ὀλυν̇ L), an 'Ολύνθιος by Ath. 3.75b (167(162K).14–16; the whole fr. is cited without play title by Epit. at Ath. 2.54f–55a), and an 'Ολυνθία by Photius and *Suda* s.v. εὐημερία (166(161K)). Alexis could have written more than one play about Olynthians of different sexes and numbers, but the variations in the endings here more probably result from haphazard expansion (in at least two cases) of titles abbreviated in transmission, as often elsewhere (cf. especially introduction to 'Αποκοπτόμενος or -ομένη); certainly frs. 164(159K) and 167(162K) presuppose an identical dramatic background. Certainty over the correct form of the title is unachievable; my preference for 'Ολυνθία springs from the subject matter of 167(162K).

This is the longest and most informative of the frs. It consists of fifteen

479

anapaestic dimeters, a metre whose popularity in 4th-century comedy as a vehicle for the individual actor (cf. Meineke 1.302f., Körte in *RE* s.v. *Komödie (mittlere)* 1265.24ff., Nesselrath, *MK* 267ff., R. Pretagostini, *Dioniso* 57 (1987) 246ff.) may have been due partly to a desire for rhythmical variety after the decline of the chorus. The fr. combines features typical in comic anapaests of the period (food listing in 11–13, cf. also Hunter on Eubulus 63, but whereas other poets emphasise gastronomic delights, Alexis' list ironically picks out the foods of indigence; poetic elevation of style 6–7, 14–16, perhaps parodying tragedy: so Nesselrath 271, but see also my introduction to comm. on fr. 124(119K)) with an expository function that suggests we may be reading part of a chanted or sung prologue (cf. in later comedy also Menander fr. 258 from his Λευκαδία, patterned like and probably influenced by examples in Attic tragedy: e.g. Eur. *Andromeda*, cf. Σ Ar. *Thesm.* 1065; *IA*, whoever wrote vv. 1–48, 115–63;[1] but probably not *Rhesus*[2]). Its speaker is an old woman (vv.1–2), probably Athenian by nationality (cf. 14–16 and comm.). She has an impoverished husband (1: also old presumably), a daughter (probably in her late teens by comedy's two-generation norm) and a son who was still a 'boy' (παῖς 2). How many of these had speaking parts we do not know; from the way they are described, none of the three has yet been seen by the audience. A fifth member of the household is presented to the audience as ἥδ' ἡ χρηστή (3), which suggests that she was there on stage with the speaker (in that case might she have shared in the expository anapaests? But see comm. *ad loc.*), but in all likelihood not closely related by blood to the other four. We are not told her status or place of origin, but the conjecture first advanced by Grotius that she was the Ὀλυνθία of a play so titled is attractive, although unsupported by hard evidence. In that case, whether she was slave (so Desrousseaux) or free, it would be easy to incorporate her and the other four in one of the familiar

---

[1] The extremes of modern opinion are represented by E. Fraenkel, *Gnomon* 37 (1965) 235, B. M. W. Knox, *YCS* 22 (1972) 239ff. = *Word and Action* (Baltimore and London 1979) 274ff. and H. Erbse, *Studien zum Prolog der euripideischen Tragödie* (Berlin 1984) 269ff., who believe that the anapaestic opening of *IA* is substantially by Euripides, and J. Diggle, *CR* 21 (1971) 179f. and D. Bain, *CQ* 27 (1977) 10ff., who do not. Cf. also the useful survey by W. Stockert in his edition of the play (Vienna 1992) 1.66ff., 2.157ff., 209ff.

[2] Cf. W. Ritchie, *The Authenticity of the Rhesus of Euripides* (Cambridge 1964) 101ff., setting out the evidence for an original iambic opening now lost, and Fraenkel's review (*loc. cit.* in n. 1 above).

later-comedy patterns of love-affair and ἀναγνώρισις (cf. Webster), but we should be wiser not to write Alexis' plot for him.[1]

The speaker of 167(162K) emphasises her family's harsh poverty throughout her speech; she is likely therefore to have been the addressee also of fr. 164(159K) (so first Meineke), whose husband is also called poor by an almost certainly female and possibly wealthier friend (comm. *ad loc.*). The other two frs. add little. 165(160K) is a general reflection on the superiority of actions to oaths, 166(161K) probably part of a prayer to the Muses and the goddess Prosperity perhaps voiced at the end of the play in the hope of the poet's victory (comm. *ad loc.*).

Fr. 164(159K) also refers to the 'everlasting' (cf. comm. on v. 3) presence in Athens of the parasite Tithymallus, whose activities spanned the second half of the 4th century (see introduction to Μιλήσιοι); Ὀλυνθία accordingly was probably written in that period. If Alexis sought plausibility by tying his plot to a firm historical background, he could have explained the presence in Athens of a native of Olynthus by reference to that city's destruction by Philip in 348, when (e.g.) a baby girl might have been sold into slavery or brought to Athens as a free refugee, becoming dramatically nubile by *c.* 333 (so Edmonds). Yet it would be absurd to pin Alexis' play to the latter date on such evidence. Menander's Ὀλυνθία, whose plot is unknown, seems to have been produced in 313 or shortly afterwards (Körte's edition, 2.110f., cf. Webster, *SM* 104); an Ὀλυνθία (or -ίαι, -ιοι, -ιος) is also attributed to Philippus (or Philippides), cf. Hense on Stob. *Anth.* 4.49.1, Kassel–Austin 7.354f.

164 (159K)

Meineke 3.457 (II), Kock 2.355, Edmonds 2.450, Kassel–Austin 2.114. One woman (almost certainly: see on ὦ γλυκεῖα v. 1) addresses another, who is described as a poor man's wife and probably identical with the speaker of 167(162K) (see introduction to Ὀλυνθία). Her choice of phrase in v. 1 ('but/and yours, i.e. husband, is poor') suggests that the speaker too is married, but to a wealthier man (so Kock), and the slant of the ideas expressed in frs. 164(159K) and 167(162K) makes it likely that the contrast between rich and poor was a motif in the play.

1 ὁ δὲ σὸς πένης ἔστ': the words may have been inspired by some remark from the poor wife about her husband's mortality. Was he ill and not expected to live long?

1–3 ἔστ', ὦ (1) and **ἀθάνατος** (3) are corrections first appearing in

---

[1] The perils are well illustrated by Mras, who by misinterpreting frs. 164(159K) and 167(162K) turns the needy old woman's husband into a parasite and both girls into her daughters now practising as *hetairai*.

COMMENTARY

Casaubon's text of A's (at Ath. 6.240c: Epit. omits the fr.) undivided ἔστω and pointless θάνατος (a corruption doubtless influenced by the correct appearance of this word in the preceding verse).

ὦ γλυκεῖα: a form of address used predominantly by women either to women (e.g. γλυκεῖα Men. *Epitr.* 862, Habrotonon to Pamphile; (ὦ) γλυκυτάτη Ar. *Lys.* 79, *Eccl.* 124, 241; the speaker at Apollodorus of Carystus 5.13 is uncertain) or affectionately to men (ὦ γλυκύτατε Men. *Epitr.* 143 probably Habrotonon to Chairestratos, 953 Habr. to Charisios; on *Heros* fr. 5 see Gomme–Sandbach, *Comm. ad loc.*, on Men. fr. 396 T. Williams, *Hermes* 91 (1963) 311 and 320 n. 1) and babies (ὦ γλυκύτατον σὺ τεκνίδιον Ar. *Lys.* 889, cf. Theoc. 15.13). On the rare occasions when these vocatives are used by men in comedy, the tone is one of either overwhelming affection for a wife (ὦ γλυκυτάτη Men. *Epitr.* 888, Charisios apostrophising) or sycophantic wheedling to a man (ὦ γλυκύτατ' Εὐριπίδη Ar. *Ach.* 462, 467). Cf. D. Bain, *Antichthon* 18 (1984) 36f. and my comm. on 91(87K).4.

2 Death's alleged reluctance to snatch away the poor (a cliché of the time, if ὥς φασιν is taken at face value; cf. also comm. on 37(36K).4) is more picturesquely described in Antiphanes 86 (cf. especially v. 6 ὁ δὲ λιμός ἐστιν ἀθανασίας φάρμακον). In S. *Phil.* 445ff. it is τὰ ... πανοῦργα καὶ παλιντριβῆ that are turned away. The wittiest variant on the conceit is perhaps Plaut. *Pseud.* 792ff., where Ballio claims that Orcus has rejected *coquom ... hunc ... | multiloquom gloriosum insulsum inutilem.* Cf. O. Crusius, *Philologus* 44 (1888) 608, W. Headlam, *CR* 13 (1899) 7.

ὁ Θάνατος would be better here; Alexis is talking about the divinity, not the condition.

3 The conceit about Death's fear of the poor is introduced in v. 2 in order to prepare the ground for the joke on Tithymallus that follows; on this parasite see introduction to Μιλήσιοι and comm. on 155(151K). We must assume that a remarkable durability in the public gaze lay behind Alexis' quip about Tithymallus, which is based on the double meaning in ἀθάνατος (with its first syllable scanned long, as always: cf. R. Porson on Eur. *Med.* 139–40 § 1, K.B. 1.308f., LSJ s.v. and on ἀ- 1), (i) literally 'eternal', (ii) 'lasting so long as to seem eternal' (e.g. Hyperides *Lyc.* 2, Men. fr. 479, Philemon 165(196K)). A parallel joke with θεός about Androcles is made by Menander in *Sam.* 606ff. (cf. Sandbach *ad loc.* and C. Dedoussi's commentary (Athens 1965) on 257, 262f., her numbering). Cf. also Plaut. *Trin.* 55f. *eho tu, tua uxor quid agit? :: immortalis est, | uiuit uicturaque est.*

This v. is probably spoken by the character who spoke 1–2, but the possibility that it is an aside by a third person overhearing the two women cannot be ruled out.

ΟΛΥΝΘΙΑ

165 (160K)

Meineke 3.458 (III), Kock 2.356, Edmonds 2.450, Kassel–Austin 2.114. Speaker and situation are unknown. The unreliability of oaths was a platitude in later comedy, and characters are advised to avoid them totally (also e.g. monost. 592 Jäkel) or at least to place no trust in those sworn by unsavoury classes of people (e.g. the wicked, Antiphanes 230(233K), monost. 26; adulterers, Philonides 7; politicians and *hetairai*, Diphilus 101; male lovers, Plaut. *Cist.* 472f.; cf. also Xenarchus 6 ~ S. fr. 811). Alexis combines the cliché with the injunction to rely rather on actions, thus rephrasing (perhaps unconsciously) Eur. *Suppl.* 907f. φιλότιμον ἦθος πλούσιον, φρόνημα δὲ | ἐν τοῖσιν ἔργοις οὐχὶ τοῖς λόγοις ἴσον, cf. also 745ff. and fr. 583.

166 (161K)

Meineke 3.458 (IV), Kock 2.356, Edmonds 2.450, Kassel–Austin 2.114. The speaker is unknown and the context uncertain, but the mention together of 'Lady Good Fortune and Dear Muses', presumably in the vocative (if the nouns were nominatives, we should expect a definite article at least with Μοῦσαι), makes one wonder whether they are being asked in a prayer, most appropriately at the end of the play, to grant it victory, just as in the closing formula at Men. *Dysk.* 968f. = *Mis.* 465f. = *Sik.* 422f. = com. adesp. fr. 249.20f. Austin ἡ δ᾽ εὐπάτειρα φιλόγελώς τε παρθένος | Νίκη μεθ᾽ ἡμῶν εὐμενὴς ἔποιτ᾽ ἀεί, with the variations at Men. *Sam.* 736f. and Posidippus 6.12f. Kassel–Austin = 218.12f. Austin.

Εὐημερία: personified elsewhere as a medical divinity in Tanagra (E. Schwyzer, *Dialectorum graecarum exempla epigraphica priora* (Leipzig 1923) 462, A6f.; cf. her male counterpart Εὐαμερίων at the shrine of Asclepius in Titane west of Sicyon, Paus. 2.11.7), and the name of an Athenian trireme (*IG* ii².1611.h429, 357/6 BC). A woman of this name lived on Paros (Collitz, *GDI* 5437.29, Bechtel, *Personennamen* 614). The same range of applications is found for the basically synonymous Εὐδαιμονία, Εὐετηρία and Εὐτυχία. Cf. Waser in *RE* s.vv. *Eudaimonia* 892.4ff., *Euemeria* 2, 952.7ff., *Eueteria* 982.5off., *Eutychia* 1530.4off.,T. B. L. Webster, *Journal of the Warburg and Courtauld Institutes* 17 (1954) 10ff. and *Art and Literature in Fourth Century Athens* (London 1956) 39ff.

Μοῦσαι φίλαι: as e.g. at Herodas 3.1 and the refrain in Theoc. 1 (v.64 + 6 other times).

483

COMMENTARY

167 (162K)

Meineke 3.456 (1), Kock 2.356, Edmonds 2.450, Kassel–Austin 2.115; cf. Nesselrath, *MK* 271 and n. 82. An old woman describes her family and its poverty in anapaestic dimeters (the metre here was first identified by Grotius, *Exc.* 597, 975, cf. Schweighaeuser, *Animadv.* 1.367), perhaps designed to combine expository prologue (see introduction to Ὀλυνθία) with parody of a tragic θρῆνος (so Nesselrath, but see comm. on 6–7 below). The whole fr. is found in Ath. 2.54f–55a (only Epit., without play title), vv. 14–16 again in 3.75b (A with, Epit. without title), and can be printed (after two desirable corrections in vv. 4, 11) as either fourteen perfect dimeters (all with median diaeresis) or thirteen dimeters and two interlarded monometers (κύαμος, θερμός 11, μελέδημ' ἰσχάς 15), followed in both arrangements by a paroemiac that ends the speech, or at least a major section of it.

2 θυγάτηρ: this separate mention of a daughter precludes any possibility that ἥδ' ἡ χρηστή, listed separately in v. 3, was also (so far as the speaker then knew) her daughter.

παῖς υἱός: see comm. on fr. 117(112K). 2–3. The addition of παῖς to υἱός indicates that the son was no older than a μειράκιον (cf. comm. on 37(36K).2). On its own παῖς is as imprecise as the English 'boy/girl' in regard to age. Although some ancient writers tried to lay down strict parameters (cf. Gomme–Sandbach on Men. *Dysk.* 27, citing Hippocrates in Philo *De opificio mundi* 36 παῖς δ' ἄχρι γονῆς ἐκφύσιος, ἐς τὰ δὶς ἑπτά· μειράκιον δ' ἄχρι γενείου λαχνώσιος, ἐς τὰ τρὶς ἑπτά, and Epictetus *Diss.* 3.9.8), popular usage was far looser, and a male παῖς could range in age from a baby (e.g. Men. *Epitr.* 321, 398) up to and including a μειράκιον of marriageable age (e.g. Gorgias at Men. *Dysk.* 27f., old enough to farm independently, or Moschion at *Sam.* 585, old enough to have performed a liturgy and commanded cavalry, cf. Gomme–Sandbach on *Sam.* 13), while a female παῖς was often of marriageable age (e.g. *Asp.* 258, 262, 333, *Dysk.* 50, 73, 672, 938, *Sam.* 433, 676, cf. 591).

3 χἤδ' ἡ χρηστή: see introduction to Ὀλυνθία. The demonstrative pronoun probably implies a gesture towards a character on stage (yet a possibility that she was not actually present, but had either just left or only been vividly described in the preceding context, cannot be excluded; see the discussions cited in comm. on fr. 19.1). The girl's description as ἡ χρηστή is intriguing. This adjective indicates conformity to the standards expected of (particularly free) women in contemporary society (skill in and devotion to household chores, chastity, a committed loyalty to the family: e.g. A. W. H. Adkins, *Merit and Responsibility* (Oxford 1960) 36f., 161ff., writing on Homer and 5th-century Athens, but the values still held in Alexis' time, cf. Dover, *GPM* 51ff., 62f., 69; monost. 155 γυνὴ δὲ χρηστὴ

484

πηδάλιόν ἐστ' οἰκίας), but the absence of any noun defining consanguinity or affinity probably means that she was not related (or known to be related) to members of the household with whom she lived.

4 CE here write τούτων οἱ τρεῖς δειπνοῦμεν, which is objectionable on two counts. It provides a catalectic dimeter which is totally spondaic and continues its sentence into the following line, against the rules for comic non-melic systems (cf. Schweighaeuser, *Animadv.* 1.367f., J. W. White, *The Verse of Greek Comedy* (London 1912) 109). Secondly, its sense is contradicted by what follows. In this impoverished household three of the five 'dine' while the other two can afford only to share with them a bit of unbaked barley-cake, the staple food of the poorest (cf. comm. on 145(141K).7). This pair are the 'we' of vv. 5–6, i.e. the speaker and most probably ἡ χρηστή of v. 3, especially if the latter was also on stage (these are the two whom in any case we should have expected to go short: the mother who puts the other members of the family first, and a girl of extra-familial status, see on v. 3: did she partly owe her designation as χρηστή to a willingness to make such sacrifices?). The other trio by contrast appears to include nobody present on stage, and so become not 'we three' but 'they three' (hence Grotius' conjecture δειπνοῦσιν, *Exc.* 597, 975 has won deserved support and ought to have been printed by Kassel–Austin). Total correction of Alexis' verse and explanation of its corruption can be made without recourse to the exotic remedies of e.g. S. A. Naber, *Mnemosyne* 8 (1880) 261f., H. Weil, *Revue critique d'histoire et de littérature* 20 (1885) 277, Richards, *AO* 85. We assume simply that a scribe saw, in the text from which he was copying, a μέν (balancing the δ' of v. 5) and a δειπνοῦσιν, which he conflated by a psychological homoeoteleuton into δειπνοῦμεν (note too that two verb endings in -οῦμεν follow in quick succession vv. 5–7). But where was that original <μέν> placed? Least probably after δειπνοῦσιν (so Kaibel), for this produces an unbalanced antithesis without any compelling justification (cf. Denniston, *GP* 371ff.); the normal position would be after τρεῖς (Schweighaeuser) or οἱ (R. Walpole, *Comicorum graecorum fragmenta quaedam* (Cambridge 1805) 89: preferable here because median diaeresis is so preserved, cf. West, *Greek Metre* 94f.).

6–7 φθόγγους δ' ἀλύρους θρηνοῦμεν: the tone changes from the everyday and prosaic to one whose lyricism comes somewhere between tragic parody and a sympathetically serious portrayal of a desperate situation in appropriate language (cf. F. H. Sandbach, *Entr. Hardt* 16 (1970) 124ff. on similar passages in Menander). The notes (φθόγγους: often musical sounds of voice or instrument, mainly in high poetry; in comedy elsewhere only Ar. *Av.* 681, 1198; in prose used as a technical term for the 'notes', i.e. strings or stops, of musical instruments, e.g. Pl. *Leg.* 7.812d τοῖς φθόγγοις τῆς λύρας, Dio Chrys. 10.19, Philostratus

COMMENTARY

VA 5.21, cf. LSJ s.v.) of lament are 'lyreless' (ἀλύρους: only here in comedy) because dirges were associated particularly with αὐλοί and not stringed instruments like the λύρα, and so ἄλυρος in Greek tragedy (its predominant home, LSJ s.v.; especially the later lyrics of Euripides, *IT* 146, *Hel.* 185, *Phoen.* 1028; cf. also A. *Ag.* 990ff. τὸν δ᾽ ἄνευ λύρας ὅμως ὑμνῳδεῖ | θρῆνον ... | θυμός, A. M. Dale, comm. (Oxford 1954) on Eur. *Alc.* 447) became little more than a picturesque synonym for 'sad'. In comedy θρηνῶ makes several (but θρῆνος no) appearances, always apparently with paratragic or high poetic intent (Ar. *Nub.* 1260, *Av.* 211, Phrynichus 74(69K).1, Men. *Dysk.* 214 and Gomme–Sandbach, *Comm. ad loc.*). The passages of Ar. *Nub.* and Men. suggest that Alexis' speaker is simply poeticising her family's habit of crying οἴμοι and ἰώ μοί μοι.

8–9 Cf. Ar. *Plut.* 422 (Chremylos to Penia on her entry) σὺ δ᾽ εἶ τίς; ὠχρὰ μὲν γὰρ εἶναί μοι δοκεῖς and Σ (especially V, ὠχροὶ γάρ εἰσιν οἱ πένητες διὰ τὸ μὴ ἔχειν αὐτοὺς ἴσως φαγεῖν).

γίγνεται: see comm. on 37(36K).7.

9–10 τὰ μέρη δ᾽ ἡμῶν χἠ σύνταξις τοῦ βίου: 'our portions and system of life'. μέρη is ambiguous, perhaps designedly: both 'portions' allotted by fate (cf. F. Marx, comm. (Leipzig 1928) on Plaut. *Rud.* 189) and *ciborum portiones* (cf. Schweighaeuser, *Animadv.* 1.368). The plural here is not a poetic licence (cf. comm. on vv. 14–16(c)) but simply reflects the fact that each member of the household has his/her own μέρος.

11–13 The whole fr. is cited by Ath. 2.54f and vv. 11–13 (without the author's name) by Eustath. 948.41 in order to illustrate Alexis' mention of ἐρέβινθος. This is one item in a list probably of eleven (not twelve: see on v. 11 below) foods that the poorest peasant could grow for himself or collect wild in the countryside. Plato includes βολβός, ἐρέβινθος, κύαμος, λάχανα and φηγός among the foods of his most primitive form of society (*Resp.* 2.372c); cf. also Poliochus 2 (λάχανα, μᾶζα and σῦκα in a list whose context suggests poverty), Archestratus fr. 192.13ff. Lloyd-Jones–Parsons, *SH* 73f. (ἐρέβινθοι, ἰσχάδες, κύαμοι are πτωχείης παράδειγμα κακῆς); μᾶζα and βολβός form part of a wretchedly impoverished life at Antiphanes 225(226K), ἐρέβινθος at Crobylus 9 is fit only for an 'unfortunate monkey', θέρμος means poverty at Lycophron fr. 2 (*TrGF* 1 pp. 267f.), cf. Timocles 20(18K).4. Cf. E. Fournier in Dar.–Sag. s.v. *Cibaria* 1141B ff.

11 κύαμος: the broad bean (*Vicia faba*), still an important source of protein for the poorer countries around the Mediterranean. Phaenias (fr. 29 *FHG* 2.300, cited by Ath. 2.54f directly before Alexis 167(162K)) writes τραγήματος ἔχει χώραν ἀπαλὰ μὲν ὦχρος, κύαμος, ἐρέβινθος· ξηρὰ δὲ ἑφθὰ καὶ φρυκτὰ (cf. Alexis 139(134K).2) σχεδὸν τὰ πλεῖστα. Varieties with black seed-coats existed (e.g. Hom. *Il.* 13.589, Ar. *Lys.* 690: genetically dominant) side by side with the recessive cream-coloured ones (cf.

486

André, *Alimentation* 35) more familiar to us. Cf. also Olck (excellent and full as usual) in *RE* s.v. *Bohne* 602.45ff., D. A. Bond in N. W. Simmonds (ed.), *The Evolution of Crop Plants* (London and New York 1976) 179ff.

θέρμος: the lupin, divided by the ancients only into cultivated and wild forms (Dioscorides 2.109, Pliny *HN* 22.154, 156). Four species are native to Greece: *Lupinus micranthus** (formerly *hirsutus*), *L. albus* ssp. *graecus*, *L. varius* ssp. *orientalis* and *L. angustifolius** (cf. T. G. Tutin and others, *Flora Europaea* 2 (Cambridge 1968) 105f.; photographs of the asterisked species in A. Huxley and W. Taylor, *Flowers of Greece and the Aegean* (London 1977) nos. 95, 96). The seeds were eaten both in Greece (e.g. Alexis 268(266K).2, Timocles 20(18K).4, Alciphr. 3.24.2, 31.2, cf. Lucian *Ver. Hist.* 2.28; still in the poorer villages of the south, cf. P. Leigh-Fermor, *Mani* (London 1958) 73f.) and Italy (André, *Alimentation* 39), but they are slightly poisonous in their raw state and must be boiled and strained to remove the bitter taste before being eaten (Varro *Rust.* 1.13.3); cf. also Steier in *RE* s.v. *Lupine* 1845.9ff., L. S. Cobley, *An Introduction to the Botany of Tropical Crops* (London 1956) 160ff.

CE here jointly write κύαμος θέρμος λάχανον, which (after the colometry of the rest of the fr. has been established) leaves these three words as a separate metrical unit, half a metron short for an anapaestic dimeter, half a metron too much for a monometer, in a comic system which avoids such anomalies (cf. White, *loc. cit.* on v. 4). Either a lacuna (by scribe or epitomist, cf. Nesselrath, *MK* 271 n. 82) must be posited after λάχανον, ranging in length from half a metron to that plus one or more complete dimeters (so Dindorf in his edition of Ath.), or λάχανον ought to be deleted (so with greater probability P. Elmsley, *Ed. Rev.* 3 (1803/4) 189). In the plural λάχανα is the regular term for pot-herbs in general, but the singular is rarely used except in passages where a named plant is identified as a λάχανον (e.g. Eubulus 13(14K).3, Epicrates 10(11K).25, LSJ s.v.). The likeliest explanation of its presence in the Epit. MSS here is that a marginal or suprascript gloss on θέρμος or (more probably: see on v. 12) ὦχρος, added to prevent any confusion with the differently accented homonym, was erroneously interpreted by a scribe as part of Alexis' text. Without λάχανον either v. 11 becomes a monometer (like μελέδημ' ἰσχάς below), or vv. 11–15 may be reconstructed as four dimeters. There is no way of inferring Alexis' own intention from MSS which print all frs. as prose.

γογγυλίς: see on fr. 92(88K).

12 ὦχρος, λάθυρος: two pulses belonging to the *Lathyrus* genus. λάθυρος is correctly identified as *Lathyrus sativus*, the chickling vetch or grass pea, still grown in the Middle East, where 'it serves as forage and as a pulse, usually for the poorer classes' (Cobley, *op. cit.* on v. 11, 151ff.). The seeds, which are brown or grey with black mottling, need careful boiling (like those of lupins) before consumption, since they contain an alkaloid which can cause paralysis of the lower body. Cf. André, *Alimentation* 38. ὦχρος was tentatively identified by Linnaeus as *L. ochrus* (a bluish-grey annual with pale yellow flowers), but although the identification is endorsed by Sir Arthur Hort (index to his Loeb edition of Theophr. *HP* (London and New York 1916) II p. 484) and LSJ, there are at least 25 species of *Lathyrus* native to Greece (Tutin, *op. cit.* on v. 11, 2.136ff.), of which one or more others could be the ancient ὦχρος. Any echo with ὠχρόν in v. 9 is probably unintentional, but this repetition of homonyms could well have led to the glossing of ὦχρος here as λάχανον and the textual problem discussed on v. 11.

φηγός: both the tree and (here) the acorn of (almost certainly) the valonia oak (*Quercus macrolepis*, formerly *Q. aegilops*; Tutin, *op. cit.* on v. 11, 1 (Cambridge 1964) 63). This is the common oak of Greece, and its acorns, sweet in taste, were eaten raw as τραγήματα or roasted in ashes (e.g. Ar. *Pax* 1137, Pl. *Resp.* 2.372c, [Theoc.] 9.20 and Gow, comm. *ad loc.*, Dio Chrys. 6.20). They are still eaten in Greece by country folk, 'apparently ... in times of food shortage' (O. Polunin and A. Huxley, *Flowers of the Mediterranean* (London 1965) 55). Cf. also *RE* s.vv. *Eiche* 2030.18ff., 62ff. (Olck) and *Buche* 972.51ff. (Schmidt).

13 βολβός: = Latin *bulbus*, the edible bulb of several *Liliaceae*, but in particular the tassel hyacinth (*Muscari comosum*: illustrated in Huxley and Taylor, *op. cit.* on v. 11, pls. 374, 375) and some other species of *Muscari* (ten are native to Greece: Tutin, *op. cit.* on v. 11, 5 (Cambridge 1980) 46ff.), which are still collected and eaten, especially during Lent (Huxley and Taylor 150). The ancient world recognised different kinds (Theophr. *HP* 7.13.8, Ath. 2.64b, Dioscorides 2.170, Ovid *Rem. Am.* 797, Columella *Rust.* 10.106, Pliny *HN* 20.105), which have not been reconciled with modern systematics. Some types were sweet enough to be eaten raw (Theophr. *loc. cit.*), but they were often boiled (cf. Diocles in Ath. 2.61c). Alexis elsewhere refers to their use as (male) aphrodisiacs (frs. 175(170K).3, 281(279K).2); cf. also Ar. *Eccl.* 1089ff. and Σ on 1092, Xenarchus 1.4ff., Ath. 2.63f–64b citing Heraclides of Tarentum, Diphilus of Siphnos and the proverb οὐδέν σ' ὀνήσει βολβὸς ἂν μὴ νεῦρ' ἔχῃς; Galen 11.851 Kühn; Ovid, Columella, Pliny *locc. citt.*, Petronius 130, Martial 3.75.3, 13.34. See also Olck in *RE* s.v. Βολβός 669.35ff., Hehn, *Kulturpflanzen* 203, Gow on Theoc. 14.17, André, *Alimentation* 20f., P. Gray, *Honey from a Weed* (London 1986) 190, 202.

τέττιξ: at first sight the cicada (see comm. on 96(92K.2–4)) seems an odd entry in a list otherwise restricted to plants and their produce, and Eustath. 948.41ff. (after citing vv. 12–13 (ὦχρος – ἀχράς)) presumably felt qualms over its interpretation when he defined τέττιξ simply as βρώσιμόν τι.[1] Yet there are several references to its use as food in ancient Greece (Ar. frs. 53(51K), 581(569K).4, Ath. 4.133b, Arist. *HA* 5.30, 556ᵇ7, 13f.; at Anaxandrides 42(41K).59 the τέττιξ may be not a cicada but the crayfish *Scyllarus arctus*) and elsewhere (Pliny *HN* 11.92), and doctors even recommended patients with disorders of the bladder to eat broiled cicadas (Dioscorides 2.51, cf. Oribas. *Ecl. Med.* fr. 63(64), p. 227.26 Raeder); cf. Casaubon, *Animadv.* 111, Schweighaeuser, *Animadv.* 1.368. It is absurd therefore to suspect corruption (so Meineke, *Anal. Crit.* 28 conjecturing πέζιξ, a *vox nihili*; the accusative plural πέζιας is once recorded = 'puffballs' in Epit. of Ath. 2.61e citing Theophr. fr. 168 Wimmer, where CE correct their joint reading πέζικας to πέζιας suprascript; whatever the correct form of that noun's nominative singular (πέζις LSJ), it was not πέζιξ).

ἐρέβινθος: the chick pea or Bengal gram, *Cicer arietinum*, cf. Theophr. *HP* 8.6.5, Pliny *HN* 18.124, cultivated today in the Middle East as its most important pulse, with seeds that vary in colour from white through red and brown to black. In Alexis' Greece they were eaten raw when fresh (Phaenias, *loc. cit.* on v. 11) or boiled (Archestratus fr. 192.14 Lloyd-Jones–Parsons) or roasted (Ar. *Pax* 1136, *Eccl.* 45 and Ussher *ad loc.*, Pherecrates 170(159K)), cf. Xenophanes fr. 22.3 Diels. See also Hehn, *Kulturpflanzen* 215f., W. B. Turrill, *The Plant Life of the Balkan Peninsula* (Oxford 1929) 241, Cobley, *op. cit.* on v. 11, 150f., André, *Alimentation* 37f., H. Gams in *Kleine Pauly* s.v. *Erbsen* 349.41ff., P. Gray, *Honey from a Weed* (London 1986) 69f.

ἀχράς: the wild pear, with several species native to Greece (*Pyrus pyraster*, *P. amygdaliformis*, *P. elaeagrifolia*: cf. Tutin, *op. cit.* on v. 11, 2.65f.), which (as Theophr. *HP* 1.4.1, cf. 3.2.1, notes) produce abundant fruit but with a flavour inferior to the cultivated species (*P. communis* of hybrid origin, see comm. on 34(33K).2–3). Cf. Olck in *RE* s.v. *Birnbaum* 491.39ff., Hehn, *Kulturpflanzen* 626, 628, Handley on Men. *Dysk.* 99ff., Ussher on Ar. *Eccl.* 355.

14–16 The last item in Alexis' list of foods for the impoverished (ἰσχάς: see comm. on 122(117K).1–2) introduces a climactic burst of lyrical ecstasy which poses severe problems of text and interpretation. These lines are cited by (i) Epit. of Ath. 2.55a and Eustath. 1572.62ff. (the latter not naming the author) with θειοπαγὲς (14), ἰσχάς (15) and an unmetrical εὕρημα συκῆς (16); (ii) Ath. 3.75a where A and Epit. MSS unite with θειοφαγὲς (Kaibel's apparatus is inaccurate here, see Peppink, *Observ.* 21),

---

[1] Eustathius' autograph (L) has τέττιξ here twice, correctly spelled (see M. van der Valk *ad loc.*). Its mistranscription as τέτιξ in the first printed edition of the Homeric commentaries (Rome 1542–50) deceived scholars from Casaubon (*Animadv.* 110f.) up to the present day.

ἰσχάδας and εὕρεμα συκῆς. Although establishment of the text and interpretation of its puzzling allusions are obviously interlinked, it will be more convenient to tackle the textual problems first on their own.

(a) θειοφαγὲς ('god-eaten') is nonsensical in this context, θειοπαγὲς ('god-planted: cf. LSJ s.v. πήγνυμι I and e.g. Theophr. *HP* 6.6.9, 7.4.3, 10, 7.5.3) comprehensible but here (*pace* Kassel–Austin, who print it) inappropriate. In the version of the myth apparently followed by Alexis the goddess Demeter did not 'plant' the fig tree but 'revealed' (ἔφηνε) it to the Athenians, as we shall see; accordingly. θειοφανὲς, a conjecture in B (*Laurentianus, pluteus* LX, 1: an apograph of the *Marcianus*; cf. also Casaubon, *Animadv.* 111), must restore what Alexis wrote, even it is a coined *hapax legomenon.*

(b) After a long list of foodstuffs in the nominative singular, a metrical ἰσχάς requires no defence against the unmetrical ἰσχάδας.

(c) Following Φρυγίας neither εὕρημα συκῆς nor εὕρεμα συκῆς completes the paroemiac desired at the close of a long speech (or section of it) in anapaestic dimeters, and εὕρεμα is a form foreign to Attic Greek (cf. LSJ s.v.). Porson (in J. Toup, *Emendationes in Suidam et Hesychium et alios lexicographos graecos* 4 (Oxford 1790) 502, cf. Schweighaeuser, *Animadv.* 1.370) recognised that Alexis is most likely to have written εὑρήματα,[1] which was then corrupted to the two singular forms by scribes who neither understood metre nor appreciated how common the poetical use of plural abstract and concrete nouns is in place of the singular, especially when that plural is in apposition (as here) to another noun (K.G. 1.18f., Porson, comm. on Eur. *Or.* 1051); for εὑρήματα so used cf. e.g. S. fr. 432, Eur. *Hec.* 250, *Cycl.* 465, *Bacch.* 59 τύμπανα, Ῥέας τε μητρὸς ἐμὰ θ' εὑρήματα. Alexis' choice of the plural here, together with that of two unusual words in his lyrical coda – the (?) coinage θειοφανές, and μελέδημα, elsewhere confined to serious poetry (LSJ cite instances from epic, lyric and tragedy, e.g. Eur. *Hipp.* 1104 μελεδήματα as poetic plural like εὑρήματα) – marks an elevation of style clearly influenced by the melic anapaests of tragedy.

Even when corrected vv. 14–16 still contain three puzzling allusions: to the fig tree's divine revelation (θειοφανές), its connection with a mother and/or the Great Mother (μητρῷον 14), and its description as Phrygian (16). Earlier attempts to explain them have lacked credible coherence or supporting evidence,[2] and I venture a new interpretation here. It is

---

[1] C. Austin informed me of M. L. West's unpublished conjecture εὕρημά <τι> συκῆς here, comparing Tinnychus fr. 1 Page, *PMG* p. 366 εὕρημά τι Μοισᾶν, possible but palaeographically and stylistically less attractive than Porson's εὑρήματα.

[2] Meineke suggested that the speaker may have been Phrygian or had a mother who grew figs. Although it cannot be proved that the allusions

based on Pausanias' account of the fig's arrival in Attica (1.37.2), cited by Schweighaeuser, *Animadv.* 1.369 and Meineke without full realisation of its significance: ἐν τούτῳ τῷ χωρίῳ (sc. on the Sacred Way from Athens to Eleusis) Φύταλόν φασιν οἴκῳ Δήμητρα δέξασθαι, καὶ τὴν θεὸν ἀντὶ τούτων δοῦναι οἱ τὸ φυτὸν τῆς συκῆς· μαρτυρεῖ δέ μοι τῷ λόγῳ τὸ ἐπίγραμμα τὸ ἐπὶ τῷ Φυτάλου τάφῳ (= epigr. 203 in T. Preger, *Inscriptiones graecae metricae ex scriptoribus praeter Anthologiam collectae* (Leipzig 1891) p. 162)·

> ἐνθάδ' ἄναξ ἥρως Φύταλός ποτε δέξατο σεμνὴν
> Δημήτραν, ὅτε πρῶτον ὀπώρας καρπὸν ἔφηνεν,
> ἣν ἱερὰν συκῆν θνητῶν γένος ἐξονομάζει·
> ἐξ οὗ δὴ τιμὰς Φυτάλου γένος ἔσχεν ἀγήρως.

---

in these vv. are external to the plot, the facts militate against the theory. Phrygians in comedy tend to be slaves, not mothers of families (e.g. Men. *Asp.* 206, cf. Ar. *Vesp.* 433, Eur. *Or* 1366ff., introduction to Φρύξ); figs do not grow in Phrygia (Olck in *RE* s.v. *Feige* 2119.10ff., A. Boulanger, comm. (Paris 1947) on Cic. *Flacc.* 41). Wilamowitz (in Kaibel's edition of Ath. at 2.54f and *Hermes* 35 (1900) 557 n. 4 = *Kleine Schriften* 4 (Berlin 1962) 135 n. 2) believed that Φρυγίας συκῆς referred not to Asian Phrygia but to an area of level ground in Attica known as τὰ Φρύγια, sited a few miles north-east of Athens in the Athmoneis deme according to *P.Oxy.* 853, xiii.16 (a comm. on Thuc. 2.22.2, cf. Gomme *ad loc.*, but Steph. Byz. s.v. Φρύγια places it less accurately 'between Attica and Boeotia', cf. Kirsten in *RE* s.v. *Phrygia* 891.6off.). Admittedly figs were believed to grow best on low-lying, level ground (Theophr. *HP* 2.5.7), but this particular area was connected in antiquity with sheep-grazing (Σ Ar. *Av.* 493), not figs, and it is likely to have been fairly free of trees if cavalry in the Peloponnesian War could fight across it (Thuc. *loc. cit.*). J. Murr, (*Die Pflanzenwelt in der griechischen Mythologie* (Innsbruck 1890) 35) advanced a theory that Alexis refers to a myth in which a 'Phrygian heroine' named Syke presented mankind with the fig as a divine gift. The only myth, however, in which Syke appears as a nymph is an aetiological compilation of Hellenistic times (Ath. 3.78b citing Pherenicus fr. 672 Lloyd-Jones–Parsons, *SH* p. 318; cf. Müller-Graupa in *RE* s.v. *Oxylos* 3, 2040.29ff., Schmid-Stählin II.i.332), and this Syke is not known to have had Phrygian connections. Finally A. M. Desrousseaux (on Ath. 2.55a) claimed that with a word-play worthy of a dithyrambic poet Alexis called the dried fig a Μητρῷον because its conservation was comparable to the use of the Athenian temple of Cybele for preserving Athenian records. I doubt whether an Athenian audience would appreciate a pun so far-fetched, obscure and unfunny, and in any case Cybele's temple could hardly be styled θειοπαγές (as Desrousseaux prints).

COMMENTARY

The date of the epigram is uncertain, but if Δημήτραν is correct in v. 2 (so V: -μητρα FPL, hence Δήμητρ' <ὁππ>ότ' Dindorf), it is unlikely to go back to the classical period; yet the story itself may well be early, since the area was called Ἱερὰ Συκῆ in classical times (cf. Ath. 3.74d, Philostr. *VS* 2.20; *RE* s.vv. *Feige* 2145.36ff. (Olck) and *Lakiadai* 524.64ff. (Th. Kock), W. Judeich, *Topographie von Athen*² (Munich 1931) 411), and an old-established shrine of Demeter and Kore was situated nearby (Paus. 1.37.2). The presence of θειοφανές in Alexis' dimeters is confirmed and explained by the story and vv. 2–3 of the epigram, while the descriptions of the dried fig as μητρῷον . . . μελέδημ' and of the fig tree as Phrygian are a further witness to the syncretisation of Demeter and the Phrygian 'Great Mother' goddess Cybele, which already in the 5th century was widely enough accepted (or at least known) for Euripides to exploit in a celebrated choral ode of *Helen* (1301ff., where Demeter is variously μάτηρ, μάτηρ θεῶν and μεγάλα μάτηρ; cf. in addition to A. M. Dale's (Oxford 1967) and R. Kannicht's (Heidelberg 1969) editions *ad loc.*, L. R. Farnell, *The Cults of the Greek States* 3 (Oxford 1907) 31f., N. M. P. Nilsson, *Geschichte der griechischen Religion* 1³ (Munich 1967) 725ff., M. J. Vermaseren, *Cybele and Attis* (London 1977) 32ff., 82f.). Alexis' own exploitation of the syncretisation was neither capricious nor dramatically inept; his speaker is presented as a mother, and so μητρῷον . . . μελέδημ' may well be deliberately ambiguous, applying to herself as well as to the goddess; his evocation of a local myth kowtows also to Attic chauvinism (cf. fr 122(117K) and comm.), whether or not the speaker is portrayed as a native of Athens (cf. introduction to Ὀλυνθία).

14 μητρῷον: although technically a derivative of μήτρως rather than μήτηρ, the adjective was always used in the sense of 'mother's/ maternal'; cf. similarly πατρῷος and J. Wackernagel, *Kleine Schriften* 1 (Göttingen 1954) 477ff.

15 ἰσχάς: see comm. on 122(117K).1–2.

Ὁμοία

Meineke 1.392, H. Usener, *Rh. Mus.* 28 (1873) 404ff., Webster, *SLGC* 67f. Ath. 14.642d introduces the one fr. (168(163K)) preserved from this play with the note τὸ δ' αὐτὸ δρᾶμα καὶ ὡς Ἀντιδότου φέρεται. Possible explanations for such cases of disputed authorship are given in the introduction to Ἀλείπτρια (= 'False or Doubtful Attributions' I, pp. 813 f.). About Antidotus *pauca sunt quae tenemus*, Meineke 1.415f., cf. Kaibel in *RE* s.v. *Antidotos* 3, 2398.38ff. His name has been plausibly supplied on a dramatic inscription (*IG Urb. Rom.* 221 Moretti = VI A 6.6 Mette = 2.308 Kassel–Austin); of the two titles

OMOIA

assigned to him without demur one (Πρωτόχορος) is shared with Alexis. The plural title Ὅμοιοι is attested for Ephippus and (in Magnesia) Metrodorus (II B 2a.7 Mette), Ὅμοιοι and/or Ὅμοιαι for Antiphanes and Posidippus; such titles probably imply plots involving confusions between identical twins (cf. Plaut. *Bacch.*, *Men.*) or unrelated doubles (cf. *Amph.*: so Webster). A singular Ὁμοία (if A's -οίᾳ at Ath. 14.642d is not an error for e.g. -οίαις: so Daléchamp, *Auctorum Index* attached to his Latin translation, cf. Schweighaeuser, *Animadv.* 7.517) may mean that Alexis directed particular attention on to one of a female pair.[1]

168 (163K)

Meineke 3.458, Kock 2.357, Edmonds 2.452, Kassel–Austin 2.116. Speakers and context are uncertain, but a character who enthuses about τραγήματα and skilfully leads the conversation towards a triumphant παρὰ προσδοκίαν (cf. the MS note by Wilamowitz cited by Kassel–Austin) about food (v.7) is most likely to be a parasite or (cf. e.g. Plaut. *Stich.* 683ff., *Trin.* 474ff.) slave, while the reference to τοῖς νυμφίοις μετιοῦσι τὴν νύμφην (v.4) may be inspired by a wedding occurring or planned in the plot. This fr. is preserved only by the *Marcianus* (and its progeny: see on v. 3), as usual without any attempt at part-division; Daléchamp was the first to realise the presence of a second speaker, but the correct assignments were made by Meineke.

1 οὐδὲ φιλόδειπνός εἰμι: presumably a negative statement (e.g. οὐ βουλιμιῶ) originally preceded. φιλόδειπνος occurs only here in Attic Greek, although its inclusion in Phryn. *Praep. Soph.* 123.1f. de Borries virtually guarantees that it was used by good Athenian authors, cf. G. Kaibel, *De Phrynicho sophista* (Progr. Göttingen 1899) 18.

μὰ τὸν Ἀσκληπιόν: a standard male oath in later comedy, employed in a wide variety of contexts (Men. *Dysk.* 666, *Pk.* 336, *Sam.* 310, fr. 85, com. adesp. fr. 262.8 Austin). On its position in the sentence cf. K. J. Dover, *CQ* 35 (1985) 330.

2 τραγήμασιν χαίρω δέ: Scaliger's correction (in Canter, Paris MS 44ᵛ; well before Erfurdt, *Obs.* 456) of A's unmetrical τραγήμασι δὲ χαίρω

---

[1] Usener's suggestion of a parallel singular male title Ὅμοιος by an unknown comedian is based on misinterpretation of a passage in an anon. commentary on Arist. *Eth. Nic.* 4.12, 1127ᵃ10 (*Comm. in Arist. Gr.* xx ed. G. Heylblut (Berlin 1892) p. 196.24ff.) ὁ δὲ πᾶσι δυσχεραίνων ὁ τοῖς ὑπὸ τῶν κωμῳδῶν <παραγομένοις> (add. Diels) ὅμοιος ὂν καὶ δύσκολόν φασιν εἶναι, where ὅμοιος is not a title (translate 'the man like those [introduced] by the comic poets') and the reference is clearly to Knemon in Men. *Dysk.*

493

COMMENTARY

(-ήμασιν already Musurus), where a scribe has removed postponed δέ back to its normal prose position as second word in its clause (see comm. on fr. 4.1).

τραγήματα (like τρωγάλια, as the derivation from τρώγω, -έτραγον indicates) are basically foods that can be gnawed or munched (cf. Arist. fr. 104 Rose), either raw or cooked, savoury or sweet, e.g. fruit, vegetables with a crunchy seed-case (cf. Σ Ar. *Vesp.* 545), nuts, eggs, small portions of meat and various cakes (see on v. 5). They were often served with wine (e.g. Ar. *Ran.* 510f., Alexis 190(185K), Amphis 9, Mnesimachus 7, Alciphr. 3.39, 4.14.3) at the end of a δεῖπνον as a δευτέρα τράπεζα ('second meal' rather than 'second course'), and this practice explains why Ath. (correctly: see on v. 4) includes this fr. of Alexis in a section on δευτέρα τράπεζα, despite vv. 4–5. Cf. Hermann–Blümner, *Privatalterthümer* 240ff., Mau in *RE* s.v. *Comissatio* 611.7ff.

εὖ πάνυ: correctly interpreted (first by Daléchamp: see introduction to this fr.) as a formula of assent by the second speaker, cf. Men. *Sik.* 356; elsewhere more fully εὖ πάνυ λέγεις Theopompus com. 15(14K).3, Ar. *Plut.* 800, cf. 198. Similarly εὖ γε... εὖ σφόδρα Nicostratus 7(8K).1, εὖ γε καὶ παλαιστρικῶς com. adesp. fr. 239.22f. Austin = 'False or Doubtful Attributions' v 22f. p. 834. Cf. H. Thesleff, *Studies on Intensification in Early and Classical Greek* (Helsinki 1954) 62ff., K. J. Dover, *CQ* 35 (1985) 332ff.

3 The first speaker resumes. On the postponement of γάρ to third word see comm. on fr. 37(36K).1. νομίζεται, the correction in B (an apograph of A: see on fr. 167(162K).14–16(a); cf. Peppink, *Observ.* 87) of A's νομίζετε, is adopted by most editors (but not Kassel–Austin) because the construction of νομίζεται as impersonal passive with (acc. and) infinitive ('it is the custom (for X) to ...') is standard in Attic: e.g. Ar. *Nub.* 498, 1420, Ephippus 3.4ff., Thuc. 2.15, Xen. *Hell.* 2.4.36, *Mem.* 4.4.19, 20), while that of νομίζω as personal active with infinitive ('I am accustomed to ...') is confined to the Ionic of Herodotus (LSJ s.v. 1.4). Otherwise νομίζετε would be attractive if addressed to (e.g.) an old man celebrating or about to celebrate his daughter's wedding (2nd p. pl. = 'people like you').

4 The *Marcianus* has μετιοῦσι· τὴν νύμφην λέγεις, of which some editors (Schweighaeuser, Dindorf, Gulick) try to make sense by giving the last three words to the second speaker as a question ('Do you mean the bride?'). In comic usage, however, such interruptions do not anticipate an interlocutor's next word in this way, but either demand (in a question) clarification of a puzzling remark (e.g. Antiphanes 127(129K).7), or add (in a statement) a comment on the other speaker's words (e.g. Alexis 223.11–12(221.5–6K), 224(222K).4). More probably all v. 4 is spoken by one person with τὴν νύμφην governed by μετιοῦσι (despite A's raised point), and λέγεις interpreted as a corruption impossible to remedy with

494

confidence, since removal of the word from the text leaves a gap in metre but not in sense. Conjectures are legion and mainly futile: e.g. γονεῖς (O. Crusius, *Philologus* 46 (1886) 680) needs the article; ἔδειν (Edmonds) is an implausible form (at this stylistic level Alexis would have used ἐσθίειν);[1] λέγειν (Richards, *AO* 85) = '(it is the custom) to order (men to provide)', but this places emphasis on the ordering and not where it is wanted, on the provision; τὴν γαμουμένην (Herwerden, *NAC* 32) seeks to explain τὴν νύμφην λέγεις as corruption of a marginal gloss τὴν νύμφην λέγει, but would a gloss be needed for so obvious an expression as τὴν γαμουμένην? Only one conjecture is reasonable: Meineke's ἀεί, which offers a colourless word at home in the context without jarring the sense, and at the same time palaeographically credible (→ ΑΕΙΕΙ by dittography → ΛΕΓΕΙC by misreading and subsequent adjustment). Plausibility is a long way from certainty, however, and Kassel–Austin rightly obelise λέγεις.

τοῖς νυμφίοις μετιοῦσι τὴν νύμφην: at an Athenian wedding the bridegroom and his groomsmen (this, rather than 'bridegrooms' in general, for otherwise the singular νύμφην would be illogical) came to the house of the bride and her parents, where they were entertained to a festal dinner (with τραγήματα such as those listed in v. 5 forming the δευτέρα τράπεζα) before the groom took his bride to their new home at eventide in a cart drawn by mules or oxen, lit by torches and escorted by musicians (cf. W. Erdmann, *Die Ehe im alten Griechenland* (Munich 1934) 250ff.). μετέρχομαι/μέτειμι is the technical expression for the bridegroom thus 'fetching' his bride, e.g. Men. *Sam.* 159, 433, 610, 676, possibly *Phasm.* 69. The reference here to such festivities would have greater immediacy if the addressee were the father of a (prospective) bride.

5 ἄμητας καὶ λαγῷα καὶ κίχλας: although Trygaios at Ar. *Pax* 1195f. includes λαγῷα and κίχλαι among the delicacies to be served at his wedding-feast, none of the three titbits listed is restricted to such an occasion. All three are τραγήματα: (1) ἄμης (defined by Σ Ar. *Plut.* 999 as εἶδος πλακοῦντος γαλακτώδους), cf. e.g. Ar. *Plut.* 995ff., Amphis 9.3, Ephippus 8.3, but the cake especially associated with weddings was the σησαμοῦς, see comm. on 132(127K).3 and Erdmann 260; (2) λαγῷα (on the word's formation see comm. on 159(155K).5), cf. e.g. Ar. *Pax* 1150, Ath. 14.641f; (3) κίχλαι (various thrushes, including certainly the mistle, *Turdus viscivorus*, in Greece a breeder and winter visitor, and song thrush, *T. philomelos*, mainly a winter visitor; redwing, *T. iliacus* and fieldfare, *T. pilaris* are less regular winter visitors to Athens and southern Greece; cf.

---

[1] In Attic comedy ἔδω (in the active) is used by Eubulus 27(28K) in a parody of an oracle (dactylic hexameter), and perhaps by Alcaeus if fr. 30(36K) is justly ascribed to him (but see Meineke, *Anal. Crit.* 139, A. Nauck, *MGR* 6 (1894) 89).

COMMENTARY

Olck in *RE* s.v. *Drossel* 1721.63ff., Thompson, *Birds*[2] 148ff., A. Kanellis and others, *Catalogus Faunae Graeciae*, II: *Aves* (Thessaloniki 1969) 129ff., and W. G. Arnott in J. Tatum (ed.), *The Search for the Ancient Novel* (Baltimore and London 1994) 204f.), cf. e.g. Ar. *Pax* 1149ff., Men. fr. 451.13, Ath. 14.641f.

6–7 τοῖς δὲ κεκαρυκευμένοις ὄψοισι καὶ ζωμοῖσιν: both ὄψα and ζωμοί (see comm. on 47(46K).6 and 145(141K).8) are heavily spiced with καρύκη, a sauce defined by Zenobius 5.3 as βρῶμα Λύδιον ἐκ πολλῶν ἡδυσμάτων συνεστὸς καὶ αἵματος, cf. also Ath. 12.516c. Men. fr. 451.6–8 names σεμίδαλις (cf. comm. on 102(97K).4), honey and eggs as three of its ingredients. Cf. Neil on Ar. *Equ.* 343, Bruhn, *Wortschatz* 13, Durham, *Vocabulary* 68.

7 ἥδομ', ὦ θεοί: this correction of A's wrongly divided and unaccented ηδ' ομω θεοι first appears in Musurus. Because ἥδομ' logically contradicts all that has gone before in the fr., a singular succession of humourless scholars has suspected further textual corruption and produced a string of alternative conjectures (e.g. ζωμοῖς ἀνήδομαι Meineke, *Quaest. Men.* 25f., ζωμοῖσιν ἥδομ' as a deliberative question Jacobi in Meineke 5.90, μηδάμ' Kock) that restore logic and destroy the joke. For six and a half verses the main speaker has orchestrated his joke by seducing the audience into the belief that he is a fussy eater, fond only of τραγήματα. At ζωμοῖσιν doubtless he paused, and the spectators (like our humourless scholars) expected some verb expressing detestation to govern the datives. Instead the speaker (whether he was parasite or slave: see introduction to this fr.) changed his tone, reverted to stereotype and admitted that he *adored* spiced ὄψα and ζωμοί. The joke is skilfully organised. The word that produces the παρὰ προσδοκίαν is delayed for maximum effect to very near the end of its sentence (cf. the numerous parallels in Aristophanes: Starkie's edition of Ar. *Ach.* p. lxvii, my paper in *Drama* 2 (1993) 18ff.). In the vv. that prepare the way for the joke Alexis uses the verb χαίρω twice (2, 6) so that the more emotive word ἥδομαι can be reserved for the climax. It is to ἥδομαι and its congeners that the 'naughtier' aspects of pleasure belong, as the history of Greek philosophy in general and the persuasive definitions of the Stoics in particular indicate (Plut. *Mor.* 449a, cf. *Suda* s.v. χαρά); χαίρω seems to lack any such element of 'sensuous impulse' (see Jebb on S. *Ant.* 648). Cf. *Hermes* 93 (1965) 305f.

Ὀπώρα

Meineke 1.401, cf. 404, 3.320f., E. von Leutsch, *Philologus* 3 (1848) 572f., Breitenbach 136, B. Warnecke, *Hermes* 41 (1906) 158f., G. W. Elderkin, *AJA* 40 (1936) 348ff., W. G. Arnott, *Rh. Mus.* 98 (1955) 312ff. and *PCPS*

196 (1970) 8f., Nesselrath, *MK* 199 n. 51 ~ 319 n. 97. Athenaeus twice (10.443e, 13.567c–d) says that the title figure of Alexis' Ὀπώρα was a *hetaira*, and there is no reason to doubt the reliability of his information; but was she (i) a caricature of a real person, like the heroines of Eubulus' Κλεψύδρα and Νάννιον, Timocles' Νέαιρα (cf. Ath. 13.567c–d, 587a, 593f–594a; Hunter's edition of Eubulus pp. 141, 152f., my comm. on Alexis 225(223K); women named Opora, from Acanthus and Miletus, lived in Athens, *IG* 11².7998, 9829, cf. Bechtel, *Personennamen* 610 and *Frauennamen* 128); or (ii) a deglamorisation of the goddess who symbolised the fruit harvest (especially the vintage), portrayed on three vases with other (mainly wine) divinities,[1] and already put on the stage by Aristophanes in *Pax*, where she combines the functions of goddess (e.g. 726, 847, 852ff.), bride for Trygaios (706f., 844, 859, 868ff., 1192, 1316, 1329ff.) and *hetaira*/harlot (726ff., 849; cf. Σ 706 she and Theoria ἑταῖραι, Σ 842 and 849 πόρναι); or (iii) a *persona ficta* in a plot of unknown type? We cannot know for certain, but although direct evidence about Alexis' play is meagre, the indirect, circumstantial (and admittedly not wholly reliable) pointers are extensive and suggest interesting conclusions.

The direct evidence (additional to Ath.'s statements on the heroine's profession) consists of the one fr. (169(164K)) securely ascribed to the play by Ath. 10.443e, in which the speaker expresses amazement that the male addressee can drink a vast quantity of wine without vomiting it up. The background to this remark is likely to be a continuing or recently ended party/κῶμος, but the identity of the characters involved is unknown, however appropriate their circumstances may be to a play about a *hetaira* and/or a wine deity.

---

[1] On two 5th-century Athenian vases Opora appears in Dionysus' train: a volute-krater by the Kadmos painter in the Jatta collection at Ruvo, and a kalyx-krater by the Dinos painter in Vienna (Beazley, *ARV*² 2.1184 no. 1, 1152 no. 8). On the former she has long hair, wears a chiton and fawn-skin, and holds grapes in her left hand and a wine-cup in her right; she is accompanied by eleven other figures including Oinopion, Silenos (the world of wine), Eros, Himeros and Pothos (sex). On the Vienna vase Dionysus offers a wreath to Himeros; Opora is one of four female and four male attendants who include Komos, Hedyoinos, Oinanthe (wine) and most strikingly Eirene. It would be interesting to know if this vase influenced – or was influenced by – Ar. *Pax* of 421; the careers of the comic poet and the Dinos painter appear to have coincided (cf. R. M. Cook, *Greek Painted Pottery* (London 1960) 184). Finally, on a Sicilian kalyx-krater by the Maron painter in Lipari (A. D. Trendall and T. B. L. Webster, *Illustrations of Greek Drama* (London 1971) 114f. = III.6.2), Opora and Ampelis attend Maron as he

COMMENTARY

The indirect evidence, however, may add to the play further frs., as well
as throwing light on characters and plot.

(1) Aelian *Epist.* 7 and 8 are an imaginary exchange between a naive
rustic Derkyllos and a greedy *hetaira* Opora who rejects his advances.
Comparison of Aelian *Epist.* 13–16 with Men. *Dysk.* (cf. I. L. Thyresson,
Eranos 62 (1964) 7ff., W. G. Arnott, *YCS* 27 (1982) 292, 302) confirms that
this epistolographer at times takes the names of his imagined correspond-
ents from characters in a comedy, paraphrases speeches and expressions
in it (not always spoken by their counterparts in the play), and combines
some of the dramatic background with ideas of his own. He seems to have
acted similarly with *Epist.* 7 and 8, deriving Derkyllos and Opora from a
comedy probably titled Ὀπώρα (a title Δέρκυλλος is not attested, and no
character with either of these two names is recorded from a play with a
different title). Aelian's source will not have been Amphis' Ὀπώρα (the
only other like-named comedy known), since that play apparently travestied a myth of the dog-star Sirius' infatuation for the goddess Opora (Σ
Germanicus *Arat.* in K. Robert, *Eratosthenis Catasterismorum reliquiae*²
(Berlin (1878) 168.7–28, Σ Aratus Latinus in E. Maass, *Commentariorum in
Aratum reliquiae* (Berlin 1895) 215.19–252.18),¹ but rather Alexis' play
(so first Warnecke), and a reasonable observation of the way in which
Aelian elsewhere exploits his sources may help us to assign two further
frs. to Alexis' Ὀπώρα with varying degrees of likelihood.

(a) The stronger case can be made for an unattributed proverb

---

presents Odysseus with wine. This may portray a scene from a play, not
necessarily local. Cf. also Türk in *RE* s.v. *Opora* 697.38ff.
¹ I formerly argued (in the *Rh. Mus.* article cited) for the attribution of
Amphis' Ὀπώρα to Alexis. However, even though all the MSS of the
citing scholia (except one: B of Aratus Latinus) corrupt Amphis' name
in various ways (*amphiam* BP, *amphyanus* U of German., *amphys* P of Arat.
Lat.), and then misrepresent him as *tragoediarum scriptor* (Σ German.) or
carminum poeta (Σ Arat. Lat.), Meineke's correction to *Amphis comoediarum scriptor* or *poeta* must be right, for more than one reason. In the
extant scholia to Aratus and his Latin translators, as well as in related
works like Hyginus' *Astronomica*, Alexis' name is never mentioned, but
that of Amphis is, correctly spelled and normally identified as the comic
poet (Σ Arat. *Phaen.* 42, Σ German. *Arat.* p. 50 Robert, Hyg. *Astron.* 2.1;
but note that Σ Arat. Lat. 181a.14 Maass repeats the description
carminum poeta). Secondly, the *excerpta e Catasterismis Marciana* (Maass
579) report that Ἄμφις ὁ τῶν κωμῳδιῶν ποιητής wrote about the rising of
the dog star, presumably mentioned or described in his Ὀπώρα. Lastly,
the evidence of Aelian *Epist.* 7 and 8 (see below) seems to indicate that
Alexis' play had a different, non-mythological plot. On the coincidence
of titles between Alexis and Amphis see introduction to Ἀμπελουργός.

498

(Macarius 4.3) which curses an Opora, πᾶσι γὰρ χαρίζεται. Aelian's Derkyllos writes to his Opora (*Epist.* 7) πολλοὺς ἐραστὰς λέγεις ἔχειν. The occurrence of the woman's name in the proverb led Leutsch to suggest that Alexis' Ὀπώρα was its source, with the endorsement of subsequent editors of the comic frs. (hence = Alexis 170(165K)); the partial paraphrase in Aelian provides additional evidence in support of the attribution.

(b) Aelian's Opora replies to Derkyllos (*Epist.* 8) with a boast that she has expensive tastes, ἐγὼ δὲ Λέσβιον πίνω καὶ Θάσιον (sc. οἶνον). This sequestered pairing of the two named wines occurs only once in extant comedy, at Alexis 277(275K) Θασίοις οἰναρίοις καὶ Λεσβίοις ... ὑποβρέχει, cited by Epit. of Ath. 1.28e, cf. 2.47d, characteristically without play-title; admittedly twice elsewhere the two wines are listed along with others, at Eubulus 121(124K) (with Χῖον) and Plaut. *Poen.* 699f. (with *Leucadio* and *Chio*, in a play almost certainly adapted from an original by Alexis, see introduction to Καρχηδόνιος, but the contexts of Alexis 277(275K) and the Plautine passage are very different). The evidence suggests but does not prove that Alexis 277(275K) derives from Ὀπώρα (cf. *PCPS* 196 (1970) 8f.), and Kassel–Austin are accordingly wise still to include it among the *incertarum fabularum fragmenta*.

(c) Δέρκυλλος (so spelled) is not otherwise attested as a character name in comedy, but an unattributed comic trimeter cited by Ath. 10.458b solely because it begins with an epsilon runs εὐκαταφρόνητόν ἐστι πενία, Δερκύλε (adesp. fr. 230 Kock). The remark – a poor man's response presumably to somebody wealthier (cf. Men. *Dysk.* 285f., fr. 8 ~ Ter. *Ad.* 605ff.; Dover, *GPM* 270, W. G. Arnott, *Philologus* 125 (1981) 220, 225) – might just possibly derive from Alexis' Ὀπώρα: in the vocative the endings of Greek proper names are often varied to suit either a mood (e.g. wheedling diminutives, cf. Dover on Ar. *Nub.* 80, V. Schmidt, *Sprachliche Untersuchungen zu Herondas* (Berlin 1968) 108) or perhaps occasionally the metre (cf. Headlam on Herodas 4.20). Yet I have not noticed any such fluctuation between -υλλε and -ύλε with the same person's name, and Δερκύλος exists as a *nomen proprium* in its own right (e.g. Ar. *Vesp.* 78; Kirchner, *PA* 1.213, nos. 3247–50); accordingly attribution of adesp. fr. 230 Kock to Alexis' Ὀπώρα is not justified on present evidence.

The information given by Aelian's two letters and the frs. assigned to Ὀπώρα suggests that one theme of the play was a relationship or clash between a self-seeking, extravagant and promiscuous *hetaira* and a rustic admirer; other lovers of Opora may have featured in the plot. Heartless *hetairai* with many lovers were commonplace in New Comedy (cf. H. Hauschild, *Die Gestalt der Hetäre in der griechischen Komödie* (Diss. Leipzig 1933) 23ff.; the closest parallel to the situation envisaged for Alexis here is Plaut. *Truc.*, where the rustic Strabax is one of three lovers whom the *meretrix* Phronesium plays against each other to her financial advantage.

COMMENTARY

The Greek original of *Truc.* is unknown (useful discussions in P. J. Enk's edition 1 (Leiden 1953) 9ff. and Webster, *SLGC* 147ff.; P. Grimal, *REL* 47/2 = *Mélanges offerts à M. Durry* (1970) 85ff. is less convincing), and Strabax's complaint about Phronesium *uolgo ad se omnes intromittit* (944) ties perfectly with Alexis 170(165K) πᾶσι γὰρ χαρίζεται; too little is known for certain about Ὀπώρα, however, for a case to be made for it as the Plautine original.

(2) A mosaic of the 3rd century AD in a villa at Syrian Daphne (W. A. Campbell, *AJA* 40 (1936) 4f. and fig. 7, Elderkin, *ibid.* 346ff., D. Levi, *Antioch Mosaic Pavements* (Princeton 1947) 1.186ff., 2.pl.XLII a, b) portrays an entertainment with three figures whose names are inscribed above their heads. On a couch, half-reclining and half-sitting, are a woman (Opora) and a man (Agros: on the name see Levi 1.187 n. 31) gazing at each other. Agros has his right arm around Opora's shoulders and in his left hand holds a wine-cup. On a low table before them rests another wine-cup. To their right stands a Silenus-like figure (Oinos), aged, bearded and bald, although his face is badly damaged; with his right hand he holds out a wine-cup to Agros, in his left is a Dionysiac thyrsus. At first glance Elderkin's suggestion that the mosaicist has depicted an incident from Alexis' Ὀπώρα looks attractive; sex and wine were presumably motifs of some consequence in the play, the presence of Oinos and Opora in the same scene might be used to support a theory that Alexis' Οἶνος and Ὀπώρα were alternative titles of the same play (see introduction to Οἶνος), and mosaics of the imperial period commonly took their inspiration from scenes in later Greek comedy (cf. Charitonidis and others, *Mosaïques* 26ff., 97ff.). Even so, although in the plots of Old Comedy ordinary humans intermingle with personified abstractions like Δῆμος (Ar. *Equ.*), Πόλεμος (*Pax*), Πενία (*Plut.*), Μέθη and Κωμῳδία (Cratinus' Πυτίνη), a juxtaposition of the mosaic's symbolic and Aelian's bourgeois figures in one plot of Alexis' time seems harder (though not entirely impossible) to imagine. Hence I am inclined to interpret the mosaic as either an allegory of the vintage or, if dramatically inspired, portraying some other comedy (Levi suggests Amphis' Ὀπώρα).

169 (164K)

Meineke 3.459, Kock 2.358, Edmonds 2.452, Kassel–Austin 2.117. The fr., cited by Ath. 10.443e (A and Epit.), consists most probably of $1\frac{1}{4}$ trochaic tetrameters (but see below on v. 2), in which the speaker's question (hardly a statement: so Kaibel and Gulick) conveys both surprise (or admiration) at the addressee's alcoholic tolerance (cf. introduction to Ὀπώρα) and probably also the average Greek's reaction to a man drinking wine unmixed with water (cf. comm. on 9.3–4).

ΟΠΩΡΑ

2 Erfurdt (*Obs.* 440 n. 9) added σύ before πίνεις to fill the metrical gap (∪) left by A and Epit. The supplement is plausible (in minuscule π and the συ ligature look very similar, so the omission would be virtually haplography; on this unemphatic use of σύ in later comedy see G. Zuntz, *PBA* 42 (1956) 212 and n. 1) but by no means certain. Scaliger (in Canter, Paris MS 44ᵛ) preferred a different supplement, reshaping the fr. as iambic trimeters (οἶνον οὐ κεκρ. | πολύν <γε> πίνεις); another possibility is that πίνεις glossed a less usual word, e.g. καταντλεῖς (cf. comm. on 88(85K).3).

μεστὸς ὤν: sc. οἴνου. Cf. Ar. *Plut.* 694f. κἀγὼ τότ᾿ ἤδη τῆς ἀθάρης πολλὴν ἔφλων, | ἔπειτ᾿ ἐπειδὴ μεστὸς ἦν, ἀνεπαλλόμην.

170 (165K)

Meineke 5.ccx, Kock 2.358, Edmonds 2.452, Kassel–Austin 2.118; cf. E. von Leutsch, *Philologus* 3 (1848) 572f. The reasons for accepting Leutsch's identification of the source of this proverb (which may be a trochaic tetrameter or the end of one and the whole of a second iambic trimeter) are given in the introduction to Ὀπώρα. Macarius' plausible claim (4.8), that the adage properly applied to loose women but was extended to people who are everybody's friends and damn that sort of friendship, tells us nothing of its original dramatic context, but the words suit a *hetaira*'s rejected lover, like the Derkyllos of Aelian *Epist.* 7 and 8.

μέλαιν᾿ Ὀπώρα: as Leutsch first saw, the phrase makes sense only if Ὀπώρα is a proper name; then μέλαιν᾿ = 'dark-complexioned', cf. comm. on 103(98K).17–18.

πᾶσι γὰρ χαρίζεται: the standard denunciation of *hetairai* and promiscuous women, e.g. Plaut. *Truc.* 943 (quoted in introduction to Ὀπώρα), Cic. *Cael.* 13.32 *ea* (sc. Clodia) *quam omnes semper amicam omnium ... putauerunt*, Agath. Schol. in *Anth. Pal.* 16.80.1f. μαχλὰς ἐγὼ γενόμην ... | ὠνητὴν φιλίην πᾶσι χαριζομένη. Pasicompsa is the name of a *meretrix* in Plaut. *Merc.*, cf. perhaps also Πασιχάρηα Alcman fr. 107 Page, Πασιφίλη Archilochus fr. 331 West. In Philippus 52 Gow–Page = *Anth. Pal.* 9.416 a boat accounts for its name Ἑταίρη with εἰμὶ γὰρ πᾶσιν φίλη. Cf. K. J. McKay, *Mnemosyne* 27 (1974) 413f.

Ὀρέστης

Meineke, *ed. min.* 731; cf. Kock 2.358, Körte, *RE* s.v. *Komödie (mittlere)* 1263.18, Schmid–Stählin I.iii.622f. Of Alexis' Ὀρέστης not a single word survives (but see comm. on fr. 269(267K)). We do not know if the play directly parodied a recently staged tragedy (Eur. *Or.* was performed again at the Dionysia of 340, *IG* ii².2320.18f. = III A 2 col. 2.20f. Mette; cf.

COMMENTARY

G. Xanthakis-Karamanos, *Studies in Fourth-Century Tragedy* (Athens 1980) 28ff., W. G. Arnott, *Antichthon* 17 (1983) 13. Theodectes produced an Ὀρέστης at some point between 370 and 340, cf. Solmsen in *RE* s.v. *Theodektes* 1, 1722.59ff., T. B. L. Webster, *Hermes* 82 (1954) 303f., Xanthakis-Karamanos 63f.), or simply burlesqued episodes in the story of Orestes without reference to any previous tragedy. Meineke (*ed. min.* 731) first linked tentatively with Alexis' Ὀρέστης a reference in Arist. *Poet.* 13, 1453ᵃ35ff. ἔστιν δὲ οὐχ αὕτη ἀπὸ τραγῳδίας ἡδονὴ (sc. produced by endings which meet the desires of the audience) ἀλλὰ μᾶλλον τῆς κωμῳδίας οἰκεία· ἐκεῖ γὰρ οἳ ἂν ἔχθιστοι ὦσιν ἐν τῷ μύθῳ, οἷον Ὀρέστης καὶ Αἴγισθος, φίλοι γενόμενοι ἐπὶ τελευτῆς ἐξέρχονται καὶ ἀποθνήσκει οὐδεὶς ὑπ' οὐδενός. If this remark is inspired by a real comedy (and not by Aristotle's own imagination: cf. M. E. Hubbard in D. A. Russell and M. Winterbottom (eds.), *Ancient Literary Criticism*[1] (Oxford 1972) 108 n. 1), the referential scene looks far more like a parody of the ending of Sophocles' *Electra* (cf. Webster 296) than anything else, although it might have been incorporated into a comedy titled Ὀρέστης (or even Timocles' Ὀρεσταυτοκλείδης, the only other known[1] Athenian comic title linked with the story of Orestes, see introduction to Ἀσκληπιοκλείδης; Dinolochus wrote a Doric comedy (Austin, *CGFP* 50 fr. 78 = *P.Oxy.* 2659), Rhinthon and Sopater of Paphos phlyax farces with the title Ὀρέστης). Cf. also L. Cooper, *An Aristotelian Theory of Comedy* (Oxford 1924) 31f., S. Halliwell, *Aristotle's Poetics* (London 1986) 272 n. 28.

---

[1] An Apulian bell-krater, however, now in New York (Fleischman collection F 93; first published by A. D. Trendall in T. Rasmussen and N. Spivey (eds.), *Looking at Greek Vases* (Cambridge 1991) 164 and pl. 67; cf. also A. D. Trendall and A. Cambitoglou, *The Red-Figured Vases of Apulia*, Suppl. ii = *BICS Suppl.* 60/1 (1991) 7f. (1.6.124) and pl. 1.3–4, O. Taplin, *Comic Angels* (Oxford 1993) 55ff. and pl. 9.1) and dated on stylistic grounds to *c.* 400–380, portrays four named characters on a low stage with a half-open door to the left: one elderly and one younger ΧΟΡΗΓΟΣ (where the Η suggests dramatic origins in Attica rather than South Italy), ΠΥΡΡΙΑ[Σ] standing on an upturned bucket or basket, and ΑΙΓΙΣΘΟΣ wearing a conical cap, tunic and cloak and holding two spears in his left hand. The interpretation of the scene is puzzling. Taplin suggests a comedy with two opposed semi-choruses of Athenian χορηγοί (in the normal classical sense of financial backers for choruses), with Pyrrhias representing the world of comedy, Aegisthus that of tragedy. Alternatively the χορηγοί could have led the semi-choruses (e.g. Pl. *Leg.* 2.654a, cf. *Gorg.* 482b) in a myth travesty where Aegisthus was attended by a slave Pyrrhias (cf. Dionysus and Xanthias in Ar. *Ran.*), but the dating of the vase prevents any connection with Alexis' play.

ΟΠΩΡΑ

171 (166K)

Meineke 3.459, Kock 2.358, Edmonds 2.452, Kassel–Austin 2.118. In a passage marred by careless abbreviation or excision since its original composition, our text of Ath. 6.247e names Ἄλεξις ἐν ᾽Ορέστῃ Νικόστρατός τε ἐν Πλούτῳ Μένανδρός τε ἐν Μέθῃ καὶ Νομοθέτῃ without quoting any fragments. Before and after this point several extracts from Attic comedy are cited in which various characters (not necessarily themselves parasites) περὶ παρασίτων εἰρήκασι (246f). Accordingly we are not entitled to assume (pace e.g. Kock) that Alexis introduced a parasite into the story of Orestes, only that by some talk about parasites he introduced once again (cf. introductions to ᾽Οδυσσεὺς ὑφαίνων and frs. 9, 140(135K)) contemporary themes into the world of myth.

᾽Ορχηστρίς

Cf. W. Süss, De personarum antiquae comoediae atticae usu atque origine (Diss. Bonn 1905) 129ff.; H. G. Oeri, Der Typ der komischen Alten in der griechischen Komödie (Basle 1948) 34f. Although Alexis' ᾽Ορχηστρίς is the only comedy known with this title, plays regularly took their names from female musicians (e.g. Αὐλητρίς by Antiphanes, Diodorus, Αὐλητρίδες by Phoenicides, Αὐλητρίς and/or Αὐλητρίδες by Menander, cf. Körte–Thierfelder 2.33ff. and Austin, CGFP pp. 122, 127f., Κιθαρίστρια by Anaxandrides, Ψάλτρια by Eubulus, Dromon; Titinius wrote a Tibicina). In Men. Epitr. the hetaira Habrotonon was a ψάλτρια (cf. 477, fr. 1), the intrigues of Plaut. Epid. (47ff.) and Ter. Eun. (457, 985) both involved a fidicina, and Phaedria fell in love with a citharistria in Ter. Phorm. (8off.).

The role of Alexis' title figure is unknown, as is her connection (if any) with the two characters who discuss a future carouse in the one fr. (172(167K)) preserved from the play. The second speaker here (vv.2–5) is an old woman (v.6) whose enthusiastic (and riddling: see comm. ad loc.) description of the wine suggests that Alexis portrayed her as a tippler, like many old women (especially bawds, midwives, nurses, slaves) in ancient comedy (e.g. Ar. Nub. 555, Philyllius 5, Dionysius 5, Men. Sam. 302f., Perinth. fr. 4 Sandbach, Plaut. Asin. 799ff., Cist. 17f., 120ff., 149, 542, in particular Curc. 96ff., the closest scenic parallel to the fr. of Alexis, with a pimp's old female slave singing a eulogy of wine in the presence of a young lover and his slave, Ter. Andr. 228ff.; Süss 121ff., Oeri 13ff., 39ff., Webster, SM 165f., cf. Charitonidis and others, Mosaïques 41ff. and pl. 5) and elsewhere (e.g. Herodas 1.78ff. and P. Groeneboom (Groningen 1922) ad loc., Headlam–Knox p. xxxiii, Anth. Pal. 7.353, 455 =

503

COMMENTARY

Antipater 27, Leonidas 68 Gow–Page, Lucian *Dial. Meretr.* 4.4, Propertius 4.5.75, Ovid *Am.* 1.8, *Fast.* 3.765f., Petronius 79, 136, 138; K. Mras, *Wien. Stud.* 38 (1916) 326), always presented from a male viewpoint. The age, sex and status of the other character on stage with the old woman is not clear from the words of the fr. (*pace* Süss, who gratuitously assumes the presence of two old women). A wine-party involving women of varied status ends several Greco-Roman comedies (e.g. Men. *Dysk.*, Plaut. *Asin.*, *Bacch.*, *Stich.*) and opens at least one by Menander (Συναριστῶσαι) adapted by Plaut. (*Cist.*, cf. 17f.).

172 (167K)

Meineke 3.459, Kock 2.358, Edmonds 2.454, Kassel–Austin 2.118; cf. W. G. Arnott, *GRBS* 11 (1970) 43ff. The fr. is cited by Ath. 10.441d (A and Epit.; vv. 3 καὶ μάλα–6 δαιμονίως also in Eustath. 1449.7ff.[1]); the correct part-divisions between the two speakers (cf. introduction to Ὀρχηστρίς) were first indicated by Schweighaeuser (v. 2) and Daléchamp (v. 5).

1–2 The comic stereotype of inebriate hags (see introduction to Ὀρχη-στρίς) is only a particularised exemplification of the general Greek belief that φίλοινον τὸ τῶν γυναικῶν γένος (Ath. 10.440e, citing from comedy in addition to the present fr. Alexis 56(55K), Antiphanes 25(24K), 58(56K), 163(165K), Axionicus 5, Xenarchus 5, 6; also an epigram by Phalaecus = 1 Gow–Page). The belief, which seems to be attested already in Anacreon (fr. 82 Page) and to have flourished most vigorously in comedy (also e.g. Ar. *Vesp.* 1402, *Lys.* 116, 195ff., 395, 465f., *Thesm.* 393 (pillorying Euripides as its disseminator, cf. *Bacch.* 26off.), 63off., 689ff., *Eccl.* 14f., 43ff., 133ff., *Plut.* 644f., 972, Eubulus 42(43K).3f., Plaut. *Pers.* 170, *Pseud.* 221, *Truc.* 903ff.; cf. Lucian *Dial. Meretr.* 5, Alciphron 4.13, 14) was probably a crude male generalisation from instances produced by the cloistered loneliness and boredom of a free woman's life and the professional demands on courtesans and slaves; cf. V. Ehrenberg, *The People of Aristophanes*[2] (Oxford 1951) 201f., J. Henderson (Oxford 1987) on Ar. *Lys.* 113f.

For the structure of the remark cf. e.g. Eur. *Hec.* 317f. καὶ μὴν ἔμοιγε

---

[1] The beginning of Eustathius' citation (οἶνος καὶ μάλα πολύς γε) is a loose but metrical paraphrase of vv. 1–4 of the fr. (οἶνος ... ὅσον ἂν βουλώμεθ᾽ ... καὶ μάλα ἡδύς γε) without authority for the establishment of Alexis' text. Scholars who use those words of Eustathius as a basis for their own conjectures (e.g. J. Pierson, edition of Moeris (Leiden 1759) 353 πολιός γ᾽, ὀδόντας or πολιός, γέρων γε, cf. Jacobs, *Addit.* 236) accordingly waste time and effort.

ζῶντι μὲν καθ' ἡμέραν | κεῖ σμίκρ' ἔχοιμι πάντ' ἂν ἀρκούντως ἔχοι, Α. *Ag.*
1574ff.

2 διαρκής: only here in comedy, and not recorded elsewhere governing
an infinitive ('enough to drink'), but its construction is analogous to that of
other adjectives indicating sufficiency and suitability (e.g. ἱκανός, ἐπι-
τήδειος, χρήσιμος), cf. Goodwin, *MT* §§ 758, 762, K.G. 2.9ff.

νὴ τὼ θεώ: in Attic usage the oath 'by the two goddesses' (Demeter,
Persephone) was peculiar to women (or men pretending to be women), cf.
Rutherford, *NP* 281, F. W. Wright, *Studies in Menander* (Baltimore 1911)
28f., Ussher on Ar. *Eccl.* 155.

3-5 The old woman's description of the wine continues in language
reminiscent of an αἴνιγμα or conundrum, as the other character recognises
(vv.6f.); cf. fr. 242(240K) and comm. *ad loc.* Conundrums were a
traditional part of the entertainment at symposia (cf. e.g. Hes. fr. 266 (c)
Merkelbach–West, Ar. *Vesp.* 20ff., Ath. 10.448b–459b), and seem to have
enjoyed a particular vogue in 4th-century comedy, to judge from the
number of examples preserved there (cf. Meineke 1.277f., Schultz in *RE*
s.v. *Rätsel* 99.22ff., Hunter on Eubulus 106(107K); the most comprehen-
sive studies are still W. Schultz, *Rätsel aus dem hellenistischen Kulturkreis*
(Leipzig 1909–13) and C. Ohlert, *Rätsel und Rätselspiele der älteren Griechen*[2]
(Berlin 1912). The present passage (along with αἰνίγματα in general)
differs from an εἰκών (cf. introduction to fr. 46(45K)) in that it does not
identify at the outset both the object described and the object of
comparison (as happens e.g. in the two straightforward εἰκόνες of Alexis
surviving, 46(45K) and 280(278K)), but names only the former of these
(here wine, as also in 46 and 280: an appropriate theme for a word-game
with symposiac associations). Even so, although Alexis here employs the
same techniques of mystification as appear in other αἰνίγματα (and indeed
in some εἰκόνες: comm. on 46(45K)), attaching to the object described a
series of adjectives or qualifying phrases which are ambiguous or properly
belong to the object of comparison, on this occasion at least (contrast fr.
242(240K)!) he makes only minimal demands on his listeners' intelligence,
because the choice of qualifying expressions (ὀδόντας οὐκ ἔχων, σαπρός,
γέρων) makes the implied comparison of wine with an old man (cf. again
frs. 46(45K), 280(278K)) absolutely obvious. On the general use by later
Greek comedy of affected language in descriptions of wine, parties and
feasting see introduction to 124(119K); the stylistic influence of dithyramb
is particularly clear when passages such as the present fr. are compared
with e.g. Philoxenus fr. 18 Page εὑρείτας οἶνος πάμφωνος.

4 ὀδόντας οὐκ ἔχων: literally 'toothless' (and so applicable to an old
man), but probably also by a colloquial metaphor 'without an astringent
taste' (and so applicable to wine and other liquids). I can trace no parallel
for this personalisation in Greek, but at Plaut. *Poen.* 700 (a play almost

COMMENTARY

certainly adapted from Alexis' Καρχηδόνιος, see introduction to that title) a pimp similarly refers to *uetustate uino edentulo*, 'wine toothless with age', and at Petronius 42.2 Seleucus (whose name suggests Greek ancestry) alleges as his excuse for not bathing daily that *aqua dentes habet*, 'water has a bite'. Cf. the parody by J. B. Morton ('Beachcomber') of modern writing about wine, 'In youth Corton is a savage wine, insolent, loud-voiced and blustering, but after seven years or so he has learnt manners, and can come into a room like an educated gentleman' (*A Bonfire of Weeds*, London 1939) 20; and my discussion in *GRBS* 11 (1970) 43ff.

4–5 Of the other expressions chosen by Alexis to describe wine and old age with dual appropriateness σαπρός and γέρων cause no problems. σαπρός = (i) 'decrepit', applied in comedy (often offensively) to old people (e.g. Ar. *Vesp.* 1380, *Pax* 698, *Lys.* 378, *Eccl.* 884, Eupolis 237(221K), Hermippus 9(10K), cf. Oeri, *op. cit.* in introduction to 'Ορχηστρίς, 41), and (ii) 'mellow' of wine (Philyllius 23(24K).2, cf. Ar. *Plut.* 1068), The noun γέρων ('old man') often stands in apposition to another noun denoting a person (e.g. πατήρ Hom. *Il.* 1.358, Eur. *Alc.* 820, γριπεύς Theoc. 1.39, cf. K.G. 1.271f.), and this use is extended adjectivally (cf. Gow on Theoc. 7.17) to other creatures (e.g. ἵππος S. *El.* 25) and inanimate objects (e.g. σάκος Hom. *Od.* 22.184, οἶνος etc. Eubulus 121(124K).2 and Hunter *ad loc.*, Epinicus 1.6, Men. *Dysk.* 946 and Handley *ad loc.*, Longus 4.16, Lucian *Lex.* 6). Cf. the similar application of πολιός (? playing on the analogy between grey hair and frothy bubbles) and γεραιός to wine (Men. *Dysk.* 946, Archestratus fr. 190.2 Lloyd-Jones–Parsons, Nicander *Ther.* 582).

In the half-metron between σαπρός and γέρων the *Marcianus* has λέγων, which Epit. and Eustathius omit. λέγων scans but is implausible as a further example of ambiguous attribute to οἶνος. Old men can be garrulous, and wine may be termed 'vocal', either with reference to the noise it makes when poured or by hypallage (with the actions of its users transferred to the object itself), e.g. οἶνος πάμφωνος Philoxenus fr. 18 Page, εὔγλωσσον ... οἶνον Maccius (Μακκίου P, but Μαεκίου Stadtmüller) in *Anth. Pal.* 9.403.5f. Yet if Alexis intended this hypallage and ambiguity here, why should he select λέγων when the idiomatic λάλος was available (applied to living creatures, cf. LSJ s.v. and comm. on Alexis 96(92K).2–4, and also to liquids, e.g. λάλον ὕδωρ Anacreont. 12.7 Preisendanz = West, cf. Ach. Tat. 2.14.8 τὸ ῥεῦμα λαλεῖ)? If λέγων in A had replaced λάλος as a gloss, it would have been unusually naive. More probably λέγων is corrupt for either an ambiguous adjective/participle parallel to the others in the passage (but not Emperius' πέπων (349), which Kassel–Austin print, nor Bergk's palaeographically ingenious γελῶν, *Zeitschrift für die Alterthumswissenschaft* 4 (1837) 48, because they lack specific applicability to *aged* men), or a relatively colourless filler (but not

Heimsoeth's γεγώς, *Comm. Alt.* xviii, a form of the perfect participle alien in Attic to comic iambics, although in lyrics at Ar. *Lys.* 641; nor Hirschig's ἤδη, *Diss.* 60, whose corruption to λέγων would be hard to explain; nor Bothe's λέγω, *PCGF* 554, since in this idiom (where λέγω = 'I mean', cf. LSJ s.v. III.9) the word qualified by λέγω is normally in the accusative and always explains a vaguer or puzzling expression, e.g. A. *Ag.* 1035 εἴσω κομίζου καὶ σύ, Κασσάνδραν λέγω, but never a further instance in a series). One conjecture, G. Burges' <γέρων>, γέρων γε δαιμονίως[1] (*praef.* to his edition of Eur. *Tro.* (Cambridge 1807) p. xvi n., anticipating Meineke), avoids the pitfalls of all its rivals; it makes excellent sense, characterising the speaker's enthusiasm, and is close to the *ductus* in A while making its omission by haplography in Epit. and Eustath. readily comprehensible. For the repetition cf. Eur. *Andr.* 678 γέρων γέρων εἶ.

5 δαιμονίως: the adverb, literally 'by divine power' (e.g. Aeschines 3.133, Pl. *Tim.* 25e, Plut. *Mor.* 683a), was used in Attic also as a vivid intensifier, like the English 'divinely' (e.g. Ar. *Nub.* 76 δαιμονίως ὑπερφυᾶ, *Pax* 541, *Plut.* 675, Pl. *Phdr.* 234d, Aeschines 1.41, cf. Plut. *Mor.* 108d; H. Thesleff, *Studies on Intensification in Early and Classical Greek* (Helsinki 1954) 188.

5–6 ἀσπάζομαι γραῦν σφίγγα: an ironic use of the normal formula of greeting (e.g. Ar. *Av.* 1377, *Nub.* 1145 and Starkie *ad loc.*, *Plut.* 1042 and C. von Holzinger, V. Coulon *ad loc.*). The old woman is saluted as if the greatest riddler of them all; cf. Anaxilas 22.22ff. σφίγγα Θηβαίαν δὲ πάσας ἔστι τὰς πόρνας καλεῖν, | αἳ λαλοῦσ' ἁπλῶς μὲν οὐδέν, ἀλλ' ἐν αἰνιγμοῖς τισιν, | ὡς ἐρῶσι, Straton 1.1f. = Philemon 114(123K).1f. σφίγγ' ἀρρέν', οὐ μάγειρον, εἰς τὴν οἰκίαν | εἴληφ', spoken by the hirer of a cook who loaded his speech with exotic epicisms (cf. Austin, *CGFP* no. 219, R. Kassel, *ZPE* 14 (1974) 121ff.). On the Sphinx of legend see especially J. Ilberg in Roscher s.v. 1298ff., Robert, *GH* 3.1.891ff., and Herbig and Lesky in *RE* s.v. 1703.1ff.

6–7 After σφίγγα A and Epit. continue with πρὸς ἐμὲ ὡς αἰνίγματα (AE: ἐνί- C) λέγε καὶ τὰ λοιπά, before the next fr. (Alexis 56(55K)) is introduced. Dindorf interpreted these words as a gloss subsequently added to an abridged version of Ath.'s original text, explaining that further vv. (τὰ λοιπά) of the Alexis fr. had now been omitted; Meineke and Kock were persuaded and left the words out of their texts of the fr. They were wrong. The passage does not lend itself to Dindorf's interpretation, which is based on the wilful alteration of the transmitted λέγε to λέγει

---

[1] It was itself partly anticipated by Scaliger (in Canter, Paris MS 40), who also doubled the γέρων but (ingeniously but less effectively) assigned the first one to the other speaker as a questioning gloss on σαπρός.

(presumably a conjecture by Daléchamp, who translates with *loquitur*), and ignores both the iambic metre of the words and the presence of πρὸς ἐμέ. It is wiser to assume that here we have a continuation of the first speaker's response to the old woman, commenting on her 'riddles to me' and bidding her 'tell me the rest too' (sc. of her story about the preparations for the party); for λέγε καὶ τὰ λοιπά in such a context cf. e.g. Men. *Dysk.* 942 πρόσεχε καὶ τὰ λοιπά (also before the continuation of a narrative), *Epitr.* 877, *Kith.* 50, Straton 1.29 = Kassel–Austin 7.622.

The preceding four words are lacunose in both sense and metre, with the gap (probably half a metron) either before or after ὡς. Missing is a verb to govern αἰνίγματα: not σφίγγα· <προσβάλλει γὰρ> ὡς (Kaibel: but Greek uses προβάλλω, cf. LSJ s.v. 5, Pl. *Charm.* 162b, with αἰνίγματα, not προσβ.; and exclamatory ὡς, cf. LSJ s.v. D.2, normally precedes the verb), nor <προσίεμαι γὰρ> (Peppink, *Observ.* 61: ὡς again wrongly placed, and -γα προσί- splits the anapaest after the first short, but see *CQ* 7 (1957) 189); more probably πρὸς ἐμέ <γ'> ὡς <λέγεις> (Edmonds, cf. Lucian *Vit. Auct.* 14, *Dial. Meretr.* 9.2) or <γ'> ὡς <πλέκεις> (Arnott, cf. Plut. *Mor.* 988a, cf. *P.V.* 610).

Παγκρατιαστής

Meineke 3.462, 505, T. B. L. Webster, *CQ* 2 (1952) 21f., T. Williams, *Rh. Mus.* 105 (1962) 209; cf. Hunter, comm. on Eubulus' Πένταθλος. Athletes are title figures in several 4th-century comedies (Παγκρατιαστής also by Philemon and Theophilus, one of the three doubtless the model for Ennius' *Pancratiastes*; Πένταθλος by Eubulus, Xenarchus; cf. Alexis' Ἀποβάτης, Epicharmus' Ἐπινίκιος), possibly with stock characteristics (e.g. gargantuan appetite, cf. Theophilus 8). The παγκρατιαστής (or πάμμαχος Pl. *Euthyd.* 271c, cf. Fraenkel, comm. on A. *Ag.* 169) engaged in the παγκράτιον, a brutal form of physical combat that won high esteem in ancient Greece, combining features of wrestling and boxing (cf. Plut. *Mor.* 638d) which brought it closer to kung-fu and judo than to traditional European types of prize-fighting; kicking and choking were allowed, and victory was achieved only when one combatant was forced into total submission. A good account of the contest is given by Philostratus *Imag.* 2.6.3; cf. also E. N. Gardiner, *JHS* 26 (1906) 4ff. and *Athletics in the Ancient World* (Oxford 1930) 212ff., B. Schröder, *Der Sport im Altertum* (Berlin 1927) 152ff., Jüthner in *RE* s.v. *Pankration* 619.35ff., H. A. Harris, *Greek Athletes and Athletics* (London 1964) 105ff., M. I. Finley and H. W. Pleket, *The Olympic Games: The First Thousand Years* (London 1976) 40f., 56 and pl. 22a,b, D. J. Kyle, *Athletes in Ancient Athens* (*Mnemosyne Suppl.* 95, 1987) 184, M. B. Poliakoff, *Combat Sports in the Ancient World* (New Haven 1987) 54ff.

Ath. 6.242d cites the only fr. (173(168K)) definitely attributed to this play. In it a woman describes to somebody of unspecified sex[1] a συμπόσιον at which six contemporary celebrities, each with a name or nickname suggesting a foodstuff, were allegedly present. This party could have been an off-stage adjunct to the plot (i.e. imagined as occurring in the house of one of the characters), or an extra-dramatic allusion with or without reference to some recent event; we have no means of deciding whether anything more than a comic point based on the homogeneity of the names was ever intended.[2] The description and tone are closely similar to fr. 102(97K) from Ἰσοστάσιον (see introduction to that play), and three of the people named as party guests (Callimedon, Cobius, 'Semidalis') are common to both frs. Of the six names listed in 173(168K), four are attached to Athenians known to have been prominent in the second half of the 4th century: Callimedon (fl. c. 345–318: introductions to Δορκίς and fr. 57(56K)), Eucrates ὁ Κόρυδος (fl. c. 345–c. 305: introductions to Δημήτριος and fr.48(47K)), Cobius (a lover of Pythionice before 330/29: introduction to Ἰσοστάσιον) and Cyrebion (mentioned in the embassy speeches of Dem. 19.287 and Aeschines 2.151f. dating to 344/3: comm. on 173(168K).2); and if, as seems likely, Σκόμβρος was a nickname given to one of the sons of Chaerephilus (active at Athens in the 320s: introduction to Ἐπιδαύριος, comm. on frs. 6, 77.2–4), we have a fifth man in the list datable to the same period. Alexis' Παγκρατιαστής then is likely to have been produced between c. 345 and c. 320; Webster's preference for the late 340s (loc. cit.) is too restrictive.

With characteristic acumen Meineke (3.462, 505) suggested that frs.274(272K) and 275(273K), quoted together by Epit. (Ath. 2.49e–f) as usual without play-title, may originally have belonged to Παγκρατιαστής. In 274(272K) somebody describes a 'victory dream' in which an opponent, while γυμνός in the stadium, crowned him with a garland of plums. Fr. 275(273K) compares a person's forehead to 'prepared tripe, a baked

---

[1] Williams' claim (loc. cit.) that the two persons involved are a husband and his wife appears to be based on a mistaken assumption that γύναι (v. 6) can be addressed only by a husband to his wife. In comedy, however, this vocative is used also by one woman to another (Men. Epitr. 858–66), a male to a tradeswoman (Ar. Vesp. 1399, Ran. 555), Euripides to his male in-law disguised as a woman (Thesm. 902, 909).

[2] We must beware of assuming from their appearance at Alexis' imagined συμπόσιον that these six figures drank together in real life or even knew each other. At Av. 1291ff. Aristophanes makes a similar collection of Athenians with bird names or nicknames for purely comic purposes, and there is no implication that the men there mentioned were acquaintances.

stuffed spleen or a basket of ripe plums'. The location and the state of undress in the former fr. indicate an athletic, not a musical or dramatic, occasion, and the comparison in the latter points to the description of a fighter's bruised and battered face, as Casaubon (*Animadv.* 101) first noted. Although the method of presentation of these two frs. in Epit. may suggest that they came from one play (see introduction to 274(272K), Alexis could have written plays other than Παγκρατιαστής (and Ἀποβάτης) with athletes dreaming of victory and battered bruisers as characters, appearing in either unknown plays named after them or plays whose titles did not reflect their presence in cast-lists; and the contused forehead of fr. 275(273K) may suit a boxer better than a pancratiast. Kassel–Austin wisely retain 274(272K) and 275(273K) among the frs. of unknown title.

173 (168K)

Meineke 3.461, Kock 2.359, Edmonds 2.454, Kassel–Austin 2.119, cf. Fraenkel, *MNC* 27f. The dramatic situation of the fr. (cited by Ath. 6.242d, A and Epit.; Daléchamp first assigned the words correctly to the two speakers in his Latin translation) is uncertain (above, introduction to Παγκρατιαστής), but similar lists of party guests are found in Aristophanes (e.g. *Vesp.* 1299ff.) and Plautus (e.g. *Asin.* 864ff., *Trin.* 1018ff.); cf. Fraenkel.

1–2 Although alliteration as a stylistic device is much rarer in ancient Greek than in early Latin literature, its employment in a list of personal names here (Κ x 5, Σ x 2) and at 223(221K).15–16 (Φ x 3) is designed presumably for comic effect. The subject has a large bibliography; see e.g. Fraenkel, *MNC* 27f. and comm. on A. *Ag.* 268, J. D. Denniston, *Greek Prose Style* (Oxford 1952) 126ff., Barrett on Eur. *Hipp.* 22–3 (appendix p. 432).

1 πρῶτον (A), not πρῶτος (Epit.), is the normal form in a sequence continued by ἔπειτα (LSJ s.v. πρότερος Β.ΙΙΙ.3a).

Καλλιμέδων ὁ Κάραβος: see introductions to Δορκίς and fr. 57(56K).

2 Κόρυδος: see introductions to Δημήτριος and fr. 48(47K).

Κωβίων (A) or **Κωβιός** (C of Epit.; E seems to have -ιούς)? Elsewhere this name (a real one) always appears as Κωβιός (our man in Alexis 102(97K) (see introduction to Ἰσοστάσιον), Antiphanes 27(26K).19, Ath. 8.339e, ? an ancestor in Archippus 27), hence Th. Bergk's suggestion (*Commentationum de reliquiis comoediae Atticae antiquae libri duo* (Leipzig 1838) 379) that we should adopt C's reading here (with A's -ίων explained as an error of assimilation before the next word Κυρηβίων) is attractive. Yet Κωβίων can be defended; the -ων (-ίων) suffix is often attached to nouns to produce nicknames where the person has some (generally disapproved) connection with the root object: e.g. Κυρηβίων v. 2, Γάστρων Ar. *Ran.* 200, Κορακίων Archippus 27, Ἰχθύων Teleclides 9(8), Πατανίων

ΠΑΓΚΡΑΤΙΑΣΤΗΣ

Philetaerus 14(15K), Λαγυνίων Ath. 13.584f, all people concerned with or about food; cf. especially Bechtel, *Personennamen* 58off., C. W. Peppler, *Comic Terminations in Aristophanes and the Comic Fragments* (Baltimore 1902) 35f., Starkie on Ar. *Nub.* 134 and introduction to *Ach.* p. liii, P. Kretschmer, *Glotta* 7 (1915/16) 34f., P. Chantraine, *La Formation des noms en grec ancien* (Paris 1933) 16off., Buck–Petersen, *Reverse Index* 247. In Ar. *Plut.* the title figure is normally called Πλοῦτος (thirty-five times, including a vocative at 230), but at 727 this is replaced by Πλούτων (cf. Σ: εἶπε παίζων, ἢ ... ὑποκοριστικῶς, cf. Holzinger *ad loc.*).

Κυρηβίων: after citing the fr. Ath. explains that this was the nickname of Epicrates, the kinsman of Aeschines whom Demosthenes savaged (19.287 τοῦ καταράτου Κυρηβίωνος, ὃς ἐν ταῖς πομπαῖς ἄνευ τοῦ προσώπου κωμάζει) and Aeschines defended (2.151 τὴν Ἐπικράτους εὐαγωγίαν, τοῦ Φίλωνος ἀδελφοῦ, ἐπανάγεις εἰς ὄνειδη. καὶ τίς αὐτὸν εἶδε πώποτε ἀσχημονήσαντα, ἢ μεθ' ἡμέραν, ὡς σὺ φῄς, ἐν τῇ πομπῇ τῶν Διονυσίων, ἢ νύκτωρ;) in their embassy speeches of 344/3. Around this time the celebrated Athenian dining-club of wits was flourishing (see comm. on 102(97K)), and although no direct evidence links Epicrates with it, the younger Chaerephon's dedication to him of a book about δεῖπνα (Ath. 6.244a, cf. 242f ff.) may point in that direction. The Demosthenes scholia (2.84 Dilts) derive his nickname from τὰ κυρήβια, variously explained by the ancient lexica as bran from wheat and barley (e.g. *Suda*, Phot. s.v. κυρήβια 1, cf. Σ on Ar. *Equ.* 254 and Dem. 19.287) and/or bean-pods (Phot. s.v. κυρήβια 2, *Et. Mag.* s.v. Κυρηβίων 512.8); could Epicrates have received his nickname from a commercial interest in the production of flour or bread? Cf. A. Schäfer, *Demosthenes und seine Zeit*[2] 1 (Leipzig 1885) 231, Kirchner, *PA* 1.304 no. 4908, Ribbeck, *Kolax* 71. Xen. *Mem.* 2.7.6 tells of a wealthy baker at Athens called Κύρηβος (cf. Bechtel, *Personennamen* 532, 608), who may have begun life as a slave, been given the name as a sobriquet, and kept it after winning freedom and success.

3 ὁ Σκόμβρος: 'Mackerel' was presumably the nickname of a contemporary Athenian, perhaps one of the sons of Chaerephilus, the fish merchant (comm. on fr. 6); these sons were described as 'Chaerephilus' two big mackerels' by Timocles (15(17K); cf. Alexis 77.2–4 and comm.), and this comic witticism may have given rise to such a nickname, popularised it or merely reflected one already in use.

ἡ Σεμίδαλις: see comm. on 102(97K).3–4.

Ἡράκλεις φίλε: invocations to Heracles in Greek comedy take various forms (Ἡράκλεις, ὦ Ἡρ., Ἡρ. ἄναξ, ὦναξ Ἡρ. commonly, ὦ πολυτίμηθ' Ἡρ. Ar. *Ach.* 807, Ἡρ. φίλε only here), but when they introduce a pointed remark (like this) or question or command, any original feeling of direct address has dwindled away and the words have become expletives

COMMENTARY

signalling amazement, irritation or a mixture of both. The present passage is remarkable only because the non-addressing vocative Ἡράκλεις is followed at so short a distance by a second, addressing vocative in γύναι; cf. Wilamowitz's edition of Eur. *Her*. II² (Berlin 1895) 36f., F. W. Wright, *Studies in Menander* (Baltimore 1911) 42ff., T. Williams, *Rh. Mus.* 105 (1962) 209, 221 n. 44.

Παλλακή

The title is shared with Menander, and Diphilus wrote a Παλλακίς (or less probably -ακή[1]); one of the Greek plays may have been the model for Naevius' *Paelex*. In Athens a παλλακή lived in more or less permanent union with a man whom she could not marry if she was non-Athenian or a slave; sometimes previously she had been a *hetaira* (cf. H. J. Wolff, *Tradition* 2 (1944) 65ff., A. R. W. Harrison, *The Law of Athens* 1 (Oxford 1968) 13ff., 61ff., Gomme–Sandbach, *Comm.* p. 30). Chrysis in Men. *Sam.*, who came from Samos and was a *hetaira* before Demeas fell in love and set up house with her (19ff.), is the best example in extant comedy, although the term παλλακή is used only once (508) in the preserved portions of the play and then not with direct reference to her.

174 (169K)

Meineke 3.460, Kock 2.359, Edmonds 2.454, Kassel–Austin 2.120. Translate 'I haven't another word/phrase fit to describe a voice raised/caterwauling like that', the remark of one character to another (both of unknown sex, age, status) in an unknown situation; one possibility would be a row between the title figure and her partner.

τοναίας: 'raised' (voice: sc. φωνῆς; cf. the definition in Photius and *Et. Mag.* s.v. ἡ ...ἐπὶ πολὺ τῆς φωνῆς ἀπότασις). The ellipse of φωνῆς turns the adjective into a noun; cf. K.G. 1.265f., pointing out that in everyday speech all consciousness of an ellipse would probably have been lost. For the corresponding use of the verb τείνω cf. A. *Pers.* 575 (αὐδάν), Eur. *Med*, 201 (βοήν); of the adjective ὑπέρτονος cf. Phrynichus com. 48(46K) (βοάν, quoting S. fr. 491).

---

[1] The one surviving fr. (58(59K)) is cited with author and play-title by *Et. Gen.* (β 195 G. Berger (Meisenheim am Glan 1972): Παλλακίδι Β, cf. Miller, *Mélanges* 68, ? πολλιακοὶ Α) and *Et. Mag.* (206.15: Παλλάκι D, Παλλακῆ other MSS apparently).

Παμφίλη

Breitenbach 117ff. Theopompus com. also (before Alexis was born) wrote a Παμφίλη, in which a woman who liked to drink wine and so became garrulous may have been a character (frs. 41(40K), 42(41K)); the suggestion that she was the title figure and a *hetaira* (so Breitenbach; cf. Kock 1.744, Webster, *SLGC* 22) is merely an attractive speculation.

The role of Alexis' heroine is likewise uncertain. The name Παμφίλη well suits a *hetaira* (cf. the real-life mistress of the actor Satyrus in the mid–4th century, Ath. 13.591e, whose activities could have inspired Alexis; in its Latin form the name of a *fidicina* in Ter. *Phorm.* 310, 510, 517; cf. also comm. on 170(165K)), but in later comedy was given to women of different status: a virtuous young wife (Men. *Epitr.*; on Plaut. *Stich.* see *BICS* 19 (1972) 74 n. 2), a free girl who marries at the end of the play (Austin, *CGFP* 250.8; cf. Ter. *Eun.* 440ff., 624, 796, 827, 1036, *Ad.* 619). One (175(170K)) of the two frs. preserved from Alexis' play implies that either the unnamed speaker or his addressee (Kteson: but see comm. on v. 1) was in love, but we do not know whether Pamphile was the sweetheart. The other fr. (176(171K)) describes a meal or party.

175 (170K)

Meineke 3.461 (1), Kock 2.360, Edmonds 2.456, Kassel–Austin 2.120. The speaker appears to be returning home from market with a collection of foodstuffs, mainly noted aphrodisiacs. Marketers are normally free men or slaves (not cooks, *pace* A. Giannini, *Acme* 13 (1960) 161).

1 Κτήσων: the name was borne by real Athenians, some in Alexis' day (Kirchner, *PA* 1.600f. nos. 8905–14, 2.471 nos. 8904a, 8912a, Fick–Bechtel 179f.; Davies, *APF* 338 discusses a wealthy example, 8908 = 8910), but here it is the *nomen fictum* of a character in the play. If the name's significance ('man of possessions', from κτῶμαι) was intended to match the status and/or personality of its bearer, as sometimes happened in later Greek comedy, Kteson will have been more probably rich than poor, old perhaps than young (? and so less likely than the speaker to have been in love).

2 ὧν νῦν φέρων πάρειμι: cf. Philyllius 4.1f. αὐτὸς φέρων πάρειμι ... κολλάβους θερμούς, Men. *Sik.* 247f. πάρεστι δ' οὑτοσί μοι νῦν φέρων | μητρὸς διαθήκας καὶ γένους γνωρίσματα.

2–3 Three of the foods listed were considered aphrodisiacs. (1) The κῆρυξ (a general term for the larger Mediterranean whelk-shaped gastropods, especially in the genera *Charonia*, *Ranella*, *Cymatium*, such as the triton, *Charonia nodifera*, with tough flesh; see Gossen–Steier in *RE* s.v. *Schnecke* 587.28ff., Thompson, *Fishes* 113f., Campbell, *Guide* 140ff.) is

513

COMMENTARY

included in Alexis' other list of aphrodisiacs at fr. 281(279K) and Alciphron's sex feast (4.13.16), although Galen 14.487 Kühn recommends it as an anaphrodisiac. (2) On βολβός and the belief in its aphrodisiac power for males see comm. on 167(162K).13. (3) πουλύπους (the common octopus, *Octopus vulgaris*, and other smaller Mediterranean species such as *O. macropus* and *Eledone cirrosa*, the curled octopus; here the addition of μέγαν confirms that Alexis has in mind *O. vulgaris*, which can grow up to a metre in length; see Steier in *RE* s.v. *Tintenfische* 1395.21ff., Thompson 204f., Palombi–Santorelli 301ff., Campbell 180f., Davidson, *Seafood* 213ff.; on its orthography see below) is named as an aphrodisiac also by Xenarchus 1.8, Diocles and Mnesitheus in Ath. 7.316c and 8.357d respectively. Probably (4) the κτείς (a general name for the eight or so species of scallop found in the Mediterranean, including *Pecten jacobaeus* = pilgrim scallop or St James's shell, *Chlamys opercularis* = queen scallop, *C. varia* = variegated scallop, and *Proteoplecten glaber*; see Steier in *RE* s.v. *Muscheln* 788.28ff., Thompson 133f., Palombi–Santorelli 324ff., Campbell 162f., Davidson 200ff.) was also believed to stimulate sexual desire, although I have not traced any other such indication in ancient texts.

3 πουλύπουν: the MSS of Ath. here (A at 8.356e; Epit. omits the fr.) and occasionally elsewhere (e.g. Epit. at 2.64a citing Xenarchus 1.8, A and Epit. at 7.316f citing Diphilus 33(34K).1) preserve the correct Attic orthography, attested by Aristophanes and the tragedians in the 5th century, and by all the Attic comic poets down to the time of Diphilus in the 4th century, although scribes often corrupt it to the later spelling πολύπους even where that is *contra metrum* (e.g. Antiphanes 95, cf. Anaxandrides 42(41K).39). πολύπους begins to appear in Athens about the time of Aristotle (cf. LSJ s.v. πολύπους B), but is never used even by later comedians there for the cephalopod (at Posidippus 20(19K) it is adjectival, 'many-footed'). Attic's adoption of the form πουλύπους (with its irregular accusative singular -πουν) is hard to explain, but it is more probable that 5th-century literature (following or leading popular usage) was influenced by epic (e.g. Hom. *Od.* 5.432), cf. M. Leumann, *Homerische Wörter* (Basle 1960) 317f., than that an attempt was being made to naturalise a foreign word. Such a borrowing would have had to antedate Mycenaean Greek (cf. M. G. F. Ventris and J. Chadwick, *Documents in Mycenaean Greek*[2] (Cambridge 1973) 345f. no. 246), but the idea that Greek might need to seek a word from abroad for a creature so abundant in Greek waters, and then to find one whose sound corresponded so exactly in Greek to the octopus' eight arms, strains credulity.

ἁδρούς: of fish, 'solid-fleshed' rather than 'fat'; cf. Antiphanes 27(26K).21 (applied to a slim goby), Dionysius com. 3.9.

176 (171K)

Meineke 3.461 (II), Kock.2.360, Edmonds 2.456, Kassel–Austin 2.121. The fr. is broken off by the excerptor (Ath. 9.380e) in mid-sentence (cf. Herwerden, *Coll. Crit.* 126).

1 παρέθηκε τὴν τράπεζαν … παραφέρων: cf. comm. on 98(152K).2. Normally in a culinary context παρατίθημι = 'I serve (food) on to' the table, but here and occasionally elsewhere (e.g. Antiphanes 143(145K), Chariton 1.13.2) it has a noun like τράπεζα or τρίπους as its object (or as subject when passive) in the sense 'I put (the table) down by (the guests)'.

2 ἀγαθῶν ἁμάξας: 'cartloads of goodies'. The phrase, which I have not found elsewhere, could be proverbial or (less probably) a comic coinage on the analogy of similar expressions (e.g. ἀγαθῶν ἀγαθίδες/θάλασσα/ θησαυρός/μυρμηκία/πόντος/σωρός, all in Leutsch–Schneidewin, see *CPG* 1.490, 2.58f., 790; ἀ. ἀγαθίδες also Phryn. *Praep. Soph.* 13.13ff. de Borries, ἀ. πόντος Sophron fr. 159 Kaibel, ἀ. σωρός Ar. *Plut.* 804, Ach. Tat. 6.4.2; cf. πλοῦτον ἀθρόον ἀγαθῶν Alciphron 1.1.3). Alexis' metaphor is founded on the extended use of ἅμαξα to mean 'cartload', e.g. Xen. *Anab.* 4.7.10, *Cyr.* 2.4.18, Pl. *Euthyd.* 299b, LSJ s.v. I.2; cf. also Plaut. *Pers.* 782 *uehiclum argenti*.

Παννυχὶς ἢ Ἔριθοι

Meineke 1.401, 490, Kock 2.241, 3.274, W. Bender, *De graecae comoediae titulis duplicibus* (Diss. Marburg 1904) 53, Breitenbach 161ff., Kann, *De iteratis* 73, N. Terzaghi, *Fabula* I (Milan 1912) 29ff., 80f., K. Mras, *Wien. Stud.* 38 (1916) 330f., A. M. Desrousseaux in *Mélanges offerts à M. Octave Navarre* (Toulouse 1935) 141f., Ziehen in *RE* s.v. Παννυχίς 629.61ff., Webster, *SLGC* 83, A. Giannini, *Acme* 13 (1960) 161f., Dohm, *Mageiros* 103f., 137f., Hunter 175, Nesselrath, *MK* 303f., 319 n. 97. Six frs. are cited from the play by Ath., three with the heading ἐν Παννυχίδι ἢ 'Ερίθοις (178(172K), 179(174K), 182(177K) = 12.516d, 4.170b, 6.248a respectively), one with ἐν Παννυχίδι only (177(173K) = 9.386a, one with 'Ερίθοις only (181(176K) = 11.483e, and one which the *Marcianus* introduces with παννυχίδι ἐρίθοισιν, where ἐρίθοισιν is either the first word of the fr. or <ἢ> has been omitted before it (180(175K) = 3.96a; see comm.). There is no evidence here (*pace* Bender) to suggest that a second production of the play accounted for the alternative title; more probably (cf. introduction to 'Αγωνίς) Ἔριθοι was added later, perhaps in Alexandria by a grammarian who wished thereby to distinguish it from the other three[1] comedies named Παννυχίς: by Pherecrates ('Ιπνὸς ἢ Παννυχίς), Hipparchus (whose title is given as Παννυχίς by Ath. 15.691c citing fr. 4, as Παννυχίδες by Pollux 10.108 with fr. 5) and Eubulus.

Pannychis is occasionally recorded as a woman's name (*hetaira*, Lucian *Dial. Meretr.* 9; concubine, Josephus *BJ* 1.511; maiden, Petronius 25; ? nymph, vases from Agrigento and Apulia, D. Raoul-Rochette, *Lettres archéologiques sur la peinture des grecs* 1 (Paris 1840) 172 n. 1, E. Maass, *JDAI* 21 (1906) 89ff.), and so the possibility that in Alexis it was the name of a human character (*hetaira*: so Nesselrath 319 n. 97) or prologue divinity (so Webster) cannot be ruled out. Yet (with or without such a divine prologue) the title may more reasonably be interpreted as referring to one of the night festivals in Attica where the participants were entirely or predominantly women, and (at least in later comedy, and literature influenced by it) free girls were raped under the cover of darkness and general revelry by drunken young men (e.g. Men. *Epitr.* 451ff. and *Phasm.* 95ff., Tauropolia; *Sam.* 38ff., Adonia; *Plokion*, see Aul. Gell. 2.23.15 citing Men. fr. 335; cf. Aelian *NA* 7.19 τὰ τοῦ Μενάνδρου ἐν ταῖς παννυχίσιν ἀκόλαστα, Philostratus *Epist.* 47; Ziehen, *loc. cit.*, Radermacher on Ar. *Ran.* 440–5, J. Martin (Paris 1961) on Men. *Dysk.* 857, T. Williams, *Hermes* 91 (1963) 304f., Gomme–Sandbach, *Comm.* on Men. *Epitr.* 451, P. G. McC. Brown, *CQ* 43 (1993) 196ff.). If Alexis' plot was a conventional type of New-Comedy intrigue revolving round the consequences of such a rape, what was the role of the ἔριθοι who provide the alternative title? This word (also the title of a play by Amphis: see introduction to Ἀμπελουργός) denotes 'hired workers', especially women (probably both free and slave) employed to spin and weave wool in private houses and public workshops (LSJ s.v., e.g. Dem. 57.45, *P.Hibeh* 121.34 (mid-3rd century), Heliodorus 1.5; cf. Blümner, *Technologie* 166, K. Latte, *Nachr. Göttingen* (1953) 84f. = *Kleine Schriften* (Munich 1968) 513f.); were they the chorus (cf. Eubulus' Στεφανοπωλίδες and Hunter p. 191), a group of people with a minor role (cf. the witnesses in Plaut. *Poen.*, the advisers in Ter. *Ad.*), or a pair of unrelated women perhaps closely involved in the plot (cf. e.g. Plaut. *Cist.*, *Rud.*)?

Unfortunately the extant frs., generous though they are in number and extent (almost fifty vv. of the play are preserved), help us neither to answer these questions nor to uncover Alexis' plot. The three longest (177(173K), 178(172K), 179(174K)) appear to come from a pair of scenes in which a typical Athenian μάγειρος (cf. introduction to fr. 24) amuses the audience

---

[1] Not four, for the Παννυχίς by 'Callippus' (Meineke 1.490, 4.561, Kock 3.378) is a chimaera, springing from a corruption in the *Marcianus* (Ath. 15.668c) of Callimachus' name (cf. Wilamowitz, *SB Berlin* (1912) 537f., Pfeiffer on Call. fr. 227).

with a series of conventional boasts and complaints, to the boredom and annoyance of the man who hired him for a now unknown celebration. Frs. 177(173K) and 178(172K) probably both belong to the scene in which the hirer brings the cook to his house, and since the last three lines of 178 include an order for the cook to remove himself from his hirer's presence (ἀπαλλάγηθί μου v. 16) and presumably go indoors, it seems likely that this fr. comes in the closing section of the scene when the cook makes his exit into the hirer's house (so Dohm 103f., Nesselrath 303 n. 48; cf. e.g. Athenion 1.45f., Nicomachus 1.41f., Sosipater 1.57), and so follows 177(173K) at some incalculable interval. Fr. 179(174K) seems to originate from a different and later scene (cf. Nesselrath 304) where the μάγειρος has emerged from the house after investigating an allegedly inadequate kitchen and finds his hirer already outside (cf. comm. on 179(174K).3 ἤδη παρελθών). The other three frs. are much briefer. In 180(175K) the μάγειρος again appears to be involved (as speaker or subject of accusation), but its message (that preparations for a meal are going badly, with one dish already cooked, one being spoiled and two not ready) may be a real one, caused perhaps by the host's demand that the food should be served before the cook is ready, but it could just as well be imaginary, with the cook describing the sort of situation he faces when the diners arrive too early or too late (cf. another cook's lecture on καιρός at fr. 153(149K)). Fr. 181(176K) reports an incident at a party (? the one for which the cook was hired) possibly involving a soldier. Fr. 182(177K) appears to predict a parasite's life for the addressee (? a young wastrel).

177 (173K)

Meineke 3.464 (II), Kock 2.361, Edmonds 2.458, Kassel–Austin 2.121; cf. M. Treu, *Philologus* 103 (1956) 220f., Dohm, *Mageiros* 154ff., Gil 324f., Bain, *Actors* 225, Nesselrath, *MK* 303f. and n. 48. A fr. of dialogue between the cook and the man who has hired him, taken probably (see introduction to Παννυχίς) from an earlier part of the same scene as 178(172K). The initial entry of cook and hirer (or hirer's slave) on their way from market to the hirer's house (or the place where the meal is to be served, if different) is a stereotyped feature in later comedy (Dohm 137f., Handley on Men. *Dysk.* 393f., my introduction to 115(110K)), exploited with a series of variations on the cook's ἀλαζονεία. Here the cook, who is accompanied up to v. 12 at least by one or more assistants (cf. comm. on 178(172K).2), asks questions about the meal he has been engaged to prepare and the facilities of his host's kitchen; the enquiries and complaints by μάγειροι about their hirers' facilities were a stock feature in later comedy (cf. e.g. Alexis 179(174K): the same cook in a later scene probably, see introduction to Παννυχίς), 132(127K), Diphilus 18, Men. *Sam.* 285ff.,

COMMENTARY

Sosipater 1.48ff., Dohm, *Mageiros* 154ff.). The combination of this cook's garrulous importunity and affected expressions (vv.2–3, 10), which are a feature of fr. 178(172K) also, already irritates his hirer by v. 11. Full appreciation of Alexis' stylistic touches in this scene, however, is severely handicapped by the vile condition of the text in frs. 177(173K) and 178(172K), cited by Ath. 9.386a (A only: omitted in Epit.) and 12.516e (A mainly: only the word κάνδαυλος and v. 5 in Epit.) respectively. Since (i) the corruptions in the two frs. contain striking similarities (e.g. short lacunae) and (ii) the context surrounding the citations in the two widely separated passages of Ath. is free from such damage, it seems likely that Ath. (or his immediate source) had access only to a text of the Alexis scene that was already lacunose and corrupt. The *Marcianus*, as always, gives minimal help with part-division (but see comm. on 177(173K).2). In its elucidation here Daléchamp, Casaubon, Schweighaeuser, the two Kock brothers and Capps all played a part; at 178(172K) the credit, it seems, is due to Daléchamp alone.

1 Despite the qualms of Kaibel and Kassel–Austin, Musurus' correction of A's χαιρεοις ἀιεὶ to χαίρεις ἀεὶ is virtually certain. Confusion in this MS and others written in early minuscule between ἀεί and ἀιεί (cf. comm. on 76.1) springs from the misreading of alpha with its long vertical tail as αι and *vice versa*, and χαιρεοις is more satisfactorily explained as homoeoteleuton induced by θερμοτέροις ... τοῖς ὀψαρίοις in the immediate context than as a conflation of alternative readings (-εις, -οις: so Kaibel, conjecturing χαίροις σύγ᾽ ἂν; but this removes an idiomatic use of ἀεί with the present indicative, 'do you enjoy ... every time you have dinner', and is unnecessarily far from the *ductus*).

2 ὀψαρίοις: cf. comm. on 47(46K).6. At this point the cook resorts to punctilious expressions which mystify his hirer: 'do you always enjoy your fish hotter/quite hot, or medium, or at a lower/quite low level (sc. temperature)? The drawing of such distinctions is a conventional characteristic of cooks and gourmands in comedy (e.g. Eubulus 6(7K).1f. θερμότερον ἢ κραυρότερον ἢ μέσως ἔχον, | τοῦτ᾽ ἔσθ᾽ ἑκάστῳ μεῖζον ἢ Τροίαν ἑλεῖν, spoken by Heracles, cf. Hunter *ad loc.*; Sosipater 1.51ff. καὶ πότε | εὔκαιρον αὐτῶν ἐστι τῶν ὄψων τὰ μὲν | θερμὰ παραθεῖναι, τὰ δ᾽ ἐπανέντα, τὰ δὲ μέσως, | τὰ δ᾽ ὅλως ἀποψύξαντα, a cook; com. adesp. fr. 343 Kock οὔτ᾽ ἄγαν ὀπτοῖσιν οὔθ᾽ ἑφθοῖς ἄγαν, | οὔθ᾽ ἧττον οὔτε μᾶλλον οὔτε διὰ μέσου | ἠρτυμένοισι), but some of the vocabulary used by Alexis' cook may be intended to parody the technical jargon of philosophy or medicine. τὸ μέσον (adverbial accusative, equivalent to Eubulus' μέσως ἔχον, Sosipater's μέσως and the anon. διὰ μέσου, cf. K.G. 1.317f.) was unconvincingly interpreted by Treu as an echo of Aristotle's doctrine on the mean, but the use of μέσος exemplified here is too widespread in all sorts of context (e.g. Eur. *Hel.* 1137, Hippocr. *Artic.* 77, Arist. *IA* 4, 706ᵇ3) for such an idea to be sustained. κατωτέρω, on the other hand ('lower' = 'less hot': I know of no parallel for this use), is an unexpected word to apply to the measurement of temperature before the invention of the thermometer, and it defeats the man questioned (v.3). With this adverb in all probability the cook, like his counterpart in fr. 129(124K), apes a contemporary usage in medicine or philosophy, influenced perhaps (at whatever remove) by such theories of heat's upward and cold's downward movement as lie at the heart of Heraclitus' philosophy (cf. G. S. Kirk, *Heraclitus* (Cambridge 1954) 272ff., 325ff. on fr. 31, 105ff. on fr. 60; note that the change from cold sea to hot fire was later termed ἀναθυμίασις). Such theories, whether based on observations that (i) heat rises from a fire and (ii) flames which climb higher are hotter, or linked with such observations by a popular pattern of thought that crudely misrepresented the original ideas, were an obvious source of material for a comic poet who wished to ridicule the scientific aspirations of his stage cooks.

After κατωτέρω (v.2) A has a dicolon: a vestige of ancient practice in marking part-division? Cf. comm. on 129(124K).2 and my general introduction, ii.i.a.

3–4 In the second and third metra of v. 3 the *Marcianus* writes τί λέγεις δέσποτα· πῶς οὑτοσί, where δέσποτα betrays its corruptness doubly by its scansion (dactyls are not allowed in the second half of a metron) and inapplicability (μάγειροι are normally free men, cf. comm. on 134(129K)). As Dobree first saw (comm. on Ar. *Plut.* 48, Cambridge 1820), the *Marcianus* scribe mangles and wrongly divides τί λέγεις δέ; ποταπὸς οὑτοσί, probably with σύ written above δέ as variant or correction, in the MS he was copying. τί λέγεις σύ; was preferred by Dobree, τί λέγεις δέ; by V. Schmidt (in C. Austin's edition of Men. *Asp.* and *Sam.* 2 (Berlin 1970) 25 on *Asp.* 241); both are possible, with σύ defended as the unemphatic use of the pronoun so common in later Greek (cf. comm. on 169(164K).2), δέ as a typical connective in indignant questions (cf. Denniston, *GP* 173ff.). The expression itself is used to similar effect (seeking an explanation of another speaker's strange usage which he first reiterates as a question) at e.g. Ar *Av.* 1650f. νόθος γὰρ εἶ κοὐ γνήσιος. | :: ἐγὼ νόθος; τί λέγεις;

ποταπός may be Alexis' own spelling (so e.g. Meineke, cf. Austin, *loc. cit.*) or a scribal substitution of the post-classical form for the correct Attic ποδαπός (so e.g. Dobree); it is uncertain which spelling Alexis would have favoured here or elsewhere (cf. comm. on 94(90K).1). After οὑτοσί the *Marcianus* has ἄνθρωπος, which Dobree rectified to ἄνθρωπος; when οὑτοσί qualifies a noun in later Greek comedy, the noun always has the definite article (e.g. Men. *Dysk.* 212f., same phrase, same *sedes*, 480, *Epitr.* 320f.); cf. comm. on 88(85K).3–5.

COMMENTARY

The correct assignment of parts in v. 3 was first seen by E. Capps (in Gulick's edition of Ath.);[1] after the cook has finished his question at the end of v. 2, his hirer picks up κατωτέρω in puzzlement and asks 'What do you mean?' Thereupon the cook, either addressing his παῖδες (cf. v. 12) or in an aside to the audience, contemptuously responds with 'Where can this fellow here have come from?' (with the implication that a man who didn't understand this technical use of κατωτέρω could hardly have been raised in Athens). Then if the *Marcianus* correctly preserves ἐπίστασαι in v. 4, the cook now turns to address his hirer with the same arrogant bluntness as in his immediately previous remark; yet there is much to be said for Jacobs' conjecture ἐπίσταται (*Addit.* 205), which confines the cook's open rudeness to remarks not addressed to his paymaster, and thus makes him address his hirer next with ψυχρά σοι ἅπαντα παραθῶ;

4 ζῆν: in the sense of εὖ ζῆν, here and commonly elsewhere with hedonistic overtones (e.g. Alexis 236(234K).1, 237(235K).2, Men. *Pk.* 183, Chaeremon 24, Dio Cass. 69.19 Σίμιλις ἐνταῦθα κεῖται βιοὺς μὲν ἔτη τόσα (so MSS generally, but πεντήκοντα exc. Vat., exc. Salm.), ζήσας δὲ ἔτη ἑπτά; cf. also my comm. on Alexis 28.4). In Latin *uiuere* is similarly used, e.g. Plaut. *MG* 678 *me uolo uiuere*; cf. C. J. Fordyce (Oxford 1961) on Catullus 5.1.

5 παραθῶ: see comm. on fr. 98(152K).2.

6 Ἄπολλον: i.e. may Apollo protect me from the situation implied by your question. The apostrophe to Ἀπόλλων ἀποτρόπαιος, sometimes expressed in full (e.g. Ar. *Vesp.* 161, *Av.* 61, *Plut.* 359, 854) but in later comedy usually abbreviated to Ἄπολλον as here (e.g. Eubulus 89(90K).4, Men. *Asp.* 86, *Dysk.* 293, 415, *Sam.* 100, 570, com. adesp. fr. 258.35 Austin), normally expresses surprise or alarm; as a response to a question is either equivalent to (so here) or reinforced by (e.g. Ar. *Plut.* 359) a vehement negative. Cf. F. W. Wright, *Studies in Menander* (Baltimore 1911) 16ff., Handley on Men. *Dysk.* 290ff.

τὸ μέσον: here as subject. δηλαδή must be the hirer's reply to the cook's last suggestion, as Meineke first realised; otherwise this would be the only place where he fails to make any response. In confirmatory answers δηλαδή is written as a single word (cf. LSJ s.v.) on the authority of the ancient grammarians (e.g. Herodian 1.489.8 Lentz, cf. 2.28.26, Σ Dionys. Thrax 150.4f. Hilgard, cf. 584.9).

---

[1] Previously Schweighaeuser's assignment was generally accepted, giving κατωτέρω (v.3) to the hirer as an answer to the cook's question, and τί λέγεις σύ; to the cook. This is clearly wrong; it makes the hirer understand the cook's odd use of κατωτέρω and choose to have his fish served at the lower temperature, in contradiction to v. 6, where he opts for the intermediate (= lukewarm) one, like so many modern Greeks.

ΠΑΝΝΥΧΙΣ

7–8 *Cook*: 'This (sc. giving the choice of temperature at which the food is to be served) is something that no other of my colleagues does.' *Hirer*: 'I imagine not – nor any other of the things you're now doing (e.g. asking ridiculous or incomprehensible questions).' Cf. the cook in Plaut. *Pseud.* 810 *non ego item cenam condio ut alii coqui* (and J. C. B. Lowe, *CQ* 35 (1985) 413). Here the *Marcianus* writes ποιεῖ (7) and ποιεῖς (8), followed by Kassel–Austin, but see my comm. on fr. 16.2.

9 A's text (ἐγὼ δ' ἐρῶ τοῖς γὰρ ἐστιωμένοις) is one syllable short, most probably ∪ before τοῖς. The gap is small, but surprisingly awkward to fill with anything approaching certainty. If ἐγὼ δ' ἐρῶ is correctly transmitted, Kaibel's ἐρῶ <σοι> (virtual haplography before τοῖς) is preferable to Musurus' τοῖσ<ιν> (removing penthemimeral caesura), and may be right, but Cobet's ἐγὼ δὲ <π>ρῶ<τος> (haplography again: *NL* 34f., cf. Meineke, *Anal. Crit.* 169 ten years later; in this idiom appositional πρῶτος normally dispenses with the definite article, e.g. Antiphanes 121(123K).1, Men. *Georg.* 45, *Epitr.* 313, *Mis.* 307, *Sam.* 509) has an imaginative vigour more in keeping with Alexis' comic style in general and his portrayal of this cook in particular as a πρῶτος εὑρετής (cf. 178.(172K).4 and comm. *ad loc.*).

9–10 The cook explains his alleged distinctiveness: 'You see, to the feasters I render as their due the appropriate/correct synthesis.' All he really means is that he gives his clients a choice between hot, cold and lukewarm food, but if he had expressed this idea in simple language (repeating or rephrasing vv. 1–2), he would have betrayed the banality of an observation that when hot and cold liquids are mixed, the resulting temperature depends on the original temperatures of the unmixed liquids and the proportions in which they are mixed. Accordingly Alexis' cook dresses up his statement with pseudo-scientific trimming, postponing here for maximum effect the key word συγκράσεως to the end of the sentence. Although the idea of 'mingling hot and cold' played a major role in 5th-century cosmological theorising (e.g. Anaxagoras fr. 2 Diels–Kranz = 468 Kirk–Raven–Schofield ἡ σύμμιξις ... καὶ τοῦ θερμοῦ καὶ τοῦ ψυχροῦ, with W. K. C. Guthrie, *A History of Greek Philosophy* 2 (Cambridge 1965) 294ff.; cf. Empedocles fr. 21.13f. Diels–Kranz = 425 K.–R. using κρῆσις, with Guthrie 2.148ff.), it seems more likely that the present cook's phraseology (like that of his counterpart in Λέβης, see introduction to that play and comm. on fr. 129(124K)) is designed to mimic the language and thought of contemporary medicine; Hippocr. *Vict.* (a work now dated to the end of the 5th or beginning of the 4th century: cf. R. Joly and S. Byl's edition, *CMG* 1.2.4 (Berlin 1984) 28ff., 44ff.) repeatedly emphasises πυρὸς καὶ ὕδατος σύγκρησιν, 1.7, 25, 32, 35, 36; cf. also Asclepiades med. in *Placit.* 5.21.2 p. 433 Diels. Although by the time of later Greek comedy abstract nouns in -σις had generally passed from intellectual into everyday speech (cf. E. W. Handley, *Eranos* 51 (1954) 129ff.), σύγκρασις itself may have retained its scientific aura longer than most (? up to Men. fr. 376), and it is notable that when this abstract is used in non-philosophic contexts during the 5th and 4th centuries (e.g. Eur. fr. 21, Alexis 242(240K).1f.), it tends to be qualified by τις as an indicator that the noun's normal use belongs to one or more specialised fields.

10 τὸν καιρόν: here in its earliest and more general, non-temporal sense (contrast 151(147K).1, 153(149K).9), 'the appropriate/proper/ correct measure'; cf. especially Wilamowitz, *Hermes* 15 (1880) 506ff. = *Kleine Schriften* 1 (Berlin 1935) 42ff., F. Pfister in *Würzburger Festgabe H. Bulle dargebracht* (Stuttgart 1938) 131ff., Barrett, comm. on Eur. *Hipp.* 386–7, J. R. Wilson, *Glotta* 58 (1980) 177ff., W. H. Race, *TAPA* 111 (1981) 197ff. The importance of καιρός in cookery is maintained by other μάγειροι at Sosipater 1.49 and Alexis 153(149K), cf. introduction to that fr. and Dohm, *Mageiros* 192ff.

11 A's text σὺ πρὸς θεῶν ἔθυσας τὸν ἔριφον is defective by half a metron, but as its meaning seems satisfactory and complete, the better supplements have been inessential words yielding few criteria for editorial judgement: e.g. <ἤδη> Schweighaeuser (before τόν) and Meineke (before σύ), <οἶμαι> τόν Kaibel, <ἡμῶν> ἔθυσας Peppink, *Observ.* 57. All of these are possible, none palaeographically convincing. Elsewhere, however, this cook is twice addressed by his hirer with exasperated impatience as ἄνθρωπε (178(172K).7, 16), as indeed are several of his comic colleagues (sometimes with the same criticism as here, e.g. Men. *Dysk.* 410 ἄνθρωπε, μή με κόπτε, cf. *Mis.* 323), and the insertion here of ἄνθρωπ' (so W. Headlam, *JPhil.* 30 (1907) 318[1]), ὤνθρωπ' or μάγειρ' before ἔθυσας has an attractiveness based partly on the cited comic parallels, partly on the fact that a scribe might easily have omitted ἄνθρωπ' by haplo- graphy (especially if written ῎ΑΝ(Ε) or ? ῎ΩΝ(Ε) with the *nomen sacrum* abbreviation between θεῶΝ and ῎Εθυσας, cf. Cobet, *NL* 612, *VL²* 14f., O. Lehmann, *Die tachygraphischen Abkürzungen der griechischen Handschriften* (Leipzig 1880) 1f.), and partly on A's parallel omission of μάγειρε at Ath. 9.382e in the citation of Strato 1.24 (where *P.Cairo* 65445 preserves the correct text). Cf. also the following note.

πρὸς θεῶν: since in drama this oath characteristically reinforces emotional questions, entreaties, commands and prohibitions, but not

---

[1] In a MS note on his copy of Kaibel's edition of Ath., now in King's College Library, Cambridge, pressmark K.31.19–21, Headlam sug- gested as an alternative supplement ἄπελθ' (also after πρὸς θεῶν and taken in conjunction with it, cf. Men. *Pk.* 481); the imperative is plausible in sense, but its omission by a scribe harder to explain.

simple statements,[1] πρὸς θεῶν here must be taken with μὴ κόπτ' ἔμ' (cf. e.g. Ar. *Vesp.* 1418, *Eccl.* 562f., Men. *Dysk.* 750f., *Her.* 14), and the intervening ἔθυσας τὸν ἔριφον be either (i) regarded as parenthetic (cf. Eur. *Hipp.* 215ff. πέμπετέ μ' εἰς ὄρος· εἶμι πρὸς ὕλαν καὶ παρὰ πεύκας . . .· πρὸς θεῶν and Barrett's comm. *ad loc.*, F. W. Wright, *Studies in Menander* (Baltimore 1911) 9f., or (ii) adjusted to θύσας τὸν ἔριφον (? after a now unelided vocative in -ε: see previous note).

12 μὴ κόπτ' ἔμ', ἀλλὰ τὰ κρέα: A writes κόπτε με, but the expressed contrast between 'me' and 'the meat' demands a different word-division with emphatic ἔμ' (so first Dindorf). The pun on two different meanings of κόπτω and its compound κατακόπτω: (i) 'cut/chop (κατα- up)', (ii) 'weary/bore/annoy (this sense first recorded in 4th-century Attic comedy and Dem. *Proem.* 29): becomes so hackneyed a joke in scenes involving a garrulous cook (also Men. *Dysk.* 398, *Sam.* 284f., 292f., Anaxippus 1.23, all with κατακόπτω) that on its own the mere command μὴ κόπτε ('stop being a bore') when addressed to a cook may be considered to imply the pun and be designed to evoke laughter (Men. *Dysk.* 410, Hegesippus 1.3, Sosipater 1.20, com. adesp. fr. 261.2 Austin, *P.Cologne* 203 c.i.17). Cf. especially Dohm, *Mageiros* 213 and n. 1, 218f., Gomme–Sandbach on Men. *Sam.* 285.

παῖδες, παράγετε: Schweighaeuser assigned vv. 11–12 entirely to the hirer, but the command that closes v. 12, 'Servants, on your way!' is perhaps more likely to have been voiced by the cook, as Kock first suggested. In the scene from which frs. 177(173K) and 178(172K) appear to derive, it is the cook and not his hirer who refers to himself indiscriminately in both the plural and the singular (see comm. on 178(172K).2), and the simplest explanation of this variation would be the presence with him of two or more assistants (cf. Rankin, ΜΑΓΕΙΡΟΙ 67f.). The intransitive use of παράγω in the sense 'go along' (LSJ s.v. B.I.1) is so common in later Greek comedy (normally of movement into a stage house: often with εἴσω, e.g. Men. *Epitr.* 405, *Sam.* 295; often on its own, also e.g. *Dysk.* 556, *Pk.* 525) and relatively so rare elsewhere that it may have been a colloquialism, perhaps taken from military terminology (cf. Xen. *Cyr.* 5.4.44, Polyb. 4.44.3).

13 The *Marcianus* gratuitously repeats παῖδες at the beginning of this v. and corrupts ὀπτάνιον to -νειον (proparoxytone), thus producing an incongruous trochaic tetrameter in the midst of iambic trimeters; the corrections were made by Schweighaeuser. ὀπτάνιον is confirmed as the Attic spelling by both the dactylic scansion of its first three syllables in

---

[1] Ar. fr. 53(51K) at first sight appears an exception to this rule, but see Barrett on Eur. *Hipp.* 215ff. and Kassel–Austin *ad loc.*

comedy (also e.g. Ar. *Pax* 891, *Equ.* 1033, Men. *Sam.* 291) and the ordinances of grammarians (Phryn. *Ecl.* p. 276 Lobeck, q.v. = 85.64ff. Fischer, Herodian 1.375.26ff. Lentz); it is often corrupted in MSS to the post-classical form ὀπτανεῖον (perispomenon) which superseded it (e.g. A and Epit. at Ath. 3.102f and 7.291b citing Damoxenus 2.45 and Nicomachus 1.25). In Athens the word seems always to have meant 'kitchen' as the room or space for cooking (in Ar. *Equ.* and Damoxenus one goes into it, cf. Alciphron 3.17.1; in Men. *Sam.* it has a roof; cf. Pollux 1.80, 6.13, identifying it as a μαγειρεῖον, and Phryn. *loc. cit*). See Rankin, ΜΑΓΕΙΡΟΙ 45.

κάπνην: not just the hole in the kitchen roof through which the smoke escaped (so LSJ s.v. καπνοδόκη), but also the pipe (cf. Σ Ar. *Vesp.* 143 τι σωληνοειδὲς ἐπὶ τῶν μαγειρείων) linking the stove to that hole.

13–15 *C(ook)*: 'Is there a kitchen?' *H(irer)*: 'There is.' *C*: 'And does it have an outlet for smoke?' *H*: 'Obviously.' *C*: 'Don't 'obviously' me! But does it have an outlet for smoke?' *H*: 'It has.' *C*: 'A nuisance if it's smoky!' *H*: 'This fellow here will be the death of me.' Appreciation of these lively exchanges was long impaired by faulty part-assignments; those in vv. 13 and (up to δῆλον) 14 were worked out by Schweighaeuser, the rest by Th. and (v.15 after ἔχει) his brother K. Kock.

14 μή μοι δῆλον: for the ellipse cf. comm. on 132(127K).1. This response picks up the key element in the hirer's δῆλον ὅτι, but does not necessarily imply that as an unqualified answer (cf. e.g. Alexis 34(33K).6, Men. *Dysk.* 913) δῆλον ὅτι was in Alexis' day still felt to be two separate words, cf. comm. on 179(174K).10 and 185(180K) (κατὰ μόνας).

15 κακόν, εἰ: punctuation (or break in sense) between the second and third syllables of a split anapaest is rare but not unparalleled (e.g. Ar. *Lys.* 731 πάλιν; :: ἀλλά, Dionysius 2.19 τόπον, ὥραν); cf. *CQ* 7 (1957) 195.

178 (172K)

Meineke 3.462 (1), Kock 2.360, Edmonds 2.456, Kassel–Austin 2.122; cf. Dohm, *Mageiros* 103, 137f., Nesselrath, *MK* 303f. and n. 48. On the source, textual condition and dramatic situation of this fr. see introduction to fr. 177(173K). Here (and sometimes elsewhere: e.g. 129(124K), 138(133K)) Alexis confines the cook's boasting to his professional expertise in the kitchen, expressed in typically (cf. introductions to frs. 24, 129(124K)) outrageous and affected language (e.g. the claim to have invented the Lydian κάνδαυλος v. 4, the conceit προσκατέδει τοὺς δακτύλους 5, the use of βατανίων 9 and ἐπιπαίζεται 15, the pretentious miniaturisations of 10–14: all this probably continued from earlier in the scene, cf. 177(173K).2f., 10).

1 ὅτι δέ σοι: so A, with a syllable (⏑) missing at the beginning of the verse. In the absence of preceding context we do not know whether the previous clause (structured e.g. λέγω . . . ὅτι μέν . . .) ended with the initial syllable of v. 1, or whether (more probably) ὅτι itself is corrupt (best <προσ>έτι Schweighaeuser after Musurus's ἔτι, thus complementing παρὰ τοῦτο).

κάνδαυλον: the fr. is cited by Ath. 12.516d to illustrate Athenian familiarity with the dish κάνδαυλος, which (like the word: cf. Chantraine 1.491 s.v., tentatively associating it with Κανδαύλης, the Lydian name for Hermes, Hipponax 3a.1, and for one of their kings, Hdt. 1.7ff.) seems to have originated in Lydia (cf. Ath. 516c–d). The *Marcianus* here preserves for Alexis the Attic spelling, which remained in use until the time of Menander (also Nicostratus 16(17K).2, Philemon 63(60K).3, Menander fr. 397.11 on the evidence of A correct at Ath. 12.517a ~ corrupt at 4.132f), when it began to be replaced by κάνδυλος (Men. fr. 451.6, Evangelus 1.8, a choliambic poet in Powell, *Coll. Alex.* 216f. = fr. 18.15, Plut. *Mor.* 664a, Pollux 6.69, Hesych. and *Suda* s.v.,[1] Σ Ar. *Pax* 123); *Et. Mag.* 488.53 records a variant κονδύλη. Ath. 516e claims that the dish had three (different) forms, without specifying them. One clearly was a sweet cake (πλακοῦς Σ Ar.) whose ingredients were listed as milk and honey (*Et. Mag.*, *Suda*), milk, fat and honey (Phot., first recipe), milk, honey, flour, cheese (Pollux). A second type is implied by the ingredients listed by Hegesippus of Tarentum in Ath. 516d: boiled meat, grated breadcrumbs, cheese, dill and a rich ζωμός (see comm. on 145(141K).8); these would produce a glutinous stew or pilaff, with cheese as the thickening agent. Photius' alternative recipe (bread, cheese, meat) is an abbreviated version of that in Hegesippus, whether or not it derives from Ath. Hesychius mentions cheese, milk, honey and hare, which suggest a sweeter variety of pilaff. We have no means of knowing what kind Alexis had in mind here. Cf. Durham, *Vocabulary* 68.

2 παραθήσομεν: the plural could be a majestic generalisation ('we μάγειροι'), but here more probably is a reference to the fact that on entry the cook was accompanied by two or more assistants (cf. fr.177(173K).12 and comm.). The switch from plural to singular (4, 5), then back to plural (6), possibly back again to singular (11) is *in der griechischen Sprache . . . ungemein häufig* (K.G. 1.86, cf. 83ff.). On the use of παρατίθημι here and later in this fr. (vv.5, 10, cf. end of comm. on vv. 6–11) see comm. on 98(152K).2.

---

[1] Probably also Photius, if Dindorf's correction of the lemma (κάνδυτος in the *Galeanus*) is accepted. When Photius goes on to cite Aristophanes for the use of the word, the reference is most probably to *Pax* 123, where κόνδυλος ('knuckle') puns on κάνδαυλος, cf. Kassel–Austin on Ar. fr. 947(791K).

COMMENTARY

2–3 After ἐδήδοκα A writes v. 3 in lacunose form: <∪–∪> οὐδ᾽ ἀκήκο᾽ οὐδε<–>ποτε (? or οὐδέποτε <∪ ∪>). The first gap may have been caused by omission of e.g. a vocative (but nothing suitable suggests itself), a verbal expression parallel to οὐδ᾽ ἀκήκο᾽ (but not Jacobs's οὐδ᾽ εἶδον, *Addit.* 280f., with the aorist hardly acceptable between two perfects) or an object accusative (κάνδαυλον Meineke, *Cur. Crit.* 50; τοιοῦτον Kock). κάνδαυλον has appropriate punch and is more likely to have been omitted by haplography after two appearances already in the previous six words; cf. A's similar omission of the repeated μῆλα πρόβατα at Ath. 9.382e citing Strato 1.23, where *P.Cairo* 65445 preserves the correct text. That οὐδε<πώ>ποτε plugs the second gap most effectively was first seen by J. Pierson in his edition of Moeris (Leiden 1759) p. 461.

4 θαυμαστὸν ἐμὸν εὕρημα: in apposition to κάνδαυλον. The cook's claim to have invented the dish (on the motif see comm. on 27.1–2) chimes in better with the comic ἀλαζονεία of his class than with historical reality (the dish originated in Lydia, according to Ath.: see on v. 1); it does not warrant any assumption that the cook here was conceived of as Lydian (so A. Giannini, *Acme* 13 (1960) 161).

πάνυ πολὺν δ᾽: sc. κάνδαυλον. Here A punctuates with a raised point after, not before, πάνυ, thus making the adverb qualify θαυμαστόν and not πολύν. Although this would be stylistically possible (cf. K. J. Dover, *CQ* 35 (1985) 332ff., showing that in comedy πάνυ follows the word it qualifies x 88, precedes it x 59), the sense here clearly links πάνυ with πολύν ('if I serve you a very big helping, you'll still be gnawing your fingers as well'), as Casaubon first saw, *Animadv.* 831. The scribal mispunctuation was probably due to a reluctance to accept postponement of δέ to third word in its clause (but see comm. on fr. 4.1 and Dover, *op. cit.* 337f.).

5 προσκατέδει τοὺς δακτύλους: the cook's boast is that his κάνδαυλος will be so delicious that even when his host has consumed an enormous helping, he will additionally (προσ-) eat his own fingers as he licks them clean in the desire to taste every last morsel of this wonder dish. Guests used their fingers in eating and their mouths to lick them clean in a society which had neither forks nor napkins, as Gulick well notes. Alexis' idea here is a comic commonplace, perhaps rooted in popular speech (so Kann, *De iteratis* 68); cf. Aristophon 9.8ff. ἐπεὶ παράθες αὐτοῖσιν ἰχθῦς ἢ κρέας, | κἂν μὴ κατέσθιωσι καὶ τοὺς δακτύλους, | ἐθέλω κρέμασθαι δεκάκις, Plaut. *Pseud.* 881ff. *nam ego ita conuiuis cenam conditam dabo | hodie atque ita suaui suauitate condiam, | ut quisque quicque conditum gustauerit, | ipsus sibi faciam ut digitos praerodat suos*, possibly also Hermippus 23(24K).

On the orthography προσκατέδει see comm. on 182(177K).

6 σαυτῷ γε χαίρων: so A here, preserving Alexis' gruesome wit; you will be 'taking pleasure in *yourself*' (the italics convey the effect of γε intensive,

ΠΑΝΝΥΧΙΣ

Denniston, *GP* 122f.), partly at least because you will be eating a portion of yourself. Failure to appreciate the joke led to numerous conjectures (e.g. αὐτῷ Dobree, *Adv.* 2.338, but the presence of the unemphatic third-person pronoun in an oblique case at line beginning would be suspicious).

6–11 These vv. are vilely corrupt; lacunae, obscure references and textual errors here combine to produce logical and syntactical chaos. Sequential analysis, however, may help us to fix the borders of our ignorance and peer through the glass darkly.

(a.i) In vv. 6–7 after χαίρων A writes ἔρια μὲν ποιήσομεν ἄνθρωπε ποιει (without accent) λευκὰ καὶ βλέπεις, with a gap of half a metron at (or before) the end of v. 7. Kock (cf. my discussion in *Hermes* 93 (1965) 396ff.) well notes that vv. 16–18 of this fr. seem to be structured in a fashion very similar to that of vv. 4–7. In both passages the cook describes his intentions in imaginative language (finger-eating 5 ~ ἐπιπαίζεται 15). At v. 16 the hirer ripostes addressing the cook as ἄνθρωπε, takes up one of the cook's expressions (ἐπίπαιζε ~ ἐπιπαίζεται) turning it into a command, and then adds a further brusque command (ἀπαλλάγηθι). Accordingly it seems sensible to assign v. 7 (so first Daléchamp) also to the hirer, with its introductory ἄνθρωπε, its possibly imperatival (? ποίει) but obscure reference to the cook's equally obscure statement at the end of v. 6 and its probable final command, if A's βλέπεις is rightly emended to βλέπ᾽ εἰς (so first Dobree, *Adv.* 2.338; cf. also Men. *Epitr.* 987 and Gomme–Sandbach, *Comm. ad loc.*). The sequence 'do something and . . .' is normally followed by either another imperative or (in cases where the initial imperative is equivalent to a conditional protasis) a second-person future indicative, but the latter alternative here seems less likely if the *ductus* is close to what Alexis wrote.

(ii) If ποίει λευκά in v. 7 is rightly interpreted as a command ('make them white') which picks up the cook's ἔρια (?) ποιήσομεν of v. 6, one of two conclusions appears inescapable. One is that Alexis' text is correct and its references to 'bands of wool' and their whitening need to be explained as the metaphorical language of a now unknown proverb. By their profession μάγειροι were involved in the religious ceremony of sacrifice (cf. in this scene 177(173K).11; Rankin, ΜΑΓΕΙΡΟΙ 55ff., Dohm, *Mageiros* 38ff., Gomme–Sandbach, *Comm.* on Men. *Dysk.* 646, G. Berthiaume, *Les Rôles du mágeiros* (*Mnemosyne Suppl.* 70, 1982) 17ff.), and objects used on these occasions might be decorated with bands of white wool as symbols of purity and for apotropaic purposes (e.g. S. *OC* 475, Autoclides in Ath. 11.473b = *FGrH* 353 F 1, *Geop.* 15.8; A. Tresp, *Die Fragmente der griechischen Kultschriftsteller* (Giessen 1914) 45ff., W. Burkert, *Homo Necans* (tr. P. Bing, Berkeley 1983) 170). Yet in the absence of evidence for the hypothetised proverb the alternative conclusion that ἔρια is a corruption for some culinary dish seems more likely. Hence ἴτρια *'quidam'* in Daléchamp,

Annot. 782, χόρια Herwerden, *NAC* 32; best θρῖα Jacobi in Meineke 5.ccx, since it alters only one letter (cf. also v. 1 of the new gold page from Hipponion, where M. L. West corrects εριον to θρῖον, *ZPE* 18 (1975) 230f., and Men. *Her.* 38, where G. Lefebvre misread ΕΡΙΑ as ΘΡΙΑ in the first edition of the papyrus (Cairo 1907); cf. also Cobet, *NL* 547) and yields more pointed sense. In Euphron 1.7 an Athenian cook named Chariades (cf. Sosipater 1.11) is credited with the invention of θρῖον τὸ λευκόν as a specially fine dish. In Alexis' time an ordinary θρῖον was still apparently a dish of cooked meat, fish, eggs and/or vegetables wrapped in a fig-leaf (a good account in Σ Ar. *Equ.* 954; cf. comm. on 179(174K).5); we are not told how Chariades improved on this for his white version, but its very existence gives extra support to Jacobi's conjecture. If the cook says he is going to make θρῖα, we might well expect his hirer to riposte 'you'd better make the best kind – white like those of Chariades'.

(iii) In Attic βλέπω εἰς + accusative = most commonly 'I pay attention to/rely on' (LSJ s.v. II.2); something like Meineke's <ὃ δεῖ> is more likely to have fallen out after εἰς (v. 7) than e.g. Dobree's <τὸ πῦρ> (which would perhaps require a fire to be visible on stage, but there is no evidence that the cook was carrying a brazier) or Kock's <φθόρον> (which requires the replacement of βλέπ' by τρέχ' or βάλλ').

(b) Vv.8–9 contain a lacuna of at least one metron, most probably at the end of v. 9; whether one or more lines have additionally been lost, we cannot be certain (but see b.iii below). The gap would be less of a problem if the text presented by A in vv. 8–10 (ἐπᾶν (*sic*) ἀπὸ τῶν κοινῶν ταρίχους ἰχθύων κρεῶν βατανίων εὐθέως δίπυρον παραθήσεις ᾠὸν . . .) construed as coherently as it scanned. It does not, but tentative interpretation and reconstruction are better postponed until some foundations have been laid.

(i) The foodstuffs, of which vv. 8–14 list a remarkable collection. In the defective vv. 8–9 these are 'main-course' foods (fish, meat) mainly in the plural, but the items named in vv. 10–14 are all lighter fare, with small quantities (11, 13f.) and diminutives (τροφάλια 12, βοτρύδιον 13) introduced, and singulars preferred to plurals (except for the cheeses in v. 12, and even they are cut up into smaller pieces); the cook concludes his list by identifying the items in vv. 10–14 as *hors-d'œuvres* (14f.). A distinction is being made apparently between main-course and lighter food.

(ii) The μάγειρος himself, who habitually uses the first person (singular or plural: see on v. 2) when describing his preparations. How then are we to account for the use of the second person in παραθήσεις (v.10)? One possibility is that παραθήσεις is corrupt (hence Kock's παραθήσω κῴόν, i.e. ΗϹΩΚΩΙ → ΗϹΕΙϹΩΙ; or ? παραθείς, εἶτ'); another, that δίπυρον παραθήσεις is an interjected question by the hirer after a verse spoken by the

528

cook and beginning with δίπυρον παραθήσω had been omitted by a scribal *saut du même au même*.

(iii) The opening of v. 8 (ἐπὰν ἀπὸ τῶν A). The cook's previous remark in v. 6 (θρῖα (?) μέν ...) leads us to expect a responsive δέ (or its equivalent), but none appears in v. 8. Although δ' can easily be added after ἐπάν (so Bothe, *PCGF* 555), or ἐπάν be altered to εἶτ' ἄν (given the common confusion between Π and ΙΤ), the possibility that one or more lines have been lost between vv. 7 and 8 must be left open.

(iv) βατανίων in v. 9. The noun's presence here (if not its ending) is guaranteed by the reference back to it in v. 18.

(v) ἀπὸ τῶν κοινῶν ταρίχους ἰχθύων κρεῶν βατανίων in vv. 8–9. When τάριχος and ἰχθῦς appear side by side elsewhere (e.g. Crates 19(17K).2), they are contrasted as pickled/dried and fresh fish respectively. When τάριχος is qualified, it is normally by an adjective (e.g. ἀντακαῖον Antiphanes 78(77K).1, 184(186K); τιλτόν Plato com. 211(193K)), not by a dependent genitive (the expression τάριχος ἰχθύων, being tautologous, never occurs); cf. comm. on 191(186K).5. Accordingly it seems best to interpret τῶν κοινῶν here as a headline and the other genitives as examples in apposition ('everyday foods – pickled/dried fish, fresh fish, meat, Sicilian dishes'). The fact that meat and Sicilian dishes were not everyday foods merely underlines this cook's ἀλαζονεία (see on v. 4).

On these foundations the following text of vv. 8–10 might be constructed with the fewest alterations to the *ductus*:

(A.) ἐπὰν <δ'> ἀπὸ τῶν κοινῶν – ταρίχους, ἰχθύων,
κρεῶν, βατανίων – εὐθέως <ἀπαλλαγῶ>,
<δίπυρον παραθήσω— ∪ — × — ∪ ⏟>.
(B.) δίπυρον παραθήσεις; (A.) ᾠόν κ. τ. λ.

<ἀπαλλαγῶ> is inserted *exempli gratia* to make the transition from main-course to lighter foods more comprehensible. If it happened to be what Alexis wrote, it would add one more word to the list of the cook's expressions picked up by the hirer in vv. 16–18.

9 βατανίων: 'Sicilian dishes' (cf. comm. on 24.3), here presumably with the contents rather than the containers in mind. The cook's choice of this exotic (cf. introduction to this fr.) synonym for the standard Attic diminutive λοπαδίων is angrily attacked by the hirer in v. 18.

10 δίπυρον: sc. ἄρτον, 'biscuit rusk', cf. Alcaeus com. 2(5K), Eubulus 17(18K), Pollux 7.23, Hesych. s.v. δίπυροι ἄρτοι.

ᾠὸν ἐπιτετμημένον: ἐπιτέμνω literally = 'I make a superficial cut in/into' (LSJ s.v., cf. Herwerden, *Coll. Crit.* 127; usually of wounds and gashes, to hands Hdt. 3.8, a vein Hippocr. *Aer.* 22, head Aeschines 2.93), and its use here in a somewhat strained expression ('cut egg' presumably = 'sliced (hard-boiled) egg') is better interpreted as a further instance of this cook's affected language than suspected of corruption (εὖ τετμημένον Blaydes, *Adv.* 2.163; ᾠὰ δίχα τετμημένα or διατετμ. Herwerden, in the plural because a single egg would hardly suffice, but Alexis' cook here deliberately chooses singulars and unrealistic quantities: cf. the quarter kotyle of honey in v. 11, the tiny bunch of grapes and the single pudding in v. 13, which together account for the description of this microcookery as ἐπιπαίζεται in v. 15: one would hardly 'play' with larger amounts).

11 πυόν: τὸ πρῶτον γάλα, ὃ πήγνυται ἑψόμενον (Σ Ar. *Vesp.* 710). Cf. Kock on Cratinus 149(142K).2.

ὀξύβαφον: a small open flattish bowl (see Sparkes–Talcott, *Agora* XII.132ff. and pls. 33, 59, nos. 843–89), used also as a liquid measure = $\frac{1}{4}$ kotyle (68.4 cm³, cf. Lang–Crosby, *Agora* x.39ff.).

ἀποταγηνιῶ: so A (but without accent). If this is correctly transmitted, it is best (*pace* Kassel–Austin) taken with v. 12: 'after cutting fresh pieces of Cythnian cheese, I'll grill them', although one cannot exclude the possibility that the honey mentioned just before was either cooked with or poured on the cheese (on the ancient Greek practice of thus sweetening savouries see Dohm, *Mageiros* 34 n. 4). Toasted cheese makes an excellent light delicacy to set beside the beestings, grapes, etc., and the modern method of preparation coincides exactly with the cook's description. For the use of ἀποταγηνίζω/ἀποτηγανίζω (on the spelling variation see comm. on 115(110K).12) cf. Pherecrates 128(123K), Phrynichus com. 60(57K), Sotades 1.1*, Machon 421 Gow*; the evidence from Alexis here and the asterisked passages (cf. also Phryn. *Praep. Soph.* 16.15 de Borries ἀποταγηνίσαι· ἀντὶ τοῦ ταγηνίσαι) indicates that the verb's meaning is always (*pace* LSJ s.v. and Gow on the Machon passage) 'I grill in a τάγηνον.'

12 τυροῦ τροφάλια χλωρὰ Κυθνίου: the key-word (here Κυθνίου) is postponed to the end of its phrase, as commonly in long comic ῥήσεις (e.g. Ar. *Ach.* 1ff.), where such delaying tactics are deliberately employed in order to retain the audience's attention.[1] Cheese from the island of Cythnos was celebrated and costly (90 drachmas for a talent's weight, Aelian *NA* 16.32 citing Aeschylides περὶ γεωργίας, cf. F. Susemihl, *Geschichte der griechischen Literatur in der Alexandrinerzeit* 1 (Leipzig 1891) 837f.; Pollux 6.63, Steph. Byz. s.v. Κύθνος, cf. Pliny *HN* 13.134; Bürchner in *RE* s.v. *Kythnos* 1, 221.3ff.). The diminutive τροφάλιον, which occurs

---

[1] Hence Dindorf's transposition of Κυθνίου here to second word in the verse, in order to smooth out the rhythm after the caesura, must be resisted. On the failure of some 19th-century scholars to appreciate this comic technique K. J. Dover's remarks in *Fifty Years (and Twelve) of Classical Scholarship* (Oxford 1968) 125 are paradigmatic.

only here, may be the poet's own coinage, designed to emphasise the smallness of the cheeses mentioned (cf. comm. on vv. 10, 13); both it and its primitive τροφαλίς denote the object one handles, while τυρός = the actual substance, cf. Ar. *Vesp.* 838 τροφαλίδα τυροῦ Σικελικήν and Σ *ad loc.* χλωρός applied to cheese = 'fresh' (Phryn. *Praep. Soph.* 127.7 de Borries, cf. e.g. Ar. *Ran.* 559 and Σ, Antiphanes 131(133K).7).

13 βοτρύδιον: with long υ, as most other -ύδιον diminutives in comedy where the text is sound and the length of the vowel can be checked (ἰχθύδιον, cf. comm. on 115(110K).5; ἀφύδιον, ἐγχελύδιον, καρύδιον), but note χλαμύδιον with short υ at Men. fr. 375 (at Antidotus 2.2 the length is uncertain); the length of the υ in the primitive seems immaterial. Cf. P. Chantraine, *La Formation des noms en grec ancien* (Paris 1933) 70. In its literal sense ('tiny bunch of grapes') the word occurs only here in Attic;[1] in later Greek e.g. Longus 2.13, Dioscorides 4.159.1, 181, Artemidorus in Ath. 14.663e. βοτρύδιον τι could be governed here by ἀποταγηνιῶ (cf. Artemidorus' recipe, *loc. cit.*), but more probably it and two following comestibles (χόριον, γλυκύν) are accusatives without an expressed governing verb, with παραθήσω to be supplied by an audience remembering the frequent use of this verb by the cook in the lines preceding (vv. 2, 5, 10, see also end of comm. on vv. 6–11).

χόριον: Schweighaeuser's correction of A's unaccented χορειον. In normal use the singular χόριον = the foetal envelope (especially of sheep and goats) or any similar membrane (LSJ s.v., cf. Gow on [Theoc.] 9.19), but the plural was used also for a sort of pudding made with milk and honey and boiled in one of these membranes (Ath. 14.646e, Σ [Theoc.] *loc. cit.*, Hesych. s.v. χόρια). Hence in culinary contexts like the present we should expect and usually find the plural (Ar. fr. 581(569K).4, ? Cratinus 507(326K), Anaxandrides 42(41K).44, Eubulus 109(110K).4; at Ar. fr. 333(318K).5 cited by Ath. 3.104e–f A has οὐδὲ χόριον οὐδὲ unmetrically in an iambic list of foodstuffs, where both οὐδὲ χόρι' (Dobree, *Adv.* 2.302) and οὐ χόριον (Porson, *Adv.* 63) may be supported as conjectures). Here the cook's unorthodox choice of the singular is clearly part of his affected reduction to the smallest terms of everything that he mentions.

14 γλυκύν: sc. οἶνον, cf. comm. on fr. 60(59K).1.

14–15 It is best (*pace* Kassel–Austin[2]) to punctuate these vv. with a

---

[1] At com. adesp. fr. 962 Kock βοτρύδια = 'ear-rings' (presumably shaped like bunches of grapes); could this have been the normal meaning of the diminutive in Attic Greek, with Alexis introducing its new sense in order to illustrate his cook's linguistic affectations?

[2] Kassel–Austin punctuate with a full stop at the end of v. 15, thus turning τὸ τοιοῦτον μέρος (the τραγήματα) into both 'aftersport' and also the chief part of the dinner. Yet it would be inconsistent if a cook

COMMENTARY

dash (so Kock) at the end of v. 15, and translate 'For such items as these always form, as it were, the aftersport, but the main course of the dinner consists of –.' Thus the ambiguous phrase τὸ τοιοῦτον μέρος is interpreted as the grammatical subject of its clause (with reference to that 'portion' of the dinner in which the guests were served dessert and/or hors-d'œuvres: sc. τραγήματα, cf. comm. on 168(163K).2, 252(250K).1–2) rather than as an internal accusative (= 'in such a way', with μέρος virtually pleonastic, as often in Hellenistic Greek, cf. LSJ s.v. III.2 and Sandbach, *Comm.* on Men. *Epitr.* 234ff., and the verb an impersonal passive, 'there is aftersport'). As subject and in its emphatic position at the beginning of the sentence τὸ τοιοῦτον μέρος leads an audience to expect something striking (and equally affected?) as subject of the balancing clause that follows, but this is never divulged, being forestalled by the hirer's angry interruption in vv. 16–18. Consequently ἐπιπαίζεται is the final example in the fr. of this cook's idiosyncratic use of words (was the verb perhaps adopted by μάγειροι as a cant term for the preparation and serving of τραγήματα?); its use, on top of the cook's other affectations, inflames his hirer into an interruption which prevents our hearing the cook's further plans for the main course.

γίγνεται: see comm. on 37(36K).7.

16–18 The hirer throws back in the cook's face four of his expressions: ἐπίπαιζε (with a play on the word's regular meaning 'mock/laugh at'), the exotic κανδαύλους and βατάνια, and χόρια (now reinstated in its normal culinary plural). W. Headlam, *CR* 10 (1896) 438 aptly compares A. *Sept.* 1045 and Ar. *Equ.* 470.

16 μόνον ἀπαλλάγηθί μου: Casaubon deleted the unmetrical ἀλλ' which A inserts after μόνον (presumably by dittography before ἀπαλλ-). For the use of μόνον with the imperative cf. e.g. Pl. *Phdr.* 262d μόνον δήλωσον ὃ φῄς, Men. *Dysk.* 905 λαθεῖν μόνον προμηθοῦ (so Fraenkel: επιθυμου B), *Mis.* 447 μόνον ἀπόδος, LSJ s.v. μόνος B.II. M. Schmidt, *Philologus* 18 (1862) 231 cites Moeris 190.11 Bekker ἀποφθάρηθί μου, Ἀττικοί· ἀπαλλάγηθί μου, Ἕλληνες (similarly Thomas Magister 16.9f. Ritschl, cf. Hesych. s.v. ἀποφθάρηθί μου) in support of a conjecture that Alexis wrote ἀποφθάρηθί μου here, but his argument fails for two reasons. Moeris' allegation must be considered of doubtful validity so long as similar expressions are attested for Aristophanes (*Vesp.* 484 (ἆρ' ἄν, ὦ πρὸς τῶν θεῶν, ὑμεῖς ἀπαλλαχθεῖτέ μου;) and Plato (*Gorg.* 491c, cited on vv. 17–18 below). Secondly, uses of the imperative ἀπαλλάγηθι/-γητε are familiar in Menander (*Asp.* 245f. ἐκποδὼν ἀπαλλάγηθ' ἀπὸ τῆς θύρας, *Dysk.* 926, *Mis.* 141).

---

who in the earlier part of the fr. praised his κάνδαυλος so extravagantly then claimed a few lines later that in fact the τραγήματα were the real κεφαλὴ δείπνου.

ΠΑΝΝΥΧΙΣ

17–18 The two vv. at the end of the fr. are defective in A, with losses of ¾ metron at the beginning of 17 and after penthemimeral caesura in 18. There is little doubt that Dobree's supplements, *Adv.* 2.338 <τοὺς σοὺς δὲ> κανδαύλους and πᾶσαν <ἀφανιεῖς> τὴν ἡδονήν restore the sense, if not the precise wording, of what Alexis originally wrote. Even so, the idiomatic use in Attic of ἀπαλλάττομαι + participle in the sense 'stop –ing' (e.g. Pl. *Gorg.* 491c εἰπὼν ἀπαλλάγηθι; to the passages cited by LSJ s.v. ἀπαλλάσσω B.II.7d may be added from comedy Ar. *Eccl.* 1082, *Plut.* 271) leads me to believe Dobree's text requires slight alteration and repunctuation: ἀπαλλάγηθί μου | <τοὺς σούς γε> κ. λέγων καὶ χ. καὶ | βατάνια· πᾶσαν <ἀφανιεῖς> τὴν ἡ.; cf. *Hermes* 93 (1965) 308f. For the epexegetic use of γε with participles see Denniston, *GP* 139; for asyndeton in explanatory clauses, K.G. 2.344.

179 (174K)

Meineke 3.465 (III), Kock 2.362, Edmonds 2.458, Kassel–Austin 2.124, cf. Nesselrath, *MK* 304. This fr. is the whole or part of a speech addressed by the cook (as Ath. himself states at 4.170b when introducing it[1]) to his hirer after (but perhaps only shortly after) the scene (or scene portion) from which frs. 177(173K) and 178(172K) derive. In the interim the cook has had time to enter his hirer's kitchen and explore its many deficiencies. The speech, which lists twenty-one items needed by but apparently unavailable to the speaker, draws most of its humour (like many such catalogues in ancient comedy, cf. introductions to frs. 84 and 132(127K)) from the opportunity it affords for patter delivery, but it contrasts with the norm (as do e.g. the briefer lists at Alexis 96(92K) and Men. *Dysk.* 505ff., cf. Gomme–Sandbach *ad loc.*, spoken by an old husband and Knemon respectively) in one particularity: each item in the list is (here asyndetically) negatived.

1 κύκλῳ δεήσει περιτρέχειν: see comm. on 138(133K).3. One of the cooks in Plaut. *Aul.* 335ff. (adapted from Alexis' Λέβης? See introduction to that play) makes a similar complaint: *huccine detrusti me ad senem parcissimum? | ubi si quid poscam, usque ad rauim poscam prius | quam quicquam detur.* Could the hirer in Alexis' Παννυχίς with his allegedly inadequate kitchen also have been portrayed as *senex parcissimus*?

2 δεῖπνον αἰτήσεις: the asyndeton emphasises the quick succession of the actions described in vv. 1–2a and 2b–3a: cf. K.G. 2.340ff.

3 ἤδη παρελθών: sc. 'as soon as you've entered the house'. The

---

[1] The fr. and its introductory comment appear in A's carefully transmitted text (only one error in eleven vv.), but are omitted by Epit.

533

COMMENTARY

transmission is correct; the cook describes a situation where his hirer demands that a dinner be served immediately on his arrival, before the cook is ready. It is not clear whether the cook's words imply that his hirer left the stage by one of the side entrances after the scene containing frs. 177(173K) and 178(172K), or whether the latter's sudden arrival is merely imagined as a future possibility. The cook himself on the other hand must have entered his hirer's house after his earlier conversation with him, otherwise he would not have known about his hirer's kitchen. παρέρχομαι and πάρειμι (εἶμι *ibo*) occur often in drama with εἴσω (and synonymous expressions) in the sense 'I go inside (a stage-house)', e.g. A. *Choeph.* 849, S. *El.* 1337, Eur. *Hel.* 451, Ar. *Nub.* 853, Men. *Asp.* 95, *Kol.* 149 Austin (*CGFP* p. 178), *Pk.* 349; here and at Men. *Sam.* 75 the same meaning is conveyed by παρελθών on its own. Cf. also R. Renehan, *Glotta* 47 (1969) 231f.

οὐκ ἔχων δέ: the particle is postponed (as commonly elsewhere in Attic prose and verse: cf. Denniston, *GP* 186f.) in order to avoid the juxtaposition of οὐ and δέ.

4 ἄνηθον ... ὀρίγανον: see comm. on 132(127K).5, 7.

5 θρῖον: in a list of ingredients θρῖον must be the leaf (normally a fig-leaf; when rarely from a different plant, the fact is deemed worthy of comment by ancient grammarians, e.g. Ath. 15.684a on Nicander fr. 74.48 Gow–Scholfield) rather than the food wrapped in it (cf. comm. on 178(172K).6–11, a.ii).

ἀμυγδάλας: almonds (the tree now *Prunus amygdalus*; cf. Wagler in *RE* s.v. Ἀμυγδαλῆ 1090.51ff., Hehn, *Kulturpflanzen* 393ff., W. K. Pritchett, *Hesperia* 25 (1956) 182, André, *Alimentation* 85f., R. Watkins in N. W. Simmonds (ed.), *Evolution of Crop Plants* (London and New York 1976) 242ff.). Accentuation of the word was disputed in antiquity; according to Herodian 1.321.21ff. Lentz and Ath. 2.52f–53b the fruit was ruled paroxytone by Aristarchus, Pamphilus and Tryphon, perispomenon by Philoxenus, oxytone by 'others'.

σκόροδον: garlic (*Allium sativum*), a plant of central-Asian origin, known only in cultivation; cf. Stadler in *RE* s.v. *Lauch* 986.61ff., Hehn 193ff., André 20, G. D. McCollum in Simmonds, *op. cit* on v. 5, 53ff.

σίραιον: see comm. on 132(127K).8.

6–7 Dobree's transposition (*Adv.* 2.308) οὐχὶ βολβὸν οὐ | γήτειον eliminates A's unacceptable scazon in v. 6 (οὐχὶ γήτειον | οὐ βολβὸν) by a minimal change (for a parallel error, see comm. on 140(135K).6; for οὐ at line-end negativing a following word, 96(92K).3), and is preferable to Meineke's conjecture (printed by Kassel–Austin) replacing γήτειον by γήθυον, with the suggestion that the former word had supplanted the latter in A as a gloss. Both words designated the same vegetable, but γήτειον was already obsolete in Lucian's day (see comm. on 132(127K).7)

534

and so must be considered an unlikely choice for a glossator's explanation; γήτειον in any case is attested for Alexis, but not γήθυον. On the identifications of γήτειον and βολβός see comm. on 132(127K).7 and 167(162K).13 respectively.

7 κύμινον: see comm. on 132(127K).6.

ἅλας: plural, cf. on 138(133K).6.

8 ξύλ': 'firewood', a widespread usage (Homeric, e.g. *Il.* 8.507, 547, 24.778, *Od.* 14.418; Attic, also Ar. *Vesp.* 301, *Pax* 1133, *Thesm.* 726, cf. Theophr. *Char.* 30) by the side of the more precise καύσιμα ξύλα (Alexis 308(307K) and comm.).

σκάφην: a large, circular or rectangular receptacle of wood, stone or terracotta, often (but not always: cf. Plut. *Rom.* 3, two boys could hide in one) shallow, used for a wide variety of purposes: e.g. holding milk (Hom. *Od.* 9.222f. using the form σκαφίς) or honey (Antiphanes 224(225K).3, cf. σκαφίς Theoc. 5.59); cooking (here and Pollux 10.102, cf. σκαφίς Anaxippus 6.3); kneading dough (Pollux 6.64, 7.22); holding freshly baked bread (Timocles 35(33K)); washing the person (A. fr. 225, Hippocr. *Steril.* (2.)234, Pollux 10.77); washing grain (Hesych. s.v. πύελος); carrying objects in religious processions (*IG* i².844.6, ii².1388.46, *Et. Mag.* 155.7ff. s.v. ἀσκοφορεῖν). Cf. Leonard in *RE* s.v. *Skaphe* 1, 439.34ff., D. A. Amyx, *Hesperia* 27 (1958) 231f., B. A. Sparkes, *JHS* 82 (1962) 126f.

τήγανον: on the object and its orthography see comm. on 115(110K).12.

9 ἱμονιάν: the Attic word (cf. Moeris s.v.) for τὸ σχοινίον εἰς ὃ δεσμεῖται ὁ κάδος δι' οὗ τὸ ὕδωρ ἐκ τῶν φρεάτων ἀνέλκουσιν (Σ Lucian p. 54 Rabe). Cf. W. Headlam, comm. on Herodas 5.11.

λάκκον denoted both a wide underground pit for storing wine, olive-oil, etc. (e.g. Xen. *Anab.* 4.2.22, *Suda* s.v. λ 60 Adler) and a water cistern (Apollodorus of Gela 1, cf Anaxilas 3 ὕδατος . . . λακκαίου). The placing of the word here between well-rope and well suggests that Alexis had the second meaning in mind. Ar. *Eccl.* 154f. plays maliciously on the double usage when placing ἐν τοῖς καπηλείοισι λάκκους . . .ὕδατος, cf. Ussher, comm. *ad loc.* and Gow on Machon 282. εἶδον after λάκκον provides a welcome second verb to help in governing the long list of accusatives in vv. 4–9; A. Palmer's conjecture ἔνδον (in Blaydes, *Adv.* 1.113) is both unnecessary and tempting, since wells and cisterns were often so described, being placed in the interior courtyards of real and stage houses (see comm. on 184(179K).3).

10 στάμνος: apparently in ancient Athens a general term for a large earthenware amphora in various shapes, used for water, wine or oil; there is no evidence to link it exclusively (or even at all!) with the shape that modern scholars have labelled 'stamnos' (sc. a high-shouldered, short-necked jar with two handles normally set vertical or at a slant on the

COMMENTARY

shoulder, cf. Richter–Milne, *Shapes* 8f. and figs. 64–8). See also D. A. Amyx, *Hesperia* 27 (1958) 190ff., B. Philippaki, *The Attic Stamnos* (Oxford 1967), Sparkes–Talcott, *Agora* XII.187 n. 1.

At fr. 133(128K) the cook's list contains 20 items, here 21; only five are common to both.

Although διὰ κενῆς is more correctly spelled as two words (cf. LSJ s.v. διακενῆς) than as one (only if διά here functions independently as a preposition – presumably indicating manner, LSJ s.v. A.III.1.c – does the genitival ending become explicable), it is doubtful if there was any clear conception in the minds of most ancient authors (as they wrote their scripts without word-division) whether the expression was one word or two; cf. Schwyzer 1.625 and my comm. on 185(180K) (κατὰ μόνας) and 177(173K).14. In such phrases (e.g. διὰ πάσης, ἀπὸ πρώτης, ἐκ καινῆς, ἐξ ἡμισείας) ellipse of a feminine noun is normally – but not always legitimately – assumed, cf. comm. on 116(111K).1.

11 ἔχων μάχαιραν: cooks characteristically appear carrying one or more μάχαιραι, large knives capable of use also as choppers (cf. G. Berthiaume, *Les Rôles du mágeiros* (*Mnemosyne Suppl.* 70, 1982), especially 109f. n. 14, 106 n. 126), mentioned in Attic comedy (e.g. also Ar. *Pax* 1017f., Men. *Asp.* 222, *Sam.* 284, Philemon jun. 1.7*, Posidippus 1.9f. com. adesp. frs. 289a.7 Austin* and 599 Kock; asterisked references have ἔχων μάχαιραν; cf. also Plaut. *Aul.* 417, Euclio: *cultrum habes*. Congrio: *coquom decet*, at v. 398 a cook's assistant has the name Machaerio) and portrayed on vases earlier than any extant comedy (e.g. Attic black-figure olpe in Heidelberg inv. 253, 6th century, plate 5.2 in B(erthiaume); Boeotian lekanis lid in Schloss Fasanerie, Adolphseck inv. 120, *c.* 500, pl. 6 B.; Attic red-figure lekythos at von Schoen collection in Munich, formerly Lugano, inv. 62, 480–470 BC = Beazley, *ARV*² 691.19, pl. 15.1 B.; Attic red-figure pelike in Erlangen inv. 486, *c.* 470 = *ARV*² 250.21, pl. 14.1 B.; Boeotian red-figure pelike in Munich inv. 2347, second quarter of 5th century, pl. 14.2 B.; black-figure pelike in Fondation Custodia, Paris inv. 3650, pl. 19 B.). Chopping knives suit μάγειροι particularly well in their sacrificial and butchering roles (Berthiaume 17ff.); although neither μάγειρος nor μάχαιρα has an assured derivation (cf. especially P. Chantraine, *La Formation des noms en grec ancien* (Paris 1933) 234 and *Dict. Etym.* s.vv., Frisk s.vv.), V. Pisani's suggestion that the two words may be etymologically linked (*Revue internationale des études balkaniques* I/1 (1934) 255ff.) has attracted even if it has not totally convinced philologists (e.g. P. Kretschmer, *Glotta* 26 (1936) 38f., cf. Dohm, *Mageiros* 72ff., Ch. B. Dedoussi, comm. (Athens 1965) on Men. *Sam.* 69, her numbering).

περιεζωσμένος: the *Marcianus* here has the Ionic form (cf. Hippocr. *Artic.* 14 = 4.124 Littré, probably Hdt. 2.85, 7.69) of the perfect passive/ middle participle of ζώννυμι and its compounds, with intrusive sigma, which prevailed in *Koine* and post-classical Greek (cf. K.B. 2.437). In its place H. van Herwerden, *Mnemosyne* 14 (1886) 186 substituted the Attic form -εζωμένος, which is attested on inscriptions down at least to the end of the 4th century (Meisterhans–Schwyzer 185). He may be right to suspect the MS of a modernising corruption (cf. Thuc. 1.6 διεζωσμένοι MSS, -ωμένοι Phot. and *Suda* s.v. σέσωται), but it is impossible to be sure which form an author like Alexis, who wrote in the period when the *Koine* was developing, would have used in an undated play.

The interpretation of περιεζωσμένος here and elsewhere (e.g. Ar. *Av.* 1148, Ezekiel *Exag.* 180, LXX *Exod.* 12.11, Paus. 1.44.1, Plut. *Mor.* 168d; cf. περιεζῶσθαι Anaxandrides 42(41K).12) is disputed,[1] but the evidence from literature and art generally supports a translation (when the participle/verb is passive or intransitive middle) 'with the tunic supported by a waist-belt' (cf. Dedoussi on Men. *Sam.* 68, her numbering). In this style of dress the χιτών was apparently drawn up above the knees (Lady M. M. Evans, *Chapters on Greek Dress* (London 1893) 45 and fig. 39) and then either a loose fold (κόλπος) was formed above the belt and the lower legs were left unencumbered, or alternatively the χιτών was worn like a modern bath-towel, doubled and hanging down over the belt, with the arms and upper body left free. Although the former style may be identified on two statues of (?) cook-sacrificers from Cyprus now in the Ringling Museum of Art, Sarasota, Fa. (O. Masson, *BCH* 30 (1966) 17ff. and figs. 12, 13), the latter one was clearly more appropriate for a cook working in a hot kitchen; we find it portrayed on the Adolphseck, von Schoen, Erlangen and (inv. 2347) Munich vases discussed in the preceding comment; the well-known Myrina terracotta figurine of a comic cook (Berlin inv. 7953; C. Robert, *Die Masken der neueren attischen Komödie*

---

[1] Most scholars (e.g. Dindorf in *TGL* s.v. περίζωμα, Meineke 3.186, Rankin, ΜΑΓΕΙΡΟΙ 71f., LSJ s.v. περίζωμα, Dohm, *Mageiros* 71) interpret περιεζωσμένος here as equivalent to ἔχων περίζωμα (cf. Hegesippus 1.7) or περιζώστραν (Anaxandrides 70(69K)), with the assumption that these nouns denote an apron rather than a style of dress. In ancient art, however, there is no certain example of a cook represented as wearing an apron (the garment identified as an apron on the Heidelberg olpe e.g. by B. Schweitzer, *JDAI* 44 (1929) 117ff. could be a loin-cloth; that on the Berlin terracotta could be a ἱμάτιον doubled over a waist-belt and not the apron which most interpreters assume). περίζωμα and περιζώστρα might logically denote any article of clothing secured by a belt; in post-classical Greek it was generally restricted to the loin-cloth (= *subligaculum*; cf. Dindorf *loc. cit.*, E. Saglio in Dar.–Sag. s.v. *Cinctus* 1172B), but Attic writers normally called that garment διάζωμα (Thuc. 1.6.5) or ᾦα λουτρίς (Hermippus 76(53K), Pherecrates 68(62K)).

COMMENTARY

(Halle 1911) fig. 26, M. Bieber, *Die Denkmäler zum Theaterwesen im Altertum* (Berlin and Leipzig 1920) fig. 72.2 and *History of the Greek and Roman Theater*² (Princeton 1961) fig. 379) is perhaps an example of a ἱμάτιον worn similarly (see p. 537 n. 1 above); cf. also Pollux 4.119 τῷ δὲ μαγείρῳ (sc. in comedy) διπλῆ ἄγναπτος ἡ ἐσθής, a reference doubtless to the bath-towel doubling of the garment. The same style of dress is adopted by a fishmonger on a Campanian krater of the mid-4th century from Lipari now in Cefalú (G. E. Rizzo, *Dedalo* 7 (1926) 403ff., A. D. Trendall, *The Red-figured Vases of Lucania, Campania and Sicily* 1 (Oxford 1957) 207f. no. 54 and *The Red-figured Vases of Paestum* (British School at Rome 1987) 39 no. 82; frontispiece of Thompson, *Fishes*), a shepherd boy on an Attic red-figured krater in Boston, end of 5th century (Beazley, *ARV*² 1149.9; figured in K. Schefold, *Die Bildnissen der antiken Dichter, Redner und Denker* (Basle 1943) 223, a carpenter on an early Attic red-figured cup in London (*ARV*² 179.1, fig. 124 in J. Boardman, *Athenian Red Figure Vases* (London 1975), and a sculptor on a late-archaic Attic red-figured cup in Munich (*ARV*² 401.2, fig. 264 in Boardman).

To be περιεζω(σ)μένος in classical Athens implied the status of an artisan (cf. the bricklaying ducks at Ar. *Av.* 1148) and so brought disrepute to Cleon ([Arist.] *Ath. Pol.* 28.3), yet for a μάγειρος the dress symbolised his craft (Hegesippus 1.6ff., cf. the anecdote in Plut. *Mor.* 182d).

180 (175K)

Meineke 3.466 (IV), Kock 2.363, Edmonds 2.460, Kassel–Austin 2.124; cf. A. M. Desrousseaux in *Mélanges offerts à M. Octave Navarre* (Toulouse 1935) 141f. Ath. 3.96a introduces this fr. with the words ἄλεξις ... κἂν παννυχίδι ἐρίθοισιν ἡμίοπτα ... (so exactly A: Epit. omits both fr. and reference). In view of Ath.'s three citations of this play elsewhere (12.516d, 4.170b, 6.248a = frs. 178(172K), 179(174K), 182(177K): see introduction to Παννυχίς) with both alternative titles, Musurus' conjecture here κἂν Παννυχίδι <ἢ> 'Ερίθοισιν (with the fr. beginning at ἡμίοπτα) seemed intelligent, but Ath. never uses the -οισι(ν) form of the dative plural when citing Attic titles. Hence Dindorf suggested either deletion of -ιν or its interpretation as ἴν' = the first word of the fr. It is, however, possible to accept A's text here just as it stands, with Παννυχίδι as the only title named (cf. Ath. 9.385f introducing fr. 177(173K)) and ἐρίθοισιν the fr.'s opening word (so Desrousseaux: such people were likely to be named in a comedy which took its alternative title from them). Desrousseaux construed ἐρίθοισιν (as a dative of advantage) with the remainder of v. 1 and the first three words of v. 2, suggesting that the hired workers were the intended recipients of the meal which was being prepared; this is improbable, since such workers (of either sex) did not belong to the class of people normally invited in later Greek comedy as we know it (cf. Men. *Dysk.* 563ff., 607ff.) to dinners for which cooks had been engaged. If ἐρίθοισιν is part of the citation, it is more likely to be the last word of an otherwise lost preceding clause, clumsily included in the citation (a not infrequent habit in Ath., cf. *PCPS* 196 (1970) 2f.).

The speaker seems to be the cook once again, at a later stage in the action than frs. 177(173K), 178(172K) and 179(174K), with the meal now in active preparation.[1]

2 κρεᾴδι': for the spelling see comm. on 27.5.

περίκομμ': see comm. on 137(132K).

ἀπόλλυται: 'is being spoiled', sc. by overcooking, which would leave the meat dry or charred. This culinary use of ἀπόλλυμι is unparalleled, so far as I know, in Greek comedy or elsewhere doubtless through the accidents of preservation, but cf. *corrumpo* in Roman comedy (a meal Plaut. *Pseud.* 892, Ter. *Ad.* 588; fish *Ad.* 421). The lack of Greek parallels led Desrousseaux to condemn ἀπόλλυται as corrupt and to conjecture in its place ἀπολέλυται; but this verb is not used of meat, single words scanning ∪ ∪ ∪ ∪ — are avoided in later comedy at the end of iambic trimeters and the conjecture destroys a neat chiastic sequence: underroasted, overroasted, boiled, underboiled.

3 ὁ γόγγρος: see comm. on 83.

ἀκροκώλι': pigs' trotters were generally boiled in the ancient world (e.g. Ar. fr. 4, Pherecrates 113(108K).14, Teleclides 51(48K)) just as they are today.

181 (176K)

Meineke 3.466 (v), Kock 2.363, Edmonds 2.460, Kassel–Austin 2.125. The fr. (cited by Ath. 11.483e, in A but not Epit.) describes an incident involving two unidentified (but see below on κώθωνα v. 1) characters at a party.

1 A begins the verse unmetrically[2] εἶτ' εν (*sic*) τετρακότυλον; Porson's

---

[1] There would be one other possibility if Dindorf were right in beginning the fr. with ἵν' (= 'where'). In that case the cook could be describing a situation where the occurrences described in the fr. had previously occurred or could be imagined to occur, and then the fr. might belong to the sequence of scenes from which frs. 177–9 derive.

[2] In the second half of the first metron it produces a proceleusmatic which is foreign to Attic comedy; see especially the judicious and thorough study of H. J. Newiger, *Hermes* 89 (1961) 175ff., effectively demolishing the arguments of C. von Holzinger in its favour, comm. on Ar. *Plut.* 1011

COMMENTARY

conjecture εἶτα τετρακότυλον (his edition of Eur. *Med.* (Cambridge 1801), comm. on v. 48, his numbering) is preferable to Th. Bergk's εἶτεν τρικότυλον (in Meineke 5.ccxi, long before Kaibel in his edition of Ath.). Up at least to the end of the 4th century the forms εἶτεν and ἔπειτεν were confined to dialects other than Attic (e.g. Doric: stage Megarian in Ar. *Ach.* 745; Messenian, Boeotian: Schwyzer 1.629; Pindar has both ἔπειτα and -τεν; Ionic: *SIG*³ 57.29, Miletus, 5th century, cf. Aelius Dionysius ε 25 Erbse citing Hdt., but the MSS of Hdt. give ἔπειτα normally, -τε occasionally, -τεν never, those of the Hippocratic corpus virtually always εἶτα and ἔπειτα, -τεν once and an error implying -τεν once, cf. H. Diels, *Hermes* 46 (1911) 267, 283f.; see also F. Bechtel, *Die griechischen Dialekte* 3 (Berlin 1924) 231) and condemned by Atticists (Ael. Dion., Phrynichus *Ecl.* p. 69.3 Fischer) without any sign of dissent from e.g. the Antiatticist. The spread of εἶτεν to *Koine* Greek (e.g. Machon 458, cf. Headlam on Herodas 2.52 and Schwyzer *loc. cit.*) doubtless accounts for its presence here in A as a modernising substitution.

ἐπεσόβει: 'he (?) was passing', perhaps a colloquialism when the object is a cup, not attested elsewhere with this compound to my knowledge, but cf. Philostratus jun. *Imag.* 3 σοβεῖν ... τὴν κύλικα, Amphis 18 ὁ παῖς σοβείτω τοῖς ποτηρίοις συχνούς (where lack of context makes both text and meaning doubtful), Men. *Theoph.* fr. 3 τὸ πρῶτον περισοβεῖ ποτήριον, similarly Alciphron 3.19.6, 39.2; intransitive 4.13.11 περιεσόβουν αἱ κύλικες, evidencing a wide range of constructions.

κώθωνα: a type of cup allegedly originating in Sparta and particularly associated with soldiers (presumably because it was portable and did not spill readily: e.g. Ar. *Pax* 1094, Critias in Ath. 11.483b = *FHG* 2.66f. fr. 3 = Diels–Kranz 2.39f. β 34, Plut. *Lycurgus* 9, cf. Theopompus com. 55(54K).1: even on sea voyages, Archilochus fr. 4.6 West, Ar. *Equ.* 600; could it perhaps identify presenter and/or recipient here in Alexis as soldiers? Cf. Nesselrath, *MK* 262f.). Ath. 11.483b–484c assembles interesting material about its shape and function, but neither the information given there and elsewhere in ancient literature (e.g. Heniochus 1.2f. κυκλοτερῆ βραχύωτον παχύστομον | κώθωνα; Theopompus com. 55(54K) κώθωνος ἐκ στρεψαύχενος, 'twisting the neck' because the drinker needed to tilt his head backwards to drink from it; Polemon in Ath. 484b–c = *FHG* 3.133 fr. 60 κ. μόνωτον ῥαβδωτόν, a common shape; Critias *loc. cit.* ἄμβωνας ἔχων, 'with lips (? curving inwards)', cf. R. C. Ross, *Glotta* 49 (1971) 251ff.; in Xen. *Cyr.* 1.2.8 small enough for boys to carry, here in Alexis more precisely τετρακότυλον = 1094.4 cm³ or nearly two pints, comm. on

---

(*SB Vienna* 218/3 (1940) 276ff.), cf. L. Strzelecki, *Eos* 51 (1961) 261ff., West, *Greek Metre* 89.

116(111K).2, p. 326 n. 1) nor the evidence from archaeology (a fragment of a one-handled cup from Isthmia stamped κοθον on its base, O. Broneer, *Hesperia* 28 (1959) 335 and pl. 70, B. A. Sparkes, *JHS* 95 (1975) 129; a series of cups with rattling pebbles concealed within the fabric, one of which Eubulus 56.3 describes as κωθωνοχειλῆ, cf. Hunter *ad loc.*, B. B. Shefton, *Arch. Rep.* 16 (1969/70) 61f. and figs. 19, 20, M. Vickers, *JHS* 90 (1970) 199ff. and pls. iv, v, A. Seeberg, *JHS* 92 (1972) 183f. and pl. xxv; all two-handled cups) enables us to link the term κώθων securely with any one ancient shape or style of vase, although many attempts have been made (e.g. (i) the shape labelled 'kothon' by modern art-historians, illustrated at the end of vol. 5 of Gulick's Loeb edition of Ath., pl. 3, but this type of cup was almost certainly used for other purposes, such as carrying perfume, see Richter–Milne, *Shapes* 21f., Sparkes–Talcott, *Agora* xii.180f.; (ii) the 'lakaina', E. Kirsten in K. Schauenburg (ed.), *Charites. Studien zur Altertumswissenschaft, E. Langlotz gewidmet* (Bonn 1957) 110ff., but see Ross, *loc. cit.*; (iii) more promisingly the 'pilgrim's flask', which tilts the neck backwards for drinking, P. Mingazzini, *Arch. Anz.* (1967) 344ff.; 'yet no one shape will meet all the literary requirements' B. A. Sparkes, *JHS* 95 (1975) 129 in a judicious survey).

2 Porson (*loc. cit.* on v. 1) recognised that παλαιὸν (his correction of A's πλέον) οἴκων κτῆμα here echoed the opening words of the tutor's entrance speech at Eur. *Med.* 49, with its application humorously switched from the nurse (in Eur.) to a drinking-cup. Philemon 82(79K).1–2 parodies part of the nurse's response to the tutor (*Med.* 57f.), but both the burlesqued passages with their memorable phraseology could have been well-known tags, and so there is no call to assume that a new production of *Med.* must have been mounted shortly before either of the comedies.

182 (177K)

Meineke 3.467 (vi), Kock 2.363, Edmonds 2.460, Kassel–Austin 2.125.

ἔσῃ: here A (Ath. 6.248a: Epit. omits the fr.) has ἔσῃι, for which Dindorf substituted ἔσει. The MSS of the Alexis frs. (A of Ath. in the following list except where otherwise stated) give the second person singular indicative middle/passive of thematic verbs sometimes as -ει/ -εῖ (ὠνεῖ 16.10, βούλει 140(135K).2 and 17, ἀναγνώσει 140(135K).3), sometimes as -ῇ/-ηι (γνώσῃ 1.2 = all MSS of Diog. Laert. 3.37), εὔχῃ 205.7(202.3K), παύσῃ 287(286K).2 = Epit. MSS of Ath. 1.34d), once both forms conflictingly (at 178(172K).5 = Ath. 12.516c προσκατεδεῖ AC, -εδῇ E). The variations can be explained in different ways: (1) Alexis (originating outside Attica) was inconsistent in his orthography (with -ει contemporary Attic, -ῃ generally non-Attic), and the scribes preserve or compound the inconsistency; (2) Alexis wrote -ει and the variations were introduced by

COMMENTARY

Hellenistic scribes who in *Koine* Greek generally preferred -η but commonly wrote βούλει and allowed both ἔσει and ἔση. Here Kassel–Austin opt for ἔση, other editors (with my hesitant support) for -ει. See K.B. 1.184, 2.60f., Meisterhans–Schwyzer 165, Schwyzer 1.668, Mayser 1.128f., 328, Threatte 1.368ff.

περιπατῶν: see comm. on 91(87K).2.

σιτόκουρος: Ath. 6.248a–b cites the three known occurrences of the adjective (also Men. frs. 207 ὀκνηρός, πάντα μέλλων, σιτόκουρος, ὁμολογῶν | παρατρέφεσθαι, 352.2f. σιτόκουρον ἄθλιον | < × – ∪ > εἰς τὴν οἰκίαν εἰλήφαμεν) and defines its meaning as ἄχρηστον καὶ μάτην τρεφόμενον (whence Hesych. s.v., cf. Eustath. 1854.5 ὃς ἄεργος χοίνικος ἐθέλει ἅπτεσθαι, καὶ μάλιστα νέος ὤν, κληθείη ἂν σιτόκουρος) expressly with the help of the Menandrean contexts. Probably either contemporary slang or a comic coinage (? by Alexis here) from σῖτος and κείρω (cf. Blaydes, *Adv.* 2.163), 'bread-cutting/ravaging', it more probably (*pace* Ath.) describes a parasite's ravenous appetite than a sluggard's uselessness. Cf. Durham, *Vocabulary* 91. Compare *cibicida* in Lucilius 718 Marx (with reference to the parasites of his own country), coined perhaps by analogy with σιτόκουρος (cf. Kappelmacher in *RE* s.v. *Lucilius* 4, especially 1621.41ff.).

Παράσιτος

Casaubon, *Animadv.* 417, Meineke 1.339, 377, 381, Kock 2.363f., Ribbeck, *Kolax* 1ff., 18, 20f., Kaibel in *RE* s.v. *Alexis* 9, 1470.6ff., J. M. E. M. Brinkhoff, *Neophilologus* 32 (1948) 127ff., in *RE* Ziehen s.v. Παράσιτοι 1377.61ff., Wüst and Hug s.v. *Parasitos* 1381.4ff., Webster, *SM* 164, *SLGC* 50, 64f., *CQ* 2 (1952) 17f., W. G. Arnott, *GRBS* 9 (1968) 161ff., Nesselrath, *LP* 102ff. and n. 314, *MK* 312ff. From Alexis' Παράσιτος, a title shared with Antiphanes and Diphilus, three frs. are preserved (183(178K), 184(179K) in Ath. 10.421d, 3.123f; 185(180K) in Diog. Laert. 3.28). These tell us nothing about the plot, but 183(178K) (part of an expository monologue, which may or may not have been the prologue) identifies and describes at some length the title figure, while 184(179K) and 185(180K) yield some information about the play's date. The combined data enable us to uncover an interesting detail in the history of 4th-century Attic comedy and language.

 Fr. 185(180K) refers to Plato in terms which suggest that the philosopher was still alive, and 184(179K) implies that comedies by Araros, the son of Aristophanes, were still being produced. Plato died in 348/7, and the career of Araros extended from at least 387 (*IG* ii².2318.196 = III B 1 col. 2.44 Mette, cf. Pickard-Cambridge, *DFA*² 105, 107, where the text after secure supplementation commemorates a victory at the Dionysia of

ΠΑΡΑΣΙΤΟΣ

that year, but whether this was a production of one of Araros' own plays or of one of his father's, is unknown; Araros produced Aristophanes' last two plays Κώκαλος and Αἰολοσίκων after 388, according to Ar. *Plut.* hypothesis 4 Hall–Geldart = 3 Coulon) to overlap Alexis' early career. Alexis' Παράσιτος accordingly must have been produced in the 350s or very early 340s (cf. Webster, *locc. citt.*, Nesselrath, *MK* 313f.).

Before Alexis' play it seems that the word for 'parasite' in everyday use was still κόλαξ, as it had been in the late 5th century (e.g. in Eupolis' Κόλακες of 421 named after its chorus of parasites; in Aristophanes κόλαξ occurs four times, κολακεύω twice, παράσιτος never; cf. Ribbeck 1ff., Starkie on Ar. *Vesp.* 45, Durham, *Vocabulary* 85, W. G. Arnott, *GRBS* 9 (1968) 161 n. 3; Phrynichus, *Ecl.* 70.68 Fischer παρασίτους οὐκ ἔλεγον οἱ ἀρχαῖοι ἐπ' ὀνείδους, ὡς νῦν, ἀλλὰ κόλακας), while παράσιτος existed only as a technical term in certain cults (e.g. of Heracles at Cynosarges) for 'companion of the feast', sc. a man who received free board in return for the performance of sacred duties (see especially Ath. 6.234d–235d citing Polemon fr. 78 Preller and Müller, *FHG* 3.137f. = A. Tresp, *Die Fragmente der griechischen Kultschriftsteller* (Giessen 1914) 209ff.; Ribbeck 18ff., Ziehen 1377.61ff.).

The opening words of Alexis 183(178K) (καλοῦσι δ' αὐτὸν πάντες οἱ νεώτεροι | Παράσιτον ὑποκόρισμα) contain a formula of introduction for the parasite as a character in later comedy (cf. Leo, *Plaut. Forsch.*[2] 106, Brinkhoff 131, *GRBS* 9 (1968) 165ff.) which is repeated elsewhere at least four times: Antiphanes 193(195K).10f. (from the Πρόγονοι, an undatable play) καὶ καλοῦσί μ' οἱ νεώτεροι | διὰ ταῦτα πάντα Σκηπτόν; Anaxippus 3 (from the Κεραυνός) ὁρῶ γὰρ ἐκ παλαίστρας τῶν φίλων | προσιόντα μοι Δάμιππον. :: <ἦ> τοῦτον λέγεις | τὸν †πέτρινον;† :: τοῦτον οἱ φίλοι καλοῦσί σοι | νυνὶ δι' ἀνδρείαν Κεραυνόν; Plaut. *Capt.* 69f. *iuuentus nomen indidit Scorto mihi,* | *eo quia invocatus soleo esse in conuiuio; Men.* 77f. *iuuentus nomen fecit Peniculo mihi,* | *ideo quia mensam, quando edo, detergeo.*[1] In Alexis and Antiphanes the parasite is described by another character, elsewhere he describes himself (in the two Plautine passages at the very beginning of his first entrance monologue), but on all five occasions the descriptions highlight an imaginative nickname given to the parasite by his younger associates. We do not know whether the formula was first adapted from its Homeric source (*Od.* 18.6f. Ἶρον δὲ νέοι κίκλησκον ἅπαντες, | οὕνεκ' ἀπαγγέλλεσκε κιών, ὅτε πού τις ἀνώγοι, cf. R. L. Hunter, *CR* 43 (1993) 18) by Alexis or by some other poet, but of far greater consequence is the

[1] On the relation of the two Plautine passages to their Greek models see especially W. G. Arnott *GRBS* 6 (1968) 166 n. 18, with the bibliography cited there. Cf. also comm. on Alexis' Ἀδελφοί, pp. 71f. n. 1, and Αἰχμαλωτός, p. 80 n. 1.

543

COMMENTARY

fact that each nickname illustrates by a vivid image an important aspect of the parasite's character, especially his voracity (Κεραυνός in a play titled – like Alexis' Παράσιτος – after the nickname, Σκηπτός, Peniculus). Alexis hit upon the nickname Παράσιτος, a *nomen proprium* likewise to be spelled with an initial capital (as Kaibel first saw, his edition at Ath. 10.421d), thus symbolising his parasite's edacity by a sobriquet taken from the world of religious ritual. Up to the moment when Alexis produced his comedy the term παράσιτος was presumably reserved for the priestly dignitary who received free meals. The nickname which Alexis chose may well have evoked for his audience a picture in particular of gormandisers at Cynosarges in the service of Heracles, the archetypal glutton and patron of parasites (cf. Diodorus com. 2.23ff., Plaut. *Curc.* 358, *Stich.* 232f., 386, 395); we may guess that the name's appropriateness so impressed the audience that they began to use παράσιτος thereafter as the *mot juste* for the type as a whole.[1]

If the line of reasoning developed above is acceptable (but see Nesselrath, *LP* 102f. n. 314), two further conclusions may be drawn. First, Alexis' Παράσιτος would necessarily be the earliest play with this title (thus antedating Antiphanes' as well as Diphilus' homonym: cf. Meineke *locc. citt.*, Kock 2.85, 363f., Kaibel in *RE* s.v. *Alexis* 9, 1470.6ff., Nesselrath, *MK* 312), and also precede any comedy in which the word παράσιτος appeared in its new, more general sense (e.g. Antiphanes 80.1, 3 from his Δίδυμοι, Araros 16 from his Ὑμέναιος[2]). Secondly,in the ancient scholarly controversies surrounding the invention of various aspects of the parasite's role (cf. *GRBS* 9 (1968) 161ff.), the claim recorded by Ath. 6.235e and then rejected by him as a maverick τὸν δὲ νῦν λεγόμενον παράσιτον Καρύστιος ὁ Περγαμηνὸς ἐν τῷ περὶ διδασκαλιῶν (*FHG* 4.359 fr. 17) εὑρεθῆναί φησιν ὑπὸ πρώτου Ἀλέξιδος, ἐκλαθόμενος ὅτι Ἐπίχαρμος ἐν Ἐλπίδι ἢ Πλούτῳ παρὰ πότον αὐτὸν εἰσήγαγεν (frs. 34, 35) can be vindicated provided we suppose that Carystius of Pergamum was referring to the parasite under his later name παράσιτος, and not to the role itself

---

[1] κόλαξ and its congeners did not thereby become obsolete, however; cf. e.g. Alexis 262(260K).1f. using κόλαξ and παράσιτος synonymously in succeeding lines, Diphilus 23(24K).1, Men. Κόλαξ as a title and v. 94, *Theoph.* fr. 1.16, Ath. 6.258e introducing Alexis 233(231K); Nesselrath, *LP* 104f., *MK* 312 n. 73.

[2] This fr. is introduced by Ath. 6.237a with the words τοῦ δὲ ὀνόματος τοῦ παρασίτου μνημονεύει Ἀραρὼς ἐν Ὑμεναίῳ διὰ τούτων, thus avoiding any claim that Araros originated the new use of the word. Casaubon, *Animadv.* 417 and Meineke 1.377, supported by Nesselrath, *LP* 102f. n. 314, seem to me mistaken in their assumptions upon this point.

irrespective of the name attached to it.[1] Carystius' work, dated to the end of the 2nd century and based presumably on Aristotle's lost διδασκαλίαι, seems to have been a literary-historical compilation marked more by factual accuracy than by critical acumen (Jacoby in *RE* s.v. *Karystios*, 2254.33ff., cf. Nesselrath, *MK* 187 n. 108).

183 (178K)

Meineke 3.467 (1), Kock 2.364, Edmonds 2.460, Kassel–Austin 2.126; cf. W. G. Arnott, *GRBS* 9 (1968) 161ff. On the significance and dramatic function of this fr., which is cited in full by both A and Epit. at Ath. 10.421d, see introduction to Παράσιτος.

1–2 See introduction to Παράσιτος. ὑποκόρισμα here implies 'pet-name/nickname' (cf. e.g. Aeschines 1.126) rather than 'euphemism' (cf. e.g. Alexis 222(219K).4ff., life a ὑποκόρισμα for μοίρα); it may be construed either (like ὄνομα frequently, cf. H. W. Smyth, *Greek Grammar* (Cambridge Mass. 1920) p. 360 § 1601, b) as an accusative of specification or (more plausibly) as in apposition to Παράσιτον (cf. K.G. 1.45, cf. 320ff.).

2 μέλει: so correctly CE, μέλλει unmetrically and senselessly A. The corruption is common (cf. Diggle, *Studies* 82); in Eur. alone one or more MSS at *Alc.* 726, *Andr.* 850, *Her.* 772, *IT* 909, *Phoen.* 1084, cf. Ar. *Av.* 1636, *Ran.* 257; the reverse error at Eur. *Hcld.* 755, *Tro.* 1258.

3 δειπνεῖ δ' ἄφωνος Τήλεφος: in Aeschylus' lost Μυσοί Telephus apparently remained speechless for a considerable part of the play because he was polluted after killing his mother's brothers in Tegea and then journeying to Mysia in search of his parents, for οἱ ἐναγεῖς οὔτε ἐν ἱερῷ προσῇεσαν οὔτε προσέβλεπον οὐδὲ διελέγοντό τινι (Σ A. *Eum.* 276); cf.

---

[1] The role itself appears to have originated with Epicharmus in Sicily, (cf. E. Wüst, *Rh. Mus.* 93 (1950) 359ff.). Pollux 6.35 ἐπὶ μέντοι τοῦ παρασιτεῖν, κατὰ λιχνείαν ἢ κολακείαν πρῶτος 'Επίχαρμος τὸν παράσιτον ὠνόμασεν, εἶτα "Αλεξις and the Towneley Σ Hom. *Il.* 17.577 τὸ δὲ ὄνομα τοῦ παρασίτου εἴρηται ἐν 'Ελπίδι παρ' 'Επιχάρμῳ make allegations that are now recognised (e.g. by Casaubon, *Animadv.* 417, Meineke 1.377, Wilamowitz in Kaibel, *CGF* p. 97 on Epicharmus fr. 36, H. W. Prescott, *CPhil.* 12 (1917) 415f.) to result from careless misinterpretation of the material given fully and assessed more accurately by Ath. in his long discussion (234e–245b). There is no evidence that Pollux and the scholiast had access to information over and above that preserved by Ath., and neither of the pair supports his allegation by verbal quotation. Ath. on the other hand is careful to avoid saying that Epicharmus used the word παράσιτος, and the word certainly does not occur in the frs. of Epicharmus.

COMMENTARY

Robert, *GH* 3.2.1.1146, S. Radt, *TrGF* 3.257f., H. J. Mette, *Der verlorene Aischylos* (Berlin 1963) 77ff., O. Taplin, *The Stagecraft of Aeschylus* (Oxford 1977) 423f., R. Parker, *Miasma* (Oxford 1983) 390f.). Aeschylus' fondness for long-silent characters was notorious already by the time of Ar. *Ran.* (911ff., instancing Niobe in the play named after her and Achilles in Μυρμιδόνες; cf. also Cassandra in A. *Ag.* 783–1071; Taplin, *op. cit.* 305f., 318f. and *HSCP* 76 (1972) 57ff.), but in the middle of the 4th century it was Telephus' speechlessness that had achieved the status of popular example: cf. Amphis 30.6f. ἔκυψεν ὥσπερ Τήλεφος | πρῶτον σιωπῇ, Arist. *Poet.* 24, 1460ᵃ32 ἐν Μυσοῖς ὁ ἄφωνος ἐκ Τεγέας εἰς τὴν Μυσίαν ἥκων. By a common construction ἄφ. Τήλ. here stands in apposition to the subject and so is vividly identified with it, instead of being introduced by ὥσπερ as a simile, cf. Alexis 47(46K).5 and comm. *ad loc.*

4 πρὸς τοὺς ἐπερωτῶντας τι, ὥστε: so A, raising doubts at two points. (i) The hiatus after indefinite τι (so also CE here) may be metrically acceptable in view of Alexis' apparent practice elsewhere, cf. comm. on 27.7–8. (ii) For A's ἐπερωτῶντας CE have ἐρωτῶντας, which at first sight seems a careless blunder, a quasi-haplographic replacement of the compound by the commoner simple verb (in Attic comedy elsewhere ἐρωτᾶν at least x 35, ἐπερωτᾶν x 7; for the construction of ἐπερωτᾶν with τι here = 'to ask a question', cf. e.g. Amphis 30.3 ὧν ἂν ἐπερωτᾷ τις), but it could just as well be the correct reading where A had corrupted the simple verb to a compound in line with *Koine* and post-classical predilections (cf. K. Zepernick, *Philologus* 77 (1921) 340; at Ath. 5.188a ἐφέλκεται A misquoting εἷλκε at Xen. *Symp.* 1.9, 9.400f. ἐπαναιρέεται A for ἀναιρέεται Hdt. 3.108).

5 τὰ Σαμοθρᾴκι' εὔχεται: the man who has invited Parasitos to a meal 'utters the Samothracian prayers' that his guest may stop blowing a gale and eventually calm down; Kock has a useful note on the construction. τὰ Σαμοθρᾴκι' is an internal accusative closely related to the cognate (e.g. εὐχὰς εὔχεσθαι Dem. 19.130, Aeschines 3.18), expressing instead an attribute of the cognate noun; expressions such as Ὀλύμπια νικᾶν, τὰ Παναθήναια πέμπειν and (Xen. *Anab.* 1.2.10) τὰ Λύκαια ἔθυσε provide exact parallels; cf. K.G. 1.305ff. There is thus no need to emend to τοῖς Σαμόθραξιν εὔχεται (so Grotius, *Exc.* 583, 973, cf. com. adesp. fr. 255.15 Austin). 'Samothracian prayers' were addressed to the μεγάλοι θεοί of Samothrace, often called the Κάβειροι, whose cult by the time of Alexis was already widespread especially in the Aegean islands but also in the Troad and mainland Greece. The belief that they would preserve those initiated in their mysteries from shipwreck is often reflected in Greek literature from the end of the 4th century on, e.g. com. adesp. fr. 255.15 Austin, Theophr. *Char.* 25, Call. epigr. 47 Pfeiffer = 28 Gow–Page (see their comm. *ad loc.*), Diod. Sic. 4.43, 48, Orphic *Argonautica* 466ff.; cf.

ΠΑΡΑΣΙΤΟΣ

Dittenberger, *OGIS* 69, a dedication found at Coptos on the Nile θεοῖς μεγάλοις Σαμόθραξι Ἀπολλώνιος Σωσιβίου Θηραῖος, ἡγεμὼν τῶν ἔξω τάξεων, σωθεὶς ἐγ (*sic*) μεγάλων κινδύνων ἐκπλεύσας ἐκ τῆς Ἐρυθρᾶς θαλάσσης, εὐχήν. Sometimes, however, these gods are invoked for general succour, e.g. Ar. *Pax* 277ff., Diod. Sic. 5.49, Σ Ap. Rhod. 1.916ff. See especially O. Kern in *RE* s.v. *Kabeiros und Kabeiroi* 1430.33ff., Preller–Robert, *GM* 2.862ff., B. Hemberg, *Die Kabiren* (Uppsala 1950) 49ff., 100ff., 212ff., cf. E. K. Borthwick, *CQ* 18 (1968) 201.

The image of the voracious parasite as a violent storm, which is implied by vv. 4–6 and made explicit in v. 7, seems to have been a cliché with roots in Old Comedy and probably popular speech; cf. comm. on 47(46K).4, where a character named Phayllos, probably a parasite, is similarly described as χειμὼν τρίτος· | ἐπὰν γὰρ ἐκνεφίας καταιγίσας τύχη | εἰς τὴν ἀγοράν, τοὔψον πριάμενος οἴχεται | φέρων ἅπαν τὸ ληφθέν (vv.4–7). Parasite nicknames such as Κεραυνός and Σκηπτός (Anaxippus 3, Antiphanes 193(195K).10f.: cf. introduction to Παράσιτος) are alternative exploitations of the image.

6 γαληνίσαι: intransitive, 'to become calm' (*pace* C. A. Lobeck, comm. on S. *Aj.* 268, Leipzig 1835[2] pp. 198f., Berlin 1866[3] pp. 164f.) as occasionally elsewhere in Greek of the period, e.g. Hippocr. *Vict.* 2.56.6 θερμαινόμενα δὲ καὶ διαχεόμενα (sc. τὰ γλυκέα καὶ τὰ πίονα καὶ τὰ λιπαρὰ) πληροῖ τὸ θερμὸν ἐν τῷ σώματι καὶ γαληνίζειν ποιεῖ, possibly the anonymous citation in Phryn. *Praep. Soph.* 57.11 de Borries γαληνίζει καὶ διεσκέδασται τὰ μέτωπα, if its author is Attic and neither τὰ μέτωπα nor some unquoted accusative was originally intended as the verb's object.[1]

7 χειμών: cf. fr. 47(46K).3f. νυνὶ δὲ πρὸς τοῖς πνεύμασιν | τούτοις Φάϋλλος προσγέγονε χειμὼν τρίτος and monost. 823 Jäkel χειμὼν κατ' οἴκους ἐστὶν ἀνδράσιν γυνή, a line preserved in several variant forms (χ. κ. ο. ἀνδράσιν κακὴ γ., χ. μέγιστος οἰκίας κακὴ γ.), which suggests widespread familiarity at least in later antiquity, if not necessarily Menandrean authorship. Asyndeton is normal in such explanatory clauses, cf. Alexis frs. 41(40K).2–3 and comm., 63(62K).8.

184 (179K)

Meineke 3.468 (II), Kock 2.364, Edmonds 2.462, Kassel–Austin 2.126. A speaker boasting to another about his (probably: but the words of the fr.,

---

[1] LSJ's treatment of the intransitive occurrences of γαληνίζω (s.v. 2) is inadequate. The parallels given above are omitted, and in their place is cited Hippocr. *Morb. sacr.* 13.5 H. Grensemann (Berlin 1968), where γαληνίζει (Θ) is probably a corrupt variant for λαγανίζει (M supported

COMMENTARY

cited by A but not Epit. at Ath. 3.123f, do not indicate the speaker's sex) splendid well is most likely to have been the head of one of the stage-houses (cf. comm. on ἔνδον v. 3), but addressee and situation are unknown.

2–3 πρᾶγμα ... μέγα φρέατος: J. Toup's μέγα for A's μετὰ (*Emendationes in Suidam et Hesychium et alios lexicographicos graecos* 2 (Oxford 1790) 142) is certain; for the error cf. Pl. *Resp.* 6.487b μέγα rightly FD ~ μετὰ A, Eur. *Hyps.* 60.8 Bond = 839 Cockle μέγα Wilamowitz ~ μετα *P.Petrie*, Fraenkel on A. *Ag.* 1271. If the three words cited correctly reproduce Alexis' text, they can be explained only as a variation or extension with defining genitive of an idiom common to Attic and Ionic Greek, μέγα πρᾶγμα = 'a thing of consequence' (cf. LSJ s.v. πρᾶγμα II.4.c), elsewhere always predicated of its referent, e.g. Eubulus 115(117K).9f. and Hunter *ad loc.*, [Dem.] 35.15, Hdt. 3.132; at Men. *Sam.* 390 the expression is an exclamatory substitute for a predicate, equivalent to 'she is a μέγα πρᾶγμα', see Gomme–Sandbach, *Comm. ad loc.*; cf. also other phrases where a noun is either predicated as a πρᾶγμα + adjective in agreement (in comedy e.g. Ar. *Eccl.* 441f., Antiphanes 239(245K).4, Amphis 17.1, Men. *Dysk.* 122f., 772, *Kith.* fr. 8) or occasionally defined by πρᾶγμα + adjective in apposition (e.g. Men. *Dysk.* 797). In several Greek dialects, however, including 5th-century Attic, it is not μέγα πρᾶγμα but the synonymous μέγα χρῆμα that is idiomatically constructed with a defining genitive, cf. Starkie on Ar. *Vesp.* 933, L. Bergson, *Eranos* 65 (1967) 88f. and 90 n. 44, P. T. Stevens, *Colloquial Expressions in Euripides, Hermes Einzelschr.* 38 (Wiesbaden 1976) 21, e.g. Ar. *Lys.* 1031 ἦ μέγ', ὦ Ζεῦ, χρῆμ' ἰδεῖν τῆς ἐμπίδος ἔνεστί μοι, Teleclides 1.15 μέγα χρῆμα γιγάντων, S. fr. 401 Pearson συὸς μέγιστον χρῆμα, Hdt. 1.36, Theoc. 18.4 and Gow *ad loc.*; cf. also (i) the related phrase ὅσον τὸ χρῆμα + genitive, e.g. Ar. *Ach.* 150, *Equ.* 1219, *Ran.* 1278, (ii) (παμ)πολύ (τι) χρῆμα + gen., Ar. *Plut.* 893f., Xen. *Cyr.* 2.1.5, Hdt. 3.109, 130, 4.81, 6.43, (iii) τοσοῦτον χρῆμ' ὄχλου Ar. *Eccl.* 394. Admittedly in a few Attic idioms πρᾶγμα seems to have replaced χρῆμα during the 4th century (Bergson 88f.), yet given the absence of any exact parallel for the expression πρᾶγμα ... μέγα φρέατος, Th. Bergk's suggestion (in Meineke 5.ccxi; cf. Kock, Blaydes, *Adv.* 1.113, 2.163) that πρᾶγμα may be a transmissional error for χρῆμα cannot be ruled out; for confusion between these two words cf. Theogn. 472 χρῆμ' ~ Evenus 8 πρᾶγμ' in versions of the same line.

3 ἔνδον: in Athenian houses wells and the bottle-shaped cisterns which began to replace them during the 4th century were normally sunk in the interior courtyards (A. Jardé in Dar.–Sag. s.v. *puteus* 780A, Thompson–

by Erotian), see Grensemann p. 48. Cf. also Plut. *Mor.* 1088e ψυχὴ ... πέφυκε χαίρειν καὶ γαληνίζειν (= Epicurus fr. 429 Usener).

548

ΠΑΡΑΣΙΤΟΣ

Wycherley, *Agora* XIV.197, J. McK. Camp in *Studies in Athenian Architecture, Sculpture and Topography presented to Homer A. Thompson, Hesperia Suppl.* 20 (1982) 12f.). Comedy thus reflects reality, with the door of the stage house representing ἡ αὔλειος θύρα; the well in Knemon's house is similarly placed, Men. *Dysk.* 67off., cf. Ar. *Plut.* 1168f., Plaut. *Rud.* 430ff. (note *ecferre* 439). Cf. also comm. on 179(174K).9.

ψυχρότερον Ἀραρότος: this is the only extant judgement on Araros' comic skills (on the career of this uniquely named son of Aristophanes see introduction to Παράσιτος, cf. Kaibel in *RE* s.v. *Araros* 2, 380.66ff., Kirchner, *PA* 1.109 no. 1579), but the frs. cited from his plays are too few and scanty to indicate whether Alexis' jibe was justified criticism or simply frivolous deflation of a rival, inspired by the opportunity for a pun. Theophrastus (fr. 94 Wimmer = 686 Fortenbaugh) defined τὸ ψυχρόν in its literary application as τὸ ὑπερβάλλον τὴν οἰκείαν ἀπαγγελίαν, and the ancient stylistic discussions (Arist. *Rhet.* 3.3, 1405ᵇ35ff., Demetrius *Eloc.* 2.114ff., [Longinus] *Subl.* 4) explained it more expansively as the stylistic result of choosing e.g. inappropriate, bathetic or strained images. The term was applied by comic poets and other wits (sometimes, as here, with a pun on the word's root meaning 'cold': the passages are asterisked) to the general style of dramatists (the tragedian Theognis, Ar. *Thesm.* 170, cf. *Ach.* 138ff.; Diphilus, Machon 259ff.*; prologues, 279ff.*), to single plays (Euripides' Παλαμήδης, Ar. *Thesm.* 848), and to individual jokes (Eupolis 261(244K)), especially those depending on strained puns (Timocles 19.3–6 Kassel–Austin = 222b.3–6 Austin, *CGFP* Τηρεύς/τηρεῖν, Πρόκνη/κνώμενος); cf. Plaut. *Poen.* 759f. (the parallel use of *frigefactas*). See also K. Gutzwiller, ψυχρός *und* ὄγκος (Diss. Basle 1969) 16ff.

A cold well was doubly advantageous; chilled water was prized as greatly as snow, especially for cooling the wine with which it was regularly mixed before being drunk (see comm. on 145(141K).10), and the well itself served as a refrigeration chamber for storing wine and comestibles (e.g. Strattis 60(57K).3, Lysippus 1; cf. Gow on Machon 259, O. Broneer, *Hesperia* 16 (1947) 239).

185 (180K)

Meineke 3.468 (III), Kock 2.364, Edmonds 2.462, Kassel–Austin 2.127. Speaker, situation and even grammatical context (does the initial ἤ mean 'either/or' or 'than'?) are unknown, but a reference to 'prattling with Plato' can hardly be complimentary (cf. comm. on fr. 1 and R. Fenk, *Adversarii Platonis quomodo de indole ac moribus eius iudicaverint* (Diss. Jena 1913) 42).

ἀδολεσχεῖν: comedy typically dismisses philosophic activity as

COMMENTARY

ἀδολεσχία ('idle talk ... and sometimes [it] implies that the talk is mischievous or foolish or both' Dover on Ar. *Nub.* 1478ff.) and its congeners, with reference elsewhere to Socrates and his associates (Ar. *Nub.* 1480, 1485, Eupolis 386(352K).1–2) or sophists like Prodicus (Ar. fr. 506(490K), Eupolis 388(353K)). Cf. Astydamas fr. 7 Nauck² defining ἀδολεσχία as γλώσσης περίπατον, Phot. s.v. ἀδολεσχεῖν (p. 48 Chr. Theodoridis, no. 372) σημαίνει μὲν τὸ φιλοσοφεῖν περί τε φύσεως καὶ τοῦ παντὸς διαλεσχαίνοντα. οἱ μέντοι ἀρχαῖοι κωμικοὶ λεσχαίνειν ἔλεγον τὸ διαλέγεσθαι (new fr.); cf. Phryn. *Praep. Soph.* 36.5 de Borries; R. Helm, *Neue Jahrb.* 5(9) (1902) 199, A. Weiher, *BBG* 65 (1929) 26.

κατὰ μόνας: 'in private'. The phrase, which is complete in itself (no ellipse of a noun need be assumed, cf. C. A. Lobeck, *Paralipomena* (Leipzig 1837) 363, Wilamowitz on Eur. *Her.* 681, Fraenkel on A. *Ag.* 916), occurs first in Thuc. 1.32, 37 and is common in 4th-century prose (see Kock *ad loc.*; add e.g. Arist. *Pol.* 3.6, 1281ᵇ34, *HA* 9.43, 629ᵃ34) and later comedy (e.g. Men. *Epitr.* 988, fr. 146, com. adesp. fr. 297.1 Austin = Men. fr. 722.1 Körte–Thierfelder). Convention prints κατὰ μόνας as two words, but see comm. on 179(174K).10 and 177(173K).14.

Πεζονίκη

Meineke 1.401, Breitenbach 136, Edmonds 2.463 note d. The title is probably the proper name (cf. Meineke), occurring only here in Greek, of a *hetaira* (cf. Breitenbach). The adjective πεζός was applied to certain courtesans and prostitutes not merely because they plied their business on foot (LSJ s.v. I.a) but also (? in consequence of a comic pun on another sense of πεζός = '(verse) unaccompanied by music', LSJ s.v. II.2, III.2) because they did not back up their sexual services with any performance on a musical instrument (Phot. s.v. πεζὰς μόσχους citing Arist. ἐν τῇ Πολιτείᾳ, Plato com. 170(155K) (or Cantharus, cf. Kassel–Austin IV.59), Eupolis 184(169K); also s.vv. πεζῇ citing com. adesp. fr. 601 Kock, πεζῷ γόῳ; Hesych. s.vv. πεζὰς μόσχους, πεζῷ γόῳ; Σᴮ Eur. *Alc.* 447; Theopompus in Ath. 12.532c = *FGrH* 115 F 213; Procopius *Anecd.* 9.11; see Porson, *Adv.* 298, H. Herter, *JAC* 3 (1960) 97, W. G. Arnott, *Glotta* 58 (1990) 91f.). The play's single fr. is dramatically uninformative.

186 (181K)

Meineke 3.468, Kock 2.365, Edmonds 2.462, Kassel–Austin 2.127. See comm. on fr. 29.2 (μᾶλλον μᾶλλον).

Ποιηταί[1] (and/or Ποιητής)

Meineke 1.389. Ath. 3.74e cites Ἄλεξις ἐν Ποιητῇ (fr. 187(182K)), 6.241d Ἄλεξις ἐν Ποιηταῖς (188(183K)).[2] These could be references to two different plays, or in one of the two passages Ath. (or the paradosis) could have corrupted the ending of the title in a familiar way (see introduction to Ἀποκοπτόμενος or -ομένη). A Ποιητής was written by Plato com. (frequently cited, always in the singular), Biottus (167 BC, *IG* ii².2323.iv; Pickard-Cambridge, *DFA*² 111, Mette III B 3 col. 4a, 23) and (?) Phoenicides (284 BC Φο]ινικ[ίδ]ης *IG* ii².2319.i.12; Pickard-Cambridge 109, Mette III C 2, 18). Ποιηταί in the plural is attested by the *Suda* (s.v. Πλάτων π 1708 Adler) as the alternative title to Plato's Λάκωνες, but the numerous frs. are always cited as from Λάκωνες simply.

Fr. 188(183K).3 refers to the Athenian parasite nicknamed Κόρυδος, who was active from *c.* 345 to *c.* 305 (see introductions to Δημήτριος and fr. 48(47K)), and was clearly spoken by a stage parasite. Fr. 187(182K) discusses the word συκοφάντης, and since in later Greek (and Roman) comedy the parasite sometimes acts as informer and/or blackmailer (e.g. Plaut. *Curc.*, *Men.*, *Pers.*, Ter. *Phorm.*, influenced perhaps by real-life practice in the Athens of the Greek originals; cf. Legrand, *NGC* 72f., J. O. Lofberg, *CPhil.* 15 (1920) 61ff., Wüst in *RE* s.v. *Parasitos* 1392.43ff. and E. Woytek's edition of Plaut. *Pers.* (Vienna 1982) pp. 54ff.), it is likely to have referred to the speaker of fr. 188(183K), but this does not necessarily mean that fr. 187(182K) was actually spoken (like Plaut. *Pers.* 62ff., Saturio himself attacking informers) by the parasite.

187 (182K)

Meineke 3.468 (1), Kock 2.365, Edmonds 2.462, Kassel–Austin 2.128. The fr. presents a speaker (see introduction to Ποιηταί) baffled by the question why the term συκοφάντης should denote a certain type of villain: sc. 'a πολυπράγμων with extra energy and with malevolence into the bargain – always prosecuting or threatening to prosecute prominent persons. As some would accept money to desist (or so their enemies said), the term often comes close to meaning blackmailer' (Gomme–Sandbach, *Comm.* on Men. *Pk.* 377f.). Precise definition of a word found, with its congeners, many times in Attic comedy (first in Ar. *Ach.* 559, 725, 840, but cf. Cratinus 70(69K) with the comments of its citer Σ^VEΘM Ar. *Equ.* 529b),

---

[1] Kassel–Austin, like all the other editors of the comic fragments, accept for Alexis only the plural title without prior justification.

[2] In both places ποιητ- is transmitted, but Alexis is perhaps more likely to have spelled the title Ποητής, cf. comm. on 16.2.

the orators and elsewhere, often a powerfully emotive term of abuse, is impracticable; in different contexts it may be translated 'informer', 'false accuser', 'swindler' or even generally 'scoundrel'. See especially J. O. Lofberg, *Sycophancy in Athens* (Menasha Wisc. 1920), Latte in *RE* s.v. Συκοφάντης 1028.67ff. The word's derivation from σῦκον + φαίνειν seems obvious, but the link between literal meaning ('revealer/denouncer of figs') and everyday usage has puzzled etymologists since antiquity. Ister of Cyrene (3rd century) suggested that the common use originated from the denunciation of illegal exports of figs (in Ath. 3.74e = *FGrH* 334 F 12; cf. also Plut. *Solon* 24, *Mor.* 523b, Σ Ar. *Plut.* 31, 873, *Et. Mag.* 733.39 s.v. συκοφαντία, Σ Pl. *Resp.* 1.340d = *Suda* s.v. συκοφαντεῖν), but there is no evidence for a ban on such exports from Athens at any time; other (highly improbable) explanations are provided by Philomnestus (in Ath. 3.74f–75a = *FGrH* 527 F 1) and the *Suda* s.v. συκοφαντεῖν = Σ Ar. *Plut.* 31, cf. Festus p. 393 Lindsay. In modern scholarship the most persuasive suggestion was made by E. Gernet, *Mélanges Émile Boisacq* 1 (Brussels 1937) 393, viz. that the popular use developed from the discovery of stolen figs concealed in the clothes of delinquents; less plausible explanations appear in e.g. A. Boeckh, *Die Staatshaushaltung der Athener*[3] 1 (Berlin 1886) 54ff., A. B. Cook, *CR* 21 (1907) 133ff. and P. Girard, *REG* 20 (1907) 143ff. Cf. also Frisk s.v. συκοφάντης, Chantraine s.v. σῦκον E, Latte *loc. cit.*, LSJ s.v. συκοφάντης and my comm. on fr. 4.2.

An interest in etymologies, shown especially by the desire to explain the names of mythical heroes and heroines as signifying their characters and/or experiences, goes back in literature to Homer and Hesiod, is widespread in Pindar and Greek tragedy (a selection of examples in J. H. L. Lersch, *Die Sprachphilosophie der Alten* 3 (Bonn 1841) 3ff.), and reaches a parodic climax in Plato's *Cratylus*. Underlying many of the literary etymologies (including that of Alexis' speaker here) is the feeling, developed into a much debated dogma by sophists and philosophers from the 5th century onwards, that a word's sound or apparent derivation should convey its meaning. See e.g. Schwyzer 1.29ff., W. K. C. Guthrie, *A History of Greek Philosophy* 3 (Cambridge 1969) 204ff.

1 ὁ συκοφάντης ... τοὔνομα: a noun in apposition to τὸ ὄνομα may either itself have the definite article (cf. e.g. Pl. *Crat.* 395a–b ὅτι οὖν ἀγαστὸς κατὰ τὴν ἐπιμονὴν οὗτος ὁ ἀνὴρ ἐνσημαίνει τὸ ὄνομα ὁ Ἀγαμέμνων, Men. *Mis.* 301 τοὔν[ομ]α λέγει γὰρ οὑτοσὶ τὸν Δημέαν) or rather more commonly be unarticled (e.g. Pl. *Polit.* 279e τούτοισι δὴ τοῖς ... ἀμυντηρίοις καὶ σκεπάσμασι τὸ μὲν ὄνομα ἱμάτια ἐκαλέσαμεν, Isaeus 3.30 τὸ τῆς τήθης ὄνομα Κλειταρέτην τὸν πατέρα ἐμαρτύρησαν θέσθαι αὐτῇ).

2 ἐν τοῖσι μοχθηροῖσιν: so the paradosis (A and Epit. MSS at Ath. 3.74f), which Kock correctly interpreted as 'among the vile (names)', supplying ὀνόμασι. There is, however, much to be said for Herwerden's replacement of ἐν by ἐπί (*NAC* 32f., cf. *Coll. Crit.* 127), 'the name συκοφάντης is applied to scoundrels', which strengthens the sense with an idiom much favoured in 4th-century Athens (Herwerden noted only Xen. *Cyr.* 2.2.12 ὁ μὲν γὰρ ἀλαζὼν ἔμοιγε δοκεῖ ὄνομα κεῖσθαι ἐπὶ τοῖς προσποιουμένοις καὶ πλουσιωτέροις εἶναι ἢ εἰσὶ καὶ ἀνδρειοτέροις; cf. also *Oec.* 6.12 ... τούτων τῶν ἀνδρῶν, ἐφ' οἷς τὸ ὄνομα δικαίως ἐστίν ὃ καλεῖται καλός τε κἀγαθὸς ἀνήρ, Pl. *Parm.* 147d ἕκαστον τῶν ὀνομάτων οὐκ ἐπί τινι καλεῖς;, Arist. *PA* 1.2, 642ᵇ15f. ... τὸ ἔναιμον καὶ τὸ ἄναιμον· ἐφ' ἑκατέρῳ γὰρ τούτων οὐ κεῖται ἓν ὄνομα; other passages cited by LSJ s.v. ἐπί Β.ΙΙΙ.5). ἐπί and ἐν are frequently confused by scribes (e.g. Hom. *Il.* 16.488, 23.693, Eur. *Tro.* 542, cf. Cobet, *VL*² 281f.).

ἐστὶ κείμενον: see comm. on 2.9.

3–4 'The noun "figs", when joined (sc. with another word to form the compound συκοφάντης), ought to have indicated the character (of a man) who was good and pleasant'; the correct interpretation of Alexis' words was first given by Schweighaeuser (*Animadv.* 2.14), thus displaying by his refinement of Casaubon's cruder version (*Animadv.* 151) an excellent (*pace* Wilamowitz on Eur. *Her.* 283) understanding of Greek idiom. When a relative clause has an indefinite antecedent, commonly that clause precedes its main clause and the antecedent is either not expressed or (as here: ἀνήρ: cf. Pickard-Cambridge, *GCP* 191) attracted into the relative clause. The article with τρόπον consequently gains almost demonstrative force. Cf. e.g. S. *Ant.* 35f. ἀλλ' ὃς ἂν τούτων τι δρᾷ, | φόνον προκεῖσθαι (sc. λέγω) δημόλευστον ἐν πόλει and Jebb *ad loc.*, *Trach.* 350 ἃ μὲν γὰρ ἐξείρηκας ἀγνοίᾳ μ' ἔχει, K.G. 2.402f.

5–6 The absence in the paradosis of a personal object to πεποίηκε (so A, Epit., but see comm. on 16.2) is striking. Palaeographically the most plausible addition would be μ' after προστεθέν (easily omitted by haplography if the participle had been spelled -τεθέμ by assimilation before it, cf. e.g. Schwyzer 1.213f., Mayser–Schmoll 1.1.203f., Threatte 1.588ff., 616ff.), but that would produce the anomaly of a postpositive elided at verse-end (rare in drama: only Ar. *Ran.* 298 μ'; S. *OR* 1184, ? Eur. *IT* 961 τ'; S. *Ant.* 1031, *OR* 29, 785, 791, 1224, *El.* 1017, *OC* 17, Ar. *Av.* 1716, *Eccl.* 351, Dionysius 2.33 δ'; cf. Descroix 292ff., West, *Greek Metre* 90). Could Alexis perhaps have written πεπόηκέ μ' (cf. comm. on 16.2) ἀπορεῖν?

188 (183K)

Meineke 3.469 (ΙΙ), Kock 2.365, Edmonds 2.462, Kassel–Austin 2.128. The stage parasite who speaks the fr. (cf. introduction to Ποιηταί) presents himself as a γελωτοποιός (= in Roman comedy *ridiculus homo*: cf.

COMMENTARY

F. Ritschl, *Opuscula philologica* 2 (Leipzig 1868) 411f., H. Petersmann's edition of Plaut. *Stich.* (Heidelberg 1973), comm. on 171, Nesselrath, *LP* 26f.). This function of the parasite (cf. Pollux 6.122), exploited already in real-life Athenian parties at the beginning of the 4th century (cf. Xen. *Symp.* 1.11ff., 2.21f., 4.50; Ribbeck, *Kolax* 15f.), was reproduced by the comic poets of Greece and Rome in various ways; the parasite might be given one or more entrance monologues, in which he entertained the audience with his wit and jokes (thus continuing and adapting the techniques of the opening monologues of βωμολόχοι in the Old Comedy of Aristophanes), before he enlivened the subsequent dialogue with witty comments (e.g. Plaut. *Capt.*, *Men.*, *Pers.*, *Stich.*, cf. *BICS* 19 (1972) 64ff.); or he might appear as the humorously deflating companion of a braggart soldier (e.g. Men. *Kol.* frs. 2, 3 ~ Ter. *Eun.* 232ff., cf. Gomme–Sandbach, *Comm.* pp. 420ff., Plaut. *MG*).

1 πάνυ τοι βούλομαι (A at Ath. 6.241d) rather than πάνυ τι βούλομαι (Epit.); τι and τοι are frequently confused with each other in MSS through itacism (e.g. Men. fr. 408.1 cited by Stob. 4.18.14, cf. Porson, *Adv.* 110), but though both scan here, τοι is particularly appropriate as indicating the speaker's emotional state (Denniston, *GP* 541f.),[1] while τι seems unidiomatic (the negative collocation οὐ πάνυ τι is common, cf. Cobet, *VL*² 222, LSJ s.v. πάνυ 1.3, but I can find no parallel for a positive πάνυ τι when the adverb qualifies a verb, as here; cf. also H. Thesleff, *Studies on Intensification in Early and Classical Greek* (Helsinki 1954) 58, K. J. Dover, *CQ* 35 (1985) 332ff.).

2 A and Epit. here read οὗτος γελᾶσθαι, which Kassel–Austin print, but when οὗτος is used of the first person, it is always predicative in a meaning close to τοιοῦτος (e.g. Dem. 18.173 ἐφάνην τοίνυν οὗτος ἐν ἐκείνῃ τῇ ἡμέρᾳ ἐγώ;, Pind. *Ol.* 4.24 Snell–Maehler οὗτος ἐγὼ ταχυτᾶτι; cf. E. des Places, *Le Pronom chez Pindare* (Paris 1947) 63), and never attributive in the sense of ὅδε (*pace* Gulick's translation of Ath. here; the use of οὗτος in the meaning 'the person present' is confined to the second and third persons, c.f. LSJ s.v. c.1.5). Corruption must be assumed, of either an original οὗτως (Musurus: ? or -τω), implying that the speaker had already cracked a joke in the previous sentence, or (preferably) αὐτός (Peppink, *Observ.* 39).

γελᾶσθαι καὶ γέλοι' ἀεὶ λέγειν: so also the parasites Eucrates ὁ Κόρυδος in Alexis 229(227K).1–2 ὁ τὰ γέλοι' εἰθισμένος | λέγειν and Philippus in

---

[1] τοι is sometimes used by Aristophanes in asides and soliloquies (Denniston, *GP* 538, citing *Lys.* 919, *Thesm.* 904, *Eccl.* 321); could the present fr. be part of a parasite's initial entry monologue, in which he defined and explained his role in the plot?

ΠΟΙΗΤΑΙ

Xen. *Symp.* 1.14 γέλοιόν τι ... ἐπεχείρει λέγειν, cf. also e.g. Ar. *Ran.* 6, Anaxandrides 10.2.

γέλοι᾿ or γελοῖ? The accentuation has been disputed since antiquity, and there is as much confused inconsistency in MSS (thus e.g. proparoxytone ACE here, properispomenon R at Ar. *Ach.* 1058, *Nub.* 1241) as in the old grammarians, who attempt without success to distinguish the two accentuations sometimes by meaning (proparoxytone = καταγέλαστος, properispomenon = γελωτοποιός: so Aelius Dionysius p. 113.5 Erbse, Ammon. *Diff.* 119, *Et. Mag.* 224.36, *Suda* s.v. γέλοιος, Σ Lucian 105.5 Rabe; but *Et. Gud.* s.v. states the exact opposite, cf. Eustath. 205.45; Σ Ar. *Ran.* 6 correctly points out that the accent does not affect the meaning), sometimes more plausibly by dialect (proparoxytone Attic, properispomenon *Koine*: Apollon. Dysc. 50.4f., Moeris s.v., Σ Ar. *Ran.* 6) or period (properispomenon earlier Attic, proparoxytone late Attic: Ael. Dion. *loc. cit.* = 'Herodian' 1.137.14 Lentz, but see A. Nauck, *MGR* 6 (1894) 58f.; cf. the change of ἑτοῖμος to ἕτοιμος in 5th-century Attic, as against that of old Attic ὅμοιος to ὁμοῖος).

3 τὸν Κόρυδον: see introductions to Ποιηταί, Δημήτριος and fr. 47(46).

Ποιήτρια

It is vain to speculate about the title of a play from which less than a single line survives (T. Hemsterhuys's conjecture, in his and J. H. Lederlin's edition (Amsterdam 1706) at Pollux 9.153, that this title could have been an alternative to Ποιηταί or -τής, is unsupported by evidence and unlikely), but Heliodorus 2.8.2 τὴν τῶν εἰς αὐτὸν ἐπιβουλῶν ... ποιήτριαν, where ποιήτρια is used in its literal sense 'female contriver', not noticed by LSJ s.v.) should act as a warning against the automatic assumption that Alexis' title figure was a poetess rather than e.g. a scheming female slave like Habrotonon in Men. *Epitr.* On the spelling of the title (? preferably Ποήτρια) see n. 2 on p. 551 and comm. on fr. 16.2.

189 (184K)

Meineke 3.469, Kock 2.365, Edmonds 2.464, Kassel–Austin 2.129. Pollux 9.153 cites Alexis' use of ὡς ἐπὶ τὰ πολλά ('for the most part') in this play as a variant for the expressions standard in Attic and later Greek ὡς ἐπὶ τὸ πολύ and ὡς ἐπὶ τὸ πλῆθος (cf. comm. on fr. 53(54K), section (a)) without either condemnation or comment on its rarity (no Attic parallel is known to me, but cf. ὡς τὰ πολλά in a similar sense, e.g. [Xen.] *Cyneg.* 7.12, Hippocr. *Progn.* 23, *Coac.* 2.272), resulting perhaps

555

from the accidents of preservation or even a nonce coinage (? for a joke, or because of the metrical inconvenience of ὡς ἐπὶ τὸ πολύ).

Pollux completes his citation with τοῦτο (so FS: CL have οὕτω, which also scans but removes the caesura) ποιῶ, on which two words Kock writes '*dubium uidetur utrum Alexidis sint an Pollucis dictionem exemplo inlustrantis*'. However, although Pollux may sometimes break off his shorter quotations in mid-sentence (cf. comm. on 136(131K), possibly 61(60K)), there is no evidence that he ever completed them with words of his own.

Πολύκλεια

Bechtel, *Frauennamen* 21, Radke in *RE* s.v. *Polykleia* 1, 1695.58ff. and 2, 1699.1ff., Nesselrath, *MK* 315. Ath. 14.642c, citing the one fr. (190(185K)) from this play, identifies its title figure as a *hetaira* (most probably a *persona ficta* in a conventional type of intrigue plot; no real-life courtesan with this name is known, and the tone and subject of fr. 190(185K) point to a parasite as speaker, cf. Nesselrath). An alternative theme would be a parody of the myth about the Heraclid siblings Polycleia and Aeatus chronicled by Polyaenus 8.44 (cf. Radke): when an oracle had predicted that the first Heraclid to lead an army across the River Achelous would become ruler of the Boeotians, Polycleia reached the far bank ahead of her brother by a trick, but then married her brother and ruled jointly with him.

190 (185K)

Meineke 3.469, Kock 2.366, Edmonds 2.464, Kassel–Austin 2.129. On the speaker see introduction to this play.

1 ὁ πρῶτος εὑρών . . . τραγήματα: cf. comm. on frs. 27.1–2, 168(163).2. – Hyberbaton, by which a participle and its object are separated by intervening matter of variable extent, is not rare in drama: e.g. Men. *Dysk.* 236ff. τοῦτο τοῦ λοιποῦ χρόνου | εἰπεῖν θ' ὅπως μηδείς ποτ' αὐτὸν ὄψεται | ποιοῦντα, *Pk.* 493f. τουτί με τῶν | πάντων λελύπηκας μάλιστ' εἰπών, S. *Phil.* 618f., Eur. *Or.* 749, 1100, cf. especially Handley, comm. on Men. *Dysk.* 223ff., Sandbach on *Dysk.* 235. The effect is normally to throw emphasis (cf. J. D. Denniston, *Greek Prose Style* (Oxford 1952) 47ff., 54f.) on the object of the participle, whether that comes first (as in the passages quoted) or last (as here, where the speaker delays it to the end of his sentence in order to tease his audience and keep their attention until the key word is spoken: cf. v. 3 below and comm. on 168(163K).7). See also K.G. 2.600ff., L. Lindhamer, *Zur Wortstellung im Griechischen* (Diss. Munich 1908), Schwyzer 2.697f.with full bibliography, and J. H. Kells, *CR* 11 (1961) 188ff.

ΠΟΛΥΚΛΕΙΑ

2–3 The *Marcianus* here (at Ath. 14.642c–d) has ἐξεῦρε κὰρ γοὺς (*sic*: scanning a syllable short at the end of v. 2), while Epit. (and Eustath. 1394.10) paraphrases v. 2 before accurately quoting virtually all v. 3 (τοῦ συμποσίου διατριβήν φησι τὰ τραγήματα, ὥστε ἀργοὺς κ. τ. λ.). The gap was plugged by Musurus (probably from his apograph of A) with πως (a metrical stopgap favoured elsewhere in MSS: cf. D. Kovacs, *GRBS* 29 (1988) 125), and by Wilamowitz (in Kaibel's apparatus) with separated καὶ | ἀργούς, but the resultant construction would require ἐξεῦρε to govern both the accusative διατριβήν and the infinitive ἔχειν ('he discovered a pastime... and how to keep occupied'). Such a use of ἐξευρίσκω + infinitive, however, is unparalleled (LSJ wrongly cite Hdt. 1.196.5 ἄλλο δέ τι ἐξευρήκασι νεωστὶ γενέσθαι and S. *OR* 120 ἓν γὰρ πόλλ' ἂν ἐξεύροι μαθεῖν, cf. *P.Oxy.* 1588.10, where the accusatives are direct objects of the main verbs and the infinitives epexegetic; in Alexis here the presence of (i) καί and (ii) a second accusative σιαγόνας as object of ἔχειν makes an epexegetic interpretation impossible), as similarly of the simple verb εὑρίσκω in the active. Yet εὑρίσκομαι in the middle can govern an infinitive in the sense 'I discover how to', e.g. Eur. *Med.* 195ff. στυγίους δὲ βροτῶν οὐδεὶς λύπας | ηὕρετο μούσῃ καὶ πολυχόρδοις | ᾠδαῖς παύειν, Hdt. 9.28.3 παρὰ δὲ σφίσι εὕροντο παρὰ Παυσανίεω ἑστάναι Ποτειδαιητέων τῶν ἐκ Παλλήνης τοὺς παρεόντας τριηκοσίους; could Alexis then have written ἐξεύρε<το> | κἀργοὺς with the same construction? Otherwise a more deep-seated corruption would have to be posited: such as a one-line lacuna between vv. 2 and 3 in which the speaker enlarged on the benefits of the discovery of τραγήματα (e.g. ἐξεύρε<το | ὥστ' + infinitival phrase> | κἀργούς ...).

The *Marcianus* spells ἐξεῦρε, but whether correctly is uncertain in an undated play, see comm. on fr. 9.2.

2 διατριβήν: see comm. on fr. 222(219K).3–6.

3 τὰς σιαγόνας: much rarer in Attic comedy (elsewhere only Cratinus fr. 174(163K), Ar. fr. 300(287)) than its synonym τὰς γνάθους (thirty-eight times including Alexis 133(128K).7), and perhaps on that account placed at the end of its clause for greater impact (cf. comm. on v. 1), yet cf. Ath. 10.416b quoting Clearchus (*FHG* 2.307 fr. 12) ὁπότε κοπιάσειε τὰς σιαγόνας ἐσθίων, Libanius *Decl.* 28.12 (a parasite) τὰς σιαγόνας κινῶν, τὰς γνάθους ἐξασκῶν; cf. Headlam, comm. on Herodas 3.49.

Πονήρα (or -ηρά)

Meineke 1.402, 3.470, Kock 2.366, F. Leo, *Der Monolog im Drama* (*Abh. Göttingen* 10, Berlin 1908) 45, Webster, *SLGC* 66 and *CQ* 2 (1952) 15, Edmonds 2.465 note c, A. Giannini, *Acme* 13 (1960) 162, Dohm, *Mageiros* 24 n. 2, 54, 83 n. 2, 101, Nesselrath, *MK* 304f. Seven frs. (191–7(186–92K)) are cited from this play by Ath. (3.117c–d, 7.324b–c, 4.170c,

14.655f, 2.46a + 15.687d (+ also Clem. Alex. *Paed.* 2.8.68), 3.127c, 9.385b respectively). The title, which is unique among those known,[1] is best interpreted as an adjective (*pace* Meineke 1.402, who thought it a woman's name, cf. Edmonds; no such name is recorded, nor do the word's negative associations make one likely) now ambiguous in sense, with the play's heroine either 'wicked' or 'wretched' (cf. Daléchamp's translation), the only meanings attested in common use (LSJ s.v. πονηρός ΙΙ, ΙΙΙ). 'Wretched' is perhaps the more likely alternative, if the preponderant accentuation of the title in the *Marcianus* (paroxytone five times, unaccented 9.385b, -ήρᾳ 15.687d) reflects the decision of an Alexandrian scholar with the play text before him to endorse its presentation of the heroine as wretched by an accentuation of the title that was generally accepted at that time for that meaning.[2]

The play is undatable[3] and its plot unknown, although five of the frs.

---

[1] A comedy presented at the Dionysia towards the end of the 3rd century (ΙΙΙ B 3 col. 1 c, 23 Mette) had a title ending].ηραι, but the traces of the letter preceding eta do not match nu, rather kappa or chi (hence Χήρᾳ S. A. Kumanudes, Ἀθήναιον 6 (1878) 474ff., cf. *CR* 20 (1970) 50).

[2] The accentuation of πονηρός was disputed by ancient and Byzantine grammarians. Ammonius 104.11ff. Nickau (citing Tryphon fr. 15 Velsen) and Eustath. 341.14f. (citing 'Herodian') claim that the word should be oxytone in both senses; Arcadius 71.16 Barker, 'Herodian' 1.197.19ff. Lentz (but see my comm. on fr. 188(183K).2), the Tzetzes scholia on Ar. *Nub.* 102 and *Plut.* 127, and anon. in Cramer, *Anecdota, Graeca Oxon.* 1.272.29ff. argue for oxytone = 'wicked', (pro)paroxytone = 'wretched/sick/toiling' in Attic. This accentual differentiation, which was widespread in the *Koine*, may have developed in late Attic. Cf. LSJ s.v. μοχθηρός, *fin.* Cramer's Byzantine grammarian (*loc. cit.*) goes on to say οἱ μέντοι νεώτεροι τῆς κωμῳδίας ποιηταί ... διαλύσαντες τὸ ὄνομα πονηροὺς (*sic*: by his accent here contradicting his earlier assertion) ἐξήνεγκαν τοὺς ἐρῶντας παρὰ τὸ πονεῖν ἐν τῷ ἐρᾶν. Kock unwisely assumes from this that in New Comedy πονηρός could also mean 'lovesick' and that Alexis' title figure was so portrayed. A more plausible source for the grammarian's explanation is some passage in a lost comedy where a character suggested the false etymology πονεῖν + ἐρᾶν for πονηρός (cf. introduction to fr. 187(182K)). Aristophanes had already linked πόνος with πονηρός (*Vesp.* 466, *Lys.* 350), and the association of πονεῖν/πόνος with love was a widespread τόπος not confined to comedy (cf. Alexis 236(234K).3 and introduction to fr., 247(245K).12f. and comm. on vv. 10–13). Cf. also Schwyzer 1.380 and Hunter on Eubulus 68.2.

[3] Webster's attempt (*locc. citt.*) to date the play to the 360s on the assumption that the reference to χόνδρος ... Θετταλικός in fr.

(191–4(186–9K), ? 196(191K) can be assigned with more or less plausibility to a scenic context. Ath. identifies the speaker of frs. 191(186K) and 192(187K) as a μάγειρος, and Meineke 3.470 may be right in suggesting that frs. 191–4(186–9K) all come from one long ῥῆσις on the cook's first entry alone (or believing himself alone: cf. 191(186K).1 λογίσασθαι πρὸς ἐμαυτὸν βούλομαι), listing the ingredients he has purchased[1] (cf. introduction to the fr.) for a meal he has presumably been hired to prepare, and discussing how each ingredient is to be treated (cf. Dohm 24 n. 2, 83 n. 2, 101, Nesselrath). Fr. 191(186K), beginning with a general statement about the cook's intentions, is likely to have come early in the speech, but the relative positions of 192–4(187–9K) are unknown. Fr. 196(191K) could have been spoken by the same cook after he had been indoors (ἔνδον), but more probably was uttered by the hiring householder, describing one of the comestibles in his store cupboard. The contexts of frs. 195(190K) and 197(192K) are uncertain.

191 (186K)

Meineke 3.470 (1), Kock 2.366, Edmonds 2.464, Kassel–Austin 2.130; cf. Dohm, *Mageiros* 83, Nesselrath, *MK* 292f. n. 20. The fr.'s dramatic context is discussed above (introduction to Πονήρα): a μάγειρος (so identified by Ath. 3.117c–d introducing the fr.) reckons up purchases and plans their preparation for the table. The speech combines three comic τόποι: (i) calculation of money spent in the market (cf. introduction to comm. on fr. 15), detailing of recipes, and (more unusually) presentation of the cook as usurper of his hirer's or hirer's slave's normal role by doing his own marketing (but cf. Alexis 115(110K).1–3, 8, 9, Archedicus 3 parallel in structure and content to Alexis 191(186K), cf. the introductory words of Ath. 7.294b, Sotades 1, Lynceus 1.20, Dionysius 2.20; Dohm 83 and his n. 2[1]). Both A and Epit. cite the fr., but Epit. abbreviates vv. 1–2 to λογίσασθαι βούλομαι τὴν ὀψωνίαν.

196(191K) was inspired by Alexander of Pherae's despatch of wheat to Athens in that decade (cf. Ephippus 1 and Kock *ad loc.*, also *Rh. Mus.* 37 (1882) 132f., H. D. Westlake, *Thessaly in the Fourth Century* (London 1935) 142 and n. 4, 154f.) is backed by no supporting evidence (the availability of Thessalian χόνδρος in Athens was presumably not confined to one special shipment; an alternative reason for its mention in fr. 196(191K) is suggested in comm. *ad loc.*), and would in any case put the opening years of Alexis' career back too far (cf. my general introduction, 1.iii). See also p. 570 n. 1.

[1] Nesselrath, *MK* 292f. n. 20 argues against Dohm that the purchases need not have been made by the cook, but in that case how could the

COMMENTARY

1 A's text ὅμως λογίσασθαι πρὸς ἐμαυτὸν βούλομαι is metrically defective, but sense is perfect and the error or omission likely to be trivial. Three remedies deserve mention. Meineke's λογίζεσθαι replaces the commoner penthemimeral with a rarer but acceptable medial caesura (Descroix 257, 259, 263f., West, *Greek Metre* 88), but the transmitted aorist infinitive is more appropriate to a simple action with no reference to its duration or repetition (Goodwin, *MT* 22f., 28ff.). Better are Jacobs' πρός <γ'> ἐμαυτόν (*Addit.* 81: on the position of γε before the word emphasised see Denniston, *GP* 146f.) with penthemimeral caesura, and Dindorf's ὅμως <δέ>, which Kassel–Austin print, with medial caesura (in Attic comedy ὅμως δέ x 13, δ' ὅμως x 4, ὅμως without particle x 8); δέ is sometimes omitted by excerptors or scribes at the beginning of citations, either carelessly or with intent to remove links with an unquoted preceding context (e.g. Men. *Epitr.* 252 ~ *Et. Gud.* 222.40ff. Sturz, monost. 222, cf. K. Zepernick, *Philologus* 77 (1921) 343).

λογίσασθαι: 'to reckon up', the root meaning, common in comedy both transitive (as here: e.g. Ar. *Nub.* 20, *Vesp.* 656, *Ran.* 1263, *Plut.* 381, cf. fr. 481(465K)) and intransitive (e.g. Eriphus 2.5, Men. *Epitr.* 140). The speaker could have used ψῆφοι with or without an abacus (cf. comm. on fr. 15.3), or simply his fingers (ἀπὸ χειρός Ar. *Vesp.* 656).

2 καθεζόμενος: 'having sat down', participle of second aorist ἐκαθεζόμην (cf. LSJ s.v. καθέζομαι, K.B. 2.407f. s.v. ‘ΕΔ-).

τὴν ὀψωνίαν: the speaker goes on to list in the extant frs. of his speech (see introduction to Πονήρα) four separate items that he has purchased (191(186K).5, 8, 192(187K).1, 194(189K).1–2), of which the first three are fish (the predominant ὄψον, see comm. on fr. 47(46K).6), and the last pork.

3 οἰστέον: the prices given by the speaker in 191(186K).6, 192(187K).2 and 194(189K).1 indicate that the purchases have been paid for and presumably brought to the door of the hirer's house; accordingly the verbal here must express the cook's need to carry them not *domum e foro* (so Herwerden, *Coll. Crit.* 127) but simply from where he stands (probably near or in front of the hirer's door) to the kitchen work-surface.

5 For the first two and a half metra A and Epit. have only τάριχος πρῶτον ὡραῖον. Musurus' <ἐστί> provides the obvious supplement,[1]

---

cook have known the cost of individual purchases (191(186K).6, 192(187K).2 and 194(189K).1) and so been able to reckon up (see comm. on v. 1 λογίσασθαι) expenditure?

[1] In his edition of Ath. Kaibel objected to this supplement because the word already appears in vv. 4 and 6 of the fr., but unemphatic words are idly repeated in adjacent lines as frequently by Alexis as by more affected authors (cf. *CQ* 21 (1971) 156). Examples include frs. 9.8/11,

although his placing of it after τάριχος is less satisfactory than Desrousseaux's (*Obs.* 52f.) at the beginning of the line (with modification to <ἔστιν>, cf. 15.4 ἔστ' ὠμοτάριχος πέντε χαλκῶν at the head of a similar list of charged items, 167(162K).1).

τάριχος . . . ὡραῖον: fish preserved (by drying/smoking/pickling, cf. LSJ s.v. τάριχος, Blümner in *RE* s.v. *Salsamenta* 2011.32ff., André, *Alimentation* 111ff.) 'in season', sc. at its best, when the species caught had just reached maturity in the spring of the year after spawning (hence Hesych. s.v. ὡραῖον· . . . καὶ ὁ τάριχος ὁ κατὰ τὸ ἔαρ συντιθέμενος, cf. Hicesius as cited by Ath. 3.116e–f), with firm flesh (leaner species seem to have been preferred, cf. Diocles in Ath. *loc. cit.* = fr. 136 Wellmann; Ath. 3.120e citing Diphilus of Siphnos). The full expression (also e.g. Pollux 7.27, Aretaeus 7.3.12) is sometimes shortened to τὸ ὡραῖον (cf. Ath. 3.116a, e–f, Diphilus of Siphonos *loc. cit.*, Archestratus fr. 169.9 Lloyd-Jones–Parsons; hence *horaeum* in Latin, Plaut. *Capt.* 851); cf. also ταρίχους ὡραῖα τεμάχη, ὡραῖαι ταρίχους σαργάναι Pollux 7.27.

5–6 τοδί· διωβολοῦ: Dindorf's correction of haplography in the MSS (τὸ διοβολου A, τοδί· ὀβολοῦ CE) restores sense and metre.

6 εὖ μάλα: 'thoroughly' as at e.g. Hom. *Od.* 22.190, Xen. *Anab.* 6.1.1, Pl. *Theaet.* 156a, Aelian *Epist.* 10; cf. H. Thesleff, *Studies on Intensification in Early and Classical Greek* (Helsinki 1954) 187. The need for thorough washing before cooking is also emphasised by Archestratus frs. 143.3, 144.2 Lloyd-Jones–Parsons.

7–9 The recipe for boiled τάριχος shows Alexis' customary expertise in culinary matters (cf. comm. on frs. 84, 115(110K), 129(124K), 138(133K), 192–3(187–8K); first the seasonings (ἡδύσματα: comm. on 84.4–5) are sprinkled in the bottom of (ὑπο-, as in fr. 193(188K).2, cf. Herwerden, *Coll. Crit.* 127) the λοπάδιον (comm. on 115(110K.22), then the fillet (τέμαχος: cf. Phryn. *Ecl.* p. 61.21f. Fischer τόμος κρέως ἢ πλακοῦντος· τὸ δὲ τέμαχος μόνον ἐπὶ ἰχθύος λέγεται, rightly: cf. Rutherford, *NP* 72ff., Neil on Ar. *Equ.* 283, my comm. on Alexis 92(88K)) of fish is inserted, white wine (cf. on v. 8 below) is poured over it and olive oil splashed on top. Herb garnitures and oil are commonly mentioned elsewhere in ancient recipes for boiled fish (e.g. Sotades com. 1, Archedicus 2), sometimes with the addition of wine (Archestratus fr. 179 Lloyd-Jones–Parsons, cf. Apicius 4.2.17). Davidson's modern recipe (*Seafood* 25)

46(45K).2/3, 255(253K)2/4 (ἐστί), 103(98K).6/7 (οὖσα, οὖσας), 115(110K).21/22, 178(173K).7/8 (parts of ποιῶ), 103(98K).10/12/13/ 16/19/20/25, 264(262K).1/3/4 (parts of ἔχω). A word thus repeated, whether unemphatically or for some designed effect (cf. J. D. Denniston, *Greek Prose Style* (Oxford 1952) 78ff.), is easily omitted in MSS by haplography; see also comm. on 178(172K).2–3.

COMMENTARY

for sea lamprey (*Petromyzon marinus*) is remarkably close to Alexis here in method and language: 'Lay these (three-inch sections of fish), with a bouquet garni and garlic, on a bed of thinly sliced onion and carrot, all in a buttered oven dish. Add red wine to cover and cook vigorously for 10 minutes. Remove the fish.'

8 λευκὸν οἶνον: the standard expression for pale wine made by the separation of the grape juice from the crushed pulp immediately after pressing (cf. comm. on 124(119K).2), used widely in comedy (Anaxandrides 42(41K).70, cf. Cratinus 195(183), Plaut. *Men.* 915), medical writers (over 130 times in the Hippocratic corpus, e.g. *Morb.* 2.38, 39, *Epid.* 5.70, 7.67.2, *Liqu.* 5; Mnesitheus in Ath. 1.32d, Galen *Comm. Hippocr. de vict. acut.* 3.1, Dioscorides 5.6.2) and elsewhere (e.g. Arist. *HA* 7.12, 588ᵃ6, Ath. 1.26c, Longus 1.16, cf. Ach. Tat. 2.2.2). Some dark wines, however, allegedly turned white after a few years (Ath. 1.27c); there were recipes for hastening this process (cf. Apicius 1.6). Cf. C. T. Seltman, *Wine in the Ancient World* (London 1957) 138ff., A. D. Fitton-Brown, *CR* 12 (1962) 192ff., M. Lambert-Gócs, *The Wines of Greece* (London and Boston 1990) 52f.

9–10 ἐπεσκέδασα τοὔλαιον ... πῶ ... ἀφεῖλόν τ': so Epit. and A (but ἀφειλοντ' A, without accents). In a cook's recipe the sandwiching of a present tense between two aorists (on the use of the latter tense see comm. on fr. 84.5) can be paralleled (e.g. παρέθενθ' ... ἐπικνῶσιν ... κατεσκέδασαν Ar. *Av.* 532–6, ἔρριψα ... παρατίθημ' ... προσέλαβον, ἐμόλυν' ... πέμπω ... ἐσπαργάνωσα Sotades com. fr. 1.12–14, 24–8; cf. Dohm, *Mageiros* 105 n. 2), but the presence of a particularising article with ἔλαιον in mid-recipe is unusual (thus unarticulated at Euphron 10(11K).9, Archedicus 2.5, com. adesp. fr. 289b.12 Austin, Archestratus fr. 168.4 Lloyd-Jones–Parsons). If there is corruption here, the first part of Kock's palaeographically neat conjecture ἐπισκεδάσας τ' ἔλαιον ... ἀφειδῶς is worth considering (on the use of τε to join the last two items in an otherwise asyndetic series see Denniston, *GP* 501, e.g. Men. *Dysk.* 26); ἀφειδῶς, however, is an unacceptable substitute for the transmitted *mot juste* ἀφεῖλον (= 'I removed' from the fire, cf. e.g. Ar. *Ach.* 1119, *Ran.* 518).

ἕψων πῶ μυελόν: despite being handicapped by a faulty text (with Musurus's ποτε for πῶ), Schweighaeuser, *Animadv.* 2.318 correctly interprets '*coquens ut sit molle et tenerum veluti medulla*'. Although no exact parallel for this use of μυελός is recorded (elsewhere the noun's metaphorical application is confined to the 'inmost part' Eur. *Hipp.* 255 and Σ, and the 'finest part' Theoc. 28.18), the softness of marrow is emphasised at e.g. A. *Ag.* 76 (see Fraenkel *ad loc.*) and Catullus 25.1, while the adjective μυελινός (= 'soft like marrow', of the buttocks) occurs in Dioscorides 10.2 Gow–Page = *Anth. Pal.* 12.37.

10 ἐπιγανώσας σιλφίῳ: 'glazing with silphium'. The compound occurs only here, but γανόω = 'I give a shiny surface to' at e.g. Plut. *Mor.* 74e, Crito med. in Galen 12.490 Kühn. Silphium juice is elsewhere described as clear, transparent (καθαρός . . . καὶ διαφανής Theophr. *HP* 9.1.7; *tralucente gutta* Pliny *HN* 19.46) and sparkling (ἀκτῖσι θείαις σιλφίου Antiphanes 216(217K).14 and Gulick's note b on Ath. 14.623b). See also comm. on 132(127K).5.

192 (187K)

Meineke 3.471 (III), Kock 2.367, Edmonds 2.464, Kassel–Austin 2.130. Before citing this fr., a recipe for cuttlefish, Ath. 7.324c identifies its speaker as a μάγειρος. The dramatic context is discussed in the introduction to Πονήρα.

1–2 The *Marcianus* opens the fr. with σηπίαι τόσους δραχμῆς μιᾶς τρις, five words which (i) are incomplete in sense (perhaps because the citation begins in mid-sentence, like many in Ath. and other excerptors (cf. e.g. Men. *Epitr.* 691f. ~ Harpocration and *Suda* s.v. ματρυλεῖον; comm. on Alexis 77, 106(101K), 128(123K), 178(172K), 194(189K) and my general introduction, II.i, p. 35; presumably here the resultant mangling of sense induced Epit. to omit these words from an otherwise complete citation of the fr.), and (ii) contain one clear indication of corruption in τόσους, a form alien to Attic comedy (τοσοῦτος occurs x 68, τοσουτοσί x 12, τοσόσδε x 2 in Ar. but not in Alexis 16.11 where see comm., τόσος transmitted only here, cf. Herwerden, *Coll. Crit.* 127). A wholly convincing restoration of Alexis' words seems impossible, but interpretations (e.g. W. Morel, *Rh. Mus.* 77 (1928) 167f.) and conjectures (e.g. σηπίας τόσας Schweighaeuser, *Animadv.* 4.428, printed by Meineke and Kock) which retain some part of τόσος may be ruled out. An alternative approach, which assigns the opening two words, variously emended and/or supplemented (e.g. σηπίας πόσας; Herwerden, <αἱ δὲ> σηπίαι πόσου; Peppink, *Observ.* 50, both with debts to Musurus's πόσου and Conti's translation '*quanti sepiae? unius dragmae*'), to a second speaker as a question and δραχμῆς μιᾶς τρεῖς (so plausibly Casaubon for τρις) to the cook in reply, would be more attractive if we had any evidence that two characters were involved here (but Ath. mentions only the μάγειρος, and see introduction to Πονήρα).

2 AE have τωνδε unaccented as one word, C τῶν δὲ as two; Kassel–Austin's apparatus is inaccurate. τῶν δέ (which Kassel–Austin print) is much inferior to τῶνδε (cf. Meineke 5.90), because (i) the demonstrative use of the article when coupled with δέ is in Attic generally confined to occasions where the referent (here σηπίαι as transmitted in v. 1) is not the subject of the preceding sentence (cf. Gildersleeve, *Syntax* 2.220f., LSJ s.v. ὁ, ἡ τό A.vi.6, Schwyzer 2.208), and (ii) the cook has been doing his own marketing (see introduction to 191(186K) and Πονήρα, pp. 559f. n. 1), so presumably he is carrying the cuttlefish with him and can point to them ('these fish here': cf. τάριχος ... τοδί in 191(186K).5, probably earlier in the same speech) as he describes what he is going to do. On the frequent confusion between ὁ δέ, ὅδε, ὅδε δέ in MSS (e.g. Eur. *IT* 918, *IA* 1373, Pl. *Resp.* 10.604a) see especially Fraenkel on A. *Ag.* 57.

2–3 The various species of cuttlefish and squid that go under the name of σηπία (see comm. on 159(155K).3 and the bibliography there) have around the mouth eight short (= πόδες) and two long, usually retractable (= προβοσκίδες) tentacles which are indiscriminately termed πλεκτάναι (cf. Arist. *PA* 4.9, 685ᵃ22ff.; in comedy Eubulus 148(150K).7 of a sepia, Diphilus 33(34K) of an octopus, cf. Crobylus 7.1). πτερύγια are the winglike lateral fins (Arist. *PA* 685ᵇ16ff.; in comedy Alexis 84.3, Sotades 1.16).

2–5 Alexis' recipe again shows culinary competence (cf. comm. on 191(186K).7–9). Davidson's 20th-century recipe for *seiches à l'Aigue-mortaise* (*Seafood* 294f.) corresponds closely: 'Clean your cuttlefish and cut them into pieces the size of ravioli. Put these into a casserole with a tumbler of water and cook them for 20 to 35 minutes ... Heat some olive oil in a pan and cook the pieces of cuttlefish gently in this ... Season with salt, pepper and a touch of cayenne.'

3 ἐφθάς: Dindorf's correction of ACE's ἐφθά, where the ending has been unmetrically assimilated to that of the nearer πτερύγια. In such predications of two (or more) nouns with different genders, the adjective may agree with either the nearer or the more dominant noun, cf. Gildersleeve, *Syntax* 2.197f.

4 For the double object with verbs of cutting etc., where one accusative identifies the creature or thing to be cut and the other the pieces into which it is divided, cf. e.g. Ephippus 22.2 τὴν βατίδα τεμάχη κατατεμών, Euphron 10(11K).7 ταύτην (sc. γογγυλίδα) ἔτεμε λεπτὰ καὶ μακρά, K.G. 1.323, W. J. M. Starkie on Ar. *Ach.* 302.

6 ἐπεισιών: so ACE, printed by Kassel–Austin, but this participle (i) produces an anapaest split after the first short in the second half of the second metron, a rare though not unparalleled licence in a verse with penthemimeral caesura (cf. my discussion in *CQ* 7 (1957) 195f., instancing from earlier comedy Ar. *Av.* 442, 1644, *Ran.* 652, 658, *Eccl.* 998, Plato 27(28K).1, perhaps Eupolis 99.35 Kassel–Austin = 92.35 Austin, *CGFP*, but only Antiphanes 85.2 from Alexis' own generation), and (ii) yields less than perfect sense (ἐπεισιών in Attic = (a) 'coming in additionally', (b) 'coming in after/next, cf. LSJ s.v. ἐπείσειμι: here neither meaning is particularly apt, but the latter is possible since the cook's entry would follow that of the diners of v. 5). Meineke's brilliant conjecture ἐπισείων (first advanced at 1.380 n. 75) normalises metre and restores the *mot juste*:

translate 'while they are at dinner I bring them (the chunks of cuttlefish), shaking them on to the grill-pan (ἐπὶ τὸ τάγηνον, governed jointly by the two verbs of movement φέρω and ἐπισείων, and so any replacement by ἐπὶ τοῦ ταγήνου, suggested by Cobet in Peppink, *Observ.* 50 and by R. Ellis, *AJP* 6 (1885) 298, is unwarranted; on τάγηνον see comm. on 115(110K).12) as it sizzles (cf. τὸ μὲν τάγηνον ... σίζον Ar. *Equ.* 929f.)'.

Although no exact parallel for the literal use of ἐπισείω in this construction (accusative + ἐπί with accusative) is cited (thus Kock's '*exempla desidero*' is legitimate), any objection to it can hardly be sustained when (i) the related literal use 'shake at/against' with accusative and dative occurs from Hom. *Il.* 4.167 onwards (on the metaphorical use derived from this see comm. on Alexis 3.1), (ii) literal uses are common with other compounds of σείω, e.g. ἐκ-, ἐν-, παρα-, προσ-, and (iii) at Pollux 4.147 the mask name ἐπίσειστος is explained by ἐπισείονται αἱ τρίχες.

193 (188K)

Meineke 3.471 (II), Kock 2.367, Edmonds 2.466, Kassel–Austin 2.131. This puzzling fr., cited by Ath. 4.170c (complete in A, merely τρῖμμα and vv. 4–5 in Epit.) as a catalogue of ἡδύσματα (less appropriately than the other two frs. quoted with the same heading – Alexis 132(127K), 179(174K)), comprises part only of a complete sentence (cf. introductions to comm. on 192(187K), 194(189K)), to which (i) a main verb, probably in the present tense and first person singular if the fr. was spoken by the cook and derives from the same speech as frs. 191(186K), 192(187K) and 194(189K), and possibly (ii) a word or words governing the opening genitive τῆς ὀριγάνου (but see below, comm. on v. 1) need to be supplied. These deficiencies make an unambiguously convincing account of the fr. impossible, and in the circumstances it may be useful to provide a translation of the fr. with the alternative possibilities indicated: 'First, having put into the bottom of a hefty stewing/boiling-dish

(EITHER)	(OR)
(? some of) the marjoram (? already mentioned); having coloured the ingredients for the *court-bouillon*, soaked evenly on top with wine-vinegar and must;	the marjoram *court-bouillon* (? already mentioned) evenly soaked on top, with wine-vinegar; having coloured it with must;

and having beaten this with a firm (stalk/root of) silphium ...'.

Despite the incompleteness and ambiguity, fr. 193(188K) to all appearance describes a sauce or *court-bouillon*, perhaps for the cuttlefish of fr. 192(187K) (cf. comm. on v. 3). There is, however, no way of deciding

COMMENTARY

whether 193(188K) preceded or followed 192(187K); the two frs. neither dovetail nor overlap.

1 τῆς ὀριγάνου: A's reading can be defended. ὀρίγανος is feminine in comedy also at Ar. *Eccl.* 1030 (cf. *Suda* s.v., Choerilus in *Et. Mag.*630.47) and Plato com. 169(154K), cf. Ath. 2.68b; see comm. on 132(127K).7, 138(133K).6; and although definite articles are sometimes corruptly added by scribes (e.g. in comedy Ar. *Nub.* 1352 and Dover, Men. *Dysk.* 18 and Sandbach *ad loc.*, W. G. Arnott, *CQ* 7 (1957) 197 n. 1, 198 n. 2 and comm. on Alexis frs. 145(141K).9, 259(257K).2), τῆς here is justifiable as confirming that another mention of the same marjoram had just preceded. The genitive either (i) is partitive (directly with ὑποθείς, cf. Ar. *Eccl.* 1030, or dependent on an accusative in the unquoted context governed by the participle), or (ii) goes with τὸ τρῖμμα in v. 3, defining its main ingredient (other varieties of τρῖμμα were similarly named: see below). With the former interpretation, commas are needed at the end of v. 2 (so first Musurus); with the latter, only after ὄξει (so first Meineke).

2 The two favoured corrections of A's hypermetrical πρώτιστον ὑποτιθείς are Jacobs's πρώτισθ' ὑποτιθείς (*Spic.* 23, cf. *Addit.* 111) and Casaubon's πρώτιστον ὑποθείς; the latter is preferable because it provides an aorist participle to match those in vv. 4 and 5, but cannot be considered certain, since the paradosis (-τιθείς εἰς) may point to a more deep-seated dittographic corruption. Cobet's suggestion ὑπόθες (in Peppink, *Observ.* 31) would be more attractive if the fr.'s context proved not to be one of first-person singular indicative statements (but see introduction to Πονήρα).

λοπάδα νεανικήν: in the sense of 'hefty/large' the adjective occurs first (? as a lively colloquialism) in Attic comedy (κρέας Ar. *Plut.* 1137, where the scholia explain its use as a metaphor from the size of a young man's appetite, ποτοί Antiphanes 188(190K).20), but its appearance with the same meaning in later 4th-century scientific writing (πόροι = 'ducts' Arist. *PA* 3.9, 671^{b}16, τὰ τοῦ δένδρου Theophr. *HP* 5.1.11) suggests that by then 'the metaphor had ... become worn and the colloquial flavour had disappeared' (P. T. Stevens, *Colloquial Expressions in Euripides* (*Hermes Einzelschr.* 38, Wiesbaden 1976) 49f., cf. also Casaubon, *Animadv.* 303, Barrett on Eur. *Hipp.* 1203–5). On λοπάδα, see comm. on 115(110K).21–3; the dish was used particularly for cooking fish (cf. Ch. Dedoussi (Athens 1965) on Men. *Sam.* 150, her numbering; and introduction to comm. on this fr.).

3 τὸ τρῖμμ': although scribes have been proved guilty of adding supernumerary articles in MSS (see above on v. 1: hence here Blaydes' unnecessary ὑπότριμμ' first *Adv.* 1.113, and καὶ τρῖμμ' *Adv.* 2.164), there is no call to reject A's reading just because it requires us to assume that the

566

τρῖμμα (like the marjoram in v. 1) had already been mentioned by the speaker. The definition of τρῖμμα given by Ath. 1.31e πόματί τινι ἐξ ἀρωμάτων κατασκευαζομένῳ (cf. Pollux 6.18, Hesych. and *Suda* s.v.), is misleading if not entirely inaccurate (*pace* LSJ s.v.); in culinary contexts τρῖμμα is always a spiced sauce/stock/*court-bouillon* (or ingredient thereof) served with some sort of fish (at Sotades com. 1.17f. a sauce for cuttlefish, which supports the suggestion advanced in the introduction to this fr. that here Alexis' cook may be describing the *court-bouillon* for the σηπία of fr.192(87K)). There were different sorts of τρῖμμα, sometimes identified by the name of an ingredient (e.g. συκαμίνινον Sotades 1.4), flavour (ὀξυλίπαρον Timocles 3.2, ? ἄνθινον Sotades 1.17f.) or colour (χλωρόν Axionicus 4.8), and this fact makes the interpretation of τῆς ὀριγάνου in v. 1 here as a comparable descriptive label more attractive. The diminutive τριμμάτιον seems not to have been differentiated in any culinary sense from τρῖμμα, but in our ignorance of so many ancient Greek cooking practices it would be foolhardy to assume (as Kock and V. Bevilacqua, *Dioniso* 7 (1939) 33 do) that ὑπότριμμα also was identical, although the recipes in Ath. 7.324a (with boiled wine, wine-vinegar and silphium!) and Apic. 1.23 (with wine, wine-vinegar) suggest something closely related. The name τρίμμα is now applied in the Epirote marches to a dish of finely chopped liver and cabbage stuffed into intestines and oven-roasted, see M. Lambert-Gócs, *The Wines of Greece* (London and Boston 1990) 250.

εὐρύθμως διειμένον: 'soaked evenly'. The adverb (properly 'rhythmically/gracefully') is used here either loosely (? as a vogue word of contemporary slang) or perhaps as an example of the oddly precious vocabulary adopted by comic μάγειροι (see introductions to frs. 24, 129(124K), 178(172K)). In comic culinary contexts the participle occurs elsewhere in the active (ἐλαδίῳ δ. Sotades 1.27; cf. οἴνῳ λευκῷ δ. Hippocr. *Intern.* 52 and with the same construction over seventy times in the corpus, Arist. *HA* 7.3.1, 583ª24) and middle (ὄξει δ. Ar. *Plut.* 720).

4 ὄξει: see comm. on 286(285K).3.

σιραίῳ χρωματίσας: cf. the use of *coloro* in Apic. 4.2.20 etc. With the punctuation offered here (see introduction and comm. on v. 1) the tinting was done not with the wine-vinegar (which goes with διειμένον) but only with the σίραιον, the boiled-down new (and here presumably red, providing colour) wine (cf. comm. on 132(127K).8).

4–5 σιλφίῳ πυκνῷ πατάξας: πυκνῷ probably refers to the close-packed pith of the root or stalk of the silphium plant (cf. comm. on 132(127K).5); both parts were used in cooking, and both were big, thick and pithy (Theophr. *HP* 6.3.1, the root πολλὴν καὶ παχεῖαν while the stalk is compared in size and thickness to the giant fennel, *Ferula communis*). In such a context πατάξας is the *mot juste* (the qualms felt by Kock and Herwerden, *Coll. Crit.* 127 are nonsensical); Meineke well compares Alexis

COMMENTARY

138(133K).5 σ. μάστιξον (see my comm. *ad loc.*) and Axionicus 8.3f. σ. σφενδονῶν.

194 (189K)

Meineke 3.472 (IV), Kock 2.367, Edmonds 2.466, Kassel–Austin 2.132. The text of this fr., which has been mishandled by the editors of Ath. (at 14.655f) and the comic fragments from Musurus to Edmonds, is (like that of 193(188K)) syntactically incomplete, consisting solely of a noun phrase and a temporal clause attached to it without any main verb. Its subject matter – a purchase of food, on this occasion roast pork – links it with frs. 191–3(186–8K), and it most probably comes from the same scene and speaker, perhaps even the same speech (cf. Meineke, *ad loc.* and my introduction to Πονήρα).

1 κρεΐσκον: a ἅπαξ λεγόμενον,[1] but comedy's fondness for diminutives of this form (over twenty examples in Old Comedy, eleven in Middle and New including γλαυκίσκος Philemon 82(79K).21, Damoxenus 2.18, ἱππίσκος the alternative title of Alexis' 'Αγωνίς, μειρακίσκος Alexis 37(36K).2, Men. *Asp.* 128, *Georg.* 4, νεανίσκος Men. *Asp.* 133, *Dysk.* 39, etc., χιτωνίσκος Antiphanes 35(33K).3, Apollodorus 12) is a warning (cf. Jacobi at Meineke 5.ccxi f.) against its replacement here by some other conjectured form.

2–3 Scholars hitherto (with the exceptions of Kassel–Austin and possibly Korais[2]) have mistranscribed the clear ἐγχυλότερον in A (our sole witness: Epit. omits the fr.) as εὐχυλό-, and most editors from Dindorf on have sought to convert the paradosis (ὀπτὸν καὶ θερμὸν ἐγχυλότερον ὅταν ᾖ προσφέρων) into a continuous metrical text by deleting the καί (so first

---

[1] From nominative masculine κρεΐσκος or neuter κρεΐσκον? Lexicographers (e.g. LSJ s.v. κρεΐσκος; Buck–Petersen, *Reverse Index* 638), editors and commentators generally assume the former, but (i) the verbless context of κρεΐσκον in Ath.'s citation affords no clue; (ii) the only known parallel formation from a neuter primitive in -ας is σφελίσκον (also a *hapax*, C. Michel, *Recueil d' inscriptions grecques* (Paris 1900) p. 679 no. 832.50); (iii) although the gender of -ισκ- diminutives is commonly identical with that of their primitives, there are too many anomalies for any assumption that κρέας *must* produce a diminutive in -ίσκον to be sustainable: e.g. ἀλθαία/-ίσκος, ἀσκέρα/-ίσκον, κάρυον/-ίσκος, λοπάς/ -δίσκος, μῦς/-ίσκη, σελήνη/-ίσκος, φιάλη/-ίσκος. Cf. *Glotta* 69 (1991) 187ff.

[2] Schweighaeuser's apparatus notes *ad loc.* 'ἐγχυλότερον corr. Corays', but this may imply that an unpublished note of Korais which pointed out the correct MS reading was misinterpreted by Schweighaeuser as a new conjecture.

Casaubon) and/or accepting Porson's implausible conjecture εὔχυλον, τέρεν[1] (*In Xenophontis Anabasin addenda et corrigenda* (London 1810) xliii). Such fiddling with the text takes little account of common practices among excerptors when quoting relatively short frs. (cf. my paper in Flores 362ff.). They reproduce with reasonable accuracy that part of the citation which is immediately relevant to the excerptor's purpose (here κρεῖσκον ... ὕειον ὀπτόν, cf. Ath.'s lemma), but the remainder of the citation, included to fill in the context or for other reasons, may be quoted very carelessly and is prone to three predominant types of error: (i) the replacement of an original word or phrase by a roughly synonymous equivalent (the result doubtless of imprecision or faulty memory: e.g. Clem. Alex. *Paed.* 2.8.68 χεῖρας for ῥῖνας in Alexis 195(190K).2), (ii) the omission of words or phrases and (iii) changes in word-order (e.g. for ii and iii John Philoponus on Arist. *Meteor.* p. 94 Hayduck citing Men. *Pk.* 533f.). In view of this, the paradosis of fr. 194(189K) is likely to be sound as far as ὀπτόν (the part relevant to the citer's purpose), with the speaker describing some pork he's bought already roasted (for purchases of roasted meat and fish, cf. e.g. Alexis 15.16, 27.7, Philemon 83(80K)); thereafter a lacuna ('*aliquid excidisse videtur*', Kock) covering the rest of v. 2 (and perhaps one or more subsequent verses); the remaining words of the fr. (as cited in A) then form an acceptable comic trimeter: καὶ θερμόν, ἐγχυλότερον ὅταν ᾖ, προσφέρων, 'and serving it (the pork?) hot, when it will be more juicy'. The cook presumably bought his roast pork cold in the market and reheated it.

3 ἐγχυλότερον: so A (see above, on vv. 2–3). ἔγχυλος and εὔχυλος are virtually synonymous ('juicy/succulent'), occurring most frequently in medicine (e.g. ἔγχ- Hippocr. *Vict.* 2.45, *Affect.* 59, *Intern.* 20; εὔχ- Ath. 2.62c and 7.282d citing Diphilus Siph. and Hicesius, Archigenes in Galen 12.460 Kühn) and botany (e.g. ἔγχ- Theophr. *HP* 3.7.2, 7.9.5, *CP* 4.12.11; εὔχ- *HP* 7.4.4, *CP* 2.6.1, 3.10.2, 4.13.2). ἔγχυλος occurs elsewhere in Alexis (129(124K).12), cf. also Agatharchides 40 Müller and Alciphron fr. 5 (coining ἰσχνέγχυλος to describe female beauty). Cf. *Glotta* 69 (1991) 189f.

195 (190K)

Meineke 3.472 (v), Kock 2.368, Edmonds 2.466, Kassel–Austin 2.132; cf. A. Olivieri, *Dioniso* 7 (1939) 292. The text of this fr. is cobbled together

---

[1] The adjective τέρην is at home in epic, lyric and tragedy, but its only occurrence in Attic comedy (trochaic tetrameter at Cratinus fr. 335(302K)) belongs to a context where high poetry and obscenity are

from three separate citations: in Ath. 2.46a (Epit. naming author but not
title, vv. 2–3), 15.687d (A naming author and title, Epit. only author,
ὑγιείας v. 2 to end), and Clem. Alex. *Paed.* 2.8.68 (P naming source as ὁ
κωμικός, the whole fr.). Speaker and dramatic context in this description
of a man anointing his nostrils with perfume (? a soldier: cf. fr. 63(62K)
and comm.) cannot be identified, but the explanation that this action aids
health by producing excellent odours for the brain clearly alludes (cf.
Olivieri), possibly with comic ridicule, to the theory that the brain was the
central organ of perception and the other senses. This theory, pioneered
by Alcmaeon of Croton (Theophr. *Sens.* 25f. = Alcmaeon 24 A 5 Diels–
Kranz ὀσφραίνεσθαι δὲ (sc. Ἀλκμαίων φησὶν) ῥισὶν ἅμα τῷ ἀναπνεῖν ἀνά-
γοντα τὸ πνεῦμα πρὸς τὸν ἐγκέφαλον ... ἁπάσας δὲ τὰς αἰσθήσεις
συνηρτῆσθαί πως πρὸς τὸν ἐγκέφαλον ... ἐπιλαμβάνεσθαι γὰρ τοὺς
πόρους δι' ὧν αἱ αἰσθήσεις) and Diogenes of Apollonia (Theophr. *Sens.*
39ff. = 64 A 19 Diels–Kranz = T 8 in A. Laks, *Diogène d'Apollonie* (Lille
1983) 106ff., 112ff., 116f.; cf. G. S. Kirk, J. E. Raven, M. Schofield, *The
Presocratic Philosophers*[2] (Cambridge 1983) 447ff.), and in its turn ridiculed
by Aristophanes in *Nub.* 227ff. (cf. Dover on 230), was further developed
by physicians like the author of *Morb. sacr.* in the Hippocratic corpus (cf.
H. Grensemann in the preface to his edition (Berlin 1968) 27ff.), who
regarded the brain as the centre of consciousness (17, 19f.) and suggested
that epileptic convulsions were caused by the descent of phlegm into the
veins, thus preventing the passage of air to the brain (10).[1] Alexis'
reference to the promotion of health by the practice described in fr.
195(190K) suggests that contemporary medical theory, which had doubtless filtered through to non-specialists in a garbled form, may have
influenced the remark. It would not be the only such allusion in the extant
frs.; 219(216K).3f. mentions the physician Mnesitheus with some knowledge of his ideas, and the pretentious cook who speaks 129(124K) seems to
be compared to the physician Glaucias (v.13, see comm. *ad loc.*) because he
loads his language with medical terminology.

1 μύροις, cited as the fr.'s opening word only by Clement, may have

---

juxtaposed in a way familiar from Aristophanes but not so far recorded
for Alexis.

[1] In the early 3rd century, when Alexis was an old man, Herophilus of
Alexandria attempted to confirm by dissection that the brain was the
central organ of sensation and to argue that health was the foundation
of all happiness (Galen *UP* 8.11, 10.12, *Loc. Affect.* 3.14 = 3.667, 813,
8.212 Kühn, [Rufus], *Anat.* 74 p. 185 Daremberg, Aëtius 4.5.4), but it
would be wrong to conclude without further and more reliable evidence, even though Πονήρα is undatable, that fr. 195(190K) was in any
way a reflection of his views.

preceded ἐναλείφεται (? directly) in Alexis' continuous text; it suits sense (cf. comm. on 63(62K).8) and metre, but we should be warned against its uncritical acceptance into the text by Clement's habitual inaccuracy in quotations (cf. comm. on vv. 2–3 below).

1–2 For both custom and idiom cf. Hipponax fr. 104.21f. West βακκάρει δὲ τὰς ῥῖνας | ἤλειφον (B. ten Brink, *Philologus* 6 (1851) 48, S. Lilja, *The Treatment of Odours in the Poetry of Antiquity* (Helsinki 1972) 62f.).

2 ἐναλείφεται (CE, Ath. 2) or ὑπαλείφεται (P, Clem.)? Both are possible (*pace* Cobet, *NL* 33, wrongly describing the former as '*vox nihili*'); the two verbs occur in good Attic (ἐν- Pl. *Resp.* 4.420c, ὑπ- Pl. *Lach.* 185c, Ar. *Pax* 898, fr. 132(129K) etc.), are basically synonymous and share the same constructions (for middle + accusative and instrumental dative cf. ἐν- Plut. *Mor.* 771b, ὑπ- Xen. *Oec.* 10.5), but here the palaeographic argument supports ἐν-. This compound is recorded less frequently than ὑπ- (cf. the *TGL* entries) in ancient texts (even the Hippocratic corpus: x 9 against x 18, although Pollux 4.180 includes ἐν- in his list of medical terms), and appears to have become obsolete in Byzantine Greek (it does not appear in the lexica of E. A. Sophocles (New York 1900) and I. D. Stamatakos (Athens 1971)). The likelihood that it was replaced with the more familiar ὑπ- by Clement himself or a later scribe is increased by the fact that P (the *codex unicus* of *Paed.*) corrupts two of fr. 195(190K)'s next six words (ὀσμάς, ὑγιείας) to post-classical forms (ὀδμάς: cf. Phryn. *Ecl.* 62 p. 65.35ff. Fischer = 71 pp. 16off. Rutherford, LSJ s.v. ὀσμή; ὑγιείας, with Epit. MSS of Ath. 15.687d: cf. LSJ s.v. ὑγίεια 'from about ii BC written ὕγεια', Mayser 1.1.92 n. 5, Mayser–Schmoll 1.1.126, Schwyzer 1.194, Threatte 1.416ff.), as well as introducing its habitual assortment of other errors (2 χεῖρας for ῥῖνας, 3 ἐγκεφάλων for -λῳ; cf. the introduction to comm. on fr. 103 (98K)).

2–3 The text is unexceptionable (Meineke aptly compares Philyllius 19(20K).2 ὅπερ μέγιστόν ἐστιν ὑγιείας μέρος), but without further context its punctuation is uncertain: after ῥῖνας either colon, with the rest of the fr. a separate clause ('It's the most important contribution to health, to make . . .': so Stählin, Kaibel, Edmonds, Kassel–Austin) perhaps even interjected by a second speaker; or comma, with μέρος μ. then in apposition to an unexpressed internal object in its clause (K.G. 1.284f.), and ὀσμὰς ἐγκεφάλῳ χρηστὰς ποιεῖν (on the orthography, see comm. on 16.2) epexegetic (K.G. 2.4f.: so Kock). CE's variant ποιῶν at Ath. 2.46a can probably be dismissed as a copyist's or reader's attempt to simplify the syntax; Desrousseaux's conjecture (his edition of Ath. 1–2, *ad loc.*) μέγιστον <ὂν> seeks with parallel pointlessness to ease the construction of the noun phrase ὑγιείας μέρος μέγιστον into an accusative absolute, but at the cost of introducing a doubly split anapaest into the second half of the first metron, an anomaly more tolerable when transmitted than when conjectured in an iambic trimeter with penthemimeral caesura (cf. *CQ* 7 (1957) 189).

196 (191K)

Meineke 3.473 (VI), Kock 2.368, Edmonds 2.466, Kassel–Austin 2.133. Speaker and scene are discussed above in the introduction to Πονήρα. The Thessalian χόνδρος here described as 'inside' is perhaps an ingredient for (? part of) the dessert to be served at the meal for which the cook who speaks frs. 191–4(186–9K) has been hired. In this type of context χόνδρος = groats made from various wheats and barleys (cf. [Arist.] *Probl.* 21.21, 929^{b}1ff., Theophr. *HP* 4.4.9) but especially from emmer (*Triticum durum*: see N. Jasny, *The Wheats of Classical Antiquity* (Baltimore 1944) 14ff., 54f., and L. A. Moritz, *Grain-mills and Flours in Classical Antiquity* (Oxford 1968) 147ff.; here Blümner, *Technologie* 55ff., Olck in *RE* s.v. Χόνδρος 2372.22ff. and LSJ need correction), which were boiled (e.g. Ar. fr. 208(203K).1, Men. fr. 451.10, Hippocr. *Vict.*2.42, *Mul.* 2.110), usually with water but in wealthier households (Pherecrates 113(108K).18, cf. Eubulus 89(90K).4f.) and for the sick-bed (Hippocr. *Acut.(Sp.)* 53) apparently with an admixture of milk, to make something akin to modern porridge that might be served μετὰ δεῖπνον (Ephippus 13.1ff.). Megara and especially Thessaly were noted for the quality of their groats (Antiphanes 36(34K).2–3 from his Ἄντεια, see below, 'False or doubtful attributions', II; possibly Hermippus 63.6, if the unmetrical Ἰταλίας there is a corruption of Θετταλίας: so Kock).

ἔνδον: cf. comm. on 184(179K).3.

197 (192K)

Meineke 3.473 (VII), Kock 2.368, Edmonds 2.466, Kassel–Austin 2.133. Context and speaker are unknown.

ἀκρολίπαροι: a vivid coinage (? by Alexis), 'glistening on the surface', sc. like athletes who have oiled themselves before leaving the *palaestra* (e.g. Theoc. 2.79f., 102f.). As the forepart of a compound adjective ἄκρος commonly takes the meaning 'at the edge': e.g. ἀκροβαφής (of a robe, Nonn. *Dion.* 48.339), -καρπος (Theophr. *HP* 1.14.2), -θιγής (of a kiss, Meleager 112.10 Gow–Page = *Anth. Pal.* 12.68), -κομος (of Thracians, Hom. *Il.* 4.533, Hipponax 115.6 West; of the hair growing from the bottom of an elk's dewlap, Polyb. 34.10.8–9), -σχιδής (of a lobed leaf, Theophr. *HP* 3.11.1).

ὑπόξυλον: so A and Epit. here (Ath. 9.385b), but Meineke's conjecture ὑπόξυλοι, based on an assumption of scribal assimilation of the ending to the case of the juxtaposed noun, is tempting if unverifiable without more

ΠΟΝΗΡΑ

context. The adjective's range of meaning is well explained by Phryn. *Praep. Soph.* 115.12ff. de Borries, ὑπόξυλος ποιητής, ῥήτωρ, φίλος καὶ τὰ ὅμοια· εἴρηται κατὰ μεταφορὰν τῶν ἀπὸ ξύλου πεποιημένων σκευῶν, οἷς ἐπιπολῆς ἐπελήλαται ἄργυρος ἢ χρυσός. καὶ τίθεται ἐπὶ τῶν πονηρῶν μὲν ἔνδοθεν, ἐντυχεῖν δ' ἐπιεικῶν; similarly Σ Hermogenes, *Rhetores Graeci* 5.486, 7.973 Walz, and cf. *Et. Mag.* 783.17 (citing Ar. fr. 911(881K)) and Phot. s.v. The literal meaning is well exemplified by Attic inscriptions of the late 5th/early 4th centuries listing a variety of such objects in the temple inventories: ἀσπίδες, διόπαι, κανοῦν, κοίτη, μήλω, ὅρμω, ὑποδερίς (*IG* i³.349.53f., 350.72ff., 351.10f., ii².1388.76f., cf. Xen. *Oec.* 10.3). According to Pollux 3.56 the adjective was applied metaphorically by the poets of New Comedy to one type of κίβδηλος above all: a man who had obtained Athenian citizenship illegally. Whether this allegation was borne out by the present fr. or Men. *Perinth.* fr. 9 Sandbach (the one other comic passage recorded where the adjective certainly described living beings[1]) we have no means of knowing. Cf. also (i) Plato's figurative use of ὑπόχαλκος, ὑποσίδηρος, ὑπόχρυσος and ὑπάργυρος at *Resp.* 3.415b–c, and A. Körte, *Hermes* 64 (1929) 267ff., and (ii) the related use of *ligneus* in Latin, e.g. Catullus 29.8 and W. Kroll. comm. (Leipzig and Berlin 1923) *ad loc.*, Lucretius 4.1153.

Ποντικός

Meineke 1.330, 387f., T. B. L. Webster, *CQ* 2 (1952) 22. The title, which is shared with Antiphanes, Epigenes and Timocles, most probably (cf. W. Dittenberger, *Hermes* 42 (1907) 6ff.) indicates a man (? a Greek colonial) from either the territory along the north coast of Asia Minor which went by the name of Pontus many years before Mithridates I established his kingdom there in 301 (thus e.g. Xen. *Anab.* 5.6.15, 6.2.4, *Hell.* 2.2.1), or any one of the other coastal regions around the Black Sea (cf. Chr. M. Danoff in *RE Suppl.* ix s.v. *Pontos Euxeinos* 866.31ff., 1046.32ff., Sandbach on Men. *Sam.* 98–101). Inhabitants of these areas were ridiculed in cities like Athens (? and possibly in this play) for graceless stupidity (Meineke 1.330 cites Ath. 8.351c, 13.580c = Machon 327ff. Gow, Diog. Laert. 6.3; cf. also Men. *Sam.* 98ff., 417, Lucian *Alex.* 17). On ethnic titles generally in Alexis see the introductions to Ἀτθίς, Ἐπιδαύριος, on those in -κός introduction to Ἐρετρικός.

The play can be dated to the period between *c.* 345 and 318 by the

---

[1] LSJ s.v. mistakenly cites fr. 197(192K) as a literal use of the adjective, ignoring Ath.'s introductory statement that Alexis there was talking about ἀνθρώπους, not inanimate objects.

reference in fr. 198(193K) to Callimedon ὁ Κάραβος (cf. Meineke1.387f., Webster, my introductions to Δορκίς, Κράτεια and to comm. on fr. 57(56K)).

198 (193K)

Meineke 3.473, Kock 2.368, Edmonds, 2.466, Kassel–Austin 2.133. The fr. and its citer (Ath. 3.100c) give no clue to speaker or dramatic situation.

1 πάτρας: in Attic largely confined to serious poetry (e.g. Eur. *Tro.* 387 ὑπὲρ πάτρας ἔθνῃσκον, fr. 120.3), but used by comic poets in place of the more mundane πατρίδος either in tragic parody (Ar. *Thesm.* 136, *Ran.* 1163, 1427) or (*pace* LSJ s.v.) for puns (here on πάτρας/μήτρας, Ar. *Ach.* 147 πατέρ'/πάτρᾳ).[1]

2–3 μήτρας ... ἐφθῆς: sow's womb, which has disappeared from modern cookery in the west, was frequently mentioned from the 4th century onward as a delicacy (e.g. ἥδιστον κρέας Antiphanes 219(220K).3, cf. Alciphron 3.37.1, Plut. *Mor.* 733e), served boiled (also Sopater frs. 8, 18, 21, Kaibel) with silphium juice and wine vinegar (Lynceus of Samos in Ath. 3.100e–f).[2] Callimedon's (cf. introduction to Ποντικός) fondness for it is attested also by Euphron 8(9K) and possibly Dioxippus 3 (if ἐκεῖνον v. 2 is rightly identified as the politician by Kock *ad loc.* and Kaibel on Ath. 3.100e).

3 The corruption in A's nonsensical ισωσ προσ ιταλων here (Epit. ends the quotation at ἐφθῆς) has led to a rash of ingenious conjectures, most of which fail to meet with equal persuasiveness the two essentials of accounting for the paradosis and producing a valid punch line for the joke whose foundations have been laid in vv. 1–2. Schweighaeuser's προσεῖτ' ἄν (after Casaubon's προσίετ' ἄν, cf. *Animadv.* 197f.) ἄλλως (*ad loc.* and *Animadv.* 2.183f.), assuming faulty word-division, the common confusion of I and EI, and lipography (AN before ΑΛΛ), has rightly convinced subsequent scholars up to the ἄν ('would be ready ...'), but its ἄλλως (? 'in vain') would make a feeble climax to Alexis' joke. Emperius' πρ. ἐλών ἄν ἀπ. (*Adv.* 346) is close to the *ductus* but ἐλών lacks point and the position of ἄν is unattractive although not unparalleled (cf. J. Wackernagel, *Indogermanische Forschungen* 1 (1892) 392ff. = *Kleine Schriften* 1 (Göttingen

---

[1] Cf. the puns on μήτρα in Antiphanes 219(220K) (~ ἔμμητρος, μητρόπολις, Μητρᾶς ὁ Χῖος) and Ath. 3.96e (~ μητρόπολις, μητήρ).

[2] For its popularity with imperial Roman gourmets see e.g. Hor. *Epist.* 1.15.41, Pliny, *HN* 11.37.210 (or 84), Juvenal 11.81, Pliny the Younger *Epist.* 1.15.3, Martial 13.56.2; several recipes in Apic. 2.3.1, 7.1.1–4, 6. According to *Ed. Diocl.* 4.4. it cost 24 denarii a pound. Cf. André, *Alimentation* 141; H. McGee, *On Food and Cooking* (London 1984) 84.

ΠΟΝΤΙΚΟΣ

1954) 6off., M. H. B. Marshall, *Verbs, Nouns, and Postpositives in Attic Prose* (Edinburgh 1987) 35ff.). Herwerden (*Mnemosyne* 14 (1886) 187), after demolishing Kock's ἁλοῶν with the demonstration that this participle cannot simply mean '*vorans*' without contextual support (as Kock alleged), cleverly proposed πρ. ἂν εἷς ὢν ἀπ. on the assumption that a scribe had abbreviated εἷς to A (cf. in the *Marcianus* e.g. Δ for τέτταρας at Ath. 15.691e = Alexis 63(62K).2); in Greek MSS, however, A is more commonly an abbreviation for πρῶτος (cf. C. G. Cobet, *Collectanea Critica* (Leiden 1878) 170, *NL* 212), and μόνος (not εἷς) would be the contrast expected here to πᾶς τις in v. 1. Kaibel indeed conjectured ἂν ἀπ. μόνος, excellent in sense but palaeographically inexplicable. With remarkable ingenuity Peppink (*Observ.* 24) suggested that the paradosis in A might have resulted from a scribal misreading of a gloss; if ἴσως λοι had been written above προσεῖτ' ἂν, offering προσέλοιτ' ἂν as a variant reading ('would prefer'), it could have been taken as a missing part of the continuous text; unfortunately I cannot trace any parallel in A for such an abbreviated gloss. The only emendation that builds convincingly on Schweighaeuser's foundations is Desrousseaux's πρ. ἂν <ἄλλον> ἀπ. in *Mélanges offerts à M. Octave Navarre* (Toulouse 1935) 140f., which is palaeographically neat (ΑΛΛΟΝ → ΑΛΩΝ, with haplography and the common confusion between Ο and Ω) and turns v. 3 into a witty παρὰ προσδοκίαν joke: 'would be ready – *for another man* to die!'[1] The point would be all the more effective if Callimedon had gained at some time a reputation for cowardice; none, however, is alleged in our sources. Cf. also Nesselrath, *LP* 484f.

Προσκεδαννύμενος

The title's import is uncertain. Periplectomenus (? -ecomenus; see F. Ritschl, prolegomenon to his edition of Plautus I (Bonn 1848) lxxxviii and *Opuscula Philologica* 3 (Leipzig 1877) 326, K. Schmidt, *Hermes* 37 (1902) 377f.) in Plaut. *MG* provides us one instance of a participle used (at least in Roman comedy) as a proper name, and Προσκεδαννύμενος would fit – as either *nomen proprium* or more probably participial description – a character who swept all before himself or out of his way as he entered in the role of parasite (cf. e.g. Plaut. *Capt.* 790ff., *Curc.* 28off.) or *seruus currens* (e.g.

---

[1] W. S. Gilbert's libretto for *Iolanthe* provides a close parallel for this witticism, when Phyllis in act II says to the two noblemen whom she has promised to marry, 'If one of you would forgo his title, and distribute his estates among his Irish peasantry, why, then, I should then see a reason for accepting – the other.'

Merc. 111ff., *Stich.* 284ff.; at *Amph.* 984ff. Mercury mimics the convention) with news, or alternatively as he bought up provisions at the market or demolished the food at dinner (like the parasites at Alexis 47(46K).3ff., 183(178K).3ff. (market), 263(261K) dinner)).[1]

199 (194K)

Meineke 3.473, Kock 2.369, Edmonds 2.468, Kassel–Austin 2.134. C. A. Lobeck's implicit correction (edition of Phrynichus (Leipzig 1820) p. 228; cf. also Meineke, *Quaest. Scen.* 3.30) of ἰσχυρίσκος in the MSS of the Antiatticist (100.13 Bekker), Photius and the *Suda* (s.v.) to -ικός is likely to be right for three major reasons. (1) The MS of the Antiatticist is full of such errors, involving one or two letters only (Bekker lists at *Anecd.* 3.1074–7 those he recognised; cf. also *Hermes*, 117 (1989) 374f.; e.g. 81.23 Bekker = Alexis 79 ἐγώ and αἰτεῖ παῖ for ἔγωγ' ὤ and αἰτεῖται, 86.18 γενεσθαῖον for γενέθλιον, 96.12 ἐπισάτης for ἐπιστάτης, 98.17 = Alexis 158(154K) ἥδιον for ἴδιον; here presumably -ισκ- by assimilation to the initial ἰσχ-), and the presence of the same reading in the MSS of Photius and the *Suda* is of no independent value, since their wording here and general practice elsewhere together suggest that they are simply copying a MS of the Antiatticist (cf. Adler's edition of *Suda*, I.xvii). (2) The form ἰσχυρίσκος would be an anomaly (all other diminutives in -ίσκος are nouns deriving from noun stems, not adjectives from adjectives: see the list in Buck–Petersen, *Reverse Index* 675f.), but ἰσχυρικός (on the formation and use of adjectives in -ικός in comedy, see comm. on 31(30K).6–7) is exactly the type of word condemned by stricter grammarians for its rarity in Attic (elsewhere only Pl. *Theaet.* 169b) and defended by the Antiatticist here as elsewhere from later comedy and not from its occurrences in Attic prose (cf. e.g. 103.15 Bekker, citing Antiphanes 16(15K) for κατάλυσις but not Pl. *Protag.* 315d, *Leg.* 11.919a, 12.953a = 'lodging', cf. Alexis 2.2, nor Pl. *Leg.* 9.856b, 864d = 'dissolution'). (3) The entry before ἰσχυρίσκος in the Photius lexicon correctly runs ἰσχυρικοί· ἰσχυροί.

Πρωτόχορος

Porson, *Adv.* 93, Meineke 1.392f., Kaibel in *RE* s.v. *Alexis* 9, 1469.15ff. At Ath. 7.287f a play with this title is attributed to Alexis, at 3.109c and 6.240b to Antidotus. Porson's suggestion that there may have been only

---

[1] Parallel (masculine singular middle or passive) participles as titles in Alexis include certainly Εἰσοικιζόμενος, Κηρυττόμενος (or Ἐκκηρ-), Καταψευδόμενος, possibly Ἀποκοπτόμενος, Ψευδόμενος.

one Πρωτόχορος of uncertain authorship was taken up by Meineke; alternatively, one comic poet could have plagiarised the other. Yet Ath. himself advances neither of these explanations, as he did over the authorship of Alexis' or Antidotus' Ὁμοία at 14.642d, and so it may be wiser (with Kaibel) to assume two distinct plays.

The meaning of Πρωτόχορος is not clear. LSJ suggests 'the first chorus', but more probable is 'first in the dance/chorus' or 'chorus leader' (for this use of πρωτο- in compounds many – often admittedly late – examples are listed in LSJ, e.g. πρωτόκοσμος = leader of the Cretan κόσμοι, *SIG* 524.3, 3rd century), as in the fragmentary 5th-century dramatic inscription from Icaria, *IG* i³.254. 15, 17 (cf. Pickard-Cambridge, *DFA*² 48f.), where it is uncertain how – if at all – the term differed from κορυφαῖος. Alternatively Πρωτόχορος could have been the name of a *persona ficta*; it is not recorded in Attica, but for parallel formations cf. Πρωτόμαχος, -νικος, Kirchner, *PA* 2.233ff. Here the one fr. surviving from the play (a dialogue involving a parasite) gives no help.

200 (195K)

Meineke 3.474, Kock 2.369, Edmonds 2.468, Kassel–Austin 2.134. Vv. 1–4 of the fr. are addressed to an unidentified character by a parasite (v. 3) who has 'taken a job' (vv. 1–2), sc. attached himself to a patron who seems to be Greek but not Athenian (v. 4, cf. Kock), most probably a *miles gloriosus*. The task of endorsing and amplifying the vainglorious boasts of military patrons who lack wit and polish (cf. comm. on v. 4; at Ter. *Eun.* 1079 Gnatho describes Thraso as *fatuos ... insulsus, tardus*) is typically identified as hard labour by their parasites (e.g. Plaut. *MG* 33, *uenter creat omnis hasce aerumnas*, Ter. *Eun.* 1085, possibly Men. *Kol.* 32f.). Cf. also Nesselrath, *MK* 314.

1–2 ἐπιπονώτερον <ἔργον> ... εἴληφ': Porson's supplement (*Adv.* 93: omitted by haplography after -ερον) restores the *mot juste*. Cf. Phot. s.v. ἔργον· ὁ μισθός. καὶ λαβεῖν ἔργον· τὸ μισθῶσαι ἑαυτόν; e.g. Amipsias 1.2 spoken by some sort of parasite, Apollodorus 2. Similarly ἐκλαμβάνω ἔργον Hdt. 9.95. The compounds ἐργολαβεῖν, -λαβία, -λάβος, -λήπτης appear in Attic (see LSJ s.vv.) to have originated as technical terms in the field of contracting, and λαμβάνω itself is commonly used of 'taking/hiring' an employee (e.g. a cook: Alexis 216(213K).1 and comm.).

ἐπιπονώτερον <ἔργον>: similarly Pl. *Leg.* 7.801e ἔργα ἐξειργασμένοι καλὰ καὶ ἐπίπονα, Dio Chrys. 29.9, Xen. Eph. 5.8.3, cf. Isoc. 12.179 ἐπιπόνως ἐργαζομένους.

3 ἀφ' οὗ παρασιτῶ: 'ever since I've been a parasite'. In classical Attic (and Ionic) Greek both ἀπό and ἐξ + relative (οὗ, οὗπερ, ὅτου) introduce such temporal clauses, usually with the present indicative (ἀπό:

COMMENTARY

e.g. A. *Pers.* 177, Thuc. 1.14, Hdt. 2.44; ἐξ: S. *Ant.* 1092, *Trach.* 326, Ar. *Ach.* 17, 596f., *Plut.* 85, Xen. *Cyr.* 8.2.16, Isoc. 6.7, Hdt. 6.109), although in Homer only ἐξ is so used (cf. H. Ebeling's lexicon 2 (Leipzig 1880) 87) while in later Greek ἀπό gains the ascendance (A. N. Jannaris, *An Historical Greek Grammar* (London 1897) 424: hence Blaydes's conjecture ἐξ οὗ here, *Adv.* 2.164, is defensible). Cf. Headlam on Herodas 4.40, Schwyzer 2.653.

μεμβράδας: cited here by Ath. (7.287f) along with Eupolis 31(28), Antiphanes 123(125K) and Alexis 260(258K) to exemplify the orthography with initial μ ~ β. As the word may be a foreign importation (P. Chantraine, *La Formation des noms en grec ancien* (Paris 1933) 352, Schwyzer, 1.507 n. 7: this seems more probable than Strömberg's suggestion, *Fischnamen* 67f., of a relation to βράζω and the sound allegedly made by fishes, cf. Chantraine s.v. μεμβράς, and Frisk s.v. β-), a definitively correct spelling for Attic Greek is unlikely (Ath. 287d cites Ar. fr. 140(137K) for β-, but the MSS of *Vesp.* 493f. give μ-). μεμβράς seems to be applied to both the sprat (*Sprattus sprattus*) and the anchovy (*Engraulis encrasiolus*), cf. Thompson, *Fishes* s.v. β-); both species are πολιόχρωτες (Ar. fr. 140(137K)), but χρυσοκέφαλοι (Phrynichus com. 52(50K)) suits the anchovy better (cf. Campbell, *Guide* 266f. ~ 264f.). Alexis singles it out here because it was the poor Athenian's food (several could be bought for an obol, Aristomenes 7, cf. Ar. *Vesp.* 493f., Timocles 11.9, P. Gray, *Honey from a Weed* (London 1986) 126f.). See also comm. on fr. 18.2.

4 ἔχειν: 'to have served up as food', possibly a colloquialism of the time; Meineke well compares Anaxilas 18.3f. βολβοὺς τρώγων, τυροὺς κάπτων, | ᾠὰ κολάπτων, κήρυκας ἔχων, where ἔχων finds its place as one of four synonyms for ἐσθίων. Conjectures (e.g. ἔψειν Bothe, *PCGF* 560; ἔσθειν Blaydes, *Adv.* 2.164) are accordingly not required (cf. Korais in Schweighaeuser, *Animadv.* 4.136).

μετ' Ἀττικιστὶ δυναμένου λαλεῖν: like ἀφ'οὗ v. 3 and ὀνησίφορον v. 5, λαλεῖν might at first sight appear an example of what Kock (at v. 5) terms '*serior graecitas*', since in *Koine* Greek it usurps the place of λέγειν as the common verb 'to say/speak'. Yet here in fact λαλεῖν retains its precise Attic sense 'to engage in conversation'; cf. the clear distinction between the two verbs in Dem. 21.118 εἰ δὲ λαλῶν μὲν καὶ ὁμωρόφιος γιγνόμενος ὡς οὐδὲν εἰργασμένῳ φανήσεται, λέγων δὲ καὶ καταιτιώμενος ταῦθ' εἴνεκα τοῦ συκοφαντεῖν ἐμέ, πῶς οὐ δεκάκις, μᾶλλον δὲ μυριάκις δίκαιός ἐστ' ἀπολωλέναι; The parasite's point is not that his (? non-Athenian: see introduction to the fr.) patron cannot *speak* Attic properly (thus λέγειν ἀττικιστὶ at Dem. *Prooem.* 8, cf. Antiphanes 97), but rather that he cannot *converse* with the appropriate Attic wit (τὸν ἐπιχώριον ἀττικισμόν Alciphron 4.19.1, cf. 3.34.1 ἀττικῆς στωμυλίας, so famous that at 4.19.4 the author can talk of αἰγυπτίοις ἀττικισμοῖς: cf. Lucian *Prometheus es* 1, Plaut. *Pers.* 394f., Cic.

ΠΡΩΤΟΧΟΡΟΣ

De or. 2.54, 217, *Ad fam.* 9.15.2, Martial 3.20.9; A. Otto, *Die Sprichwörter und sprichwörtlichen Redensarten der Römer* (Leipzig 1890) 44).

5 ὀνησιφόρον ἦν τοῦτο: as Kock notes, a feeble repetition of κρεῖττον ἦν in v. 3 if construed as a continuation of the parasite's speech, and so better taken as a confirmatory comment by a second speaker. Yet Ath. regularly chops off in the middle, abridges or otherwise corrupts final sentences in his citations (cf. comm. on e.g. 38(37K), 89(86K), 93(89K), 123(118K), 193–4(188–9K), and so a secure interpretation of these words may be unachievable; thus an ἄν might have been omitted (ὀνησιφόρον ἦν τοῦτ' ἄν Kock, preferable to τοῦτ' ἦν ἄν ὀνησιφόρον Blaydes, *Adv.* 2.164, cf. *CQ* 7 (1957) 189), or the cited words have been merely the opening of a new sentence.

τὸ ὀνησιφόρον is condemned by Pollux 5.136 as μοχθηρόν (? with reference to Alexis' use here, also in neuter singular); the comic poet may have been introducing into literature a new vogue word (but cf. com. adesp. fr. 109.11 Kock, undatable but apparently New Comedy; Hippocr. *Praec.* 14, probably a work of imperial Rome, cf. W. H. S. Jones' Loeb edition (London and New York 1923) 310f.), which proved popular in *Koine* Greek (e.g. Lucian, *Vit. auct.* 26, Rufus in Oribasius 8.24.34, Agatharchides fr. 99 Müller; adverb in Plut. *Mor.* 71d, Cyrill. *Psalm.* 32.8 = 69.873B Migne).

Πυθαγορίζουσα

Meineke 1.389f., cf. T. B. L. Webster, *CQ* 2 (1952) 20ff. and *SLGC* 50ff., K. von Fritz, *Pythagorean Politics in Southern Italy* (New York 1940) 76f., W. Burkert, *Lore and Science in Ancient Pythagoreanism* (Cambridge Mass. 1972) 198ff. Alexis' Πυθαγορίζουσα belongs to a group of plays (with Aristophon's Πυθαγοριστής, the younger (?) Cratinus' Πυθαγορίζουσα;[1] perhaps also his Ταραντῖνοι and Alexis' Ταραντῖνοι, but see introduction to the latter play) taking their titles from disciples of Pythagoreanism who, preferring the religious side of their heritage to the scientific and philosophic, founded communities in South Italy (that at Tarentum apparently

---

[1] Both title and authorial identity, however, are uncertain. The one extant fr. (6) is cited by both Diog. Laert. 8.37 and *Suda* s.v. Ξενοφάνης, and two MSS. (VM^pc) of the latter give the title in the dative as Πυθαγορίζουσι not -ουση (cf. A. Weiher, *Philosophen und Philosophenspott in der attischen Komödie* (Diss. Munich 1913) 60). In the play, furthermore, we are told by Diog. Laert. that Pythagoras and by the *Suda* that Xenophanes were ridiculed, and so a play by the elder poet with an agon between these two philosophers cannot be ruled out.

proved the most tenacious: cf. the introduction to Ταραντῖνοι) and (after many had fled from the west probably between 390 and 360: cf. von Fritz 68ff. on the chronology) mainland Greece, where they practised ascetic and vegetarian regimes in accordance with what they considered to be Pythagoras' own teachings (ἀκούσματα or σύμβολα: cf. Burkert 166ff.; G. S. Kirk, J. E. Raven and M. Schofield, *The Presocratic Philosophers*[2] (Cambridge 1983) 229ff.). In the plays listed – and elsewhere too in other comic frs. (Antiphanes 133(135K), 158(160K), 166(168K), 225(226K + ? 227K), Mnesimachus 1, probably Alexis 27, see comm. on vv. 1–2; cf. Diog. Laert. 8.37–8, Ath. 4.160f–162b) – the practices of these cults are ridiculed in a way that reminds us of the attacks on Socrates in Aristophanes (cf. T. Gelzer, *Mus. Helv.* 13 (1956) 67ff., Dover's edition of Ar. *Nub.* pp. xxxii ff.), with no attempt at accurate discrimination between the regimes of Pythagorist and other sects (cf. especially my comm. on 201.5–6(197K)). A warning here is needed against two common assumptions: (1) that because some of the relevant comedies and references can be dated to the period *c.* 350–320 (Antiphanes 166(168K) comes from the same play as 167(169K), which refers to the Halonnesos quibble, cf. introduction to Alexis' Ἀδελφοί; Aristophon's Πυθαγοριστής refers in fr. 10.2 to Tithymallus and Philippides, cf. introduction to Alexis' Μιλήσιοι and comm. on fr. 2.8; Alexis' Ταραντῖνοι mentions Nannion in fr. 225(223K), cf. introduction to the play), all the Pythagorist titles and allusions must necessarily belong to the same period (so e.g. Meineke, Webster); (2) that the depiction of Pythagorists as title figures in some of the listed comedies necessarily means that ridicule of their cults was the only or most important element in the plots (so e.g. Kock 2.290). At some point admittedly Alexis' Πυθαγορίζουσα must have highlighted a woman who followed – or pretended to follow – a Pythagorist (I use this term throughout to denote the religious and largely non-philosophical ascetic; on the precise significance of the various Greek terms, see comm. on 201(196K).3) way of life, but whether the whole play was focused on the cult, or its practices rather formed merely a minor but colourful embroidery in an otherwise conventional plot of New-Comedy intrigue, we can no longer say. The extant frs. 201–3(196–9K) here afford slight help; 201.1–3, 5–6(196.1–3K, 197K) seem to have been spoken by a man who was previously an adherent, perhaps to the title figure before she joined the cult (see comm. *ad loc.*).

201 (196 + 197K)

Meineke 3.474 (ii, iii), Kock 2.370, Edmonds 2.468, Kassel–Austin 2.135; cf. Diels–Kranz, *Vorsokr.* 1.479. The speakers in this fr. are discussed on v. 2.

ΠΥΘΑΓΟΡΙΖΟΥΣΑ

(a) (196K)

1–3 Antiphanes 225(226K).3f. exemplifies Pythagorist vegetarianism (cf. comm. on 27) with βολβὸς εἷς τις (comm. on 167(162K).13) καί ... σόγχος τις ἢ μύκης τις. According to Diog. Laert. 8.12 Pythagoras once recommended a regime of dried figs and cheese to athletes. When in Philemon 88(85K) the Stoic Zeno is presented with a diet of εἷς ἄρτος (cf. Alexis 223.10(221.4K) ὄψον, ἰσχάς, ἐπιπιεῖν ὕδωρ (cf. Alexis 202(198K), Aristophon 10.3, 12(13K).8), it seems that he was being classed as a Pythagorist (on the confusion, see comm. on 5–6 below).

1 στέμφυλα: in Attic Greek a cake of olives from which the juice has been pressed out (Σ Ar. *Nub.* 45, Ath. 2.56d, Phryn. *Ecl.* 385 p. 103 Fischer, cf. Neil, comm. on Ar. *Equ.* 806), i.e. ἐλαῖαι τετριμμέναι (Ath.) or θλασταί (Ar. fr. 408(391K + 393K), Poliochus 2.7), normally (apart from Ar. *Equ.* 806) in the plural.

2 ἔσται: so A (Ath. 4.161c). If tense and text are correct (ἐστι would be an easy conjecture), we must assume that the male (cf. ὦ βέλτιστ᾽ v. 4) first speaker warns the second (? the title figure) about the fate in store for her or him on joining the Pythagorists. However, if Ath.'s claim that vv. 5–6(197K) followed vv. 1–4(196K) μετ᾽ ὀλίγα is not an under-statement,[1] and if the speaker of 201(196K).1–3a goes on to deliver 201.5–6(197K) (as seems likely), ἔδει in v. 5 will imply that he was previously a Pythagorist himself.

θύειν: Diog. Laert. 8.20 claims that Pythagoras himself θυσίαις ... ἐχρῆτο ἀψύχοις, and in the catechism preserved in Iamblichus *Vit. Pyth.* 18.82 the response to the versicle τί τὸ δικαιότατον; is θύειν.

3 τοῖς Πυθαγορείοις: the precise meaning and colour of the three terms (Πυθαγόρειος, -ρικός and -ριστής) commonly applied to Pythagoreans/ -rists at Alexis' time were already disputed in antiquity. Iamblichus *Vit. Pyth.* 18.80 identified -ρειοι as the genuine philosophers, -ρισταί their imitators; one scholion on Theoc. 14.5 makes -ρικοί concerned about their physical appearance, -ρισταί squalid and dirty, adding that others identify -ρικοί as real adherents of Pythagoras, -ρισταί as imitators of the ideas but lacking in the true faith; a further scholion, however, admits that ἕτεροι ... ἐναντία περὶ τοῦ Πυθαγορικοῦ καὶ Πυθαγοριστοῦ λέγουσιν. In fact our texts reveal that (1) -ρικός and -ρειος are synonymous, often neutral in tone (e.g. -ρικός Arist. frs. 202, 203 Rose, Diog. Laert. 8.7, 50,

---

[1] We cannot, however, be certain of this. On the nine occasions where Ath. uses this expression to introduce a second fr. from a work just quoted (also 1.5c, 2.56b, 68e, 6.244e with Alexis 205(201, 202K), 9.385f, 11.474c, 14.653a, 15.667a), that work is not extant and so Ath.'s reliability cannot be checked.

COMMENTARY

56, Iambl. *Comm. math.* p.42 Ast, *Protr.* 21 κ, Sext. Emp. *Math.* 4.11; -ρειος
Pl. *Resp.* 6.530d, Arist. *Metaph.* 1.5, 985ᵇ23, Diog. Laert. 5.86, 8.15, 46,
Hierocles *CA* 2.4; in comedy also Alexis 223(220K).5), but occasionally
coloured by the context (e.g. dismissive in Arist. *De an.* 1.3, 407ᵇ22 τοὺς
Πυθαγορικοὺς μύθους, cf. Philoponus 140.5, Phot. s.v. Ἰταλιώτης· ὁ
ἀλαζὼν ἀπὸ τῶν Πυθαγορικῶν); (2) -ριστής is the term applied by Attic
comedy usually with contempt to beggarly ascetics (Aristophon 9.2, 12.3
and title; cf. Theoc. 14.5), but elsewhere is not always pejorative (e.g. Σ
Theoc. 14.5: Plato a -ριστής because influenced by Pythagoras). Cf. also
πυθαγορίζω ('I practise as a -ριστής', Antiphanes 133(135K).1,
225(226K).8, Alexis 223(220).1 and title there, Cratinus title), -ρίδες
(= women genuinely studying the philosophy, Iambl. *Vit. Pyth.* 36.267),
-ρισμοί (the rhetorical tricks, Alexis 223(220K).7, q.v.; ? -ριστί (= like a
-ριστής, F at Diog. Laert. 8.37 = Mnesimachus 1.1, -ριστῇ BP, -ρισταί
Menagius; omitted in LSJ). See especially Gow on Theoc. 14.5, K. von
Fritz, *Mathematiker und Akusmatiker bei den älteren Pythagoreern*, SB Munich
(1960/11) 4ff.

4 ὁποῖον ἂν κάλλιστον, ὦ βέλτιστ', ἔχῃ: Casaubon (*Animadv.* 293)
corrected A's οὖν (? slip induced by οὖν two words before) to the syntactically needed ἄν, but is further emendation required? Editors have assumed
here that the transmitted ἔχη (*sic*) must be impersonal, and so have either
changed κάλλιστον to the adverbial -στα (necessitating further changes:
-στά γ' Kaibel, -στα καὶ βέλτιστ' Diels) in order to accommodate the
καλῶς ἔχει idiom (LSJ s.v. ἔχω, B.2), or conjectured ἔχῃς (Bothe, *Griech.
Kom.* 55; Cobet in Peppink, *Observ.* 30). It is just as likely that Ath. ended
his citation in mid-sentence (cf. e.g. frs. 89(86K), 123(118K), 126(121K),
176(171K), 193(188K), and comm. *ad locc.*), leaving out the subject of ἔχη
(? ἡ πόλις Ἀθηνῶν, adding point to the second speaker's response, since
Attic ἰσχάδες had a high reputation, cf. fr. 122(117K).7 and comm., and
Athenian συκοφάνται an even higher one). Cf. also *Hermes* 93 (1965) 309.

(b) (197K)

5–6 These vv. provide a list of six discomforts that must be tolerated
by Pythagorists. The list does not specifically include vegetarianism
(presumably because it had already been discussed; the idea is implicit at
201(196K).1–2) or abstention from wine (cf. comm. on 202(198K)), but
several of the items mentioned are endorsed elsewhere in comedy (μικροσιτία Antiphanes 133(135K), 158(160K), 166(168K).7f., Aristophon
10.1ff.; ῥύπος/ἀλουσία Aristophon 10.4, 12.5f., 12(13K).9f.; ῥῖγος Aristophon 10.5) and their accuracy confirmed by later Pythagorean
(admittedly unreliable: cf. von Fritz, *Pythag. Politics*, 19ff., on their
tendency to muddle material from sources of the 4th century with much

that is later) writers like Iamblichus and Porphyry. Thus (i) ῥῖγος: in the 4th century Pythagoreans adopted the threadbare τρίβων (a poor garment to withstand winter cold, cf. Σ^V Ar. *Nub.* 416) of the Cynics in place of the sparkling white dress worn earlier, following a fashion set by Diodorus of Aspendos (Ath. 4.163e–164a, citing Timaeus and Sosicrates as his sources). (ii) ἀλουσία, ῥύπος: Pythagoreans were forbidden to use the public baths, in order to avoid ritual impurity (Iambl. *Vit. Pyth.* 18.83); in a society where public bathing was normal, the combination of this restriction with tattered dress easily accounts for the comic charges; cf. Ath. 4.163e on Diodorus of Aspendos, Πυθαγορικός ... δόξας εἶναι ... τῶν κυνικῶν τρόπον ἔζη, κομῶν καὶ ῥυπῶν καὶ ἀνυποδητῶν. (iii) σιωπή: at Croton Pythagorean novices were bound to five years' silence, in order to gain mastery over their tongues (Iambl. *Vit. Pyth.* 17.72); cf. the less strict injunctions in the ἀκούσματα against λαλιά (Iambl. *Protr.* 21.6, Porph. *Vit. Pyth.* 42, cf. Isoc. 11.29 and Alciphron 3.19.4). (iv) στυγνότης: the charge of sullenness (on the meaning, see comm. on v. 6) doubtless originates from membership of a restrictive cult, avoidance of chatter, and obedience to ἀκούσματα such as 'avoid public roads', 'don't laugh unrestrainedly', 'don't clasp everybody's right hand lightly' (Iambl. *Protr.* 21.4, 26, 28; Porph. *Vit. Pyth.* 42). Yet such characteristics were not unique to the Pythagorists; in the 5th and 4th centuries accusations were made by the comic poets against a number of philosophic schools, indiscriminately alleging μικροσιτία (generally, Antiphanes 120(122K).3f.; Socratics, Ar. *Nub.* 414ff., 440ff., *Av.* 1281ff.; Zeno, Philemon 88(85K), see my comm. on v. 5 below; cf. Alciphron 3.19.5, Cynics) and ῥύπος/ ἀλουσία (Socratics, Ar. *Nub.* 837, cf. *Av.* 1554f.; Cynics, Men. fr. 215.6, cf. Lucian *Cyn.* 17, Alciphron 3.19.2, Stoics; Lucian *Par.* 50, philosophers as a group; Nesselrath, *LP* 451ff.), while toleration of cold was described as an ordeal of the Socratic syllabus (Ar. *Nub.* 416, 442). In all probability this diffusion of targets was due as much to a comic poet's lack of concern over precise distinctions between different schools of philosophy as to the presence of shared features in them; cf. especially A. Weiher, *Philosophen und Philosophenspott in der attischen Komödie* (Diss. Munich 1914) 57f., Hunter on Eubulus 137(139K).

5 ἔδει: cf. comm. on v. 2 above.

μικροσιτίαν: Porson's correction (*Adv.* 72) of A's μικρὸν ἀσιτίαν (Epit. omits μικρόν) produces a *hapax*, but several compounds of this type were coined in Alexis' time and later (presumably on the analogy of μικρολογία, μικροψυχία) mainly by philosophers/scientists (e.g. μικρομέρεια, -πρέπεια, -φωνία Arist., -καρπία, -φιλοτιμία Theophr.) and physicians (e.g -σφυξία Galen).

ῥύπον: cf. Phryn. *Ecl.* 120 p. 71 Fischer (and C. A. Lobeck's comm., (Leipzig 1820) 150f., Rutherford, *NP* 238ff.)

COMMENTARY

6 στυγνότητ': so A, Epit.; Eustathius' substitution of γυμνότητ' (1560.60) when quoting this passage may well come from a lapse of memory or a maverick variant in his MS of Epit. of Ath. rather than from his own emendation (cf. C. Aldick, *De Athenaei Dipnosophistarum epitomae codicibus* (Diss. Münster 1928), C. Collard, *RFIC* 97 (1969) 164ff., Hunter's edition of Eubulus, p. 32: all countering P. Maas, *BZ* 35 (1935) 299ff.). It is probably an accident that this is the first appearance of a noun otherwise confined to the *Koine* (in the same sense, 'sullenness': e.g. Polyb. 3.20.3, Plut. *Marius* 43, cf. *Thes.* 20), since the use of στυγνός = 'sullen' (especially in look) is common in Attic (e.g. A. *Ag.* 639, but see Fraenkel *ad loc.*, S. *OR* 673, Eur. *Alc.* 777, *Hipp.* 172, 290, Xen. *Anab.* 2.6.9, 11). Herwerden's objection to the noun here (*Mnemosyne* 4 (1876) 301) is groundless and his conjecture στρυφνότητ' (cf. Plut. *Marius* 2) unnecessary.

ἀλουσίαν: Lobeck's claim (*Parerga* to edition of Phrynichus, p. 507) that the correct Attic form of this noun is ἀλουτία, which should be accepted in passages such as Eupolis fr. 280(251K) (cited by Pollux 7.168, where S has ἀ. λουτίαν), is false. In MSS the word is normally spelled with -σ-: e.g. FA at Pollux 7.168, Alexis here, Aristophon 12(13K).9 quoted by Diog. Laert. 8.38, com. adesp. fr. 115.3 Kock quoted by Σ Eur. *Or.* 234, Eur. *Or.* 226, Hesych. s.v. See K.B. 2.275, '*ein T-Laut geht bevor dem -ια gewöhnlich in σ über*', e.g. ἀδύνατος/ἀδυνασία, ἀθάνατος/-σία, ἄκριτος/-σία, ἀσύνετος/ -σια; P. Chantraine, *La Formation des noms en grec ancien* (Paris 1933) 83f., Schwyzer 1.270.

202 (198K)

Meineke 3.474 (1), Kock 2.370, Edmonds 2.468, Kassel–Austin 2.135. Ath. 3.122f introduces the fr. with the words καὶ ὁ Κύνουλκος (a deipnosophist, cf. B. Baldwin, *Acta Classica* 20 (1977) 42), ἀλλὰ προπίνω σοι, ἔφη, φιλοτησίαν, διψᾷς γὰρ λόγων, παρ' Ἀλέξιδος λαβὼν ἐκ Πυθαγο-ριζούσης, ὕδατος κ.τ.λ. From this and Ath.'s occasional practice else-where (e.g. 12.510a/Alexis 241(239K) and comm., 14.622f/Antiphanes 216(217K), 623f/Theophilus 5) it is sensible to assume that, before the precisely transcribed citation of the comic fr. begins at ὕδατος (v.1 Kassel–Austin, v. 2 Kock), Ath.'s introductory words quote or adapt part of the sentence in Alexis immediately before the main body of the citation. Ath. confesses to having 'taken' φιλοτησίαν from that sentence; it would not be surprising if he had also taken προπίνω σοι, since Alexis writes at 293(291K) φιλοτησίαν σοι ... κύλικα προπίομαι, cf. 59(58K) and Theo-pompus 33(32K).9. Placing and supplementation of these words in the verse are uncertain, but there would be nothing syntactically objectiona-ble in taking κύαθον as appositive to a preceding noun or (with e.g. κύλικα supplied) adjective φιλοτησίαν, cf. e.g. Men. fr. 443.2, ἄκρατον ἐβόων, τὴν μεγάλην (sc. κύλικα). In this way the opening words of the fr. gain comic point; the speaker (clearly a Pythagorist of indeterminate sex[1]) proposes a loving cup (cf. comm. on 59(58K).1), but the rigour of the cult according to Alexis compels him/her to drink the toast in a ladleful of water instead of the customary wine (cf. also Alexis 223(220, 221K).3 and 10f., Aristophon 12(13K).8. Wine-drinking is not specifically banned in the Pythagorean ἀκούσματα, although water is an integral part of the recommended diet, cf. Diog. Laert. 8.13. Teetotalism was also foisted by Aristophanes on the Socratic school, *Nub.* 417).

1 **ὕδατος ἀπέφθου**: why 'boiled' water? For two comic reasons, apparently. The expression prepares the way for (i) a comic contrast with the ludicrous concept of ὠμὸν ὕδωρ (cf. Arist. *Meteor.* 4.3, 380^{b}10, τὸ ὕδωρ ἑφθὸν μὲν λέγεται, ὠμὸν δ' οὔ, ὅτι οὐ παχύνεται), and (ii) parody of an alleged Pythagorean predilection for scientific (and especially medical: cf. Iambl. *Vit. Pyth.* 18.82 τί σοφώτατον τῶν παρ' ἡμῖν; ἰατρική, cf. Diog. Laert. 8.12) terminology in the use of κοπώδης = 'causing fatigue/debilitating,' very rare (along with its by-form κοπιώδης) outside medical writers (e.g. Hippocr. *Epid.* 6.7, *Reg. acut.* 16, *Humor.* 7, *Prorrhet.* 1.38, *Aphor.* 4.31, Galen, *In Hippocr. Prorrhet.* 3.49).

πίῃ: Musurus' correction of A's πίνηι (note that three of the four preceding words end in nu).

203 (199K)

Meineke 3.475 (IV), Kock 2.370, Edmonds 2.470, Kassel–Austin 2.136; cf. J. Haussleiter, *Der Vegetarianismus in der Antike* (Berlin 1935) 97ff.; W. K. C. Guthrie, *A History of Greek Philosophy* 1 (Cambridge 1962) 187ff.; W. Burkert, *Lore and Science in Ancient Pythagoreanism* (Cambridge Mass. 1972) 190f. In Alexis' time the attitude of Pythagoras and his early followers to meat-eating was a subject of lively controversy. Aristoxenus, the pupil of Aristotle and musical theorist, sponsored the view that Pythagoras was no vegetarian (eating young pigs and goats, according to Gellius *Noct. Att.* 4.11.4–6; other animals except plough oxen and rams, Diog. Laert. 8.20; cf. also Plut. fr. 182 Sandbach, Porph. *Vit. Pyth.* 36 and perhaps 15, although the identity of the Pythagoras mentioned there was disputed, cf. Iambl. *Vit. Pyth.* 25, Diog. Laert. 8.12), and indeed many Pythagorean sources claim that the cultic abstention from meat was limited to certain animals (Arist. fr. 195 Rose in Diog. Laert. 8.34, cf.

---

[1] λαβών at Ath. 3.122f (*pace* Kock) is not part of the Alexis fr., and in any case its gender is controlled by the sex of its subject Cynulcus.

COMMENTARY

Iambl. *Vit. Pyth.* 85) and to certain parts of animals (Arist. fr. 194 in Diog. Laert. 8.19, Porph. *Vit. Pyth.* 43, 45, Iambl. *Protr.* 21.30, 31). Eudoxus on the other hand maintained that Pythagoras abstained from eating meat (Porph. *Vit. Pyth.* 7), and Onesicritus that he recommended such abstinence (Strabo 15.1.65, 716c). This was the line generally reflected in Athenian comedy (e.g. Alexis 201(196K), 223(220K).1–3, probably 27, Antiphanes 133(135K), Mnesimachus 1), cf. also Archestratus fr. 154.18ff. Lloyd-Jones–Parsons.

In its context Gellius' statement about Alexis (*Noct. Att.* 4.11.6–8) implies that somebody in Πυθαγορίζουσα described Pythagoras as a meat-eater. Such an allegation might have been part of a joke like that in Alexis 27 (see comm.) or of a more or less serious argument about Pythagoras' personal diet. Yet Gellius was careless in his use of sources and quotations (e.g. at 1.15.19 he illustrated the theme of idle prattling with Ar. *Ran.* 837–9, a description of Aeschylus, not Euripides), and it is just as likely that he inaccurately attributed a statement about Pythagorists in Alexis' play (which he is unlikely to have known at first hand: cf. L. Holford-Strevens, *Aulus Gellius* (London 1988) 174, 210) to Pythagoras himself.

Πυλαία (or -αῖαι)

Meineke 1.402, 5.90. The one fr. (204(200K)) from this play is cited as Ἄλεξις ἐν Πυλαίαις (so A at Ath. 6.225f). If the transmission here is correct, the title is more probably an ethnic from Πύλαι, the local name for Thermopylae (Hdt. 7.201 καλέεται δὲ ὁ χῶρος ὑπὸ μὲν τῶν πλεόνων Ἑλλήνων Θερμοπύλαι, ὑπὸ δὲ τῶν ἐπιχωρίων καὶ περιοίκων Πύλαι, cf. LSJ s.v. πύλη II.2) than for Πύλος, one of the three Peloponnesian cities recorded with this name, most familiarly the one in Messenia. Despite the statement of Steph. Byz. s.v. Πύλος· πόλις ἐν Μεσσήνῃ . . . τὸ ἐθνικὸν Πύλιος καὶ Πυλαῖος. λέγεται καὶ θηλυκῶς καὶ ἀρσενικῶς, place names in -ος, irrespective of gender (e.g ὁ Σφηττός, ὁ/ἡ Ὀρχομενός, ἡ Σάμος), normally form their derivatives in -ιος, and names in -η/-αι derivatives in -αιος (the apparently exceptional Σαμαῖος from the Homeric Σάμη, cf. LSJ s.v.); cf. Schwyzer, 1.466ff. Alexis' title figures would then be two or more girls/women either from or associated with Thermopylae.

Female plural ethnics are, however, relatively rare as titles (cf. Δηλιάδες of Cratinus, Λήμνιαι of Aristophanes, Nicochares, Antiphanes, Diphilus, cf. Turpilius' *Lemniae*, Λοκρίδες of Anaxandrides, Posidippus), and Meineke's suggestion (1.402) '*uidendum ne apud Athenaeum pro* Πυλαίαις *scribendum sit* Πυλαίᾳ, *qui Cratineae fabulae titulus fuit* (cf. J. Th. M. F. Pieters, *Cratinus* (Leiden 1946), 172), *de panegyri Pylaica interpretandus*', deserves

586

serious consideration.[1] The twice-yearly meetings of the Amphictyonic League organised originally around the temple of Demeter Pylaea at Anthela near Thermopylae but later also around the temple of Apollo at Delphi were always named Πυλαῖαι (e.g. Hdt. 7.213, Dem. 18.154, Aeschines 3.124, Theophr. *HP* 9.10.2, Strabo 9.3.7, 4.17, cf. S. *Trach.* 633ff.; G. Busolt and H. Swoboda, *Griechische Staatskunde* 2[3] (Munich 1926) 1292ff., 1303ff., Schaefer in *RE* s.v. πυλαία 3, 2098.4ff., Wankel on Dem. 18.148, D. Müller, *Topographischer Bildkommentar zu den Historien Herodots: Griechenland* (Tübingen 1987) 369ff.). They would have provided a suitable background for a conventional New-Comedy type of plot, with opportunities for nocturnal rape (cf. the introduction to Παννυχίς) or the kidnapping of a small child (e.g. Plaut. *Men.* 24ff., cf. *Poen.* 66f., Men. *Sik.* 1ff.), and Demeter Pylaia might even have spoken the prologue. The surviving fr. (see below) unfortunately offers no help with title or plot.

204 (200K)

Meineke 3.475, Kock 2.370, Edmonds 2.470, Kassel–Austin 2.136. An attack on the high prices charged by fishmongers (not necessarily at a time of food shortages), in the vein of frs. 16 (see comm.), 76, 78, 130(125K) and 131(126K), all cited by Ath. 6.224f–228b. One of the two speakers here – the first certainly (see on v. 1), the other probably, male – has presumably just returned from market in disgust at these prices (cf. Euclio in Plaut. *Aul.* 371ff.).

1 νὴ τὴν Ἀθηνᾶν, ἀλλ': the oath by Athena is confined to males in extant passages of comedy (Ar. *Pax* 218, Men. *Asp.* 319, *Kol.* fr. 2.4f., *Pk.* 302f., *Sam.* 213, *Sik.* 116, frs. 333.13f., 656.1, com. adesp. fr. 239.21f., 255.8, 257.41, 258.37 Austin; cf. F. W. Wright, *Studies in Menander* (Diss. Princeton 1911) 13ff.). If the text here is correct, the oath either introduces the speaker's words with an endorsement of what the previous speaker has just said but then goes on to qualify the endorsement (but other sentences of this form run (οὐ) μὰ Δί' (etc.) ἀλλά, rejecting and then correcting the previous speaker's words, e.g. Ar. *Equ.* 85, *Vesp.* 297, *Eccl.* 532f.: could Alexis have written μὰ τὴν Ἀθηνᾶν here?), or belongs as a closing endorsement to a clause in the lost preceding context.

1–2 τεθαύμακα τοὺς ἰχθυοπώλας, πῶς ποτ'...: a less usual variant of the normal construction θαυμάζω (LSJ s.v. 6) εἰ, but cf. Ar. *Equ.* 211, *Av.* 1255 (θ. ὅπως), com. adesp. fr. 257.46f. Austin (ὅπως ποτ' ἐπιτρέπει ... πολλάκις τεθαύμακα), Ar. *Ran.* 1257 (θ. ὅπη). For the common idiom

---

[1] Edmonds 2.470 (note a) suggests that the plural title too can be accepted in the sense of 'League meetings': theoretically possible but unlikely when compared with the run of known titles of 4th-century comedies.

COMMENTARY

with this verb (LSJ s.v. 6.b) of expressing as its object the subject of the subordinate clause cf. e.g. Men. *Dysk.* 78f. καὶ τὴν διατριβὴν ἥτις ἔστ' αὐτοῦ πάλαι | τεθαύμακ'.

3–4 λαμβάνοντες βασιλικοὺς φόρους: whether Alexis wrote this play before, during or after Alexander's conquest of the Persian empire, it is likely that the enormous tributes paid by the Persian satrapies to their king (Hdt. 1.192, 3.89–96; cf. A. H. Sayce's edition of 1–3 (London 1883) pp. 442f., W. W. How and J. Wells, comm. 2 (Oxford 1912) 404, E. Herzfeld, *The Persian Empire* (Wiesbaden 1968) 295ff.) lie behind this comment, although the Athenians considered that the tributes paid to the kings of Sparta were also very high (Pl. *Alc.* 1.123a, ἔτι δὲ καὶ ὁ βασιλικὸς φόρος οὐκ ὀλίγος γίγνεται, ὃν τελοῦσιν οἱ Λακεδαιμόνιοι τοῖς βασιλεῦσιν, cf. Busolt–Swoboda, *Griechische Staatskunde* 2.665f. n. 6). βασιλικός here is used in its literal sense, without any apparent trace of the slang development detected in Plautus' use of *basilicus/-ice* in Roman comedy = 'very splendid(ly),' cf. Fraenkel, *EP* 183ff., H. Haffter, *SIFC* 27/8 (1956) 135ff.

4 For this verse both A and Epit. transmit φόρους μόνον οὐχὶ δεκατεύουσι γὰρ, which is defective by half a metron (cf. Grotius, *Exc.* 974, Casaubon, *Animadv.* 399). Of the many supplements suggested only φόρους. (B.) <φόρους> μόνον; οὐχὶ δ. γ. (so Cobet, *NL* 35f., improving on Bothe's earlier φόρους. (B.) <φόρους;> μόνον οὐχὶ δ. γ., *Griech. Kom.* 55) merits serious consideration. Its interposition of a second speaker with his repetition of the noun appropriately enlivens the point being made, while Cobet's assumption of an exactly parallel haplography in the *Marcianus* at Ath. 9.382e = Strato 1.23f. was later confirmed by *P.Cairo* 65445; cf. also Kaibel on Ath. 4.145c, 11.501b, 13.561f.

4–5 Once Cobet's supplement, part-division and punctuation in v. 4 have been accepted, there is no need to tinker further (*pace* Meineke, *Anal. Crit.* 97, Kock 2.371 but cf. 3.743, O. Crusius, *Philologus* 46 (1888) 621, Blaydes, *Adv.* 2.164, Herwerden, *Coll. Crit.* 128) with the subsequent text of the fr. The fishmongers, selling their wares as they sit in the city fish-markets (cf. 131(126K).5 and comm.; both καθήμενοι and ἐν ταῖς πόλεσι here clearly refer to the ἰχθυοπῶλαι), do not remove from their customers merely one tenth of their money, like tax-collectors (yet taxes at so high a rate, e.g. on the transport of goods through the Hellespont at certain periods, were relatively rare, cf. H. Michell, *The Economics of Ancient Greece* (Cambridge 1940) 256f.) and those temple functionaries who imposed tithes (see especially Koch in *RE* s.v. Δεκάτη 2423.10ff., G. Busolt, *Griechische Staatskunde* 1³ (Munich 1920) 610 n. 2), but with their extortionate prices take it all away. Here in Alexis (cf. also e.g. Dem. 22.77) there seems to be no reference to any specific tax or tithe, whereas Diphilus 32(33K).2–4 plays wittily on the idea of Poseidon (as god of the sea) forcing the fishmongers to pay tithes to him: Πόσειδον, εἰ δεκάτην

ΠΥΛΑΙΑ

ἐλάμβανες | αὐτῶν ἀπὸ τῆς τιμῆς ἑκάστης ἡμέρας, | πολὺ τῶν θεῶν ἂν ἦσθα πλουσιώτατος, and Roman comedy introduces native allusions to tithes to Hercules (e.g. Plaut. *Bacch.* 665f., *Stich.* 232ff. and H. Petersmann, comm. (Heidelberg 1973) *ad loc.*, 386, *Truc.* 562, Naev. *Colax* fr. I Ribbeck; Fraenkel, *EP* 21f.).

Πύραυνος (or -ον)

Meineke 1.394, Webster, *SLGC* 107f., Nesselrath, *MK* 199. From this play Ath. cites three frs. certainly (206–8(203–5K): 6.258b, 13.590b, 14.663f–664a respectively), and two others (205(201–2K)) if Dindorf's plausible correction of A's παρυνωι at 6.258f to Πυραύνῳ[1] is accepted. The title, which is recorded also for Aristophon (Δίδυμοι ἢ Πύραυν-) and probably Euphanes,[2] is always cited in the dative; hence it is uncertain whether Alexis and/or the other comic poets named their plays Πύραυνος or -ον. In a list of τά . . . μαγείρου σκεύη at Pollux 6.88–9 πύραυνοι are identified as ἀγγεῖα . . . ἐν οἷς τοὺς ἐμπύρους ἄνθρακας κομίζουσιν (cf. Herodian 1.178.10 Lentz, describing it as ὁ χυτρόπους), but at 10.104 a similar definition is attached to πύραυνον (so MSS CL: but see n. 1), while Hesych. s.v. gives only the neuter form with a broader explanation: εἰς ὃ ἂν πῦρ ἐναύηται, δᾳδίον ἢ βόλβιτον (i.e. dung used as fuel) ἢ τοιοῦτόν τι· οἱ δὲ τὴν θέρμαυστριν. Apparently the noun (in both -ος and -ον) could be applied to any means of carrying fire around, but was perhaps more often restricted to portable containers of burning charcoal, from a cook's brazier on which pots could be placed (cf. B. A. Sparkes, *JHS* 82 (1962) 130 and pl. v.4, B. A. Sparkes and L. Talcott, *Pots and Pans of Classical Athens* (Princeton 1958) fig. 40, *Agora* XII.232f. and fig. 19, pl. 97) to a pair of

---

[1] A word clearly unfamiliar to copyists and elsewhere regularly corrupted: e.g. at Pollux 9.70: πυραύλῳ CL, οὐλαυρῷ F, 10.104: πυράνου AB, παρ' αὐτῶν FS, Steph. Byz. s.v. Πάρνης: πυραινῷ P after correction. At Ath. 14.663f Alexis' title appears as τυράννῳ in A's Laurentian apograph (B), but this may be a Renaissance conjecture rather than a copying error. At Ath. 6.244d editors before Dindorf printed Musurus's conjecture Παροίνῳ, attractive palaeographically but yielding a title attested only for Philemon.

[2] The MSS of Steph. Byz. s.v. Πάρνης attribute the one known fr. of this play to an otherwise unknown Emphanes (ἐμφ- P, ἐνφ- QR), but Meineke's early correction to Εὐφάνης (*Cur. Crit.* 45) has subsequently been supported by epigraphical evidence (*IG Urb. Rom.* p. 221.5 = VI A 6.5 Mette, Εὐφά]νης Πυ[ραύνωι, suppl. Moretti; cf. *IG* ii².2325.149); Kassel–Austin 5.280f.).

COMMENTARY

tongs. Yet according to Phot. s.v. (cf. also Eustath. 1547.64f.) the form in -ος might also denote a person, ὁ τὸ πῦρ ἐναυόμενος.

Although the frs. from Alexis' play do not help to establish the identity or function of its πύραυνος/-ον, they introduce characters, character names and situations which would be typical in a comedy produced between c. 305 and c. 295.[1] This dating is secured by a reference in fr. 207(204K).3 to the tiger which Seleucus Nicator sent to Athens (cf. Philemon 49(47K), the only other mention of this gift). Even in antiquity the western range of the tiger (*Panthera tigris*) is unlikely to have extended beyond its 19th-century boundaries (eastern Turkey, north Iran, Russia between the Caspian and Black Seas; cf. G. Mountfort, *Saving the Tiger* (London 1981) 16, P. Jackson, *Endangered Species: Tigers* (London 1990) 23f.), and accordingly Seleucus' tiger is most likely to have been either a product of the Indian campaign halted by Chandragupta Maurya c. 305 or more probably one of the presents made subsequently by the Indian leader before his death in 297 to Seleucus or his envoy Megasthenes (F. W. Thomas in E. J. Rapson (ed.), *The Cambridge History of India* 1 (Cambridge) 472f., R. K. Mookerji in R. C. Majumdar and others (edd.), *The History and Culture of the Indian People* II[4] (Bombay 1968) 60f., cf. also W. S. Ferguson, *Hellenistic Athens* (London 1911) 69, A. Bouché-Leclercq, *Histoire des Seleucides* 1 (Paris 1913) 27ff., H. H. Schmitt, *Die Staatsverträge des Altertums: III. Die Verträge der griechisch-römischen Welt von 338 bis 200 v. Chr.* (Munich 1969) 441, Webster), since before 301 the relations beteen Athens and Seleucus were less than cordial (Ferguson 124ff., cf. Wilamowitz, *Schiedsg.* 161f. n. 1). Fr. 205(201–2K) probably comes from a single conversation between a disgruntled parasite named Stratios and his patron, whom at v. 3 he appears to name 'Demeas son of Laches, the Eteobutad'. The men with whom parasites associate in later comedy and related literature (cf. the introduction to Παράσιτος and Nesselrath, *LP* 23ff.), however, are normally young (e.g. Men. *Dysk.*, Plaut. *Asin.*, *Capt.*, *Curc.*, *Men.*, *Stich.*, Ter. *Phorm.*; soldiers: Men. *Kol.*, *Sik.*, Plaut. *Bacch.*, *MG*, Ter. *Eun.*; exceptionally a slave: Plaut. *Pers.*), and Demeas elsewhere in comedy is always an old man's name (see comm. on v. 3). Alexis here must have either introduced an unusual pairing or (? more probably) attached his parasite to Demeas' son and named the father because he was head of

---

[1] The lower date is based on two probabilities: that an exotic gift which could have been made as late as 297 would have ceased to be newsworthy by c. 295, and that a tiger would not have survived long in captivity with keepers almost certainly ignorant of life-preserving regimens. In today's zoos, even with the back-up of modern science and veterinary medicine, tigers normally die well before their late teens (cf. Jackson 48).

the household (? cf. Plaut. *Capt.* 172ff., Ter. *Phorm.* 1050ff.). Frs. 206(203K) and perhaps also 208(205K) (on 207(204K) see introduction to that fr.) were spoken (? in the same speech or scene) by a man who used to be dissolute but presumably no longer is; it is not possible to say whether this character was a *senex* or a reformed *adulescens*, or indeed one of the men featured in fr. 205(201–2).

205 (201 + 202K)

Meineke 3.476 (I, II), Kock 2.371, Edmonds 2.471, Kassel–Austin 2.137. Ath. 6.244d names the speaker as Stratios the parasite, disgruntled with a patron (on his identity see introduction to this play) for hurrying him through the streets, presumably to perform some urgent service on that patron's behalf (cf. also comm. on vv. 5–8) – hardly attendance at a dinner (no parasite would then complain of undue haste), more probably participation in a ruse.[1] A close analogy is provided by the speech of the *aduocati* at Plaut. *Poen.* 515ff. (cf. especially 522ff.), adapted in my view at least partly from a passage in Alexis' Καρχηδόνιος (q.v., and comm. on fr. 265(263K)); prolific playwrights are likely to have dealt with recurrent situations in identical ways.

(a) (201K)

1 **κρεῖττον ἦν**: cf. comm. on fr. 241(239K).5.

1–2 τῷ Πηγάσῳ ἢ τοῖς Βορεάδαις: papyrus discoveries have confirmed that myth comparisons, whether at the beginning of a speech as here (cf. e.g. Men. *Dysk.* 153ff., *Sam.* 589ff., Anaxilas 22, Eubulus 6(7K).2 citing Eur. *Andr.* 369), or embedded in it (e.g. Men. *Epitr.* 326ff., *Kol.* 124), are a standard feature of later Greek as well as of Roman comedy; hence it is reasonable to suppose that some of those Plautine examples whose point does not depend on particularities of Roman life and the Latin language (e.g. at the beginning of a speech: *Stich.* 1ff., ? *Bacch.* 21ff. = fr. xv.1ff.; in conversation *Men.* 714ff.) may derive from their Greek originals (cf. N. Zagagi, *Tradition and Originality in Plautus* (Göttingen 1980) 26ff., 40ff., 63, opposing Fraenkel's dogmatism, *EP* 7ff., but contrast E. Stärk, *Die Menaechmi des Plautus und kein griechisches Original* (Tübingen 1989) 50, 100f.). Pegasus, the horse born from Medusa's head (Hes. *Theog.* 280f.) and ridden by Bellerophon (W. Lermann and F. Hannig in Roscher s.v. *Pegasos* 1727.8ff., G. Türk in *RE* s.v. *Pegasos* 1, 56.58ff.), and Calais and

---

[1] Nesselrath's suggestion (*LP* 37) that Alexis is rather emphasising the parasite's bad physical condition seems less plausible.

Zetes, the two sons of Boreas by Oreithyia (Rapp in Roscher s.v. *Boreaden* 797.24ff., Wernicke in *RE* s.v. *Boreas* 2, 721.62ff.), were portrayed with wings in both art and literature (Pegasus: e.g. Pind. *Ol.* 13.86, *Isthm.* 7.44, Eur. *Ion* 202, Ar. *Pax* 76 and 135 citing Eur. fr. 306, *Pax* 160, Strabo 8.6.21, Apollodorus myth. 2.3.2, 4.2, Palaephatus 27; Boreadai: e.g. Pind. *Pyth.* 4.183f., Ap. Rhod. 1.219ff., Antipater Thess. 94 Gow–Page = *Anth. Pal.* 9.550, *Orph. Arg.* 221f., Apollodorus myth. 1.9.21, 3.15.2, Ovid *Met.* 6.712f., Hyginus 14.18 (32), Serv. on V. *Aen.* 3.209 = *Mythographi Vaticani* 1.27, 2.142), and became standard exemplars of speed (Pegasus: e.g. Hes. fr. 43a.84f. Πήγασο[ν] ... ὠκύτατον, Cic. *Quinct.* 80; Boreadai: e.g. Theogn. 715f. ὠκύτερος ... πόδας ... παίδων Βορέω, Ap. Rhod. 2.273ff., 427f., Dio Chrys. *Or.* 4.117). For Boreas himself as such a symbol, cf. Tyrtaeus fr. 12.4 West, Nonnus 33.211; for the winds in general, Call. *H. Art.* 3.94, Plaut. *Bacch.* 290, *neque aues neque uenti citius* and J. Barsby, comm. (Warminster 1986) *ad loc.*

2 ἢ εἴ τι θᾶττον ἔτι τρέχει: this correction of A's unmetrical and unsyntactical ἤ τι θᾶττον ἔτι τούτων τρέχει cures the ills most simply and satisfactorily[1] with Schweighaeuser's (cf. *Animadv.* 3.444) deletion of τούτων (? added by a pedant to clarify the construction) and the substitution of Epit.'s ἢ εἴ (whether Byzantine conjecture – so P. Maas, *BZ* 35 (1935) 302 n. 1 – or transmitted reading; cf. H. Papenhoff, *Zum Problem der Abhängigkeit der Epitome von der venezianischen Handschrift des Athenaios* (Diss. Göttingen 1954), C. Collard, *RFIC* 97 (1969) 157ff. and my general introduction, II.i.b) for A's ἤ; for the resultant idiom, with εἴ τις introducing the last in a series of items linked by a succession of either καίs or ἤs, cf. e.g. Longus 2.5 δυσθήρατος ἐγὼ καὶ ἱέρακι καὶ ἀετῷ καὶ εἴ τις ἄλλος τούτων ὠκύτερος ὄρνις. εἰ could easily have been omitted in A after its homophone ἤ especially in a synizesis which a scribe with an insufficient knowledge of metrics might have found unacceptable (cf. e.g. Ar. *Thesm.* 1224 δ' ὤξεις R corrected to διώξει; εἰς by Cobet; Men. *Dysk.* 949 ωσπερεις B needing correction to ὡσπερεὶ εἰς, cf. Gomme–Sandbach, *Comm ad loc.*[2]). 'A final diphthong or long vowel ... may form one syllable

---

[1] The other conjectures here proposed (G. Kaibel, *Hermes* 19 (1884) 259 τοῖς Βορ. ἢ θᾶττον ὅτι τούτων τρέχει, deleting the first ἤ and the τι before θᾶττον; W. Headlam, *CR* 13 (1899) 7 κεῖ τι θᾶττον ἔτι τρέχει, deleting τούτων with Schweighaeuser; Peppink, *Observ.* 40 ἤ τι θᾶττον εἰ τρέχει) restore metre at the expense of Attic idiom; the sequences in the first two (A, B ἤ C; A ἤ B καὶ C), and the position of indefinite τι before εἰ in the third, are alien to good Attic usage.

[2] Synecphonesis of -ει εἰς is now usually printed in the form -ει 'ς, as if it were an instance of prodelision or haplology (cf. Schwyzer 1.264), but it

with an initial vowel. The great majority of instances fall into two classes: (*a*) the first word is a monosyllable (especially the article, καί, ἤ, δή, μή, ὦ), or ἐπεί or ἐγώ; or (*b*) the second word is enclitic ἐστι, or begins with an ε which is not part of a declinable root,' M. L. West, *Greek Metre* (Oxford 1982) 13; examples of η + ει include Ariphron fr. 1.6 Page, Theoc. 11.81 (and Meineke *ad loc.*) ἢ εἰ ; Hom. *Il.* 5.466 ἢ εἰς; S. *Trach.* 321, Eur. *Hipp.* 1335, *Or.* 478 μὴ εἰδέναι; *IT* 1048 ἢ εἰδότος; *Rhes.* 683 χρὴ εἰδέναι.

3 Δημέα Λάχητος 'Ετεοβουτάδη: on the question whether a character with this appellation was really the parasite's patron, see above, introduction to the play. The names Demeas and Laches were both common in real-life Athens (Kirchner, *PA* 1.218ff. nos. 3307–26, 2.6ff. nos. 9009–27), and adopted by later Greek comedy, always for free old men (Demeas: Men. *Mis.*, *Sam.*, fr. 212, possibly *Dis ex.*, but see the note on fr. 2 in my Loeb edition (Cambridge Mass. and London 1979), but not fr.276.5, see Körte *ad loc.*; com. adesp. frs. 244.193 etc., 252.16, 258.40 Austin; Demea in Ter. *Ad.*; Laches: Men. *Her.*, *Kith.*, *Perinth.*, *Fab. inc.*, frs. 572, 663, com. adesp. frs. 250.2, 255.24, 266.5 Austin, Philemon 28, 136(149K), Crobylus 5; Ter. *Hec.*, Caecilius, *Obolostates* fr. v, pall. adesp. fr. ix, xi Ribbeck, cf. x, *Lachetem audiui percussisse Demeam*). The designation as an Eteobutad would turn this Demeas into a member of one of Athens' most aristocratic families, claiming descent from Erechtheus and holding the hereditary priesthoods of Athena Polias and Poseidon Erechtheus (Aeschines 2.147 and Σ; cf. Harpocration, Hesych., Phot., *Et. Mag.*, *Et. Gen.* = Bekker, *Anecd.* 257.4, *Suda*, all s.v. 'Ετεοβουτάδαι, describing the family as λαμπρόν, ἐπίσημον and the like; Davies, *APF* 169ff., 348ff.). Alexis' purpose in ascribing such ancestry to his Demeas may have been partly ridicule of upper-class extravagance (cf. the portrayal of Pheidippides as a Megaclid in Ar. *Nub.* and Dover on v. 46 and p. xxvii; Alciphron 3.25.2), partly emblematic emphasis on background and wealth (cf. Alciphron 3.2.1).

4 πέτεται: an appropriate metaphor for a man compared to Pegasus and the Boreadae, although the use is common (e.g. Alexis 213(210K).2, Ar. *Lys.* 55, 321, Antiphanes 227(229K).2, Pl. *Resp.* 8.567d; E. W. Whittle, *CQ* 9 (1959) 58 n. 4; cf. Ach. Tat. 7.15.2 εἶχον οἱ πόδες μου τότε πτερά). The *Marcianus* here strangely writes πετεγαρ (*sic*!) with no indication of error or abbreviation, while the Epit. MSS (CE) are correct; this is one of four differences in reading between A and Epit. in vv. 1–4 (in v. 2 besides ἢ εἰ also θᾶσσον and τούτων ἔτι CE ~ θᾶττον and ἔτι τούτων A), a cluster

---

seems preferable to spell both syllables out in full, as in other examples of synizesis.

COMMENTARY

of minor testimonies that need to be weighed carefully by those who still believe that the Epit. derives directly from the *Marcianus*.

οὐχ οἷον: 'not just/merely', a usage which arose in Hellenistic Greek and was roundly condemned not just by Phryn. *Ecl.* 348 p. 98 Fischer κίβδηλον ἐσχάτως, μάλιστα δ᾽ ἁμαρτάνεται ἐν τῇ ἡμεδαπῇ, οὐχ οἷον καὶ μὴ οἷον λεγόντων, ὅπερ οὐ μόνον τῷ ἀδοκίμῳ, ἀλλὰ καὶ τῷ ἤχῳ ἀηδές. λέγειν δὲ χρὴ οὐ δήπου καὶ μὴ δήπου, but even by the Antiatticist 110.13 Bekker οὐχ οἷον ὀρ<γ>ίζομαι (corr. C. A. Lobeck, edition of Phrynichus (Leipzig 1820) p. 373), οὐχ οἷον ἁλίσκω (βαδίζω A. Nauck, *MGR* 3 (1869–74) 52f., cf. 5 (1888) 236 and 6 (1894) 98f., assuming a reference to Alexis here), καὶ τὰ ὅμοια· σὺ δὲ <λέγε> (Nauck), πολὺ ἀπέχω τοῦ ὀρ<γ>ίζεσθαι (corr. Lobeck). The usage forcefully reverses the normal order of 'not X but Y' (in Attic Greek simply οὐ ... ἀλλά, e.g. S. *Ant.* 523, Dem. 1.5, Denniston, *GP* 1) in order to give extra emphasis to Y ('Y, not just X'), presumably originating in popular speech to fill a gap in idiom (Phrynichus' claim that οὐ δήπου was the Attic equivalent is not borne out by existing evidence, cf. Denniston, *GP* 267f.). In non-purist writers of *Koine* Greek (e.g. Polyb., Diod. Sic. ∼ Lucian, Plut.; cf. *TGL* s.v. οἷος col. 1831) the use of οὐχ οἷον was further developed in a variety of ways: (i) 'not only not', followed by ἀλλ᾽ οὐδέ (most common), e.g. Polyb. 1.20.12, Diod. Sic. 3.18.2, (ii) 'not only' + ἀλλὰ καί, (iii) 'not only not' + ἀλλὰ καί, (iv) 'not only not' + τὸ δ᾽ ἐναντίον, etc.; in many of these idioms οὐχ οἷον replaced Attic οὐχ ὅπως/μὴ ὅτι, cf. K.G. 2.258ff., Schwyzer 2.670. Cf. also the related use of οὐδ᾽ οἷον at Alexis 18.2 and comm. there.

βαδίζει τὰς ὁδούς: similarly e.g. Xen. *Oec.* 3.7 πάνυ μακρὰν ὁδὸν βαδίζοντα, *Mem.* 2.1.11, Hippocr. *Intern.* 44, *Acut. (Sp.)* 7 Kühlewein = 5 Littré, *Dieb. Judic.* 3, Plut. *Artax.* 24.6 ἐβάδιζε πρῶτος ὁδοὺς ὀρεινὰς καὶ προσάντεις, cf. Arist. *HA* 9.38, 622ᵇ25 ἀεὶ μίαν ἀτροπὸν πάντες βαδίζουσι.

(b) (202K)

5–8 These vv., which according to Ath. 6.244e follow on 1–4 μετ᾽ ὀλίγα (i.e. probably but not verifiably a few lines later in the same scene, see comm. on 201(196K).2 and n. 1 there), seems to be a dialogue (part-assignments worked out by Daléchamp, vv. 5, 7a; Meineke, v. 7b) between Stratios the parasite and his patron. The latter's need to be reassured about the parasite's love and good wishes (this love being a standard theme of later comedy: e.g. Plaut. *Capt.* 144f., 148ff., *Stich.* 372, 465f., 583f.; cf. introduction to fr. 149(145K)) may well be a preliminary to a request for the service whose urgency has already forced the patron to hurry the remonstrating parasite along in vv. 1–4.

5 Στράτιε: in introducing this fr. Ath. 6.244d identifies (? just from the

594

context of the quotations themselves) Stratios as a parasite. The name is not rare among real-life Athenians (cf. Kirchner, *PA* 2.271f., nos. 12913–20), but unparalleled for a character in comedy.

5, 7 φιλεῖς δήπου με ... εὔχει τ᾽ ἀεί με ζῆν;: the first of the patron's two interjections is best interpreted (with Bothe, *PCGF* 562) as a statement ('of course you love me': δήπου is normally thus used in statements and negative, not positive questions, cf. Denniston, *GP* 267f.), but the second is more lively and pointed if taken as a question (so Meineke). On what may have followed the parasite's responses, see introduction to fr.

5 μᾶλλον τοῦ πατρός: Stratios' father or his patron's? Although the Greek is ambiguous, in this idiom the article is most commonly a substitute for a first-person possessive or a possessive of the same person as the subject of the sentence (e.g. Theogn. 277, Andocides 1.47, Xen. *Oec.* 7.4; cf. Cobet, *NL* 614, Gildersleeve, *Syntax*, 2.227f. § 534).

6 τρέφει ... τρέφεις: ὁ τρέφων becomes the technical term for the parasite's patron, e.g. Ath. 6.244d introducing this fr., Timocles 8.8, Nicolaus 1.11, Machon 236 and Gow *ad loc.*, 48, Alciphron 3.42, cf. Diodorus com. 2.31ff.; Nesselrath, *LP* 23ff., *MK* 314.

λαμπρῶς: appropriately, since the patron appears to have been an Eteobutad (cf. comm. on v. 3).

7 Dindorf's εὔχει (for εὔχη(ι) A and Epit.) seems preferable, cf. comm. on 182(177K). The prayer ἀεί με ζῆν appears to have been conventional if absurd in such contexts (e.g. Men. *Sam.* 728 ἀεὶ ζῴην, Eur. *Alc.* 713, Ter. *Ad.* 874).

ἅπασι τοῖς θεοῖς: sc. εὔχομαι; cf. Dem. 14.39, Men. *Sam.* 614 and H. Wankel, comm. on Dem. 18.1 (Heidelberg 1976).

8 πάθῃς τι: the conventional euphemism for 'die/suffer some appalling fate' from Homer onwards (e.g. *Il.* 5.567, 11.470, *Od.* 17.596, Callinus 1.17, Hdt. 8.102.3, Lysias 19.51, Ar. *Vesp.* 385, *Eccl.* 1105, Hermippus 45(44K).1, Antiphanes 216(217K).26). For the idea cf. the parasite in Lucian *Dial. meretr.* 13.2 ἀβίωτα γὰρ ἦν μοι σοῦ ἀποθανόντος.

206 (203K)

Meineke 3.476 (III), Kock 2.372, Edmonds 2.470, Kassel–Austin 2.138. On the speaker see introduction to Πύραυνος.

1 ἐπεθύμουν: the imperfect presumably refers to a former period in the speaker's life (? cf. ἐλάνθανον 207(204K).1, aorist ἀνέκραγον 208(205K).2, perhaps from the same speech or scene); assumption of corruption (hence ἐπιθυμῶν S. A. Naber, *Mnemosyne* 8 (1880) 262f.) is unjustified.

θατέρου βίου: sc. 'the other way of living', as e.g. in Alciphron 2.10.3 μετιτέον μοι ἐφ᾽ ἕτερον βίον, cf. Page on Eur. *Med.* 1039.

2 ὑγρόν: Ath. 6.258b cites the fr. to illustrate the expression ὑγρὸς βίος ('dissolute life'), which apparently came into vogue during the 4th century and survived into the Roman and Byzantine empires (e.g. Pollux 6.126, Philo *Vit. contempl.* 47 ὑγρὸς ... καὶ ἄσωτος βίος, John Chrysostom *Hom. xxiv in Epist. ad Rom.* 60.624 Migne, cf. Plut. *Mor.* 751a, *Suda* = Phot. and other lexica s.v. ὑγρός; cf. δίυγρος in Eustath. 827.3, ὑγρότης in Crobylus 4, Lycurg. *Leoc.* 33; cf. Hadrianus Junius, *Adagiorum Centuria vii.*xvii (Basle 1574) 245). These usages can clearly be linked with others which developed earlier (ὑγρός = (i) 'supple/ flexible' of limbs, movement, etc., e.g. Ar. *Vesp.* 1213, Xen. *Equ.* 1.6, Pl. *Symp.* 196a; (ii) 'soaked in wine' and so 'tipsy', e.g. Heraclitus 117 Diels–Kranz, Plut. *Mor.* 713a) or contemporaneously (ὑ. = (iii) 'moistly languishing/seductive' of glances, e.g. Antipater Sid. 15.3, Leonidas 31.3 Gow–Page = *Anth. Pal.* 7.27, 16.306, Lucian *Imag.* 6, *Anacreont.* 16.21, cf. -ῶς Philostratus *Epist.* 33), but it is difficult to say which of these (? or other: e.g. ὑ. = literally 'wet' in sexual union) applications sparked off the extension exemplified in Alexis here. Cf. also in contemporary comedy the synonymous (? and politer) τὸν ἡδὺν λεγόμενον τοῦτον βίον (Men. *Epitr.* 680).

3 ἐν Κεραμεικῷ: the Cerameicus, which extended from the north side of the Athenian Agora in a north-westerly direction up to and beyond the Dipylon Gate, and so was split into two sections (ἐντός, ἐκτός) by the Themistoclean wall (cf. W. Judeich, *Die Topographie von Athen*[2] (Munich 1931) 175f., 328f., J. Travlos, *Pictorial Dictionary of Ancient Athens* (London 1971) 299ff.), included inside the wall the city's main markets and was a notorious red-light district (*Lex. rhet.* 275.19 Bekker Κεραμεικός· τόπος ἐν ᾧ αἱ πόρναι ἑστήκασιν, cf. Hesych. = Σ Pl. *Parm.* 127c, Phot., *Suda* s.v., Σ Ar. *Equ.* 772.c.ii, Alciphron 2.22.2 ἀκούω γάρ σε τὰ πολλὰ ἐπί ... Κεραμεικοῦ διατρίβειν, οὗ φασι τοὺς ἐξωλεστάτους σχολῇ καὶ ῥαστωνῇ τὸν βίον καταναλίσκειν, 3.12.3 τὸ ἐκ Κεραμεικοῦ πορνίδιον, 28.3; W. Peek, *Kerameikos: Ergebnisse der Ausgrabungen* 3 (Berlin 1941) *Fluchtafel* c.3.29ff., R. E. Wycherley, *Agora* iii.221ff., H. Herter, *JAC* 3 (1960) 86, H. Lind, *Mus. Helv.* 45 (1988) 158ff.), where the speaker found his thirty prostitutes to act as teachers of the ὑγρὸς βίος.

4 ἐξηῦρον: cf. comm. on fr. 9.2.

5 τριάκοντ' ἀφ' ἑνὸς ἐργαστηρίου: 'thirty from one shop', where the noun is a very thinly veiled euphemism for 'brothel', cf. [Dem.] 59.67 ὁπόσαι ἂν ἐπ' ἐργαστηρίου καθῶνται ... ἐργαστήριον φάσκων καὶ τοῦτο εἶναι, τὴν Στεφάνου οἰκίαν, Alciphron fr. 5.1. The wording in the [Dem.] passage led Meineke, *Anal. Crit.* 112 to conjecture ἐφ' ἑνὸς here, but ἀφ' is perfectly acceptable in its context, cf. e.g. Ar. fr. 156(149K).2 ἕνα ... ἀφ' ἑκάστης τέχνης and expressions such as οἱ ἀπὸ τοῦ δήμου (Thuc. 4.130), οἱ ἀπὸ τοῦ περιπάτου (Lucian *Symp.* 6).

ΠΥΡΑΥΝΟΣ

207 (204K)

Meineke 3.477 (IV), Kock 2.372, Edmonds 2.472, Kassel–Austin 2.138. The male (v. 2 περιπατῶν) speaker urgently requests to enter one of the stage-houses. His admission that he had long been a paragon of insensitivity and/or ignorance suggests that he has now seen the light, but the dramatic context cannot be identified with any security. He could have been (i) the reformed debauchee of 206(203K) (? from the same speech; cf. the imperfects in 206(203K).1, 207(204K).1), (ii) a man bent on exploring the ὑγρὸς βίος (at a brothel presumably rather than a formal school, *pace* Kock, who nevertheless aptly compares Ar. *Nub.* 181: ? the speaker of 206(203K) *before* reform) or (iii) a slave whose sudden idea for a ruse leads him to despise his previous stupidity (cf. e.g. Plaut. *Trin.* 1008f.)

1 ἄνοιγ' ἄνοιγε τὴν θύραν: repetition of an imperative (cf. e.g. *carmen populare* 2.18 Page, *PMG* 450f. ἄνοιγ' ἄνοιγε τὰν θύραν, Ar. *Nub.* 181 ἄνοιγ' ἄνοιγ' ἀνύσας τὸ φροντιστήριον (Strepsiades to a pupil of Socrates), *Ach.* 1054, *Equ.* 107, *Pax* 1119, Eubulus 14(15K).11) indicates urgency; on other kinds of anadiplosis in Greek drama see W. Breitenbach, *Untersuchungen zur Sprache der euripideischen Lyrik* (Stuttgart 1934) 214ff., Fraenkel on A. *Ag.* 1101, Bond on Eur. *Her.* 763ff., Handley on Men. *Dysk.* 574. For the action and phrasing cf. also Men. *Dysk.* 454 ἄνοιγε θᾶττον τὴν θύραν (Knemon unexpectedly returning home), *Asp.* 303 μᾶλλον δ' ἄν. τὰς θ. (Daos to Chairestratos in a state of collapse indoors).

2–3 The speaker emphasises his earlier stupidity by comparing himself to a series of chosen objects and creatures which imaginatively varies the standard yardsticks (similarly Ar. *Nub.* 1201ff., addressed to the audience τί κάθησθ' ἀβέλτεροι, | ἡμέτερα κέρδη τῶν σοφῶν, ὄντες λίθοι, | ἀριθμός, πρόβατ' ἄλλως, ἀμφορῆς νενησμένοι; cf. Plaut. *Bacch.* 1087ff., Ter. *HT* 877) and closes with a topically striking exemplar. The list comprises:

(i) ἀνδριάς (strictly a likeness of the same sex as the speaker: Trypho 8.731.9ff. Walz): as a symbol of stupidity/insensitivity also at *App. Prov.* 1.27 ἀνδριὰς σφυρήλατος· ἐπὶ τῶν ἀναισθήτων, cf. Arrian *Epict.* 3.2.4; similarly βρέτας at Anaxandrides 11. Elsewhere a symbol of uselessness (e.g. Eur. *El.* 388, fr. 282, Metagenes 10, Dem. 18.129, Arrian *Epict.* 3.9.12) or of immovability/silence (Lucian *Imag.* 1, *Vit. auct.* 3, Synesius *Dion* 66.1149a Migne; cf. εἰκών Ar. *Ran.* 537, *statuae* Hor. *Sat.* 2.5.40, *Epist.* 2.2.83).

(ii) ἀλέτων ὄνος (upper millstone, see comm. on fr. 13): cf. Pl. *Hipp. mai.* 292d εἴ μοι παρεκάθησο λίθος, καὶ οὗτος μυλίας, μήτε ὦτα μήτε ἐγκέφαλον ἔχων. More usually the non-specific terms λίθος (λίθινος) and πέτρα/-ος (in Latin *lapis, saxum*) are chosen as symbols of stupidity (e.g. Ar. *Nub.* 1202, Plaut. *MG* 236, 1024, *Most.* 1073, *Poen.* 291, Ter. *HT* 831, 877, 917, *Hec.* 214 = Apollodorus Car. 9, Herodas 6.4, 7.109, Arrian *Epict.*

597

3.22, Clem. Alex. *Protrept.* 1.4.1), insensitivity or heartlessness (e.g. *P.V.* 242, Eur. *Med.* 1279f., *Her.* 1397, *Cycl.* 596, Plaut. *Curc.* 197, *Poen.* 290, Theoc. 3.18, Alciphron 4.16.7, Lucian *Dial. meretr.* 12.2, *Anth. Pal.* 11.253 Lucillius, cf. 255 Palladas), uselessness (e.g. Arrian *Epict.* 3.9.12) and silence (Theogn. 568f.); cf. O. Crusius, *Untersuchungen zu den Mimiamben des Herondas* (Leipzig 1892) 114, Headlam–Knox on Herodas, P. Groeneboom on *P.V.* (Groningen 1928), Seaford on Eur. *Cycl.*, *locc. citt.*

(iii) ποτάμιος ἵππος (the classical name, e.g. Hdt. 2.71, Arist. *HA* 2.7, 502ᵃ9; ἱπποπόταμος first in Dioscorides 2.23): included because of its exceptionally thick skin (5 cm in places; cf. Hdt., Arist., *locc. citt.*), since παχύδερμος could mean 'stupid' (Men. *Epitr.* 1114 παχύδερμος ἦσθα καὶ σύ, νοῦν ἔχειν δοκῶν, Lucian *Tim.* 23), but the elephant was a more common exemplar (Epinicus 2.7, cf. Diogenian 4.43, *Suda* s.v. ἐλέφαντος οὐδὲν διαφέρεις, Plaut. *MG* 235f.).

(iv) τοῖχος: not itself (but cf. Hesych. s.v. δίτοιχος· ἀναίσθητος) found elsewhere as a symbol of stupidity, but chosen presumably because a house wall consists of stones (see ii), bricks (cf. Aelian *Epist.* 19 οὐ μὴν εἰς τὸ παντελές μου καταφρονήσουσιν ὥσπερ οὖν πλινθίνου) and/or wood (cf. e.g. *Anth. Pal.* 11.275 = ? Ap. Rhod. epigr. 1 Page ὁ ξυλινὸς νοῦς, Ach. Tat. 5.22.5).

(v) τίγρις: deliberately chosen as the climactic *pièce de résistance*, cf. the widespread use of the lion as an example of insensate savagery (but not stupidity), e.g. Hom. *Il.* 5.782ff., 18.161ff., A. *Ag.* 717ff., Eur. *Med.* 1342, *Her.* 1211ff., *Suppl.* 1222f. and Collard *ad loc.*, *IT* 297, Ar. *Ran.* 1431f., Men. *Mis.* 311; cf. Breitenbach, *op. cit.* on v. 1, 150, J. Taillardat, *Les Images d'Aristophane* (Paris 1962) 168.

The list is organised informally but skilfully, with the fourth item splitting the two animals at the end and by the alternation of object and creature increasing the climactic surprise. Herwerden's suggested transposition of τοῖχος before ποτάμιος ἵππος (*Coll. Crit.* 128) and S. A. Naber's χοῖρος for τοῖχος (*Mnemosyne* 8 (1880) 263) would not improve the effect.

3 ὁ Σελεύκου τίγρις: see also introduction to Πύραυνος. Here and commonly elsewhere (Arist. *HA* 8.28, 607ᵃ4, Theophr. *HP* 5.4.7, Strabo 15.1.37, Aelian *NA* 8.1, 15.4) τίγρις is masculine, but at Philemon 49(47K) (the same individual as here!), Plut. *Mor.* 144e and Arrian *Ind.* 15.1, 3 feminine. The reason for the variation may possibly have been confusion between sex and grammatical gender in an unusual creature.

208 (205K)

Meineke 3.477 (v), Kock 2.372, Edmonds 2.472, Kassel–Austin 2.139. A short and puzzling fr. whose speaker and context cannot be determined with certainty, although clues to both are provided by (i) Ath.'s comments when citing this fr. (14.663f–664a Ἄλεξις ... ἀμφιβόλως εἴρηκεν (sc. the word ματτύη(ς)) ... ὥσπερ ἂν εἰ τὸ δεῖπνον ἔλεγεν); (ii) possibly fr. 206(203K) (and less probably 207(204K)), in which a man's past quest (n.b. the imperfects in 206.1, 207.1 ~ the ? gnomic aorist ἀνέκραγον in 208(205K).2) for a life of debauchery is described; and (iii) the meanings of ματτύη(ς), where our evidence comes mainly from this section of Ath. (662e–664f), supplemented by 640d (citing Sophilus fr. 5(4K)) and 4.141e (from Molpis: = FGrH 590 F 2), Pollux 6.70, Hesych. and Phot. s.v. ματτύης. ματτύη (fem.: so Nicostratus fr. 7(8K), Sophilus 5(4K).5, Machon com. 1, Ath., Artemidorus and Dorotheus in Ath. 662e ff.), ματτύης (masc.: Philemon 11(12K), Artemidorus in Ath. 663d–e, Phot. and Hesych.) and ματύλλη (fem.: Pollux 6.70) are variant forms of a Macedonian word (? related to μάσσω: so Ath. 663b, cf. T. Kalén, *Quaestiones grammaticae graecae* (Göteborg 1918) 91ff., Frisk 2.185f., but contrast Chantraine 2.672) properly used for a Thessalian (so Dorotheus in Ath. 662f) dish which became popular in Athens during the Macedonian hegemony[1] and was assumed by some (e.g. Pollux, cf. Machon com. 1) to have been a Macedonian invention. The name was given to a wide variety of costly ἐδέσματα including fish, meat, fowl, geese, game birds, vegetables, fruit and cakes, cooked in a highly spiced way (Artemidorus in Ath. 663c–f) and normally eaten during the drinking bouts that followed the main meal (Philemon 11(12K), Ath. 141d–e, 664b–c, e–f, Pollux), when its spiciness increased the thirst (Pollux). Ath. goes on (663f) to claim that from its association with such parties the word gained a secondary meaning (coyly explained as ὁ τρόπος τῆς τοιαύτης εὐωχίας), although in all three passages cited as illustration (Philemon 8(9K), 11(12K), Alexis 208(205K)) ματτύη(ς) can[2] (and at Philemon 8(9K) must) be understood in its primary meaning. Even so, Ath.'s claim is at least tenable; the dish itself was associated with ἀκολασία (Ath. 663b–c), the related verb ματτυάζω seems to have had indelicate overtones (see fr. 50(49K).3 and comm.), and fr. 206(203K) indicates that lechery was one theme of Alexis' play. It is unlikely that the secondary meaning of ματτύη(ς) was simply 'prostitute' (the use of the masculine form in Philemon 11(12K) makes this implausible, even though male

---

[1] Bentley's conjecture ματτυολοιχός at Ar. *Nub.* 451 (ματιο- most MSS, ματτιο- NO⁷) would presuppose that it was already known at Athens in the previous century, cf. Dover on 445–51.

[2] As Ath. himself admits (664a, πιθανὸν δὲ καὶ ἰδίως ἐπὶ τῶν ἐδεσμάτων ἀναφέρειν: so A defensibly, with ἐπί + genitive as commonly in lexica and paroemiographers when introducing explanations, cf. e.g. comm. on 207(204K).2–3 (i); Kaibel's addition of <τι> after ἐπί is unnecessary).

prostitutes undoubtedly existed, cf. K. J. Dover, *Greek Homosexuality* (London 1978) 20ff.), yet some kind of sexual innuendo could well have been involved. Sexual favours were, like the titbits of μ.'s primary sense, enjoyed as ἐπιδορπίσματα during the drinking bouts, and the suggested extension of μ.'s use (? in ephemeral slang) might have been inspired by either a witty appreciation of the parallel or a punning association with words like ματρυλεῖον ('tavern-cum-brothel', e.g. Dinarchus fr. 43.5, Men. *Epitr.* 692 and Gomme–Sandbach, *Comm. ad loc.*, lexica such as Harpocration, Hesych., *Suda*, s.v.), μάτρυλλος and -λλα ('pimp', Phryn. *Praep. Soph.* 84.4 de Borries, Eustath. 380.5), or both.

The speaker of Alexis 208(205K), who describes either himself or some 'busy' (ἀσχολουμένους) men (see below) calling on more than one occasion for a ματτύη(ς) (the accusative case makes the form which Alexis used uncertain), was clearly bent on pleasure; he could have been e.g. the lecher of fr. 206(203K) (in which event the alleged second meaning of μ. would be particularly appropriate) or (so Gulick) Stratios the parasite of 205(201–2K), but speculation beyond that (e.g. on the activity occupying the ἀσχολουμένους of fr. 208(205K)) would be unprofitable.

1–2 'Whenever I have found them occupied, I (so all translators from Conti and Daléchamp to Gulick, but 'they' is also possible) have shouted . . .' If Ath.'s text here (14.663f) is correctly transmitted (and there is no valid reason to question it, *pace* O. Crusius, *Philologus* 46 (1888) 621, whose conjecture ἐπείνων ἀσχολούμενος λαλῶν κἀνέκραγον rashly rewrites the fr. and destroys any possibility of the alleged *double entendre*), it provides a rare but paralleled (e.g. S. *El.* 89ff., Lysias 12.41; K.G. 2.449 n. 3, J. M. Stahl, *Kritisch-historische Syntax des griechischen Verbums* (Heidelberg 1907) 135 s 3, J. Wackernagel, *Vorlesungen über Syntax* (1 Basle 1920) 176ff., Schwyzer 2.282f. § 5) sequence of aorist in main clause + subjunctive with ἄν in subordinate temporal clause, which implies here continuation of the described event into the present. For the use of λαμβάνω here (rather than the commoner καταλαμβάνω, LSJ s.v. ii.2) + object participle cf. e.g. Ar. *Vesp.* 758f., Pl. *Resp.* 3.389d, Dem. 21.97, LSJ s.v. i.4.

ἀσχολουμένους: the verb, both in the middle and intransitively in the active, occurs elsewhere in later comedy (also Alexis 263(261K).12, Men. *Dysk.* 294, fr. 828, Philemon 184(220K), cf. Alciphron 3.17.1), and appears in prose first in Aristotle (*EN* 10.7.6, 1177^b4, *Pol.* 4.12.8, 1299^b33, 7.13.9, 1333^a41, etc., cf. Theophr. *Char.* 12.2, Epicurus fr. 204 Usener); cf. Bruhn, *Wortschatz* 51, Durham, *Vocabulary* 46f.

Ῥόδιον ἢ Ποππύζουσα

See Δορκὶς ἢ Ποππύζουσα.

Σικυώνιος

Σικυώνιος, like Menander's Σικυώνιος (or -ιοι, attested by *P.Brit.Mus.* 2562, the subscription in *P.Sorb.* 2272–3, and a wall-painting in Ephesus figured in Charitonidis and others, *Mosaïques* pl. 27.2, and defended by A. M. Belardinelli, *Corolla Londiniensis* 2 (1982) 15ff., opposing Gomme–Sandbach, *Comm.* p. 632, cf. *Drama* 2 (1993) 29) and most of the other titles in Alexis consisting of a male ethnic (cf. introduction to Ἐπιδαύριος), is most likely to have featured a man visiting or living in a city other than that of his origin. The one short fr. tells us nothing about the play.[1]

209 (206K)

Meineke 3.477, Kock 2.372, Edmonds 2.472, Kassel–Austin 2.139. This fr., if we accept the text (Antiatticist, 84.1–3 Bekker) of the MS that quotes it, comprises (as Meineke first saw) most of a Eupolidean verse ([ŏ o] ⁓ × − ∪ ∪ − / ŏ o − ∪ − ∪ ⊔) of a standard type, ending with a lekythion (cf. J. W. White, *The Verse of Greek Comedy* (London 1912) §§ 508, 528f., Wilamowitz, *Griechische Verskunst* (Berlin 1921) 228f., West, *Greek Metre* 95f., R. Pretagostini, *Dioniso* 57 (1987) 258f., L. P. E. Parker, *PCPS* 34 (1988) 115ff.). Yet although Eupolideans are fairly common in Old Comedy (e.g. Ar. *Nub.* 518–62, Cratinus 75(74K), 105(98K), Pherecrates 70(64K), probably com. adesp. frs. 53–6 Kock; a complete list in Parker 116), where in checkable passages they are confined to the chorus, they are very rare in 4th-century drama (satyr play: Astydamas fr. 4; comedy: elsewhere possibly only Alexis 239(237K), delivered apparently to the chorus in a play from the beginning of Alexis' career, cf. comm. *ad loc.* and introduction to Τροφώνιος, but Marius Victorinus, *Gramm. Lat.* 6.104 Keil alleges examples in Diphilus and Men.). Here, where less than one line is preserved in a notoriously corrupt MS (cf. comm. on frs. 10, 108(103K), 127(122K), 158(154K), *Glotta* 68 (1990) 91f.), the

---

[1] When Pollux 4.119 writes πορφυρᾷ δ' ἐσθῆτι χρῶνται οἱ νεανίσκοι, οἱ δὲ παράσιτοι μελαίνη ἢ φαιᾷ, πλὴν ἐν Σικυωνίῳ λευκῇ, ὅτε μέλλει γαμεῖν ὁ παράσιτος, the reference is more probably to Menander's play, which was celebrated in antiquity (cf. Alciphron 4.19.19) and is known to have included a parasite named Theron, than to Alexis', cf. Körte on Men. fr. 337 = now *Sik.* fr. 9 and Gomme–Sandbach, *Comm. ad loc.*, R. Kassel, *Eranos* 63 (1965) 7. Bridegrooms regularly wore a garland and a white ἱμάτιον (Plut. *Mor.* 771d, cf. Eur. *Alc.* 923, Plaut. *Cas.* 446; Hermann–Blümner, *Privatalterthümer* 274; W. Erdmann, *Die Ehe im alten Griechenland* (Munich 1934) 255 n. 25).

COMMENTARY

Eupolidean could well be a chimaera, misbegotten from an original οὐχὶ τῶν | μετρίων <γάρ εἰσιν/ἐστιν/ἦσαν>, ἀλλὰ τ. β. β.[1]

τῶν "βαβαὶ βαβαί": sc. λεγόντων. For this ellipse Meineke aptly compares Ar. *Vesp.* 666f. εἰς τούτους τοὺς 'οὐχὶ προδώσω τὸν Ἀθηναίων κολοσυρτόν, | ἀλλὰ μαχοῦμαι περὶ τοῦ πλήθους ἀεί'; he could have added e.g. *Ran.* 223, ὦ 'κοὰξ κοάξ'. Commonly quotations of, and references to, other people's words are introduced by τό: e.g. Men. *Pk.* 1006, πάνυ σοῦ φιλῶ τὸ 'νῦν διαλλαχθήσομαι', Ar. *Nub.* 1173f., Heliodorus 1.18.5, but contrast Philostratus *Epist.* 29, ἡ 'ἤ μ' ἀνάειρ' ἤ ἐγώ σέ' (= Hom. *Il.* 23.724) πρὸς τὸν ἀντεραστὴν μάχη. As an interjection βαβαί expresses surprise or pleasure (singly: common in comedy, e.g. Ar. *Ach.* 806, *Av.* 272, Timocles 24(22K).2, cf. Plaut. *Stich.* 771 and in Plato, e.g. *Phd.* 84d, *Phdr.* 236e, Eur. *Cycl.* 156, Heliodorus 9.2.1; doubled as here: Achaeus fr. 28, Chrysippus in Ath. 4.158b, βαβαὶ βαβαιάξ Ar. *Pax* 248); thus οἱ βαβαὶ βαβαί = those who go round effusively expressing astonishment at every new thing they see or hear (so Meineke rightly, 3.478[2]), contrasted with οἱ μέτριοι, those able to control their emotions.

Σκίρων

O. Jahn, *Arch. Zeit.* 23 (1865) 26. Alexis' Σκίρων (this, not Σκεί-, is the better attested Attic orthography[3]) was most probably a burlesque (? in

---

[1] Alternatively οὐ τῶν μετρίων <ἤν/ἔστ'> is possible (Blaydes, *Adv.* 2.164: οὐ already Dindorf, *TGL* s.v. βαβαί); but not τῶν οὐχὶ μετρίων (S. A. Naber, *Mnemosyne* 8 (1880) 263), because that sequence would normally be balanced by ἀλλά + anarthrous attribute.

[2] But elsewhere (*Philologicarum exercitationum Athenaei specimen primum* (Berlin 1827) 18, *FCG* 5.90, *Anal. Crit.* 75) he interpreted the phrase as referring to those who aroused admiration because of their pomp and majesty, without being able to cite any parallels for such an elliptic usage.

[3] Attic vases (P. Kretschmer, *Griechische Vaseninschriften* (Gütersloh 1894) 131ff. and *Wien. Stud.* 22 (1900) 179f.; cf. J. D. Beazley, *AJA* 39 (1935) 479 n. 2), Callimachus in the *Hecale* (fr. 296 Pfeiffer = 59 Hollis), the Athenian Tower of the Winds (1st century; A. Boeckh, *CIG* 518, figured in Roscher, s.v., 1013), and the London papyrus at Bacchylides 18.25 (probably 2nd century AD, cf. the Snell–Maehler edition (Leipzig 1970) ix f.) spell the name Σκίρων, but medieval MSS vary between -κεί- and -κί-. Possibly an original and correct formation in -κί- was corrupted in late Hellenistic or imperial times to -κεί- (cf. Meisterhans–Schwyzer 49), perhaps partly influenced by a false Alexandrian (? by Ar. Byz.: *Et. Mag.* 716.47, cf. Wilamowitz, *GGA* (1893) 739 n. 1) derivation from

the Middle-Comedy period) of the Athenian version of the saga in which Sciron (cf. Waser and Höfer in Roscher s.v., 1004.3ff., van der Kolf in *RE* s.v. 1, 537.39ff., Robert, *GH* 2.715ff.), a brigand who waylaid travellers between the Corinthian isthmus and Athens as they crossed the rocky ledge some seven kilometres west of Megara (the Σκιρωνίδες πέτραι of Eur. *Hipp.* 979f., *Hcld.* 860; cf. especially J. G. Frazer's comm. on Pausanias (London 1898) 2.546ff., D. Müller, *Topographischer Bildkommentar zu den Historien Herodots: Griechenland* (Tübingen 1987) 713f.), forced them to wash his feet and as they did it threw them over the cliff to provide food for a giant turtle[1] below. He was eventually killed by Theseus and met the same fate as his previous victims. The one fr. (210(207K)) of Alexis' play, which describes a man or object 'being raised aloft like a garland you can roll', is best interpreted as part of a description (? in a speech by Theseus or a messenger) of Sciron being hoisted by Theseus before being thrown over the cliff (so first Jahn; Kock's alternative suggestion of a reference to Sinis tying one of his victims to a pine tree is an aberration). A mid-4th-century bell-krater now in Naples (K. Schefold, *Untersuchungen zu den kertscher Vasen* (Berlin and Leipzig 1934) iii and fig. 51; H. Metzger, *Représentations dans la céramique attique du IVe siècle* (Paris 1951) 318 no. 30; other vases discussed by T. Ely, *JHS* 9 (1888) 272ff., T. B. L. Webster, *JHS* 59 (1939) 115 and pl. xi.b, W. T. Magrath, *TAPA* 107 (1977) 221 and n. 48; Beazley, indexes of *ABV* and *ARV*[2], ii s.v. Theseus and Skiron) portrays this moment, with Sciron gripped by the forehead and right leg; could the painter have been influenced by a recent play such as Alexis' Σκίρων? The same title was used also by Euripides (a satyr play: pp. 572ff. Nauck + 94f. Austin, *NFEP*; H. J. Mette, *Mus. Helv.* 21 (1964) 71f., B. Snell, *Aegyptus* 47 (1967) 184ff., D. F. Sutton, *The Greek Satyr Play* (Meisenheim am Glan 1990) 62ff.) and Epicharmus (frs. 125, 126 Kaibel), but we do not know whether Alexis' play parodied earlier material.

210 (207K)

Meineke 3.478, Kock 2.373, Edmonds 2.472, Kassel–Austin 2.140. If Alexis here compares Theseus' mighty feat of hoisting Sciron into the air

---

κείρω; see also J. Wackernagel, *Indog. Forsch.* 25 (1909) 328 = *Kleine Schriften* 2 (Göttingen 1954) 1024, Threatte 1.193. In the citation of Alexis' title at Ath. 15.678e the *Marcianus* has -κεί-, corrected to -κί- by Kaibel.

[1] This part of the legend (*pace* O. Keller, *Die antike Tierwelt* 2 (Leipzig 1913) 253f.) is less fanciful to those who are aware that the Leatherback (or Leathery) Turtle (*Dermochelys coriacea*) still inhabits the Mediter-

COMMENTARY

(see introduction to Σκίρων), before he threw him down the cliff, to the mundane action of lifting and poising a κυλιστὸς στέφανος (a garland for rolling, whirling or throwing: see comm. on 4.2) most probably before it was hurled in competition, Alexis employs a standard technique of the myth-parodist in Middle Comedy: that of reducing heroic behaviour to the level of everyday life (cf. introduction to 140(135K), *G and R* 19 (1972) 72f., Webster, *SLGC* 18f., 85).

Σπονδοφόρος

T. B. L. Webster, *CQ* 2 (1952) 19. Σπονδοφόροι (cf. e.g. Pind. *Isthm.* 2.23, Ar. *Ach.* 216 playing on the word's derivation, Aeschines 2.133, Pausanias 5.15.10, Pollux 1.35 and 8.137, where all the MSS record the term correctly, but at 4.94 σπενδο- FS, at 10.111 with the citation of this fr. -φορικῶ FSL; see Ch. Michel in Dar.–Sag. s.v. *Spondophoroi* 1441b f., Latte in *RE* s.v., especially 1849.12ff.) carried the libation cups and wine in festivals such as the Eleusinia. As they were also charged with proclaiming throughout Greece the dates of these festivals and the sacred truces in force during them, they enjoyed the status of heralds, with the privileges of wearing garlands, carrying wands and receiving lavish hospitality in the cities through which they passed. Alexis' title figure was presumably so depicted, but his role in the plot and the plot itself are uncertain.

The one surviving fr. (211(208K)) refers to Aristogeiton ὁ ῥήτωρ (see comm. on v. 1). His political career in Athens seems to have extended from *c.* 340 to the late 320s, and Alexis' play is probably to be dated within these limits (so Webster).

211 (208K)

Meineke 3.478, Kock 2.373, Edmonds 2.474, Kassel–Austin 2.140. Speaker and context are unknown.

1–2 Ἀριστογείτονα τὸν ῥήτορ': see A. Schaefer, *Demosthenes und seine Zeit* 3.2 (Leipzig 1858) 113ff., F. Blass, *Die attische Beredsamkeit*[2] 3 (Leipzig 1898) 278ff., Thalheim in *RE* s.v. *Aristogeiton* 2, 931.53ff., Kirchner, *PA* 1.123f. no. 1775, R. Sealey, *BICS* 7.1960, 33ff., Davies, *APF* 476. Aristogeiton son of Cydimachus (probably not to be identified with A. of

---

ranean, reaches a length of over 180 cm and a weight of over 450 kg, and is carnivorous (cf. A. Carr, *Handbook of Turtles* (Ithaca N.Y. 1952) 442ff., R. Bustard, *Sea Turtles* (London 1972) 34f. W. G. Arnott, *LCM* 16 (1991) 111f.).

ΣΠΟΝΔΟΦΟΡΟΣ

Aphidna, see Davies countering Sealey) was politically active (allegedly as a συκοφάντης, but our main sources, [Dem]. 25 and 26, Dinarchus 2, are biased against him; cf. J. O. Lofberg, *Sycophancy in Athens* (Diss. Chicago 1917) 78ff.) up to the time of the Harpalus affair (324–3, cf. comm. on 143(139K)). The *Suda* (s.v.) attributes seven speeches to him, including κατὰ Φρύνης and κ. Ὑπερείδου (cf. Ath. 13.591e; frs. in Baiter-Sauppe 2.309f. and K. Jander, *Oratorum et rhetorum graecorum fragmenta nuper reperta* = *Kleine Texte* 118 (Bonn 1913) 15); estimates of his oratorical ability range from condemnation of his incorrigible τραχύτης, misplaced invective and vehemence, and general ὕθλοι ἄλογοι (Hermogenes *Id.* 257.22f., 377.21ff. Rabe, Syrianus *in Hermog.* 1.56.9ff., 2.3.21f. Rabe) to modest praise (Quintilian 12.10.22, placing him among the better Attic orators).

2–3 The speaker claims to have seen Aristogeiton 'wearing a basket of the sort used for charcoal'. This is far less likely to have been a description of some surrealist dream (so tentatively Kock) than a slur by innuendo on Aristogeiton's social status, of a kind familiar from Old Comedy (e.g. Ar. *Ach.* 457, 478, *Thesm.* 387, 456, *Ran.* 840: Euripides' mother as a seller of vegetables; *Equ.* 44, *Nub.* 581: Cleon as a tanner; *Nub.* 1065: Hyperbolus as a lamp-maker; cf. especially K. J. Dover, *Aristophanic Comedy* (London 1972) 97, showing that this type of abuse was not confined to comedy or the 5th century). The λάρκος, specifically a large basket for carrying charcoal (Ar. *Ach.* 333 and Σ 351, cf. λαρκίδιον 340; Pollux here), was essential equipment for the ἀνθρακεύς, whom we can imagine going out to work each morning at daybreak with his basket on his back and his head protruding through or rising above the handle (hence Alexis' imaginative ἠμφιεσμένον here, as if the charcoal-burner were actually dressed in it). The ἀνθρακεύς was often a slave (e.g. Syros in Men. *Epitr.*, cf. *ZPE* 70 (1987) 27); hence the speaker's allegation here of having seen Aristogeiton equipped as a charcoal-burner is tantamount to calling him a slave ([Dem.] 25.65 asserts – probably with equal unreliability – that his mother was a freedwoman, whence *Suda* s.v.) or at least a free manual worker of the lowest social status. [Dem].25.54, 65, 77 and Dinarchus 2.8, 18 maintain that Aristogeiton's father was condemned to death and died ignobly in exile.

Στρατιώτης

H. F. Clinton, *Fasti Hellenici* 2 (Oxford 1834) 142f., Meineke 1.387, Breitenbach 60 n. 148, Webster *SM* 171, *SLGC* 64, *CQ* 2 (1952) 15f., Nesselrath, *MK* 190f., 199, 282 n. 1, 327f. This was a favourite title in later Greek comedy (also Xenarchus, Philemon; Antiphanes Στρατιώτης ἢ Τύχων, Diphilus Εὐνοῦχος ἢ Σ.; Menander's Στρατιῶται may be comparable, but hardly Hermippus' in Old Comedy). A soldier played the title role also in Alexis' Θράσων, Menander's Θρασυλέων, Μισούμενος, Σικυώνιος (or -ιοι, see introduction to Alexis' Σικυώνιος), probably Ψευδηρακλῆς, and in the anonymous Ἀλαζών which formed the Greek original of Plaut. *MG* (v.86). On soldiers in other plays see Ribbeck, *Alazon* 28ff., W. Hofmann and G. Wartenberg, *Der Bramarbas in der antiken Komödie* (Berlin 1973) 9ff., Webster, *SLGC* 64 and my introduction to Alexis' Θράσων.

Whether Alexis' soldier participated in the lively dialogue of the one fr. preserved from the play (212(209K)) is uncertain. In it two speakers, one of them (A.) certainly male (ἀποφέρων ἥκω v. 3) and both in all probability either accompanied by or involved with a spouse or other member(s) of a household (otherwise the references of both to themselves in the plural vv. 2, 5–7, as well as in the singular are hard to explain), discuss the ownership of a baby (παιδάριον v. 3). (A.) previously received it from (B.) but now wishes to return it to him (? her), but (B.) disclaims ownership as strongly as (A.). One possibility is that the baby was a foundling, discovered by (A.) when he was out walking with (B.), but picked up first and taken home by (B.); such a background makes the best dramatic sense of the various exchanges in the fr., including the cryptic v. 7 (where (B.)'s topical reference in ἀπεδώκαμεν, see below, must presumably also be dramatically meaningful). Such a scenario inevitably brings to mind the scene in Men. *Epitr.* 218ff. (cf. Nesselrath 282 n. 1) where two slaves (Daos the shepherd, Syros the charcoal-burner) dispute the possession of an exposed baby which Daos found but passed on to Syros without the tokens originally left with it, but it would obviously be rash to force an interpretation on to the Alexis fr. from this.[1] Webster (*SLGC* 64) suggested a totally different scenario, with a borrowed baby which its previous owner refuses to take back (? a prefiguration of the incident in Plautus' *Truculentus* (389ff.) where the *hetaira* borrowed a baby in order to extract more money from a soldier lover induced to believe that he was the baby's father). Webster's suggestion is more ingenious than plausible (the person returning the baby in Alexis is male, the baby borrower in Plautus is female), but it usefully demonstrates that different situations may be extrapolated from the Alexis fr.

Even so, title and fr. between them provide two staples of a typical New-Comedy plot, all the more remarkably in a play of the Middle-Comedy period. Vv. 5–7 of the fr. echo Demosthenes' famous quibble with Philip in 343 about Halonnesos (cf. fr. 7 and comm., introduction to

---

[1] Yet dramatically influenced terracottas in Athens of men holding babies were already being produced in the second quarter of the 4th century (Webster, *MIOMC*[3] AT 59, 60, 67).

Ἀδελφοί), and thus date Στρατιώτης to *c.* 342–340 (so first Clinton, *loc. cit.*; cf. my introduction to Ἀδελφοί); topical jokes of this sort quickly grow stale.

212 (209K)

Meineke 3.478, Kock 2.373, Edmonds 2.474, Kassel–Austin 2.141. In this fr., cited by Ath. 6.223e–f (*Marcianus* only, not Epit.), the correct part-assignments were worked out by Daléchamp (vv. 1–5 ἡμέτερον, 6 (B.) οὐκ – 7 (B.) ἀπεδώκαμεν) and Schweighaeuser (the rest, cf. *Animadv.* 3.280). The identity and situation of the two speakers are discussed in the introduction to Στρατιώτης; their dispute centres on the legal ownership of a baby, with (A.) claiming that he is rightfully restoring (note ἀπόλαβε, 1: = 'receive what is one's due', LSJ s.v.) a child which was not 'properly' his to take (τὸ μὴ προσῆκον ... λαβεῖν 7) in the first place, and (B.) responding that it was his duty to give it to (A.) (ἀπεδώκαμεν 7, cf. LSJ s.v.). Use of these ἀπο- compounds (cf. also ἀποφέρων 3) is partly dictated by the legal situation, as it is in other dramatic disputes about responsibility for a dependant (e.g. baby also at Men. *Epitr.* 278–89, 346–61; woman at Eur. *Hel.* 911–16, 963–74 and R. Kannicht, comm. (Heidelberg 1969) on 909–18, cf. Men. *Sik.* 236f. with ἀφίημι in addition, cf. R. Kassel (Berlin 1965) *ad loc.*), but partly also by a desire to prepare the way for the joke in vv. 5–7 on Demosthenes' Halonnesos quibble.

2 τουτί. **(B).** τί τοῦτο δ' ἐστίν; **(A).** ὃ ... is G. Hermann's correction (*Epitome doctrinae metricae²*, Leipzig 1844, xvi f.; cf. Meineke, *ed. min.* 742, Kock 3.743) of A's unmetrical transposition τουτί· τοῦτο δ' ἔστι τί ὃ ..., where the error presumably originated in haplography (τί after τουτί) and subsequent replacement of the missing word after the wrong -τι.

6 Kock's τότ' for A's τοῦτ' is no improvement; this baby is relevant to the context, but the time of its delivery to the speaker is not.

6–7 According to the *Marcianus*, (B.)'s two remarks are οὐ δεδώκαμεν and ἀποδεδώκαμεν, where the latter does not scan and so must be corrupt, most probably (? by dittography: ΑΠΕΔ → ΑΠΕΔΕΔ → ΑΠΟΔΕΔ) for ἀπεδώκαμεν (so Casaubon); consequently the preceding δεδώκαμεν must also be altered to the same tense (ἐδώκαμεν), for otherwise the remarks would lose half their pungency, and pungency is essential here where topical play is being made on Demosthenes' quibble with these two words (see above). The negative before ἐδώκαμεν is better οὐκ (first Meineke in 1847, *ed. min.* 742; cf. *FCG* 5.91 and (Jacobi) ccxiii, Hirschig, *Annot.* 9) than οὐδ' (first Hirschig in 1840, *Diss.* 27; cf. Meineke, *ed. min.* xviii and *FCG* (Jacobi) 5.ccxiii); although there is nothing to choose between them palaeographically (for as soon as ἐδώκαμεν was altered by a scribe to δεδώ-, in order to balance the previously corrupted ἀποδεδώ-, the correct οὐκ would swiftly have been replaced by οὐ), οὐ provides more appropriate sense ('we did *not* give' as opposed to 'we didn't give, either').

τί δαί: Hermann's correction (in Erfurdt, *Observ.* 434 n.) of the *Marcianus*' τί δε. None of the four idiomatic uses of τί δέ; in Attic (i, exclamation of surprise or incredulity, usually introducing a further question by the same speaker; ii, formula of resignation, 'What of that?'; iii, formula of transition, 'And what about the following?'; iv, picking up the previous speaker's question, 'You ask what?'; Denniston, *GP* 175f.) would be relevant here, but the commonest use of τί δαί; (lively or suprised question, not introducing a further query, Denniston, *GP* 262f.) most certainly is. Scribal confusion between AI and E is too common to need comment or exemplification, but cf. Cobet, *NL* 333f.

7 τὸ μὴ προσῆκον ἐμοὶ λαβεῖν in the *Marcianus* produces a split anapaest in the first half of the third metron with no elision at the break (cf. *CQ* 7 (1957) 196f.). The one defensible parallel known to me[1] is Ar. *Eccl.* 219 (οὐκ ἂν ἐσῴζετο all MSS except Λ οὐκ ἀνεσώ-, where the three words form an integrated unit). Most probably Alexis here wrote not ἐμοί but μοι or ἐμέ (so Meineke); the latter perhaps would be a likelier candidate for corrruption by a copyist unaware that in Attic impersonal προσήκει can take acc. + infinitive (LSJ s.v., II.2.b; cf. Pl. *Gorg.* 491c–d τούτους γὰρ προσήκει τῶν πόλεων ἄρχειν BTP corrupted in F[1] to τούτοις γ. π.). Translate the verse: '(A.) We restored (the baby to you) as yours by right. (B.) What I had no right to take.' Kock's wish to substitute λάβω (in a deliberative question) for the transmitted λαβεῖν is palaeographically unacceptable and does nothing for the sense (cf. Herwerden, *Coll. Crit.* 128).

Συναποθνήσκοντες

Meineke 1.402, F. Olivier, *Revue de théologie et de philosophie* 17 (1929) 103ff. = *Essais dans le domaine du monde gréco-romain antique et dans celui du nouveau testament* (Geneva 1963) 155ff., T. B. L. Webster, *CQ* 2 (1952) 22. The title is shared with Philemon and Diphilus; from the latter's play Plautus adapted his *Commorientes* and Terence took a scene (155ff.) for his *Adelphoe* (cf. 6f.; K. Dziatzko and R. Kauer (Leipzig 1903), comm. on 11ff.; H. Drexler, *Philologus Suppl.* 26/2 (1934) 1ff., Webster, *SM* 87, E. Fantham, *Philologus*, 112 (1968) 196ff., H. Lloyd-Jones, *CQ* 23 (1973) 279ff., R. H. Martin's edition (Cambridge 1976) 242ff., A. S. Gratwick's

---

[1] On cases like Ar. *Nub.* 1192 and *Av.* 90 see Radermacher on Ar. *Ran.* 1220; on *Av.* 23 and 93, Antiphanes 146(148K).6 see *CQ* 7 (1957) 197 n. 1.

(Warminster 1987) 43ff.). Neither the Terentian scene nor the extant frs. from the Greek plays and the Plautine adaptation shed any light on the title, but no character actually dies in what remains of later Greek and Roman comedy (cf. A. G. Katsouris, *Dioniso* 47 (1976) 30, K. Treu, *JAC Suppl.* 9 (1982) 21ff.), and the probability must be that in each of the Συναποθνήσκοντες two (or more) characters pretended to die as part of a ruse (like Chairestratos in Men. *Asp.*, cf. 381; see also introduction to Μανδραγοριζομένη), or in grief or despair threatened suicide (see Katsouris 24ff., listing the New-Comedy instances: mainly lovers, e.g. Thrasonides at Men. *Mis.* 309f., ? 394, Polemon at *Pk.* 504f., cf. 977f., and their Roman counterparts, but note too the mourning Glycerium at Ter. *Andr.* 134, 140, and Gelasimus the parasite at Plaut. *Stich.* 639f., cf. *BICS* 19 (1972) 73f.), or were mistakenly reported dead (like Kleostratos in Men. *Asp.*, ? Krateia's brother in *Mis.*, cf. *Arethusa* 3 (1970) 54ff., Gomme–Sandbach's *Comm.* 438ff.).

Three frs. are cited from Alexis' play. Fr. 213(210K) refers to the real-life parasite Chaerephon in Corinth and the pleasure of dining at another's expense, fr. 214(211K) alleges that seafaring is a sign of madness, poverty or a death-wish, 215(212K) bewails the misery caused by man's belly. A stage parasite is the likeliest person both to enthuse over free meals and at a time of despair (cf. Dobree, *Adv.* 2.325, Ribbeck, *Kolax*, 34 n. 2) to condemn the tyranny of the belly, although the remarks in 215(212K) could also perhaps be imagined on the lips of a puritanical servant or an ex-patron rejecting a parasite's request to his face or behind his back. 214(211K)'s mention of seafaring may imply that during the play one or more characters propose(s) to undertake or has/have undertaken a voyage. 213(210K)'s reference to Corinth, however, need not mean that this city was in any way involved in the plot (e.g. as scene or voyager's goal: see comm. on fr.), nor need the allusion to a death-wish in 214(211K).2 have any thematic connection with the title of the play. Yet each piece of information provided by the frs. would fit snugly into a typical but (since most of the jigsaw is missing) mysterious New-Comedy plot staged between *c.* 325 and 310, the period when Chaerephon is known to have been active (cf. Webster and comm. on 213(210K).1).

213 (210K)

Meineke 3.480 (II), Kock 2.374, Edmonds 2.474, Kassel–Austin 2.141. This fr., spoken most probably by a parasite (cf. introduction to Συναποθνήσκοντες), begins in mid-sentence, like many others in Ath. (cf. comm. on 192(187K).1–2); the main verb (? some part of φοιτῶ, cf. Cratinus 47(45K) ἄκλητος φοιτᾶς ἐπὶ δεῖπνον, cf. 46(44K)) is lost in the preceding context.

COMMENTARY

1 εἰς Κόρινθον ἐλθὼν Χαιρεφῶν: so A (Ath. 4.165a), but Epit.'s transposition ἐλθὼν εἰς Κ. is equally possible.

Information about this Chaerephon, an Athenian who became notorious as a παράσιτος for dining uninvited at others' expense and who wrote a short prose essay entitled Δεῖπνον in the form of an epistle (cf. Call. fr. 434 Pfeiffer), comes virtually all from Ath. (especially 6.242f–246a, but also 4.135d citing Matron 534.8–10 Lloyd-Jones–Parsons, 164f–165a citing also Alexis 259(257K), 13.584e citing Lynceus of Samos, 15.685e–f); cf. Ribbeck, *Kolax* 76ff., Wellmann in *RE* s.v. *Chairephon* 4, 2029.1ff., editors and commentators on Men. *Sam.* 603, especially E. Capps (Boston 1910) 231f., A. Körte 1³ (Leipzig 1938) xl–xli, Sandbach, V. Bevilacqua, *Dioniso* 7 (1939) 42f., Gow on Machon 11. The earliest datable reference to him seems to be Men. fr. 304 from Ὀργή (325–320, see my Loeb edition of Men. 1 (Cambridge Mass. and London 1979) xiv f.), and the latest Apollodorus ? of Carystus[1] fr. 29(24K) (in which a second Chaerephon is alleged to have gatecrashed Ophellas of Cyrene's wedding-feast some time before the groom's death in 309, cf. W. S. Ferguson, *Hellenistic Athens* (London 1911) 110f.); all the other mentions either demonstrably fall in the period *c.*325–*c.*310 (e.g. Men. fr. 245 from the same play as fr. 238 with its allusion to Demetrius of Phalerum's sumptuary legislation; cf. Lynceus in Ath. 245a), or can be accommodated there plausibly if roughly (e.g. Men. *Sam.* 603f., cf. D. M. Bain's edition (Warminster 1983) p. xii, Gomme–Sandbach, *Comm.* 542f.; Lynceus in Ath. 245f associates Chaerephon with Corydus, cf. introduction to Alexis 48(47K), and in Ath. 584e with Gnathaena, cf. T. B. L. Webster, *CQ* 2 (1952) 13 and *SLGC* 152 and n. 3; Chaerephon's Δεῖπνον was dedicated to Cyrebion, cf. introduction to Παγκρατιαστής and comm. on 173(168K).2; see also Alexis 259(257K)). It is unclear whether the visit to Corinth alleged by Alexis here was a historical reality (Capps' suggestion that Chaerephon could have migrated there during the unrest in Athens between 323 and 317 would be more persuasive if we had for him any evidence of pro-Macedonian affiliations; for a parasite a major attraction of Corinth would have been its reputation for sexual and other pleasures, cf. Alexis 255(253K) and comm., Göbel, *Ethnica* 37f., H. Herter, *JAC* 3 (1960) 71 and n. 8, R. Renehan, *Studies in Greek Texts* (Göttingen 1976) 105) or just a figment of Alexis' imagination, designed to show the lengths to which Chaerephon would go in order to get a free dinner.[2]

---

[1] Of Carystus according to Ath. 6.243d, but the play from which the fr. is cited (Ἱέρεια) is attributed to his earlier namesake from Gela by the *Suda*.

[2] The references to Chaerephon and Corinth here must not be used as evidence that Corinth was the scene of the play, with the parasite a

ΣΥΝΑΠΟΘΝΗΙΣΚΟΝΤΕΣ

2 ἄκλητος: a term applied to both genuine gatecrashers (such as parasites, e.g. Philippus in Xen. *Symp.* 1.11ff., Corydus in Timocles 11.3, and especially Chaerephon: ἄκλητος also in Apollodorus Car. 29(24K), 31(26K), Lynceus in Ath. 245a, 584e; ἀσύμβολος Alexis 259(257K), Men. *Sam.* 603; παράβυστος Timotheus 1. Cf. also Antiphanes 193(195K).7 and *inuocatus* at Plaut. *Capt.* 69f. ~ introduction to Alexis' Παράσιτος) and also those who came to a dinner without a personal invitation from the host but as friends of an invited guest (e.g. Aristodemus at Pl. *Symp.* 174b with R. G. Bury's comm. (Cambridge 1932²) *ad loc.*). Cf. Plut. *Mor.* 706e–710a, noting that the practice of gatecrashing goes back to Homer (Menelaus at *Il.* 2.408), Lucian *Conv.* 12; A. Hug, *De graecorum proverbio* αὐτόματοι δ' ἀγαθοὶ ἐπὶ δαῖτας ἴασιν (Festprogr. Univ. Zurich 1872) 1ff., Mau in *RE* s.v. *Convivium* 1204.40ff.

πέτεται: cf. comm. on fr. 205(201K).4.

3 οὕτω τι τἀλλότρι' ἐσθίειν ἐστὶν γλυκύ: 'The τι has the effect of gently toning down, almost in the same way as a πως, and it is suitably added to an adjective which serves as predicate when the subject of the sentence is an infinitive,' Fraenkel on A. *Ag.* 884; cf. Men. *Kith.* fr. 7 οὕτω τι πρᾶγμ' ἐστ' ἐπίπονον τὸ προσδοκᾶν and Gomme–Sandbach, *Comm. ad loc.*, *P.V.* 536, Ar. fr. 633(622K), Blaydes, *Adv.* 1.115.

τἀλλότρι' ἐσθίειν: this expression (cf. Ephippus 20.2 ἀλλότριον ... ὄψον ἐσθίειν), like the commoner τἀλλότρια δειπνεῖν (cf. Eubulus 72.1 and Hunter *ad loc.*, Nesselrath, *LP* 57, 65f. and n. 172, 100, *MK* 310f.), identifies the successful parasite's *modus uiuendi*.

ἐστὶν γλυκύ: the nu ephelkystikon, present in A but omitted by CE, was defended by I. Hilberg, *Das Princip der Silbenwägung* (Vienna 1879) 207 (cf. also A. Nauck, *MGR* 6 (1894) 94f., Herwerden, *Coll. Crit.* 128), on the ground that open final vowels in trochaic disyllables such as ἐστί are allegedly not lengthened before either mute + liquid or other consonantal combinations at the beginning of the following word. Hilberg's mandate (cf. 207ff.) has too many exceptions in comic texts for automatic acceptance; more relevant here are (1) the total unreliability of A's scribe with regard to paragogic nus (in citations of Alexis, e.g. wrongly omitted at 9.1*, 167(162K).10*, 212(209K).2*, 215(212K).2*, 16.9, 77.2, 164(159K).2, 168(163K).2, 223(221K).13; wrongly added at 91(87K).3* (*pace* Kassel–Austin), 191(186K).6*, 212(209K).4*, 41(40K).1, 103(98K).2, 17, 131(126K).7, 150(146K).7, 11, 243(241K).2; asterisked are instances with ἐστί(ν); cf. also L. Radermacher (Vienna 1954²) on Ar. *Ran.* 1220, Handley on Men. *Dysk.* p. 65, and my discussion

---

character and indeed the voyager of fr. 214(211K) (despite Plaut. *Curc.* 28off.).

in *CQ* 7 (1957) 191), and (2) the general reluctance of comic poets to lengthen syllables with short vowels before any mute + liquid combination unless tragic rhythm is being deliberately imitated (cf. Handley on Men. *Dysk.* 414, Gomme–Sandbach, *Comm.* p. 38).

214 (211K)

Meineke 3.480 (III), Kock 2.374, Edmonds 2.476, Kassel–Austin 2.142.The folly and dangers of seafaring are a frequent theme in Greek literature from Homer onwards (e.g. *Od.* 5.100f., 174f., 8.138f., Hes. *Op.* 687ff., S. *Ant.* 332ff., Alex. Aet. fr. 18 Powell, Quint. Smyrn. 7.296f.; cf. W. C. Greene, *North American Review* 199 (1914) 433ff., Kroll in *RE* s.v. *Schiffahrt* 412.3ff., A. Lesky, *Thalatta* (Vienna 1947) 26ff.), but in later Greek comedy and the Roman adaptations this theme is often woven into speeches by men who directly after a voyage thank the gods for safe arrival (e.g. Plaut. *MG* 411ff., *Most* 431ff.; thanks without the dangers, *Bacch.* 172ff. *Rud.* 906ff., *Stich.* 402ff., *Trin.* 820ff.) or greet joyfully their first contact with land (e.g. Plaut. *Men.* 226ff., possibly Men. *Asp.* 491ff.; greetings without dangers, Men. fr. 1, Plaut. *Bacch.* 170f., *Stich.* 649f.), while the shipwrecked Labrax at Plaut. *Rud.* 485ff. whines *qui homo sese <esse>* (corr. G. Hermann: *<esse> sese* Bentley) *miserum et mendicum uolet,* | *Neptuno credat sese atque aetatem suam*, in terms similar to Alexis 214(211K), cf. also Antiphanes 100, 202(204K).7, 290(101K), Philemon 51(183K). Yet the wording of Alexis 214(211K) neither necessitates a parallel context nor identifies the speaker (cf. introduction to Συναποθνήσκοντες); similar ideas are voiced by e.g. a fisherman bent on retiring from the sea at Alciphron 1.3.

1 The unanimous reading of the MSS (SMA at Stob. *Anth.* 4.17.2 Hense) διαπλεῖ θάλασσαν requires only the correction of the noun to the normal 4th-century Attic orthography with -ττ- (? so first Hense). διαπλεῖν with direct object is good Attic (Pl. *Phd.* 85d δ. τὸν βίον) and regular in *Koine* (e.g. Plut. *Mor.* 206c δ. τὸ πέλαγος, Lucian *Hermot.* 28 τὸν Αἰγαῖον ἢ τὸν Ἰόνιον δ., *IG* xiv.1976 from a late Roman cemetery πέλαγος δ.; cf. similarly διαπλώω in e.g. Ap. Rhod. 2.628f., *Anth. Pal.* 7.23b), so there is no need for Hirschig's conjecture δὲ πλεῖ (*Annot.* 13, supported by Cobet, *NL* 120 and Blaydes, *Adv.* 1.115).

μελαγχολᾷ: from at least the time of Aristophanes onwards (*Av.* 14, *Eccl.* 251, *Plut.* 12, 366, 903; cf. e.g. Pl. *Phdr.* 268e, [Dem]. 48.56, Men. *Dysk.* 89, *Sam.* 563[1]) a popular expression for 'is mad', since 'an excess of black bile

---

[1] At Men. *Asp.* 306 μελαγχολῶ = 'I am depressed.'

ΣΥΝΑΠΟΘΝΗΙΣΚΟΝΤΕΣ

was supposed to produce mental derangement, of a manic as well as of a depressive type' (Sandbach in an excellent note, *Comm.* on *Dysk.* 88; cf. also H. Flashar, *Melancholie und Melancholiker*(Berlin 1966) 37f.).

2 θανατᾷ: here 'wishes to die', as elsewhere in Attic (Pl. *Phd.* 64b and Σ *ad loc.*, *pace* J. Burnet's note in his edition (Oxford 1911), and *Axioch.* 366c), although in post-classical Greek the verb appears also with the non-desiderative sense 'is at death's door' (cf. LSJ s.v. ι, ιι). On verbs in -<ι>ᾶν see especially Rutherford, *NP* 152ff.

τούτων τῶν τριῶν: so SMA unmetrically, but Gesner's correction τούτων τριῶν is certain, for when οὗτος introduces or accompanies a numeral in Attic it dispenses with the article (e.g. cardinals: Pl. *Gorg.* 463b τέτταρα ταῦτα μόρια, Dem. 27.23 ταύτας ... τριάκοντα μνᾶς, possibly Lysias 7.10 ταῦτα τρία ἔτη (so MS X); ordinals: Lysias 24.6, Dem. 3.4, 8.2, Men. *Epitr.* 243f.; LSJ s.v. οὗτος в.ιv). The error here in the MSS of Stobaeus was due presumably either to dittography or to scribal ignorance of this anarthrous use of οὗτος.

3 SMA's ἑνός τ' produces a nonsensical connection; Meineke's γ' restores the *mot juste*, which is then further underlined by the following τοὐλάχιστον. Confusion in MSS between τε and γε is inveterate; see e.g. comm. on frs. 46(45K).3, 129(124K).18, 138(133K).5, J. Adam's edition of Pl. *Resp.* 2² (Cambridge 1963) p. 524.

τοὐλάχιστον: i.e. the voyager cannot fail to be victim to one of three afflictions 'at the very least'; cf. in 4th-century Attic e.g. Xen. *Anab.* 5.7.8, Dem. 4.21, Antiphanes fr. 145(147K).5, Axionicus 6.5, Diphilus 74(73K).8. The accusative is adverbial (cf. K.G. 1.317 n. 21).

215 (212K)

Meineke 3.479 (1), Kock 2.374, Edmonds 2.476, Kassel–Austin 2.142; cf. M. P. Paoletta, *Annali della Facoltà di Lettere e Filosofia dell'Università di Napoli* 26 (1983–4) 27f. Attacks on the tyranny of man's belly are a comic cliché (cf. Diphilus 60; contrast [Alexis] 25.6) suiting equally the jaded or rejected parasite (e.g. Plaut. *MG* 33, cf. [Diphilus] 2.579.133 Kock = falsely *carm. pop.* 15 Diels, Alciphron 3.3.1, 3, 3.42.1), the priggish slave (e.g. Plaut. *Men.* 970f.) and the parasite's ex-patron (cf. introduction to Συναποθνήσκοντες). How far these attacks are inspired by contemporary gnomologists (cf. Paoletta), and how far by a long literary tradition going back to Homer (*Od.* 7.216, 17.286, cf. Heliod. 2.22; Archilochus 124b.4f. West, Eur. *Suppl.* 865f., frs. 49, 201, 915, the moralist Chares in Stob. *Anth.* 3.17.3 = falsely fr. 1 in Nauck p. 826; cf. Wilamowitz, *Analecta Euripidea* (Berlin 1875) 226ff., K. J. McKay, *Erysichthon* (*Mnemosyne Suppl.* 7, 1962) 103 and n. 3, West, comm. on Hes. *Theog.* 26, G. Xanthakis-Karamanos, *Studies in Fourth-Century Tragedy* (Athens 1980) 141), it is impossible to establish. On the use of trochaic tetrameters for such topics, see the introduction to 'Ισοστάσιον.

1 Without the preceding context there is no way of deciding whether Alexis here wrote τ' ἂν (τ'ἂν *sic* A at Ath. 10.422a, ἂν CE) or τἂν (Blaydes, *Adv.* 2.165). Thereafter ἀνθρώποις κακόν is G. Morel's transposition (133, before Canter, Paris MS p. 49 and Grotius, *Exc.* 974) of ACE's κακὸν ἀνθρώποις, an error introduced probably by some scribe who preferred normal prose order to metre (cf. W. Headlam, *CR* 16 (1902) 243ff.).

1–2 The sequence τε (?: see above, on v. 1) . . . δὲ . . . τε is irregular and may be a product of excerptor's or scribe's carelessness, but it is attested in the MSS of Attic authors with sufficient frequency for cautious acceptance, δέ presumably replacing an expected τε in order to introduce an element of contrast (see comm. on fr.2.8).

3 I see no compelling reason to tamper with the transmitted text εἴ τις ἀφέλοι τοῦτ' (so CE and Eustath. 1837.20: ταῦτ' A) ἀφ' ἡμῶν τὸ μέρος ἀπὸ τοῦ σώματος, despite the proliferation of 19th-century conjectures (Jacobs, *Spic.* 53, Meineke, Bothe, *PCGF* 563, Herwerden, *NAC* 33, Kock, Kaibel in Ath., Blaydes, *Adv.* 2.165). The construction of ἀφαιρεῖν + accusative and ἀπό with genitive is a well-attested Attic variation (e.g. in comedy Ar. *Vesp.* 883f., Diocles 9(8K), Men. *Pk.* 999f., cf. com. adesp. fr. 239.3f. Austin sometimes attributed to Alexis = 'False or doubtful attributions' v in this edition) of the more usual ones with (i) two accusatives and (ii) accusative + genitive of separation; the addition of ἀπὸ τοῦ σώματος after the vaguer ἀφ' ἡμῶν is more likely here to be a colloquial boost to precision (cf. e.g. Pl. *Lach.* 190b, τοῖς ὑέσιν αὐτῶν ἀρετὴ παραγενομένη ταῖς ψυχαῖς) than a deliberate imitation of the poetic σχῆμα καθ' ὅλον καὶ μέρος, with which formally it has much in common (cf. K.G. 1.289f.).

4 A textually corrupt verse (MSS οὐδ' ἂν ἀδικοῖτ' οὐδὲν οὐδεὶς οὔθ' ὑβρίζοιτ' ἂν CE/ -ζοιτ ἂν A ἑκών), whose restoration to metrical sense can be confidently argued. (i) οὔθ' (fourth word from verse-end) must be corresponsive to οὔθ' (first word), not οὐδ' (corrected by Dindorf, cf. Denniston, *GP* 508ff.); doubtless the erring copyist (or excerptor) was psychologically influenced by the deltas in οὐδὲν and οὐδεὶς. (ii) The two verbs in the disjunctive clauses will probably have expressed contrasted, if not necessarily mutually exclusive, ideas. The presence of volitive ἑκών in apposition to the subject of the second verb makes it more likely for that verb to have been active than passive. H. L. Ahrens's conjecture ὑβρίζοι τἂν (*De crasi et aphaeresi* (Stolberg, Harz 1845) 9 = *Kleine Schriften* (Hanover 1891) 62) admirably satisfies the conditions of metre, palaeography (this type of faulty word-division is common in MSS: e.g. Alciphron 2.15.2 ἀτιμάζοι τὸ Γ for -οιτο, Heliod. 8.63 μαλάσσοι τὸ S for -οιτο), and sense.

ΣΥΝΑΠΟΘΝΗΙΣΚΟΝΤΕΣ

Passive ἀδικοῖτ' (Ahrens's conjecture ἀδικοῖ γ' removes the element of contrast and introduces a less regular form, cf. K.B. 2.72) and active ὑβρίζοι (reinforced by ἑκών, *pace* Richards, *AO* 86: compare v. 2, the belly *forces* mankind into all manner of crimes, and v. 5, it is the *active* cause of all our troubles) provide the strongest sense: 'nobody would be either the victim or the intentional and arrogant perpetrator of any injustice'. For the contrast cf. e.g. Alexis 150(146K).7f. and an anonymous pipe-song (Powell, *Coll. Alex.* 199, 37.1) μηδ' ἀδικεῖν ζήτει, μηδ' ἂν ἀδι[κῇ πρ]οσερίσῃς; for the linkage of theme and syntactical structure cf. Gomme–Sandbach, *Comm.* on Men. *Dysk.* 743.

On the meaning of ὑβρίζοι, cf. especially Arist. *Rhet.* 2.2.5, 1378ᵇ22ff., ὁ ὑβρίζων δ' ὀλιγωρεῖ· ἔστι γὰρ ὕβρις τὸ πράττειν καὶ λέγειν ἐφ' οἷς αἰσχύνη ἐστι τῷ πάσχοντι, μὴ ἵνα τι γένηται αὐτῷ ἄλλο ἢ ὅτι ἐγένετο, ἀλλ' ὅπως ἡσθῇ· οἱ γὰρ ἀντιποιοῦντες οὐχ ὑβρίζουσιν ἀλλὰ τιμωροῦνται. αἴτιον δὲ τῆς ἡδονῆς τοῖς ὑβρίζουσιν, ὅτι οἴονται κακῶς δρῶντες αὐτοὶ (H. Richards, *Aristotelica* (London 1915) 107: αὐτοὺς MSS) ὑπερέχειν μᾶλλον. διὸ οἱ νέοι καὶ οἱ πλούσιοι ὑβρισταί; D. M. MacDowell, *G and R* 23 (1976) 14ff., N. R. E. Fisher, *G and R* 23 (1976) 177ff., 26 (1979) 32ff. and his exhaustive study *Hybris: A Study in the Values of Honour and Shame in Ancient Greece* (Warminster 1992), M. Gagarin in G. W. Bowersock and others (edd.), *Arktouros, Hellenic Studies Presented to Bernard M. W. Knox* (Berlin 1979) 229ff., Dover, *GPM* 54f., 110f., 147, and *Greek Homosexuality*, (London 1978) 34ff., Hunter on Eubulus 67.9.

5 Alexis' words echo – or are echoed by – Diphilus 60.11f. πανταχοῦ | διὰ τὴν τάλαιναν πάντα ταύτην (sc. τὴν γαστέρα, cf. vv. 2–3) γίνεται, from an undatable play; cf. Nesselrath, *MK* 315.

Συντρέχοντες

Meineke 1.387f., cf. 3.382 (on συντρέχειν), J. Toeppel, *De fragmentis comicorum graecorum quaestiones criticae, Specimen 3* (Progr. Neubrandenburg 1867) 13, Kock 2.375. The interpretation of this title, which Alexis shares with Sophilus, is uncertain. Kock suggested *aequales aetate*, comparing Afranius' *Aequales* (cf. Ribbeck, *CRF*³ 194), but neither the participle nor any other part of the verb appears to bear this meaning. One or both Greek titles could be intended literally, implying a scene (on the general implications of present-participle titles see introductions to Μανδραγορι-ζομένη, Συναποθνήσκοντες) in which two or more characters 'ran together' for some purpose (e.g. competitively: so Toeppel, cf. Edmonds' translation 'Neck and Neck'; or to announce news, ? as *serui currentes*). Alternatively συντρέχοντες might be used in the secondary sense 'going along with/

COMMENTARY

agreeing' (LSJ s.v. -ἔχω 3, citing Hdt. 1.53, Xen. *Cyr.* 8.2.27; also e.g. Lucian *Demon.* 24, Heliod. 4.13, 15, 7.18; Meineke 1.387f. notes Phot. s.v. συνᾴδων· ἁρμόττων, συντρέχων, συμφωνῶν).

The three frs. from Alexis' play (and fr. 6(5K) from Sophilus', involving a pimp and apparently a cook) in no way elucidate the title. In Alexis 216(213K) the speaker intends to hire two cooks (like e.g. Megadorus in Plaut. *Aul.* ii.4; cf. Rankin, ΜΑΓΕΙΡΟΙ 67f., A. Giannini, *Acme* 13 (1960) 162, Dohm, *Mageiros* 244ff., my introduction to Λέβης), because he is entertaining a man from gluttonous Thessaly (see comm. on v. 3). One possible background would be a wedding-feast at the end of a New-Comedy type of plot where a character had been reunited with a relation previously resident in Thessaly. Some sort of love intrigue is implied by fr. 217(214K), where the male (see comm.) speaker can describe himself as 'Aphrodite's white dove' only if at this point of the play some amour is proceeding satisfactorily to him. The play can be dated roughly between *c.* 345 and 318 by its allusion in fr. 218(215K) to Callimedon (see introduction to Δορκίς).

216 (213K)

Meineke, 3.480 (1), Kock 2.375, Edmonds 2.476, Kassel–Austin 2.143. The fr., cited by Ath. 4.137d (all of it in A, only vv. 4 and 6 in Epit.) to illustrate the modest size of Attic dinners, is irremediably garbled in vv. 5–6. A possible scenic context is suggested above in the introduction to Συντρέχοντες.

1 δύο μαγείρους: see introduction to Συντρέχοντες.

λαβεῖν: 'to hire', as elsewhere of cooks (e.g Posidippus 1.1, Sosipater 1.6) and other servants (e.g. προσλαβεῖν | τραπεζοποιόν Men. *Sam.* 289f., λαβεῖν αὐλητρίδα. τραπεζοποιόν, δημιουργὸν λήψομαι Alexander com. 3). This use of λαμβάνω is closely related to another (predominantly 4th-century) use, 'I buy', cf. comm. on 15.18; neither meaning is noted in LSJ. Cf. also ἔργον λαμβάνω, 'I (= the hireling) take a job', and comm. on 200(195K).2.

3 μέλλοντα δειπνίζειν γὰρ: on the postponement of γὰρ see comm. on 37(36K).1.

ἄνδρα Θετταλὸν . . .: Alexis points the contrast between (i) the voracity and large meals of the Thessalians, amply attested in ancient literature (e.g. εὐτράπεζοι Ath. 4.137d citing Eriphus 6 as well as Alexis 216(213K), πολυφάγοι 10.418c–e citing Crates 21(19K), Ar. fr. 507(492K) δεῖπνα . . . καπανικώτερα, Hermippus 42(41K), Philetaerus 10; 14.662f–663a; cf. also Antiphanes 249(276K), Mnesimachus 8, Phot. and Hesych. s.v. Θετταλικὴ ἔνθεσις, Eustath. 857.28ff.; Rankin, ΜΑΓΕΙΡΟΙ 39, Göbel,

Ethnica 69), and (ii) the reputation of Athenians for serving small portions and generally poor fare (e.g. Eubulus 11(12K).2f. and Hunter *ad loc.*, Lynceus 1.3ff. οὐδέτερος ἡμῶν ἥδεται τοῖς ἀττικοῖς | δείπνοις, Alciphron 3.15, possibly Eubulus 9(10K).6f. as a subtext for the city's groundless optimism; Antiphanes 170(172K) says Greeks but seems to mean Athenians; cf. also Rankin 38), although a few Attic dishes won high praise (e.g. the θρῖον: Ar. *Ach.* 1102 and Σ, Dionysius com. 2.36ff., Euphron 1.7; on Alexis 178(172K).6 see comm.).

4 ἀττικηρῶς: only here in literature, but the formation is recognised by Phot. (Zavorda MS s.v. ἀττικὴ φωνή· ... καὶ ἀττικηρῶς ἐπιρρηματικῶς ἀντὶ τοῦ ἀττικῶς ˝Αλεξις, cf. K. Tsantsanoglou, *New Fragments of Greek Literature from the Lexicon of Photius* (Athens 1984) 105); possibly a nonce coinage by Alexis (*'vox ... iocosa efficta ... ad formam vocis* λυπηρῶς' Schweighaeuser, *Animadv.* 2.446; cf. *TGL* s.v.), since there are no parallel formations of ethnic adjectives in -ηρής, -ηρός (cf. P. Kretschmer and E. Locker, *Rückläufiges Wörterbuch der griechischen Sprache* (Göttingen 1963) 265f., 468f.).

ἀπηκριβωμένως: 'in precisely calculated portions', a euphemism for *parce* (cf. Schweighaeuser, *Animadv.* 2.446). The adverb occurs only here indisputably (at Plut. *Agis* 2 ὁ μὲν γὰρ ἀπηκριβωμένος GPR / -νως L καὶ τελείως ἀγαθός there is nothing to choose between the readings), but the participle is regular in the sense of 'consummate/near-perfect' (e.g. people, Isoc. 12.28; other creatures, Arist. *PA* 3.4, 666^{a}28; things, Pl. *Tim.* 29c, Isoc. 4.11, 15.190).

5–6 A's text here (Epit. in 6 as A) is a shambles, with (i) lacunae of $\frac{3}{4}$ metron after παρελθεῖν in 5 and probably παρατιθέντα in 6, (ii) παρελθεῖν unintelligible in its context, (iii) the plural αὐτοῖς in 6 awkward after the singular Θετταλόν in 3 (but see below), and (iv) μεγαλείως δέ (with which the citation seems to close) not scanning at either the end of 6 or the beginning of 7. The multiplicity of faults, which is best explained by the assumption of both mechanical errors in the transmission and careless or wilful abbreviation at the end of a fr. by copyist or excerptor, should signal caution to editors and commentators (*pace* Herwerden, *Obs. Crit.* 74 and *Mnemosyne* 6 (1878) 70f., Heimsoeth, *Comm. Crit.* 1.xvii, Toeppel, *loc. cit.* in introduction to Συντρέχοντες, Kock, Blaydes, *Adv.* 2.165, Edmonds, and myself below); even so, some idea of the original sense, if not of Alexis' precise words, can be gleaned from careful assessment of the surviving text (cf. Herwerden, *Obs. Crit.*). Vv.5–6 belong to a sentence starting in vv. 3–4. Its construction appears to be δεῖ (cf. Musurus) or χρή (Edmonds) + accusative (μέλλοντα in v. 3, referring to the speaker) and infinitive (-ειν v. 5): 'For a man who's going to entertain a Thessalian oughtn't to torture (?) him with hunger in the Attic fashion – *moderato* –

serving the necessaries (unless ἃ δεῖ in 6 is corrupt) portion by portion, . . . but majestically . . .'. Four points merit further discussion. (i) Any infinitive governed by δεῖ/χρή must be construed with λιμῷ, whose aptness in a context ridiculing Attic frugality speaks for itself, and mean something like 'to torture/destroy': thus not παρελθεῖν but e.g. παραπολέσαι, παρακινεῖν or (best) παρατείνειν (so Herwerden, *Mnem.*, without noting Pl. *Symp.* 207b, αὐτὰ (sc. τὰ θηρία) τῷ λιμῷ παρατεινόμενα). (ii) Is δεῖ in v. 5 the governing impersonal verb (in which case the preceding ἃ must be deemed corrupt), or was there (more probably) a δεῖ/χρή lurking in one of the two lacunae (so first Herwerden, *Obs. Crit.*)? E.g. (v.5) λιμῷ παρ<ατείνειν δεῖ> θέλειν, ἃ δεῖ κ.τ.λ. (iii) αὐτοῖς in 6 are the plural guests invited to dinner, but v. 3 specifies a single Thessalian; the clash in numbers is due to textual corruption (Herwerden αὐτῷ for αὐτοῖς, *Mnem.*, or <τοὺς ξένους> in the v. 5 lacuna, *Obs. Crit.*), or authorial carelessness (cf. Schweighaeuser, *Animadv.* 2.445 *facile intelligi poterit, Thessalum non sine sociis ad coenam fuisse vocatum*). (iv) μεγαλείως δέ apparently closes the citation, making good but unmetrical sense at the end of v. 6. Either a scribe/abbreviator/ excerptor omitted half a verse or more after παρατιθέντα and quoted only what was necessary to complete the sense (e.g. παρατιθέντα <κατὰ μέρος/ ἅπαντα,> μεγαλείως δέ . . .), or these last two words are a paraphrase (so Herwerden). Attempts were made to retain μεγ. δέ at the end of v. 6 by Kaibel (μ. δὲ <δεῖ>) and Peppink, *Observ.* 28 (μ. δέ <πως>), but neither fits metrically after παρατιθέντα. Kock more ingeniously interpreted μεγ. δέ as the opening words of Ath.'s next sentence, but this would require a further emendation (μ. δὲ εὐτράπεζοί {δ'} εἰσι).

παρατιθέντα: see comm. on 98(152K).2.

μεγαλείως: cf. Durham, *Vocabulary* 76f.

217 (214K)

Meineke 3.481 (II), Kock 2.375, Edmonds 2.476, Kassel–Austin 2.143. The speaker's (on his identity, see introduction to Συντρέχοντες) contrast of Aphrodite and Dionysus was presumably intended (note γάρ in v. 1) to explain a previous remark, but in the absence of context its point is enigmatic. The implication may be that success in love is the privilege of youth (cf. Kock), whereas drunkenness has no age barriers; the speaker could have been a young lover with an older rival (like e.g. Plautus' Lyconides in *Aul.*, Charinus in *Merc.*, the unnamed son in *Cas.*; cf. G. E. Duckworth, *The Nature of Roman Comedy* (Princeton 1952) 165ff.), or just have been debating the rival pleasures of sex and wine.

1 λευκὸς Ἀφροδίτης ... περιστερός: here A writes ὁ before λευκὸς (Ath. 9.395a: an abbreviated version in Epit., cf. Eustath. 1712.45, 1770.13; A. Nauck, *Philologus* 6 (1851) 419), unmetrical and unidiomatic with the predicate (cf. K.G. 1.591), but commonly added by scribes (cf. Cobet, *NL* s.v. *Articulus perperam additus* in index; W. G. Arnott, *CQ* 7 (1957) 197 n. 1, 198 n. 2) and here deleted by Scaliger (in Canter, Paris MS, 49: before Schweighaeuser, cf. *Animadv.* 5.178).

The bird in question is the all-white variety of the domesticated pigeon, descended originally from the Rock Dove, *Columba livia* (W. M. Levi, *The Pigeon* (Sumter and Columbia S.C.) 1957, 53f., 60, 74f., 89, 313ff., D. Goodwin, *Pigeons and Doves of the World*[3] (London 1983) 57, S. Cramp and others, *The Birds of the Western Palaearctic* 4 (Oxford 1985) 285), and first bred perhaps in Babylon (cf. Hehn, *Kulturpflanzen* 347ff., Thompson, *Birds*[2] 242); progeny can still be seen in Greece, e.g. around the Temple of Apollo at Delphi. Pigeons in general were associated with Aphrodite, in temple worship (e.g. *IG* ii[2].659.23f., 287/6 BC; cf. Ath. 9.394f-395a), art (e.g. Furtwängler in Roscher s.v. *Aphrodite* 408f. section c, L. R. Farnell, *Cults of the Greek States* 2 (Oxford 1896) pl. xli/a-c) and literature (e.g. Pherecrates 143(135K), Ap. Rhod. 3.541ff. and Σ, Plut. *Mor.* 379d, Aelian *VH* 1.15; V. *Aen.* 6.190ff., Prop. 3.3.31, 4.5.65, Ov. *Met.* 14.597ff.); the white variety, which is alleged to have reached Greece first at the time of the Persian War (Charon of Lampsacus in Ath. 9.394e/Aelian *VH* 1.15 = *FGrH* 262 F 3a-b), is linked with the goddess also by Aelian *NA* 10.33 (where the bird is misidentified as a turtle dove), Catull. 29.8, Tibull. 1.7.18, Ov. *Fast.* 1.451f. (see J. G. Frazer (London 1929) *ad loc.*), Martial 8.28.13, Apul. *Met.* 6.6, cf. also e.g. Hdt. 1.138, Ov. *Met.* 2.536f.; O. Gruppe, *Griechische Mythologie und Religionsgeschichte* 2 (Munich 1906) s.v. *Taube* in index, Farnell 2.674f., in *RE* Tümpel s.v. *Aphrodite* 2767.23ff., Steier s.v. *Taube* 2496.28ff., 2497.48ff., Thompson, *Birds*[2] 244ff.

The fr. is cited for the use of the second-declension form in -ρός, which occurs also in Pherecrates 38(33K), cf. Σ Aristides p. 263 Frommel, Phot. s.v. περιστερόν (? correct to ός), but is condemned as unattic by Lucian *Sol.* 7. It was doubtless here preferred by Alexis to the normal (e.g. Alexis 58(57K).1 and comm., 63(62K).3) first-declension form in -ρά (applied to male and female: sexual differentiation is indicated by ὁ ἄρρην, ἡ θήλεια or τὸ ἄ., τὸ θ., e.g. Arist. *HA* 6.2, 560[b]20ff., 9.7, 612[b]31ff., Aelian *VH* 1.15, *HA* 3.5, Ath. 9.394b-d) in order to stress humorously by means of the masculine ending the sex of a speaker whose identification of himself with Aphrodite's pet bird is itself an amusing conceit. Cf. also 88(85K).3-5 and comm.

γάρ (fourth word in its clause): see comm. on 37(36K).1.

2 ὁ δὲ: Schweighaeuser's correction of A's ὁιδε, anticipating the following οἶδε.

οἶδε τὸ μεθύσαι μόνον: οἶδα commonly governs an infinitive without the article in the sense 'I know how to' (e.g. Hom. *Il.* 7.238 νωμῆσαι βῶν,

COMMENTARY

S. *Phil.* 1010 τὸ προσταχθὲν ποεῖν, Eur. *Med.* 664 προσφωνεῖν φίλους, *Tro.* 85 εὐσεβεῖν, Ar. *Ran.* 740 πίνειν ... καὶ βινεῖν μόνον, Dem. 4.40 προβάλλεσθαι ... ἢ βλέπειν ἐναντίον, LSJ s.v. *εἴδω* B.2, Goodwin, *MT* 363 § 915.2a), but adding an article to the infinitive alters both construction and meaning (at least slightly: → 'I know about'). I am unaware of exact parallels with οἶδα, but cf. e.g. A. *Ag.* 1290 τλήσομαι τὸ κατθανεῖν, Xen. *Oec.* 13.4 (τοὺς ἐπιτρόπους) τὸ ἀρχικοὺς εἶναι ἀνθρώπων παιδεύεις, Goodwin, *MT* 316f. § 791.

3 νέον ἢ παλαιόν: the explanations of reference suggested by Meineke (τὸ μέθυ) and Kock (ungrammatically ἑταῖρον) show remarkable insensitivity to linguistic usage. The neuters *syntactically* pick up τὸ μεθύσαι (v.2), but Alexis is writing colloquial Greek, with quick shifts of emphasis and telescoping of thought sequences, and the idea of being drunk suggests the individuals involved, both young and old.

218 (215K)

Meineke 3.481 (III), Kock 2.376, Edmonds 2.476, Kassel–Austin 2.144. For Callimedon see especially introductions to Δορκίς and fr. 57(56K), and comm. on 117(112K).1–2.

Σύντροφοι

A. Croiset, *Revue des cours et conférences* 5/1 (1896–7) 515; Fraenkel, *MNC* 29. In Alexis' time and subsequently σύντροφος was the standard word for 'foster-child': someone of either sex (in the following references an asterisk denotes female) brought up in a man's home along with his own child(ren) but of different parentage (nobles as companions to princes in royal households: e.g. Polyb. 5.9.4 and F. W. Walbank (Oxford 1957) *ad loc.*, 15.33.11*, 32.15.10, Dittenberger, *OGIS* 247.2 and n. 2, 372.2; in ordinary families: *PSI* 584.5 (3rd century), *P.Oxy.* 1034.2*, *P.Rylands* 106.3; cf. Preisigke, *Wörterbuch* 2.555, C. Brescia in *Menandrea: miscellanea philologica* (Genoa 1960) 123). Its popularity in the plural as a title for New-Comedy plays (also Damoxenus, Diphilus, Posidippus) is hardly surprising, given the frequency with which extant plots involve the discovery of true parents or parentage by children separated from them early in life (e.g. in Men. *Her.* Gorgias and Plangon, *Mis.* Krateia, *Pk.* Moschion, *Sik.* Stratophanes and (?) Philoumene; in Plaut. *Cist.* Selenium = σύντροφος of Gymnasium).

The one fr. (219(216K)) of Alexis' Σύντροφοι is spoken by a man (vv.1–3; not necessarily a parasite, *pace* Croiset) about to leave the stage (see comm. on v. 2) after a party which had presumably been held either on stage or in one of the stage-houses. In support of his temperance the

ΣΥΝΤΡΟΦΟΙ

speaker cites the Athenian doctor Mnesitheus (see comm. on v. 3), whose *floruit* is too uncertain to provide even a rough dating for Alexis' play.[1]

219 (216K)

Meineke 3.481, Kock 2.376, Edmonds 2.478, Kassel–Austin 2.144; cf. H. Hohenstein, *Der Arzt Mnesitheos aus Athen* (Diss. Berlin 1935) fr. 43, J. Bertier, *Mnésithé et Dieuchès* (*Philosophia Antiqua* 20, Leiden 1972) fr. 21, 178f. Speaker and situation are discussed in introduction to Σύντροφοι and comm. on v. 3.

1 ὡς ἡδύ: ὡς exclamatory, as commonly at the beginning of speeches (e.g. Ar. *Nub.* 1399*, *Pax* 819, 1210, *Thesm.* 130*, *Plut.* 1, 802*: where * denotes ὡς ἡδύ).

1–2 οὔθ' ὑπεργέμων ἀπέρχομαι νῦν οὔτε κενός: the reference could be to food (*'cibo onustus'*, Casaubon, *Animadv.* 714) or drink (cf. on v. 3) or both. For the expression cf. e.g. Ar. *Equ.* 280f. κενῇ τῇ κοιλίᾳ | εἰσδραμὼν εἰς τὸ πρυτανεῖον, εἶτα πάλιν ἐκθεῖ πλέα.

2 ἀπέρχομαι: elsewhere in Greek drama (both tragedy and comedy) ἀπέρχομαι and ἄπειμι indicate a speaker's intention to leave the stage (cf. F. Ellendt, *Lexicon Sophocleum* (Berlin 1872) s.v. ἄπειμι *abeo 'omnia tralaticiam hominis abeuntis significationem habent'*, K. B. Frost, *Exits and Entrances in Menander* (Oxford 1988) 121); the intention may be carried out

---

[1] Apart from the reference here, there are two snippets of evidence which provide treacherous clues to Mnesitheus' period of activity. (1) A scholiast to Oribasius, *Libri incerti*, 37 (*CMG* VI.II.2.135; Mnesitheus fr. 20 Bertier = 37 Hohenstein) says that Mnesitheus' περὶ παιδίου τροφῆς ἢ νηπιοτροφικός was written as an ἐπιστολὴ πρὸς Λυκίσκον; several Athenians bore the name Lyciscus in the 4th century (cf. introduction to Λυκίσκος) but only one (the eponymous archon of 344/3: 9214 Kirchner) appears to have achieved any distinction, and so is the most likely (but by no means certain) addressee of Mnesitheus' treatise. (2) An ex-voto dedication to Asclepius found on the south slope of the Acropolis (*IG* ii².4359) names two of its five donors as Διάκριτος Διεύχος and Μ[ν]η[σ]ί[θεος Μν]ησιθέο; the orthography with o for ου almost certainly dates this inscription before 355 (cf. Threatte 1.350ff.), but although some linkage with the families which produced the cele- brated physicians Dieuches and Mnesitheus seems assured (cf. P. Girard, *BCH* 2 (1878) 87ff.), we cannot be certain that the latter (rather than e.g. a homonymous son: so W. Jaeger, *Aristotle*² (tr. R. Robinson, Oxford 1948) 407ff.) was the inscriptional donor. Neither clue helps to date Mnesitheus' *floruit* any more precisely than the whole period covered by Alexis' career. Cf. Deichgräber in *RE* s.v. *Mnesitheos* 3, 2281.28ff., Bertier, *op. cit.* in introduction to fr. 219(216K), 1ff.

COMMENTARY

immediately (e.g. Ar. *Av.* 948, *Eccl.* 936, Men. *Sik.* 271), shortly afterwards (e.g. Men. *Pk.* 481) or be delayed by some intervening idea/event (e.g. Ar. *Ach.* 465). Thus dramatic convention rules out Fraenkel's suggestion (*MNC* 29) that Alexis' speaker was about to launch out into a long descriptive narrative about the previous festivities.

2–3 ἡδέως ἔχων ἐμαυτοῦ: for the idiom cf. e.g. Ar. *Lys.* 1125 αὐτὴ δ' ἐμαυτῆς οὐ κακῶς γνώμης ἔχω, Philemon 3(4K).11 οὐκ εὖ σεαυτοῦ τυγχάνεις ἔχων, Pl. *Resp.* 9.571d ὅταν ... ὑγιεινῶς τις ἔχῃ αὐτὸς αὑτοῦ καὶ σωφρόνως, where the genitives are perhaps best explained by analogy with partitives after πῶς (ποῦ γῆς; → ποῦ/πῶς γνώμης; cf. K.G. 1.382f., LSJ s.v. ἔχω β.ΙΙ.2.b), although superficially similar passages in which the genitives are not reflexive (e.g. Machon 351ff. διὰ τό πως | τὸν Ἀνδρόνικον ἡδέως αὐτῆς ἔχειν | τὸν ὑποκριτήν, and Gow on 176f., Men. *Dysk.* 44 (νεανίσκον) [αὐτῆ]ς ἔχειν πως ἐνθεαστικῶς ποῶ, Pl. *Symp.* 222c ἐρωτικῶς ἔχειν τοῦ Σωκράτους) may be influenced rather by the construction of ἐρᾶν with the genitive.

Porson (edition of Eur. *Med.* (Cambridge 1801) comm. on 139–40, section x) was the first to see that the Alexis fr. continued after ἐμαυτοῦ for a further one and a half verses (cf. Schweighaeuser, *Animadv.* 5.341).

3 Μνησίθεος: the Athenian physician, a contemporary of either Alexis or his parents. Highly regarded by Galen (ἀνὴρ τά τε ἄλλα ἱκανὸς πάντα τὰ τῆς τέχνης καὶ εἰς ὅσον χρὴ μεθόδῳ τὴν ἰατρικὴν ἀσκεῖν, οὐδενὸς ἐπιγνῶναι δεύτερος *ad Glauc. de medendi meth.* 1 = Kühn, 11.3), he was an expert dietician writing major works on the subject (περὶ ἐδεστῶν, so Ath. 2.54b, 59b–c + 8 other passages, or ἐδεσμάτων, so Galen *CMG* v.4.2, 321.22, περὶ παιδίου τροφῆς, περὶ κωθωνισμοῦ ἐπιστολή). An extract from π. κωθ. cited by Ath. 11.483f (= fr. 45 Hohenstein and Bertier) runs συμβαίνει τοὺς μὲν πολὺν ἄκρατον ἐν ταῖς συνουσίαις πίνοντας μεγάλα βλάπτεσθαι καὶ τὸ σῶμα καὶ τὴν ψυχήν, and the need for moderation in food and drink may have been a keynote in Mnesitheus' teaching. Yet it is difficult to see why the comic poet should have singled out this one physician here as authority for a doctrine which permeated Greek thought at least from Hesiod's time onwards (cf. M. L. West (Oxford 1978) on Hes. *Op.* 694, H. Fränkel, *Early Greek Poetry and Philosophy* (tr. M. Hadas and J. Willis, Oxford 1975) 127, 474 n. 11), was supported generally by medical writers (e.g. Hippocr. *Affect.* 47, 61, *Epid.* 6.6, *Artic.* 49), and was elsewhere mentioned by Alexis without named attestation (with reference to wine frs. 82, 160(156K), 257(255K); to expenditure 256(254K), 261(259K)),[1] unless at the time of the play Mnesitheus was so fashionable

---

[1] An anonymous comic fr. (3.423, 106–7 Kock = Mnesitheus fr. 41 Hohenstein and Bertier) quoted by Ath. 2.36a (Epit.), which also cites Mnesitheus for the doctrine that wine brings ἀγαθὸν μέγιστον (v.3) to

ΣΥΝΤΡΟΦΟΙ

in Athens that a mere mention of his name would guarantee an audience's approval. Cf. also Deichgräber (*op. cit.* at p. 621, n. 1) and Bertier. **δεῖν:** the anon. conjecture for A's δεῖ (first in its apograph B: cf. Peppink, *Observ.* 60) is probably right, but Men. *Dysk.* 433f. (σιωπῇ, φασί, τούτῳ τῷ θεῷ/οὐ δεῖ προσιέναι the papyrus correctly, but cited by Σ Ar. *Lys.* 2 and *Suda* s.v. Πανικῷ δείματι with δεῖν; see my comments in Flores 363) shows that a parenthetic construction here cannot be totally ruled out.

4 ὑπερβολάς: cf. Durham, *Vocabulary* 98, F. Stoessl, *Kommentar zu Menander Dyskolos* (Paderborn 1965) on v. 326.

ἀεί: cf. comm. on 76.1.

Συρακόσιος[1]

Meineke 1.402, G. Kaibel in *RE* s.v. *Alexis* 9, 1470.18ff., 1471.11f. A further ethnic title (cf. e.g. the introductions to Ἐπιδαύριος, Ἀτθίς),[2] but the one brief platitude preserved from the play (fr. 220(217K)) implies only that the speaker or his addressee is in some trouble.

Nonius (96.30, 176.29, 391.30 Merc.) cites three frs. from a comedy by Caecilius Statius (81f. Ribbeck) with the probable title *Syracusii* (but the MSS twice give *Syracusis*, once *-usi* in the ablative); the plural would exclude an adaptation of Alexis' singular title, if the modern attempts to heal corrupt transmissions were accepted. Yet fr. III of Caecilius' play presupposes a situation (a man in love, families starving and farmwork neglected) compatible with that of the Alexis fr., and the two playwrights have six other titles in common (Kaibel notes *Epistula, Exul*/Φυγάς; add *Epicleros, Fallacia*/Ψευδόμενος, *Titthe, Hypobolimaeus*).

---

those who use it correctly, sc. τοῖς ... μέτριον πίνουσι καὶ κεκραμένον (10), was first assigned to Alexis by Schweighaeuser, *Animadv.* 5.341 (cf. C. G. Cobet, *Mnemosyne* 12 (1884) 447f., Bertier 57ff.). Despite a few parallels with Alexis in everyday phraseology (τοῖς χρωμένοις 2, 4 ~ Alexis 140(135K).16 and comm.; καθ' ἡμέραν 9 ~ Alexis 145(141K).6, 223(221K).9; the fr.'s style does not strike me as characteristic of Alexis, and Meineke (3.482) was wise to banish it to comic anonymity.

1 In Attic inscriptions this ethnic is always spelled Συρακόσιος (Meisterhans–Schwyzer 27 and n. 140, Threatte 1.219, 524), and although a form in -κούσι- is occasionally presented by medieval MSS (e.g. MA in Stob. *Anth.* 4.44.41 here; Pl. (?) *Epist.* 7, 326b, 327c ~ -κόσι- 324b, 333b and c), this is best treated simply as a corruption induced by the ου- in Συράκουσαι.

2 Meineke's idea of a pleasure-loving titular hero is pure speculation, although founded on Syracuse's popular reputation for self-indulgent luxury (cf. Göbel, *Ethnica* 121f., cf. 126).

COMMENTARY

220 (217K)

Meineke 3.482, Kock 2.376, Edmonds 2.478, Kassel–Austin 2.145. The idea that 'those who don't struggle against their troubles deal with them most easily' rephrases prosaically the proverb πρὸς κέντρα μὴ λάκτιζε (cf. in comedy Plaut. *Truc.* 768, *si stimulos pugnis caedis, manibus plus dolet*; Ter. *Phorm* 77f., *namque inscitiast* | *aduorsum stimulum calces*; elsewhere e.g. Pind. *Pyth.* 2.94f., A. *Ag.* 1624, *P.V.* 322f., Eur. *IT* 1396, *Bacch.* 795, fr. 604, iamb. adesp. fr. 13 Diehl, N.T. *Act. Ap.* 26.14).

Σώρακοι

Meineke 1.402. Σώρακος is a container for (1) actors' equipment (Pollux 10.129f., καὶ τὰ ἀγγεῖα τὰ ὑποδεχόμενα τὴν ὀπώραν . . .· τάχα δὲ καὶ σώρακος, εἰ καὶ παρὰ τοῖς κωμῳδιοποιοῖς οὕτως ὀνομάζεται, τὸ ἀγγεῖον ἐν ᾧ τὰ σκεύη τῶν ὑποκριτῶν. Ἀριστοφάνης δὲ ἐν Δαναῖσιν (258(249K)) ἔφη, κακῶν τοσούτων ξυνελέγη μοι σώρακος. Ἀλέξιδος δὲ καὶ δρᾶμα Σώρακοι); (2) arrows (*IG* ii².120.36f., 1649.14: mid-4th century); and (3) figs (*Suda* s.v. σωράκους, citing Babrius 108.17f.; cf. Hesych. s.v. σώρακον, adding the alternative definition ξυλοκανθήλια, wooden pack-saddle). The function of the containers in Alexis' play is unknown (the Pollux passage does not identify Alexis' use, and even if it did, its reliability would be impaired by its citing a verse where σώρακος is metaphorical in order to illustrate use (1)): were they for treasure (cf. the Assteas vase, Berlin F3044, A. D. Trendall, *The Red-figured Vases of Paestum* (Rome 1987) no. 125, pp. 84 and 86f., pl. 44) or for recognition tokens in an intrigue plot of New-Comedy style?

The one fr. (221(218K)) describes Phidippus, the son of the salt-fish importer Chaerephilus, as a ξένος. Members of the family were granted Athenian citizenship, possibly for services to Athens in the food shortages of *c.* 330–*c.* 326, but the temptation thereby to date Alexis' play prior to that award must be resisted (see comm. on fr. 6).

221 (218K)

Meineke 3.482, Kock 2.376, Edmonds 2.478, Kassel–Austin 2.145. See comm. on frs. 6 and 77.

Ταραντῖνοι

Meineke 1.388, A. Weiher, *Philosophen und Philosophenspott in der attischen Komödie* (Diss. Munich 1913) 66ff., T. B. L. Webster, *CQ* 2.1952, 21, and

SLGC 53; cf. G. Zuntz, *PBA* 42 (1956) 234ff., Gil 339f. Alexis and Cratinus (? *minor*: so Meineke 1.412f., but see below) wrote comedies with this title[1] in which Pythagorist practices were ridiculed (the introduction to Πυθα-γορίζουσα lists with bibliography the other known plays containing parallel raillery). Nowhere in Alexis' time had Pythagoreanism a stronger hold than in Tarentum (Strabo 6.3.4, Iamblichus *Vit. Pyth.* 269 naming 43 Pythagoreans from this one city; cf. J. Burnet, *Early Greek Philosophy*[4] (London 1930) 276, P. Wuilleumier, *Tarente des origines à la conquête romaine* (Paris 1939) 563ff., von Fritz in *RE* s.v. *Pythagoreer* 217.12ff. and *Pythagorean Politics in South Italy* (New York 1940) 95, 97, G. S. Kirk, J. E. Raven and M. Schofield, *The Presocratic Philosophers*[2] (Cambridge 1983) 223), and this fact appears to provide an obvious explanation for the choice of title. Yet any assumption that the two plays were primarily anti-philosophical entertainments comparable to e.g. Ar. *Nub.* is insecure; the surviving frs. are neither extensive nor explicit enough to substantiate theories about their plots, although one enigmatic remark (224(222K).7–9, see comm.) *can* be interpreted as an angry reaction to a confidence trick on the speaker by an old man and a parasite.

The one fr. (7) of Cratinus' play, in which the sophistries of a group of people identified as Pythagorists only by the citer (Diog. Laert. 8.37) – and that implicitly – yields no clues to speaker, plot or date; there is indeed nothing absolutely to forbid ascription to the elder Cratinus. Some forty-four verses (? 4–5%) of Alexis' Ταραντῖνοι are preserved in six or seven frs. 222–7(219–25K), of which one (225(223K)) dates the play roughly between *c.*345 and *c.*320 by a present-tense reference to the real-life *hetaira* Nannion, who flourished at that time.[2] In fr. 222(219K) an

---

[1] Naevius wrote a *Tarentilla* (Ribbeck, *CRF*[3] 21ff., E. V. Marmorale's edition (Florence 1950[2]) 170ff., 219ff.; cf. Kock 2.377, J. Wright, *Rh. Mus.* 115 (1972) 239ff., M. von Albrecht, *Mus. Helv.* 32 (1975) 230ff.; M. Barchiesi, *La Tarentilla rivisitata* (Pisa 1978) largely confines his comments to questions of metatheatre), adapted from an unknown Greek original (not one of the two Ταραντῖνοι: the Latin title differs crucially in number and gender, and the Naevius frs., which contain no anti-Pythagorean tags, point to a plot in which two young men spend money abroad on a young Tarentine *meretrix*). Titles like *Tarentilla* also normally present a heroine whose national origin differs from that of all or most of the other characters and from the city where she now finds herself (cf. e.g. the introductions to Ἀτθίς, Ἀχαΐς, Βρεττία, Κνιδία, Λημνία, Ὀλυνθία, and von Albrecht 230 n. 5).

[2] Nannion must have been celebrated in her profession already in the 340s, since Eubulus' Νάννιον (a title explicable only as a reference to the historical figure) cannot be dated any later than that if its reference to 'Cydias the admiral' (fr. 67.11) is linked with the man who made a

unspecified man (v.8) maintains that men like him are harmless, and he supports the claim by a series of philosophical clichés reflecting a Greek tendency to fatalistic pessimism. Several of those clichés appear to have been associated with contemporary Pythagorean beliefs (see comm. *ad loc.*), but Alexis has adapted them, doubtless with conscious irony, to the enunciation of an opposing hedonistic view that people should laugh, drink and make love, for life is short. Such a message in the second half of the 4th century could have been voiced on the comic stage by a variety of characters, including a typical Tarentine burgher (his love of pleasure was notorious: e.g. Pl. *Leg.* 1.637b, Ath. 4.166e–f and 12.522d–e citing Theopompus, *FGrH* 115 F 100 and 233 and Clearchus, *FHG* 2.306 fr.9, Aelian *VH* 12.30, Hor. *Sat.* 2.4.34, Σ Serv. to V. *Aen.* 3.551 *Tarentum, in quo molles et luxoriosi nascuntur*; Weiher 67 and n. 1, Göbel, *Ethnica* 123f.; Wuilleumier, 229ff.) or a parasite (Weiher 66ff.,Webster, *SM* 164). The two sections of fr. 223(220 + 221 K) appear to derive from a single scene involving at least two characters, one of whom humorously (vv.4–5, 7ff.) disparages the vegetarianism, sophistry and poverty of (? two: see comm. on v. 10) Pythagoreans. In these three frs., the only ones preserved from the play with any 'philosophical' content, there is notably no trace of a Pythagorean on the stage; references to the cult are uniformly critical, hedonistic, even if knowledgeable. There is nothing to prevent their being explained as incidental and scenically appropriate comments in an intrigue plot of New-Comedy type (cf. e.g. Men. *Sam.* 96ff., 603ff.; H.-D. Blume, *Menanders 'Samia'* (Darmstadt 1974) 36ff., 240ff.), nor anything either to hinder the references to drinking and parties in frs. 224(222K) and 225(223K) (whether those come in one scene or two) from

---

speech opposing a cleruchy in Samos (Arist. *Rhet.* 2, 1384ᵇ32) probably between 365 and 352 (J. K. Davies, *Historia* 18 (1969) 309ff., and Hunter's edition of Eubulus, introduction to Νάννιον). Nannion was still remembered in Menander's time (i.e. after 324–320, cf. my Loeb edition, vol. 1 (Cambridge Mass. and London 1979) xv), but if still alive no longer practising (fr. 456, *Kol.* fr. 4: note the tone and tenses). Comedies that allude to her in the present tense with no mention of her age must presumably have appeared between *c.* 345 and *c.* 320. Alexis' Ταραντῖνοι falls into this category; the allegation there (fr. 225(223K)) that Nannion μαίνεται ἐπὶ Διονύσῳ does not necessarily stigmatise her as an old hag (so H. G. Oeri, *Der Typ der komischen Alten* (Basle 1948) 43, T. B. L. Webster, *CQ* 2 (1952) 21); aged *hetairai* may characteristically have been portrayed on the comic stage as topers, but it is fallacious to infer from this that drunken *hetairai* were all old, in real life or literature, as Alciphron 4.14 makes perfectly clear. Cf. also Fensterbusch in *RE* s.v. *Proskenion, Nachtrag* 1290.54ff., Gow on Machon 423, G. M. Sifakis, *Studies in the History of Hellenistic Drama* (London 1967) 128 n. 1.

being associated with a conventional New-Comedy symposium at the beginning (cf. e.g. Plaut. *Cist.*), middle (Men. *Epitr.*) or end (*Dysk.*, Plaut. *Bacch.*, *Pseud.*, *Stich.*) of the play. In fr. 224(222K).1–2 one speaker addresses the other with the words σοι | ἐν ταῖς Ἀθήναις, which indicates that he was not, but his addressee was, Athenian, in a scene less likely to have been Athens than some other city, although the phraseology does not entirely rule out Athens (cf. introduction to Αἴσωπος and comm. on frs. 9.1–2, 224(222K).1–2): perhaps Tarentum?

222 (219K)

Meineke 3.484 (III), Kock 2.377, Edmonds 2.478, Kassel–Austin 2.146; G. Zuntz, *PBA* 42 (1956) 234ff.; cf. R. Fenk, *Adversarii Platonis quomodo de indole ac moribus eius iudicaverint* (Diss. Jena 1913) 51f. n. 1, A. Weiher, *Philosophen und Philosophenspott in der attischen Komödie* (Diss. Munich 1913), 66ff., W. Burkert, *Hermes* 88 (1960) 165 n.3, M. Kokolakis, Ὁ Ὑποβολιμαῖος τοῦ Μενάνδρου (Athens 1962), 48f., 52f., 56ff., Gil 339. The fr., cited by Ath. 11.463c–e (A and – vv. 3 to end – Epit.), is a pessimistic hedonist's (on its speaker, see also introduction to Ταραντῖνοι) defence of his philosophy. It rambles, as Zuntz notes in his penetrating analysis of this and the superficially similar Men. (?: see below) fr. 416.8ff., but its lack of logical tautness may not be the result of slipshod composition, but rather an attempt to reproduce the thought processes of an unintellectual average man in Alexis' time (in Menander cf. Gorgias' speech at *Dysk.* 271ff. with Gomme–Sandbach, *Comm. ad loc.*, L. A. Post, *AJP* 80 (1959) 410, W. G. Arnott, *Philologus* 125 (1981) 223ff.). Alexis introduces into the speech the four following slogans:

(i) the word βίος is a euphemism for man's μοῖρα (vv. 3–6);
(ii) human affairs are μανιώδη (9);
(iii) life is (a) an ἀποδημία, resembling (b) a visit to a πανήγυρις, (c) on our release from death and darkness into the light of day (10–14);
(iv) the most agreeable existence is one of laughter, drink, sexual indulgence ... (14–17).

Alexis selects and organises his slogans with fine comic irony. The first three incorporate, with the intention of misleading the listener, philosophic sentiments promoted (iii a,b,c certainly, i very probably) by, or at least congruous (ii) with, contemporary Pythagorean doctrine, before the climactic surprise of the fourth endorses a support for hedonism diametrically opposed to Pythagorean asceticism (cf. Burkert). Although the παρὰ προσδοκίαν climax is a common element in the recorded humour of

COMMENTARY

Athens from Old Comedy onwards, its employment here clearly illustrates Alexis' skill in the preliminary concealment (when the Pythagorean allusions are being interlarded) of the direction in which the argument is to be steered. It is not until vv. 14ff. that the audience realises how Pythagorean texts have been inserted into a hedonistic sermon. The whole fr. reveals too in exemplary form some other of Alexis' comic talents, so far as they can be judged from the meagre remains that have survived: vigorous and imaginative language, even if the most memorable tropes are second-hand; a full command of the techniques and structures of humour, wit and irony; and perhaps also, in both his choice of themes and the (?) embryonic attempt to individualise a character by his fashion of speech, his influence on Menander.

This fr., more certainly than any other passage in Alexis or in the Roman comedies adapted from his originals (e.g. Plaut. *Poen.* 1099ff., 1296ff., possibly *Aul.*; cf. introductions to fr. 35(34) and Λέβης), demonstrates an influence by the older poet on his alleged pupil Menander (see my general introduction, 1.iii and 1.v.iii). We cannot now know whether Gorgias' incoherence in philosophising at Men. *Dysk.* 271ff. was modelled on Alexis fr. 222(219), but the similarities between this fr. (see comm. on 10–14, 15–16) and Men. fr. 416.8ff. Körte–Thierfelder = 416b.1ff. Sandbach are too close to be coincidental. Zuntz's arguments for the separation of this fr. from 416.1–7 seem unanswerable (*pace* A. W. Gomme, *CQ* 10 (1960) 103ff.), but its ascription to an unidentified play by Menander is justified on grounds of style and quality. If Menander was once trained by Alexis, the pupil here outshone the master, producing a passage of profound beauty far beyond anything that has survived from Alexis (cf. Zuntz 236).

1–2 Ath. 11.463c (= A only; Epit. omits vv. 1–2) introduces the directly quoted vv. of the fr. with διόπερ συνιοῦσι καὶ ἡμῖν ἐπὶ τὰς Διονυσιακὰς ταύτας λαλιὰς οὐδεὶς ἂν εὐλόγως φθονήσαι (Musurus: -ῆσαι A) νοῦν ἔχων, κατὰ τοὺς Ἀλέξιδος Ταραντίνους· οἳ τῶν πέλας (v.2) κ.τ.λ. These words, as Grotius first noted (*Exc.* 589, 974), appear to include paraphrase or quotation of words in the fr. just before οὐδὲν in 3, on the evidence both of rhythm (e.g. φθονῆσαι νοῦν ἔχων) and aptness in the comic context. Yet any attempt to restore Alexis' precise words here is foolhardy; Ath. may have cut out phrases, altered moods and tenses, and ruined its original character in order to accommodate his tediously pretentious lead-in. It is likely enough that νοῦν ἔχων directly preceded οἳ τῶν πέλας in v. 2, but details such as the tense and mood of φθονεῖν (? φθονῆσαι: for this form of the 3rd p. s. aor. opt. act. in later comedy cf. e.g. Men. *Dysk.* 203, *Sam.* 685; for -αις in 2nd p. s. e.g. *Dysk.* 511, *Epitr.* 224; K.B. 2.74 refuting Rutherford, *NP* 429f.; or ? -ῆσει CE (cf. Rutherford), -οίη), the identity and position of that verb's object (Grotius' transfer of ἡμῖν

directly before φθον-, *Exc.* 589, is only one possibility), and the position of
οὐδείς (? οὐδὲ εἷς, Dobree, *Adv.* 2.329) remain unsure.

3 οὐδὲν ... οὐδένα is given by the MSS (A, Epit.), and there is no need
to transpose to οὐδέν' ... οὐδέν (so Grotius before Kock and S. A. Naber,
Mnemosyne 8 (1880)., 264; cf. Peppink, *Observ.* 63). Both sequences are
common, choice being dictated by emphasis, metre or whim. Contrast e.g.
Alexis 215(212K).4 οὔτ' ἂν ἀδικοῖτ' οὐδὲν οὐδείς, Philemon 102(101K).5
οὐδὲν ... πρὸς οὐδένα, Pl. *Resp.* 6.495b οὐδὲν ... οὐδέποτε οὐδένα, Dem.
21.157 οὐδὲν ... ὑπ' οὐδενός, with Ar. *Lys.* 1043ff., οὐ παρασκευαζόμεσθα
| τῶν πολιτῶν οὐδέν', ὦνδρες, | φλαῦρον εἰπεῖν οὐδὲ ἕν, Thuc. 2.3.1 ἐς
οὐδένα οὐδέν, Xen. *Mem.* 1.2.8 ἐπηγγείλατο μὲν οὐδενὶ πώποτε τοιοῦτον
οὐδέν.

ἆρ' <οὐκ> οἶσθ': Dobree's prior supplement (*Adv.* 2.329) of ACE's
deficient text is superior (the question is rhetorical, demanding a positive
response, cf. Denniston, *GP* 46f.) to his alternative suggestion (ἆρά <γ'>
(Denniston 50).

3–6 The transmitted text (A, Epit. agreeing) presents two difficulties.
(i) A logician might justifiably object that ὄνομ' in v. 5 is otiose; with
ὑποκόρισμα (5) as second predicate and τὸ καλούμενον ζῆν (4) as subject
there is a surfeit of words meaning 'name'. But Alexis is not compiling a
dialectical treatise but attempting to reproduce colloquial speech, which is
at times repetitive and wayward. Furthermore ὄνομα has overtones of its
own which are particularly relevant to the present context, hinting at the
emptiness of a name in opposition to the reality of the thing itself (cf.
e.g. Eur. *Hipp.* 501f., *Or.* 454, Kannicht's edition of *Hel.* (Heidelberg
1969) 1.57ff.). With ὄνομα the sentence breaks up into more easily spoken
phrases, with a pause after ἐστίν. In its place Madvig's conjecture μόνον
(*Adv. Crit.* 3.67) is palaeographically ingenious (confusion of μ and ν in
minuscule; a scribe predisposed in such a context to words meaning
'name'), sensible but inessential.
(ii) διατριβῆς χάριν (4) is troublesome (hence Grotius's conjecture
χαρίεν διατριβῆς, *Exc.* 974) mainly because of the difficulty in identifying
the precise overtones of διατριβή,[1] a noun of vague ambience with one

---

[1] LSJ s.v. διατριβή is not always accurate in its listings (thus Ar. *Plut.* 923
is classified under 'pastime', against Σ), and it fails to discuss one
common idiom where δ. is coupled with another noun which defines
more precisely the manner in which time is passed: e.g. διατριβαὶ καὶ
λόγοι Pl. *Apol.* 37d, *Gorg.* 484e, Arist. *Cat.* 10, 13ᵃ24, γέλωτα καὶ δ.
Aeschines 1.175, συνουσία καὶ δ. Dem. 21.71, δ. καὶ μέλλησις Thuc.
5.82, δ. ἀγωνίαν τε Men. *Asp.* 388f., δ. καὶ παιδιᾶς Plut. *Mor.* 512d, cf.
Alexis 222(219K).13, Baton 2.4, Thuc. 5.38, Pl. *Theaet.* 172c, Plut. *Mor.*
342c, 710d, *Per.* 16. On the secondary development of διατριβή =

basic meaning ('passage/passing of time': neutrally e.g. at Ar. *Plut.* 923, Men. *Dysk.* 41) at the heart of several of its more specialised applications. Of these the commonest are (a) '(pleasant) pastime/amusement' (e.g. Alexis 190(185K).2, 228(226K).4, Timocles 8.12, Men. *Asp.* 388, *Dysk.* 669, 890, 939), (b) '(serious) occupation' (e.g. Ar. *Nub.* 1055, *Plut.* 923 and Σ, Pl. *Apol.* 37d, *Theaet.* 172c), (c) 'waste of time/delay' (e.g. Ar. *Ach.* 193, *Ran.* 1498, Men. *Asp.* 76, *Dysk.* 78, com. adesp. fr. 339b.11 Austin), although the boundaries between each nuance are often not clearly defined. Here in Alexis 222(219K).4, where the speaker is stressing the bleakness of human life, the most appropriate classification of διατριβή is under (c), and we should translate the sentence 'Don't you know that this thing called "living" is an empty name idly given, a euphemism for man's fate?' Other translations of διατριβῆς χάριν, however (e.g. 'a mocking misnomer' Zuntz 235, '(Life), as we amusingly call it' G. Norwood, *Greek Comedy* (London 1931) 52, cf. Edmonds and Kokolakis 52f. n. 1, *en chanza* Gil: all based on Dobree, *Adv.* 2.330 *ludi jocique causa*, and classifiable under (a) above), are also possible.

5–6 ὑποκόρισμα τῆς ἀνθρωπίνης μοίρας: for the idiom LSJ cites Plut. *Galba* 20 (a provincial appointment = φυγῆς ὑποκόρισμα), *Mor.* 807e (σεισάχθεια = ὑπ. χρεῶν ἀποκοπῆς); cf. also Eustath. *Opuscula* 98.8f. (ὑπόκρισις = τὸ ἀγεννὲς τῆς ἀρετῆς ὑπ.), 259.1 (a fresh-picked fig is μέλιτος ὑπ.).

μοίρας: the best discussion of it in Greek thought is still M. P. Nilsson, *Geschichte der griechischen Religion* 1[3] (Munich 1967) 361ff.; cf. also W. C. Greene, *Moira: Fate, Good and Evil in Greek Thought* (Cambridge Mass. 1944), B. C. Dietrich, *Death, Fate and the Gods* (London 1965) 59ff. At this point in the speech it is uncertain – perhaps deliberately so, given the direction of the argument (see above, introduction to fr.) – whether τῆς ἀνθρωπίνης μοίρας is intended to convey the whole of man's allotted portion, from birth to death (which would make the slogan a banal truism), or whether uppermost is the idea of death as the final dispensation (a usage familiar from Homer onwards, e.g. *Il.* 16.334, πορφύρεος θάνατος καὶ μοῖρα κραταιή, 18.115ff., cf. Hes. *Theog.* 217, 220–2 and M. L. West *ad loc.*, Wilamowitz, *Glaube* 1.359f., Zuntz 235). The latter interpretation brings the meaning very close to two traditional Greek paradoxes (a) about the identity of life and death, allegedly formulated by Thales (A 1 Diels–Kranz, *Vorsokr.*[6] 1.71) according to Diog. Laert. 1.35; cf. also Heraclitus в 88 Diels-Kranz (G. S. Kirk, *Heraclitus. The Cosmic Fragments* (Cambridge 1954) fr. 88 pp. 135ff., M. Marcovich (Merida,

---

'diatribe' see Ἀσωτοδιδάσκαλος ('False or Doubtful Attributions' III, p. 821 n. 1).

Venezuela 1967) fr. 41 pp. 216ff.), Eur. frs. 361, 638, 833, the parody in Ar. *Ran.* 1477, cf. 1082, the quotation in Pl. *Gorg.* 492e with E. R. Dodds, comm. (Oxford 1959) *ad loc.*, Sext. Emp. *Pyrrh.* 3.230, [Plut.] *Mor.* 106f; F. Cumont, *Rev. Phil.* 44 (1920) 230ff.; and (b) about the living body being the tomb of the ψυχή, an idea shared apparently by Pythagoreans (Ath. 4.157c citing Clearchus) and Orphics (Pl. *Crat.* 400b–c); at *Phd.* 62b it is described as ἐν ἀπορρήτοις, but the Pythagorean Cebes appears to hold to it. The Pythagorean connection almost certainly accounts for its insertion by Alexis here (see introduction to this fr.).

7 ACE's φήσειε produces an objectionably divided resolution (cf. *CQ* 7 (1957) 189). Dobree's φήσει (*Adv.* 2.330) gives perfect sense and metre with a minimum of change, and is generally accepted, but φῆσαι (as 3rd p. s. aor. optative: cf. on v. 2 above) cannot be ruled out. At the end of the line Dobree's supplement οὐκ ἔχοιμ' ἂν <σοι> φράσαι of ACE's defective text is virtually certain; 2nd p. pronouns are often omitted by scribes (cf. comm. on fr. 169(164K).2), and a quickly written σοι in minuscule could easily be misread as φ and overlooked by quasi-haplography before φράσαι.

8 ἔγνωκα: 'I have come to realise', as e.g. *P.V.* 51, S. *OC* 553, Eur. *Alc.* 1080, *IT* 934, *Hyps.* fr. 21.9 Bond, Ar. fr. 231(209K), com. adesp. fr. 257.51 Austin; Cobet, *N.L.* 7. Directly thereafter γοῦν (A) or δ'οὖν (Epit.)? On the confusion between these particles in MSS see Denniston, *GP* 467f.; here δ'οὖν, leading back to the main topic after the detour of vv. 6–7 (ἐγὼ γὰρ - φράσαι), has a relevance denied to γοῦν (cf. Denniston 463f. ~ 450ff.).

9 The key-word in the second slogan (cf. introduction to this fr.) is μανιώδη, which here implies irrational judgement rather than raving madness, as Zuntz points out (235 n. 2), citing as parallels Eur. *Andr.* 52, *Bacch.* 399, *Cycl.* 168, *Hcld.* 904, fr. 640; cf. also e.g. Ar. *Vesp.* 1496 (Philocleon's dancing μανικὰ πράγματα), Pl. *Protag.* 343c (the first part of Simonides fr. 37 Page appears μανικόν). The idea itself is attested for the Pythagoreans by Iamblichus *Vit. Pyth.* 31.207 (cf. Weiher 67) (sc. οἱ Πυθαγόρειοί φασι) μανικόν τε καὶ πολύμορφον εἶναι κατὰ τὴν τῆς ψυχῆς κίνησιν τὸ ἀνθρώπινον φῦλον. This is of course only a variation or development of vv. 4–6; if life is identified with fate viewed as an external, superhuman agency, then the latter's effect on human affairs will inevitably appear irrational.

τἀνθρώπων: so A, but Epit.'s τἀνθρώπει' is just as likely (cf. S. *Aj.* 132, Antiphanes fr. 251(240b K)).

10–14 (i) The speaker's third slogan in which he (a) compares life to an ἀποδημία, where, (b) as in a visit to a πανήγυρις, (c) we are released from darkness and death to pass our time in the light of day. The vividness of these images need not blind us to the apparently clumsy way (? designed to illustrate the speaker's incoherence: see introduction to the fr.) in which traditional ideas have been strung together into a single picture, yet all three (a, b, c) have been selected primarily for their Pythagorean affiliations.

(a) The equation of life with an ἀπο-, ἐν- or (most frequently) ἐπιδημία, already hackneyed in Alexis' own day ([Pl.] *Axioch.* 365b τὸ κοινὸν δὴ τοῦτο καὶ πρὸς ἁπάντων θρυλούμενον, παρεπιδημία τίς ἐστιν ὁ βίος, cf. also e.g. *Phd.* 67b–c, Men. fr. 416.9 Körte–Thierfelder = 416b.2 Sandbach and comm. below, N.T. *2 Ep. Cor.* 5.6, *Hebr.* 11.13, *1 Pet.* 2.11, Marc. Aurel. 2.17.2; Zuntz 229ff.), was endorsed by a tract ascribed in Stob. 4.7.64 to the 4th-century Pythagorean Ecphantus but now believed to be a much later compilation of the sect (cf. Wellmann in *RE* s.v. *Ekphantos* 3, 2215.52ff.), and repeated in other works which seem to incorporate (neo-)Pythagorean ideas (e.g. Hipparchus in Stob. 4.44.81, Philo *Conf. Ling.* 77f., [Plut.] *Mor.* 117f).

(b) The idea that birth is a release from the murk of death into the world of light is consistent with, even if it does not inevitably presuppose, the doctrine of metempsychosis. Although this in Alexis' day was espoused by sects like the Orphics and philosophers like Plato as well as by the Pythagoreans, with a considerable interweaving of accessories,[1] in the context of our fr. there can be little doubt that the Pythagorean associations (cf. e.g. Arist. *De An.* 1.3, 407[b]20ff. = Pythag. school B 39 Diels–Kranz 1.462, Diod. Sic. 10.6.1–3, Diog. Laert. 8.4–5, 13, 31 = Alex. Polyh., *FGrH* 273 F 93 = 58.B1a Diels–Kranz 1.418ff., Iamblichus *Vit. Pyth.* 14.63) were uppermost in the author's mind, even if the wording may perhaps have been influenced by memorable expressions in other sources (popular or literary: e.g. Pl. *Resp.* 7.518c, in the allegory of the cave, ὄμμα ... στρέφειν πρὸς τὸ φανὸν ἐκ τοῦ σκοτώδους).

---

[1] The bibliography here is enormous. I confine myself to listing a small sample of works dealing with Orphic and Pythagorean presentations of metempsychosis, and with the question of interrelationships between them and with Platonic teaching: E. Rohde, *Psyche* (English translation, London 1925) 344ff., 374ff., 598ff., A. Dieterich, *Nekyia* (Leipzig 1893) 113ff., K. Ziegler in *RE* s.v. *Orphische Dichtung* 1370.45ff., H. S. Long, *A Study of the Doctrine of Metempsychosis in Greece: From Pythagoras to Plato* (Diss. Princeton 1948) 89ff., but see D. Tsekourakis, *Aufstieg und Niedergang der römischen Welt* 11.36.1 (Berlin and New York 1987) 371 n. 23, K. Kerényi, *Pythagoras und Orpheus*[3] (Zurich 1950), W. K. C. Guthrie, *Orpheus and Greek Religion*[2] (London 1952) 148ff., E. R. Dodds, comm. on Pl. *Gorg.* (Oxford 1959), introduction to 523a, W. Burkert, *Lore and Science in Ancient Pythagoreanism* (Cambridge Mass. 1972) 120ff., von Fritz in *RE* s.v. *Pythagoreer* 234.43ff., 242.52ff., M. P. Nilsson, *Geschichte der griechischen Religion* 1[3] (Munich 1967) 691ff., 699ff., M. L. West, *The Orphic Poems* (Oxford 1983), index s.v. 'metempsychosis'.

(c) Evidence for Pythagorean associations in the comparison of life to a πανήγυρις and/or a ἑορτή (just as hackneyed as (a), cf. e.g. Men. fr. 416.8 K.T. = 416b.1 Sandbach and comm. below = monost. 627 Jäkel, Teles p. 15.9ff. Hense[2] citing Bion, Arrian *Epict.* 2.14.23, 28, 3.5.10, 4.1.105, [Lucian] *Am.* 25, Xen. Eph. 1.10.2, [Longinus] *Subl.* 35.2, Photius *Ross. Inc.* p. 205.8f. Nauck, *Lex. Vind.*; cf. Zuntz 226ff.) is even more compelling; Heraclides Ponticus, an older contemporary of Alexis, actually ascribed its formulation to Pythagoras himself (fr. 88 Wehrli, Cicero *Tusc.* 5.3.9, Iamblichus *Vit. Pyth.* 12.58, Synesius *De Prov.* 8, 1280A Migne; Diog. Laert. 8.8 names Sosicrates as an intermediary source (cf. A. Rostagni, *Il verbo di Pitagora* (Turin 1924) 276f. n. 1, Burkert 165 n. 3, H. B. Gottschalk, *Heraclides of Pontus* (Oxford 1980) 23ff.)). Whatever may have been the authority for Heraclides' claim, its existence points to a 4th-century link between the comparison and the Pythagoreans strong enough for Alexis to exploit directly before his παρὰ προσδοκίαν in vv. 14ff.

(ii) At v. 10 begins the passage of Alexis imitated (but with typical Hellenistic *uariatio*) in Menander fr. 416.8–10 K.T. = 416b.1–3 Sandbach:

> πανήγυριν νόμισόν τιν' εἶναι τὸν χρόνον
> ὃν φημι τοῦτον, τὴν ἐπιδημίαν ἄνω·
> ὄχλος, ἀγορά, κλέπται, κυβεῖαι, διατριβαί.

Two fundamental differences between the two passages need to be stressed. (1) When Menander compares life to a πανήγυρις, he plants his feet firmly on our earth, considering death presumably as a leap away from it into the unknown. For him, as for most users of the comparison, life is an ἐπιδημία, a residence on that same earth. Alexis by contrast takes his imaginary stand in the dark place that is before birth and after death, from which man is released for his attendance at the festival of life. This interval is accordingly viewed by the older playwright as an ἀποδημία (cf. also Pl. *Phd.* 67b–c, Philo *Conf. Ling.* 77, [Ecphantus] in Stob. 4.7.64 p. 275.2 Hense; Durham, *Vocabulary* 44), a spell spent abroad from the home station of non-existence. Failure to appreciate this distinction led C. J. Blomfield (*Glossarium* on A. *Sept.* 206 (Cambridge 1812) p. 120) to conjecture ἐπιδημία inappropriately in Alexis here. (2) To Alexis (as to other writers: e.g. Dio Chrys. 8.9, 9.1, 27.5ff., [Lucian] *Am.* 25; cf. Zuntz 227) the πανήγυρις was an occasion for enjoyment and self-indulgence; there is therefore – despite the Pythagorean overtones – a certain logic in the speaker's development of his comparison into the sponsorship of hedonism with which the fr. closes. Menander's picture of a πανήγυρις, on the other hand, concentrates on its discomforts: 'crowds, buying and selling, thieves, gambling, pastimes (διατριβαί: ? or 'delays'). Hence Menander's conclusion is radically different from Alexis': if life includes such tribulations, the best thing is to end it as early as possible (cf. comm. on 145(141K).14–16).

COMMENTARY

10 ἀεί: so CE, corrupted to unmetrical ἀιεί in A, cf. comm. on 76.1.

12 ἀφειμένους: the form is always passive in Attic, e.g. v. 16 ἀφεῖται, Posidippus 25(23K).3 (cf. Alciphron 2.7.2) ἀφεῖσαι, Jebb on S. *Ant.* 1165, Fraenkel on A. *Ag.* 412.

13–14 εἰς τὴν διατριβὴν εἰς τὸ φῶς τε τοῦθ', ὃ δὴ ὁρῶμεν: 'into the time we spend in this daylight here that we see'; see above on v. 3–6 and n. 3.

14–17 The exhortation to crass hedonism – a commonplace in comedy and popular literature of the time (cf. e.g Alexis 273(271K) and the introduction to comm. on fr. 25), and particularly apropos if voiced here by a parasite (see the introduction to Ταραντῖνοι) – wittily defies expectations by changing the speech's apparent direction (cf. introduction to this fr.), although there is still one further humorous surprise in store (v. 16 ἐράνου τινός and comm.).

14–15 The absence of eating from Alexis' catalogue of pleasures is worthy of note, but hardly a reason for doubting the accuracy of the transmission (Hirschig's substitution of φαγῆ τε for γελάσῃ, *Annot.* 13, is palaeographically implausible, metrically objectionable with its split anapaest, and – because more hackneyed – dramatically less pungent).

15 τῆς Ἀφροδίτης ἀντιλάβηται: metonomy (cf. comm. on 153(149K).16) of Aphrodite for the sexual act/love-affair (cf. *Glossary of Useful Terms* 173.5f. Bachmann Ἀφροδίτης· ἀντὶ τοῦ Ἀφροδισίων) is common; e.g. Alexis 273(271K).4 τὸ τῆς Ἀφροδίτης τυγχάνειν, Hom. *Od.* 22.444f., Pind. *Ol.* 6.35 γλυκείας ... ἔψαυσ' Ἀφροδίτας, Men. *Mis.* A1f., Oppian *Hal.* 1.499, 525, Nonnus *Dion.* 4.325f. κούρης | μυρομένης ... ἀναγκαίην Ἀφροδίτην.

15–16 τὸν χρόνον τοῦτον: the phrase is taken over in Men. fr. 416.8f. K.T. = 416b.1f. Sandbach, cf. above on vv. 10–14 (ii).

16 καὶ τύχῃ γ' ἐράνου τινός, Musurus's correction of ACE's nonsensical τ' ἐρ., is all that is needed to restore the final παρὰ προσδοκίαν joke in the passage; Meineke's κἄν (for καί: '"*si res ita tulerit*", *ut* ἐράνου *pendeat ab* ἀντιλάβηται', printed by Kassel–Austin) unnecessarily spoils the balance of the clause. The speaker lists his pleasures in ascending order with four parallel subjunctives linked by καί (the last one with emphatic γε added, cf. Denniston, *GP* 157f., to mark the unexpected climax: 'laughs, and drinks, and enjoys sex during the time he's released, and – yes – secures an interest-free loan'). We must presume that at the time of Alexis' Ταραντῖνοι the practice of making ἔρανοι (primarily such loans, but also favours or services done with no eye on profit, cf. comm. on 145(141K).5) was so much in vogue that receipt of one could be ridiculed as the pinnacle of human pleasure.

17 πανηγυρίσας ... ἀπῆλθεν οἴκαδε: drawing the attention back to the image of v. 11, with its implication (cf. comm. (i.a) on vv. 10–14) that

634

man is in his real home only before birth and after death. ἀπῆλθεν, as a gnomic aorist, takes primary sequence (cf. comm. on 153(149K).9).

223 (220 + 221K)

Meineke 3.483 (I, II), Kock 2.378, Edmonds 2.480, Kassel–Austin 2.147. This fr., cited by Ath. 4.161b–c (all in A; vv. 1–3, δεσμωτηρίου 11– διάγουσι 13, paraphrase of vv. 10–ὕδατος 11 in Epit.), is really two frs. (vv.1–6 ἔμψυχον, vv. 7 πυθαγορισμοί–17) separated by Ath. with the words προελθών (the normal formula: so Musurus for A's προσελθών) τέ φησι. Although this formula does not necessarily mean that the two frs. so linked originally came near to each other in the same scene (see introduction to Λέβης), here both subject matter (Pythagorist sophistry and asceticism) and dialogue structure make it probable that they derive from one dialogue involving at least two speakers. The most satisfactory part-division was worked out by Jacobs, *Addit.* 102 (vv.1–6), Daléchamp and Grotius, *Exc.* 579 (v.11) and Kock (vv.12–13, after Schweighaeuser in v. 12).

(a) (220K)

1 οἱ πυθαγορίζοντες: see comm. on fr. 201(196K).3.

2–3 Pythagorist abstention from eating flesh – both fish (ὄψον v. 2, see comm. on fr. 47(46K).6) and animal – is attested by contemporary comedy and later writers about the Pythagoreans (see comm. on frs. 27.1–2, 201(196K).1–3), but the claim that the sects rejected wine totally (in comedy elsewhere at Aristophon 12(13K).8, cf. 10.3 and Alexis 202(198K)) exaggerates the known facts (comm. on 202(198K)).

4 Epicharides is not an uncommon name in Attica; Kirchner, *PA* 1.330 lists five certain instances (5005–9: 5008 fathered a syntrierarch of 334/3, cf. Davies, *APF* 184, 468) and one doubtful (5004) between 437 and 270. Whether the man here, reduced to eating dog-meat (see below), was identical with the Ἐπ. ὁ μικρός of fr. 248(246K), who had allegedly run through his patrimony in five days, is uncertain, although Alexis' two references could fit different stages in a spendthrift's career. We are not of course obliged to take seriously the assertion that this Epicharides was a Pythagorist (v.5); it could simply be a comic conclusion based on a major premise that all poor men must be Pythagorists.

μέντοι κύνας: A has μὲν τὰς κύνας, but (1) μέν is inappropriate (μέν *solitarium* rarely has the adversative force required here, cf. Denniston, *GP* 368f.), and (2) the presence of the article (rather than its gender: of the 69 checked passages in Attic comedy where κύων = 'dog/bitch', in 29 it is masculine, 16 feminine, 24 unspecified) is malapropos. Jacobs' μέν τοι (so

COMMENTARY

Addit. 102, but in 4th-century Attic μέντοι appears as one word, cf. Denniston, *GP* 397f.) removes the two objections (on μέντοι adversative, Denniston 404ff.) with palaeographic aplomb (confusion of οι and α, homoeoteleuton).

In ancient Greece[1] dog-meat was not normally eaten by humans (e.g. Porph. *Abst.* 1.14, Sext. Emp. *Pyrrh.* 3.225) except in a mince for ἀλλᾶντες by the poorest (Ar. *Equ.* 1398f.); it was not banned, however, by medical writers (e.g. Hippocr. *Vict.* 2.46, *Morb. sacr.* 2 Jones) or in sacrifices (e.g. Sophron fr. 8, Ar. fr. 209(204K), Theocr. 2.12, Pliny, *HN* 29.58).[2]

5 τῶν Πυθαγορείων εἷς: see comm. on v. 4 and 201(196K).3,

ἀποκτείνας γέ που: Kock's brilliant correction (without knowing G. Morel's γε μὴν p. 135, however) of A's ἀπ. γενοῦ, 'Yes – after killing them, I presume', with γε affirmative + που 'used ironically, with assumed diffidence' (Denniston, *GP* 490f., cf. 494) in a riposte (cf. e.g. Pl. *Phdr.* 262c, *Polit.* 259e, *Theaet.* 147c) which exploits the ambiguity of ἔμψυχος to make the joke (see comm. on 27.2, 4). Confusion between Π and Ν is easy in papyrus uncial when the cross stroke of Ν meets the right-hand upright near the top (good examples in e.g. *P.Oxy.* 2460, 1st century AD = Eur. Τήλεφος, plates in E. W. Handley and J. Rea's edition (*BICS Suppl.* 5 (1957); 2078, 2nd century AD = Eur. ? Πειρίθους, and 2654, 1st century AD = Men. *Karch.*, pls. 33 and 41 in E. G. Turner, *Greek Manuscripts of the Ancient World* (Oxford 1971)). The consequences of this confusion often disfigure medieval MSS: e.g. Xen. *Hell.* 5.2.42, CF ἀνεχώρουν for ἀπ-; Ap. Rhod. 3.397 LASG ἐπὶ for ἐνὶ; Macrobius 1.18.22 citing *Orph.* fr. 238 Kern, vv. 6, 7, 9; cf. comm. on v. 13 below.

6 ἔμψυχον: see comm. on fr. 27.4, where the same joke appears.

(b) (221K)

7–8 The charge of logic-chopping levelled against the Pythagorists is of doubtful validity. A similar accusation was made by Cratinus (? jun.) fr. 7

---

[1] More recently westerners have eaten dog-meat knowingly only through extreme poverty or in dire emergencies (e.g. Captain James Cook in Tahiti 1769, Roald Amundsen in Antarctica 1910), but in the far east such meals have never been tabu. China bred the chow for the table, and dog-meat continues there to be a favoured item on menus (e.g. J. Boswell, *Life of Johnson*, 1.467 in the Dent Everyman edition; P. Thorogood, *The Listener*, 2 March 1967, 306; C. Thubron, *Behind the Wall* (London 1987) 184f., 265, cf. 141).

[2] Ananius in Ath. 7.282b (= fr. 5.5 West) is sometimes cited (e.g. by Meineke, E. Cougny in Dar.–Sag. s.v. *canis* (890A on *cynophagie*)) as evidence of dog-eating, but even in a general culinary context the

in his Ταραντῖνοι against an unnamed sect identified as the Pythagorists implicitly by Diog. Laert. 8.37 and plausibly by the play-title (cf. introduction to Alexis' Ταραντῖνοι). Evidence in Pythagorean sources for the sect's teaching of rhetoric and logic is skimpy, vague and unreliable: Iamblichus *Vit. Pyth.* 29.158 claims that Pythagoras τὰ φυσικὰ πάντα ἀναδιδάσκει, τήν τε φιλοσοφίαν καὶ τὴν λογικὴν ἐτελειώσατο, cf. 17.79 τιμήν τε ἐξαίρετον ἐτίθετο καὶ ἐξέτασιν ἀκριβεστάτην περὶ τὴν διδασκαλίαν καὶ μετάδοσιν τῶν αὐτῷ δεδογμένων, βασανίζων τε καὶ διακρίνων τὰς τῶν ἐντυγχανόντων ἐννοίας διδάγμασί τε ποικίλοις καὶ θεωρίας ἐπιστημονικῆς μυρίοις εἴδεσι; a monograph with the title περὶ τῶν ἀντικειμένων, attributed (falsely, in the view of Diels–Kranz 1.439) to the 4th-century Pythagorean Archytas, presumably attempted a logical refutation of the sect's opponents; and the strong denunciation of sophistic λόγοι in the περὶ πολιτείας of another Pythagorean cited by Stob. 4.1.95, p. 34.11ff. Hense (Hippodamus, according to Stob., but see A. Delatte, *Essai sur la politique pythagoricienne* (Liège and Paris 1922) 125ff., 146ff.) may perhaps imply that some Pythagoreans at least had been infected with the sophistic virus. Yet in view of Attic comedy's tendency, in a tradition extending back to the attacks on Socrates in Ar. *Nub.* (and elsewhere) and embracing both Plato and the Pythagoreans in the 4th century (cf. comm. on fr. 1, and introduction to Πυθαγορίζουσα), to assign a common stock of attributes to different philosophic sects with no regard for accurate distinctions, it would be unwise here to place too much trust in a comic poet's prejudiced allegations. After all, the terms chosen by Alexis in vv. 7–8 might well reflect those of a philistine Athenian's dismissive response to any Pythagorean defence of ascetic practices which seemed to him outlandish.

πυθαγορισμοί: 'Pythagorean/-orist quiddities of expression', a hapax that presumably refers to the strange metaphors in the σύμβολα (e.g. Porph. *Vit. Pyth.* 41 ἔλεγε (Pythagoras) δέ τινα καὶ μυστικῷ τρόπῳ συμβολικῶς ... οἷον ὅτι τὴν θάλατταν μὲν ἐκάλει εἶναι δάκρυον, τὰς δ' ἄρκτους Ῥέας χεῖρας, τὴν δὲ Πλειάδα Μουσῶν λύραν, τοὺς δὲ πλανήτας κύνας τῆς Φερσεφόνης; Diels–Kranz 1.462f.).

λόγοι λεπτοί: '(over-)subtle arguments/niceties of phrasing', where the use of λεπτός is designed to prejudice the hearer against those who so reason; cf. especially Ar. *Nub.* 153 and Dover *ad loc.*, 229f., 359, 740f., 1404, *Ran.* 956, 1108, 1111, Antiphanes 120(122K).3f., Amphis 33.4ff., Pl. *Resp.* 10.607c; J. D. Denniston, *CQ* 21 (1927) 119.

διεσμιλευμέναι ... φροντίδες: 'finely chiselled thoughts', repeating the

---

reference there to autumn as the season for dogs, hares and foxes suggests hunting rather than the kitchen.

COMMENTARY

idea implicit in λόγοι λεπτοί but without overtly prejudicial overtones. Other metaphorical applications to literary contexts of technical terms from carving (the chisel, it must be remembered, was used also for cutting inscriptions) include Cometas in *Anth. Pal.* 15.38 εὑρὼν Κομητᾶς τὰς ʽΟμηρείους βίβλους | ἐφθαρμένους τε κοὐδαμῶς ἐστιγμένας, | στίξας διεσμίλευσα ταύτας ἐντέχνως, Ar. *Ran.* 819 σμιλεύματα τʼ ἔργων, 901f., ἀστεῖόν τι λέξειν | καὶ κατερρινημένον.

9 τὰ δὲ (καθ' ἡμέραν): Musurus' correction of A's τα δει. At Pl. *Resp.* 10.617e ἒ δὲ is similarly corrupted in A² to ἔδει; cf. also A. *Suppl.* 765, οὗ δεῖ Bamberger for οὐδὲ ME, but see H. Friis Johansen and E. W. Whittle (Copenhagen 1980) *ad loc.*

10–11 Alexis distorts the Pythagorean tabu on meat and wine (cf. introduction to Πυθαγορίζουσα and comm. on 223(220K).2–3 above, 27.1–2, 201(196K).1–2, 202(198)) into a diet limited to bread and water; Philemon 88(85K).3 similarly restricts Zeno the Stoic to εἷς ἄρτος, ὄψον ἰσχάς, ἐπιπιεῖν ὕδωρ.

ἄρτος καθαρός: white (as opposed to wholemeal) bread, although this product of presumably second-grade σεμίδαλις flour (see comm. on fr. 102(97K).3–4) is likely to have been greyish or grey in colour and much heavier and coarser than a modern white loaf. In the late 1st and early 2nd centuries AD at Ephesus καθαρός bread was priced at 2 obols per Roman pound, whole-wheat (αὐτόπυρος: see comm. on fr. 126(121K)) 2 obols per pound and one ounce, speckled (ῥαντός) 2 obols per 9 ounces, and best white bread (σιλιγνίτης) 3 obols per 9 ounces (J. Keil, *JÖAI* 23 (1926) *Beibl.* 279ff., T. R. S. Broughton in Tenney Frank and others (edd.), *An Economic Survey of Ancient Rome* 4 (Baltimore 1938) 879f.). Cf. also e.g. Hdt. 2.40, Galen *De bonis malisque sucis* 2.3 p. 394.21 Helmreich, Blümner, *Technologie* 75, L. Mitteis and U. Wilcken, *Grundzüge und Chrestomathie der Papyruskunde* 1.2 (Leipzig and Berlin 1912) p. 50 no. 30.i.17 (a papyrus of *c.* 200), N. Jasny, *The Wheats of Classical Antiquity* (Baltimore 1944) 68f. and *Osiris* 9 (1950) 227ff.

10 ἑκατέρῳ: presumably the ἐκείνους of v. 9, whose standing in the play is unknown (they could have been characters in the plot or merely the subjects of a passing discussion), were two in number.

11 τοσαῦτα ταῦτα: 'that's all'; compare the much commoner summation τοιαῦτα ταῦτα, e.g. *P.V.* 500, S. *El.* 696, Eur. *Andr.* 910.

11–12 δεσμωτηρίου λέγεις δίαιταν: so CE (λέγειν A, the scribe's eye having wandered to the end of the following word). The phraseology (cf. e.g. Ar. *Plut.* 922 προβατίου βίον λέγεις, Pl. *Gorg.* 494b χαραδριοῦ τινα αὖ σὺ βίον λέγεις, Men. *Dysk.* 116f., fr. 334.6, Alexis 224(222).4, 228(226K).3, 248(246K).1, 249(247K).4; A. Oguse, *REA* 67 (1965) 131f.) indicates that the comment was interjected by a second speaker (cf. introduction to this fr.). This appears to be the only passage in Greek

638

literature identifying bread and water as the prison diet; Alexis might of course be exaggerating. Cf. E. Caillemer in Dar.–Sag. s.v. *carcer* 916A ff., R. J. Bonner and G. Smith, *The Administration of Justice from Homer to Aristotle* 2 (Chicago 1938) 275f., D. M. MacDowell, *The Law in Classical Athens* (London 1978) 256f.

12–14 πάντες – ὅτι: the transmission here has one possible and three certain corruptions. In v. 12 ACE's οὗτοι (homoeoteleuton and hiatus before οἱ σοφοί) was corrected to οὕτως by Villebrune, in 16 A's ἄρισθ' (wrong word-division and iotacism) brilliantly to ἆρ' οἶσθ' in Musurus's edition. Before the latter A writes τρυφῶσιν ἕτεροι πρὸς ἑτέρους, 'some people live in luxury compared with (πρός + acc., LSJ s.v. c.4, cf. Alexis fr. 150(146K).6) others': which would be feeble even as a generality summing up an argument, but all the more so as a link statement when only one group has yet been mentioned. Cobet's οὗτοι (for ἕτεροι: *NL* 120f.) is almost certainly right, requiring a scribe's eye to have wandered ahead to ἑτέρους and combined its stem and the correct word's ending.

Part-division is uncertain. There are at least four possibilities:

(a): δεσμωτηρίου (v. 11) to the *Marcianus'* που (13) all to the second speaker, with πάντες to που punctuated as a question, then vv. 14–17 to the first speaker (so Cobet, Kaibel);

(b): δεσμωτηρίου to δίαιταν (v.12) to the second speaker, and the rest of the fr. to the first (Daléchamp);

(c): as (b), but with the last word of v. 13 interpreted as a questioning ποῦ; and given to the second speaker (Schweighaeuser);

(d): Kock conjectured that κακοπαθοῦσί που (13) was corrupted from -οῦσιν; (A.) οὔ· (for scribal confusion between Π and N see comm. on v. 5), with δεσμωτηρίου to κακοπαθοῦσιν assigned to the second speaker (πάντες–κακοπαθοῦσιν as a question), the first speaker answering οὔ· (= 'No', cf. e.g. Pherecrates 87(82K) (A.) μάχαιραν ἆρ' ἐνέθηκας; (B.) οὔ, S. *Trach.* 415) and continuing to the end of the fr. This yields the most lively dialogue, and is printed by Kassel–Austin.

15–16 It is sometimes assumed (e.g. by W. Pape and G. Benseler, *Wörterbuch der griechischen Eigennamen*[3] (Brunswick 1911) s.vv. Μελανιππίδης 2, Φᾶνος 2, Φάων 2, Φυρόμαχος 4, in *RE* Nestle s.v. *Melanippides* 3, 423.48ff. and von Fritz s.v. *Phanos* 3, 1785.68ff.) that all four men here described as ἑταῖροι were 4th-century Pythagorean/-orist ascetics. This seems highly unlikely. None of the names occurs in Iamblichus' long list of Pythagorean disciples (*Vit. Pyth.* 36.267), and the assumption takes no account of the techniques of ridicule in Attic comedy. Alexis is more likely to have been chaffing contemporary Athenians, some of them at least beggars or paupers whose paraded impoverishment allowed a comic poet to explain their circumstances ludicrously as due to Pythagorist asceticism. Unfortunately only one of the four can be identified with any plausibility. Melanippides and Phaon are not mentioned by any other comic poet of the time, and neither name is listed in Kirchner (*PA*) or recorded on Attic inscriptions, although Ath. 8.350e–f (citing Stratonicus' ἀπομνημονεύματα) refers to an allegedly bad piper of the 4th century called Phaon, and Galen mentions an early doctor with this name as a possible author of the Hippocratic περὶ διαίτης (*In Hippocr. de Vict. Acut.* 1.17, p. 135.3 Helmreich = 15.455 Kühn). In Athens Phaon could have been a nickname given to a pale, handsome youth, after the mythological counterpart whose adventures seem to have been popular in Athens at the beginning of the century (cf. Webster, *SLGC* 18f., Stoessl in *RE* s.v. *Phaon* 1790.67ff.). Phanus (Φᾶνος[1]) is a rare Athenian name (five examples in Kirchner, *PA* 2.344, 14078–82, but omitting Demetrius of Phalerum, who was said to have originally been called Phanus, cf. *Suda* s.v. Δημήτριος, E. Bayer, *Demetrios Phalereus der Athener* (Stuttgart and Berlin 1942) 109, in *RE* Martini s.v. *Demetrios* 85, 2818.51ff. and H. Herter s.v. *Phanos* 2, 1785.63ff.). If these three were impoverished Athenians inserted into Alexis' list in order to ridicule both themselves and Pythagorist asceticism, the addition of Phyromachus could be a stroke of comic genius (cf. Edmonds p. 483 note c). A man with this name was ridiculed as a gluttonous parasite in comedy by Euphanes 1.6 (misattributed as Euphron 8.6 in Kock), in epigram (quoted by Ath. 10.414d) by Posidippus 16 Gow–Page (cf. H. W. Prescott, *CP* 5 (1910) 494ff., A. S. F. Gow, *CR* 41 (1954) 199f.) and in anecdote (according to Ath. 6.245e) by his contemporary Corydus (*floruit c.* 350–320: see introduction to Δημήτριος). It would be an improbable coincidence if two men bearing this rather unusual name (seven instances collected by Kirchner, *PA* 2.400f. nos. 15052–8, 15056 being father to an ephebe of 334/3) were mocked on dietary grounds at the same time, and the identification of Alexis' Phyromachus with the parasite appears tempting. In that case he was either (like the other three in Alexis' list) a hungry pauper at the time of Ταραντῖνοι, or – the more appealing alternative – a glutton perhaps of Falstaffian girth included in the list παρὰ προσδοκίαν in order to raise a laugh at the incongruity.

On the alliteration of three names with Φ see comm. on 173(168K).1–2.

16 The unmetrical and nonsensical μιᾶς that follows ἡμέρας in A,

---

[1] The *nomen proprium* Φᾶνος carries no accent here in A, but in medieval MSS it usually appears oxytone like its common-noun and adjectival homonyms (e.g. Ar. *Equ.* 1256 RVΦS, *Vesp.* 1220 VΓ ~ Φάνος R, *Suda* s.v., Eustath. 1607.16). According to Arcadius 63.10 Barker, however, τὰ εἰς ΑΝΟΣ δισύλλαβα κύρια ὄντα ... βαρύνεται ... Φᾶνος ...· τὰ μέντοι ἐπιθετικὰ ... ὀξύνεται, φανός (cf. [Herodian] 1.175.31 Lentz, K. Lehrs, *De Aristarchi studiis homericis*[3] (Leipzig 1882) 277).

combining its ending with the stem of the last word in v. 17 (cf. comm. on vv. 12–14), was deleted by Musurus.

δι' ἡμέρας ... πεμπτῆς, sc. 'every *four* days', since ancient Greeks habitually included in such computations both the starting and the final day/year etc. (cf. e.g. Ar. *Plut.* 583f. τὸν Ὀλυμπικὸν ... ἀγῶνα, ... δι' ἔτους πεμπτοῦ, Hdt. 2.4.1, 37.2, Eubulus 92(93K).2; B. B. Rogers' edition of Ar. *Thesm.* (London 1904) xxxviii f., LSJ s.v. διά A.3).

17 ἀλφίτων: hulled barley coarsely ground in its natural state and then most commonly mixed with water and cooked in a container over an open fire to produce the staple Athenian food of μᾶζα (see comm. on 145(141K).7). One κοτύλη amounted to about a quarter of a litre (273.6 cm³, cf Κράτεια, p. 326 n. 1), and a daily ration of one quarter of that would come to no more than a single portion of shredded wheat. Four kotylai appear to have been the normal daily allotment of wheat grain for free men (cf. Hdt. 7.187, Diog. Laert. 8.18) and of ἄλφιτα for slaves (cf. Thuc. 4.16, with twice that amount for free men, Ath. 6.272b); at Syracuse the Athenian prisoners were allowed daily only two kotylai of wheat grain and one of water (Thuc. 7.87). Cf. Blümner, *Technologie* 51f., M.-C. Amouretti, *Le Pain et l'huile dans la Grèce antique* (Paris 1986) 123f., 218f., 288ff.

224 (222K)

Meineke 3.485 (iv), Kock 2.379, Edmonds 3.480, Kassel–Austin 2.148. The fr., transmitted very corruptly in Ath. 4.134a (all in A, but Epit. omits ἄκραν 4–end of 5, παραμασύντην 8, 9 and beginning of 10, partly at least through incomprehension), comes from a dialogue between a non-Athenian and an Athenian, possibly in Tarentum (see introduction to Ταραντῖνοι and vv. 1–2 below).

1–2 σοι ἐν ταῖς Ἀθήναις ταῖς καλαῖς: see above. Without further context it is impossible to know whether the praise of Athens (cf. e.g. Eupolis 316(290K).1 ὦ καλλίστη πόλι πασῶν ὅσας Κλέων ἐφορᾷ, com. adesp. fr. 44 Kock; E. Kienzle, *Der Lobpreis von Städten und Ländern in der älteren griechischen Dichtung* (Diss. Basle 1936) 86, P. Walcot, *Greek Drama in its Theatrical and Social Context* (Cardiff 1976) 96ff.) is typical dramatic jingoism or here a sarcastic jibe.

3 ἄπαντες ὀρχοῦντ': comm. on 102(97K).1–2.

εὐθύς: so correctly MSS of Epit.; A's unmetrical εὐθέως reflects the tendency of -έως to supplant -ύς in the *Koine* (L. Rydbeck, *Fachprosa, vermeintliche Volkssprache und Neues Testament* (Uppsala 1967) 167ff., Mayser–Schmoll 1.1.216).

4 ὀσμὴν ἴδωσιν: so A correctly (ἴσχωσι nonsensically and unmetrically

COMMENTARY

C and perhaps E[1]). The use of verbs/nouns/adjectives of sight in conjunction with other senses such as smell and hearing is a striking but natural consequence of verbs like ὁρῶ extending their meanings metaphorically to 'I understand/notice'; examples include (a: smell) Eur. *Cycl.* 153f. (Od.) ἰδού. (Sil.) παπαιάξ ὡς καλὴν ὀσμὴν ἔχει. | (Od.) εἶδες γὰρ αὐτήν; (Si.) οὐ μὰ Δί᾽, ἀλλ᾽ ὀσφραίνομαι (cf. Seaford *ad loc.* and R. Kassel, *Maia* 25 (1973) 102f.), Ar. *Av.* 1715f. ὀσμὴ ... χωρεῖ, καλὸν θέαμα, Theoc. 1.149 θᾶσαι ... ὡς καλὸν ὄζει (with Gow *ad loc.*); (b: sound) Hom. *Il.* 16.127 λεύσσω ... ἰωήν, *Od.* 9.166f. ἐλεύσσομεν ... φθογγήν, A. *Sept.* 103 κτύπον δέδορκα, S. *Phil.* 216 τηλωπὸν ἰωάν, *OC* 138 φωνῇ ... ὁρῶ, LXX *Exod.* 20.18 πᾶς ὁ λαὸς ἑώρα τὴν φωνήν, Ach. Tat. 1.7.3 οἱ ὀφθαλμοί σου λέγουσιν. Rarely in the Greek (above, Eur. *Cycl.*, S. *OC*) is a verbal point made about an incongruity which in English at least is normally a springboard for a joke (e.g. *Punch* 87 (1884) 38, 'Don't look at me, Sir, with – ah – in that tone of voice'). See further C. A. Lobeck, ῬΗΜΑΤΙΚΟΝ (Königsberg 1846) 332ff. and E. Norden (Stuttgart 1926³) on V. *Aen.* 6.257.

4–5 After ἴδωσιν the *Marcianus* has συμφορὰν λέγεις ἀρ᾽ ἂν φαίης ἂν εἰς συμπόσιον εἰσελθὼν ἄφνω. Daléchamp was the first to assign συμφορὰν λέγεις to a second speaker: (B.) *Calamitosum ac miserandum quod refers*; for this type of interjection cf. comm. on 223(221K).11–12, 228(226K).3); but ἀρ᾽ ἂν is impossible either appended to present indicative λέγεις, or prepositive (with duplicated ἂν) to φαίης ἄν, since ἄρ᾽ can never be first word in its clause and ἆρ᾽ would introduce unmetrically an unwanted question. Remedies making συμφοράν the direct object of a verb of seeing (e.g. Casaubon's σ. σέ γ᾽ ("*voluit* σύ γ᾽" Kaibel) εἰσορᾶν φαίης ἄν ... , *Animadv.* 253, rejecting the second speaker, or Dindorf's σ. λέγεις ὁρᾶν) are far less convincing than Dobree's interjected σ. λέγεις ἄκραν (*Adv.* 2.305), which is close to the *ductus* and scores highly for idiomatic and lively appropriateness ('A *perfect* disaster, you say': for this non-personal application of ἄκρος LSJ s.v. III.2 cites Diphilus 53(54K).2 νηστείας ἄκρας and Pl. *Phlb.* 45a τὰς ἀκροτάτας (ἡδονάς), cf. also Eur. *Ion* 776f. ἄκρον ἄχος; cf. H. Thesleff, *Studies on Intensification in Early and Classical Greek* (Helsinki 1954) 182). Alternatively σ. λέγεις πικράν might perhaps be considered; although a little further from the *ductus*, πικρά is closely related to the family of attributes regularly attached to συμφορά in Attic drama (ἀθλία Eur. *Hel.* 483, βαρεῖα S. *Trach.* 746, Eur. *Alc.* 405, δεινή S. *OR* 1527, κακή A. *Pers.* 445, Eur. *El.* 69, fr. 286.15, σκληρά Eur. fr. 684.2f., τάλαινα S. *El.* 1179, Ar. *Ach.* 1204), and regularly appears in this *sedes* (second half of the third metron) in comedy (Theopompus 8(7K).2, Anaxandrides 81(78K) =

---

[1] E abbreviates to ἴσχω(σι), where the second letter is better read as σ (with its tail raised to link with χ) than as δ.

642

Diphilus 134(136K), Men. *Dysk.* 21, *Georg.* fr. 3.3 Sandbach, frs. 11, 154, 543, 589, 619, 733, Philemon 113(122K).4). Emperius (*Adv.* 311) deletes the first ἄν as a dittography and suggests σ. λέγεις ἄρα as B.'s rejoinder: simple, effective (συμφορά often = 'disaster' without adjectival qualification, LSJ s.v. II.2), but less pointed than the two previous conjectures.

6 τοῖς μὲν ἀγενείοις: those in their late teens, being no longer παῖδες but not yet ἄνδρες (the 17–20 age group apparently in those games – Panathenaea, Nemea, Pythia – which included separate events for ἀγένειοι, *IG* ii/iii².2311.38ff., 3125.17ff. = L. Moretti, *Iscrizioni agonistiche greche* (Rome 1953) no.22; cf. e.g. Pind. *Ol.* 8.54, 9.89 and Wilamowitz, *Pindaros* (Berlin 1922) 350 n. 2, Lysias 21.4; H. A. Harris, *Greek Athletes and Athletics* (London 1964) 154f.); juxtaposition of Pl. *Leg.* 8.833c and Xen. *Symp.* 4.17 suggests that this term and μειράκια were interchangeable in everyday use.

A's unmetrical and nonsensical σοι after τις was presumably a scribe's unconscious echo of the ending of v. 1 (Kaibel).

7–8 The ἤ in v. 8 (there is no need to suspect corruption with Hirschig, *Diss.* 40f., *Annot.* 14, and Meineke, *Anal. Crit.* 61) indicates that τὸν γόητα Θεόδοτον and τὸν παραμασύντην . . . τὸν ἀνόσιον are different individuals, but why then is Theodotus mentioned by name and the other only by profession? One cannot exclude a possibility that some real-life Theodotus of Alexis' generation who had attained celebrity was always accompanied by the same parasite, but no Theodotus is mentioned by other writers of or about the period (Kirchner, *PA* 1.440ff., 2.464 lists 41 Theodoti: 6771–808, 6773a, b, 6802a, none of any distinction in the second half of the 4th century; Collitz, *GDI* 2563–5 lists a Θεύδοτος Θευδότου Ἀθηναῖος as a comic χορευτής at the Delphic Soteria in the 270s). It seems far more likely that the duo mentioned in vv. 7–9 were characters in Alexis' Ταραντῖνοι. The accusations that (i) Theodotos was a fraud (for this meaning of γόης cf. especially Dem. 19.109, ἐπίστευσ᾽, ἐξηπατήθην, ἥμαρτον . . . τὸν δ᾽ ἄνθρωπον, ἄνδρες Ἀθηναῖοι, φυλάττεσθε· ἄπιστος, γόης, πονηρός; cf. W. Burkert, *Rh. Mus.* 105 (1962) 50f., H. Wankel, comm. (Heidelberg 1976) on Dem. 18.276) and (ii) the parasite was ἀνόσιος need not be taken as objective comments but rather as the angry and prejudiced outburst of (perhaps) the victim of a swindle engineered by them; thus Pyrrhias' description of Knemon as ἀνόσιος γέρων at Men. *Dysk.* 122f. is a rueful reaction to his recent experiences (but cf. *G and R* 22 (1975) 146 and 148). If Alexis' Theodotos had organised or participated in a deceitful stratagem, we should perhaps expect him to be a trickster slave or a *leno*, but names beginning with Theo- in later comedy are invariably given to free old men (Theodotus in Naevius' *Tunicularia* fr. 1, Theodoromedes in Plaut. *Capt.* 288, 635, 973, Theophilos in Men. fr. 286.2, Theotimos/-mus in Men. *Dis Ex.* 55f./Plaut. *Bacch.* 308, etc.,

COMMENTARY

Theopropides in Plaut. *Most.*), some of whom engage in trickery (e.g. Chairestratos in Men. *Asp.*) or carouse and wench (e.g. Demaenetus in Plaut. *Asin.*, Nicobulus and Philoxenus in *Bacch.*). A παραμασύντης portrayed in comedy as older than οἱ ἀγένειοι would be unusual (cf. Alexis 262(260K).2; Ribbeck, *Kolax* 41) but not unparalleled; Peniculus was over thirty (Plaut. *Men.* 446) and Saturio old enough to have a nubile daughter (*Pers.*, see E. Woytek's edition (Vienna 1982) p. 53 n. 271).

8 παραμασύντην: so A here; cf. Ephippus 8.6 (cited by Ath. 14.642e, where A's παρὰ μασυλτας was corrected to παραμασύντας by Casaubon, *Animadv.* 914) and Hesych. s.v. μασύντης· παράσιτος. All other formations in -ύντης/-υντής derive from verbs in -ύνω (e.g. εὐθυντής, λαμπρυντής, φαιδ(ρ)υντής; Buck–Petersen, *Reverse Index* 561), but (παρα-)μασύνω does not exist: only μασάομαι, from which παραμασήτης is correctly formed (Alexis 238(236K).2, Timocles 9.6). The -ύντης form is accordingly either a *vox nihili* to be eliminated as corrupt for -ήτης wherever it occurs (so first G. Dindorf in *TGL* s.v. παραμασήτης; cf. A. Nauck, *MGR* 6 (1894) 95), or a deliberate coinage (by popular analogy or creative wit making a point now lost; cf. Nesselrath, *MK* 309) against philological norms. The latter is more likely; it would be hard to account for corruption of H to YN independently in two MSS traditions.

9 βαυκιζόμενον: = τρυφερὸν καὶ ὡραϊστήν (Hesych. s.v.; Bekker, *Anecd.* 1.225.26), presumably because the person so described is performing a βαυκισμός, an Ionic (Hesych. s.v.) and effeminate (Σ Hom. *Il.* 22.391) dance; cf. Sittl, *Gebärden* 229. The adjective βαυκός, linked by Araros fr. 9 with μαλακός, τερπνός and τρυφερός, and defined as the last of these terms by *Et. Mag.* s.v. βαύκαλον, may have been a vulgar back-formation (*pace* Pollux 4.100, claiming that the dance took its name from one Baucus).

τὰ λευκά τ᾽ ἀναβάλλονθ᾽: emended by Jacobs, *Addit.* 93, from A's faultily divided τον αβαλλονθ, but first correctly explained by Hirschig (*Diss.* 41, *Annot.* 14). τὰ λευκά are the whites of the eyes, e.g. Hippocr. *Progn.* 2 = 1.80.12 Kühlewein, *Et. Mag.* s.v. λογάδες· ἐπὶ τῶν ὀφθαλμῶν, τὰ λευκά, cf. Alciphron fr. 5.4 τὸ κύκλῳ λευκόν; in full τὰ λευκὰ τῶν ὀφθαλμῶν/τοῖν ὀφθαλμοῖν/τῶν ὀμμάτων, e.g. Hippocr. *Epid.* 7.25, *Mul.* 1.7, *Steril.* 215 = 5.396, 8.32 and 416 Littré, Ath. 12.529a and Pollux 2.60, citing Ctesias, *FGrH* 688 F 1 p, α and γ. Thus (ἐπ-)ἀναβάλλειν τὰ λ. (τοῖν ὀφθαλμοῖν) is to roll the eyes until the whites are visible (Ctesias, Hippocr. *Mul.* 1.32 = 8.76 Littré); similarly ἀναβάλλειν τὰ ὄμματα [Arist.] *Probl.* 4.1, 876ª31f.

10 After ἥδιστον (A only) ACE give ἀναπήξαιμ᾽ ἂν αὐτὸν ἐπὶ τοῦ ξύλου λαβών, where ἥδιστον is meaningless (the adverb ἥδιστα is required), αὐτόν just tolerable (as a reference to the parasite with Theodotus now forgotten) and the rest of the quotation unmetrical. Jacobs (*Addit.* 94) changed the opening word to ἥδιστ᾽ ἂν and Dobree (*Adv.*

2.305) deleted ἂν αὐτόν, thus restoring sense and metre with palaeographic credibility (once ἥδιστ' ἂν had been misread as ἥδιστον, a scribe of linguistic soundness, metrical ignorance and no imagination might well add the needed ἂν after the verb and supply a singular object in line with the singulars of v. 9).

What is the punishment wished on the parasite (? and Theodotos) by the angry speaker? ἀναπήγνυμι normally means 'I transfix/impale' (e.g. Ar. *Eccl.* 843, Plut. *Artax.* 17.5 διὰ τριῶν σταυρῶν ἀναπῆξαι), and this led Herwerden (*Mnemosyne* 4 (1876) 299f.) to interpret a reference here to ἀνασκολόπισις. ξύλον, however, is not the normal word for 'impaling stake', and it is unlikely that Alexis would have used it in an unusual sense to denote an unattic penalty when the word was used in Athens for a variety of punishments. There τὸ ξύλον was basically a flat piece of wood (i.e. a σανίς), with or without holes, to which malefactors could be fastened in various ways: by nailing (προσπασσαλεύειν, for crucifixion: Hdt. 7.33, 9.120, both punishments inflicted by Athenians), binding (δεῖν: Ar. *Equ.* *367, *705, *Thesm.* 930ff. and Σ on 940, Plut. *Pericl.* 28.2) and muzzling (φιμοῦν, the neck: Ar. *Nub.* *592). The different verbs suited different types of ξύλον; binding was appropriate for stocks (= ἡ ποδοκάκκη), in which a malefactor's feet were secured (Lysias 10.16, Dem. 24.105), and muzzling for the pillory (= ὁ κύφων), where the neck was held (Cratinus fr. 123(115K) with the explanation of Pollux 10.177, Ar. *Nub.* *592, *Lys.* 68of.); feet, hands and head were all fixed in a πεντεσύριγγον ξύλον (Ar. *Equ* 1048f.). In Alexis here the use of ἀναπήξαιμ' and the general tone of anger suggest something more vicious than whipping in stocks or pillory: perhaps ἀποτυμπανισμός, where a criminal was executed by being fixed naked to an upright plank on which iron bands encircled ankles, wrists and neck (cf. A. D. Keramopoullos, Ὁ ἀποτυμπανισμός (Athens 1923), L. Gernet, *REG* 37.1924, 261ff., R. J. Bonner and G. Smith, *The Administration of Justice from Homer to Aristotle*, 2 (Chicago 1938) 279ff., D. M. MacDowell, *Athenian Homicide Law in the Age of the Orators* (Manchester 1963) 110ff.). In the asterisked passages above (cf. also Ar. *Ran.* 736) ξύλον appears with the article; thus there is no call to delete τοῦ in v. 10, as suggested first by Jacobs (in Schweighaeuser, *Animadv.* 2.425).

225 (223K)

Meineke 3.486 (v), Kock 2.379, Edmonds 2.482, Kassel–Austin 2.149. On the *hetaira* Nannion, see introduction to Ταραντῖνοι, especially pp. 625f. n. 2. Our main source of information is Ath., and especially the section of *Deipn.* from which this fr. derives (13.587a–c, citing Antiphanes – not the comic poet – περὶ Ἑταιρῶν, who says Προσκήνιον ... ἐπεκαλεῖτο ἡ Νάννιον, ὅτι πρόσωπόν τε ἀστεῖον εἶχε καὶ ἐχρῆτο χρυσίοις καὶ ἱματίοις πολυτελέσι, ἐκδῦσα δὲ ἦν αἰσχροτάτη; cf. also 558c citing Anaxilas 22.15ff., 567e–f citing Timocles 27(25K) and Amphis 23, Harpocration s.v.). This is the only place where an accusation of bibulousness – true or otherwise[1] (cf. introduction to Ὀρχηστρίς, comm. on fr. 172(167K).1–2 and H. G. Oeri, *Der Typ der komischen Alten in der griechischen Komödie* (Basle 1948) 43) – is laid against Nannion.

1–2 μαίνεται ἐπὶ τῷ Διονύσῳ: for the verbal play, by which Dionysus is two things at once: a person (with whom the *hetaira* is fancifully imagined to be in love) and a metonymy (cf. comm. on fr. 153(149K).16) for wine, cf. especially (serious) Eur. *Bacch.* 284f. οὗτος (Dionysus) θεοῖσι σπένδε-ται θεὸς γεγώς (with Dodds's comm.: the verb is passive, and the ambiguity possibly an echo of traditional religious belief); (comic) *Cycl.* 525ff. θεὸς δ' ἐν ἀσκῷ πῶς γέγηθ' οἴκους ἔχων; ... οὐ τοὺς θεοὺς χρὴ σῶμ' ἔχειν ἐν δέρμασιν, Xenarchus 9 μὰ τὸν Διόνυσον, ὃν σὺ λάπτεις ἴσον ἴσῳ, Plaut. *Stich.* 661 *fero conuiuam Dionysum,* 699f.; cf. also e.g. Philostratus *Epist.* 33, Julian *Epist.* 45.3 Hercher = 46 Hertlein = 4 Bidez, Heliod. 5.16.1. The equation is ambiguous when the god's name is either in the genitive (possessive or material? e.g. Eur. *IA* 1061 κρατῆρά τε Βάκχου, *Cycl.* 415 Διονύσου γάνος, Matron in Ath. 4.137a = 534.109 Lloyd-Jones–Parsons κρητὴρ δὲ Βρομίου, Plaut. *Curc.* 97a *Liberi lepos*) or adjectival (e.g. βάκχιος Ar. *Eccl.* 14, Antiphanes 234(237K).1, βρομιάς Antiphanes 55(52K).12, Βρόμιος Eur. *Cycl.* 63, Alexis 232(230K).3, 278(276K).1, 285(283K).2, Philodemus 23.4 Gow–Page = *Anth. Pal.* 11.44.4, εὔιος Men. *Dysk.* 946).

μαίνεται ἐπί (τῷ Διονύσῳ), 'is madly fond of', possibly a 4th-century extension (with ἐπί + causal dative, cf. Gow on Theoc. 13.49), first here in Greek, of earlier colloquial uses of μαίνομαι intransitive in Attic (e.g. Ar. *Ran.* 103, 751; ? with infinitive in Eur. *Cycl.* 164, ἐκπιεῖν γ' ἄν ... μαινοίμην L, but see Seaford *ad loc.*); cf. e.g. Theoc. 10.31, 20.34, Lucian *Dial. Meretr.* 12.2, Ach. Tat. 5.19.4, Xen. Eph. 1.4.6, and the parallel expressions ἔρως ... φρένας ἐξεφόβησεν Ἀργείῳ ἐπὶ παιδί Theoc. 13.48f., ἐπὶ τήνῳ πᾶσα καταίθομαι 2.40, τι ἔπαθον ἐπ' αὐτῷ Lucian *Dial. Meretr.* 10.2, τετηκυῖαν ἐπὶ σοί 12.1.

226 (224K)

Meineke 3.487(VII), Kock 2.380, Edmonds 2.482, Kassel–Austin 2.149. The Antiatticist (100.31 Bekker) cites Alexis here and Diphilus fr. 8

---

[1] Ath.'s words about this (Ἄλεξις ... κωμῳδῶν αὐτὴν ὡς μεθύουσαν: so Cobet in Peppink, *Observ.* 80 for A's μεθυσσαν, better than Musurus' μέθυσον) are wisely non-committal.

presumably to defend the shortened form κάθου in Attic (side by side with κάθησο) as second person singular present imperative of κάθημαι. He did not fight alone; cf. Σ Hom. *Il.* 2. 191a¹ κάθου Ἀττικῶς, a² οἱ Ἀττικοὶ κάθου λέγουσιν, Cramer, *Anecdota Graeca* 2.381.11 κάθου· Ἀττικῶς, Orus A 57 Alpers κάθου καὶ κάθησο, ἄμφω Ἑλληνικά (= Attic: Alpers p. 68); for the opposition e.g. Moeris 234 Pierson κάθησο, Ἀττικῶς· κάθου, κοινῶς. κάθου flourished in *Koine* Greek (e.g. LXX *Ps.* 109.1, N.T. *Ep. Jac.* 2.3, W. Bauer, *Griechisch–deutsches Wörterbuch zu den Schriften des Neuen Testaments*⁶ (revised K. and B. Aland, Berlin and New York 1988) s.v. κάθημαι), but in Attic was probably a colloquialism, confined so far to comedy (also Ar. fr. 631(620K), Anaxandrides 14(13K), Men. fr. 853, possibly *Dysk.* 931 with F. H. Sandbach *ad loc.* and *PCPS* 193 (1967) 38f.). Cf. O. Lautensach and J. Wackernagel in *Glotta* 9 (1918) 88 and 14 (1925) 56 respectively.

227 (225K)

Meineke 3.487 (VI), Kock 2.380, Edmonds 2.482, Kassel–Austin 2.149. When citing Alexis for what seems the first attested use of οἰκοδεσπότης, both Pollux (10.21 τὸ κοινότατον τουτὶ καὶ μᾶλλον τεθρυλημένον, τὸν οἰκοδεσπότην καὶ τὴν οἰκοδέσποιναν, οὐκ ἀποδέχομαι τοὔνομα) and Phrynichus (*Ecl.* p. 98 Fischer οἰκίας δεσπότης λεκτέον, οὐχ ὡς Ἄλεξις οἰκοδεσπότης, cf. Thom. Mag. p. 259.3 Ritschl) reject these and parallel (e.g. οἰκοδεσποτεῖν, -ποτικός) forms as non-Attic. οἰκίας(1)/οἴκου(2) δεσπότης(a)/δέσποινα(b) remained the accepted forms (e.g. 1a: Pl. *Leg.* 12.954b, Themistius *Or.* 11.150d, Heliodorus 5.1; 1b, Longus 3.25; 2a, Eur. *Alc.* 681, Xen. *Mem.* 2.1.32), but from the 3rd century the οἰκο-compounds became very common in literature (-δεσπότης e.g. in Plut. *Mor.* 271e, pleonastically οἰκοδ. τῆς οἰκίας N.T. *Ev. Luc.* 22.11; long lists in C. A. Lobeck, *Phrynichus* (Leipzig 1820) 373 and Bauer, s.v.; add now the 5th-century Mani codex = *P.Cologne* inv. 4780, p. 100.21f., A. Henrichs and L. Koenen, *ZPE* 44 (1981) 208f.) and everyday use (e.g. *SIG* 888.57f. = AD 238, *PSI* 158.80 = 3rd century AD, B. Boyaval, *ZPE* 17 (1975) p. 235, VII/VIII.31 = ? 4th century AD).

Τίτθη (or Τίτθαι)

T. B. L. Webster, *CQ* 2 (1952) 22, Hunter 209. Of the four frs. preserved under the title(s), one is cited grammatically in the singular (229(227K): Ath. 6.241b), two corruptly but apparently in the singular (228(226K): Ath. 10.426c τιθεῖ altered to Τιτθῇ by Schweighaeuser, *Animadv.* 5.381; and 230(228K): Stob. *Anth.* 4.50b.54 τιθῆς MA altered to Τιτθῆς by

Gaisford[1]), and one grammatically in the plural (231(229K): Antiatticist 85.14 Bekker). Such variations, which plague citations (see especially introduction to Ἀποκοπτόμενος), make a decision here for Τίτθη as Alexis' title probable rather than certain. Menander also wrote a Τίτθη (with a reference to a baby which the title figure presumably nursed and fed, fr. 396; speculations about its plot in T. Williams, *Hermes* 91 (1963) 287ff. and Webster, *IM* 193), from which Caecilius' *Titthe* (where the baby was the result of a rape or seduction at unidentified mysteries, fr. III Ribbeck) is perhaps more likely to have been adapted than from Alexis'. Eubulus wrote a Τίτθαι (or Τίτθη: frs. 109–11(110–12K) cited by Ath.7.311d, 3.106a, 15.685d–e with the title in the plural, 112(113K) by the Antiatticist 108.28 Bekker, contradictory again, in the singular).

In extant comedy the (wet-)nurse[2] plays a minor role from time to time, for instance as the slave-attendant of kidnapped children (Giddenis in Plaut. *Poen.* 83ff., 120ff.), identifying tokens (Ter. *HT* 614ff., *Eun.* 807f., 913ff.), helping at childbirth (*Ad.* 288ff.); in Men. *Sam.* the comments of Moschion's old nurse, now free but still working for Demeas, awaken suspicions about the baby in the house (236ff.). They seem generally to have enjoyed a bad stage-reputation (cf. Men. *Dysk.* 384ff.) for chattering (e.g. Men. *Sam.* 260f.), malicious gossip (e.g. Antiphanes 157(159K).4) and a tendency to indulge themselves – especially with alcohol – while starving their charges (Ar. *Equ.* 716ff., cf. Arist. *Rhet.* 3.4.3, 1407[a]6ff., Eubulus 80(80–2K), Men. fr. 454, Plaut. *Poen.* 28ff., Ter. *Hec.* 768f.); cf. H. Oeri, *Der Typ der komischen Alten in der griechischen Komödie* (Basle 1948) 53ff., M. Bieber, *The History of the Greek and Roman Theater*[2] (Princeton 1961) figs. 165, 185, H.-D. Blume, *Menanders "Samia"* (Darmstadt 1974) 105 n. 45, Hunter 209.

The frs. of Alexis' Τίτθη involve an old man or woman (230(228K)) and

---

[1] Although τίτθη is normally spelled correctly in MSS (but with accentuation oscillating between oxytone and paroxytone: the latter is endorsed by (?) Herodian 1.311.29f. Lentz) and inscriptions, instances with omission of the second tau (whether due to lazy articulation, confusion with τήθη, vulgar simplification of the τθ combination or carelessness) turn up at all periods: e.g. *IG* ii[2].12559 (before 350, cf. Threatte 1.545), Men. *Sam.* 85 (B, 3rd/4th century AD), com. adesp. fr. 272.16 Austin (τιθθας, 5th century AD), Hesych. s.v. τιθή ; cf. the MSS of Nonius, corrupting Caecilius' title to *Tite* at 483.4 (fr. 1 Ribbeck), *Tithae* 258.34 (II), *Tithe* 270.6 (VI).

[2] Ammonius *Diff.* 470 p. 122 Nickau distinguishes between τιτθή (*sic*) as ἡ μαστὸν παρέχουσα (cf. Choerob. *Orthogr.* 2.226.33f. Cramer) and τιθήνη/τροφός as the nurse who took over after weaning, but popular usage was less strict (thus a wet-nurse continued to be so labelled even after her charge had grown up: e.g. Men. *Sam.* 237, 258, 276).

a scene in which two men (228(226K): ? one possibly named Kriton: see comm. on vv. 1–2) prepare to carouse. If they and the nurse of the title were involved in the kind of intrigue associated with New Comedy, it must have been an early example. Fr. 229(227K) refers to Eucrates ὁ Κόρυδος and Blepaeus as living personalities. The former is a parasite who flourished in Athens c. 345–c. 305 (see introductions to Δημήτριος and fr. 48(47K)), and Blepaeus (whom Alexis calls wealthy, πλουτεῖ v. 3) can hardly be any other than the banker who made a loan to Mantitheus before 356 ([Dem.] 40.52), approached Demosthenes prior to the Meidias case of 347/6 (Dem. 21.215 and D. M. MacDowell (Oxford 1990) ad loc., A. Schaefer, *Demosthenes und seine Zeit* 3.2 (Leipzig 1858) 224) and acted as contractor for temple work at Eleusis c. 337/6 (*IG* ii².1675.32, cf. L. D. Caskey, *AJA* 9 (1905) 147ff.; Kirchner, *PA* 1.190 no. 2876 suggests persuasively that the contractor's father, Socles by name, was the banker named in Dem. 36.29). It is reasonable to suppose that Blepaeus' activities were confined to the earlier part of Corydus' career, and that Alexis' play dates to between c. 345 and c. 335 (cf. Webster, *CQ* 2 (1952) 22). Cf. also R. S. Stroud, *Hesperia* 41 (1972) 429f.

228 (226K)

Meineke 3.487 (1), Kock 2.380, Edmonds 2.482, Kassel–Austin 2.150. A brief extract from a conversation between two men, one a sobersides and the other a tippler, directly before a carousal (cf. introduction to Τίτθη). Like many short frs. in Ath. (here 10.426c, all fr. in A; ἐγχέωμεν (see on vv. 1–2) + v. 2 ἕνα to the end, Epit.) torn away from their original contexts (cf. e.g. comm. on 192–4(187–9K)), the text bristles with errors both petty and baffling, with at least one lacuna; partly because of these corruptions and partly because in its transfer from dramatic script to book of excerpts all dicola and paragraphi have been expunged, it is difficult to assign the various remarks to their original speakers.

1 ἰδού, πάρεστιν οἶνος: A's dittographic insertion of γὰρ before πάρεστιν, which ruins both metre and idiom (ἰδού is normally followed directly by an asyndetic statement, command or question: e.g. Ar. *Equ.* 87 ἰδού γ' ἄκρατον. περὶ πότου γοῦν ἐστί σοι: which incidentally shows that Blaydes' (*Adv.* 1.116) suggested change to ᾦνος in Alexis here is unnecessary), was removed by Musurus.

οἶνος: possibly followed by a change of speaker (so first Daléchamp), if the opening three words were uttered by the sobersides.

1–2 A's text οὐκοῦν ἐγχέω (ἐγχέωμεν CE) κρίτωνα πολὺ βέλτιον ἕνα καὶ τέτταρας) scans but does not make connected sense; even so, part of Alexis' original idea may be glimpsed. οὐκοῦν ἐγχέω is clearly (? part of) a question (cf. Denniston, *GP* 433ff.) by the tippler, 'Then am I to pour (the water: see comm. on fr. 116(111K).1) in (the wine)?' – with βέλτιον ἕνα καὶ τέτταρας (? part of) the sobersides' response (so first Schweighaeuser, *Animadv.* 5.382), 'Better one (part wine) and four (parts water).' For this exchange (and the tippler's succeeding remark, 'That's a watery (mixture) you're stipulating', v. 3) to be viable in the context, the tippler must have intended to pour a stronger mixture than the 'one and four' preferred by the sobersides, but it is difficult to achieve convincingly any expression of such an objective from A's corruptly transmitted text in the first metron of v. 2. Dobree (*Adv.* 2.326) conjectured οὐκοῦν ἐγχέω, Κρίτων, πολύν; as the whole of the tippler's question, thus identifying the sobersides as Kriton (cf. Diodorus com. 1, the addressee in a speech about drinking; an old man in Alciphron 3.28, like Crito in Ter. *Andr.* 796ff., cf. *Phorm.* 456ff., *HT* 498; recipient of a *hetaira*'s letter in Alciphron 4.15), but it is uncertain whether πολύν on its own (referring just to the wine) would imply clearly to an audience that the mixture was to be strong rather than merely copious. Kaibel (edition of Ath., vol. 3 p. x) made a brilliant attempt to solve that problem by suggesting οὐκοῦν ἐγχέω Τρίτωνα; for the question and πολὺ βέλτιον κ.τ.λ. for the answer; this would assume that Τρίτων was in use as a punning name for a mixture of one-third wine to two-thirds water (= ἕνα καὶ δύο, cf. Alcaeus z.22.4 Lobel–Page with D. L. Page, *Sappho and Alcaeus* (Oxford 1955) 308, and Anacreon 11a Page, *PMG*: a relatively strong mixture). Yet although the divine names Τρίτων and Τριτογένεια/-γενής (= Athena) were sometimes linked with τρεῖς and τρίτος by both ancient etymologisers (e.g. -ων Plut. *Mor.* 381f; -γένεια/ γενής Democritus 68 F 2 Diels–Kranz 2.132, *Suda* s.vv., *Et. Mag.* s.v. -γένεια, Harpocration s.v. τριτομηνίς, Choerob. 2.264.16ff. Cramer) and Aristophanes (symposiac pun at *Equ.* 1187ff., (ΑΛ.) ἔχε καὶ πιεῖν κεκρα-μένον τρία καὶ δύο. | (ΔΗ.) ὡς ἡδύς, ὦ Ζεῦ, καὶ τὰ τρία φέρων καλῶς. | (ΑΛ.) ἡ Τριτογενὴς γὰρ αὐτὸν ἐνετριτώνισεν, with Neil *ad loc.*; cf. also the pun on Οἰνόμαος and οἶνος at Nicochares 2(1K), with the comment by Ath. 10.426e), there is still no hard evidence that Τρίτων by itself was a nickname for a particular wine mixture. Neither Kaibel's nor Dobree's conjecture can be discounted, but it is also possible that the corruption here may conceal a lacuna (thus e.g. οὐκοῦν ἐγχέω, | Κρίτων; ἅ<λις σοί γ' ἴσον ἴσῳ κεκραμένον; | ΚΡ. ἄγαν> πολύν· βέλτιον . . ., cf. comm. on fr. 59(58K)).

2 ἕνα καὶ τέτταρας: elliptical phrases indicating the proportions of wine and water in the mixture are sometimes masculine as here (with κύαθον/-άθους something added, e.g. Men. fr. 2, Ion of Chios in Ath. 10.426c = *FHG* 2.50 fr. 14), but more often neuter (without any need to supply a noun such as μέρη: e.g. Ar. *Equ.* 1187, Cratinus 195(183K), Diocles 7(6K), Anaxilas 23, Ephippus 11.2). The proportion for wine is normally given first, but there are enough exceptions to this (e.g. Hes. *Op.* 596, Anacreon 11a Page, Ar. *Equ.* 1187ff., Anaxilas 23, Philetaerus 15(16K), Ath. 10.426e-f on Ameipsias 4, Eupolis 6(8K),

Hermippus 24(25K).4 and Nicochares 2(1K)) for unexplained expressions like τέτταρα καὶ δύο in Diocles 7(6K) to be ambiguous. The proportions suggested by Alexis' sobersides here are remarkably weak and probably a comic exaggeration; the most temperate drinkers seem to have opted for 1 measure of wine to 3 of water (ἀρχόντων τινῶν ... νοῦν ἐχόντων ἢ διαλεκτικῶν τὰς ὀφρῦς ἀνεσπακότων ... νηφάλιος καὶ ἀδρανὴς κρᾶσις Plut. *Mor.* 657c, cf. e.g. Hes. *Op.* 595f., Evenus 2 West = 6 Gow-Page = *Anth. Pal.* 11.49, Pollux 6.18, Hesych. s.v. ἆρ' οἴσει τρία;, Ath. 10.426e citing Ion) or 2 wine and 5 water (Ath. 426e ff., Hesych. s.v. τρία καὶ δύο). See especially Ath. 10.426b–427a, 430a–431b, 11.782a–b, Plut. *Mor.* 657b–e, Dar.–Sag. s.vv. *symposium* 1579A ff. (O. Navarre) and *vinum* 921A ff. (A. Jardé), Mau in *RE* s.v. *Comissatio* 612.17ff., Page, *Sappho and Alcaeus* 308; F. Lissarrague in O. Murray (ed.), *Sympotica* (Oxford 1990) 201ff.

3 ὑδαρῆ λέγεις: a natural rejoinder (cf. on v. 2 above; division of speakers before ὑδαρῆ first Daléchamp); for the form of the expression, see comm. on 223(221K).11–12. Comic applications of ὑδαρής (the standard Attic form:[1] e.g. A. *Ag.* 798, in addition to the passages cited below) to wine are regularly contemptuous (cf. Alexis 232(230K).2, Antiphanes 25(24K).4, Ephippus 11.2, Pherecrates 76(70K).2), but note also e.g. Xen. *Lac.* 1.3, Hippocr. *Reg. Acut.* 37, Arist. *GC* 1.5, 322ᵃ32, *HA* 7.12, 588ᵃ7, [Arist.] *Probl.* 3.3, 871ᵃ22, 18, 873ᵇ 24, 35.

3–5 After λέγεις in v. 3 interpretation and speech-assignments are uncertain, partly because of a lacuna of half a metron in the first half of v. 4 (A, Epit.) and a possible presence of further minor corruptions (4, A's καὶ διατριβήν τε corrected by Epit. to καὶ δ. γε; 5, A and Epit.'s active ποιῶμεν). Attempts to fill the lacuna so far (e.g. <κομψὸν> λ. τε κ. δ. γε Porson, *Adv.* 118, <πιθανὸν> λ. τε κ. δ. γε Dobree, *Adv.* 2.326, λέγε τι καλὸν σὺ δ. τε Herwerden, *Anal. Crit.* 42,γρῖφον or μῦθον λέγ' ἵνα κ. δ. γε Kock, λέγ' εἴ τι Kaibel with καὶ<νὸν> Wilamowitz, then δ. τε) seem unacceptable because they fail to provide the kind of sense demanded by the context and the speakers. Attempts at plausible restoration need to pay more attention to three things:

(i) there is nothing inherently objectionable or incomplete in the transmitted λέγε τι, provided it is rightly understood as an impatient command by the toper, 'talk sense' (cf. LSJ s.v. λέγω III.6, citing S. *Ant.* 757, *OT* 1475, Pl. *Crat.* 404a, Xen. *Mem.* 2.1.12);

---

[1] Its replacement by ὑδαρός in Byzantine Greek – note Hesych. s.v. ὑδαρές· τὸ ὑδαρόν and LSJ s.v. – has led to corruption of the acc. sing. form -αρῆ to -αρήν wherever it occurs in the *Marcianus* (e.g. 10.430e =

COMMENTARY

(ii) division and assignment of speeches require sensitivity to the different presentations of the tippler and the sobersides. Thus perhaps:
3 (A.) ὑδαρῆ λέγεις. (B: ? = Kriton). ὅμως δὲ ταύτην ἐκπιὼν –
4 (A.) <ὦ τᾶν or a name like Λάχης>, λέγε τι καὶ δ. γε . . .
The second and third metra of v. 3 seem more appropriate in sobersides' mouth (ταύτην = τὴν κύλικα, cf. Eustath. 1624.48ff. and Schweighaeuser, *Animadv.* 5.383), just as the opening of v. 4 better suits the tippler's brusqueness;

(iii) when a verb such as διατρίβω is replaced periphrastically by its verbal noun in the accusative (διατριβήν) + governing *uerbum faciendi*, the middle ποιοῦμαι is used more often than the active ποιῶ (LSJ s.v. ποιέω A.II.5, K.G. 1.106; cf. e.g. Lysias 16.11 τὰς διατριβὰς ποιούμενοι, Isaeus 11.37, Arist. *HA* 1.1, 487ᵃ19f., *Respir.* 474ᵇ26, Alciphron 3.29.2); thus in v. 5 here we might expect ποιώμεθ', not the transmitted -ῶμεν, if Alexis originally intended διατριβήν here to be the object of that verb. Yet Heliodorus 5.16 ὡς διατριβὴν τῷ πότῳ χόρειαν ἐστήσαντο should act as a warning that ποιῶμεν could still be retained for Alexis, if his sentence continued after that verb with a different object (e.g. ἀφροδίσια cf. Diphilus fr. 42(43K).22, σπονδάς cf. Men. fr. 239.2) to which διατριβήν . . . τῷ πότῳ was in apposition.

4 διατριβήν: comm. on fr. 222(219K).3–6 (ii.a).

229 (227K)

Meineke 3.487 (II), Kock 2.380, Edmonds 2.482, Kassel–Austin 2.150. The fr., cited by Ath. 6.241b (A, Epit.), comes from a conversation between two unidentified characters (so Jacobs, *Addit.* 148f., but part-assignments first combined with correct text in Meineke) about the parasite Corydus (see introductions to Τίτθη and Δημήτριος and comm. on fr. 48(47K)). If the lost preceding context contained an allusion to Corydus seeing or looking at (with the verb βλέπειν) somebody or something, the first speaker's claim (vv. 1–2) that Corydus wishes to be the banker Blepaeus (see introduction to Τίτθη) would gain in point by paronomasia, as would the second speaker's reply (vv. 2–3) by its diversion of that claim into a different but equally relevant direction.

1–2 ὁ τὰ γέλοι' εἰθισμένος λέγειν: see comm. on fr. 188(183K).2.

Βλεπαῖος βούλετ' εἶναι: Schweighaeuser's transposition (cf. *Animadv.* 3.416) of ACE's unmetrical B. εἶναι βούλεται (a *simplex ordo* corruption,

---

Pherecrates 76(70K).2, 430f = Ephippus 11.2, 431a = Alexis 232(230K).2.

652

juxtaposing predicate and infinitive, cf. W. Headlam, *CR* 16 (1902) 243ff.).

3 ὁ Βλεπαῖος: see comm. on fr. 89(86K).3.

230 (228K)

Meineke 3.488 (III), Kock 2.381, Edmonds 2.484, Kassel–Austin 2.150. In his discussion of verbal imagery Aristotle (*Poet.* 21, 1457ᵇ19ff.) illustrates a particular type of metaphor (καὶ ἐνίοτε προστιθέασιν ἀνθ' οὗ λέγει πρὸς ὅ ἐστι, 'correlative substitute') with the examples ἑσπέρα βίου and δυσμαὶ βίου (= τὸ γῆρας). The former doubtless had become a cliché[1] long before the time of Aristotle,[2] but strangely its only other recorded appearance in ancient Greek literature is the present line of Alexis, although the play on it in Macedonius' epigram (*Anth. Pal.* 5.233.5f.) τί δ' ἕσπερός ἐστι γυναικῶν; | γῆρας ἀμετρήτῳ πληθόμενον ῥυτίδι, implies its familiarity. δυσμαὶ βίου were associated with Epicharmus in a story of doubtful authenticity by Aelian (*VH* 2.34: *test.* 12 in Kaibel, *CGF*); cf. also A. *Ag.* 1123 and Fraenkel *ad loc.*, Pl. *Leg.* 6.770a, Ath. 13.592b quoting Hegesander, *FHG* 4.418 fr. 27). The analogous trope from autumn in the proverb τῶν γὰρ καλῶν καὶ τὸ μετόπωρον καλόν ἐστι (Plut. *Mor.* 177b) seems to derive from Euripides (Plut. *Mor.* 770c, *Alcib.* 1.3, Aelian *VH* 13.4).

---

[1] Its popularity in English-language literature (a sample of instances: 'my night of life', Shakespeare *Comedy of Errors* v.1.315; 'in life's cool evening', Pope *Imitations of Horace, Epistle 1.1.9*; 'the evening of my age', Nicholas Rowe *The Fair Penitent* IV.1; 'the chill, cloudy, and comfortless evening of life', Scott *The Antiquary* ch. XVI; 'the pleasant morning time of life; the hot, weary noon, the sad evening, the sunless night', C. Bronte *Shirley* ch. XXI; 'as the sun is falling in the heavens and the evening lights come on', Trollope *Ralph the Heir* ch. XI in relation to old age; 'two old codgers ... as they sat on the evening verandahs of their lives', Salman Rushdie *The Satanic Verses* (London 1988) p. 341) may have been increased by two influential texts which until recently many schoolboys and schoolgirls knew by heart: J. H. Newman's prayer, 'May He support us all the day long, till the shades lengthen, and the evening comes, and the busy world is hushed, and the fever of life is over, and our work is done'; and H. F. Lyte's hymn 'Abide with me, fast falls the eventide'.

[2] Aristotle *may* imply that this or a closely related metaphor was used by Empedocles (31 B 152 Diels–Kranz, *Vorsokr.* 1⁶.371), but neither text nor interpretation is certain at that point (24); see especially A. Gudeman, comm. (Berlin and Leipzig 1934) *ad loc.*, and E. B. England (Manchester 1921) on Pl. *Leg.* 6.770a.

COMMENTARY

231 (229K)

Meineke 3.488 (IV), Kock 2.381, Edmonds 2,484, Kassel–Austin 2.151. The MS of the Antiatticist (85.14 Bekker) has βαβαλίσαι· ἀντὶ τοῦ βαυκαλίσαι. Ἄλεξις Τιτθαῖς (on the title's number and accent see introduction to Τίτθη and n. 1). Bekker himself corrected the *uox nihili* βαβαλίσαι to βαυβα- (the frequent confusion in MSS between β and υ may be explained by similarity both of pronunciation in post-classical Greek and of letter-form in minuscule, cf. Cobet, *VL* 219, R. Browning, *Medieval and Modern Greek*² (Cambridge 1983) 26f.). The Antiatticist presumably defends βαυβαλίζω as Attic ('I lull to sleep'; here clearly relevant to the tasks of the nurse of the title, but not necessarily referring to her) against opponents who required βαυκαλίζω (cf. Hesych. s.v. βαυκαλι-ζόντων· τιθηνούντων, where the definition implies the nurse's task of lulling her charge to sleep); neither form is attested in surviving Attic or *Koine* literature, but συοβαύβαλος (= 'pig-sty') occurs in Cratinus 345(312K) (cf. Hesych. and Phot. s.v. -λοι), κατεβαυκάλισε in com. adesp. fr. 1030 Kock (3.581, from *Et. Mag.* 192.18) and βαυκαλισμός in the 5th-century AD Mani codex, *P.Cologne* inv. 4780, 103.1–2 (A. Henrichs and L. Koenen, *ZPE* 44 (1981) 210f. and 243 n. 330). Similarly βαυβᾶν ('to sleep': Ar. Byz. fr. 15A Slater, Herodian 2.461.7, 1.432.14 Lentz, Choerob. *Orthogr.* 2.218.31 Cramer, Hesych. s.v.) appears in Attic (Eur. fr. 694, tr. adesp. fr. 165, Cantharus fr. 3: all cited by the Antiatticist 85.10, with MS similarly corrupted to βαβᾶν, corr. Bekker) side by side with βαυκαλᾶν (defended as Attic by Moeris s.v.; a now obsolete Atticism in Lucian *Lex.* 11, but post-classical in e.g. Origen *Cels.* 6.34, 37, Aretaeus 4.11 p. 82.4 Hude, and [Crates of Thebes] *Epist.* 33 Hercher; and explained by Σ Orib. *inc.* 38.26 = 4.138 Raeder as τὸ κατακοιμίζειν τὴν τίτθην τὸ παιδίον μετ᾽ ᾠδῆς τινος, cf. Hesych. and *Suda* s.v.).

Τοκιστὴς ἢ Καταψευδόμενος

Schweighaeuser, *Animadv.* 9.24, Meineke 1.402, C. A. Dietze, *De Philemone comico* (Diss. Groningen 1901) 8off., Nesselrath, *LP* 448f., *MK* 315. Two frs. are cited from Alexis' Τοκιστὴς ἢ Καταψευδόμενος (232(230K), 234(232K): by Ath. 10.431a, 15.692f), two others simply from Καταψευδόμενος (233(231K), 235(233K): by Ath. 6.258e and *Suda* s.v. ἀνάριστος).[1] The reason for alternative titles (? a second production in a revised

---

[1] Two further frs. are cited from Alexis' Ψευδόμενος (261(259K), 262(260K) by Ath. 10.419b, 6.255b), which is better interpreted as a separate play (see pp. 729f.) despite Schweighaeuser's sugestion

version, a Hellenistic scholar's addition of Τοκιστής for clearer definition of a main character, or less plausibly perhaps an attempt to avoid confusion with dramatic homonyms such as Nicostratus' Τοκιστής, Menander's or Philemon's or Sosipater's Καταψευδόμενος, and Chaerion's Αὑτοῦ καταψευδόμενος in *IG* ii².2323 = iii B 3 Mette, col. 5a.22; cf. Plautus' *Faeneratrix*, Caecilius Statius' *Obolostates* or *Faenerator* (probably alternative names of the same play, see J. J. Scaliger, *Coniectanea in M. Terentium Varronem De Lingua Latina* (Paris 1565) 164, F. Ritschl, *Parerga zu Plautus und Terenz* (Berlin 1845) 157f. and Ribbeck, *CRF*³ 64ff.; cf. also the introduction to *Agonis*) is unclear, but their attachment to one and the same play rather implies a plot of New-Comedy type, with a money-lender playing a key but not necessarily large role (? advancing money for the purchase of a slave girl loved by an impoverished young hero: so Plaut. *Epid.* 620ff., *Most.* 532ff.) and a (probably different[1]) character concocting a stratagem based on a lie. The four surviving frs. would fit neatly into such a scenario. Fr. 233(231K) is spoken by a parasite (λέγοντά τινα κόλακα, Ath. 6.258e) who intends to enjoy himself ἐν τοῖς γάμοισιν (v. 3), where the celebration for the wedding (or -ings: see comm. *ad loc.*), if Alexis' play followed New-Comedy norms, would have formed the play's happy ending. Frs. 234(232K) (where the parasite is almost certainly the second speaker) and 232(230K) (where the part-division is uncertain but one or more unidentified males – the one probably foreign – and a girl named Tryphe are involved: see comm. *ad loc.*) may come from these or earlier celebrations. In fr. 235(233K) the speaker claims that he will be totally unable 'to survive a day like that' (διακαρτερῆσαι τηλικαύτην ἡμέραν) without lunch; this can hardly be anybody but the parasite (cf. Lucian *Par.* 49 οὐχὶ πρῶτον μὲν ὁ τοιοῦτος (sc. ὁ παράσιτος) ἀριστοποιησάμενος ἔξεισιν ἐπὶ τὴν παράταξιν; with Nesselrath, *LP* 448f., *MK* 315), and if the ordeal inferred from his words was that of mounting or assisting in the stratagem implied by the play's title, we have the elements of a plot that in several particulars could have approached that of Plautus' *Curculio*, where the title figure was a gluttonous (313, 316ff., 366ff., 384ff., 66of.) parasite who organised and carried through the ruse which enabled Phaedromus to secure from a pimp the girl he loved. The ruse involved Curculio in forging a letter ostensibly from Therapontigonus, a soldier and Phaedromus' rival for the girl's affections, and affixing to it a seal stamped

---

(*Animadv.* 9.24: cf. Meineke 1.402) that in those two places of Ath. Ψευδο- might be corrupted from Καταψευδο-.

[1] Different, because money-lenders were loathed, not heroised, for their dishonesty in 4th-century Athens (e.g. Pl. *Alc. 2.* 149e ὑπὸ δώρων παράγεσθαι οἷον κακὸν τοκιστήν, Arist. *EN.* 4.1.40, 1121ᵇ34) and on the comic stage (Plaut. *Most.* 626 *danista . . . genus quod improbissimum est*).

with the soldier's ring which Curculio had stolen. The letter authorised Curculio as Therapontigonus' agent to pay for the girl with money previously deposited with a banker. In carrying through the stratagem the parasite was clearly 'lying against' the soldier (καταψευδόμενος + genitive, the common construction: LSJ s.v. -ομαι, cf. also e.g. Chariton 4.6.9, Ach. Tat. 8.5.3). The stolen ring finally proved that the girl was Therapontigonus' lost sister, and so (being free) she was able to marry Phaedromus at the end of the play (728).[1]

The date (? -s) of Alexis' play, and any possible relationship to its Greek homonyms, are unknown.

232 (230K)

Meineke 3.488 (1), Kock 2.381, Edmonds 2.484, Kassel–Austin 2.151; cf. Gomme–Sandbach, *Comm.* p. 631. The fr., cited by Ath. 10.431a (all in A, only v. 4 δίκαιον to the end in Epit.) to illustrate the wine mixture ἴσον ἴσῳ (v.2 and comm.), comes from a scene of revelry (a possible scenario is suggested in the introduction to Τοκιστής), but appreciation of its vigour and character-presentation is seriously marred by uncertainty about part-division and identity of speakers. Editors now generally assign vv. 1–2 to one male reveller (but there is doubt whether he or Tryphe speaks the final word of v. 2), v. 3 to a second (so first Schweighaeuser; probably non-Athenian, see comm. on vv. 4–5), Θάσιος in v. 4 to Tryphe

---

[1] The Greek author adapted in Plautus' *Curculio* is unknown, although many suggestions have been made (including Alexis: Dietze 8off., noting some of the similarities between Τοκιστής and *Curculio*; Diphilus, F. Marx's edition of Plaut. *Rud.* (Leipzig 1928) pp. 306f.; Menander, G. Capovilla, *Menandro* (Milan 1924) 68f., 297, Webster, *SLGC*[1] 196ff. = [2] 217ff., cf. C. Questa, *Dioniso* 39 (1965) 244f., but opposed by E. Fantham, *CQ* 15 (1965) 100; Philippides, G. W. Elderkin, *AJA* 33 (1934) 29ff.; Posidippus, O. Ribbeck, *Geschichte der römischen Dichtung* 1 (Stuttgart 1887) 125, F. Groh, *Listy filolog.* 19 (1892) 13, cf. P. Grimal in R. Chevallier (ed.), *Mélanges d'archéologie et d'histoire offerts à André Piganiol* 3 (Paris 1966) 1731ff. See also Enk, *Handboek* 2.1.28off. and G. Monaco's edition of *Curc.* (Palermo 1969) pp. 7ff.). The case for Alexis is as doubtful as that for any Greek comic poet. Structural and other parallels between Plaut. *Curc.* and *Poen.* were already noted by Dietze, cf. now especially O. Zwierlein, *Zur Kritik und Exegese des Plautus, I: Poenulus und Curculio, Abh.* Mainz (1990). Yet Alexis' Τοκιστής is unlikely to have been *Curc.*'s model; there are no verbal ties between the Greek frs. and the Plautine text, and the function of Lyco the banker in *Curc.* is not to act as money-lender but simply to pass money deposited with him by the soldier over to the pimp.

(so Dobree, *Adv.* 2.326 and Meineke, *Men. et Phil.* 154 independently) and the rest of the fr. to the second (so Meineke) reveller. Other distributions, however, are feasible. If Tryphe (? as a *hetaira*: on her identity see below) was orchestrating the revels (e.g. like the Bacchis sisters at Plaut. *Bacch.* 1149ff., or Stephanium at *Stich.* 673ff.), she could have given the instructions in vv. 1–2 (so Edmonds, but dividing the parts with Kaibel before καλῶς, not after), with one male reveller responding in vv. 3 and 4–5 (from ὅμοιον). In that event, however, αὐτῷ (v.1) would be harder to explain: as the recipient of the drink being poured in vv. 1–2, he is then presumably the person who gives his approval in v. 3, and this would fit more snugly into a context where Tryphe received, but did not give, the order expressed in vv. 1–2. Cf. also comm. on 234(232K).2.

1 αὐτῷ: see above.

2 ὑδαρῆ: so the Bedrotus edition (A -ην): see comm. on fr. 228(226K).3 and Τίτθη, p. 651 n. 1.

κατανοεῖς;: parenthetical, like μανθάνεις; (fr. 98(152K).3, 129(124K).15) and συνιεῖς; (129(124K).6).

ἴσον ἴσῳ μικροῦ: if the text here is transmitted correctly, presumably 'about an equal <amount of wine mixed> with an equal <amount of water>'. On the expression ἴσον ἴσῳ, see comm. on fr. 59(58K).2. Nowhere else is it qualified with μικροῦ (hence Blaydes' conjecture μίγνυ, *Adv.* 1.116, before W. Morel, *Rh. Mus.* 77 (1928) 168; but normally in later comedy the verb used for mixing wine and water is κεράννυμι, e.g. Antiphanes 137(139K) κέρασον εὐζωρέστερον, Alexis 9.5, 59(58K), 169(164K), 246(244K).4, Men. *Her.* fr. 4 Gomme–Sandbach, *Sam.* 673, with μ<ε>ίγνυμι substituted for it only in the dithyrambic extravaganza of Men. *Dysk.* 946f.), but although the most common use of μικροῦ (later comedy, prose from 4th century onward) and ὀλίγου (poetry and prose, older comedy) in the sense of 'almost' (the genitive explained as elliptical for μ./ὀλ. δεῖν: LSJ s.vv. μικρός III.2, ὀλίγος IV.1) is to qualify verbs in the indicative (aorist e.g. Hom. *Od.* 14.37, Lysias 14.17, Xen. *Cyr.* 1.4.8 (earliest record of μ.), Dem. 18.151, Ar. *Ach.* 348, 381, *Vesp.* 829, *Thesm.* 935, Alexis 107(102K).2, Men. fr. 688, K.G. 1.204; perfect Ar. *Nub.* 722, Men. *Dysk.* 438, 669, 681, cf. Dem. 19.334; imperfect *Dysk.* 687f.), both forms occasionally qualify nouns and adjectives expressing quantity (e.g. Thuc. 4.124 ὀλ. ἐς χιλίους, Pl. *Apol.* 22b ὀλ. αὐτῶν ἅπαντες οἱ παρόντες, *Protag.* 361b ὀλ. πάντα, Men. fr. 264.6 μ. ταλάντου = 'costing nearly a talent').

καλῶς: clearly an approving comment (after the order to serve the drink has been carried out), voiced possibly by the speaker of v. 1 and the rest of v. 2 (= 'Splendid!'; cf. Men. fr. 257 ἐπίθες τὸ πῦρ, ἡ ζάκορος· οὑτωσὶ καλῶς, if that whole verse belongs to one speaker, and *Kol.* fr. 1.2f. σπονδή. φέρ', ὦ παῖ Σωσία· σπονδή. καλῶς | ἔχει), but more plausibly

657

assigned to a new speaker (so Kaibel, though wrongly introducing Tryphe here for just one word; better Edmonds, with καλῶς and v. 3 all given to one speaker), signifying ('Thank you!') and then explaining his approval ('Yes, it's nice, the drink'); cf. especially Ar. *Equ.* 23 πάνυ κ., *Nub.* 848 κ. γε, *Ran.* 512 πάνυ κ., after an order has been obeyed. See comm. on fr. 116(111K).4.

3 ποδαπὸς ('from what country?'): so Dindorf for A's ποταπὸς, but see comm. on fr. 94(90K).1.

ὁ Βρόμιος: facetious metonymy for 'wine', as also in frs. 278(276K).1, 285(283K).2; see comm. on fr. 225(223K).2.

Τρύφη: Meineke first recognised that A's unaccented τρυφη was a woman's name. In real life it was borne by a member of a θίασος in the Piraeus (*IG* ii².2357, 3rd/2nd century: as a *hetaira*? so Gomme–Sandbach, *Comm.* p. 631), in literature by slaves (Men. *Sam.* fr. 1: a doubtful attribution) and menials (a saucy rustic with upper-class lover: Aelian *Epist.* 11, 12), cf. Müller-Graupa in *RE* s.v. 2, 714.65ff, and in later Hellenistic art by the personification of Luxury, dressed as a young courtesan (Antioch: D. Levi, *Antioch Mosaic Pavements* (Princeton 1947) 206, 224, 254; Emesa, now in Toronto: N. Leipen, *Archaeology* 22 (1969) 231, cf. G. Downey, *TAPA* 69 (1938) 360 and the editorial entry s.v. *Tryphe* in *Enciclopedia dell'arte antica, suppl.* (Rome 1970) 872a).[1] In Alexis' Τοκιστής Tryphe could have been a minor slave girl or e.g. major *hetaira* (with foreign or military lover: so Sandbach, with a possible but risky interpretation of vv. 4–5, but that would rule her out of the marriage in fr. 233(231K).3). Tryphera similarly is a *hetaira*'s name in Asclepiades 26.6 and possibly Meleager 63 (*Anth. Pal.* 5.185, 154), but a beautiful and virtuous young wife of the 3rd/4th century AD in *IG* ii/iii².12828 = W. Peek, *Versinschriften* (Berlin 1955) no. 746.8.

4 Θάσιος: cf. also Alexis 277(275K).1. The wine of Thasos was highly praised in antiquity (Ath. 1.28d–29e, 31a–b, f–32a, citing notably Antidotus fr. 4 and Archestratus fr. 190.15f. Lloyd-Jones–Parsons Θάσιος πίνειν γενναῖος ἐὰν ᾖ | πολλαῖς πρεσβεύων ἐτέων περικαλλέσιν ὥραις; Ar. *Lys.* 196, Men. *Kol.* 48, Machon 266 and Gow *ad loc.*; second only to Chios, Hermippus 77(82K).3ff.); it was dark red (Ar. fr. 364(350K)), its fine bouquet (Ar. *Lys.* 206, *Eccl.* 1118f., *Plut.* 1021, cf. Clem. Alex. *Paed.* 2.2.30) suggested apples (Hermippus), and its sweetness was increased by the

---

[1] It has been suggested (first by Leo, *Plaut. Forsch.*² 202; cf. also Stoessl in *RE* s.v. *Prologos* (23.2 *Nachtrag*) 2401.48ff., E. Fantham, *Hermes* 105 (1977) 408 n. 10) that the prologue-figure Luxuria in Plaut. *Trin.* was taken over from the Philemon original and there called Tryphe.

insertion of dough kneaded with honey into the jars (Theophr. *Odor.* 51); cf. F. Salviat, *BCH Suppl.* 13 (1986) 145ff. with full source material at times inaccurately cited, and M. Brunet in M.-C. Amouretti and J.-P. Brun (edd.), *La Production du vin et d'huile en Méditerranée* (*BCH Suppl.* 26, 1993) 201f. The island imposed strict laws regulating sale and export (G. Daux, *BCH* 50 (1926) 214, von Hiller von Gärtringen in *RE* s.v. *Thasos* 1, 1317.48ff., J. Pouilloux, *Recherches sur l'histoire et les cultes de Thasos* 1 (Paris 1954) 130f.).

4–5 ὅμοιον καὶ δίκαιον τοὺς ξένους πίνειν ξενικόν: Dobree (*Adv.* 2.326), followed by e.g. Meineke, Kock (text), Wilamowitz (*Schiedsg.* 110), Fraenkel (on A. *Ag.* 1239) and Kassel–Austin, punctuates with a stop after ὅμοιον (proparoxytone: cf. K.B. 1.326f., Schwyzer 1.383), taking it as a one-word response in the sense of 'All one', i.e. 'I have no objection'; Eur. *Suppl.* 1068f. (Ιφ.) ἀλλ' οὐδέ τοι σοὶ πείσομαι δρώσῃ τάδε. | (Ευ.) ὁμοῖον, would provide the perfect parallel, and for the meaning of ὅμ. cf. also e.g. A. *Ag.* 1239, 1403f. σὺ δ' αἰνεῖν εἴτε με ψέγειν θέλεις, | ὁμοῖον, Hdt. 8.80, possibly Men. *Epitr.* 1088 and Sandbach *ad loc.* Yet such an interpretation here seems less in keeping either with the presentation of the speaker, who elsewhere in the fr. is an interested and approving, not an indifferent or surly, toper, or with the quality of the wine being served. Hence I prefer (with Kaibel and O. Crusius, *Philologus* 46 (1888) 621f., cf. Edmonds) punctuation with no stop between ὅμ. and καί, translating 'It's reasonable and right for foreigners (or 'guests': see below) to drink foreign wine', cf. e.g. Men. fr. 153.4 καὶ τοῦθ' (sc. the make-up of a chorus) ὁμοίως πως ἔχει. It is doubtful whether ὅμ. on its own in this sense could govern an infinitive, but δίκαιον in the neuter commonly does (e.g. *P.V.* 611, Hdt. 1.39*, Men. *Dysk.* 293ff.*, elliptically *Asp.* 168f.: * = acc. and inf.), and the coupling effectively removes any suspicion of syntactical anomaly. For the collocation cf. e.g. Call. fr. 433 Pfeiffer ὅδε ὁ νόμος ἴσος ἐγράφη καὶ ὅμοιος.

τοὺς ξένους … ξενικόν: if τοὺς ξένους is intended to mean 'foreigners' here, as seems most likely (ξένος = 'foreigner/stranger' most commonly in unambiguous and unbroken passages of comedy), the speaker by implication will be non-Athenian at a party where the other person or persons present (τοὺς ἐγγενεῖς: the plural could be generalising) is/are Athenian. It is, however, just possible that Alexis is playing on the different meanings of ξένος (foreigner, guest/host), with only the wine 'foreign' (cf. Alexis 292(290K).1, Diphilus 31(32K).27: being from Thasos), and the speaker just a 'guest' (hardly here the 'host', for it is the fr.'s first speaker who gives the orders and so is likely to be the host). So long as this possibility exists, conjectures about the nationality of the present speaker (and its implications for the plot) are unwise.

COMMENTARY

233 (231K)

Meineke 3.489 (II), Kock 2.381, Edmonds 2.484, Kassel–Austin 2.152. The speaker, identified by Ath. 6.258e when citing the fr. (all in A, but Epit. omits καὶ τὴν Ἀθ. in v. 2; cf. Eustath. 1598.31, εὐδ. ἐγώ, οὐχ ὅτι – end of v. 4, and O. Kaehler, *Woch. Klass. Phil.* 2 (1885) 903f.) as a κόλαξ (cf. Παράσιτος, p. 544 n. 1), looks forward to attending a wedding feast. His speech is probably a monologue (see on v. 5).

1–2 μὰ τὸν Δία τὸν Ὀλύμπιον καὶ τὴν Ἀθηνᾶν, οὐχ ὅτι: the same two deities are coupled (in the same *sedes*, by metrical constraints) in oaths at Men. frs. 87 and 333.13f., and com. adesp. fr. 239.21f. Austin (often wrongly attributed to Alexis, see 'False or Doubtful Attributions' V). In normal Attic usage μά (when not coupled with ναί or οὐ) + acc. (1) implies or reinforces a negative response to a preceding question, or (2) reinforces (i) an immediately preceding (cf. e.g. Alexis 63(62K).4 with comm.) or (ii) following negative statement: see especially J. Werres, *Die Beteuerungsformeln in der attischen Komödie* (Diss. Bonn 1936) 4f., W. S. Barrett on Eur. *Hipp.* 306ff. (usefully correcting LSJ s.v. III.1.a and K.G. 2.148), K. J. Dover, *CQ* 35 (1985) 328ff. In many examples of (2.ii), as here, the oath is immediately followed by the negative (e.g. Eur. *Med.* 1059f., Ar. *Ran.* 508f., Men. *Asp.* 306f., *Dysk.* 666ff., *Mis.* 314f., *Sam.* 283, 306f., 668), but occasionally is separated by a few emphatic words (e.g. *Dysk.* 459f.) or even a parenthesis (e.g. *Dysk.* 718ff.). The comic papyri in particular now provide such a plethora of parallels as to show that earlier attempts by scholars (such as S. A. Naber on the present passage, *Mnemosyne* 8 (1880) 264) to replace μά by νή in the circumstances outlined above actually contravene Attic idiom. In later Greek μά came to be used (like ναὶ μά) affirmatively (cf. LSJ s.v. III.2); whether Men. *Dysk.* 151f. is an early example, or B's μά there is a copyist's modernising adjustment, remains uncertain (cf. Handley and Sandbach *ad loc.* and on *Dysk.* 639).

3 ἐν τοῖς γάμοισιν: one or more marriages, to close the play? Since comedy followed the normal Greek habit (cf. LSJ s.v. γάμος) of using both singular and plural indiscriminately for the same single wedding (e.g. Ar. *Av.* 1724 -ος ~ -οι 1689, 1740, 1755, Men. *Sam.* 64, 220 -ος ~ *Sam.* 71, 211 -οι), the odds favour just one, but how (or if) Tryphe and the presumed foreigner of fr. 232(230K) were involved remains a mystery.

ἄνδρες: probably, but not certainly in the absence of further context (cf. Bain, *Actors* 190 n. 4), addressed to the audience in a monologue (cf. comm. on 63(62K).7).

4 διαρραγήσομ': 'I shall burst' (sc. through over-eating). The word which conveys the παρὰ προσδοκίαν joke is delayed for maximum effect until late in its sentence, as elsewhere (cf. comm. on 168(163K).7, 236(234K).6). For the use of διαρρήγνυμαι in this sense cf. (in addition to the passages cited by LSJ s.v. -υμι and Alexis here) Men. fr. 353.2, Lucian *Hist. Conscr.* 20. It implies for a parasite the happiest of deaths while engaged in the activity he enjoys most, cf. Lucian *Paras.* 57 παρασίτου δὲ θάνατον ... εὐδαιμονέστατον φαγόντος καὶ πιόντος with Nesselrath, *LP* 484f., Men. fr. 23.

ἂν θεὸς θέλῃ: also e.g. Eur. *El.* 638, *Antiope* 10.43 Page = fr. xlviii.46 Kambitsis (Athens 1972), Ar. *Pax* 1187, *Plut.* 347, 1188, Men. fr. 39 ('*saepius trimetros uel tetrametros claudit*', A. Körte); alternatively ἦν/ ἂν (οἱ) θεοὶ θέλωσι, Ar. *Plut.* 405, Alexis 249(247K).1, Men. *Georg.* 44f., cf. S. *OR* 280f.; εἰ θεὸς θέλοι, Ar. *Ran.* 533; θεοῦ θέλοντος, Eur. *Suppl.* 499, fr. 397 = monost. 349 Jäkel. These expressions, like the Moslem's *in sha'llah* in Arabic, are largely a convention, implying a popular belief that the course of events was – or could be – directed by the gods; cf. Dover, *GPM* 133ff.

5 τούτου ... τοῦ θανάτου τυχεῖν: cf. e.g. Xen. *Apol.* 32 τῶν δὲ θανάτων τοῦ ῥᾴστου ἔτυχεν, Pl. *Tim.* 41b οὐδὲ τεύξεσθε θανάτου μοίρας, S. *Ant.* 465 τοῦδε τοῦ μόρου τυχεῖν, Eur. *Alc.* 523, *Hec.* 773.

μοι γένοιτο: cf. comm. on fr. 112(107K).3–4.

234 (232K)

Meineke 3.489 (III), Kock 2.382, Edmonds 2.484, Kassel–Austin 2.152. Cited by Ath. 15.692f (A: omitted by Epit.; part-division by Schweighaeuser, cf. *Animadv.* 8.237), this fr. in all probability comes from the same drinking-party (? and scene) as fr. 232(230K), with the same characters involved (see on v. 2), but slightly earlier (so Kock, rightly; the toast to Zeus the Saviour (234(232K).1–2) was drunk in unmixed wine directly after the meal had ended, before further wine was mixed (232(230K).1–2) and drunk in the carousal, cf. e.g. Philochorus in Ath. 2.38c, 15.693d–e = *FHG* 1.387). The man who makes the witty and irreverent (cf. Gil 335f.) comment on bursting (v.4) is most likely to be the parasite who used the same word of himself in fr. 233(231K).

1–2 ἀλλ' ... Διός γε τήνδε Σωτῆρος: if this combination of particles is correct (and it is hard to see from what it could have been corrupted; for γε Dobree, *Adv.* 2.353 suggested σύ, Cobet, *NL* 121 ἔτι, both implausible palaeographically), it implies that speaker (A.) is trying to cajole a (B.) reluctant to take part in the drinking-bout (in that case less likely to be a parasite!) with 'Well, at least pour him the toast to Zeus the Saviour' (cf. Denniston, *GP* 119). For τήνδε without noun expressed, see comm. on frs. 116(111K).1 and 59(58K), for the 'genitive of the toast' comm. on 59(58K). 'Custom prescribed that at a banquet libation should be made from the first mixing-bowl to Zeus *Olympios* and the Olympians, from the second to the Heroës, from the third to Zeus *Soter*, otherwise styled *Teleios*' (A. B. Cook, *Zeus* 2 (Cambridge 1925) 1123, with abundant references

COMMENTARY

from ancient literature (cf. e.g. in comedy Antiphanes 3(4K).2, cf. 163(165K).3; Diphilus 70(69K), Eriphus 4, Eubulus 56.7, Xenarchus 2.4f.; cf. Alexis 272(270K).5), scholia and lexica); see also Höfer in Roscher s.v. *Soter* 1262.53ff., H. Sjövall, *Zeus im altgriechischen Hauskult* (Lund 1931) 85ff., M. P. Nilsson in A. Nelson (ed.), *Symbolae philologicae O. A. Danielsson octogenario dicatae* (Uppsala 1932) 227ff., Dornseiff in *RE* s.v. Σωτήρ 1212.26ff., Fraenkel on A. *Ag.* 1387, H. Schwabl in *RE Suppl.* 15 s.v. *Zeus* 1056.56ff.).

2 αὐτῷ: if 'he' is identical with the αὐτῷ of fr. 232(230K).1, here also the command could be addressed by the first speaker of 232(230K).1 to Tryphe.

3 χρησιμωτάτου: Meineke's correction of A's -ώτατον. Confusion in MSS between -ου and -ον is not uncommon, but explicable more often by assimilation to the case or ending of a neighbouring word (e.g. Eur. *Hipp.* 338 ταῦρον O, *Ion* 1227 Φοῖβον L) than by a presumed misreading of minuscule υ (as here) or ν (e.g. Pl. *Resp.* 3.396d ἑαυτοῦ A for -ὸν). Alexis may have chosen the adjective here partly because in general Zeus ἐν ... νόσοις καὶ πᾶσι καιροῖς βοηθῶν Σωτὴρ (κέκληται), Aristides 43.30 Keil, cf. also e.g. *SIG* 985.61ff. of the 2nd/1st century, but partly too because this third toast to him was proverbially associated with good luck (e.g. Pl. *Charm.* 167a, *Phileb.* 66d, *Epist.* 7.340a, cf. 334d; Höfer and Schwabl, *opp. citt.* on vv. 1–2, 1263.52ff. and 1056.41ff. respectively).

4 ἂν ἐγὼ διαρραγῶ: cf. comm. on frs. 48(47K).4, 233(231K).4. At 233(231K).4 the parasite looked forward to bursting; here either he is less sanguine or another character is speaking.

5 A's corruptions to μο ν ησ ει (*sic*) and πειθει were emended first by J. Pierson (edition of Moeris (Leiden 1759) 72) and Canter, *Nov. Lect.* 167 respectively. Cf. e.g. Eur. *Andr.* 161 κοὐδέν σ' ὀνήσει, Pl. *Resp.* 4.426b οὐδὲ ἄλλο τῶν τοιούτων (αὐτὸν) οὐδὲν ὀνήσει.

235 (233K)

Meineke 3.489 (IV), Kock 2.382, Edmonds 2.484, Kassel–Austin 2.153. Context and speaker (? a parasite typically needing lunch before being able to engage in some stressful, difficult or laborious activity) are discussed in the introduction to Τοκιστής.

1 πάντως does not qualify ἀναρίστητος (*pace* LSJ s.v. 1) but, as commonly from Homer onwards (e.g. *Il.* 8.450f., *Od.* 19.91, *P.V.* 333, Eur. *Hipp.* 1062, Ar. *Ach.* 956, *Pax* 1194, *Eccl.* 704, Pl. *Gorg.* 497b), at a clause's opening emphasises a following negative, although the degree of emphasis may vary from 'not at all' to 'not entirely' according to context, speaker and tone (cf. K. J. Dover's parallel comment on the use of οὐ + πάνυ, *CQ*

35 (1985) 332f.): here 'I'll not *at all* be able to endure a day as important as this right to the end without having lunch.'

ἀναρίστητος: the fr. is cited by the *Suda* s.v. ἀνάριστος (along with Ar. fr. 470(454K), Antiphanes 139(141K), Timocles 26(24K); also without the author's name Polyb. 3.71.10) for the preferability of the -ητος form to ἀνάριστος (for which Men. fr. 821 is cited). Photius s.v. (b = p. 120.10 R. Reitzenstein (Leipzig and Berlin 1907), z = p. 165 Chr. Theodoridis (Berlin and New York 1982) α 1632) has an abbreviated version of the entry (naming but not quoting Alexis); cf. also Ath. 2.47e (citing Eupolis: ? fr. 77(68K).1), *Et. Sym.* in T. Gaisford's edition (Oxford 1848) of *Et. Mag.* 266D. ἀνάριστος was rejected presumably because it was Ionic (x 8 Hippocr., including *Reg. Acut.* 32, *Vict.* 3.70) and *Koine* (e.g. Polyb. 3.71.10, Theoc. 15.147; Bruhn, *Wortschatz* 39, Durham, *Vocabulary* 42), although Xenophon used it (x 6, including *Anab.* 1.10.19, *Hell.* 4.5.8).

2 διακαρτερῆσαι: 'to endure to the end' rightly LSJ, transitive here and at Polyb. 36.16.4 καὶ τὴν ἐπὶ τῶν ἱππικῶν κακοπάθειαν ἡμέραν καὶ νύκτα συνεχῶς διακαρτερῶν οὐδὲν ἔπασχεν, but more commonly either intransitive (but often then with an expression of time as accusative of extent, e.g. Plut. *Mor.* 770f ἡμέρας τρεῖς καὶ νύκτας ἄσιτος διεκαρτέρησε, *Crass.* 30) or with participle (e.g. Xen. *Hell.* 7.4.8, Plut. *Mor.* 239d, *Arat.* 22).

Τραυματίας

Meineke 1.519ff.; cf. Schweighaeuser, *Animadv.* 7.31, Fraenkel, *MNC* 86, A. Spies, *Militat omnis amans* (Diss. Tübingen 1930) 32, C. A. P. Ruck, *IG II² 2323: The list of the Victors in Comedies at the Dionysia* (Leiden 1967) 51f. In Alexis' time τραυματίας seems always to have denoted a soldier or sailor wounded on war service (e.g. Hdt. 3.79, Thuc. 7.75, 8.27, Theophr. *Char.* 25; cf. the metaphorical use in Pindar fr. 223 Schroeder/Snell–Maehler = 210 Bowra), and such a figure must have been the eponymous hero of the three comedies known to have borne this title: besides Alexis', an undatable play by Antiphanes with two frs. (205(207K) drinking-party, 206(208K) description of a doctor's surgery!) and one by Philocles that won first prize at the Dionysia of 154 (*IG* ii².2323.234, Ruck 16, Pickard-Cambridge, *DFA*² 111, Mette III B 3 col. 5a.20; on the date cf. B. D. Meritt, *Historia* 26 (1977) 183) with no frs. preserved. From Alexis' Τραυματίας we have one certain fr. (237(235K)) in which an old man appears to express a desire to enjoy the remainder of his life, and one plausibly assigned to it (236(234K)) where an unidentified character (? the titular hero in love, cf. Fraenkel) discusses the

habits of lovers in language at times (e.g. στρατευτικωτάτους 2, ἰταμούς
5) most appropriate to a military man (cf. Spies).

Fr. 236(234K) occurs in a confused section of Ath. 13 where the
assignments do not always correspond with the facts. At 562d Alexis'
Ἀποκοπτόμενος is cited (fr. 20), followed by a reference (562e) to
Theophrastus' *Erotikon* (fr. 107 Wimmer = 559 Fortenbaugh) in which a
passage of Chaeremon is paraphrased (cf. Nauck[2] p. 785, *TrGF* 1.215, 71
T 1 and n.), thirdly a quotation from ὁ ποιητὴς οὗτος which logically
should be Chaeremon but turns out to be Eur. *IA* 548ff. and finally (562f)
our fr. 236(234K) presented as ὁ ... αὐτὸς οὗτος ποιητής (logically
again Chaeremon, and so identified by most[1] earlier scholars, cf.
Schweighaeuser, *loc. cit.*, despite the error over the preceding ascription)
... ἐν τῷ ἐπιγραφομένῳ Τραυματίᾳ. Meineke (1.519ff.) convincingly
explained the errors and confusion by suggesting that Ath. had inserted
the passage from Theophrastus (which probably paraphrased or quoted
Eur. *IA* 548ff. as well as Chaeremon) into a previously written text, with
equal carelessness misidentifying the Euripidean source and failing to
realise that the insertion now made the following ὁ ... αὐτὸς οὗτος
ποιητής (originally a back-reference to Alexis fr. 20 cited in 562d)
incorrect. In support of his suggestion Meineke showed that (i) our fr.
236(234K), whose style and metre are comic (vv. 1, 4, 5 break Porson's
Law, v. 6 has an anapaest in the second half of the first metron), is unlike
anything correctly assigned to Chaeremon, a tragic poet (*pace* the *Suda* s.v.
and comm. anon. on Arist. *Rhet.* 3.12, 1413^{b}13, 21.ii.220.27f. Rabe, claiming that Chaeremon wrote comedies: possibly a false deduction from the
present passage of Ath., cf. C. Collard, *JHS* 90 (1970) 24, *TrGF* 1 71 T1)
whose diction and metre seem never to have departed from the norms of
his genre (Collard 27ff.); and (ii) the title Τραυματίας is attested elsewhere
(Stob. *Anth.* 4.52a.15 = fr. 237(235K)) for Alexis but not for Chaeremon.
Additionally, the παρὰ προσδοκίαν joke in 236(234K).6 is of a type
apparently favoured by Alexis (cf. e.g 168(163K).7 and comm.).

236 (234K)

Meineke 3.490 (II), Kock 2.382, Edmonds 2.486, Kassel–Austin 2.153; cf.
A. Spies, *Militat omnis amans* (Diss. Tübingen 1930) 30ff., Webster. *SLGC*
54f. The speaker (cf. introduction to Τραυματίας) analyses the characteristics demanded of lovers. Webster usefully draws attention to the simi-

---

[1] But not all: Schweighaeuser himself notes that a *Gallicus Athenaei interpres*
(= Lefebvre de Villebrune in his French translation of the passage (Paris
1791) 5.26f.) had already attributed the fr. to Alexis, thus anticipating
Meineke.

larity of some of Alexis' ideas here to those in Diotima's account of Eros as
the child of Πενία and Πόρος at Pl. *Symp.* 203b–e, but a direct link between
philosopher and comic poet need not necessarily be inferred. Plato and
Alexis could be drawing independently on a common stock of images and
conceits, some of them perhaps originating in the sophistic writings about
love so popular in the first half of the 4th century (see introduction to
comm. on fr. 20) and others going back even further (cf. F. Lasserre,
La Figure d'Éros dans la poésie grecque(Paris 1946) 111ff.). Much of this
source material is now lost, so that it is impossible to pinpoint the πρῶτος
εὑρετής of these ideas, but their triteness is easily demonstrated by tabu-
lation of the known occurrences in Greek literature of Alexis' time and
before (verbal correspondences with the comic poet are asterisked):

	Alexis	Others
2	στρατευτικωτάτους	Eur. *Hipp.* 525ff., Pl. *Symp.* 178e (Pausanias, cf. Xen. *Symp.* 8.32), 196c–d (Agathon), 203d (Diotima), *Phdr.* 239d.
3–4	πονεῖν δυναμένους τοῖς σώμασιν μάλιστα	Aristarchus trag. 2.4f.
5	ποιητικούς	*Eur. fr. 663 ποιητὴν δ' ἄρα | Ἔρως διδάσκει, Pl. *Symp.* 197a (Agathon).
5	ἰταμούς, προθύμους	Eur. fr. 430, *Pl. *Symp.* 203d (Diotima) καὶ ἴτης καὶ σύντονος (sc. Ἔρως).
5–6	εὐπόρους ἐν τοῖς ἀπόροις	*Eur. fr. 430 διδάσκαλον | ἐν τοῖς ἀμηχάνοισιν εὐπορώτατον, | Ἔρωτα *Aristarchus trag. 2.4f. οὗτος γὰρ ὁ θεὸς (sc. Ἔρως) ... τίθησι ... τὸν ἄπορον εὑρίσκειν πόρον, *Pl. *Symp.* 203d–e (Diotima) πόριμος (sc. Ἔρως) ... τὸ δὲ ποριζόμενον ἀεὶ ὑπεκρεῖ, ὥστε οὔτε ἀπορεῖ Ἔρως ποτὲ οὔτε πλουτεῖ.

No parallels are presented for Alexis' προσεδρεύειν ἀρίστους τῷ πόθῳ,
because beneath the phrase's imaginative distinction lies nothing more

than a restatement of other ideas in the sequence (στρατευτικωτάτους, ἰταμούς, εὐπόρους). Only three things in the passage can be claimed by the poet as his own: the elegance of arrangement and diction, the transfer of the images from Eros the god to his human devotees (cf. also fr. 20, although here Alexis is forestalled by e.g. Aristarchus and Pausanias in Pl. *Symp.* 178e), and the addition of the comic sting in the tail at the end of v. 6.

1 τίς οὐχί φησι τοὺς ἐρῶντας ζῆν μόνους;: the parallel phraseology in Theophilus 12.1 τίς φησι τοὺς ἐρῶντας οὐχὶ νοῦν ἔχειν;, cited in the same section of Ath. (13.563a, A and Epit. + Stob. *Anth.* 4.20a.12 ~ 562f for Alexis 236(234K), A without Epit.), confirms the correctness of A's φησι in Alexis (replaced by φήσει or a further corruption in editions of Ath. up to Dindorf and the comic frs. up to Kock, but see Meineke, *Anal. Crit.* 260), yet it raises suspicion about the transmitted word order in Theophilus (? transpose οὐχί there to precede φησι).

ζῆν: 'enjoy life', cf. frs. 28.4, 177(173K).4 (both with comm.), 237(235K)), 271(269K).5.

2 A's ἔδει γε πρῶτον is hardly tolerable; an imperfect is unnatural in this context, and connection with the preceding verse is inadequate. There is little to choose between the two conjectures which solve both problems with palaeographic credibility: Casaubon's οὓς δεῖ (haplography after μόνους, cf. Schweighaeuser, *Animadv.* 7.31) and Dobree's εἰ δεῖ (*Adv.* 2.342). For the idiomatic use of γε in both relative (= *ut qui/quippe qui*) and conditional (= *si quidem/quippe cum*) clauses see Denniston, *GP* 141ff.

2–4 πρῶτον μὲν ... πονεῖν τε ... προσεδρεύειν τ': the connective sequence is worthy of note but not suspicion, although this variant of the regular μέν ... δέ ... is often 'needlessly altered by editors' (Denniston, *GP* 374ff. with examples). For the particular organisation of the present passage cf. e.g. S. *Phil.* 1424f. πρῶτον μὲν ... ἀρετῇ τε, Pind. *Ol.* 6.88ff., Eur. *Hcld.* 337ff., *Ion* 401f., *IA* 1148ff.

στρατευτικωτάτους: the formation occurs only here in extant classical literature. The idea that Ἔρως/*Amor/Cupido*, along with his human votaries, resembled a soldier on campaign became a hackneyed motif in later Greek and in Roman literature (for Eur. down to Alexis, see introduction to this fr.; a rich collection of passages in Spies' dissertation): e.g. (Ἔρως) Ach. Tat. 4.7.3 στρατιώτης με πορθεῖ τόξον ἔχων; (human lover) Lucian *Dial. Meretr.* 10.4 συστράτευε, Ach. Tat. 2.5.1 στρατιώτης ἀνδρείου θεοῦ, cf. 2.10.3; Ovid *Am.* 1.9.1f. *militat omnis amans* and the whole poem, *Ars Am.* 2.33ff.; witty or obscene exploitations in Men. *Pk.* 482ff., Machon 341ff.

3–4 πονεῖν τε δυναμένους τοῖς σώμασιν μάλιστα: like e.g. Sostratos in Men. *Dysk.*, who toiled with a mattock φιλοπόνως (528, cf. 862), if only for a short time in the hope of forwarding his plan to marry the girl for whom

666

he had fallen, or Clinia in Ter. *HT*, who because of an infatuation was pressured by his father to toil abroad as a mercenary (102ff., cf. 399: his *labores*); cf. also Men. *Kon.* 16, *Sam.* 623ff., Plaut. *Merc.* 857ff. Alexis may also have had in mind the numbing, all-night θυραυλίαι καὶ χαμαικοιτίαι (Philostr. *Epist.* 29) of the *exclusus amator*, which were not confined to comedy (contrast Men. *Mis.* Aiff. and Theoc. 7.122ff., with Gow's introduction to idyll 3, Headlam on Herodas 2.34ff., and F. O. Copley, *TAPA* 73 (1942) 96ff.).

4 προσεδρεύειν τ᾽ ἀρίστους τῷ πόθῳ: 'and best at persevering with their desire'. For ἄριστος + infinitive cf. e.g. Hom. *Od.* 8.123 θέειν ὅχ᾽ ἄριστος, Eupolis 116(95K) λαλεῖν ἄρ., Thuc. 3.38 ἀπατᾶσθαι ἄρ., Xen. *Cyr.* 5.4.44 ἄρ. ... μάχεσθαι, LSJ s.v. ι.d, Goodwin, *MT* 305, K.G. 2.9ff. προσεδρεύειν + dative = literally 'to sit by' (e.g. a person being watched, Dem. 34.26; a city under siege, Polyb. 8.7.11, cf. Dio Cass. 75.13.1), metaphorically (as here) 'to persevere with' (e.g. τοῖς πράγμασιν Dem. 1.18, ταῖς φιλοπονίαις Arist. *Pol.* 8.3, 1338ᵇ25).

5 ποιητικούς: probably 'artistically creative', if Alexis intends here to echo the idea expressed in Eur. fr. 663, Pl. *Symp.* 197a (see above, introduction to 236(234K)) and later writers (e.g. Theoc. 11 with Σ quoting Nicias' response οἱ γὰρ Ἔρωτες | ποιητὰς πολλοὺς ἐδίδαξαν τοὺς πρὶν ἀμούσους = fr. 566 Lloyd-Jones–Parsons), but a more general sense 'inventive' cannot be ruled out (cf. Spies 31f.). Literary history (for the former meaning) and contextual appropriateness (for both) make Meineke's suspicion of corruption here (5.91, cf. Kock) hard to understand. On the word's spelling see comm. on fr. 16.2.

ἰταμούς: cf. Alexis 110(105K).3 and comm., 248(246K).4. Menander applies the adjective to the drunken rapist Charisios (*Epitr.* 528, cf. Moschion at *Pk.* 713) and the soldier Thrasonides (*Mis.* 399). Soldiers in later Greek comedy often bore names signifying impetuosity (also Thrason, Thrasyleon: cf. introduction to Alexis' Θράσων), and it is by no means impossible that Alexis' title figure (possibly the speaker of this fr.: see introduction to Τραυματίας) was named in this way.

5–6 εὐπόρους ἐν τοῖς ἀπόροις: the popularity of this quasi-proverbial idea in both erotic (see introduction to this fr.) and non-erotic (e.g. *P.V.* 59 and C. J. Blomfield (Cambridge 1810) *ad loc.*, Ar. *Equ.* 758f., *Eccl.* 236, Dion. Hal. *Ant. Rom.* 7.36 δεινὸς ἀνὴρ ... πόρους εὑρεῖν ἐν ἀπόροις, *Thuc.* 5, Stephen Sgouropoulos' encomiastic verses to Alexius Comnen., vv. 71f. in A. Papadopoulos-Kerameus, *Analecta Hierosolymitikes Stachyologias* 1 (St Petersburg 1891) 431ff.; cf. also the wording of Alexis 78.2) contexts makes it highly probable that these four words form a syntactical unit separated from what follows.

6 βλέποντας ἀθλιωτάτους: Kassel–Austin print A's reading, which can mean only 'most miserable men with sight', a pointless climax to

Alexis' sentence. Emenders here (e.g. Dobree, *Adv.* 2.342, Emperius 158, Bothe, *PCGF* 569, I. G. Patakis, *Philologus* 8 (1853) 523, Herwerden, *Obs. Crit.* 75f., R. Ellis, *AJP* 6 (1885) 290, Blaydes, *Adv.* 1.116, 2.166, Edmonds) prefer to remove ἀθλιωτάτους altogether, thereby failing to observe a comedian's habit of closing a list of parallel adjectives and participles with one implicitly contradicting all that goes before and so providing a παρὰ προσδοκίαν joke. Hence my conjecture βλέποντας ἀθλιώτατον (cf. *Hermes* 93 (1965) 310, and V. Schmidt's βλ. ἀθλιώτατα in Kassel–Austin): '... inventive – impulsive – resourceful in impossible situations – looking absolutely MISERABLE!' In this sense βλέπω may be construed (cf. LSJ s.v. II, K.G. 1.309) with an internal accusative (e.g. Anacreon 15.1 Page, Ar. *Ach.* 254, Euphron 9(10K).16, Men. *Dysk.* 147, *Epitr.* 900, with neuter singular adjective, probably the commonest construction; Pind. *Nem.* 4.39, Theoc. 20.13, neuter plural adj.; A. *Sept.* 498, Ar. *Equ.* 631, sing. noun; Ar. *Vesp.* 455, 643, plural noun; Eur. *Alc.* 773, Ar. *Vesp.* 900, sing. participle), adverb (not always directional: e.g. Ar. *Equ.* 855, *Ran.* 804) or infinitive (see comm. on 102(97K).1–2). A scribe ignorant of the idiom presumably adjusted the -ώτατον ending to that of the adjoining word.

237 (235K)

Meineke 3.490 (1), Kock 2.383, Edmonds 2.486, Kassel–Austin 2.154; cf. Webster, *SLGC* 131 n. 4. If ζῆν in v. 2 (see comm.) = 'to enjoy life', the speaker may be an old man with a philosophy (as well as an image!) comparable to those of Demipho in Plaut. *Merc.* 544ff. (cf. Webster; note 547f. *decurso spatio, breue quod uitae relicuomst | uoluptate, uino et amore delectauero*) and Demea in Ter. *Ad.* 859f. (*nam ego uitam duram quam uixi usque adhuc | prope iam excurso spatio omitto*).

1–2 τὸν γὰρ ὕστατον τρέχων δίαυλον τοῦ βίου: the δίαυλος was a race of between 340 (Delphi) and 420 (Pergamum) metres, in which the runners ran the length of the stadium, round a turning-post (καμπτήρ) at the end and then back to the original starting line (cf. Jüthner in *RE* s.v. *Diaulos* 2, 354.15ff. and *Die athletischen Leibesübungen der Griechen* (*SB* Vienna 249.2 (1968) 102ff., E. N. Gardiner, *Athletics of the Ancient World* (Oxford 1930) 136f., H. A. Harris, *Greek Athletes and Athletics* (London 1964) 64ff., D. J. Kyle, *Athletics in Ancient Athens* (*Mnemosyne Suppl.* 95, 1987) 178ff.), and so became a convenient metaphor for any phenomenon or activity that had an outward passage followed by a return: e.g. the ebb and flow of (non-tidal) waves (Eur. *Hec.* 29), the movement of passengers from one side to the other of a storm-tossed ship and back (Ach. Tat. 3.1.6), return home after a long absence (A. *Ag.* 344, Eur. *Her.* 1102), return to earth after death (*Her.* 662), a wife's return to her husband after leaving him (Anaxandrides 57(56K).4). Human life is frequently imaged as a race in ancient literature, with emphasis normally on the later stages when the καμπτήρ has been turned and the finish is in sight (e.g. S. *OC* 91, Eur. *Hipp.* 87 and Barrett *ad loc.*, *El.* 955f., *Hel.* 1666 and R. Kannicht (Heidelberg 1969) *ad loc.*, Herodas 10.3, Plaut. *Stich.* 81 and the two other passages of Roman comedy cited in introduction to this fr., Varro in Nonius p. 284.10 Lindsay = fr. 544 Bücheler, Cic. *Pro Archia* 28), but only here are man's declining years called his last δίαυλος, only at Epicrates 3.14 an ageing *hetaira* δόλιχον (the long-distance race, varying from 7 to 24 stades) τοῖς ἔτεσιν ἤδη τρέχει.

2 ζῆν: almost certainly here (cf. Herwerden, *Coll. Crit.* 129) 'to enjoy life', as in frs. 28.4, 177(173K).4 (both with comm.) and 236(234K).1, especially if the context reflects that of Plaut. *Merc.* 544ff. and Ter. *Ad.* 859f., cited above. Even so, neither Kock's suggestion that ζῆν could originally have been qualified by words in the lost following context (e.g. μετὰ σοῦ or ἐν ἡσυχίᾳ), nor A. C. Pearson's (comm. on S. fr. 298) that the speaker might simply be preferring 'to live' rather than to die (like Pheres at Eur. *Alc.* 681ff.), can altogether be ruled out.

Τροφώνιος

Meineke 1.392, Kann, *De iteratis* 77f., Fraenkel, *MNC* 27 n. 1, Körte in *RE* s.v. *Komödie (mittlere)* 1262.52ff., K. J. Maidment, *CQ* 29 (1935) 14, Pickard-Cambridge, *TDA* 164 n. 1, Schmid–Stählin 1.iv.45 n. 1, T. B. L. Webster, *CQ* 2 (1952) 18 and *SLGC* 6of., 65, cf. *SM* 100 n. 1, Gil 333, G. M. Sifakis, *AJP* 92 (1971) 421ff., R. L. Hunter, *ZPE* 36 (1979) 35f. The celebrity of the oracle of the Boeotian seer Trophonius in a still unlocated cave at or near Lebadeia[1] is proved by the frequency of references to it in 5th-century literature (e.g. Hdt. 1.46, 8.134, Eur. *Ion* 300, 393f., 404, Ar.

---

[1] In addition to the commentaries on Pausanias (H. Hitzig and H. Blümner 3 (Leipzig 1910) 510ff., J. G. Frazer, vol. 5 (London 1898) 196ff.) and the standard encyclopaedias (Radke in *RE* s.v. *-ios* 1, 678.26ff., Gruppe in Roscher s.v., 1265.59ff.), see F. Wieseler, *Das Orakel des Trophonios (Programm d. arch. Inst. Göttingen* 1848), L. Deubner, *De incubatione* (Leipzig 1900) 8ff., 39ff., Robert, *GH* 1.133f., P. Philippson, *Griechische Gottheiten in ihren Landschaften (Symb. Osl. Suppl.* 9, 1939) 11ff., M. P. Nilsson, *Geschichte der griechischen Religion* 2 (Munich 1950) 450, D. Kouretas, *Medical Annals* 6 (Athens 6 1966) 935ff. and *British Journal of Psychiatry* 113 (1967) 1441ff., D. Müller, *Topographischer Kommentar zu den Historien Herodots: Griechenland* (Tübingen 1987) 520ff. The volume of A. Schachter's *Cults of Boeotia (BICS Suppl.* 38, 1981 onwards) dealing with Trophonius has not yet appeared.

COMMENTARY

Nub. 508) and later (Paus. 9.39–40, the major ancient source of information, supplemented by Philostratus *Vit. Apoll.* 8.19, and Σ^{RVE} Ar. *Nub.* 508 citing the Pergamene historian Charax, *FGrH* 103 F 5; cf. also e.g. Plut. *Mor.* 590a–592e, Lucian *Dial. Mort.* 10 Macleod, *Nec.* 22, *Deor. Conc.* 12, Strabo 9.2.38; Dicaearchus wrote a treatise περὶ τῆς εἰς Τροφωνίου καταβάσεως, F. Wehrli² (Basle and Stuttgart 1967) pp. 16f., 46ff., frs. 13–22).

Cephisodorus, Cratinus and Menander joined Alexis in naming comedies after the vatic hero. If Cratinus' Τροφώνιος ridiculed the oracle's elaborate ritual (frs. 236(221K), 241(225K)) in an episodic Old-Comedy satire (cf. J. Th. M. F. Pieters, *Cratinus* (Leiden 1946) 172f.), Menander's play, from which a brief but conventional snatch of a cook scene is preserved (fr. 397), may have used the Boeotian cave (? like Pan's grotto in *Dysk.* or the temple of Aphrodite in Diphilus' original of Plautus' *Rudens*) as the exotic background to a New-Comedy intrigue.

Both date and plot of Alexis' play are unknown. In fr. 238(236K) ὁ Μοσχίων ὁ παραμασήτης ... αὐδώμενος is more likely to have been a reference to a real-life contemporary than to a dramatic character (if the latter, would the identification tag παραμασήτης have been added to a name already familiar enough to be accompanied by the article?),¹ but any attempt to identify him with one of the Moschions who stalk through the gastronomic history of Athens during Alexis' career is baulked by a lack of reliable information. Moschion was a common name in Athens (Kirchner, *PA* 2.105f., 476 = nos. 10431–53, 10432a, cf. Davies, *APF* 178ff.), and it is difficult to distinguish individuals from the casual inscriptional (*PA* 10432, -44, -52, -53) and literary (e.g. Dion. Hal. *Dinarch.* 11) evidence. Alexis' Moschion is more likely to be identical with the man described in an undated play (*pace* Maidment, Webster, Sifakis) by Axionicus (*fl. c.* 350–315²) as fond of rich foods and the pipes (fr.

---

¹ Fraenkel's suggestion (*MNC* 27 n. 1) that fr. 238(236K), couched as it is in paratragic language, may come from the opening of a narrative about a dinner-party, is probably to be rejected because of its implicit assumption that Moschion was a *dramatis persona*. An alternative (but equally speculative) context for the fr. would be an account of an oracular consultation at Lebadeia, with Moschion ridiculed as one of the alleged participants; cf. the references to Neoclides in the narrative about Plutus' visit to the shrine of Asclepius in Ar. *Plut.* 665f., 716ff., 745ff.

² Cf. Meineke 1.417f. Axionicus fr. 6.2 mentions Philoxenus, a friend of Eucrates ὁ Κόρυδος (*fl. c.* 345–305, see introduction to Δημήτριος), fr. 2 Gryllion, the parasite of Menander, Alexander's general, and of Phryne the *hetaira* (Ath. 6.245a, 13.591d–e), and fr. 1 the *hetaira* Ischas (mentioned also by Men. *Kol.* fr. 4). Edmonds 2.563 seems to link Axionicus'

4.12ff.), by Machon as a rich hag's parasite (46ff., cf. Gow *ad loc.*), and who is possibly also the title figure of a comedy by Callicrates (cf. comm. on 238(236K).1), than with e.g. either the shadowy and undatable comic poet (Körte in *RE* s.v. 4, 347.67ff., C. Austin, *ZPE* 14 (1974) 216 = no. 164) or a cook with a high reputation in the time of Demetrius of Phalerum (Ath. 12.542f, cf. Bux in *RE* s.v. 6, 348.21ff.).

One of the other two extant frs. from Alexis' play (239(237K)), however, perhaps points to the earlier part of Alexis' career. In Eupolidean metre three or more (cf. ἅπαντες v. 5) Boeotian men are ordered to be vigorous (vv.1–4) and strip (γυμνοῦθ') themselves with all speed (5). This exhortation has reminded modern scholarship (e.g. Kann 77f., cf. A. Körte, *RE* s.vv. *Komödie (attische)* 1258.52ff., *(neue)* 1267.61ff., Maidment 1ff., Schmid–Stählin, R. Pretagostini, *Dioniso* 57 (1987) 258f.) of commands to the chorus at the beginning of Old-Comedy parabases (Ar. *Ach.* 627, *Pax* 729f. and Σ, *Lys.* 615) to remove such outer clothing as might hamper their dancing (e.g. Neil on Ar. *Equ.* 891, Pickard-Cambridge, *DFA*[2] 245, G. M. Sifakis, *Parabasis and Animal Choruses* (London 1971) 105f., R. C. Ketterer, *GRBS* 21 (1980) 217ff.). Eupolideans are particularly associated with the parabasis (of all the surviving passages certainly in this metre, apart from fr. 239(237K) here, only Cratinus fr. 75(74K) comes from another part of the play, but Marius Victorinus *Gram. Lat.* 6.104 alleges without citation that Diphilus and Menander used Eupolideans; for a list of passages see L. P. E. Parker, *PCPS* 214 (1988) 116; on Alexis 209(206K), see comm. *ad loc.*). Yet Alexis' play must have been written half a century or more after the last surviving parabasis, at a time when the chorus had lost its political importance and become little more than a picturesque accessory, singing one or two specially composed songs directly on and sometimes also shortly after entry, engaging then through the coryphaeus in a few exchanges with the actors, and marking the later act-divisions with lyrics whose words were deemed unworthy of preservation (cf. introductions to Alexis' Κουρίς, fr. 112(107K) and 'False or Doubtful Attributions' V). Unless Alexis' Τροφώνιος was a resuscitated fossil, composed for some obscure special purpose (cf. E. Capps, *AJA* 10 (1895) 321f., Schmid–Stählin, *loc. cit.*), the metre and contents of fr. 239(237K) need to be explained in a way appropriate to what little we know about 4th-century comedy. In the parodos of Aristophanes' *Plutus* (388 bc) Karion addresses the chorus of countrymen on their joint entry with instructions (vv.254–6) similar to those expressed in Alexis

---

title Φίλιννα with the mistress of Philip of Macedon (Ath. 13.578a, cf. 557d), but that could well be a *nomen fictum* (an old ? nurse in Men. *Georg.*; cf. [Aristaen.] 2.3).

239(237K) and in a metre (iamb. tetr. catal.) no less lively than Eupolideans:

> ἄνδρες φίλοι καὶ δημόται καὶ <u>τοῦ πονεῖν ἐρασταί</u>,
> ἴτ᾽, ἐγκονεῖτε, σπεύδεθ᾽, ὡς ὁ καιρὸς οὐχὶ μέλλειν,
> ἀλλ᾽ ἔστ᾽ ἐπ᾽ αὐτῆς τῆς ἀκμῆς, ᾗ δεῖ παρόντ᾽ ἀμύνειν.

If in the parodos of Alexis' Τροφώνιος a parallel character used Eupolideans to introduce a chorus of Boeotians who responded in the same metre, the resultant scenario might possibly match that of Eubulus' contemporary (?) Στεφανοπωλίδες (where frs. 102(104K), 103(105K) could be sung either by an actor addressing the chorus or by the chorus themselves, *pace* Hunter in his edition) and also convincingly explain the use in Alexis 239(237K) of second-person-plural commands (rarely ever used by a chorus addressing its own members, cf. R. L. Hunter, *ZPE* 36 (1979) 35f.); cf. Maidment, Pickard-Cambridge, Sifakis, Gil and Hunter (*locc. citt.* at the head of this introduction).

The presence of a chorus of Boeotians makes a Boeotian scene (probably before or near the oracle of Trophonius) likely for Alexis' play, but the frs. give no clues to its plot. The possibilities include (1) comic burlesque, treating the story and/or the conduct of the oracle at Lebadeia with the same irreverence (so Meineke, 1.392, cf. Körte, *RE* s.v. *Komödie (mittlere)* 1262.53ff.) as the therapeutic techniques at the shrine of Asclepius in Ar. *Plut.* 627–770, and (2: but not necessarily alternatively) an embryonic romantic intrigue, played out before the Lebadeian cave.

238 (236K)

Meineke 3.492 (II), Kock 2.383, Edmonds 2.486, Kassel–Austin 2.154. Possible contexts for this fr., cited by Ath. 6.242c (A only), are sketched in n. 1 on p. 670. Why is Moschion described in tragic language and metre (ἐν βροτοῖς αὐδώμενος: ? quotation from a lost tragedy = fr. trag. inc. 20 Nauck[2], cf. Meineke, *Anal. Crit.* 105, F. Selvers, *De mediae comoediae sermone* (Diss. Münster 1919) 28)? Why is he styled outlandishly παραμασήτης (? a soubriquet habitually applied to and/or by himself) rather than παράσιτος?

1 ὁ Μοσχίων: on his identity see introduction to Τροφώνιος. Why this name was commonly given in New Comedy to young men of licentious habits or desires (Choricius 32.73 τῶν Μενάνδρῳ πεποιημένων προσώπων Μοσχίων μὲν ἡμᾶς παρεσκεύασε παρθένους βιάζεσθαι, e.g. Men. *Kith.*, *Pk.*, *Sam.*, *Fab. Inc.*, frs. 428 = *Hypobolimaios*, 951, cf. Strato fr. 1.13, com. adesp. frs. 242.66, 251.10 and 255.4 Austin; cf. Breitenbach 45 n. 92, K. Gatzert, *De nova comoedia quaestiones onomatologicae* (Diss. Giessen 1914) 23, F. Poland, *Neue Jahrb.* (1914) 590 n. 2, A. Körte in *RE* s.v. *Komödie* *(neue)* 1274.22ff., Webster, *SM* 100 n. 1) rather than to young rustics (cf. Alciphr. 2.21) remains a mystery; if Callicrates' Μοσχίων (cf. introduction to Τροφώνιος, Meineke 1.418, Breitenbach 45f., A. Körte in *RE* s.v. *Komödie (mittlere)* 1262.12, Webster, *SLGC* 65) portrayed the real-life parasite as a young libertine, however, it might have served to introduce the later stereotype.

2 ὁ παραμασήτης ἐν βροτοῖς αὐδώμενος: 'the man styled among mortals fellow-chewer'. αὐδᾶν is a favourite word in tragedy (x 7 A. + 2 *P.V.*, x 30 S. at least, over 40 Eur.; in this usage e.g. S. *Trach.* 1106 ὁ τοῦ κατ' ἄστρα Ζηνὸς αὐδηθεὶς γόνος, *Phil.* 240f., 430, cf. *El.* 1148, Eur. *Phoen.* 125, LSJ s.v. II.3), but alien to Attic prose; in comedy elsewhere with its compounds it is largely confined to paratragic or mock-solemn contexts, Ar. *Ach.* 1183, *Av.* 556, *Ran.* 369 ~ *Equ.* 1072). For βροτοῖς cf. comm. on fr. 86(66K).2; for παραμασήτης (only here and Timocles 9.6), comm. on 224(222K).8.

<h2 style="text-align:center">239 (237K)</h2>

Meineke 3.490 (1), Kock 2.383, Edmonds 2.486, Kassel–Austin 2.155. The fr.'s context (? an unidentified character's address to a chorus of Boeotian men in Eupolidean metre at the parodos) is discussed in introduction to Τροφώνιος. The chorus are requested not to behave like typical Boeotians: stolid, fit only for physical labour (if A's πονεῖν is correct, but see comm. on v. 3) and gluttonous at all hours (4). This was a view disseminated particularly by the Athenians, their neighbours and traditional enemies. Ath. 10.417b–418b collects eleven passages mainly from comedy (besides the present fr., Eubulus 11(12K), 33(34K), 38(39K), 52(53K), 66, Diphilus 22, Mnesimachus 2, Achaeus fr. 3 Nauck², Eratosthenes p. 199 Bernhardy, Polyb. 20.4.1, 6.5; cf. also e.g. Demonicus 1, Polyb. 20.6.6, Plut. *Mor.* 995e) to show that ἔθνη . . . ὅλα εἰς πολυφαγίαν ἐκωμῳδεῖτο, ὡς τὸ Βοιωτόν, but he does not stress the frequency and unusual timing of the meals (τὴν νύχθ' ὅλην Alexis 239(237K).4 and Eubulus 52(53K).1, δι' ἡμέρας ὅλης Eubulus 66.2f., cf. 33(34K).2, 52(53K).2, πρὸ ἡμέρας ... πρὸς ἡμέραν Diphilus 22, cf. Polyb. 20.6.6). The willingness to toil hard (cf. e.g. Eubulus 11(12K) καρτερεῖμεν v. 2, πονεῖν A and Epit. MSS v. 1 at Ath. 417c, as also A at 417e citing v. 3 of Alexis 239(237K).3, but see comm. below *ad loc.*) went with a national reputation for physical strength and fitness (e.g. Satyrus in Ath. 12.534b = *FHG* 3.160 fr. 1), boorishness, insensitivity and a mental slowness (e.g. Dem. 5.15, 18.35, 43 and H. Wankel (Heidelberg 1976) *ad loc.*, Isoc. 15.248, Lucian *Jup. trag.* 32, Plut. *Mor.* 995e, Dio Chrys. 64.13; cf. Corn. Nep. *Alcib.* 11.3 *omnes enim Boeotii magis firmitati corporis quam ingenii acumini inseruiunt, Epam.* 5, Tertullian *Anim.* 20) that was sometimes put down to the oppressively humid

climate (e.g. Cic. *Fat.* 7, Hor. *Epist.* 2.1.244); hence the proverb Βοιωτία ὗς (e.g. Pind. *Ol.* 6.89f., Plut. *Mor.* 995e, *Suda* s.vv.; cf. συοβοιωτοί Cratinus 77(310K)). See H. Steiger, *Der Eigenname in der attischen Komödie* (*Acta Semin. Philolog. Erlangensis* 5, 1891) 50f., W. Rhys Roberts, *The Ancient Boeotians, their Character and Culture and their Reputation* (Cambridge 1895), Göbel, *Ethnica* 57ff. with the richest collection of material, Hunter, comm. on Eubulus 11(12K).

2 τοῖς διασύρειν ὑμᾶς εἰθισμένοις: possibly a double reference to (a) the prevalent dislike and disparagement of Boeotians at Athens, and (b), metatheatrically, the performance of an Athenian chorus playing its role of Boeotians. The consequences of a slipshod performance in the Theatre of Dionysus are clearly illustrated by the fate of the tragic actor Hegelochus (Σ Eur. *Or.* 279, Ar. *Ran.* 303 and Σ, Strattis 1, 63(60K), Sannyrion 8; cf. Pickard-Cambridge, *DFA*² 170). διασύρειν in its metaphorical sense ('to ridicule/disparage', cf. Alexis 145(141K).11, Diphilus 76(75K)) is a favourite word of Demosthenes in his attacks on Aeschines (e.g. 18.27 and Wankel *ad loc.*; cf. e.g. Anaximenes *Rhet.* 12.14, 33.1, 36.19 pp. 48, 70, 84 Fuhrmann, Philodemus *Poet.* 19.19, p. 45 Jensen).

3 A Eupolidean verse normally consists of two polyschematic choriambic dimeters, the second being cataleptic (ŏ o $\overset{\times}{-}$ × – ∪ ∪ – ¦ ŏ ¦ o – × – ∪ ⊔): cf. comm. on fr. 209(206K)), and this is the form in vv. 1–2, 4–5 of the present fr. In v. 3, however, A gives ὡς ἀκίνητοι νῦν εἶναι βοᾶν καὶ πονεῖν μόνον, with a presumably corrupt νῦν εἶναι in place of the expected ∪ ∪. Whether corruption has spread beyond these two words is uncertain. ἀκίνητοι before νῦν fits metre and sense (here 'sluggish/insensitive' rather than 'steadfast', cf. e.g. Arist. *Eth. Eud.* 3.2.4, 1230ᵇ13f. τοὺς γὰρ ἀκινήτως ἔχοντας δι᾿ ἀναισθησίαν πρὸς ταύτας τὰς ἡδονὰς οἱ μὲν καλοῦσιν ἀναισθήτους, thus chiming with the common slur against Boeotian stolidity, cf. comm. on v. 1 above) equally well, despite Sylburg's wish (in Casaubon, *Animadv.* 712) to substitute for it ἀνίκητοι. After εἶναι, however, βοᾶν καὶ πονεῖν, though metrical, is less attractive. Boeotians are not elsewhere pilloried for shouting, and although πονεῖν receives some support from the MSS at Eubulus 11(12K).1 (see above, comm. on 239(237K).1), J. Palmerius, *Exercitationes in optimos fere auctores graecos* (Leiden 1688) 513 conjectured πίνειν[1] in its place with some plausibility (note καὶ δειπνεῖν at the beginning of v. 4).

---

[1] Kaibel's adjustment to πώνειν here was unworthy of a fine scholar; Alexis uses Attic, not Aeolic (cf. N. Hopkinson, comm. (Cambridge 1984) on Call. *H. Dem.* 95), Greek to disparage the Boeotians. Edmonds' attempt to defend πονεῖν as a euphemism for βινεῖν is rightly dismissed by Hunter on Eubulus 11(12K).1, showing that Hesych.'s definition of πονεῖν (s.v.; cf. also the following entries πονέεσθαι, πον-

3–4 There are four possibilities of interpreting the structure and syntax of these verses: (i) ὡς + participle (either ἐπιστάμενοι alone, or with an additional participle removed by corruption) providing an alleged reason; (ii) ὡς + second-person-plural indicative verb (now corrupted out) in an explanatory clause, with ἐπιστάμενοι in agreement with the subject; (iii) ὡς ἀκίνητοι + noun (corrupted out) as a comparison, followed by ἐπιστάμενοι as explanatory participle; (iv) ὡς ἀκίνητοι νῦν εἶναι corrupted from a form of vocative address (e.g. ὦ συκινοί...), with the following words interpreted as in (iii). Conjectures are legion and unconvincing. Those upholding (i) are too far from the ductus (φρεσὶ καί Kaibel), unidiomatic (ξυνέσει Kock, but ὄντες would also be required) or objectionable for other reasons (ἀκίνητοι ∪ ∪ νοῦν Peppink, *Observ.* 60, after Bothe, *PCGF* 569, but what could be fitted in the gap?). Supporters of (ii) (e.g. ἀνίκητοί 'στε βοᾶν νυνὶ Porson on Ar. *Nub.* 518, ἀνίκητοί τε βοᾶν ἔστε Meineke, after Sylburg in Casaubon, *Animadv.* 712) convince in neither palaeography nor idiom (? ἀκίνητος/ἀνίκητος + infinitive at this stylistic level). Although I am tempted provisionally to suggest (= i) ὡς ἀκινητοῦντες ἀεί (ἀεί already Erfurdt, *Obs.* 443), it seems best to obelise νῦν εἶναι (with Kassel–Austin) and suspend judgment over ἀνίκητοι ... βοᾶν καὶ πονεῖν.

4 τὴν νύχθ' ὅλην: cf. introduction to this fr.

γυμνοῦθ' αὐτούς: cf. introduction to Τροφώνιος.

θᾶττον: commonly from Homer onwards (*Od.* 7.151f., 10.72) this form is used with the imperative (e.g. S. *Aj.* 581, *OC* 838f., Eur. *Andr.* 551, *Med.* 100, Ar. *Vesp.* 180, 187, *Thesm.* 1186, *Plut.* 604, Eubulus 98(100K), Men. *Asp.* 222, *Dysk.* 430, *Sam.* 574) and other expressions implying a need for urgent action (οὐ + second-person future indicative in questions, e.g. Ar. *Nub.* 505f., *Pax* 1126, Men. *Pk.* 526, *Sam.* 678f.; jussive subjunctives, e.g. Ar. *Lys.* 686; verbals in -τέος/-τέον, e.g. Ar. *Lys.* 320) without obvious comparative significance, although 'very quickly' is not far removed from 'quicker (than you/we are now doing)'. Cf. K.G. 2.306, H. Thesleff, *Studies on Intensification in Early and Classical Greek* (Helsinki 1954) 123.

240 (238K)

Meineke 3.492 (III), Kock 2.384, Edmonds 2.488, Kassel–Austin 2.155. The Antiatticist's citation (110.15 Bekker) of Alexis' Τροφώνιος for the use of ὀφθαλμὸν ἐπιβάλλειν in the sense of περιέργως θεᾶσθαι, repeated by Phot. and the *Suda* (s.vv.) without naming the play and with θεᾶσθαι altered (? by dittographic slip) to the aorist, is presumably intended to

---

ἐόντο) as ἐνεργεῖν need have no sexual implications; significantly there is no entry for πονεῖν in J. Henderson, *The Maculate Muse* (New Haven and London 1975[1], Oxford 1991[2]).

support a claim that the phrase was good Attic. No evidence survives for or against, but in later Greek Stob. *Flor.* 3.10.60 gives Διογένης ὁ κύων θεασάμενός τινα πλουσίας γραίας προσποιούμενον ἐρᾶν ἔφη· ταύτη οὐ τὸν ὀφθαλμὸν ἀλλὰ τὸν ὀδόντα ἐπιβέβληκεν, and [Lucian] *Asin.* 4 πᾶσι τοῖς νέοις ἐπιβάλλει τὸν ὀφθαλμόν; cf. τὰ ὄμματα ἐπιβάλλειν [Aristaen.] 2.1.23, and τὰς ὄψεις ἐπιβ. e.g. Herodian 7.6.8, Synesius *Epist.* 66 p. 114.16 Garzya.

Τυνδάρεως

On this title, possibly an alternative to Ἑλένης μνηστῆρες, see the introduction to the *Helen* titles.

241 (239K)

Meineke 3.492, Kock 2.384, Edmonds 2.488, Kassel–Austin 2.156; cf. C. Dobias-Lalou, *Rev. Phil.* 55 (1981) 309ff. At the end of book 11, Ath. grows bored for a while with his imaginary background of a scholar's banquet and begins to discourse in his own name, apostrophising there (11.509e) the Timocrates to whom the work was addressed at the outset (1.1a, cf. B. Baldwin, *Acta Classica* 19 (1976) 28). Book 12 then commences with the first verse of Alexis 241(239K),[1] followed by a statement of that verse's source (κατὰ τὸν Ἀλέξιδος Τυνδάρεων), a further address to Timocrates such as is prefixed to twelve of the fifteen books (the exceptions are 2, 3, 7), and thereafter the five remaining verses of the Alexis fr. It is probable that there was no other reason for this curious separation of the fr. into two pieces than a desire not to delay the address to Timocrates, although the possibility of a private allusion on Ath.'s part cannot entirely be ruled out: for example, could Timocrates have been a native of Cyrene?

Ath.'s version of the opening line of this fr. ἄνθρωπος εἶναί μοι Κυρηναῖος δοκεῖς (so A, Epit.) requires Κυρηναῖος to scan with its first syllable short, but elsewhere in Attic this syllable always scans long (see comm. on fr. 37(36K).3). Is Ath.'s version then wrong? The presence of

---

[1] Cf. Meineke, *Cur. Crit.* 33 (after Hertel 398). There can be no doubt that the opening words of Ath. 12 form (or are based on) the first line of the Alexis citation; without them the subsequent reference to ἐκεῖ (v. 2 Kock = 1 Kassel–Austin) is unintelligible. For other examples of divided citations in Ath. see e.g. 14.622f (Antiphanes 216(217K)), 623f (Theophilus 5) and probably 3.122f (Alexis 202(198K), cf. comm.). Kassel–Austin's failure to print the opening line here as part of the fr.'s text is to be deprecated.

the metrical anomaly, combined with a suspicion of editorial tinkering in order to insert Timocrates' salutation, has led several scholars to think so. Edmonds prints the transposition δοκεῖς Κυρηναῖος, which is found in two Byzantine quotations of the line (Eustath. 1148.32, Σ Lucian *Symp.* 12[1]). The ultimate source of these two quotations can only be Ath., but we cannot eliminate a faint possibility that one of the quoters may have had access to an earlier or better MS of Ath. than the *Marcianus.* Edmonds' text involves the correption of the αι in Κυρηναῖος, in itself legitimate (cf. particularly Ἀθηναῖος at Eupolis 37(35K), Pherecrates 39(34K), Polyzelus 12(11K).3, and my note on Alexis 247(245K).1, but unparalleled with this word). Herwerden's conjecture ἄνθρωπε, Κυρηναῖος εἶναί μοι δοκεῖς (*Obs. Crit.* 76ff.) has deservedly won support for its avoidance of all anomaly while enlivening the sentence and producing a more idiomatic word order with its juxtaposition of μοι δοκεῖς.[2]

This reputation of the men of Cyrene for bringing uninvited guests with them to dinner engagements (on their general τρυφή cf. Eupolis 202(189K), Göbel, *Ethnica* 119, Dobias-Lalou) seems to have been shared with the inhabitants of Myconos (*Suda* s.v. Μυκόνιος γείτων, cf. Ath. 1.7f).

1 (2 **Kock**) ἐπὶ τὸ δεῖπνον is the reading of A here, but the normal Attic locution (in circumstances where the article has no obvious demonstrative force) is ἐπὶ δεῖπνον (e.g. Ar. *Ach.* 1085, *Vesp.* 1005, *Pax* 1192, Alexis 213(210K).1, Pl. *Symp.* 174a, Dem. 21.73), and intrusive articles are a notorious blight in MSS. Hence Blaydes (*Adv.* 2.166) conjectured ἕνα τιν' ἐπὶ δεῖπνον κ., unaware that the Epit. MSS here also omit the article in their mangled and unmetrical version of the line. Nevertheless ἐπὶ τὸ δεῖπνον does incontrovertibly occur in 4th-century Attic as an exact equivalent of ἐπὶ δεῖπνον, e.g. at Ar. *Eccl.* 1128 (where there is no previous mention of a specific meal), cf. 1135, 1165 (where the presence of the article might now be conditioned by the previous reference(s)), and the plural ἐπὶ τὰ δεῖπνα occurs frequently with implications indistinguishable from ἐπὶ δεῖπνον (e.g. Ephippus 9, Men. *Sam.* 393, Isaeus 3.14, [Dem.] 59.33). It may be that by analogy with this plural expression a generalised ἐπὶ τὸ δεῖπνον had a temporary vogue in Attic. Clearly there is no warrant

---

[1] 3.426 in T. Hemsterhuys' edition of Lucian (Amsterdam 1743), 4.243 in K. J. Jacobitz's (Leipzig 1836–41). H. Rabe's edition (Leipzig 1906) wilfully omits this scholion (which is found in a late 15th-century MS (G)) presumably because (cf. *Nachr. Gött.* (1902) 719) its source was extant.

[2] Thus in Aristophanes juxtaposed μοι δοκεῖς occurs eleven times, μοι ... δοκεῖς only once (*Av.* 935), δοκεῖς δέ μοι once (*Eccl.* 920); in Menander, juxtaposed μοι δοκεῖς eight times, and δοκεῖς γέ μοι (*Sam.* 286), δοκ]εῖς ... μοι (*Pk.* 341), μοι ... δοκεῖς (fr. 538.1) all once.

for tampering with A's text here, in a contextless fr. where we do not know whether or not a specific dinner had been mentioned in the preceding verses now lost.

2–3 (3–4K) Kassel–Austin aptly cite [Dem.] 42.24 (the young and wealthy Phaenippus) ὄχημ' αὑτῷ ... ἐώνηται, ἵνα μὴ πεζῇ πορεύηται· τοσαυτῆς οὗτος τρυφῆς ἐστι μεστός as a further expression of Athenian attitudes to this use of carriages (yet contrast Göbel, *Ethnica* 13f.). Cyrene and Libya were celebrated for their horses (e.g. Pind. *Pyth.* 4.2 and Σ (4.1a), 9.4, 123, Call. fr. 716 Pfeiffer, Strabo 17.3.21, Arrian *Cyn.* 1.4, 24.1, Aelian *NA* 3.2, Oppian *Cyn.* 1.172, 2.253; cf. Hdt. 2.50, 4.188f. on the Libyan worship of Poseidon), and according to Hdt. 7.86 ἤλαυνον ... οὗτοι πάντες (sc. Libyans) ἅρματα (cf. 4.189, 7.184); W. Ridgeway, *The Origin and Influence of the Thoroughbred Horse* (Cambridge 1893) 238ff., 470f., O. Keller, *Die antike Tierwelt* I (Leipzig 1909) 221, Broholm in *RE* s.v. *Kyrene* 2, 168.14ff. Although Alexis' figures for diners, carriages and horses here may be exaggerated for comic reasons, they are calculated precisely, as Dobias-Lalou demonstrates. There are ten carriages, fifteen συνωρίδες (cf. e.g. *Rhesus* 987, Ar. *Nub.* 1302, cf. 15, Antiphanes 88.3, Pl. *Phdr.* 246b, *Critias* 119b) = thirty horses, one invited and eighteen other guests. Three horses (either two yoked and one in traces, or all three yoked) draw each carriage; one will contain the invited guest, each of the other nine a pair of gatecrashers.

4 (5K) τούτοις ... τἀπιτήδει' ἐμβαλεῖν: 'to throw in the food for them', where 'them' = the horses; ἐμβάλλω is the usual word for stocking the mangers, cf. Xen. *Cyr.* 8.1.38, Theophr. *Char.* 4.8.

5 (6K) ὥστ' ἦν κράτιστον: 'and so it would have been best', cf. Isoc. 20.14. On the idiomatic use of the imperfect indicative without ἄν in such clauses depending on an unrealised wish, obligation, etc., see K.G. 1.204ff., Goodwin, *MT* 151ff., and cf. fr. 205(201K).1.

Ὕπνος (? and Ὑπόνοια)

Schweighaeuser on Ath. 15.671d, cf. *Animadv.* 8.54, Meineke 1.392f., Kann, *De iteratis* 69ff., cf. also 'False or Doubtful Attributions' 1 (introduction to Ἀλείπτρια and the works cited in p. 813 n. 1). Ath. 10.449d cites Ἄλεξις ἐν Ὕπνῳ (fr. 242(240K)), 13.572c Ἄλεξις ἢ Ἀντιφάνης ἐν Ὕπνῳ (fr. 244(242K)) and 15.671d ἐξ Ὑπονοίας (so the *Marcianus*) Ἀλέξιδος· ... τὰ αὐτὰ ἰαμβεῖα φέρεται καὶ παρ' Ἀντιφάνει ἐν Ὕπνῳ (fr. 243(241K)).[1] Clearly

---

[1] Meineke's suggestion (1.393), accepted by Kock and Edmonds, that a further fr. (3.494 (IV) Meineke = 243 Kock) should be attributed to

ΥΠΝΟΣ

Alexis' and Antiphanes' names were both attached in Ath.'s time to one
Ὕπνος title, although whether this was because Alexis e.g. (i) had made a
διασκευή of a play by Antiphanes presumably after the latter's death (cf.
Meineke, Kann 71: such major plagiarism is less likely when both poets
were still alive), or (ii) had acted as διδάσκαλος for one of Antiphanes'
plays, remains uncertain (cf. introduction to Ἀλείπτρια). If Alexis was a
plagiarist here, the presence of identical passages in the two versions would
be explicable, and Schweighaeuser's suggested substitution of ἐξ Ὕπνου
for ἐξ Ὑπονοίας at Ath. 15.671d (cf. Animadv. 8.154) acceptable. Yet
Ὑπόνοια is a plausible title in later Greek comedy (cf. e.g. Μέθη, Ὀργή by
Menander, Ἄγνοια by Diphilus or Calliades, by Machon (Gow's edition
of Machon p. 137, Webster, SLGC 118), suggesting a plot based on
suspicion[1] with its title figure perhaps delivering the prologue as a divine
personification (cf. e.g. Agnoia in Men. Pk., Elenchos in Men. fr. 717,
Phobos in com. adesp. fr. 154 Kock; Auxilium in Plaut. Cist., Inopia and
Luxuria in Trin.; F. Stoessl in RE s.v. Prologos (23.2 Nachtrag) 2372.43ff.).
Despite this, I hesitantly accept Schweighaeuser's conjecture because of
(i) its palaeographic plausibility (the abbreviation of titles on didascalic
records and in MSS often produces corrupt endings; cf. introduction to
Ἀποκοπτόμενος) and (ii) the other evidence connecting Alexis' and
Antiphanes' Ὕπνος.

Xenarchus also wrote a Ὕπνος, which appears to have featured the
stock situation of a husband with a talkative wife (fr. 14). No fr. is cited
independently of Alexis frs. 243(241K) and 244(242K) for Antiphanes'
play. If we assume that frs. 242–4(240–2K) all derive from Alexis'
undatable (but see introduction to 242(240K), comm. on 243(241K).1)
version, we gain references to a stingy man (243(241K): ? a character in
the play, cf. n. 1 below) and a homosexual πόρνος (244(242K): ? a parasite, see comm.), and an interesting dialogue in which an older woman (if
γύναι is correctly transmitted at 242(240K).6, but see comm. ad loc.)

Alexis' Ὕπνος, must be rejected; see introduction to Οἶνος and comm.
on fr. 162(243K).
[1] If Alexis' Λέβης (see introduction to that play, and Appendix III) was
the Greek original of Plautus' Aulularia, Ὑπόνοια would have been an
appropriate alternative title for it; Euclio's suspicions were central to
the Plautine plot, Hyponoia might have spoken the prologue of the
Greek original and Alexis fr. 243(241K) (with its description of a
character so parsimonious that he could be compared to a Triballian
host who at his dinner parties only showed to his guests the food that he
went on to sell for money the next day) would fit neatly into a scene that
exemplified or caricatured the stinginess of Euclio's original (cf. e.g.
Aul. 296ff.).

COMMENTARY

propounds to a girl (κόρη v. 9) a conundrum about sleep. Subject matter here and play-title together imply the importance to the plot of some character's sleep (? on lines similar to those suggested for Alexis' Μανδραγοριζομένη); could Sleep as a divine personification have delivered the prologue?[1]

242 (240K)

Meineke 3.493 (1), Kock 2.385, Edmonds 2.489, Kassel–Austin 2.157. The fr., cited by Ath. 10.449d (complete in A, the words between ἀεί v. 6 and τίς v. 8 omitted in Epit.; Eustath. 1336.15ff. cites vv. 1–6 and refers to v. 9), is a dialogue here involving two speakers (on their identity, see introduction to Ὕπνος; correct part-division first by Daléchamp, but note the dicolon in A at the end of v. 4). The first speaker propounds a conundrum in which a well-known thing (here Sleep) is described in extravagant and paradoxical language (hence correctly identified in v. 6 as αἴνιγμα: cf. Arist. Poet. 22, 1458ᵃ26ff., αἰνίγματός τε γὰρ ἰδέα αὕτη ἐστί, τὸ λέγοντα ὑπάρχοντα ἀδύνατα συνάψαι). Conundrums and other word-games were a pastime at symposia (e.g. Antiphanes 122(124K), Diphilus 49(50K)), and although they featured already in 5th-century comedy (e.g. Epicharmus' Σφίγξ, Cratinus' Κλεοβουλῖναι), they seem to have been especially popular during the period of Middle Comedy (Hunter on Eubulus 106(107K)). In Alexis 242(240K) the language and metre of both conundrum (vv.1–5) and solution (9) are notably paratragic, perhaps reflecting parallel (but non-riddling) descriptions of sleep in Attic tragedy (cf. e.g. S. Aj. 675f., Eur. Or. 174ff., 211ff.). In a riddle attributed to Simonides (fr. 69 Diels) by Chamaeleon (Ath. 10.456c) Sleep is παῖδα ... νυκτός. See especially W. Schultz, Rätsel aus dem hellenischen Kulturkreise (Leipzig 1909) and in RE s.v. Rätsel 62.15ff., K. Ohlert, Rätsel und Rätselspiele der alten Griechen² (Berlin 1912); cf. also R. Merkelbach and M. L. West, Rh. Mus. 108 (1965) 313ff., D. L. Clayman, Callimachus' Iambi (Mnemosyne Suppl. 59, 1980) 32f. Cf. also my introduction to Alexis' Κλεοβουλίνη and comm. on 172(167K).3–5.

1 οὐ θνητὸς οὐδ' ἀθάνατος: just like Eros in Pl. Symp. 202d–203e, who οὔτε ὡς ἀθάνατος πέφυκεν οὔτε ὡς θνητός, and so by his intermediate position is identified as δαίμων μέγας (on this interpretation of δαίμων, which, originating perhaps in folk belief, goes back in literary texts to Hes. Op. 122ff. with West ad loc., cf. Theog. 991, and was popularised in the 4th century especially by Plato and Xenocrates, see e.g. Andres in RE Suppl. 3

---

[1] At Paus. 2.31.3 Hypnos is called θεός in the description of an altar erected to him and the Muses at Troezen.

ΥΠΝΟΣ

s.v. *Daimon* 282.30ff., 283.51ff., 293.53ff., H. Usener, *Götternamen*[3] (Frankfurt 1948) 292ff., M. P. Nilsson, *Geschichte der griechischen Religion* 1[3] (Munich 1967) 217, 2 (1950) 200, 243ff., G. François, *Le Polythéisme et l'emploi des mots* ΘΕΟΣ, ΔΑΙΜΩΝ (Paris 1957) 337ff., W. Burkert, *Greek Religion* (English tr., Oxford 1985) 179ff., 331f.). That Alexis knew the passage of *Symp.* is clearly shown by fr. 247(245K) (see comm. and introduction to Φαῖδρος), and Plato's words may have influenced the comic poet here also. Yet fr. 242(240K) (unlike 247(245K).5 and Plato) does not identify its anomalous being as a δαίμων, and Alexis' inspiration could equally well have been non-literary folk ideas of the time; cf. e.g. the Sibylline oracle cited by Paus. 10.12.3 about Herophile εἰμὶ δ᾽ ἐγὼ γεγαυῖα μέσον θνητοῦ τε θεᾶς τε.

ἀθάνατος: cf. comm. on 164(159K).3.

1–2 ἔχων τινὰ σύγκρασιν: a collocation (together with σύγκ. λαμβάνειν) particularly common in Hippocr. *Vict.*, e.g. 1.7 ψυχὴ πυρὸς καὶ ὕδατος σύγκρησιν ἔχουσα.

2–3 μήτ᾽ ἐν ἀνθρώπου μέρει μήτ᾽ ἐν θεοῦ: the use of ἐν μέρει + genitive ('in the class/category of') is particularly favoured by 4th-century Athenian orators (e.g. Dem. 3.31 ἐν ὑπηρέτου καὶ προσθήκης μ., 23.56 ἐν ἐχθροῦ μ., 148 ἐν σφενδονήτου καὶ ψιλοῦ μ., Isoc. 9.24 ἐν ἰδιώτου μ.), side by side with the less common ἐν τάξει (e.g. Dem. 23.89, Hyperides *Eux.* 30), ἐν μοίρᾳ (e.g. Dem. 23.61) and ἐν μερίδι (e.g. Dem. 18.176); cf. Kock's note *ad loc.*, Rehdantz–Blass, *Index* 71 and LSJ s.v. μέρος IV.3.

3–4 ἀλλὰ φύεσθαί τ᾽ ἀεὶ καινῶς φθίνειν τε τὴν παρουσίαν πάλιν: the transmitted text (with A's ἀιεὶ (*sic*) corrected in Epit. MSS and Eustath. to ἀεὶ: cf. v. 6 and comm. on fr. 76.1) entails an awkward switch of subject from the nominative masculine singular (i.e. ὕπνος) of the fr.'s opening two and a half lines to τὴν παρουσίαν in v. 4 (cf. Richards, *AO* 66f.), but this may be acceptable in a conundrum designed to tease addressee and audience with its unexpected turns and poetic phraseology masking an as yet mysterious subject whose 'presence' is said 'to be born afresh and perish every time' that we fall asleep and subsequently awake. The awkwardness of the interposed τὴν παρουσίαν is perhaps also lessened by the idiomatic use of phrases such as ἀνδρῶν ... παρουσία in the sense of ἄνδρες παρόντες (especially in tragedy: cf. e.g. S. *El.* 948, Eur. *Alc.* 606, perhaps S. fr. 451a Radt = 459 Pearson, LSJ s.v. παρουσία). Attempts to ease the construction by conjecture have rarely been felicitous, but Herwerden's μετὰ παρουσίαν (*Coll. Crit.* 129) deserves mention if only because his supporting argument demolishes Kock's τὴν παροῦσαν αὖ and Richards' τὴν ἐπιοῦσαν αὖ (a genitive or dative, not accusative, would be required to express time when or within which); alternatively one might hazard ἐκ τῆς παρουσίας.

Alexis' coupling of φύεσθαι and φθίνειν varies the cliché coupling growth

681

COMMENTARY

or bloom with death (e.g. S. *Trach.* 547f. ἕρπουσαν πρόσω ... φθ., fr. 718 Pearson ἀνθεῖ ... φθ., Eur. fr. 330.5, 9 ζῆν ... φθ., 415 αὔξεται ... φθ., cf. Pl. *Phd.* 71b, *Theaet.* 155a, *Parm.* 157b, Hippocr. *Loc. Hom.* 24 θάλλει ... φθ., cf. trag. adesp. fr. 574, Arist. *Meteor.* 1.14, 351ª29f. ἀκμάζειν καὶ φθ.), but cf. e.g. Hom. *Il.* 6.149 φύει ... ἀπολήγει.

5 ἀόρατος ὄψιν: elsewhere τὴν ὄψιν is normal in this accusative of specification (e.g. Alexis 60(59K).3; K.G. 1.315ff., LSJ s.v. ὄψις 1.a), but omission of the article here adds to the tragic flavour.

6 The victim turns on her torturer. Epit. again (see on vv. 3–4 above) corrects A's ἀιεί (inexplicably retained by Kaibel in a line spoken not by the grandiloquent riddler but by the verbally less affected victim) to ἀεί; thereafter A reads (and Epit. omits) σὺ χαίρεις ὦ γύναι μ' αἰνίγμασιν. Since χαίρω is normally intransitive (except in the idiom with personal object and participle, LSJ s.v. 1.2), μ' provides a problem. Wilamowitz (in Kaibel's apparatus) defends the transmission by assuming that the speaker's words are interrupted by the riddler in mid-sentence (before the participle governing/governed by μ' is expressed), but in Greek drama 'truly incomplete utterances ... due to ... hasty interruption by the dialogue-partner, are exceedingly rare' (D. J. Mastronarde, *Contact and Discontinuity* (U. Cal. Publications in Classical Studies 21, Berkeley, Los Angeles, London 1979) 73, cf. 63ff., in a full discussion of the tragic instances; cf. Barrett on Eur. *Hipp.* 1049, Garvie on A. *Choeph.* 117–21, 1042f.; I know of no comparable studies for comedy, although the same conclusion is valid[1]). Corruption must be posited: possibly in αἰεί/ἀεί σὺ (hence παίζουσα L. K. Valckenaer, comm. (Franeker 1755) on Eur. *Phoen.* 497f., ἀνιῶσα Kock) or χαίρεις (hence e.g. τείρεις Emperius 311, πειρᾶς Meineke, *Anal. Crit.* 203, παίζεις Kock, *Rh. Mus.* 30 (1875) 402) or both (hence ἀπολεῖς σὺ χαίρουσ' Richards, *AO* 86), or even in ὦ γύναι μ' (? with -ναι influenced by the following αἰνί-: thus tentatively I suggest ὦ Γελάσιμ', which would make the riddler male and a parasite; ὦ τάλαιν' Blaydes, *Adv.* 1.117); A. H. Sommerstein orally to me suggests a lacuna after αἰνίγμασιν.

αἰνίγμασιν: see above, introduction to this fr.

7 καὶ μὴν ... γε: adversative, 'on the contrary/and yet', with γε emphasising ἁπλᾶ, cf. Denniston, *GP* 120, 351, 357f.

---

[1] Normally in comedy the interrupter continues his or her partner's construction (e.g. Ar. *Ach.* 45ff., 414ff., Men. *Dysk.* 410ff., *Epitr.* 391ff.), or the missing word(s) can be readily supplied by the audience (e.g. the obscenity at Ar. *Vesp.* 1178, cf. my introduction to Ἀγκυλίων). At first sight Ar. *Ach.* 55, where Amphitheus' appeal περιόψεσθέ με; is cut off before he can add a participle or adjective in agreement with με, might appear to support Wilamowitz' interpretation of Alexis 242(240K).6,

μαθεῖν: epexegetic with both ἁπλῆ and σαφῆ, K.G. 2.13f.

8 τοιαύτην: cf. comm. on fr. 140(135K).11.

ἔσται: future, because the speaker is asking who this prodigy will turn out to be when her tormentor deigns to give the answer to the puzzle.

9 ὕπνος, βροτείων . . . παυστὴρ κακῶν: possibly a quotation from a lost tragedy, possibly Alexis' own parody of tragic language. For the idea and expression cf. e.g. Men. monost. 76 = Pap. xiv.2 Jäkel ἀνάπαυσίς ἐστι τῶν κακῶν πάντων ὕπνος, Nicander Ther. 746 ἐσχάτιον κακοεργὸς ἄγων παυστήριον ὕπνος, H. Orph. 85.5 (ὕπνε) κόπων ἡδεῖαν ἔχων ἀνάπαυσιν, Nonnus 27.1 λυσιπόνοιο . . . ὕπνου; for this and related ideas see e.g. Eur. Or. 159, 174f., 211, Ach. Tat. 4.10.3; for its expression e.g. S. Phil. 1437f. Ἀσκληπιὸν . . . παυστῆρα . . . σῆς νόσου, Men. Asp. 11f. τῶν μακρῶν πόνων τινὰ | ἀνάπαυσιν.

243 (241K)

Meineke 3.494 (ii), Kock 2.385, Edmonds 2.489, Kassel–Austin 2.157. On the attribution of this fr. (cited by Ath. 15.671d: only in A) to Alexis' Ὕπνος rather than Ὑπόνοια, and its link with Antiphanes' Ὕπνος, see introduction to Ὕπνος. Preserved are four imaginative trimeters with an amusing παρὰ προσδοκίαν at the end; it is no surprise that they should invite plagiarism, especially since they would suit most contexts where a gourmand (not necessarily a parasite, but cf. e.g. Plaut. Men. 487ff., Stich. 497ff., 631ff.) felt he had cause for complaint.

1 Τριβαλλοῖς: a tribe of Illyrian (Ar. Av. 1520f., Steph. Byz. s.v.) or Thracian (Strabo 7.3.13, 5.6, 11, cf. 3.8, Diod. Sic. 15.36.1, Paus. 10.19.7, Σ Dionys. Perieg. 323) origin living between Macedonia and the Danube, with a reputation for uncouthness (Ar. Av. 1520ff., especially 1568, 1573) and savagery that led aristocratic hooligans in 4th-century Athens to adopt this name for one of their gangs (Dem. 54.39, cf. Eubulus 75.3 and Hunter ad loc.; J. E. Sandys and F. A. Paley, Select Private Orations of Demosthenes 2³ (Cambridge 1896) 241ff.).[1] Such behaviour underpinned Greek confidence in the superiority of their own ethical and social codes to those operating elsewhere, with the result that exceptional violations by

---

but περιοράω is found elsewhere in Attic with an unqualified personal object (e.g. Men. Perinth. 6, LSJ s.v. ii.1).

[1] In their entries for Τριβαλλοί the ancient lexica seem often to describe the characteristics of the Athenian hooligans rather than the northern tribe: e.g. συκοφαντία (Hesych., Lex. Rhet. in Bekker, Anecd. 307.3), lounging at the public baths (Phot., Hesych., Et. Mag.), scrounging (Hesych.); cf. the reference to paederasty in Σ Aeschines 1.52).

COMMENTARY

Greeks might be (especially in Euripides) either compared to (e.g. *Hcld.* 131, *Tro.* 764) or (as here) described as exceeding (e.g. *IT* 1174) barbarian conduct (cf. especially E. Hall, *Inventing the Barbarian* (Oxford 1989) 187ff., 201ff.). The belligerence (Isoc. 12.227) of the Triballi made news several times during Antiphanes' and Alexis' lives: in 376–375 they terrified Greece with two attacks on Abdera (Diod. Sic. 15.36.1–4 alleging starvation as the cause, Aen. Tact. 15.8–9, Σ Aristid. *Panath.* 172.3), in 339 they mauled Philip on his return from Scythia (Justinus 9.2.14–3.3, Orosius 3.13.6–8) and in 335 they were finally subjugated by Alexander (Arrian *Anab.* 1.1.4, 2.1–7, Strabo 7.3.8, Ps.-Callisth. 1.26, Aphthon. *Progymn.* p.29.17ff. Rabe); the reference here and/or in Antiphanes was possibly but not necessarily prompted by one of these events. Cf. E. Polaschek in *RE* s.v. *Triballi* 2392.63ff., N. G. H. Hammond with G. T. Griffith and F. H. Walbank respectively, *A History of Macedonia* 2 (Oxford 1979) 196, 581ff., 3 (1988) 32ff.

2 τὸν θύοντα: sc. the host, with a sacrifice celebrating a wedding or some other special event, as commonly in later Greek comedy (e.g. fr. 177(173K).11, Men. *Asp.* 216ff., *Georg.* 9, *Dysk.* 260, *Pk.* 996, *Sam.* 399f.; G. Berthiaume, *Les Rôles du mágeiros* (*Mnemosyne Suppl.* 70, 1982) 32ff.).

3 δείξαντ᾽ ἰδεῖν is printed by Kassel–Austin (δείξαντα ἰδ. A), but this bungles both syntax and joke, and needs to be be replaced by Kaibel's brilliant correction δείξαντα δεῖν. ἰδεῖν could be construed only as epexegetic after δείξαντα, and its insertion here (by a scribe misreading presumably an alpha with raised tail as αι and/or subconsciously looking ahead to the end of v. 4) spoils a joke depending on the παρὰ προσδοκίαν appearance of this infinitive (for its syntax cf. 260(258K).1 and comm.) as its final and key word (cf. comm. on 168(163K).7): 'they say that the sacrificer is obliged to show the dinner to his guests, before offering for sale on the morrow what he had served up for them, unfed, to *see*'. Cf. the behaviour of the ἀνελεύθερος in Theophr. *Char.* 22.4 καὶ ἐκδιδοὺς αὑτοῦ θυγατέρα τοῦ μὲν ἱερείου πλὴν τῶν ἱερέων τὰ κρέα ἀποδόσθαι, τοὺς δὲ διακονοῦντας ἐν τοῖς γάμοις οἰκοσίτους μισθώσασθαι. Does Alexis' witticism (first explained by Hirschig, *Annot.* 14) imply a slur not merely on Triballian uncouthness, but also on their food shortages (cf. comm. on v. 1)?

εἰς τὴν αὔριον: sc. ἡμέραν, cf. e.g. Philemon 178(213K).12, Pl. *Menex.* 234b, Polyb. 1.60.5, N.T. *Act. Apost.* 4.3, side by side with the Homeric and classical Attic unarticled ἐς/εἰς αὔριον. Forms with preposition + article became increasingly common in 4th-century Attic and the *Koine*: e.g. ἀπὸ τῆς αὔριον Plut. *Mor.* 214c, ἐν τῷ αὔρ. LXX *Genes.* 30.33, ἐπὶ τὴν αὔρ. LXX *Esther* 5.8, N.T. *Act. Apost.* 4.5.

244 (242K)

Meineke 3.494 (III), Kock 2.385, Edmonds 2.490, Kassel–Austin 2.158. On the attribution of this fr., cited by Ath. 13.572c (only in A), see introduction to Ὕπνος. Its unidentified speaker describes a πόρνος who, in order to keep his breath fresh when kissing his male lover, avoids eating leeks (a τόπος of anecdotal literature: leeks, also Martial 13.18 *fila Tarentini grauiter redolentia porri | edisti quotiens: oscula clusa dato*; onions, Ar. *Lys.* 797f. and J. Henderson (Oxford 1987) *ad loc.*, cf. Xen. *Symp.* 4.8; garlic, Hor. *Iamb.* 3.1ff., 19ff., cf. Ar. *Thesm.* 494f.). Although this πόρνος is said to have dined with the speaker, it is uncertain whether he was a character in the play (if so, hardly a φιλοσοφομειρακίσκος as identified by Ath. 13.572b, cf. Cobet in Peppink, *Observ.* 78; more probably a parasite, cf. e.g. Ephippus 20, Aeschin. 1.75f., Ath. 572c–d), or some contemporary Athenian cited here as an instance (cf. e.g. Men. *Sam.* 603ff., Chaerephon introduced similarly with οὗτος).

1 πόρνος: when precisely used, a male prostitute, normally young and engaging in homosexual acts (e.g. Ar. *Plut.* 155, Xen. *Mem.* 1.6.13, [Dem]. *Epist.* 4.11, Polyb. 12.15 citing Timaeus, *FGrH* 566 F 124b, Lucian *Adv. Indoct.* 25; K. J. Dover, *Greek Homosexuality* (London 1978) 19ff., 29), but also applied more loosely where the catamite is older and/or the payment is not monetary (e.g. Aeschines 1.75, 157 citing com. adesp. fr. 298 Kock, cf. Dover 39); on Eupolis 99.26 Kassel–Austin = 92.26 Austin, *CGFP*, see A. W. Gomme (Oxford 1956) on Thuc. 2.40.2, p. 122 n. 2.

τῶν πράσων: see comm. on 132(127K).8. The genitive is partitive (K.G. 1.345); the presence of the article implies there was one particular meal at which the πόρνος refused leeks on every occasion that they were offered.

2 ἐπεδείπνει: Bothe's correction (*PCGF* 570; also independently Cobet, see Peppink, *Observ.* 78) of A's ἐπιδειπνεῖ is attractive but not certain; A's tense sits awkwardly with the following ἦν and the secondary sequence in v. 3, but could possibly be defended as a historic present (? the last of a series in a vivid description of the meal), in which case juxtaposition of present and imperfect would accord with Attic usage (examples in K.G. 1.157f.). The verb here is used in its proper sense, of eating ὄψον (the leeks of v. 1) along with bread (cf. Ar. *Eccl.* 1178, *Equ.* 1140 with Neil *ad loc.* and on vv. 706f.).

3 φιλῶν: 'kissing' (cf. Kock and LSJ s.v. φιλέω 1.4).[1]

---

[1] For comm. on fr. 243 Kock see Οἶνος (fr. 162 Kassel–Austin).

*245 (342K)

Meineke 3.513 (xix), Kock 2.408, Edmonds 2.308 (= Antiphanes fr. 212(331K)), Kassel–Austin 2.158; cf. Meineke 3.142 (xix). Under this title Kassel–Austin print a fourth fr., asterisked in order to indicate doubt over the attribution. Meineke 3.142 (Antiphanes inc. fab. fr. xix) suggested that the fr., cited by Epit. at Ath. 2.66f as Ἀντιφάνης ἢ Ἄλεξις (characteristically without play-title) may derive from Ὕπνος, simply because the Ὕπνος title was disputed between these two playwrights. Yet so too were Ἀλείπτρια and Ἄντεια (see 'False or doubtful attributions' I, II), some of the twenty other titles shared by the two poets may have involved plagiarism on Alexis' part (cf. Kann, De iteratis 69), and other explanations for ancient uncertainty over the authorship of fr. *245 are possible (e.g. Alexis could have acted as διδάσκαλος for one or more plays of Antiphanes). Accordingly commentary on this fr. is removed to 'False or Doubtful Attributions' VI.

Ὑποβολιμαῖος

Meineke 1.374f., cf. 3.495, J. G. Droysen, *Geschichte des Hellenismus* 3.1² (Gotha 1877) 268 n. 3, Th. Bergk, *Rh. Mus.* 35 (1880) 259f. and *Griechische Literaturgeschichte* 4 (Berlin 1887) 151f., C. Haeberlin, *Philologus* 50 (1891) 697ff., Kaibel in *RE* s.v. *Alexis* 9, 1468.51ff., W. S. Ferguson, *Hellenistic Athens* (London 1911) 171, T. B. L. Webster, *CQ* 2 (1952) 16 n. 1 and *SLGC* 108f., P. M. Fraser, *Ptolemaic Alexandria* (Oxford 1972), index at 3.65, H. Heinen, *Untersuchungen zur hellenistischen Geschichte des 3. Jahrhunderts v. Chr.* (Wiesbaden 1972) 135ff. One fr. (246(244K)) survives from Alexis' Ὑποβολιμαῖος, cited in full by the *Marcianus* (beginning of fol. 240) at Ath. 11.502b, but with the playwright's name and the first three letters of his title lost when the previous folio went missing (cf. comm. on fr. 293(291K) and general introduction, II.i.a); correct supplementation (first by Daléchamp in his Latin translation; cf. Casaubon, margin of text and *Animadv.* 820) was eased by Epit.'s quotation of parts of the fr. with author's name and by the further citation of v. 3 ἀπνευστί–end of v. 4 with author and title in A at Ath. 10.431a-b.

The fr. proposes toasts successively to 'Ptolemy the king' (v.1), 'the sister of the king' (2–3) and τῆς ὁμονοίας (5). The one Ptolemy in the 4th or early 3rd century who became king, had a sister important enough to be mentioned alongside him and fomented friendly relations with Athens was Philadelphus,[1] who became co-ruler of Egypt in 285/4, was married to his sister Arsinoe II from between 279 and 273[2] to her death in July 268,[3]

---

[1] So Meineke 1.374f. and most scholars (e.g. Droysen, Bergk, Kaibel, Ferguson, Webster), but in his comm. at 3.495 Meineke identified the sister(-wife) as Berenice, who married Ptolemy Soter in 317. Droysen pointed out (3.1.268 n. 3) that at the time of this wedding there was no rapport between Egypt and Athens, and that Berenice was not Ptolemy's full sister (they had different mothers; Soter's father was Lagus, Berenice's more probably Magas than Lagus, cf. Σ Theoc. 17.34, Βερενίκην λέγει τὴν †βάγα† (K: γαμάου the other MSS; Μάγα conj. F. Bücheler, *Rh. Mus.* 30 (1875) 59, Λάγου apogr. Ambros.; cf. Heinen 136). On Philadelphus see especially E. H. Bevan, *A History of Egypt under the Ptolemaic Dynasty* (London 1927) 56ff.; Volkmann in *RE* s.v. *Ptolemaios* 19, 1645.21ff., B. J. Müller, *Ptolemaios II. als Gestetzgeber* (Diss. Cologne 1968), Fraser, see index at 3.65.

[2] The termini for the wedding are 279 (Arsinoe's return to Egypt: J. G. Droysen, *SB Berlin* (1882) 226ff.; cf. K. J. Beloch, *Griechische Geschichte*[2] 4.2 (Berlin and Leipzig 1927) 182) and 273 (the Pithom stele records visits by Ptolemy in 279 without Arsinoe, and in 273 with her as queen; cf. H. Brugsch and A. Erman, *Zeitschrift für ägyptische Sprache und Altertumskunde* 32 (1894) 74ff., E. Naville, *ibid.* 41 (1903) 66ff. and *The Store-city of Pithom and the Route of the Exodus*[4] (London 1903), U. Köhler, *SB Berlin* (1895) 965ff.). Attempts to narrow down these limits have been numerous but insecure (e.g. 279–278 Beloch; early 278 A. M. Honeyman, *JEA* 26 (1940) 57ff.; 278–277 J. P. Mahaffy, *The Empire of the Ptolemies* (London 1895) 137ff.; 276–275 W. W. Tarn, *JHS* 46 (1926) 161 and *CAH*[1] 7.703; 274 Köhler 971; cf. R. Pfeiffer, comm. (Oxford 1949) on Call. fr. 392, Fraser 2.367 n. 228), although the remarkable impression that Arsinoe as Philadelphus' queen made on the Hellenistic world (cf. Dorothy B. Thompson, *Ptolemaic Oinochoai and Portraits in Faience* (Oxford 1973) 4 and n. 2) would be more comprehensible if she survived nearer to eleven than five years in this marriage. On Arsinoe see also e.g. Bevan, *op. cit.* above in n. 1, 59ff., 64ff., D. B. Thompson, *AJA* 59 (1955) 199ff., L. Robert, *Hellenica*, 11/12 (1960) 156ff., S. Sauneron, *Bull. Inst. Arch. Orient.* 60 (1960) 92ff., E. Longega, *Arsinoe II* (Rome 1968), Fraser, index at 3.12, J. Quaegebeur in H. Maehler and V. M. Strocka (edd.), *Das ptolemäische Ägypten* (Mainz 1978) 245ff., H. Hauben in E. van't Dack and others, *Egypt and the Hellenistic World* (Leuven 1983) 99ff.

[3] See E. Grzybek, *Du calendrier macédonien au calendrier ptolémaïque: problèmes de chronologie hellénistique* (Basle 1990) 103ff., correcting earlier identifications of the date as 270 (e.g. F. von Bissing in H. von Prott, *Rh. Mus.* 53 (1898) 464 and n. 1, K. H. Sethe, *Hieroglyphische Urkunden der griechisch-römischen Zeit* 2 (Leipzig 1904) 40, Fraser 2.937f. n. 415).

and bolstered his Athenian alliance with gifts of corn, money and mercenaries which the city commemorated by the erection of statues of the king and his wife in the Agora (Paus. 1.8.6) and by public expressions of gratitude (e.g. (i) the Callias decree of 270/69, published by T. L. Shear, *Kallias of Sphettos and the Revolt of Athens in 286 B.C.* (*Hesperia* (Suppl. 17, 1978) 2ff., referring to (lines 22f.) τεῖ τοῦ βασιλέως Πτολεμαίου πρὸς τὸν δῆμον εὐνοίαι; (ii) the treaty between Athens and Sparta of either 267/6 or 266/5 (*IG* ii².687 = *SIG* ³ 434/5, cf. W. S. Ferguson, *The Athenian Archons of the Third and Second Centuries B.C.* (New York 1899) 28, W. W. Tarn, *JHS* 40 (1920) 150ff.); which hoped that (31ff.) κοινῆς ὁμονοίας γενομένης τοῖς Ἕλλησι ... πρόθυμοι μετὰ τοῦ βασιλέως Πτολεμαίου καὶ μετ' ἀλλήλων ὑπάρχωσιν ἀγωνισταὶ καὶ τὸ λοιπὸν μεθ' ὁμονοίας σώιζωσιν τὰς πόλεις; or (iii) the Plataean decree of between 263 and 246, cf. R. Étienne and M. Piérart, *BCH* 99 (1975) 1ff., 58, praising Glaucon's association with Ptolemy and – as a cult – τῆι τῶν Ἑλλήνων Ὁμονοίαι, p. 15.10f., 18, 20; cf. also Chr. Habicht, *Untersuchungen zur politischen Geschichte Athens* (Munich 1979) 85, G. A. Lehmann, *ZPE* 73 (1988) 146 n. 51). Such expressions make it likely that Alexis also in fr. 246(244K).5 celebrates international ὁμόνοια rather than primarily the more limited fellowship between husband and wife, although of course in a comedy the presence of an ironic subtext, hinting at the unconventionality of Ptolemy's incestuous marriage, cannot be ruled out for either τῆς ὁμονοίας or (in v. 4) ἴσον ἴσῳ κεκραμένον, where malicious intent cannot actually be proved against the author.[1]

If one accepts the available evidence (see my general introduction, i.iii, pp. 15ff. and *Studi di filologia in onore di Giusto Monaco* 1 (Palermo 1991) 333ff.) that Alexis apparently (i) began competing in the dramatic festivals at Athens during the 350s (cf. introductions to Ἀγκυλίων, Ἀποβάτης, Μεροπίς, Παράσιτος), possibly as a young man in his twenties,[2] (ii) lived to a very great age (105 or 106, according to Plut. *Mor.* 420d, *testimonium* 4, cf. Diog. Laert. 10.23; compare the anecdote, doubtless apocryphal,

---

[1] Cf. here e.g. Webster, *SLGC* 108 and Longega, *op. cit.* on p. 687 n. 2, p. 94f., interpreting τῆς ὁμονοίας in Alexis as a reference to international relations, while Heinen 135f. follows Meineke 3.495 in supposing they are conjugal. Heinen sees a touch of irony in ὁμονοίας, Droysen (see comm. on 246(244K).4) and Haeberlin 700) in ἴσον ἴσῳ κεκραμένον. At this time ὁμόνοια was an important rallying-cry in Greece; see especially Zwicker in *RE* s.v. *Homonoia* 2265.6off., N. Kramer, *Quid valeat ὁμόνοια in litteris Graecis* (Diss. Göttingen 1915), J. de Romilly in *Mélanges de linguistique et de philologie grecque offerts à Pierre Chantraine* (Paris 1972) 199ff., Étienne and Piérart 71ff., W. C. West, *GRBS* 18 (1977) 307ff.

[2] There is no indication that he produced plays in his late teens, unlike Menander according to anon. *De comoedia Graeca*, 17 p. 9 Kaibel = *test.* 2 Körte-Thierfelder, or Eupolis according to the *Suda* s.v.

ΥΠΟΒΟΛΙΜΑΙΟΣ

attributed to [Arist.] *Chreiai* in Stob. *Flor.* 4.50b.83 = *Gnom. Vat.* 46 p. 23 Sternbach = *Apophthegm. Vind.* 36 Wachsmuth, *test.* 15), and (iii) died while competing and winning a victor's garland (Plut. *Mor.* 785b, *test.* 5), it is hard to reject at least the possibility that the comic poet successfully produced his *Hypobolimaios* in the 270s as a centenarian or thereabouts, although Plutarch's source(s) may well have exaggerated Alexis' age at death. Bergk's claim that fr. 246(244K) must have been added by an unknown hand to the text of the Ὑποβολιμαῖος for a posthumous second production was founded partly on an incorrect belief that its praise of Ptolemy, Arsinoe and ὁμόνοια belonged to the times of the Chremonidean War in the mid–260s, but this scholar added a further supporting argument (*Gr. Lit.* 4.150f.) that still merits consideration: the presence of numerous references in Alexis' frs. to events and personalities between the 350s and the 300s (or possibly 290s: cf. introductions to Ἱππεύς, Κράτεια, Πύραυνος; on the reference to an unspecified Ptolemy in fr. 92(88K) see introduction to Θεοφόρητος), and the absence of anything comparable between the 290s and fr. 246(244K)'s allusion to the 270s. Yet this chronological distribution of references can be explained in other ways than by Bergk's theory of a posthumous performance for Ὑποβολιμαῖος: by accidents of selection and preservation in the frs. of Alexis, for instance, by the decline in allusions to contemporary persons and situations in later Greek comedy, or perhaps even by Alexis' return to the theatre after retirement in order to celebrate a special event (? his hundredth birthday) with one final, victorious performance (Plut. *Mor.* 785b).

Plays with the same title were written also by Eudoxus, Philemon, Menander (cf. Webster, *SM* 100f., *IM* 152f., G. Zuntz, *PBA* 42 (1956) 236ff.) and Caecilius (Ribbeck, *CRF*[3] 54ff., cf. *Agroikos* 10), probably adapting Menander); a Ψευδυποβολιμαῖος is attested for Crobylus and (? along with a Ὑποβολιμαῖος: cf. Kassel–Austin 4.343f.) Cratinus jun. In the 270s Alexis' title would imply a New-Comedy intrigue focused on a supposititious child and probably its identification (cf. e.g. Plaut. *Truc.* 85ff., 194ff., 389ff., 501ff., 775ff., where the baby boy which the *meretrix* Phronesium passes off as her and Stratophanes' child turns out to be the son of Callicles' daughter and Diniarchus; cf. Legrand, *NGC* 211 and my introduction to Στρατιώτης); it is uncertain whether the daytime revelling proclaimed by the unidentified speaker on entrance at fr. 246(244K), cf. fr. 91(87K) and comm., Fraenkel, *MNC* 29f., is part of conventional celebrations after the play's dénouement.

246 (244K)

Meineke 3.494, Kock 2.386, Edmonds 2.490, Kassel–Austin 2.158. The fr.'s transmission, possible context and historical references are discussed in the introduction to Ὑποβολιμαῖος.

689

COMMENTARY

1 Πτολεμαίου τοῦ βασιλέως: 'genitive of the toast', like τῆς ἀδελφῆς τῆς τ. β. (2f.) and τῆς ὁμονοίας (5), see comm. on fr. 59(58K).

2 ἀκράτου: neat wine, drunk in toasts: cf. comm. on frs. 5 and 9.3–4.

προσλαβών: sc. 'having *drunk* in addition'; this (doubtless colloquial) use of (προσ)λαμβάνω is commoner than the entry in LSJ s.v. λαμβάνω 1.8b (citing only medical writers) suggests. Cf. e.g. Eriphus 4.1 ἐκπεπήδη-κας πρὶν ἀγαθοῦ πρῶτα δαίμονος λαβεῖν (with a similar genitive), Baton 3.2 Λεσβίου χυτρίδε λαμβάνειν δύο.

3 ταῦτ': A (Ath. 11.502b) has neither accent nor breathing, but the preceding τ' (v.2) helps to endorse Kaibel's interpretation here ('the same number' as for Ptolemy).

ἀπνευστί τ' ἐκπιών: ἀπνευστί τ' correctly A at Ath. 10.431b ~ ἐκπνευστ' A at 11.502b from anticipation of the following ἐκπιών. Cf. e.g. Hippocr. *Intern.* 12 τοῦτο δὲ κέλευε ἀπνευστὶ πιεῖν, Antiphanes 75(74K).14 ἕλκειν ἀπνευστί.

4 I.e. 'as happily as one would (sc. drink: supply ἐκπίοι) wine mixed like with like'. The difficulties which Porson (*Adv.* 119) and Meineke felt over syntax and meaning disappear as soon as we take due account of (i) the correct accentuation of ταῦτ' in v. 3, (ii) the point that the toasts are here drunk in neat wine, so that the reference to 'wine mixed like with like' (on the expression see comm. on 59(58K).2; toasts were often drunk also in this mixture) must be part of the comparison, and (iii) the reason for this apparently banal comparison, which Droysen (*Geschichte des Hellenismus*[2] 3.1.268 n. 3) first revealed. Alexis here is praising in what supporters would call patriotic, and denigrators sycophantic, fashion Ptolemy, Arsinoe and their *entente* with Athens (cf. introduction to Ὑποβολιμαῖος). At the same time many Athenians (like later Greeks: e.g. Plut. *Mor.* 736e–f, Lucian *Icar.* 15, Paus. 1.7.1, Herodian hist. 1.3.3, [Maneth.] *Apotelesm.* 5.208) would have been offended by the incestuous marriage of full brother and sister (see especially J. G. Droysen revised by E. Bayer, *Geschichte des Hellenismus*[3] 3 (Tübingen 1952 and Basle 1952–3) 171 and n. 173, J. Seibert, *Historische Beiträge zu den dynastischen Verbindungen in hellenistischer Zeit* (Wiesbaden 1967) 81ff., E. Longega, *Arsinoe II* (Rome 1968) 74, Fraser 1.117f. and 2.209f., nn. 201–6), with the result that the pen of Alexis the satirical moralist might have wished to move in the opposite direction to that of Alexis the patriotic spokesman. He effected a clever compromise by inserting into the middle of his encomium a few words which seem harmless at face value but which, given a particular delivery, might hint at the marriage of 'like with like'. The obliqueness of the reference is easily understood if we pay attention to the fate of the iambic poet Sotades of Maroneia, whose criticism of the marriage was direct and crude (fr. 1 Powell; Plut. *Mor.* 11a, Ath. 14.620f–621a).

For the idiom here cf. e.g. Thuc. 6.57 προσπεσόντες καὶ ὡς ἂν μάλιστα δι' ὀργῆς (sc. προσπέσοιεν) ... ἔτυπτον, Dem. 1.21 οὐδ' ὡς ἂν κάλλιστ' (sc. ἔχοι) αὐτῷ τὰ παρόντ' ἔχει, K.G. 1.243f.

5 καὶ τῆς ὁμονοίας, διὰ τί is A's text (Ath. 11.502b), which makes excellent sense; the speaker is thus interpreted as coupling ὁμόνοια with the toasts to Ptolemy and Arsinoe, not proposing a third and separate toast to the concept. Yet Meineke's καὶ τῆς ὁμ. δύο, τί ..., based on Epit.'s lacunose προσλαβὼν δύο νῦν μὴ κωμάσω κ.τ.λ. and printed by Kassel–Austin, is attractive and possibly right.

κωμάσω: cf. comm. on 112(107K).1.

6 λυχνούχου ... τηλικοῦτο: Porson's correction (*Adv.* 119) of A's haplography λύχνου (cf. the related error at 107(102K).1, see comm.) and (with Jacobs, *Spic.* 71: the priority is uncertain[1]) unmetrical -κοῦτον. In Attic comedy τηλικοῦτο (also Men. *Asp.* 215, *Dysk.* 209), τοιοῦτο and τοσοῦτο are metrically convenient but slightly less common (*c.* 45 ~ *c.* 53) alternatives to forms of the neuter nom. and acc. sing. in -τον (but -τον always Ar., nearly always tragedy: exceptions τοιοῦτο *P.V.* 801, MSS SMA of Stob. *Flor.* 4.22.136 at Eur. fr. 1059.5, MAV at Eur. *Andr.* 173). For the corruption cf. e.g. Antiphanes 55(52K).15 (the culprit again A, Ath. 10.449c), Philemon 94(90K).6. Cf. also K.B. 1.606f.

πρὸς τὸ τηλικοῦτο φῶς: '(why shouldn't I revel...) out into daylight as bright as this?' The words imply that the speaker has just entered from one of the stage houses, cf. e.g. Ar. *Nub.* 632 αὐτὸν καλῶ θύραζε δευρὶ πρὸς τὸ φῶς.

Φαιδρίας (? or Φαίδρια)

See Φαίδων ἢ Φαιδρίας.

Φαῖδρος

L. Spengel, Συναγωγη Τεχνων, *sive artium scriptores* (Stuttgart 1828) 135, Th. Bergk in C. Schiller's edition of Andocides (Leipzig 1835) 132ff. and *Griechische Literaturgeschichte* 4 (Berlin 1887) 153 n. 109, Meineke 1.381ff., Wilamowitz, *Aus Kydathen* (Berlin 1880) 221f. and *Platon*[2] (Berlin 1920) 1.363 n. 2, Breitenbach 90ff. and 176, A. Hug and E. Schoene, edition of Pl. *Symp.*[3] (Leipzig and Berlin 1909) xxxi, R. Fenk, *Adversarii Platonis quomodo de indole ac moribus eius judicaverint* (Diss. Jena 1913) 27ff.,

---

[1] Jacobs' *Spicilegium* was published in 1805, Porson's *Adversaria* in 1812 four years after his death.

COMMENTARY

G. Coppola, *RIGI* 7 (1923) 55ff., A. Weiher, *Blätter für das Bayerische Gymnasialschulwesen* 65 (1929) 27, A. Olivieri, *Dioniso* 7 (1939) 291, F. Lasserre, *La Figure d'Éros dans la poésie grecque* (Paris 1946) 114ff., T. B. L. Webster, *CQ* 2 (1952) 25 and *SLGC* 55, G. J. de Vries, *Hermeneus* 27 (1955) 7, Gil 337f., cf. Hunter's edition of Eubulus pp. 132f.

Two frs. (247(245K), 248(246K)) from the play[1] are preserved by Ath. (13.562a, 4.165e). In 248(246K) an unidentified character appears to be mitigating (most probably) some young man's extravagance (cf. Eustath. 1554.2ff. πέπαικται ... εἰς ἄσωτον βραχυήλικα; Bergk in Schiller) by citing the example of the even more prodigal Epicharides. If the named figure was a contemporary Athenian and identical with the pauper mentioned (fr. 223(220K).4 and comm.) in Alexis' Ταραντῖνοι (? *c.* 345–*c.* 320: introduction to that play), there would perhaps be grounds for assigning Φαῖδρος to a similar period.

Although such a dating is based on uncertain premises, it may gain some support from ostensible Platonic allusions in fr. 247(245K). Here an unidentified speaker claims that on a journey from the Piraeus his troubles and inability to cope with them set him thinking about the nature of Ἔρως, whom he characterises as an amalgam of (a) qualities that do not fit into conventional files of opposites (vv.6–9), (b) qualities that normally typify different beings, moods and states (10–13). Spengel first noted that two striking oppositions in (a) (Eros οὔτε θεὸς οὔτ' ἄνθρωπος, οὔτ' ἀβέλτερος οὔτ' αὖθις ἔμφρων vv. 6–8) also occur in Diotima's speech at Pl. *Symp.* 203d–e (οὔτε ὡς ἀθάνατος πέφυκεν οὔτε ὡς θνητός ... σοφίας τε αὖ καὶ ἀμαθίας ἐν μέσῳ ἐστίν, sc. ὁ Ἔρως, cf. 202d–e). These may be supplemented (cf. Fenk 28, de Vries 7) with other links (of varying strength) between fr. and dialogue: πορευομένῳ δ' ἐκ Πειραιῶς v. 1, ἀνιὼν Φαληρόθεν 172a; the ἀπορία of Alexis' speaker v. 2, of Eros' mother 203b (Diotima); φιλοσοφεῖν v. 2, Ἔρωτα φιλόσοφον εἶναι 204b (Diotima); Eros a δαίμων v. 5, 202d, cf. 203a (Diotima); E. neither female nor male v. 6, 189c–e (Aristophanes; cf. Gil); E. an amalgam vv. 8–9, 202a ff. (Socrates); E.'s boldness and vehemence vv. 10, 12, 203d (Diotima), cf. 196cd (Agathon); E.'s rationality vv. 11f., 203d (Diotima); E.'s φιλοτιμία 13, 178d (Phaedrus; cf. Olivieri); cf. also comm. on 247(245K).2 (with p. 696 n. 1), 10–13 and ? 16. Since the historical Phaedrus, son of Pythocles (cf. L. Parmentier, *Bulletin Budé* 10 (1926) 8ff., von Fritz, *RE* s.v. *Phaidros* 7, 1555.62ff., Davies, *APF* 201), is also πατὴρ τοῦ λόγου (177d) and first speaker in *Symp.*, as well as presenter of an essay on love (230e ff.) in the

---

[1] On the tentative suggestion advanced by Meineke, Breitenbach and Coppola that frs. 247–9(245–7K) might all derive from a single play titled Φαιδρίας, Φαῖδρος or Φαῖδρος ἢ Φαιδρίας, see introduction to Φαίδων (? Φείδων) or Φαιδρίας.

Platonic dialogue named after him, Bergk (in Schiller; cf. Wilamowitz, *Aus Kyd.* 221f., Fenk 27f.) suggested that he too must have been the subject of Alexis' play, describing (as the speaker of fr. 247(245K)) in vv. 1–2 his own poverty after the confiscation of his property as a result of alleged involvement in the Hermocopid scandal of 415 (*IG* i³.422.229ff., Andocides 1.15, Lysias 19.15). Bergk's theory was energetically opposed by Meineke, arguing that (i) the historical Phaedrus' disgrace, which had occurred some sixty years before Alexis began writing, would no longer have been newsworthy; (ii) the subject matter of fr. 247(245K) implied that its speaker's troubles were amatory rather than political; and (iii) if Alexis had intended to portray the Platonic Phaedrus, why did so many of the ideas in fr. 247(245K) reflect Diotima, Socrates and symposiasts in the dialogue other than Phaedrus?

Although Meineke's first argument is flawed, failing as it does to take account of the likelihood that the composition of Pl. *Phdr.* not many years perhaps before Alexis' play (*pace* Diog. Laert. 3.38: e.g. ? *c.* 359, cf. O. Regenbogen, *Miscellanea academica Berolinensia* 2 (Berlin 1950) 198ff. = *Kleine Schriften* (Munich 1961) 247ff.; ? 362–353, W. Jaeger, *Paideia* 3 (English translation, Oxford 1945) 320 n. 109; 'relatively close to, but still some distance from, the end of (Plato's) life', C. J. Rowe, *PCPS* 212 (1986) 120f.; but the date is much disputed) would have reawakened Athenian interest in the historical Phaedrus (cf. Gil 337f.), it persuaded Bergk into partial retraction (*Gr. Lit.*) and can be substantially reinforced. First, the Platonic parallels in 247(245K) are easily overstressed (cf. e.g. Fenk, Lasserre 114ff., Webster, *SLGC*). Precise verbal and conceptual links with *Symp.* are confined to barely a quarter of the fr. (vv. 6–8, 11–12), and even these are not necessarily direct borrowings. *Symp.* and *Phdr.* (along with Xen. *Symp.*, *Cyr.* 5.1.1–17 and [Dem.] 61) are the sole survivors of numerous enquiries into the nature of Eros circulating in the late 5th and early 4th centuries (cf. Meineke 1.384, Lasserre 110ff., Hunter and my introductions to frs. 20, 236(234K)), and parallels for two of the ideas linking *Symp.* and Alexis (vv.6f., 12) can be found in (i) Gorgias' *Helen* 19 (the question whether love is θεός, ἔχων θείαν δύναμιν or an ἀνθρώπινον νόσημα, cf. Lasserre 116) and (ii) Eur. fr. 430 (the vehemence of lovers, cf. comm. on 236(234K)). Secondly, if the two Alexis frs. are considered without any reference to Platonic parallels, they can be seen to point to situations and behaviour characteristic in New Comedy. Fr. 247(245K)'s opening reference to the speaker's journey from the Piraeus groups it with a serious of entrance monologues (e.g. Plaut. *Amph.* 153ff. ~ 148f., *Capt.* 768ff. ~ 869, *Merc.* 111ff. ~ 109, 161, *Most* 348ff. ~ 363, *Stich.* 274ff. ~ 295, 338; Ter. *Eun.* 292ff. ~ 290; cf. the variant in com. adesp. fr. 257.73ff. Austin) in which the entrant has normally (*Eun.* and fr. 257 Austin are here the exceptions) either himself just landed or seen someone who has landed at a nearby harbour. Alexis' speaker proceeds to mention his troubles and ἀπορία (1–2) and then to analyse the nature of Ἔρως (3ff.) without explaining this transition. As Meineke saw, its obvious implication was the speaker's involvement in an unhappy love affair; wretched lovers in comedy habitually soliloquise about their love (e.g. Men. *Asp.* 286ff., *Mis.* A1ff., Plaut. *Cist.* 203ff., Ter. *Andr.* 26off., *Eun.* 629ff., cf. the dialogue speech at *Hec.* 281ff., where the speaker has also just come from the harbour; Webster, *SM* 166; P. Flury, *Liebe und Liebessprache bei Menander, Plautus, Terenz* (Heidelberg 1968) 2off., 7off.). It is tempting to speculate that the impoverishment hinted at in fr. 248(246K) might have been that of 247(245K)'s speaker as a result of an affair with a grasping *hetaira* (cf. Coppola) who had relieved him of all his money, but other scenarios are possible (cf. Breitenbach).[1]

The cited comic parallels suggest that Alexis' play most probably was, along with e.g. Ἀγωνίς, an early example of a plot-type much favoured in New Comedy, with a young man in love, a ? *hetaira* as inamorata, and a critic and/or defender of profligacy. Why then did Alexis choose Φαῖδρος for his title (? and the name of his young lover, although this is no certain equation), and season at least one speech with philosophic tags reminiscent of Plato's *Phdr.* and *Symp.*? The generally accepted view since Meineke is that Alexis was inspired by these two dialogues to portray the hero of a conventional love intrigue as a romanticised and youthful[2] Platonic Phaedrus (so e.g. Breitenbach, Coppola, Gil; cf. Lasserre's unevidenced variation, that after the facts about the historical Phaedrus' career had been blurred by time, Alexis fictionalised the story of his downfall with a love affair replacing the Hermocopid scandal). Yet Phaedrus was not a rare name in Athens (17 examples in Kirchner, *PA* 2.336f., 485), and it was used by Terence without any philosophical reference as a stock name for a young lover (*Andr.* 86f.); could then the Platonic associations in Alexis 247(245K) have been no more than fashionable arabesques added to give swagger to a standard lover's monologue?

---

[1] Equally uncertain is Spengel's (cf. also Breitenbach 91 and Lasserre 118 n. 1) guess that fr. 247(245K) opened Alexis' Φαῖδρος. Of parallel monologues, one or two begin plays (e.g. Men. *Mis.* A1ff.), but most come later.

[2] The impression given by Plato in *Phdr.* is that its titular hero was callow and enthusiastic, but not necessarily young. Although it is difficult to reconcile the historical and personal allusions in the dialogue with any precise scenic date (cf. K. J. Dover, *Lysias and the Corpus Lysiacum* (Berkeley and Los Angeles 1968) 28ff., C. J. Rowe's edition (Bristol 1986) 13), the period 418–416 (so Dover 43) best fits the data, when Phaedrus would have been over 30 (cf. Davies, *APF* 201).

247 (245K)

Meineke 3.495 (1), Kock 2.386, Edmonds 2.490, Kassel–Austin 2.160. The speaker, context and Platonic allusions of this fr. are discussed, and its extensive bibliography listed, in the introduction to Φαῖδρος. Ath. 13.562a ff. cites it (all in A, vv. 3–13 in Epit.; 3–12 φρονοῦντος in Eustath. 988.14ff. with the same textual variants as Epit.), along with Alexis 20, 70, 236(234K), Amphis 15, Aristophon 11, Eubulus 40(41K) and Theophilus 12 (all single speeches) in a section on Ἔρως and ἐρῶντες.

1 A's πορευομένων *fortasse seruari potest, si Phaedrum* [if he is the speaker] *cum sodalibus ex Piraeo ad urbem accessisse putas* (Meineke), in which case ἡμῶν could have been written in a preceding verse or be supplied from the general sense (cf. K.G. 2.81 *Anm.* 2, and especially δεομένων at Thuc. 3.55); yet Kock's objection (*philosophatur sine dubio solus ambulans*) is reinforced by consideration of the scenic situation: if the speaker is soliloquising directly after his walk, what has he done with his companions? πορευομένῳ (-ένω Musurus, -ένῳ Bedrotus) is the obvious correction, and A's corruption explained by homoeoteleuton with κακῶν later in the line.

ἐκ Πειραιῶς: why the speaker should have come from the harbour is uncertain (but see introduction to Φαῖδρος). Correption of αι before a long vowel or diphthong in this word is common in comedy (1st metron: Ar. *Pax* 145, fr. 683(608K), Philiscus 2, cf. Machon 388; 3rd metron: Criton com. 3.4, Men. *Epitr.* 752, com. adesp. fr. 340.3 Kock; only here in 2nd metron), as it is in the penultimate syllable of a number of adjectives and one pronoun in comedy, occasionally also where the final syllable is short or *anceps* (e.g. Ἀθηναῖος Eupolis 37(35K), Pherecrates 39(34K), Polyzelus 12(11K).3; ? φιλαθηναῖος Ar. *Vesp.* 282; γεραῖέ Men. *Sik.* 169; δείλαϊος especially in the exclamation οἴμοι δ. at line end, x 10 in Ar. e.g. *Equ.* 139 and Neil *ad loc.*, Eubulus 115.13(117.8K), cf. Ar. *Plut.* 850; probably not δίκαιον at Men. *Epitr.* 348, see *ZPE* 24 (1977) 16f.; αὑταῖί Ar. *Av.* 1018). Scansion in all the authentic cases and the orthography Πειραεύς (especially common in 4th-century inscriptions: cf. Meisterhans–Schwyzer 32 n. 173, Threatte 1.279ff. and 292) clearly reflected contemporary pronunciation, which glided over or totally suppressed the ι. Cf. K.B. 1.312f., Descroix 24, West, *Greek Metre* 11f.; on comic practice, Starkie, comm. on Ar. *Vesp.* 40, Handley on Men. *Dysk.* 230–2, pp. 172f., Sandbach on Men. *Epitr.* 348; on tragic, especially Jebb on S. *Ant.* 1310f., Denniston on Eur. *El.* 497.

The commonest examples of correption in Alexis affect οι before a long vowel or diphthong: τοιοῦτος (οι short: frs. 4.3, 103(98K).14, 113(108K).2, 133(128K).6; *anceps*: 35(34K).1, 91(87K).4, 223(221K).13, 247(245K).16, 275(273K).4, 304(301K).1; long: 178(172K).14,

265(263K).7; cf. Hunter, comm. on Eubulus 67.5) and πο(ι)ῶ, where orthography may reflect the scansion (cf. comm. on 16.2; ο(ι) always short or *anceps* except 178(172K).7, 189(184K)).

1–2 ὑπὸ τῶν κακῶν καὶ τῆς ἀπορίας: the troubles of love and a shortage of money for conducting the affair, in all probability (see introduction to Φαῖδρος).

2 φιλοσοφεῖν ἐπῆλθέ μοι: 'the idea of playing the philosopher entered my head'. The construction (impersonal ἐπέρχεται + dative and infinitive) occurs first in 5th-century Greek (Ionic: Hdt. 6.107; Attic: S. *Trach.* 134f.) in the sense 'X happens to . . .', but in 4th-century Attic the related meaning 'it enters X's mind to . . .' generally takes over: e.g. Xen. *Mem.* 4.3.3, Pl. *Crat.* 428c, *Symp.* 197c,[1] *Gorg.* 485e, *Resp.* 7.524c, Isoc. 12.96, *Epist.* 9.8, Dem. 14.29, 18.263, 20.52, 23.5, 24.195; cf. Rehdantz–Blass, *Index* 77f. φιλοσοφεῖν occurs several times in later (never Old) comedy in the sense 'to theorise like a (professional) philosopher', usually with a pejorative implication that such activity is ill-judged, ill-timed, useless, irrelevant or bogus (Men. *Asp.* 340, *Mis.* A17, Anaxippus 4.1, Theognetus 1.9, com. adesp. fr. 248 Kock, Xen. *Mem.* 1.2.19, [Lysias] 8.11, Isoc. 8.5, Lucian *Nigr.* 24); when such implications seem absent (here, Alexis 37(36K).2, Men. *Sam.* 725), a touch of self-deflating or captious ridicule may be sensed; lack of context makes a verdict on Men. fr. 204 impossible, but cf. Lysias 24.10. In Alexis here and at Men. *Mis.* the subject of the speculations is love; cf. later e.g. Chariton 2.4.5, Ach. Tat. 1.12.1.

3–5 The accusation that artists were ignorant of the true appearance of Eros was a commonplace of the time: cf. Eubulus 40(41K) and Hunter *ad loc.*, Alexis 20 and comm.

ζωγράφοι (so A, Epit.), not ζῳ- (Blaydes, *Adv.* 2.167), appears to have been the accepted orthography (sc. as derived from ζωός or ζωή, not ζῷον, + γράφω), on the evidence of Ptolemaic papyri (e.g. *PSI* 4.346.4, 407.2, mid–3rd century), inscriptions (e.g. *SIG* 682.3, Pergamum 140/39 BC) and at least one grammarian (*Et. Mag.* 412.53, s.v. -ος, . . . οὐκ ἔχει τὸ ι προσγεγραμμένον); similarly ζωγραφία (e.g. Philodemus, *Rhet.* fr. xxx.9, 2.166 Sudhaus, *SIG* 960.13, Magnesia 2nd century).

---

[1] ἐπέρχεται δέ μοί τι καὶ ἔμμετρον εἰπεῖν, which comes towards the end of Agathon's λόγος and is followed by a peroration on Ἔρως in some respects stylistically akin to Alexis 247(245K), with balanced antitheses (e.g. πραότητα μὲν πορίζων, ἀγριότητα δ' ἐξορίζων) and lists of characteristics (e.g. θεατὸς σοφοῖς, ἀγαστὸς θεοῖς· ζηλωτὸς ἀμοίροις, κτητὸς εὐμοίροις), although its rhymes and contrived word-play are alien to Alexis here. Even if this passage directly inspired 247(245K), however, we are still a long way from knowing whether Platonic influence extended beyond the one fragment (see introduction to Φαῖδρος).

4 Epit.'s συντομώτερον δ' εἰπεῖν is correct and A's συντομώτατον δ' εἰπεῖν (*pace* Kassel–Austin) unidiomatic, the comparative form in -ον being adverbial, the superlative in -ον adjectival. Such absolute uses of the infinitive, whether or not introduced by ὡς (K.G. 2.17f., 508ff., Goodwin, *MT* 310ff.) are regularly accompanied by an adverb (e.g. συντόμως Xen. *Oec.* 12.19, Pl. *Tim.* 25e, ἁπλῶς Dinarchus 1.31, 2.19), adverbial equivalent (e.g. σὺν θεῷ Pl. *Prot.* 317b, *Theaet.* 151b, *Leg.* 9.858b), or accusative neut. sing. of an adjective with article (e.g. τὸ ξύμπαν Thuc. 1.138, 7.49, τὸ ὀρθόν S. *OR* 1220f.), but not acc. neut. sing. of adj. alone. MSS commonly confuse comparative and superlative forms: see comm. on 283(281K).2.

5 τοῦ δαίμονος τούτου: cf. introduction to Φαῖδρος and comm. on 242(240K).1.

εἰκόνας: i.e. both pictures and other sorts of representation such as statues; the clause ὅσοι–εἰκόνας is added simply to extend the range beyond the painters (ζωγράφοι) of v. 3.

6–7 οὔτε θῆλυς οὔτ' ἄρρην, πάλιν οὔτε θεὸς οὔτ' ἄνθρωπος: on Alexis' likely source here and in vv. 7–8, see introduction to Φαῖδρος. ACE's ἄρσην was corrected by Dindorf to ἄρρην, the Attic form during Alexis' lifetime (cf. Meisterhans–Schwyzer 100, Threatte 1.536, Hunter on Eubulus 106(107K).1). It is possible to construe πάλιν with either (a) the preceding or (b) the following phrase. In favour of (a) (so Bothe, *PCGF* 571, Richards, *AO* 67, Edmonds) is the common adhesion of πάλιν/αὖ/ αὖθις to the second element in conjunctive and disjunctive clauses: e.g. S. *El.* 370f. εἰ σὺ μὲν μάθοις | τοῖς τῆσδε χρῆσθαι, τοῖς δὲ σοῖς αὔτη πάλιν, monost. 396 Jäkel καλὸν τὸ γηρᾶν καὶ τὸ μὴ γηρᾶν πάλιν; Eur. *Andr.* 866ff., *Hec.* 956f., Aristonymus com. fr. 2(3K), Dem. 27.49 οὔτε ... οὔτε + αὖ; Alexis 247(245K).7f. οὔτ' ... οὔτ' αὖθις, cf. Ar. *Vesp.* 58ff. In favour of (b) is a use of πάλιν that becomes increasingly common in later Greek but is not well treated by the lexica, whereby the adverb introduces a clause in the sense of 'next/furthermore', sometimes with a connecting particle (e.g. καὶ π. Alexis 146(142K).5, Plut. *Mor.* 36c; π. δέ Men. *Epitr.* 890, *Sam.* 275) and sometimes without (e.g. Pl. *Resp.* 10.612d, Damoxenus 2.18, Sosipater 1.36, Plut. *Mor.* 33a, 54e, 533b). I opt for (b) partly because A and CE have a raised point after ἄρσην, thus indicating that at some time between Alexis' original manuscript and the early 10th century a conscious decision was taken so to interpret an ambiguous text.

8 συνενηνεγμένος: L. K. Valckenaer's correction (in Peppink, *Observ.* 77, forestalling Kock) of the unmetrical gibberish of A (συνενηγμένος) and CE (συνηνεγμενος without accent) scores over the other suggestions (συμπεπηγμένος Grotius, *Exc.* 593, 974, συννενημένος Schweighaeuser, συμμεμιγμένος Bailey, *CGF* (Cambridge 1840) 39, before Herwerden, *Obs. Crit.* 79, συνενηνησμένος and <που> συνηγμένος Meineke 3.496 and *Anal.*

COMMENTARY

Crit. 260) because it provides ideal sense (cf. e.g. Hesych. s.v. συνενηνεγμέ-νος· συνελθών, Eur. *Her.* 488, Dem. 24.74; LSJ s.v. συμφέρω A.I.1) and the most plausible explanation (haplography) of the corruptions in both A and Epit.

9 ἐνὶ τύπῳ <τε> πόλλ' εἴδη φέρων: Schweighaeuser's supplement of the short syllable omitted (by quasi-haplography: ΤΕΠ) in ACE and Eustathius between τύπῳ and πόλλ' provides the desired connection for the two participles in 8–9, but τύπῳ as instrumental ablative worried Meineke ('*fortasse* ... πάντοθεν, ἐν ἐνὶ τύπῳ τε' *Anal. Crit.* 260, after Casaubon; palaeographically neat, and for πάντοθεν in comedy cf. Men. fr. 510.1 and monost. 103 = *Comp. Men. et Phil.* 1.153 Jäkel, *pace* LSJ s.v.), and φέρων worried Herwerden (hence φορῶν, *Mnemosyne* 4 (1876) 317); yet 'supporting/enduring many forms with/by means of one containing shape' (cf. LSJ s.v. τύπος VI.2) seems satisfactory if not elegant Greek for the concept Alexis wishes to convey.

10–13 A more sophisticated version of εἰκών (cf. comm. on 46(45K), 242(240K)) in which Alexis, instead of comparing one object directly to another, describes it (here Ἔρως) by attributing to it a series of qualities that normally typify other objects or beings; his most celebrated precedent in extant comedy was Aristophanes' description of Cleon at *Vesp.* 1030ff. = *Pax* 752ff. Some of the qualities chosen by Alexis for his identikit of Ἔρως are clearly contemporary commonplaces (cf. F. Lasserre, *Mus. Helv.* 1 (1944) 175):

(i) τόλμα: Eur. fr. 430 τόλμης καὶ θράσους διδάσκαλον | Ἔρωτα, Aristophon 11.4f. (Ἔρως) λίαν ἦν θρασὺς καὶ σοβαρός; cf. A. *Choeph.* 597 γυναικῶν ... παντόλμους ἔρωτας.

(ii) δειλία: a characteristic particularly of some lovers in later comedy (e.g. Ctesipho, Antipho in Ter. *Ad.*, *Phorm.*; G. E. Duckworth, *The Nature of Roman Comedy* (Princeton 1952) 239ff.); ? cf. also Pl. *Symp.* 179d μαλθακίζεσθαι ἐδόκει (Pausanias on Orpheus).

(iii) ἄνοια: Theognis 1231 σχέτλι' Ἔρως, μανίαι σε τιθηνήσαντο λαβοῦσαι, Anacreon 53 Page ἀστράγαλοι δ' Ἔρωτός εἰσιν | μανίαι τε καὶ κυδοιμοί; cf. Hom. *Il.* 3.442, 14.294, Pind. *Nem.* 11.48, S. *Ant.* 790, Eur. *Hipp.* 214, 232, 240f., 398, fr. 161 ἥρων· τὸ μαίνεσθαι δ' ἄρ' ἦν ἔρως βροτοῖς, Pl. *Phdr.* 231d (lovers, cf. 249d–251a), *Leg.* 8.839a λύττης ἐρωτικῆς καὶ μανίας, Arist. *EE* 3.1.17, 1229ᵃ21, Theophr. fr. 115 Wimmer, Men. *Pk.* 494ff. (with J. van Leeuwen's ἐρᾷς, cf. *CQ* 18 (1968) 237), fr. 79, Plaut. *Curc.* 177, *Merc.* 443ff., *Truc.* 47; F. Lasserre, *Mus. Helv.* 1 (1944) 176f.

(iv) λόγος: Pl. *Symp.* 196d–197b σοφία of Ἔρως (Agathon), 203d (Ἔρως) φρονήσεως ἐπιθυμητής, cf. 184d–e (Pausanias of lovers), [Dem.] 61.37 (their διάνοια).

698

ΦΑΙΔΡΟΣ

(v) σφοδρότης: closely related to τόλμα above, but note also Pl. *Symp.*
203d (Ἔρως) ἀνδρεῖος ὢν καὶ ἴτης καὶ σύντονος (Diotima's
account); cf. Alexis 236(234K).5 (lovers) ἰταμούς, προθύμους, and
comm. *ad loc.*, Men. *Epitr.* 527f. (Habrotonon's description of a rape)
ὡς ἀναιδὴς ἦσθα καὶ | ἰταμός τις ... κατέβαλες δέ μ' ὡς σφόδρα, *Pk.*
172 (Polemon) ὁ σοβαρός.

(vi) πόνος: cf. Aristarchus trag. fr. 2.4f. (Ἔρως) καὶ τὸν ἀσθενῆ σθένειν |
τίθησι, Pl. *Phdr.* 231b, 232a (τοὺς ἐρῶντας) ἐπιδείκνυσθαι πρὸς
ἅπαντας ὅτι οὐκ ἄλλως αὐτοῖς πεπόνηται, [Dem.] 61.26, 37, 56
(lovers' φιλοπονία), Alexis 236(234K).3f. πονεῖν τε δυναμένους τοῖς
σώμασιν | μάλιστα (lovers) with comm.

(vii) φιλοτιμία: cf. Pl. *Symp.* 178e (lovers φιλοτιμούμενοι πρὸς ἀλλήλους:
Phaedrus' speech), *Phdr.* 232a, 234a; [Dem.] 61.29; F. Lasserre, *La
Figure d'Éros dans la poésie grecque* (Paris 1946) 113, *Mus. Helv.* 1
(1944) 174.

With the loss of so many of the ἐρωτικοὶ λόγοι composed in the 4th and
late 5th centuries, it is difficult to estimate how far vv. 10–13 were inspired
directly by Pl. *Phdr.* and *Symp.* (which provide close or rough parallels for
five or perhaps even six of the seven items in Alexis' list), and how far both
Plato and Alexis were indebted to literary (including comic: e.g. (ii) and
(v) above) or popular tradition. Even the structure of the list, which opens
with two paradoxical pairs of opposites, may be influenced less by Plato
than by philosophic (cf. e.g. Heraclitus fr. 61 Diels–Kranz 1.164 and G. S.
Kirk (Cambridge 1954) 74f. = fr. 35 M. Marcovich (Merida Venezuela
1967) 177ff.; W. K. C. Guthrie, *A History of Greek Philosophy* 3 (Cambridge
1969) 166), sophistic and rhetorical practices going back to the 5th
century.

10–11 ἡ τόλμα μὲν γὰρ ἀνδρός, ἡ <δὲ> δειλία γυναικός: so Musurus; δὲ
was omitted in A by haplography and misplaced after δειλία in Epit. and
Eustath. τόλμα/θράσος and δειλία are regularly presented as the vices at
opposite extremes to the virtue ἀνδρεία (e.g. Arist. *EN* 2.7.2, 1107^{b}2ff.,
3.6.1–9.7, 1115^{a}5ff., cf. Thuc. 3.82.4, Pl. *Tim.* 87a, *Leg.* 1.648b, Σ T Hom.
13.289 citing ? Men. fr. 942), and the association of the former vice
particularly with men and δειλία with women (in a literature almost
entirely written by males) is largely taken for granted (but cf. e.g. A. *Sept.*
191f., S. *El.* 995ff., Eur. *Med.* 263ff. γυνὴ γὰρ τἄλλα μὲν φόβου πλέα | κακή
τ' ἐς ἀλκὴν καὶ σίδηρον εἰσορᾶν, *Andr.* 757 γυναικῶν δειλὸν ... λόγον,
Arist. *Pol.* 3.2.10, 1277^{b}2off.; Dover, *GPM* 98ff., R. Just, *Women in Athenian
Law and Life* (London and New York 1989) 153ff.).

11 ἡ δ' ἄνοια μανίας: contrasted here as it is with ὁ λόγος φρονοῦντος
(where λόγος clearly = 'rational thought', see LSJ s.v. iv.1; cf. the similar
polarity of νοῦς and ἄνοια in Arist. *HA* 9.3, 610^{b}2off.), this expression

seems odd in a list where the other six genitives predicated as typical owners of Eros' qualities all denote concrete creatures or things. Such inconsistency can be defended for Alexis here (cf. comm. on vv. 12f.), however, by the fact that elsewhere ἄνοια is used as the general term for a state ('want of understanding') of which μανία is one specific part (cf. Pl. *Tim.* 86b νόσον μὲν δὴ ψυχῆς ἄνοιαν συγχωρητέον, δύο δ' ἀνοίας γένη, τὸ μὲν μανίαν, τὸ δὲ ἀμαθίαν, *Resp.* 2.382c διὰ μανίαν ἤ τινα ἄνοιαν). Even so, the possibility that μανίας (so AE, Eustath.: μανοίας C influenced by the preceding ἄνοια) is a scribal error (? substitution of a marginal gloss on ἄνοια) cannot be ruled out; in that case Herwerden's παιδός (*Mnemosyne* 14 (1886) 195f.) is a plausible speculation.

12 ἡ σφοδρότης δὲ θηρός: the point presumably is that the behaviour of a male lover (cf. in comedy especially Men. *Epitr.* 527f., cited above on 10–13 (v)) can resemble the uncontrolled violence of wild beasts (e.g. Arist. *HA* 9.1, 610ᵃ15 μάχονται δὲ καὶ ἐλέφαντες σφοδρῶς πρὸς ἀλλήλους; cf. 6.21, 575ᵃ14, on the mating bull).

12–13 ὁ δὲ πόνος ἀδάμαντος: five of the other combinations in Alexis' list (10–13) involve nominative and subjective genitive ('his A belongs (typically) to a B'), one involves nom. and defining gen. (ἡ ἄνοια μανίας 11, see *ad loc.*), but the relationship between πόνος and ἀδάμαντος here is looser and the genitive needs to be grouped with those extensions of the objective gen. where the controlling noun expresses a feeling or activity (K.G. 1.335f., with a good collection of examples): translate 'his toil is that associated with (working) ἀδάμας' (i.e. indefatigable, see below).[1] The closest parallel is A. *Ag.* 53f. δεμνιοτήρη | πόνον ὀρταλίχων ὀλέσαντες, 'having lost the couch-guarding toil associated with their nestlings' (see Fraenkel *ad loc.*, but ignore his incorrect interpretation of A. *Pers.* 751, where see H. D. Broadhead, comm. (Cambridge 1960) *ad loc.*). ἀδάμας in Greek authors from the time of Hesiod (*Op.* 147, *Theog.* 239; cf. e.g. Pind. *Pyth.* 4.71, fr. 123.4 Snell–Maehler = 108.3 Bowra, *P.V.* 6, 64, Hdt. 7.141, Eur. *Cycl.* 596, Antipater Sid. 44.4 Gow–Page = *Anth. Pal.* 16.167.4, Diod. Sic. 16.5.4., [Lucian] *Asin.* 11) was a symbol of indestructible permanence and indefatigability, but its identification is not always clear. Up to the end of the 5th century it seems to have denoted some compound of iron (cf. Hesych. s.v. ἀδάμας· γένος σιδήρου) such as cementite (cf. Forbes, *Technology* 9.195ff., 206ff.[1] = 207ff., 218ff.[2]; cf. Forbes in C. J. Singer and others, *A History of Technology* 1 (Oxford 1954) 55ff.), or smelted manganese-bearing iron ores (cf. J. F. Healy, *Mining and Metallurgy in the Greek and Roman World* (London 1978) 215), but thereafter also some other very hard

---

[1] Although the transmitted text thus makes acceptable sense, Meineke's conjecture Ἄτλαντος (in place of ἀδάμαντος, *Anal. Crit.* 260) is well worth considering, before it is rejected.

ΦΑΙΔΡΟΣ

materials (but down to Roman times almost certainly not diamonds, *pace* LSJ s.v. and Blümner in *RE* s.v. *Diamant* 322.19ff.; these were not known in classical Greece, cf. R. A. Higgins, *Greek and Roman Jewellery*² (London 1980) 36f. The identity of the ἀδάμας labelled in Pl. *Tim.* 59b as χρυσοῦ ὄζος is unknown; that in Theophr. *Lapid.* 19, 44, cf. Pliny, *HN* 37.55–61, is probably native crystalline aluminium oxide, i.e. corundum, particularly the mixture known as emery, see E. R. Caley and J. F. C. Richards, comm. (*Theophrastus on Stones*, Columbus OH 1956) *ad loc.*).

13 ἡ φιλοτιμία δὲ δαίμονος: the final item provides an effective climax (cf. G. Coppola, *RIGI* 7 (1923) 57). The φιλοτιμία of lovers is essentially competitive (cf. Dover, *GPM* 229ff., 236), a pride in the success of an *amour* that excites the envy of others (of the passages cited above on vv. 10–13 (vii), cf. especially Pl. *Phdr.* 232a, [Dem.] 61.29). Divine φιλοτιμία, on the other hand, is simply and literally (cf. M. Landfester, *Das griechische Nomen <<philos>> und seine Ableitungen* (Hildesheim 1966) 148ff.) the desire to receive from mortals the honour that gods and goddesses claim as their due: evidenced throughout the literary versions of Greek myth (e.g. Aphrodite, Eur. *Hipp.* 7f. ἔνεστι γὰρ δὴ κἂν θεῶν γένει τόδε· τιμώμενοι χαίρουσιν ἀνθρώπων ὕπο, cf. 107; Tiresias on Dionysus, *Bacch.* 321 κἀκεῖνος ... τέρπεται τιμώμενος, cf. 208f.; Thanatos, *Alc.* 53 τιμαῖς κἀμὲ τέρπεσθαι δοκεῖ; cf. A. W. H. Adkins, *Merit and Responsibility* (Oxford 1960) 63f., 80 n. 4)[1] and popular belief (e.g. Hippocr. *Aër.* 22 εἰ δὴ τιμώμενοι χαίρουσιν οἱ θεοὶ καὶ θαυμαζόμενοι ὑπ' ἀνθρώπων, and expressions such as φθόνος θεῶν, A. *Ag.* 946f., *Pers.* 362, Eur. *Alc.* 1135, cf. Pind. *Isthm.* 7.39, so widespread that it could be reduced comprehensibly to just φθόνος, e.g. S. *Phil.* 776, Dem. 18.305, cf. Fraenkel on A. *Ag.* 762). We cannot know how far Alexis, in his clever combination of the two concepts of φιλοτιμία that seem here to filter through the text, intended his audience to remember that he had already (5, 7) described Ἔρως as neither god nor man, but a δαίμων.

14–15 καὶ ταῦτ' ἐγώ, μὰ τὴν Ἀθηνᾶν καὶ θεούς, οὐκ οἶδ' ὅ τι ἐστίν: the same oath is sworn in com. adesp. fr. 258.37 Austin by a young man who may have fathered an illegitimate baby and is being advised by an old man to leave on a journey (cf. Webster, *SLGC* 172f.). Oaths invoking Athena elsewhere in later Greek comedy are sworn regularly by men, usually Athenians, to emphasise the truth of a statement (also e.g. *Asp.* 319, *Pk.* 303, *Sam.* 213, com. adesp. frs. 255.8, 257.41 Austin, cf. Alexis 204(200K).1, 233(231K).2; F. W. Wright, *Studies in Menander* (Baltimore 1911) 13ff.).

---

[1] In the extant Greek romances Ἔρως himself is characteristically described as φιλόνικος (e.g. Xen. Ephes. 1.2.1 φιλόνικος ... καὶ ὑπερηφάνοις ἀπαραίτητος, Chariton 1.1.4, 6.4.5).

701

If καὶ ταῦτ' (so A: Epit. ends its citation at v. 13, Eustath. at v. 12) is correctly transmitted, the pronoun is best interpreted as the subject of ἐστίν removed from its clause to become the object of οἶδ' (on this common idiom, K.G. 2.577ff.): 'And these things – I don't know ... what they amount to, but even so they involve something like this.' For ταῦτα predicated by the singular ὅ τι cf. e.g. Antiphanes 120(122K).15 ταυτὶ δ' ὅ τι ἐστὶν οὐδ' ἂν 'Απόλλων μάθοι, Men. Epitr. 309 τὰ χρυσῖ' ἢ ταῦθ' ὅ τι ποτ' ἐστί, Ar. Ach. 899f., Nub. 348 (similarly τί in direct questions, cf. Gildersleeve, Syntax 1.59). Meineke's conjecture διὰ ταῦτ' (Anal. Crit. 260) here weakens the connection by removing the subject of ἐστίν.

15–16 ἔχει γέ τι τοιοῦτον: 'they (the ταῦτα of v. 14, rather than Ἔρως or a vague 'it') involve something like this'. The vagueness of the words perfectly reflects the speaker's uncertainty. I see no reason to alter the text to ἔχω γέ or ἔχει μέ (Richards, AO 67f.).

16 ἐγγύς τ' εἰμὶ τοὐνόματος: this correction of A's ἐ. τ' εἰμη (εἰμὶ B, an apograph of A, before Causabon) τοῦ ὀνόματος (τοὐν- Dindorf) satisfies both metre (with the citation ending at the second element of the third metron) and sense.[1] The speaker sums up his investigation with an amusingly banal conclusion, 'I'm close to the name', sc. to the concept of Ἔρως that the name indicates. His words imply acceptance of the naturalistic view of names which maintained that a name contained a clue to the real nature of the creature or thing it denoted (cf. J. H. Lersch, Die Sprachphilosophie der Alten 3 (Bonn 1841) 3ff). Plato's Cratylus, in which the title figure attempts to defend this view against the theory of Hermogenes that names are just conventional labels (cf. e.g. Guthrie 3.204ff., J. Derbolav, Platons Sprachphilosophie im Kratylos und in den späteren Schriften (Darmstadt 1972), with full bibliography 234ff., K. Gaiser, Name und Sache in Platons <Kratylos> (Abh. Heidelberg 1974), J. K. Rijlaarsdam, Platon über die Sprache (Utrecht 1978)) shows the liveliness of the issue in the first half of the 4th century. Since Ἔρως, the subject of Alexis' investigation here, is one figure whose name clearly defines his sphere of interest, the speaker's conclusion is presumably intended as a comic dig at the triviality of some of the current theorising.

248 (246K)

Meineke 3.496 (II), Kock 2.387, Edmonds 2.492, Kassel–Austin 2.161. On a possible context for the fr. (cited by Ath.4.165e, all in A, vv. 2–4 in Epit. and Eustath. 1554.2ff.) see introduction to Φαῖδρος and comm. on v. 1.

---

[1] Of the many other conjectures proposed (a sample: Dobree, Adv. 2.341, Emperius 350, Blaydes, Adv. 1.117), only two are worth recording: τοῦ νοήματος A. Emperius, Rh. Mus. 1 (1842) 462 = Opuscula 158, 311 and

ΦΑΙΔΡΟΣ

1 σχολῇ γε, νὴ τὸν Ἥλιον, σχολῇ λέγεις: probably the opening words of one speaker's riposte to another's criticism of the speed with which some young man in the play has dissipated his fortune. The use of γε with an adverb at the opening of a sentence is exclamatory and emphatic (Denniston, *GP* 126f.), and the repetition of σχολῇ also emphatic (cf. comm. on 207(204K).1), the more so when reinforced by an oath as here (cf. in later comedy e.g. Men. *Epitr.* 878 ὑπομαίνεθ' οὗτος, νὴ τὸν Ἀπόλλω, μαίνεται, *Theoph.* 29f. νὴ Δί', εὖ γε, Λυσία, | ὑπέρευγε, *Phasm.* 90 ἐγώ σε· μὰ τὸν Ἀπόλλω, 'γὼ μὲν οὔ, com. adesp. fr. 251.1 Austin οὐκ ἔσ]τι, μὰ τὸν Ἥφαιστον, ἀλλ' οὐκ ἐ[στί μοί, 255.8 Austin δειλὸ]ς εἶ, νὴ τὴν Ἀθηνᾶν, δειλὸς εἶ). The oath νὴ τὸν Ἥλιον is common in New (but absent from Old) Comedy and confined to men (*senex*: Men. *Sam.* 323; *adulescens*: *Sik.* 273, *Fab. Inc.* 25, ? *Epitr.* 631; parasite: ? *Sik.* 117; slave: *Asp.* 399, *Epitr.* 525, *Mis.* 285); cf. Wright, *op. cit.* in comm. on 247(245).14–15, 39ff., Gow on Call. epigr. 12.1. On λέγεις see comm. on fr. 223(221K).11–12.

2 Ἐπιχαρίδης ὁ μικρός: possibly the same person as the pauper described eating dog flesh at fr. 223(220K).4 (see comm., and introduction to Φαῖδρος). In place of Ἐπιχαρίδης (so A, CE) Eustathius has Χαρίδης, which induced Meineke (before retraction in his edition of Callimachus (Berlin 1861) 273f.) to conjecture ἐπεὶ Χαρίδης here (at Ath. 8.387a, A conversely corrupts ἐπικεχοδὼς to ἐπεὶ κεχ. when citing Ar. *Av.* 68) and so remove any link with fr. 223(220K).4; against this, however, (i) ἐπεί would not improve grammatical connection with v. 1, as Meineke claimed, because asyndeton is a regular feature of explanatory clauses such as v. 2 here (K.G. 2.344f. with examples; in Alexis e.g. 35(34K).1f. τοιοῦτο τὸ ζῆν ἐστιν· ὥσπερ οἱ κύβοι, οὐ ταῦτ' ἀεὶ πίπτουσιν and comm., 9.8, 27.4, 41(40K).2, 179(174K).2, 224(222).3); (ii) Χαρίδης is not a known Attic name (as Χάρης, Χαριάδης, Χαρίας, Χαρίδημος are: Kirchner, *PA* 2.416ff., 489; cf. Herwerden, *Coll. Crit.* 129f., Blaydes, *Adv.* 2.167).

ὁ μικρός: presumably a nickname given to him because of small stature (cf. Bechtel, *Spitznamen* 8); similarly also Cleigenes (Ar. *Ran.* 709), Aristodemus (Xen. *Mem.* 1.4.2, cf. Pl. *Symp.* 173b, Plut. *Mor.* 607a), Amyntas (Arist. *Pol.* 5.8.10, 1311^{b}3).

ἐν πένθ' ἡμέραις: more probably a colloquial way of saying 'very quickly' than a precise calculation, cf. e.g. Herodas 5.59f. <σ>έ, μᾶ, ... / ... Κύδιλλ' ἐπόψεθ' ἡμερέων πέντε and Headlam *ad loc.*, Lucian *Merc. Cond.* 17 πέντε οὐδ' ὅλων ἡμερῶν ὄψεσθε αὐτὸν ἐνταῦθά που ἐν ἡμῖν τὰ ὅμοια ποτνιώμενον.

3 σφαῖραν ἐποίησε τὴν πατρῴαν οὐσίαν: in fr. 110(105K).2 Alexis has

---

τοῦ 'ννοήματος Meineke, *Anal. Crit.* 260, but even these lack the topicality of the adopted text.

COMMENTARY

σφ. ἀπέδειξε τ. π. οὖσ., where see comm. Such repetitions of a vivid image in different plays are hardly surprising in a prolific author: cf. comm. on 24.2–4. On ἐποίησε (-οι- ACE) see comm. on 16.2.

4 συνεστρόγγυλεν exactly repeats the metaphor of σφαῖραν ἐποίησε (comm. on 110(105K).2).

ἰταμῶς: comm. on 110(105K).3.

Φαίδων (or Φείδων) ἢ Φαιδρίας (or? Φαίδρια)

Meineke 1.384f., Breitenbach 93f., G. Coppola, *RIGI* 7 (1923) 58, W. G. Arnott in Flores 368. Ath. 8.340b identifies the source of Alexis fr. 249(247K) with the words ἐν ... Φαίδωνι ἢ Φαιδρίᾳ. The similarity of both these alternative titles to Φαῖδρος led Meineke to suspect that the *Marcianus* here had doubly corrupted an original ἐν Φαίδρῳ (-δρῳ → -δρία → -δωνι ἢ -δρία, ? by confusion with the two similarly named Platonic dialogues: an improbable sequence of mischances that it would be hard to parallel[1]). Variations of this theory appear (1) in Breitenbach, suggesting that in the citations of frs. 248(246K) (cf. 247(245K)) at Ath. 4.165e (cf. 13.562a) Φαίδρῳ could have been a simple, and at Ath. 8.340b

---

[1] Meineke 1.385 n. 80 supports his conjecture with two alleged instances of parallel corruption: (i) Σ^V Ar. *Pax* 528 citing Εὐριπίδου ἐκ Τηλέφου ἢ Τληπολέμου (fr. 727 Nauck² = 135 Austin, *NFEP*, where Dindorf's deletion (p.471) of ἢ Τληπολέμου is totally convincing (there is no other evidence that Euripides wrote a Τληπόλεμος, and the cited fr. 727 (ἀπέπτυσ' ἐχθροῦ φωτὸς ἔχθιστον τέκος) would have been appropriately spoken by Telephus (directly or in a messenger's report) to Agamemnon after the former had snatched up the baby Orestes; cf. e.g. E. W. Handley and J. Rea, *BICS Suppl.* 5 (1957) 37, T. B. L. Webster, *The Tragedies of Euripides* (London 1967) 47); and (ii) less plausibly Hesych. s.v. Κανδαύλας· Ἑρμῆς ἢ Ἡρακλῆς, where Meineke deleted ἢ Ἡρακλῆς on the grounds that Κανδαύλας (a Maeonian epithet of Hermes in the sense of 'dog-strangler' according to Hipponax fr. 3a.1 West, but meaning and origin are disputed; cf. P. Kretschmer, *Einleitung in die Geschichte der griechischen Sprache* (Göttingen 1896) 388f., Prehn in *RE* s.v. *Kandaulas* 1860.28ff., Schwyzer 1.65, O. Szemerényi in *Studi linguistici in onore di V. Pisani* 2 (Brescia 1969) 980f.) suited only Hermes (sc. as Ἀργειφόντης), but Meineke forgets that Heracles (while in Lydia as Omphale's slave; Hdt. 1.7.3 equates Lydia and Maeonia) slew Orthrus, the two-headed dog of Geryones, and later carried off Cerberus from the underworld with his hands squeezing the dog's throat (ἄγχων Ar. *Ran.* 467f.); cf. especially O. F. Gruppe, *Griechische Mythologie und Religionsgeschichte* 1 (Munich 1906) 497 and *RE Suppl.* iii s.v. *Herakles* 972.31ff.

Φαίδωνι a dittographic, corruption of a single title Φαιδρίᾳ; and (2) more intricately in Coppola, suggesting that frs. 247–9(245–7K) derive from one play titled Φαῖδρος ἢ Φαιδρίας, with Φαίδωνι substituted for -δρῳ at Ath. 8.340a (? again by confusion of the two Platonic dialogues) and the alternative titles explained by a supposition that the central character in a typical plot of later comedy was named Phaedrias but modelled on the Platonic Phaedrus. Although none of the three theories can be disproved, they are all based on a series of speculations implausible in individual detail (e.g Coppola's binominal Phaedrias/Phaedrus is not convincingly supported by Old-Comedy parallels such as Dionysus/Paris/Pericles in Cratinus' Διονυσαλέξανδρος or Paphlagon/Cleon in Ar. *Equ.*) and even more so in combination.

It is safer to rely on facts and probabilities:

(1) Since fr. 249(247K) (a conversation between two unidentified characters, the first perhaps a parasite, but yielding no clues about the plot; Plaut. *Capt.* 813ff., where a parasite's attack on fishmongers is followed by a reference to market-inspectors, suggests one possible context) ridicules the ὀψοφαγία of Callimedon, who was active in Athenian politics between *c.* 345 and 318 (cf. introduction to Δορκίς), Alexis' play is likely to have been produced during this period (see also comm. on v. 5).

(2) The nominative of Φαιδρίᾳ is (i) probably the name Φαιδρίας (not uncommon in Athens: Kirchner, *PA* 2.336 nos. ? 13933–45, *SEG* 28 (1978) 155.8, 36 (1986) 155.17, ? 21 (1965) 911), which was borne characteristically in later comedy and related literature by young men (lovers of courtesans in Ter. *Eun.* and *Phorm.*, ? enslaved victim of pirates in Turpilius' *Lemniae* fr. II, husband of a wife who had a baby five months after marriage in Alciphron 3.27, a farmer in Aelian *Epist.* 20, unidentifiable in Turpilius' *Paraterusa* fr. III; contrast Ar. *Lys.* 356, old man in the chorus; see K. Gatzert, *De nova comoedia quaestiones onomatologicae* (Diss. Giessen 1913) 25), but (ii) the female name Φαίδρια cannot be excluded (Phaedria = Euclio's daughter in Plaut. *Aul.*; in Greek Φαίδρια is not attested, but Φα[ίδ]ρα *IG* ii/iii².7565, Φαῖδρον 6963, 12841, and Φαίδρυλλα 12842, 128423 are the names of free Athenian women, Φαίδριον Epicurus' slave in Diog. Laert. 10.21; cf. Bechtel, *Frauennamen* 34).

(3) There is no evidence elsewhere for Φαίδων as a comic name (it is rare in real life; for Athens only nos. 13967–8 in Kirchner, *PA* 2.338, but see also *SEG* 21 (1965) 667.7, 23 (1968) 102.17; Plato's Phaedo came from Elis, Diog. Laert. 2.105, cf. 126). Yet the very similar Φείδων (not uncommon in Athens: Kirchner, *PA* 2.348f., 14177–85) was a standard name in comedy etymologically appropriate for avaricious old men (Antiphanes 189.22(191.21K), Mnesimachus 4.7 and Meineke *ad loc.*; cf. Alciphron 2.32 Φείδωνες ... μικροπρεπέστεροι, 4.2.5, Nicarchus in *Anth.*

Pal.. 11.170 Φ. ὁ φιλάργυρος; cf. in Ar. *Nub.* 65 Strepsiades' father; W. Süss, *De personarum antiquae comoediae Atticae usu atque origine* (Diss. Giessen 1905) 103, 114, Gatzert 7, 11f.). Whether or not Φαίδωνι in Ath. 8.340a is corrupted from Φείδωνι (so my paper in Flores) under the influence of either the following Φαιδρίᾳ or the Platonic title,[1] a play with two major characters (? miser, young man/woman) could have taken its original title from one of their names, like many plays in later Greek comedy (young men: e.g. ? Alexis' Δημήτριος, Φαῖδρος, Eubulus' Πάμφιλος and Hunter *ad loc.*, Menander's Θρασωνίδης = alternative title of Μισού-μενος, Θρασυλέων; old men: ? Alexis' Δρωπίδης, Ἰμίλκων; young free woman: ? Alexis' Κράτεια; *hetairai*: Alexis' Ἀγωνίς, Δορκίς, Ἰσοστάσιον, etc.). An alternative title could then have been attached to the play for a variety of reasons: most probably perhaps as a later critic's identification of the principal character (cf. the introduction to Ἀγωνίς), possibly also for a second production in a revised version (of which, however, there is no record), least credibly because some scholar had attempted to fill out an ambiguously contracted Φαιδ in his source (but in that event why was Φαῖδρος not included as a possibility?).

(4) Plays of New Comedy where different characters bore similar names may not have been unusual (e.g. in Men. *Asp.* Chaireas, Chaires-tratos; *Epitr.* Charisios, Chairestratos), perhaps thus aiming to reflect an oddity of real life.[2]

249 (247K)

Meineke 3.497, Kock 2.388, Edmonds 2.492, Kassel–Austin 2.162. Part-division in this dialogue between two unidentified speakers (Ath. 8.340b, only in A) was correctly established by Daléchamp, although A's dicola at the ends of vv. 3 and 4 could just possibly be taken to indicate a text where v. 5 was incorrectly returned to the first speaker. After citing

---

[1] A possibility of more serious corruption here cannot be ruled out. A scribe could have introduced one of the Φαιδ syllables into his text by an ill-timed *saut des yeux* to (or memory of) the other, in which case the original titles would have been -ων (? Μίδων, Ἰμίλκων) ἢ Φαιδρίας/ Φαίδρια, or Φαίδων/Φείδων ἢ -ρίας/ρια (? Ἀλείπτρια, Ποιήτρια).

[2] The same practice operated in Hellenistic poetry. For instance, in Theoc. 5 the shepherd Lakon mentions *en passant* a Lykon (8) and a Lykopas (62), and is described as both τὸν Συβαρίταν (1) and δῶλε Σιβύρτα (5). In Herodas 1 Gyllis mentions a man called Gryllos (50), in 3 both a Kottalos (48, 62, 74, cf. 72) and a Kokkalos (60, 87) appear, and in 4 (cf. *Coroll. Lond.* 4 (1984) 10ff.) Kottale (88) appears to have a slave named Kokkale (19).

249(247K) Ath. goes on to say that τὰ αὐτὰ ἰαμβεῖα φέρεται κἀν Τῇ ἐπιγραφομένῃ εἰς τὸ φρέαρ, which indicates that Ath. lacked either the means or the inclination to verify a statement that he found in his own source (cf. I. Düring in *Apophoreta Gotoburgensia Vilelmo Lundström oblata* (Göteborg 1936) 252f.). Yet there seems no reason to doubt the accuracy of the claim: cf. comm. on fr. 24.2.

1 ἀγορανομήσεις: cf. ἀγορανόμων v. 4, Plaut. *Capt.* 823f., *Curc.* 285. The basic facts about the appointment and duties of ἀγορανόμοι (a variant spelling -ορονο- appears on lead tokens which they issued, cf. Lang–Crosby, *Agora* x.79 n. 6) in Attica are given by [Arist.] *Ath. Pol.* 51 κληροῦνται δὲ καὶ ἀγορανόμοι <ι΄> (add. P. N. Papageorghiou, ᾿Αθηνᾶ 64 (1892) 590f.), πέντε μὲν εἰς Πειραιέα, ε΄ δ᾿ εἰς ἄστυ. τούτοις δὲ ὑπὸ τῶν νόμων προστέτακται τῶν ὠνίων ἐπιμελεῖσθαι πάντων, ὅπως καθαρὰ καὶ ἀκίβδηλα πωλήσεται (so G. Kaibel, *Stil und Text der* Πολίτεια ᾿Αθηναίων *des Aristoteles* (Berlin 1893) 220f., cf. 76 n. 1: πωλῆται P); see especially Rhodes, comm. *ad loc.* Yet although the ἀγορανόμοι were responsible for maintaining order in the Agora (Arist. *Pol.* 4.12.6, 1299ᵇ16f., 6.5.2, 1321ᵇ12ff., cf. Ar. *Ach.* 968) and heard accusations within their remit (cf. Ar. *Vesp.* 1407), they were clearly not empowered (as v. 4 shows) to prevent a citizen such as Callimedon from buying up large quantities of fish for his personal disposal. Cf. also U. Kahrstedt, *Untersuchungen zur Magistratur in Athen* (Stuttgart 1936) 191, 193f., 213f., 233, A. H. M. Jones, *The Greek City from Alexander to Justinian* (Oxford 1940) 215ff., MacDowell, comm. on Ar. *Vesp.* 1407.

ἂν θεοὶ θέλωσι: see comm. on 233(231K).4.

1–2 θέλωσι, σύ, ἵνα: Musurus' correction of A's θέλωσιν | συινα. Although σύ more commonly in Attic is placed early in its sentence (cf. K. J. Dover, *Greek Word Order* (Cambridge 1960) 20ff.), there are enough examples in comedy of emphatic postponement to last word of clause and/or verse, especially in questions (e.g. Ar. *Ach.* 993, *Nub.* 858, perhaps Alexis 177(173K).3 and frequently), to justify the correction (but not punctuation as a question at the end of v. 3). Alternatively perhaps θέλωσι, νῦ<ν>, ἵνα?

2 Καλλιμέδοντ᾿: see introductions to Δορκίς, Φαίδων, and fr. 57(56K). **εἰς τοὔψον:** see comm. on fr. 47(46K). 6 and 8. **εἰ φιλεῖς ἐμέ:** normally appended to a request or command (e.g. Ar. *Pax* 118, Men. fr. 612.1, Herodas 6.43, cf. Ar. *Nub.* 1488; *si me amas* similarly Ter. *HT* 1031), here to a more indirect equivalent (= 'I'd like you to be an ἀγ. and stop C.'), at com. adesp. 131.1 Kock to a first-person promise.

3 καταιγίζοντα: see comm. on Alexis 47(46K).5. **δι᾿ ὅλης ἡμέρας:** cf. e.g. Ar. *Pax* 27, Eubulus 66.2–3. Kock points to a logical flaw in this verse ('*cum uersari in foro per totum diem possit,* *inruere in forum non possit'*), but this is a sign not of corruption (thus δὶς τῆς ἡμ. Kock, πρῷ τῆς ἡμ. Peppink, *Observ.* 52, needlessly) but of comically extravagant colloquialism, the implication being simply that at whatever time you go to the market, you are sure to find Callimedon there bearing down on the fish stalls like a hurricane.

4 λέγεις: see comm. on fr. 223(221K).11–12.

5 In vv. 1–4 Callimedon is an object of ridicule and perhaps even veiled animosity, but here 'You see, the man's (ἀνήρ Valckenaer before Dindorf: see Peppink, *Observ.* 52) a fighter, but a benefit to the city' at face value indicates positive praise. Webster (*SLGC* 46) rightly detected irony without investigating its probable background. In Alexis 57(56K) (see comm.) the speaker reports a decision of the city's fishmongers to erect a bronze statue of Callimedon holding a crayfish (κάραβος, also his nickname). Although the details there are doubtless comic fantasy, it is possible that in the years before Δορκίς (? and Φαίδων) a public decree had rewarded some public service(s) of Callimedon (? in the early 320s, when prices were high in a period of food shortages) with the honour of a bronze statue. Such awards were a feature of public life in late 4th/early 3rd-century Athens (cf. W. Larfeld, *Griechische Epigraphik*[3] (Munich 1914) 390f.; A. S. Henry, *Honours and Privileges in Athenian Decrees* (Hildesheim 1983) 294ff., lists ten to foreigners and six to Athenians), and the decrees which ratified them praised the qualities of the honorands in stock phrases such as εὔχρηστος/πρόθυμος/φίλος/ χρήσιμος τῷ δήμῳ/τῇ πόλει: e.g. *IG* ii².356.28f. (327 BC) χρήσιμοι ὄντες ... τῷ δήμῳ, 584.21 (end 4th century) χρῆ]σιμος ἔσεσθαι τῇ[ι πόλει, 498.19 (303/2) χρήσιμος ἦν καὶ εὔνους τῇ τοῦ δήμου [σ]ωτηρίᾳ; cf. Larfeld 355ff., 370f., 432ff.; the index volume of *IG* ii/iii² p. 66). This particular cliché, which apparently was already circulating in the 5th century (cf. Eur. *Suppl.* 887, *Or.* 910f., Eupolis 129(118K).2), also appeared frequently in the political speeches of e.g. Dem. (4.7, 18.257, 19.277, 281, 25.42, 36.56, 57, 58.64; cf. 34.38, 42.22, Lysias 14.43, Isaeus fr. 22 Thalheim = 1 Forster, Aeschines 3.161; Dover, *GPM* 296ff.). Yet if Alexis' speaker in 249(247K).5 was ironically quoting the jargon of a recent laudatory speech and/or decree, why was the banal χρήσιμος τῇ πόλει contrasted with an untypical μάχιμος? Callimedon could have been an arrant coward, and this description a vicious joke; the adjective could have been an unusual insertion in the supposed decree (in that event Kock's τε would be preferable to A's δέ); or (perhaps most probably) Callimedon was known to be aggressive in his general behaviour (cf. v. 3). Whatever the correct explanation, there is no good reason to suspect corruption in μάχιμος (λιχνός Emperius 358, δόκιμος Kock).

ἀνήρ: Dindorf's correction of A's ἀνὴρ, cf. comm. on 88(85K).3–5.

ΦΑΡΜΑΚΟΠΩΛΗΣ

Φαρμακοπώλης ἢ Κράτεια

See Κράτεια ἢ Φαρμακοπώλης.

Φιλαθήναιος

The normal use of φιλαθήναιος (e.g. Ar. *Ach.* 142, Pl. *Tim.* 21e, Dem. 19.308) suggests that Alexis' title figure is likely to have been not a patriotic Athenian but a friendly foreigner (cf. D. M. MacDowell, comm. (Oxford 1971) on Ar. *Vesp.* 282), but speculation is futile when so little of this play (fr. 250(248K) = three words, 251(249K) = one) and of Philippides' homonym (restaged at the Dionysia in 154: *IG* ii².2323.486 in C. A. P. Ruck, *IG II² 2323: The List of the Victors in Comedies at the Dionysia* (Leiden 1967) = III B 3 col. 5a, 19 Mette[1]) survives.

250 (248K)

Meineke 3.498 (1), Kock 2.388, Edmonds 2.494, Kassel–Austin 2.162; cf. Sicking, *Annotationes* 122. The Antiatticist's citation of Alexis here was presumably intended as a counterblast to some Atticist(s) who required verbs containing no notion of movement to be constructed with παρά + dative. Whether or not the construction of verbs like οἰκεῖν with παρά + accusative implied a combination of prior movement to, and present rest at, a point, it was a standard usage in Attic (e.g. Eur. fr. 403.3f. οἰκεῖ, Ar. fr. 466.5 Kassel–Austin εἶναι, Timocles 11.4 ὠψώνει, Demetrius com. II 1.4 ἐγενόμην, Men. *Dysk.* 162f. διατρίβειν, *Epitr.* 434f. κατακεῖσθαι, *Pk.* 768ff. ἕστηκεν, Dem. 15.7 ὄντα, Aeschines 3.90 ᾤκει, Isaeus 8.16 καθήμενοι, cf. Xen. *Anab.* 7.1.12 εἰστήκει, *Cyr.* 1.4.18 μένειν) and other (Epic: e.g. Hom. *Od.* 12.32 κοιμήσαντο; Ionic: e.g. Hdt. 4.87; Doric: e.g. *IG* vii.3171.18ff. from Orchomenos, Ar. *Ach.* 759) dialects (K.G. 1.513). The fact that the Antiatticist cited Alexis rather than an orator indicates his confidence in the comic poet's Atticism.

---

[1] At col. 2b, 24 in the same inscription a third place in the Dionysia of *c.* 193 is recorded for a comedy of whose title only]αθηνα[is preserved; A. Wilhelm, *Urkunden dramatischer Aufführungen in Athen* (Vienna 1906) 71 supplemented with Φιλ]αθηνα[ίῳ or Μισ]αθ., but the latter title is unparalleled; Ἀθηνα[ίῳ cannot be ruled out as a third possibility for the title, but this (cf. Wilhelm, and Ruck 43) would require the unknown comic poet's name that originally preceded the title to have filled a space of about thirteen letters.

251 (249K)

Meineke 3.498 (II), Kock 2.388, Edmonds 2.494, Kassel–Austin 2.162. In Athens the adjective παιδικός covered a range of meanings from 'of children' (applied to children's possessions, behaviour, etc.: LSJ s.v. 1.1), to 'childlike' (of adult behaviour: cf. Phot. and *Suda* s.v. παιδικά = *Glossary of Useful Terms* 1.325.10ff. Bachmann, λέγεται δὲ παιδικὸν καὶ τὸ παιδα-ριῶδες, οἷον τὸ ἁρμόζον παιδί;[1] sometimes neutrally in contrast to σπουδαῖος, e.g. Xen. *Ages.* 8.2, Pl. *Crat.* 406c, *Lys.* 211a; sometimes pejoratively, e.g. Pl. *Phlb.* 49a, *Epin.* 974a, Arist. *Eth. Nic.* 10.6.6, 1176^{b}33). The abbreviated form in which the Antiatticist's note here has been preserved leaves it altogether uncertain why he should have felt obliged to defend the latter usage.

Φιλέταιρος

See Δημήτριος ἢ Φιλέταιρος.

Φιλίσκος

Kock 2.105, Breitenbach 54f., Kann, *De iteratis* 69. An unusual title, shared by Antiphanes (fr. 215(216K): three unmetrical words) and Alexis (fr. 252(250K): just over three iambics about preparations for a party); with so little preserved from either play, it would be foolish to speculate about the possibility that Alexis' Φιλίσκος was a διασκευή of Antiphanes' (cf. Kann).

The title suggests at least three possible types of plot for either comedy. (1) Φιλίσκος (originally a hypocoristic diminutive of φίλος: cf. Buck-Petersen, *Reverse Index* 638) was an established name in Athens (cf. Kirchner, *PA* 2.363, 487: nos. 14119–30, 14120a), but of those known there perhaps only Philiscus of Abydos (14430; Lenschau in *RE* s.v.

---

[1] The entry continues ἡ δὲ λέξις ὡς ἐπὶ πολὺ ἐπὶ τῶν ἀσελγῶς ἐρωμένων; this may be a reference to an occasional use in the *Koine* of the neuter singular παιδικόν (e.g. *P. Tebt.* 104.20, 91 BC; cf. *P. Geneva* 21.4f., 2nd century) in place of the plural παιδικά for (usually) 'boy/youth loved by an older man', but there is no way of interpreting the Antiatticist's note at 112.3 Bekker as a defence of such a use by Alexis here.

ΦΙΛΙΣΚΟΣ

Philiskos 2, 2378.58ff.) was sufficiently important and interesting,[1] with his peace mission to Delphi in 368 as hyparch of the Persian satrap Ariobarzanes and his subsequent award of Athenian citizenship (Xen. *Hell.* 7.1.27, Diod. Sic. 15.70.2, Dem. 23.141–3, 202), to provide material for a political plot by Antiphanes in the early 360s (so Kock; cf. Legrand, *NGC* 28f., T. B. L. Webster, *CQ* 2 (1952) 18f.), before Alexis came on to the scene (cf. my general introduction, I.iii, pp. 16f., and introduction to Ὑποβολιμαῖος).

(2) According to Diog. Laert. 6.75 (cf. 80) λέγεται γοῦν Ὀνησίκριτόν τινα Αἰγινήτην πέμψαι εἰς τὰς Ἀθήνας δυοῖν ὄντοιν υἱοῖν τὸν ἕτερον Ἀνδροσθένην, ὃν ἀκούσαντα τοῦ Διογένους αὐτόθι προσμεῖναι· τὸν δ' ἐπ' αὐτὸν καὶ τὸν ἕτερον ἀποστεῖλαι τὸν πρεσβύτερον Φιλίσκον ... ὁμοίως δὲ καὶ τὸν Φιλίσκον κατασχεθῆναι· τὸ τρίτον αὐτὸν ἀφιγμένον μηδὲν ἧττον συνεῖναι τοῖς παισὶ συμφιλοσοφοῦντα. τοιαύτη τις προσῆν ἴυγξ τοῖς Διογένους λόγοις. Breitenbach's comment '*haec comoediam sane sapere videntur*' (55)[2] receives partial support from Alciphron 2.38, a letter ostensibly addressed to (presumably) the same Philiscus by a farmer Euthydicus, describing how the farmer's son had been sent to Athens to sell wood and barley in the market, but had been bewitched by the Cynic philosophers. Alciphron characteristically develops in his letters (but with more creative imagination than Aelian and [Aristaenetus]) material derived from comedy (cf. e.g. W. Volkmann, *Studia Alciphronea, partic.1: de Alciphrone comoediae imitatore* (Diss. Breslau 1886), Th. Kock, *Hermes* 21 (1886) 403ff. and *Rh. Mus.* 43 (1888) 35ff., falsely assuming that Alciphron was a slavish imitator; cf. in *RE* Schmid s.v. *Alkiphron* 1548.40ff., and Gerth, *RE Suppl.* VIII s.v. *Zweite Sophistik* 735.27ff.), and indeed portions of Alciphron 2.38 slip into iambic rhythm. If Diogenes Laertes and Alciphron here depended on a comic source, the Φιλίσκος of Alexis and/or Antiphanes are

---

[1] It is unlikely that either play took its title from e.g. the comic poet Philiscus (Körte in *RE* s.v. *Philiskos* 5, 2381.62ff.; Kassel–Austin 7.356ff.), or the αὐλητὴς παραδοξότατος (*Suda* s.v. Φιλίσκος) who became a pupil of Isocrates (Solmsen in *RE* s.v. 9, 2384.53ff., L. Radermacher, *Artium scriptores* (*SB Vienna* 227.3, 1951) 194f.).

[2] On Diog. Laert.'s sources see especially Schwartz in *RE* s.v. 40, 738.11ff. and K. von Fritz, *Quellenuntersuchungen zu Leben und Philosophie des Diogenes von Sinope* (*Philologus suppl.* 18.2, Leipzig 1926) 1ff. and (on 6.74–8) 10ff. Diog. Laert. himself and/or his sources frequently cite Athenian comic poets by name (including Alexis frs. 1, 151(147K), 163(158K), 185(180K), but not Antiphanes): 1.12, 62, 89, 2.18–28, 108, 120, 3.26–8, 4.18–20, 6.83, 87, 93, 7.27, 68, 8.34, 37–8. In the anecdote cited from 6.75 λέγεται is all we are given (cf. also in this section λέγεται 76, διάφοροι λέγονται λόγοι 76, ὥς φασιν 78).

711

likely candidates,[1] perhaps embroidering with fantasy (cf. Ar. *Nub.*) real-life events (cf. von Fritz in *RE* s.v. *Philiskos* 6, 2382.45ff.), although there is now no way of knowing whether Alciphron's Euthydicus too was a character in the same play.

(3) A third possibility is that one Φιλίσκος or both conformed to New-Comedy patterns, with the title figure a *nomen fictum*. Names beginning Phil- are given to many such characters in later comedy and literature influenced thereby: e.g. Philainion/-aenium (*meretrix* Plaut. *Asin.*, ? *Anth. Pal.* 6.284 = anon. 40 Gow–Page; young girl 7.487 = Perses 6), Philainis (bawd in Men. Συναριστῶσαι, cf. Charitonidis and others, *Mosaïques* 41ff. and pl. 5.1; *hetaira Anth. Pal.* 5.162, 186, 202, 6.206 = Asclepiades 8, Posidippus 2, ? Asclepiades 35, Antipater 6; servant girl 5.4 = Philodemus 1); Philainis or -ainion (bawd Herodas 1.5, where the papyrus offers both names); Philinna (old nurse Men. *Georg.*, see Gomme–Sandbach, *Comm.* on v. 22; title figure of comedies by Hegemon, Axionicus; cf. [Aristaen.] 2.3); Philinos (*senex* named in Men. *Pk.* 1026, cf. Strato 1.13, com. adesp. fr. 131.2 Kock, ? Apollodorus 7.1, Lucian *Dial. Meretr.* 6.1; character in cast list, *P.Antinoop.* 15 = Austin, *CGFP* fr. 240); Philon (Men. fr. 215); Philotis (*meretrix* Ter. *Hec.*, cf. com. adesp. fr. 284.3 Austin = ? Apollodorus' *Hekyra*, Alciphron 4.9.4; title of Antiphanes); Philoumene/-lumena (free girl Men. *Sik.* 378, cf. Ter. *Andr.* 306 and *alter exitus* 20; name of young wife Ter. *Hec.* 191, 219; *hetaira* ? Crobylus 5, cf. *Anth. Pal.* 5.40 = Nicarchus; Men. fr. 489; title of Caecilius, p. 68 Ribbeck).

252 (250K)

Meineke 3.498, Kock 2.389, Edmonds 2.494, Kassel–Austin 2.163. An unidentified speaker either orders or describes the preparations for serving δευτέρα τράπεζα (cf. comm. on 168(163K).2), itemising the duties asyndetically (as in actual descriptions of parties: Fraenkel, *MNC* 23, 24ff., 39, 41f., 51, Hunter on Eubulus 111(112K)) and so turning the fr. into that favoured form, the list (comm. on 84). The relation of fr. to plot is uncertain; although revelry is a characteristic way of ending comedies (cf. introduction to fr. 54(52K)), preparations for it often come much earlier in the play (e.g. Getas' description, Men. *Dysk.* 546ff.; Erotium's orders, Plaut. *Men.* 351ff.).

1–2 The *Marcianus* (Ath. 14.642f) opens its citation faultily (cf. comm.

---

[1] The arrival of Diogenes in Athens would obviously provide a *terminus post quem* for such a play/plays, but that date is itself disputed (? before Antisthenes' death in the 360s; ? just before 340: see D. R. Dudley, *A History of Cynicism* (London 1937) 54f. n. 3).

on frs. 192–4(187–9K) ἄρτεον τράπεζαν ἀπονίψασθαι δοτεον προσοισ-τέος, where (if ἀρτέον ends a trimeter) the two words at the beginning of the following verse have a syllable too many. The neatest conjecture is undoubtedly Meineke's ἀρτέα | τράπεζ᾿ (*Anal. Crit.* 313, cf. *FCG* 5.91, after Dobree, *Adv.* 2.349), which would imply corruption of a less to a more common construction of the verbal adjective (cf. C. E. Bishop, *AJP* 20 (1899) 10: *c.* 900 instances of impersonal construction, c. 90 of personal); even so, Meineke's earlier approach (*FCG* 3.498) with transposition τράπεζαν ἀρτέον | × – ἄπον deserves serious consideration, with the postulated lacuna more plausibly filled with a form of address (e.g. ὦ τᾶν, cf. comm. on fr. 16.11; or ἄνθρωπ᾿, cf. A's parallel omission at 9.382e = Strato 1.24, where *P.Cairo* 65445 supplies μάγειρε) than with Meineke's ὕδωρ or χεῖρας, both unnecessary to the idiom. αἴρειν τράπεζαν is 'to lift up (and remove the) table (on which the main course of a meal has been served)', as an indication that the stage for dessert and post-prandial drinking has been reached: cf. e.g. Men. frs. 239 τὰς τραπέζας αἴρετε· | μύρα, στεφάνους ἑτοίμασον, σπονδὰς πόει and 385, the joke at Timocles 13 and Σ^{Tr} Ar. *Vesp.* 525 (but probably not Eubulus 111(112K).3, where see Hunter), and Plaut. *Truc.* 364 *auferte mensam.*

The fr. is one of many passages (cf. e.g. Pl. *Symp.* 176a, Xen. *Symp.* 2.1, Matron 534.104ff. Lloyd-Jones–Parsons, Plut. *Mor.* 645d–648a, Ath. 9.408b–409f, 11.462c–463a, 14.639b–643e, 15.665a–d, 692f–693f, citing Xenophanes fr. 1 West, Achaeus fr. 17, Philoxenus Leuc. *Deipn.* fr. e Page, Theophr. fr. 123 Wimmer = 572 Fortenbaugh, Dicaearchus fr. 71 and Philochorus fr. 18 = *FHG* 2.266, 1.387, from comedy also Ar. *Vesp.* 1216, Anaxandrides 2, Antiphanes 172(174K), Clearchus 4, Dromon 2, Ephippus 8, Philyllius 3, Nicostratus 19(20K), Plato com. 71(69K), Men. fr. 239) indicating the sequence of rituals that precedes an Athenian drinking-party. After removal of the tables host and guests wash their hands (see on v. 2), garlands (comm. on 4.2) and μύρον (comm. on 61(60K).1) are distributed, wine and water are mixed in the κρατήρ, and a toast (σπονδή v. 3) is drunk either to Zeus Soter (so e.g. Philochares fr. 19 = *FHG* 1.387, Philonides in Ath. 15.675c) or in sequence to Zeus Olympios, the Heroes and Zeus Soter (Σ Pind. *Isthm.* 6.10, Σ Pl. *Phlb.* 66d, Pollux 6.15, cf. 100) while a paean is sung, often to the accompaniment of αὐλοί. Cf. in *RE* Mau s.v. *Comissatio*, 611.7ff., Ganszyniec s.v. *Kranz*, 1602.18ff. and *RE Suppl.* iii s.v. *Agathodaimon* 40.34ff., M. Blech, *Studien zur Kranz bei den Griechen* (Berlin and New York 1982) 63ff.

2 ἀπονίψασθαι[1] **δοτέον**: sc. ὕδωρ, '(water) must be provided for

---

[1] Since the use of the middle here is canonical, as Ar. Byz. and the passages cited in LSJ s.v. ἀπονίζω 1.4, clearly show, Porson's attempt

COMMENTARY

washing'. The noun is normally omitted in this colloquial expression (cf. Antiphanes 134(136K).1f. ~ 2) as with the corresponding κατὰ χειρός/ -ῶν (e.g. Alexis 263(261K).2 κατὰ χειρὸς ἐδόθη, Antiphanes 280(287K), Archedicus 2.3). ἀπονίψασθαι (the infinitive here governed by δοτέον, cf. Goodwin, *MT* 300f., K.G. 2.6ff.) normally refers in Attic usage to the practice of washing the hands clean at the end of the main course, κατὰ χειρός/-ῶν to that of washing them before the meal has started (so e.g. Ar. *Vesp.* 1216f. ὕδωρ κατὰ χειρός· τὰς τραπέζας εἰσφέρειν | δειπνοῦμεν· ἀπονενίμμεθ'· ἤδη σπένδομεν, Ar. Byz. fr. 368 Slater = Ath. 9.408f, cf. 410b; cf. Cobet, *NL* 4f., Neil on Ar. *Equ.* 357), but contrary instances are not unknown (e.g. Ar. *Vesp.* 608, ἀπονίζῃ before the meal).

3 λιβανωτός: frankincense, the bitter aromatic resin exuded as a shiny reddish or yellowish globule (cf. Pind. fr. 122.3 Snell–Maehler = 107.3 Bowra χλωρᾶς λιβάνου ξανθὰ δάκρη) from the shrub *Boswellia sacra* (and related species) growing naturally in southern Arabia and East Africa, from where it was imported into Greece in Alexis' time through Syria (cf. Eur. *Bacch.* 144, Hermippus fr. 63.13, Σ A. *Ag.* 1312); cf. R. Sigismund, *Die Aromata* (Leipzig 1884) 6ff., D. L. Page, *Sappho and Alcaeus* (Oxford 1955) 36, Gow, comm. on Leonidas 28.1. Alexis here conforms to the rule prescribed by Phryn. *Ecl.* 157 p. 75 Fischer (but see C. A. Lobeck's edition (Leipzig 1820) p. 187) that λιβανωτός should be used of the product, λίβανος of the tree. Other passages of Attic comedy show that incense was burnt during wine-parties: e.g. Plato com. 71(69K).9, Men. *Sam.* 158 and the fr. attributed to that play, probably wrongly, by Phryn.; cf. also Xenophanes fr. 1.7 West, Alciphron 4.13.5.

ἐσχαρίς: this diminutive of ἐσχάρα (first here, LSJ s.v.) in the same sense of 'brazier' (cf. comm. on 106(101K).2), would be used (as Schweighaeuser, *Animadv* 7.523 noted) for burning the incense: cf. e.g. Heliod. 4.5.2 τρίποδά τις καὶ δάφνην καὶ πῦρ καὶ λιβανωτὸν παραθέσθω, 18.6 τήν τε ἑστίαν ἐσχάραν ... ἀνάψαντος καὶ λιβανωτὸν ἀποθύσαντος.

4 The *Marcianus* begins the verse with τραγήματα δοτέον ἔτι, but this (i) ruins a probably intentional sequence of singular nouns in vv. 2–4 (for this preciosity of style elsewhere in later comedy cf. e.g. Alexis 132(127).4– 8, Mnesimachus 4.29–31, 37–44), and (ii) produces an ugly rhythm with no caesura, eight successive short syllables and a divided resolution in the second half of the second metron. Although none of these features is wholly objectionable in itself (on split anapaests in this *sedes* cf. *CQ* 7 (1957) 189; for a longer sequence of short syllables cf. e.g. Men. *Dysk.* 450), in combination they arouse suspicion. Porson's τράγημα (*Adv.* 141) removes

---

(*Adv.* 141) to remove A's superfluous syllable in v. 2 by conjecturing ἀπονίψαι proves vain.

714

all the anomalies at one blow; corruption to the commoner plural form would be easy for a scribe who had just written that form seven times in the immediately preceding lines (642c–f) without any instance of the singular.

δοτέον, ἔτι: this punctuation (so only Schweighaeuser; Kassel–Austin and most other editors punctuate after ἔτι) provides a pause at the penthemimeral caesura and allows ἔτι idiomatically (= 'furthermore') to introduce a new item (cf. e.g. Philemon 79(76K).3 ἔτι ταῦτα προσετίθην).

πλακοῦντος: cf. comm. on 22.3.

Φιλόκαλος ἢ Νύμφαι

The sole fr. (253(251K)) preserved from the play has one character asking another, whom he labels a skinflint (v.3), to 'invite' (κάλει) some girls (presumably *hetairai*) to a party. The simple use of this imperative may imply that the girls lived nearby (possibly in one of the stage-houses), operated independently (like e.g. the title figures of Plaut. *Bacch.* and Phronesium in *Truc.*), and that one at least had a relationship with a character in the play.

Why the play should have received alternative titles (both unparalleled in later Greek comedy) is unknown (cf. introduction to Ἀγωνίς). In Alexis' time φιλόκαλος was a word whose precise reference depended largely on its user's concept of καλός and τὸ καλόν (cf. LSJ s.v.), but in everyday speech it was commonly applied to a person with a taste for or pretension to elegance (e.g. Xen. *Cyr.* 1.3.3, 2.1.22, *Mem.* 3.11.9, Isoc. 1.10, 27, 10.57; possibly, *pace* LSJ, com. adesp. fr. 249.18 Austin; Arist. *HA* 1.1, 488^{b}24 so characterises the peacock); such a character, whether old or young, could easily be accommodated as an interesting eccentric (cf. e.g. Knemon in Men. *Dysk.*, Euclio in Plaut. *Aul.*) within the framework of a more or less conventional love intrigue.[1] The νύμφαι of the second title pose more of a problem: perhaps two newly wedded wives (? rivals to the *hetairai* in a pluralistic version of the story line of Men. *Epitr.* or Ter. *Hec.*), more probably immortal nymphs with a shrine on stage (as in Men. *Dysk.*: cf. Gomme–Sandbach, *Comm.* on vv. 1–49) but not necessarily also a visible role (as chorus or divine prologue).

---

[1] Φιλόκαλος is listed once as an Athenian proper name in Kirchner, *PA* 2.366 no. 14506 (inspector of shipyards 349/8 BC, *IG* ii/111^2.1620.46ff.; cf. Edmonds, 2.495 note c), but interpretation of Alexis' title as a reference to a contemporary figure or a *nomen fictum* seems most implausible.

COMMENTARY

253 (251K)

Meineke 3.499, Kock 2.389, Edmonds 2.494, Kassel–Austin 2.163. The fr.'s possible background and speaker are discussed above, introduction to Φιλόκαλος. It is cited by Ath. 8.365b (only A).

1 κἀκείνας κάλει: see introduction to the play.

2 συναγώγιμον: '(drinking-)party' rather than 'picnic' (LSJ s.v.), derived (along with συναγώγιον Men. fr. 147*) from συνάγειν, which was commonly used in 4th-century and later Greek in the sense 'to assemble for a party' (transitively: e.g. Men. *Dysk.* 566, *Pk.* 175, fr. 384; intransitively e.g. Ath. 365c ἔλεγον δὲ συνάγειν καὶ τὸ μετ' ἀλλήλων πίνειν καὶ συναγώ-γιον τὸ συμπόσιον ... μήποτε δὲ τοῦτ' ἐστὶ τὸ ἀπὸ συμβολῶν καλούμενον, directly after quoting Alexis 253(251K), Hesych. s.v. συνάγειν, συν-άγουσι, συναγώγιον; cf. e.g. Men. *Epitr.* 412, fr. 146, Sophilus 5(4K).2, Theophr. *Char.* 30.18*, probably Euphron 1.10* despite possible corruption later in the line). Ath.'s final comment is justified by the fact that shared contributions (ἀπὸ συμβολῶν, cf. introduction to comm. on fr. 15) often financed such parties (so the passages asterisked).

ἀλλ' εὖ οἶδ': from Musurus onwards all editors (except Kassel–Austin) give all the fr. to one speaker, but R. Kassel suggests that here a second man interjects, thus identifying the proposer of the party as a skinflint. Admittedly, instances where ἀλλά expresses opposition or contrast, as here, 'occur most frequently in answers, less frequently in continuous speech' (Denniston, *GP* 7), but in Alexis the instances balance out (answers: 2.8, 132(127K).2 and 4; continuous speech: 84.2, 224(222K).7; I exclude the numerous cases where ἀλλά follows a negative clause in continuous speech, or opens a fr.), and there are close parallels enough outside Alexis (e.g. Ar. *Pax* 1061, Pl. *Euth.* 3c) to justify assigning all fr. 253(251K) to one speaker.

On the hiatus in εὖ οἶδ', see comm. on fr. 1.1 and A. C. Moorhouse, *CQ* 12 (1962) 239ff.

3 κυμινοπρίστης: cummin seeds (cf. comm. on 132(127K).6) are so small and cheap that sawing them in half in order to make them go farther is a mark of extreme parsimony: hence the proverb κύμινον ἔπρισεν (if rightly conjectured at Sophron fr. 110 Kaibel, cf. Theoc. 10.55) and the coinages κυμινοπρίστης ('skinflint' also e.g. Posidippus 28(26K).12, Arist. *Eth. Nic.* 4.1.39, 1121[b]27, cf. Ar. *Vesp.* 1357; O. Crusius, *Untersuchungen zu den Mimiamben des Herondas* (Leipzig 1892) 115; but 'pettifogger' Dio Cass. 70.3.3; B. Baldwin, *Glotta* 60 (1982) 244f.) and κυμινοκίμβιξ (? com. adesp. fr. 1055 Kock from Eustath. 1828.6ff.), cf. also Men. fr. 864. George Eliot provides a modern parallel (*Middlemarch*, heading to ch. 6): 'Nice cutting is her function: she divides | with spiritual edge the millet-seed, | and makes intangible savings.'

716

ΦΙΛΟΤΡΑΓΩΙΔΟΣ

Φιλοτραγῳδός

A unique title, but several characters in Menander could be described as φιλοτραγῳδοί: Daos at *Asp.* 407ff., Syros (on the name, cf. *CQ* 18 (1968) 227ff., and Gomme–Sandbach, *Comm.* on *Epitr.* 270) and Onesimos at *Epitr.* 325ff., 1123ff. respectively.

254 (252K)

Meineke 3.499, Kock 2.389, Edmonds 2.494, Kassel–Austin 2.164. The need for wisdom to cope with (bad) fortune was a cliché (also e.g. S. fr. 947 Pearson, Radt = 861 Nauck², Eur. fr. 37 τὰς δὲ δαιμόνων τύχας | ὅστις φέρει κάλλιστ' ἀνὴρ οὗτος σοφός, cf. Men. fr. 634, possibly Cratinus 184(172K)). Coping well was the mark of a real man or woman (Antiphanes 320(278K) ἀνδρὸς... ὀρθῷ τρόπῳ, Men. *Dysk.* 767ff., fr. 650, cf. Ar. *Thesm.* 198f.) and showed nobility (Theognis 657f., Pind. *Pyth.* 3.82ff., S. fr. 319 Pearson, Radt = 296 Nauck², Eur. *Her.* 1227ff., frs. 505, 572, Lysias 3.4, Antiphanes 321(281K), Men. *Dysk.* 280ff.). Cf. Dover, *GPM* 120, 167ff.

ὀρθῶς: so MA in Stob. *Anth.* 4.44.44, cf. Antiphanes 320(278K) cited above; S's unmetrical synonym εὖ reminds one of the frequency of such substitutions in familiar quotations (cf. e.g. H. W. Fowler, *Modern English Usage*² (Oxford 1965) 367f.).

Φιλοῦσα

Herwerden, *Coll. Crit.* 130, Nesselrath, *MK* 282 n. 1. Ath. 13.574b and 10.419b quotes the two frs. (255(253K), 256(254K)) certainly preserved from this play (on fr. 292(290K) see comm. *ad loc.*). The speaker of 256(254K) condemns excess because it is expensive; the reasoning implies that he is an (? elderly) miser. Fr. 255(253K) informs the audience that ἡ πόλις (v.1) celebrates two festivals of Aphrodite, one for free girls and one in which *hetairai* take part μεθ' ἡμῶν (v.4). In citing the fr. Ath. states that the city in question was Corinth, and although we do not know the evidence on which Ath. or his source based this claim, there seems little reason to doubt its accuracy; Corinth was notorious for its *hetairai* (including those in the Temple of Aphrodite dedicated to sacred prostitution, cf. Strabo 8.6.20; Göbel, *Ethnica* 37f., H. Herter, *RAC* 3.1177 and *JAC* 3 (1960) 70ff., R. Renehan, *Studies in Greek Texts* (Göttingen 1976) 105, Hunter, comm. on Eubulus 54, Kassel–Austin on Ar. fr. 928(902K), J. B. Salmon, *Wealthy Corinth* (Oxford 1984) 398ff.). The scene of Φιλοῦσα would then be Corinth, and the speaker of fr. 255(253K) presumably

717

somebody (possibly but not certainly female and free: cf. comm. on vv. 1–2) able to associate with courtesans there. The fr. breaks off before we are told what happened during the courtesans' festival of Aphrodite, but the presentation of material here suggests a prologue speech (cf. Herwerden, Nesselrath), and festivals such as the Aphrodisia had two main (but not exclusive: cf. Plaut. *Poen.* and comm. on 255(253K).1–2) dramatic functions in later Greek comedy: they provided occasions at night for rape leading to the victim's pregnancy (e.g. Men. *Epitr.*, *Sam.*, probably *Kith.*, see Gomme–Sandbach, *Comm.* pp.411f., Plaut. *Aul.*; cf. Nesselrath) and during daylight for a young man's first encounter with a girl who attracted him (e.g. Plaut. *Cist.* 89ff. = Men. *Synaristosai*, fr. 382 Körte; contrast Theoc. 2.66ff.).

The title Φιλοῦσα is either a participle, referring to an incident in or immediately before the action when the heroine kissed some man (not necessarily a lover: cf. Men. *Pk.* 156), or a proper name. Phil(o)usa is a common name of Romanised Greek women in Latin inscriptions (cf. W. Pape and G. E. Benseler, *Wörterbuch der griechischen Eigennamen*³ 2 (Brunswick 1911) 1629, *CIL* vi.7.6 p. 6783), and although there is no record of its occurrence in Attica or Corinth, such a formation has many parallels (e.g 'Αρέσκουσα, Παίζουσα, Ποθοῦσα, Τρυφῶσα; Pape–Benseler s.vv.), and the passive form Φιλουμένη was in common use as a *nomen fictum* in comedy (cf. introduction to Φιλίσκος). Herwerden's suggestion that in Alexis' play Philousa was the name of a *hetaira* is only one of many possibilities.

255 (253K)

Meineke 3.499 (1), Kock 2.389, Edmonds 2.494, Kassel–Austin 2.164. Context and speaker of this fr., cited by Ath. 13.574b (only A), are discussed in the introduction to Φιλοῦσα and comm. on vv. 1–2.

1–2 Our information about festivals of Aphrodite in the various Greek cities (cf. especially Stengel in *RE* s.v. *Aphrodisia* 4, 2725.38ff., M. P. Nilsson, *Griechische Feste von religiöser Bedeutung mit Ausschluss der attischen* (Leipzig 1906) 337f., L. Deubner, *Attische Feste* (Berlin 1932) 215f.) comes largely from literary sources, which reflect practices in Athens (e.g. Ath. 14.659d citing Men. *Kol.* fr. 1 Sandbach, Alciphron 4.16.3, Machon 262ff., probably Lucian *Dial. Meretr.* 14.3, Ath. 3.101f, 4.128b), Corinth (also Chamaeleon in Ath. 13.573c, fr. 31 Wehrli) and ostensibly Calydon (Plaut. *Poen.* 190ff., 256, 497ff., 758, 1131ff., 1174ff., which is scened there; yet if Alexis wrote the Greek original, cf. introduction to Καρχηδόνιος, and was responsible for choosing the Aphrodisia at Calydon as the plot's background, it is reasonable to guess that he modelled the festival details there on those he knew at Athens, cf. Deubner 216 n. 4). Plautus describes a daytime festival in which crowds of *meretrices* visited the shrine of the goddess, made offerings to her and prayed for good fortune; Lucian indicates that a lover could make offerings on the *hetaira*'s behalf; successful *hetairai* (according to Alciphron and Machon), rulers like Antigonus (Ath. 3.101f, 4.128b) and τετραδισταί (Ath. 659d citing Men., cf. my comm. on fr. 260(258K)) celebrated the festival with private dinner-parties. Since Chamaeleon (*loc. cit.*) attests the presence of both *hetairai* and free women at the Corinthian Aphrodisia (Alexis is the sole evidence for the existence of two festivals), it would be attractive to interpret v. 4 of Alexis here correspondingly, with ἡμῶν = 'us (free women)', but the fr. nowhere indicates the speaker's sex, and males were not excluded from the Athenian festivities.

1 Ἀφροδίσι' ἦγε: the normal expression, cf. e.g. Pherecrates 181(170K), Diphilus 42(43K).39f. (Ἀδώνια), Men. fr. 796.3f. (ἑορτήν), *Sam.* 681 (τοὺς γάμους), LSJ s.v. ἄγω IV.1. The imperfect implies that while the festival was being celebrated something happened, but the speaker breaks off in order to describe the organisation of Aphrodisia festivals in Corinth before explaining what that something was (cf. introduction to Φιλοῦσα). Conjectures such as Kaibel's ἄγει <μέν> and Blaydes' ἄγει <γάρ> (*Adv.* 117), both introducing a divided resolution, miss the point.

ἡ πόλις: cf. introduction to Φιλοῦσα. The phraseology here seems to imply that the courtesans' Aphrodisia was organised by the state. The relation between the two festivals is uncertain. If the speaker and the ἡμῶν of v. 4 are free women, both festivals could have been held at the same time, with *hetairai* and free women participating together as in e.g. the Attic Tauropolia (cf. Men. *Epitr.* 471ff.); but see above on vv. 1–2.

3–4 These verses were savaged by earlier critics, arguing from various arbitrary postulates. (i) Hirschig, *Annot.* 14f. ends the fr. at ἐλευθέραις in v. 2, interpreting what follows as Ath.'s commentary; but ἐνθάδε ... μεθ' ἡμῶν then becomes meaningless (cf. Kock) and the iambic rhythm hard to explain, while the postponement of δέ (v.3) to fourth word in its clause is an anomaly of comic style in Alexis' time (cf. comm. on fr. 4.1) but not of prose in Ath.'s. (ii) Herwerden, *Coll. Crit.* 130 closes the fr. with ἔθος | ἐνθάδε μεθ' ἡμῶν, deleting ἔστιν, νόμος τε τὰς ἑταίρας in v. 4 and converting the speaker to a *hetaira*; but he fails to account for the erroneous insertion into the text of five words that scan perfectly. (iii) Bothe, *PCGF* 573 anticipated an alternative idea of Herwerden, *NAC* 33f. by suggesting the deletion of just νόμος τε in v. 4 and transferring μεθ' ἡμῶν into its place; this provides both good sense and one (but not, I believe, correct) solution to the problem of A's lacuna near the end of the fr. (see below), but it assumes too intricate a series of errors (νόμος as a gloss on ἔθος; juxtaposition of gloss and glossed word rather than substitution of the former for the latter; displacement of μεθ' ἡμῶν). One faulty postulate unites all three scholars: that v. 4 cannot belong to the Alexis fr. because they partially repeat the information given by v. 3; such repetition, however, is a normal feature in New-Comedy prologues (cf. introduction to Φιλοῦσα), helping audiences to remember expository data (e.g. Men. *Asp.* 125/130, 117/139f., *Dysk.* 1–3, 19/30, *Mis.* A4–5, *Pk.* 128f./151).

4 A's ἐνθάδε μεθήμῶν (*sic*) at the end of the fr. most probably (but cf. above on vv. 3–4) indicates a lacuna of either $\frac{3}{4}$ metron ($-\cup-$) before, or $\frac{1}{2}$ metron ($\underline{\cup}-$) after, ἐνθάδε. Supplementation is uncertain, but if the missing word(s) = a verb parallel to κωμάζειν in v. 3, Porson's <μεθύειν> μεθ' ἡμῶν (*Adv.* 137) is most attractive for both sense (cf. comm. on 112(107K).1 s.v. κῶμον) and palaeography (haplography of μεθ/ν).

256 (254K)

Meineke 3.500 (II), Kock 2.390, Edmonds 2.496, Kassel–Austin 2.164. The platitude here expressed, which was repeated elsewhere in Alexis (frs. 219(216K), 261(259K)) and fathered on Pittacus by Plutarch (*Mor.* 155d = Stob. *Anth.* 4.28.14 ὁ δὲ Πιττακὸς εἶπεν ὡς ἄριστος οἶκός ἐστιν ὁ τῶν περιττῶν μηδενὸς δεόμενος καὶ τῶν ἀναγκαίων μηδενὸς ἐνδεόμενος), is rooted in two traditional Athenian antipathies: to the acquisition of wealth by dishonourable means, and to expenditure on personal pleasures like sex, good food and gambling rather than on the family, friends and the state (cf. Dover, *GPM* 171ff., 177ff., with abundant illustration). Even so, the emphasis here on πολυτέλεια may well give a clue to the character and perhaps also the age of the speaker (see introduction to Φιλοῦσα).

1–2 τοῦ τὰ δέοντ' ἔχειν τὰ περιττὰ μισῶ: so A at Ath. 10.419b correctly (cf. Emperius 161, Meineke 5.91f., Richards, *AO* 87), 'I hate possessions in excess of having what you need'; for the genitive (of implied comparison) with περιττός cf. e.g. Xen. *Cyr.* 8.2.21 τῶν ἀρκούντων περιττά, 22 π. τῶν ἐμοὶ ἀρκούντων, *Hier.* 1.19 π. τῶν ἱκανῶν, Σ^{vet.} Ar. *Ach.* 579a περισσόν τι τοῦ δέοντος ἐλάλησα, and K.G. 1.391f.

Φρύξ (or Φρύγιος)

Meineke 1.403, Kock 2.390, Th. Bergk, *Griechische Literaturgeschichte* 4 (Berlin 1887) 155 n. 117, Breitenbach 107, S. L. Radt, *Mnemosyne* 42 (1989) 87, Nesselrath, *MK* 199 n. 51. At 10.429e Ath. cites Ἄλεξις ἐν τῇ τοῦ Φρυγίου διασκευῇ (fr. 257(255K); on διασκευή cf. introduction to Δημή-τριος), at 7.307d Ἄλεξις Φρυγί (258(256K)). It seems less probable that even a productive author wrote two different plays with titles so similar than that Ath., his source or the *Marcianus* in one of the two passages corrupted a single title's ending. Although Φρύγιος is palaeographically the likelier victim of scribal error,[1] both Φρύξ and Φρύγιος would be plausible titles in later Greek comedy.

(i) Φρύξ (but virtually never Φρύγιος: cf. Radt) is the noun in use for a male (∼ Φρυγία for a female, cf. Dion. Hal. 2.19.4) Phrygian, with a general reputation for spinelessness, cowardice and effeminacy (e.g. Eur. *Or.* and Σ on 1483, Ar. *Av.* 1244, com. adesp. fr. 814 Kock; cf. Headlam–Knox on Herodas 2.37, C. Austin (*Menandri Aspis et Samia* II: *subsidia interpretationis*, Berlin 1970) on Men. *Asp.* 242, K. Gaiser, *Grazer Beiträge* 1 (1973) 128 n. 40, M. Fantuzzi, *Ancient Society* 15–17 (1984–6) 113ff.). In Greek drama, related literature and real life it appears as both an ethnic (e.g. Eur. *Or.* 1369ff., Daos in Men. *Asp.*, Apollodorus 6, Alciphron 4.19.15) and a proper name (Ar. *Vesp.* 433, Turpilius' *Leucadia* fr. 11 Ribbeck, Rychlewska; cf. Bechtel, *Personennamen* 544 citing *IG* iv.348 from archaic Corinth and A. Plassart and Ch. Picard, *BCH* 37 (1913) 221ff. citing 30a.15 from Chios, 1st-century AD) for slaves;[2] as the title of a comedy where such a slave played a leading role it could be either.

(ii) A myth relates (Plut. *Mor.* 253f–254b, Polyaenus 8.35, [Aristaen.] 1.15; cf. Höfer in Roscher s.v. *Phrygios* 1, 2470) how Phrygius, a son of Neleus who ruled Miletus, fell in love with Pieria of Myus, a city in conflict with Miletus, and at her request made peace between the two cities. The source of this myth is unknown, but as a comic title Φρύγιος would best fit a parody of the story itself or of a lost literary predecessor in tragedy or dithyramb (cf. Kock 2.390, Nesselrath).

The two frs. give no clues to title or plot; 257(255K) is a bromide on hangovers, 258(256K) a stale witticism possibly spoken by a parasite who

---

[1] Corruption of Φρυγίῳ to -γί is easier to explain than that of -γίου to -γός; for a parallel error, cf. the mistaken appearance of both Φρύγες and Φρύγιοι in M's catalogue of Aeschylus titles (τ 78.18a and b, S. Radt *TrGF* 3 (Göttingen 1985) pp. 58f.). Radt's defence of Φρύξ as Alexis' title, which has persuaded Kassel–Austin, is unsound because it neglects the evidence for the existence (at least in myth) of Phrygios as a proper name.

[2] Similarly the feminine Φρυγία (Men. fr. 928, Aelian *Epist.* 19 with article; Aelian *Epist.* 8, on which see introduction to Ὀπώρα, Theoc. 15.42 without article; Plaut. *Aul.* 333, Ter. *HT* 731, *Ad.* 973), and many other ethnics that also doubled as slave names: e.g. in comedy Γέτας, Καρίων, Λυδός/Lydus, Mysis, Παφλαγών, Σκύθαινα, Σκύθης, Σύρα/Syra, Σύρος/Συρίσκος/Syrus, Thessala, Θρᾷττα (cf. Breitenbach, M. Lambertz, *Die griechischen Sklavennamen* (Vienna 1907) 10ff., Headlam on Herodas 1.1 with abundant references, Neil's edition of Ar. *Equ.* p. 6 making the point that it is often difficult to distinguish between name and ethnic, although the presence or absence of the article may help).

COMMENTARY

has been refused an invitation to dinner (cf. e.g. Plaut. *Stich.* 400f., 498ff.).

257 (255K)

Meineke 3.500 (1), Kock 2.390, Edmonds 3.496, Kassel–Austin 2.165; cf. Kann, *De iteratis* 65f. The speaker of this sermon on one penalty of drunkenness is unknown, but the unfulfilled present condition which opens the fr. presumably implies that somebody in the play was now experiencing a hangover. Clearchus fr. 3 expresses the same sequence of ideas (cf. e.g. Casaubon, *Animadv.* 724, Meineke, Blaydes, *Adv.* 1.117f., Kann) with parallel syntactical structures but largely different vocabulary (apart from τοῖς μεθυσκομένοις 1, τὸν ἄκρατον and οὐδὲ εἷς … ἄν 3, νυνὶ δέ 4). If here there was *imitatio cum uariatione*, we have no means of identifying who was model, who copier;[1] yet both could have independently developed a platitude that goes back to passages like Theogn. 479f., 485f. (both familiar enough to have been cited by Ath. 10.428c–d and Stob. *Anth.* 3.18.13), 498.

1 τὸ κραιπαλᾶν: see comm. on fr. 287(285K).1.

2 A's reading παρεγίνεθ<'> (Ath. 10.429e) is probably correct, corrupted to προσεγίνεθ' by Epit. MSS doubtless from a *saut des yeux* to προσίετο at the beginning of the next verse. On the orthography with -γιν- ~ γιγν- (which Dindorf conjectures and Kassel–Austin print here) see comm. on 37(36K).7.

3 A's text προσίετο πλεῖον τοῦ μετρίου has two anomalies: one of metre (an anapaest split after the second short in the second half of the first metron – rare but with several parallels where the two component words are verb + subject/object/word in agreement with either, e.g. Ar. *Av.* 1022, 1228, *Eccl.* 1027, Eubulus 123(126K).2; *CQ* 7 (1957) 195, 197), one of form (πλεῖον a rare alternative in comedy to the regular Attic πλέον, see comm. on 160(156K).3; hence Bothe's transposition (*PCGF* 573) προσίετο τοῦ μετρίου πλέον, but keeping the split anapaest and removing the caesura). One anomaly might be tolerated, two in one word arouse suspicion; hence Epit.'s πλείω (as attribute of οἶνον) must be preferred: 'nobody would ever accept (LSJ s.v. προσίημι II.2.b, although it is hard to detect a substantial

---

[1] The career of Clearchus as a comic poet seems to have fallen entirely within that of Alexis. In the list of victors at the Lenaea (*IG* ii/iii².2325.154 = v c i col. 4.3 Mette) Κλέ[αρχ]ος (suppl. Wilhelm) appears eight places after Alexis and five before Menander, and the scanty remains (three titles, five frs.) suggest a short career. Kann's claim that the presence of alleged infelicities in the Clearchus version shows that he was the imitator is a subjective evaluation and logically unsound; botching is not confined to the copier.

difference between b and c) more wine than was moderate/reasonable'. Cf. Herwerden, *Coll. Crit.* 130.

3–4 τὴν | τιμωρίαν: see comm. on 20.4.

5 τοὺς ἀκράτους πίνομεν: so acceptably ACE, provided we can assume the presence of οἴνους or some other masc. plur. noun in the following context. When ἄκρατος/-τον appears elsewhere as a substantive, it is always in the singular, normally masculine but occasionally neuter (see comm. on fr. 5.1). The lack of plural parallels has inflamed a rash of conjectures: e.g. τὰς ἀκράτους Meineke (sc. κύλικας, but cf. comm. on fr. 116(111K).1), προχείρως πως or προχειρότερον Kock (leaving the plural), τοῦδ' ἀκράτου Kaibel (but the article is needed), πρόχειρον οἶνον ἀκρατῶς Herwerden, *Mnemosyne*, 14 (1886) 188 (hard to justify palaeogaphically), τὰς ἀκράτου Blaydes (*Adv.* 1.117: sc. κύλικας); I once toyed with χοῦν (for the form, cf. *IG* ii².1366.23, 1st century AD) or χοῦς ἀκράτου, but in Attic comedy only third-declension forms of χοῦς are attested (e.g. Alexis 15.19).

258 (256K)

Meineke 3.500 (II), Kock 2.390, Edmonds 2.496, Kassel–Austin 2.166; cf. Kock 1.430 on Ar. fr.159(156K), Ribbeck, *Kolax* 71, E. Woytek, *Wien. Stud.* 86 (1973) 69ff. For a possible context and speaker see introduction to the play.

κεστρεὺς νῆστις: κεστρεύς = grey mullet (see comm. on 16.8–11), whose reputation for going without food for long periods and afterwards guzzling insatiably on other things than fish[1] was well known in Alexis' Athens (e.g. Arist. *HA* 8.2, 591ᵃ17, ᵇ1 cited in Ath. 7.307a–308b, Plato com. 28(29K), Antiphanes 216(217K).9f.; hence the proverbial application of κ. νῆστις to hungry humans (Phot. and Hesych. s.v. κεστρεῖς, *Suda* s.v. κεστρεὺς νηστεύει, Zenobius 4.52, Diogenian 5.53) such as comic parasites (Ar. fr. 159(156K), Ameipsias 1.3, Theopompus 14(13K), Antiphanes 136(138K), Anaxandrides 35(34K).8, Eubulus 68.2, Diphilus 53(54K), Euphron 2 and com. anon. in Ath. 7.307f, cf. Kaibel's editions of Ath.,

---

[1] Modern studies have shown that various species of grey mullet migrate in winter offshore to deeper and warmer waters where they hibernate; at this period no residue of food is found in their remarkable two-part gut, comprising a thick-walled crop and a long intestine more than twice the length of the fish. With the springtime rise in temperature feeding recommences, mainly on diatoms, epiphytic algae and larval gastropods (τρέφεται ... φυκίοις καὶ ἄμμῳ, Arist. *HA* 8.2, 591ᵃ22). Cf. A. Wheeler, *The Fishes of the British Isles and North-west Europe* (London, Melbourne, Toronto 1969) 462f.

vol. 3, p. viii; A. Nauck, *MGR* 6 (1894) 174). A speaker's identification with something as exotic as a 'starving mullet' was originally striking and bold, however tedious it may have become by repetition; how far such identifications influenced a favourite Plautine type of expression is still disputed, cf. Fraenkel, *EP* 21ff., H. W. Prescott, *TAPA* 63 (1932) 110ff., Woytek).

Φυγάς

L. von Spengel, *Caii Caecilii Statii deperditarum fabularum fragmenta*(Munich 1829) 6, T. B. L. Webster, *CQ* 2 (1952) 22 (with *Phygas* miscopied as *Phryges*), Nesselrath, *MK* 295. The reason why the title figures of Alexis' Φυγάς, Ἐκκηρυττόμενος (see introduction to that play) and Philemon's Ἄπολις became willing or forced exiles from their native cities is as much a mystery as is the plots of these comedies. Caecilius Statius' *Exul* (p. 48 Ribbeck) was possibly adapted from one of the trio, but there are no verbal or character links to determine its source (Spengel's choice of Φυγάς is based solely on exact identity of titles).

Alexis' Φυγάς may be dated between *c.* 325 and *c.* 310, the period when the parasite Chaerephon, described in the present tense by the play's one extant fr. (259(257K)), was active in Athens (Webster and my comm. on fr. 213(210K).1).

259 (257K)

Meineke 3.501, Kock 2.391, Edmonds 2.496, Kassel–Austin 2.166. The fr. is cited by Ath. 4.164f (all: A + Epit.) and 6.229b (vv.3–4 μαγείροις: only A). Speaker and context (*pace* Nesselrath, *MK* 295) are unknown.

1–2 The transmitted text ἀεί (CE ~ αἰεί A, see comm. on fr. 76.1) γ' ὁ Χαιρεφῶν τιν' εὑρίσκει τέχνην· καὶ νῦν πορίζεταί γε τὰ δεῖπν' ἀσύμβολα yields good sense, but may benefit from two minor adjustments.

(i) Loss of the preceding context makes the function of γ' after ἀεί uncertain (? emphasising a response to a previous speaker's comment on parasitical expertise, 'At any rate Ch. always' or 'Yes, Ch. always'; cf. Denniston, *GP* 120f, 130ff.; or could it be a corruption for τ'? Cf. comm. on fr. 64(63K)). Paired clauses such as this, where the first states a general rule and the second a specific instance of it, are frequently linked by τε . . . τε, τε . . . καί, καὶ . . . καί (e.g. Eur. *Alc.* 222f. καὶ πάρος γὰρ . . . καὶ νῦν . . ., Ar. *Thesm.* 576ff. γυναικομανῶ γὰρ προξενῶ θ' ὑμῶν ἀεί· καὶ νῦν ἀκούσας . . .ἥκω φράσων τοῦτ', Alexis 131(126K).2ff. τά τ' ἄλλα γὰρ νενομοτέθηκε . . . νυνί τε καινὸν εἰσφέρει νόμον τινά).

(ii) γε τὰ δεῖπν' in the second half of the second metron of v. 2, with the anapaest split after the first short and no close connection between γε and τὰ, is unusual, but can be paralleled (e.g. Ar. *Lys.* 760 γε τάλαιν', same *sedes*); even so, γε δεῖπν' may represent what Alexis wrote, since γε is appropriately emphatic and articles are often added superfluously by scribes (cf. comm. on 145(141K).9 and *CQ* 7 (1957) 197f.).[1]

ὁ **Χαιρεφῶν**: see comm. on 213(210K).1.

τέχνην: derogatory ('trick'), as commonly from Homer (e.g. *Od.* 4.455, 529) onwards (e.g. Hes. *Theog.* 160 and West *ad loc.*, 770, S. *Phil.* 88, Eur. *Suppl.* 381 and Collard *ad loc.*, Pl. *Leg.* 11.919e, 936d).

2 δεῖπν' ἀσύμβολα: i.e. dinners which have been organised ἀπὸ συμβολῶν (see introduction to fr. 15) are successfully gatecrashed by Chaerephon without him paying his share of the cost. Such behaviour, allegedly typical of Chaerephon (e.g. Alexis 213(210K), Men. *Sam.* 603, Apollodorus Car. 29(24K), 31(26K)) and parasites in general (e.g. Epicharmus fr. 35 Kaibel, Phrynichus 60(57K), Eubulus 20(21K), Timocles 8.10 and 18f., Diodorus 2.13, Ephippus 20.3, Diphilus 74(73K).8, Ter. *Phorm.* 339, Lucian, *Dial. Meretr.* 12.1), prompted vigorous complaints (e.g. Dromon 1.1ff., Aeschines 1.75). Cf. Nesselrath, *LP* 66 and n. 178.

3–4 'You see, where the cooks find pottery for hire.' For this use of κέραμος as a collective singular (= τὰ κεράμεια σκεύη, Alciphron 2.14.1) cf. e.g. Hdt. 3.6.1, 5.88.2, Ar. *Ach.* 902, Men. *Sam.* 290, Ath. 6.229c–d citing Ptolemy VII = fr. 7 in *FHG* 3.187, and comm. on Alexis 15.3. The implication is that μάγειροι regularly hired pottery for their engagements (cf. Chr. Dedoussi, comm. (Athens 1965) on Men. *Sam.* 290 = '75' in her numbering), but whether the place (also called ὁ κέραμος, according to the difficult and probably corrupt Diphilus 42(43K).28f., cf. Dohm, *Mageiros* 70 n. 2 and see comm. on fr. 47(46K).8) where they hired it was identical to that part of the market (near the shrine of Eurysaces, Pollux

---

[1] Hence deletion of γε (so Meineke, K. Bernhardi, *De incisionibus anapaesti in trimetro comico graecorum* (Diss. Leipzig 1872) 22 = *Acta Soc. Phil. Lipsiensis* 1 (1872) 264) must be resisted. S. A. Naber's conjecture (*Mnemosyne* 8 (1880) 264, anticipating Kaibel and printed by Kassel–Austin) τέχνην καινὴν πορίζεταί τε ..., was presumably inspired by the existence of expressions like δεῖ μ' ἀεὶ καινὸν πόρον | (?) εὑρεῖν (Antiphanes 253(244K) and αἰεί μέν ... τι καινὸν εὑρίσκει (Herodas 6.89 and Headlam-Knox *ad loc.*; cf. also e.g. Ath. 14.623e, 15.665a), but it ignores ACE's colon after τέχνην and destroys the idiomatic structure of vv. 1–2 with paired clauses (i) contrasting general ἀεί and specific νῦν/νυνί (cf. e.g. Hom. *Il.*˙1.107ff., S. *Aj.* 1ff., Ar. *Nub.* 1288ff., *Vesp.* 719ff., *Thesm.* 576f., Pl. *Symp.* 212b) and (ii) emphasising (καί) νῦν/νυνί characteristically with γε (cf. e.g. S. *Aj.* 1376, Eur. *Alc.* 374, *El.* 1057, *IA* 661, Ar. *Vesp.* 442, *Pax* 326, 337, *Ran.* 276; Denniston, *GP* 291f., 157f.).

COMMENTARY

7.132f.; cf. Thompson–Wycherley, *Agora* XIV.170f.) where the cooks themselves were hired (= τὰ μαγειρεῖα, Antiphanes 201(203K) cited by Pollux 9.48, Theophr. *Char.* 6.9; *forum coquinum* in Plaut. *Pseud.* 790) is uncertain. Cf. Meineke, *Men. et Phil.* xviif., Rankin, ΜΑΓΕΙΡΟΙ 42ff., Dohm 70f.

3 μισθώσιμος: cf. Machon 54 κατάλυσιν ... μισθωσίμην.

4 τοῖς μαγείροις: the dative of the person interested (K.G. 1.420f.) is closely akin to that of the agent (1.422f.) in contexts like this, where ἐστιν ... μισθώσιμος replaces a passive (μισθοῦται) or verbal (μισθωτέος); cf. e.g. S. *Aj.* 440 ἄτιμος Ἀργείοισιν.

εὐθὺς: corrected from A and Epit. MSS's εὐθέως (cf. comm. on fr. 224(222K).3) by Scaliger in Canter, Paris MS 53, long before either Porson, *Adv.* 142, or Jacobs, *Addit.* 104.

ἐξ ἑωθινοῦ: 'from dawn', standard in Attic, e.g. (comedy) Ar. *Thesm.* 2, Pherecrates 95(90K), Men. *Sam.* 511; (prose) Xen. *Hell.* 1.1.5, Pl. *Phdr.* 227a, 228b, *Symp.* 220c, *Leg.* 4.722c.

5 ἕστηκεν (cf. 8 **εἰσελήλυθεν**): the perfect vividly represents one instance of a habitual action or situation as if it has already been completed (cf. Kock on Antiphanes 202(204K).3, K.G. 1.150); whether it can be labelled 'gnomic' (cf. Goodwin, *MT* 53ff.) when a specific individual's behaviour (as here) is concerned, is open to question. Comedy has many examples: e.g. Ar. *Equ.* 718 with Th. Kock (Leipzig 1853) and Neil *ad loc.*, *Vesp.* 561 with Starkie *ad loc.*, 591, *Ran.* 970, Antiphanes 202(204K).3 (ἥρπακεν), 7, 8, Anaxandrides 35(34K).4–7, Theophilus 4.2; cf. also Pl. *Protag.* 328b.

μισθούμενον: middle, 'a man hiring (a μάγειρος)', as elsewhere (in comedy: e.g. Men. *Dysk.* 264, 665, Philemon 176(210K), Nicomachus 1.5; cf. Diog. Laert. 2.72, Pollux 9.48). Kock's addition of τιν' before ἤδη to clarify the participle's reference is gratuitous and, with its split anapaest, metrically unattractive.

6–7 τοῦ μαγείρου πυθόμενος τὸν ἑστιῶντα: 'having learnt from the cook who's giving the dinner'; construction with accusative and simple genitive is less common than with acc. and διά/παρά/πρός + gen., but cf. A. *Ag.* 599, Ar. *Ach.* 204f. καὶ τὸν ἄνδρα πυνθάνου | τῶν ὁδοιπόρων ἁπάντων, *Av.* 1119f. ἄγγελος ... ὅτου πευσόμεθα τἀκεῖ πράγματα, *Ran.* 1417, Hdt. 1.111 πυνθάνομαι πάντα τὸν λόγον θεράποντος, 7.43, LSJ s.v. πυνθάνομαι 4.

7 τῆς θύρας χασμωμένης: the attribution of human functions and qualities to inanimate objects or concepts is more characteristic of the Old Comedy of Aristophanes and the Roman adaptations of Plautus (cf. Fraenkel, *EP* 95ff., H. J. Newiger, *Metapher und Allegorie* (Munich 1957)) than of the New Comedy of Menander. This is Alexis' most striking

726

ΦΥΓΑΣ

example[1] (cf. Favorinus *Ecl.* 175a = W. Dindorf, *Grammatici Graeci* (Leipzig 1823) 1.450.7 χασμᾶσθαι, ὅπερ οὐκ ἐπὶ στομάτων μόνον λέγεται, ἀλλ' ἤδη τροπικῶς καὶ ἐπὶ θύρας ἠνεῳγμένης, citing this passage; O. Kaehler, *Woch. Klass. Phil.* 2 (1885) 905), but cf. also Alexis 115(110K).2, 153(149K).16f., 172(167K).4f. (the last two couched in riddling language). More commonly in the extant frs. inanimate or bestial existence is assigned to humans: 47(46K).3ff., 88(85K).3ff., 113(108K).5, 140(135K).17, 183(178K).7, 207(204K), 217(214K).1, 258(256K).

Χορηγίς

Schweighaeuser, *Animadv.* 9.24, Meineke 1.403, Kaibel in *RE* s.v. *Alexis* 9, 1469.54ff., Breitenbach 165, Nesselrath, *MK* 319 n. 97. The title may be interpreted in two ways. It could be the name of a woman, possibly (but not necessarily: cf. *IG* ii².13068 Χορηγὶς Χορηγίωνος on a 4th-century tombstone) a *hetaira*, like Choregis the alleged mistress of the Athenian politician Aristophon (so Carystius[2] in Ath. 13.577c = *FHG* 4.358 frs. 11, 12; cf. Meineke, Kaibel, Breitenbach, Nesselrath, Bechtel, *Personennamen*

---

[1] Since χασμᾶσθαι is applied to an inanimate object only here, it seems safe to assume that the metaphor is not a dead one.

[2] Carystius' claim, however, that Aristophon ἀπεδείχθη ὑπὸ Καλλιάδου τοῦ κωμικοῦ ἐκ Χορηγίδος τῆς ἑταίρας παιδοποιησάμενος poses chronological problems. Aristophon died in the 330s in his 100th year (Σ Aesch. 1.64; cf. Davies, *APF* 65, R. Develin, *Athenian Officials 684–321 B.C.* (Cambridge 1989) p. 446 no. 462), but his political activity seems to have been concentrated in the period between *c.* 410 and 390 (Miller in *RE* s.v. 3, 1005.59ff.). The comic poet Calliades appears in the Lenaea victors' list two places after Diphilus and five after Menander (*IG* ii².2325.166 = v c 1 col. 4, 15 Mette), and so can hardly have begun producing before the last decade of the 4th century (Körte in *RE* s.v. *Kalliades* 4, 1612.51ff.). The suggestion that Carystius' Καλλιάδου may have been an error (so Meineke 1.450) for, or a by-form (so A. Wilhelm, *Urkunden dramatischer Aufführungen in Athen* (Vienna 1906) 133; cf. Gulick's note on Ath. *ad loc.*) of, Καλλίου does not remove the difficulty, for the career of Callias the comic poet does not appear to have extended beyond the 420s (cf. frs. 15(12K), 17(13K), 20–1(14–15K); Meineke 1.214, P. Geissler, *Chronologie der altattischen Komödie* (Berlin 1925) 27, Körte in *RE* s.v. *Kallias* 20, 1627.33ff.). It seems more probable either that Carystius was right, and Calliades for some reason had referred to events of a century or so earlier, or that in one of his comedies a fictive character named Aristophon (with an equally fictive mistress Choregis) was misidentified as the Athenian politician by Carystius.

COMMENTARY

67); in this case Choregis is likely to have been a *nomen fictum* and the title perhaps comparable to Ἀγωνίς, Δορκίς/Ῥόδιον, Ἰσοστάσιον, Ὀπώρα, Παμφίλη, Πεζονίκη, Πολύκλεια (see introductions to those plays). Alternatively χορηγίς could be a female χορηγός (cf. Schweighaeuser, Meineke, LSJ s.v.), the heroine of a fantasy in which a woman took over a role traditionally confined (cf. Paramonus' Χορηγῶν of 169: *IG* ii².2323.202 = III B 3 col. 4a, 13 Mette) to men; in that event cf. e.g. Ar. *Lys.*, *Eccl.*, possibly Theopompus' Στρατιωτίδες, Alexis' and Amphis' Γυναικοκρατία. The one short fr. preserved from Alexis' Χορηγίς (260(258K)), a reference to some unknown (? real-life, ? stage) skinflint who served inferior food to his dining-club colleagues, gives no help to the title's interpretation.

260 (258K)

Meineke 3.501, Kock 2.391, Edmonds 2.498, Kassel–Austin 2.167.

1 ὅς: the name of the skinflint host (cf. introduction to Χορηγίς) was presumably given in the preceding context.

τοῖς τετραδισταῖς: the fourth day of the month was popularly believed to have been the birthday of Hermes (*H. Merc.* 19, Ar. *Plut.* 1126 and Σ, Plut. *Mor.* 738f) and Heracles (cf. the proverb τετράδι γέγονας Zenobius 6.7, Apostolius 16.34, Miller, *Mélanges* 366, Phot. and *Suda* s.vv.),[1] and was associated in some way with Aphrodite Pandemos (Ath. 14.659d citing Men. *Kol.* fr. 1 and Gomme–Sandbach, *Comm. ad loc.*; cf. Ziehen in *RE* s.v. Παννυχίς 1, 630.67ff., West, comm. on Hes. *Op.* 770), and men who dined together each month on that day (Men. fr. 265; contrast Theophr. *Char.* 16.10) were called τετραδισταί (Ath. *loc. cit.*, Hesych. s.v.; cf. R. Renehan, *Glotta* 50 (1972) 177f.). Similar formations include δεκαδιστής (? Theophr. *Char.* 27.11 and R. G. Ussher (¹London 1960, ² Bristol 1993) *ad loc.*), εἰκαδιστής (celebrating Epicurus' death on that day, Ath. 7.298d), νουμηνιαστής (Ath. 12.551f citing Lysias fr. 53) = κακοδαιμονιστής (cf. Starkie, comm. on Ar. *Ach.* 999) and ἀγαθοδαιμονιστής (Arist. *Eth. Eud.* 3.6, 1233ᵇ3).

παρέθηκεν: see comm. on 98(152K).2.

ἐσθίειν: Schweighaeuser's conjecture (*Animadv.* 4.135, but cf. Daléchamp's translation *edenda ... apposuit*) in place of ACE's inappropriate ἐσθίων (Ath. 7.287f); we do not expect to be told what the host himself ate

---

[1] This proverb, which referred to those who (like Heracles) worked mainly to benefit others, was applied to Aristophanes by his rivals (Ameipsias 27(28K), Aristonymus 3(4K), cf. Plato com. 107(100K)) because Callistratus and Philonides sometimes acted as διδάσκαλοι for his plays.

while serving dinner to his guests, but what he gave them to eat. For the infinitive of purpose (K.G. 2.16f., Goodwin, *MT* 308ff.) with παρατίθημι cf. Alexis 243(241K).4, with προτίθημι cf. Ath. 3.110b citing Diocles fr. 116 Wellmann (J. Meyer, *Emendationes et observationes in novissimam Athenaei editionem* (Progr. Regensburg 1897) 30). Yet Villebrune's conjecture ἑστιῶν seems equally good in sense, palaeography and idiom; for παρατίθημι with nominative present participle cf. e.g. Ar. *Equ.* 778.

2 The three foods were typically the fare of Athens' poor. As a feminine λέκιθος = egg yolk, masculine = porridge of cereals (barley, Hippocr. *Mul.* 1.109) or thick soup of pulse (lentils, 1.52; chick-peas, 2.192; cf. Cantharus fr. 13(10K)); Galen's description runs λέκιθον δὲ (ὀνομάζω) τὸ ἐκ τῶν ἀλεσθέντων ἄλευρον ἑψόμενον ἐν ὕδατι, προσεμβαλλομένου τινὸς λίπους 6.782 Kühn. In Alexis (and e.g. Ar. *Lys.* 562, *Eccl.* 1178, Pherecrates 26(22K)), as prepared food it can mean only porridge/soup; elsewhere a lack of gender indication (e.g. Metagenes 18(16K)) can make interpretation more difficult.

μεμβράδας: see comm. on fr. 200(195K).3.

στέμφυλα: see comm. on fr. 201(196K).1.

Ψευδόμενος

Schweighaeuser, *Animadv.* 9.24, Meineke 1.402, T. Mantero in *Menandrea: Miscellanea philologica* (Genoa 1960) 129ff. and *Maia* 18 (1966) 392ff., W. Kraus, *Anz. Alt.* 28 (1975) 6; cf. Th. Bergk, *Griechische Literaturgeschichte* 4 (Berlin 1887) 154f. n. 116 and my comm. on Τοκιστής, pp. 654f. n. 1. Schweighaeuser (followed tentatively by Meineke) suggested that the title Ψευδόμενος, cited twice for Alexis by Ath. (10.419b = fr. 261(259K), rephrasing fr. 256(254K).2–3 and presumably also spoken by a character who disliked spending money; 6.255b = fr. 262(260K), spoken about and probably by a parasite), might be an error for Καταψευδόμενος, the alternative title for Τοκιστής which is twice cited (by Ath. 6.258e = fr. 233(231K); *Suda* s.v. ἀνάριστος = fr. 235(233K)) on its own as the name of the play. In support of this suggestion it may be argued (i) that Τοκιστής features a parasite (identified by Ath. as the speaker of fr. 233(231K)) and that the usurer is traditionally portrayed on stage as sordidly mercenary (e.g. Plaut. *Most.* 532ff., with his repeated demands for interest payments); and (ii) that Pollux 9.50 provides a parallel for the alleged transcriptional error by corrupting the title of Euripides' Ἱππόλυτος κατακαλυπτόμενος to -τῳ καλυπτομένῳ (fr. 442; cf. Barrett's edition of Eur. *Hipp.* p. 10 n. 1). Ultimately, however, the suggestion seems to me misguided. A scribal error of this kind is comprehensible if committed once, less so if repeated and then set against the three places in the same author (6.258e, 10.431a,

COMMENTARY

15.692f = frs. 232–4(230–2K) where Καταψευδ- is correctly transcribed; cf. also introduction to 'Εκκηρυττόμενος. And the uncompounded Ψευδόμενος makes an excellent title, whether for a character study of a habitual liar, or for a plot in which a male character told one or more lies in furtherance of an intrigue (cf. e.g. Men. *Asp.*, *Dis Ex.*/Plaut. *Bacch.*, *Epid.*, *Merc.*, *Most.*, *Pseud.*, Ter. *Phorm.*).

More recently Teresa Mantero has argued that Alexis' Ψευδόμενος was the – or a – model for Plautus' *Pseudolus*. Starting from the similarity of the two titles and a possibility that the Roman playwright could have been prompted by the description of a scheming slave in Alexis' cast list as θεράπων ψευδολόγος, she claims that *Pseud.* 822 (*hic quidem homines tam breuem uitam colunt*) is a rough translation of Alexis 262(260K), and that the Plautine conversation between Ballio and the cook (790ff., cf. especially the cook's remark at 804ff. *cum extemplo ueniunt conductum coquom,* | *nemo illum quaerit qui optimus et carissimust:* | *illum conducunt potius qui uilissimust*) could have been adapted from the Alexis scene containing fr. 261(259K). Kraus succinctly noted the flaws in Mantero's theory. Alexis 262(260K) complains about the short life of parasites, *Pseud.* 822 about the short life of diners poisoned by the herbal seasonings of rival cooks. The speaker of Alexis 261(259K) apparently dislikes extravagance, but such a trait is not characteristic in *Pseud.* of either the cook (a conventional braggart who takes pride in his expensiveness, 803ff., 848) or Ballio (a profit-seeking villain who is nevertheless willing to spend money freely in order to attract potential clients, 167; he is called lots of names, but never miser, 359ff., 975f.). The Plautine cast in fact has neither skinflint nor parasite.

261 (259K)

Meineke 3.502 (i), Kock, 2.392, Edmonds 2.498, Kassel–Austin 2.168. In this fr. v. 1 reproduces fr. 256(254K).2 exactly, v. 2 paraphrases 256(254K).3; for the use of the same material in different plays, see comm. on fr. 24.2–4. Though the context of fr. 261(259K) is unknown, its speaker is likely to have been similar in character to that of fr. 256(254K).

262 (260K)

Meineke 3.502 (ii), Kock 2.392, Edmonds, 2.498, Kassel–Austin 2.168; cf. Nesselrath, *MK* 314. The fr. consists of a pair of hexameters, a metre employed in comedy particularly for riddles, oracles and parodies of literature using that metre (cf. introductions to 'Αρχίλοχος and fr. 22, F. Selvers, *De mediae comoediae sermone* (Diss. Münster 1919) 23, R. Pretagostini, *Dioniso* 57 (1987) 249ff., Nesselrath). Without context it is impossible to know why Alexis chose the metre here; one possibility is that the speaker (probably himself a parasite) was giving 'Parasite' as the answer to a riddle (? inspired by Hom. *Il.* 6.146ff., 21.464ff., Mimnermus 2.1ff. West), 'Whose life most resembles that of leaves and flowers?' Stage parasites characteristically talk about themselves and their profession: e.g. Alexis 121(116K), Men. *Dysk.* 57ff., Plaut. *Capt.* 69ff., *Men.* 77ff., 446ff., *Pers.* 53ff., *Stich.* 155ff. They associate with young men, and the frequency with which they describe the rough treatment meted out to them (Epicharmus fr. 35 Kaibel, Antiphanes 193(195K).3, Aristophon 5(4K).6, Axionicus 6, Plaut. *Capt.* 88ff., 472, Ter. *Eun.* 244f.; cf. Alciphron 3.3.1, 13.2, 32.1) implies possession of juvenile vigour and fitness; Pollux 4.146 lists the masks of κόλαξ and παράσιτος under νεανίσκοι (cf. Ribbeck, *Kolax* 41). In literature older parasites are rare; Peniculus is just over 30 (Plaut. *Men.* 446) but still addressed as *adulescens* (494); Saturio uniquely has a daughter old enough to be a *hetaira* (*Pers.*, cf. Webster, *SLGC* 81); Capnosphrantes in Alciphron 3.13.2 is μεσαιπόλιος (so S. Bergler (Leipzig 1715); -πονος MSS, -πολος F. H. Fobes (London and Cambridge Mass. 1949)).

1 κόλακος: so A (Ath. 6.255b), but CE's κολάκων may be preferable, at least palaeographically (? → -ακος by assimilation to the ending of βίος).

2 πολιοκροτάφῳ παρασίτῳ: one whose hair is just beginning to turn grey, cf. Arist. *HA* 3.11, 518ᵃ16f. πρῶτον δὲ πολιοῦνται οἱ κρόταφοι τῶν ἀνθρώπων. The adjective goes back to Homer (*Il.* 8.518, cf. epigr. 12.3 in D. B. Monro's edition (Oxford 1896), Hes. *Op.* 181, Bacchylides fr. 52; Gow on Theoc. 14.68) and may have been chosen for its appropriateness to (? riddling) style and metre.

παρασίτῳ: here κόλαξ and παράσιτος are used as interchangeable synonyms; similarly at fr. 121(116K) παράσιτοι (v. 1, cf. 4, 5) engage in a κολακείας ἀγών. At 183(178K).2 Alexis uses Παράσιτος as a proper name (see introduction to the play), 200(195K).3 παρασιτῶ, 224(222K).8 the coinage παραμασύντης, 238(236K) παραμασήτης. Ath. 6.258e claims that a κόλαξ is the speaker of Alexis 233(231K), a typical parasite's speech. How far the interchangeability of κόλαξ and παράσιτος in Alexis reflected the general usage of his time and later is now disputed; Ribbeck, *Kolax*, *passim*, A. Giese, *De parasiti persona capita selecta* (Diss. Kiel 1908) 3 n. 3 and Wüst in *RE* s.v. *Parasitos* 1389.45ff. take it for granted; L. Gil, *Est. Clas.* 25 (1981–3) 39ff. and Nesselrath, *LP* 88ff. (but compare 104, *MK* 311f.) argue for a distinction between a voracious but otherwise harmless παράσιτος and a more ambitious and sinister κόλαξ in New Comedy; see also P. G. McC. Brown, *ZPE* 92 (1992) 98ff.

731

COMMENTARY

INCERTARUM FABULARUM FRAGMENTA

263 (261K)

Meineke 3.502 (1), Kock 3.392, Edmonds 2.500, Kassel–Austin 2.168; cf. Bothe, *PCGF* 574f., Jacobi in Meineke 5 p. ccxv, Fraenkel, *MNC* 14ff., 26f. A banquet is described by an uninvited guest (ἔλαθον v. 1, cf. Diodorus com. 2.14–17; Bothe, Kock) whose voracity identifies him as either a parasite or a mythical glutton such as Heracles, but attempts to name the play from which the fr. came ('Ησιόνη Jacobi in Meineke 5. p. ccxv, cf. my p. 233 n. 1; Παράσιτος Bothe, *PCGF* 574f.) are idle in the absence of supporting evidence. The speaker's style – vivid, quick-moving and asyndetic – is typical in such narratives (cf. Fraenkel 23, 39, 41f., 51), but (unlike Alexis 124(119K)) it does not rise here to dithyrambic burlesque. The highlight of the description, which follows the normal sequence of events at a dinner-party (comm. on v. 2), is a dish representing τὸ τοῦ πόλου τοῦ παντὸς ἡμισφαίριον (6), with the comestibles symbolising two signs of the zodiac (*Pisces* 12th, *Scorpio* 8th: v. 9) and other stars such as the Kids (ἔριφοι, v. 9). Although knowledge of the zodiac first reached Greece in the 6th or 5th centuries, a wider interest in it may have been disseminated during the 4th century by the studies of Eudoxus of Cnidos and its appearance as a motif of popular art (e.g. Alexander the Great's shield as depicted on the Aboukir medallions, if these are genuine; Demetrius of Phalerum's cloak, Plut. *Dem.* 41.4, Duris in Ath. 12.535f = *FGrH* II A fr. 14 p. 142; Menedemus of Eretria's hat, Diog. Laert. 6.102; H. Thiersch, *JDAI* 26 (1908) 163, A. J. Wace, *Jahreshefte des Öst. Arch. Inst.* 39 (1952) 114f); but it is uncertain whether Alexis' inclusion of the non-zodiacal Kids (*Haedi*, η and ξ in the *Auriga* constellation, close to *Capella*; cf. Gow, comm. on Theoc. 7.53f.) in his list was a mistake caused by confusion with *Capricorn* (αἰγόκερως, tenth sign of the zodiac), a constellation in a totally different part of the sky (so Gundel, *RE* s.v. *Zodiakos* 602.32ff.), or whether Alexis' dish was not intended to be exclusively zodiacal (Casaubon, *Animadv.* 123, J. A. E. Bethe, *Buch und Bild im Altertum* (Leipzig and Vienna 1945) 124 n. 8), unlike the dish at Trimalchio's feast fully and explicitly detailed in Petronius *Sat.* 35:

rotundum enim repositorium duodecim habebat signa in orbe disposita, super quae proprium conuenientemque materiae structor imposuerat cibum: super arietem cicer arietinum, super taurum bubulae frustum, super geminos testiculos et rienes, super cancrum coronam, super leonem ficum africanam, super uirginem steriliculam, super libram stateram in cuius altera parte scriblita erat, in altera placenta, super scorpionem pisciculum marinum, super sagittarium oclopetam, super capricornum locustam marinam, super aquarium anserem, super pisces duos mullos; cf. K. F. C. Rose and J. P. Sullivan, *CQ* 18 (1968) 180ff. Sosipater 1.25ff. brings on stage a cook who claims to know astronomy and the zodiac; the speaker praising astronomical discoveries in Alexis 31(30K) is unknown, but may have been a scheming slave (see introduction to Ἀχαΐς). See especially Gundel and Böker, *RE* s.v. *Ζodiakos* 462.14ff.; cf. also A. Bouché-Leclercq, *L'Astrologie grecque* (Paris 1899) 52ff., 130ff., Fr. Cumont in Dar.–Sag. s.v. *Ζodiacus* 1046A ff. and *Astrology and Religion among the Greeks and Romans* (New York and London 1912), A. M. J. Festugière, *L'Astrologie et les sciences occultes* (Paris 1944), O. Neugebauer, *A History of Ancient Mathematical Astronomy* 2 (Berlin 1975) 593ff., H. Lloyd-Jones, *Myths of the Ζodiac* (London 1978), W. Hübner, *Die Eigenschaften der Tierkreiszeichen in der Antiken* (Wiesbaden 1982).

1 οὗ τὸ πρᾶγμ' ἠβούλετο: absence of preceding context makes an assured interpretation more difficult, but τὸ πρᾶγμ' here is clearly a (? colloquially) imprecise substitute for something like δεῖπνον (cf. e.g. Ar. fr. 174(165K).1f. ἦν δὲ | τὸ πρᾶγμ' ἑορτή). Daléchamp (*Annot.* 715, followed by Casaubon, *Animadv.* 122) took τὸ πρᾶγμ' as the subject of ἠβούλετο and translated *quo res ipsa uolebat*, but parallels for such a use of βούλομαι with inanimate subject are hard to find. τὸ πρᾶγμ' is better construed as an object: 'where he (sc. the host) intended the party (to occur)'. This construction of βούλομαι is well explained and illustrated in LSJ s.v. 1 1: 'when β. is followed by an acc. only, an inf. may generally be supplied', here γενέσθαι (cf. Herwerden, *Coll. Crit.* 131) as also at e.g. Hom. *Il.* 15.51, Pl. *Euthphr.* 3a, Philemon 72(69K).2. In post-Homeric Greek βούλομαι, δύναμαι and μέλλω appear with augments in ἠ- (side by side with the more regular ἐ-), probably by popular analogy with ἤθελον, ἠθέλησα, but the examples transmitted in Attic drama are only twice (Ar. *Ran.* 1038, *Eccl.* 597) guaranteed by metre and greatly outnumbered by examples in ἐ-. Forms in ἠ- appear on Attic inscriptions first in the 280s (e.g. *IG* ii.² 657.25; cf. Meisterhans–Schwyzer 169), and were strongly favoured in second-sophistic Greek (W. Schmid, *Der Atticismus* 4 (Stuttgart 1896) 590). Grammarians identified the forms variously as Attic (Moeris 198.18, [Herodian] 2.326.4, 354.14 and *passim* Lentz), Ionic (anon. in Cramer, *Anecd. Oxon.* 2.374.32f.) or barbaric (the author of περὶ βαρβαρισμοῦ in L. K. Valckenaer's edition of Ammonius (Leiden 1739) 195. Cf. especially Veitch, *Greek Verbs*⁴ s.v. βούλομαι, K.B. 2.9, A. Debrunner in *Festschrift für Friedrich Ζucker* (Berlin 1954) 108f., J. K. Elliott, *Ζeitschrift für die neutestamentliche Wissenschaft* 69 (1978) 249ff.

2 κατὰ χειρός: sc. ὕδωρ, water being poured over the hands as the customary preliminary to a meal (cf. e.g. Teleclides 1.2 εἰρήνη μὲν πρῶτον

COMMENTARY

ἁπάντων ἦν ὥσπερ ὕδωρ κατὰ χειρός; Ath. 9.408e–f citing Ar. Byz. fr. 368 Slater, see his note *ad loc.*; my comm. on Alexis 252(250K).2). With this expression (and the parallel κατὰ χειρῶν, normally referring to hand-washing after a meal, like ἀπονίψασθαι) ὕδωρ is normally added in earlier comedy (e.g. Ar. *Vesp.* 1216, *Av.* 464, fr. 516(502K).1, Alcaeus com. 16, Ameipsias 20(21K), Eupolis 320(298K), Teleclides 1.2; but also Clearchus 4.1), omitted in later (also e.g. -ός Archedicus 2.3, Demonicus 1.3f., Nicostratus 26(25K), -ῶν Antiphanes 280(287K), Men. fr. 405, Philyllius 3.3).

ἦx': sc. ὁ οἰκέτης, the subject being omitted (cf. K.G. 1.32f.) when implied by predicate or context.

3 οὐδ' ἐλαῶν γένη: of the olive (*Olea europaea*) Macrob. *Sat.* 3.20.6 lists sixteen cultivars, Pliny *HN* 15.4.13ff., 6.20 fifteen; cf. also Cato *Agr.* 6.1 = Varro *Rust.* 1.24.1f., V. *Georg.* 2.85f., Columella 5.8.3, Palladius 3.28.4, Isid. *Etym.* 17.7.63ff.; Hehn, *Kulturpflanzen* 103ff., Pease in *RE* s.v. *Ölbaum*, 1998.1ff.

If ἐλαῶν is rightly transmitted here (Epit. of Ath. 2.59f, CE), its penult must be shortened before the following long vowel (cf. comm. on 247(245K).1), as occasionally elsewhere (comedy: possibly Evangelus 1.5; other genres: Philippus in *Anth. Pal.* 4.2.12, 6.102.6 = 1, XVII Gow–Page; the pun on Hom. *Il.* 5.366 etc. in Ath. 6.246a and Diog. Laert. 6.55, cf. Eustath. 572.34f., 860.21ff.; oracle in Phleg. *Mir.* 10, p. 79.1 Keller; cf. Meineke). Yet normally the penult of both ἐλάα and ἐλαία (the two forms are used indiscriminately in Attic for tree and fruit, *pace* *Suda* s.vv. ἐλάα, ἐλαία and Thom. Mag. p. 120.10f. Ritschl: cf. Threatte 1.278) is scanned long (cf. for ἐλαῶν in drama e.g. Eur. fr. 360, Ar. *Ach.* 550, *Pax* 578, *Ran.* 995), and this prompted L. Dindorf (*TGL* s.v. ἐλαία) to conjecture in Alexis here a disyllabic form ἐλῶν, attested as Attic by Ael. Dion. ε 29 Erbse and found occasionally in papyri (e.g. *P.Rylands* 97.7, 130.11 = 2nd and 1st centuries AD). Cf. also Schulze, *QE* 51 n. 1.

4 κνῖσαν: Dindorf's correction of CE's misspelling (cf. Herodian 1.266.13ff., 445.28f., 2.12ff., 536.11f.) -ισσ-, which occurs elsewhere in MSS (and cf. κνισσᾶν transmitted at Eur. *Alc.* 1156). Since the word generally implies the steam and smell from freshly roasted meat (cf. LSJ s.v. κνῖσα; in Attic comedy also Ar. *Ach.* 1045, *Pax* 1050, *Av.* 193, 1517, Ephippus 3.3), at first sight vv. 4–5 appear to be contradicted by ἔριφοι in v. 9, but the presence also of σκορπίος in the latter verse implies that the three items listed there were not the real thing but rather imitations moulded in their shapes from other comestibles (cf. Gow on Theoc. 15.118); accordingly emendation (e.g. T. G. Tucker's κνισμόν, *CQ* 2 (1908) 187) is not required.

πλείονα: more steam and smell than what? Meineke's conjecture πίονα (3.503 and *Anal. Crit.* 32), which Desrousseaux prints, is particularly

INCERTARUM FABULARUM FRAGMENTA

attractive, since κνῖσα is elsewhere described as rising from μηρία (e.g. Ar. *Av* 193, 1517) which are typically πίονα (e.g. Hom. *Il.* 1.40, 11.773, *Od.* 4.764, cf. Theoc. 17.126).

5 παροψίδες: 'courses', see comm. on 89(86K).2.

καὶ λῆρος: this coda to a string of nouns implies that they are all trumpery; cf. e.g. Dem. 3.29 τὰς ἐπάλξεις ἃς κονιῶμεν καὶ τὰς ὁδοὺς ἃς ἐπισκευάζομεν καὶ κρήνας καὶ λήρους copied in [Dem.] 13.30, Philostratus *VA* 5.14 (on Aesop's fables) βάτραχοι . . . καὶ ὄνοι καὶ λῆροι, Longinus in Euseb. *Praep. Evang.* 15.21.3, cf. Archestratus fr. 166.7 Lloyd-Jones–Parsons; Jacobs, *Addit.* 49.

παρετέθη: see comm. on 98(152K).2.

6 ὑπερηφάνως: this correction of CE's -ος, necessitated by sense and metre, was made by Casaubon (margin at Ath. 2.60a) long before Jacobs (*Addit.* 50), to whom it is usually ascribed.

ὄζουσα τῶν Ὡρῶν λοπάς: Eustathius' claim (1349.4f.) that τὸ . . . ὄζουσα Ὡρῶν παραπεποιῆσθαι δοκεῖ ἐκ Θεοκρίτου (1.150, on the goatherd's cup: Ὡρᾶν πεπλύσθαι νιν ἐπὶ κρανᾶῖσι δοκησεῖς) is ruled out less by chronology (compare Gow 1.xvii, K. J. Dover (London 1971) xxi f. in their editions of Theoc., and introduction to Ὑποβολιμαῖος) than by differences in phraseology, but in both passages the Ὧραι appear as the goddesses who, by making flowers and plants grow at the appropriate times (hence Θαλλώ and Καρπώ as the Attic names of two, Paus. 9.35.2), are the creators of seasonal fragrances; cf. J. A. Hild in Dar.–Sag. s.v. *Horae* 249ff., L. R. Farnell, *The Cults of the Greek States* 5 (Oxford 1909) 426f., Jolles, *RE* s.v. *Horai* 2300.27ff., G. M. A. Hanfmann, *The Season Sarcophagus in Dumbarton Oaks* 2 (Cambridge Mass. 1951) 129ff. (a *catalogue raisonné* of appearances of the Ὧραι in Greco-Roman art), E. Simon, *EAA* s.v. *Stagioni* 468ff. Alexis' present mention of the Ὧραι, however, in a context which explicitly contrasts their fragrance with the the κνῖσα of roasted meat in vv. 4f., may possibly have been influenced also by a fact recorded by Philochorus (in Ath. 14.656a, = *FGrH* 3B.328.F171): in Athens the meat from sacrifices to the Ὧραι was boiled, not roasted, and so less productive of reeking steam and odour.

λοπάς: see comm. on 115(110K).21ff.

7 τὸ τοῦ πόλου τοῦ παντὸς ἡμισφαίριον: although Alexis does not identify precisely the actual dish served on the λοπάς, whether dessert or savoury (cf. comm. on v. 4), it was clearly moulded into a hemisphere representing that half of the celestial sphere visible to an observer imagined at its centre. The concept of a spherical sky, which originated in early Babylonian astronomy (Neugebauer 2.575ff.), had already become familiar to Greeks by the 5th century (Hdt. 2.109; ? first in the Parmenidean enigma of a sphere-like boundary to the universe, 28 B8.42ff., cf. Anaxagoras 59 A 9 Diels–Kranz, G. E. L. Owen, *CQ* 10 (1960) 95ff.,

COMMENTARY

W. K. C. Guthrie, *A History of Greek Philosophy* 2 (Cambridge 1965) 43ff., 304ff., K. Bornmann, *Parmenides* (Hamburg 1971) 171ff., G. S. Kirk, J. E. Raven, M. Schofield, *The Presocratic Philosophers*[2] (Cambridge 1983) 252ff.). In poetry and popular speech πόλος was the word used for the celestial sphere (e.g. *P.V.* 429, Eur. *Ion* 1154, *Or.* 1685, frs. 594.5, 839.11, [Eur.] epigr. 2 p. 156 Page, Ar. *Av.* 179, Timotheus frs. 24.1, 27.1 Page, Limenius p. 149.7 Powell, Cleanthes 1.16 Powell, fr. adesp. 1051 *SH*), while philosophers and scientists (e.g. Parmenides, Anaxagoras, *locc. citt.*, Pl. *Resp.* 10.616b–617d, *Tim.* 33b–34c, Hipparchus fr. 37 Dicks) employed other expressions for this and restricted πόλος to the axis (e.g. Pl. *Tim.* 40c) or the pole of the axis (Arist. *Cael.* 2.2, 285ᵇ8ff.), cf. Σ Ar. *Av.* 179. See especially E. Maass, *Aratea* (Berlin 1892) 124ff., Neugebauer 2.575ff., 3.1077.

8 γάρ: fifth word in its clause, see comm. on 37(36K).1 and K. J. Dover, *CQ* 35 (1985) 338ff.

9 ἰχθῦς, ἔριφοι ... σκορπίος: see introduction to fr. 263(261K). The MSS correctly preserve the spelling ἰχθῦς for the nominative plural, cf. Gomme–Sandbach, *Comm.* on Men. *Sam.* 98.

διέτρεχε τούτων σκορπίος: with the verb governing the genitive ('ran through these'); cf. in a similar context Diphilus 120(121K) ᾠῶν ἐν αὐτῇ (sc. λοπάδι: Meineke 4.427) διέτρεχεν νεόττια, Plut. *Alex.* 68, *Pyrrh.* 13. Presumably in the dish *Scorpio* seemed to be darting through the other two constellations like a shooting star (διατρέχοντες ἀστέρες Ar. *Pax* 838, cf. διαθεόντων ἁ. Arist. *Meteor.* 1.5, 342ᵇ21; most commonly διάττοντες ἁ. e.g. Arist. *Meteor.* 1.4 341ᵇ34f., *Mund.* 4, 395ᵃ32, Plut. *Lys.* 12.3).

10 ὑπέφαινεν: 'suggested' (LSJ s.v. ὑποφαίνω 1.2).

ᾠῶν ἡπίτομα: only here (its rarity noted elsewhere by Ath. 2.57e, yet formation of the phrase is regular, e.g. τὸ ἡ.τοῦ ποδός Hdt. 9.37, τὸ νότιον τῆς γῆς ἡ. Lucian *Navig.* 44), but cf. Alexis 178(172K).10 ᾠὸν ἐπιτετμημένον.

11 ἐπεβάλομεν τὰς χεῖρας: the normal expression from the 5th century onwards (e.g. A. *Choeph.* 395, Cratinus 309(277K), Ar. *Nub.* 933, *Lys.* 440, Polyb. 3.2.8, 5.5, Lucian *Tim.* 4).

12 διανεύων: also with ἐμοί, cf. e.g. N.T. *Ev. Luc.* 1.22, Lucian *VH* 2.25 διένευον ἀλλήλοις ἐν συμποσίῳ, Alciphron fr. 5.2 = [Aristaen.] 1.1.

ἠσχολεῖθ'· ὁ πᾶς δ' ἀγών: Herwerden's correction (*Anal. Crit.* 41, but Eustath. 1349.2 already gives ὁ πᾶς) and repunctuation of CE's wrongly divided -εῖτο πᾶς C/πᾶν E. Definite article in attributive position with πᾶς is needed here, emphasising totality: 'absolutely the whole enterprise' (Gildersleeve, *Syntax* 2.309ff.; LSJ s.v. πᾶς II).

12–13 ἠσχολεῖθ' ... κατήντα: neither ἀσχολέω (cf. Philemon 184(220K)) /-έομαι (cf. Men. *Dysk.* 294, fr. 828; Bruhn, *Wortschatz* 50, Durham, *Vocabulary* 46f., with a long list of *Koine* passages) nor καταντάω (only here in comedy) is recorded in good Attic authors. Elsewhere

736

καταντάω with ἐπί + accusative usually has a personal subject (e.g. Epicurus *Epist.* 3 p. 63.3f. Usener, LXX *2 Regg.* 3.29, Polyb. 10.37.3, 14.1.9, Diod. Sic. 1.79.2, 3.27.3, Vett. Val. 6.15, 7.12).

13 τὸ πέρας: adverbial, 'to conclude', used either internally in the sentence (e.g. Lysias 9.17) or initially as here (e.g. τὸ πέρας asyndetic, also Men. *Epitr.* 287, Apollodorus 13.13, Evangelus 1.9; πέρας asyndetic, Aeschines 1.61; τὸ δὲ πέρας Men. *Dysk.* 117, *Epitr.* 891, Polyb. 1.48.9, 3.48.3, cf. τὸ πέρας δὲ πάντων Men. *Epitr.* 533; καὶ πέρας Polyb. 2.55.6, Alciphron 4.17.3, *Anth. Pal.* 11.92.3, 212.5 (Lucillius)).

οὐκ ἀνῆκ': this intransitive use of ἀνίημι is particularly common with a negative, 'I didn't give up', e.g. Hdt. 2.121.β*, 3.109.1, 4.28.2*, 125.2*, Eur. *IT* 318f.*, Xen. *Hell.* 2.3.46, 5.3.2*, Pl. *Legg.* 5.741a* (examples with a participle asterisked).

14 ὀρύττων: metaphorically 'digging into the plate' (with the fingers), like a wrestler digging into the vulnerable parts of his opponent's body (Ar. *Av.* 442f., *Pax* 899, cf. Antiphanes 117(119K)).

ἀποδέδειχα κόσκινον: expression and idea are characteristic of Alexis, cf. comm. on frs. 110(105K).2 = 248(246K).3, 115(110K).21ff. = 24.2ff. For the construction cf. e.g. Pl. *Theaet.* 166a γέλωτα δὴ τὸν ἐμὲ ἐν τοῖς λόγοις ἀπέδειξεν, *Phd.* 72c. The perfect tense (in place of a more normal aorist) emphasises the present result of the action: 'until I made it the sieve it now is' (cf. K.G. 1.167f.). Casaubon, *Animadv.* 123 compares Lucian *Epist. Sat.* 24 τὴν ἐσθῆτα... κοσκινηδὸν διατετρυπῆσθαι ὑπὸ τῶν ... μυῶν.

264 (262K)

Meineke 3.519 (xxxiv), Kock 2.393, Edmonds 2.502, Kassel–Austin 2.169. The fr. is a collection of clichés (cf. comm. on vv. 1 ὑγιαίνων, 2, 3–6, 7–8, 8) on the hackneyed theme of marital misery (cf. comm. on 150(146K)). Here context and speaker are uncertain, but similar attacks elsewhere in comedy are normally made either (i) by disillusioned husbands, not always elderly (cf. e.g. Plaut. *Men.* 114ff.) but often with rich wives whom dowries have turned into tyrants (e.g. Men. frs. 333–5, Plaut. *Asin.* 87ff.) or spendthrifts (e.g. Ar. *Nub.* 42ff.), or (ii) by elderly bachelors warning against marriage (e.g. ? Men. fr. 59.1–3, 5–9, Philippides 6) or the extravagance of wealthy women (Plaut. *Aul.* 478ff., 532ff.) or both (Plaut. *MG* 678ff.).

1 τίς δῆθ': 'δῆτα denotes that the question springs out of something which another person (or more rarely, the speaker himself) has said' (Denniston, *GP* 269).

ὑγιαίνων νοῦν τ' ἔχων: here probably 'of sound mind (ὑγ.) and judgment (ν. ἔχ.)', although in Attic with νοῦν ἔχειν the meanings 'to be sane' and 'to be sensible' often overlap. ὑγιαίνων: e.g. Ar. *Plut.* 1066, Pl.

COMMENTARY

Theaet. 190c τινα ... ὑγιαίνοντα ἢ μαινόμενον, *Phlb.* 29d. νοῦν ἔχων = 'sensible': e.g. Pl. *Phdr.* 276b, *Resp.* 1.331b, Dem. 18.256; with overlap e.g. v. 3 of this fr., Eur. *IA* 1139, Xen. *Mem.* 3.12.7, Men. fr. 59.1, Varro *infra*). The idea that getting married betokens male insanity is a commonplace in such contexts: e.g. Men. fr. 59.1f. οὐ γαμεῖς ἂν νοῦν ἔχῃς, | τοῦτον καταλείπων τὸν βίον (Blaydes, *Adv.* 2.337), 335.2 a poor man who marries ἀλόγιστός ἐστ' ἀνήρ; Varro contradicts the cliché, *Sat. Men.* fr. 167 Bücheler *ego, unus scilicet antiquorum hominum, subductis superciliis dicam* γαμήσει ὁ νοῦν ἔχων, while the husband who married late in life in Ar. *Eccl.* 323ff. claims that it is his wife who does οὐ ... ποθ' ὑγιὲς οὐδέν.

2 γαμεῖν διαπραξάμενος ἥδιον βίον: so the MSS (SMA, Stob. *Flor.* 4.22.2.89), with the scansion indicating either (i) a lacuna of $\frac{1}{4}$ metron before or after διαπρ., or (ii) corruption in διαπρ. and/or ἥδιον. Evaluation of the numerous conjectures is easier if three points are borne in mind.

(i) If the lacuna/error comes before or in the stem of διαπρ., the verse then has a more attractive rhythm with hephthemimeral caesura, and this militates against suggestions such as διαπρ. < ἂν> ἥδ. β. (Richards, *AO* 87) and διαγραψάμενος <τὸν> ἡδίω β. (H. van Herwerden, *Mnemosyne* 21 (1893) 162 and *Coll. Crit.* 131, after διαγρ. S. A. Naber, *Mnemosyne* 8 (1880) 265, and <τὸν> ἡδίω Bailey, *CGF* 36).

(ii) Attempts to replace ἥδιον with ἤθεον (e.g. Meineke 5.ccxvii προδιαπραξάμενος ἤθεον βίον, Madvig, *Adv. Crit.* 1.719 διαλλαξάμενος ἤθ. β., C. G. Cobet, *Mnemosyne* 2 (1874) 426 διαπρ. <τὸν> ἤθ. β.) must be rejected because ἤθεος is not normally found in Attic or *Koine* Greek 'as epithet of anything but a person' (Edmonds 2.502 n. 6; the one exception is Porphyr. *Marcell.* 55 ἐκ παρθένου ... ψυχῆς καὶ ἠθέου νοῦ, where the abnormality of the adjectival use is underlined by the parallel anomaly with παρθένου).

(iii) ἥδιον (or Bailey's ἡδίω) is supported by the existence of parallel clichés in similar comic contexts: e.g. Philippides 6.1 ἔλεγον ἐγώ σοι μὴ γαμεῖν, ζῆν δ' ἡδέως, Men. fr. 576 ὅστις πενόμενος (Bentley = 'Phileleutheros Lipsiensis', *Emendationum in Menandri et Philemonis reliquias* (Utrecht 1710) 85: γεν- MSS) βούλεται ζῆν ἡδέως, | ἑτέρων γαμούντων αὐτὸς ἀπεχέσθω γάμου, Apollodorus Car. 5.1, Apollodorus 16(15K).2, fr. adesp. (? trag., ? com.) 1207.2 Kock = 95.2 Nauck[2], Snell–Kannicht.

The most promising suggestions have been G. Hermann's διαπραξάμενός <τιν'> ἡδίω βίον (in Meineke 3.519 after ἡδίω Bailey) and Meineke's προδιαπραξάμενος (but with MSS ἥδιον); they do not depart implausibly (contrast A. Nauck, *Philologus* 6 (1851) 449; F. W. Schmidt, *Kritische Studien* 3 (Berlin 1887) 55) from the *ductus*, and although διαπράττομαι βίον ('I go through life') is an unparalleled idiom in Attic (and προδιαπράττω an unrecorded compound), Homer's ἤματα δ' αἱματόεντα διέπρησσον πολεμίζων (*Il.* 9.326) provides something of a precedent. Alternatively, if the occasion for this speech was an old man's plan to marry, perhaps διαπερανάμενος (cf. e.g. Pl. *Epist.* 7.338a) or διαπερασάμενος (cf. e.g. Xen. *Oec.* 11.7) ἥδιον βίον?

3 εἶτ' οὐχί: indignant questions so introduced more commonly open a speech (cf. comm. on 44(43K).1).

3–4 κρεῖττόν ἐστι . . . μᾶλλον ἤ: the redundant addition of μᾶλλον to a comparative adjective or adverb is particularly common in Attic and elsewhere when there is enough distance between the original comparative and ἤ for the addition to clarify the construction: e.g. Ar. *Nub.* 1215f. κρεῖττον εὐθὺς ἦν τότε | ἀπερυθριᾶσαι μᾶλλον ἢ σχεῖν πράγματα, Xen. *Anab.* 4.6.11 πολὺ οὖν κρεῖττον τοῦ ἐρήμου ὄρους καὶ κλέψαι τι πειρᾶσθαι λαθόντας καὶ ἁρπάσαι φθάσαντας, εἰ δυναίμεθα, μᾶλλον ἢ πρὸς ἰσχυρὰ χωρία καὶ ἀνθρώπους παρεσκευασμένους μάχεσθαι, *Cyr.* 2.2.12, Pl. *Phd.* 79e, *Protag.* 317b, *Hipp. Ma.* 284e–285a, Isoc. 6.89 πολὺ γὰρ κρεῖττον ἐν ταῖς δόξαις αἷς ἔχομεν τελευτῆσαι τὸν βίον μᾶλλον ἢ ζῆν ἐν ταῖς ἀτιμίαις, 10.53, Hdt. 1.31.3. Contrast those passages where a merely intensifying μᾶλλον directly precedes or follows a comparative adjective/adverb (e.g. A. *Sept.* 673, *Suppl.* 279, S. *Ant.* 1210, Eur. *Hipp.* 485, *Hec.* 377, *El.* 222, Pl. *Gorg.* 487b, *Legg.* 6.781a, Arist. *Top.* 3.1, 116[b]24). Cf. K.G. 1.26, LSJ s.v. μάλα II.2.

3–6 A wife's tyranny over her husband, especially when she holds the purse strings, is a comic commonplace (cf. e.g. Alexis 150(146K).3 γυναιξὶ δοῦλοι ζῶμεν, Anaxandrides 53(52K).5f. ἔχει δέσποιναν ... ἧς ἐστὶ δοῦλος, Men. frs. 333.6ff., 334.2f.), but Alexis develops it by the introduction of politics (cf. Alexis 150(146K).9 ὧν οὐκ ἐχρῆν ἄρχουσιν, Plaut. *Asin.* 87 *dote imperium uendidi, Men.* 114ff., cf. comm. on v. 8) and a comparison between a wife's domestic ἀρχή (unsanctioned by Attic law) and the ineligibility of an ἄτιμος for political ἀρχή (legally prescribed): e.g. Aeschines 1.19 μὴ ἐξέστω αὐτῷ τῶν ἐννέα ἀρχόντων γενέσθαι ... μηδὲ ἀρξάτω ἀρχὴν μηδεμίαν μηδέποτε ... μήτε κληρωτὴν μήτε χειροτονητήν, cf. Arist. *Pol.* 3.1.4, 1275[a]19ff.; U. Kahrstedt, *Staatsgebiet und Staatsgehörige in Athen* (Stuttgart and Berlin 1934) 106ff., 116ff., E. Ruschenbusch, *Untersuchungen zur Geschichte des athenischen Strafrechts* (Cologne 1968) 16ff., A. R. W. Harrison, *The Law of Athens* 2 (Oxford 1971) 169ff., M. H. Hansen, *Apagoge, Endeixis and Ephegesis against Kakourgoi, Atimoi and Pheugontes* (Odense 1976) 75ff., D. M. MacDowell, *The Law in Classical Athens* (London 1978) 73ff., P. J. Rhodes (Oxford 1981) on *Ath. Pol.* 8.5 (p. 158), 16.10 (p.222), 53.5.

3–4 τῷ γ' ἔχοντι νοῦν ἄτιμον εἶναι: in constructions with dative and infinitive, predicates and appositional phrases may be attracted from dative into accusative, e.g. κύριον v. 7, S. *El.* 959ff., Eur. *Med.* 659ff., 743f., 814f., 1236ff., Xen. *Hell.* 4.1.35, 8.4, 6.3.9, Pl. *Gorg.* 492b, *Resp.* 5.469c–d, *Leg.* 9.858e, Aeschines 2.108, Dinarchus 1.112, Hdt. 1.37.2; cf.

COMMENTARY

K.G. 2.24ff., J. M. Stahl, *Kritisch-historische Syntax des griechischen Verbums der klassischen Zeit* (Heidelberg 1907) 63f.

5 πολλῷ γε: sc. κρεῖττον, 'a great deal better' (LSJ s.v. πολύς III.2.a). Meineke's correction of SMA's odd πτωχῷ – presumably a misreading of similar letters (π/πτ; minuscule λ/χ, cf. e.g. Eur. *Alc.* 905, *Hipp.* 1002, Cobet, *NL* 204) co-operating with a thought (beggary as a result of ἀτιμία) suggested by the context: cf. Fraenkel on A. *Ag.* 1391, 3.655 n. 1 – is palmary.

7–8 By Attic law a free woman passed on marriage from her father's to her husband's legal control (cf. MacDowell, *op. cit.* 84ff.), but that did not prevent one henpecked husband in later comedy (Men. fr. 334.2f.) from complaining that κυρίαν τῆς οἰκίας | καὶ τῶν ἀγρῶν καὶ <τῶν ἀ>πάντων ἀντικρυς | ἔχομεν, and κυρία appears to have been used loosely in the sense of κεκτημένη (Antiatticist 102.20 Bekker, citing Philemon 190(223K)). Elsewhere in comedy only goddesses (Men. *Asp.* 147, *Theoph.* fr. dub. = fr. 145.25 Austin) and perhaps non-Athenian mistresses (Men. *Pk.* 497, possibly *Mis.* Α45) could strictly be described as κύριαι in any legitimate sense.

8 τὰς γὰρ εὐθύνας μόνον: εὔθυναι = (i) the public examination that all Athenian magistrates underwent in Alexis' time before the ten λογισταί at the end of their office, and (ii) interim checks held every prytany (e.g. Lysias 30.5, *Ath. Pol.* 48.3 and Rhodes *ad loc.*, 54.2; see also Wilamowitz, *Aristoteles und Athen* 2 (Berlin 1893) 231ff., G. Busolt, *Griechische Staatskunde* 2² (Munich 1926) 1032f., 1076ff., D. M. MacDowell, comm. (Oxford 1962) on Andocides 1.73, M. Piérart, *Ant. Class.* 40 (1971) 526ff.). The reference to εὔθυναι follows on naturally (but with some logical inconsistency) from the mention in v. 6 of state office (for which the ἄτιμοι of vv. 4–5 were ineligible). A similar comparison between inquisitions in marriage and in officialdom is made by an errant husband to his wife in Plaut. *Men.* 114ff. *rogitas* | *quo ego eam, quam rem agam, quid negoti geram,* | *quid petam, quid feram, quid foris egerim.* | *portitorem* (customs officer) *domum duxi, ita omnem mihi* | *rem necesse eloqui est, quidquid egi atque ago.* Here SMA have μόνον, which Kassel–Austin print, but Dobree's μόνοι (*Adv.* 2.359) must be right; the point is the contrast between husbands alone and magistrates (cf. Kock), not the fact that the only result of marriage for husbands is daily audits (so Meineke); the MSS error originates in an ancestor of SMA where each line of verse quotations was vertically separated (cf. Hense's edition of Stob. 3.xviii f., xxxv), with the scribe's eye wandering to the end of the previous verse (κύριον).

265 (263K)

Meineke 3.506 (VII), Kock 2.393, Edmonds 2.502, Kassel–Austin 2.170. Although Kassel–Austin print this fr. among the *incertarum fabularum fragmenta*, my reason for attributing it to Καρχηδόνιος is given briefly in the introduction to that play, and at greater length in *Rh. Mus.* 102 (1959) 252ff. The whole fr. is cited by the Epitome of Ath. (1.21d) and the *Suda* s.v. ἀναλαμβάνειν (1.172f. Adler), while vv. 1–2 and 5 (φέρει δὲ) to 7 (τῷ βίῳ) are paraphrased or quoted by Eustathius 1164.33ff. In all three places the fr.'s author is named but not the play title. This form of presentation is normal for the Epit. of Ath., which was the source here certainly for Eustath. and possibly also for the *Suda*, although the latter's compiler seems at times to have had access to a fuller version of Ath. 1–3.73e than we possess today (cf. G.Kaibel, *Hermes* 22 (1887) 323ff.).[1] Certainly the *Suda*'s text of fr. 265(263K) gives evidence of a transmission independent from that of the extant Epit. MSS of Ath.

If Plaut. *Poen.* 522ff. accurately reflects Alexis' original context, the fr. will form part of a speech addressed to the young lover by one of a group of men (possibly, but not necessarily, the chorus) called in to act as witnesses of a confidence trick (see introduction to Καρχηδόνιος). It emphasises the need for free men to walk in public with a measured gait. This was a generally accepted rule of deportment in classical Athens: cf. Pl. *Charm.* 159b (to walk κοσμίως καὶ ἡσυχῇ a mark of σωφροσύνη: so also Ar. *Nub.* 964f., S. *El.* 872, Philemon 4(5K), Dem. 37.55 (a man can walk ἀτρέμας and still be a blackguard), Arist. *Eth. Nic.* 4.3.34, 1125ᵃ12ff. (κίνησις βραδεῖα a sign of the μεγαλόψυχος); even a *hetaira*'s βάδισμα τεταγμένον, βραχὺ δέ wins commendation, [Aristaen.] 1.1. Cf. also Casaubon, *Animadv.* 55, and J. F. Boissonade's edition of [Aristaen.] (Paris 1822) 508f.

1–2 ἐν γὰρ νομίζω τοῦτο τῶν ἀνελευθέρων εἶναι, τὸ βαδίζειν κ.τ.λ.: for the idiom, with an articulated infinitive or subordinate relative clause in epexegetic apposition to a predicative ἕν, cf. e.g. Eur. *El.* 815ff. ἐν τῶν καλῶν κομποῦσι τοῖσι Θεσσάλοις | εἶναι τόδ', ὅστις ταῦρον ἀρταμεῖ καλῶς | ἵππους τ' ὀχμάζει, Aelian, *VH* 13.5 τοῖς Θηβαίοις ἐν τῶν καλῶν ἐδόκει τὸ τῶν ὡραίων ἐρᾶν, W. Headlam, *JPhil.* 23 (1895) 289.

2 ἀρρύθμως: so correctly *Suda*, Eustath.; ἀρύ- C, ἀρί- E of Epit. Plautus appears to take this in the sense 'too fast' (*festinantem*, *Poen.* 523), since it was a slow gait that generally won approval (see above), but the word strictly means 'irregularly', implying that the paces were uneven and not in time (ἐν ῥυθμῷ, Pl. *Leg.* 2.670b, Xen. *Anab.* 5.4.14, *Cyr.* 1.3.10) with each other.

3–5 These lines pose several problems, mainly because of severe textual

---

[1] There can be no doubt that some version of Ath. 1.21d, whether (i) Epit. or (ii) Ath.'s original text, was the *Suda*'s source here, for the lexicon's entry includes other material from Ath. 1.21b–d, including a quotation from Pl. *Theaet.* 175e.

COMMENTARY

corruption in both Epit. and *Suda* that clearly originates in a MS of their common ancestor, but also partly because Alexis seems to have expressed himself in this of all contexts with insufficient care and grace. In vv. 4–5 the *Suda* MSS give μηδὲν γὰρ ἡμᾶς, μήτε δι' ἑτέρων λαβεῖν τιμὴν δόντας, and those of Epit. μηδεὶς ἡμᾶς μήτε μὴν δόντας δι' ἑτέρων λαβεῖν. These readings point to a common source with μηδεὶς or μηδὲν ἡμᾶς μήτε τιμὴν δόντας δι' ἑτέρων λαβεῖν (less probably μήτε δι' ἑ. λ. τ. δόντας: see below); μὴν in Epit. is simply a haplographical slip (after μήτε) for τιμὴν. Any attempt to cure the corruption with a restoration of sense and metre needs first to take account of the syntactical structure of vv. 3–8 of the fr.

(i) In v. 3 οὗ must introduce a subordinate relative clause (= 'in cases where', cf. S. *Phil.* 1049 οὗ γὰρ τοιούτων δεῖ, τοιοῦτός εἰμ' ἐγώ) which continues down to τῷ βίῳ in v. 7, before the main clause begins with τὸ τοιοῦτον γέρας. The alternative interpretation of οὗ here as a connecting relative ('of which' = 'and of this', where 'this' = τὸ βαδίζειν καλῶς) is ruled out by the presence of the negative forms μήτε . . . μήτε and μηδείς, which are normal in a generic relative clause (K.G. 2.185), but would be hard to justify under any other circumstances. With the preferred explanation of the οὗ clause, we must print a comma after βίῳ in v. 7, not a colon (Desrousseaux's edition of Ath.) or a dash (Kaibel); and we are entitled to accept the *Suda*'s γάρ (second word in v. 4) as part of the tradition rather than as a Byzantine conjecture on a par with later suggestions at this point (e.g. ποθ' Scaliger and Grotius, *Exc.* 596f., 975). This particle is the appropriate connective, and its postponement to sixth word in its clause, although a typical feature of later comedy (see on fr. 37(36K).1, and K. J. Dover, *CQ* 35 (1985) 338ff.), could easily have puzzled an Epit. scribe and led him to omit it.

(ii) Choice between the *Suda*'s μηδὲν and Epit.'s μηδεὶς in v. 4 is difficult. With the former, τέλος μηδὲν will be subject, πράττεται passive and ἡμᾶς the retained accusative normal in the passive with verbs that can govern two accusatives in the active (K.G. 1.326f. n. 7: 'no tax is exacted from us'). With the latter, πράττεται is middle and governs two accusatives (cf. the examples cited by LSJ s.v. πράσσω vi). Here perhaps μηδεὶς is more likely to have been corrupted to μηδὲν than vice versa, by assimilation to the gender of the preceding noun.

(iii) The text between ἡμᾶς (4) and λαβεῖν (5) cannot be restored with certainty. If Ath.'s epitomist was here paraphrasing or abridging the words of a citation (a common practice: cf. Peppink, *Observ.* 4), recovery of Alexis' original verse would be inconceivable. Yet as a paraphrase neither the Epit. nor the *Suda* version makes even prosaic sense (δι' ἑτέρων is odd, and the accusative and infinitive construction in vv. 4–5 lacks a governing verb). Good sense and acceptable metre can in fact be achieved by three small changes: Casaubon's δεῖ for δι' (providing the needed main verb), and Dobree's δόντα (for δόντας, preceding δεῖ) and ἑτέρῳ (for -ρων: in his and Porson's edition of Ar. *Plut.* (Cambridge 1820) p. 30, on v. 256).[1] Translate 'nor must one acquire it by paying a fee to a second man'; τιμὴν δοῦναι is the standard phrase in contemporary Attic (e.g. Pl. *Leg.* 11.914a), and λαβεῖν unexceptionable in a sense close to that of μαθεῖν (LSJ s.v. λαμβάνω A.1.9.b). Could there be a slight dig at the practice (and high cost: cf. Dover's edition of Ar. *Nub.* (Oxford 1968) p. xxxix) of sophistic training here?

(iv) If Alexis wrote the text supported here and independently printed by Kassel–Austin, he could be accused of slipshod expression. The logical subject switches awkwardly from μηδείς (? μηδέν) in v. 4 to an unexpressed 'someone' (4–5), then to an equally unexpressed τὸ βαδίζειν καλῶς (supplied from vv. 2–3) in 5–7. There is, however, no difficulty in following the argument, and passages of careless writing like this and fr. 103(98K).10ff. (q.v.) are hardly surprising in a playwright of Trollopian productivity.

5 τοῖς μὲν χρωμένοις: see comm. on 140(135K).16.

6 δόξης τιν' ὄγκον: i.e. an impression of the dignity that goes with a high reputation. Cf. S. *Trach.* 817f. ὄγκον γὰρ ἄλλως ὀνόματος τί δεῖ τρέφειν | μητρῷον, Eur. (?) *Rhes.* 760 ὄγκος καὶ δόμων εὐδοξία, Chaeremon fr. 36.1f. πλοῦτος . . . οὐκ ἔσχεν ὄγκον ὥστε καὶ δόξης τυχεῖν.

7 κόσμον: here not 'gloss', as Edmonds translates, but rather the outward sign of orderly behaviour (LSJ s.v. κόσμος I.2) indicating that a person is κόσμιος (cf. Pl. *Charm.* 159b, Philemon 4(5), Lucian *Tim.* 54 κόσμιος τὸ βάδισμα).

8 αὐτῷ κτῷτο: G. Morel's correction in 1563 (cf. *PCPS* 196 (1970) 3f.) of the *Suda*'s αὐτὸ κτ. and Epit. of Ath.'s transposition κτ. αὐτῷ (C: αυ- E).

266 (264K)

Meineke 3.508 (x), Kock 2.394, Edmonds 2.504, Kassel–Austin 2.171. The fr. appears in Ath. 13.565b (A and Epit.; vv. 6–7 cited also by Eustath. 1910.3) as part of a quotation from the Stoic philosopher Chrysippus (H. von Arnim, *Stoicorum veterum fragmenta* 3 (Leipzig 1903) 198, cf. Schweighaeuser, *Animadv.* 7.43; Kaibel's suggestion that Ath. himself interpolated the fr. into the Chrysippus quotation is unwarranted

---

[1] The postulated MSS errors are easily explained, δόντας as an assimilation to the ending and number of ἡμᾶς, and ἑτέρων as a homoeoteleuton error before λαβεῖν. Many editors keep the ἑτέρων of the MSS, without attempting to explain its syntax (? a price belonging to others; hardly 'from others', which would require παρ' ἑτέρων in the idiom of comedy).

and implausible), and blame for the failure to record Alexis' play-title is probably to be laid on the philosopher. The subject of Ath., Chrysippus and Alexis is clean-shaven chins. Up to the later part of the 4th century most Athenian men wore beards, and those who shaved them off (to prolong youthful appearances, according to e.g. Philostratus *Epist.* 58, Dio Chrys. 33.63) were subject to raillery and accusations of effeminacy (e.g. Ar. *Thesm.* 191f., 218, Σ Ar. *Equ.* 1374, Timocles fr. 5); cf. also Archilochus fr. 114 West. The rise of Macedon and a tradition of beardlessness among its leaders, especially Alexander the Great (reflected in his portraits: M. Bieber, *The Portraits of the Greeks* 3 (London 1965) figs. 1714–40), led to a similar fashion among the young, first in Alexander's army (at the battle of Gaugamela in 331: Synesius *Enc. Calv.* 15, cf. Plut. *Mor.* 180b, *Thes.* 5.4 = Polyaenus 4.3.2, allegedly for military reasons) and then by the end of the century throughout Greece, although puritanical philosophers and doubtless too the older generation opposed the new trend as a denial of manhood (cf. E. Saglio in Dar.–Sag. s.v. *Barba* 669a f., Mau, *RE* s.v. *Bart* 31.47ff., W. Headlam, *CR* 15 (1901) 393ff., Webster, *SLGC* 121f.). Accusations of effeminacy (e.g. Men. *Sik.* 264, Lucian *Demon.* 50, *Merc. Cond.* 33, *Rhet. Praec.* 23, Palaephatus 32 Festa) and immorality (com. adesp. fr. 339.6f. Kock, Chrysippus in Ath. 565c; cf. Clem. Alex. *Paed.* 3.60.3–61.1) still continued; the present fr. of Alexis belongs with them. It is most likely to have been spoken (presumably in the last thirty years of the 4th century) by an old-school *senex* or *paedagogus* criticising (before an unidentified character) some beardless *adulescens* (not necessarily a soldier) in the play.[1]

1 <ἄν>: in the MSS the fr. begins with πιττοκοπούμενον at the second element of the first metron, and the most convenient way of linking πιττ.– ὁρᾷς with the remainder of v. 2 is to treat it as a conditional protasis; hence the need to supply either Meineke's <ἄν> here or Dobree's <ἐάν> (*Adv.* 2.342) at the end of the preceding verse with e.g. <σύ> at the beginning of this (but not Jacobs' <εἰ>, cf. Schweighaeuser, *Animadv.* 7.44, since the protasis required is an indefinite present, cf. Goodwin, *MT* 141f.).

πιττοκοπούμενον ... ἢ ξυρούμενον: the reference with both participles

---

[1] Archaeological evidence clearly shows that in (? later) Middle Comedy young men were sometimes presented as bearded, sometimes as clean-shaven (T. B. L. Webster, *Monuments Illustrating Old and Middle Comedy*[3], revised J. R. Green, *BICS Suppl.* 39 (1978), 16ff.), but in New Comedy young men (and soldiers) were always clean-shaven (Webster, *MINC*[2] 17); cf. A. C. H. Simon, *Comicae tabellae* (Emsdetten 1938) 94. Portraits of Menander always show him without a beard (Bieber, *op. cit.* in the introduction to fr. 266(264K), figs. 1510–643).

is to the beard (cf. v. 4). Πιττοκοπούμενος is the title of a play by Philemon (7.260 Kassel–Austin); cf. also com. adesp. fr. 339.6f. Kock κιναίδους ... πεπιττοκοπημένους. The verb is used in the middle, like πιττοῦμαι (e.g. Theopompus, *FGrH* 2.115 F204 πάντες δὲ οἱ πρὸς ἑσπέραν οἰκοῦντες βάρβαροι πιττοῦνται καὶ ξυροῦνται τὰ σώματα, Lucian *Merc. Cond.* 33 κίναιδόν τινα τῶν πεπιττωμένων τὰ σκέλη καὶ τὸν πώγωνα περιεξυρημένων, *Demon.* 50, *Rhet. Praec.* 23), in the sense 'I use pitch as a depilatory on' the beard and other parts of the body. In ancient Greece pitch (πίττα) was made by heating resin from various conifers (e.g. Theophr. *HP* 9.2.2–3.4, Pliny *HN* 16.52ff., 23.46, 24.38, 28.137; Schramm in *RE* s.v. *Pech* 1.4ff., J. André, *Ant. Class.* 33 (1964) 86ff.), and although we are not told by the ancient authors how pitch was used as a depilatory, it is unlikely that the method in Alexis' day differed much from that adopted today, in which a mixture of resinous substances and wax is gently warmed, attached to the hair, allowed to cool and then pulled off, bringing the hair with it.[1] That this operation was (? normally) conducted by professional barbers is suggested by the existence of terms like πιττοκόπος, -οπική (Pollux 7.165, cf. U. E. Paoli, *A&R* 5 (1924) 204ff.).

ξυρούμενον: from ξυρέω, the Attic form (LSJ s.v., Frisk 2.340, Chantraine 2.769, cf. Phot. ξυρεῖσθαι, οὐδὲ ξυρᾶσθαι λέγουσιν).

2 After ὁρᾷς the MSS give τούτων (CE) / τοῦτον (A) ἔχει τι θάτερον, producing a line defective by half a metron but (with τούτων accepted and τι rejected as incompatible with θάτερον) adequate in sense: 'he's involved in one of these two things'. Conjectures are numerous, none convincing (e.g. Jacobs, *Addit.* 298 <σὺ> τοῦτον <ἴσθ'> ἔχοντα θάτερον, Cobet, *NL* 36 <δυοῖν> τούτων ἔχειν δεῖ θάτερον after Erfurdt's <δυοῖν> τ. in Meineke 5.92), and Kassel–Austin are right to obelise; one possibility that has not so far been considered, however, is that the excerptor has omitted a name in the vocative (often corrupted in quotations: cf. my examples in Flores 362, 364): e.g. ὁρᾷς, <Λάχης,> τούτοιν ἔχει τὸ θάτερον (τούτοιν already Edmonds; for superfluous τό with θάτερον cf. e.g. Men. fr. 710, Chrysippus in Pausanias gram. fr. 82 Schwabe = θ 2 Erbse).

3–4 Kassel–Austin wrongly obelise στρατεύειν (v.3); the transmitted text makes perfect sense. The speaker's first interpretation of a (clearly young) man's beardlessness is an intention to go campaigning (like one of Alexander's warriors) and consequently to commit soldierly misdemeanours which run 'counter to the beard': sc. misdemeanours which (in the old and puritanical speaker's view) would not have been committed by bearded young men when *he* was young. The speaker has in mind popular

---

[1] Other ancient methods for removing unwanted hair included singeing (e.g. Ar. *Lys.* 828 and Wilamowitz *ad loc.*, *Thesm.* 216, 236ff., *Eccl.* 12f.) and some fishy depilatories (Aelian *NA* 13.27).

ideas (which are clearly reflected in Greek and Roman comedy) about the bad behaviour of soldiers: indiscriminate womanising (e.g. Plaut. *MG* 58ff., 775f.), adultery (*MG* 802, 972), physical violence against women (Men. *Pk.*, Plaut. *Poen.* 1288ff.) and attacks on their property (Men. *Pk.* 467ff., Ter. *Eun.* 771ff.), perhaps even (but in this context not predominantly) homosexuality (Plaut. *MG* 1111ff., Ter. *Eun.* 479). Hence conjectures replacing στρατεύειν (e.g. Jacobs, *Addit.* 299 ἢ μαστροπεύειν, but γάρ is needed and μαστρ. is not intransitive, cf. Meineke 3.509; Herwerden, *NAC* 34 ἤτοι γὰρ ἑταιρεῖν with an anapaest split after the first short; W. Headlam, *CR* 15 (1901) 395f. ἢ γὰρ ἐρατεύειν, but the verb in use is ἐραστεύειν) or postulating an obscene meaning for στρατεύειν (e.g. Gulick on Ath. 565b cites Hesych. s.v. στάτη· πόρνη, where στάτη is M. Schmidt's correction of MS τάτη and πόρνη is corrupt for πάρνη, see Hesych. s.v. στατή· πάρνη, κάρδοπος) may be discounted.

5 ἢ πλουσιακόν τούτῳ <τι> προσπίπτει κακόν: Meineke (*Cur. Crit.* 65) restored the τι (lost by haplography before π, cf. Cobet, *NL* 346) to its right place; earlier scholars (first Daléchamp according to Schweighaeuser's edition, *Animadv.* 7.45; cf. Casaubon, *Animadv.* 864 and the marginal comment to his text of Ath.) had supplied it before a then unmetrical τούτῳ. The suggestion that 'some depravity of wealth' may lie behind or be associated with (non-military) smooth chins inevitably remains imprecise in our ignorance of the speech's dramatic context, although Casaubon's interpretation (*loc. cit.*) of πλ. κακόν as a euphemism for pathic homosexuality receives some support from the implications of vv. 6–7. It is possible that the habit of shaving the beard began in Athens with young, wealthy and trendy patrons of the κουρεῖα; at any rate the fashion is described by the speaker as a symbol or example of the depravities that had been linked in popular thought for centuries to both the misuse of wealth (i.e. κόρος leading to ὕβρις: as early as Solon frs. 4.1ff., 6.3f. West, cf. Theogn. 153f., 605f.) and the leisure that wealth made possible (in comedy e.g. Men. *Dysk.* 293ff, 341ff., cf. fr. 616; Dover, *GPM* 111f., W. G. Arnott, *Philologus* 125 (1981) 219f., 224).

πλουσιακός first occurs here and is rare elsewhere (Plut. *Mor.* 528b, M. Ant. 1.3), but such formations are regular in Attic (-ιακός replacing -ικός in adjectives derived from -ιο- stems, cf. ἀφροδισιακός, Ὀλυμπιακός, πεδιακός, ταμιακός, Buck–Petersen, *Reverse Index* 637), widespread in the *Koine*, and apparently lacking (*pace* W. Headlam, *CR* 15 (1901) 394f.) in stylistic or technical overtones.

6 τί γὰρ αἱ: cf. *CQ* 7 (1957) 189.

ἡμᾶς (A, Eustath.; Kassel–Austin and editors since Dindorf) or ὑμᾶς (Epit.; editors up to Schweighaeuser)? A decision is difficult. ἡμᾶς links neatly with ἡμῶν in v. 7 (but note the singular μοι in v. 3; cf. e.g. Men. *Sam.* 431ff.), and elsewhere in the fr. (vv.2, 8) the speaker uses the second person singular. On the other hand ὑμᾶς is more likely to have been corrupted to ἡμᾶς by assimilation to v. 7's ἡμῶν than vice versa, and interchanges between second person singular (= addressee) and plural (= addressee + companion(s)/family/friends) are common in comedy (e.g. Men. *Dysk.* 512f., *Epitr.* 430f., *Sam.* 292ff., 480f.).

πρὸς θεῶν: see comm. on 91(87K).3.

7 'through which each of us shows that he's a man', with ἀνήρ predicate. The idea of the beard as an emblem of maleness and virility was a commonplace: e.g. Musonius in Stob. *Ecl.* 6.24 = fr. xxi Hense τὸν δὲ πώγωνα καὶ σύμβολον γεγονέναι τοῦ ἄρρενος, Timocles 5, Theoc. 10.40, 14.28, Chrysippus in Ath. directly after this fr. = H. von Arnim, *SVF* 3.198, Julian *Misopogon* 339AB Spanheim, Palaephatus 32 Festa; cf. Headlam, *op. cit.* on v. 5.

8 ἀντιπράττεσθ' ὑπονοεῖς: '(unless) you suspect that (some) action is being taken that contradicts (these hairs)'. The speaker rather inconsequentially admits that bearded men too can be immoral. ἀντιπράττεσθ' here is clearly passive (with τι as its subject; W. Headlam, MS note *ad loc.* on his copy of Kaibel's edition of Ath., now K.31.21 in King's College Library, Cambridge; cf. Headlam, *op. cit.* on v. 5, p. 395) and not middle (so LSJ s.v.); when construed elsewhere with the dative, it is always active (e.g. [Xen.] *Ath. Pol.* 2.17, Pl. *Resp.* 4.440b, Aeschines 2.29, 3.167, 259, Dinarchus 1.102; hence L. Dindorf's conjecture -πράττειν here, in *TGL* s.v., 977A), and occurrences in the middle are rare and absolute (Xen. *Hier.* 2.17, Hesych. s.v. ἀντιπράττεται). ὑπονοεῖς, as commonly, comes very close here to a neutral 'you conjecture'; when Schweighaeuser suggested in its place ἐπινοεῖς (later -νοεῖ Meineke), he misinterpreted both point and construction.

267 (265K)

Meineke 3.507 (VIII), Kock 2.394, Edmonds 2.504, Kassel–Austin 2.172. An unidentified speaker requires those who enjoy good fortune to show their appreciation of it publicly, otherwise they may lose all they have. The vagaries of fortune are a commonplace of Greek thought and literature (e.g. J. D. Denniston, comm. (Oxford 1939) on Eur. *El.* 943f., Dover, *GPM* 138ff.) that surfaces particularly often in later Greek comedy (Alexis: frs. 35(34K), 283(281K), 289(288K), 341(340K), possibly 254(252K), 288(287K); Menander: Handley on *Dysk.* 271–87, W. G. Arnott, *Philologus* 125 (1981) 219, 223ff., G. Vogt-Spira, *Dramaturgie des Zufalls* (Munich 1992) 55f.); similar sermons on the preservation of wealth and good fortune are preached in Men. *Dysk.* by Gorgias to Sostratos (271ff., comparable to the present fr. in both argument and structure; cf. also *Phoenix* 18 (1964) 110ff.) and by Sostratos to his father (797ff.,

COMMENTARY

comparable to Alexis 283(281K)). Alexis' speaker has four main (all trite) points:

(i) The need for beneficiaries of fortune (here interpreted in materialistic terms) to live ἐπιφανῶς ('publicly'), cf. Men. *Dysk.* 286f. τοῦ διευτυχεῖν δ' ἀεὶ | πάρεχε σεαυτὸν τοῖς ὁρῶσιν ἄξιον. In such contexts 'publicly' seems to imply a use of wealth to benefit φίλοι (cf. *Dysk.* 800ff., 805ff.; Theophr. paraphrased by Hieron. *Adv. Iovinian.* 1.47 = fr. 486 W. W. Fortenbaugh (but L46 in his *Quellen zur Ethik Theophrasts* (Amsterdam 1984) 35ff., 207ff.) = Migne, *PL* 23.290f.; Wilamowitz, *Glaube* 2. 285 n. 1, Webster, *SM* 201 nn. 1, 4, Handley on *Dysk.* 807–10).

(ii) A divinity (ὁ θεός v. 2, cf. also comm. on vv. 3–5) is responsible for man's good fortune, cf. Eur. *Phoen.* 555f., Men. fr. 358, [Dem.] *Prooem.* 54 τῶν θεῶν διδόντων τἀγαθά, Plaut. *Trin.* 346ff., 355. Τύχη itself/herself is often described as ruling over human affairs (e.g. Chaeremon fr. 2 = Men. *Asp.* 411, Men. frs. 295, 417, 630 Körte and 110, 113 Austin, *CGFP*, Antiphon 6.15, Lysias 24.22, Isoc. 4.26, Dem. 18.306), in later comedy sometimes identified as the presiding deity (Men. *Asp.* 97ff., cf. ταὐτόματον as controller *Sam.* 163f.), sometimes with that divinity challenged (e.g. Men. fr. 468 Körte, Philemon 125(137K)).

(iii) The need to thank the divinity, e.g. Dem. 1.11 ἂν μὲν γάρ, ὅσ' ἂν τις λάβῃ, καὶ σώσῃ, μεγάλην ἔχει τῇ τύχῃ τὴν χάριν, cf. Men. *Epitr.* 1098f.

(iv) Concealment of wealth (and so failure to help φίλοι) will make the god take away (ἀφείλεθ') all he originally bestowed, e.g. Eur. *Phoen.* 557 (the gods ἀφαιροῦνται πάλιν), S. fr. 588.4f., Men. *Dysk.* 803ff. (Fortune ἀφελομένη B, better παρελομένη MSS of Stob. *Anth.* 3.16.14); cf. Ar. *Plut.* 237ff.

1–2 ἐπιφανῶς . . . **ζῆν:** Men. *Theoph.* fr. 1.19 ζῶντας ἐπιφανέστερον.

2–3 τὴν δόσιν τὴν τοῦ θεοῦ: stereotyped phrasing, as in e.g. A. *Choeph.* 782, S. *OR* 1518, Eur. *Alc.* 1071, Pl. *Apol.* 30d, *Phlb.* 16c, cf. S. fr. 588.5, Pl. *Phdr.* 244a.

3–5 ποιεῖν: comm. on fr. 16.2. Thereafter the MSS (Epit. of Ath. 2.40e) have ὁ γὰρ δεδωκὼς τἀγαθὰ τῶν (C: τὸν E) μὲν ὦν πεποίηκεν οἴεται χάριν τινὰ (τινα E, τιν' C) ἔχειν αὐτῶ with half a metron omitted in v. 3, corruption certainly at the beginning of 4 and possibly later in the verse, and unmetrical nonsense at the beginning of 5. Both typology and frequency of error (four more in vv. 6–7!) are unhappily characteristic of the Epit. MSS (cf. Peppink, *Observ.* 4f.), and confident restoration of Alexis' words is impossible.

In v. 3 the commonly printed supplement is G. Hermann's ὁ γὰρ <θεὸς> (*Elementa doctrinae metricae* (Leipzig 1816) 140), plausible in sense and palaeography (? haplography after θεοῦ in 2), but by no means certain; other options include <δαίμων> in the same *sedes* (Casaubon, *Animadv.* 84 supplied it elsewhere in the verse) and <δὴ δια>δεδωκὼς

748

(T. G. Tucker, *CQ* 2 (1908) 186f.; unacceptable are Cobet's <θεὸς ὁ> δεδωκώς (*NL* 121: introducing a divided resolution rare in this *sedes* after the second short of a tribrach, cf. Handley's edition of Men. *Dysk.* p. 67) and Desrousseaux's <δόσει> δεδωκώς (edition of Ath.: see D. Eichholz, *CR* 7 (1952) 218).

Vv.4–5 are better obelised. With CE's τῶν/τὸν deleted at the beginning of 4 (P. Elmsley, *Ed. Rev.* 3 (1803–4) 188), metre is restored but not tolerable sense. οἴεται χάριν τινὰ ἔχειν inappropriately means 'thinks he *does* receive[1] some gratitude', when the context requires either 'thinks he *ought to* receive ...' (hence δεῖν ὦν ... οἴεται or ὦν ... ἀξιοῖ H. van Herwerden, *Mnemosyne* 6 (1878) 71 and *Coll. Crit.* 131, the latter preferable since the Epit. MSS frequently substitute near-synonyms for the correct word; οἴεται χρῆναι χάριν | ἔχειν Tucker 186f.) or 'thinks he *will* receive ...' (hence οἴεται χ. | ἕξειν Meineke, *Anal. Crit.* 22). ὦν μὲν πεποίηκεν (? -όη-: see comm. on 16.2) seems acceptable, but Meineke's πεπόρικεν (*FCG* 5.92) is worth considering; Dobree's replacement of μέν by εὖ (*Adv.* 2.296), Hirschig's τούτους μὲν ὦν with deletion of τινά (*Annot.* 16) and Schmidt's ἥκειν ἑαυτῷ (*Krit. Stud.* 3.54) are neither demanded by sense nor palaeographically plausible. After ἔχειν Musurus' ἑαυτῷ (for CE's αὐτῷ) restores sense and metre.

5 τοὺς ἀποκρυπτομένους δέ: cf. e.g. Pind. *Nem.* 1.31 πολὺν ἐν μεγάρῳ πλοῦτον κατακρύψαις ἔχειν, Men. *Dysk.* 812 πλοῦτος ἀφανής, ὃν σὺ κατορύξας ἔχεις, Dem. 27.53, and (on the risks involved by burying valuable goods in the earth) Ar. *Av.* 599ff., Plaut. *Aul.* 673ff., 705ff.

On the position of δέ, see comm. on 4.1.

6 πράττειν μετρίως: G. Morel's (p.142) transposition of CE's unmetrical μ. πρ. anticipated both Grotius (*Exc.* 597) and Casaubon (*Animadv.* 84). Cf. e.g. Men. fr. 8.3 ὁ γὰρ μετρίως πράττων, 24.1 εὐποροῦμεν, οὐδὲ μ., Hdt. 1.32 μ. ἔχοντες βίου, Xen. *Hier.* 1.8 τῶν μ. διαγόντων ἰδιωτῶν.

ἀχαρίστους: Elmsley's brilliant correction[2] of CE's ἀχρήστους restores the *mot juste* (cf. χάριν in v. 4). The same error is found in some MSS of monost. 49 Jäkel = Men. fr. 476.1.

---

[1] In Attic Greek 'χάριν ἔχειν more often means "feel" than "receive" gratitude ... but χάρις can be either a favour done or one received' (A. Andrewes (Oxford 1981) on Thuc. 8.87.5, cf. LSJ s.v. II.2; in comedy 'feel gratitude' at Eubulus 26(26–7K).2, Men. *Epitr.* 280f., *Sam.* 614, 'receive gr.' at Ar. *Thesm.* 601f. and presumably here). Kock's mistaken assumption that τινά is the subject of ἔχειν in Alexis' line here stems presumably from ignorance of the second meaning.

[2] He alternatively suggested ἀχαρίστως (anticipating Desrousseaux), but the -τους ending is supported by CE here and C's error ἀνελευθέρους in v. 6, caused by assimilation to the -τους ending just before.

COMMENTARY

7 ἀνελευθέρως τε ζῶντας: so correctly E (-ρως C: see p. 749 n. 2). For the adverb see e.g. Xen. *Apol.* 9, Plut. *Lucullus* 19.7, Pollux 3.113.

ἐπὶ καιροῦ τινός: 'at an appropriate time'. Musurus deleted CE's unmetrically superfluous καί before ἐπί (presumably a scribe's eye had wandered to the first syllable of καιροῦ). The expression (not noticed by LSJ s.v. καιρός III.b) is popular in 4th-century orators: e.g. Dem. 23.105 (exactly the same wording), 19.258, 20.90, 21.204, Aeschines 2.27, 3.178, 220, 226, 234.

8 ἀφείλεθ': a true gnomic aorist (Goodwin, *MT* 53f., K.G. 1.158ff.), to be distinguished from the (probably related) examples in some speeches by Alexis' cooks (comm. on 84.5).

δεδωκὼς ἦν πάλαι: on the periphrasis for pluperfect, see comm. on 2.9. The transmitted πάλαι is unexceptionable; Meineke's πάλιν (5.92) would be more attractive if it stood next to ἀφείλεθ' (cf. Eur. *Phoen.* 557).

268 (266K)

Meineke 3.507 (IX), Kock 2.395, Edmonds 2.504, Kassel–Austin 2.172. The fr., cited in its entirety (but anonymously) by Epit. of Ath. 2.55c (vv. 2 τοὺς θ.–3 κατέλιπεν also in Pollux 6.45, identifying the author; vv. 6 οὐδενός–7 λέπος anonymously in Eustath. 1863.58, cf. Meineke, *ed. min.* xviii, O. Kaehler, *Woch. Klass. Phil.* 2 (1885) 904), has the lacunae (certainly vv. 1–2 and 7, possibly between 4 and 5) typical in this transmission, and these make it uncertain whether the fr. comes from a single speech or a dialogue (see on vv. 4–6). Lupin pods have been scattered in front of one or more of the stage-houses (v. 3, see comm.) by a previous character (? a member of the impoverished family in Ὀλυνθία, cf. 167(162K).11; ? a poor parasite, cf. Alciphron 3.31.2), and the speaker(s) of the fr. is/are annoyed by the litter.

1–2 μὴ ὥρασι ⟨⏕⟩ | μετὰ τῶν κακῶν ἵκοιθ' ὁ τοὺς θέρμους φαγών: this imprecation ('may the man . . . not come in season/time' = 'bad luck to him') is recorded in various forms: (subject +) μή + 2nd or 3rd person optative of ἱκνοῦμαι +

(i) ὥρασι (Ar. *Lys.* 391 with ellipse of verb, see Henderson, comm. *ad loc.*, ? Men. *Phasm.* 43f.: originally a locative form, like θύρασι, Ὀλυμπίασι, Πλαταιᾶσι, cf. K.B. 2.309, Schwyzer 1.559, but corrupted here by CE to ὥραισϊ, cf. MSS of Lucian *Salt.* 5, *Dial. Meretr.* 10.3, *Dial. Deor.* 9.4 Macleod – unless ὥραισι had already replaced ὥρασι in popular use by Alexis' time, cf. Σ Lucian, *locc. citt.* ὥρασι was conjectured in Alexis here first by Dindorf in his edition of Ath., not by Hermann, as several scholars claim);

(ii) ὥρας (Men. *Pk.* 321f., Lucian, *locc. citt.*, Theophylact. *Epist.* 17

750

INCERTARUM FABULARUM FRAGMENTA

Hercher; ? Men. *Phasm.* 43f.: presumably explained as accusative of goal of motion, but perhaps originating from juxtaposed ὥρασ' ἵκοι- with elided iota, e.g. Ar. *Lys.* 1037);

(iii) εἰς ὥρας (Babrius 53.7, cf. *Milet.* 2(3) no. 406 with ἔλθοιεν and Eustath. 1619.62: acting as the negative of good-luck wishes with ἱκνοῦμαι, e.g. *H. Hom.* 26.12, Theoc. 15.74 with ellipse of verb, Diog. Laert. 2.32); cf. Wilamowitz, comm. (Berlin 1927) on Ar. *Lys.* 391, Gomme–Sandbach, *Comm.* on Men. *Pk.* 321f.

The passages of Ar. and Men. cited confirm the legitimacy of hiatus between μή (scanned long) and ὥρασι/-ρας in comedy (cf. K.B. 2.579 on 1.197, my comm. on fr. 1.1). CE's text here is problematical; with ὥρα ι σι in v. 1 a lacuna of at least one syllable must follow, and μετὰ τῶν κακῶν at the beginning of v. 2 is highly suspicious. W. Headlam (*JPhil.* 30 (1907) 318) tried to defend the latter phrase ('with all his mischief') by citing Libanius *Decl.* 27.11 ἀλλὰ κακὸς κακῶς ἀπόλοιο μετὰ τῶν καλῶν διδασκάλων (but 'you along with your ... teachers' is no parallel for the neuter τῶν κακῶν), and V. Schmidt (in Kassel–Austin) by citing Plaut. *Rud.* 1225 *Hercules istum infelicet cum sua licentia* (but Greek has no corresponding idiom, and *cum sua licentia* is a Latin joke on the repeated use of *licet* in vv. 1212–27). More probably μετὰ τῶν κακῶν is a gloss on μὴ ὥρασι (so first Casaubon, *Animadv.* 112; for other examples in Epit. see Peppink, *Observ.* 4); if so, Bergk's simple transposition (*Zeitschrift für die Althertums- wissenschaft* 4 (1837) 47) ἵκοιτο μὴ ὥρασιν (better ὥρασ' or -ας: cf. L. Radermacher, comm. (Vienna 1954²) on Ar. *Ran.* 1220) ὁ τοὺς θ. φ. yields an acceptable text and (unlike H. van Herwerden's ἵκ. ὁ τοὺς θ. φ., <ὅστις ποτ' ἦν>, *Mnemosyne* 19 (1891) 202) disposes of the lacuna alleged at the end of v. 1, for which all other suggestions (ὥρασι <μέν> J. G. Hermann, *Epitome doctrinae metricae* (Leipzig ¹1818, cf. ²1844) xix; <δή> Casaubon, cf. *Animadv.* 112; <γε> Edmonds) add unconvincing fillers to the curse.

2 τοὺς θέρμους: comm. on 167(162K).11.

3 ἐν τῷ προθύρῳ (Epit. of Ath.) or ἐπὶ τῶν προθύρων (Pollux)? It is impossible to say, without context specifying whether the litter was scattered before one or more stage houses. In ancient use πρόθυρον was the *'space before a door*, whether or not it is a *porch* or *portico'* (LSJ s.v. I.3), and neither here nor in any other passage of Greek drama (A. *Choeph.* 966f., Eur. *Alc.* 98ff., *Hyps.* fr. 1.ii.15ff., Ar. *Vesp.* 802ff., 875, *Eccl.* 709, Cratinus 42, Eupolis 192.90, Theopompus com. 64(63K)) does the context inform us whether the doors of stage-houses were (1) recessed behind the wall of the σκηνή, (2) decorated with porches projecting in front of the wall or (3) simply flat with the wall; the evidence from vase-painting, mosaics and Roman drama is also inconclusive. The

COMMENTARY

arguments for the existence and theatrical use of recesses and/or porches are unconvincingly put by Kelley Rees, *CPhil.* 10 (1915) 117ff. and C. O. Dalman, *De aedibus scaenicis comoediae novae* (*Klassisch-Philologische Studien* 3, Leipzig 1929) 22ff.), and effectively countered by Pickard-Cambridge, *TDA* 75ff.; cf. also e.g. Fensterbusch in *RE* s.vv. *Proskenion* (xxiii.1 *Nachtrag*) 1287.66ff. and *Theatron* 1394.13ff., T. B. L. Webster, *Greek Theatre Production* (London 1956) 24f., Legrand, *NGC* 346ff., M. Bieber, *The History of the Greek and Roman Theater*[2] (Princeton 1961) 64f., W. Beare, *The Roman Stage*[3] (London 1964) 279ff., S. Melchinger, *Das Theater der Tragödie* (Munich 1974) 193, C. W. Dearden, *The Staging of Aristophanes* (London 1976) 29f., 50f., E. Billig, *Opuscula Atheniensia* 13 (1980) 65ff.

τὰ λέμμαθ' ὁτιὴ κατέλιπεν (so Pollux: -έλιπε Ath.): apparently λέμμα was the standard Greek and λέπος (cf. v. 7 here) the *Koine* word (cf. Moeris s.v. λέμμα) for the inedible covers also e.g. of (1: λέμμα) gourds (Hippocr. *Mul.* 2.117), cucumbers (Arist. *Plant.* 1.5, 820ᵃ38f.), nuts (Eustath. *Opusc.* 259.62), eggs (Ar. *Av.* 674, Aelian *NA* 4.12), fish (Pollux 6.51), even the human body (Pl. *Tim.* 76a); (2: λέπος) pulses in general (v.7 of this fr.), broad beans (Lucian, *Icar.* 19), stavesacre (Nicander *Ther.* 943) and again fish (Pollux 6.51, 94). In Alciphron 3.24.2, however, lupin seed-pods are called φλοιοί.

4 ἀπεπνίγη: 'he choked (to death)', as in Pherecrates 170(159K) τρώγων ἐρεβίνθους ἀπεπνίγη; cf. also e.g. Hippocr. *Epid.* 5.37 ὁ Συμμάχου παῖς ὑπὸ χολῆς ἀπεπνίγη νύκτωρ καταδαρθών.

4–6 The Epit. MSS CE write a continuous text (μάλιστα δὲ Κλεαίνετος μὲν οὐκ ἐδήδοκ' οἶδ' ὅτι ὁ τραγικὸς οὗτος) which is accepted by some editors (e.g. Meineke, Kock, Desrousseaux) without any change of speaker, although it would be interpreted more effectively as a topical interjection by a second speaker playing the βωμολόχος (cf. e.g. Men. *Sam.* 599ff.): 'But in particular it won't have been Cleaenetus ... who ate them ... he's εὐχερής' (see on v. 8). Even so, Dobree's suggestion of a lacuna between vv. 4 and 5, with change of speaker at 5 (*Adv.* 2.298), has much to recommend it, although its length (? one line or more) and contents are debatable. Dobree proposed a single line with a further curse: <πρώτιστος ἐξόλοιτο πολὺ Κλεαίνετος>, but when a speaker doubles or multiplies his imprecations, μάλιστα (with μέν) is normally attached to the first, not the closing, curse (e.g. S. *Phil.* 1285ff., cf. Dem. 20.25), and there seems to be no good palaeographical reason why Dobree's line should have been omitted. Edmonds fills the lacuna with <Κλεαίνετος, εἴπερ οὗτός ἐσθ' ὁ καταλιπών>, with the line omitted by a *saut du même au même* (cf. e.g. Mosch. *Europa* 81f., 114–17 in the σ group of MSS); this would turn one Cleaenetus (with whom the tragedian of vv. 5f. would then be contrasted) into a fictive play character (like the old men in Men. *Georg.*, *Fab. Inc.*, cf. Alciphron 3.36). Yet clauses introduced by μάλιστα δέ

752

normally give a particular example, illustration or explanation of a preceding idea (e.g. Eur. *Hcld.* 456, Ar. *Nub.* 1509, *Av.* 1347, Antiphanes 254), and something like <Κλεαίνετος θυμοῖτ' ἄν, εἰ μάθοι, σφόδρα> might be a more suitable supplement if the fictive Cleaenetus owned the property with litter in front, but was then away from home.

Κλεαίνετος ... ὁ τραγικός: this Cleaenetus won third prize at the Lenaea of 363 with a Ὑψιπύλη (*TrGF* 1 p. 342 Snell = III D 1 col. 6.17 Mette); two brief frs. from unnamed plays are cited by Stob. *Anth.* 4.25.5, 35.2 = p. 807 Nauck², 251 Snell). Philodemus in *P.Herculaneum* 994 (π. ποιημάτων [1], col. 25.10 Sbordone) called him and Carcinus incompetent (πονηρούς). He may have been the χοροδιδάσκαλος mentioned by Aeschines 1.98 (testimonia in Snell, 250f.). Alexis identifies him as ὁ τραγικός here (i) most probably because at least three other Cleaeneti won some prominence during Alexis' lifetime (Kirchner, *PA* 1.566f., nos. 8459, 8462, 8461): an Ἰκαριεύς and a Μελιτεύς as διατηταί in 325/4 (*IG* ii².1926.40, 122), the former having been trierarch in 342/1 (*IG* ii².1622.613), while a Κυδαθηναιεύς (? a descendant of Cleon) rescued his father from a crippling fine in 304/3 by prostituting himself with Demetrius Poliorcetes (Plut. *Dem.* 24), but also (ii) perhaps to distinguish him from a *persona ficta* in the play (see above on vv. 4–6).

οἶδ' ὅτι: often placed, like δηλονότι, in the middle or at the end of the clauses that it would be expected to introduce (cf. Rehdantz–Blass, *Index* 108, K.G. 2.368). In comedy it usually comes at the end of a line as here (Ar. *Vesp.* 1348, *Nub.* 1175, *Pax* 365, cf. *Lys.* 154); in Attic prose its position is less standardised (contrast e.g. Dem. 6.30 with 19.273, 309).

7 After οὐδενὸς γὰρ πώποτε (-ποτ' CE) at the end of v. 6 Epit. of Ath. and Eustath. write just ἀπέβαλεν ὀσπρίου λέπος in 7, with a lacuna of one metron most probably before or directly after ἀπέβαλεν but no obvious gap in sense. Accordingly supplementation can only be *exempli gratia*; neatest is Meineke's <μὰ τὸν Δί' οὗτος> ἀπ. (*Anal. Crit.* 28), and worst Kock's <οὐδ' ἂν> ὀσπρίου λεπύχανον (for here Eustath. cites this passage for the use of λέπος and Theopompus 34(33K) for the use of λεπύχανον, cf. Kaehler 904). The MSS correctly give ὀσπρίου (cf. *Et. Mag.* 635.48 ὄσπριον δεῖ λέγειν καὶ οὐκ ὄσπρεον, the latter being a vulgar by-form in e.g. *P.Oxy.* 494.10, 2nd century AD); ὄσπριον (or more commonly the pl. ὄσπρια: cf. LSJ s.v.) is the general term for pulses (cf. Xen. *Anab.* 4.4.9, Theophr. *HP* 8.1.1), of which θέρμοι were one type. On λέπος see above on v. 3.

7 'He's just such an omnivorous fellow,' with εὐχερής (the joke's key-word) placed near the end of the sentence for maximum effect. The adjective and its congeners are well discussed by M. Leumann, *Philologus* 96 (1944) 161ff. = *Kleine Schriften* (Zürich 1959) 207ff., although he misinterprets this line of Alexis (*Kl. Schr.* 211 n. 1) through assuming that its subject is the litter lout of vv. 1–4 and not the tragic Cleaenetus. In general use εὐχερής meant 'complaisant/ good-natured/easy-going' (e.g. S. *Phil.* 519, Aristophon fr. 12.5f., Arist. *Pol.* 8.3.4, 1338ᵇ21), but in 4th-century Athens it was particularly applied to a person who would eat anything (e.g. Xen. *Lac.* 2.5 εὐχερέστερον δὲ πρὸς πᾶν ἔχειν βρῶμα, Arist. *HA* 8.6, 595ᵃ18 (describing the pig) εὐχερέστατον πρὸς πᾶσαν τροφὴν τῶν ζῴων, *Eth. Eud.* 2.3, 1221ᵇ2 εὐχερὴς ὥσπερ οἱ γαστρίμαργοι πρὸς τροφήν). We may safely guess that the tragic Cleaenetus had such a reputation for gormandising on every dish put before him that he would even consume lupin seeds, pods and all (and so never drop the pods as litter).

269 (267K)

Meineke 3.519 (xxxv), Kock 2.395, Edmonds 2.506, Kassel–Austin 2.173. This fr., cited by Stobaeus 4.25.13 in a section (on the honour due to parents) where all ten comic citations come from unidentified plays, was probably spoken by a free, young, conventionally dutiful young man or woman. Expressions of respect for parents are a commonplace in drama, but mothers are more rarely singled out (e.g. Eur. frs. 358 Nauck² = *Er.* fr. 48 Austin, 1064, Philemon 143(156K), Ter. *HT* 991ff, *Hec.* 301ff., 481), presumably because in most comedies they played a less significant role (cf. Legrand, *NGC* 127ff., G. E. Duckworth, *The Nature of Roman Comedy* (Princeton 1952) 256ff.). The opening words of the fr. ('I thought it right not to desert my mother, but to save her first') imply a situation more precarious than that of Gorgias at Men. *Dysk.* 617ff., where an invitation to lunch can be accepted only on condition of μηδαμῶς τὴν μητέρα | οἴκοι καταλείπων; one possibility would be the rescue or preservation of an endangered mother in a tragic burlesque (e.g. (i) Orestes in Ὀρέστης explaining a decision not to kill Clytemnestra – especially if he also befriended Aegisthus, cf. the introduction to that play; or (ii) Telemachus in Ὀδυσσεὺς ὑφαίνων).

2 πρώτην δὲ σῴζειν: with δέ cancelling the negative, cf. Denniston, *GP* 167f. Without further context πρώτην remains mysterious (but not corrupt, *pace* Bothe, *PCGF* 582); it implies the presence of other people in danger too, but who?

σῴζειν: 'with ι whenever ζ follows ω ... and so (written σωιζ-) in Inscriptions and Papyri down to iii BC' (so LSJ s.v.; also H. Usener, *Neue Jahrb.* 35 (1865) 238ff., G. Curtius, *The Greek Verb* (English tr. London 1880) 532f., K.B. 2.544f., Meisterhans–Schwyzer 65f., 179, Schwyzer 1.736; cf. Threatte, 1.358f.), although *Et. Mag.* 741.27ff. notes that σῴζω χῶρις τοῦ ι λέγει ὁ Δίδυμος ... ἀλλ' ἡ παράδοσις ἔχει τὸ ι.

3 μεῖζον: so A, the *difficilior lectio*, rightly printed by Meineke (with the correct interpretation of vv. 2–3, *iis qui recte aestimant res divinas, nihil matre sanctius esse dicit*; cf. Blaydes, *Adv.* 2.169) and Kassel–Austin. Failure to realise that τὰ θεῖα was the object of (τοῖς ... ὀρθῶς) εἰδόσι induced a corruption of μεῖζον to μείζω in SM that turns a speaker elsewhere consistently reverent into a blasphemer at v. 3. For the idiom cf. e.g. Ar. *Nub.* 1185f. οὐ ... τὸν νόμον | ἴσασιν, *Av.* 691f. φύσιν οἰωνῶν γένεσίν τε θεῶν ... | εἰδότες ὀρθῶς.

4–6 In a play most probably written for an Athenian audience Alexis would primarily have in mind the ἱερὸν μητρός in the south-western part of the Agora, described by Paus. 1.3.5 (cf. J. G. Frazer's comm., vol. 2 (London 1898) 66ff.) and excavated in the 1930s (T. L. Shear, *Hesperia* 4 (1935) 350ff., H. A. Thompson, *ibid.* 6 (1937) 115ff., 172ff.; cf. Wycherley, *Agora* III.150ff., Thompson and Wycherley, *ibid.* XIV.29ff, J. Travlos, *Pictorial Dictionary of Athens* (London 1971) 352ff.). This temple, first built around 500, destroyed by the Persians in 480, then rehoused in the Old Bouleuterion until construction of a new shrine *c.* 200, was dedicated to (τῆς) Μητρὸς (τῶν) θεῶν (so e.g. Aeschines 1.60, Dem. *Prooem.* 54, Dinarchus 1.86, Theophr. *Char.* 21.11, Paus. 1.3.5, *IG* ii².1257.1–2: i.e. Cybele, sometimes identified with Rhea and/or Demeter: cf. e.g. L. R. Farnell, *The Cults of the Greek States* 3 (Oxford 1907) 289ff.; in Roscher, Rapp s.v. *Kybele* 1638.33ff., Höfer and W. Drexler s.v. *Meter* 11, 2849.64ff.; Schwenn in *RE* s.v. *Kybele* 2250.27ff., 2254.21ff., s.v. *Meter* 1372.15ff.; R. Kannicht, comm. (Heidelberg 1969) on Eur. *Hel.* 1301–68), but the shrine's name was abbreviated to (i) Μητρὸς ἱερόν or ἱερὸν Μητρὸς as here (also e.g. Plut. *Them.* 31.1 and the rock inscription in W. Peek, *Ath. Mitt.* 67 (1942) 149f. no. 323, cf. Paus. 10.32.3) and (ii) most commonly (especially with reference to the shrine's use from the 4th century onwards as a repository of official records: cf. Wycherley, collecting the references) Μητρῷον – forms which aided the speaker's claim here that the temple honoured human motherhood.

The origin of this cult in Athens was traditionally associated with a begging priest from Phrygia who initiated Athenian women into its rites (*Suda* s.vv. βάραθρον σ 99 Adler and μητραγύρτης = Phot. s.v. Μητρῷον, Σ Ar. *Plut.* 431 and 431a, Apostol. 11.34, Julian *Orat.* 8(5).1 Rochefort, 159a–b). The anonymity of this priest in our records is particularly unfortunate, because Alexis' account of the temple's foundation is corruptly transmitted at the opening of v. 4 (ὅθεν ὁ πρῶτος SMA unmetrically), and G. Wakefield (see Meineke 3.520) may well be right in suggesting that a proper name is concealed by the corruption (hence ὅθ. ὁ Προμηθεύς G. Hermann in Meineke 3.520, but Promethus is not associated with this cult; ὅθ. Βροτέας ποτ' Kock citing Paus. 3.22.4, who names Broteas as the creator of the oldest known statue of the μητὴρ θεῶν in a temple on Mt Sipylus, but it is unlikely that this would be common knowledge in

COMMENTARY

Athens). Other conjectures are unconvincing (e.g. ὅθεν γ' ὁ πρ. Bothe, *PCGF* 582, where ὅθεν γ' = 'for precisely which reason', cf. Denniston, *GP* 127f., but ὁ πρῶτος is implausibly vague; ὅθ. βροτῶν τις O. Hense, *Acta soc. phil. Lips.* 2 (1872) 75; ὅθενπερ οὗτος R. Ellis, *AJP* 6 (1885) 290; πρὸ τοῦ τις Richards, *AO* 87); ? perhaps ὅθεν γε Φρύξ τις.

4 οὐκ ἀπαιδεύτως ἔχων: as in Eur. *Ion* 247 τὸ μὲν σὸν οὐκ ἀπαιδεύτως ἔχει, cf. Pl. *Resp.* 8.559d (τεθραμμένος).

5–6 οὐ δείξας σαφῶς ποίας: 'not indicating distinctly what (mother's temple)', as he would if he had added e.g. τῶν θεῶν (comm. on 4–6 above), Ἰδαία (Eur. *Or.* 1453, Ap. Rhod. 1.1128), Φρυγία (Pollux 3.11), μεγάλη (*SIG* 1014.83, Erythrae 3rd century) or ὀρεία (Ar. *Av.* 746).

6 ὑπονοεῖν εἰς τοὔνομα: 'to guess with regard to the name'; cf. e.g. Ar. *Plut.* 361 σὺ μηδὲν εἰς ἔμ' ὑπονόει τοιουτονί. This idiom with εἰς is so common with verbs of speech and thought (cf. LSJ s.v. εἰς, IV) that conjectures such as ὑπονοῆσαι (Emperius 311) or ὑπονοεῖσθαι (Kock) τοὔν. seem aberrations.

270 (268K)

Meineke 3.517 (xxx), Kock 2.396 (misprinted '936'), Edmonds 2.506, Kassel–Austin 2.174; cf. W. H. Roscher, *Die Sieben- und Neunzahl im Kultus und Mythos der Griechen*, and *Die Hebdomadenlehre der griechischen Philosophen und Ärzte* (*Abh.* Leipzig 24.1 (1904) 4ff., 24.6 (1906) 7ff., 179ff.), W. L. Lorimer, *Some Notes on the Text of Pseudo-Aristotle 'De Mundo'* (Oxford 1925) 79f., W. H. Mineur, comm. (Leiden 1984) on Call. *H. Del.* 19f. The fr., cited in full by (1) ? an unepitomised version of Stephanus of Byzantium, *Ethnica* 567.14 (s.v. Σικελία) in Constantinus Porphyrogenitus, *De Thematibus* 2.10 p. 95 Pertusi, (2) Σ^TW Pl. *Menex.* 242e p. 185 Greene and (3) Eustathius' commentaries on Dionysius Periegetes, 580 = K. Müller, *Geographi Graeci Minores* 2 (Paris 1882) 329,[1] was preserved because it lists the seven largest islands in the Mediterranean. Lists of seven have been popular since remotest antiquity (e.g. the seven gates of Thebes, wise men, wonders of the ancient world), partly perhaps because the uniqueness of the one number between one and ten that was neither a factor

---

[1] The transmissional relationship (if any) between the three versions is uncertain (*pace* Müller in his apparatus). Even if all derive from Stephanus' *Ethnica* in the 6th century AD, it is most likely that this author's source was a work already excerpting the Alexis fr., not an original play text that would hardly have survived to this date. The three versions differ substantially and often in their readings, which make it impossible to restore the correct text with any confidence, although the general line of the argument remains clear.

756

INCERTARUM FABULARUM FRAGMENTA

nor a product of the others appealed to philosophers and mystics, more probably because seven was a popular limit of items to memorise (cf. Roscher, *locc. citt.*). By Alexis' time these seven islands had evidently become a canon (and cf. the later references to αἱ λεγόμεναι ἑπτά [Arist.] *Mir. Ausc.* 88, 837ᵃ31; αἱ ἑπτά Strabo 14.2.10, Diod. Sic. 5.17.1, Σ Ar. *Ach.* 112), but although the identity of the seven was generally agreed, the order of listing (usually based on size) varied from author to author:

Si(cily) Sa(rdinia) Co(rsica) Cr(ete) Eu(boea) Cy(prus) Le(sbos): Alexis and [Arist.] *Mund.* 3, 393ᵃ12ff.
Si Sa Cy Cr Eu Co Le: Diod. Sic. 5.17.1 and (with Rh(odes), the eighth largest, added) anon. *Geog. Comp.* 8(27) in K. Müller, 2.501.
Sa Si Cy Cr Eu Co Le: Timaeus (*FGrH* 3в p. 620, 566 F65) in Strabo 14.2.10 (but Si Sa Co Strabo 2.5.19).
Si Cr Rh Le Eu Si Sa Co: Appian *Praef.* 5.17 (with Rhodes added).
Eu Cr Si (Sa Cy) Co (Le): verse inscription in Chios (C. A. Trypanis, *Hermes* 88 (1960) 69, 73: order dictated by metrical constraints).

The inaccuracy of large-scale areal measurement in the ancient world may account for most of the above variations, but it is perhaps surprising that none of those recorded is fully correct (Si 25460, Sa 24090, Cy 9251, Co 8700, Cr 8400, Eu 3600, Le 1650, Rhodes 1400 km², +/− 100 km²).

In this fr. speaker and dramatic situation are unidentifiable.

1 δέδειχεν: correctly Σ Pl. and Const.; Eustath.'s ἔδειξεν probably reflects the confusion between perfect and aorist in medieval Greek (cf. P. Chantraine, *Histoire du parfait grec* (Paris 1927) 244f.).

2 ὡς λόγος: 'as is (generally) reported', common in this shorthand form from the 5th century on (e.g. A. *Suppl.* 230, Eur. *IT* 534, *Phoen.* 396, Eubulus 13(14K).3, Pl. *Phil.* 65c, *Symp.* 196d, *Critias* 120d, Dem. 23.66, [Arist.]. *Mund.* 6, 398ᵃ13, Philo *De Spec. Legg.* 3.3.13, Aelian, *NA* 6.51, *VH* 2.21) as well as in expanded versions (both without verb expressed, e.g. ὡς ὁ (τῶν σοφῶν) λ., ὡς λ. τις; and with, e.g. ὡς λ./ὁ λ. ἔχει/φησί/ἐστίν/ἦν/ ἔσπαρται; cf. Fraenkel on A. *Ag.* 264, R. Renehan, *Studies in Greek Texts* (Göttingen 1976) 138ff., with full references).

3 ἔστιν μεγίστη: so Σ Pl.; Eustath.'s πρώτη μ., which removes a needed verb, is presumably a corruption influenced by the succession of ordinals in vv. 3–6. Worried by the repetition of the adjective in vv. 2–3, Kock here conjectures κρατίστη, but the islands appear to be listed in order of size, not importance or excellence.

δευτέρα: the reading of Eustath., generally the least reliable of the three sources (∼ unmetrical καὶ δ. in Const.), perhaps rightly printed by Kassel–Austin, since the variant readings in Σ Pl. (καὶ δὲ Σαρδὼ δ. W, πρὸς δὲ Σάρδος δ. T) (i) introduce a juxtaposed καὶ δέ which would be unique for Alexis (cf. Denniston, *GP* 199) and (ii) assume a lacuna of two metra after τροφός (marked in T by a gap of some eight letters).

4 δ' (Eustath., δὲ Const.) or θ' (τε Σ Pl.)? Despite the μέν in v. 2 it is hard to decide.

ἡ Διὸς Κρήτη τροφός: cf. Eur. *Hyps.* fr. 1.iii.22 Διότροφον Κρήταν, *Bacch.* 121f. ζάθεοί τε Κρήτας Διογενέτορες ἔναυλοι, Call. *H. Zeus* 6, 42ff. On the legend of Zeus' infancy in Crete see especially L. R. Farnell, *The Cults of the Greek States* 1 (Oxford 1896) 36ff., A. B. Cook, *Zeus*, 2.2 (Cambridge 1925) 932ff., R. F. Willetts, *Cretan Cults and Festivals* (London 1962) 207, 231ff., 239ff. and *The Civilization of Ancient Crete* (Berkeley 1977) 200ff., C. Kerényi, *Zeus and Hera* (English tr., London 1975) 28f. and H. Veerbruggen, *Le Zeus crétois* (Paris 1981) 27ff.

5 Εὔβοια πέμπτη στενοφυής: Const. transposes Εὔοια (*sic*) and π.; thereafter στενο- Eustath., στεινο- Const. and Σ Pl. T, στηνο- Σ Pl. W, revealing uncertainty over the spelling of this hapax, 'physically narrow'. Euboea is 175 km long, 6–50 km broad but at its narrowest in the portion nearest to Athens. Cf. Ar. *Nub.* 211f. ἡ δέ γ' Εὔβοι', ὡς ὁρᾷς, | ἡδί παρατέταται μακρὰ πόρρω πάνυ.

6 τάξιν ἑβδόμην λαχοῦσ' ἔχει: cf. in a military context Xen. *Cyr.* 7.1.16 εἰ μὴ ἔλαχον τήνδε τὴν τάξιν.

Substitution of ἔχω (used as an auxiliary verb) + aorist participle for a resultative perfect is an idiomatic feature of classical Attic (cf. Σ Eur. *Hipp.* 932 διαβαλὼν ἔχει· ἀττικόν), especially Greek tragedy (e.g. A. *Sept.* 947 ἔχουσι μοῖραν λαχόντες), where nevertheless most frequently the participle precedes ἔχω, and the *sedes* extends over the last metron of an iambic trimeter as here in Alexis). The usage may ultimately derive, but in the classical period needs to be distinguished, from passages like Hom. *Il.* 1.356 etc. ἑλὼν γὰρ ἔχει γέρας and Hes. *Op.* 42 κρύψαντες γὰρ ἔχουσι θεοὶ βίον ἀνθρώποισι, where ἔχει/ἔχουσι retain the basic meaning 'possess' (in later Greek cf. e.g. Dem. 9.12 Φεράς . . . ἔχει καταλαβών, Men. *Dysk.* 812 πλοῦτος ἀφανής, ὃν σὺ κατορύξας ἔχεις). See especially W. J. Aerts, *Periphrastica* (Amsterdam 1965) 128ff.; cf. K.G. 2.61f., Schwyzer 1.812f.

In place of ἑβδόμην (Σ Pl., Const.) Eustath. has ἐσχάτην, probably a trivialising variant.

271 (269K)

Meineke 3.509 (XI), Kock 2.396 (misprinted '936'), Edmonds 2.506, Kassel–Austin 2.174. An imaginative comment, inspired probably by some character's refusal or inability to enjoy life to the full, but neither speaker nor situation can be identified.

1 ἰδιώτην: here presumably with the basic meaning ('private person, individual . . . one in a private station, opp. to one holding public office or taking part in public affairs' LSJ s.v., unnecessarily here subdividing the meaning), but the contrast with ποιητήν in v. 2 may have been (? subconsciously) suggested by its less frequent application 'prose writer' (cf. Pl. *Phdr.* 258d ἐν μέτρῳ ὡς ποιητὴς ἢ ἄνευ μέτρου ὡς ἰδιώτης, *Symp.* 178b, *Legg.* 10.890a).

μονοσιτοῦντ': elsewhere in unambiguous contexts μονοσιτεῖν = 'to eat one meal (a day)', e.g. Hippocr. *VM* 10, *Acut.* 11, 28 τοῖσι δὶς σιτεομένοισι τῆς ἡμέρης καὶ τοῖς μονοσιτέουσιν, 32, *Epid.* 7.3, Xen. *Cyr.* 8.8.9, Plato com. (?) fr. 296(207K) and Ath. 2.47d citing it, Phylarchus in Ath. 2.44b = *FGrH* 2A 81 F13; cf. Plaut. *Men.* 456 *hominum in dies qui singulas escas edint*; similarly μονοσιτία/-ίη at e.g. Hippocr. *Vict.* 3.68, Galen 10.544 Kühn, Philumenus in Oribas. *Coll. Med.* 45.29.55 τὸ δὲ δὶς σιτεῖσθαι μονοσιτίας αἱρετώτερον. That is likely to be the meaning in Alexis here (so Casaubon, *Animadv.* 95f.), since such a regime would contrast well with that of a *bon viveur* (cf. e.g. Pl. *Epist.* 7.326b); even so, LSJ's translation (s.v., after Daléchamp) of the passage here as 'eating alone', though unsupported by parallels, cannot be ruled out, since compounds such as μονοτράπεζα (Eur. *IT* 949), μονοφάγος (e.g. Plut. *Mor.* 301d) and -φαγία (e.g. LXX *4 Macc.* 1.27, 2.7) undoubtedly bear that meaning; on the practice see Nesselrath, *LP* 487.

2 ποθοῦντ': so CE (Ath. 2.47c) correctly; cf. K. Zacher, *BPW* 22 (1902) 1221f., *so verliert der Dichter sein halbes Leben wenn er nicht nach Lied und Gesang Sehnsucht hat, d.h. nicht ins Theater und Konzert geht, sondern nur mit seinen eigenen Liedern zufrieden ist.* Grotius' conjecture (*Exc.* 974, long before Meineke) ποιοῦντ' is better forgotten (corruption of ποθ- to common ποι- would be more likely than the reverse), as are Kaehler's πονοῦντ' (*Annot.* 16), Herwerden's προτιθέντ' (*Mnemosyne* 14 (1886) 188) and J. Meyer's δηλοῦντ' or πλέκοντ' (*Emendationes et observationes in Athenaei novissimam editionem* (Progr. Regensburg 1896/7) 11).

ᾠδάς . . . καὶ μέλη: the two terms were virtually synonymous in everyday usage, with ᾠδή embracing both words and music of a song (cf. e.g. Xen. *Symp.* 6.4) and μέλος words, music and rhythm (so Pl. *Resp.* 3.398d), although when juxtaposed as here (also e.g. Pl. *Resp.* 3.398c, 399c, *Legg.* 2.654e, [Mosch.] 3.12, Josephus *AJ* 8.44, Plut. *Mor.* 396d, 1026a) ᾠδή probably stresses the sung words, μέλος the tune. Cf. S. Michaelides, *The Music of Ancient Greece: An Encyclopaedia* (London 1978) 202, 223.

ποιητήν: this correction of CE's ποιητὰς (assimilation to the ending of the preceding word) is usually attributed to Casaubon (margin of text, *Animadv.* 96), but Grotius (*Exc.* 974) claims it for Scaliger. The orthography ποιητήν would here be preferable: cf. comm. on 16.2.

4 νόμιζε: common in drama as an exhortation to individual addressees (e.g. S. *Aj.* 497, Eur. *Alc.* 703, *Hel.* 1657, frs. 142.4, 941.3, Anaxilas 3.2,

COMMENTARY

Antiphanes 202(204K).14, Aristophon 10.2, Ephippus 20.4, Hegesippus 1.5, Men. *Karch.* 34, Philemon 99(97K).2, com. adesp. fr. 244.348 Austin; νόμισον Men. (?) fr. 416.8); similarly νομίζετε directed to chorus and/or characters (e.g. Eur. *Hcld.* 315, *Tro.* 510; *Rhes.* 819), to audience (e.g. Men. *Dysk.* 1, Heniochus fr. 5.8). Cf. Dobree, *Adv.* 2.138 on Ar. *Plut.* 361, Headlam, comm. on Herodas p. 407, G. Zuntz, *PBA* 42 (1957) 233 n. 3.

5 ζῶσι ... μόλις: cf. frs. 28.4 and 177(173K).4 with comm., 236(234K).1, 237(235K).

272 (270K)

Meineke 3.510 (XII), Kock 2.397, Edmonds 2.506, Kassel–Austin 2.175; cf. Nesselrath, *MK* 282 n. 1. Because of A's loss of several folios at Ath. 11.466d (cf. the editions of Schweighaeuser 1.xxviii and xci, Kaibel 1.ix, my general introduction II.i.a), the lemma (just Ἄλεξις) and vv. 1–2 (up to ἦν γάρ) of this fr. are preserved only in Epit. (= Casaubon, *Animadv.* 784); A returns at στρογγύλον (v.2). A and Epit. continue together up to γράμματ' (-τα) in v. 4, where Epit. ceases its citation; ἔχον–γράμματα (v.4) is also found in Eustath. 1960.13).

The fr. comes from a conversation (part-division first in Schweighaeuser) about a γραμματικὸν ἔκπωμα with crushed handles, which the second speaker recognises partly from its inscription Διὸς σωτῆρος in gilt letters. The dramatic context is presumably a recognition scene (cf. Nesselrath) with the cup helping to confirm the identity of a long-lost relative. Even though in extant scenes of ancient comedy no comparable use of a vase can be instanced (but ? cf. Ar. fr. 634(623K); Hähnle 141ff.), the precise description of other objects – e.g. clothes and fabrics (A. *Choeph.* 231ff. ~ Eur *El.* 539ff., *Ion* 1421ff., Men. *Sik.* 280ff.), rings (Men. *Epitr.* 386ff.; cf. S. *El.* 1222f., Plaut. *Curc.* 653ff., Ter. *Hec.* 572ff., 811f.), jewellery (Men. *Pk.* 768ff.) sometimes inscribed with names (Plaut. *Rud.* 1156ff.) – often establishes a person's identity. The Alexis fr. apes tragic rhythms (regular caesurae, Porson's law observed, no resolutions) and avoids overt comic play, just like the recognition scene of Men. *Pk.* (Legrand, *NGC* 220f., Webster, *SM* 160, F. M. Sandbach, *Entr. Hardt* 16 (1970) 126ff.).

Meineke (3.511) tentatively assigns this fr. to the Ἱππεύς because two frs. from that play have descriptions of vases with gold or gilt decoration (κυμβία 100(95K), κύλιξ 101(96K)). All three frs. may derive from the same scene, but vases were featured in Alexis' Ἀγωνίς (fr. 2), Κύκνος (fr. 124(119K)) and doubtless many other plays.

1 εἴπω: could be (i) jussive, in which case an imperative such as λέγε is likely to have preceded in the unquoted preceding context (cf. e.g. Pl. *Phd.* 86e, *Resp.* 5.457c, K.G. 1.219f.), or (ii) deliberative (and punctuated as a question: so first Meineke), either on its own (e.g. Ar. *Ran.* 1) or

INCERTARUM FABULARUM FRAGMENTA

introduced by e.g. θέλεις (so Kock; θέλεις was conjectured by Blaydes, *Adv.* 2.169 in place of CE's γέ σου, which is better explained as an assimilation to the ending of the preceding word and corrected with Schweighaeuser to γέ σοι) or βούλει (K.G. 1.221f.), or (iii) in a final clause after ἵνα (so also Kock).

2 πρώτιστον: in adverbial use πρώτιστον/-τα often come at or near the beginning of the clause, but there are enough instances of late or end position (e.g. Alexis 46(45K).4 ~ 193(188K).2, S. *Trach.* 1181 ἔμβαλλε χεῖρα δεξιὰν πρώτιστά μοι, Ar. *Plut.* 791f. ἐμοῦ γὰρ εἰσιόντος εἰς τὴν οἰκίαν | πρώτιστα) to justify punctuating after rather than immediately before it.

3 ὦτα συντεθλασμένον: 'with crushed handles', implying that the cup was metal, not ceramic (see on vv. 4–5); Arist. *Meteor.* 4.9, 386ᵃ9ff. carefully distinguishes things like κέραμος that can be broken into pieces (θραυστά) and those like χαλκός that can be pressed and crushed (θλαστά) but not broken (ἄθραυστα). Cf. *IG* ii².1544.20f. (late 4th century, Eleusis temple records) ἐνώδια δύο χρυσᾶ συντεθλασμένα, Machon 108 συγκατέθλα ('he crushed, *not* smashed, the cup to pieces', *pace* Gow *ad loc.* and LSJ s.v. συγκαταθλάω).

ὦτα is one of a series of nouns in common use which Attic employs indiscriminately with and without the definite article (cf. e.g. Ar. *Plut.* 287 ἢν ὦτ' ὄνου λάβητε, Cratinus 257(239K), Pl. *Phdr.* 253e περὶ ὦτα λάσιος, *Protag.* 342b; Gildersleeve, *Syntax* 2.259ff., § 568–72).

4–5 ἔχον κύκλῳ τε γράμματ' (Kassel–Austin with ACE, cf. Fraenkel, *MNC* 25) wins over ἔχ. κ. τὰ γρ. (Meineke, Kock with Eustath.) because (i) a definite article is inappropriate at first mention of the letters, (ii) when postponed, particles such as τε are often corrupted (comm. on fr. 4.1). Alexis clearly imagined a silver cup with gilt letters in relief, as Ath. here recognised, following his citation with τοιοῦτον εἴδομεν ποτήριον γραμματικὸν ... ἐν Καπύῃ τῆς Καμπανίας ... ἀργυροῦν ... καὶ ἐντετυπωμένα ἔχον τὰ ἔπη χρυσοῖς γράμμασιν. Few such cups may have been preserved (F. Courby, *Les Vases grecs à reliefs* (Paris 1922) 189; cf. D. E. Strong, *Greek and Roman Gold and Silver Plate* (London 1966) 19ff., 80, 108f.); far more common from the 4th century onwards are ceramic vases (especially black lustre-ware: cf. Sparkes–Talcott, *Agora XII.1: Black and Plain Pottery* 2of.) with inscriptions gilded on added clay, painted in white or incised with a pointed tool, including dedications in the genitive to deities invoked in toasts (cf. comm. on fr. 59(58K)). These include Ἀγαθοῦ δαίμονος, Ἀφροδίτης, Διονύσου, Ἔρωτος and Ὑγιείας as well as Διὸς σωτῆρος, and are collected by W. H. D. Rouse, *Greek Votive Offerings* (Cambridge 1902) 279 n. 12, C. Picard, *Mélanges d'archéologie et d'histoire* 30 (1910) 104ff., P. Wolters, *MDAI (Ath.)* 38 (1913) 193ff., cf. H. A. Thompson, *Hesperia* 3 (1934) 339 and F. Benoit, *L'Épave du grand*

761

COMMENTARY

congloué à Marseille (Gallia Suppl. 114, Paris 1961) 78. Διὸς σωτῆρος (cf. comm. on 234(232K).2) appears on e.g. (i) a 4th-century krater or stamnos from Apulia (British Museum F548; H. B. Walters, *Catalogue of the Greek and Etruscan Vases* 4 (London 1896) 226, H. Bulle, *Festschrift für James Loeb* (Munich 1930) 25f., figs. 11, 11a, cf. P. Wuilleumier, *Tarente des origines à la conquête romaine* (Paris 1939) 467, T. B. L. Webster, *JHS* 71 (1951) 222), (ii) a fragment from the top of a pot from Cyprus (British Museum 91.8–6.79; J. A. R. Monro and H. A. Tubbs, *JHS* 12 (1891) 144f.), (iii) a Hellenistic kantharos from Corinth (O. Broneer, *Hesperia* 16 (1947) 240 and pl. LIX.14) and (iv) a fragment of a late 4th-century kantharos from the Athenian Agora (G9; M. Lang, *Agora, XXI: Graffiti and Depinti* (Princeton 1976) 54); cf. also (v) a cup reported by M. Collignon, *Rev. Arch.* 32 (1876) 184 and (vi) κέρας ἐπιγεγραμμένον Διὶ σωτῆρι ἕν in the list of consecrations from Didyma, 288/7 BC (A. Boeckh, *CIG* 2852 = A. Rehm, *Didyma* 2 (Berlin 1958) 255 no.424 = J. Pouilloux, *Choix d'inscriptions grecques* (Paris 1960) 237, line 43). Ath. here collects several references to γραμματικὰ ἐκπώματα (also Ar. fr. 634(623K), Eubulus 69, Achaeus trag. 33); add Plaut. *Rud.* 478 (a pitcher inscribed with Venus' name).

ἀρά γ' ἕνδεκα χρυσᾶ, Διὸς σωτῆρος; (Kassel–Austin) or ἀρά γ' ἕνδεκα; χρυσᾶ; Δ. σωτῆρος; (Kock)? Kock's pernickety punctuation may indicate how some actors would have delivered these words, but there is no way of knowing how they were voiced at the original production.

οὐκ ἄλλου μὲν οὖν: clearly a statement = 'precisely that', with ἄλλου referring back to ποτηρίου in v. 1 and μὲν οὖν strongly confirmatory (W. Headlam, *CR* 10 (1896) 437, Denniston, *GP* 477). Cf. e.g. Longus 4.21 οὐκ ἄλλα μὲν οὖν ἀλλ' αὐτὰ ταῦτα, Pl. *Resp.* 4.443b τοῦτο μὲν οὖν καὶ οὐδὲν ἄλλο, Men. *Sam.* 406f., Lucian *Timon* 54, *Nec.* 1 οὐ μὲν οὖν ἄλλη/-ος.

273 (271K)

Meineke 3.518 (XXXI), Kock 2.397, Edmonds 2.508, Kassel–Austin 2.176; cf. M. P. Paoletta, *Annali della Facoltà di lettere dell'Università di Napoli* 26 (1983/4) 25f. The whole fr., cited by Plut. *Mor.* 21d (πῶς δεῖ τὸν νέον ποιημάτων ἀκούειν 4; cf. especially D. Wyttenbach *ad loc.*, *Animadv.* 1 (Oxford 1810) pp. 217ff.) as an instance τῶν ἀτόπως εἰρημένων (vv.4–5 also in *Mor.* 445e (περὶ τῆς ἠθικῆς ἀρετῆς 6) as an instance of ἀκολαστία), is an encouragement to self-indulgence (like Alexis 222(219K).14ff. and [Alexis] 25, cf. comm. *ad locc.*, the latter = 'False or Doubtful Attributions' III) that could have been spoken by any hedonist in a myth travesty (cf. Polyphemus in Eur. *Cycl.* 316ff., 336ff.) or New-Comedy intrigue (cf. *senex* in Plaut. *MG* 677,, *aduocati* in *Poen.* 600ff., *adulescens* in Men. 473ff., *leno* in *Pseud.* 1132ff., slave in *Most.* 20ff., *Stich.* 446ff.). Wyttenbach tentatively suggested as source Ταραντῖνοι, and G. R. Holland (*De Polyphemo et Galatea* (*Leipziger Studien* 7 (1884) 222) Γαλάτεια, with Polyphemus speaking as in Eur. *Cycl.*

1 τὰς ἡδονὰς . . . συλλέγειν: elsewhere συλλέγω is more commonly used of collecting unpleasant things (e.g. ἀλγήματα Eur. fr. 507.2, ἁμαρτήματα Dem. 10.1, κακά Philemon 94(90K).8f., πολὺν κυφῶν᾿ Men. *Dysk.* 101f.: see Handley and Sandbach *ad loc.*, συμφοράς Lucian *Luct.* 20, ὕβρεις and ἀτιμίας Dem. 21.23), but cf. Ar. *Pax* 1326f. τἀγαθὰ πάνθ᾿ . . . συλλέξασθαι.

2 τρεῖς δ᾿ εἰσὶν αἵ γε: so all the MSS, with γε presumably to be interpreted in its general emphatic sense (Denniston, *GP* 116ff., e.g. S. *Trach.* 945 οὐ γάρ ἐσθ᾿ ἥ γ᾿ αὔριον, Ar. *Pax* 625 τἀκείνων γε κέρδη τοῖς γεωργοῖς ἦν κακά), but Herwerden's conjecture αἵδε (*Anal. Crit.* 41) is very attractive. Wyttenbach sees here a possible parody of Eur. fr. 853 (? from *Hcld.*: see Wilamowitz, *Hermes* 17 (1882) 345 = *Kl. Schr.* 1 (Berlin 1935) 89f., with n. 3) τρεῖς εἰσὶν ἀρεταὶ τὰς χρεών σ᾿ (so Dindorf: χρήσεις M, χρή σ᾿ A of Stob. *Anth.* 3.1.80) ἀσκεῖν, τέκνον, | θεούς τε τιμᾶν τούς τε θρέψαντας γονῆς | νόμους τε κοινοὺς Ἑλλάδος.

2–3 τὴν δύναμιν . . . τὴν . . . συντελοῦσαν τῷ βίῳ: 'the capacity of contributing to life'. The construction of συντελεῖν intrans. + dative in this metaphorical meaning, which is unparalleled in extant comedy (for another sense and construction, cf. Alexis 153(149K).12), doubtless develops from the verb's more literal use in political contexts = 'to make financial contributions to (a more powerful state, and so become a dependent ally)': intrans. e.g. in Isoc. 14.8), and becomes relatively common in the *Koine*, both intrans. (e.g. Galen on Hippocr. *Acut.* 3.29 τῇ πέψει δ᾿ ἀεὶ τὸ μὲν θερμὸν συντελεῖν, cf. 4.40, 44) and trans. (e.g. Lucian, *Alex.* 36 οὐδὲν τῷ χρησμῷ . . . συντελοῦντες, Galen, *Vict. atten.* 6 ἡ τοῦ πεπέρεως μίξις . . . οὐ σμικρὰ τῇ λεπτυνούσῃ διαίτῃ συντελεῖ, cf. on Hippocr. *Acut.* 14).

4 τὸ πιεῖν τὸ φαγεῖν: all MSS at *Mor.* 21d (except Z) + G at 445e give τὸ πιεῖν τὸ φαγεῖν, but Z at 21d + all MSS at 445e (except G) τὸ φαγεῖν τὸ πιεῖν; the same problem occurs at Xen. *Cyr.* 7.1.1 (ἐμπιεῖν καὶ φαγεῖν CAEGH, ἐμφαγεῖν καὶ πιεῖν V^cor.) and [Simonides] epigram 37 in Page, *Further Greek Epigrams* (Cambridge 1981) 252f. (πολλὰ πιὼν καὶ πολλὰ φαγών ACE at Ath. 10.415f + P at *Anth. Pal.* 7.348, where Pl has π. φαγὼν κ. π. πιών). In Xen. and Alexis the correct original text cannot be determined. When eating and drinking are mentioned together in ancient literature, eating is more commonly written first (? because it preceded drinking in δεῖπνα/συμπόσια): e.g. with ἐσθίειν/πίνειν, Hom. *Od.* 15.373, 16.143, 18.3, Ar. *Pax* 1351f., com. adesp. fr. 230.19f. Austin, Pl. *Symp.* 211d, Isoc. 7.49, [Alexis] 25.11, Phoenix Col. fr. 1.9 Powell, Aristobulus 139 F 9 Jacoby in Ath. 12.530c and Strabo 14.5.9 (cf. Arrian *Anab.* 2.5.4), Σ Ar. *Av.* 1021b citing Apollodorus, LXX *Is.* 22.13 = *1 Ep. Cor.* 15.32, *Ev. Luc.* 12.19, Ath. 10.415f,

Socrates' apophthegm in Plut. *Mor.* 21e = *Gnomol. Vat.* 479 Sternbach, Nicostratus in Stob. *Anth.* 4.23.64, Palladas in *Anth. Pal.* 10.47, Hesych. s.v. δίαιτα τοῦ ἀνθρώπου; with compounds or other verbs, Epicharmus 35.7, Ar. *Ach* 78, *Equ.* 354, Diodorus com. 2.12. Yet the usual order is often reversed (by whim or by metrical exigence): e.g. with πίνειν/ἐσθίειν, Hom. *Od.* 10.386, Theogn. 33, Antiphanes 226(228K).5, Epicrates 3.2, Ath. 12.529f citing Amyntas 122 F 2 Jacoby, 8.336d citing 'Bacchidas' = W. Peek. *Griechische Versinschriften* (Berlin 1955) 1368.1; with compound, Eur. *Cycl.* 336.[1] A. Nauck, *MGR* 6 (1894) 99 collects some of the above passages, but his conclusion that Alexis here wrote τὸ φ. τὸ π. is based on incomplete and ill-arranged material (cf. Kassel–Austin).

τὸ τῆς Ἀφροδίτης τυγχάνειν: on the metonymy (Ἀφροδίτη = sexual act or love affair) see comm. on 222(219).15. Sex, as the third pleasure commonly linked with eating and drinking (and often following them at συμπόσια) in popular thought (cf. introduction to fr. 25), is sometimes named specifically in such triads as these (e.g. Alexis 222(219).15, Plaut. *Men.* 476, 1141f., *Pseud.* 1134, *Stich.* 447; cf. ἡφροδίσιασα, ὄχευε and μετ' ἔρωτος | τέρπν' ἔπαθον in different versions of the Sardanapalus epitaph, see introduction to [Alexis] fr. 25), and sometimes euphemised or vaguely generalised (e.g. Aristobulus' version of the Sard. epitaph παῖζε, 'Bacchidas' πάντα τᾷ ψυχᾷ δόμεν, *Ev. Luc.* εὐφραίνου).

5 τὰ δ' ἄλλα προσθήκας ἅπαντα χρὴ καλεῖν: as in Arist. *Rhet.* 1.1.3, 1354ᵃ13ff. αἱ γὰρ πίστεις ἔντεχνόν ἐστι μόνον, τὰ δ' ἄλλα προσθῆκαι; cf. Wyttenbach's comm. on Plut. *Mor.* 21e, F. Marx, comm. (vol. 2, Leipzig 1905) on Lucilius 1208. Here Kassel–Austin print ἅπαντα χρὴ καλεῖν (= all MSS at *Mor.* 21e, except Xυ with δεῖ for χρή), but the reading at 445e (ἅπανθ' ἐγὼ καλῶ all MSS) is more likely to have been what Alexis wrote, depersonalised at 21e so as to be more suitable to a quoted gnome (for this sort of trivialisation, cf. my paper in Flores 363).

274 (272K)

Meineke 3.503 (II), cf. 3.462, Kock 2.397, Edmonds 2.508, Kassel–Austin 2.176; cf. Schweighaeuser, *Animadv.* 8.402. Frs. 274(272K) and 275(273K) are cited together by Epit. of Ath. 2.49e–f with only the word πάλιν intervening. Ath. regularly uses this adverb when citing two frs. from the same work, but not necessarily in their original order (thus from Alexis' Ἀπεγλαυκωμένος, fr.17 before 18 at 7.301ab, but see introduction to the play; contrast Ath.'s use of καὶ προσελθὼν δέ φησιν, Alexis 130/131 (125/

---

[1] In Plautus too *edo* precedes *bibo* commonly (*MG* 677, *Poen.* 313, *Pseud.* 1134, *Trin.* 258ff., cf. *Men.* 476, 1141f.) but not exclusively (cf. *Most.* 64f., *Stich.* 447).

126K) and 223(220/221K), and καὶ μετ' ὀλίγα, 201(196/197K) and 205(201/202K)), and so it may be less surprising that the two frs. here seem to share a common subject matter: the plum-complexioned and battered face of a pancratiast, wrestler or (cf. Casaubon, *Animadv.* 101) boxer. Meineke's suggestion that both frs. derive from Παγκρατιαστής is ingenious, uncertain (cf. introduction to that play), but preferable to Schweighaeuser's that 274(272K) could have come from Ἀγωνίς because fr.4.2 (like 274(272K).5) mentions a στέφανος κυλιστός.

1–2 The main speaker describes a dream about his award of a victory garland at some games, with brief comments from a companion (λέγ' αὐτό v. 2, Ἡράκλεις 5: the correct part-division first in Daléchamp's translation, long before Schweighaeuser) to enliven the narrative (cf. Men. *Dysk.* 407ff. narrating a dream, 97ff.). Such a dream would most obviously be interpreted as a portent of future success, but the presence of plums in the garland (v.5: an unusual component, but Ath. also cites Hipponax fr. 60 West directly before Alexis) may be both comic (reflecting the colour of the speaker's face) and sinister (cf. Artemidorus 1.77 οἱ δὲ (sc. στέφανοι) ἐκ τῶν πορφυρῶν καὶ θάνατον σημαίνουσιν). Symbolic dreams predicting future and/or describing past events unknown to the dreamer are a common feature of ancient theatre (future: Eur. (?) *Rhesus* 780ff., Plaut. *Curc.* 253ff., *Merc.* 225ff. with P. J. Enk's edition, vol. 1 (Leiden 1932) 7ff.), *Rud.* 593ff. with F. Marx's edition (Leipzig 1928) *ad loc.*; past: A. *Pers.* 176ff. (L. Belloni, Milan 1988), *Choeph.* 526ff. (and A. F. Garvie, Oxford 1986, xix ff.), S. *El.* 410ff. (G. Kaibel, Leipzig 1896), Men. *Dysk.* 407ff. (Handley, Sandbach); both: Eur. *Hec.* 68ff., *IT* 42ff., cf. Herodas 8). None of these dramatic dreams involves athletic games, but Heliodorus 4.16 describes a Tyrian's dream (which is fulfilled) of winning a victory at wrestling in the Pythian games, and Artemidorus 4.52 has Zoilus dreaming about his sons competing at Olympia and being garlanded on their ankles, which implied that they would die before the contest. The subject has a massive literature; see e.g. Leo, *Plaut. Forsch.*[2] 162ff., Hopfner in *RE* s.v. *Traumdeutung* 2233.51ff., E. R. Dodds, *The Greeks and the Irrational* (Berkeley 1951) 102ff., G. Devereux, *Dreams in Greek Tragedy* (Oxford 1976), A. G. Katsouris, *Dodoni* 7 (1978) 43ff., A. H. M. Kessels, *Studies on the Dream in Greek Literature* (Utrecht 1978), R. G. A. van Lieshout, *Greeks on Dreams* (Utrecht 1980), in addition to the commentaries on the passages identified above. Cf. also comm. on 108(103K).

1 καὶ μὴν ἐνύπνιον οἴομαί <γ'> ἑορακέναι: almost certainly what Alexis wrote here, but (i) ἐνύπνιον is a conjecture first made by Schweighaeuser (*Animadv.* 1.509), correcting C's ἐν ὕπνοις (E typically, cf. Kaibel's edition of Ath. 1.xv, abbreviates to ἐνυ^πν', which more probably represents ἐν ὕπνοις with rough breathing carelessly omitted than an intended ἐνύπνιον); (ii) γ' after οἴομαι (removing CE's hiatus and enlivening the idiom,

COMMENTARY

cf. Denniston, *GP* 120) was first suggested by an unnamed *vir doctissimus* in Schweighaeuser, *Animadv.* 8.402 (? = de la Porte Dutheil: see introduction to Schweighaeuser's edition, 1.cxvii); (iii) ἑορακέναι is Elmsley's correction (in his unsigned review of Schweig., *Ed. Rev.* 3 (1803) 188) of C's ἑωρακέναι (which will not scan) and E's ὡρακ- (which will); similarly at 275(273K).1 ἑόρακας Elmsley for unmetrical ἑώρακας CE and Eustath.

ἑόρακα, the earlier Attic orthography for the perfect active of ὁρῶ, is (apart from one instance of ἑώρακεν confirmed by metre at Men. fr. 208.2) universal in Attic comedy, where the omicron is frequently preserved in papyri and demanded by the metre (cf. Σ^R Ar. *Plut.* 1045 διὰ τοῦ ο μικροῦ τὸ ἑορακέναι, διὰ τὸ μέτρον, contradicting Theognostus *Can.* 2.150.23ff. Cramer), although medieval MSS tend to corrupt to the forms presented by CE here. Cf. T. Tyrwhitt in R. Dawes, *Miscellanea Critica²* (Oxford 1781) 454f., LSJ s.v. ὁράω, K.B. 2.504, Veitch, *Greek Verbs⁴* 495.

ἐνύπνιον ... ἑορακέναι: the standard expression (e.g. Ar. *Vesp.* 25, Pl. *Crit.* 44a, *Polit.* 290b, Men. *Dysk.* 407, 409, *Pk.* 359f., fr. 620.10, Hippocr. *Intern.* 48, *M. sacr.* 15 Littré = 18 Jones, cf. P. Leigh Fermor, *Mani* (London 1958) 68), with ἐνύπνιον the prosaic equivalent to ὄνειρος (cf. Kessels 190ff.).

2 λέγ' αὐτό: as Heniochus 4.6, cf. Ar. *Eccl.* 1014.

3–5 Realistic features in Alexis' dream narrative include (i) the crowning of the victor in the stadium, e.g. the inscription (*IG* xiv.1102 = *IGR* i.153 = *IAG* 79 Moretti, 16) describing Asclepiades, victor in the παγκράτιον at Olympia in AD 181, ἐν αὐτοῖς τοῖς σκάμμασιν στεφανωθείς, cf. Pind. *Pyth.* 1.32, Xen. *Hell.* 3.2.21, Philostratus jun. *Imag.* 2.6.1, M. Blech, *Studien zum Kranz bei den Griechen* (Berlin 1982) 109ff.; and (ii) description of one's competitors as ἀνταγωνισταί (the correct term, appearing seven times in lines 23–32 of the Asclepiades inscription; also e.g. Xen. *Cyr.* 3.3.36, Pl. *Leg.* 8.830a).

γυμνὸς προσελθών: thereafter in the Epit. MSS a lacuna of ¾ metron (— ∪ ⊔) at the end of the verse. Supplements suggested include <ὡς ἐμέ> Casaubon (cf. *Animadv.* 101), <παγκάλῳ> Herwerden (*Coll. Crit.* 132) and most ingeniously γυμνῷ (*sic*! γυμνὸν would have been better) προσελθών <γυμνὸς ὤν> Kaibel. Victorious competitors were still γυμνοί when crowned (as e.g. the youth on a red-figure psykter in New York, Metr. Mus. 10.218.18, figured in Blech 216), but not the officials performing the ceremony (Ἑλλανοδίκαι), who were dressed in crimson (*Et. Mag.* 331.20, cf. Oehler in *RE* s.v. *Hellanodikai* 155.45ff., Blech 110f.).

5 στεφάνῳ κυλιστῷ (Casaubon's correction of -στῆ CE): see comm. on 4.2.

κοκκυμήλων: as the remarks of Epit. here make clear, κοκκύμηλα are commonly 'plums' (from cultivars of *Prunus domestica domestica*), but sometimes also 'damsons' (properly Δαμασκηνά, from *P. domestica insititia*);

766

both subspecies seem to have originated in western Asia but to have been known in Greece at least from archaic times (Archilochus fr. 241, Hipponax fr. 60, both West); cf. Steier in *RE* s.v. *Pflaume* 1456.22ff., F. Lasserre, *Les Épodes d'Archiloque* (Paris 1950) 245.

6 πεπόνων: as often in comedy, the key word that makes the joke is delayed to the very end. The mention of plums (an unusual component in garlands: comm. on vv. 1–2) was intended to puzzle the audience, until the added πεπόνων made all clear. The plums were ripe: not green but purple, i.e. the colour of the speaker's face (and presumably mask). A symbolic interpretation of the dream, concentrating on the colour of the plums (see above, comm. on vv. 1–2), might well have followed. Dobree's proposal to delete πεπόνων here (as a scribal error induced by κοκκυμήλων ... πεπόνων in the following fr. 275(273K).3, *Adv.* 2.297) shows a failure to grasp the comic point.

275 (273K)

Meineke 3.504 (III), Kock 2.398, Edmonds 2.508, Kassel–Austin 2.177. If this fr., with its amusing comparison of a bruiser's battered forehead to three items of food, derives from the same play as 274(272K), q.v., it might form part of (1) an interpretation of the dream there described (but not addressed to the main speaker of 274(272K), if ἔχει is correct at 275(273K).4) later in the play; or (2) an earlier description of him presumably before he first appeared on stage. Eustath. 211.16ff. cites vv. 1 (to πώποτε) and 3 (from κοκκυμήλων) to the end.

1 ἑόρακας <ἤδη> πώποτ': Kassel–Austin print Dobree's supplement (*Adv.* 2.297), extending his list of comic parallels for the collocation of ἤδη and πώποτε (legitimately Ar. *Nub.* 370, 1061, Eupolis 226(214K), 329(306K), Plato com. 102(95K), Amphis 27.4, Men. fr. 63). Although this idea is better than Desrousseaux' ἀσκῷ (cf. D. Eichholz, *CR* 7 (1957) 218), no supplementation is needed, since both fr. and question could have begun in the second half of the first metron; for the phrasing cf. e.g. Ar. *Ach.* 86, *Nub.* 1061, *Thesm.* 32, 33, Nausicrates 2(3K). On ἑόρακας, see comm. on 274(272K).1.

1–2 ἐσκευασμένον ἤνυστρον: Casaubon's transposition (cf. *Animadv.* 101) of CE's ἤν. ἐσκ. is plausible but not certain in a passage transmitted corruptly and with one certain lacuna (v.3). ἤνυστρον (the correct Attic orthography: Phryn. *Ecl.* p. 72.22 Fischer) is the bovine fourth stomach (abomasum, reed, rennet-bag; Arist. *HA* 2.17, 507^{b}9ff., cf. *PA* 3.14, 674^{b}16), although on undisclosed grounds (? following some alternative nomenclature in the food trade) Pollux 2.204 and Hesych. s.v. identify it as the first (paunch, rumen). It was (and is still) generally a food of the poor (Ar. *Equ.* 356 and Neil *ad loc.*, 1179, Mnesimachus 4.14, Dioxippus

COMMENTARY

1.2, Hor. *Sat.* 2.5.40f., *Epist.* 1.15.34f.; André, *Alimentation* 151); although we do not know how Alexis imagined it to be 'prepared' (ἐσκευασμένον, cf. frs. 50(49K).2, 138(133K).1, 153(149K).6), its similarity to a fighter's forehead is likely to have lain less in its colour (reed tripe is normally white, other tripes range from white to pale grey or fawn; there is no evidence that reed was ever dyed red or purple by the liquids in which, or the ingredients with which, it was cooked) than in the 'repellent slithery' (E. David, *Italian Food* (London 1954), recipe for *Florentine Tripe*) and slightly ridged surface.

σπλῆν' ὀπτὸν ὠνθυλευμένον: with Elmsley's emendation (*Ed. Rev.* 3 (1803) 188) of CE's μεμονθυλευμένον, restoring both metre and the normal Attic form (Phryn. *Ecl.* p. 96.38f. Fischer μονθυλεύω· ... ἔστι δυσχερές· ἀπόρριπτε οὖν καὶ τοῦτο; in MSS of comedy forms in ὀνθ- correctly appear at Alexis 38(37K).1, where see comm., 84.6, Athenion 1.28, Diphilus 90.2, 118(119K), cf. ὀνθύλευσις Men. fr. 397.7, but at com. adesp. fr. 289b.15 Austin a 3rd-century papyrus gives ἐμονθύλευσα metrically correct; cf. Pollux 6.60, Σ Ar. *Equ.* 343). Alexis' 'roasted stuffed spleen' (stuffed also at Antiphanes 221(222).8, cf. Ar. fr. 520(506K).6) would resemble a haggis with meat etc. cooked inside a (?) sheep's spleen, whose purplish colour was intended to remind the audience of a prizefighter's complexion just as strongly as the basket of ripe plums mentioned next in v. 3, where Meineke excellently compares Arist. *Rhet.* 3.11 Kassel, 1413ᵃ19ff. εἰσὶ δὲ καὶ <αἱ> (suppl. H. Richards, *Aristotelica* (London 1915) 112) εὐδοκιμοῦσαι ὑπερβολαὶ μεταφοραί, οἷον εἰς ὑπωπιασμένον "ᾠήθητε δ' αὐτὸν εἶναι συκαμίνων κάλαθον"· ἐρυθρὸν γάρ τι τὸ ὑπώπιον, ἀλλὰ τὸ πολὺ σφόδρα.

3 κοκκυμήλων ... πεπόνων: see comm. on 274(272).5–6. After πεπόνων in CE and Eustath. there is a lacuna at verse-end of ¾ metron, supplemented *ex gratia* with <νὴ Δία> as a second speaker's interjection by ? Dobree (so claims Kock, but I cannot trace it in *Adv.* or elsewhere) or <ἐμπλέων> (Desrousseaux).

4 τοιοῦτ': so Meineke for CE and Eustath.'s -οῦτον, which would provide a divided resolution; confusion between the two forms of nom. and acc. neut. sing. is common in MSS (e.g. -τον for -το Antiphanes 55(52K).15, Men. *Dysk.* 489, cf. Philemon 94(90K).6; -το for -τον Men. fr. 635.2, possibly *Dysk.* 76; divided transmission Eur. *Andr.* 173, Ar. *Ran.* 1399). See also comm. on 246(244K).6 and K.B. 1.606f.

μέτωπον: so CE; Eustath.'s πρόσωπον carelessly substitutes a commoner near-synonym, exactly as Crates 362 F 11 Jacoby in Ath. 9.367a when citing Ar. *Equ.* 631, and MSS AB at [Xen.] *Cyneg.* 4.8, cf. Diggle's apparatus at Eur. *Cycl.* 227.

INCERTARUM FABULARUM FRAGMENTA

276 (274K)

Meineke 3.505 (IV), Kock 2.398, Edmonds 2.508, Kassel–Austin 2.178. In
a discussion about wines from the Greek islands, Epit. of Ath. 1.28e cites
frs. 276–8 (274–6K) all together, identifying the author (φησὶν Ἄλεξις) at
the end of 276 (cf. in Epit. e.g. 1.28e where φησὶ Κλέαρχος similarly
follows the citation immediately preceding Alexis 276(274K), 33c, 2.39b,
40c, 52e, 71f; cf. also comm. on Alexis 2.9; note that here C has a dicolon, E
a space, after Ἄλεξις), omitting any ascription either before or after 277,
but prefixing ὁ αὐτός to 278. Alexis' authorship of 277, however, is
confirmed later in Epit. (2.47d, on νωγαλεύματα) when most of the fr. is
again cited, but now with Alexis' name attached. At 1.28e, presumably
between the end of 276 and the beginning of 277, Epit.'s original linking
words (most probably καὶ πάλιν, cf. 1.21f, 29d, 2.57d, 63a, 70f, 71a, or just
πάλιν, cf. 2.49e–f linking Alexis 274(272K) and 275(273K), 2.66d) were
carelessly omitted. It is far less likely that 276 and 277 join together as one
continuous fr., with the author's name interposed (like that of Antiphanes
at Ath. 2.45a, fr. 240(246K)), since 276 finishes at line-end, while 277
begins at the fourth element of the first metron; on the other hand 276
could possibly have followed (as another speaker's comment) directly after
277 (so Kock; see comm. on 276.1), although the situation and identity of
the speakers in these two frs. is unknown.

1–2 Lesbian wine, produced primarily from grapes grown in the north
and west of the island around Methymna and Eresus (Galen, *Meth. Med.*
12.4, *Comp. Medic.* 1.8 = 10. 832, 13.405 Kühn), was generally considered
(with Chian and Thasian) one of the three finest in ancient Greece
(e.g. Antiphanes 172(174K).3, Clearchus 5, Ephippus 28, Eubulus
121(124K).2; Call. epigr. 68 Gow–Page, Archestratus 190.19 *SH* οὐδὲν . . .
ἁπλῶς πρὸς Λ. οἶνον making the same point as Alexis, Donatus on Ter.
Andr. 226 *a Lesbo insula, quae ferax est suauissimi candidissimique uini*, Longus
4.10 ἀνθοσμίας οἶνος Λέσβιος, ποθῆναι κάλλιστος οἶνος, Pliny *HN* 14.73;
cf. Hermesianax 7.55 Powell), fragrant (Clem. Alex. *Paed.* 2.2.30, Galen
locc. citt.), not astringent and easily digested (Ath. 1.32f, 2.45e), but *sponte
suae naturae mare sapit* (Pliny, *loc. cit.*; cf. Galen *Meth. Med.* 12.4); it didn't go
to the head (Philodemus 21 Gow–Page = *Anth. Pal.* 11.34.7) or cause a
hangover (Philyllius 23(24K)). Cf. Bürchner in *RE* s.v. *Lesbos* 2118.59ff.,
R. Nisbet and M. Hubbard (Oxford 1970) on Hor. *Od.* 1.17.21, Hunter on
Eubulus 121(124K).2, B. G. Clinkenbeard, *Hesperia* 54 (1982) 254ff.
(useful but less accurate over the comic frs.), M. Lambert-Gócs, *The Wines
of Greece* (London and Boston 1990) 30.

1 Λεσβίου <δὲ> πώματος: Porson's supplement and correction of CE's
Λεσβίου πόματος (*Adv.* 218, cf. his comm. on Eur. *Hec.* 392). πώματος is
clearly right (πῶμα is Attic, see LSJ s.v.; πόμα Ionic and *Koine*). The

infiltration of a *Koine* form into the MSS is helped here by the common scribal confusion between O and Ω, cf. S. *Phil.* 715, Eur. *Hipp.* 209, 227, *Hec.* 392, *Bacch.* 279, *Cycl.* 123, 139, Epinicus 1.10 with πῶμα A, πόμα Epit. at Ath. 10.432b), but <δὲ> is an uncertain addition; <γὰρ> is equally likely (? a response to 277(275K), if that fr. immediately preceded 276(274K)); Desrousseaux' <τοῦ> can be discounted (Λεσβίου is not predicative).

2 ἡδίων πιεῖν: the adjective (like ἀρίστους at 236(234K).4) governs an infinitive which limits the meaning to one particular action; to the examples cited by LSJ s.v. ἡδύς may be added e.g. Eur. fr. 358.2–3 οὐκ ἔστ' ἔρως ... ἡδίων ἐρᾶν, Hdt. 4.53 Βορυσθένης πίνεσθαι ἥδιστός ἐστι, Xen. *Mem.* 3.8.8, *Vect.* 3.1, cf. Goodwin, *MT* §763 pp. 306f., K.G. 2.13f., Headlam–Knox on Herodas 4.94f.

277 (275K)

Meineke 3.505 (v), Kock 2.398, Edmonds 2.508, Kassel–Austin 2.178; cf. W. G. Arnott, *PCPS* 196 (1970) 8f. and introduction to Ὀπώρα, where the argument for assigning this fr. (albeit tentatively) to that play is set out. Speaker and person described are both unknown.[1]

1 Θασίοις οἰναρίοις καὶ Λεσβίοις: Scaliger's correction (in Canter, Paris MS. 54ᵛ, long before Porson, *Adv.* 50) restores metre convincingly at the beginning of the fr. (Θ. καὶ Λ. οἰναρίοις CE at Ath. 1.28e, Θ. οἰναρίοις B / οἰνάρ(οις) C / οἰνάροις E at 2.47d), good examples of Epit.'s tendency to omit words and adjust unmetrically to *simplex ordo*). On the wines of Thasos, see comm. on 232(230K).4; on those of Lesbos, comm. on 276(274K).1; on their juxtaposition here, introduction to Ὀπώρα.

2 ὑποβρέχει: here probably transitive and metaphorical, 'wets (i.e. tipples away) the rest of the day', cf. the literal use 'moisten' in an anonymous epigram, *Anth. Pal.* 11.3; but just possibly intransitive, 'becomes tipsy' over the stated period, cf. *Suda* s.v. ὑπέβρεχον· οἴνῳ ἐμεθύσκοντο. Much commoner is the use of the perf. pass. participle ὑποβεβρεγμένος = 'tipsy' (e.g. in the formula for introducing the chorus at Men. *Dysk.* 231, *Epitr.* 170; cf. also Alciphron 4.13.12, Heliod. 1.15, 3.10. Longus 2.32, Lucian *Dial. Deor.* 3.2 Macleod, *Gall.* 8, *Icarom.* 27, *Philopatr.* 4, cf. *Asin.* 51, Pollux 6.25). Cf. Durham, *Vocabulary* 98f.

3 νωγαλίζει: 'nibbles'. The nouns (neut. pl.) νώγαλα (Antiphanes

---

[1] If the fr. does derive from Alexis' Ὀπώρα, the person described could be Opora herself or possibly the male drinker addressed in fr. 169(164K). The quaffer of Lesbian and Thasian wines in Aelian *Epist.* 8 is Opora herself, but the imagined penners of these letters do not always coincide with the original dramatic characters whose words are being quoted or paraphrased by Aelian (see introduction to Ὀπώρα).

66(65K), Ephippus 24.1 = ἡδέα βρώματα, Ath. 2.47d) and νωγαλεύματα (Araros 8.1) are used particularly of nuts and fruits with pips or stones (dates, grapes, pomegranates) eaten with wine, so here the verb νωγαλίζει presumably refers to such desserts; but at Eubulus 14(15K).7 the food eaten is a black pudding (cf. Hunter *ad loc.*). The nouns are virtually synonymous with τραγήματα (see comm. on 168(163K).2), the verb with τρώγω.

C's grossly aberrant text at the end of this fr. in Ath. 2.47d (ὑποβρέχων ... ἐνωγαλίζει) probably arose from a copyist misreading an abbreviated form of καί (ϗ) as epsilon, and then adjusting ὑποβρέχει to the participle. Desrousseaux' theory (app. crit. to his edition of Ath.) that C's reading may point to a correct ἐννωγαλίζει here is ingenious but wrong: this compound is not recorded, and the conjecture accounts less satisfactorily for the paradosis.

278 (276K)

Meineke 3.505 (VI), Kock 2.398, Edmonds 2.508, Kassel–Austin 2.178; cf. H. Weil, *Revue critique d'histoire et de littérature* 20 (1885) 276, Leo, *Plaut. Forsch.*[2] 123 n. 1. Further praise of Lesbian wine, in which the speaker (cf. frs. 130(125K), 131(126K)) at a party imagines himself proposing legislation (cf. Weil, Leo) in favour of those who import this wine (presumably to Athens, although in our ignorance of the fr.'s source and context we cannot know whether its scene was Athens) and against its export from Lesbos to any other city.

1–4 At several points the fr. (cited by Epit., Ath. 1.28e) is inaccurately transmitted, but the needed corrections are easy (fewer than the text of Kassel–Austin indicates) and better discussed together:

(a) 1 ἡδύς <γ'> (add. Porson, *Adv.* 50) ὁ Βρόμιος: cf. Alexis 232(230K).3, where a speaker says ἡδύ γε τὸ πῶμα in response to an offer of wine; on the use of the particle to emphasise a predicative adjective in such expressions with ellipse of ἐστι see Denniston, *GP* 127.

(b) 1–2 CE has τὴν ἀτέλειαν Λεσβίου | ποιῶν; Kaibel conjectured χρῆν ἀτ. Λεσβίοις | ποιεῖν (Λεσβίοις already Casaubon, margin and *Animadv.* 66), which Kassel–Austin print; Dobree conjectured Βρόμιός ἐστ'· ἀτέλειαν, *Adv* 2.295. τὴν ἀτέλειαν Λεσβίου, however, can be defended. Although in epigraphical formulas (and here Alexis' speaker apes their language) ἀτέλεια often appears without the article, instances with the article can be found (e.g. *IG* ii[2].33.7, 37.16, 245.10, probably 1172.32f.: end 5th/beginning 4th centuries) in a sense appropriate here ('the usual exemption awarded in such circumstances', A. S. Henry, *Honours and Privileges in Athenian Decrees* (Hildesheim 1983) 243). And although genitives attached to ἀτέλεια most frequently identify the tax or duty from which a beneficiary is being exempted, they do occasionally also indicate the objects exempted from tax (e.g. *OGIS* 10.13 ἀτέλειαν ὧν ἂν εἰσάγῃ ἢ ἐξάγῃ: see below). If CE's ποιῶν is replaced by ποῶ (on the orthography, comm. on 16.2; ? with CE's -ῶν here, like E's -ων at v. 4, explained as assimilation to the endings of the words immediately following), we have perfect sense: 'I create the (usual) tax exemption for Lesbian (wine) for those importing the wine here.'

On ἀτέλεια in Athens see especially Oehler in *RE* s.v., 1911.6ff., G. Busolt, *Griechische Staatskunde* I (Munich 1920) 300f., P. J. Rhodes, comm. on [Arist.] *Ath. Pol.* (Oxford 1981) 58.2, Henry, *op. cit.* 241ff., 255f. n.41. It was specifically granted by Athens to a 2nd-century Messenian for exports (*IG* ii².986.80), by Ephesus to Nicagoras of Rhodes in the 3rd century for imports and exports (*OGIS loc. cit.*). Cf. also comm. on 77.2.

(c) 3 ὃς δ᾽ ... ληφθῇ unmetrically CE, corrected to ὃς ... ληφθῇ δ᾽ by Porson, cf. comm. on 4.1.

(d) 4 ἐγγράφω C correctly (parallel to ποῶ v. 4), -ων E.

1 ὁ Βρόμιος: comm. on frs. 225(223K).2, 232(230K).3.

3-4 The speaker's proposal is prompted by (and phrased analogously to) current laws forbidding or restricting exports of certain goods: wine from islands such as Thasos (where any transgressor ἔκτην κατ᾽ ἀμφορέα ἕκα[στον ὀφελέτω ἱρὴν τῇ Ἀθ]ηναίῃ τῇ πολιόχῳ, J. Pouilloux, *Recherches sur l'histoire et les cultes de Thasos* I (Paris 1954) 37ff., inscr. 7.5f.; cf. e.g. *IG* xii.8.263.5 = 412/11 BC, 264.15 early 4th century); corn from Athens and the Piraeus (e.g. [Dem.] 34.37, 35.50, Lycurgus 27, [Arist.] *Ath. Pol.* 51.4 and Rhodes *ad loc.*, J. Hasebroek, *Trade and Politics in Ancient Greece* (tr. L. M. Fraser and D. C. Macgregor, London 1933) 112, 149). Wine in fact was a major Athenian export (cf. Hasebroek 60, 92ff.; H. Michell, *The Economics of Ancient Greece* (Cambridge 1940) 293f.). Confiscation of goods in Athens was normally an accessory punishment (added to death, enslavement or banishment) for serious crimes against the gods (e.g. sacrilege, cf. Xen. *Hell.* 1.7.22, Pollux 10.97), the state and the person; ἱεράν here, with its implication that all the proceeds from the confiscation (not merely the customary tithe: e.g. Ar. *Equ.* 300ff. καί σε φαίνω τοῖς πρυτάνεσιν, ἀδεκατεύτους τῶν θεῶν ἱερὰς ἔχοντα κοιλίας) should be forfeit to Athena, stresses the enormity of the imagined crime; cf. especially J. H. Lipsius, *Das attische Recht und Rechtsverfahren* (Leipzig 1915) 299ff., Thalheim in *RE* s.v. Δημιόπρατα 2854.10ff., G. Busolt, *Griechische Staatskunde* 2³ (Munich 1926) 848 n. 2, 1211, A. M. Andreades, *A History of Greek Public Finance* (tr. C. N. Brown, Cambridge Mass. 1933) 276, A. R. W. Harrison, *The Law of Athens* 2 (Oxford 1971) 178f., 212ff., Rhodes on *Ath. Pol.* 52.1.

3 ἀποστέλλων: replacing ἐξάγων, the normal term for 'exporting', perhaps because ἐξάγουσιν had already been used in the previous verse.

4 κᾶν κύαθον: cf. e.g. Ar. *Plut.* 126 ἐὰν ἀποβλέψῃς σὺ κᾶν μικρὸν χρόνον, Dem. 2.14 ὅποι τις ἄν ... προσθῇ κᾶν μικρὰν δύναμιν. The addition of a second ἄν in crasis with καί (= 'even') becomes an idiomatic formula, cf. K.G. 1.244f. On κύαθον cf. comm. on 2.5–7 and p. 326 n. 1 on Κράτεια.

ἐγγράφω: either 'I inscribe on stone' or 'I enter in the (appropriate) register'; for the application to a prescribed punishment cf. e.g. the ἔγκλημα inserted in Dem. 37.22 αἴτιος ἐμοὶ γενόμενος ἐγγραφῆναι τὸ διπλοῦν τῷ δημοσίῳ; Lipsius, *op. cit.* on vv. 3–4, 944f.

279 (277K)

Meineke 3.511 (XIII), Kock 2.399, Edmonds 2.510, Kassel–Austin 2.179. The fr., cited by Epit. of Ath. 1.23c (vv.1–4 in C, only v. 1 in E) to illustrate the use of κατακεῖσθαι (v.1), remains a puzzle in our ignorance of its speaker and context (see on v. 1).

1 ὡς ἔστι: so CE (unobjectionable: conjectures such as Hirschig's ὅση 'ὅτι, *Annot.* 16, are not needed, cf. Kock), but is ὡς (1) the conjunction introducing indirect speech, governed by a verb in the unquoted previous context, or (2) exclamatory, as often in comedy (cf. frs. 29, 70.1 and comm.)? If the former, the speaker could be either supporting the expressed view (another character's? a contemporary doctor's?) that reclining on the couch before dinner was a mistake, or criticising it; if δήπουθεν in v. 2 is ironic (cf. Denniston, *GP* 267ff.), the second is the more likely possibility, and the speaker might then be a parasite who prefers to arrive well in advance of a meal to which he has been invited (cf. Eubulus 117(119K), Men. fr. 304, Alciphron 3.1; Ribbeck, *Kolax* 35).

συμφορά: 'a disaster' (cf. 224(222K).4), commonly in this meaning as predicate in nom. and acc. singular, e.g. Eur. *Alc.* 802, *Med.* 54, *Hcld.* 607, trag. adesp. fr. 376, Ar. *Eccl.* 488, Antiphanes 2.1, Xen. *Ages.* 7.4, 11.9, Pl. *Phd.* 84e, Isaeus 1.6.

2 ὕπνος: so B; C's corruption δεῖπνος conflates the correct ending with remembered δείπνου from the line before. ὕπνος λαμβάνει + acc. is a standard phrase, e.g. S. *Phil.* 766f., Eur. *Ion* 315, Hippocr. *Epid.* 5.2, Arist. *Probl.* 916ᵇ1, 917ᵃ18; with ἐπιλαμβάνει Hippocr. *Epid.* 5.28, ὑπολαμβάνει *Aer.* 22.

οὐδέν': Musurus' correction of C's οὐδὲν.

3 οὔθ' ἄν: Jacobs' correction (*Addit.* 14; ἄν already *Spic.* 3) of BC's οὐδ' ἄν, a common error (cf. comm. on Alexis 160(156).4–5).

μάθοιμεν: so B; C's μάθοιμ' probably comes from misreading the common contraction for μὲν/-μεν as μ'.

4 For the idiom Blaydes, *Adv.* 2.169 compares Ar. *Pax* 669 ὁ νοῦς γὰρ ἡμῶν ἦν τότ' ἐν τοῖς σκύτεσιν, and Kassel–Austin Ter. *Eun.* 816 *iamdudum*

COMMENTARY

animus est in patinis; cf. also Damocharis in *Anth. Pal.* 7.206.5 σὺ μὲν ἐν πέρδιξιν ἔχεις νόον, Plaut. *Men.* 584, *Pers.* 709, *Pseud.* 34.

280 (278K)

Meineke 3.512 (xv), Kock 2.399, Edmonds 2.510, Kassel–Austin 2.179; cf. A. M. Desrousseaux's edition of Ath. 1–2 (Paris 1956) p. 91 n. 1. The fr. is an εἰκών which emphasises one difference between old men and old wine, and so contradicts Alexis 46(45K), q.v., as Epit. of Ath. 2.36f (followed by Eustath. 1449.23) points out when citing the two frs. together. Desrousseaux' suggestion that this fr. could have been a response by another speaker to fr.46(45K) in the same scene of Δημήτριος is attractive but uncertain. Grotius' assignment of v. 4 to a second speaker (*Exc.* 595) is best ignored.

1 The unmetrical opening in Epit. and Eustath. results from a slight lacuna. One of οὐδέν <γ'> ἔοικ' Musurus, <ἄρ'> S. A. Naber, *Mnemosyne* 8 (1880) 265 (comparing Ar. *Vesp.* 20), <δ'> (omitted by haplography in the sequence δενδεοι) or <προσ>έοικε both Blaydes, *Adv.* 2.169, is likely to be right.

2 The transmitted text ὁ μὲν γὰρ ἀπογηράσκων has a syllable too many. Porson deleted μέν (*Notae in Aristophanem* (Cambridge 1820, edited by Dobree) 34, comm. on *Nub.* 893), Meineke γάρ (4.423, cf. 5.92; followed by Kassel–Austin); P. Elmsley conjectured ἀπογηρὰς (*Ed. Rev.* 3 (1803) 187), Kock μέν γ'. However, if the history of γηράσκω/γηράω and their compounds is considered, another solution emerges. γηράσκω is the older form (Hom. *Il.* 2.663, *Od.* 4.210, etc., poetry and drama until the end of the 5th century); it was invariable in Ionic and – until the early 4th century – Attic, and remained common thereafter in Attic and *Koine* Greek. γηράω appears first in Xen. *Cyr.* 4.1.15 (γηρᾶν CDF: ? a back-formation based on the misinterpretation of ἐγήρα in Hom. *Il.* 7.148, 17.197, *Od.* 14.67 as imperfect from γηράω rather than as aorist from γήραμι, cf. the participle γήρας at *Il.* 17.197; LSJ s.v., H. W. Smyth, *The Sounds and Inflections of the Greek dialects: Ionic* (Oxford 1894) 493, V. Schmidt, *Sprachliche Untersuchungen zu Herondas* (Berlin 1968) 15ff., C. R. Barton, *Glotta* 60 (1982) 31ff.), then e.g. Pl. *Crit.* 112c (καταγηρῶντες), Isaeus 2.22 (καταγηρᾶν A), Arist. *EN* 5.8, 1135ᵇ2, Men. fr. 416.14 (against γηράσκω fr. 408) and *Koine*. Both forms were used (e.g γηράσκω x 5 Xen., x 2 Plato, x 3 Arist.) with no apparent distinction of meaning (*pace* Ammon. s.v. γῆρας 121 Nickau) until the end of the 3rd century AD, but in Byzantine Greek γηράσκω dominated, γηράω disappeared. Could Alexis have written ὁ μὲν γὰρ ἀπογηρῶν, and a Byzantine scribe have substituted the form in -άσκων with which he was more familiar?

γίγνεται: see comm. on 37(36K).7.

3 Cf. Alexis' words in 46(45K) and 284(282K). The use of σπουδάζ-ομεν with accusative (as direct object of the thing enthusiastically desired) is much less common than the intransitive use with infinitive or περί and accusative, but in Attic cf. e.g. Eur. *Her.* 507 τό ... αὐτοῦ, Xen. *Symp.* 8.17 τὰ ἑαυτοῦ ἡδέα, Pl. *Phd.* 114e τὰς ... ἡδονάς.

4 ὁ μὲν δάκνει γάρ: an old man may 'bite' one's head off, like Knemon (Men. *Dysk.* 467) and Demeas (*Sam.* 384, 387, with Chr. Dedoussi's comm. *ad loc.* (Athens 1965), v. 169 in her edition); cf. Ar. *Thesm.* 530.

ποιεῖ: comm. on 16.2.

(278b K)

See fr. 53(54 + 278b K) above.

281 (279K)

Meineke 3.513 (xviii), Kock 2.399, Edmonds 2.510, Kassel–Austin 2.180; cf. T. Hemsterhuys on Ath. 2.63e in Dindorf's edition (1.145, see also *praef.* xviii). This fr., cited by Epit. of Ath. 2.63e–f to illustrate τὴν τῶν βολβῶν πρὸς τὰ ἀφροδίσια δύναμιν, lists seven aphrodisiacs and implies that the speaker has used or will use them in prosecuting an affair with a *hetaira*. Hemsterhuys' suggestion that the fr. *fortasse* came from Alexis' Παμφίλη is unprovable but attractive; the title figure in that play may have been a *hetaira* (but see introduction to Παμφίλη), and its one assigned fr. (175(170K)) is a lover's confession that he is carrying a load of six named aphrodisiacs, two of them (κήρυκες, βολβοί) mentioned also in 281(279K).

1–2 The list of aphrodisiacs:

(i) πίννας (so Kassel–Austin with C: πίννες E, πίνας more correctly B): fan mussels, see comm. on 84.1. They are not elsewhere named as an aphrodisiac, although they belong to τὸ τῶν μαλακίων γένος which is said by Mnesitheus in Ath. 8.357c–d to stimulate sexual desire (cf. Dohm, *Mageiros* 157). Artemidorus 2.14 (131.1 Pack) claims that a dream about πῖνα ... καὶ ὁ λεγόμενος πινοφύλαξ κάρκινος is a good omen for marriage because of those creatures' goodwill and fellowship.

(ii) κάραβον: see introduction to 57(56K). Not elsewhere recorded as a sexual stimulant, but Philyllius 12(13K) links it with fan mussels in a list of comestibles, Ar. fr. 164(158K) with βολβοί and ἀκροκώλια.

(iii) βολβούς: often mentioned as an aphrodisiac, see comm. on 167(162K).13.

(iv) κοχλίας: Heraclides of Tarentum (in Ath. 2.64a) states that βολβὸς καὶ κοχλίας καὶ ᾠὸν καὶ τὰ ὅμοια δοκεῖ σπέρματος εἶναι ποιητικά; at Alciphron 4.13.16 ἐπιχώριοι κοχλίαι and κήρυκες are foods at a sexual orgy, at Theocr. 14.17 (cf. Gow *ad loc.*) and Petronius 130.8 they are singled out as aphrodisiacs along with βολβοί/*bulbi*. Galen's remark κοχλίας ... ὁσημέραι πάντες Ἕλληνες ἐσθίουσιν (6.669 Kühn) was probably true also in Alexis' time (cf. e.g. Philyllius 26(27K), Poliochus 2.5f., but see Thompson, *Fishes* 129); various species of edible snail are still common throughout Greece and the Aegean, including *Helix aperta*, *H. aspersa* (Common Garden Snail), *H. cincta*, *H. lucorum* and even (*pace* Thompson) *H. pomatia* (Roman or Edible Snail), and shells are frequently found in the kitchen waste of classical sites (but not always correctly identified by the archaeologists: cf. A. E. Ellis, *British Snails* (Oxford 1926) 232ff. and pl. XI); see also O. Keller, *Die antike Tierwelt* 2 (Leipzig 1913) 522ff., Thompson, *Fishes* 129ff., Gossen and Steier in *RE* s.v. *Schnecke* 589.44ff., V. Pfleger and J. Chatfield, *A Guide to the Snails of Britain and Europe* (tr. M. Schierlová, Oxford 1988) 168ff., M. Mylonas in A. Solem and A. C. van Bruggen (edd.), *World-wide Snails* (Leiden 1984) 249ff.

(v) κήρυκας: aphrodisiacs at Alexis 175(170K).2 (see comm.) and apparently also Alciphron 4.13.16.

(vi) ᾠά: named as sexual stimulants by Heraclides of Tarentum (cited above, iv) and (with *bulbi*) Ovid *Ars Am.* 2.421ff., and eaten at the sexual orgy in Alciphron 4.13.10.

(vii) ἀκροκώλια: cf. fr. 123(118K).2. Normally pigs' trotters (e.g. Archippus 10(11K).1f., Strattis 5(4K), Antiphanes 124(126K).1f.), but Galen 14.241 identifies τὸν ἀστράγαλον τῆς βοός as an aphrodisiac.

3–4 The text of the Epit. MSS here is probably less corrupt than has sometimes been alleged, but there are three areas of dispute.

(a) τοσαῦτα CE: Meineke's conjecture τοιαῦτα is tempting at first sight (confusion between the two words is common in MSS: e.g. Eur. *Alc.* 551, Phoenix of Colophon 2.21 p. 233 Powell, p. 248 Knox, possibly Phoenicides 3.4; cf. comm. on 140(135K).11), but the length of Alexis' list here itself justifies τοσαῦτα as it does at fr 223(220–1K).11 also.

(b) Thereafter the MSS write τούτων ἄν τις εὕρη (*sic* C after correction, E: εὕροι C before corr., apparently B); with the minor adjustment to εὕρη we have the protasis of an indefinite or open future condition ('if anybody (? ever) finds other remedies more serviceable than these'), and must then assume that either the fr. breaks off without quoting the apodosis[1] or an interruption prevented the speaker from appending it. The reading εὕροι is best interpreted as an adjustment by a scribe who

---

[1] In frs. where both A and Epit. MSS survive, Epit. often omits the closing line(s) (e.g. Alexis frs. 70, 115(110K), 150(156K), 160(156K), 204(200K), 223(220–1K), 247(245K)), and even A sometimes breaks off a citation in mid-sentence (e.g. Alexis 89(86K), 193(188K), 194(189K); see comm. *ad locc.*).

failed to understand the incomplete syntax; scholars who print it are then normally obliged to change τις to τίς (first Korais in his edition of Xenocrates, Περὶ τῆς ἀπὸ τῶν ἐνύδρων τροφῆς (Paris 1814) 134) and to place ἄν unidiomatically before the interrogative pronoun; Herwerden, *Obs. Crit.* 79f. and Jacobs, *Addit.* 50f. attempt to wriggle out of this difficulty by suggesting τίς ἂν <ἂν>εύροι and τοσαῦτ' ἀτονούντων ἄν τις εὔροι respectively, both unconvincing.

(c) CE open v. 4 with ἐρῶντι ἑταίρας, which produces in addition to a split anapaest either hiatus or elision of the final iota of a dative singular, both unparalleled in Attic drama (cf. *CQ* 7 (1957) 198). Jacobs' conjecture ἐρῶν ἑταίρας (*Animadversiones in epigrammata anthologiae graecae* 2.1 (Leipzig 1799) 234; cf. Meineke's refinement ἐρῶν γ') removes all the difficulties; the MSS corruption could have arisen from a scribe's wish for an apparently simpler syntax with a dative depending on χρησιμώτερα rather than a nominative agreeing with τις.

For the idea and the idiom, cf. Chariton 6.3.7, where the king, in love with Callirhoe, tells Artaxates σκεπτέον οὖν πῶς ἂν ἀπαλλαγείην τῆς ἀνίας. ζήτει πανταχόθεν εἴ τι ἄρα δυνατόν ἐστιν εὑρεῖν φάρμακον, and Artaxates replies φάρμακον ... ἕτερον Ἔρωτος οὐδέν ἐστι, πλὴν αὐτὸς ὁ ἐρώμενος.

282 (280K)

Meineke 3.522 (XLVII), Kock 2.400, Edmonds 2.510, Kassel–Austin 2.180. A father addresses his son about their mutual obligations, presumably after some favour has been requested, granted or turned down; one contextual possibility is a scene where a father and son agree over the latter's marriage (cf. e.g. Men. *Dysk.* 784ff., *Sam.* 694ff., Ter. *Ad.* 637ff.). The idea expressed here that the greatest favour (ἔρανος: cf. fr. 145(141K).5 and comm., 222(219).16) any father can bestow on a son is to bring him up properly, thus repaying his own father's services to himself, was clearly an article of popular faith in 5th/4th-century Athens: e.g. Eur. *Suppl.* 361ff. τοῖς τεκοῦσι γὰρ | δύστηνος ὅστις μὴ ἀντιδουλεύει τέκνων, | κάλλιστον ἔρανον· δοὺς γὰρ ἀντιλάζυται | παίδων παρ' αὐτοῦ τοιάδ' ἂν τοκεῦσι δῷ; Dem. Phal. citing Thales (1.64.5 Diels–Kranz) in Stob. *Anth.* 3.1.172 (cf. Diog. Laert. 1.37) οἵους ἂν ἐράνους ἐνέγκῃς τοῖς γονεῦσιν, τούτους αὐτὸς ἐν τῷ γήρᾳ παρὰ τῶν τέκνων προσδέχου; cf. the related uses of the ἔρανος metaphor in Dicaeogenes fr. 4 αὐτὸς τραφεὶς δὲ τῶν φυτευσάντων ὕπο | καλῶς, τὸν αὐτὸν ἔρανον αὐτοῖσιν νέμεις, [Dem.] 10.40 δεῖ γάρ, οἶμαι, τοῖς γονεῦσι τὸν ὡρισμένον ἐξ ἀμφοτέρων ἔρανον, καὶ παρὰ τῆς φύσεως καὶ παρὰ τοῦ νόμου, δικαίως φέρειν καὶ ἑκόνθ' ὑποτελεῖν. A similar point to that of Alexis, but without use of ἔρανος, is made by Isaeus 8.32 κελεύει γὰρ (ὁ νόμος) τρέφειν τοὺς γονέας ... ἐκεῖνοι γὰρ ἀρχὴ τοῦ γένους εἰσὶ καὶ τὰ ἐκείνων παραδίδοται τοῖς ἐγγόνοις· διόπερ ἀνάγκη τρέφειν αὐτούς ἐστι. The idea complements the general Athenian belief that parents must be honoured (e.g. Eur. frs. 852, 853, cf. 1064) and looked after when old (so Isaeus 8.32 above, Eur. *Med.* 1032ff., Lysias 13.45, but Athenian law imposed a condition, see Alexis 305(304K) and comm.); cf. Headlam–Knox on Herodas 3.29, A. R. W. Harrison, *The Law of Athens* 1 (Oxford 1968) 77f., W. K. Lacey, *The Family in Ancient Greece* (London 1968) 116ff., Dover, *GPM* 218f., 273ff., cf. 302f.

2 θρέψαι: as in Isaeus 8.32 above, Plut. *Solon* 22; cf. the use of compounds in γηροβοσκ-, γηροτροφ- (e.g. Alexis 305(304K). 313(312K) and comm.); cf. also C. Moussy, *Recherches sur* ΤΡΕΦΩ *et les verbes grecs signifiant "nourrir"* (Paris 1969) 37ff.

2–3 ὃν γὰρ αὐτὸς ἀπέλαβον παρὰ τοῦ πατρός, δεῖ τοῦτον ἀποδοῦναί με σοί: for ἀποδίδωμι τὸν ἔρανον e.g. [Dem.] 59.8 (cf. 53.11), Plut. *Mor.* 631d, Dio Chrys. *Or.* 44.5, and although I can trace no other example of ἀπολαμβάνω τὸν ἔρανον (but ἀντιλαμβάνω Arist. *Pol.* 7.13, 1332ᵇ40), ἀποδίδωμι and ἀπολαμβάνω are commonly contrasted (e.g. Eur. *Hel.* 912f., 954ff., Ar. *Nub.* 1274ff., 1283ff., Alexis 212(209K), Philemon 76(74K).3, Men. *Epitr.* 277ff., Pl. *Resp.* 1.332b, *Legg.* 12.964a, Isaeus fr. 129 Thalheim; *TGL* s.v. ἀπολαμβάνω 1511D). For ἀπολαμβάνω + παρά with gen. cf. e.g. Thuc. 5.30.2, 39.2, Xen. *Symp.* 3.3, Pl. *Legg.* 12.964a, Aeschines 2.117, 3.27, 58, 168. Kock's conjecture παρέλαβον (the legal term for *hereditate accipere*: to replace ἀπέλ.) is not needed; everyday idiom does not always use technical terminology.

283 (281K)

Meineke 3.520 (xxxvii), Kock 2.400, Edmonds 2.510, Kassel–Austin 2.181; cf. Gil 343f., G. Vogt-Spira, *Die Dramaturgie des Zufalls* (Munich 1992) 56 and n. 141. This reflection on the impermanence of wealth (see introduction to fr. 267(265K)), cited by Stob. 4.32a.8, is similar in both concept and wording to the opening of Sostratos' speech to his father in Men. *Dysk.* 797ff. περὶ χρημάτων λαλεῖς, ἀβεβαίου πράγματος. | εἰ μὲν γὰρ οἶσθα ταῦτα παραμενοῦντά σοι | εἰς πάντα τὸν χρόνον, φύλαττε μηδενὶ | τούτων (Jacques, Steffen: τούτου B, ἄλλῳ MSS of Stob. 3.14.16) μεταδιδούς: see especially Handley's comm. *ad loc.* Here one passage (but which?) might have been influenced by the other, but the subject matter is too hackneyed for the likelihood of conscious dependence of either or both on an earlier source such as Eur. *El.* 941ff.

2 ἀβεβαιότατον correctly SM, -ότερον A. *Incredibile dictu est quam saepe hae formae inter se mutent locum et apud caeteros scriptores et in Comicis* (Cobet, *NL* 119); cf. e.g. (i) superlative corrupted to comparative: Ar. *Plut.* 67 βέλτιστον VAMU rightly, βέλτιον R (see C. von Holzinger's comm.

INCERTARUM FABULARUM FRAGMENTA

(*SB Vienna* 218.3, 1940) *ad loc.*), Diphilus 32(33K).4 πλουσιώτατος
Meineke rightly, -ώτερος MSS; (ii) comp. corrupted to superl., Alexis
247(245K).4 and comm., Ar. *Nub.* 507, Men. *Dysk.* 128 πρακτικώτατον
corrected to -ώτερον B, Pl. *Gorg.* 489d. Cf. also Richards, *AO* 229, 313f.

3 τὰ δ' ἄλλ' ἐπιεικῶς ... παραμένει: 'the others (sc. ἀγαθά) last pretty
well'. ἐπιεικῶς is treated unsatisfactorily by lexica; in colloquial Attic of
Alexis' time ἐπιεικῶς is a limiting adverb of imprecise meaning, most
commonly qualifying an adjective (e.g Men. *Asp.* 24f. ἐπ. πολλαῖς |
μάχαις 'quite a lot of battles', 35, *Dysk.* 8 and Handley *ad loc.*, *Epitr.* 423,
Xen. *Hell.* 5.4.50, *Oec.* 2.1, Pl. *Gorg.* 485e and Dodds, *Dem.* 19.340),
slightly less often a verb as here (= 'fairly well/to a reasonable degree', e.g.
Isoc. 10.5, Pl. *Symp.* 201a, *Resp.* 4.431e, Isaeus 6.18). Understatement,
however, is at times a feature of such colloquialisms, with the result that
'quite a lot/fairly well' can grade into 'very many/very well' (e.g. Pl. *Gorg.*
449d, Xen. *Oec.* 11.25 in the expression πάνυ ἐπιεικῶς).

παραμένει: 'the *mot juste* by sense and usage' (Handley, *loc. cit.* in
introduction to fr. 283(281K)); of money also at Men. *Dysk.* 798 (cited
above), Timocles 9.1f.

284 (282K)

Meineke 3.512 (XIV), Kock 2.400, Edmonds 2.512, Kassel–Austin 2.181;
cf. Kann, *De iteratis* 6of., Hunter, comm. on Eubulus 122(125K). Epit. of
Ath. 1.25f (cf. Eustath. 1422.47) cites Eubulus 122(125K) with the
comment τὸ αὐτὸ δὲ καὶ "Αλεξις σχεδὸν ἀπαραλλάκτως τοῦ σφόδρα
μόνου κειμένου ἀντὶ τοῦ ἀεί. Neither fr. is assigned to a play-title, and it is
impossible to know (*pace* Kann, identifying Alexis as the plagiarist) who
copied whom. Theft of other dramatists' lines was common in later Greek
comedy (examples include Antiphanes 212(331K)/Alexis 243(241K): cf.
introduction to "Υπνος, Antiphanes 89/Epicrates 5, Antiphanes 59(58K)/
Eriphus 2, Eubulus 109(110K).1f./Ephippus 15.3f., Philemon 114(123K)/
Strato 1.1–4 (cf. the bibliography in Austin, *CGFP* p. 205, Kassel–Austin
7.617), Mnesimachus 4.34–6/Men. *Kol.* fr. 7 (and Gomme–Sandbach,
Comm. ad loc.): the order of names in this list is not intended to indicate
priority); it was not surprising given the huge output of many comic poets,
especially at a time when 'the idea was steadily developing that verses
were not in any way the "private property" of the original poet' (Hunter,
comm. on Eubulus 67.4). Cf. also, in addition to Kann, E. Stemplinger,
Das Plagiat in der griechischen Literatur (Leipzig and Berlin 1912) 128ff.,
A. C. Pearson, comm. on S. fr. 565, D. L. Page, *Actors' Interpolations in
Greek Tragedy* (Oxford 1934) 18f., R. Renehan, *Studies in Greek Texts*
(Göttingen 1976) 105f.

Speaker and dramatic situation in this Alexis fr. are uncertain; it could have been a comment on an older man's defeat by one younger (? his son) in his pursuit of a *hetaira*. The comment links two comic clichés: the εἰκών comparing or contrasting man and wine (Alexis 46(45), 280(278) and comm.), and the fondness of *hetairai* for wine. Ath. 10.440e registers the stereotyped male view of female bibulousness (ὅτι ... φίλοινον τὸ τῶν γυναικῶν γένος κοινόν; cf. J. Henderson, comm. on Ar. *Lys.* 113f. and cf. H. G. Oeri, *Der Typ der komischen Alten in der griechischen Komödie* (Basle 1948) 13ff., 39ff.), and *hetairai* could be singled out because attendance at symposia was an essential feature of their profession (e.g. Machon 174ff., 252ff., 258ff., 376ff., 441ff., Lucian, *Dial. Meretr.* 1.1, 3.1, 6.3, 9.5, 11.1, 12.1, 13.4, 15.1, Ath. 13.583e, 584b, 585de, Alciphron 4.8.2, 13.6, 9–19, 14.3–4, 7–8; cf. Alexis 60(59K), 225(223K) and comm.; S. B. Pomeroy, *Goddesses, Whores, Wives and Slaves* (London edition 1976) 143).

1 ἄτοπόν γε: so Eustath., ἄτοπον δὲ CE (but ἄτοπόν C!). γε is particularly common in such reflections (cf. Hunter, comm. on Eubulus 122(125K).1), especially when stressing as here a predicative adjective at sentence beginning (with ellipse of ἐστί), cf. Denniston, *GP* 127; even so Epit.'s δέ is easily defended as introducing a counter to a different view. On ἄτοπον, 'odd/strange', see *Phoenix* 18 (1964) 119ff. and n. 38.

εὐδοκιμεῖν σφόδρα: cf. Xen. *Cyr.* 1.6.38, H. Thesleff, *Studies on Intensification in Early and Classical Greek* (Helsinki 1954) 92ff. It is difficult to see how Alexis' σφόδρα here is less appropriate than Eubulus' ἀεί (so Kassel–Austin on Eubulus 122(125K)).

1–2 The pre-eminence of old wine is maintained also in frs. 46(45K), 280(278K). Pliny *HN* 14.79 implies that Greek wines required seven years to achieve *uestustatem mediam*; ten-year old wine was drunk from the πίθος in Hom. *Od.* 3.391, four-year old in Theoc. 7.147 and Gow *ad loc.*, cf. 14.16.

285 (283 + 284K)

Meineke 3.512 (XVI + XVII), Kock 2.400, Edmonds 2.512, Kassel–Austin 2.181. Epit. of Ath. 2.39b cites frs. 283K and 284K without implying that they came together in one scene; they are better treated as separate frs.

(a) (283K)

A type of drinker's slogan in comedy, paralleled e.g. at Ar. *Equ.* 91–4, Diphilus 86, Baton 2.9, Ion fr. 26.12 West, and countered by Ar. *Vesp.* 79f. χρηστῶν ... ἀνδρῶν ἡ νόσος, cf. *Equ.* 88. The presence of parodic language in v. 2 (see *ad loc.*) induced Nauck (Nauck² 843) and Snell (*TrGF* 2.26), in my view wrongly, to identify all three vv. as trag. adesp. fr. 21.

INCERTARUM FABULARUM FRAGMENTA

1 φιλοπότης: see Kassel–Austin on Eupolis 221(208).1.

ἐστὶν ἄνθρωπος: Hertel's transposition (402: thirty-seven years before Casaubon, margin of his text of Ath. and *Animadv.* 81) of MSS's unmetrical ἄνθ. ἐστὶ, but Nauck's ἄνθρωπος οὐδεὶς φ. ἐ. κ. (*MGR* 5 (1884–8) 236, cf. *TGF*[2] 843) is equally plausible.

2 ὁ γὰρ διμάτωρ Βρόμιος: the Doric form διμάτωρ suggests parody of Greek lyric or tragedy (so Meineke; cf. O. Ribbeck, *Zeitschrift für das Gymnasialwesen* 17 (1863) 327f., F. Selvers, *De mediae comoediae sermone* (Diss. Münster 1909) 28). On Βρόμιος see comm. on 232(230K).3. Dionysus is διμάτωρ because 'Semele was pregnant by Zeus with D., and as she perished she gave birth prematurely; Zeus took the foetus and sewed it in his own thigh, and thence after the full time D. was born by a second birth' (Barrett on Eur. *Hipp.* 559ff.; the story is told by Eur. *Bacch.* 88–100, see Dodds *ad loc.*); cf. also Voigt in Roscher s.v. *Dionysos* 1045, Kern in *RE* s.v. 1014.64ff., 1034.63ff., Preller–Robert, *GM* 1[4] 660ff., L. R. Farnell, *The Cults of the Greek States* 5 (Oxford 1909) 110, J. G. Frazer on [Apollodorus] myth. 3.4.3 n. 1. The god is διμήτωρ/-μάτωρ also at *Orph. H.* 50.1, 52.9, Diod. Sic. 3.62.5, 4.4.5, δίγονος Eur. *Hipp.* 560, *Anth. Pal.* 9.524.5 (anon.), δισσοτόκος Nonnus 1.4, *bimater* Ovid *Met.* 4.12, Caesius Bassus poet. 2.3 Baehrens, Hyginus, *Fab.* 167.

3 πονηροῖς: perispomenon here in CE with the meaning 'wicked', but MSS in general do not always uphold the accentual distinction (that πόνηρος = 'wretched', -ός = 'wicked') alleged by some ancient grammarians: see introduction to and p. 558 n. 2 on Πονήρα.

ἀπαιδεύτῳ βίῳ: similarly ἀπ. τύχη (? Τύχη) Apollodorus Car. 5.26, τροφήν Pl. *Tim.* 86e, ὁρμαῖς Plut. *Mor.* 37e.

(b) (284K)

Another slogan, apparently upholding wine's ability to make people wordsmiths, cf. Horace *Epist.* 1.5.19 *fecundi calices quem non fecere disertum?*; on a similar plane e.g. Cratinus (if really Cratinus: see Kassel–Austin *ad loc.*) 203(199K), Amphis 41 ἐνῆν ... κἂν οἴνῳ λόγος, cf. Ar. *Equ.* 349, Phrynichus com. 74(69K), Ion fr.5.4f. Page, the proverb οἶνος ...καὶ ἀλαθέα with Gow on Theoc. 29.1, Maccius in *Anth. Pal.* 9.503 = 10 Gow–Page vv. 5f. εὔγλωσσον ... οἶνον, and in opposition e.g. Eubulus 133(135K) (the supremacy of water), Ar. *Vesp.* 87 (drunkenness not creative), Theogn. 479ff., 503ff. (wine destroys control of the tongue).

Epit. MSS so mangle the text here (with corruption and/or omissions) that it is impossible to restore Alexis' original wording, although Meineke's suggestions (καὶ φιλολόγους πάντας ποιεῖ (but see comm. on 16.2) τοὺς πλείονα | πίνοντας αὐτόν and οἶνος φ. | πάντας ποιεῖ τοὺς πλείον αὐτὸν — ∪ ⊔ | πίνοντας) take account of CE's malpractices elsewhere.

φιλολόγους: E's corruption to φιλοπότους (*sic*: not -πότας, as stated by Kaibel, Kassel–Austin) is clearly inspired by the surrounding subject matter. In Alexis' time φιλόλογος meant 'fond of talk, dispute, dialectic, in a wide and rather vague or ironical sense' (R. Pfeiffer, *History of Classical Scholarship* 1 (Oxford 1968) 159), cf. Phryn., *Ecl.* 372 p. 101.69ff. Fischer φιλόλογος ὁ φιλῶν λόγους καὶ σπουδάζων περὶ παιδείαν; the word's ambivalence is best exemplified in Plato, e.g. the playful *Theaet.* 161a φιλόλογός γ' εἶ ἀτεχνῶς ... ὅτι μ' οἴει λόγων τινὰ εἶναι θύλακον, cf. *Phdr.* 236e, *Lach.* 188c, e, *Leg.* 1.641e.

286 (285K)

Meineke 3.514 (xx), Kock 2.400, Edmonds 2.512, Kassel–Austin 2.182. In citing the fr. to show how Decelean ὄξος was admired (ἐθαυμάζετο), Ath. 2.67e (Epit.) here (as elsewhere: see introduction to Ἀγωνίς and comm. on frs. 89(86K).2 and 147(143)) misinterprets Alexis' point, as Meineke first noted (*apertum est (Decelicum acetum) in vilissimis fuisse habitum*: see on v. 3). Speaker, situation and play are unrecorded, but in the second act of Plaut. *Most.* Callidamates lies fast asleep after a drunken orgy when Theopropides, the father of his host, unexpectedly returns from abroad, and after being roused by Tranio he complains at being hurried out of the way (cf. 383f.). It is a remote possibility that the fr. derives from Καλάσιρις, if fr. 104(99) involves the same speaker in the same scene.

1 κοτύλας τέτταρας: P. Brunck's transposition (in Schweighaeuser, cf. *Animadv.* 1.453 '*Brunck in ora sui exempli*') of CE's τέττ. κοτ. is plausible but hardly certain in the mangled state of the transmission at vv. 1–2. On κοτύλη see comm. on 223.17(221.11K).

2 ἀναγκάσας με †μεστὰς αὑτοῦ† σπάσαι: so CE[1] unmetrically and one element short; Kassel–Austin are possibly right to obelise, but plausible corrections have been suggested: (i) Brunck's transposition (*loc. cit.*) μεστὰς ἔμ' has won much support (? dittography through misreading μεστὰς as με μεσ-) and is clearly superior to Kaibel's μ' ἑστῶτα (hardly consistent with the movement implied in ἄγεις v. 3, while μεστάς receives some support from parallel phraseology in fr. 5). (ii) Brunck's αὐτόθεν provides the needed extra syllable, but is awkward in its context (whether translated 'from the spot' or 'immediately': LSJ s.v.), and Kock's αὑτίτου (*Rh. Mus.* 30 (1875) 401) remains the most attractive suggestion (with αὑτοῦ a telescopic error, cf. comm. on frs. 31(30K).6, 148(144K).1 and my paper in Flores 368ff.), despite a dispute over its meaning (here LSJ

---

[1] Desrousseaux claims that E first wrote μυστὰς and then corrected it to με-, but my photograph of E appears not to confirm this.

s.v. is inaccurate and incomplete) that goes back to Hellenistic scholarship on medical writing such as Hippocr. *Morb.* 3.14 οἶνον αὐτίτην: (i) Galen *Gloss. Hippocr.* 19.87 Kühn τὸν ἐκ τοῦ ἐνεστῶτος ἔτους (on the textual transmission see A. A. Nikitas, "Ἔρευναι ἐπὶ τῶν πηγῶν τοῦ Λεξικοῦ τοῦ Ἐρωτιανοῦ (Athens 1971) 144ff.), (ii) Erotian *Voc. Hippocr.* δ 23 τὸν ἀπαράχυτον citing Polyzelus 1, cf. Ath. 1.31e, (iii) Pollux 6.18 αὐτίτης δ' οἶνος ὁ ἐπιχώριος, *Glossary of Useful Terms* 1.165 Bachmann = *Suda* s.v. αὐτίτην· τὸν αὐθιγενῆ οἶνον, citing Teleclides 10(9K); cf. A. A. Nikitas, *Würz. Jahrb.* 4 (1978) 87f.

3 σπάσαι: comm. on 5.1.

ὄξους Δεκελεικοῦ: so first Musurus; C has -λεικ- in the lemma (but its abbreviation omits the penultimate syllable in the text), E has -λικ- both times. ειк- is supported by most MSS of some 4th-century Attic authors (e.g. Isoc. 8.37, Dem. 57.18; cf. Schwyzer 1.380, but Threatte 1.304 notes a tendency to drop the iota in Δεκελειεύς after 350), and by a number of parallel formations (e.g. βοεικός, (ἡμι)δαρεικός, Κεραμεικός, ὀρεικός, Ap. Dysc. *Adv.* 166.29, Herodian 2.416 Lentz). ὄξος is strictly wine-vinegar, i.e. impure acetic acid made from wine under the action of the fungus *Mycoderma aceti* and characterised by a strong sour taste, commonly mentioned in recipes and medical treatments (e.g. Ar. *Av.* 534, *Plut.* 720, Alexis 129(124K).5, 7, 193(188K).4, Diphilus 42(43K).35f., Archestratus 153.6, 167.4, 192.8 *SH*; cf. Xen. *Anab.* 2.3.14), but it was also applied as an abusive colloquialism to bad wine of sour taste (e.g. Eupolis 355(326K), Eubulus 65.3f., 136(138K).3 and Alexis here). If Decelean wine was generally reckoned of inferior quality, its failure to be mentioned elsewhere (e.g. in Pliny's lists of Greek wines, *HN* 14.73ff., 96f.) is readily explained. Cf. Hermann–Blümner, *Privatalter-thümer* 232 and n. 1.

287 (286K)

Meineke 3.515 (xxII), Kock 2.401, Edmonds 2.512, Kassel–Austin 2.182. Epit. of Ath. 1.34c appears to be citing the fr. (BC: omitted by E) to illustrate the use of boiled cabbage in preventing intoxication, but Alexis' speaker is suggesting it to remedy a hangover.

1 ὑπέπινες: the literal meaning is 'you had a little drink' (e.g. Anacreon 11b Page μηκέτ'... | Σκυθικὴν πόσιν παρ' οἴνῳ | μελετῶμεν, ἀλλὰ ... | ὑποπίνοντες, Pl. *Resp.* 2.372d μετρίως ὑποπίνοντες, cf. Plut. *Mor.* 615e), but the word was often used colloquially as a euphemism for drinking a great deal (especially in comedy, e.g. here and Nicophon 19(11K); cf. Pl. *Lysis* 223b, probably Xen. *Anab.* 7.3.29 about himself, Antiatticist 115.10 = Phot., *Suda* s.v. ὑποπίνειν· μεθύσκεσθαι).

κραιπαλᾶς: here 'you're suffering from a hangover (κραιπάλη, see comm.

COMMENTARY

on fr. 9.8)', as in fr. 257(255K).1f. εἰ τοῦ μεθύσκεσθαι πρότερον τὸ κραιπαλᾶν | παρεγίγγνεθ᾽ ἡμῖν, Pl. *Symp.* 176d κραιπαλῶντα ἔτι ἐκ τῆς προτεραίας; elsewhere often more loosely 'to suffer from the effects of drink', especially from a spectator's viewpoint, e.g. Polyb. 15.33.2, Epicurus fr. 114 Usener, Plut. *Demosthenes* 7. Cf. *Suda* s.v. κραιπάλη· ὁ ἐκ πολλῆς οἰνώσεως παλμός· καὶ κραιπαλῶν<τα>· ἀντὶ τοῦ ἐκ μέθης ἀτακτοῦντα, μεθύοντα.

2 κατανύστασον: 'take a nap', intransitive only here in literary use (but cf. Pollux 2.67 καὶ συνελεῖν βλέφαρον τὸ κατανυστάσαι; 3.122f. may imply a metaphorical extension, 'to be idle').

2–3 Boiled cabbage as remedy against a hangover: comm. on 15.7.

288 (287K)

Meineke 3.522 (XLIII), Kock 2.401, Edmonds 2.512, Kassel–Austin 2.182; cf. G. Vogt-Spira, *Dramaturgie des Zufalls* (Munich 1992) 41. The speaker (cf. Men. fr. 630) considers the present misfortune(s) of some character (cf. e.g. Chaireas or Pataikos, Men. *Asp.* 284ff., *Pk.* 802ff.) undeserved. The irrationality of fortune is a commonplace of comedy (e.g. in Men. ἄνοια fr. 632, ἀσυλλόγιστον fr. 295, δυσπαρακολούθητον fr. 424, οὐδὲν κατὰ λόγον fr. 464, πλάνον *Kith.* fr. 8, *insanam* Pacuvius, inc. fab. fr. 14.1 Ribbeck[2]; cf. μανιώδη in Alexis 222(219K).9 with comm.) and contemporary belief (e.g. Arist. *Magn. Mor.* 2.8, 1207[a]1ff. ἡ δέ γε τύχη ... ἀτάκτως καὶ ὡς ἔτυχεν ... οὗ δὲ πλείστη τύχη, ἐνταῦθ᾽ ἐλάχιστος νοῦς); cf. Dover, *GPM* 140f., Vogt-Spira 37ff.

1 ἔχουσιν ... φρένας: 'are sensible/reasonable', a common expression when applied to people (e.g. S. *OR* 1511, Ar. *Ran.* 534 ἀνδρὸς ... νοῦν ἔχοντος καὶ φρένας, Polyb. 7.12.2, Plut. *Mor.* 116b, Rutherford, *NP*9f.); here even in the plural τύχαι are personalised (like the deified Τύχη), cf. e.g. Eur. *Med.* 198, *Her.* 1396, *Tro.* 1204, ? Ar. *Nub.* 1264).

2 οὐδεὶς γὰρ <ἂν> τοιοῦτος ἠτύχει ποτέ: 'for otherwise nobody like him would ever be unfortunate'. Gesner's supplement (in his first edition of Stobaeus, Zurich 1543) restores the common idiom (e.g. Pl. *Symp.* 222c οὐ γὰρ ἄν ποτε οὕτω κομψῶς ... ἐνεχείρεις, *Crat.* 413e, Hdt. 1.124; Jebb's edition of S. *OR*, pp. 220f., Denniston, *GP* 62f.).

289 (288K)

Meineke 3.521 (XLII), Kock 2.401, Edmonds 2.512, Kassel–Austin 2.183. A further warning (? to a man who is prosperous or greedy) about the instability of fortune, cf. especially fr. 267(265K) and comm. In a brief couplet the speaker makes the same point as Gorgias' rambling sermon at Men. *Dysk.* 271ff. (where note τοῖς τ᾽ εὐτυχοῦσιν 272, τῷ μὲν εὐτυχοῦντι

274, βελτίον' εἶναι μερίδα προσδοκᾶν τινα 283, μήτ' αὐτὸς ... | πίστευε
τούτῳ 284f., and cf. *Philologus* 125 (1981) 215ff.).

290 (289K)

Meineke 3.520 (xxxviii), Kock 2.401, Edmonds 2.514, Kassel–Austin
2.183; cf. F. Lasserre, *La Figure d'Éros dans la poésie grecque* (Paris 1946) 111.
When citing this fr., the MSS of Stob. *Anth.* 4.20.1.13 add to its end the first
five vv. of Men. fr. 198 before prefixing the lemma Μενάνδρου Θησαυρῷ (so
M: ἐν Θ. S, θησαυρῶν A) to the remaining four vv. of that fr.; T. Tyrwhitt
(in T. Gaisford's edition of Stob., vol. 2 (Oxford 1822) 457 note b) first
corrected the error.

1 The conceit of Ἔρως as instructor is a commonplace going back at
least to Euripides (fr. 663, cf. Alexis 236(234K).5 and comm., Anaxandrides 62(61K), Nicias 566 *SH*; Lasserre 111). Although παιδαγωγός was
strictly the slave who accompanied a free boy to and from his lessons, the
term came to be both coupled with διδάσκαλος (e.g. Plut. *Alexander* 5,
Aratus 48, *Galba* 17) and even sometimes loosely substituted for it, as here
(cf. also e.g. Pl. *Resp.* 3.390e, Phoenix the παιδαγωγός of Achilles; Hesych.
s.v., Donatus on Ter. *Andr.* 54), partly because παιδαγωγοὶ were often
educated men (e.g. Daos in Men. *Asp.*) who acted as tutors of good
manners and morality to their charges (e.g Lydus in Plaut. *Bacch.* 132ff.,
148, 152ff., 163ff., 419ff., Plut. *Mor.* 439f, 452d).

2 οὐδεὶς ἄλλος ἐπιμελέστερος: with ἄλλος redundant, in an idiom that
goes back to Homer (*Il.* 15.569 οὔτις σεῖο νεώτερος ἄλλος, 22.106 μή ποτέ
τις εἴπῃσι κακώτερος ἄλλος; cf. e.g. Isaeus 2.11 εὕρισκεν οὖν οὐδένα ἄλλον
οἰκειότερον ὄνθ' ἡμῶν ἑαυτῷ; Jebb on S. *OR* 7, Page on Eur. *Med.* 945, LSJ
s.v. ἄλλος ii.8).

291 (302K)

Meineke 3.521 (xxxix), Kock 2.403, Edmonds 2.516, Kassel–Austin
2.183. The female speaker (cf. Fraenkel, *EP* 177) who testifies to her own
shamelessness as typical of the sex is perhaps most likely to have been
either a *hetaira* or a mythical villainess like Anteia or Helen. Greek
literature is often misogynistic from the earliest times (e.g. Hom. *Od.*
11.424ff., 456, Hes. *Op.* 77ff., 375, *Theog.* 590/1ff. with West *ad loc.*), and
it is a notable feature of plays written by men for predominantly male
audiences that some of the harshest remarks are voiced by female
characters (e.g. Eur. *Med.* 263ff., 407ff., *Hipp.* 406f., *Andr.* 269ff., 353, *El.*
1035, Ar. *Lys.* 460, *Thesm.* 531f., cf. Plaut. *Aul.* 135ff.). On this dramatic
prejudice see especially P. Decharme, *Euripides and the Spirit of his Dramas*
(tr. J. Loeb, New York and London 1906) 93ff., Legrand, *NGC* 116ff.,

COMMENTARY

Fraenkel, *Kl. Beitr.* 1.511ff., Stockert on Plaut. *Aul.* 135ff. with bibliography; V. Ehrenberg, *The People of Aristophanes*[2] (Oxford 1951) 192ff., and S. B. Pomeroy, *Goddesses, Whores, Wives, and Slaves* (London 1976) 103ff. provide useful correctives. For allegations of shamelessness in particular cf. especially Ar. *Lys.* 369 οὐδὲν γὰρ ὧδε θρέμμ' ἀναιδές ἐστιν ὡς γυναῖκες, 456ff. ὦ ξύμμαχοι γυναῖκες ... οὐκ ἀναισχυντήσετε;, 1014f. οὐδέν ἐστι θηρίον γυναικὸς ἀμαχώτερον | ... οὐδ' ὧδ' ἀναιδὴς οὐδεμία πόρδαλις, *Thesm.* 531f. ἀλλ' οὐ γάρ ἐστι τῶν ἀναισχύντων φύσει γυναικῶν | οὐδὲν κάκιον εἰς ἅπαντα πλὴν ἄρ' εἰ γυναῖκες. Cf. also Alexis 150(146K), 264(262K), 340(339K).

1 οὐθέν: see comm. on fr. 15.5.

1–2 The paradosis here (SMA, Stob. 4.22.7.149) θηρίον εἰσορᾶν (εἰσ ὁρᾶν M, εἰσορᾶν superscript S) γυναικὸς has been explained in five different ways, three implausible.

(1) Meineke (*ed. min.* 765) identified the fr. as the remains of two trochaic tetrameters with θηρίον ending v. 1, εἰσορᾶν beginning v. 2, but then both tetrameters would lack the regular median diaeresis of later Greek comedy (invariable elsewhere in Alexis, regular in Menander, cf. F. Perusino, *RCCM* 4 (1962) 52f., Handley's edition of Men. *Dysk.*, pp. 59f., West, *Greek Metre* 92).

The other suggestions assume a fr. in iambic trimeters (cf. A. Nauck, *MGR* 6 (1894) 99): (2) Meineke (3.521) conjectured θρέμμ' ὁρᾶν at the end of v. 1, too far from the *ductus* but given some support by Ar. *Lys.* 369 above. (3) A badly written εἰσορᾶν | οὐκ ἔστ' ἀναισχυντότερον οὐθὲν θηρίον | γυναικὸς κ.τ.λ. in an earlier MS of Stob. could possibly account for the readings in SMA, but in such predications οὐκ ἔστι normally opens its clause.

More probably either εἰσορᾶν or θηρίον is an interpolation. (4) θηρίον was deleted first by Bailey *CGF* 33, anticipating Meineke 3.521), and (5) εἰσορᾶν by G. Morel 137 (? added from Stob. 4.22.7.143 = Eur. *Med.* 264, so Hense). There is little to choose between them, but a retained θηρίον not only enlivens the image but also matches better the stereotyped phraseology of comic misogyny, e.g. Ar. *Lys.* 1014f. above, Anaxilas 22.30f. οὐδὲ ἕν | ἔσθ' ἑταίρας ὅσα πέρ ἐστιν θηρί' ἐξωλέστερον, Men. fr. 422.2 κάκιστόν ἐστι θηρίον γυνή, cf. monost. 342 Jäkel, [Epicharmus] 90.1f. Austin (*CGFP* p. 82) [χείρω γυναῖ]κά φαμ' ἐγὼ τῶν θηρ[ίων] | [εἶμεν].

2 ἀπ' ἐμαυτῆς ... τεκμαίρομαι: a common construction with the verb (i) intransitive, as here (also e.g. Hippocr. *Aer.* 24, Xen. *Equ. Rat.* 1.14, Pl. *Resp.* 6.501b, *Theaet.* 206b), (ii) transitive (e.g. Ar. *Vesp.* 76, Xen. *Mem.* 3.5.6, Pl. *Resp.* 3.409a), (iii) introducing indirect speech (ὅτι e.g. Thuc. 4.123). Similarly with ἐκ + genitive, (i) intrans. (e.g. Pl. *Resp.* 2.368b, *Symp.* 204c), (ii) trans. (e.g. Hippocr. *Acut. (Spur.)* 19, Xen. *Mem.* 4.1.2), (iii) introducing indirect speech (ὅτι e.g. Xen. *Cyr.* 7.5.62, infinitive 8.1.28, Pl. *Resp.* 9.578c).

292 (290K)

Meineke 3.515 (xxiii), Kock 2.401, Edmonds 2.514, Kassel–Austin 2.184. The speaker describes an occasion when 'foreign wine' was drunk because that of Corinth was undrinkable (cf. J. B. Salmon, *Wealthy Corinth* (Oxford 1984) 126f., 136). Meineke may be right (cf. also Desrousseaux on the fr.'s citer Ath. 1.30f) to assume from this that the scene of the play to which the fr. belongs was Corinth (? perhaps Φιλοῦσα, see *ad loc.*), but Kock's warning that the fr.'s source could have been a narrative in which past experiences abroad were described (cf. e.g. Men. *Sam.* 98ff., Demeas on the Pontus, or Plaut. *Bacch.* 251ff., Chrysalus on Ephesus, in two plays where the scene was Athens) must be heeded.

1 οἶνος ξενικός: cf. comm. on 232(230K).5.

ὁ γὰρ **Κορίνθιος**: Kassel–Austin print Eustathius' conjecture (953.32ff.: in the Laurentian autograph) for Epit.'s transmitted ὁ γὰρ κορίνθια (E), τὸ γὰρ κορίνθια (C). This may be correct (ος and α are often very similar in these MSS), but Kaibel's alternative suggestion τὰ γὰρ Κορίνθια ('the things you get in Corinth') is even more attractive (the neuter plural puzzling scribes who expected a masculine singular agreeing with οἶνος and βασανισμός).

2 βασανισμός: literally the torture suffered by Athenian slaves when required to give evidence (A. R. W. Harrison, *The Law of Athens* 2 (Oxford 1971) 147ff.), but here contemporary slang for an experience considered by the speaker to be equally painful. In N.T. *Apoc.* 9.5 the word is applied to a scorpion's sting; comparable colloquialisms in Attic comedy would be ἀγχόνη (Ar. *Ach.* 125, something as bad as a noose) and possibly κύφων (Men. *Dysk.* 102 with Handley and Sandbach *ad loc.*, ? something as bad as a pillory), while in Latin Lucilius 1146 Marx has *uinum crucium*, explained by Paulus (epitome of Festus p. 53m) as *quod cruciat ... uinum insuaue* (cf. J. J. Scaliger, *In Sex. Pompei Festi libros de verborum significatione castigationes recognitae et auctae* (Paris 1576) p. lii).

293 (291K)

Meineke 3.515 (xxiv), Kock 2.402, Edmonds 2.514, Edmonds 2.184. The fr. is cited at Ath. 11.502b only by the Epit. MSS at a point where the relevant folio of the *Marcianus* is missing (cf. introduction to Ὑποβολιμαῖος); cf. also Harpocration s.v. φιλοτησία (φ 21 J. J. Keaney in his edition (Amsterdam 1991) p. 261). The occasion for the toast proposed by the fr.'s speaker is unknown.

COMMENTARY

1 **φιλοτησίαν**: see comm. on 59(58K).1, 202(198K).

2 The Epit. MSS here write ἰδίᾳ τε καὶ κοινῇ τὴν κύλικα προπίνομεν (with identifiable tachygraphs for -εν, cf. O. Lehmann, *Die tachygraphischen Abkürzungen der griechischen Handschriften* (Leipzig 1880) 58ff. and pl. 5; Kaibel's apparatus at Ath. 11.502b is both inaccurate and incomplete, cf. Peppink, *Observ.* 67), which is unmetrical (dactyl in 3rd/4th elements of 2nd metron, followed by anapaest split after first short) and ungrammatical (singular subject, plural verb). Editors of Ath. since Dindorf and of the comic fragments from Meineke to Kassel–Austin accept Jacobs' deletion of τὴν (*Spic.* 71) and Schweighaeuser's conjecture προπίομαι (cf. *Animadv.* 6.301), but neither proposal is satisfactory. (1) ἰδίᾳ τε καὶ κοινῇ (here 'individually and all together') normally implies action by more than one person (e.g. καὶ ἰ. καὶ κ. with plural subject, [Arist.] *Ath. Pol.* 40.2; καὶ κ. καὶ ἰ. with plural, Xen. *Hell.* 1.2.10, *Mem.* 2.1.12, ~ Pl. *Resp.* 1.333d; καὶ ἰ. καὶ δημοσίᾳ with plural, Thuc. 3.45, Pl. *Apol.* 30b; καὶ κ. πᾶσι καὶ χωρίς Arist. *Pol.* 3.4.3 1278ᵇ23). (2) K.G. 1.627ff. lists the cases where a definite article can be omitted with a demonstrative pronoun, and this is not one of them (cf. Gomme–Sandbach, *Comm.* on Men. *Dysk.* 568, correcting Handley). It is impossible to know what Alexis originally wrote here; could perhaps τὴν κύλικα be deleted as a gloss explaining an original <τὴν> φιλοτησίαν (for the substantival use of φιλοτησία, see comm. on fr. 59(58K).1), and προπίνομεν be retained with ἐγώ (v.1), then interpreted as part only of a plural subject expressed or implied in the lost context?

294 (292K)

Meineke 3.522 (XLVI), Kock 2.402, Edmonds 2.514, Kassel–Austin 2.184. A comment presumably on a character's (? the speaker's) mental collapse after some grievous event or news. Cf. also fr. 298(296K), Antiphanes 287(295K), Men. *Asp.* 336ff., Philemon 106.2f., monost. 602, 440 = Eur. fr. 1071, S. fr. 602 Nauck² = 663 Pearson, Radt. In Men. *Asp.* 305ff. Chairestratos describes such a breakdown with the words Δᾶε παῖ, κακῶς ἔχω· | μελαγχολῶ τοῖς πράγμασιν· μὰ τοὺς θεούς | οὐκ εἴμ' ἐν ἐμαυτοῦ, μαίνομαι δ' ἀκαρὴς πάνυ· | ὁ καλὸς ἀδελφὸς εἰς τοσαύτην ἔκστασιν | ἤδη καθίστησίν με τῇ πονηρίᾳ; in Ter. *Ad.* 197 Sannio reflects after a thrashing *minime miror qui insanire occipiunt ex iniuria*.

The most popular explanation of insanity in ancient Greece was divine possession (cf. E. R. Dodds, *The Greeks and the Irrational* (Berkeley 1951) 64ff., Barrett on Eur. *Hipp.* 141–4, Dover, *GPM* 126ff.), although attempts at rational interpretation (e.g. excess of black or more rarely yellow bile, Ar. *Nub.* 832f., *Pax* 65f., Dem. 48.56, Men. *Asp.* 305ff., 422, *Epitr.* 880f., cf. Galen, 14.740, 15.370, 16.14f.; brain injury, Ar. *Nub.* 1275f.; heavy drinking, Hdt. 6.84) were not confined to the medical profession.

INCERTARUM FABULARUM FRAGMENTA

2 τοῦ φρονεῖν μετάστασιν: 'dislocation of sanity', with μετάστασιν a euphemistic substitute for ἔκστασις or ἔκπληξις. It is a favourite term in the Hippocratic corpus, applied to changes in blood (*Morb.* 1.18, *Ulc.* 2), progress of disease (*Prorrh.* 2.29, *Coac.* 7.575, *Affect.* 12), physical condition (*Aer.* 16, with ἔκπληξις the corresponding term for mental) and once mental state (*Morb. sacr.* 18 Jones). The presence of medical (or at least scientific and/or philosophical) overtones may account for the word's unique appearance here in extant comedy, although it occurs several times (with the general sense of 'change') in tragedy (e.g. S. *Ant.* 718, Eur. *Andr.* 1003, *Hec.* 1266, *IT* 816, fr. 554).

295 (293K)

Meineke 3.516 (xxvi), Kock 2.402, Edmonds 2.514, Kassel–Austin 2.185; cf. R. Seaford, comm. (Oxford 1984) on Eur. *Cycl.* 499f. In a confusingly arranged section Epit. of Ath. 1.23b-e claims that ἀναπίπτειν is used κυρίως ἐπὶ ψυχῆς ... οἷον ἀθυμεῖν, ὀλιγοδρανεῖν (wrongly instancing Thuc. 1.70, where the meaning is 'give ground'; better would be Dem. 19.224, cf. Polyb. 20.4.6) and then goes on to cite this brief fr. of Alexis for the sense 'recline'. Commonly in good 5th/4th-century Attic ἀναπίπτω means 'I fall/lean backwards' literally, both in general contexts (e.g. A. *Ag.* 1599, Eur. *Cycl* 410, cf. Plut. *Mor.* 992b) and as a technical term in rowing (e.g. Cratinus 332(345K), Xen. *Oec.* 8.8, cf. Polyb. 1.21.2) and riding (Xen. *Equ. Mag.* 3.14, Pl. *Phdr.* 254b). Use in the related meaning 'I recline' (at banquets, symposia) would hardly have come under attack from stricter Atticists (e.g. Phryn. *Ecl.* s.v. ἀναπεσεῖν p. 79.3 Fischer, Phot. p. 118.12 and 14ff. Reitzenstein, *Suda* = Aelius Dionysius s.v. ἀναπίπτειν p. 106 Erbse; for the defence, Antiatticist 77.10 Bekker) if it had not become so popular in the *Koine* (e.g. N.T. *Ev. Matt.* 15.35, *Marc.* 6.40, 8.6, *Jo.* 21.20, Lucian *Asin.* 23; ? com. adesp. fr. 638 Kock) and been transformed there into a euphemism for 'I make love' (e.g. LXX *Susanna* 37 καὶ ἦλθε πρὸς αὐτὴν νεανίσκος ... καὶ ἀνέπεσε μετ' αὐτῆς). Whether (or how far) any euphemistic use is felt in the present fr. of Alexis is uncertain without more context, but an order (given here by the speaker, if ἐκέλευον = 1st person singular; by others, if 3rd person plural) for a girl (presumably a *hetaira* at a symposium) to recline by the speaker's side presumably had erotic implications; cf. e.g. Eur. *Cycl.* 499f. (Seaford *ad loc.*), Men. *Epitr.* 434f. οὐκέτι μ' ἐᾷ ... οὐδὲ κατακεῖσθαι ... | παρ' αὐτόν (spoken by the *hetaira* Habrotonon); for the portrayal of such scenes on Attic vases see e.g. B. Fehr, *Orientalische und griechische Gelage* (Bonn 1971), 100ff., O. Murray (ed.), *Sympotica: A Symposium on the Symposion* (Oxford 1990), pl. 16a (Attic red-figure cup, New York 20.246), *EAA* s.v. *Simposio* 317f.

COMMENTARY

296 (294K)

Meineke 3.516 (xxv), Kock 2.402, Edmonds 2.514, Kassel–Austin 2.185. Context and speaker are unknown, but the arrangements for the betrothal party at the end of Men. *Dysk.* are couched in a similar way, 855ff. δεῖ ποτὸν | ἡμῶν γενέσθαι ... νυνὶ καλὸν | καὶ τῶν γυναικῶν παννυχίδα.

1 σύντομον: so Kassel–Austin (with the other modern editors of Ath. and the comic frs.), thus expanding CE's abbreviation here (Epit. of Ath. 2.47e) συντμ´ (with τμ superscript, ´ clearly angled to the right and so interpretable only as an acute accent). The adjective σύντομος, however, is not elsewhere to my knowledge linked with nouns designating meals or food, and earlier editors may well have been right to follow Musurus in printing συντόμως, in the very appropriate sense of 'shortly/quickly', which had developed from the root meaning 'concisely' already in the 5th century (A. *Eum.* 415 is ambiguous, but cf. e.g. S. *OT* 810, Xen. *Hell.* 3.4.15, Machon 110, Hippocr. *Aph.* 3.12, *Epid.* 5.49).

ἀριστόδειπνον: cf. Hesych. s.v., ὅταν τὸ ἄριστον τῷ δείπνῳ συνάψωσιν. The word seems to have been a 4th-century coinage, perhaps by Alexis here or (cited by Pollux 6.102) Menander fr. 827, turning up again as late as John Malalas, *Chronogr.* 18, p. 4734.3f. L. Dindorf. Cf. Bruhn, *Wortschatz* 19, Durham, *Vocabulary* 45, Gow on Machon 312ff.

297 (295K)

Meineke 3.522 (xLIV), Kock 2.402, Edmonds 2.514, Kassel–Austin 2.185. This iambic trimeter, attributed by Stob. 3.6.7 to Alexis and by the unknown collectors of monostichs (with characteristic inaccuracy) to Menander (no. 806 Jäkel: comic lines by Anaxandrides, Antiphanes, Diphilus and Philemon are also inserted into these collections, cf. Jäkel 143ff.), varies a banal cliché that was assumed to originate with Solon (one of the apophthegms collected by Dem. Phal., Stob. 3.1.172β, cf. 3.6.25; cf. Martini in *RE* s.v. *Demetrios* 85, 2835.51ff., E. Bayer, *Demetrios Phalereus der Athener* (Stuttgart and Berlin 1942) 138ff.) in the form ἡδονὴν φεῦγε ἥτις λύπην τίκτει, and was taken up by e.g. Antiphon (fr. 131 Blass², fr. 49 Diels–Kranz = Stob. 3.6.45) ἀκολουθοῦσιν αὐταῖς (sc. ταῖς ἡδοναῖς) λῦπαι καὶ πόνοι, [Isoc.] 1.46f. εὐθὺς αἱ λῦπαι ταῖς ἡδοναῖς παραπεπήγασι ... πρότερον ἡσθέντες ὕστερον ἐλυπήθημεν, Epicurus *Epist.* 3.129 οὐ πᾶσαν ἡδονὴν αἱρούμεθα, ἀλλ᾽ ἔστιν ὅτε πολλὰς ἡδονὰς ὑπερβαίνομεν ὅταν πλεῖον ἡμῖν τὸ δυσχερὲς ἐκ τούτων ἔπηται, cf. frs. 181, 442, monost. 250, 302, 863 Jäkel and (with comm. there) the differently pointed Alexis 68 (= Antiphanes 270 Kock). Alexis' present trimeter would be appropriate advice from a *paedagogus* or father to a pleasure-seeking son, but is

INCERTARUM FABULARUM FRAGMENTA

not confined to such situations (cf. e.g. Plaut. *Amph.* 635 *ita diuis est placitum, uoluptatem ut maeror comes consequatur*, spoken by Alcumena after Jupiter has left her).

φέρουσαν: so SMA (Stob.), B (monost.), but ἔχουσαν the other MSS (monost.). Both verbs are thus used with βλάβην (e.g. S. *El.* 1042 ἔνθα χἠ δίκη βλάβην φέρει, Eur. fr. 253.1f. τὸ γὰρ λέγειν | εὖ δεινόν ἐστιν εἰ φέρει τινὰ βλάβην, cf. Hippocr. *Acut.* 39, 40; Eur. *Ion* 1350 ἔχει δέ μοι τί κέρδος ἢ τίνα βλάβην;, cf. Arist. *Pol.* 2.1, 1261ᵇ32, 7.13, 1333ᵇ31), but here φέρουσαν is more reliably attested.

298 (296K)

Meineke 3.522 (xlv), Kock 2.402, Edmonds 2.514, Kassel–Austin 2.185. A comic cliché (cf. 294(292K) and comm.) precisely linking λύπη and μανία (like Antiphanes 287(295K) and monost. 602 Jäkel), and enlivened only by an imaginative use of κοινωνία (cf. Ar. *Thesm.* 140 τίς δαὶ κατόπτρου καὶ ξίφους κοινωνία;).

299 (297K)

Meineke 3.518 (xxxiii), Kock 2.402, Edmonds 2.514, Kassel–Austin 2.186; cf. Legrand *NGC* 233. A slave's greeting to a master who has just arrived, probably after a long absence abroad (cf. Plaut. *Most.* 447f., *Trin.* 1072f., Ter. *Phorm.* 286; Plaut. *Poen.* 1127ff. is a variant, a slave greeting her master after a long separation caused by her abduction).

ὦ δέσποθ', ὑγίαιν': in his short essay ὑπὲρ τοῦ ἐν τῇ προσαγορεύσει πταίσματος Lucian cites this fr. (allegedly from ἀρχαία κωμῳδία) and Achaeus fr. 44 σὺ δ' ὑγίαινέ μοι (from tragedy) as literary precedents for the use of ὑγίαινε as a greeting. Conventionally for both sexes χαῖρε was the formula of greeting (e.g. Ar. *Ach.* 176, *Pax* 582, *Ran.* 184, Men. *Epitr.* 860, *Sam.* 296, fr. 280.1), ὑγίαινε of parting (e.g. Ar. *Ran.* 165, *Eccl.* 477), cf. Plut. *Mor.* 508b, Lucian *Laps.* 14, but neither imperative was limited to the one situation by basic meaning, and χαῖρε was occasionally used at parting (e.g. Men. *Dysk.* 512f.), ὑγίαινε elsewhere too at first meeting (Lucian *Laps.* 8 has an anecdote about Hephaestion greeting Alexander with ὑγίαινε, βασιλεῦ and thereby causing a commotion). In letters similarly χαίρειν commonly appears as a greeting, ὑγιαίνειν as a closing formula (Preisigke, *Wörterbuch* 2.632, Mayser 2.1.146; cf. also H. Koskenniemi, *Studien zur Idee und Phraseologie des griechischen Briefes bis 400 n. Chr.* (Helsinki 1956) 128ff.), but Lucian's essay quotes instances of reversed usage (5–6, Pythagoreans, Epicurus; 10, Ptolemy I beginning a letter to Seleucus with ὑγιαίνειν, ending with χαίρειν), and the combination χαίρειν καὶ ὑγιαίνειν is a familiar alternative opening (e.g. *SIG* 1259,

COMMENTARY

P.Oxy. 3806). See also F. V. Fritzsche's fine discussion in his comm. on Ar. *Ran.* 164, 165 (Zürich 1845) pp. 110ff.

ὡς χρόνιος ἐλήλυθας: 'how long it is since you've been here', normally implying a protracted absence, e.g. Hom. *Od.* 17.112 ἐλθόντα χρόνιον, S. *Phil.* 1446, Eur. *Ion* 403 χρόνιος ἐλθών, *Hel.* 566 = Ar. *Thesm.* 912 ὦ χρόνιος ἐλθών, Cratinus 237(222K).2f., Men. fr. 280, Theoc. 14.2 ὡς χρόνιος, 15.1.

300 (298K)

Meineke 3.524 (LXII), Kock 2.403, Edmonds 2.516, Kassel–Austin 2.186. A puzzling and perhaps corrupt trimeter, but best interpreted as a command that some music should be played. The addressee (perhaps named: see below) could be another character in the play (e.g. Men. *Dysk.* 432f. αὔλει, Παρθενί, | Πανός*) or the official αὐλιστής (e.g. Epicharmus fr. 127*, Ar. *Thesm.* 1186*, Men. *Theoph.* 28* and fr. dub. 17*); cf. Pickard-Cambridge *DFA*² 156ff., 165ff., O. Taplin, *Comic Angels* (Oxford 1993) 70ff.

Photius s.v. παναρμόνιον (between παραρρήτοις and παράρρυμα ποδός; in the lemma παραρμ- MS with a superscript correction misplaced above the second ρ) introduces the fr. with Ἄλεξις ἐν ὧι, where ὧι may be a corruption of the original play-title (ἐν Ὕπνῳ or more appropriately ἐν Λίνῳ Dobree, *Adv.* 1.606; Linos was a citharist and music-teacher, see introduction to that play), but Meineke's ἐν τῷ (sc. ἀποσπάσματι) is also plausible.

τὸ παναρμόνιον τὸ καινόν: identified by Phot. here as ὄργανον μουσικόν (cf. also Hesych. s.v. παναρμόνιον· εἶδος ὀργάνου, ἐξ ὅλου τεταγμένον), but this may result from an incorrect reading of this line and other passages such as Pl. *Resp.* 3.399c and d, where Adam in his comm. convincingly identifies παναρμόνιον as 'a style of composition, in which the *Tondichter* passed freely from δωριστί to φρυγιστί and λυδιστί and as many others as he chose. The name may even have been given to well-known compositions in this style'; cf. here Phot.'s other gloss (directly after πανάπυστος) on παναρμόνιον· παντόθεν ἡρμοσμένον. With ἔντεινον as an imperative parallel to those asterisked above (which make M. Schmidt's conjecture ἐντείνων (*Diatribe in dithyrambum poetarumque dithyramborum reliquias* (Berlin 1845) 260) quite unnecessary), translate 'Play the new panharmonic (tune) *con brio*'; for this use of ἐντείνω Adam cites Dion. Hal. *Dem.* 48 τὸ κάλλιστον ἐντείνας μέλος, cf. also Ar. *Nub.* 968 ἐντειναμένους τὴν ἁρμονίαν.

At the end of the verse Kassel–Austin print τεχνῶν (MS τεχν(ων) unaccented), with the genitive plural assuming dependence on words in the lost context. Meineke's brilliant suggestion Τέχνων (the addressee's name) seems preferable, since Clearchus (fr. 58 Wehrli) in Ath. 8.344c identified a man with this name as ὁ παλαιὸς αὐλητής, and pipers are the musicians normally addressed in comedy; cf. Kirchner, *PA* 2.306, no. 13556. Other conjectures (τέχνη Dobree, *Adv.* 1.606; τρέχων S. A. Naber, edition of Phot., vol. 2 (Leiden 1865) 59 n. 1 and *Mnemosyne* 8 (1880) 265; τέκνον M. Schmidt) are less good.

301 (300K)

Meineke 3.516 (xxviii), Kock 2.403, Edmonds 2.516, Kassel–Austin 2.186. Context and speaker are uncertain, but the idea of diving into a swimming-pool (? full) of perfume is worthy of boasting soldiers and their parasites. Another extravagant use of μύρον is described in fr. 63(62K) from the Εἰσοικιζόμενος, but there is no way of knowing whether the present fr. also came from that play.

κολυμβήθραν: a swimming-bath or reservoir, sometimes of extravagant size and luxury (e.g. Diod. Sic. 4.78 near Megaris, 11.25.4 = Ath. 12.541f at Acragas with a circumference of 7 stades and a depth of 30 feet, Plut. *Alexander* 76 at Babylon; cf. also e.g. Pl. *Resp.* 5.453d, Paus. 4.35.9, Plut. *Mor.* 487f, Galen 6.23 Kühn); see Mehl in *RE Suppl.* v s.v. *Schwimmen* 852.10ff., R. Ginouvès, *Balaneutikè* (Paris 1962) 134 n. 12.

After μύρου the citer (Epit. of Ath. 1.18c, cf. Eustath. 1842.20) writes ἀρκεῖσθαί τις ἂν δύναιτο, φησὶν Ἄλεξις, thus implying that he has either unmetrically transposed the last four words of the fr. (hence δύναιτ' ἂν ἀρκεῖσθαι Meineke, δ. ἂν ἀρκεῖσθαί τις Kock, cf. Peppink, *Observ.* 4; but at this stylistic level ἀρκεῖσθαι is more commonly constructed with the participle, not the infinitive, cf. Dobree, *Adv.* 2.294, LSJ s.v. ἀρκέω III), or so paraphrased or garbled his source that reconstitution of Alexis' original text is impossible.

302 (306K)

Meineke 3.526 (lxxii), Kock 2.404, Edmonds 2.518, Kassel–Austin 2.187; see also Chr. Theodoridis' edition of Photius I (Berlin and New York 1982) 218 s.v. ἀπειλεῖταί μοι, and K. Tsantsanoglou, *New Fragments of Greek Literature from the Lexicon of Photius* (Athens 1984) 79f. The Zavorda MS (S^z) of Photius expands this fr. from the two words (διηπειλεῖτό σοι) cited by the Antiatticist (82.25 Bekker) to either a complete trochaic tetrameter or the ending of an iambic trimeter with a complete second one (ἀρτίως | ἐνταῦθ᾽ ἐπῆδα καὶ διηπειλεῖτό μοι). The speaker describes a recent physical and verbal assault on himself (cf. e.g. Pyrrhias in Men. *Dysk.* 110ff., Sosia in Plaut. *Amph.* 606, 624, Congrio in *Aul.* 409ff., Sannio in Ter. *Ad.* 196ff.).

COMMENTARY

ἐπήδα: 'he (or she) sprang (at me)'. The meaning of πηδῶ and its compounds progresses naturally from a literal 'I jump/leap' to a (? more colloquial) 'I move quickly' (with or without an initial leap): cf. in drama e.g. (πηδῶ) Eur. fr. 323.2, Ar. *Vesp.* 227, possibly Men. *Sam.* 606 (cf. Gomme–Sandbach, *Comm. ad loc.*); (εἰσ-) Men. *Dysk.* 602, *Sam.* 564; (ἐκ-) Eubulus 1.2(2K), Men. *Perinth.* fr. 6 Sandbach, *Pk.* 527, *Theoph.* 26; (ἐπανα-) Ar. *Nub.* 1375; (ἐπι-) Ar. *Vesp.* 705; (ἐπεισ-) Ar. *Equ.* 363; (παραπ.) Men. *Sik.* 259; (προ-) ? A. fr. 23; (προσ-) Alexis 129(124K).16; cf. also Tsantsanoglou.

διηπειλεῖτό μοι: Phot.'s μοι here fits the extended context better than Antiatticist's σοι. The latter's explanatory note (ἀπειλοῦμαι· ἀντὶ τοῦ ἀπειλῶ) implies an attempt to defend the use of the middle form ἀπειλοῦμαι as Attic (wrongly: only *Koine*, e.g. aorist Appian *Bell. Civ.* 3.29; the passive at Xen. *Symp.* 4.31 is misread by the Antiatticist as middle; at Lysias 12.72 Cobet's correction of MSS ἀπειλοῖτο to διαπειλοῖτο (haplography after μηδὲ) is generally accepted), and fails to distinguish between the (active) simple verb and the (middle) compound διαπειλοῦμαι in Attic (+ dative also in Aeschines 1.43, cf. *P.Petrie* II.1.14, 3rd century), although Ionic (e.g. Hdt. 2.121γ, 7.15) and *Koine* (e.g. Plut. *Otho* 16.3) sometimes used the active. Cobet, *NL* 625 noted that *verba cum δια composita quae certamen et contentionem significant solent ferme medii formam induere*, citing numerous instances (e.g. ἀκοντίζω βοῶ κελεύω κολακεύω λοιδορῶ τοξεύω).

303 (299K)

Meineke 3.516 (XXVII), Kock 2.403, Edmonds 2.517, Kassel–Austin 2.187. Either the first part of an iambic trimeter or the last metron of one and the beginning of a second (Kassel–Austin). Euboean wine was apparently excellent and expensive (cf. Apollodorus Car. 5.25f. κεραννύναι τὸν οἶνον Εὐβοῆς (*sic* A at Ath. 7.281a). τρυφὴ / καὶ βίος ἀληθῶς); cf. Philippson in *RE* s.v. *Euboia* 855.43ff. and *Die griechischen Landschaften* I.2 (Frankfurt 1952) 632.

πιών: Musurus' correction of CE's ποιῶν (Epit. of Ath. 1.30f). Confusion between ι and οι is common at all periods, and so cannot always be explained by itacistic pronunciation of οι (which was not stabilised until the 10th century AD, cf. L. R. Palmer, *The Greek Language* (London 1980) 177); examples may be cited from the classical period (e.g. Thuc. 2.54.2–3, commenting on confusion between λοιμός and λιμός in an old prophecy), early papyri (e.g. *P.Tebt.* 61b.17, 18 ἀσπερμοί by the side of correct -μί 307, 118/17 BC; cf. Mayser–Schmoll 1.1.91), and medieval MSS (e.g. Eur. *Med.* 1096 AP οὐχ οἱ for οὐχί, Pl. *Resp.* 1.345c A πιαίνειν for ποιμαίνειν).

794

304 (301K)

Meineke 3.514 (xxi), Kock 2.403, Edmonds 2.516, Kassel–Austin 2.187. Two trochaic tetrameters, spoken by someone protesting his[1] sobriety after drinking too much at a party.

1 CE here (the fr. is cited by Epit. of Ath. 2.40c) open the citation with οὐ μεθύω, but the υ of μεθύω is short in Attic (cf. Schulze, *QE* 346; in comedy after the 5th century e.g. Ar. *Eccl.* 139, *Plut.* 1048, Alexis 15.18, 113(108K).4, Men. *Dysk.* 60, *Epitr.* 522; hence presumably short also when in *anceps* position, e.g. Alexis 44(43K).1, 91(87K).2), and so a syllable is probably omitted here in the paradosis. Hence οὐχὶ μ. Dindorf (printed by Kassel–Austin), οὐδὲ μ. Schweighaeuser (*Animadv.* 8.399), οὐ μ. γάρ Kaibel (with an opening dactyl, very rare in comic troch. tetr., cf. e.g. F. Perusino, *RCCM* 4 (1962) 55ff., Handley's edition of Men. *Dysk.*, pp. 71ff.), οὐ με-μεθύω with το-τοσοῦτον later T. G. Tucker (*CQ* 2 (1908) 186, with the speaker stammering like the drunken Callidamates at Plaut. *Most.* 319, 331; cf. also *Rud.* 528ff. and E. A. Sonnenschein's comm. (Oxford 1891) *ad loc.*); Tucker's conjecture is the most ingenious, Dindorf's the most plausible (for οὐχί corrupted to οὐ cf. e.g. Eur. *Or.* 97 A, 107 L, Ar *Equ.* 904 VAΓ^ac, Antiphanes 58(56K).3 ACE at Ath. 10.441d, Diphilus 88.1).

μεθύω τὴν φρόνησιν: cf. Theophr. *Odor.* 46 ὥσπερ μεθύσκων τὴν αἴσθησιν.

τὸ τοιοῦτον μόνον: 'only in this kind of way'. Casaubon's tentative suggestion τοσοῦτον (*Animadv.* 83) was worth advancing, but the speaker is as concerned to describe one particular effect of his drinking as to minimise its extent.

Kaibel and Kassel–Austin fail to note that CE here write τοιοῦτο, corrected by Musurus.

2 CE have τὸ διορίζεσθαι βεβαίως, which makes perfect sense: the speaker claims not to be drunk as regards control over his senses, only as regards the clear articulation of words. Meineke's alteration to -εσθ' οὐ βεβαίως (with the crasis -εσθἀβεβαίως as an alternative) misreads the limiting function of the accusatives of respect in vv. 1–2 (cf. H. W. Smyth, *Greek Grammar* (Cambridge Mass. 1920) 360) and fails to observe the idiomatic preference of Greek for μή over οὐ with all expressions linked to an articulated infinitive (Goodwin, *MT* p. 270, K.G. 2.197ff., A. C. Moorhouse, *Studies in the Greek Negative* (Cardiff 1959) 37). Fourth-century Attic favoured the use of the middle of διορίζω (cf. LSJ s.v., 1.4), as of

---

[1] Probably: similar characters in later comedy are male, whether slave (e.g. Plaut. *MG* 818ff. with speech affected, *Pseud.* 1246ff. staggering) or free (e.g. *Most.* 313ff. stammering, Ter. *Eun.* 727ff. staggering).

other δια- compounds (comm. on 302(306K)). τὰ γράμματα here = the sounds made by the letters of the alphabet, cf. Posidippus 30(28K).4, Pl. *Phlb.* 18c, *Crat.* 390e, Arist. *PA* 2.16, 660ᵃ5 φθέγγεσθαι τὰ πλεῖστα τῶν γραμμάτων, cf. [*Probl.*] 10.39, 895ᵃ8 and (for the question διὰ τί τῶν μεθυόντων ἡ γλῶττα πταίει;) 3.31, especially 875ᵇ21f. ἡ γλῶττα ... οὐ δύναται τὴν λέξιν διαρθροῦν: cf. also Bywater, comm. on Arist. *Poet.* 20, 1456ᵇ22 (Kassel–Austin).

305 (304K)

Meineke 3.527 (LXXXI), Kock 2.404, Edmonds 2.518, Kassel–Austin 2.188. This fr., preserved only in Latin prose paraphrase (Vitruvius 6 *praef.* 3... *Alexis, qui Athenienses ait oportere ideo laudari, quod omnium Graecorum leges cogunt parentes <ali>* (the haplography corrected by a later hand in E) *a liberis, Atheniensium non omnes nisi eos, qui liberos artibus erudissent*; Edmonds attempts a metrical translation into Greek[1]), confirms that a law attributed to Solon (cf. Plut. *Solon* 22.1 (Σόλων) νόμον ἔγραψεν υἷῳ τρέφειν πατέρα μὴ διδαξάμενον τέχνην ἐπάναγκες μὴ εἶναι) was still in force; cf. also Socrates' question in Pl. *Crit.* 50d οὐ καλῶς προσέταττον ἡμῶν οἱ ἐπὶ τούτῳ τεταγμένοι νόμοι, παραγγέλλοντες τῷ πατρὶ τῷ σῷ σε ἐν μουσικῇ καὶ γυμναστικῇ παιδεύειν;. See J. H. Lipsius, *Das attisches Recht und Rechtsverfahren* 2 (Leipzig 1908) 505, cf. 343f., A. R. W. Harrison, *The Law of Athens* 1 (Oxford 1968) 78, D. M. MacDowell, *The Law of Classical Athens* (London 1978) 92 and my comm. on Alexis 282(280K). Alexis' comment will perhaps have come in a speech or debate about the education of young men, a favourite topic in later comedy (commonly broached by the father, e.g. Alexis 282(280K), Men. *Sam.* 698ff., Ter. *HT* 102ff., *Ad.* 48ff., 72ff., but by the son in Men. *Sam.* 9ff.). Meineke suggested that both frs. 282(280K) and 305(304K) may have come from the same play, but their themes are neither so related nor so dissimilar as to constitute evidence either way.

306 (305K)

Meineke 3.526 (LXXIX), Kock 2.404, Edmonds 2.518, Kassel–Austin 2.188. Zenobius* (Athos rec. 1.58 = vulgate rec. 2.17, Leutsch–Schneidewin 1.p.36 = Bodleian rec. 148; cf. W. Bühler, *Zenobii Athoi proverbia* 1

---

[1] Vitruvius presumably did not cite Alexis independently, but took the reference and quotation from one of his Greek sources, ranging in date from contemporaries of the comic poet such as Pytheus or Satyrus of Paros to Ctesibius or Hermogenes a century or more later, cf. P. Fleury's edition of Vitruvius, vol. 1 (Paris 1990) xxxix ff.

(Göttingen 1987) 41ff., 91ff., 126ff.) cites Men. fr. 31, Sophron fr. 169 and Alexis here for the use of the proverb ἀληθέστερα τῶν ἐπὶ Σάγρᾳ (if verbatim in iambic trimeters, presumably e.g. κἀληθέστερα | or ∪ ∪ ἀληθέστερα | τῶν ἐ. Σ.), adding a long explanation from an unidentifiable source (the Atthidographer Demon, suggests O. Crusius, *Analecta critica ad paroemiographos Graecos* (Leipzig 1883) 147, but a western Greek historian such as Timaeus is perhaps more likely, cf. L. Pearson, *The Greek Historians of the West* (Atlanta 1887) 108ff.). The proverb is listed in several paroemiographic collections (also Macarius 1.84*, Apostolius 2.12*, Arsenius 38*), Byzantine lexica or commentaries (*Suda** and Phot.* (1.100.11ff. Theodoridis = 73.27ff. Reitzenstein) s.v., citing Men. with a play-title, cf. Phot. s.v. Σάγρα, 2nd entry; Eustath. 278.4ff.* citing Paus. gr. 157f. Erbse, Σ Clem. Alex. *Protr.* 9.307.11f. Hense), referred to by earlier writers (e.g. Strabo 6.1.10*, Aelian *NA* 11.10, Cic. *ND* 3.13), and generally interpreted as ἐπὶ τῶν ἀληθεστάτων (or πάνυ ἀληθῶν), οὐ πιστευομένων δέ; Phot. s.v. Σάγρα (1st entry: citing Cratinus 488(442K), cf. 238(223K) and Kassel–Austin *ad loc.*) may imply that this proverb was so familiar that the word Σάγρα on its own could be used as a picturesque synonym for ἡ ἀλήθεια. The proverb was inspired by a battle (accounts in the works asterisked above and Plut. *Aem. Paull.* 25.1, Cic. *ND* 2.6, see Pease's comm. *ad loc.*, Justin 20.2.10–3.9, *Suda* s.v. Φορμίων citing Theopompus, *FGrH* 115 F 392) fought between Croton and Epizephyrian Locri at the river Sagra (now generally identified as the Allaro); although heavily outnumbered, the Locrians were victorious, attributing their success to the help of the Dioscuri. A rumour of the Locrian success allegedly reached Sparta on the very day of the battle, but was not believed until messengers arrived later to confirm it. The more fanciful elements in the story have with some plausibility been ascribed to the poet Stesichorus (cf. Wilamowitz, *Sappho und Simonides* (Berlin 1913) 234, Oldfather in *RE* s.v. *Lokroi* 1328.17ff.), but precise facts here are as hard to identify as the date of the battle, which 'may be anywhere between the late 7th and early 5th centuries' (A. J. Graham, *CAH* 3.3² (1982) 193f.; cf. also E. Meyer, *Geschichte des Altertums* 3² (Stuttgart 1937) 629 and n. 1, T. J. Dunbabin, *The Western Greeks* (Oxford 1948) 358f., P. Bicknell, *Phoenix* 20 (1966) 294ff.).

On this form of expression (comparative adjective + genitive of comparison), which is common in proverbs (e.g. ἀκαρπότερος ἀγρίππου, ἀμουσότερος Λειβηθρίων, εὐγενέστερος Κόδρου, Ἰαλέμου ψυχρότερος, Zen. vulg. 1.60, 79, 4.3, 39; ἀμ. also [Aristaen.] 1.27, εὐγ. Lucian *Timon* 23, *Dial. Mort.* 19(9).4), see especially P. Martin, *Studien auf dem Gebiete des griechischen Sprichwortes* (Programm/Diss., Gymnasium zu Plauen i. V. 1889) 11, Netta Zagagi, *Tradition and Originality in Plautus* (Göttingen 1980) 20f.

307 (1 Demiańczuk, 305A Edmonds)

Demiańczuk 7, Edmonds 2.518, Kassel–Austin 2.188. In a confused note Phot. s.v. ἀνάστατα ποιεῖν (122.19 Reitzenstein = 1 (Berlin 1982) 168.15 Chr. Theodoridis) cites Plato (with quotation: *Soph.* 252a), Alexis, Menander (without play-title: ? *Epitr.* 165f.), Euripides (without title: ? *Andr.* 1249) and Demosthenes (ἐν τῷ περὶ τῆς παραπρεσβείας with quotation: 19.39) for two uses of ἀνάστατος: as predicate of γίγνεσθαι (= 'to become devastated') and as predicate to the object of ποιεῖν ('to devastate (cities)' or 'to expel from their homes (people)'). It is not clear which use Alexis chose, but both are common in good Attic and elsewhere: (a) pred. of γίγνεσθαι: e.g. Eur. *loc. cit.*, Antiphon 5.79, Isoc. 12.70, Pl. *Legg.* 6.770e, *Epist.* 8.353a, Dem. 19.39, 327, Hdt. 1.178, 7.118, 9.106; Polyb. 2.9.8, Plut. *Mor.* 613b; (b) pred. to obj. of ποιεῖν: e.g. Thuc. 6.76, 8.24 ἀνάστατα ἐποίησαν τὰ ταύτῃ χωρία, [Andocides] 4.31, Xen. *Hell.* 6.5.35, Isoc. 4.37, 108, 5.20, 44, 6.27, 12.89 and elsewhere, Pl. *Legg.* 3.682d, 4.716b, Aeschines 2.115, 3.80; Men. *Epitr.* 165f.; Hdt. 1.76, 155, 177 τὰ μὲν νυν κάτω τῆς Ἀσίης ... ἀνάστατα ἐποίεε, 7.56; Paus. 1.4.1.

308 (307K)

Meineke 3.526 (LXXIII), Kock 2.404, Edmonds 2.518, Kassel–Austin 2.188. The Antiatticist's citation καύσιμα ξύλα· Ἄλεξις (105.4 Bekker) implies a defence of the expression's Atticism which is supported by its appearance on the confiscation stelae of the late 5th century (*IG* i³.425.9). Presumably some Atticist had misidentified it as a *Koine* innovation (cf. e.g. *P.Strassburg* 2.117.3, 1st century AD) and recommended instead either the expression καύσιμος ὕλη (Pl. *Legg.* 8.849d) or words such as ἐκκαύματα (S. fr. 225 Pearson = 205 Nauck²), κληματίδες (Ar. *Thesm.* 728, 739, Thuc. 7.53, Wilamowitz's supplement at Men. *Perinth.* 2), σχίζα, -ζαι (Ar. *Pax* 1024, 1032, *IG* ii².1366.11) and φρύγανον, -να (Ar. *Pax* 1026, *Av.* 642, Teleclides 41(39K), Thuc. 3.111, Xen. *Anab.* 4.3.11, *IG* i³.429.9f.); cf. the lists in Pollux 10.110f. Cf. also W. K. Pritchett, *Hesperia* 25 (1956) 296f.

309 (308K)

Meineke 3.523 (LV), Kock 2.404, Edmonds 2.518, Kassel–Austin 2.189. Pollux 6.104 quotes νάρδον Βαβυλωνικήν (so FSC: -νικόν AB, but the noun is always feminine, cf. *Suda* s.v.) from Alexis. νάρδος (a Semitic loan-word, cf. É. Masson, *Recherches sur les plus anciens emprunts sémitiques en grec* (Paris 1967) 56) is the name of both a perfumed oil and the plant(s) from which it derives: especially (i) spikenard, *Nardostachys jatamansi*, providing oil most abundantly from its root (cf. Theophr. *Odor.* 6.28) but no longer used commercially (cf. M. Zohany, *Plants of the Bible* (Cambridge 1982) 205); and (ii) several grasses predominantly of the *Cymbopogon* genus (e.g. *C. nardus*) that are still a prime source of citronella oil (L. S. Cobley, *An Introduction to the Botany of Tropical Crops* (London 1956) 339ff.). Although these plants basically belong to the Indian subcontinent, attempts were made in antiquity to identify spikenard as 'Syrian', the grasses as 'Indian' (e.g. Dioscorides 1.7, Galen 12.84f. Kühn, Pliny *HN* 12.42–5), either thus reflecting centres of manufacture and/or trade, or in confusion over geographical boundaries. Spikenard itself was variously labelled as 'Babylonian' (also Posidonius in Ath. 15.692c–d = fr. 179 Theiler, 71 Edelstein–Kidd, 87 F 20 Jacoby), 'Syrian' (e.g. Dioscorides 1.7, Tibullus 3.6.63f.) and 'Assyrian' (e.g. Hor. *Od.* 2.11.16, Sil. Ital. 11.402, Seneca *Hipp.* 393, Martial 8.77.3f.), cf. T. Nöldeke, *Hermes* 5 (1871) 443ff. Nard oil was the finest and most expensive of perfumes in antiquity (e.g. N.T. *Ev. Marc.* 14.3, Plut. *Mor.* 990b, Pliny *HN* 12.42f.), and was sprinkled on hair and garlands at extravagant banquets (e.g. Posidonius *loc. cit.* ἐν Συρίᾳ ἐν τοῖς βασιλικοῖς συμποσίοις ὅταν τοῖς εὐωχουμένοις δοθῶσιν οἱ στέφανοι, εἰσίασίν τινες μύρων Βαβυλωνίων ἔχοντες ἀσκίδια καὶ πόρρωθεν ἐκ τούτων περιπορευόμενοι τοὺς ... στεφάνους τῶν κατακειμένων δροσίζουσι τοῖς μύροις, ἄλλο μηδὲν ἔξωθεν παραρραίνοντες, *id.* in Ath. 2.46a = fr. 116 Theiler, 283 Edelstein–Kidd, 87 F 72 Jacoby (omitting the end of the fr.), Hicesius in Ath. 15.689d, Hor. *Od.* 2.11.16f., *Epod.* 13.8f., Tibullus 2.2.7, [Lygdamus] 3.6.63f., Martial 8.77.3f.). See in *RE* especially Steier s.v. *Nardus*, 1705.67ff., also Hug s.v. *Salben*, 1864.57ff., Forbes, *Technology* 3.35f.[1] = 36f.[2], J. I. Miller, *The Spice Trade of the Roman Empire* (Oxford 1969) 27, 88ff., 94ff., S. Lilja, *The Treatment of Odours in the Poetry of Antiquity* (Helsinki 1972) 86ff.

310 (309K)

Meineke 3.525 (LXV), Kock 2.404, Edmonds 2.518, Kassel–Austin 2.189. Photius and the *Suda* here (s.v. σπουδάζω περὶ τὸν ἄνδρα) cite authors for various uses of σπουδάζω before quoting Alexis' use of τίνι σπεύδεις; ἀντὶ τοῦ τίνι σπουδάζεις. The likeliest interpretation of Alexis' phrase is 'For whom are you siding?' (cf. Chariton 6.1 οἱ μὲν Χαιρέᾳ σπεύδοντες ... οἱ δὲ Διονυσίῳ σπεύδοντες); for the intransitive use of σπουδάζω with the dative in the same meaning cf. in *Koine* Greek Plut. *Artaxerxes* 21 σπουδάσας βασιλεῖ, Arrian *Epict.* 1.11.27 τοῦ ἵππου ᾧ ἐσπουδάκει, 3.4.1 σπουδάσαντος κωμῳδῷ τινι, Epict. *Ench.* 33.10 μηδενὶ σπουδάζων φαίνου ἢ σεαυτῷ. Yet the possibility that τίνι may have been neuter in Alexis here ('For what are you eager?') cannot be ruled out (cf. Edmonds), in view of parallel uses of σπουδάζω with a non-personal dative (e.g. Lucian *Par.* 37 φιλοσόφους ... παρασιτίᾳ σπουδάσαντας, where Nesselrath's doubts

COMMENTARY

about the idiom (*LP* 397f.) spring from inadequate knowledge of the parallels, e.g. [Aristaen.] 2.3 σπουδάζω γάμῳ).

311 (310K)

Meineke 3.525 (LXIX), Kock 2.404, Edmonds 2.519, Kassel–Austin 2.189. An anonymous Homeric commentator (Cramer, *Anecdota Graeca*, 1. 224.31ff.; cf. A. R. Dyck, *Epimerismi Homerici* 1 (Berlin and New York 1983) 1ff.) seeks to explain Κηφισίδι at *Il.* 5.709 by citing several parallels for the co-existence of feminine formations in -ίς (-ίδος) and masculine in -ός from the same root, including φορμίς and -ός (cf. here Schwyzer 1.464f.). φορμίς is less common (also Ar. *Vesp.* 58, Arist. *HA* 5.15, 547ª2) than φορμός (e.g. Hes. *Op.* 482, Ar. *Thesm.* 813, frs. 168(172K) and Kassel–Austin *ad loc.*, 591.96 = 63.96 Austin, *IG* i³.421.126ff.) in the sense of 'basket'; the extant passages point to no obvious distinction in meaning between the two forms.

ἰσχάδων: Meineke's conjecture (for MS ἰσχάδιον) is supported by many parallels for the use of genitive of contents with container noun (e.g. Ar. *Av.* 1325 κάλαθον ... πτερύγων, *Thesm.* 813 φορμὸν πυρῶν, cf. *IG loc. cit.*, K.G. 1.333, H. W. Smyth, *Greek Grammar* (Cambridge Mass. 1920), 318). See also comm. on 122(117K).1.

312 (311K)

Meineke 3.523 (LI), Kock 2.404, Edmonds 2.518, Kassel–Austin 2.189. Pollux 2.110–13 lists adjectives in -φωνος and nouns in -φωνία, noting that many of the adjectives lack the corresponding noun (cf. Meineke), but that by the side of βαρύφωνος (e.g. Ar. fr. 793(753K), Men. fr. 209.7, Arist. *GA* 5.7, 786ᵇ31; Bruhn, *Wortschatz* 39, Durham, *Vocabulary* 49) we find τὴν βαρυφωνίαν παρ' Ἀλέξιδι (cf. also Arist. *GA* 5.7, 786ᵇ35, Hippocr. *Aer.* 8).

313 (312K)

Meineke 3.522 (XLVIII), Kock 2.404, Edmonds 2.518, Kassel–Austin 2.189. Pollux 2.14 cites Alexis for the use of γηροβοσκεῖα (so all the MSS), which would be a *hapax*, but Plut. *Mor.* 111e, Theon *Progymn.* 1.249.14 Walz and *P.Oxy.* 1210.5 (1st century BC/AD) have γηροβοσκία = 'care of the aged'. If Pollux (or his copyists) did not simply mistranscribe -βοσκίαν here (so '*corrigitur*' in *TGL* s.v. γηροβοσκία, but Meineke assigns the conjecture to Schneider; thereafter LSJ), we must assume that γηρο-βοσκεῖα was used (or even coined) by Alexis in the sense of 'homes for the aged' (cf. γηροτροφεῖον, γηρωκομεῖον (not -ροκ-, *pace* LSJ; cf. ps.-Herodian *Epimerismi*, p. 205 Boissonade) attested by Zonaras and *Suda* s.v. the latter form), by analogy with forms like πορνοβοσκεῖον (Σ^{VΓLhAld} Ar. *Vesp.* 1353), ? χηνοβοσκεῖον (so L at *Geop.* 14.22.1, other MSS -σκιον), cf. ὀρτυγοτροφεῖον ([Arist.] *Probl.* 10.12, 892ª11), χοιροτροφεῖον (Phrynichus com. 45(43K), ? Eupolis 493(453K)). The application of βόσκω, its compounds and congeners to human beings in comedy often implied contempt (see Starkie on Ar. *Ach.* 678, Neil on Ar. *Equ.* 256), but not in tragedy (e.g. γηροβοσκός S. *Aj.* 570, Eur. *Suppl.* 923, -βοσκεῖν *Alc.* 663, *Med.* 1033).

314 (313K)

Meineke 3.523 (L), Kock 2.405, Edmonds 2.518, Kassel–Austin 2.189. Pollux 2.64 cites Alexis for δακρυρροοῦντα. This verb is particularly common in tragedy in its basic sense 'shed tears' (S. *OR* 1473, *Trach.* 326, 796, *El.* 1313, fr. 910.3 Pearson, Radt = 824.3 Nauck², Eur. *Alc.* 137, 826, *Med.* 1012, *Suppl.* 289, *Her.* 1114, 1181, *Ion* 246, 967, *Phoen.* 370, *IA* 889, adesp. fr. 447.2), and Alexis may have been guying tragic vocabulary, but Ionic (Hippocr. *Epid.* 4.25) and *Koine* (e.g. Herodian 6.9.1; + accus. = 'weep for' Philo *Vit. Mos.* 291, 4.268 Cohn) prose uses the verb without any such colour; cf. also a technical use in horticulture, 'bleed', of vines (Theophr. *CP* 3.13.2, *Geop.* 5.38 heading).

315 (314K)

Meineke 3.523 (LIII), Kock 2.405, Edmonds 2.518, Kassel–Austin 2.190. Pollux 3.42f. lists two verbs with the meaning τῆς παρθένου παρθενίαν ἀφελέσθαι: διακορεῦσαι (but not διακορῆσαι) and διαπαρθενεῦσαι. For the latter verb he cites Herodotus (passive διαπαρθενεύεται, 4.168), Diocles com. fr. 16 (-πεπαρθενευμένη), Alexis here (-πεπαρθενευκότα: presumably with *sedes* directly after penthemimeral caesura), and ? Antiphanes 76(75K) (διεπαρθένευσα A, -σε(ν) FSBC; MSS identify the source as Ἀριστοφάνης (-άνου A) ... Γλαύκῳ, cf. Meineke 3.43); cf. also e.g. Alciphron 4.17.4, Herodorus (*FGrH* 31 F 20) in Ath. 13.556f.

If Alexis used the participle to describe some incident in a myth travesty or a plot of New-Comedy type, the speaker's reference to a maiden's rape was explicit, as e.g. in Plaut. *Aul.* 28, 33, 689, *Cist.* 158, 178, 616, *Epid.* 540, Ter. *Hec.* 828, all with *comprimere*, Ter. *Ad.* 686 *uirginem uitiasti*, *Hec.* 383 *uitiumst oblatum uirgini*, and not cloaked by euphemism or aposiopesis, as e.g. in Men. *Sam.* 47f., cf. Plaut. *Aul.* 745, *Truc.* 828, Ter. *Eun.*604ff.

COMMENTARY

316

Kassel–Austin 2.190; see also K. Tsantsanoglou, *New Fragments of Greek Literature from the Lexicon of Photius* (Athens 1984) 56f. In addition to Alexis, the Zavorda MS of Photius (S^z) cites for the use of the form ἐνῴδια (so Tsantsanoglou: ἐνώδια S^z; the spelling with ῳ/ωι is supported by Attic inscriptions, e.g. *IG* ii².1388.17, 1544.20, both 4th century; cf. Meisterhans–Schwyzer 65 n. 558) A. fr. 424b Radt and Philemon fr. 187 Kassel–Austin. Photius' intention may have been to oppose Moeris' allegation that ἐνώτια Ἀττικοί, ἐνῴδια Ἕλληνες (for the survival of ἐνῴδια in *Koine* Greek, e.g. *IG* xi.2.199.B46 (Delos), *P.Petrie* xii.24, both 3rd century; *P.Rylands* 124.30f., 1st century AD). The derivation of ἐνῴδιον remains disputed. An ancient guess (*Et. Gen.*^AB in R. Reitzenstein, *Geschichte der griechischen Etymologika* (Leipzig 1897) 292 ~ *Et. Mag.* 345.4 ~ *Et. Sym.* V ~ Cramer, *Anecdota Graeca* 2.433.11 ~ *Suda* and Zonaras s.v. ἐνῴδιον) possibly originating with Oros (but ignored by K. Alpers in his edition, Berlin and New York 1981), that the noun is perhaps connected with ἐνοιδεῖν, may safely be ignored; modern scholarship generally supports J. Wackernagel's derivation from *ἐνου(σ)ίδιον (*Philologischer Anzeiger* 15 (1885) 199f. = *Kleine Schriften* 3 (Göttingen 1979) 1769f.), but this has been challenged by O. Szemerényi (*Studi Micenei* 3 (1967) 54, 87f. = *Scripta Minora* 3 (Innsbruck 1987) 1280, 1313f.), proposing a sequence *ἐνώειος - *ἐνώειον - *ἐνωείδιον; Chantraine's suggestion (*Dictionnaire*, 2.340a s.v. οὖς) of syncopation from ἐνωτίδιον seems simpler.

ἐνῴδια are earrings, and in a plot of New-Comedy type they might possibly have functioned as recognition tokens, like other small pieces of jewellery (cf. Hähnle 142ff.).

317 (315K)

Meineke 3.525 (LXVIII), Kock 2.405, Edmonds 2.518, Kassel–Austin 2.190. Aristophanes' syncopation ἐπιλησμότατον (in place of -λησμονέστα-τον, the regular form of this superlative) at Ar. *Nub.* 790 is compared by Σ^REM *ad loc.* and the *Suda* s.v. to Alexis' ἐπιλήσμη here and to Cratinus' ? ἐπιλῆσμον, -λήσμονι or -λησμονή (fr. 451(410K): hardly -λησμοσύνη: so *Suda* MSS, -λησμ*** Σ^R where A. Martin, *Les Scolies du manuscrit d'Aristophane à Ravenne* (Paris 1882) 47 claims to decipher -λησμοσυνη, cf. Starkie on Ar. *Nub.* 790; -λήσμονι Σ^Ald·, cf. ἐπιλήσμοσι at Cratinus fr. 162(154K); ἐπιλησμονή conj. F. L. Abresch, cf. Kock). If the *hapax* ἐπιλήσμη is correctly transmitted for Alexis, it is impossible to account for in the absence of context; possibilities include a syncopation in contemporary colloquial use (? cf. πλήσμη for πλημυρίς, if correctly transmitted in Σ Ap. Rhod. 1.757 (p.65 Wendel), citing Hes. fr. 320 Merkelbach–West), or a comical nonce coinage. It could also be a telescopic corruption for ἐπιλησμονή (so Meineke 5.92; ἐπιλησμονή occurs in *Koine* Greek at e.g. LXX *Ecclesiasticus* 11.27, N.T. *Epist. Jacob.* 1.25).

318 (317K)

Meineke 3.526 (LXXVIII), Kock 2.405, Edmonds 2.518, Kassel–Austin 2.190. *Et. Mag.* 462.22f. (s.v. θυσία) correctly notes that compounds of φυή normally take the ending -φυῖα (so εὐφυῖα: Attic/*Koine*, e.g. [Pl.] *Def.* 412e, 413d, Arist. *Rhet.* 1.6.15, 1362ᵇ24, *Poet.* 22, 1459ᵃ7, Theophr. *CP* 1.2.3, Polyb. 2.68.5, Diod. Sic. 1.97.6, Plut. *Solon* 1.2; Ionic -φυΐη, e.g. Hippocr. *Offic.* 4, *Artic.* 82, *Mochl.* 26), but that Alexis has the form εὐφύεια. εὐφύεια is transmitted also in the anonymous commentary on Pl. *Theaet.* (H. Diels and W. Schubart, *Berliner Klassikertexte* 2 (1905), e.g. 4.43, 47f., 9.39f., 11.15) and Philodemus *Rhet.* 12.12 = 2.p.3 Sudhaus, cf. W. Croenert, *Memoria Graeca Herculanensis* (Leipzig 1903) 33); whether Alexis used it as a colloquial by-form (cf. ὑπερφύεια Dittenberger, *OGIS* 666.26, Egypt, 1st century AD ~ ὑπερφυῖα *Suda* s.v.), or for metrical convenience, is as uncertain as its precise meaning in the comic context.

319 (318K)

Meineke 3.527 (LXXX), Kock 2.405, Edmonds 2.518, Kassel–Austin 2.190. Eustath.'s commentary on the *Iliad* (859.51) cites Ael. Dion. (123.15 Erbse) for ἰατρὸν γυναῖκα and Alexis for the *hapax* ἰάτριαν. ἰατρός is occasionally found in the feminine as (i) an attribute of goddesses (Artemis: Diogenes Ath. trag. fr. 1.5; Aphrodite: Plut. *Mor.* 143d; nymphs in Elis: Hesych. s.v. ἰατροί), (ii) 'female doctor' (Helladius in Phot. *Bibl.* 104.308B Migne = 8.173 Henry; elsewhere μαῖα occurs with this sense, Galen 14.641 Kühn), (iii) 'midwife' (Hesych. s.v. μαῖα). If Alexis coined ἰάτρια, it could have been any of these: e.g. a prologue goddess describing her activities, a woman taking over a position normally held by a man (? in a play like Γυναικοκρατία), or a midwife summoned in a New-Comedy plot (cf. Ter. *Ad.* 353f., *Andr.* 228ff., 459ff., ? Men. *Perinth.* fr. 4 and Gomme–Sandbach, *Comm.* p. 534).

320 (319K)

Meineke 3.525 (LXXI), Kock 2.405, Edmonds 3.518, Kassel–Austin 2.191. Apocope of κατα- in compounds (with assimilation of τ to the following consonant) is familiar in epic (e.g. κάββαλε Hom. *Od.* 6.172, Hes. *Theog.* 189, κακκείοντες *Il.* 1.606, κάμμορος *Od.* 11.216, Ap. Rhod. 4.1318, καννεύσας *Od.* 15.464, κάτθανε *Il.* 21.107), in Aeolic and Doric (e.g. in

COMMENTARY

literature κάββαλε Alcaeus 338.5 Page, κάββας Pind. *Nem.* 6.51, καλλίπη Alcaeus 207.5, καππυρίσασα Theoc. 2.24, κατθανοῖσα and καττύπτεσθε Sappho 55.1 and 140.2 Page), and in the iambics of Attic tragedy (mainly future and aorist of καταθνήσκω: e.g. A. *Ag.* 1553, S. *Ant.* 464, Eur. *Alc.* 291, *Or.* 1150, but also κάππεσε A. *Ag.* 1553); cf. especially K.B. 1.176ff. Phrynichus' condemnation of such an apocope in καμμύειν as ἡ βαρβαρία and its use by Alexis as ἠμελημένως ἐσχάτως (*Ecl.* 94.1ff. Fischer, cf. the discussions in the editions of C. A. Lobeck (Leipzig 1820) 339ff., Rutherford, *NP* 426f.), which is echoed by the Antiatticist without any reference to Alexis (103.27 Bekker, καμμύειν οὔ φασι δεῖν λέγειν, ἀλλὰ καταμύειν), doubtless sprang from the frequent use of the apocopated form in *Koine* Greek (e.g. Philo *De Somniis* 1.26 = 1.645 Cohn, Hero *Autom.* 22.1, Paul. Aegin. 3.22.29, *P.Mag.Lond.* 121.855 3rd century AD) with its illiterate treatment as an uncompounded verb (e.g. ἐκάμμυον LXX *Isaiah* 6.10, ἐκάμμυσαν N.T. *Act. Ap.* 28.27, cf. Ap. Dysc. *Synt.* 4.36 = 2.465.5 Uhlig citing the form κεκάμμυκα; if Alexis had used such a form, the severity of Phrynichus' condemnation would be more explicable). However, what governed Alexis' choice here (? contemporary usage; imitation of a non-Attic dialect; parody of epic, lyric or tragedy, cf. e.g. κατθανεῖν in Ar. *Ran.* 1477) remains uncertain.

321 (320K)

Meineke 3.524 (LX), Kock 2.405, Edmonds 2.518, Kassel–Austin 2.191. Pollux 7.161 cites Dinarchus (fr. 89.18 Sauppe, incert. 22 Conomis) for the use of κεραμοπῶλαι, -πωλεῖον, -πωλία, Alexis for κεραμοπωλεῖν (all *hapax legomena*). Similarly formed compounds of πωλεῖν are scattered throughout Attic comedy (ἀλλαντο- Ar. *Equ.* 1242, 1246, 1398, γελγο- Hermippus 11(13K), λιβανωτο-, λοφο- Ar. frs. 845(807K), 850(812K), μυρο- Ar. fr. 856(821K), Pherecrates 70(64K).1, παντο- Men. *Pk.* 283, τυρο- Ar. *Ran.* 1369, Men. *Pk.* 290, φαρμακο- Ar. fr. 28.3) and other Attic writers (λαφυρο- Xen. *Anab.* 6.6.38, οἰνο- Theophr. *Char.* 30.5, cf. [Arist.] *Mirab.* 32, 832^b22, πυρο- Dem. 19.114, ταριχο- Pl. *Charm.* 163b).

322 (321K)

Meineke, *ed. min.* 768 (LXXXII), Kock 2.405, Edmonds 2.518, Kassel–Austin 2.191. Eustathius' commentary on *Il.* (863.29ff., deriving from Suetonius περὶ βλασφημιῶν 53f., p. 415 Miller, *Mélanges* = p. 51 Taillardat) cites λευκόπυγον (= τὸν ἄνανδρον) in Alexis, and notes by contrast μελαμπύγους (= τοὺς ἀνδρείους). These usages derived from the belief that οἱ πονοῦντες ἔντριχον ἔχουσι τὴν πυγήν (*App. Prov.* 3.62, cf. 4.35);

INCERTARUM FABULARUM FRAGMENTA

see also e.g. Σ^{RΓ} Ar. *Lys.* 802 τοὺς λευκοπύγους ὡς γυναικώδεις ἐκωμῴδουν, Σ^V Ar. *Pax* 1310, Hesych. (~ Phot. = *Suda*) s.v. λευκόπυγος, Zenob. 5.10, Eustath. 455.37ff. citing Ael. Dion. p. 127.25 Erbse; cf. O. Kaehler, *Woch. Klass. Phil.* 2 (1885) 902. λευκόπυγος is not known to occur elsewhere, although it was boldly supplemented at Herodas 7.12 by O. Crusius in his first edition (Leipzig 1892), cf. Headlam's comm. *ad loc.*; λευκόπρωκτος has similar connotations at Callias com. fr. 14(11K), but see A. Nauck, *MGR* 6 (1894) 86f.; λευκός on its own may imply effeminacy, e.g. Ar. *Thesm.* 191, *Ran.* 1092, Men. *Sik.* 200, 258, possibly *Sam.* 607 but see Gomme–Sandbach, *Comm. ad loc.*, Sosicrates fr. 1.1, Xen. *Hell.* 3.4.19, [Arist.] *Physiogn.* 6, 812^a13f., 812^b4f., Pollux 4.147, cf. μῦς λευκός at Philemon 65(126K).1. See also E. Fraenkel, comm. on A. *Ag.* 115, Nesselrath, *LP* 406ff.

323 (322K)

Meineke 3.524 (LXI), Kock 2.405, Edmonds 2.518, Kassel–Austin 2.191. In Photius' gloss Νήστης· Σικελικὴ θεός. Ἄλεξις, the lemma was corrected by Meineke to Νῆστις from Eustath. 1180.15 (καὶ Σικελικὴ δέ τις, φασί, θεὸς Νῆστις ἐλέγετο: *fons est ignotus, nisi forte e Lex. Attic.* M. van der Valk (vol. 4, Leiden 1987) *ad loc.*). This goddess is known elsewhere only from the Sicilian Empedocles, who gave her name to the deified element of water (Νῆστίς θ' ἣ δακρύοις τέγγει κρούνωμα βρότειον 31 в 6.3, cf. в 96 Diels–Kranz), since Νῆστις (like Νηίδες, Ναιάδες) seems to be derived from νάω; cf. Wagner and Drexler in Roscher s.v. *Nestis* 287.60ff., L. Preller and C. Robert, *Griechische Mythologie* 1⁴ (Berlin 1894) 555 and n. 1, Wilamowitz on Eur. *Her.* 625, Preisendanz in *RE* s.v. *Nestis* 108.18ff. Why Alexis should have introduced or mentioned her is a mystery; one possibility is that she was an exotic divine prologue for a play set in Sicily (? Γαλάτεια) or southern Italy (? Βρεττία, Λοκροί, Ταραντῖνοι).

324 (323K)

Meineke 3.523 (LII), Kock 2.406, Edmonds 2.518, Kassel–Austin 2.191. Pollux 2.149 cites Men. fr. 891 for ὀξύχειρ (cf. e.g. A. *Choeph.* 23, Lysias 4.8, Nicomachus 1.33, Theoc. epigr. 22.2 with Gow's note, Lucian *Dial. Deor.* 11(7).2, Pollux 4.97) and Alexis for ὀξυχειρία (elsewhere only in *Koine* Greek: e.g. Sext. Emp. *Math.* 2.39 οἱ ψηφοπαῖκται τὰς τῶν θεωμένων ὄψεις δι' ὀξυχειρίαν κλέπτουσιν, Philo *Vit. Mos.* 1.44, 4.130 Cohn). Cf. in Attic authors also αὐτοχειρία (e.g. [Dem.] 25.57, Pl. *Legg.* 9.872b), ἐκεχειρία (e.g. Ar. *Pax* 908, Thuc. 4.58), πολυχειρία (Thuc. 2.77, Xen. *Cyr.* 3.3.26).

COMMENTARY

325 (324K)

Meineke 3.522 (XLIX), Kock 2.406, Edmonds 2.518, Kassel–Austin 2.192. Alexis' use of οὐλόκομος is cited by Pollux 2.23 (in a list of words connected with hair) and Phot. s.v. (with incorrect paroxytone accent in MS); Pollux goes on to cite οὐλοκέφαλος in Pherecrates 257(223K) and οὐλοκίκιννος in Telesilla fr. 8 Page. οὖλος itself is applied to hair in the sense 'woolly/curly' as early as Homer[1] (*Od.* 6.231 οὔλας ... κόμας, cf. e.g. Hdt. 7.70 (a black African's) οὐλότατον τρίχωμα, Clem. *Paed.* 3.11.60, *Geop.* 16.1.19), spawning many compound adjectives: οὐλόθριξ (e.g. Arist. *GA* 5.3, 782^{b}18, *Probl.* 33.18, 963^{b}10, Strabo 15.24; comparative in -τριχώτερος at Arist. *HA* 8(9).44, 629^{b}34) and the incorrectly formed nominative -τριχος (*Cod. Astr.* 12.177.23, cf. Phot. s.v. οὐλόθριξ· οὐχὶ οὐλότριχος), -κάρηνος ('woolly-headed' Hom. *Od.* 19.246, but = ὅλα κάρηνα *H.Merc.* 137), -κέφαλος (also Ptol. *Tetr.* p. 143, *Cod. Astr.* 12.177.23), -κίκιννος (*sup.*), -κόμης (Plut. *Aratus* 20.1, Aristides *Or.* 50(26).40), -κομος ('woolly-haired' also Sext. Emp. *Dogm.* 1. = *Math.* 7.268, Heph. Astr. 1.1.52, 2.2.41, epit. 4.31, but at LXX *Levit.* 23.40 οὐλοκόμους = *varia lectio* for δασεῖς in the sense 'thickly foliaged') and -κρανος (Arrian *Ind.* 6.9).

326 (325K)

Meineke 3.525 (LXX), Kock 2.406, Edmonds 2.518, Kassel–Austin 2.192. Phrynichus (*Ecl.* p. 81.33 Fischer; cf. the discussions in the editions of Lobeck 242, Rutherford 314) writes under the heading παλαιστρικός· ᾿Αλεξίν (so most MSS, but ἀλέξανδρον EF) φασιν εἰρηκέναι, ὁ δὲ ἀρχαῖος παλαιστικὸν λέγει (similarly Thom. Mag. 290.5). No occurrence of the word in either form is recorded before Alexis and/or Aristotle, but in stricter *Koine* writing there seems to have been some attempt to confine παλαιστικός to the meaning '(of) wrestling' (e.g. Arist. *Rhet.* 1.5.14, 1361^{b}24, Plut. *Mor.* 130ab, Paus. 1.39.3, cf. Pollux 3.149), and to use παλαιστρικός in senses ranging from 'of the palaestra' (the adverb -τρικῶς Σ Ar. *Vesp.* 1212, cf. Nonius 1.226 Lindsay (citing Afranius'*Exceptus* XIV) and Plaut. *Rud.* 296 *exercitu gymnastico et palaestrico*) to the more general 'athletic/energetic' (adverb in com. adesp. fr. 239.23 Austin). Yet since wrestling took place in the palaestra, the -τρικός form could easily subsume the meaning '(of) wrestling' (e.g. Arist. *Cat.* 8, 10^{b}4f., Plut. *Mor.*

---

[1] On the various meanings of οὖλος in Homer see especially P. Buttmann, *Lexilogus* 1^4 (Berlin 1865) 173ff., 2^2 (1860) 141; cf. also F. Williams, comm. (Oxford 1978) on Call. *H.Ap.* 76.

639f, as transmitted), and it is often difficult both to identify the precise meaning intended (e.g. -τικός Diog. Laert. 6.4, -τρικός Galen 6.158 Kühn) and to be certain about the form transmitted (e.g. Lucian *Dear. Iudic.* 14, Helen described as παλαιστική most MSS, -τρική γ group). Without context we cannot know how Alexis used the τρ- form, but if in Phrynichus the adjective (rather than the adverb) is correctly cited for the comic poet, one argument for ascribing com. adesp. fr. 239 Austin (*P.Berlin* 11771) to Alexis is thereby removed (see below, 'False or Doubtful Attributions' v, 838f.). Cf. also Hermann–Blümner, *Privatalterthümer* 312, 336ff., J. Delorme, *Gymnasion* (Paris 1960) 253ff.

327 (326K)

Meineke 3.526 (LXXIV), Kock 2.406, Edmonds 2.518, Kassel–Austin 2.192. The Antiatticist (113.20 Bekker) cites συμπατριώτης for Archippus (fr. 61(64K)) and πατριώτης for Alexis without comment. πατριώτης is defined by ancient lexicographers and grammarians (Pollux 3.54, Ammonius s.v. p.103 Nickau, Steph. Byz. s.v. πατρίς, Σ Lucian *Soloec.* 5, cf. Phot. and Hesych. s.v.) as the term used in place of (συμ)πολίτης by non-Greeks and slaves for a fellow-countryman, and most extant texts bear this out (e.g. Pl. *Leg.* 6.777c, Lucian *Soloec.* 5, Dio Cass. 40.9; thus Pherecrates 11.2 a slur on Lycurgus' parentage, cf. Meineke 2.257f., Nicon com. 1.2 presumably spoken by slave or non-Greek; ? Alexis here; cf. also Nicostratus' title Πατριῶται 7.85f. Kassel–Austin), although occasionally it is applied by Greeks to fellow-Greeks (Iambl. *Vit. Pyth.* 5.21), or non-humans (Dionysus, Plut. *Mor.* 671c; horses, Xen. *Cyr.* 2.2.26; Cithaeron, S. *OT* 1090).

328 (327K)

Meineke 3.524 (LXIII), Kock 2.406, Edmonds 2.518, Kassel–Austin 2.192. Phot. s.v. cites Alexis for the use of πίσον (πῖσον MS) apparently as a neuter (elsewhere for certain only Eustath. 802.3); masculine πίσος is normal (e.g. Theophr. *HP* 8.1.4, Ath. 9.406c citing Phaenias of Eresos fr. 48 Wehrli, *Geop.* 2.13.3, *P.Tebtunis* 9.11 = 2nd century, Pollux 6.60, Arcadius 75.4, Herodian 1.205.28ff., Hesych. s.v. ὄσπριος); form ambiguous at Ar fr. 22, Eupolis 323(321K), Galen 6.532 Kühn = the common pea, *Pisum sativum*, still wild as well as a cultivar throughout Greece (Olck in *RE* s.v. *Erbse* 392.22ff., O. Polunin, *Flowers of Greece and the Balkans* (Oxford 1980) 299). If the paroxytone accent is correct (so Herodian; cf. *P.Tebtunis*), the first syllable will scan short (at Ar. fr. 22 πίσοις may end one trimeter or begin the next, cf. Kassel–Austin *ad loc.*), but MSS commonly give πισ(σ)ός (cf. Schwyzer 1.516).

COMMENTARY

329 (328K)

Meineke 3.524 (LVIII), Kock 2.406, Edmonds 2.518, Kassel–Austin 2.192. Pollux 7.35 cites Alexis for ποικιλεύς; the form used elsewhere is ποικιλτής (e.g. Aeschines 1.97, Arist. *Meteor.* 3.4, 375ᵃ27, Plut. *Pericles* 12.6, LXX *Exod.* 26.36, 28.6, 15; cf. Hesych. s.v. ποικιλεύς· ποικιλτής) = ὁ τὰ ποικίλα ποιῶν ἔργα, ἃ νῦν φαμὲν ψυχροβαφῆ· ἢ ὁ τὰ ποικίλα ἔργα ὑφαίνων (*Lex. Rhet.* 295.25 Bekker), rightly (*pace* Hermann–Blümner, *Privatalterthümer* 414f., Blümner, *Technologie* 218ff.) indicating that normally (a) pictures and patterns were either woven on the loom or dyed into the material, and (b) the professional worker was male (though the form ποικίλτρια is found at Strabo 17.1.36, and women practised the craft from childhood, e.g. Eur. *Ion* 1417ff., Theoc. 15.35f.). See especially M. Besnier in Dar.–Sag. s.v. *Phrygio* 446A ff., Forbes, *Technology* 4.183ff., 207ff., 230f.[1] = 186ff., 211ff., 235f.[2], and cf. T. B. L. Webster, *Everyday Life in Classical Athens* (London 1969) 35.

330 (329K)

Meineke 3.523 (LIV), Kock 2.406, Edmonds 2.518, Kassel–Austin 2.193; cf. Nesselrath, *MK* 99f. Among the ἐργαλεῖα τῶν ἰατρῶν Pollux 4.182 includes λεκάνη, ἧς τὸν πυθμένα Ἄλεξις πτερνίδα καλεῖ; similar statements (without reference to Alexis) are made about λεκάνια (Eustath. 870.28 citing Ael. Dionys. s.v. πτερνίδες, p. 138 Erbse, cf. Phot. s.v.) and λεκανίδες (Pollux 2.197 citing ἡ μέση κωμῳδία, cf. Nesselrath, Hesych. s.v. πτερνίς adding that μέχρι νῦν προσδέουσιν (sc. the bottoms of these bowls) ἁλυσειδίοις μακραῖς ἐν τοῖς ἰατρ<ε>ίοις). On λεκάνη, -άνιον and -ανίς see comm. on fr. 129(124K).5; the bowl sat securely on a flat surface because its flared base or 'heel' (Alexis' πτερνίς) was flat underneath. πτέρνα is commonly used in a similar sense (e.g. bottom of πύργοι Lycophron 442, cf. Eustath. 310.10, siege engine Polyb. 8.6.2, a torsion-engine's arms Philo mech. *Bel.* 4.21, 35 = 59.30, 66.2 Wescher, surgical machine Oribas *Coll. Med.* 49.4.9, ship's mast Ath. 11.474f citing Asclepiades of Myrlea, ploughshare Hesych. s.v. πτέρνα). If Alexis mentioned the heel of a medical λεκάνη, could it have belonged to the φαρμακοπώλης in the play named after him?

331 (330K)

Meineke 3.524 (LIX), Kock 2.406, Edmonds 2.518, Kassel–Austin 2.193. In his list of carpentry tools Poll. 7.113 includes ῥίνη (the Attic form ~ ῥῖνα *Koine*, so Moeris s.v. -νη; cf. J. Pierson's edition (Leiden 1759), comm. on θοίνη, pp. 183f., and F. Solmsen, *Beiträge zur griechischen Wortforschung* 1

(Strasbourg 1909) 255), for its use citing Xenophon (*Cyr.* 6.2.33) and Alexis, the latter in a way (καὶ τὰ Ἀλέξιδος ἂν θείης followed directly by the infinitives of eight carpentry verbs) implying that θείης originally introduced a quotation from the comic poet which has now fallen out of the MSS (so first G. Jungermann in J. H. Lederlin and T. Hemsterhuys, edition of Pollux (Amsterdam 1706)). ῥίνη is a standard word for a metal file (cf. e.g. [Arist]. *Aud.* 803ᵃ2, Leonidas in *Anth. Pal.* 6.205 = 8 Gow–Page, *IG* xi(2).173.11 (Delos, 3rd century BC), Aen. Tact. 18.5). Presumably this was Alexis' meaning, although ῥινή (oxytone: cf. Arcadius 111.24 Barker) is the name of an edible fish (Monkfish/Angel Fish, now *Squatina squatina*; Thompson, *Fishes* 221f., Campbell, *Guide* 260, 263, Davidson, *Seafood* 32; cf. Epicharmus fr. 59.2, Archippus 23(25K).2, Anaxandrides 42(41K).53, Ephippus 12.2 = Mnesimachus 4.32 in comedy, Archestratus 177.2 *SH*, Matron 534.56f. *SH* in gastronomy) whose rough skin when dried was used in ancient and modern times by cabinet makers for polishing (Matron *loc. cit.*, Pliny *HN* 9.14.40; cf. W. Yarrell, *A History of British Fishes*³ 2 (London 1859) 538); hence its name (cf. Frisk 2.657, Chantraine 2.974).

332 (331K)

Meineke 3.525 (LXIV), Kock 2.406, Edmonds 2.518, Kassel–Austin 2.193. Photius cites Alexis for using Σκυθαίνας as the feminine of Σκύθας (he could have cited Ar. *Lys.* 184); Σκυθίδας is the commoner form (e.g. Aeschines 3.172, Lucian *Contemp.* 13, Libanius *Arg. Dem.* 3 = 8.601 Förster). On feminines in -αινα see Schwyzer 1.455f., 475, and cf. Henderson, comm. on Ar. *Lys.* 184.

333 (332K)

Meineke 3.525 (LXVI), Kock 2.407, Edmonds 2.518, Kassel–Austin 2.193. Photius cites Alexis for στόλον in the sense of τὰ πλοῖα. This is far more likely to be the accusative of στόλος (cf. LSJ s.v., 3) in a sense ('expedition consisting of ships') that is standard in Attic historians (e.g. Thuc. 1.31, Xen. *Hell.* 3.4.1) and tragedy (e.g. A. *Ag.* 45, S. *Phil.* 270, 547, 561, Eur. *IT* 10) than an unparalleled comic neuter coinage in the same sense.

334 (333K)

Meineke 3.526 (LXXV), Kock 2.407, Edmonds 2.518, Kassel–Austin 2.193. The Antiatticist (115.14 Bekker) implicitly defends the use of ὑπόμακρον in Attic by citing Alexis; he could have cited Ar. *Pax* 1243. The word also occurs in Ionic (e.g. Hippocr. *Prorrh.* 1.144) and *Koine* (e.g. [Arist.]

COMMENTARY

Physiogn. 3, 807ᵇ26, Galen 16.808 Kühn commenting on the passage of Hippocr., *Geop.* 10.68.2). Here ὑπο- qualifies the adjective ('fairly/quite long', LSJ s.v. ὑπό F.II, Schwyzer 1.436); cf. e.g. ὑπομήκης (Antiatticist's definition here; also e.g. Arist. fr. 339 Rose), ὑπόπλατυς (e.g. Hippocr. *Liqu.* 6, *Coac.* 410), ὑπόπλεως (e.g. Timocreon 1.10 Page), ὕπορθος, ὑποτετράγωνος.

335 (334K)

Meineke 3.526 (LXXVI), Kock 2.407, Edmonds 2.518, Kassel–Austin 2.193. The Antiatticist (115.26 Bekker) cites Alexis for φιλαδελφία and φιλεταιρία (φιλαιτερία MS transposing ε and αι, homophonous and confused from 4th century on, cf. Mayser–Schmoll 1.1.85f., J. Perpillou, *Glotta* 62 (1984) 152ff.; corr. Bekker, cf. 3.1077). φιλαδελφία is elsewhere common in *Koine* Greek (e.g. Lucian *Dial. Deor.* 26(25).2, Babrius 47.15, περὶ φ. titles by Plut. *Mor.* 478a ff., Hierocles in Stob. *Anth.* 4.27.20 Hense = p. 59 von Arnim; Philo 2.558 Mangey = 2.171.23 Cohn, *ed. mai.*, Josephus *Ant. Jud.* 2.6.9; N.T. *Epist. Rom.* 12.10, *Thess.* 1.4.9, *I Petr.* 1.22); φιλεταιρία occasionally in 4th-century Attic (Xen. *Ages.* 2.21 (-αιρείᾳ MSS), Arist. *Rhet.* 1.7, 1364ᵇ2, with τὸ φιλέταιρον in the same sense at Timocles fr. 8.4, cf. Plut. *Lysander* 5.

Although the Antiatticist here names no play or plays in which these two words appeared, it is worth guessing that φιλεταιρία at least occurred in Δημήτριος ἢ Φιλέταιρος (cf. p. 155 n. 1).

336 (335K)

Meineke 3.523 (LVI), Kock 2.407, Edmonds 2.518, Kassel–Austin 2.194. In his list of over seventy φιλο- compounds (including Alexis here and 337(336K), but not the Homeric φιλοκτέανος *Il.* 1.122, cf. Schwyzer 1.442 n. 3) Pollux 6.166 couples φίλερις ('contentious/quarrelsome', a common adjective: e.g. Axionicus fr. 6.9, Arist. *Soph. Elench.* 11, 171ᵇ26, Philodemus *Piet.* 95, Musonius fr. 16 p. 86 Hense, Philo 1.360 Mangey = 2.173 Cohn *ed. mai.*) and Alexis' φιλεριστήν, a *hapax* possibly coined by the comic poet (but cf. also φιλέριστος in Justin *Dial. Tryph.* 161B).

337 (336K)

Meineke 3.523 (LVII), Kock 2.407, Edmonds 2.518, Kassel–Austin 194. In the list discussed above on 336(335K), Pollux 6.166 notes that Alexis used φιλοθέωρον (acc. masc.) in place of φιλοθεάμονα (misprinted -άμον in Bethe's edition). φιλοθεάμων is good Attic (Pl. *Resp.* 5.476a, b) and *Koine* (e.g. Philo 1.38 Mangey = 1.55 Cohn *ed mai.*, Ath. 4.179a, Epict. *Diss.*

INCERTARUM FABULARUM FRAGMENTA

2.14.25, Lucian *Herod.* 8, Plotinus 3.8.4, Plut. *Mor.* 410a); φιλοθέωρος first here and Arist. *Eth. Nic.* 1.8.10, 1099ᵃ10, then *Koine* (e.g. Alex. Aphr. on Arist. *Top.* p. 245.18, Dion. Hal. *Ant. Rom.* 1.6.4, Plut. *Mor.* 604c, 1095c, Cicero *Ad Fam.* 7.16.1).

338 (337K)

Meineke 3.526 (LXXVII), Kock 2.407, Edmonds 2.518, Kassel–Austin 2.194. The Antiatticist (116.10 Bekker) cites Alexis for χαλκίζειν· ἀντὶ τοῦ χαλκῷ κυβεύειν. Pollux 7.105 is more explicit, χαλκίζειν δὲ παιδιᾶς τι εἶδος ἐν ᾗ νομίσματι ἠρτίαζον ('they used to play 'odds or evens' with/for money': one player held out a closed hand and the other had to guess whether that hand concealed an odd or even number of objects: e.g.coins at Ar. *Plut.* 816, knucklebones at Pl. *Lys.* 206e), cf. Pollux 7.206 and Herodas 3.64f. (a mother questioning her delinquent son) πρὸς δὲ τὴν παίστρην | ἐν τοῖσι προυνείκοισι χαλκίζεις φοιτέων;

This game needs to be distinguished from χαλκισμός (where the verbal phrase is χαλκίνδα παίζειν, Hesych. s.v.), described by Pollux 9.118 ὄρθον νόμισμα ἔδει συντόνως περιστρέψαντας, ἐπιστρεφόμενον ἐπιστῆσαι τῷ δακτύλῳ, cf. 7.206, Eustath. 986.41ff. (adapted from Suetonius περὶ παιδιᾶς 16, cf. J. Taillardat, *Suétone* Περὶ βλασφημιῶν, Περὶ παιδιῶν (Paris 1967) p. 66), 1409.17ff. Cf. L. Grasberger, *Erziehung und Unterricht im klassischen Alterthum* 1 (Würzburg 1864) 70, 159, L. Becq de Fouquières, *Les Jeux des anciens*² (Paris 1873) 298, Hermann–Blümner, *Privatalterthümer* 296f.

339 (338K)

Meineke 3.525 (LXVIIa), Kock 2.407, Edmonds 2.518, Kassel–Austin 2.194. Photius and the *Suda* s.v. ψυχικός note that in Alexis the adjective designated τὸν ἀνδρείόθυμον (so MSS of *Suda*: ἀνδρόθυμον Phot.; 'virile/brave').[1] Elsewhere in Greek ψυχικός has as wide a variety of nuances as ψυχή, the noun from which it was derived, but no exact parallel for the meaning alleged in Alexis seems to have survived. If it was a contemporary colloquialism, presumably it developed out of a positive view of the ψυχή

---

[1] The medieval lexica here (*Glossary of Useful Terms* 1.420.12 Bachmann, *Et. Mag.* (MS V), along with Phot. and *Suda*) define ψυχικός as σαρκικός, influenced by its use in N.T. (e.g. *1 Epist. Corinth.* 2.14, *Jud.* 19, cf. S. A. Naber's edition of Phot., vol., 2 (Leiden 1865) 271 n. 1 and W. Bauer, *A Greek–English Lexicon of the New Testament* (English translation², tr. W. F. Arndt and F. W. Gingrich, Chicago and London 1979) s.v. ψυχικός).

as the seat of qualities such as endurance (LSJ s.v., IV.2; e.g. Pind. *Pyth.* 1.48 τλάμονι ψυχᾷ, Ar. *Ach.* 393 καρτερὰν ψυχὴν λαβεῖν, Lysias 10.29 τοῖς μὲν σώμασι δύνανται, τὰς δὲ ψυχὰς οὐκ ἔχουσιν; the contrast between σωματικός and ψυχικός later became a cliché, e.g. Arist. *Eth. Nic.* 3.10.2, 1117ᵇ28, Polyb. 6.5.7 with τὸν τῇ ψυχικῇ τόλμῃ διαφέροντα, Josephus *Bell. Jud.* 1.430, Plut. *Mor.* 1092d).

345 Kock (37.6 Kassel–Austin)

Kock 2.408, cf. Meineke 3.400, Edmonds 2.392, Kassel–Austin 2.44f. If the form ἀκολασίᾳ is correctly transmitted at fr.37(36K).6 by the MSS (A, Epit.) of Ath. 12.544f (cf. comm. *ad loc.*), the statement (s.v. ἀκολασία) of Photius (p.62 Reitzenstein, 1.84 Theodoridis) = *Glossary of Useful Terms* (1.57.11 Bachmann, 367.24 Bekker) ἀκολασία Θουκυδίδης ἔφη, ἀκολαστία δὲ Ἄλεξις must refer to another passage in Γαλάτεια or to some other play. ἀκολασία is the form used normally in 5th- and 4th-century Athens (LSJ s.v., citing Antiphon 4.1.6, Thuc. 3.37, Lysias 16.11, Pl. *Gorg.* 505b, *Leg.* 10.884, Arist. *EN* 2.7.3, 1107ᵇ6), existing like many other abstract nouns in -ασία (e.g δικασία, δοκιμασία, εἰκασία, ὀνομασία) side by side with congeneric verbs in -ζω/-ζομαι and nouns or adjectives in -στης/-στος (cf. E. Fränkel, *ZVS* 45 (1912) 160ff., A. Debrunner, *Griechische Wortbildungslehre* (Heidelberg 1917) 143, P. Chantraine, *La Formation des noms en grec ancien* (Paris 1933) 83ff., Buck–Petersen, *Reverse Index* 120ff., Schwyzer 1.468f.). The very presence of -στ- in congeners, however, must have influenced a parallel formation of abstract nouns in -αστία (e.g. in good Attic ἀναρμοστία, ἀνηκουστία, ἀπαστία, ἀπληστία, ἀρρωστία, εὐαρμοστία, εὐλογιστία, παιδεραστία, φιλεραστία; in Homer ἀκομιστίη *Od.* 21.284; note particularly φιλογυμναστία Pl. *Symp.* 182c, 205d alongside ἀγυμνασία Ar. *Ran.* 1088, Arist. *EN* 3.5.15, 1114ᵃ24 and later ἀγυμναστία Porph. *Abst.* 1.37).

FALSE OR DOUBTFUL ATTRIBUTIONS

I Ἀλείπτρια

Meineke 1.377. In his discussion of earlier Greek references to hot water, Ath. 3.123b introduces Antiphanes 26(25K) with the words Ἀντιφάνης δ' ... ἐν δ' Ἀλειπτρίᾳ, φέρεται τὸ δρᾶμα καὶ ὡς Ἀλέξιδος. The terms in which Ath. expresses himself suggest that uncertainty over the play's authorship went back certainly to Ath.'s immediate source, and very probably beyond that to Hellenistic scholarship.[1] It could have originated in several ways. Alexis might have revised one of Antiphanes' comedies and produced it as his own, probably after the other playwright's death when charges of plagiarism would have been more difficult to sustain (so basically Meineke). This kind of theft was alleged against Menander (Porph. in Euseb. *Praep. Evang.* 10.3.12–13 = Menander, Test. 51 Körte–Thierfelder; cf. E. Stemplinger, *Das Plagiat in der griechischen Literatur* (Leipzig 1912) 7f., Ziegler in *RE* s.v. *Plagiat* 1979.18ff., P. M. Fraser, *Ptolemaic Alexandria* 2 (Oxford 1972) 1055f. n. 271), and may account for at least some of the cases of disputed attribution. An alternative source of confusion could have been provided by a dramatic production in which the author used somebody else, perhaps another comic poet, as his διδάσκαλος. This happened to our knowledge with eight of Aristophanes' plays (Βαβυλώνιοι, *Ach.*, *Vesp.*, *Av.*, *Lys.*, *Ran.*, Κώκαλος, Αἰολοσίκων), and the same practice was adopted by several other comic poets including Eupolis (Ath. 5.216d = *test.* 15 Kassel–Austin), Plato (fr. 106(99K)), Eubulus (the Arethas Σ of Pl. *Apol.* 19c = *test.* 4, cf. Hunter 13f.) and probably Anaxandrides (*IG* xiv.1098 = VI A 4.9 Mette, cf. Hunter 13 n. 2). Although there is no documentary proof that this practice ever led to a disputed attribution, a plausible case for its occurrence can be made with at least one 4th-century comedy, the Νάννιον. According to Ath. 13.568f

---

[1] There are similar uncertainties over the authorship of Ἄντεια, Ὕπνος (both Alexis or Antiphanes), Ὁμοία (Alexis or Antidotus); cf. also Alexis' Πρωτόχορος, frs. 245(342K), 284(282K), 341(340K). The problem of disputed authorship in comedy has often been discussed: e.g. Meineke 1.31f., 377, Kaibel, *Hermes* 24 (1889) 35ff. and *RE* s.v. *Alexis* 9, 1469.6ff., G. Lafaye, *Rev. Phil.* 40 (1916) 25ff., E. Mensching, *Mus. Helv.* 21 (1964) 17ff., R. Kassel, *ZPE* 14 (1974) 125ff., Hunter 12, 13ff. Kann, *De iteratis* is often cited as the basic work in this field, but it is marred by a tendency to unsupported subjectivity.

the authorship of this play was disputed between Eubulus and (almost certainly[1]) Philippus, the playwright son of Aristophanes who (according to the Plato scholiast cited above) produced more than one of Eubulus' plays.

Two other possible explanations that might account for disputed attributions elsewhere may perhaps be safely eliminated in the case of Ἀλείπτρια. It is unlikely that a text of the play had survived without its author's name and in consequence some ancient scholar had picked out the options from existing didascalic records. In such an event how could the names of Amphis and Diphilus have been excluded? Both were known to have written an Ἀλείπτρια, and the absence of citations from their two plays is best explained by an assumption that the texts had been lost (cf. Kock 2.236, 543, Kaibel, *Hermes* 24 (1889) 43f.). Secondly, the abbreviation of authors' names which occurs sometimes in didascalic inscriptions (e.g. *IG* ii².2323.101, 2323a.40 = III B 3 col. 1.18, B 2 col. 1.15 Mette) and MSS (e.g. Hense's introduction to the edition of Stob. 3.xxi f., Gow–Page, *Hellenistic Epigrams* (Cambridge 1965) 1.xxx ff.) might cause confusion between names as similar as Anaxilas and Anaxandrides, but hardly between Alexis and Antiphanes.

An ἀλείπτρια would be the female counterpart of an ἀλείπτης, who took his name from the task of anointing athletes in the ἀλειπτήριον (cf. Alexis 106(101K).2) of the gymnasium, although in practice the range of activities extended far beyond that, to judge from the word's use in many passages of literature (LSJ and Passow–Crönert s.v.; add also e.g. Plut. *Mor.* 133b, Epict. 3.10.8, 20.10, 26.22; cf. E. N. Gardiner, *Greek Athletic Sports and Festivals* (London 1910) 506, H. A. Harris, *Greek Athletes and Athletics* (London 1964) 171), and the job seemed to have differed little from that of a γυμναστής. ἀλείπτρια occurs as the title of three Attic comedies (cf. also Pollux 7.17 ἀλείπτριαν εἰρήκασιν οἱ μέσοι κωμικοί), and was mentioned in an unknown context by Lysias fr. 88 Sauppe. The one fr. extant from Antiphanes' or Alexis' play (= Antiphanes 26(25K), II.322 Kassel–Austin) gives a little direct information: the speaker is a female (βάψασα v. 3) slave (vv.4–5) in charge of an ἐργαστήριον, addressing two or more people (ποιῆτε v. 2, ὑμῶν v. 3). Was she the ἀλείπτρια herself, or a slave assistant? Was the ἐργαστήριον just a normal gymnasium with its attendant foot-baths (see below on vv. 2ff.), or could ἀλείπτρια have also been a euphemism for ἑταίρα, supplementing the gymnastic services to her clients with sexual favours (cf. the modern misuse of *masseuse* in English)?

---

[1] Ath.'s comment runs <εἰ> (add. Korais) Εὐβούλου τὸ δρᾶμα καὶ μὴ Φιλίππου (so the *recentiores*: φιλιππιδου A); cf. Meineke, *Men. et Phil.* x, Hunter 13ff.(the latter with a more sceptical view about the grounds for the dispute over the Νάννιον).

In this connection note especially Plaut. *Bacch.* 66 (the *hetaira*'s house a *palaestra*), 421ff. (Lydus comparing gymnastic exercise with that in a *hetaira*'s establishment), and Gymnasium as the name of a *meretrix* in Plaut. *Cist.*; cf. also Eubulus 82(84K).2 (*hetairai* as πώλους Κύπριδος ἐξησκημένας). To whom was this slave overseer speaking? To a κῶμος of young men banging on her doors (so Casaubon, *Animadv.* 236)? The visit of a κῶμος to a *hetaira*'s house was a familiar theme in ancient literature (references in Headlam–Knox on Herodas 2.34ff.; add now Men. *Dysk.* 58ff.). Could such a κῶμος have formed a chorus of New-Comedy type, and this speech have announced their entry at the end of the first act (cf. the introduction to Κουρίς and comm. on fr. 112(107K))?

Antiphanes 26(25K)

Meineke 3.11, Kock 2.19, Edmonds 2.170, Kassel–Austin 2.322. Iambic tetrameters catalectic are not attested elsewhere for Alexis, but they are for Antiphanes (293(300K))* and other comic poets at all periods from Cratinus down to Diphilus and Menander. In those passages which date roughly to the time of Alexis (e.g. also Anaxandrides 35(34K), Anaxilas 38(39K), Diphilus 1, Men. *Dysk.* 880ff.*), a mood of revelry or boisterous energy can sometimes be identified (the references asterisked) or at least sensed (e.g. here) in the use of the metre, whether the speculations outlined above about the fr.'s context are acceptable or not. Cf. J. W. White, *The Verse of Greek Comedy* (London 1912) 62ff., F. Perusino, *Il tetrametro giambico nella commedia greca* (Rome 1968), Handley and Sandbach on Men. *Dysk.* 880–958.

1 τοὐργαστήριον: here presumably the gymnasium (see on vv. 2ff.), although the word is occasionally used (euphemistically?) of a *hetaira*'s establishment or brothel, see comm. on 206(203K).5.

περιβόητον: here in a bad sense, 'notorious', as Casaubon saw (*Animadv.* 236), see LSJ s.v. 2.

2–4 The speaker threatens to dip her ἀρύταινα (a big ladle especially associated with bath houses, Pollux 7.166, 10.63) into a cauldron of boiling water and empty it over the people she is addressing. Small bath houses were regularly attached to gymnasia from the 4th century on, with the water circulating through a series of floor basins into which the bathers dipped their feet while the attendant used the ladle to pour cold water over their bodies (cf. Theophr. *Char.* 9). See R. Ginouvès, *Balaneutikè* (Paris 1962) 37, 212ff. The speaker's words here are curiously echoed in the description of an accident (?) that befell a woman of the Fayûm at the end of the following century (*P.Magd.* 33 = *P.Enteux.* 82): λουομένης γάρ μου ἐν τῷ βαλανείῳ . . . παραχέων (sc. the bath-attendant) ἐν τῷ γυναικείῳ [θό]λῳ, ἐκβεβηκυίας (εγβ- Π) μου ὥστε ζμήσασθ[αι], εἰσενέγκας θερμοῦ τὰς ἀρυταίνας κα{σ}τεσκέδασέν μου κ[. . .] καὶ κατέκαυσεν τήν τε κοιλίαν καὶ τὸν ἀρίστερον μηρὸν ἕως τοῦ γόνατος, ὥστε καὶ κινδυνεύειν με.

2 νὴ τὴν φίλην Δήμητρα: this precise oath occurs twice in later comedy, both times in the mouth of a *hetaira* (Men. *Epitr.* 955, Philippides 5.4–5), which might be of some significance in the present context, but cf. F. W. Wright, *Studies in Menander* (Baltimore 1911) 26.

3 βάψασα: sc. 'having dipped and drawn up (the biggest ladle from the middle of the cauldron of boiling water).' The expression amalgamates two common constructions of βάπτω: (1) + accusative of the object dipped (LSJ s.v. 1.1), e.g. Theophr. *Char.* 9.8 βάψας ἀρύταιναν, often with εἰς ὕδωρ, ἐν ὕδατι, etc. added; (2) + accusative of the liquid drawn up (LSJ s.v. 1.3), often with a dative of the vessel dipped (e.g. Theoc. 5.127 τᾷ κάλπιδι κηρία βάψαι, Eratosthenes in Ath. 11.482b), occasionally with ἐκ + genitive of the liquid (e.g. Ap. Rhod. 4.157 βάπτουσ' ἐκ κυκεῶνος). Cf. also Eur. *Hec.* 609f. σὺ δ' αὖ λαβοῦσα τεῦχος . . . βάψασ' ἔνεγκε δεῦρο ποντίας ἁλός (where π. ἁ. = partitive genitive, 'some sea water', unlike ζέοντος ὕδατος in v. 4 of the Ἀλείπτρια fr., which = genitive of the material or contents with λέβητος, cf. Alexis 223(221K).10f. ποτήριον ὕδατος and 202(198K).1; K.G. 1.333e). See also Rutherford on Babrius 71.2 and A. W. Bulloch, comm. (Cambridge 1985) on Call. *Lav. Pall.* 45.

4–5 ὕδωρ πίοιμ' ἐλεθεύριον: the phrase may be elucidated from the combined testimonies of (1) Paus. 2.17.1 ῥεῖ δὲ κατὰ τὴν ὁδόν (sc. the road from Mycenae to the Heraeum) ὕδωρ Ἐλευθέριον καλούμενον· χρῶνται δὲ αὐτῷ πρὸς καθάρσια αἱ περὶ τὸ ἱερὸν καὶ τῶν θυσιῶν ἐς τὰς ἀπορρήτους; (2) Hesychius (and other unpublished sources, cf. K. Latte *ad loc.*) s.v. Ἐλευθέριον (-ερον *Marcianus* of Hesych., -έριον S of *Prov. Par.*) ὕδωρ· ἐν Ἄργει ἀπὸ τῆς Κυνάδρας (Συναγείας *Marcianus* of Hesych., corr. Eustath.) πίνουσι κρήνης <οἱ> (add. *Prov.*, *Phot.*) ἐλευθερούμενοι τῶν οἰκετῶν, διὰ τὸ καὶ τὸν Κέρβερον κύνα ταύτη διαδρᾶναι καὶ ἐλευθερωθῆναι; (3) Eustath. 1747.11 ἐν Ἄργει Κυνάδρα κρήνη, ἐξ ἧς ἔπινον οἱ ἐλευθερούμενοι. ὅθεν τὸ ἐν Κυνάδρα ἐλευθέριον ὕδωρ παροιμιακῶς ἐπὶ τῆς κατ' ἐλευθερίαν ζωῆς. The detailed interpretation of these passages bristles with problems (cf. Hitzig–Blümner on Paus. *ad loc.*, J. G. Frazer, *Pausanias' Description of Greece* 3 (London 1898) 179ff.), but behind them clearly lies a tradition that at Argos and/or Mycenae the ceremony in which slaves were freed included a ritual drink from the spring Cynadra. Kock and Edmonds assume that an identical ceremony existed in Athens; there is no evidence, however, for any Athenian 'water of freedom', and indeed no need to import into Attica the explanatory origin of a phrase that was probably proverbial throughout Greece. Cf. Xenarchus fr. 5 ἐμοὶ γένοιτο σοῦ ζώσης, τέκνον, | ἐλευθέριον (-θερον A and Epit. MSS, Ath. 10.440e: corr. Meineke 3.12) πιοῦσαν οἶνον ἀποθανεῖν, a bibulous old slave's joke on the phrase, Petronius 71.1 where Trimalchio claims that his servants *aquam liberam gustabunt*, and Ovid *Am.* 1.6.26.

II Ἄντεια

Meineke 1.32, 322f., Breitenbach 125ff., R. Kassel, *ZPE* 14 (1974) 126 n. 19. After quoting a fr. (36(34K)) from Antiphanes' Ἄντεια, Ath. 3.127b continues with the allegation τὸ δ' αὐτὸ τοῦτο δρᾶμα φέρεται καὶ ὡς Ἀλέξιδος ἐν ὀλίγοις σφόδρα διαλλάττον. The statement is couched in substantially the same terms as the one made by Ath. shortly before (123b) on the Ἀλείπτρια, and we are probably justified in drawing the same conclusions about possible grounds for the disputed authorship of Ἄντεια. Some work of Alexandrian scholarship is likely to have been the source of Ath.'s allegation, but without the evidence of the lost play texts we have no means of knowing whether the claim that Alexis' comedy differed from Antiphanes' 'in exceedingly few' particulars (cf. here Kassel) was literally true, or a further example of the tendency of some ancient commentators to wild exaggeration when they compared similar treatments of a comic subject. None the less, the most plausible interpretation of Ath.'s words remains the one voiced by Meineke, that Alexis here adapted an earlier play by Antiphanes for one of his own productions.

The three frs. remaining from the play are all quoted with an undisputed attribution to Antiphanes (36–8(34–6K)); we are unable to say whether any or all of them featured in the version ascribed to Alexis.[1] These frs. yield no precise information about the plot of the play, although one of them (37(35K)), with its reference to the perfumes of the dealer Peron which a man 'is probably bringing to you' (v.2), suggests the world of the expensive courtesan. In Athens during the first half of the 4th century there was a celebrated *hetaira* by the name of Anteia (Breitenbach 119ff., Wissowa in *RE* s.v. 2, 2348.64ff.), contemporary with the Peron of the fr.; Breitenbach's suggestion that this *hetaira* was the main subject of Antiphanes' play is very tempting. Here Breitenbach was countering Meineke's alternative idea that the play was a myth burlesque about the daughter of Iobates who tried to seduce Bellerophon. Yet both theories are open to objection as they stand. Against Meineke Breitenbach argued that a burlesque about Iobates' daughter written in the 4th century was more likely to have been called Σθενέβοια, since Beller-

---

[1] Detailed commentary on them seems inappropriate here in a work devoted to Alexis.

ophon's temptress usually went by that name then in Athens.[1] Against the simple identification of Antiphanes' heroine with the real-life *hetaira* Meineke made the (admittedly not conclusive) point that in Ath.'s list of comedies about famous *hetairai* (13.567c; cf. Wehrli, *Motivstudien* 28) the Ἄντεια of Eunicus or Philyllius is found but not Antiphanes'. Only one explanation fits the facts and meets the objections: Antiphanes' play combined myth burlesque and ridicule of the contemporary *hetaira* by portraying the temptress of the Bellerophon myth as a (perhaps veiled) caricature of the courtesan. This would account for the choice of Ἄντεια rather than Σθενέβοια as title, and for the play's absence from Ath.'s list. As precedents for this type of burlesque may be instanced Cratinus' Διονυσαλέξανδρος and Νέμεσις, in both of which Pericles seems to have been ridiculed in the guise of a myth figure (cf. especially J. Th. M. F. Pieters, *Cratinus* (Leiden 1946) 117ff., 121ff., W. Luppe, *Philologus* 110 (1966) 169ff., 124 (1980) 154ff. and *Halle W.Z.* 23 (1974) 4, 49ff., J. Schwarze, *Die Beurteilung des Perikles durch die attische Komödie* (Munich 1971) 6ff., E. W. Handley, *BICS* 29 (1982) 109ff., Hunter 25f.). And in Plato's Φάων, a comedy produced only twenty or so years before Antiphanes' Ἄντεια,[2] it appears that Aphrodite was vulgarised into a procuress and Phaon into a male prostitute (Kock 1.645ff., Webster, *SLGC* 18f.).

It would have been useful to know if Alexis turned Antiphanes' play into pure myth travesty at a time when the *hetaira* Anteia had ceased to be of topical interest, and if tragedies on the Bellerophon myth such as Euripides' Σθενέβοια and Βελλερόφων or Astydamas' Βελλερόφων (cf. Webster, *Hermes* 82 (1954) 296ff.) influenced comic presentations of the myth. But further speculation is futile.

---

[1] She was called Anteia by Homer (*Il.* 6.160) but Stheneboea by Hesiod (frs. 129.16ff., 131 Merkelbach–West), and the latter name was standardised in Athenian usage by the 5th-century tragedians, especially Euripides in his notorious Σθενέβοια (cf. T. B. L. Webster, *The Tragedies of Euripides* (London 1967) 80ff.). On the names, pedigrees and legends of Anteia/Stheneboea see especially the entries s.vv. *Anteia, Bellerophon* and *Stheneboia* in *RE* (2348.53ff.: Wernicke, 241.48ff. and 2468.37ff.: Bethe) and Roscher (364.32ff.: Engelmann, 757.50ff.: Rapp and 1506.42ff.: Buslepp), Robert, *GH* 1.182f., and cf. M. L. West, *The Hesiodic Catalogue of Women* (Oxford 1985) 78 and index s.v. *Stheneboea*).

[2] Plato's Φάων was produced in 391, if Clinton's plausible emendation of Φαίδρῳ to Φάωνι at Σᴱ Ar. *Plut.* 179 (p.334.41 Dübner: citing Plato fr. 196(179K)) is accepted. Antiphanes' Ἄντεια has been dated with some plausibility to the 370s (Webster, *CQ* 2 (1952) 15; cf. Edmonds 2.178 note b).

III Ἀσωτοδιδάσκαλος

C. Burney, *Monthly Review* 29 (1799) 436f., Porson in R. Walpole, *Comicorum Graecorum fragmenta quaedam* (Cambridge 1805) 88, Meineke 1.397f., H. van Herwerden, *Mnemosyne* 14 (1886) 184, G. Kaibel, *Hermes* 24 (1889) 43 n. 2, E. Bignone, *L'Aristotele perduto* (Florence 1936) 1.335, 2.228ff. (in 1973 reprint 1.308, 2.577ff.), W. Süss, *Gnomon* 13 (1937) 599, W. G. Arnott, *CQ* 5 (1955) 210ff., H. Wankel, *Hermes* 111 (1983) 151f. and n. 58, Nesselrath, *MK* 69f. Only one fr. (25 Kassel–Austin, 2.37ff.) of an Ἀσωτοδιδάσκαλος attributed to Alexis now survives, and although some scholars continue to believe in its authenticity (e.g. in addition to Bignone, Nesselrath and Kassel–Austin cited above, A. Giannini, *Acme* 13 (1960) 159, A. Barigazzi, *La formazione spirituale di Menandro* (Turin 1965) 131), the evidence that the fr. was a deliberate forgery composed some time in the 3rd or 2nd century still seems to me overwhelming. A full review of that evidence is presented in my 1955 paper; here it is enough to summarise the main argument.

(1) Ath. 8.336d–f, quoting the fr., claims to owe all his information about the play and its one fr. to the writings of Sotion, the Peripatetic historian of philosophy who lived early in the 2nd century.[1] According to Ath. the play was not one of the 800 or more plays of Middle Comedy which he (or to be more precise, the deipnosophist Democritus who is imagined to be speaking at this point in Ath.'s work) had read and excerpted, nor had it been catalogued in the library at Alexandria by Callimachus (fr. 439 Pfeiffer) or Aristophanes of Byzantium (fr. 402 Slater, p. 246 Nauck), or at Pergamum by the cataloguers there. Sotion was himself a native of Alexandria, and it seems remarkable that he – working on philosophy, not comedy – should have had access to a genuine comic text that neither Callimachus nor Aristophanes – the latter an expert in comedy and a contemporary of Sotion working presumably in the same library – had listed for Alexandria. It seems wiser to assume that a spurious text, of either a complete play or (more probably) one or more passages from it, had been palmed off on Sotion.

(2) Analysis of the fr. itself reveals traits that are not merely unparalleled in Alexis (this would be a point of trivial value when we possess only a

---

[1] The frs. of Sotion have been conveniently collected by F. Wehrli (*Schule des Aristoteles*, Suppl. 2, Basle and Stuttgart 1978); the Ἀσωτοδιδάσκαλος citation appears as fr. 1 of περὶ τῶν Τίμωνος Σίλλων pp. 31, 68. See also Stenzel in *RE* s.v. *Sotion* 1, 1235.61ff., W. von Kienle, *Die Berichte über die Sukzessionen der Philosophen in der hellenistischen und spätantiken Literatur* (Diss. Berlin 1961) 79ff., M. Di Marco, *Timone di Fliunte, Silli* (Rome 1989) 54, Nesselrath 69 n. 13.

fraction of 1 per cent of the poet's total output) but also unlikely for any Attic comedian writing at the time of Alexis. One may instance here the reference to the gates of the Odeon as a haunt of philosophers (v.2: on this and the other topics, see comm. *ad loc.*), the shortening of the iota in ἥδιον (6), the use of τύρβαζε (6) and ψύξει (10), the clumsiness of expression in vv. 1–3 and 8–9, and perhaps also the repetition πίνωμεν, ἐμπίνωμεν (4). The density and variety of these anomalies make attempts to explain them away as possibly due to *natürliche Korruptelen* (so Nesselrath 69 n. 13) of excerptor or scribe misguided.

In 1955 it appeared to me that the most likely motive for such a forgery was a hope of financial gain; of this I am now less convinced. The starting-point for reconsideration must be Bignone's stimulating discussion of the fr., even though his arguments are blemished by the failure to recognise its spuriousness and by a tendency to force too much evidence into the straitjacket of his case. Bignone sees everywhere in this fr. an attempt to ridicule by satirical parody the language and ideas which were used in the 3rd century and later to promote hedonistic philosophy in general and Epicureanism in particular. He would have justified his interpretation more effectively if he had been content to recognise the undifferentiated hedonistic drift of most of the fr.'s language, and to emphasise the one place where Epicureanism specifically is called to mind: the reference in vv. 8ff. to the vanity of public office, which echoes this philosophy's rejection of political activity as a desirable ambition. Bignone weakens his argument by trying to identify particularised Epicurean allusions in contexts too general for such equations. Two instances may be given. First, the commendation of the stomach at vv. 6f. is linked by Bignone with Epicurus' words ἀρχὴ καὶ ῥίζα παντὸς ἀγαθοῦ ἡ τῆς γαστρὸς ἡδονή (fr. 409 Usener = 59 Bailey). This comparison is interesting, but in the absence of any direct verbal tie it is more important to remember that the belly was praised in Attic drama too (e.g. Cratinus 349(317K), Eur. *Cycl.* 334ff.) long before Epicurus. Secondly, Bignone compares the fr.'s last two lines with the strikingly similar phraseology of the Sardanapalus epitaph (see comm. on vv. 11–12), but he fails to prove any positive relationship between Epicurus and epitaph beyond their common hedonism, or to mention that the 'eat, drink and be merry' motif is also an early comic platitude (see below, introduction to fr. 25). Yet it would be wrong to make too much of such criticisms of detail; they qualify but do not seriously impair the plausibility of Bignone's general thesis that we are intended here to see an amusing travesty of a hedonistic sermon tinged with Epicurean colour. This explanation suits my own scenario and suggested date of the postulated forgery no less well than does the fr.'s style, to which attention must now be directed.

In my earlier paper some of the significant features in that style were analysed: the shortness of the phrase units, the asyndetic structure, the triads of nouns. It may be rash to call these uncharacteristic of Alexis in view of the scantiness of the remains; but the first two of these features, together with some others recognisable in the fr. (a jerky, unargued series of assertions; the address now to one hearer (Sikon), now to another (Manes, if his name is rightly conjectured in v. 6); a use of vivid, earthy images), are very characteristic of a form of literature which came into vogue in the early years of the 3rd century and dealt predominantly with ethical matters: the so-called 'diatribe'.[1] This was a favourite literary weapon of at least some Cynics, and it is a well-known fact that the sect conducted an active campaign against hedonism and its philosophic votaries in the Hellenistic period; two books of Menippus' satires, for instance, directly opposed Epicureanism (Diog. Laert. 6.101).[2] I am now inclined to believe that this alleged fr. of Ἀσωτοδιδάσκαλος formed part of the Cynics' war on hedonism, and that its forger[3] fabricated it as a bogus quotation designed to illustrate the enemy viewpoint in an anti-Epicurean pamphlet composed in the 3rd or 2nd century. Such a theory would explain how the passage came to be known to a historian of philosophy such as Sotion, but escaped the notice (or authenticating approval) of experts in comedy like Aristophanes of Byzantium. It would also perhaps help to account for the lack of fluency and of structured

---

[1] These stylistic features are well illustrated and analysed in the opening chapter of R. Bultmann, *Der Styl der paulinischen Predigt und die kynisch-stoische Diatribe* (*Forschungen zur Religion* 13, Göttingen 1910); cf. also E. Norden, *Die antike Kunstprosa* (Leipzig and Berlin 1909) 129f., W. Capelle and H. I. Marrou, *RAC* s.v. *Diatribe* 902f. Recently, however, the legitimacy of identifying a homogeneous genre in this type of literature and of labelling it διατριβή has once more been vigorously challenged (see especially H. D. Jocelyn, *LCM* 4 (1979) 145f., 7 (1982) 3ff. (with a useful survey of earlier discussions), 8 (1983) 89ff., D. Tsekourakis, *Hellenika* 32 (1980) 61ff., C. O. Brink, *Horace on Poetry* 3 (Cambridge 1982) 300) and defended (H. B. Gottschalk, *LCM* 7 (1982) 91f., 8 (1983) 92f.).

[2] Cf. D. R. Dudley, *A History of Cynicism from Diogenes to the 6th Century AD* (London 1937) 103ff.

[3] On the practice of forgery in the ancient world see especially E. Stemplinger, *Das Plagiat in der griechischen Literatur* (Leipzig 1912), Ziegler in *RE* s.v. *Plagiat* 1956.26ff. (comedy is discussed at 1969.7ff.), J. A. Sint, *Pseudonymität im Altertum* (*Commentationes Aenipontanae* 15, Innsbruck 1960), W. Speyer, *Die literarische Fälschung im heidnischen und christlichen Altertum* (Munich 1971), cf. his articles in *JAC* 8/9 (1965/6) 88ff. and *RAC* 7 (1969) 236ff.; *Entr. Hardt* 17 (1972), and P. M. Fraser, *Ptolemaic Alexandria* 2 (Oxford 1972) 1055f. n. 271.

clarity in the writing, to which attention is drawn in the following commentary.

[Alexis] 25

Meineke 3.394, Kock 2.306, Edmonds 2.306, Kassel–Austin 2.38; cf. the works cited at the beginning of the introduction to Ἀσωτοδιδάσκαλος. The peculiar circumstances of this fr.'s composition, hypothesised and argued above, make a detailed commentary desirable, even if Alexis is not its author.

The writer has envisaged a scene, according to Sotion (Ath. 8.336e), in which a slave, plausibly named Xanthias (the plays or frs. in which a character with this name appears are conveniently listed by V. Ehrenberg, *The People of Aristophanes*[2] (London 1951) 173 n. 1; up to now they all belong to Old Comedy, but this may be an accident of preservation, cf. Austin, *CGFP* p. 123 fr. 106.118), preaches to an unspecified number of his fellows (a Sikon and probably a Manes are named in the fr.), urging them to a life of pleasure. 'Eat, drink, and be merry, for tomorrow we die' is his general theme; this may have fitted into the broad framework of Epicurean belief, yet taken by itself it is as inadequate a diagnostic of such belief as are its other occurrences in ancient writings, where it is often nothing more than a general hedonistic motto (e.g. the Sardanapalus epitaph in its different versions (Apollodorus in Σ Ar. *Av.* 1021b; Amyntas in Ath. 12.529f = *FGrH* 122 F 2; Aristobulus in Ath. 12.530b–c and Strabo 14.5.9 = *FGrH* 139 F 9, cf. Arrian *Anab.* 2.5.4; Choerilus in Strabo 14.5.9, cf. Polyb. 8.10(12).3, Dio Chrys. 4.135, Clem. Alex. *Strom.* 2.20, 118.6, Σ Ar. *Av.* 1021c), Eur. *Alc.* 788ff., the skolion in Ameipsias 21(22K).4–5, the inscription on one of the Boscoreale goblets in the Louvre, εὐφραίνου ὃ(ν) ζῆς χρόνον (cf. A. M. A. Héron de Villefosse, *Mon. Piot* 5 (1899) 64ff.), although in comedy it often represents the philosophy of parasites and other voluptuaries (e.g. Epicharmus frs. 34, 35, where the speaker is a parasite by nature if not by name; Alexis 222(219K).14ff., possibly spoken by a parasite, cf. the introduction to Ταραντῖνοι, and 273(271K), Philetaerus 7, com. adesp. fr. 1203 Kock, Plaut. *Bacch.* 1193ff. spoken by a *meretrix*, Men. 473ff., 1140ff., *Stich.* 447 and the variation in *Trin.* 258ff.; cf. G. Giangrande, *Entr. Hardt* 14 (1969) 104f., 165f., W. Fauth, *Wien. Stud.* 86 (1973) 42ff., Dover, *GPM* 269, Lloyd on Hdt. 2.78). If the forger of the present fr. needed a model for his efforts, it would doubtless have been in passages such as these that he found it.

1 φληναφῶν: at first sight, a good imitation of comic language; the verb is used intransitively at Ar. *Equ.* 664, *Nub.* 1475 (see Starkie *ad loc.*), and the noun φλήναφος occurs in Menander in the senses of 'chatter' (fr. 417.6) and 'chatterer' (fr. 97.4; *Kol.* 22 is too mutilated for a decision between these two meanings), although it is condemned by strict Atticists (Durham, *Vocabulary* 100). λῆροι καὶ φλήναφοι are coupled by Lucian *Somn.* 7 (cf. the imitation in [Aristaen.] *Epist.* 2.17). Yet the construction here poses problems: see on v. 3.

2 Λύκειον, Ἀκαδήμειαν, Ὠιδείου πύλας: the Lyceum, where Protagoras (Diog. Laert. 9.54), 4th-century 'sophists' (Antiphanes 120(122K).3) and Aristotle (cf. Gow on Machon 47) taught, and the Academy, where Plato established his school (E. Zeller, *Plato and the Older Academy* (London and New York, 1888 edition of the English translation by S. F. Alleyne and A. Goodwin) 25; on its site see J. Travlos, *Pictorial Dictionary of Ancient Athens* (London 1971) 48ff.), could clearly have been described by Alexis as sophistic haunts, but the Odeon (W. Judeich, *Die Topographie von Athen*[2] (Munich 1931) 306ff., O. Broneer, *U.Cal.P.C.A.* 1 (1944) 305ff., J. A. Davison, *JHS* 78 (1958) 33ff., Travlos 387ff.) is not mentioned as attracting philosophers before the time of Chrysippus, who did not arrive in Athens until after Alexis' death (Diog. Laert. 7.184, cf. Plut. *Mor.* 1033d–e). The reference to the Odeon's *gates* is puzzling; the author may have had in mind the Propylon on the east side of the building (Judeich 308), or alternatively he may have introduced the idea of the gates merely as a metrical stopgap, being ignorant or careless about the true facts.[1] Given the probable circumstances of composition, there is no reason to postulate corruption, as do some scholars: (i) Ὠιδεῖον, Πύλας Daléchamp after the *recentiores* and Musurus, but Casaubon, *Animadv.* 585 notes that there were no philosophers at Thermopylae, and Meineke's suggestion that Πύλας could be a loose designation of the Propylaea on the Acropolis is unsupported by evidence for either the usage or the presence of sophists there; (ii) Ὠιδεῖον, πύλας | λήρου σοφιστῶν F. Wieseler, *Schedae criticae atque exegeticae* (*Index Scholarum*, Göttingen 1869) 8, on the analogy of Pind. *Ol.* 6.27, Bacchylides fr. 5 Blass: stylistically incongruous; (iii) Ὠιδεῖον πάλιν H. Sauppe in C. Wachsmuth, *Die Stadt Athen im Altertum* 1 (Leipzig 1874) 635 n. 1, and (iv) Ὠιδεῖον, στοάν Blaydes, *Adv.* 2.153 after Kock's στοάς: good sense, but palaeographically unconvincing.

Ἀκαδήμειαν (scanning ∪ ∪ – – ∪) is the correct orthography for the Athenian site (cf. Meisterhans–Schwyzer 41 and 50, Threatte 1.128), but the medieval MSS here and elsewhere (e.g. Alexis 99(94K).1, Ar. *Nub.* 1005, cf. Dover *ad loc.*) corrupt it to the unmetrical form ∪ ∪ – ∪ – (-ημ(ί)αν).

3 λήρους σοφιστῶν: for the phrase cf. Alciphron 3.19.10 ὁ τῶν σοφιστῶν

---

[1] In view of my suspicions about this fr.'s composition, I am inclined to discount any possibility that Ὠιδείου πύλας was coined as a comic parody of the poetic cliché Ἅιδου πύλας (of which Barrett collects instances in his commentary on Eur. *Hipp.* 56f.).

λῆρος; for the use of λῆροι to dismiss derisively a string of place names see comm. on 263(261K).5.

The syntactical difficulties of the fr.'s opening sentence (cf. also vv. 8–9), which is foggily conceived and clumsily expressed, arise almost certainly from its author's ineptitude, not from any fault in the transmission. The presence of ἄνω κάτω in v. 1, along with the string of accusatival place names that follow in v. 2, would lead one to expect some such governing particle as περιπατῶν, but instead of this we find φληναφῶν, which elsewhere in Greek is always used intransitively in the active (e.g. in addition to the passages cited above on v. 1 Meletius in Cramer, *Anecdota Graeca* 3.5.20, Oenomaus in Euseb. *Praep. Evang.* 5.24.5, Proclus on Pl. *Tim.* 1.90 Diehl). There appear to be two alternative ways of construing the sentence: either (1) φληναφῶν here is transitive, governing the v. 2 triad ('chattering about . . .').; such an anomaly might perhaps be defended by the verb's personal use in the passive in Philodemus *Rhet.* 1.246 Sudhaus and *Ir.* p. 69 Wilke; or (2), if φληναφῶν is intransitive, the three place names would then be in apposition to ταῦτα (v.1); I think this the less probable option. In either case ἄνω κάτω would be attached to φληναφῶν by a slender thread of association, 'chattering up and down' because philosophical conversation in ancient Athens was commonly linked to a stroll (cf. my note on 151(147K).2).

4 πίνωμεν, ἐμπίνωμεν: this kind of repetition, in which a compound *directly* follows the simple verb merely to reinforce the meaning ('let's drink, let's drink *up*'), is contrary to normal Attic idiom, where either the chosen word is exactly repeated (e.g. Alexis 207(204K).1, Men. fr. 674) or the simple verb follows the compound (e.g. Eur. *Alc.* 400, *Bacch.* 1065); cf. Fraenkel, *Kl. Beitr.* 1.441f., R. Renehan, *Greek Textual Criticism* (Cambridge Mass. 1969) 83ff. and (the fullest discussion) *Studies in Greek Texts* (Göttingen 1976) 11ff., Diggle, *Studies* 18.[1] Where the simple verb does precede its compound directly in an uninterrupted sentence of Attic Greek (I have noticed few instances), a substantial modification of the verbal meaning is detectable: Antiphanes 146(148K).1f. ἔρχεται, | μετέρχετ' αὖ, προσέρχετ' αὖ, μετέρχεται, Men. *Dysk.* 818 δίδου, μεταδίδου, cf. Ar. *Ran.* 369. Accordingly, in a careful Attic author there would be grounds for considering emendation (ἐντράγωμεν after πίωμεν would perhaps be preferable to Blaydes' ἐσθίωμεν, *Adv.* 1.105); here, however, it is more appropriate to accept ἐμπίνωμεν and compare two very late parallels: the formula δεδεμένον συνδεδεμένον καταδεδεμένον

---

[1] For the practice in Roman comedy see O. Raebel, *De usu adnominationis apud Romanorum poetas comicos* (Diss. Halle 1882) 24ff.

which appears misspelled on magic tablets *c.* AD 400 (Audollent, *Defix.* 155, A.36, B.6) and [Aristaen.] *Epist.* 2.4. μεῖνον ἀνάμεινον (a girl to her lover).

ὦ Σίκων, <Σίκων>: Casaubon's supplement (cf. *Animadv.* 585) is plausible enough, although such repetition of vocatives usually belongs to a more impassioned context: of either solemn warning (Headlam–Knox on Herodas 10.2, cf. Pl. *Tim.* 22b; not relevant in this fr. before v. 10) or regretful disapproval (e.g. Ar. fr. 402(387K).1, Theoc. 11.72, Plaut. *Rud.* 1235, *Trin.* 1094, Ter. *Andr.* 282). Sikon was a common name of slaves in real life (Zwicker in *RE* s.v. Σίκων 2527.6off., M. Lambertz, *Die griechischen Sklavennamen* (Vienna 1907) 15), and so was used for them at least in early 4th-century comedy (Ar. *Eccl.* 867, cf. the title Αἰολοσίκων and Kassel–Austin 3.2.34, Meineke 3.264 on Eubulus 123(126K).1, T. B. L. Webster, *CQ* 42 (1948) 25); by the end of the 4th century it seems to have become the standard name for the hired cook (Handley on Men. *Dysk.* 889, Gomme–Sandbach, *Comm.* p. 131). Ancient etymologists connected the word with Σικελός (cf. Zwicker); on the name's formation see A. Debrunner, *Griechische Wortbildungslehre* (Heidelberg 1917) 313. On the use of ὦ here with the vocative, see especially Gomme–Sandbach, *Comm.* on Men. *Dysk.* 823.

5 χαίρωμεν, ἕως: not necessarily to be condemned on metrical grounds, since ἕως may be scanned by synecphonesis as one long syllable (*CQ* 7 (1957) 192, West, *Greek Metre* 12).

τὴν ψυχὴν τρέφειν: a striking expression, presumably to be interpreted as *animum lautitiis fouere ac recreare* (Daléchamp); cf. Semonides fr. 29.13 Diehl = Simonides fr. 8.13 West ψυχῇ τῶν ἀγαθῶν τλῆθι χαριζόμενος. This use of ψυχή (= the non-rational, emotional and appetitive self) seems to have developed first in Ionia (E. R. Dodds, *The Greeks and the Irrational* (Berkeley 1951) ch. 5); in Attic Greek it is found in philosophers (e.g. Pl. *Protag.* 313c τῶν ἀγωγίμων, ἀφ' ὧν ψυχὴ τρέφεται; the Socratic injunction τῆς ψυχῆς ἐπιμελεῖσθαι, cf. W. K. C. Guthrie, *A History of Greek Philosophy* 3 (Cambridge 1969) 467ff.) and tragedy (e.g. 841, Eur. *Cycl.* 340f.) as well as comedy (Diocles fr. 14.3 ἀγαθόν τι τῇ ψυχῇ παθών); cf. the Doric of Bacchidas' tomb (Ath. 8.336d) πιέν, φαγὲν καὶ πάντα τᾷ ψυχᾷ δόμεν. It would be interesting to discover whether Plaut. *Stich.* 622 *genium meliorem tuom non facies* (sc. by eating my food) and other comparable passages in Roman comedy (e.g. *Pers.* 263, Ter. *Phorm.* 44) were modelled on equivalent Greek expressions, and if they were, what these would have been.

6 The reading of the *Marcianus* τυρβαζε μανην produces no sense. One can τυρβάζειν 'stir up' mud (Ar. *Vesp.* 257) or a city (*Equ.* 310; cf. the use of the middle = 'jostle', *Pax* 1007), but hardly a μάνην, either in the sense of 'drinking cup' (LSJ s.v. μάνης 1)[1] or as part of the κότταβος stand (ibid. II);[2] and there is no evidence that here we may have to deal with the allusive language of a proverb. Hence Muretus' conjecture Μάνη (Variae Lectiones XIX.3 in J. Gruter, Lampas 2 (Frankfurt 1604) 1225) is generally accepted; it makes sense of the noun (see below), but at the expense (as Muretus himself realised) of fathering on the fr.'s author an intransitive active use of the verb presumably in the sense of 'revel' (LSJ s.v. τυρβάζω II; after Casaubon, Animadv. 585) that is unparalleled elsewhere in comprehensible Greek (P.Rylands 483.8 is unintelligible). The Suda (with other lexica cited by Adler ad loc.) has the gloss τύρβη· ἀπόλαυσις, ἢ θόρυβος, ἢ τάραξις; even if this gloss is correctly transmitted, it is still unsafe to argue from it for a similar use of the congeneric verb; yet it would be equally rash to reject the possibility of such a use, in view of our author's style (τυρβάζειν in any case appears to be a word of vulgar speech: Neil on Ar. Equ. 310),[3] and of the close semantic relationship between the ideas of 'stirring up' and 'revelling'. However, is it legitimate to conjecture τρύφαινε (cf. Handley on Men. Dysk. 830)?

With Muretus' conjecture, the addressee changes from slave (? or freedman cook) Sikon to slave Manes. The name Manes, like Sikon, has a non-Attic origin; Strabo 7.3.12 and 12.3.25 alleges that it is a Phrygian stem, and was given in Athens particularly to slaves hailing from that and the surrounding regions; cf. Ath. 13.578b. The allegation is supported by the evidence discussed by Wilamowitz, Hermes 34 (1899) 222, A. Wilhelm, Beiträge zur griechischen Inschriftenkunde (Vienna 1909) 35ff., L. Zgusta, Kleinasiatische Personennamen (Prague 1964) 287ff., cf. Gow on Machon 191.

---

[1] Wine was mixed with water in the κρατήρ, not in the ποτήριον itself; this fact rules out a possible interpretation of τύρβαζε μάνην that would, however, still give a strained sense (τυρβάζειν implies that any mixture produced by the stirring will be muddy or clouded; it might be used of adding water to ouzo, for instance, but not water to wine).

[2] See Schneider in RE s.v. Kottabos 1535.44ff., showing that the traditional interpretation of μάνης = 'figurine' is probably wrong.

[3] To explain the anomalous use of τύρβαζε here and ψύξει in v. 10, Bignone suggests that these words were chosen in order to parody Epicurus' own style, which admitted non-Attic vocabulary and usage. If Bignone is right about the parodic intent, he is wrong about the mechanics. The cited words are not themselves unattic, they are Attic words used oddly; and the explanation of the oddness may be that the author of the fr. is deliberately choosing vulgar uses, not aping a foreigner's solecisms. The vulgarity of τυρβάζειν is well argued by Neil, and the particular sense of ψύξει here may deserve the same label. The vulgarity of Epicurus' style was a byword among the ancients (Norden, op. cit. in p. 821 n. 1, 123).

Like Sikon Manes too became a stock name for comic slaves (Ar. *Pax* 1146, *Av.* 1311, 1329, *Lys.* 908, 1211, Pherecrates 10.1, Mnesimachus 4.2), along with its feminine form Μανία (Ar. *Thesm.* 728 etc., *Ran.* 1345, Ameipsias fr. 2, Pherecrates fr.130(125K), Men. fr. 873, T. Williams, *Hermes* 91 (1963) 288ff.).

γαστρὸς οὐδὲν ἥδιον: see above, introduction to Ἀσωτοδιδάσκαλος. Yet the majority of characters on the comic stage follow the example of Odysseus in Hom. *Od.* 17.286f. in bewailing rather the pangs that come from the belly (cf. comm. on fr. 215(212K).

The shortening of the iota in -ίων comparatives is a feature of epic at various periods (e.g. Hom. *Il.* 6.410, Ap. Rhod. 3.815) and poetry in the Ionic dialect influenced by epic (e.g. Mimnermus fr. 2.10 West, Semonides 7.31 West); Doric verse (e.g. *Pseudepicharmea* fr. 86.7 Austin, *CGFP* p. 89 = *P.Hibeh* 1.7), which may account for its occurrence in choral lyric (Pind. fr. 89a Snell–Maehler), copied by Ar. *Equ.* 1264 and Dionysius Chalcus fr. 6 West; and perhaps also Eur. *Bacch.* 877 = 897, where metrical laws are obeyed whether one scans the iota of κάλλιον long or short: see Dodds *ad loc.* and A. M. Dale, *The Lyric Metres of Greek Drama*² (Cambridge 1968) 148). In Attic, however, the iota is regularly long (Porson on Eur. *Or.* 499, cf. C. Burney, *Monthly Review* 29 (1799) 428ff.), and the few exceptions to the general rule (the choral anapaests of Eur. fr. 546; the iambics of Aeschylus fr. 309.3 (satyric), Eur. *Suppl.* 1101 and Collard *ad loc.*, trag. adesp. fr. 320 Nauck² = [Men.] monost. 738, Eupolis fr. 336, perhaps Men. fr. 416.11 with Gomme–Sandbach, *Comm. ad loc.*; cf. also A. Nauck, *MGR* 6 (1894) 97, Schulze, *QE* 300f. nn. 3, 4, Wilamowitz, *Hermes* 59 (1924) 257f., W. G. Arnott, *CQ* 5 (1955) 214, Diggle, *Studies* 29f., perhaps Slater on Ar. Byz. fr. 347, but he is wrong about Alexis fr. 158(154), see comm. *ad loc.*) ought to be considered rare licences influenced by the practice in other literary genres and dialects familiar to Athenians. In the present fr., whose command of Attic idiom and style is suspect, the shortening of the iota becomes an insignificant vagary, just as it is with the eclectic Herodas (βέλτῖον 2.91, but ἥδῖον 1.87: Headlam–Knox on the former passage, Cunningham on the latter).

7–9 If the *Marcianus* and Epit. preserve the correct text here (but ἀρεταί in v. 8, κενοί in v. 9 have been questioned: see below), these lines are an odd rigmarole, comprehensible only on the postulate of an author who jotted down a series of clichés without considering their logical and syntactical relationship. In v. 7 the looseness of conversational usage may explain (if it does not excuse) the organisation of thought that makes the stomach *alone* both mother and father. This *grotesquerie* is merely a comic or colloquial extension of an image that begins with γῆ πάντων μήτηρ in Hesiod (*Op.* 563; cf. in addition to the passages cited by West *ad loc.* [Men.] monost. 511, Aelian *Epist.* 20), and then is freely stretched to take in ideas where the parental metaphor is more laboured (e.g. the diatribe fr. published by V. Martin, *Mus. Helv.* 16 (1959) 83, 1 10 ἐπιθυμία μήτηρ ἐστὶ πενίας, Ach. Tat. 2.29.3 λόγος δὲ τούτων ἁπάντων (sc. emotions) πατήρ, Plaut. *Stich.* 155 *famem ego fuisse suspicor matrem mihi*, cf. Fraenkel, *EP* 278ff.). On the converse use of υἱός see Handley and Sandbach on Men. *Dysk.* 88, and cf. *Rh. Mus.* 108 (1965) 373 n. 8. The alleged relationship between the ideas in v. 7 and Epicurus fr. 409 Usener is discussed in the introduction to Ἀσωτοδιδάσκαλος.

8–9 The transmitted text of these verses[1] is normally printed as one sentence (so Kassel–Austin) without internal punctuation: 'Instances of excellence – both embassies and military commands – sound like empty vaunts, as dreams.' This may be tolerable sense, but it requires one to interpret ἀντί as 'equivalent to' rather than 'instead of', although the latter sense would be more natural in a clause apparently organised as here with a substantival predicate (κόμποι κενοί). But if one punctuates with a colon after κενοί ('. . . commands – are empty vaunts: they sound like . . .'), this difficulty is removed, the sentence construction is less clumsy and one gains in place of botchery two pithy asyndetic clauses which fit the fr.'s general style admirably. Other problems, however, remain.

(1) If ἀρεταὶ δὲ πρ. τε καὶ στρ. is correctly transmitted, it cannot mean 'instances of excellence and embassies and commands' (Denniston, *GP* 500f. cites no parallel for a triad where the second member is linked to the first by τε and the third to the second by καί; Ar. *Av.* 701f. and Lysias 2.39 are rarish examples of a related construction); the acceptable interpretation must be 'instances of excellence – both embassies and commands', with πρ. and στρ. cited as examples of ἀρεταί. This would provide an odd expression of an odd thought, but is perhaps conceivable Greek for this author in view of his clear intention at this point to parody Epicurean belief (cf. the introduction to Ἀσωτοδιδάσκαλος). Yet Jacobs' ἀρχαί for ἀρεταί (*Addit.* 184) here is an attractive conjecture; it gives the correct term for the genus of which πρ. and στρ. are species, and is fairly close to the *ductus*. Jacobs' postulate of the reverse corruption in a passage of Diotogenes at Stob. *Anth.* 4.7.62 Hense (p.266.9–10) is equally neat, equally tempting and equally perhaps to be relegated to the apparatus.

(2) Phryn. *Praep. Soph.* 83.8 de Borries has the entry κενὰ ψοφεῖν· κενῶς

---

[1] I assume (with all editors) that the *Marcianus*' ἀρεταί τε is a simple copying error, and that Epit.'s ἀρ. δὲ preserves – or reintroduces – the correct particle. δέ emphasises the strong contrast between vv. 8–9 and the preceding vv.; τε would be unsatisfactory, either as a connective (in view of that contrast) or as a preparatory corresponsive particle (τε . . . τε . . . καί being a rare, perhaps even a non-existent, sequence: Denniston, *GP* 500f., 503ff., 511f.).

κομπάζειν (καινά, καινῶς MS: corr. Meineke), and although it is unlikely that this entry was made with specific reference to the Ἀσωτοδιδάσκαλος fr. (cf. G. Kaibel, *De Phrynicho sophista* (Göttingen 1899) 18), Kaibel took his cue from the idiom illustrated in the entry when he conjectured (in his edition of Ath.) κόμποι κενὰ ψοφοῦντες here; this appears to me less plausible than κόμποι· κενὰ ψοφοῦσιν (cf. also Peppink's κενοψοφοῦσιν, *Observ.* 52). Yet κόμποι κενοί is a natural collocation (cf. Eur. *Her.* 148; Epictetus 2.6.19 ψόφος ἐστὶ πάντα ταῦτα καὶ κόμπος κενῶν ὀνομάτων), and the transmitted text, when correctly punctuated, is unexceptionable.

10 ψύξει σε δαίμων τῷ πεπρωμένῳ χρόνῳ: the line (if we ignore for a moment a possible overtone in ψύξει) has a tragic ring which suits equally well the subject of death and the homiletic style (Norden, *op. cit.* in p. 821 n. 1, 130). τῷ πεπρωμένῳ χρόνῳ recalls Euripidean language (*Ion* 1582, cf. *Alc.* 147); the solemnity of its intimations about man's inescapable doom of mortality underlies many of the seriously poetic and all the few prose and comic occurrences of πεπρωμένος (cf. LSJ s.v. *πόρω): Hdt. 1.91 (quotation of an oracle), Xen. *Mem.* 2.1.33 (Prodicus' μῦθος), Isoc. 1.43, 10.61, *Comp. Men. et Phil.* II.151 Jäkel; Antiphanes fr. 225(226 + 227 K).10 makes a joke out of the solemnity. These tragic and sombre associations will lead us to accept σε δαίμων (A, Epit.) here, and reject σ' ὁ δαίμων (Muretus' *ueteres libri*,[1] see comm. on v. 6); the article is unnecessary, unpoetical and out of keeping with the general style of the fr.

The colour of ψύξει in such a context, however, is puzzling. Kock's comparison of Pl. *Phd.* 118a (which misled Bignone: see p. 826 n. 3) is irrelevant: ψύχοιτο there refers precisely to the chilling numbness induced by the hemlock in Socrates' limbs (a normal use of this verb both transitive and intransitive: LSJ s.v. ψύχω, cf. Nicander *Alex.* 85, 192, and C. Gill, *CQ* 23 (1973) 23ff.). Better clues to the present use in a general sense of 'kill' are (1) Ap. Rhod. 4.1527 ψύχετ' ἀμηχανίῃ, 'he grew cold in his helplessness' at death's approach, where the normal use of the verb (appropriate to the cooling of the body after death) is extended to the moment when death comes; (2) Ar. *Nub.* 151 ψυχείση of a flea 'cooled' after a Socratic experiment,[2] where the participle was misinterpreted by ancient grammarians (the *Venetus* scholast, *Suda* s.v. ψυγείση) as meaning ἀποθανούσῃ. This error is easily explained if ψύχω was used, at least in Hellenistic times, as a slang expression for 'kill'; and (3) the general use of the compounds ἐκψύχω and ἀποψύχω in related senses throughout Greek literature (see LSJ s.vv.). ἐκψύχω (= 'lose consciousness', intransitive)

---

[1] On the meaning of this term see W. S. Watt, *Hermes* 93 (1965) 244ff.
[2] Aristophanes applies the participle to the flea, although it was the flea's waxen shoes that cooled, rather then the flea itself: see Dover's note *ad loc.*

appears to be Ionic and *Koine* (cf. Headlam on Herodas 4.29); ἀποψύχω (= 'breathe away' one's life, transitive; 'lose consciousness', intransitive) has no such dialectal confines (e.g. ἀποψύχοντα intrans. Hom. *Od.* 24.348, ἀπέψυξεν βίον S. *Aj.* 1031, cf. A. fr. 104, Meleager 92.2 Gow–Page = *Anth. Pal.* 12.72). Is then the use of ψύξει in the present fr. influenced by poetical usage or by contemporary slang? The limitations of our evidence preclude a firm answer, but if ψύξει *is* a vulgarism, it would not be out of place in its chosen context (cf. Norden, *loc. cit.* at the beginning of this note).

11–12 Bignone draws attention to the striking similarity of phraseology in part of the Sardanapalus epitaph: καὶ γὰρ ἐγὼ σποδός εἰμι ... κεῖν' ἔχω ὅσσ' ἔφαγον (Ath. 8.336a, Arist. fr. 90 Rose = Cic. *Tusc.* 5.35.101, *App. Anth.* 2.130 (3.110 Cougny) with the heading 'anonymous or by Choerilus'). The similarity is probably no accident; the epitaph was much quoted from the time of Aristotle onwards. Yet the σποδός image is here turned in an unexpected direction with an ironic piquancy that would not have been unworthy of Alexis himself (cf. the joke in fr. 198(193K).

12 Περικλέης, Κόδρος, Κίμων: at first sight the sandwiching of a legendary Athenian king between two 5th-century statesmen seems curious; it may, however, be an instance of pamphleteer's cunning. In his Epicurean allegation that political activity is empty show, the imagined speaker debunks the achievements of Pericles and Cimon as σποδός, just as Philodemus (*Rhet.* 2.204f. Sudhaus) attempts to deflate the reputations of the same two politicians by showing that they never enjoyed Epicurean σχολή. Here, to add emphasis to his contemptuous dismissal, the fr.'s speaker links them with an ancient Athenian hero whose name was often used to denote a doddering old fool (Phryn. *Praep. Soph.* 38.9ff. de Borries, Pollux 2.16, Hesych. s.v. Κόδρους; cf. Bühler on Zenobius 2.6, especially pp. 84f.); with this juxtaposition the speaker tries to smear off on to Pericles and Cimon some of the ridicule associated with the name of Codrus.

Περικλέης is here uncontracted, as elsewhere in comedy (Ar. *Ach.* 530, *Equ.* 283, *Nub.* 859, *Pax* 606, Cratinus 326(300K).2, Eupolis 104(100K).1); the rule is that names in -κλέης are not contracted to -κλῆς when the fourth syllable from the end is short (Kock on Ar. *Equ.* 283). This rule may mainly reflect poetic convenience, yet on Attic inscriptions of the 5th and 4th centuries uncontracted forms do occasionally occur (about 5 per cent of the instances: Meisterhans–Schwyzer 132). Cf. K.B. 1.432 n. 6, Schwyzer 1.580 (*Zusatz* 3), Dover on Ar. *Nub.* 70.

IV *P. Heidelberg* 175 (= Pack² 1639)

G. A. Gerhard, *Veröffentlichungen aus den badischen Papyrussammlungen* 6 (Heidelberg 1938) 18f., Edmonds 3A.350 fr. 103J, Austin, *FCGP* 298f.

fr. 265, Webster, *IM* 187 n. 105, W. G. Arnott, *ZPE* 72 (1988) 23ff.; cf.
A. Körte, *Archiv für Papyrusforschung* 14 (1941) 124.

>   ]τινοσ[
>   ]υσαθ' ἡ κ[όρη
>   ]s τὴν μητ[έρα
>   ]ελειν τὰ πολ[
> 5   ]ον ὅτι χαρ[
>   ]καν προσλαβ[
>   ]τ' ἔρως ἐρρωμ[έν
>   ]s. – ἃ ποίας, τάλαν,
>   ]κειν τῆς Λημνία[ς
> 10   ]τι γειτνιᾶι γέρων
>   ]τρέφων γὰρ θυγατ[έρα
>   ]ε κωλύσειν γαμεῖν

Unidentified supplements come from ed. pr. (Gerhard) **3** πρὸ]s
Gerhard **6**] κἂν προσλαβ[ῇ Edmonds **7**]τ' ἔρως ἐρρωμ[ένος or
-νως Arnott **8** ς· with lower point of dicolon perhaps lost in lacuna (so
Austin)

P. Heidelberg 175, first published by Gerhard and later re-edited by
Edmonds, Austin and myself, is a tiny scrap of papyrus from the 1st
century AD containing the ends of twelve verses (most probably iambic
trimeters) of comedy. In v. 9 of the fr. τῆς Λημνία[ς appears, and because
Alexis is the only comic poet to have written a play with the title Λημνία,
Gerhard tentatively assigned the papyrus scrap to that play; the attribution was quoted by Körte and Austin without further comment. It is,
however, almost certainly wrong. Webster (*IM* 187 n. 105) anticipated
me in observing that the twelve lines of the fr., mutilated as they are, link
up remarkably closely with a passage from Plautus' *Cistellaria*, which was
adapted from Menander's Συναριστῶσαι and treats the imagined rivalry
for Alcesimarchus' affections between Selenium and 'the Lemnian relation'. That passage is 95–103:

95   LENA: *o mea Selenium,*
     adsimulare amare oportet. nam si ames, extempulo
     melius illi multo, quem ames, consulas quam rei tuae.
     SELENIUM: *at ille conceptis iurauit uerbis apud matrem meam,*
     me uxorem ducturum esse; ei nunc alia ducendast domum,
100 *sua cognata Lemniensis, quae habitet hic in proxumo.*
     nam eum pater eius subegit. nunc mea mater iratast mihi,
     quia non redierim domum ad se, postquam hanc rem resciuerim,
103 *eum uxorem ducturum esse aliam.*

Plautus is not an exact translator of his models, as the frs. of Menander's Δὶς ἐξαπατῶν clearly show, and this fact, when added to the incoherence of a tiny mutilated scrap of papyrus, makes it impossible to prove beyond all shadow of doubt that *P.Heidelberg* 175 derives from Menander's Συναριστῶσαι. Even so, the ties between the Plautine scene and the papyrus go substantially beyond circumstances that could be explained as casual coincidence.

In the papyrus there are almost certainly two speakers, although the lower part of the dicolon in v. 8 has vanished, perhaps in a lacuna (cf. Austin *ad loc.*).[1] Of these speakers the one who speaks after the dicolon is certainly a woman, for the interjection τάλαν in that verse is confined to females (C. Dedoussi, *Hellenika* 18 (1964) 1ff., Gomme–Sandbach, *Comm.* on Men. *Epitr.* 434, D. Bain, *Antichthon* 18 (1984) 33ff.). At the beginning of the papyrus one speaker refers to 'the (or 'my/your/her', etc.) mother' (v. 3) in the accusative just after mentioning 'the girl' (v. 2) in the nominative, if Gerhard's supplement is accepted. In the passage of *Cist.* immediately preceding the one quoted, Selenium three times mentions her own mother and herself in the same phrase (83–5, 90, 92), and although in the Latin text at 95–7 the *lena* says nothing about a mother or her daughter, her Greek counterpart might well have done so in this context. At v. 7 of the papyrus a character different from the one who speaks after the dicolon in v. 8 makes a remark (if I have interpreted the line correctly) about 'powerful love' (or 'powerfully ... love'); the effect of sexual passion is precisely what the *lena* talks about at *Cist.* 95–97. The words and phrases uttered by the woman who speaks after the dicolon in v. 8 tie remarkably closely with Selenium's speech at *Cist.* 98–103. After her initial 'poor thing' she mentions 'the Lemnian (? girl)' (v.9), then says '... old man lives next door' (v.10), adds (as a reason: note γάρ in v. 11) a reference, possibly to that same old man 'rearing a daughter' (v.11), and finally, before the scrap breaks off, talks of somebody or something 'being about to prevent [someone male: γαμεῖν is active] marrying' (v. 12). At *Cist.* 98–103 Selenium refers to Alcesimarchus' female 'Lemnian relation, who lives next door here' (100: sc. next door to the old man Demipho!); she does not actually say in the Plautine version that Demipho had been 'rearing a daughter' in Lemnos, but that is the simple fact that lies behind the subterfuge of 'the Lemnian relation', and the

---

[1] We cannot be certain that the only change of speaker occurred in v. 8 of the papyrus. The comparison with Plaut. *Cist.* 98–103 suggests that everything after the dicolon was spoken by Selenium's Greek counterpart, but we should be unwise to exclude a possibility that some of the remarks made before the dicolon came from her.

determination of Alcesimarchus' father that the young man should marry the girl from Lemnos (*Cist.* 101, cf. 103) would at this stage appear to be a barrier that would prevent (the male) Alcesimarchus from marrying Selenium.

The links are sufficient in number and detail to make the identification of the papyrus scrap as Menander's Συναριστῶσαι highly probable. These links also come in the same sequence in both *Cist.* and the papyrus. In Menander's play the *lena* was named Philainis and Selenium's counterpart Plangon (cf. Charitonidis and others, *Mosaïques* 41ff.). We may therefore attach names to the speakers in this papyrus scrap with some confidence.

V *P.Berlin* 11771 (= Pack² 1641)

Wilamowitz, *SB Berlin* (1918) 743ff., E. Fraenkel in O. Morgenstern, *Sokrates* 6 (1918) 366, A. Körte, *Ber. Leipzig* 71/6 (1919) 36ff. and *Arch. Pap.* 7 (1924) 144f., cf. *RE* s.v. *Komödie* 1260.5ff., G. Vitale, *Aegyptus* 2 (1921) 82ff., E. Wüst, *Burs. Jahresb.* 195 (1924) 172, G. Norwood, *Greek Comedy* (London 1931) 56ff., M. Platnauer in J. U. Powell (ed.), *New Chapters in the History of Greek Literature* 3 (Oxford 1933) 166f., G. Zuntz, *Mnemosyne* 5 (1937) 53ff. and *Aegyptus* 31 (1951) 329ff., Page, *GLP* 232ff. no. 48, C. Ferrari, *Dioniso* 11 (1948) 177ff., Webster, *SLGC* 59, 76, K. J. Dover in M. Platnauer (ed.), *Fifty Years of Classical Scholarship* (Oxford 1954) 117f., Edmonds 2.498ff. ('Alexis' fr. 260A), Gil 333f., Austin, *CGFP* 239ff. (com. adesp. fr. 239), R. L. Hunter, *ZPE* 36 (1979) 37, W. G. Arnott, *ZPE* 102 (1994) 61ff. (with photographs).

P.Berlin 11771 was first published by Wilamowitz and subsequently re-edited by Zuntz (1937), Page, Edmonds, Austin and Arnott; the most useful other discussions come from Fraenkel, Körte, Zuntz (1951), Dover and Hunter. The papyrus, deriving from mummy cartonnage and written in a fine book-hand of the third century, contains several fragments from one comedy, three tiny but one sizable (15 x 13.3 cm). This last has (i) a whole column (fr. 1 i) of twenty-six iambic trimeters well preserved apart from the opening two to five letters which are lost in all lines except 12 to 14 and 20, and (ii) the opening letters of part of the following column (fr. 1 ii). Part-division is indicated at line beginnings by paragraphi (fr. 1 col. i 13, col. ii 27, 34, 41, 44, 51, 52, 53), and in mid-line by spaces of about one letter's width (col. i 13, 17, 21). Fr. 2 has the sign χο]ροῦ, indicating a choral song with words not recorded, as in late Aristophanes (*Eccl.*, *Plut.*) and Menander.

Fr. 1

col. i   col. ii

(A) τὸ δ]αιμόνιον τὰ τοιαῦτα το[ῖς] φ[ρονοῦσιν] ε[ὔ]   [

παρα]δείγματ' ἐκτίθησιν, ἀλλοτρίαν ὅτι   [

ζωὴ]ν ἔχομεν ἅπαντες, ἣν ὅταν δοκῇι   [

πάλ]ιν παρ' ἑκάστου ῥαιδίως ἀφείλετο.   30 [

5 ἀλλ'] εἰσιὼν μετὰ τῆς ἱερείας βούλομαι   [

τὴν] ἐπιμέλειαν τῶν προσηκόντων λαβεῖν.   [

(B) ...]γ', εὐλάβει, βέλτιστε· πρὸς θεῶν πάρες.   [

διώ]κομαι γάρ, κατὰ κράτος διώκομαι   [

ὑπὸ] τοῦ καταράτου κληρονόμου· ληφθήσομαι.   35 [

10 (C) ....] δίωκε, Σωσία, συνάρπασον   [

τὸ]ν ἀνδραποδιστήν, λαβέ, λάβ' αὐτόν. οὐ μενεῖς;   [

(B) ὦ φιλτάτη Δήμητερ, ἀνατίθημί σοι   / . [

ἐμαυτόν, ἀξιῶ τε σώιζειν. (B) ποῖ σύ, ποῖ;   λ[

(B) ἤρου με; πρὸς τὴν ἀσφάλειαν· ἐνθαδὶ   40 ω[

15 †ει...κ'† ἐμαυτὸν ἀντεταξάμην τέ σοι.   μ [

(C) οὐκ] ἔστ[ι]ν ἀσφάλειά που πεποιηκότι   δ [

τοιαῦτ'·] ἀκολ[ο]ύθει θᾶττον. (B) ἃ ἃ μαρτύρομαι,   λ [

μαρ]τύρομ' ὑμᾶς, ἄνδρες· ἂν τὴν χεῖρά μοι   θ[

πα]ρ[ὰ] τῆι θε[ῷ]ι τις προσφέρηι, πεπλήξεται   45 α[

20 παραχρῆμά τ' εὐθὺς τἀπίχειρα λήψεται.   ου[

(C) τί] φήις; ὑπὸ σοῦ, μαστιγία; (B) νὴ τὸν Δία   λ [

τὸ]ν Ὀλύμπιον καὶ τὴν Ἀθηνᾶν, εὖ γε καὶ   σο[

πα]λαιστρικῶς· πεῖραν δ' ἐὰν βούληι λαβέ.   μ [

(? Χορ.) καὶ π]άντες ἡμεῖς γ' οἱ παρόντες ἐνθάδε   50 κα[

25 νομίζ]ομέν σε παρανομεῖν εἰς τὴν θεὸν   ὑπ[

(? B) ....]ό γ', ἄνδρες, εὖ γε· προσπαίζειν δοκεῖ   τ [

ακ[

Fr. 2   Fr. 3

] .. επρ [   ]οιός γε καὶ

                   ]ην τῆς τύχης

                   ]κατὰ τὴν φ[ύσιν

XO]P OY   65].ερα δὲ

                   ]φρονεῖν

55]λέγω τρ .. [λ]ογον

]νοισι μηθεν[   ] .. αι[

]μεναπραγ[   ] .. ασ .. [

σ]υγγνωμη.[70]ουσ[

]αι γὰρ αὐτὸς[   ]α.[.]υκ.[

60]ύς εἰμ' ἀγα[ν   ]ασ.[
    ]...[   ]ροσκυν[
                                       ]ποινα[
    Fr. 4   75   ]ησινε.[

76]ραιδιων[
    ]ζουσι δελ[
78]..αυταισ[

Supplements (where unidentified) by ed. pr. (Wilamowitz). B = the
papyrus   **1** or δ]αιμόνιον· τοῦτο Handley *per epistulam*   το[ῖς] φ[ρο-
νοῦσιν] ε[ὖ] Fraenkel in Zuntz (1937)   **2** παρα]δείγματ' Körte (1919)
ματαεκ B   **6** τωμ B   **7** ἄνα]γ' Austin in *Menandri Aspis et Samia II:
subsidia interpretationis* (Berlin 1970) 72, n. on Sam. 360, ἄπα]γ' Arnott,
πάρα]γ' Zuntz (1951)   θεωμ B   **10** ἰοῦ] Wilamowitz, ἔπου] Austin, ὦ
παῖ] Arnott   **14** punctuation after ἀσφάλειαν Beazley in Page   **15**
εισ την ' apparently B: a corruption of? ἔστησ' Arnott (after Zuntz)   **19**
πα]ρ[ὰ τῆι θε[ῶ]ι Zuntz   **24** καὶ π]άντες Handley, σύμπ]αντες Zuntz
25 παρανομεν B before correction   **26** νὴ τοῦτ]ό γ', ἄνδρες, εὖ γε· (with
punctuation after γε) Arnott (or εὖ τοῦτ]ό γ', Handley)   **42** or α[, λ[
B   **43** or α[B   **57** τὸν] μὲν ἀπράγ[μονα Fraenkel in Zuntz (1937):
]μενα πράγ[ματα Wilamowitz   **59** κ]αὶ Wilamowitz   **60** ειμι B   **62**
or]ρ B

The first six lines of the well-preserved column in *P.Berlin* 11771 form
part or the whole of a man's (εἰσιών v. 5) exit monologue, reflecting on a
devastating blow of fortune (τὸ δ]αιμόνιον[1]) that has either led to the death
(if we interpret the supplement ζωή]ν in v. 3 literally as 'life', LSJ s.v. ζωή
1.1) or destroyed the livelihood (LSJ s.v. ζωή 1.2) of some other person.
Scholars have assumed that a real (so plausibly e.g. Zuntz: see further
below) or at least feigned (so Webster 76) death is here involved, but the
'livelihood' interpretation, which would turn the passage into a comic
cliché,[2] cannot be entirely ruled out. In Men. *Pk.* 802ff. Pataikos confesses
in similar terms to a double blow of fortune which made him a widower
and impoverished in two days. The identity of the *P.Berlin* speaker is
uncertain; Zuntz argues for a free old man, Fraenkel (in Zuntz 1937) for a
slave; it is perhaps at this point wiser to recognise that in the New Comedy
of Menander speeches on the mutability of fortune are made by old men
(e.g. *Pk.* 802ff.), young men (*Dysk.* 271ff., 797ff.) and slaves (*Sik.* 127f., cf.
Asp. 1ff., 399ff.). At vv. 5–6 the speaker announces his decision to go inside
and μετὰ τῆς ἱερείας ... | [τὴν] ἐπιμέλειαν τῶν προσηκόντων λαβεῖν, 'to pay

---

[1] See comm. below on vv. 1–2.
[2] See comm. below on vv. 2–4.

attention to these/my concerns with the priestess'. Fraenkel first pointed out that τῶν προσηκόντων here was neuter, not masculine as Wilamowitz had assumed. The priestess presumably was in charge of a temple visible on stage with other houses or a house (cf. Men. *Dysk.*, Plaut. *Curc.*, *Rud.*, Pickard-Cambridge, *TDA* 172f.), and the article with τῆς ἱερείας may imply that she had previously been mentioned, although whether she was a speaking character in the play is unknown.[1]

The speaker's plan to exit into the temple, however, is forestalled by the entry at speed (end of v. 6) of a new character hotly pursued by a third man, who makes his appearance at the end of v. 8 along with a slave named Sosias. The pursued character (whom I shall call the quarry) addresses the speaker intending to leave after v. 6 as βέλτιστε, but although this form of address is normally used to free men, both old (Men. *Asp.* 251; βέλτιστε on its own *Asp.* 431, *Dysk.* 476, 503, *Epitr.* 224, 244, 308, 370, *Mis.* 229) and young (*Dysk.* 338, *Sam.* 81; βέλτιστε on its own *Dysk.* 144, 319, 342), it is occasionally used unctuously to slaves (βέλτιστε *Sik.* 13, cf. *Dysk.* 497). That first speaker may have remained on stage for a further period, or departed immediately after being addressed; we cannot be sure of this, although if the silence of the pursuer's slave Sosias throughout the extant fragment is a consequence of the rule limiting speaking characters to three in Menandrean comedy at least, it may have been due to that first speaker's delayed withdrawal.

The quarry identifies his pursuer as τοῦ καταράτου κληρονόμου (9), and submits himself to the protection of the goddess Demeter (12f.), clearly the goddess of the stage temple, at whose altar the quarry now seeks asylum (13f., 17f.). The pursuer calls his quarry το]ν ἀνδραποδιστήν (11) and μαστιγία (21), and threatens violence. If the accusation that the quarry is a slave-dealer or kidnapper is correct, he is most likely to have been either a slave who kidnapped a female baby long ago, removing her from her parents, or (as Zuntz (1937) argues), a *leno* who has come into the possession of a kidnapped girl and wishes to make her a ἑταίρα. It may be noted that in New Comedy μαστιγία is applied to both slaves (*Dysk.* 473, *Epitr.* 1113, *Pk.* 324, *Sam.* 324) and *lenones* (*Kol.* 125, cf. *mastigia* in Plaut. *Curc.* 567). To be a κληρονόμος the pursuer must have been named as heir to an estate, presumably on adoption as son by an older man without male heirs.[2]

---

[1] In Men. *Sik.* 242ff. a priestess is asked to look after a κόρη of disputed background, in Plaut. *Rud.* 259ff. a priestess takes protection of two girls who have escaped from a *leno*'s clutches.

[2] Cf. A. R. W. Harrison, *The Law of Athens, I: The Family and Property* (Oxford 1968) 124, 155 and n. 1, W. K. Lacey, *The Family in Classical*

Zuntz speculates that the kidnapped girl could have been the only child of the father who had adopted the pursuer as his son; that the pursuer was in love with the girl and wished to secure her freedom; and that the father's death might have prompted the comments in vv. 1–4 of the fragment. The play could then have ended with recognition of the girl's identity and her marriage to the adopted son. These speculations would create part of a plausible New-Comedy plot, and indeed gel neatly with the hints and data provided by the papyrus fragments; yet they remain unverifiable guesswork, even when they are taken in conjunction with another speculation that I tentatively advance below, in an attempt to identify author and title of the *P. Berlin* fragments.

When the pursuer threatens violence at the end of the main fragment, he is warned off by someone who says καὶ π]άντες or σύμπ]αντες ἡμεῖς γ' οἱ παρόντες ἐνθάδε | νομίζ]ομέν σε παρανομεῖν εἰς τὴν θεόν (vv. 24–5). In v. 18 the quarry calls ὑμᾶς, ἄνδρες to witness, and in v. 26 he appears to applaud the warning given in vv. 24–5 with νὴ or εὖ τοῦτ]ό γ', ἄνδρες, if this punctuation and one of these supplements are accepted. It is clear that the speaker of vv. 24–5 has at least two and possibly more men with him whose concurrence he takes for granted, and who form the ἄνδρες addressed by the quarry. These must be either (1) the chorus, on whose behalf the coryphaeus intervenes in iambic-trimeter dialogue just as still happens in Aristophanes' *Plutus* (328ff., 631f., 962f.),[1] but is so far unparalleled in the New Comedy of Menander, or (2) the first speaker, still on stage, with other men – free or slaves – accompanying him who were played by mutes. The *aduocati* in Plautus' *Poenulus* (504–816) and the *piscatores* in *Rudens* (290–324) have seemed relevant parallels in discussions of this part of the papyrus fragment from Fraenkel down to Hunter, but without a clear distinction being drawn between the role of the *aduocati*, who appear to function in both Plautus and his Greek original[2] as a non-choral group acting like a single character in a way similar to that outlined in alternative (2) above, and that of the *piscatores*, who resemble much more the etiolated chorus of Aristophanes' *Ecclesiazusae* and *Plutus*, with the words of their entry song preserved (*Rud.* 290–305), followed by a few remarks at the beginning of the following scene before they are made

---

Greece (London 1968) 145ff. and D. M. MacDowell, *The Law in Classical Athens* (London 1978) 99ff.

[1] Choruses are addressed as ἄνδρες in Aristophanes (e.g. *Vesp.* 340, *Pax* 318).

[2] Probably Alexis; see the introduction to Καρχηδόνιος. J. C. B. Lowe's arguments opposing this view (*Rh. Mus.* 133 (1990) 274 ff.) seem to me far less convincing than those he puts forward against the identification of the *aduocati* as a chorus in the ancient sense.

to depart – by Plautus – at v. 324. It seems to me that in *P.Berlin* 11771 these ἄνδρες are more likely to be the chorus, still (through their coryphaeus) intervening occasionally in the dialogue but confined largely to singing entr'actes whose words were not preserved, as the inter-scenic χο[ροῦ of fr. 2 of the papyrus suggests.

Wilamowitz accepted the presence of such a chorus and inferred from their involvement in the dialogue that the *P.Berlin* play belonged to the period of Middle Comedy. Noting that v. 23 opens with πα]λαιστρικῶς and that vv. 22–2 contain the oath νὴ τὸν Δία | [τὸ]ν Ὀλύμπιον καὶ τὴν Ἀθηνᾶν, he went on to attribute the play to Alexis, who was criticised by Phrynichus (*Ecl.* 212 p. 81 Fischer = Alexis fr. 326(325K), see comm.) for using the form παλαιστρικός instead of παλαιστικός, and employed the oath by Olympian Zeus and Athena in his Τοκιστής (fr. 233(231K)). In supporting these conclusions, Körte (1919) drew attention to Alexis' title Ἐπίκληρος; he could also have mentioned that Alexis wrote a Βωμός and several plays whose titles denoted a woman's non-Athenian origin (e.g. Ἀχαΐς, Βρεττία), which may sometimes have featured the titular heroine's reunion with a family from which she had been separated (cf. Terence's *Andria*). Yet although this attribution has been accepted with more or less confidence by the majority of interested scholars, it is perhaps sounder to recognise its weaknesses (as in particular Fraenkel and Zuntz (1937) did) and to admit the possibility of an alternative source.

The first point that needs to be made concerns the chorus in later Greek comedy. Although the last known intervention of a coryphaeus in the iambic-trimeter dialogue of a complete play occurs in Aristophanes' *Plutus*, we must always remember how scanty the remains of Greek comedy are after 388, and it would be unwise to deny at least the possibility of similar interventions as late as Diphilus (the author of the Greek original of the *Rudens*) and Menander, even though papyri of the latter so far include no instance of one.[1] Secondly, as Körte (1919) and Zuntz (1937) noted, the oath νὴ τὸν Δία τὸν Ὀλύμπιον καὶ τὴν Ἀθηνᾶν is not confined in comedy to Alexis; it occurs twice in Menander (frs. 87.1f., 333.13f.) too.[2] Thirdly, Phrynichus accuses Alexis of using the adjective παλαιστρικός, not the adverb παλαιστρικῶς. This may at first sight seem an insignificant point, but in the *Eclogae* Phrynichus is pedantically precise, sometimes criticising the use of an adjective (e.g. βασιλικός, ἐπίτοκος, ἡμιμόχθηρον, ὄρθριος), sometimes that of an adverb (e.g.

---

[1] Cf. now K. S. Rothwell, *GRBS* 33 (1992) 252ff., collecting anew the admittedly scanty evidence in post-Aristophanic comedy for preserved choral songs and conversation (in various metres, but not iambic trimeters) between individual actors and the chorus or coryphaeus.

[2] Cf. F. W. Wright, *Studies in Menander* (Baltimore 1911) 13ff.

βραδύτερον, δαψιλῶς, εὐνοικῶς, τάχιον), and the citations that on occasions he introduces from named authors always confirm that they used the particular form, whether adjective or adverb, that he stigmatises. Accordingly, it seems unwise to use Phrynichus as evidence that Alexis used the adverbial form παλαιστρικῶς.

An alternative candidate – I claim no more than that – for the source of *P.Berlin* 11771 is Menander's *Perinthia*.[1] Körte[2] convincingly demonstrated that *P.Oxy.* 855, which contains some twenty-three partially mutilated iambic trimeters, derives from the *Perinthia*, by showing that vv. 13ff. of that papyrus deliberately and dramatically echo a boasting speech which a slave named Daos had made earlier in the play and which is partially preserved in a book fragment (3 Sandbach) cited with author's name and title. In the papyrus scene, preparations are being made to set an altar on fire and thus remove from its sanctuary that same slave Daos who has sought refuge there (1ff.). The leader of the assault on Daos is accompanied by at least three slaves (Tibeios, Getas 3, Pyrrhias 8); he is named Laches (a suprascript ΛΑΧ(ΗΣ) indicates the speaker at vv. 10 and 20). To reinforce the tentative suggestion that the *Perinthia* scene comes from a slightly later point of the same play as the main fragment of *P.Berlin* 11771, three more potential links between the two papyri may be mentioned. (1) Sosias is addressed in *P.Berlin* v. 10, and the same name appears suprascript as a speaker's name in *P.Oxy.* 855 (ΣΩΣΙΑΣ v. 21, first deciphered by Schroeder). (2) In v. 18 of *P.Oxy.* the reference to τὴν κληρονομίαν makes good and literal sense when linked with τοῦ ... κληρονόμου of *P.Berlin* v. 9. (3) In the tiny scrap (fr. 2) of *P.Berlin* that contains the inter-scenic χο]ροῦ, the third and fourth lines of the first scene after the act-break have]μεναπραγ[and σ]υγγνωμη.[(vv. 57, 58). Fraenkel noted that the remains of 57 can be divided and supplemented τὸν] μὲν ἀπράγ[μονα *ut in Perinthia Menandri v. 13*, without realising that if *P.Berlin* 11771 does derive from the *Perinthia*, this could well provide a further reference to Daos' words of *Perinthia* fr. 3, spoken either to or by Daos. If this is so, it is not surprising that there is talk in the verse immediately following of 'forgiveness', asked, given or denied either for Daos' insulting words in *Perinthia* fr. 3, or for the greater crime that led him to seek sanctuary at the altar of Demeter. At this point it is perhaps worth adding that another of the *Perinthia* book fragments (5 Sandbach) seems to allude to the death of a wealthy man. If he was the father who adopted the

---

[1] Cf. Austin's comment, *etiam de Menandro cogitare possis.*

[2] *Hermes* 44 (1909) 309ff., amplifying a suggestion already made by the first editors of the papyrus (B. P. Grenfell and A. S. Hunt, *The Oxyrhynchus Papyri* 6 (1908) 151, 154).

κληρονόμος of *P.Berlin* 11771, it would add further support to the interpretation of vv. 1–4 in that papyrus as a reference to his death.

It is of course admitted that any claim for *P.Berlin* 11771 and *P.Oxy.* 855 to derive from the same play will cause serious problems, which I should not wish to dwell on at great length here. It would not necessarily require Menander to have a coryphaeus engaging in dialogue (although such an anomaly would not worry me unduly), since Laches, the first speaker in *P.Oxy.* 855, is attended by several slaves, and he could be identical with the first speaker in *P.Berlin* 11771 and perhaps an elderly relative (? uncle) of the κληρονόμος, taking over from the latter the attempt to move away from the altar the man seeking sanctuary there. Nor would there be any insuperable difficulty in identifying the quarry of *P.Berlin* 11771 as a slave called Daos. But we should now be obliged to assume that three important features of Menander's *Perinthia* were (1) a character's κληρονομία, (2) a wealthy man's death and (3) a slave's taking refuge at an altar in order to avoid punishment for a crime of ἀνδραποδισμός.

In the prologue to his *Andria* Terence claims (9–12):

> Menander fecit Andriam et Perinthiam.
> qui utramuis recte norit ambas nouerit:
> non ita dissimili sunt argumento, sed tamen
> dissimili oratione sunt factae ac stilo.

Since neither κληρονομία nor ἀνδραποδισμός enrich the plot of Terence's *Andria*, any attempt to argue that the two papyri derive from the one play involves an accusation that Terence was economical with the truth in the *Andria* prologue. Donatus' commentary on v. 10 may well imply this: *prima scene Perinthiae fere isdem uerbis quibus Andria scripta est, cetera dissimilia sunt exceptis duobus locis, altero ad uersus XI, altero ad XX, qui in utraque fabula positi sunt.* Perhaps we should be wiser to accept the words '*cetera dissimilia sunt*' at their face value, and not attempt to interpret the fragments of the *Perinthia* as if that play was a clone of the *Andria*.

1–2 τὸ δ]αιμόνιον τὰ τοιαῦτα ... [παρα]δείγματ' ἐκτίθησιν: if this is the correct punctuation, the closest parallel to this expression appears to be Polyb. 15.20.5 (ἡ τύχη) ἐξέθηκε κάλλιστον ὑπόδειγμα πρὸς <ἐπ>ανόρθωσιν τὸν τῶν προειρημένων βασιλέων παραδειγματισμόν; cf. also 4.24.9 καλὸν δεῖγμα τῆς ἑαυτοῦ προαιρέσεως τοῖς συμμάχοις ἐκτεθειμένος, Dinarchus 1.107 ἢ πᾶσιν ἀνθρώποις παράδειγμα ἐξοίσετε κοινὸν ὑπὲρ τῆς πόλεως, ὅτι μισεῖτε τοὺς προδότας;, Herodas 5.12f. ἢν μὴ ... τῇ σ' ὅλῃ χώρῃ παράδειγμα θῶ with Headlam's commentary *ad loc*. Yet Handley's suggestion that τὸ δ]αιμόνιον may belong to the previous clause, so that τὰ τοιαῦτα becomes the subject of ἐκτίθησιν, is worth considering.

In Greek of the 4th century and later τὸ δαιμόνιον, as a vaguer substitute for δαίμων, ranged in meaning from a god one did not know or did not wish to name (e.g. Isoc. 1.13; *CIG* 2³ 539.15f., 545.14f., 601.14f., all from Delphi at the end of the 3rd or beginning of the 2nd centuries) to the concept of fate or τύχη (so here and Men. *Epitr.* 911f. εὖ μοι κέχρηται καὶ προσηκόντως πάνυ | τὸ δαιμόνιον). Cf. M. Dibelius, *Die Geisterwelt im Glauben des Paulus* (Göttingen 1909) 221ff., Andres in *RE Suppl.* III s.v. δαίμων 292.37ff., W. Ludwig, *Philologus* 105 (1961) 60f., and G. Vogt-Spira, *Die Dramaturgie des Zufalls* (Munich 1992) 170f. n. 12.

το[ῖς] φ[ρονοῦσιν] ε[ὖ]: Fraenkel supports his brilliant supplement by citing Eur. fr. 781.2, Philemon fr. 228.4 Kock (= com. adesp. 887.4 Kassel–Austin), Eubulus 93(94K).2; in Attic drama cf. also S. *Aj.* 1252, *Ant.* 904, *El.* 394, Eur. *Hipp.* 921f., Ar. *Vesp.* 1463, *Eccl.* 862, *Plut.* 577, Men. *Dysk.* 861.

2–4 For the idea Zuntz (1937) compares Lucian *Apologia pro Merc. Cond.* 8 ὡς οὐδενὸς ἡμεῖς κύριοι, ἀλλ' ὑπό τινος κρείττονος ... ἀγόμεθα οὐχ ἑκόντες, which *may* be inspired by comedy (= com. adesp. fr. 1401 Kock, but see A. Nauck, *MGR* 6 (1894) 134ff.). The mutability of fortune, when applied in particular to possessions (rather than to life or human nature: cf. Eur. *El.* 941) is a popular cliché (Dover, *GPM* 174f., W. G. Arnott, *Philologus* 125 (181) 224f.); the nearest approaches to the *P.Berlin* wording are Eur. *Phoen.* 555ff. οὔτοι τὰ χρήματ' ἴδια κέκτηνται βροτοί, | τὰ τῶν θεῶν δ' ἔχοντες ἐπιμελούμεθα· | ὅταν δὲ χρήζωσ', αὔτ' ἀφαιροῦνται πάλιν, Alexis 267(265K).3–8 ὁ γὰρ <θεὸς> ... | λαβὼν ἀφείλεθ' ὅσα δεδωκὼς ἦν πάλαι with comm. *ad loc.*, Men. *Dysk.* 803f. αὕτη (sc. ἡ τύχη) γὰρ ἄλλῳ, τυχὸν ἀναξίῳ τινί, | ἀφελομένη (so B, supported by the parallels cited: παρελ- MSS of Stob. *Anth.* 3.16.14) σου πάντα προσθήσει πάλιν.

6 τὴν] ἐπιμέλειαν τῶν προσηκόντων λαβεῖν: although exact parallels for τὴν ἐπιμέλειαν λαβεῖν cannot be cited, as Wilamowitz already realised (normal in Attic is τὴν ἐπ. ἔχειν, but ἐπιμελοῦμαι, παρέχομαι, ποιοῦμαι + accusative, τυγχάνω + genitive are also found), Isocrates in particular is fond of similar expressions with λαμβάνω: e.g. 1.47 τῆς τελευτῆς αἴσθησιν λαμβάνομεν, 5.68 τὴν γ' εὔνοιαν ... τὴν παρὰ τῶν Ἑλλήνων, ἣν πολὺ κάλλιόν ἐστι λαβεῖν, 15.123 μηδὲ μικρὰν ὑποψίαν περὶ αὑτοῦ λαβεῖν.

7 When Pyrrhias rushes on stage at Men. *Dysk.* 81f. in the belief that he is being hotly pursued, his first words are πάρες, φυλάττου, πᾶς ἄπελθ' ἐκ τοῦ μέσου, | μαίνεθ' ὁ διώκων, μαίνεται. The opening words of the new entrant in the Berlin papyrus (...)γ' εὐλάβει) may well have been similar, with the first word, if similarly a command to one or more characters already on stage, in all probability a compound of ἄγω in the imperative. P. Maas in Zuntz (1951) supplied πάρα]γ': intransitive in comedy at Ar. *Av.* 1720, Euphron 9(10K).15, Men. *Dysk.* 556, 780, *Epitr.* 405, *Mis.* 274, *Pk.* 525, with a range of meanings from 'get inside' (with εἴσω) to 'get along with you'. Austin, *Men. Asp. et Sam.* II 72 on *Sam.* 360) supplied ἄνα]γ': in comedy with σεαυτόν at Ar. *Ran.* 853, Men. *Sam.* 360, perhaps *Pk.* 406;

intransitive at Ar. *Av.* 383, 400, 1720, cf. ἀνάγ<αγ>ε Nicophon 7(16K).1. Zuntz (1937) suggested ἄπα]γ', which from its frequent use with expressions such as ἐς μακαρίαν, ἐς κόρακας, εἰς τὸ βάραθρον may imply greater force and/or vulgarity (the speaker here seems to be either a slave or a *leno*, see above): ἄπαγε is intransitive in comedy at Ar. *Equ.* 1151 (ἐς μακ.), *Pax* 1053 (+ ἀπό and genitive), Theophilus 4, Men. *Dysk.* 394 (εἰς τὸ βάρ.), 432 (ἐς κόρ.), 575 (εἰς τὸ βάρ.), 920, *Pk.* 396 (ἐς κόρ.).

εὐλάβει (= imperative of εὐλαβέω) is not found in Attic Greek, as Zuntz (1937, 1951) noted; the middle/passive εὐλαβοῦ is normal, scans identically and occurs at Ar. *Equ.* 253, Diphilus 115(116K), but there is no obvious reason why a copyist here should have corrupted it to a form so far not attested until the 1st century AD (*BGU* 665.4).[1]

πάρες: cf. Men. *Dysk.* 81 (quoted on v. 7 above), *Sik.* 189 πάρες μ', Ar. *Vesp.* 757.

8 διώ]κομαι ... διώκομαι; cf. vv. 11 λαβέ, λάβ' αὐτόν, 13 ποῖ σύ, ποῖ;, 17f. μαρτύρομαι, | [μαρ]τύρομ'. As a stylistic device to express emphasis or urgency such repetitions are found in our earliest dramatic texts (e.g. A. *Pers.* 980, 991); on their exploitation by Euripides see W. Breitenbach, *Untersuchungen zur Sprache der euripideischen Lyrik* (Stuttgart 1934) 214ff., and by Menander see Handley, comm. on *Dysk.* 596ff. Cf. also comm. on Alexis 207(204K).1.

κατὰ κράτος: cf. e.g. Men. *Pk.* 388, 479, 985.

9 καταράτου: although this adjective occurs once in Sophocles and is quite common in Euripides and Aristophanes, it is not so far recorded for Alexis or Menander.

10 Austin supplies ἕπου,] δίωκε, comparing the chorus' opening words on first entry at Ar. *Ach.* 204 τῇδε πᾶς ἕπου, δίωκε. In later Greek comedy, however, the use of ἕπομαι is confined to the closing New-Comedy formula Νίκη μεθ' ἡμῶν εὐμενὴς ἕποιτ' ἀεί (Men. *Dysk.* 969, Posidippus 6.13 Kassel–Austin, com. adesp. fr. 249.21 Austin, probably also Men. *Mis.* 466, *Sik.* 423, cf. the variation in *Sam.* 737) and to the high-flown hexameters of a riddle at Antiphanes 192(194K).4, and so is probably inappropriate in the unornamented style of the papyrus here. I should prefer something like ὦ παῖ,] δίωκε, Σωσία; for the collocation of παῖ and a name in the vocative cf. e.g. Men. *Asp.* 305, *Dysk.* 401, 959, and for the use of ὦ + vocative in the first address to a slave cf. Men. *Asp.* 19.

11 οὐ μενεῖς; is common in Aristophanes, to prevent somebody going away: *Ach.* 564, *Equ.* 240, *Av.* 354, 1055, *Thesm.* 689, *Plut.* 440, cf. the more elaborate variant at *Equ.* 1354.

---

[1] LSJ cite also Photius' entry s.v. εὐλάβησον· καὶ εὐλαβῆσαι λέγουσιν, but there is no way of deciding whether the alleged instances of the active dated to Hellenistic times (so Zuntz, 1937 and 1951) or later.

13 ποῖ σύ, ποῖ;: as in Ar. *Eccl.* 1065, Men. *Sam.* 324 and 570.

14–15 At the beginning of 15 the traces suit only an original ΕΙΣΤΗΚ᾽, thus indicating transcriptional error:[1] but error for what? Not simply for ἕστηκ᾽, which cannot be linked with the following ἐμαυτόν. Zuntz (1951) asked why the comic poet could not have written ἕστησ᾽; in fact this is what I suspect he did write, with ΕΙΣΤΗΚ᾽ showing a scribe's addition of two unwanted hastae. The aorist links far better with the following ἀντετα-ξάμην. If ἕστησ᾽ ἐμαυτόν construed with εἰς ἀσφάλειαν, Zuntz's (1937) comparison of Isoc. 5.123 ἡμᾶς εἰς ἀσφάλειαν καταστήσεις (cf. also *Epist.* 2.5 τὸ βουλευόμενον ... εἰς ἀσφάλειαν καθιστάναι) would be most appropriate, but it seems better to punctuate in v. 14 with a colon after ἀσφάλειαν (so Beazley in Page), and translate vv. 13–15 as follows: (C) '... Where to?' (B) You ask me? To safety. Here I place myself and oppose you'. (B) presumably makes his last remark directly after taking sanctuary at the stage altar, with the aorists thus referring to action of the immediate past (cf. K.G. 1.163f.).

17 ἆ ἆ: Wilamowitz cites Phot. s.v. ἆ (Α 1 Theodoridis) and Σ Pl. *Hippias* I 295a, claiming that this interjection βραχέως καὶ ψιλῶς σημαίνει ἀπόφασιν ἀρνητικήν; cf. e.g. Cassandra's cry at A. *Ag.* 1125f. ἆ ἆ ἰδοὺ ἰδοὺ· ἄπεχε τῆς βοὸς | τὸν ταῦρον, where scansion of the interjection as two shorts with hiatus between them is demanded in the dochmiacs (see Fraenkel *ad loc.*).

20 παραχρῆμά τ᾽ εὐθύς is a favourite locution in Attic oratory: e.g. Dem. 19.42, 48.40, Isaeus 1.11, Dinarchus 1.94; cf. εὐθέως παραχρῆμα in Antiphon 1.20; cf. K.G. 2.584f.

22–3 εὖ γε καὶ [πα]λαιστρικῶς: cf. e.g. Ar. *Equ.* 800 εὖ καὶ μιαρῶς, *Eccl.* 253 εὖ καὶ καλῶς, Pl. *Soph.* 236d εὖ καὶ κομψῶς, and H. Thesleff, *Studies on Intensification in Early and Classical Greek* (Helsinki 1954) 186f. Cf. also comm. on Alexis 138(133K).5.

23 πεῖραν ... λαβέ: the normal phrase; in comedy Antiphanes 159(161K).10, Alexis 18.1, 206(203K).1, Men. *Theoph.* 24, fr. 629, Philemon 178(213K).14, com. adesp. frs. 110.9 and 130.1 Kock, *P.Didot* 1.33.

25 παρανομεῖν εἰς τὴν θεόν: cf. e.g. [Dem.] 59.126 τοὺς θεούς, εἰς οὓς οὗτοι παρανενομήκασιν.

26 Once the rest of the line is correctly punctuated, supplementation of the opening five or six letters[2] is easier. εὖ γε here ought to be taken with

---

[1] Mayser–Schmoll 1.1.41f., cited by Austin *ad loc.*, quotes instances of ΕΙ for Ε in later papyri, but none of this particular misspelling of ἕστηκ᾽.

[2] On the difficulty of computing the number of letters cut off or abraded at the opening lines in the lower part of this column see especially Zuntz (1951) 321.

the words that go before, adding (? a further) endorsement of the previous speaker's statement in vv. 24–5 criticising any attempt to remove by force the person taking sanctuary at the altar; for εὖ γε thus expressing support of somebody else's words cf. Men. *Dysk.* 300f. εὖ γε, δέσποθ', οὕτω πολλά [σοι] | ἀγαθὰ γένοιτο, *Her.* 72 νὴ Δι', εὖ γ' ὦ Μυρρίνη, *Epitr.* 528, Denniston, *GP* 127; cf. my comm. on Alexis 138(133K).5. With εὖ γε so interpreted, the opening of the verse cannot be ὄλοιτ]ό γ' (Edmonds, followed by Austin: but the simple verb ὄλλυμι does not belong to the everyday vocabulary of comedy (thus only Ar. *Pax* 1013 in quoting another poet's lyrics = *TrGF* 29 F 1 Snell, *Av.* 1071 in choral lyric, Plato com. 3.3 in a hexameter oracle, Diphilus 74(73K).9 citing Eur. *IT* 535); better would be another endorsement of the last speaker, e.g. νὴ τοῦτ]ό γ' or Handley's εὖ τοῦτ]ό γ'. For the use of νή = 'yes', often coupled with a confirmatory γε, cf. Men. *Georg.* 41 and *Sam.* 129 νὴ καὶ σύ γ', *Dysk.* 510 νὴ σὺν κακῷ γ', *Sam.* 389 νὴ δικαίως γ', *Epitr.* 1120f., *Karch.* 33, probably also *Sam.* 385f. Cf. Denniston, *GP* 130f., F. M. Sandbach, *PCPS* 193 (1967) 46, Austin, *Men. Asp. et Sam.* II 59 on *Sam.* 128f.

προσπαίζειν δοκεῖ: if the line is spoken by the suppliant at the altar, the presumption must be that he is now trying to make light of the situation ('he's apparently playing games', with reference to his pursuer); whether the infinitive is on its own, or followed by the dative μοι in the following context, is uncertain.

VI Other fragments doubtfully or spuriously attributed to Alexis

*245 (342 K)

Meineke 3.513 (XIX), Kock 2.408, Edmonds 2.308 (= Antiphanes fr. 212(331K)), Kassel–Austin 2.158. Meineke's attribution (3.142 (XIX)) of this fr. to Alexis or Antiphanes' Ὕπνος, which Kassel–Austin accept, is discussed and opposed directly after comm. on Alexis fr. 244(242K). Speaker and dramatic situation of this fr., cited by Epit. of Ath. 2.66f, are uncertain: possibly a householder or his slave addressing a cook.

2 τοῦ λευκοτάτου πάντων ἐλαίου Σαμιακοῦ: A. *Pers.* 884 called the island of Samos ἐλαιόφυτος, Apuleius *Flor.* 1.15 *fecundior oliueto*; in 1886 it still had 825,544 olive trees (E. I. Stamatiadis, Σαμιακά (Samos 1881–91) 4.398); cf. von Geisau in *RE* s.v. *Samos* 4, 2182.68ff. λευκός = 'colourless/clear' when applied to liquids such as water (especially springs, e.g. Hom. *Od.* 5.70, Eur. *Her.* 573, *Hel.* 1336, and rivers, Hes. *Op.* 739, Call. *H. Zeus*

VI OTHER DOUBTFUL OR SPURIOUS FRAGMENTS

19; cf. Hom. *Il.* 23.282, A. *Suppl.* 23), wine (cf. comm. on 124(119K).2–3) or olive oil as here. See L. Foxhall in M.-C. Amouretti and J.-P. Brun (edd.), *La Production du vin et d'huile en Méditerranée* (*BCH Suppl.* 26, 1993) 184, noting that this clearer oil comes from green olives, which yield less oil than ripe black ones, and so its relative scarcity may perhaps explain why it was held to be of higher quality; cf. also Amouretti, *Le Pain et l'huile dans la Grèce antique* (Paris 1986) 180, on a similar oil from late-maturing fruit, picked in spring.

3 μετρητής: as a liquid measure = 12 χόες or 38.88–39.6 litres, e.g. [Dem.] 42.20, Dionysius 5, Polybius 2.15.1; cf. comm. on Alexis 15.19, F. Hultsch, *Griechische und römische Metrologie*[2] (Berlin 1882) 101ff., P. Tannery in Dar.–Sag. s.v. *Mensura* 1729a, W. K. Pritchett, *Hesperia* 26 (1956) 195, M. Lang, *ibid.* 26 n. 1, Lang–Crosby, *Agora* x.58, H. A. Shapiro in R. M. Rosen and J. Farrell (edd.), *Nomodeiktes: Studies in Honor of Martin Ostwald* (Ann Arbor 1993) 213ff. For liquids such as wine and olive oil an ἀμφορεύς was in classical Greece regularly the container of this size, and so came to be used also for the measure (cf. Pollux 10.70 citing Philyllius 6(7K), *pace* Wernicke in *RE* s.v. *Amphora* 1, 1970.22ff., cf. 1971.49ff.). According to Moeris ἀμφορεὺς Ἀττικῶς, μετρητὴς Ἑλληνικῶς, cf. Thom. Mag. s.v. ἀμφορεύς, but this claim seems prescriptive rather than descriptive. A μετρητής of olive oil in Alexis' time could vary in price from 12 to 55 drachmas, cf. Pritchett 184.

340 (339K)

Meineke 3.521 (XL), Kock 2.407, Edmonds 2.520, Kassel–Austin 2.194; cf. O. Hense's edition of Stob. *Anth.* 3 (Berlin 1894) lvi ff. and app. crit. on 4.22g.154. Stob. cites this fr. twice, at 4.22g.154 with the lemma Ἀλέξιδος (SMA),[1] at 4.23.13 with Εὐριπίδου Δανάη[2] (MA: S omits author and abbreviates title: = Eur. fr. 320 Nauck[2] p. 455). Hense warns against any assumption that at 4.22g.154 a fr. of Alexis has dropped out after Ἀλέξιδος and with it a following lemma Εὐριπίδου Δανάη(ς), since in this section of the anthology (ψόγος γυναικῶν, the seventh part of περὶ γάμου) between 150 and 187 nineteen frs. of Euripides are cited in alphabetical order of initial letter, deriving presumably from an earlier alphabetised collection

---

[1] Arsenius' attribution of this fr. to Alexis (41.96, 16.46 = [Apostolius] 13.51p) is of no independent value, for here clearly Stob. 4.22g.154 was the source he was following, cf. O. Hense, *Rh. Mus.* 41 (1886) 30, Crusius in *RE* s.v. *Apostolios* 183.22ff., W. Bühler, *Zenobii Athoi proverbia* 1 (Göttingen 1987) 293ff.

[2] Since titles often appear as nominatives in Stob., there is no need for Hense to alter Δανάη here to Δανάης.

845

of gnomes, and the insertion of Δανάη(ς) at 154 would be out of sequence. This leaves two possibilities: either a simple error of ascription in one of the two lemmata, or (so Kock, opposed by Hense) a case of Alexis quoting two lines from Euripides' Δανάη in one of his plays. The latter appears the better option. A fr. deploring the difficulty of guarding a woman implies a situation where a wife or daughter is believed to have left the family house and possibly suffered some misfortune such as pregnancy in consequence. In Euripides' Δανάη it could have been spoken by Acrisius (or a male associate: hardly his wife, as T. B. L. Webster, *The Tragedies of Euripides* (London 1967) 94f. suggests) on discovery that his daughter was pregnant, and a similar situation can be envisaged in a play of New Comedy, with a father, his friend or some member of the household quoting lines from the Δανάη as an apt comment on the situation. Cf. Men. *Sam.* 589ff. οὐκ ἀκήκοας λεγόντων . . . | τῶν τραγῳδῶν ὡς γενόμενος χρυσὸς ὁ Ζεὺς ἐρρύη | διὰ τέγους καθειργμένην τε παῖδ᾽ ἐμοίχευσέν ποτε;, where Demeas cites a Danae tragedy as a parallel to the experience of Nikeratos' daughter; and *Asp.* 424ff., *Epitr.* 1123ff. for comic use of tragic quotations.

2 δυσφύλακτον: 'hard to guard', also elsewhere applied to cities (e.g. Polyb. 2.55.2) and to possessions (e.g. Strabo 9.3.8), as well as to τύχη (Polyb. 15.34.2, cf. 8.20.10) and a parasite (Plut. *Mor.* 49b). In literature Athenian wives and daughters of wealthier families[1] appear isolated from contact with men who were not closely related, living in separately locked sections of the house, normally staying indoors (e.g. Xen. *Oec.* 7.30 τῇ μὲν γὰρ γυναικὶ κάλλιον ἔνδον μένειν ἢ θυραυλεῖν, cf. 7.22, Men. fr. 592.2f. πέρας γὰρ αὔλειος θύρα | ἐλευθέρᾳ γυναικὶ νενόμιστ᾽ οἰκίας, Eur. *Hcld.* 43f., *Tro.* 645ff., *Or.* 108 with M. L. West's comm. (Warminster 1987), fr. 521; Dover, *GPM* 97f., P. Walcot, *Greek Drama in its Theatrical and Social Context* (Cardiff 1976) 90f., S. B. Pomeroy, *Goddesses, Whores, Wives and Slaves* (New York 1975, London 1976) 72ff.), and leaving the house only on special occasions such as festivals, where they might fall prey to seduction or rape (a commonplace of New Comedy, see introduction to Παννυχίς, but cf. also Lysias 1.6).

οὐδὲν (SMA 23.13, S 22.154) or οὐθὲν (MA 22.154)? See comm. on 15.5.

341 (340K)

Meineke 3.521 (XLI), Kock 2.407, Edmonds 2.520, Kassel–Austin 2.195; cf. Hense in *RE* s.v. *Ioannes (Stobaios)* 18, *Nachtrag* 2570.26ff. Stob. *Anth.* 4.31c.53 cites the fr. as Ἀλέξιδος, οἱ δὲ Μενάνδρου: so MSS MA; S omits οἱ δὲ Μεν.; *Cod. Parisinus* 1168, containing extracts from Stob. (see Hense

---

[1] The error of extending this pattern of behaviour to respectable free women in Athens who were relatively poor and in a large majority is most clearly demonstrated by D. Cohen, *G and R* 36 (1989) 3ff.

3.xxxviii f.), omits the whole lemma.[1] There seems no way of deciding whether one (in this case, which one?) of the ascriptions is at fault, or whether both Alexis and Menander (in that case, who copied whom?) used this imaginative pair of lines; cf. also 'False or Doubtful Attributions' I (introduction to Ἀλείπτρια with footnotes on pp. 813f.). Speaker and situation are uncertain; one possibility is a friend advising a person dispirited after sudden impoverishment (cf. e.g. Pataikos in Men. *Pk.* 802ff.) to bear his fate bravely.

1 ψυχὴν ... πλουσίαν: ψυχή here is basically the emotional self (cf. 'False or Doubtful Attributions' III, comm. on 25.5), with πλούσιος extended metaphorically into non-material areas ('well-endowed': e.g. πλούσιος κακῶν Eur. *Or.* 394, πλουσιώτερος ... φρονήσεως Pl. *Polit.* 261e, οἱ τῷ ὄντι πλούσιοι, οὐ χρυσίου ἀλλ᾿ οὗ δεῖ τὸν εὐδαίμονα πλουτεῖν, ζωῆς ἀγαθῆς τε καὶ ἔμφρονος *Resp.* 8.521a). Eur. *Suppl.* 907f. provides a close parallel, giving to Tydeus φιλότιμον ἦθος πλούσιον, φρόνημα δὲ | ἐν τοῖσιν ἔργοις, οὐχὶ τοῖς λόγοις, ἴσον (deleting 902–6 with Diggle; Collard's deletion of 907f. (his edition) seems ill-founded). Cf. also φρένας ἄφνειος Hes. *Op.* 455 with West's comm. *ad loc.*, cf. *Philologus* 108 (1964) 164.

2 ὄψις, παραπέτασμα τοῦ βίου: material wealth is dismissed as only an (illusory) semblance of real (i.e. emotional and moral) prosperity; the idea comes very close to Pl. *Resp.* 8.521a, cited in the comm. on v. 1. Here ὄψις = '(false) appearance' as at Thuc. 6.46.3 ἐπέδειξαν τὰ ἀναθήματα ... ἃ ὄντα ἀργυρᾶ πολλῷ πλείω τὴν ὄψιν ἀπ᾿ ὀλίγης δυνάμεως χρημάτων παρείχετο; and παραπέτασμα, often elsewhere used metaphorically in the sense of '(false) cover/excuse' (εἶχεν δὲ περιπέτασμα τὴν ἐρημίαν Men. fr. 336.9; especially predicatively in the dative with χρῶμαι, e.g. ταῖς τέχναις ταύταις παραπετάσμασιν ἐχρήσαντο Pl. *Protag.* 316e, Dem. 45.19, Plut. *Mor.* 41d), here comes close to '(false) appearance' too, cf. Plut. *Mor.* 471a διαστείλας ὥσπερ ἀνθηρὸν παραπέτασμα τὴν δόξαν αὐτῶν.

342 (303K)

Meineke 3.518 (xxxii), Kock 2.403, Edmonds 2.516, Kassel–Austin 2.195. This spurious fr. is found in [Plut.] περὶ εὐγενείας 2 (in G. N. Bernardakis'

---

[1] In his first edition of the *Florilegium* (Zurich 1543) Conrad Gesner appends to this fr. a marginal note '*Alexidis, al. Antiphanes*' (f. 448ʳ), but in his app. crit. to 4.31c.53 Hense plausibly explains the alternative attribution to Antiphanes as a slip caused by the sequence of extracts in the Stobaean anthology published by Frobenius along with the Basle edition of Callimachus (1532, p. 203: cf. Hense 3.xxvi), where 4.31c.66 (Ἀντιφάνης) directly precedes 4.31c.53, which is given the lemma τοῦ αὐτοῦ. The same ordering is found in *Cod. Vossianus gr.* O.9 (f. 93ʳ), but with the lemma to 4.31c.53 omitted.

edition, 7 (Leipzig 1896) p. 202), which has been proved to be a forgery of the late 15th or early 16th century (M. Treu, *Zur Geschichte der Überlieferung von Plutarchs Moralia* 3 (Prog. Breslau 1884) 34ff., Ziegler in *RE* s.v. *Plutarchos* 2, 812.40ff. = *Plutarchos von Chaironea* (Stuttgart 1949[1], 1964[2]) 176.10ff. The single fr. in this work purporting to come from Alexis is written in prose and probably originated in the brain of the forger.

Alexis 341 Kock

Meineke 3.151 (LIII: Antiphanes), Kock 2.408, Edmonds 2.308 (fr. 329). This fr. is cited by Stob. *Anth.* 4.22f.128 as Ἀντιφάνους (SMA: = Antiphanes fr. 270(329K)), which was miscopied as Ἀλέξιδος by Arsenius (= [Apostolius] 13.39t, 2.p.584 Leutsch–Schneidewin). Cf. O. Crusius, *Philologus* 46 (1888) 622.

Alexis 343 Kock

Kock 2.408, Edmonds 2.520. This fr. is cited by Stob. *Anth.* 3.27.2 as Αἰσχύλου (SMA, but L has the compendium <Αἰ>σχίνου: = A. fr. 394 p. 114 Nauck[2], p. 437 Radt), miscopied as Ἀλέξιδος by Arsenius (= [Apostolius] 13.21a, 2.p.579 Leutsch–Schneidewin) presumably because his eye wandered to the lemma of the fr. immediately following in his Stobaean source (3.27.3 Ἀλέξιδος ἐκ Θητευόντων, fr. 95(91K)). Cf. O. Crusius, *Philologus* 46 (1888) 622.

Alexis 345 Kock

Comm. follows directly after 339(338K).

Alexis 345b Kock

Kock 3.744. In Philodemus περὶ ῥητορικῆς XLIV.23ff. (*Volumina Rhetorica* 1 (ed. S. Sudhaus (Leipzig 1892) p. 79) a reference to Ἀλεξ[....] in the genitive condemning the professors of rhetoric ὅτι πολλὰ ζητοῦσιν ἀχρήστως was originally supplemented by Th. Gomperz (*Zeitschrift f. d. Österr. Gymn.* (1865) 625) as Ἀλέξ[ιδος], but Ἀλεξ[ίνου] is correct (first A. Nauck, *MGR* 5 (1884–8) 236f., before H. von Arnim, *Hermes* 28 (1893) 67 and S. Sudhaus, *Rh. Mus.* 48 (1893) 153).

APPENDICES

I THE FRAGMENTS OF TURPILIUS' *DEMETRIUS*

Turpilius' *Demetrius* was modelled on Alexis' Δημήτριος ἢ Φιλέταιρος (see the introduction to that play). For the convenience of users of this edition the text of the frs. surviving from Turpilius' play is given here, with brief interpretative comment. Cf. H. Keil (ed.), *Grammatici Latini, I: Flavii Sosipatri Charisii artis grammaticae libri V, Diomedis artis grammaticae libri III* (Leipzig 1857), O. Ribbeck, *Comicorum Romanorum fragmenta* (²Leipzig 1873) 87ff., (³ Leipzig 1898) 100ff., W. M. Lindsay's editions of Nonius (*Nonii Marcelli de compendiosa doctrina libri XX*, Leipzig 1903: for *sigla* see I.vi–xii) and Festus (*Sexti Pompeii Festi de verborum significatu quae supersunt cum Pauli epitome*, Leipzig 1913), Webster, *SLGC* 75; L. Rychlewska, *Turpilii comici fragmenta* (Wroclaw 1962) 12, 19f., 61ff. and *Turpilius: Fragmenta* (Leipzig 1971) IX, 7ff.

I

ab initio, ut res sit gesta, enoda mihi

Nonius 15.3 *Enoda significat explana; et quae sit proprietas, manifestum est, hoc est, nodis exsolue* ... (11) *Turpilius Demetrio*

ut r. est g. or *uti r. gestast* E. Becker in W. Studemund, *Studia in priscos scriptores latinos collata* I (Berlin 1873) 158

Speaker and context are uncertain. Requests for detailed information about a plight or incident commonly introduce an account of the dramatic antecedents early in the play (Men. *Dysk.* 69f., Plaut. *Pseud.* 3ff., *Trin.* 88, Ter. *HT* 78ff., *Hec.* 103ff., cf. *Andr.* 48), and in the Latin instances the metre is normally iambic senarius, as here. Other contexts, however, cannot be ruled out (cf. Ter. *Andr.* 536f., *Hec.* 361ff., on which see W. Schadewaldt, *Hermes* 66 (1931) 10ff., along with S. Ireland's edition of *Hec.* (Warminster 1990) 11f.).

II

timere occepi, interdum oscitarier;
ineptus quid mihi uellem ex insolentia
nescibam

Nonius 322.14 *Insolens rursus non solens* ... (18) *Turpilius Demetrio*

851

1 *tumere* Ribbeck²   *occepit* B^A, *hoccoepit* L, *occepi et* J. Lipsius   *excitarier* L. Müller   **3** *nescibam* Lipsius: *nesciebam* MSS

Ribbeck's conjecture that the speaker is *adulescens imperitus et paulo stupidior* seems plausible; spineless young men in Terence are characteristically the surprised and impotent victims of circumstance (*Andr.* 256ff., *Phorm.* 282ff.).

III

pudet pigetque mei me

Nonius 423.27 *Pudet et piget. hoc distat; pudet enim uerecundiae est, pigere paenitentiae* ... (424.5) *Turpilius Demetrio*

The metre is uncertain (? part of an iambic senarius or octonarius). The person ashamed of and sorry for some past escapade or escapades may be a young man like Philolaches in Plaut. *Most.* 149, as Rychlewska suggests (cf. also Clinia in Ter. *HT* 260), but there are other possibilities (e.g. the bailiff Olympio's words at Plaut. *Cas.* 877, cf. 898ff.). Yet Plaut. *Bacch.* 1013, where the apology is part of an epistolary deception, ought to be a warning against facile interpretation of isolated, contextless phrases.

IV

(× —) *nunc me ex aliorum ingeniis iudicat*
intercapedo quorum amicitias leuat

Nonius 336.29 *Leuare etiam minuere* ... (337.4) *Turpilius Demetrio*

1 *num* L. Müller (for *nunc* MSS)

Ribbeck guesses that the speaker is the *adulescens* of fr. II, estranged from his love (? *meretrix*, ? free-born citizen) after a quarrel; cf. Thais' strikingly parallel words at Ter. *Eun.* 197f. Alternatively, the alienation referred to in the fr. could have arisen between the titular φιλέταιρος of Turpilius' model and his friend.

V

antehac si flabat aquilo aut auster, inopia
tum erat piscati

Nonius 488.17 *Piscati, pro piscatus* ... (19) *Turpilius Demetrio*

1 *fluat* C^A   **2** *tum erat* C^AH², *tum orat* L¹, *tumeor at* A^AB^A apparently

The fr. translates Alexis 47(46K).1–2. Rychlewska compares Plaut. *Rud.*

290ff. and suggests that we have here (and in the Greek model) the words *piscatoris nescio cuius uitae suae miserias querentis.* It seems to me rather more likely that this fr. and Alexis 47(46K) come from the monologue of a man (*adulescens, senex,* cook or slave) returning from market either with the provisions he had contracted to buy for a meal or (more probably: cf. Plaut. *Aul.* 371ff.) with an inferior substitute. On the contrast in style between the concrete simplicity of the Greek model and the abstract nouns of the Turpilian adaptation, see especially H. Haffter, *Untersuchungen zur altlateinischen Dichtersprache* (Berlin 1934) chapter 4.

VI

in acta cooperta †age† inoras ostreas

Nonius 216.4 *Ostrea generis feminini* ... (6) *Turpilius Demetrio*

alga J. M. Palmerius, *coge* J. H. Onions

The metre is uncertain (either troch. septen. or iamb. sen.). Corruption here increases the contextual mystery. The source could be a list of fish (cf. Plaut. *Capt.* 850f., *Rud.* 297ff.), a proverb unknown to A. Otto, *Die Sprichwörter und sprichwörtlichen Redensarten der Römer* (Leipzig 1890, reprint Hildesheim 1964 with further literature, *Nachtrag* Darmstadt 1968 by R. Häussler) or a parabolic instance (cf. e.g. the parasite in Ter. *Phorm.* 330ff.). The possibilities are legion.

VII

nec recte dici mihi quae iam dudum audio

Festus 162 Müller (158.27ff. Lindsay) *Nec coniunctionem grammatici fere dicunt esse disiunctiuam, ut 'nec legit nec scribit', cum si diligentius inspiciatur, ut fecit Sinnius Capito, intelligi possit, eam positam esse ab antiquis pro non, ut ... aput Plautum in Phasmate (Most. 240)... et Turpilium in Demetrio* Paulus 163 Müller (159.14ff. Lindsay) *Nec coniunctio disiunctiua est, ut 'nec legit nec scribit'. ponitur et pro non: Turpilius*

quae Keil: *que* MS of Festus (word omitted in Paulus)

False accusations based on the misinterpretation of outwardly suspicious events or behaviour are in Greco-Roman comedy a staple motif, variously handled. Compare and contrast Plaut. *Pseud.* 427ff., Ter. *Ad.* 98ff. (old man excusing wild oats), com. adesp. fr. 257.66ff. Austin, Plaut. *Trin.* 98f., 187f. (honourable action misconstrued), Ter. *Phorm.* 289ff. (dishonourable action defended).

VIII

etiam me inrides, pessime ac sacerrime?

Nonius 397.25 *Sacrum etiam scelestum et detestabile: ita et consecratum* ... (37) *Turpilius Demetrio*

demetrius etiam LA^A, *demetrio sed (set) iam* B^A   *inrides* H. Iunius: *inridens (irr-)* MSS

Etiam may here imply continuation or renewal of impudent mockery. An obvious context would be the riposte of a *senex* to his or another's slave engaged in duplicity or irritating activity of any kind (e.g. Plaut. *Most.* 1132, cf. Men. *Dysk.* 500f., Plaut. *Amph.* 564f., 571, 585), but what is obvious is not necessarily right. Slaves, for instance, use similar language to a cheeky *puer* (Plaut. *Pers.* 290) and to a courtesan's pert maid (*Truc.* 265).

IX

(A.) *'nam si iceris me posthac, credas mihi uelim',*
inquit, 'tum' – quid censes? (B.) *'dolebit' scilicet.*

Nonius 123.33 *Icit significat percutit, ab ictu* ... (124.12) *Turpilius Demetrio*

1 *nam* F^3, *na nam* LB^A   2 *quid c. tum* F. H. Bothe

The dramatic assignment of the words is uncertain. Either one person speaks the whole fr. (so Rychlewska), in which case the quip at the end of v. 2 will be a continuation of the quoted statement in v. 1; or alternatively – and perhaps more naturally – the last three words of v. 2 are interposed by a second speaker (so Ribbeck, Lindsay; cf. e.g. Plaut. *Poen.* 149ff.). Either way the subject matter is pretty clear. A previous event is being described. A slave or some other character exposed to a thrashing (e.g. a *leno* of Sannio's kidney, Ter. *Ad.* 197ff.) had begun to threaten his assailant, and had then either weakly withdrawn with a cynical joke (cf. Plaut. *Epid.* 147), or said something surprising but now lost in the unquoted context.

X

homo unica est natura ac singularia

Nonius 491.1 *Singularia pro singulari. Turpilius Demetrio*

If *homo* here = 'man' in the sense of 'humankind', Ribbeck and Rychlewska may be right in suggesting that this fr. is the opening line of a monologue (monologues are commonly introduced by such generalities, cf. F. Leo,

Der Monolog im Drama (*Abh.* Göttingen 10 (1908) 75ff., Fraenkel, *EP* 150ff.). It is equally possible, however, that *homo* here is specific, 'the fellow (? who last spoke, ? who had just been mentioned)'. In either case some strange event or behaviour (? that which gave rise to Alexis 46(45K) in Turpilius' model) must have triggered off the remark.

XI

> *uide mirum ingenium delenificum mulierum!*
> *commorat hominem lacrimis*

Nonius 277.39 *Delenitus, ad nostram consuetudinem* (here D^A adds *dicitur*) *placatus. Turpilius in Demetrio*

1 *uirum* L   *ingenitum* A^A *delenifica mulierem* MSS: *delenificum mulierum* H. Iunius

The captivating woman whose tears here produce their desired effect is more likely to have been Rychlewska's *meretrix* (cf. Plaut. *Pseud.* 41ff., Ter. *Eun.* 67ff.) than Ribbeck's *uirgo*. That the male victim of v. 2 is this woman's lover, persuaded into some action or belief advantageous to herself, and that the speaker of the fr. is the lover's slave, are reasonable suppositions on the analogy of the comic passages cited.

XII

> *sandalio innixa* †*dicigitis*† *primoribus*

Nonius 427.22 *Priores et primores hanc habent diuersitatem. priores enim comparatiui sunt gradus; primores summae quaeque res* ... (27) *Turpilius Demetrio* ...

dicidigitis LB^A (presumably a miscopying of *dicĭtis*), *digitulis* J. Passerat, *digitis in* Quicherat, *digitibus* Lindsay

The metre is uncertain (either troch. septen. or iamb. sen.). Rychlewska, comparing Propertius 2.28.40, thinks that the woman described here is on tiptoe because angry. This seems unlikely. A more natural explanation would be that she was straining to do something unobserved, like overhearing a secret conversation (cf. Ter. *Phorm.* 867). Her identity remains doubtful; the *meretrix* of fr. XIV and a female slave are two possibilities.

XIII

> *meos parentes careo*

Nonius 466.4 *Carere etiam re bona potest dici. Turpilius Demetrio, dolentis*

persona   477.20 *Accusatiuus uel nominatiuus pro ablatiuo. Turpilius Demetrio*
meos MSS 497, *eos* MSS 466   *doleo* (for *careo*) C^A 466, verb omitted by
C^A 497

A tantalising scrap. Ribbeck, with Rychlewska's approval (cf. also
Webster), imagines that the speaker is a *uirgo amata*, different from the
meretrix of fr. XIV. There is, however, no sure evidence that Turpilius' plot
involved such a *uirgo* in addition to its attested *meretrix*. *Meretrices* who have
not yet begun to practise their profession may turn out to be free citizens
and find the parents they previously lamented as lost (cf. Palaestra in
Plaut. *Rud.* 215ff.). Nor is the loss of parents confined to women in comedy;
the speaker of this fr. might be a counterpart to (e.g.) Stratophanes in
Men. *Sik.*

XIV

(*MERETRIX.*) *non sum iurata*

Diomedes, *Grammatici Latini* 1.402.12 Keil *Apud Turpilium* <*in*> (add. early
editors) *comoedia nobili, cuius titulus Demetrius, legimus 'iurata sum' perfecto
finitiuo dictum; iuuenis est qui consulit, meretrix respondet* (early editors: *respondit*
MSS) '*non sum iurata', pro eo sane quod est 'iurasti?' 'non iuraui'.*

(*IVVENIS.*) <*iurata es?*> (*MERETRIX.*) *non sum iurata* suppl. Rychlewska
from Diomedes' comment

The metre is troch. septen. Diomedes identifies the speakers as *meretrix* and
iuuenis. Rychlewska believes that the occasion for the courtesan's rejoinder
was a quarrel between her and the young man. The obvious (but not
inevitably correct) context for such a quarrel would be a refusal by the
meretrix to allow the young man access to her bed (cf. for instance
Phronesium and the soldier in Act II of Plaut. *Truc.*), or an allegation of
her infidelity made by the man (so Webster).

XV

numquam nimis numero quemquam uidi facere, quom facto est opus

Nonius 352.16 *Numero significat cito* . . . (20) *Turpilius Demetrio*
quom L. Müller: *quam* MSS   *fato* LG

The metre is iamb. octon. Context and speaker are uncertain.

XVI

at etiam ineptus meus mihi est iratus pater,
quia se talento argenti tetigi ueteri exemplo amantium

THE FRAGMENTS OF TURPILIUS' *DEMETRIUS*

Nonius 408.31 *Tangere etiam circumuenire. Turpilius Demetrio*

2 *amantium* Carrio: *amanti* MSS

The metre is iamb. octon. An instructive fr. The speaker (probably the *iuuenis* of fr. xiv) has, presumably with the inspiration and help of a *seruus callidus* or parasite (cf. Webster), cheated his father out of a talent. In Greco-Roman comedy no motif could be more hackneyed, as Rychlewska says; its very triteness allows us to guess by analogy that the money was required to purchase the freedom and/or services of the *meretrix* of fr. xiv (cf. e.g. Plaut. *Bacch.*, *Epid.*, *Poen.*, *Pseud.*, Ter. *Ad.*).

XVII

lec[tum tappete stratum] ueterem

Festus 351 Müller (478.12 Lindsay) *Tappete ex Graeco sum[ptum + c.* 12 letters]*tae Ennius cum ait: t[+ c.11 Turpi]lius in Demetrio . . .*

The Farnesianus has *sum[* or *sun[, lec[* or *leg[* or *leo[: [lec[tum* or *lec[ti* or *lec[to* suppl. Lindsay, *stratum* tentatively Arnott

Context and speaker are unascertainable. Cf. also Turpilius fr. inc. iii (p. 130 Ribbeck[3], p. 58 Rychlewska[2]), where the expression *glabrum tappete* is attributed to an unnamed play by Nonius 542.10 and 229.5.

These seventeen frs. suggest that Turpilius' *Demetrius* was a play of intrigue firmly rooted in the dramatic tradition of New Comedy, peopled with familiar figures like the *meretrix*, her young lover and his angry father, and exploiting conventional motifs such as a confidence trick against the lover's rich father and (probably) the discovery by an apparently orphaned child of his or her true parents. Ribbeck, Rychlewska and Webster have suggested how the play's characters and motifs could have been interlinked, but the possible permutations are too numerous and the gaps in our information too wide for an accurate reconstruction of Turpilius' plot or worthwhile comment on Turpilius' relation to his Greek original. Among the unanswerable questions three stand out. What part did Alexis' φιλέταιρος play in Turpilius' plot? Was the *meretrix* ruthless and experienced (like Phronesium in Plaut. *Truc.*), a sympathetic trainee (like Palaestra in *Rud.*), or perhaps neither? And how did Turpilius handle the luncheon-party, whose antecedents are the subject of several of the Alexis frs.?

II Alexis''Ιππεύς and the bill of Sophocles of Sunium

Sophocles' bill, of which the fullest and still the best account is to be found in W. S. Ferguson, *Hellenistic Athens* (London 1911) 103ff., did not specifically ban philosophy or expel philosophers from Athens, but required them simply to be licensed by the state. As a result Theophrastus and the Peripatetics (together apparently with all the other philosophers in the city) withdrew from Athens in protest. Alexis' use of ἐρρίφασιν in fr. 99(94K).5 (see comm. *ad loc.*) can therefore be readily understood, even if it incorrectly writes into the bill something that was only an indirect consequence of it. A year later the situation was reversed when Philon, a Peripatetic, successfully brought a γραφὴ παρανόμων against Sophocles, who was defended by the democrat Demochares. Thereupon the philosophers returned to Athens. These are the facts given by the ancient sources (Ath. 13.610e–f, Diog. Laert. 5.38, Pollux 9.42); remarkably, no date or time reference is mentioned other than the interval of a year between the bill and its repeal. However, Alexis mentions (99(94K).2) a Demetrius as the bill's champion. This can hardly have been the Phalerean, who was regent of Athens from 317 to 307, since he was a pupil of Theophrastus and a supporter of his school, which appears to have had ties with Demetrius' regime (Ferguson 104 and *Klio* 11 (1911) 268, E. Bayer, *Demetrios Phalereus der Athener* (Stuttgart and Berlin 1942) 6 and 93ff., S. Dow and A. H. Travis, *Hesperia* 12 (1943) 144ff.); and we have no reason to believe that this Demetrius ever turned against a school with which he had been so closely linked.[1] Thus Alexis' reference must be to

---

[1] Despite this, there have been a number of attempts to assign Sophocles' bill to 317, the first year of the Phalerean's regency. This date was originally proposed by J. Meursius, *Fortuna Attica* (Leiden 1622) 65, adopted by H. Fynes Clinton, *Fasti Hellenici* 3 (Oxford 1830/1) 185, supported by Meineke 1.393f., Kock, G. F. Unger, *Neue Jahrb.* 33 (1887) 755ff., Kaibel in *RE* s.v. *Alexis* 9, 1469.29 and R. Fenk, *Adversarii Platonis quomodo de indole ac moribus eius iudicaverint* (Diss. Jena 1913) 58f., and still uncritically accepted by some recent scholars (e.g. A. Presta, *Cultura e Scuola* 7 (1968) 24). Arguments for the 317 dating rest on two false premises: that Alexis' mention (99(94K).1) of Xenocrates, who died in 314 (Diog. Laert. 4.14), is explicable only if Xenocrates was still alive when the 'Ιππεύς was produced, and that Alexis' reference to the Academy in the same verse was designed expressly to contrast against the Peripatetics. The main obstacle to the 317 dating remains the fact that early in that year (Ferguson 39) the government of Athens passed into the hands of a supporter, not an enemy, of the Peripatetics.

Demetrius Poliorcetes, who overthrew the Phalerean's regime in 307. Poliorcetes left Athens in 306; hence if Sophocles' bill was passed under his aegis, as Alexis' words imply, it could have been passed only in 307. The year's interval before repeal is readily explained, as Ferguson notes; Poliorcetes' absence made repeal easier. In any case, 307 was an appropriate time for a bill directed against philosophy in general and those philosophers connected with the late regime in particular. Restored democracies had attacked philosophy before, not only with the condemnation of Socrates in 399, but more recently when Aristotle and Theophrastus were arraigned in 322 and 318 respectively, having incurred the hatred of political opponents because of their monarchic and oligarchic connections. Arguments for this dating (or thereabouts) of Sophocles' bill and its repeal were advanced long ago by J. Jonsius, *De scriptoribus historiae philosophicae* 1 (Frankfurt 1659) 103f. and C. G. Heyne, *Opuscula academica collecta* 4 (Göttingen 1796) 435; these were analysed, confirmed and expanded by F. A. Hofmann, *De lege contra philosophos* (Karlsruhe 1842). Some new points were made by Wilamowitz, *Antigonos von Karystos* (Berlin 1881) 189ff., 270ff. (but see comm. on Ἱππεύς, p. 261 n. 2); cf. also Kaerst in *RE* s.v. *Demetrios* 33, 2773.18ff., K. J. Beloch, *Griechische Geschichte*[2] 4/1 (Berlin and Leipzig 1925) 147, 422f., I. Düring, *Herodicus the Cratetean* (Stockholm 1941) 84f., 149f., Webster, *SLGC* 105, J. P. Lynch, *Aristotle's School* (Berkeley 1972) 117ff., W. Kraus, *Anz. Alt.* 28 (1975) 6f. and M. Isnardi Parenti, *RFIC* 114 (1986) 353 n. 1.

III Alexis' Λέβης and Plautus' *Aulularia*

See especially my papers in *Wien. Stud.* 101 (1988) 181ff. and *QUCC* 33 (1989) 27ff., and D. Bain, *LCM* 17 (1992) 68ff. Many attempts have been made to identify the Greek original of Plautus' *Aulularia*; W. Stockert includes in the introduction to his edition of the play (Stuttgart 1983, pp. 8–16) an excellent survey of the scholarship with an accurate bibliography, to which R. L. Hunter, *PCPS* 27 (1981) 37ff. needs to be added. So far two major landmarks have dominated the discussions. The first was J. L. Ussing's discovery (addenda in comm. on *Aul.*, 2 (Copenhagen 1878) 587f.) of a similarity between Choricius of Gaza's indignant question (32.73f. = pp. 36of. Förster–Richsteig), seeking to reject a claim that we have been made avaricious (φιλαργύρους) by characters in Menander like Σμικρίνης ... ὁ δεδιὼς μή τι τῶν ἔνδον ὁ καπνὸς οἴχοιτο φέρων, and Strobilus' statement in Plaut. *Aul.* 300f. that Euclio makes a public complaint *de suo tigillo fumus si qua exit foras*. It is injudicious, however, to conclude from this parallel that Choricius must have been referring here to the Greek model of Plaut. *Aul.*, which was therefore written by Menander with Smikrines as the leading character's name. K. Gaiser (*Menander, Der Schild oder die Erbtochter* (Zurich 1971) 11) pointed to two weaknesses in the arguments of those who assumed a verbal link (amounting to translation) between the two passages. Although in *Aul.* Euclio is described by the divine prologue as the grandson of a man *auido ingenio* (9) and *pariter moratum ut pater auosque huius fuit* (22), he is not presented generally in the play as an out-and-out miser, but rather as a decent old man (114ff., 172, 215f.) whom discovery of the family treasure has unbalanced into an obsession about protecting his gold (contrast here Stockert pp. 18ff. and Gaiser, *Aufstieg und Niedergang* 1.2 (Berlin and New York 1972) 1095f., both with useful bibliographies; especially G. Jachmann, *Plautinisches und Attisches* (Berlin 1931) 129ff., P. J. Enk, *Mnemosyne* 2 (1935) 281ff., W. Ludwig, *Philologus* 105 (1961) 55ff.). Secondly, there is a crucial difference between the Greek and Roman passages; Choricius expresses the Menandrean hero's fear that the smoke would remove some of his property, while Euclio's complaint is about the loss of the smoke itself.

Landmark number two was the publication in 1958 of the papyrus of Menander's *Dyskolos*. Many striking similarities with Plaut. *Aul.* in structure, choice and presentation of characters, and details of plotting, motif and dramatic technique were soon pointed out in a series of discussions (A. Theuerkauf, *Menanders Dyskolos als Bühnenspiel und Dichtung* (Diss. Göttingen 1960) 46ff., W. Ludwig, *Philologus* 105 (1961) 251ff. and *Entr. Hardt* 16 (1970) 71ff., W. Kraus, *Sert. Phil. Aenipont.* 7/8 (1963) 185ff., W. G. Arnott, *Phoenix* 18 (1964) 232ff., A. Schäfer, *Menanders Dyskolos: Untersuchungen zur dramatischen Technik* (Meisenheim am Glan 1965) 96ff., E. W. Handley, *Entr. Hardt* 16 (1970) 100ff., R. L. Hunter, *PCPS* 207 (1981) 41ff.), and these resemblances were generally explained by the assumption that Menander wrote both *Dysk.* and the Greek original of *Aul.*[1] Many critics were convinced (largely by Schäfer's arguments) that

---

[1] In the paper just cited I wrote (p.233): 'the circumstantial evidence [sc. for a Menandrean model of *Aul.*] is now so massive in weight and quantity that only the devil's advocate would any longer put forward the theory that ... a very clever and subtle imitator of Menandrean techniques ... might have picked the Athenian master's brain in devising the original of the *Aulularia*'. Perhaps that diabolical advocate has the better case after all, even if we must now persuade him to turn it inside out, by suggesting that *Dysk.* was the later play of the two and the young Menander himself a subtle imitator of another playwright's ideas and techniques. See below.

Aul. was the better constructed play, but F. M. Sandbach, *Entr. Hardt* 16 (1970) 97f. called attention to two alleged weaknesses in *Aul.* (Lyconides' failure to ask Euclio for his daughter's hand as soon as he made her pregnant is not explained; unimaginative repetition in ii.ii and vi, where Lyconides' slave twice overhears Euclio saying where the pot of gold is to be hidden), which made him hesitate to attribute the *Aul.*'s original to Menander. Sandbach may be right in his conclusion, but the arguments which led him to it are faulty: (i) Plautus may well have excised from his model an early scene involving Lyconides (cf. Stockert p. 10 and nn. 14, 15, with bibliography), in which the young man's failure to approach Euclio earlier could have been explained, and (ii) information vital to the plot was often repeated a second time in Greek and Roman comedy, with at least one example in Menander (*Asp.* 166ff., 310f., cf. Plaut. *Cas.* 150f., 196, 531ff., *Epid.* 40ff., 132ff., *Pseud.* 51ff., 344ff.; *Wien. Stud.* 95 (1982) 131ff., *Gnomon* 59 (1987) 18f.).

Scholars have scoured the titles and frs. of later Greek comedy in their efforts to identify the source of *Aul.*, suggesting several plays by Menander and even other playwrights like Diphilus and Philemon,[1] but before 1988 the case for Alexis' Λέβης had never been put. The evidence is not conclusive, but despite one weakness it seems stronger than that for any other Greek comedy apart perhaps from Menander's Ἄπιστος. It is conveniently collected under three headings.

(i) Alexis' title denotes a large metal or earthenware cauldron (see introduction to Λέβης) which would be normally translated into Latin by *aula*, the word that Plautus always uses in his play for the container of Euclio's treasure, and the word from which the Roman title is derived. We cannot know whether Plautus here simply translated his Greek title or

---

[1] The Menandrean candidates include three non-starters: (i) Ὑδρία (Legrand, first in *Daos, Tableau de la comédie grecque pendant la période dite nouvelle* (κωμῳδία νέα) (Lyons 1910) 218 = *NGC* 168), but fr. 401 seems incompatible with the plot of *Aul.*, cf. F. Della Corte, *Da Sarsina a Roma* (Genoa 1952) 184f.; (ii) Φιλάργυρος (Ludwig 253f.), but the title is not attested for Menander; (iii) Θησαυρός (A. Krieger, *De Aululariae Plautinae exemplari Graeco* (Diss. Giessen 1914) 91ff.), but frs. 198–200 imply a plot about a man's sexual passion (cf. also C. Garton, *Personal Aspects of the Roman Theatre* (Toronto 1972) 73ff., although it is not certain that Luscius Lanuvinus adapted Menander's Θησαυρός); and one plausible suggestion: (iv) Ἄπιστος (Webster, *SM* 120ff., K. Gaiser, *Wien. Stud.* 79 (1966) 191ff.), with the suggestion that fr. 58 might have been spoken by the Greek 'Euclio' in the original of *Aul.* iii.v, cf. 496f., 503f. The cases made for Diphilus (F. Marx's edition of Plaut. *Rud.* (Leipzig 1928) 285ff.) and Philemon (e.g. F. Blass, *Rhein. Mus.* 62 (1907) 102ff.) rest on flimsy foundations.

replaced it with one that he deemed more suitable in Rome; if he did translate it, however, the only other known title of a Greek New-Comedy play that could be accurately translated *aula* is Menander's Ὑδρία, which we have already excluded as a source for *Aul.* (p. 861 n. 1).

However, as Bain's paper acutely observes, λέβης is masculine, *aula* feminine, and one of *Aul.*'s most brilliant scenes (731ff.) is based on the cross-purposes resulting from the interpretation of feminine singular pronouns (*illa, ea, mea* in the Plautine scene) by Euclio as references to his pot (*aula*), but by Lyconides as references to Euclio's daughter. If Plautus here was following his Greek original closely, the cross-purposes in the latter could not have been based on masculine nouns like λέβης, χρυσός or θησαυρός, but only on feminines like ὑδρία or χύτρα. But need Plautus here have been slavishly copying his model? Humorous word-play and situations are often conceived independently (e.g. the jokes depending on a series of ablatives at *Amph.* 366ff.) or greatly expanded by Plautus, so that he might well have developed the equivocal exchanges of *Aul.* 731ff. off his own bat or from word-play in his Greek original that depended on some word like κληρονομία.

(ii) None of the six frs. preserved from Alexis' Λέβης yields a strong verbal tie with any portion of *Aul.* (any more than e.g. fr. 58 of Menander's Ἄπιστος does), but all of them can be fitted with remarkable smoothness into a scenic situation Romanised by Plautus. Frs. 129(124K), 132(127K) and 134(129K) involve a μάγειρος; *Aul.* has two cooks. Fr. 134 describes the μάγειρος as a scruffy citizen; this looks like some character's disparaging or angry comment of the kind made by Euclio when he returns to find a cook in his house (III.ii, 415ff.). In fr. 129 Alexis' cook explains to a παῖς his recipe for disguising the taste of burnt pork. In 132 he demands from his hirer (or hirer's slave) twenty items that he will need for the meal which he must have been contracted to prepare. It is widely suspected (see especially E. Burck, *Wien. Stud.* 68 (1956) 265ff., F. Klingner, *SIFC* 27/28 (1956) 157ff. = *Studien zur griechischen und römischen Literatur* (Zurich and Stuttgart 1964) 114ff., J. C. B. Lowe, *Class. Ant.* 4 (1985) 86ff.) that Plautus made substantial alterations to his original in the cook scenes of *Aul.* Fr. 129 would fit well into a scene rewritten by Plautus as II.iv, with the cook entering with either his own assistant or his hirer's slave. Fr. 132 would derive most naturally from one of the scenes adapted as II.v and vi: Congrio the cook at *Aul.* 336 and the slave at 341 both refer to the difficulty that cooks have when asking for things they require.

Frs. 130(125K), 131(126K) and 133(128K) are attacks on tradesmen. Frs. 130(125K) and 131(126K) assail fishmongers and couple the invective with praise of past and future legislation designed to curb their excesses. The comments in 130(125K) are practical and reasonable, while the grotesque fantasies of 131(126K) sound more like the comic arabesques of a βωμολόχος. The two frs. could have come from the Greek original of either (a) *Aul.* II.viii, the scene in which Euclio returns from market complaining that the prices of fish were too high (373f.), or (b) III.v, where Euclio overhears Megadorus attacking contemporary extravagance (at 486ff. Megadorus explains that his quarrel is with greedy people who cannot be stopped by legislation). The latter scene provides a better setting for the two frs., with Megadorus inveighing seriously and Euclio commenting always in asides. Fr. 133(128K) attacks fig-sellers for dishonest practices; the way it opens (καὶ τί δεῖ | λέγειν ἔθ' ἡμᾶς) indicates that the fr. forms a further section of a long tirade against tradesmen, and it would fit smoothly into the same scene as frs. 130(125K) and 131(126K).

There is also a remote possibility that fr. 243(241K), which is cited by Ath. 15.671d ἐξ ῾Υπονοίας ᾿Αλέξιδος (εξ υπονοίας A, but Schweighaeuser's conjecture ἐξ ῞Υπνου has much to commend it, see the introduction to ῞Υπνος), could be added to the six frs. of Λέβης, since ῾Υπόνοια would be an appropriate alternative title (? and also divine personification as prologue) for the Greek original of the *Aulularia*, where Euclio's suspicions are a dominant element of the plot. In that event fr. 243, with its description of a man so parsimonious that he outdid Triballian hosts, would sit well in a scene comparable to, or inspiring, that of *Aul.* 296ff., where a slave describes with grotesque caricature some examples of Euclio's stinginess.

Two further difficulties over the incorporation of the Λέβης frs. into the scenario of *Aul.* need to be mentioned. In the Alexis frs. only one cook is mentioned, while the scenes in Acts II and III of *Aul.* require two, divided between the houses of Megadorus and Euclio. Secondly, Alexis' cook is a free citizen (fr. 134(129K)), while the two Roman *coqui* on one occasion (*Aul.* 309f., but contrast 456ff.) admit to being slaves. These difficulties are not insuperable. The evidence (spelled out in comm. on fr. 134(129K)) seems to suggest that Plautus himself altered the status of the cooks in *Aul.* to slaves. Alexis' play might have had a second cook, of whom the extant frs. have left no trace; or Plautus could have doubled the cooks himself for comic purposes (the cook in Megadorus' house has no functional role in the plot); or the Roman dramatist could have altered Alexis' cook and assistant (? the παῖς of fr. 129(124K).14), or perhaps most probably a cook and a household slave (like Sikon and Getas in Men. *Dysk.*), into two equal cooks.

(iii) In *Aul.* the cooks are hired to prepare a banquet in celebration of Megadorus' proposed marriage to Euclio's daughter (28off., 290ff., 351ff.). In fr. 132(127K) from the Λέβης, where the cook names twenty different items that he will need, the place of honour at the head of his list goes to sesame (v.3). Sesame was an important ingredient of Athenian wedding-cakes (see comm. *ad loc.*), and it seems reasonable to suppose that it owed its privileged position in the cook's list here to the fact that he had been hired to officiate at a nuptial feast.

The evidence for Λέβης as the Greek original of *Aul.* is obviously inconclusive. If it is accepted, however, it has an interesting consequence. The allegation in the anonymous tractate on comedy (p.9 Kaibel = p. 10 Koster = 2 p. 21 Kassel–Austin *test.* 2 = p. 5 in this edition) that Menander appears to have been trained by Alexis may or may not be true, but the existence of striking parallels in motif and dramatic technique between the two dramatists cannot be denied (see my introduction to this edition, I.v.iii). The much-discussed similarities between Plaut. *Aul.* and Men. *Dysk.* would now need to be added to this list, with the important rider that if Alexis' Λέβης is correctly dated to the period immediately before 324 (see introduction to the play) and Men. *Dysk.* to 316, we have clear chronological information on which to assess originality and dependence.

ADDENDA

After this commentary was completed, several important works were published of which regrettably I found it impossible to take full account. These included editions such as M. J. Osborne and S. G. Byrne, *Lexicon of Greek Personal Names* 2 (Oxford 1994), D. J. Mastronarde's of Euripides' *Phoenissae* (Cambridge 1994), Nan Dunbar's of Aristophanes' *Birds* (Oxford 1995), and the eighth volume of Kassel and Austin's *Poetae comici graeci* (Berlin and New York 1995) which contains and renumbers the known comic fragments of unknown or uncertain authorship. Part I of the addenda lists all the references in my commentary to Greek comic adespota and adds the new Kassel–Austin numbers; its four columns give from left to right a page reference, a reference to the relevant Alexis (or other) title or fragment, the number previously assigned to the adespoton in the third volume of K(ock) or in Au(stin, *CGFP*), and finally the new number in the eighth volume of Kassel–Austin. Part II of the addenda collects some interesting suggestions, comments, references (including the relevant ones in the third edition of Webster, *MINC*: revised and enlarged by J. R. Green and A. Seeberg, 1995 = *BICS Suppl.* 50) and parallels, offered mainly by other scholars (and in particular E. W. Handley) who saw this commentary at the proof stage.

I Concordance of Greek comic adespota

59	2.6	262.7Au	1092.7
66	5.1	375K	133*
77	9.2	285.8Au	1108.8
		286.5Au	1004.5
94	15.11	257.65Au	1017.65
		257.64Au	1017.64
97	15 end	1320K	431*
112	21.2	251Au	1098
122	27.1–2	115.1K	859.1
123	27.5	255.225Au	1093.225
124 n.1	27.7–8	289a.4Au	1072.4
130	31 intro(duction)	532K	892*
138	Βωμός	239Au	1032
146	37.7	258.24Au	1014.24
154	Δακτύλιος	240Au	1084
155	44.1	44K	100
156	Δημήτριος	257.20ff., 67ff.Au	1017.20ff., 67ff.
180	57.4	Philemon 228.2K	887.2

447	151.3	208K	98
448	152 intro.	240.4ff.Au	1084.4ff.
467	159.1	253.10Au	1006.10
		233.1Au	1111.1
		P.Cologne 203.C.i.2	1147.41
472	160.3	231.7Au	1088.7
472f.	160.3	244.100Au	1093.100
483	166 intro.	249.20f.Au	(vol. VI)
493	168.1	262.8Au	1092.8
494	168.2	239.22f.Au	1032.22f.
499	'Οπώρα (c)	230K	121.3
513	Παμφίλη	250.8Au	1045.8
518	177.2	343K	719
520	177.6	258.35Au	1014.35
523	177.12	261.2Au	1081.2
		P.Cologne 203.C.i.17	1147.56
531 n.1	178.13	962K	783
536	179.11	289a.7Au	1072.7
		599K	522
546 (bis)	183.5 (bis)	255.15Au	1063.15
550	185	In Phot. s.v. ἀδολεσχεῖν	572
		297.1Au	1027.1
550	Πεζονίκη	601K	Ar. fr. 962
562	191.9–10	289b.12Au	1073.12
579	200.5	109.11K	896.6
594	201.6	115.3K	859.3
587	204 intro.	239.21f.Au	1032.21f.
		255.8Au	1063.8
		257.41Au	1017.41
		258.37Au	1014.37
587	204.1–2	257.46f.Au	1017.46f.
593	205.3 line 8	244.193Au	1093.193
		252.16Au	1008.16
		258.40Au	1014.40
593	205.3 lines 9f.	250.2Au	1045.2
		255.24Au	1063.24
		266.5Au	1010.5
601	209 intro.	53K	246
		54K	Ar. fr. 968
		55K	iamb. adesp. 37 West
		56K	555
614	215.1–2	239.3f.Au	1032.3f.

ADDENDA

622 n.1	219	106/107K	101	
630	222.3–6	339b.11Au	53.11	
631	222.8	257.51Au	1017.51	
641	224.1–2	44K	100	
648 n.1	Τίτθη	276.16Au	1046.16	
654	231	1030K	Ar. fr. 971	
660	233.1–2	239.21f.Au	1032.21f.	
672	238.1	242.66Au	1096.66	
		251.10Au	1098.10	
		255.4Au	1063.4	
679	Ὕπνος	154K	873	
685	244.1	298K	73	
693	Φαῖδρος	257.73ff.Au	1017.73ff.	
695	247.1	340.3K	155.3	
696	247.2	248K	893	
701	247.14–15	258.37Au	1014.37	
		255.8Au	1063.8	
		257.41Au	1017.41	
703	248.1	251.1Au	1098.1	
		255.8Au	1063.8	
707	249.2	131.1K	821.1	
712	Φιλίσκος	131.2K	821.2	
		240Au	1084	
		284.3Au	1117.3	
715	Φιλόκαλος	249.18Au	(vol. vi)	
716	251.3	1055K	219	
723	258	In Ath. 7.307f.	112	
744	266 intro.	339.6f.K	137.4f	
745	266.1	339.6f.K	137.4f.	
760	271.4	244.348Au	1093.348	
763	273.4	230.19f.Au	1083.19f.	
768	275.2	289b.15Au	1073.15	
789	295 intro.	638K	Ar. fr. 966	
806, 807	326	239.23Au	1032.23	
822	25	1203K	745	
830–3	P.Heid. 175	265Au	1074	
833–44	P.Berl. 11771	239Au	1032	
841	P.Berl. 11771.1	Philemon fr. 228.4K	887.4	
842	P.Berl. 11771.10	249.21Au	(vol. vi)	
843	P.Berl. 11771.23	110.9K	148.9	
		130.1K	911.1	
		P.Didot 1.33	1000.33	
853	Turp. Dem. vii	257.66ff.Au	1017.66ff.	

II ADDITAMENTA

Page 7, *testimonium* 12. E. W. Handley notes that σπερμολόγους πεφρυγμένους would scan as the end of a comic iambic trimeter or trochaic tetrameter; the anecdote is probably fictitious, but did it perhaps quote a phrase from one of Alexis' plays? See also Dunbar on Ar. *Av.* 232.

61 n.1. Cf. A. Cameron, *Callimachus and his Critics* (Princeton 1995) 488ff.

121f., fr.27.1–2. See also C. Osborne in J. Wilkins, D. Harvey and M. Dobson (eds.), *Food in Antiquity* (Exeter 1995) 214ff.

129, 'Αχαῖς intro. *MINC*² XM 1 = *MINC*³ 6DM 1.

150, Γραφή intro. Cf. com. adesp. fr. 1147.9–11 K(assel–)A(ustin).

166, fr.47.5. Cf. D. van Nes, *Die maritime Bildesprache des Aischylos* (Groningen 1963) 31ff.

166, fr.47.6. On ὄψον see also J. Davidson in *Food in Antiquity* 205ff.

173 n.2. Cf. com. adesp. fr. 1132.13κα δίδυμα θυγάτρια.

176, fr.56. Cf. also Plaut. *Curc.* 78 *quasi tu lagoenam dicas* (insulting the old drunkard Leaena).

179, fr.57.2–3. On the orthography and accentuation of ἀγαθεῖ . . . τεῖ βουλεῖ in a 3rd-century inscription see Threatte, 1.378. Cf. also τεῖ in the contemporary inscription cited on p. 688 ('Υποβολιμαῖος intro.)

192, fr.63.8. A different explanation of the corruption was suggested by Handley: ὑ's rough breathing misread as superscript θ.

201, the *Helen* titles. The Würzburg strass gem is *MINC*³ 4XJ 46.

241, fr.91 intro. On drunk scenes see also J. R. Green, *AJA* 89 (1985) 465ff.

251f., fr. 96.2–4(2). Cf. also Plaut. *Bacch.* 78 *pol ego metuo lusciniolae ne defuerit cantio*, with A. Otto, *Die Sprichwörter und sprichwörtlichen Redensarten der Römer* (Leipzig 1890) 201.

253, fr.96.2–4 (on τέττιξ). Cf. also W. Clausen, comm. (Oxford 1994) on V. *Ecl.* 2.12–13.

279f., fr.103.16–18. Cf. J. R. Green and E. W. Handley, *Images of the Greek Theatre* (London 1995) 75, 'good Athenian girls had black hair'.

298 n.2. Com. adesp. fr. 1153.8–9κα now provides a third example.

301 n.1. Bothe's supplement <ἀθρόον> (*PCGF*) can no longer be dismissed as implausible in view of the speaker's warning of an approaching chorus at com. adesp. fr. 1153.9κα προ]σιόντας . . . ἀθρόους ὁρῶ τινάς.

309ff., 314f., Κράτεια intro.; 324f., fr.116 intro. Handley ventures a scenically different interpretation of fr.116: not as a piece of staged action, but as a rehearsal for some such action by one of the characters, either alone or with a companion; cf. Bdelykleon in Ar. *Vesp.* 1208ff. This is an engaging possibility, with interesting implications: e.g. the ἄνδρες συμπόται of v.6 might then be imaginary and not physically present addressees.

347, Κυβευταί intro. Cf. also F. Williams, *Glotta* 65 (1987) 96ff.

352f., Κύπριος intro. In Menander's Κόλαξ the soldier Bias had served in Cyprus, attended by Strouthias his parasite (fr. 3 Sandbach, cf. Ter. *Eun.* 497f.; Gomme–Sandbach, *Comm.* p. 432 and my edition of the play in the Loeb series: Menander, volume 2).

366f., fr.129.1. On linguistic characterisation see now also W. G. Arnott in F. De Martino and A. H. Sommerstein (eds.), *Lo spettacolo delle voci*, 2 (Bari 1995) 147ff.

382, fr.131.9. See also D. J. Mastronarde, *Classical Antiquity* 9 (1990) 247ff.

415, fr.140.17. Cf. L. J. D. Richardson, *BICS* 8 (1961) 15ff.

425, fr.145.7. See also T. Braun in *Food in Antiquity* 25ff.

429f., fr.145.15–16. Cf. M. L. West, *CQ* 17 (1967) 433ff., especially 462.

433, fr.150.4. Although present indicative forms of φάσκω are relatively uncommon, note for the first personal plural also καταφάσκομεν in Theon, *Progymn.* 2.90.18 Spengel.

472, intro. to fr.160. On Anacharsis in Stob. 3.18.25 see F. Kindstrand, *Anacharsis* (Uppsala 1981) 114f., 141f.

472, fr.160.1–2. Cf. also Eur. *Hipp.* 384 μακραί τε λεσχαὶ καὶ σχολή.

496, fr.168.6–7; and 525, fr.178.1. See also D. Harvey in *Food in Antiquity* 277.

502 n.1. See also H. A. Shapiro, *JHS* 115 (1995) 173ff.

536., fr.179.11. See now N. Dunbar, comm. on Ar. *Av.* 1148.

560, fr.191.3. Handley wonders whether οἰστέον might mean 'serve', like φέρω in fr.192.6.

597, fr.207.1. Cf. also com. adesp. fr. 1063.2f.κα ἔγειρ' ἔγειρε δη | [νῦν σε]αυτόν.

613, fr.214.2. For demonstrative + numeral without article cf. also Ar. *Ach.* 130, 187.

631, fr.222.9. Thuc. 4.39.3 called Cleon's campaign in Pylos μανιώδης.

636, fr.223.4. See also D. Harvey in *Food in Antiquity* 282ff.

655, Τοκιστής intro. Handley writes '*Obolostates siue Faenerator* is present as the title of Caecilius' play in *P.Herculaneum* 78, a fragmentary papyrus discussed by K. Kleve at the 21st International Papyrology Congress in Berlin, 13–19 August 1995'.

667, fr.236.3–4. Cf. also F. O. Copley, *Exclusus Amator* (American Philological Association monograph 17, New York 1956).

678, fr.241.2–3. Cf. also F. Williams, *ZPE* 110 (1996) 40ff.

683f., fr.243.1. See also N. Dunbar, comm. on Ar. *Av.* 1529.

688, Ὑποβολιμαῖος intro. See above on p. 179, fr.57.2–3.

703, fr.248.1. For νὴ τὸν Ἥλιον cf. now also com. adesp. fr. 1155.6κα.

719f., fr.255.3–4. Handley tentatively conjectures ταῖς ἡμ<ετ> έραις.

760, fr.272 intro. Cf. also com. adesp. fr. 1084.28ff.κα, where letters written on some unidentified objects seem to have been παιδίου | [γ]νωρί[σματα.

762, fr.272.4–5 (ἔχον). The Apulian vase (British Museum F548) = *MIOMC*³ TV 5; illustrated in Green and Handley, *Images of the Greek Theatre*, fig. 43.

762, fr.272.4–5 (ἄρά γ'). Handley would prefer to interpret the whole fr. as uninterrupted speech, conjecturing γράμματ' αὐτά γ' ἕνδεκα and comparing Men. *Epitr.* 387f. ὑπόχρυσος δακτύλιός τις οὑτοαί, | αὐτὸς σιδηροῦς (where the function of αὐτός has a different, more appropriate relevance after ὑπόχρυσος, 'here's a ring that's gilt, iron basically'). Alternatively A. H. Griffiths suggests γράμματ' ἀρχαῖ' ἕνδεκα. Neither conjecture convinces me; the postulated interruption adds liveliness to the situation, but without more context we cannot decide whether the question is an artificial and wooden attempt to move on the plot, or whether it has a deeper significance now lost.

782, fr. 285. On φιλόλογος see H. Kuch, Φιλόλογος (*philologus*) (*Schriften der Sektion für Altertumswissenschaft, Deutsche Akedemie der Wissensch. zu Berlin*, (1965)), and O. Skutsch, *Studia Enniana* (London 1968) 6f. and comm. on Ennius (Oxford 1985), *Ann.* 209.

834–5, *P.Berlin* 1771. Handley suggests ἡμ]ῶν v.4, ἐνδείξ]ομεν v.25; the latter supplement is striking and particularly attractive.

INDICES

In all three indexes the references are to page numbers.

1 Index of passages (outside Alexis) discussed

INDICES

2 Index of subjects

INDICES

INDICES

Thericles 66–8
three ways of dying 73–4
tiger 590, 598
Timocles 212 n.1, 213–4, 298, 306
tithes 588–9
Tithymallus 449–50, 458, 465, 481, 482
tragic (or otherwise elevated)
  language and tragic rhythm 20–1,
  33, 54, 68–9, 201, 231, 232, 234–5,
  237, 244–6, 343–4, 350–2, 395, 450,
  455–7, 457, 480, 483, 484, 490,
  672–3, 680, 683, 760, 780–1, 801,
  829
transformation 439
Triballi 683–4, 870
Turpilius 31; (Demetrius) 157–9, 164, 851–7
Tyche 343; see also fortune
tyranny of the belly 613–14

unachieved aims as reason for
  character's early re-entry 288
Utopias 399, 445

vase descriptions 186, 265–6, 267,

760–2
victor garlanded in stadium 766

walking with measured gait 741
wars between slaves and masters
  174
wealth impermanent 747–8, 778
weight of objects 58–9
wells 229, 548–9
wine from: Corinth 787; Decelea 783;
  Euboea 794; Lesbos 769; Thasos
  658–9
wine: mixtures 183–4, 650–1, 657;
  prices 97; superiority when old
  160–4, 774, 780
wine-vinegar from Decelea 783
women: in theatre audiences 152;
  isolation 846; see also misogyny

Xenocrates 262

Zeus: coupled with Athena in oath
  660, 838; infancy in Crete 758; Zeus
  Soter in toast 661–2, cf. 713; Zeus
  Soter inscribed on cup 761–2
zodiac 732–3, 736

3 Index of words discussed in the commentary

ἀβυρτάκη 427
ἀγαθῶν ἅμαξαι 515
ἀγένειος 643
ἀγνεύω 90
ἀγορανόμος 707
ἀδάμας 700–1
ἀδολεσχῶ 549–50
ἀεί γε/τε … καὶ νῦν 724–5
ἀηδών 251–2
αἴθρα 456
αἴθων 55–6
αἶνος 150–1
αἴρω τράπεζαν 713
αἰσθητικός 230–1
αἰτῶ/αἰτοῦμαι 218–19, 234
Ἀκαδήμεια 823
ἄκανθα 169, 400
ἀκαρής 438
ἄκλητος 611
ἀκολασ(τ)ία 145, 812
ἄκρατος, -ον 66, 77–8
ἀκρολίπαρος 572
ἄκρος 642

ἀλάβαστ(ρ)ος 189
ἀλειπτήριον 289–90
ἀλείπτρια 814–15
ἀλέτων ὄνος 597–8; see also ὄνος
ἀληθέστερα τῶν ἐπὶ Σάγρᾳ 796–7
ἀλουσία 584
ἄλυρος 485–6
ἀλύω 344
ἀμφιτάπης 255
ἀμφωτις 83
ἀναδενδράς 81–2
ἀνακυλίω 341–2
ἀναλαμβάνω 275
ἀναπίπτω 789
ἀναρίστητος 663
ἀνασπᾶν: see τὰς ὀφρῦς
ἀνάστατος 798
ἄνδρες (vocative) 191–2, 314–15,
  324–5, 660, 837–8, 869
ἀνδριάς 597
ἄνηθον = 'dill' 386
ἂν θεὸς θέλῃ 661
ἀνθράκιον 403

880

INDICES

ἀνίημι (of fevers) 95
ἄννησον = 'anise' 388–9
ἀνταγωνιστής 766
ἀπανθῶ 163
ἀπαρύω 163
ἀπέρχομαι 621–2
ἀπηκριβημένως 617
ἀπινής 392–3
ἀποβάτης 104–5
ἀπογηράσκω/ἀπογηρῶ 774
ἀποδείκνυμι 239
ἀποδημία 627, 632, 633
ἀποδίδωμι: see δίδωμι ~ ἀποδίδωμι
ἀποζῶ 163
Ἄπολλον 520
ἀπόλλυμαι 539
ἀπολογοῦμαι, -ηθῆναι 82–3
ἀπονίζομαι 463, 713–14
ἀπὸ συμβολῶν: see δεῖπνον ἀπὸ
   συμβολῶν
ἀποταγηνίζω/ἀποτηγανίζω 530
Ἀργείους ὁρᾷς 461–3
ἀριστόδειπνον 790
ἀρύταινα 815
ἀρχιτέκτων 450–1
ἀσεβῶ 90
ἄσβολος 279–80
ἄσημον 197
ἀσύμβολος 725
ἀσχολοῦμαι 600
ἀτηρία 147
ἀτρεμά 409
ἀτρεμεί 373–4
ἀττικηρῶς 617
αὐτίτης 782–3
αὐτόπυρος 355
ἀφαιρῶ 276, 614
Ἀφροδίσια ἄγω 719
ἀφύαι 227
ἀφυβρίζω 162
Ἀχαΐς 128 n.1
ἀχράς 489

βάκηλος 287
βαλλίζω, βαλλισμός 302–3
βάραθρον 467
βασανισμός 787
βάσις 351–2
βατάνιον, πατάνιον 117–18
βαυβαλίζω/βαυκαλίζω 654
βαυκίδες 275–6
βαυκίζομαι 644

βέλτιστε 836
βεμβράς: see μεμβράς
Βεργαῖος 239–40
βιβλίον/βυβλίον 407–8
βλέπω 271, 667–8
βολβός 488, 514
βοτρύδιον 531
βούλιμος 415
βούλομαι (+ accusative) 733
βοῶ 91
βράγχια 400
Βρεττία 135 n.1
Βρόμιος 658

γέγονε = 'floruit' 4
γέλοιος/γελοῖος 555
γέρων (adjectival) 506
γηγενής 307
γηράσκω/γηρῶ 774
γηροβοσκεῖα (? -βοσκία) 800–1
γήτειον 388–9, 534–5
γί(γ)εται ἐμοί/μοι (+ infinitive) 302
γί(γ)νομαι 145–6
γι(γ)νόμενος ἀεί 190
γι(γ)νώσκω 145–6, 202–3
γλαῦκος 318
γλυκύ(ς) 185–6
γράμμα 796
γραμματικὸν ἔκπωμα 760, 761–2
γυμνός 216

δαιδάλεος, -λειος 102–3
δαιμονίως 507
δαίμων 680–1
δάκνω 775
δάκτυλος 448
δέ and τε permutated 60, 614
δεδείπναμεν 307–8
δείκνυται (+ infinitive) 473–4
δεινὸν ποῶ 99–100
δεῖπνον ἀπὸ συμβολῶν 85–6, 86–7, cf.
   271
δευσοποιός 426
δέχεται (+ infinitive) 474
δήμιος 111
διάβαθρον 276
διαπαρθενεύω 801
διαπειλοῦμαι 794
διαπλέω 612
διάπυρος 371
διασκευή 155–7, 720
διατρέχω 736

881

INDICES

INDICES